Design Studies and Intelligence Engineering

Proceedings of DSIE 2023, Hangzhou, China, 28–29 October 2023

Edited by

Lakhmi C. Jain

KES International, Selby, United Kingdom

Valentina Emilia Balas

Department of Automation and Applied Informatics, Faculty of Engineering,
Aurel Vlaicu University of Arad, Arad, Romania

Qun Wu

Institute of Universal Design, Zhejiang Sci-Tech University, China

and

Fuqian Shi

Rutgers, The State University of New Jersey, New Brunswick, USA

IOS Press

Amsterdam • Berlin • Washington, DC

ISBN 978-1-64368-488-8 (print)
ISBN 978-1-64368-489-5 (online)
Library of Congress Control Number: 2023952552
doi: 10.3233/FAIA383

Publisher
IOS Press BV
Nieuwe Hemweg 6B
1013 BG Amsterdam
Netherlands
e-mail: order@iospress.nl

For book sales in the USA and Canada:
IOS Press, Inc.
6751 Tepper Drive
Clifton, VA 20124
USA
Tel.: +1 703 830 6300
Fax: +1 703 830 2300
sales@iospress.com

Preface

The 2023 International Symposium on Design Studies and Intelligence Engineering (DSIE-2023) was held in Hangzhou, China on 28 & 29 October 2023, providing a platform for professionals and researchers from industry and academia to present and discuss recent advances in the field of design studies and intelligence engineering.

The technology applied in design studies varies from basic theory to more application-based systems, whereas intelligence engineering also plays a significant role in design science, such as computer-aided industrial design, human factor design, and greenhouse design. Intelligence-engineering technologies also include topics from both theoretical and application perspectives, such as computational technologies, sensing technologies, and video detection. The conference aims to promote cooperation between industries and universities in these fields. Renowned professors from around the world were invited to speak on these topics in greater depth and to discuss in-depth research directions with the presenters.

We received 275 online submissions from researchers. All papers were reviewed by three or four independent experts. Based on the reviewer's comments, 105 papers were accepted for publication in this book. We believe that this conference will foster cooperation among the organizations and researchers involved in these merging fields.

DSIE 2023 was sponsored by Zhejiang Sci-Tech University and co-sponsored by the Chinese Mechanical Engineering Society-Industrial Design, Aurel Vlaicu University of Arad, Techno India College of Technology, the Chinese Academy of Art, Xiamen University of Technology, and Tanta University.

We would like to thank all contributors for their efforts in submitting their manuscripts on time and we express our gratitude to the reviewers for their contribution. Thanks are also due to Mr. Maarten Fröhlich of IOS Press for accepting this volume for publication, and to his colleagues for their work during the typesetting stage of the volume.

Lakhmi C. Jain
Valentina Emilia Balas
Qun Wu
Fuqian Shi

About the Conference

The 2023 International Symposium on Design Studies and Intelligence Engineering (DSIE2023) was held successfully in Hangzhou, China on 28 & 29 October 2023. It provided a platform for professionals and researchers from industry and academia to present and discuss recent advances in the fields of design studies and intelligence engineering. The discipline of design studies applies various technologies, from basic theory to application systems, while intelligence engineering includes computer-aided industrial design, human factor design, and greenhouse design, and plays a major part within design science. Intelligence engineering technologies also include topics from theory and application, such as computational technologies, sensing technologies, and video detection. The conference fosters cooperation among the organizations and researchers involved in these merging fields and invites well-known professors worldwide to further explore these topics, also allowing for participants to discuss technical presentations with the presenters in-depth. For this collection of papers on design studies and intelligence engineering, 275 submissions were reviewed. The conference chairs selected papers based on the scores given by three or four referees, after which 105 papers were accepted for publication in this issue.

DSIE2023 was sponsored by

Zhejiang Sci-Tech University
and co-sponsored by
Chinese Mechanical Engineering Society-Industrial Design, China
Aurel Vlaicu University of Arad, Romania
Techno India College of Technology, India
Chinese Academy of Art, China
Xiamen University of Technology, China
Tanta University, Egypt

Committee

International Advisory Board

Prof. Michio Sugeno†, Tokyo Institute of Technology, Japan
Prof. Bogdan M. Wilamowski, Auburn University, USA

Conference Chairs

Prof. Jialin Li, Zhejiang Sci-Tech University, China
Prof. Lakhmi C. Jain, KES International, UK
Prof. Valentina E. Balas, Aurel Vlaicu University of Arad, Romania

Program Committee Chairs

Prof. Qun Wu, Zhejiang Sci-Tech University, China
Prof. Chunlei Chai, Zhejiang University, China
Prof. Zheng Liu, China Academy of Art, China

International Program Committee

Prof. Adina Magda Florea, Politehnica University, Bucharest, Romania
Prof. Ahmad Taher Azar, Modern Science and Arts University (MSA), Egypt
Dr. Amira S. Ashour, Tanta University, Egypt
Prof. Anca Ralescu, College of Engineering, University of Cincinnati, USA
Prof. Bernadette Bouchon-Meunier, UPMC – LIP6, Paris, France
Prof. Dan Ralescu, College of Engineering, University of Cincinnati, USA
Prof. Diego Andina, Univ. Politécnica de Madrid, Madrid SPAIN
Prof. Dragan Radojevic, Mihajlo Pupin Institute, Belgrade, Serbia
Prof. Eiji Uchino, Yamaguchi University, Japan
Prof. Emil M. Petriu, University of Ottawa, Canada
Prof. Fangyu Li, Southwest Jiaotong University, China
Dr. Fuqian Shi, Rutgers University-New Brunswick, USA
Dr. Genoveffa Tortora, University of Salerno, Italy
Prof. Hacène Habbi, University Boumerdès, Algeria
Prof. Hani Hagras, University of Essex, UK
Prof. Herchang Ay, National Kaohsiung University, Taiwan
Prof. Hideyuki Takagi, Kyushu University, Japan
Prof. Imre J. Rudas, Óbuda University Budapest, Hungary
Prof. Jair Minoro Abe, Paulista University, Sao Paulo, Brazil
Dr. Jasmko Tochiny, University Malaysia Sabah, Malaysia
Dr. Juanfang Xu, Jiangnan University, China
Prof. Jude Hemanth, Karunya University, India
Prof. Kazumi Nakamatsu, University of Hyogo, Japan
Prof. Kejun Zhang, Zhejiang University, China
Dr. Kelly Robinson, Electrostatic Answers LLC, USA
Prof. Laszlo T. Koczy, Szechenyi Istvan University, Gyor, Hungary
Dr. Lefteris Gortzis, University of Patras, Greece
Prof. Luis Gomez, Universidade Nova de Lisboa, Portugal
Prof. Marius M. Balas, Aurel Vlaicu University of Arad, Romania
Dr. Mehdi Roopaei, University of Wisconsin-Platteville, USA
Dr. Mihaela Luca, Romanian Academy, Iasi Branch, Romania
Prof. Mojtaba Agha-Mirsalim, Amirkabir University of Technology, Iran
Prof. Mokhtar Beldjehem, Saint-Anne's University, Canada
Prof. Moraru Luminita, Dunarea de Jos University, Romania
Dr. Nilanjan Dey, Techno International New Town, India
Prof. Preeti Bajaj, Galgotias University, India
Prof. S. Ablameyko, Belarusian State University, Belarus
Prof. S. Komithe, Malaysia University of Science and Technology, Malaysia
Prof. Santo Banerjee, Politecnico di Torino, Italy
Dr. Sifaki-Pistolla Dimitra, University of Crete, Greece
Prof. Sikh Namh C., University of Delhi, Indian

Prof. Ting Han, Shanghai Jiao Tong University, China
Prof. Traian Mazilu, Politehnica University, Bucharest, Romania
Prof. Tsung-Chih Lin, Feng Chia University, Taiwan
Prof. Vladimir O. Safonov, St. Petersburg University, Russia
Prof. Xiaojian Liu, Zhejiang University of Technology, China
Prof. Yew-Soon Ong, Nanyang Technological University, Singapore
Dr. Yulin Ma, Luoyang Yijia Electric Tech, China
Dr. Zenggui Gao, Shanghai University, China
Dr. Zhengyu Tan, Hunan University, China
Prof. Zhiqiang Zeng, Xiamen University of Technology, China

Organizing Committees Chairs

Prof. Ying Wang, Zhejiang Sci-Tech University, China
Dr. Xiaodong Wang, Xiamen University of Technology, China

Organizing Committees Co-Chairs

Prof. ZuyaoZhang, Zhejiang Sci-Tech University, China
Dr. Yuxiang Yu, Zhejiang Sci-Tech University, China
Dr. Baixi Xing, Zhejiang University of Technology, China
Ms. Honghuan Liao, Beijing Zisuzi Culture Co., Ltd, China
Dr. Chao Li, Zhejiang Sci-Tech University, China
Dr. Danni Shen, Zhejiang Sci-Tech University, China
Dr. Defu Bao, Zhejiang Sci-Tech University, China

Contents

Preface v
Lakhmi C. Jain, Valentina Emilia Balas, Qun Wu and Fuqian Shi

About the Conference vii

Innovative Application of a First-Class Weaving Technology Course: Visual
Error Design in Experimental Practice 1
Taohai Yan, Yajing Shi, Luming Huang, Yuxi Lin and Dongdong Lu

Exploring Innovation and Development of Yarn Spinning Through
Industry-Education Integration: A Practical Teaching Approach 10
Taohai Yan, Yu Lin, Yajing Shi, Luming Huang and Zhaoguo Wang

AI-Assisted Design for Intangible Cultural Heritage: A Study on the Tujia
Hand-Waving Dance 20
Anguo Wu and Rong Chang

Sustainable Product Design of Innovative Design Methods and Case Studies 28
Weishu Yang

Investigating Preference Factors in the Design of Shopping Carts for the Elderly:
A Miryoku Engineering Study 39
Shuai-Ke Meng, Bao-Yi Zhang and Jing-Jing Huang

Research on Innovative Design Method and Evaluation of Jewelry Based
on CiteSpace&Playgound AI 47
*Jinhong Hu, Shuwei Yu, Ming Zhang, Yue Wu, Jinwei Lu, Jiongzhou Weng,
Feiyang Liu, Hao Huo, Cheng Li and Dongfang Pan*

Virtual Reality Technology in Art Education System 58
Ruoyuan Liao

Research on the Innovation Trend Direction of Fitness Products Based on
the Construction Method of Patent Knowledge Graph 70
*Shuwei Yu, Jiongzhou Weng, Feiyang Liu, Hao Huo, Jinwei Lu,
Jinhong Hu, Ming Zhang and Yue Wu*

Sustainable Material Innovation Design for Building Construction: Exploring
Bio-Based Alternatives 81
Benyu Yang, Qun Wang and Siu Shing Man

Design of a Supernumerary Robotic Limb Based on Hybrid Control of Motion
Imagination and Object Detection 88
Zhichuan Tang, Hang Wang, Zhixuan Cui, Jun Ding and Lingtao Zhang

Measurement and Optimization of Navigation Bar Icon Design in Mental
Health Apps 97
Zihan Wei, Yuxiang Kuang and Zhanhui Gao

Research on the Application of Traditional Culture in Product Innovation
Design   108
   Jian Han and Xinran Yu

Research on Sustainable Development of Intangible Cultural Handicraft from
the Perspective of Social Innovation Design   117
   Jian Han and Weimeng Xu

Third-Person Pain Experience Exploration Based on Multimodal Physiological
Features Analysis   127
   Baixi Xing, Yuehan Shi, Kaiqi Wang, Xinjie Song and Yanhong Pan

Development and Application of Offshore Trade Authenticity Verification
Platform Based on Blockchain   137
   Hai-Feng Chen, Lv Zhang, Shuai Wang and Shan-Shan Shi

Design of Children's Artistic Creation Products Integrating AR and Tangible
Interactions   148
   Jiarui Liu and Lingyan Zhang

Digital Baseball Sport Design Based on DMC Gamification Theory   164
   Jiqing Fu, Lingyan Zhang, Xinyi Zheng, Fang'er Yang and Yongqi Lin

Power System Uncertainty Modeling Based on Gaussian Process   179
   Tianze Zhang

Digital Personality in the Voice Interaction Products Design   191
   Lingyan Zhang and Yun Wang

Construction of Intermediate Knowledge in Design: A Case Study of Cultural
and Creative Product Design   205
   Lintao Tang and Jianwei Yin

AI-Driven Interactive Painting Synthesis System for Children's Art Education   216
   *Mengyue Tang, Baixi Xing, Zhichuan Tang, Pan Zou, Jiayin Yu
   and Haojing Zhang*

"Ask Aloud Protocol": Toward a Participant-Driven Question-Asking Design
Research Method   225
   Lintao Tang and Sihang Wang

An Interactive Application for Hand Muscle Fatigue Relief Based on Gesture
Recognition   241
   *Siyu Pang, Baixi Xing, Zhichuan Tang, Pan Zou, Zhepeng Xu
   and Hailong Zhang*

Residential Spatial Layout Design Using Advanced Optimization Techniques   251
   Yalong Mao, Zhe Lai, Zitong Chen, Shaojie Wang and Lukui Huang

A Review on Vascular Biometrics for Finger Vein Authentication System   259
   D Jude Hemanth and Nisha Joy Thomas

Research on Improving the Quality of Japanese Chinese Machine Translation
Based on Deep Learning   267
   Jialing Lu and Fengxian Yin

Computer-Aided Putonghua Test: Problems and Strategies   278
    Yuhan Song

Research on Factors Influencing User Experience in H5 Interactive Advertising
Based on Flow Theory   286
    Biao Gao and Yi Hu

Research on Automotive Front Face Styling Based on Shape Grammar   295
    Lingling Liu, Biao Ma, Mengyuan Pan, Zhen Chen, Zeyu Yang
    and Xinyao He

An Overview of Deepfake Methods in Medical Image Processing for Health
Care Applications   304
    Dhanya Lakshmi and D Jude Hemanth

Optimization Analysis of Product Design Process Based on Reinforcement
Learning Algorithm   312
    Yuping Hu and Qian Li

Product Design Process Based on GANs Model   322
    Yuping Hu and Danfeng Chen

Explainable Artificial Intelligence (XAI) for Air Quality Assessment   333
    Sayan Chakraborty, Bitan Misra and Nilanjan Dey

Construction of the Place Spirit of Qianmen Street in Beijing: Historical
Performance and User Needs   342
    Zuqun Zhang, Chenggang Lu, Haotian Zhao, Qi Chen, Qiuyu Wu
    and Tingting He

Design of Intelligent Wheelchair for the Disabled Elderly of Mild and
Moderate Type   362
    Chuan-xin Sheng, Wei-liang Li, Lian-xin Hu and Ze-feng Wang

Deep Subspace K-Means Clustering for Syringe Defect Detection Without
Defective Samples   373
    Fei Yan, Xiaodong Wang, Longfu Hong and Zhiyao Xie

The Promotion of Cultural Heritage Protection Driven by Artificial
Intelligence in the Context of Hemei Rural Construction   382
    Min Ma

An Analysis and Modeling Method for Design Information Based on User
Generated Reviews Mining and Extenics   393
    Jin-juan Duan, Feng Zhang, Zhe-wen Bai and Gaofeng Li

The Application of the "Feitian" Element from the Yungang Grottoes in
Jewelry Design   404
    Jinwei Lu, Shuwei Yu, Feiyang Liu, Jiongzhou Weng, Hao Huo,
    Xiaojiang Zhou, Jinhong Hu, Ming Zhang and Yue Wu

Behavior-Oriented Low-Carbon Campus Mobile Interface Design Research   415
    Yunjia Chen and Ruiyun Feng

Interface Design of College Life Circle APP Based on Improved KJ
Method-Entropy Power Method 436
 Xiaofei Lu and Shouwang Li

Research on Rural Aged Outdoor Seating Based on Fusion Design Concept 449
 Zhixian Zhang

Effect of Music Therapy on the Rehabilitation of Elderly People with Dementia 459
 Zhenyu Liu, Cheng Yao and Fangtian Ying

Research on Intelligent Shoe Washing Machine Design and Evaluation Method
Based on AHP-DEMATEL 467
 *Feiyang Liu, Shuwei Yu, Jiongzhou Weng, Jinwei Lu, Ming Zhang,
 Jinhong Hu and Xiaojiang Zhou*

Jiangxi NanFeng Nuo's Cultural and Creative Product Design Research 478
 Xin Liu and Lei Chen

How to Use Self-Attention Mechanism Model to Improve Driving Interface
Design and Evaluation Research 486
 *Ming Zhang, Shuwei Yu, Jinhong Hu, Yue Wu, Feiyang Liu, Jinwei Lu,
 Jiongzhou Weng, Hao Huo, Cheng Li, Xiaojiang Zhou
 and Dongfang Pan*

Research on the Interactive Narrative Design of Jiangnan Sizhu Based on
the Perception of Cultural Symbols 497
 Jiang Yao and Bing Feng

Construction of User Portrait System for Online Shopping of Cultural and
Tourism Products Based on Generalized Regression Neural Network 507
 Yue Xu, Xuyan Hu and Jiande Zhang

Research and Design of Wearable Olfactory Displays 517
 Hongfang Tang, Weibin Ding and Xi Zhu

Research of Irrational User Model on Subway Emergency Product Design 524
 Xiaofan Sun, Meidan Deng and Hongbin Jiang

Research on Sustainable Reconstruction of Rural Idle Primary Schools Based
on Light Intervention: A Case Study of Nanqiang Primary School in Kaiping
Tangkou Town 530
 Zheng Li and Xiaoya Hou

Application Research of Waterborne Plastic Waste Recycling Device Based
on Green Design Principles 540
 Zheng Li and Biao Li

Research on the Design of Diet Management System for Sub-Obese People
Based on FBM Behavior Model 549
 Xiaolu Liu, Fangying Li and Yingying Huang

KYPHOTONE: Wearable Hunchback Corrector for Women 560
 *Yousheng Yao, Yuan Xie, Fangtian Ying, Zhihao Huang, E. Tang,
 Xiqin Pan, Junpeng Zheng, Junqi Zhan, Jin Peng and Haoteng Chen*

Map and Network Urban Analysis: A Case Study on Guangzhou Nanhuaxi
Street Historic District's Urban Form   571
   Hong Li and Xiaofeng Wang

Product Innovation Design Method Based on System Thinking   583
   Dehui Ye, Lingxiao Meng and Ruikai Zhang

Characteristics of Co-Design in the Context of Social Innovation   595
   Zhi Guan and Yue Qiu

Study on Signage System Design for Fashion City Construction   605
   Hong Liu and Shanshan Lu

No Driver Is Alone: A Multicentered Human-Machine System Framework
for Multitasking While Driving   614
   Min Lin, Mo Chen, Yubo Zhang, Xinying He and Fan Yang

TIP CUP: An Interactive System to Promote Tea-Drinking Activities   626
   Yousheng Yao, Zhihao Huang, Fangtian Ying, Yuan Xie, E. Tang,
   Xiqin Pan, Fengping Feng, Junpeng Zheng, Junqi Zhan, Jin Peng
   and Haoteng Chen

A Brief Discussion on How Memetics Guides the User Experience Design
of Cultural and Creative Products   635
   Dingyu Zhu, Yuxiang Kuang, Yanqing Yang and Zhanhui Gao

MyCmp: Temporomandibular Joint Disorder Monitoring and Regulation
System   641
   Yousheng Yao, Xiqin Pan, Fangtian Ying, E. Tang, Zhihao Huang,
   Yuan Xie, BinAo He, Junpeng Zheng, Jin Peng, Jiaqi Zhang
   and Haoteng Chen

Feasibility Analysis on the Design of Elderly Volunteer Maintenance Service
in Rural Cultural Facilities in Guangdong   652
   Qi Song, Yuxin Liang, Bingjie Sun and Riyang Li

Evaluation and Application of Aging-Appropriate Bathing Facilities Design
Based on Grounded Theory and Fuzzy Analytic Hierarchy Process   663
   Xinhui Hong and Shunlan Mei

Research on the Integration and Application of Design Thinking and Large
Language Models in the Innovation Design of Fintech Products   673
   Wenjing Wang and Baixi Xing

Mobile Agricultural Products Vending Vehicle with Autonomous Navigation
Selling on Town Roads   683
   Yousheng Yao, E. Tang, Fangtian Ying, Xiqin Pan, Yuan Xie,
   Zhihao Huang, Junpeng Zheng, Junqi Zhan, Jin Peng, Haoteng Chen
   and Wenjing Feng

Effects of Growth Distributions on Tensile Properties of Palm Leaf Sheath
Fibers   694
   Xin Liu, Yanxin Qi, Jianjun Hou, Zhihui Wu and Jilei Zhang

Research on Personalized Ceramic Bottle Design with Imagery and Neural
Networks 703
Yong-xin Guo, Mimi Li and Xiao-long Chen

Designing Cultural and Creative Products of Chinese Jingchu Patterns Based
on Non-Finetuned Text-to-Image Systems 713
Yijin Wang

Operation Space Optimization Design of Mobile Chinese Food Cart Based on
Ergonomics 723
Meidan Deng, Xiaofan Sun, Biyun Zhu and Jinhua Zhang

Research on Emotional Experience Design of Cultural and Creative Products
Based on User Needs 732
Donglin Cheng, Yuanyuan Tan and Shi-le Lee

Research on Renovation and Design of Urban Block Public Toilets Based on
Service Design 742
Wei Zhang, Yunjia Qiao and Zijie Zhou

Exploring the Solutions of Sustainable Product Design: An ESG Perspective 754
Wei Li and Jidong Yang

The Preliminary Validation of PCMI in the Context of Museum Creativity 764
Hui Cheng and Xiao Qiu

Research on Parameterized Design of Urban Furniture in Wuyi Overseas
Chinese Hometown from the Perspective of Digitalization and Localization 775
Liang Chen, Zhenyi Chen, Mingyuan Wu and Ze Li

Does the Manufacturing Industry Also Need Gamification? – A Gamification
Design Practice for CNC Machine Tool Skill Training 789
Tian-shu Li and Min-yang Liu

Research on Multimodal Interaction Design Patterns for Visually Impaired
People Under Sensory Compensation Theory 799
Wei Zhang and Cong An

To Improve the Students' Learning Motivation of Vocational Colleges Through
Design Thinking 809
Qianqian Lin, Zhenghong Liu and Yuanbo Sun

Research on the Color Design of Hospital Inpatient Wards Under the Concept
of Color Empowerment 820
Wei-lin Qiu

Combining Contemporary Design Principles with the Craftsmanship of Ancient
Chinese Architecture 831
Guangzhou Li and Porncharoen Ratthai

Research on the Design of Tourism Cultural and Creative Products from
the Perspective of Semiotics 841
Zhenzhen Wang and Yu Wang

Modern Design Thinking and AIGC Intervention 850
Yu Wang, Zhenzhen Wang and Ruirui Mu

Design of Fast-Growing Plant Material Woven Furniture Products Based
on Sustainable Concepts 863
    Beibei Jia

Research on Knowledge Transfer-Oriented Intelligent Assistance Design
Communication System for CNC Machine Tools 873
    Xiaoli Niu, Honghai Li and Xiaobin Shi

Laser-Induced Colourization on Metal Surface for Product Design 884
    Fangyuan Ji, Jiandan Zeng, Zhigang Tang and Xibin Wang

Application of Biofeedback Technology in Human-Computer Interaction in
Video Games 890
    Shenglin Xu, Zekun Qin and Xin Lyu

Analysis on the Predicament of Future Law and Its Solution Under
the Background of Artificial Intelligence 901
    Xiaoying Ruan and Hongfu Chen

Indoor Color Planning Based on Color Image Coordinate System 914
    Can Zhou

Artificial Intelligence Driven Promotion of Cultural Heritage Protection in
the Context of Harmony Rural Construction 923
    Xiujuan Wu

A New Bio-Inspired Tool for Visual Design: A Cognitive Protocol Analysis 934
    Yiwen Wang, Nannan Li and Biao Li

The Development of a University Express Packaging Recycling System Based
on Service Design 940
    Meidan Deng, Di Wang, Shanglu Zhao and Biyun Zhu

Computational Interpretation of the Difference Between the 5 Writing Styles
of Chinese Calligraphy 948
    Yangzi Fu, Ruimin Lyu, Guoying Yang, Baixi Xing and Lekai Zhang

Research on Creative Design Reasoning Model Based on Cultural Elements 958
    Xin Tian, Shijian Luo and Yao Wang

Study on the Design of Children's Home Oral Protection Based on Perceptual
Engineering 967
    Yanan Zhang, Weijia Guan and Yi Liu

Research on Style Transfer of Artistic Images Based on Artificial Intelligence 976
    Jian Wang

Research on the Method of Artistic Image Restoration Based on Artificial
Intelligence 989
    Jian Wang

Research on Crowdinnovation Design Methods and Models for Internet
Platforms Based on the Innovation Value Chain 1001
    Cong Gu and Fei Wang

Knowledge Collaboration Mechanism and Validity Assessment Based on
Design Awards: A Case Study of Design Intelligence Award 1013
  Jihong Zhu, Peiwen Peng, Zhouping Xu and Yixin Zhang

Research on the Elements of Tourist Experience Demands in Archaeological
Site Parks Based on Grounded Theory 1023
  Yizi Chen and Zihan Deng

Virtual Simulation Experimental Teaching Method and Practice Based on
BOPPPS Teaching Model: An Example of Virtual Simulation Experiment
Platform of Jiajiang Bamboo Paper Making Skills 1034
  Fangyu Li, Jiayi Li and Yefei Li

Requirement Analysis of Smart Kitchen Dietary and Social Service System
Based on Older Adults Mental Models 1044
  Fangyu Li, Lin Zhu, Zheng Liu and Lin Li

Research on the Performance Assessment of CMF Design Curriculum Based
on Fuzzy Comprehensive Evaluation: Taking the CMF Design of Passenger
Interface of High-Speed Train Dining Car as an Example 1052
  Jun Du, Ning Dai, Fangyu Li, Tianjiao Zhang and Xiaoyan Wang

Research on the Design of Red Cultural and Creative Products in Hongyuan
County Based on Regional Characteristics 1060
  Sinuo Chen, Ning Dai, Jun Du, Fangyu Li, Jingyu He and Yuqing Wang

The Design of Undergraduate Students' Learning Product Service System
Based on User Behavioural Persuasion 1071
  Zhule Zhang and Ningchang Zhou

Research on Intelligent Assistant Teaching System for National Musical
Instruments Based on PSS 1083
  Na Lu

Subject Index 1097

Author Index 1103

Design Studies and Intelligence Engineering
L.C. Jain et al. (Eds.)
© 2024 The Authors.
This article is published online with Open Access by IOS Press and distributed under the terms
of the Creative Commons Attribution Non-Commercial License 4.0 (CC BY-NC 4.0).
doi:10.3233/FAIA231419

1

Innovative Application of a First-Class Weaving Technology Course: Visual Error Design in Experimental Practice

Taohai YAN[a,1], Yajing SHI[a], Luming HUANG[b], Yuxi LIN[a,c], and Dongdong LU[d]

[a] *Clothing and Design Faculty, Minjiang University, Fuhzou, Fujian, China, 350108*
[b] *Chunhui Technology Group Co., Ltd, Fuzhou, Fujian, China, 350018*
[c] *Fujian Huafeng New Material Co., Ltd., Putian, Fujian, China, 351164*
[d] *Guobin Yaqi Textile Co., Ltd., Yinchuan, Ningxia, China, 751400*

Abstract. The Weaving Technology course is a first-class course at Minjiang University. After a three-year construction period, a series of teaching reform experiences have been formed. This article primarily summarizes the innovations in the practical aspects. The course includes eight experimental practice hours. In the experimental practice session, students are required to design and develop multiple series of woven fabrics with visual errors. Each design group must fully understand and appropriately apply various elements of visual illusions, combining visual illusion images to make the designed works more dynamic, novel, and artistic. This innovative practice is a comprehensive test of students' imagination and the mechanical weaving process operation, providing an interesting exploration experience for course design.

Keywords. "Mechanical Weaving Technology" course, visual errors, woven fabrics, design

1. Introduction

Weaving Technology is a basic course for textile engineering majors with a total of 54 class hours, including 48 theoretical hours and 8 experimental practice hours. The course begins with the formation principles of various fabrics, and systematically introduces the basic theories, research methods, and experimental skills of fabric formation. This enables students to master the weaving process, the main equipment configuration and working principles of each process, and the design, testing, and adjustment methods of the weaving process parameters, thereby laying a solid foundation for future production practice and scientific research. Against the background of new engineering, IEET engineering certification, and Ministry of Education engineering certification, the goal of this course is to enable students to master the equipment and process technology issues in the pre-weaving preparation and weaving processes. Moreover, the course aims to provide a comprehensive understanding of weaving technology and equipment, lay the

---

[1] Corresponding Author. Taohai YAN, Email, yantaoh@126.com

foundation for the further study of professional courses, and enable students to become advanced application-oriented talents suitable for the textile and apparel industry.

The Weaving Technology School-level First-class Course underwent a three-year construction period, thus providing a series of teaching reform experiences. In this article, the background of the Weaving Technology course construction is first introduced. With the development of the textile industry, this course was opened to train application-oriented talents. This article then elaborates on the basic ideas of course construction, including the introduction of new technologies, the strengthening of design capability training, and the organization of field trips. The innovative points of the course construction lie in building an online course platform, implementing a flipped classroom, and conducting online teaching. The promotion of the course results has achieved good effects, such as the promotion of industry-academia-research cooperation, the training of application-oriented talents, and the promotion of the local economy. However, the course construction is also characterized by some shortcomings, such as limited practical training conditions and delayed resource updates. Finally, future research directions are proposed, including the application of virtual simulation technology, interactive teaching methods, and the cultivation of self-learning ability, among other aspects. Overall, the construction of the Weaving Technology course is a systematic project that requires continuous improvement and development to adapt to the textile education situation and industry needs. The "post-00" college students entering the campus have distinctive personalities; they are good at thinking, brave in their expressions, daring to try new things, and happy to explore [1]. Visual error is a special aesthetic art; it is a unique dynamic sense generated by the combination of pattern transformation, color matching, and pattern uniqueness [2]. In the field of textiles and clothing, it has become a popular fashion pursued by a new generation of designers [3]. In the practical experiment session of this course, 24 students in the class were divided into four groups, and multiple series of woven fabrics were designed and developed with visual errors as the theme. The specific requirements were to select the most basic patterns for rotation transformation and combine contrasting and similar colors during color matching to design and develop a series of woven works. Such fabrics with visual error effects are not only a new innovation in the field of textiles, but also provide a new reference for modern woven fabric design, thus enriching the research and development and unique innovation of woven fabrics and providing a more interesting exploration for curriculum reform.

2. Purpose and Significance of Course Design

Visual error patterns provide a unique visual experience that conveys strong interest, rhythm, and texture. They are a one-of-a-kind style that can form a school of its own. Whether researching from a theoretical perspective or in practical design, the study of visual error methods, applications, and marketing is crucial. The application of visual error art in the field of textile design is a new development and innovation in textile product design and will continuously promote the innovative development of fabric design.

The first aspect of textile visual error design is color. Largely visual errors rely on rich colors to achieve an illusion effect. For example, similar and contrasting colors produce very different effects in different patterns, which also increases the difficulty of the design and development of visual error products. The second aspect is function; the effects produced by visual errors, to some extent, are unique. For instance, camouflage clothing uses irregular stripes and color combinations like wild grass and green land to confuse the enemy or achieve a concealment effect. The third aspect is patterns, which are the most important component. The essence of pattern design lies in visual art. It can create unexpected effects through the disassembly, rotation, translation, and repetition of some simple shapes according to certain rules. Pattern design has large room for development, which also provides a test of students' imagination. Rich visual error patterns can be both shocking and admirable.

3. Group Design and Development Practice

3.1. Design Principles and Concepts

Considering the equipment features of the laboratory weaving sample machine, which constitutes a small jacquard loom, the basic principles of development and design have been emphasized since the beginning of the course. First, simple, and easily transformable geometric elements should be used as the theme; these include points, lines, planes, and the minimum cycle of some patterns as the basis. The most used methods are mathematical geometric methods of translation and symmetry, which are combined with suitable color selection to form a variety of pattern effects. In this development and design work, it was recommended that each group take inspiration from the inlaid paintings of masters and Op Art styles, and continuously take new approaches and innovate to design unique visual illusion works with group characteristics [4-6].

In the group development and design process, many black and white striped twisted contrasting styles were used, including sharp left-right swinging lines, softer symmetrical wavy stripes, scaly shimmering effect patterns, and uneven grid effect patterns. Black and white can best demonstrate the effects of visual errors and are also the most suitable for this theme. Their rhythmic and slightly changing movements provide a feeling of entering a three-dimensional space. This further confirms that the design effect of visual errors has strong individual characteristics. By using different geometric shapes in a periodic arrangement, interweaving, and overlapping warp and weft yarns, and employing various artistic techniques and color matching, the patterns produce different effects under different angles of light; this imparts stimulation, impulse, vibration, and color mixing and overlapping confusion on the retina, resulting in an unstable and lasting pattern effect [7].

3.2. Experimental design

Woven fabrics are formed by the interweaving of warp and weft yarns on a loom. Before the design stage, the first step was to choose the yarn, which is crucial. After several experiments, each group chose the most suitable yarn for weaving. They chose 20s/2 and 20s/3 polyester plied yarns and some single yarns, and some functional yarns were also used in some fabrics. The yarns must have high strength; otherwise, they will easily break during the weaving process. Furthermore, the yarns should be even and free of defects. Polyester plied yarns are good for evenness, have less fluff, are smooth, and have high strength, and are mainly used for woven fabrics and thicker materials such as denim [8]. The specific parameters designed by each group for the woven fabric are reported in Table 1. Both warp and weft yarns were selected as 20s/2-ply yarn. In the fabric weaving trial of each group, the warp and weft density settings were consistent within the group.

However, the settings for warp and weft density differed between groups. Because each group had different settings for warp and weft density, the grams per square meter (gsm) of the fabric also varied. Fabric samples with a higher warp and weft density have a larger gsm.

Weaving experiments demonstrated that weaving preparations come before the actual weaving process. In the weaving preparation phase, the first step was the warp yarn preparation. About 700-800 lengths of neatly arranged yarn, each measuring 3 meters in length, were prepared as warp yarn. Following that was the process of threading the heddles, where the prepared warp yarn was divided into sections and threaded through the heddles of various harness frames based on a predetermined threading pattern. The number of harness frames ranged from 8 to 16. Next was the process of sleying the reed. After completing the threading, the yarn was systematically passed from left to right through steel reed dents according to a sleying diagram. This process involved grouping 2 or 3 warp ends per dent. Finally, there was the process of warp beaming. Once sleying was complete, the yarn ends were divided into multiple strands and tied onto a warp beam. The yarn at the back of the weaving machine was combed and organized, then tied onto the cloth beam, applying a specific tension to wind the yarn onto the cloth beam. Throughout the winding process, the warp yarn was carefully arranged to maintain consistent tension. The machine used for weaving fabric samples was the SLO-02 digital semi-automatic sample loom. The weaving settings were as follows. (1) Turn on the machine – create a sample pattern – create a new pattern (enter the number of shuttles) – draw a pattern board – set the selvage – set the weft density – save (set the file name). (2) Open the control system – open – select the target file – download. (3) Weaving: Prepare and adjust the tension of the warp yarns. Then, switch to the work button, and perform step-by-step shuttle and weft insertion. If the weaving process goes smoothly, switch to the operation button. Keep a close eye on the loom while weaving and press the stop button in case of any problems. Pay attention to weaving safety.

Table 1. The fabric and yarn specifications.

Number	Warp yarn counts (S)	Weft yarn counts (S)	Warp density (roots/10 cm)	Weft density (roots/10 cm)	Fabric weight (g/m²)
Group 1	20/2	20/2	230	248	340
Group 2	20/2	20/2	230	250	342
Group 3	20/2	20/2	250	250	370
Group 4	20/2	20/2	230	270	371

4. Visual Error Pattern Fabric Design Product Description and Exhibition

4.1. Group 1 Finished Product Presentation and Design Description

As shown in Figure 1, the machine diagram of the visual illusion fabric of the first group adopted a 12-piece comprehensive photo threading method, with two healds in one thread, and was woven with a mountain-shaped twill pattern. Figure 2 displays the front and partial views of the fabric. White was used for the warp yarn and black was used for the weft yarn. The final fabric effect is fish scale-shaped, appearing as a diagonal pattern;

however, with careful observation, a fine horizontal stripe effect can be seen. The white and black areas have different proportions, demonstrating a white bird overlapping effect with a more three-dimensional feel.

The charm of fabric often lies in its intricate texture and design. At first glance, this fish scale-patterned fabric presents a distinctive twill effect, reminiscent of fish scales in nature, arranged in a way that is both orderly and whimsical. However, as you draw closer and inspect this "ocean" carefully, you realize that behind each "scale" lies a hidden world. Those seemingly subtle horizontal stripes resemble the ripples on a beach, flowing rhythmically. The combination of white and black is an eternal classic, but in this fabric, they do not just stack upon each other in a simple manner. The white areas are reminiscent of soaring birds, spiraling in a black sky. Their wings seem to flutter softly, giving a sense of ethereal, dreamy ambiance. These white "birds," due to their contrast against the black backdrop, appear as if flying through layers of the sky, creating a visual impression of depth, with nuances ranging from the profound to the superficial, layer upon layer.

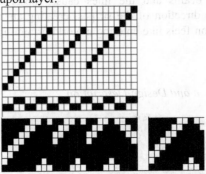

Figure 1. The machine diagram.   Figure 2. The fabric view.

4.2. Group 2 Finished Product Presentation and Design Description

Figure 3. The machine diagram.   Figure 4. The fabric view.   Figure 5. The fabric view.

Figure 3 shows the machine diagram of the visual illusion fabric of the second group. A 12-piece comprehensive photo threading method was used, with two healds in one thread. Figure 4 displays the fabric, which was woven using white as the warp yarn and sky blue as the weft yarn. The surface of the fabric shows irregular twisted lines, and the bright white color combined with the even more vivid sky-blue color creates a light, clean, and transparent beauty. Simultaneously, it presents subtle vertical stripes, which cause the eyes to move along the direction of the stripes under sunlight, leading to a dizzying feeling. Another fabric view is shown in Figure 5; like the fabric shown in Figure 4, the same threading method and machine diagram were used, with white as the warp yarn and alternating red and blue as the weft yarn. Compared to the fabric displayed in Figure 4, it has a more vivid feel with alternating red, blue, and white diagonal stripes, creating a dazzling effect. It also produces uneven vertical stripes, like an electrocardiogram pattern, intensifying the overall dizzying sensation. The contrast between red and blue further enhances this dizzying feeling.

Fabric, seemingly a simple material, in fact, carries a world filled with visual magic. This piece is a prime example. On its surface, the irregular twisted lines seem like dancers moving freely, with each line expressing its own emotions and stories. The delicate white is reminiscent of the first rays of sunlight in the morning – fresh and pure. When this gentle breeze collides with the soft sky blue, it seems to break the boundaries of the sky, making one feel as if they are immersed in an endless blue expanse, experiencing a sense of lightness, cleanliness, and transparent beauty. This is not merely a piece of fabric; it is more akin to a dreamscape. Those faint vertical stripes act as guides within this dream, subtly and quietly leading you into an even more enchanting space. Under the glow of sunlight, these stripes seem to become beams of light, directing your gaze and dazzling the eyes. The interplay between these beams and the lines causes observers to unconsciously shift their focus along the direction of the stripes, creating an almost mesmerizing effect. This dizzying sensation feels like entering a world brimming with magic.

4.3. Group 3 Finished Product Presentation and Design Description

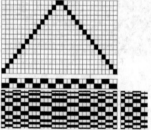

Figure 6. The machine diagram.   Figure 7. The fabric view.   Figure 8. The fabric view.

Figure 6 presents the machine diagram of the visual illusion fabric of the third group, for which a 15-piece comprehensive photo threading method, with two threads in one heald, was used, and which appears as a satin weave fabric. Figure 7 depicts the view of the fabric. White was used as the warp thread and black was used as the weft thread, which creates a striking contrast and showcases the pattern and texture of the fabric very well. As shown in the image, each white circle tends to diffuse outward, and at the edges, it interweaves with another circle. The white color gradually decreases in size from the inside out, while the black color becomes denser, creating a protruding effect. Overall, the fabric has an uneven, three-dimensional visual appearance with some areas appearing concave and others convex.

Figure 8 displays another fabric view. The same threading, heddling, and organization methods as those in the fabric shown in Figure 7 were used. The weft arrangement was as follows: 1 light purple, 6 light blue, 6 sky blue, 4 dark blue, 6 sky blue, 6 light blue, and 1 light purple. This weft arrangement creates a visually pleasing gradient effect, as well as a striped effect with alternating deep and shallow stripes, creating an optical illusion of alternating distance. Additionally, due to the pattern style, the white dots continuously attract attention, making the fabric appear rich and meaningful.

This fabric showcases a visual magic through its color coordination. The gradient from lilac to light blue is reminiscent of the sky at dawn, transitioning from the tranquil lilac to the hopeful light blue, followed by the profound deep blue, then returning to the bright sky blue and light blue, and finally culminating back to the serene lilac. This arrangement of weft threads represents not just a flow of colors but a journey of emotions. The progression from darker to lighter shades combined with the stripe effect imparts a rich layering to the fabric. The alternating dark and light stripes evoke images of undulating mountains or surging waves, providing a dynamic yet harmonious visual experience. This alternation creates an illusion as if viewers are immersed in a three-dimensional space, as though they are traversing through a tunnel of time and space, witnessing varying landscapes and emotional shifts. Meanwhile, the white dot-like patterns resemble twinkling stars in the night sky or crystalline snowflakes on snowy grounds, constantly capturing one's gaze, adding a layer of mystery and depth to the fabric. These dot patterns serve both as embellishments and highlights, endowing the fabric with an indescribable allure. Whenever sunlight or artificial light hits these white dots, they reflect a brilliance, akin to a sky filled with myriad stars, offering a dreamy sensation.

All in all, the design of this fabric ingeniously leverages the elements of color, stripes, and dot patterns, creating a visual effect that is both profound and ever-changing, making one feel as if they are in a magical artistic realm.

4.4. Group 4 Finished Product Presentation and Design Description

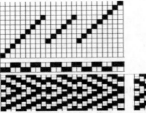  

Figure 9. The machine diagram.   **Figure 10.** The fabric view.   **Figure 11.** The fabric view.

Figure 9 presents the loom setup for the visual error fabric of the fourth group. A 12-piece heald frame threading method was used, resulting in a broken twill pattern. The fabric shown in Figure 10 serves as a comparison to the fabric presented in Figure 8, with white also used as the base color of the warp thread and alternating between sky blue and lake blue. Because these two colors are similar, they appear as a single color from a distance. This fabric uses a color illusion, with sky blue and lake blue forming an arrow together, creating a diagonal pattern from the bottom left to the top right when viewed individually. The colors of the fabric are fresh and bright, with a completely different style from the fabric shown in Figure 10. The design of this fabric ingeniously blends distinct colors and geometric patterns, offering viewers an experience brimming with visual tension. The collision of white warp and black weft is akin to lightning piercing the dark night – striking and impactful. The arrows in the pattern act as directional indicators in the wind, all pointing in one direction, evoking a sense of forward momentum and decisiveness. Each arrow aligns like soldiers in formation, exhibiting uniformity and exuding strong dynamism and vigor. However, upon closer inspection, the visual intrigue unveils itself. Despite the arrows all pointing in the same direction, they remain unconnected, thereby forming a pronounced horizontal stripe effect. This unique design allows the fabric to showcase two textures: the dynamic diagonal lines and the steady horizontal stripes. The alternating black and white stripes resemble the keys of a piano, at times soaring high and at others, dipping low. Under varying light, this interlaced visualization can easily cause dizziness, as if one is enchanted by the fabric's magic, becoming utterly captivated. This is not just a piece of fabric, but a visual feast replete with magic and dreaminess.

Figure 11 presents another fabric view, for which white was used as the warp thread and black was used as the weft thread, creating a strong contrast and easily showing the effects. The arrows in the image all point in the same direction, appearing particularly neat and spectacular. The arrows do not connect with each other, clearly demonstrating the horizontal stripe effect. The fabric displays a twill weave combined with a horizontal stripe effect, with alternating white and black stripes that can easily cause a dizzying sensation under light. This piece of fabric artfully plays with our visual perception, creating an illusion of color. Sky blue and lake blue, although distinct, visually complement each other, intertwining to form a harmony that makes them almost indistinguishable. From a distance, these two colors appear as variations of a single hue, as if nature has imprinted its unique signature on this fabric. The arrow design is especially ingenious. These two similar colors collectively form an upward-pointing arrow, adding a dynamic feel to the fabric. When you focus on just one of the colors, it seems to be revealing a secret: its movement along a diagonal line from the bottom left to the top right. This visual illusion suggests that the fabric conceals a world in motion, filled with rhythm and cadence. Overall, the colors of this fabric are reminiscent of the first rays of morning sunlight – fresh and radiant. It is as if the fabric is a visual poem, expressing the allure of nature and the vitality of life through color and shape.

5. Conclusion

The study of Weaving Technology is a foundational course for the textile engineering major and is recognized as a top-tier course by Minjiang University. In this course design for the practice of weaving technology, four groups of students were able to fully research the Op Art style and Escher's tessellation principles. In the design and development of their works, they used many mathematical methods, such as translation, offset repetition, symmetry, splicing, and rotation. In terms of color application, darker color schemes were used, such as brown, purple, dark red, and black. However, some bright colors were also adopted, such as white for the warp threads, as well as sky blue and bright yellow to form a strong contrast with the dark weft threads, to better achieve the visual error effect. Groups 2, 3, and 4 were also able to extrapolate and comprehensively use control groups, employing different materials to achieve different visual error effects. The combination of theory and practice effectively achieved the course design objectives. The practical component of the course is a test of its teaching quality. This visual "error" in fabric design is intentional by the designers. Through the skillful manipulation of color, texture, and structure, they create effects that seem to be in motion even when static. This design technique demands a high level of precision and a deep understanding of color and texture. Fabric design is often the perfect fusion of art and science. From a scientific perspective, it concerns the precise control of yarn, weaving techniques, and color. From an artistic standpoint, it delves deep into nature, emotions, and human visual experiences. These pieces of fabric are like a microcosm, filled with endless mysteries, inviting people to explore and experience.

Acknowledgment

This research was funded by Minjiang University Teaching Reform First-class Course Construction Project, grant number MJU2020KC315, China Scholarship Council, grant number 202008350058, Fujian science and technology project guidance project, grant number 2022H0049, the Open Project Program of Key Lab for Sport Shoes Upper Materials of Fujian Province, grant number SSUM2202, Fuzhou Science and Technology Major Project, grant number 2021-Z-3 and 2021-ZD-296, Fuzhou Major Science and Technology Project of Jiebang Guashuai, grant number 2022-ZD-007 and Minjiang University Science and Technology Project, grant number MJY21022.

References

[1]Wang P, Zhang M, Wang Y, et al. Sustainable Career Development of Chinese Generation Z (Post-00s) Attending and Graduating from University: Dynamic Topic Model Analysis Based on Microblogging, Sustainability **15** (2023), 1754.
[2]Galanter P. Computational aesthetic evaluation: past and future, *Computers and creativity* **10** (2012), 255-293.
[3]Bonsiepe G. Design and democracy, *Design issues* **22** (2006), 27-34.
[4]Dobrova U P. Op Art in the Works of A, Andreeva (1917-2008): Sources of the Style, *The Actual Problems of History and Theory of Art*3(2013), 332-338.
[5]Chen X, Zhang Y, Wang Y, et al. Optical flow distillation: Towards efficient and stable video style transfer, *Computer Vision-ECCV 2020: 16th European Conference, Glasgow, UK, August 23-28, 2020, Proceedings* **16** (2020), 614-630.
[6]Mikhailov S, Khafizov R, Mikhailova A, et al. Supergraphics as a project and artistic method in design of a modern city, *IOP Conference Series: Materials Science and Engineering* **890** (2020), 012003.
[7]Immelmann B. Wassily Kandinsky's Conception of a Vibration of the Soul: Art Theory at the Crossroads of Esoteric Literature, Popular Science, and Aesthetics, *Genealogy of Popular Science: From Ancient Ecphrasis to Virtual Reality* **2020** (2020), 425.
[8]Johnson S, Echeverria D, Venditti R, et al. Supply chain of waste cotton recycling and reuse: A review, AATCC *Journal of Research* **7** (2020), 19-31.

Design Studies and Intelligence Engineering
L.C. Jain et al. (Eds.)
© 2024 The Authors.
This article is published online with Open Access by IOS Press and distributed under the terms
of the Creative Commons Attribution Non-Commercial License 4.0 (CC BY-NC 4.0).
doi:10.3233/FAIA231420

Exploring Innovation and Development of Yarn Spinning Through Industry-Education Integration: A Practical Teaching Approach

Taohai YAN[a, b,1], Yu LIN[a], Yajing SHI[a], Luming HUANG[c], and Zhaoguo WANG[d]

[a] *Clothing and Design Faculty, Minjiang University, Fuhzou, Fujian, China, 350108*
[b] *Fujian Huafeng New Material Co.,Ltd., Putian, Fujian, China, 351164*
[c] *Chunhui Technology Group Co., Ltd, Fuzhou, Fujian, China, 350018*
[d] *Guobin Yaqi Textile Co., Ltd., Yinchuan, Ningxia, China, 751400*

Abstract: To cultivate outstanding engineering talent capable of both adapting to and spearheading regional economic and social progress, as well as to facilitate the transformation and advancement of local economies and to promote collaboration between universities and regional economies, practical teaching bases should be established. Through the strategic alignment and interactive development of practical teaching bases, it may be possible to deepen the integration between industry and education, as well as the interactions between universities and enterprises. Thus, successful teaching bases leverage the academic strengths of universities and the resources offered by businesses. The approach to industry-education integration revolves around refining the model of collaborative education between universities and enterprises, with a specific focus on refining the talent development process. A case of innovative yarn development design within a spinning study practice teaching base is analyzed in this study to investigate the approach. Within this base, student teams have developed ultra-comfortable yarn, stainless steel fiber/lyocell flame-retardant blended yarn, and stainless steel filament/cotton ply-twisted composite yarn. The case study exemplifies the potential for effective cooperation between universities and enterprises in nurturing talent, leveraging dual-teacher training, providing societal contributions, facilitating employment opportunities, and fostering entrepreneurial initiatives. This collaborative model shows significant potential for comprehensively enhancing the quality of talent cultivation, thereby propelling regional economic and social development.

Keywords: Industry-education integration; Craftsmanship; Yarn development; Innovative design; Practice teaching

1. Introduction

Collaborative talent cultivation through industry-education integration is a critical pathway towards the development of exceptional engineers [1]. In the midst of ongoing scientific and technological revolution coupled with industrial transformation, China's economic and societal progress has been met with significant opportunities as well as challenges [2]. Since the 18th National Congress of the Communist Party of China, General Secretary Xi Jinping has consistently stressed the significance of "key core technologies" for the nation and the persistent need to address "bottleneck" issues within

---

[1] Corresponding Author. Taohai YAN, Email, yantaoh@126.com

engineering and technology fields [3]. To effectively surmount these challenges, the country needs a substantial influx of talented, accomplished engineers with mastery over key core technologies [3]. This imperative not only aligns with President Xi's vision but also hinges upon harnessing the prevailing opportunities of the era, which will require innovation in terms of industry-education integration as well as university-enterprise cooperation [4].

Today, the training of exceptional engineers in China is guided by principles of industry-driven demand and holistic education. This paradigm balances "instrumental rationality" and "value rationality" to underpin the process of talent cultivation. The effects of collaborative talent cultivation through industry-education integration have been evaluated from multiple perspectives [5].

The spirit of craftsmanship has endured across ages. Ancient texts such as the pre-Qin "Mozi," "Zhuangzi," and "Kaogongji in Zhou Rites" encapsulate early notions of the craftsman's spirit. The Ming Dynasty's "Tiangong Kaiwu", written by Song Yingxing, is a concentrated exposition of this same spirit. Craftsmanship, in essence, is the relentless pursuit of excellence in the process of crafting products, emphasizing aspects like design and quality. It entails perpetual enhancement and innovation of skills, coupled with a meticulous and objective approach to creating superior work [6]. This ethos represents an enduring aspiration for quality. Modern applied universities bear the historical mantle of fostering the spirit of craftsmanship and nurturing artisan talents within the framework of industry-education integration and talent cultivation [7].

The present study began with an analysis of the practical teaching of spinning studies in the School of Clothing and Art Engineering, Minjiang University. By harnessing the methodologies of collaborative talent cultivation through industry-education integration, innovative yarn products are developed with the spirit of craftsmanship. Thus, the pedagogical outcomes of industry-education integration are demonstrated through cases of textile innovation.

2. Existing Issues in Collaborative Talent Cultivation via Industry-education Integration

The cotton textile industry is an essential sector in Fujian. With a cotton spinning capacity surpassing 13 million spindles (with over 7 million in the Changle area alone), Fuzhou Province is a major player in the textile industry. The province boasts nearly one hundred cotton spinning enterprises, with more than half of these concentrated in Changle and Fuzhou. Changle's cotton spinning sector is advantageous in terms of its large enterprises, exemplified by Xinhua Yuan Textile Group, Changyuan Textile (Group), and Jinyuan Textile (Group), each overseeing more than 1 million spindles. Enterprises with over 500,000 spindles include Jinyuan, Changyuan, Jinyuan, and Xianglong. The hallmark products of Fujian's cotton spinning industry include cotton, cotton blends, synthetic fibers, synthetic fiber blends; the area also leads the nation in the production of polyester, viscose, and blended yarns. Changle, Fuzhou, and their surrounding areas have become essential bases for synthetic non-cotton yarn and cotton-synthetic blended yarn production in China. Consequently, there is an urgent need to establish a spinning practical teaching base that can be seamlessly linked with enterprises to effectively cultivate applied talents.

In this context, the School of Clothing and Art Engineering, Minjiang University actively promotes university-enterprise cooperation and industry-education integration.

Deepening university-enterprise linkages is a consistent priority for institutions aiming to strengthen practical teaching, highlight the instruction of hands-on skills, and comprehensively enhance the quality of applied talents emerging from universities.

The advancement of industry-education integration and the seamless alignment of universities with enterprises have been a major challenge in terms of cooperative education. On one hand, as industry-education integration develops, university-enterprise convergence has gradually emerged as the main channel for universities to expand their professional practices and internship programs. However, due to the systemic influence of educational institutions, the nexus between universities and enterprises is often superficial, primarily confined to the realm of internships, and thus lacks depth. However, in the context of practical university instruction and teaching base establishment, the latent potential inherent in the convergence of universities with enterprises remains underutilized. Many practical teaching bases primarily serve as experiential learning platforms, with a dearth of momentum or cooperation in terms of university-enterprise integration. Hence, it is imperative to construct practical teaching bases that fully align with university-enterprise collaboration and engender interactive, practice-driven teams. Such strategic initiatives align with the overarching goal of industry-education integration and the seamless fusion of universities and enterprises.

3. Showcasing and Analysis of New Yarn Series Developed with Craftsmanship

3.1. Innovative Development of Ultra-comfortable Yarn

3.1.1. Development Process
(1) Yarn Density and Twist Design

This experiment involved a blend of polyvinyl alcohol (PVA) water-soluble fiber and long-staple cotton fiber, so the desired outcome was a lightweight, soft fabric achieved by high-temperature hydrolysis of the blended materials. Therefore, the yarn density before blending was kept relatively low. Cotton counts normally range from 10S-60S; to align better with the objectives of the experiment, the targeted line density of the blend was set to 45tex.

(2) Spinning Process

After analyzing the properties of PVA fiber and long-staple cotton fiber, and in efforts to reduce costs, appropriate adjustments were made to the production process. Equipment from Tianjin Jiacheng Mechanical and Electrical Equipment Co., Ltd. was applied to optimize resource utilization. Given the equipment's capabilities and the inherent attributes of the raw materials, a carding process was incorporated into the experiment. The formulated process sequence progressed through several steps: Raw material → fiber pretreatment → cotton blending → cotton opening and cleaning → carding → drawing-1 → drawing-2 → roving → spinning → sizing.

(3) Cotton Opening and Cleaning Process

PVA fiber and long-staple cotton fiber have strong hygroscopicity, so temperature and relative humidity are important. Excessively low temperatures or humidity levels cause the cotton fiber surface wax to solidify, weakening the fiber and generating static electricity. Conversely, elevated temperatures or humidity levels soften the cotton wax, escalate fiber friction, and hinder normal stretching; the rollers tend to wind, which causes the sliver to become uneven.

The optimal conditions for effective loosening are achieved within a temperature range of 25-26°C and relative humidity between 55-65%. These conditions balance the cotton wax properties, rendering it suitably pliable for decomposition and conducive to effective fiber opening, dust removal, and stretching. This timeframe is identified as the most opportune for loosening. The main technical parameters of loosening process in this case were a loosening roller diameter of Φ458 mm, loosening roller speed of 280 r/min, and loosening speed ratio of 369 times.

(4) Carding Process

Long-staple cotton fiber has high elasticity and a fluffy quality, so attaining a harmonious balance in the spacing of the material throughout the carding process is important. Notably, both PVA fiber and long-staple cotton fiber have strong hygroscopicity. When the temperature is maintained at 2-26°C and the relative humidity is between 55-65%, the wax on the cotton is suitably pliable, the cotton can readily decompose, and single fibers are conducive to loosening, dust removal, and stretching. These climatic conditions form a opportune juncture for carding. It is important to ensure that equipment is kept dry throughout the process to mitigate issues like winding and congestion. Prudent reduction of the licker-in and cylinder speeds is also necessary to prevent licker-in recycling and cotton knots. Strategically expanding the gap between the cover plate and cylinder also prevents fiber from winding around the cylinder and blocking the cover plate, thereby improving the quality and clarity of the cotton web. Incorporating a leather roller cotton guiding device before the doffing stage enhances the support and stretching of the cotton web, minimizes the tension of the cotton web, minimizes sliver degradation, and improves production efficiency. The main technical parameters of the carding process include a cylinder speed of 500 r/min, cylinder working width of 270 mm, surface line speed ratio (cylinder/licker-in) of 4.1 times, web output speed of 3 m/min, and total draft ratio (doffing/feeding) of 60 times.

(5) Drawing Process

The dryness factor, which is an important concern related to the hygroscopic and fluffy attributes of PVA and long-stable cotton fibers, must be properly considered throughout the drawing process. Within the temperature range of 2-26°C and relative humidity range of 55-65%, the cotton wax is suitably pliable, the cotton readily decomposes, and single fibers are conducive to loosening, dust removal, and stretching, making these the most suitable conditions for drawing. Winding caused by static electricity must also be avoided and irregularities in the sliver must be carefully monitored and prevented. Regular sliver unevenness (mechanical waves) arises due to drafting component malfunctions leading to periodic variations in thickness, while irregular sliver unevenness (drafting waves) stems from erratic movement of suspended fibers within the sliver during drafting, causing alternating thick and thin segments. Stabilizing the components during the drawing process can prevent these problems; if they do occur, the drawing process must be carried out again. To ensure uniformity, the drawing process conducted in this study was a two-pass drawing with a four-strand drawing method in each pass. The main technical parameters of the drawing process included a first pass out speed of 10 m/min, total draft ratio of 6 times, rear area draft ratio of 1.4 times, middle area draft ratio of 1.02 times, and front area draft ratio of 4.21 times.

(6) Roving Process

As mentioned above, the properties of both PVA fiber and long-staple cotton fiber make a temperature range of 25-26°C and relative humidity of 55-65% optimal. Under these conditions, the winding of the roving in the process is moderate and the roving sliver is uniform. It is important to avoid excessive elongation of the roving during this phase to prevent compromised sliver quality. Careful consideration should also be given to roving twist, striking a balance between low and high. Skillful control of temperature and humidity ensures moderate tension of the roving winding, which should not be overly lax or excessively tights. Regular cleaning of the roving machine is vital to prevent fly waste adherence and consequent fiber aggregation, which can lead to hank yarn entanglement and unevenness in the roving sliver. The main parameters of the roving process in this study include a roving count of 500 tex, twist factor of 90, twist of 40.25 T/m, theoretical bobbin speed of 400 r/min, bobbin winding speed of 300 r/min, back area draft ratio of 1.05 times, front area draft ratio of 1.2 times, and mechanical draft of 5.5 times.

(7) Spinning Process

Again, given the hygroscopicity and fluffiness of PVA and long-stable cotton fibers, the optimal temperature and relative humidity for processing are 25-26°C and 55-65%, respectively. These conditions are conducive to a smooth spinning process. Excessive total draft or back zone draft during the spinning can lead to an uneven sliver and should be carefully controlled. Similarly, inappropriate apron clamping, roller spacing, or roller pressure can lead to an uneven sliver. During the spinning process, the winding of the yarn on the bobbin and the bundling of the yarn tube should be monitored to prevent localized thick yarn. The main parameters of the spinning process included a spindle gauge of 70 mm, spindle number of 24 (on both sides), twist factor of 350, twist of 81 T/m, and twist shrinkage rate of 3%.

(8) Fabric Production

The yarn fabricated through the above processes was used to produce fabric samples on a computerized flat knitting machine (Model LXC-252SC 12G, Jiangsu Jinlong Technology Co., Ltd.). The fabric structure was 1+1 rib knitting.

(9) Hydrolysis Process

To ensure the complete dissolution of PVA fiber within the fabric and yarn, a temperature 10°C above the fiber's dissolution temperature must be sustained for a defined period. Boiling water temperature was controlled here at 95±5°C, with high-temperature hydrolysis desizing lasting approximately 120 min.

3.1.2. Tests and Analyses

(1) Yarn Mechanical Properties

The breaking strength of pure cotton yarn is 629.7 CN, corresponding to a breaking strength of 13.8 CN/tex and a breaking elongation rate of 7.6%. In contrast, the blended yarn composed of 40% PVA and 60% long-staple cotton blended yarn has a reduced breaking strength of 494.3 CN, breaking strength is 10.8 CN/tex, and breaking elongation rate of 7.6%. The breaking strength this blended yarn after PVA hydrolysis is 389.8 CN, while its breaking strength is 8.5 CN/tex and its breaking elongation rate is 2.6%. The strength of the blended yarn is lower than that of the pure cotton yarn due to the nature of short PVA water-soluble fiber, which, despite individual fiber strength exceeding that of long-staple cotton fiber, does not have robust cohesion with the long-staple cotton fiber. Consequently, during force-induced yarn stretching, fibers with weaker cohesive bonds succumb first. Notably, the mechanical properties of the blended yarn are further compromised after hydrolysis, as the water-soluble fiber dissolves during the high-temperature hydrolysis process. This reduces the density of long-staple cotton thread and increases the gap between long-staple cotton fibers thus reducing the breaking strength of the cotton fabric.

(2) Yarn Softness

The weft-knitted fabric made of pure cotton yarn has a warp elongation of 36.6 mm, a warp bending length of 18.3 mm, a warp bending stiffness of 150.7 mm, a weft elongation of 22.1 mm, a weft bending length of 11.1 mm, and a weft bending stiffness of 33.4 mm. The weft-knitted fabric of 40% PVA and 60% long-staple cotton blended yarn has a warp elongation of 32.8 mm, a warp bending length of 16.4 mm, a warp bending stiffness of 109.6 mm, a weft elongation of 19.4 mm, a weft bending length of 9.7 mm, and a weft bending stiffness of 22.5 mm. After the PVA hydrolysis process, the weft-knitted fabric of 40% PVA and 60% long-staple cotton blended yarn has a warp elongation of 29.2 mm, a warp bending length of 14.6 mm, a warp bending stiffness of 52.2 mm, a weft elongation of 16.9 mm, a weft bending length of 8.5 mm, and a weft bending stiffness of 10.6 mm. The longitudinal bending stiffness of all fabrics, regardless of blending ratio, is greater than the transverse bending stiffness. This is due to the structure of the fabric coil. The longitudinal direction of the coil consists of two ring-shaped columns, while the horizontal direction is an arc. The longitudinal load-bearing capacity is greater than the horizontal, so the bending stiffness of the fabric in the longitudinal direction is larger. The bending stiffness of pure cotton knitted fabric is relatively large due to the shorter length of PVA water-soluble fiber, which softens the cotton fiber blended yarn. However, the bending stiffness of the fabric after desizing significantly decreases as the water-soluble fiber further dissolves during high-temperature hydrolysis, which reduces the density of long-staple cotton yarn, increases the gap between the long-staple cotton fibers, and further softens the cotton fabric.

(3) Breathability

The weft-knitted fabric made of pure cotton yarn has a breathability rate of 91.7 mm·s-1. The weft-knitted fabric of 40% PVA and 60% long-staple cotton blended yarn has a breathability rate of 86.8 mm·s-1. The weft-knitted fabric of 40% PVA and 60% long-staple cotton blended yarn has a breathability rate of 153.2 mm·s-1 after the PVA hydrolysis process. The breathability rate appears to increase as the content of PVA water-soluble fiber increases. This may be due to the dissolution of the water-soluble fiber during the high-temperature hydrolysis process, which increases the gap between the long-staple cotton fibers, thus increasing the breathability of the cotton fabric.

(4) Yarn Cross-sections

Microscopic examination of yarn cross-sections offers insights into the structures of the material. The pure cotton yarn cross-section exhibits a compact arrangement. In contrast, the PVA/cotton blended yarn shows small gleaming spots on its cross-section that are attributable to the inclusion of PVA. The structure remains relatively tight, with fibers near one another. Hydrolyzed PVA/cotton blended yarn shows a looser cross-section with gaps between the fibers. These inter-fiber gaps contribute to enhanced softness and improved breathable comfort in the yarn (as shown in Fig.1-3).

  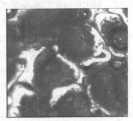

| **Figure 1.** Cross-section of pure cotton yarn | **Figure 2.** Cross-section of PVA/cotton blend yarn | **Figure 3.** Cross-section of PVA/cotton blend yarn after hydrolysis |

3.2. Yarn Innovation Practices of Other Groups

3.2.1. Stainless Steel Fiber/Lyocell Blended Flame-retardant Yarn

The welding industry plays an important role in modern industry. Increased demands for protective attire have arisen from both labor safety requisites and scientific standards. In handheld welding processes, where metal splashes and sparks land on steel or iron surfaces, the cooling impact of the air can cause these particles to contact the welder's clothing. These metal splashes can reach temperatures of 500-700°C. Additionally, iron water sparks with diameters over 1 mm are emitted within 30-50 cm from the welder's body, and can puncture clothing, creating holes or even causing burns on the skin. Considering these factors, the melting point of the fabric worn by welders must be a primary consideration when developing anti-welding spatter solutions. However, existing protective clothing options for specialized welding work rely on a limited array of high-temperature resistant fabrics.

Commonly employed high-temperature resistant fabrics in welding work attire include thick cowhide fabric (protection up to 120°C), thickened and treated pure cotton fabric (protection up to 150°C), and aramid or aramid composite fabric (protection up to 260-280°C). These fabrics are commonly used, but do not completely ensure the safety of welders as they perform necessary tasks. Stainless steel fiber fabric is a noteworthy potential candidate material for protective clothing, as it has a melting point of 1350°C and can work continuously in oxidizing environments below 600°C, giving it excellent heat resistance. Preliminary experiments have shown that 900 g/m2 pure stainless steel fiber woven fabric can effectively counter welding spatter. However, due to the inherent limitations to the spinnability of stainless-steel fiber, pure stainless-steel fabric is heavy, expensive, and has poor thermal and humidity comfort.

The roving process was conducted in this study on an FA467E-type fly frame using the parameters listed in Table 1.

Table 1. Roving frame process parameters

Yarn count (g/10 m)	Draw ratio	Twist factor	Initial tension	Twist (turns/meter)	Spindle speed (rpm)	Roller spacing (mm)	Spacer
12.5	5.2	109	800	2.7	500	12×26×40	7.5

The ring-spinning process was carried out using a BS529J-type ring-spinning machine. The specific spinning process parameters are listed in Table 2.

Table 2. Ring-spinning frame process parameters

Yarn count (tex)	Total draw ratio	Twist factor	Twist (turns/meter)	Spindle speed (rpm)	Roller spacing (mm)	Spacer	Type of steel ring
98.4	26	320	360	5000	20×45	4.5	18#

Utilizing Lyocell fiber as a primary material is a promising approach to creating innovative welding service fabrics. Lyocell fiber boasts excellent thermal and humidity comfort while remaining cost-effective. By incorporating stainless steel fiber as a supplementary component, the composite fabric has enhanced flame retardancy and resistance to holes formed by molten metal. In this study, a stainless-steel fiber/Lyocell blended yarn was spun with a 30% proportion of stainless steel and 70% Lyocell. Figure 4 shows a SEM image of this yarn, where the bright colored fiber is stainless steel short fiber, and the dark colored fiber is Lyocell. This blended material, theoretically, has robust flame retardancy and resistance to molten welding spatter.

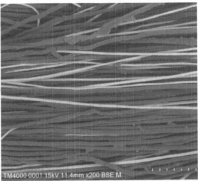

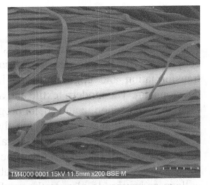

Figure 4. SEM image of stainless-steel fiber/Lyocell blend yarn

Figure 5. SEM image of stainless-steel filament/cotton composite yarn

3.2.2 Stainless Steel Filament/Pure Cotton Ply-twisted Composite Yarn

To enhance both the flame retardancy and melt-hole resistance of flame-retardant cotton, and to improve the comfort of pure stainless-steel fabric while reducing its cost, stainless steel filaments can be added to the comfortable pure cotton flame-retardant fabric. Stainless steel filaments were ply-twisted with cotton yarn in this study to create stainless steel filament/pure cotton ply-twisted composite yarn. Figure 5 shows a SEM image of this yarn, where stainless steel filaments are bright in color and pure cotton yarn is dark in color.

The manufacturing process involved two strands of stainless-steel filaments and one strand of S-twisted pure cotton yarn being ply-twisted with an S-twist on a digital sample ply-twisting machine at a speed of 300 m/min. The ply-twisted yarn was placed on a digital sample doubling machine for twisting at a twist degree to 15T/10 cm and spindle speed of 4000r/min, thus creating the composite yarn.

4. Spinning Education "Craftsman + Innovation" Practical Teaching Training based on Collaborative Industry-Education Integration Model

4.1. Deeply Integrated Collaborative Education Organization Structure

With a concentrated emphasis on the overarching framework of industry-education integration, the College of Clothing and Art Engineering, Minjiang University has established a comprehensive organizational structure for practice-based teaching. This structure is a collective endeavor shared by educational institutions and corporate entities, fostering an environment of resource synergy. The outcome is a dynamic system of multi-dimensional investments, resource harmonization, and mutually advantageous decision-making protocols. Through a meticulous delineation of roles and responsibilities, the partnership is defined to encompass policy support, funding input, daily teaching activities, and operational management. This framework has created a robust operating structure for practical teaching bases. This approach stands out as an industry-leading model in which enterprises directly participate, characterized by a symbiotic relationship generating benefits for all stakeholders. The dual-subject ethos of industry-education integration generates a virtuous cycle, where the collaborative efforts between academics and industrialists reinforce each other.

4.2. Continuous Regional Economic and Social Development

The fundamental purpose of industry-education integration and school-enterprise cooperation is to bolster industrial development, lead and support industrial transformation and upgrading, and harmonize education with economic and social development. The modern textile and apparel industry college is strategically positioned to align with economic and social progress, catering to market demands and addressing the critical challenge of supplying the industry with new talent. A key facet of this approach involves responding to the talent gap, a situation referred to as the "two skins" predicament. This entails bridging the gap between the skills sought by industries and those possessed by prospective graduates. By adopting a supply-side reform strategy, the college endeavors to elevate the quality of education, optimize the supply of skilled professionals, and nurture a cohort of technically adept and high-caliber engineers.

Central to this endeavor is a keen understanding of the evolving requirements for local economic growth. Through effective collaboration with enterprises, the college strives to equip students with robust practical competencies, foster a strong sense of professional ethics in graduates, and cultivate a well-rounded social service orientation. This holistic approach ensures that graduates are not only technically proficient, but also poised to contribute meaningfully to their communities and to the industry at large.

5. Conclusion

The spinning practice teaching model, based on the principles of industry-education integration and collaborative education, capitalizes on the current state of practical teaching. Drawing upon the strategic advantages of the college's location, this model is centered on the establishment of practical teaching bases to optimize education within universities.

The construction of a spinning teaching practice within the university analyzed in this study adheres to a central approach: Connecting classroom teaching with hands-on experimentation, linking practical training to enterprise production lines, harmonizing classroom and workshop instruction, integrating course-based scientific research with enterprise-driven technological advancements, and forging a link between experimental products and enterprise base products. This approach advances the development of the university's spinning practical teaching base, bolstered by a robust internship system in the textile industry. Students' practical spinning skills are honed through a series of innovative yarn development and design courses in alignment with the industry's needs.

Minjiang University's College of Clothing and Art Engineering, cognizant of industrial demands, is dedicated to deeply fostering industry-education integration and collaborative education. This initiative aims to seamlessly interconnect education, talent cultivation, and industrial chains for not only economic development but also the broader modernization and advancement of the textile industry. Transformation of the practical teaching base creates a hub for nurturing talent, student employment, and technological research. This also creates a center for hands-on instruction, a resource for technical consultation, and a foundation for skilled technical talents and "double-qualified" teacher development, as well as a source of industry-education integration innovation. In sum, these efforts contribute significantly to the significant advancement of the Fujian textile industry.

Acknowledgment

This research was funded by China Ministry of Education Industry-Education Cooperation Collaborative Education Project, grant number 202102647012, China Scholarship Council, grant number 202008350058, Fujian science and technology project guidance project, grant number 2022H0049, Fuzhou Science and Technology Major Project, grant number 2021-Z-3 and 2021-ZD-296, and Project of Jiebang Guashuai, grant number 2022-ZD-007.

References

[1] Lin J, Geng L. Multi-party Collaborative Education: A New Way to Train High-Quality Engineering Talents in China, *IFEES World Engineering Education Forum-Global Engineering Deans Council (WEEF-GEDC)* **1** (2020), 1-5.
[2] Wu F, Lu C, Zhu M, et al. Towards a new generation of artificial intelligence in China, *Nature Machine Intelligence* **2** (2020), 312-316.
[3] Zhang L. The application of adaptive analytic hierarchy process driven by multisource big data in the training of school-enterprise joint engineering ability, *Scientific Programming* **2022** (2022), 1-14.
[4] Chu H. Research on a New Mode of Integration of Production and Education for Applied Undergraduates, *economic and social development* **4** (2022), 68-72.
[5] Chen M. The Application of Information Technology in Classified Training and Layered Teaching of Marketing Specialty in Higher Vocational Colleges Under the Integration of Industry and Education, *International Conference on Frontier Computing* **2023** (2023): 1106-1115.
[6] Li H, Pang Z. Research on the Cultivation Path of Craftsmanship Spirit of Skilled Talents Based on Professional Post Group, *2nd International Conference on Education, Language and Art* **2023** (2023), 158-166.
[7] Maddock J T. Engineering the Body, Mind, and Soul: Engineering's Endurance in a Technoscientific Society and the Creation of New Entities Through Power/Knowledge Assemblages and Practical Scientific Technologies in Education, *The University of Wisconsin-Madison* **1** (2023), 1-24.

Design Studies and Intelligence Engineering
L.C. Jain et al. (Eds.)
© 2024 The Authors.
This article is published online with Open Access by IOS Press and distributed under the terms
of the Creative Commons Attribution Non-Commercial License 4.0 (CC BY-NC 4.0).
doi:10.3233/FAIA231421

AI-Assisted Design for Intangible Cultural Heritage: A Study on the Tujia Hand-Waving Dance

Anguo WU[a] and Rong CHANG[b,1]

[a, b] *Beijing Institute of Graphic Communication*

Abstract. Taking the Tujia hand-waving dance as an example, this study aims to apply AI technology to design to improve the design efficiency of intangible cultural heritage and promote the development and communication of related digital collections. Firstly, based on the video of inheritors' performance, the study establishes a semantic dataset of the typical postures of Tujia hand-waving dance. Then, the study tries 3D reconstruction of the human body from the single-view images using AI algorithms. Later, the designer carves the details of the 3D models generated by AI. Finally, the human-AI co-created 3D models are transformed into NFT works. This study initially confirms that not only the AI-assisted workflow may obviously reduce the workload that designers need to invest in the early stage of modeling, but also can efficiently connect the links of data collection, 3D modeling, detail carving, and morphological transformation, thus improving the design efficiency of intangible cultural heritage.

Keywords. human-AI co-creation, intangible cultural heritage, 3D modeling, NFT

1. Introduction

The Tujia hand-waving dance is an ancient sacrificial dance included in the national intangible cultural heritage list. Inheriting the hand-waving dance in a contemporary cultural environment needs the support of innovative design and communication, which is also low-cost, flexible, and efficient at the same time. To explore the role AI-assisted design can play in this area, we carried out this experimental design. As shown in Figure 1, our research frame consists of the following parts.

- Design elements extraction. At this stage, we conducted fieldwork, filmed inheritors' performance, built the image dataset, and selected the representative dance poses.
- AI-driven 3D modeling. At this stage, we constructed the computing framework, preprocessed images, and reconstructed the human body from single-view images.
- Manual refinement of the 3D model. At this stage, we drew the main view, sculpted the details of the 3D models, designed the style, and named the work series.
- NFT creation. At this stage, we casted the NFTs and authenticated them.

---

[1] Corresponding author, Beijing Institute of Graphic Communication, No. 1 (band -2) Xinghua Street, Daxing District, Beijing, China; E-mail: changrong-bj@bigc.edu.cn

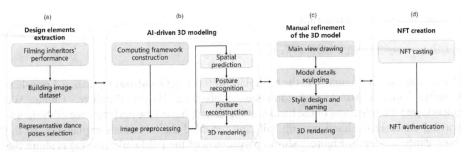

Figure 1. The research frame of AI-assisted design for the Tujia hand-waving dance.

2. Related Work

2.1. Single-view 3D dance posture reconstruction

The research reconstructs 3D model from frontal photos of the inheritors, involving algorithms such as gesture recognition, spatial prediction, and image translation. In terms of 2D posture reconstruction, previous research was based on OpenPose and image translation [1,2] to achieve the recognition and reconstruction of dance postures [3]. 3D reconstruction focuses on reconstructing pose using as little information as a single view [4,5,6,7,8,9]. Related work has initially achieved 3D reconstruction of the human body from single-view images or videos [10, 11, 12, 13, 14, 15, 16]. PIFuHD maps 2D images to 3D surfaces by predicting front and back normal maps in image space [17]. Its pre-training requires expensive computing resources and big data. But fine-tuning based on pre-trained models will be much more convenient. This research is based on PIFuHD to quickly generate 3D models, and then perform subsequent manual carving and scene rendering to realize the co-creation of humans and AI.

2.2. Blockchain-based NFTs

Previous studies have proposed that distributed protocols and cryptocurrencies can ensure the ownership of digital artworks, thereby promoting the development of the digital art market [18, 19]. Researchers believe that the art blockchain provides creators with opportunities to get closer to content consumers and buyers of cultural products [20], changing the ownership structure of digital artworks, forming two parts: collective ownership and private collections [21]. Blockchain-based NFTs present exciting opportunities for intangible cultural heritage. Traditionally, cultural products related to intangible cultural heritage are displayed and sold in tourist destinations, and most of them are physical products. For dance, this approach has many limitations. Our research attempts to digitize and transform cultural products into NFT collections and explore new ways in which intangible cultural heritage dance can be disseminated and sold in the contemporary cultural environment.

3. Design elements extraction

3.1. Inheritors interview and performance filming

We conducted a field survey in the birthplace of the Tujia hand-waving dance, Longshan County, Xiangxi Minority Autonomous Prefecture, Hunan Province, China. We interviewed the inheritors of the hand-waving dance, filmed the performance of the hand-waving dance in the hand-waving hall, and recorded the inheritor's explanation of the main dance sequence. Figure 2 shows part scenes of the fieldwork: row (a) is about the survey on the big hand-waving dance, and row (b) is about the survey on the small hand-waving dance.

Figure 2. Field survey in the birthplace of the Tujia hand-waving dance.

3.2. Representative dance poses selection

The big hand-waving dance is a dance performed by the Tujia people to worship the ancestors of the Eight Great Kings. During the big hand-waving dance, the sound of drums is deafening, and the men hold sticks or short knives, like soldiers on the battlefield. The small hand-waving dance poses are based on women's labor scenes and daily life, which are brisk and lively. We selected four representative poses from the big hand-waving dance and fourteen representative poses from the small hand-waving dance. As shown in Figure 3, these selected poses with rich narrative attributes and visual appeal are organized into four series of works.

4. AI-driven 3D modeling

The computational framework of AI-driven 3D modeling was referred to PIFuHD, which has a multi-level framework: a coarse level that integrates global geometric information by taking the down-sampled images as input and producing backbone images, and a fine level that adds more subtle details. A TelsaK80 GPU was used for computing. Figure 4 shows the process of modeling. Firstly, each single-view image was preprocessed, including cutting, binarization, denoising, and edge enhancement, to form a standard binary image of 512 * 512 pixels. After that, the frontside and backside normal maps of the single-view binary image were predicted based on the image translation algorithm pix2pixHD. Subsequently, the normal maps were converted into coordinates in 3D space, and the position of the Z-axis of each point in 3D space was calculated by the pixel-aligned depth predictor. At the same time, the single-view binary image was synchronized to the lightweight human pose function for posture recognition and extraction. When the normal maps, spatial coordinates, and posture were determined, the value was recompiled from computer language to 10000 to 100000 3D surfaces of the 3D model with the pythoch3D function. Finally, the 3D human mesh diagram was rendered and saved in obj format for the subsequent carving.

Figure 3. Representative poses of the hand-waving dance were organized into four series of works.

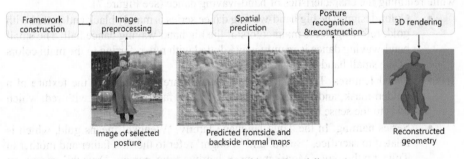

Figure 4. The process of AI-driven 3D modeling.

It can be seen from Figure 5 that the AI-driven 3D modeling, which is based on a single-view image and without any additional information, basically completed the 3D modeling tasks. However, these AI-generated 3D models also have obvious flaws, such as missing parts, rough texture, etc., which means they need to be refined.

Figure 5. Some results of AI-driven 3D modeling.

5. Manual refinement of the 3D model

When manually carving 3D models, the traditional approach is to conduct three-dimensional carving referring to the three views of the object, including the main view, side view, and top view. In the previous work step, AI-driven modeling completed the overall structure of the 3D model, which has greatly reduced the workload of human designers. At this stage, the designer only needs to perfect the frontside structure and texture of the model referring to the main view (see Figure 6).

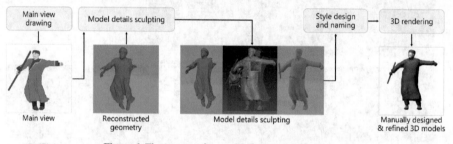

Figure 6. The process of manual refinement of the 3D model.

In terms of art style, we designed an abstract and modern appearance for the work while retaining the characteristics of hand-waving dance (see Figure 7).

- Color design. The big hand-waving dance series is mainly black and dotted with gold, referring to the main colors of the big hand-waving dance hall. The small hand-waving dance is mainly white dotted with red, referring to the main colors of the small hand-waving dance hall.
- Facial features. The abstract facial features are covered with the texture of a golden mask, and the forehead of the female faces are dotted with red, which adds to the sense of mystery.
- Series naming. In the Tujia language family, 'Wengke' means gold, which is related to sacrifice. 'Busuo' and 'Yongni' refer to the first father and mother in Tujia mythology. 'Modi' means a hardworking person. 'Yuezhi' means an excellent farmer. Combining the above words, we named the four series of works respectively as 'Wenke Busuo', 'Wenke Yongni', 'Modi Wenke Yongni', and 'Yuezhi Wenke Yongni'.

Wenke Busuo   Wenke Yongni

Modi Wenke Yongni   Yuezhi Wenke Yongni

Figure 7. The 3D works of Tujia hand-waving dance.

6. NFT creation

To develop cultural and creative products of Tujia hand-waving dance that adapt to the new cultural and technological environment, we use NFT art as a way of innovative communication and sales. The above series of works were cast, certificated, and finally released on the NFT China platform on April 8, 2023 (see Figure 8).

¥9999   ¥9999   ¥9999   ¥9999

Figure 8. The NFTs of the Tujia hand-waving dance.

7. Conclusion

How to introduce emerging technologies, such as artificial intelligence and blockchain, into the workflow to improve the design efficiency and promote communication and commercial transformation of intangible cultural heritage is the core issue of this research. Taking the Tujia hand-waving dance as an example, comprehensive AI-driven 3D modeling and manual refinement, we created 3D models from single-view images of represented dance postures of Tujia hand-waving dance and transferred them to the NFT collections. The experimental creation process and results preliminarily confirm that the human-AI co-creation could significantly reduce the workload and cost that human designers need to invest in. In addition, the digital process significantly improves the overall efficiency of the design work.

With the widespread application of AI technology in the field of art and design, human designers need to master more IT skills. AI specialists are convinced that there's some evidence that today's larger models have some creative capability, but it is still rudimentary. When designers have more aesthetic ideas to express, the role of AI is still limited. The value of art and design lies in the expression of multiculturalism and the exploration of human creativity. Under the human-AI collaborative mode, this core value remains unchanged. Future research should pay more attention to fair access to AI technology, that is, to ensure that designers of different nationalities, languages, and technical resources can more easily use the latest AI technology for creation, thereby helping designers express their culture and ideas faster and better.

Acknowledgments

Funding from the Beijing Social Science Fund Project (No.19XCB007) is gratefully acknowledged.

References

[1] D. Osokin, Real-time 2d multi-person pose estimation on CPU: Lightweight OpenPose, (2018), arXiv preprint arXiv:1811.12004.

[2] C. Chan, S. Ginosar, and T. Zhou, Everybody dance now, in: Proceedings of the IEEE/CVF international conference on computer vision, (2019), 5933-5942.

[3] T. C. Wang, M. Y. Liu, J. Y. Zhu, A. Tao, J. Kautz, and B. Catanzaro, High-resolution image synthesis and semantic manipulation with conditional GANs, in: Proceedings of the IEEE conference on computer vision and pattern recognition, (2018), 8798-8807.

[4] X. Li, S. Liu, K. Kim, S. D. Mello, V. Jampani, M. Yang, and J. Kautz, Self-supervised single-view 3d reconstruction via semantic consistency, in: Proceedings of the European Conference on Computer Vision, (2020), 677–693.

[5] D. Vicini, S. Speierer, and W. Jakob, Differentiable signed distance function rendering, *ACM Transactions on Graphics (TOG)* **41** (2022),1–18.

[6] K. Chen, C. B. Choy, M. Savva, A. X. Chang, T. Funkhouser, and S. Savarese, Text2shape: Generating shapes from natural language by learning joint embeddings, in: Proceedings of the Computer Vision–ACCV 2018: 14th Asian Conference on Computer Vision, (2018), 100-116.

[7] S. Saito, S. Huang, R. Natsume, S. Morishima, A. Kanazawa, and H. Li, PiFu: Pixel-aligned implicit function for high-resolution clothed human digitization, in: Proceedings of the IEEE/CVF international conference on computer vision, (2019), 2304-2314.

[8] Z. Zheng, T. Yu, Y. Wei, Q. Dai, and Y. Liu, Deephuman: 3D human reconstruction from a single image, in: Proceedings of the IEEE/CVF International Conference on Computer Vision, (2019), 7739-7749.

[9] R. Liu, C. Vondrick, Humans as light bulbs: 3D human reconstruction from thermal reflection, in: Proceedings of the IEEE/CVF Conference on Computer Vision and Pattern Recognition, (2023), 12531-12542.

[10] G. Pavlakos, V. Choutas, N. Ghorbani, T. Bolkart, A. A. Osman, D. Tzionas, and M. J. Black, Expressive body capture: 3D hands, face, and body from a single image, in: Proceedings of the IEEE/CVF conference on computer vision and pattern recognition, (2019), 10975–10985.

[11] G. Tiwari, D. Antic, J. E. Lenssen, N. Sarafianos, T. Tung, and G. Pons-Moll, Pose-NDF: Modeling human pose manifolds with neural distance fields, in: Proceedings of the European Conference on Computer Vision, (2020), 572–589.

[12] M. Kocabas, N. Athanasiou, and M. J. Black, Vibe: Video inference for human body pose and shape estimation, in: Proceedings of the IEEE/CVF conference on computer vision and pattern recognition, (2020), 5253–5263.

[13] N. Kolotouros, G. Pavlakos, M. J. Black, and K. Daniilidis, learning to reconstruct 3D human pose and shape via model-fitting in the loop, in: Proceedings of the IEEE/CVF International Conference on Computer Vision, (2019), 2252–2261.

[14] K. Lin, L. Wang, and Z. Liu, End-to-end human pose and mesh reconstruction with transformers, in: Proceedings of the IEEE/CVF Conference on Computer Vision and Pattern Recognition, (2021), 1954–1963.

[15] G. Moon, K. M. Lee, I2l-meshnet: Image to-lixel prediction network for accurate 3D human pose and mesh estimation from a single RGB image, in: Proceedings of the European Conference on Computer Vision, (2020), 752–768.

[16] D. Rempe, T. Birdal, A. Hertzmann, J. Yang, S. Sridhar, and L. J. Guibas, Humor: 3D human motion model for robust pose estimation, in: Proceedings of the IEEE/CVF International Conference on Computer Vision, (2021), 11488–11499.

[17] S. Saito, T. Simon, J. Saragih, and H. Joo, PIFuHD: Multi-level pixel-aligned implicit function for high-resolution 3D human digitization, in: Proceedings of the IEEE/CVF Conference on Computer Vision and Pattern Recognition, (2020), 84-93.

[18] M. McConaghy, G. McMullen, G. Parry, Visibility and digital art: Blockchain as an ownersh layer on the Internet, *Strategic Change* **26** (2017), 461-470.

[19] M. Zeilinger, Digital art as 'monetised graphics': Enforcing intellectual property on the blockchain, *Philosophy & Technology* **31** (2018), 15-41.

[20] N. Malik, Y. Wei, G. Appel, L. Luo, Blockchain technology for creative industries: Current state and research opportunities, *International Journal of Research in Marketing* **40** (2023), 38-48.

[21] A. Whitaker, Art and blockchain: A primer, history, and taxonomy of blockchain use cases in the arts, *Artivate* **8** (2019), 21-46.

Design Studies and Intelligence Engineering
L.C. Jain et al. (Eds.)

doi:10.3233/FAIA231422

Sustainable Product Design of Innovative Design Methods and Case Studies

Weishu YANG[a,b]

[a]*School of Communication & Design Art, Yunnan University of Finance and
Economics, Kunming, China,*
[b]*Faculty of Educational Sciences, University of Helsinki, Finland*
weishu.yang@helsinki.fi

Abstract. Sustainable design is an important design strategy for people to establish a healthily developmental circular economy. With the development, product design fields have changed accordingly, many successful product designs were created for sustainable effects with innovative design methods, including the designs of end-of-life treatment, product life cycle, and product-service system (PSS). There were some design solutions in design cases ranging from product itself or offered services, and these sustainable product designs utilized existing or new skills and technologies, utilizing resources and materials which were manufacturable and maintained to benefit locally, to achieve benefits on the various aspects of sustainability e.g., social, environmental, and economic. Analyzing and evaluating these design methods applied in typical design cases, assisted to summarize effective design approaches and strategies in sustainable product design. Some values behind the design were thus recognized based on the evaluated criteria which were used to judge product quality. The findings indicated the relevant design interventions in response to the design solutions could influence to reach sustainability, thereby assisting designers and researchers to learn closely.

Keywords. Product Design, Sustainable Design, Innovative Design Method, end-of-life treatment, Product Life Cycle, Product-Service System

1. Introduction

In 1972, American designer Victor Papanek first proposed in his book called "Designing for the Real World" [1], he explained "Designers should abandon those fancy and useless products, make rational use of limited resources, and create new ideas for our world. Provide rational and responsible design." This view reflects the concerns about environmental and social resource issues. At that time, the global economy benefited from the development of some applicative new technologies, materials, and energies, but people did not realize that the results of the economic growth would harm nature environment. Until global natural disasters emerged, after suffering from natural disasters and environmental pollution, people began to rethink the relationship between people and nature, and between people and products. People began to gradually shift the traditional resource-dependent economy into a circular economic model that relies on ecological resources, and circular economy has been gradually promoted globally. Sustainable design has become an important design strategy for people to establish a healthily developmental circular economy. With the development, product design fields have also changed accordingly, and many successful product designs were created in sustainable design. Our previous study [2] discussed the context that design works in the design industry have moved toward project work and more often collaborative multidisciplinary projects. Thus, the design work is to be characterized as project-based, fluid, and enhanced by design practices. In design education, requiring student designers recognize the characteristics brought by the changes with sustainable design development, and learn the increasingly innovative design methods and tools across various disciplines. This study was to analyze and evaluate the design cases, and to summarize innovative ideas and methods applied in sustainable product design e.g., the idea of end-of-life treatment, product life cycle design, and product-service system (PSS) design. To focus on analyzing the adopted ideas and approaches, those values thus were recognized based on the evaluated criteria which were used to judge product quality. The aim was to find what are the relevant design interventions in response to those design solutions, which could influence to reach sustainability.

2. Theoretical Background

Initially, sustainable design ideas came from the concept of sustainable development. In 1987, the World Commission on Environment and Development was established in the United Nations and studied the issue of "Our common future". The organization defined "sustainable development" for the first time as the development that meets the needs of the present without compromising the ability of future generations to meet their own needs. Another definition came from Paul Hawken and presented the basic assumptions of the concept in an accessible way: "Leave the world better than you found it, take no more than you need, try not to harm life or the environment, make amends if you do" [3]. The ideas behind these are to achieve economic development and prosperity in human society and require people to maintain ecosystems and make rational use of natural resources. The concept of sustainable design was grounded in the development of our society, and it was interpreted as: it is a strategic design activity that combines products and services to create and develop sustainable solutions to meet the specific needs of consumers [4].

Three design methods can be proposed into design practice for sustainable product design, namely end-of-life treatment of products, product life cycle design [4], and product-service system (PSS) design [5]. For an example of the PSS design, sustainable innovation is around one idea of changing customers' behaviours, specifically, transforming can be created by considering how products are delivered and consumed. This is exemplified by applying the PSS design method. The idea behind this is that services offered by companies will be fulfilled with people's needs, but not products; the physical artifact of a product is not necessary to customers. By focusing on functionality, product designers are required to ask whether a tangible product is needed or whether it would be added with corresponding services, to raise environmental and social benefits from the PPS design.

For study purposes, some criteria by which we judged product quality were broader and built on environmental, economic, and social [6]. The successful sustainable product designs could be evaluated with the proposed criteria: need, suitability, usability, relative affordability, local manufacture, local control and repair, advancement, and empowerment. With the criteria, the evaluated framework was structured for references (Table 1). The first set of factors is related to product itself; these reflect more approaches to products that focus on "user-orientated" ways of promoting social sustainability. The second set of factors is related to product design and production locally. The final set of factors is related to the use models, they demand diverse ways of doing things and thinking things, advancement is of adding new jobs and skills in corporations, and empowerment is to enable relevant community locally by design. The findings emphasized that the sustainable design progresses from product itself to production process, and to business model, and social sustainability become more service-focused versus user-focused.

Table 1. The evaluation framework with the criteria

Use models	Advancement: Dose it create jobs and skills in companies or communities?		Empowerment: Dose it empower people to own and develop the design solution?	
Process	Local manufacture: Can it be manufactured locally?	Local control: Can it be controlled and maintained locally?	Repairing: Can it be repaired and retrieved locally?	
Product	Needs: Do the users and the communities need it?	Suitability: Is it socially, culturally, and environmentally appropriate?	Usability: Is the solution easily understood and easy to use?	Relative Affordability: Is it accessible and affordable?

3. Innovative Design Methods and Case Studies

There were many cases of product design concerning sustainable design, some were more successful than others. These design solutions ranged from product itself or offered services, and the sustainable products utilize existing or new skills and technologies, resources, and materials, to benefit locally and its supply chains. Through exploring the applied approaches in these cases e.g., the idea of end-of-life treatment, product life cycle design, and PSS design, the interventions of the innovative design were learned closely.

3.1. The Idea of End-of-Life Treatment

The concept of end-of-life treatment refers to applying effective treatment technologies on emerging wastes at the end of product production or use process. This concerns the critical issues in developing environmental management strategies. Aiming at some possible damages from the specific products to the environment, the formulated feasible method is conducive to eliminating environmental pollution and slowing down the development of pollution and damage caused by product manufacture. This is an important design strategy. Initially, people understood the environmental pollution and damage issues, which caused people to worry about pollution effects, and thus noticed how the environment must be protected ecologically. Returning to products, "end-of-life treatment" mainly concerns how to make the emerging wastes reduce negative impacts on the environment at the end of a product's lifespan and think of the possible solutions to turn the wastes into treasure. For example, a way of combination strategy is adopted to extend product lifespan, which is utilizing the product parts design to increase the possible flexibility of a product, i.e., the multiple functions design will address the product's parts to meet opportunities of various uses under different situations.

There are many related cases in daily life, e.g., dealing with discarded plastic bottles from the ideas of the Coca-Cola company and the water brand Evian. Plastic material is difficult to degrade. If the bottles are randomly thrown into the environment, it will cause a lot of pollution. Therefore, considering how to dispose of discarded bottles is a challenge that designers need to think about. Coca-Cola used the design of end-of-life treatment, aimed at utilizing discarded plastic to transform its bottles use into interesting and practical items, to encourage consumers to recycle beverage bottles. Specifically, by repurposing the useless bottles by creating special bottle caps, the finished plastic beverage bottles were turned into bubble makers for children to play with (see Figure 1, left), brushes for painting, and other uses.

Figure 1. The bottle redesign of Coca-Cola (left) and the recycled plastic bottles of Evian (right)

To compare with the method of Coca-Cola, Evian adopted a different way to approach discarded bottles. They released a kind of label-free bottle made of recycled plastic on a recycling solution at the end of the product lifespan. To implement a fully circular bottle design they challenged the industrial restrictions in technology and production. The recyclable 400-milliliter bottle was made of recycled polyethylene terephthalate (RPET) and featured an embossed logo instead of a label, see Figure 1, right. However, the pink cap was made from virgin high-density polyethylene (HDPE) and oriented polypropylene (OPP), i.e., these were approximately fully recycled.

Evian adopts a circular method with technologies for its plastic usage, where the production of plastic material will be kept within economy and out of nature, which means the bottles will be made from recycled plastic, whereby are retrieved at the end of the product's lifespan. Additionally, considering the works for local sustainability through empowering communities and applying advanced technologies, they collaborated with other units such as governments, recycling industry partners, and consumers over the world to increase collecting plastic bottles and recycling rates. For example, in the United States, they established a Closed Loop Fund which has developed large-scale recycling infrastructure. In Indonesia, it has worked with research partners to analyse waste captured by an interceptor technology which is a way of stopping plastic waste from entering oceans. Through collaboration with a variety of units, they have been keeping on supporting recycling solutions to ensure bottles were recycled suitably.

Cozy & Green is another case of utilizing the end-of-life treatment method to treat discarded bottles for cycling use solution. With the launch of their zero-waste shopping program, they created a mobile app-based service that offered a convenient way for people to shop from refill stores. The service offline was established through they can pick up reusable bottles from customers, refill and deliver them to customers' doors. They found a lot of problems in this product delivery process with refill stores based on the research with customers, which mainly included a lack of refill and delivery services, inconvenience of the shopping experiences due to the extra effort, and difficulty to find nearby refill stores. For solving the problems, they created a mobile application that enables connecting local refill stores for making online orders for customers in the area. Based on the received information, their workers can pick up customers' bottles to refill and deliver them back to their homes.

They focused on utilizing reusable bottles and customers' needs for convenient shopping experiences. The online solution was created to suitably increase the convenience of shopping events. At the intersection of sustainability, retail, and technology, the app-based service was created to take on challenges with applied information communication technology (ICT), and out of zero-waste shopping, and achieved the sustainable product design with the evaluation framework, see Table 2.

Table 2. Evaluation of the mobile app-based service

Use models	Advancement: Created jobs and skills in the company, developing the training in the consumers.		Empowerment: Established the connection relationship among consumers, refill stores, and Cozy & Green.	
Process	Local manufacture: To produce the design with the provided service locally.	Local control: To maintain and develop the project with refill stores locally.		Repairing: No need of repairing and retrieving physical products.
Product	Needs: The consumers who own environmental consciousness were strongly desired.	Suitability: These were appropriate among consumers, refill stores, and Cozy & Green.	Usability: Created a convenient way, this was easily understood and easy to use.	Relative Affordability: It was limited by the area's size. Need the relative web services in the areas.

3.2. Product Life Cycle Design

The product life cycle design is to carry out the design intervention from the source of product production to extend to product waste e.g., considering on raw material, manufacture technology, needs from different customers, etc., and these impacts required to consider in a product's lifespan with design strategy. The obtained design concepts can be implemented in real situations and achieve sustainable goals. Compared with the end-of-life treatment strategy that occurs after environmental pollution and waste, people realize that they should notice environmental protection in the beginning. Such an idea of post-pollution treatment is viewed as a remedial measure. People realize that the applied approaches after pollution cannot completely solve those environmental problems, thus proposing the method for products' life cycle. We must pay increasing attention to the idea of clean production at the beginning so that it is possible to minimize pollution and reduce environmental impacts during product production and use process. The strategy of a product's life cycle requires considering multiple factors at the source for sustainability, i.e., approaching source control from the beginning. A loop process with the focus of the various stages is shown in Table 3.

Table 3. The stages focus on the product life cycle design

The stages	The focuses
Product planning stage	Need to consider clean, renewable, and non-polluting raw materials in the beginning.
Product production stage	A whole-process clean production method is adopted to avoid pollution and waste of resources.
Product use stage	Need to reduce environmental load to the maximum extent when using the product.
Product discarded stage	When a product reaches the end of its lifespan in service, the parts and materials can be reused to realize recycling use in the industry chain and form a sustainable production of garbage-free, pollution-free, and renewable.

In a design practice of bamboo furniture, regarding the life circle assessment theory, the study of Deng et al., (2023) proposed the process and strategy of sustainable product design as shown in Figure 2.

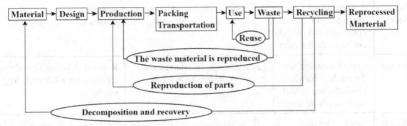

Figure 2. A sustainable product design process and strategy

One typical example of no waste and no pollution in product life cycle is from bamboo material products and the material itself. Bamboo has many advantages such as environmental protection, shorter growth cycle, higher yield, and higher strength. In this case, MOSO is an international company relying on the Chinese bamboo industry in the development of innovative and sustainable bamboo products. The range of products is divided into some product groups e.g., flooring and panels. They offered a natural, fast-growing alternative with the proven sustainable bamboo products based on publishing the environmental impacts of the bamboo products, i.e., some relative studies concerned Environmental Product Declarations (EPDs) and Life Cycle Assessment (LCA). More specifically, EPDs according to ISO 14025 standard (ISO, 2006c) nowadays is a well-acknowledged tool to communicate credible information about the environmental performance of a product based on an LCA study [7]. They are defined as "providing quantified environmental data using predetermined parameters and where relevant, additional environmental information." At that time, collaborating with the research institutes, they presented a full LCA study for partial bamboo products. With developing various verified EPDs for the product ranges reported the results about low environmental impacts in manufacture. Specifically, from the report of Laminated (EN15804), online documentation, involved the manufacture of the solid panel and beam regarding some visually appealing products. Stage A of the process involved disposing of bamboo strips by gluing together and with a hot press way. These (in Table 4) were collected to evidently evaluate for environmental impact results.

Table 4. GB, GF, GL, and respective standard deviations (partial results)

EE	Unit	A1	A2	A3	A4	A5
GB	kg CO_2 eqv.	-1.13E+3	4.29E-3	-1.08E+1	-4.75E-2	7.30E-1
GF	kg CO_2 eqv.	9.57E+1	9.28E+0	2.00E+2	1.07E+2	2.92E+1
GL	kg CO_2 eqv.	2.90E-2	3.40E-3	5.42E-2	1.14E-1	1.09E-2

EE: Environmental Effects, GB: Global warming potential - Biogenic, GF: Global warming potential – Fossil, GL: Global warming potential - Land use and land use change

In sum, through using the product life cycle design each phase of products' lifespan was involved, whereby the goal of eco-impacts could be reached. MOSO applied the product studies, as an effective way with the partners, to obtain the evaluated results where sustainability was proven within product production and achieved the sustainable product design with the evaluation framework, see Table 5.

Table 5. Evaluation of the MOSO bamboo products

Use models	Advancement: Created jobs and skills in the company, and its supply chains in the industry.		Empowerment: Empowered customers to achieve product applications with ecological and sustainable development.		
Process	Local manufacture: To produce bamboo products locally and their supply chains.	Local control: To manage and maintain the products locally.		Repairing: To repair and retrieve locally with a full recycling strategy.	
Product	Needs: Met the requirements of highest technical and quality standards, and from sustainable manufacture.	Suitability: Enabled the full life cycle of product safety, and well-being of people involved.	Usability: Provided the use of expertise and higher standards.		Relative Affordability: Offered to worldwide needs, with the backbone of the Chinese bamboo industry.

3.3. Product Service System (PSS) Design

With the development of sustainable design, designers and researchers have paid close attention to sustainable issues and environmentally friendly design, e.g., green design, low carbon, etc. Among them, the PSS design has received more notice because it has the characteristics of environmental protection, social and economic effects. What is a PSS design? According to the interpretation of the United Nations Environment Program in 2002, this can be understood as the result obtained by utilizing an innovative strategy under a new situation or context, e.g., a bike-sharing system is viewed as a typical PSS design. In this sense, the design focus is shifted from use-oriented product design to providing integrative products-service systems to meet people's needs better and effectively. The explanation highlighted such a shift in design from material products to non-material services. In other words, service design is an extension and expansion of physical product design. It is a whole-process design based on material products, and the purpose is to provide users with high-quality product services. In daily life purchasing products means gaining a lot of corresponding services from product providers. For examples, we buy cars to intend automobile sales services and buy mobile phones for mobile communication services. Designing a specific product means the corresponding services are offered by the company. The ultimate purpose of consumers buying products is not to obtain the physical product itself but the services.

In product design practice, with such shift, the product-service design not only meets users' needs, but also complies with the sustainable developmental requirements of energy saving, environmental protection, and social harmony. Service design has emphasized a concept of shared consumption to enjoy services, that is, people enjoy services a certain product brought. Regarding the case of bike-sharing services, it is convenient to meet such a need for short-distance travel. Specifically, bike-sharing services meet the users' needs in traveling at the end of public transportation, and the "last mile" issue has been addressed by the service design, which is after public transportation people need to consider choosing either walking or taking a taxi to go home. When the services provided by some companies in China initially e.g., OFO, Hellobike, and Mobike, the number of their users had shown a blowout growth. These help users obtain services in a leasing way. Users only use mobile app-based services to register an account, pay a deposit, scan the code of a bike to unlock, and then get the bike with the related riding services provided by those companies.

To meet peoples' demands of bike-sharing services requires the companies to provide a mixed offer of both products and services so that sustainability regarding both consumption and production is possible. From a PSS and innovative design perspective, a bike-sharing system should offer a "use-orientated" approach to the ownership rights of the material artifact. The companies retained the ownership in this PSS configuration and the users purchased the use of the product/system over a given period or units of service. The companies created the product-service delivery system with the service delivery process grounded on ICT technology. In the bike-sharing industry, the service delivery design process was divided into two dimensions as: online and offline service operations [8]. Specifically, these bike-sharing operations were supported by applying mobile applications for the main two services of delivering the offline ride-sharing service for users and informing the company's employees about managing and maintaining bikes. The offline bike-sharing operations were regarded as the activities of bike-sharing operations procedures on the street, and the online bike-sharing operations were supported by the technical department which aimed to provide effective guidance to the offline bike-sharing operations. A created working diagram (see Figure 3) shows a basic bike-sharing operations process for the bike-sharing PSS design. With the organization of the emerging data including material and non-material, it facilitates our understanding of how the key elements interact, support, or conflict with each other during the system working, and could support the cross-analysis in depth.

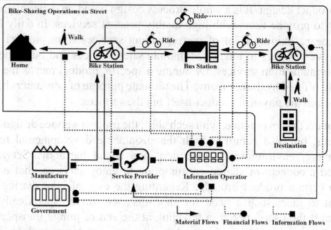

Figure 3. The working diagram of the bike-sharing operations system

In a typical case in Shanghai in 2016, the bike-sharing services in Shanghai saved 8358 tonnes of petrol and decreased CO_2 and NO_X emissions by 25,240 and 64 tonnes [9]. The study demonstrated the spatial distribution of environmental benefits of bike sharing, and indicated Hongkou district is the highest density of environmental benefits with the highest population density. For each square kilometre (km^2) in this district, bike sharing resulted in a reduction of 33 tonnes of petrol, 100 tonnes of CO_2, and 254 kg (kg) of NO_X in 2016 (Table 6), i.e., 35,000 people per km^2, bike-sharing in this district resulted in a decrease of 2.9 kg CO_2 emissions per person. Therefore, in this study bike-sharing services indicated it with great potential to reduce energy consumption and emissions to reach sustainability.

Table 6. Environmental benefits of bike-sharing services in Shanghai (partial results)

No.	District	Area (km^2)	Fuel (t)	CO_2 (t)	NO_X (t)	Fuel per unit area (kg/km^2)	CO_2 per unit area (kg/km^2)	NO_X per unit area (kg/km^2)
1	Baoshan	301	733	2214	5.6	2433	7348	19
2	Changning	37	409	1236	3.1	10,995	33,205	84
3	Chongming	1357	0	0	0	0	0	0
4	Fengxian	721	1	3	0	1	4	0
5	Hongkou	23	774	2339	5.9	33,087	99,921	254
...	...	...	...	...	...	...	...	...

Utilizing the bike-sharing PSS design which can facilitate people driving shared bikes in urban will be realized to the various aspects of sustainability. Driving bikes do not release greenhouse gases, unlike buses and cars. So, if people rent bikes from bike-sharing systems, driving bikes will reduce the carbon footprint and take measures to keep the environment safe. Moreover, the bike-sharing service delivery system can be utilized for producing economic benefits. For example, to meet people's increasing demands from these uses, participatory companies are required to guarantee that there are adequate numbers of shared bikes on the street. Thus, require the companies to spend a large amount of money to purchase many shared bikes, which the local bike manufacturers will benefit from these, and the related providers in supply chains also will benefit from these e.g., making docking stations. Finally, people who use the service will decrease the frequency of using cars because they live near the bike-sharing docking stations, then, the use of shared bikes significantly alleviates traffic congestion there, whereby social efficiency will be improved. Then, various communities were provided bike-sharing services, thereby this also is viewed as applying the way of empowerment to achieve community construction and development. In sum, with advanced technologies the bike-sharing PSS design focused on users' need to provide shared product services. Through using the bike-sharing PSS system a potential transition emerged and engaged in low-carbon mobility in urban, i.e., the PSS system supported by the bike-sharing service delivery operations, users can freely use bike-sharing services without producing any emissions, thus, the bike-sharing PSS design achieved in sustainability with the evaluation framework, see Table 7.

Table 7. Evaluation of the bike-sharing PSS services

Use models	Advancement: Created jobs in the companies, and developing app-based services with the users.		Empowerment: Empowered people to engage in low-carbon transportation.	
Process	Local manufacture: To manufacture locally and their supply chains.	Local control: To manage and maintain the products locally.	Repairing: To repair bikes and retrieve the discarded bikes locally	
Product	Needs: Most people desired to use shared bikes for low-carbon transportation.	Suitability: These were appropriate to the uses of travel and commuting.	Usability: This is convenient to use with the app-based service.	Relative Affordability: Uneven distribution, the urban centres were usually over-supply but a limited number of in the suburban.

4. Conclusion

This paper contributed to the product design fields in general and provided case studies on exploring their design methods in response to sustainable issues. Through analyzing and evaluating the applied design approaches based on the evaluation framework, from the cases including the methods of end-of-life treatment, product life cycle design, and PSS design, then, the finding indicated that some relevant design interventions enable the design solutions to achieve sustainability in various aspects. Specifically, by way of end-of-life treatment, Coca-Cola took the repurposing strategy to the useless bottles by creating special bottle caps, the useless bottles thus became recycled use, and environmental benefits were reached. Evian and Cozy & Green also adopted the ways of end-of-life treatment. MOSO used the product life cycle design in its production, i.e., by presenting the EPDs reports where sustainability was proven in those products in manufactures. Further, by using the bike-sharing PSS design and the bike-sharing service delivery system, the bike-sharing companies considered and realized sustainable goals. For design practice, the paper could provide opportunities to learn innovative design methods with sustainable issues, these might inspire designers to think and identify the appropriate approaches which will be adopted for specific sustainability challenges. In design education, educators could consider the approaches to sustainable issues with challenges in design courses, where the importance of teaching is to enable student designers to know the rich and complex concerned issues in contexts, and to explain how to use approaches individually to contribute to some sustainable developmental aspects.

References

[1] Papanek V, Fuller R B. Design for the real world. London: Thames and Hudson, 1972.
[2] Yang W, Lahti H, Seitamaa-Hakkarainen P. A cross-disciplinary workshop on 3D modelling: Students' design concepts in the bottle form design task. Journal of Design Thinking, 2023.
[3] Hawken P. The Ecology of Commerce: Doing Good Business. HarperCollins Publishers, 1993.
[4] Deng W, Lin H, Jiang M. Research on Bamboo Furniture Design Based on D4S (Design for Sustainability). Sustainability 2023 15(11): 8832.
[5] Tukker A. Eight types of product–service system: eight ways to sustainability? Experiences from SusProNet. Business strategy and the environment 2004 13(4): 246-260.
[6] Melles G, de Vere I, Misic V. Socially responsible design: thinking beyond the triple bottom line to socially responsive and sustainable product design. CoDesign 2011 7(3-4): 143-154.
[7] Del Borghi A. LCA and communication: environmental product declaration. The International Journal of Life Cycle Assessment 2013 18: 293-295.
[8] Li D, Jia F, Liu G. How do bike-sharing platform companies overcome the operational challenge? A social exchange perspective. Production Planning & Control 2022 33(14): 1355-1371.
[9] Zhang Y, Mi Z. Environmental benefits of bike sharing: A big data-based analysis. Applied energy 2018 220: 296-301.

Design Studies and Intelligence Engineering
L.C. Jain et al. (Eds.)
© 2024 The Authors.
This article is published online with Open Access by IOS Press and distributed under the terms
of the Creative Commons Attribution Non-Commercial License 4.0 (CC BY-NC 4.0).
doi:10.3233/FAIA231423

Investigating Preference Factors in the Design of Shopping Carts for the Elderly: A Miryoku Engineering Study

Shuai-Ke MENG [a], Bao-Yi ZHANG [a,1] and Jing-Jing HUANG [a]

[a] *Xiamen University of Technology, China*

Abstract. By introducing the Miryoku Engineering theory, the mapping relationship between elderly shopping cart design factors and users' perceptual imagery is explored. To design an elderly shopping cart that meets the cognitive preferences of the elderly and promotes social participation. Firstly, we collected and screened the elderly shopping carts in the market, selected representative products as experimental samples, conducted interviews and extracted design factors based on the samples. Secondly, through data analysis, specific design factors were deduced as the reference basis for the design. Finally, combined with the design orientation and analysis, the design factors were introduced to guide the innovative design of the elderly shopping cart.

Keywords. Elderly, Shopping Cart, Miryoku Engineering, Evaluation grid method (EGM), Quantification theory type I

1. Introduction

According to the report of National Bureau of Statistics, the proportion of people aged 60 and above in China reached 18.9%, among which the proportion of people aged 65 and above reached 14.2%, further deepening the degree of aging, and the elderly population will enter a period of rapid growth in the next decade [1]. The clothing, food, housing and transportation industries related to the elderly population are attracting much attention.

After the elderly retired from work, shopping has become one of the main activities of the elderly, which is the main means of communication between the elderly and the society [2]. However, as older people grow older, their shopping behavior decreases [3]. To enhance better social integration and communication among Elderly. Thus, the study of aids in their shopping behavior. According to the survey, 83% of elderly people use elderly shopping carts when they go shopping [4]. However, existing shopping carts for the elderly are relatively single in design and do not take into account the sensual psychological needs and cognitive preferences of the elderly.

The research process and method of Miryoku Engineering will focus on the perceptual psychological needs and cognitive preferences of the elderly, which can effectively explore and attract the charm factors of users. Taking the elderly shopping

---

[1] Bao-Yi Zhang 26784214@qq.com.

cart as the research object, we analyze the sensual cognition of the elderly users towards the elderly shopping cart, discover the charming factors in it, and conduct quantitative analysis. We will establish the connection between cognitive preferences and product design factors to bring users a new shopping experience. The main research methods are the Evaluation grid method and the Quantification theory type I.

2. Literature Review

2.1. Shopping behavior of the elderly

Internationally, Osmud Rahman et al. used in-depth semi-structured interviews to gain insight into how income, cognitive age, physiological changes, and life-changing events affect elderly consumers' shopping behaviors and preferences as a way to understand the changing needs of elderly consumers [5]; Chinese scholars Yuan Shu et al. used a combination of questionnaire and interview methods, observation and behavior map methods to study the Shanghai elderly [3]. Although the elderly population is only a part of the shoppers, supermarkets are an indispensable public place in the lives of all elderly people who can walk on their own.

2.2. Elderly Shopping Cart

The elderly shopping cart originated in the United States and evolved from the supermarket shopping cart. Cao, Lixiao, et al. have studied the frequency of shopping among the elderly, and found that it occurs on average 5.2 times a week, close to once a day, and has become an important part of the life of the elderly [6]. Yu, Dongjiu et al. also concluded from a survey that shopping carts for the elderly are another high-frequency life support tool in the shopping behavior of the elderly [4].

2.3. Market Status

Yang Simeng et al. pointed out that for the existing shopping carts for the elderly, there are too few types, small choices easy to be taken wrong, etc. [7]; Yang et al. used questionnaire survey method to analyze the needs of the elderly and used fuzzy comprehensive evaluation method to verify the feasibility of the elderly shopping cart design scheme [8]. However, more analysis was conducted from the behavioral experience and functional level. Wang Tiedong et al. pointed out that the emotional needs are the "first needs" of the elderly [9].

2.4. Quantification theory type I

Miryoku Engineering is a research method that captures and organizes individual cognitive concepts with the aim of "creating techniques and learning for charismatic products and spaces", which was initiated by Japanese scholar Masato Ujikawa in 1991. It is a design concept developed by consumer preference, which provides a communication interface between designers and consumers.

The Evaluation grid method is a modified version of the individual construct method proposed by Japanese scholar Junichiro Sanai, which helps to gain insight into the psychological perception of a subject [10].

Quantification theory type I is a is a type of quantitative theory that specifically studies the relationship between a set of qualitative variables independent variables X and a set of quantitative variables dependent variables Y, and uses multiple regression analysis to build a mathematical model between them to achieve the prediction of the dependent variable Y [11].

This study used the median charisma factor of elderly shopping carts as items and the specific charisma form characteristics under each median charisma factor as classes. Suppose there are m items in s samples, denoted as P_1, P_2, ..., P_m, where the gth item P_g has n classes, then $\delta i(g,k)$ ($g = 1,2,...,8$; $k = 1,2,...,n$) refers to the kth class of the gth item in the i-th sample in the i-th sample. Then.

$$\delta_i(g,k) = \begin{cases} 1 \text{ (When the } g \text{ item in the i sample is the } k \text{ class)} \\ 0 \text{ (other)} \end{cases} \tag{1}$$

$$x = \{\delta_i(g,k)\}, (i = 1,2,...,s) \tag{2}$$

Assuming a linear relationship between the perceptual evaluation value and the factors of the median item and the lower item styling design, a mathematical model can be developed as follows.

$$Y_i = \sum_{g=1}^{M}\sum_{k=1}^{n} \delta_i(g,k)b_{gk} + \varepsilon_I \tag{3}$$

In Eq. (3), Yi is the perceptual imagery evaluation value of the dependent variable y in the i sample; b_{gk} is the kth class constant that depends only on the g item; εi is the random error of the i sampling.

3. Research Process

3.1. Sample Preparation Phase

Firstly, defining the sample: The definition of the elderly shopping cart described in the study from the perspective of structure and function is; structurally the basic components contain wheels, body, and shopping bags; functionally, the sample must contain the storage function in the shopping behavior.

Secondly, sample collection and determination: The sample pictures of elderly shopping carts were collected as comprehensively as possible. After excluding the images of products with poor resolution and difficult to identify their functions. 30 sample images were finally selected as shown in Table I. In addition, the visual angles of the elderly shopping carts in the sample pictures were adjusted to the same level as far as possible, so as to improve the accuracy of the experimental results.

Table 1. Experimental samples

No	Sample	No	Sample	No	Sample	No	Sample
1		2		3		4	
5		6		7		8	
9		10		11		12	
13		14		15		16	
17		18		19		20	
21		22		23		24	
25		26		27		28	
29		30					

3.2. Identification of subjects

In order to fully understand the users' preferences for elderly shopping carts, 11 subjects were invited and divided into two groups: a user group and an expert group, the main purpose of the experiment was to extract the user's preference characteristics based on the user's perspective, so that the charm factor obtained could be more targeted and accurate.

3.3. EGM Interview Implementation

The expert group and the user group were invited to conduct one-on-one in-depth interviews, and the experimental sample cards were all disrupted before the start of each interview, and the interview steps were explained to the interviewees in detail. After obtaining the consent of the user group, shorthand plus audio recording was used to record the whole experimental process. Finally, the KJ method was applied to simplify the data derived from the in-depth interviews with the respondents.

3.4. Questionnaire

A questionnaire was created around this charm vocabulary, a seven-point Likert scale was used to rate the sample pool, and the arithmetic mean of each elderly shopping cart sample under this charm imagery vocabulary was derived.

4. Extraction of design factors

4.1. Results of EGM interviews

After counting and integrating the experimental information from the expert group and the user group in order to draw the elderly shopping cart evaluation constructs, the established elderly shopping cart evaluation constructs are shown in Figure 1.

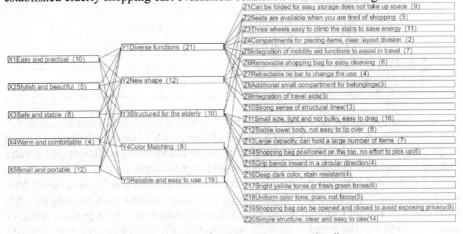

Figure 1. Elderly shopping cart evaluation construction diagram.

4.2. Discussion of results

The Quantification theory type I calculation method can be used to obtain the class score, which represents the conversion score of each class, with negative and positive class scores, where a negative number indicates that each class is negatively correlated to the overall, and vice versa.

Finally, the charm factor evaluation matrix and perceptual evaluation values were input using the formula of quantitative category I. Due to the spatial constraints, selecting the top ranked perceptual imagery for presentation. The results of the analysis are shown in Table II for the example of "easy and practical.

Table 2. Results of the "easy and practical" attractiveness factors

Item	Category	Category score	Partial correlation coefficient	Rank
	Z1	0.2673843		
	Z2	*0.9203855		
Y1	Z3	0.8740988	*0.68520	1
	Z4	-0.1953324		
	Z5	-0.3933564		

	Z6	0.5690543		
	Z7	-0.502579		
	Z8	-2.311995		
	Z9	-1.42582		
	Z2	0.05332797		
	Z5	-0.3817025		
Y2	Z7	*1.407693	0.26432	4
	Z9	1.058485		
	Z10	-2.942263		
	Z2	-0.8191635		
	Z5	*0.6538932		
	Z11	0.1686758		
Y3	Z12	0.2255301	0.47853	3
	Z13	-0.1730571		
	Z14	0.2625048		
	Z15	-0.7121359		
	Z3	-1.579481		
Y5	Z12	0.1263211	0.51481	2
	Z19	-0.8717755		
	Z20	*2.253765		
Constant	2.307542			
R==0.76480				
R2=0.58492				

(*: Maximum value)

When analyzing the data, it is found that X1>X3>X5>X2>X4, it can be concluded that older users are more inclined to X1 product type and Y1 bias correlation coefficient is greater, among which, Z2 has a higher positive correlation coefficient and greater influence weight. In addition, older users also attach great importance to X3 product type, and the difference between its complex correlation coefficient and X1 is smaller. And, when designing a product, if you want to get a certain product with an imagery style tendency, you should focus on the specific matters (lower items) with positive category scores. Except for the items with high significance, the charm factors with negative scores should be avoided in the design, so as to provide a design reference basis for design practice.

5. Design Practice

By calculating and analyzing using the Quantification theory type I, we extracted the charm factors that are more related to the imagery semantics and have the highest user recognition. In this way, the elderly shopping cart is effectively positioned and designed in a user-oriented way. Putting this design factors into the specific design will have a significant effect on the attractiveness of the elderly shopping cart.

5.1. Design Positioning

Combined with the above data analysis results, under the intention of meeting most users' demand preferences for elderly shopping cart, we segmented the design target group characteristics and drew a user journey map to explore the design requirements and pain points, and then designed the elderly shopping cart. The design analysis of the elderly shopping cart is detailed in Table III.

Table 3. Design target group and scene segmentation

Target group	Crowd characteristics segmentation	Scene segmentation
Elderly who has shopping habits and bring their own shopping tools	1. Vigorous new elderly	1.Taking care of children
	2. Poor physical strength, easily tired	2.Tired of walking without a place to sit
	3. Can't see well	3.Raining on the way
	4. Hard to hear	4.Going up and down stairs
	5. Poor memory, easy to forget things	5.Bending down to pick up things
	6. Joint and back pain	6.Crowded, difficult to pass
	7. Poor balance, unstable walking	7. Buying eggs and other fragile goods
	8. Left-behind elderly, pet companion	8. Going home for storage
		9. Caring for pets

For the design target group positioning, draw its user journey map to explore the design needs and pain points, the user journey map is shown in Figure 2.

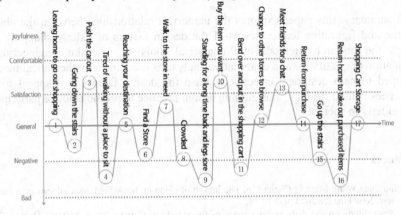

Figure 2. User Journey Map.

For elderly people with poor physical strength and balance, the journey to the grocery store is difficult and they need walking aids, and they usually get tired easily and have no place to rest. After the shopping behavior is completed, it is inconvenient for the elderly to bend down to retrieve things at home, and the storage space of the final shopping cart is also a design requirement for the elderly.

5.2. Charisma factor application

Through the results of the design analysis were summarized, and the overall demand preference was "easy and practical", which was expressed through the variety of functions that could provide seats when tired of shopping. Based on this, "safe and stable" elderly shopping cart also has a greater influence, which is expressed through its small size, lightweight and not bulky; easy to drag and easy to pick up the shopping bag. Creative design for elderly shopping cart with comprehensive design positioning crowd analysis and user journey map pain points mining. Import Rhino software to build the digital model and complete the elderly shopping cart design. The final result is shown in Figure 3.

Figure 3. Final effect.

6. Conclusions

In summary, this paper explores the numerical relationships between the abstract semantic and figurative feature levels of the design factors of elderly shopping carts through the research methods and analytical tools of Miryoku Engineering. A combination of qualitative and quantitative analysis is used and a mathematical model is developed to help designers effectively grasp the design factors that appeal to user preferences in their designs, thus guiding design practice to promote active participation of the elderly in society.

References

[1] Ba Shu Song,Wang Miao,Li Cheng Lin. The impact of aging on household asset allocation: a literature review. New Finance **2023** (03):28-34.
[2] Liu Xuan. Study on the daily activity space of the elderly in Chinese cities. Master's Degree, Peking University, 2003.
[3] Yuan Shu, Dong Hua, Liu Misty. Research on the shopping behavior of elderly people in supermarkets and design insights. Industrial Engineering and Management **9** (2014), 06, 138-143.
[4] Yu, Dongjiu, Yi, Xianqin, Wang. Research on the design of shopping cart for the elderly based on user experience. Packaging Engineering **38** (2017), 12, 99-103.
[5] Osmud Rahman and Hong Yu. Key antecedents to the shopping behaviours and preferences of aging consumers. Journal of Fashion Marketing and Management: An International Journal **23** (2019), 2, 193-208.
[6] Cao Lixiao,Chai Yanwei. Spatial study of daily shopping activities of the elderly in Shanghai. Human Geography **2006** (02), 50-54.
[7] Zhang Baoyi. Preference-based design:a study of charm engineering and its application in product design. Decoration **2017** (11),134-135.
[8] Yang Dongmei,Zhang Jiannan,Xu Xiaoyun. Design of elderly shopping cart based on fuzzy comprehensive evaluation method. Machine Design **33** (2016), 09, 117-120.
[9] Wang Tiedong. An analysis of the emotional needs of the elderly and the corresponding design issues. Art and Design (Theory) **2** (2009), 07,169-171.
[10] XI Le,WU Yixiang,YE Junnan et al. Micro electric vehicle styling design based on charm factor[Journal of Graphology, **39** (2018), 04, 661-667.
[11] Su Jianning,Li He-qi. A study on the relationship between perceptual imagery and stylistic design elements applying a quantitative category of theory. Journal of Lanzhou University of Technology **2005** (02), 36-39.

Design Studies and Intelligence Engineering
L.C. Jain et al. (Eds.)
© 2024 The Authors.
This article is published online with Open Access by IOS Press and distributed under the terms
of the Creative Commons Attribution Non-Commercial License 4.0 (CC BY-NC 4.0).
doi:10.3233/FAIA231424

Research on Innovative Design Method and Evaluation of Jewelry Based on CiteSpace&Playgound AI

Jinhong HU[a], Shuwei YU[a,1], Ming ZHANG[a], Yue WU[a], Jinwei LU[a], Jiongzhou WENG[a], Feiyang LIU[a], Hao HUO[a], Cheng LI[b], and Dongfang PAN[a]

[a] *China Jiliang Univercity, College Art and Communication*
[b] *Suzhou Ar t& Design Technology Institute*

Abstract. This study aims to propose an innovative jewelry design method that combines knowledge graph with artificial intelligence to solve the problem of relying on the experience of designers in the traditional jewelry design field, resulting in unstable design quality, difficulty in inheriting experience, and inability to evaluate innovation. The specific method is to extract research hotspots in jewelry design from the knowledge graph, and construct artificial intelligence recognizable prompt words based on the rules of prompt word formation. Use prompt words in artificial intelligence tools to generate ideas, then use AHP Analytic Hierarchy Process to screen the best ideas, and finally combine the designer's ability to output design solutions. The combination of knowledge graph and artificial intelligence can affect the working methods and efficiency in the field of jewelry design, improve design quality and innovation, and solve the problem of inheriting design experience, which is of great significance for modern jewelry design.

Keywords. Citespace, Playground Ai, Jewelry design, Knowledge map

1. Introduction and summary of jewelry design research problems

Jewelry design was developed on the basis of craftsmen in the early days. Traditional design and production are based on the experience of experienced craftsmen, which is inefficient, outdated in design form and unable to pass on design experience. Even in industrialized jewelry factories, there are a large number of design innovations that rely on designers' experience and aesthetics, and then engineers evaluate the design feasibility. This form not only can't break through the traditional innovation, but also has a bad influence on the development of jewelry industry, the introduction of new technologies and new ideas. However, with the development of new technology and new ideas, people put forward new requirements for jewelry innovation, and personalization, customization and stylization have become urgent problems for the jewelry industry. Starting from these problems, this paper uses knowledge map and artificial intelligence to innovate the innovative design method of jewelry, thus solving the above problems in jewelry industry.

---

[1] Corresponding Author: YU Shuwei,frunner@qq.com

1.1. A survey of generative artificial intelligence

The new era of artificial intelligence started in Turing Machine. At the end of 2022, with chatgpt and midjourey entering into a wide range of social applications, generative artificial intelligence rose again in society, which had a far-reaching impact on industrial design and jewelry design.

In 2014, Canadian Dr. Goodfellow proposed a generative model based on game theory - generative adversarial network.[1] So that artificial intelligence can automatically generate image classification, image synthesis, image translation, style conversion, image restoration and video prediction.[2] In June 2017, a research paper from Rutgers University introduced the Creative Adversarial Network (CAN), which enhances its style ambiguity on the basis of GAN and makes the generation effect more "creative"[3] In 2017, Google Research published an article about transformer, the attention mechanism, which brought the generative artificial intelligence into a new era.[4] In 2020, JonathanHo proposed the DDPM (Denoising Diffusivity Probabilistic Model) generation model. It can achieve sampling in complex image distribution through multi-step denoising of the denoising network during the image generation stage.[5]

Starting from 2022, generative artificial intelligence has entered an explosive era. Various AI image generation tools such as OpenAI's DALL·E2, Google's Imagen, Midjouney, Playround Ai, Stable Diffusion, DALL-E2, and Stableboost Ai provide industrial designers with textual, graphic, post-processing, and Model training and other functions. These tools have directly changed traditional innovative design methods, and jewelry design thinking and working methods must also adapt to the development of the times. Research based on this aspect is of great significance for improving jewelry design efficiency and design productivity.

1.2. Advantages of Generative Artificial Intelligence Tools in Jewelry Design

With the popularity of generative artificial intelligence, a large number of visual designs have been replaced by artificial intelligence, and the jewelry design industry has also been greatly impacted. Compared to traditional design, generative artificial intelligence tools have significant advantages in short-term creative generation, stylization, and combination of ideas. In terms of short-term creative generation, AI jewelry design can generate 4-10 sets of effect plans in 1 minute, while traditional design takes 3-7 days. Meanwhile, AI painting tools are very user-friendly, which can reduce the time cost for humans to learn jewelry design.[6]In terms of creative stylization, AI jewelry design can customize various styles such as digital, entertainment, metal, and so on through cultural and graphic forms. In terms of creative combination, AI jewelry design can generate scheme diagrams through the AI Text To Image generator. The experiments of German researchers such as STEVE GÖRING have shown that some generators can produce realistic and highly attractive images.[7]

Although AI has significant advantages in intelligent generation, how to ensure the quality of innovative jewelry design for generative AI is still a problem that most designers face. This article plans to study the literature knowledge graph of jewelry design, establish hot keywords to define product attributes, and then use artificial intelligence image generation tools to visualize rational data and keywords, generate independent creativity, and establish new jewelry design methods and processes that conform to the era of artificial intelligence, better serve society, and have pioneering significance for enhancing the depth and breadth of jewelry design.

2. Creative jewelry design method based on knowledge map and generative artificial intelligence

2.1. Jewelry design method model combined with artificial intelligence

In order to better study the influence of artificial intelligence in jewelry design and the design method of combining the two, this paper sets up the research flow, as shown in Figure 1, which can be divided into four steps.

　　1.Acquisition of frontier hotspots: use the data visualization software Citespace to study the literature knowledge map of domestic jewelry design direction, confirm the current hotspots of jewelry design through the literature knowledge map, take the research hotspots as the main design objects and creative points, analyze the hot keywords, and initially define the product theme.

　　2.Prompt word transformation: using the existing AI-generated jewelry picture prompt words and general prompt words as materials, the natural language processing model ChatGPT is trained to be a prompt word generator. Input the preliminarily defined product theme into chatGPT, and ask chatGPT to output preliminary prompts. Input the prompt words into AI image generation tool to check the effect of drawing, and manually adjust the prompt words until they are satisfied.

　　3.Scheme evaluation and screening: use AHP to screen the generated creative schemes and determine the final scheme by scientific methods.

　　4.Final scheme presentation: designers combine design tools to output excellent design schemes.

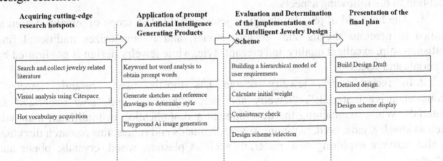

Figure 1. jewelry design method model combined with artificial intelligence

2.2. Key words construction and transformation of knowledge map

The data of this study were collected from CNKI (China National Knowledge Internet) platform, and 1671 valid literature articles were obtained from 2018.1.1 to 20123.6.30.

　　The specific operation method of literature analysis method is using the information visualization software named Citespace developed by Professor Chen Chaomei and other researchers[8] draws a knowledge map for keywords, research institutions and authors in the literature of jewelry design. Refworks format document data is exported on CNKI platform, and the data is preprocessed and format converted by CiteSpace, then the data analysis conditions are set. The time slice is set to 1, and the literature is studied at multiple levels through keyword co-occurrence and keyword time zone map. Then, according to the set output visual data map, manually adjust the chart to ensure its readability. Finally, the research hotspots and trends in the field of jewelry design are summarized, so as to get hot words.

(1) Keyword clustering vocabulary extraction

Figure 2. Keyword cluster diagram of jewelry design research field from 2018 to First half of 2023

Through cluster analysis, we can see that the field of jewelry design also pays more attention to the following aspects.

1. The hot field of jewelry design is jewelry field. The scope of jewelry design is limited to precious metals and precious stones, and it emphasizes traditional fine craftsmanship, excellent quality and elegant style, while jewelry design is not limited by materials and styles.

2. In recent years, jewelry design has mostly used "ceramic jewelry", "comprehensive materials", "jewelry and jade", "jewelry" and "new materials" as materials. While maintaining the development and application of traditional materials such as jewelry, jade, gold, platinum, silver, diamonds and rubies, this research direction is also actively exploring new materials such as plastics, wood, crystals, bones and ceramics.

3. The key aspects in the field of jewelry design are innovation, application, craft, culture, material, emotion, modeling, development, inheritance, integration, nature, tradition, art and style.

4. Jewelry field pays special attention to technology, and there are two main research directions. The traditional directions are: enamel craft, lacquer art, filigree craft and mosaic craft, which is one of the representatives of China traditional culture and an important craft of traditional luxury goods production. Emerging directions are: "3D printing", which is based on rapid prototyping and additive manufacturing technology and is a brand-new digital forming manufacturing process.

5. Cross-field: "Mineralogy" and "Gemmology" became high-intensity words in 2022. Hao Liang and other researchers used glass sponge structure, 3D printing and digital monitoring technology to design hard, lightweight, high strength and high toughness smart wearable jewelry.[9]

(2) Keyword extraction of timeline graph

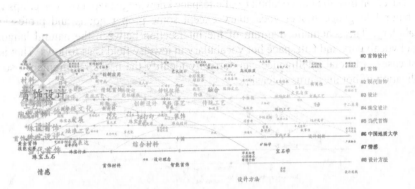

Figure 3. Timeline diagram of jewelry design and research in early 2018-2023

Based on Citespace's time-zone mapping (Figure 3) and analysis, eight cluster groups marked with "#" are extracted, which reflects the phased keywords and development direction of this research field. In order to keep up with the direction of scientific research and the development of the times, this study extracts the hot words of the main clustering groups in 2020 and beyond as the creative points and product themes of AI-generated jewelry. Artificial intelligence prompt word transformation method for creative keywords of jewelry design.

2.3. Artificial intelligence prompt word transformation method for creative keywords of jewelry design

2.3.1. Citespace vocabulary arrangement and induction

Because some words in the knowledge map are not suitable as reference hints for AI image generation tools. Therefore, it is necessary to delete words that have no reference meaning or are counterproductive when they are generated, expand and refine words that contain a wide range, and describe words that are difficult to distinguish correctly in natural language, and finally sort out and summarize them. In this study, the hot words of style from 2020 to 2022 are refined and summarized, which are mainly divided into categories, appearance attributes, culture and theme, technology, materials, scientific research and market demand, individualism and style, and interdisciplinary subjects. Finally, a small vocabulary with timeliness is obtained, which provides inspiration and direction for designers when it is generated.

2.3.2. Refer to the usage rules of artificial intelligence prompts to add commonly used prompts in jewelry field.

At present, AI drawing tools such as Midjouney use large-scale pre-training language model, also known as large language model. (LLMs), which has brought new opportunities and challenges to the field of natural language processing since 2018. Using the learning paradigm of "pre-training large model+fine-tuning large model" can achieve a leading effect in almost all natural language processing tasks, Researchers only need to fine-tune the downstream task annotation data set with pre-trained large-scale language models to obtain better task performance[10], which provides a technical basis for the transformation of hot words into hints.

Based on this, the hot vocabulary of citespace knowledge map mostly overlaps with the natural language model vocabulary except some proper nouns and professional vocabulary. The schematic diagram of the intersection between the natural language model vocabulary and Citespace hot vocabulary in jewelry field is as follows. That is, in most cases, artificial intelligence can correctly identify the user's requirements, so the application of hot thesaurus is feasible.

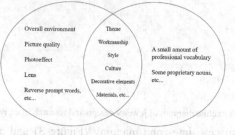

Overall environment
Picture quality
Photoeffect
Lens
Reverse prompt words, etc...

Theme
Workmanship
Style
Culture
Decorative elements
Materials, etc...

A small amount of professional vocabulary
Some proprietary nouns, etc...

Natural Language Model   Citespace Hotspot Thesaurus

Figure 4. schematic diagram of the intersection of natural language model vocabulary and citespace hot vocabulary in jewelry field.

2.3.3. General rules for AI to generate tooltips

In order to get more accurate results and good visual effects, there are many AI drawing tool users who summarize and prompt vocabulary from a human perspective.

Prompt words are generally divided into positive words and negative words. The general order formula of positive words is: prefix+subject+subject descriptor+other descriptions. In the first part, prefixes are mostly for the requirements of image quality to ensure the generated quality. The second part puts forward subjects. This study will use the hot word brooch as the subject. The third part, describing the subject or imposing requirements on the subject, this study will put forward requirements in terms of technology, theme, material and style. The fourth part, supplementary expansion, to determine the background, environment, lens and filter. Reverse words are also called negative prompts, such as: low quality, malformed hands, etc., to avoid unsuitable elements and low-quality generation.

The specific application steps are as follows:

Step 1: Preliminary generation. According to the above formula and citespace hot words, we can get the preliminary artificial intelligence tips: Masterpiece, High-quality, A Butterfly Brooch, Enamel, Gold and Silver, Chinese Style, White Background and Front View. This tip can get the works that meet the requirements in most AI drawing tools.

Step 2, expand the generation. ChatGPT can be trained by using the above prompt word method and prompt word cases, and then hot words are used as the theme to ask chatGPT to draw inferences to obtain a large number of available vocabularies, or you can query the prompt word website to supplement the vocabulary yourself.

Step 3, because the effects of different tool platforms are different, users need to fine-tune them repeatedly to get satisfactory results.

2.4. Comparison of creative graphic schemes of extracted keywords in various artificial intelligence drawing tools

2.4.1. Comprehensive comparison of artificial intelligence image generation tools

In this study, the mainstream artificial intelligence image generation tools, such as Midjourney, Stable Diffusion and Playground AI, are selected to analyze the tools themselves, the media used, the features and the generation examples. At the same time, according to the above application methods, various tools are used to generate relevant jewelry design schemes. Here, the butterfly element is taken as an example for further study, as shown in Table 1. Three preliminary tools of butterfly-shaped jewelry are generated, and then the tools are selected for in-depth design.

Table 1. Comprehensive comparison chart of artificial intelligence image generation tools

	Midjourney	Stable Diffusion	Playground AI
summarized account	Midjourney is an artificial intelligence program and service developed by Midjourney, an independent research lab based in San Francisco. Midjourney offers a service based on the Discord platform, which can generate images based on natural language descriptions (called "Prompt"), and supports picture-generated graphics.	Stable Diffusion, a deep learning text-to-image generation model released in 2022, is a potential diffusion model developed by startup Stability AI in collaboration with several academic researchers and non-profit organizations. Its source code and models are open source and are being maintained by developers around the world.	Playground AI is an online AI painting tool that generates 1,000 free images per day and is the leading platform for text-to-image generation, offering image generation, automatic art style tips, free image magnification, image saving in the cloud, and social media for AI-generated images.
Image resolution	Can only control the image aspect ratio, high resolution need to enter HD, 8K and other prompt words	self-configurable	Available in a variety of sizes
Use media	Installed on the discord website, you can get AI images directly online after sending a command from the chat interface.	It can be downloaded to the local computer. You need to select various model plug-ins and adjust various parameters before using them.	Use on an independent web platform that integrates communication and generation.
Features/ advantages and disadvantages	1. no hardware requirements, can run on almost all devices. 2. simple deployment, no threshold for use. 3. low difficulty to use, easy to master. 4. the upper/lower limit difference is very small. 5. weak controllability, no plug-in, the output of the screen style is fixed. 6. run the whole network, the data exists on the server, it is difficult to save locally. 7. Only use officially defined models.	1. high hardware requirements, the need for local independent graphics card, high hardware requirements. 2. Deployment is relatively difficult. 3. it is difficult to use, there are a lot of content in the interface, such as sampling methods, model training, etc., which requires a more complex learning process. 4. the upper/lower limit gap is very large: no special operation in the case of poor visual effect, after a certain amount of learning to generate a very high upper limit. 5. highly controllable, many plug-ins, LORA, can almost change style and form at will, the number of drawings is large. 6. can be completely local operation, data only exists locally, with hardware can be unlimited use. 7. can train the model, get a personal database, let the AI completely according to their own ideas to shape the content of the target style.	1. no hardware requirements, can run on almost all devices. 2. simple deployment, no threshold for use. 3. the use of low difficulty, but still need to learn. 4. the upper/lower limit has a certain gap. 5. strong controllability, more models and styles, there are various parameter options. 6. Untrainable model. 7. Playground combines the advantages of the first two, which is easy to use and controllable. 8. Close communication between users.
Example: Preliminary prompt word: Masterpiece, high-quality, a butterfly brooch, enamel, gold and silver, Chinese style, white background, front view			

2.4.2. Playground AI & Midjourney in-depth design

In order to obtain the preliminary design concept, this study used the prompt phrases obtained above in playground Ai and Midjourney to generate butterfly brooches, which provided inspiration and materials for designers. Examples of specific effects are shown in the figure 5. Figure 6.

Figure 5. Playground AI Generation Diagram.   **Figure 6.** Midjourney Generation Diagram.

2.4.3. Refinement of Jewelry Design for Single Element

Because the effect of artificial intelligence is uneven, this study based on visual effect, feasibility, cost and style, screened out feasible and beautiful schemes and expanded them into group-based scheme styles. The following style pictures are based on the butterfly brooch, which are generated by changing the description and order of the prompt words. After manual screening, they basically meet the requirements and meet the standards in vision and structure. See Figure 7, Figure 8, Figure 9 and Figure 10 for specific examples.

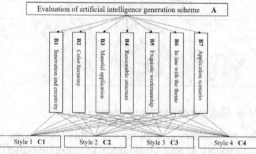

Figure 7. style I.   **Figure 8.** Style II.   **Figure 9.** Style III.   **Figure 10.** Style IV.

3. Determination and evaluation method of innovative jewelry design scheme

3.1. Construction of hierarchical model of users' jewelry innovation demand

In order to obtain the demand of Chinese jewelry design scheme based on preliminary keywords and from the designer's perspective, this study uses questionnaire and interview. Based on the comprehensive results, 7 key evaluation criteria were determined to construct a hierarchical model for jewelry design scheme evaluation, as shown in Figure 11.

Figure 11. Requirements of Chinese Jewelry Design Scheme.

3.2. Weight calculation of criterion layer

Accord to that established evaluation hierarchy model of artificial intelligence generation scheme, 8 expert user and ordinary users are invited to compare each factor with 1-9 scale method, and an initial judgment matrix Z is established as follow:

Accord to that established evaluation hierarchy model of artificial intelligence generation scheme, 8 expert user and ordinary users are invited to compare each factor with 1-9 scale method, and an initial judgment matrix Z is established as follow:

$$Z = \left(z_{ij}\right)_{m \times n} = \begin{bmatrix} z_{11} & z_{12} & \cdots & z_{1n} \\ z_{21} & z_{22} & \cdots & z_{2n} \\ \cdots & \cdots & \cdots & \cdots \\ z_{m1} & z_{m2} & \cdots & z_{mn} \end{bmatrix} \tag{1}$$

Among them, z_{ij} represents the relative importance value of factor i to factor j, satisfying $z_{ij} = \frac{1}{z_{ji}}$. Using the above judgment matrix and based on the basic principles of Analytic Hierarchy Process, the square root method is used to calculate the weight values of the evaluation criteria layer for the artificial intelligence generation scheme in this study, as shown in Table 2.

Table 2. Weight of criteria layer of jewelry design scheme generated by artificial intelligence

	Innovation and creativity	Harmonious color matching	Material application	rational construction	exquisite workmanship	Meet the theme	Application scenario	proper vector	Weight value (%)
Innovation and creativity	1	3	2	3	4	0.5	5	2.1	23.478
Harmonious color matching	0.333	1	0.5	1	2	0.25	3	0.82	9.172
Material application	0.5	2	1	2	3	0.25	4	1.292	14.442
Rational construction	0.333	1	0.5	1	2	0.333	3	0.855	9.557
Exquisite workmanship	0.25	0.5	0.333	0.5	1	0.25	2	0.521	5.825
Meet the theme	2	4	3	3	4	1	6	3.022	33.793
Application scenario	0.2	0.333	0.25	0.333	0.5	0.167	1	0.334	3.734

The weight calculation results of analytic hierarchy process show that the weight of theme is 33.793%, the weight of innovation is 23.478%, the weight of material application is 14.442%, the weight of reasonable structure is 9.557%, the weight of harmonious color matching is 9.172%, the weight of exquisite craftsmanship is 5.825%, and the weight of application scene is 3.734%.

3.3. consistency check

In order to ensure the rationality of AHP, it is necessary to check the consistency of the initial judgment matrix. The consistency ratio CR is used to measure the degree of consistency, and the formula is:

$$CR = \frac{CI}{RI} \tag{2}$$

In the formula, if CR is less than 0.1, it means that the initial judgment matrix is consistent, otherwise, the test fails and the matrix needs to be readjusted. RI is a random consistency index, and its value can be found in the average random consistency index table. CI is a consistency test index, which can be calculated by Formula (3) and Formula (4).

$$CI = \frac{\lambda_{max} - n}{n - 1} \tag{3}$$

$$\lambda_{max} = \sum_{i=1}^{n} \frac{(ZW)_i}{nW_i} \tag{4}$$

The calculation result based on the above formula shows that the maximum feature root is 7.188, and the corresponding RI value is 1.341 according to the RI table, so CR=CI/RI=0.023<0.1. The weight calculation result is valid through one-time testing.

3.4. Scheme selection and determination

According to the summary results of the scheme level judgment matrix (Figure 12, Table 3), the overall ranking of the scheme level is obtained. Based on the single ranking of index level and the total ranking of scheme level, the best scheme in the evaluation and analysis of artificial intelligence generation scheme is Style III, and its quantitative score is 1.447, so this study will choose Style III for further design. Table 3 shows the calculation results of scheme layer weight, and the CR values of seven key evaluation criteria are all less than 0.1, which passes the consistency test.

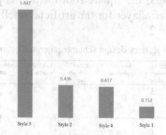

Figure 12. Quantitative score histogram of Chinese jewelry design scheme

Table 3. Weight Values and One-time Inspection Results Table

Node term	Style 1	Style 2	Style 3	Style 4	CR value	Consistency check
Innovation and creativity	0.249	0.096	0.558	0.096	0.016	Pass
Harmonious color matching	0.07	0.193	0.368	0.368	0.002	Pass
Material application	0.073	0.17	0.472	0.285	0.019	Pass
Rational construction	0.084	0.113	0.479	0.324	0.035	Pass
Exquisite workmanship	0.246	0.069	0.438	0.246	0.01	Pass
Meet the theme	0.088	0.496	0.332	0.083	0.018	Pass
Application scenario	0.061	0.311	0.495	0.133	0.03	Pass

4. Digital deepening and establishment of jewelry design scheme

In addition to drawing pictures by artificial intelligence to get inspiration quickly, designers should also give full play to their subjective initiative to avoid the problems of logic and structural details and provide a solid foundation for the landing of products. Synthesizing the ranking of key evaluation criteria, style selection, Citespace prompt thesaurus, artificial intelligence generation chart and multiple references of personal ability obtained by AHP, the final design case is as follows (Figure13). The scheme takes butterflies as the main elements, disassembling and reorganizing many elements in the pictures generated by artificial intelligence, with elegant style and compact and harmonious decoration, which meets the requirements of prompt phrases.

Figure 13. Rhino modeling.   **Figure 14.** Final Scheme Presentation.

5. Summary

In this paper, the initial jewelry scheme is designed by the innovative design method combining knowledge map with AI, and then the generated creative scheme is screened by AHP. Finally, the designer combines design tools to output excellent design schemes. The above practical operation verifies a new jewelry design method combining knowledge map with artificial intelligence, directionality and randomness, which solves the problem that the traditional jewelry design field relies on the designer's experience to design, which leads to the problem that the design experience cannot be passed down, the design level is unstable, and the design innovation cannot be evaluated. At the same time, it can effectively improve the designer's design quality and innovation. The method obtained in this study is of great significance to modern jewelry design, and can also provide some reference for other artificial intelligence drawing research.

Acknowledgments

This article is supported by the 2022 Zhejiang Province Curriculum Ideological and Political Project: A Case Study of Industrial Design Ideological and Political Teaching Based on Correct Values (project number: 113). Foundation item(s): National Social Science Foundation Art Program "Research on Contemporary Paradigm and Standard System of Traditional Chinese Crafts Inheritance" (project number:20BG137).

References

[1]   GOODFELLOW I, POUGET-ABADIE J, MIRZA M, et al. Generative adversarial nets //Advances in Neural Information Processing Systems. 2014: 2672-2680.
[2]   Zhu Xiuchang, Tang Guijin. Overview of Image Processing in Generative Adversarial Networks. Journal of Nanjing University of Posts and Telecommunications (Natural Science Edition), 2019, 39 (03): 1-12.
[3]   Ye Zhenkuan.Research on Visual Illusion Image Generation Design Based on Creative Adversarial Networks. Guangdong University of Technology, 2022.
[4]   Vaswani, A., Shazeer, N., Parmar, N., Uszkoreit, J., Jones, L., Gomez, A. N., Kaiser, Łukasz, & Polosukhin, I. (2017). Attention is all you need. Advances in Neural Information Processing Systems, 2017-December, 5999-6009.
[5]   Gu Shuyang.Image Generation and Quality Assessment Based on Deep Learning. University of Science and Technology of China, 2023.
[6]   Liu Shuliang. On the Impact of AI Painting on the Field of Cultural Creativity. Contemporary Animation, 2023 (02): 91-95
[7]   S. Göring, R. R. Ramachandra Rao, R. Merten and A. Raake, Analysis of Appeal for Realistic AI-Generated Photos, IEEE Access 2023 (11), 38999-39012.
[8]   Chen Yue, Chen Chaomei, Liu Zeyuan, et al. The methodological function of SiteSpace knowledge graph. Scientific Research 33 (2015), 02, 242 253.
[9]   Hao Liang, He Meng, Pan Ruiqi, et al. Wearing Structure Design and Additive Manufacturing Based on Geological Mineral Inspiration. Journal of Gemology and Gemology (Chinese and English) 2022 (24) 05, 258-268.
[10] Zhao Tiejun, Xu Mufan, Chen Andong. A Review of Natural Language Processing Research [J/OL]. Journal of Xinjiang Normal University (Philosophy and Social Sciences Edition): 1-23, https://doi.org/10.14100/j.cnki.65-1039/g4.20230804.001.

Design Studies and Intelligence Engineering
L.C. Jain et al. (Eds.)
© 2024 The Authors.
This article is published online with Open Access by IOS Press and distributed under the terms
of the Creative Commons Attribution Non-Commercial License 4.0 (CC BY-NC 4.0).
doi:10.3233/FAIA231425

Virtual Reality Technology in Art Education System

Ruoyuan LIAO[a, 1]

[a] *China Academic of Art, Hangzhou, China*

Abstract. Our country has always attached great importance to the cultivation of talents and the development of education. As education has now entered the information age, there have emerged more new concepts, new demands and new challenges, which require us to constantly absorb new technology to improve and optimize the education system. After studying the current application of virtual reality technology and the shortcomings of the education system, this paper tries to take the Industrial design Department of China Academy of Art as a sample to explore the new way of applying virtual reality technology in the field of art teaching. Through the combination of vision and software, we try to create a new digital system for the Industrial design department, build a personalized creation virtual space for students, and provide functions such as virtual tour, online class, virtual exhibition, space construction and alumni exchange. This research has certain social significance. It combines technology with art education and helps to enhance the efficiency of education.

Keywords. Virtual reality, art education, immersive, creativity

1. Introduction

In the rapid development of digital technology, virtual reality technology has become a hotspot for people's attention, it is a new technology of multidisciplinary cross-fertilization emerging in the field of information technology, the use of computer technology to create a digital three-dimensional spatial scene, and the experience of the person who feels the changes in the virtual world through their own senses [1]. It now permeates every aspect of our lives, bringing radical changes to our production and lives. Virtual reality technology has been involved in many fields, such as military, medical, education, culture and tourism, etc., it is through the emphasis on the experience of the user's own senses, to enhance the user's visual, tactile, auditory and other experiences, to bring the user immersive experience, so as to enhance the quality and efficiency of people's work. And for the past decade, higher education institutions have also undergone profound transformation and are facing new technological challenges in the educational arena [2]. After studying the current application of virtual reality technology and the shortcomings of the education system, this paper tries to take the Industrial design Department of China Academy of Art as a sample to explore the new way of applying virtual reality technology in the field of art teaching.

---

[1] Corresponding Author.

This thesis will use blender, c4d and unity 3d as the development software, oculus quest 2 hardware device as the carrier, and take the industrial design building of China Academy of Art as an example, to explore the new way of applying virtual reality technology in the field of art education. Through the combination of visual and software, we try to build a digital twin display system for the industrial design department of China Academy of Art, to build a personalized virtual space for students' individual creation, to strengthen the relationship between teachers and students through a new form of interaction, and to stimulate students' creativity through the construction of a virtual campus and a personal virtual space. The construction of the whole teaching display system relies on the idea of alumni association recently put forward by China Academy of Art, and in terms of visual presentation, it shows the overall appearance of China Academy of Art, which enhances the cohesion of the students and at the same time serves to promote the campus. The whole system mainly focuses on the emotional bond between teachers and students as well as the exhibition creation needs of design students, so it is not limited to the industrial design area of the China Academy of Art, but can be extended to all creative groups with group attributes, and through the incorporation of virtual reality technology, it helps people to have a more immersive touring experience and a more efficient creative workflow.

In summary, exploring the application of virtual reality technology to art education in order to construct a teaching display system will be conducive to the image promotion of the campus, strengthen the emotional attributes of the alumni group, and enhance the creative enthusiasm of industrial design students. At the same time, it is also significant for helping groups with creative needs and exploring new ways of applying innovative education.

2. Analysis of virtual reality technology

Virtual reality technology consists of several systems, including the virtual environment system, the processing system of the computer used, display equipment, etc. [3]. The implementation method primarily involves using computer programming as a foundation, combined with three-dimensional graphics and multimedia display technologies to create an immersive space, providing users with a lifelike three-dimensional experience, and even simulating various senses such as touch and smell. It is a product of the cross-application of a variety of disciplines and technologies, along with the development of various disciplines and high technology, virtual reality technology has also been a great development, and gradually be used in all aspects of our lives.

2.1. Technical overview

VR systems require harmonious coordination among interaction, locomotion, audio, visual, and task design, to provide users with a good immersive experience [4]. Virtual reality technology has the following main qualities:

- Immersion

  Immersion refers that virtual reality technology is the combination of computer systems and three-dimensional graphics or multimedia, which can allow users to feel that they are parts of the virtual space [5]. Virtual reality environment refers to the virtual environment built in the computer, through the visual, auditory, tactile, and other senses to achieve a variety of real-time means of interaction, you can realize the establishment of the virtual environment [6]. People are able to move and interact in the virtual space, experience touch and taste, smell and vision, just as in the real world. This is also the biggest feature of the virtual scene: Simulation, to achieve the restoration of the real environment [7].

- Interactivity

Interactivity refers to the fact that the users can interact with objects in the virtual environment to a certain extent in the virtual space, including but not limited to simple gravity and physical collisions. Through the setting of program triggers, it is possible for the users to get close to or touch a certain object in the virtual world, and make a certain behavior to trigger the corresponding interaction and get the corresponding feedback. For example, the virtual space scene, the transformation of objects, the flashing and disappearing of dialogue pop-ups, and so on.

- Multi-sensory

Multi-sensory refers to the ability of computer technology to support multiple human sensory modalities, such as hearing, touch, smell, and vision. The final form of virtual reality technology should be able to replicate all human perceptual functions, and provide a sense of immersion that is exactly the same as or even greater than that in the real world. However, due to the lack of technological development, especially the limitation of the current sensing technology, most of the current virtual reality technology are still limited to the senses of sight, sound and touch. Among them, vision and hearing are the core perception modules of current virtual reality technology.

- Conceivability

Conceptualization is one of the main points of distinction between virtual reality and reality. In the world of virtual reality, there can be experiences such as fully realistic gravity systems and visual effects, but it is also possible to create and realize environments that cannot exist in reality according to the human's own imagination, such as levitating buildings, glowing trees and other things that do not exist in reality.

- Autonomy

It is the extent to which objects in the virtual world act according to the laws of physics. For example, whether the objects follow the real-world gravity system, and whether rigid or flexible objects interact with each other in terms of force when they collide and undergo corresponding deformation and positional shifts.

2.2. Application status

Virtual reality technology has now been applied in the field of education. Compared to traditional offline education, through virtual reality technology, colleges can give students a more immersive teaching experience, such as learning to appreciate the "Thousand Miles of Rivers and Mountains", when the mainstream education is still through the graphic and the teachers' words to help students to understand what it means, with the addition of virtual reality technology, the teacher can take the students go back to the thousands of years ago in the midst of the verdant landscapes and feel the beauty of the mountains and forests. Virtual reality technology can also realize low-cost and low-risk experiments, remote and efficient online courses and other useful functions. For example, the Geological Crystallography Learning System developed by China University of Geosciences realizes the structural characteristics of crystals through virtual reality technology so that students can recognize and learn more clearly [8].

Virtual reality technology has already been used in the design field as well. Through virtual reality technology, people can experience the results of design in an immersive way and understand the designer's intention, for example, they can travel to roam around in a building whose design been completed but has not yet been built, and experience new products that have not yet been released. At the same time, virtual reality technology can also be applied to the designer's workflow to improve the designer's design quality and work efficiency. With the development of digital painting and design, art stylization technology, as the core of digital brush engine, is widely used in creative tool software [9]. For example, designer H.Y. Kan's team built an Internet-based virtual reality collaborative environment, Virtual Reality Based Collaborative Environment (VRCE), a working model that successfully makes collaborative design feasible for small and medium-sized enterprises with a narrow range of low-cost products [10]. VR is also used to develop and inspire communication, collaboration and other soft skillsets that are at the core of pedagogy and learning [11]. The study showed that by learning in a virtual reality environment, the testers achieved good learning outcomes in emotional adaptation skills [12], safety skills in a variety of hazardous situations [13], social skills [14], etc.

Virtual reality technology now has a more stable development mode and smooth output effect, and has been used in different areas of life, it also achieved good results. Meanwhile, with the continuous development of computer, multimedia and other fields, virtual reality technology also continues to develop at a high speed, with a very broad prospect. It is foreseeable that virtual reality technology will be highly involved in our production and lives in the future. However, while virtual reality technology plays a big role, the technology itself also has some non-negligible problems.

Some users may get dizziness, vomiting and other uncomfortable feelings when using VR equipment. Sufficient refresh rates of displays and updates in the virtual world are key factors to consider when using VR, as the user will be otherwise likely prone to motion sickness on longer exposure [15]. The perfect experience of virtual reality technology depends on the appropriate VR equipment, and the current price of VR equipment is generally expensive, common VR glasses are generally located in the price of more than three thousand, and the one VR equipment at the same time can only be used for one user to experience. The current virtual reality presents in the development also need to cooperate with the equipment model adaptation, different unsupported models in the development and the use of the process will often frequently report errors and other problems, which also enhances the development of the cost and difficulty. Reducing the price of equipment, lowering the difficulty and threshold of development, and improving the quality of the output with creative content may be the direction and goal of the development of virtual reality technology. With the progress of virtual reality technology, in the future, the virtual environment will become more realistic and better meet people's requirements for the use of virtual space [16].

Figure 1. Tilt Brush, which allows professional artists or hobbyists to realize painting in VR space

3. Integration of virtual reality technology and campus

Currently, VR and AR are setting trends with great impact on various studies and proposals applied to the field of education and its creative process [17] After analyzing the existing cases of virtual reality technology, it can be determined that the application of virtual reality technology in the education system can well enhance the students' learning efficiency and enthusiasm and optimize the college teaching experience. In the following, the industrial design department of China Academy of Art is taken as a case study, and the research and system design are attempted.

3.1. Basic campus information and user research

The Industrial Design Program of China Academy of Art was first established in 1993, and has a long history of thirty years so far. The department takes social needs, humanistic responsibility and post-industrial as the directions of discipline construction, takes new materials, new processes, new theories, new industries, new fields and new issues as the characteristics of professional research, and spans the three disciplines of arts, science and engineering to cultivate design and research talents in the fields related to industrial design and product design.

Rooted in the core concept of oriental design, based on the international vision and the forefront of the times, China Academy of Art's industrial design program adheres to the "user-centered" scientific law of art and design, takes the beauty of the local lifestyle as the source, cross-border synergy as the way, cultural creativity as the driving force, scientific and technological integration as the means, and industrial transformation and service as the key to revitalize traditional Chinese culture and to promote the development of the industry. With the revitalization of traditional Chinese culture and the equal emphasis on design creation and intellectual manufacturing, we will create a localized systematic innovation model for China's industrial design profession, establish professional characteristics combining traditional innovation and technological integration, and strive to build a new image of China's design in the era of globalization.

Through questionnaires and offline interviews, we have a certain preliminary understanding of the current industrial design education in China Academy of Art. A total of 46 questionnaires were collected, of which 44 were valid questionnaires, all of them were students studying in the Department of Industrial Design, and the grade ratio of freshman: sophomore: junior: senior was 5:3:1:1. The number of offline interviews was four, one for each grade. After summing up, we try to find out the existing shortcomings and strengths and explore feasible optimization solutions.

Table 1. What is the best way to document creativity in the learning process

Option	Quorum	Proportion
handwritten records	30	68.18%
electronic record	32	72.73%
mental note	16	36.36%
non-record	5	11.36%
others	0	0

Table 2. What are the limitations of current methods of acquiring knowledge

Option	Quorum	Proportion
similarity	31	70.45%
traceability is difficult	18	40.91%
hysteresis	16	36.36%
high landing threshold	9	20.45%
single presentation	13	29.55%
difficulty in searching	19	43.18%
others	2	4.55%

3.2. Current problems

- Teaching display form is relatively single: now the teaching method of industrial design colleges is still based on offline teaching, supplemented by a certain amount of e-learning, and e-learning is still limited to catechism, screen equipment, data statistics and other fields, which can't enhance the teaching efficiency and enthusiasm for learning.

- Teaching display limited by time and space: in the teaching of industrial design will often open physical exhibitions to explain, offline lectures and other activities limited by time and space, once the students miss, it is difficult to have the opportunity to observe and experience, the existing system cannot cross the time and space to solve this problem.

- The advantages of the alumni group are not well utilized: design is a job that requires more exchanges of ideas and more collisions of thoughts in order to come up with better ideas. In the previous research, we have found that the teachers and students of China Academy of Art have a strong willingness to share, they are willing to share their ideas with their classmates, which is a good platform in itself, but the existing system does not give good play to the advantages of the alumni group, to strengthen the exchange of teachers and students to view the exhibition and learning.

3.3. Prospects and trends of virtual reality technology used in art education

In order to cope with the new needs of art talent training, art professional education and exhibitions also need to move closer to digitalization and diversification, and the means also need to be updated. Virtual reality technology supports the systematization of the whole process of "from design to manufacturing" and "from production to marketing" simulation through the construction of a high-fidelity simulation environment. Through virtual reality, industry practice can be introduced into the learning process, guiding students' interest in learning, stimulating students' creative potential and enthusiasm for learning, helping students' sustainable innovation, increasing the possibility of improving the real world through design creativity, and helping students to continue to develop after graduation and in the longer term. By adding virtual reality technology, the college can realize immersive experience and novel interactive forms in the process of creation and teaching exhibitions, which enhances students' learning efficiency and enthusiasm for learning. Meanwhile, the digital twin world constructed by virtual reality technology can meet people's needs of visiting different times and spaces, which is a good solution to the problem of art education being limited by time and space. The addition of virtual reality technology also provides a good platform for communication between student groups, and the combination of virtual reality technology and art design education system is a feasible direction for the future. Virtual reality technology can be a good solution to the problems that occur in the art campus at this stage.

4. An attempt at intelligent art education starting with virtual reality technology

The use of virtual reality technology in the art education system not only meets the creative needs and emotional social attributes of the user group, but also solves the constraints of time and space, and improves the effectiveness of work and enthusiasm for learning. The virtual environmental characteristics such as active presentation of materials, unlimited access level to the learning materials, and presentation of the materials in a supplemental format were more effective [18]. This paper takes the Department of Industrial Design of China Academy of Art as a case study, but the idea is also applicable and can be extended to all user groups with creative needs, and has certain social value. The Fig. 2 shows the specific functions and structural framework.

4.1. Specific functions of the virtual art education creation system

- Virtual Tour: Take a virtual digital human tour of the Industrial Design Building, where experiencers can see and experience different industrial design products across time and space.

- Online Seminars: Participate in online seminars or online courses as a virtual participant, with no space limitations and permanent record keeping.

- Exchange of insights: works in the virtual space can be commented on and exchanged with the creators to produce a collision of ideas across time and space to inspire.

- Personal Creation Exhibition: You can exhibit your own works in your personal space to form your own pavilion, and you can also invite others to visit and exchange ideas.

- College business card: to make the college more cohesive, the unity of visual style will become a business card of the college and play a certain role in publicity.

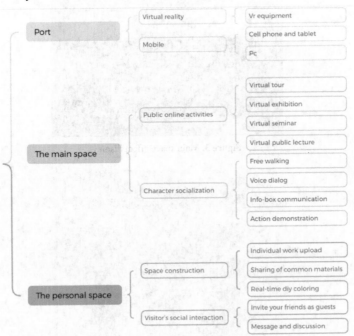

Figure 2. Illustration of the virtual art education creation system.

4.2. Initial effect projection

In order to realize the envisioned framework function, the construction of the scene chooses to be carried out in sketch up, blender and c4d first, after the scene design and intention map output, it will be transferred to the modeling software for the production of the model, and then imported into unity 3D for the rendering of the material and the atmosphere of the scene, and then after the visual effect meets the requirements, it will produce the physical collision effect through the collider plug-in that comes with unity. After the visual effect meets the requirements, the physical collision effect is made by the collider plug-in of unity, to realize the anamorphic walking experience and spatial atmosphere, and the trigger event trigger and trigger box are set to the object, to combine the interactive UI with the object space, to realize the free interaction of the virtual reality.

Figure 3. Main space effect display

Figure 4. Personal space effect display

Since the early days of VR, various locomotion techniques have been developed and studied, targeting seamless and user-friendly navigation in virtual environments [19]. Considering that users need to participate in the virtual roaming, the user's access threshold and interaction guidance are designed and optimized. After combining the use of programming scripts and unity trigger triggers, we added an air wall and delineated a certain trigger area and bound the trigger event, when the user enters the trigger area, there will be specific interactions to guide the user: when walking into the corresponding area, the corresponding cursor will appear under the feet to guide the path, and when leaving, the cursor will disappear, and the cursor will guide the path of the tour; when entering the specific area, the interactive objects will appear light effects to remind; when the object is selected, the object will appear a special light effect state. When you enter a specific area, the interactable objects will appear with light effects to remind you; when an object is selected, the object will appear with a special light effect state.

Figure 5. Pathfinder display

4.3. Summery

This chapter is an optimized design of the problems existing in the current education teaching exhibitions found in the above research results, trying to solve the deficiencies of the current teaching as well as the creative display system through the application of virtual reality technology, and realizing the integration of arts and sciences. Through learning in the virtual reality environment, students can experience the teaching process in a more immersive way, communicate their ideas more efficiently, realize the collision of thinking across time and space, and enhance the teaching efficiency while reducing the cost of practice.

The system design of applying virtual reality technology to art education is a feasible solution for the application of virtual reality technology to art education by combining the technical characteristics of virtual reality technology and the characteristics of teaching.

5. Conclusion

This paper explores the optimization of the existing art education system through virtual reality technology. In the design, taking the industrial design department of China Academy of Art as an example, the virtual teaching building and exclusive creation space for students of the National Academy of Art are built to enhance the sense of belonging and creative inspiration of the students of the Academy, and optimize the creative efficacy and experience.

Taking the comprehensive construction class as an example, the teacher can present the internal functional structure of the product to the students through the virtual environment, and the students can also carry out mechanical experiments through the virtual interaction, and even take a cloud tour of the machinery manufacturing workshop to understand the construction process. In this virtual reality technology architecture of the creation system, students can more immersive experience of the creative content, across the time and space for efficient learning and communication, more diverse interaction and interaction. The construction of the virtual teaching building makes it possible to visit and learn without regard to space and time, while the composition of personal space completely unleashes the creativity and imagination of the students. Depending on the alumni as a whole, through virtual reality technology, we can develop and tap into the huge social function and design power that has not been utilized so far, to inspire members and enhance the efficiency of work.

Virtual reality technology is rapidly changing and developing, and has been combined and utilized in every aspect of our lives. At a time when emphasis is placed on nurturing people and cultivating talent, the integration of virtual reality technology and artistic creation is an irreversible trend, and the addition of virtual reality technology will undoubtedly bring optimization and quality improvement to our creative methods. This is a process of fusion of art and technology, the successful operation of the system still needs careful design and debugging, and more unremitting efforts, but it must have corresponding social value and significance.

References

[1] Yingmiao Wu. Technical research and implementation of immersive virtual campus roaming system. Hunan University, 2018

[2] Yu-Li Chen, Chun-Chia Hsu, Self-regulated mobile game-based English learning in a virtual reality environment, Computers & Education, **154**, 2020,103910

[3] Lanju Li. Research and application of several key technologies of virtual reality in virtual campus. Liaoning: Northeastern University, 2008.

[4] Lin, C.-L.; Chen, S.-J.; Lin, R. Efficacy of Virtual Reality in Painting Art Exhibitions Appreciation. Appl. Sci. 2020, 10, 3012.

[5] Hairong He. Application of virtual reality technology in live news program. Western Radio and Television **2017** (11),14.

[6] Jiyu Wang. Application and research of virtual reality technology in industrial design teaching. Supervisor: Qu Zhenbo; Song Feng. Shandong University of Architecture, 2021.

[7] Ziyan Zhang. Research on virtual scene design Based on 3D vision. Journal of Physics: Conference Series, 2021,1848

[8] Kun Liang, Huang Xiaoli. Discussion on the application of virtual reality technology in education. Software Guide (Educational Technology) **2008** (03), 80-82.

[9] Yingjun Gong, Application of virtual reality teaching method and artificial intelligence technology in digital media art creation, Ecological Informatics **63** (2021),101304

[10] H.Y. Kan, Vincent G. Duffy, Chuan-Jun Su. An Internet virtual reality collaborative environment for effective product design. Computers in Industry **45** (2001), 2, 197-213

[11] Sarune Baceviciute, Thomas Terkildsen, Guido Makransky, Remediating learning from non-immersive to immersive media: Using EEG to investigate the effects of environmental embeddedness on reading in Virtual Reality, Computers & Education **164** (2021),104122,

[12] Horace H.S. Ip, Simpson W.L. Wong, Dorothy F.Y. Chan, Julia Byrne, Chen Li, Vanessa S.N. Yuan, Kate S.Y. Lau, Joe Y.W. Wong, Enhance emotional and social adaptation skills for children with autism spectrum disorder: A virtual reality enabled approach, Computers & Education **117** (2018), 1-15.

[13] Ünal Çakiroğlu, Seyfullah Gökoğlu, Development of fire safety behavioral skills via virtual reality, Computers & Education **133** (2019), 56-68

[14] Kyung-Min Park, Jeonghun Ku, Soo-Hee Choi, Hee-Jeong Jang, Ji-Yeon Park, Sun I. Kim, Jae-Jin Kim, A virtual reality application in role-plays of social skills training for schizophrenia: A randomized, controlled trial, Psychiatry Research **189** (2011), 2, 166-172

[15] Hilfert, T., König, M. Low-cost virtual reality environment for engineering and construction. Vis. in Eng. **4** (2016), 2, 1-18.

[16] D' Errico Maria. Immersive Virtual Reality as an International Collaborative Space for Innovative Simulation Design. Clinical Simulation in Nursing **54** (2021), 30-34

[17] González-Zamar, M.-D.; Abad-Segura, E. Implications of Virtual Reality in Arts Education: Research Analysis in the Context of Higher Education. Educ. Sci. **10** (2022), 225, 1-19

[18] Zahira Merchant, Ernest T. Goetz, Lauren Cifuentes, Wendy Keeney-Kennicutt, Trina J. Davis, Effectiveness of virtual reality-based instruction on students' learning outcomes in K-12 and higher education: A meta-analysis, Computers & Education, **70** (2014), 29-40
[19] Boletsis, C. The New Era of Virtual Reality Locomotion: A Systematic Literature Review of Techniques and a Proposed Typology. Multimodal Technol. Interact. **1** (2017), 24, 1-17

Design Studies and Intelligence Engineering
L.C. Jain et al. (Eds.)
© 2024 The Authors.
This article is published online with Open Access by IOS Press and distributed under the terms
of the Creative Commons Attribution Non-Commercial License 4.0 (CC BY-NC 4.0).
doi:10.3233/FAIA231426

Research on the Innovation Trend Direction of Fitness Products Based on the Construction Method of Patent Knowledge Graph

Shuwei YU[a], Jiongzhou WENG[a,1], Feiyang LIU[a], Hao HUO[a], Jinwei LU[a],
Jinhong HU[a], Ming ZHANG[a], and Yue WU[a]

[a] *China Jiliang University, College Art and Communication*

Abstract. To accelerate fitness product development and innovation, we propose a patent knowledge graph. Using a patent database and TF-IDF, we identify key areas and terms. This forms a keyword graph with inflation word analysis, guiding innovation direction. Applying this to fitness rowing machine innovation identifies needs. Empowering R&D for swift decisions enhances competitiveness.

Key words. Patent Knowledge, Graph Construction, Definition of Innovation Direction

1. Introduction

Defining the innovation direction for fitness products in R&D is critical yet challenging. Often, subjective decisions lead to substantial economic losses [1]. Hence, the emphasis is on scientifically and efficiently defining innovation, addressing development needs, and industrial design [2]. To achieve this, the paper will use a patent knowledge graph to enhance R&D efficiency and decision-making in fitness product innovation direction.

2. Research status of fitness product innovation methods

2.1 Current status of research and issues

Aerobic and anaerobic equipment are two main fitness product categories. Defining innovation is challenging, often relying on subjective experience and impacting profits. A scientific approach is needed. Ren Shuhao [3] proposed patent clustering. Wang Chaoxia [4] suggested mining patents for design innovation. This paper introduces a novel method using design and computer algorithms to construct a patent knowledge graph, quantitatively defining fitness product innovation for industrial design.

---

[1]Corresponding Author; E-mail: 603521575@qq.com

2.2 Patent Knowledge Graph Construction Method

Creating a knowledge graph entails data mining and information processing to visually represent scientific knowledge and activity patterns, highlighting interconnections and evolution [5]. Utilizing knowledge graphs to analyze patent data improves R&D and innovation decision-making by recognizing product evolution and technology links. Sternitzke et al. [6] underscored its importance in identifying significant technologies.

This paper employs patent data, a keyword extraction algorithm, and social network analysis to visualize the fitness product domain's knowledge map, revealing development trends and R&D focus. A thematic clustering algorithm assesses innovation viability, identifies patent gaps, and reveals R&D opportunities, defining the fitness product innovation direction.

3. Definition process of fitness product innovation direction based on patent knowledge graph construction method

The paper's research flow, depicted in Fig.1, identifies product development hotspots. This involves collecting fitness product patent data, utilizing TF-IDF [7] for keyword extraction, assessing lexical influence through knowledge graphs, and quantifying keywords with the inflated word algorithm. Gephi [8] visualizes the findings, and the LDA topic clustering model analyzes patent data for design innovation trends.

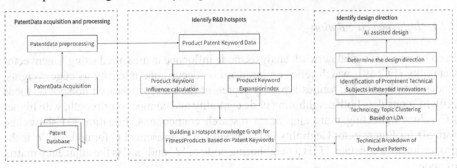

Figure 1. Flowchart of Patent Mapping Design and Evaluation Method.

3.1 Patent Data acquisition and processing

3.1.1 Patent Data Acquisition

In this paper, the search criteria listed in Table 1 are applied to the State Intellectual Property Office's patent database, yielding 6,238 records. Following the removal of unrelated data, 5,752 patent records pertaining to fitness products remain.

Table 1. Fitness Product Patent Search Criteria

Item	Search condition
Search term	Fitness Products OR Fitness Equipment OR Exercise Equipment OR Exercise Products OR Gym Product OR Gym Equipment
Patent Type	Invention Patent、Utility model patents
Patent Source	China National Intellectual Property Administration
Search time years	2011 - 2022
Data content	Title, Date, Abstract

3.1.2   Patent Data Preprocessing

Because Chinese patent data lacks keywords, keywords are extracted from patent abstracts using natural language techniques. The Jieba package in Python and a patent stopword list are used to tokenize and filter irrelevant data from the patent database.

TF-IDF (Term Frequency-Inverse Document Frequency) helps identify keywords that are distinctive within a document and suitable for categorization. It's calculated as TF (Term Frequency) * IDF (Inverse Document Frequency). TF measures a term's frequency in a document (see formula 1). Using the TF-IDF algorithm, we extract 5 keywords from the abstract, as shown in Table 2.

$$TF - IDF_{ij} = TF(d_i, t_j) \times IDF(t_j) = TF(d_i, t_j) \times \lg\left(\frac{M}{DF(t_j)}\right) \tag{1}$$

Table 2. TF-IDF algorithm keywords extraction

Patent Name	Summaries (d_i)	keywords (t_j)	$TF - IDF_{ij}$
An exercise bicycle brake-locking device	This fitness bicycle brake lock includes a fine-tuning knob, lever, and brake base. The knob is on the upper lever, connected to the brake base. One end of the fixed piece connects to the base, while the other secures to the bicycle frame. The brake base combines high-density wool and an aluminum seat for a simple, safe, and efficient design.	check	0.89838
		fine-tuning knob	0.23908
		exercise bike	0.20965
		High-Density Wool	0.12520
		aluminum collar	0.12520

3.2   Define R&D hotspots

3.2.1   Influence calculation

In co-occurrence social network analysis, node influence is measured using Eigenvector Centrality (EC) [9], which relies on keyword co-occurrence intensity as edge weights. Nodes with higher EC values typically represent the current research hotspot or focus [10]. EC considers both neighboring node centrality and connection strength, with higher EC values indicating more significant research connections. Equation (2) shows the formula for Eigenvector Centrality (EC_i), where 'x_i' represents EC for node 'I,' 'c' is the proportionality constant, 'j' is a neighboring node of 'I,' and 'a_{ij}' is the adjacency matrix of node 'i'.

$$EC_i = x_i = c \sum_{j=1}^{n} a_{ij} x_j \tag{2}$$

3.2.2   Expansion Index Calculation

In knowledge measurement, the inflation index [11] tracks keyword trend changes over time. Analyzing hot word frequency variations helps identify research evolution. For instance, formula (3) defines the inflation index, where 'a_j' is the expansion index of candidate word j, '$p_{i,j}$' is the word frequency at time 't_i,' and '$p_{i+1,j}$' is the word frequency at time 't_{i+1}' adjusted by the category's word frequency. Selecting words with a high inflation index 'a_j' within the current timeframe represents research frontiers for analysis. Frontier words are associated through keyword co-occurrence. Since we focus solely on the inflation of hotspot words '$p_{i+1,j} \leq p_{i,j}$,' their disappearance is no longer a concern when the inflation index 'a_j' is set to 0. Thus, we can recognize temporal R&D hotspot changes through the mentholated word formula's influence on patent keyword nodes.

$$a_j = \begin{cases} \dfrac{p_{i+1,j} - p_{i,j}}{p_{i,j} \times (t_{i+1} - t_i)} & p_{i+1,j} > p_{i,j} \\ 0 & p_{i+1,j} \le p_{i,j} \end{cases} \tag{3}$$

$$i = 1,2,\cdots,n; \; j = 1,2,\cdots,m$$

3.3   Design Direction Recognition

3.3.1   Latent Dirichlet Allocation

LDA [12] is a statistical model for patent data clustering, aiding structured comprehension, and accelerating knowledge discovery for innovation and decision-making. The model has three layers: topics, keywords, and documents, with Equation (4)[13] representing its complete joint distribution. $\boldsymbol{a}$ is the Delicacy prior distribution hyperparameter, and sampling $\boldsymbol{bi}$ from the polynomial distribution θA yields topic probability ' $P(\boldsymbol{bi} \mid \boldsymbol{a})$. To determine the optimal number of topics, Blei et al. [14] proposed using perplexity to assess language model quality. Lower perplexity signifies better sample prediction and determines the optimal number of topics, as per equation (5).

$$p(\omega, z, \theta_m, \varphi_k | \alpha, \beta) = \prod_{n=1}^{N} p(\theta_m, \alpha) p(z_{m,n}, \theta_m) p(\varphi_k, \beta) p(\omega_{m,n}, \theta_{z_{m,n}}) \tag{4}$$

$$perplexity(A) = \exp\left(\frac{-\sum_{a=1}^{M} ln(P(\omega_a))}{\sum_{a=1}^{M} N_a}\right) \tag{5}$$

4.   Building Fitness Product Hotspot Knowledge Graph from Patent Keywords

4.1   Building a hotspot graph for fitness products

A co-occurrence matrix derived from 5752 fitness product patents, with synonym cleaning, yielded 50 keyword nodes and 1158 edges in Gephi. Edges with weights exceeding 31.32 were used to generate the fitness product hotspot map shown in Fig. 2.

Figure 2. Fitness product hotspot graph

Fig. 2 shows fitness product hotspots: exercise bikes, rowing machines, ellipticals, dumbbells, and treadmills. Tab. 3 ranks keyword centrality, emphasizing exercise bikes, rowing machines, and ellipticals in fitness patents from 2011 to 2022.

Table 3. Node Eigenvector Centrality Data

Node Name	Eigenvector Centrality
Exercise Bike	0.91902
Rowing Machine	0.68830

Elliptical Machine	0.53097
Dumbbell	0.45127
Abdominal Exerciser	0.43000
Sit-up Machine	0.41822
Chin-up Bar	0.38957
Treadmills	0.36032

4.2   Constructing fitness product timing graphs

The fitness product chronogram reflects recent development trends, using inflation-based word calculations. We selected candidate words from Table 3's top-ranked hot product keywords and generated the chronogram, shown in Figure 3.

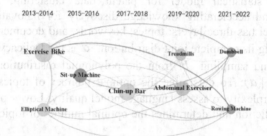

Figure 3. Fitness Product Timing Graph

Equation (2) calculated inflation indices for fitness product candidates, summarized in Tab. 4 over time. Among fitness keywords, 'exercise bike' and 'elliptical' initially grew, while 'rowing machine' and 'dumbbell' gained traction. This highlights 'rowing machine' as the recent primary research hotspot in fitness product patents, warranting further study.

Table 4. Cutting-edge Representations of The Fitness Product Sector

Time Phase	Product Name	Inflation Index (a_j)
2013–2014	Exercise Bike	2.20833
2013–2014	Elliptical Machine	1.0
2015–2016	Sit-up Machine	1.16667
2017–2018	Chin-up Bar	1.85
2019–2020	Treadmills	0.63953
2019–2020	Abdominal Exerciser	1.32
2021–2022	Rowing Machine	0.13725
2021–2022	Dumbbell	0.14329

5.   LDA-based direction recognition for rowing machine design

5.1   Technical Breakdown of Rowing Machine Patents

Using insights from fitness product hotspot mapping, we gained a quantitative understanding of fitness product design trends, with a focus on 'rowing machines.' To identify R&D hotspots in patented rowing machine technologies, we continued the method outlined earlier. We filtered 752 patents related to rowing machines from the National Intellectual Property Database, ultimately analyzing 716 patents.

Patent technology subject decomposition [15] uses specific rules to categorize technical branches, aiding designers in understanding a product's technical components.

Rowing machines were divided into five parts: resistance system, motion structure system, operation and control system, motion sensing system, and user feedback system, as depicted in Figure 4 based on patent technology composition.

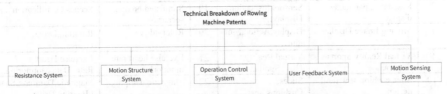

Figure 4. Technical Breakdown of Rowing Machine Patents

5.2 Technology Topic Clustering Based on LDA

Based on formula (5), perplexity calculation is used to find the optimal number of topics, and the results are presented in Fig. 5. The lowest confusion level is achieved when there are 23 topics. According to the perplexity score, the best theme clustering is achieved when 23 themes are selected from the literature.

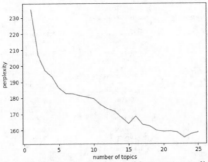

Figure 5. Rowing machine patent technology subject corresponding to the perplexity

Running the LDA topic clustering model produced technical topics and feature words for rowing machines. The output includes a 716×23 "document-topic" matrix, and Table 5 displays selected results from the "topic-feature word" matrix.

Table 5. Selected Rowing Machine Patent Technology Topics and Documents

File 1		File 2		File 3		File 4		File 5	
Topic	Probability	Topic	Probability	Topic	Probability	Topic	Probability	Topic	Probability
17	0.3798	18	0.3833	15	0.3655	2	0.4301	23	0.4839
23	0.3157	20	0.3296	13	0.2859	15	0.1457	10	0.1967
18	0.1636	17	0.1487	23	0.1462	4	0.1186	14	0.1057

Table 6. Rowing machine patent technology theme clustering and feature words

Technical topics		Feature Word	Technical topics		Feature Word
No	Topic Name		No	Topic Name	
1	of the user's movement posture	Sports;Training, Simulation…	13	Pedal structure design	Pedals,Instruments,Pedals…
2	Handle design	Handle,User,Hinge d…	14	Flywheel drag device	Resistance,Flywheel, Belt…
3	Adjustable bracket design	Bracket,Adjustable, Lift…	15	Folding structure design	Folding,Structure,Hinge d…
4	Handle reset function	Reset,Handle、,Fle xible…	16	Positioning Detection System	Detection,Hull,Motion…

5	Display Bracket Adjustment	Display,Bracket,Ad justable...	17	Structural design of the support frame	Bracket, Structure ,Bolt...
6	Provides assisted stretching	Stretching, Exercise,Trainer...	18	Provides running function	Multifunction,Treadmill ,Base...
7	Resistance parameter display	Sensors,Inspection, Display...	19	Simulated boating scenarios	Scenes,Gamification...
8	Moving Image Display	Display,Action,Mot ion...	20	Rotary drive	Rotation,Drive、 Gears...
9	Virtual Reality Sports Experience	Virtual Reality, User, Sports...	21	Exercise heart rate monitoring	Exercise,Heart Rate ,Data Monitoring...
10	Slide cushion structural design	Slides, Cushions,Seat...	22	Magnetic damping	Magnetic,Damping,Shaf t,Bearing,Drive...
11	Functional accessory combinations	Function,Compone nt,Handle...	23	Water resistance device	Tank,Paddle,Water ...
12	Provides anaerobic training function	Exercise,Multifunct ion、Strength...			

The LDA model-based topic clustering results above are summarized in the rowing machine patent tech decomposition table. The results are shown in Figure 6.

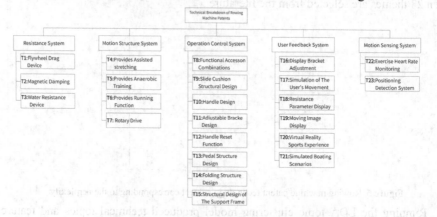

Figure 6. Rowing machine patent technology element structure

5.3　Identification of Prominent Technical Subjects in Patented Innovations

Using the 'doc-topic' matrix, we calculate topic probabilities within documents, filtering for technical topics with a probability >0.17. Then, we visualize a co-occurrence network of technical topics and measure their influence with Gephi, as seen in Fig7.

Figure 7. Rowing machine technology theme co-occurring network

Fig. 7 reveals that topics such as T11, T10, T15, and T3 hold central positions in the network, serving as key R&D hotspots in rowing machine technology.

Table 7's influence index identifies key patent tech areas for rowing machines: T8, T9, and T14, current research focuses, particularly in operation control systems. Avoiding saturated tech fields is advisable for product innovation.

Themes like T4 and T19 have lower influence. Prioritizing R&D in motion structure systems can create a 'blue ocean' opportunity in rowing machine product development, boosting innovation and competitiveness.

Table 7. Rowing machine technology theme impact table

Patented Technology Topics			Eigenvector Centrality
Secondary indicators	No.	Topic Name	
Resistance System	T$_1$	Flywheel Drag Device	0.85643
	T$_2$	Magnetic Damping	0.80573
	T$_3$	Water Resistance Device	0.87535
Motion Structure System	T$_4$	Provides Assisted Stretching	0.49364
	T$_5$	Provides Anaerobic Training Function	0.95625
	T$_6$	Provides Running Function	0.74934
	T$_7$	Rotary Drive	0.91373
Operation Control System	T$_8$	Functional Accessory Combinations	1
	T$_9$	Slide Cushion Structural Design	0.97538
	T$_{10}$	Handle Design	0.81675
	T$_{11}$	Adjustable Bracket Design	0.97538
	T$_{12}$	Handle Reset Function	0.8858
	T$_{13}$	Pedal Structure Design	0.89578
	T$_{14}$	Folding Structure Design	0.97538
	T$_{15}$	Structural Design of The Support Frame	0.93835
User Feedback System	T$_{16}$	Display Bracket Adjustment	0.82237
	T$_{17}$	Simulation of The User's Movement Posture	0.87535
	T$_{18}$	Resistance Parameter Display	0.7077
	T$_{19}$	Moving Image Display	0.478
	T$_{20}$	Virtual Reality Sports Experience	0.96163
	T$_{21}$	Simulated Boating Scenarios	0.92932
Motion Sensing System	T$_{22}$	Exercise Heart Rate Monitoring	0.80608
	T$_{23}$	Positioning Detection System	0.87302

6. Innovative directions and conclusions

This paper focuses on fitness products, utilizing patent data and knowledge graphs to analyze innovation directions, integrating results, and exploring AI software for design.

1) User Experience Innovation Direction（UX）：

Rowing machine UX design innovation centers on virtual reality sports experiences and simulated rowing scenarios, AI assists as shown in Fig.8.

Table 8. User Experience Innovation Direction Rowing Machine Innovation Ideas

Innovative Directions	AI	Topic Name	Keywords
User Experience Innovation Direction	Midjourney	Moving Image Display、Virtual Reality Sports Experience Technology、Simulated boating scenarios	Monitor、Analog、Virtual Reality、User Experience、Rowing Machine、Exercise Scenario

Figure 8. User experience innovation direction rowing machine design effect (AI)

2) Innovative Directions for Fitness Monitoring:

Rowing machine fitness innovation focuses on tech themes like simulating user training status, displaying resistance parameters, and motion images. Tab 9 outlines these themes, and AI tools and tech keywords shape Fig. 9's innovative direction diagram.

Table 9. Fitness Monitoring Innovation Directions Rowing Machine Innovation Ideas

Innovative Directions	AI	Topic Name	Keywords
Innovative Directions for Fitness Monitoring	Midjourney	Simulation of the user's movement posture、Resistance Parameter Display、Motion Picture Display、Exercise Heart Rate Monitoring、Positioning Detection System	User、Transducers、Monitor、Heart Rate、Rowing Machine

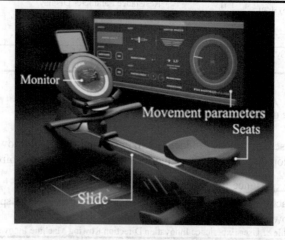

Figure 9. Fitness Monitor Innovative Directions Rowing Machine Design Rendering (AI)

3) Innovative directions for diversifying fitness functions:

Rowing machine fitness innovation diversifies with user-centric design, motion image display, and unique tech themes detailed in Table 10. AI assists in product rendering using specific keywords, as shown in Fig. 10.

Table 10. Fitness function diversification innovation direction rowing machine innovation ideas

Innovative Directions	AI	Topic Name	Keywords
Innovative directions for diversifying fitness functions	Midjourney	Provides Running Function、Slide Cushion Structural Design、Moving Image Display	Multifunctional Module、Treadmill Function、Slide、Cushion、Monitor

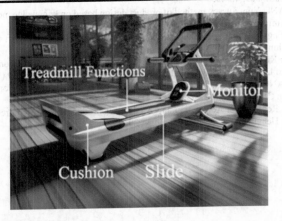

Figure 10. Fitness function diversification innovation direction rowing machine design effect diagram (AI)

The study shows that knowledge mapping reduces subjectivity, aiding in product discovery, R&D, and innovation. It speeds up trend comprehension, empowers designers, enhances competitiveness, and reduces the risk of misdirection.

Acknowledgments

Project supported by the Zhejiang Province Ideological and Political Education Research Project (Project Number: 220141), and the Zhejiang Province Philosophy and Social Sciences Annual Key Course: Research on Precise Supply of Innovative Urban Community Elderly Care Services in Standardized Format (Project Number: 22NDJC020Z)

References

[1] LIU Ji-hong. Development for Digitalized and Intelligent Product Design. Packaging Engineering 44 (2023) 08, 27-36.
[2] TAO Jiaqi,LI Xinyu,ZHENG Pai, , et al. State-of-the-art and frontier of manufacturing knowledge graph application. Computer Integrated Manufacturing Systems 28 (2022), 12, 3720-3736.
[3] REN Shuhao. Research on Product Innovation Design Method Based on Patent Data Network Cluster Analysis. Southeast University, 2021.
[4] WANG Zhaoxia,QIU Qingying,FENG Peien.Patent knowledge mining for conceptual design. Journal of Zhejiang University:Engineering Science 03 (2008), 522-527.
[5] LIANG Xiujuan. Review of Mapping Knowledge Domains. Library Journal 28 (2009), 06, 58-62.
[6] Sternitzke C, Bartkowski A, Schramm R. Visualizing patent statistics by means of social network analysis tools. World Patent Information 30 (2007), 2, 115-131
[7] HUANG Chenghui,YIN Jian,HOU Fang. A Text Similarity Measurement Combining Word Semantic Information with TF-IDF Method. Chinese Journal of Computers 34 (2011), 05, 856-864.

[8] PENG Yan, YAN Li. Visualization Analysis of Yunnan Nationality Medicine Research Based on Gephi. Journal of Medical Informatics **36** (2015), 02, 65-68+89.

[9] Liu Siwei,Zhou Lijun,Yang Jing, et al. Evolution of Standard Cooperation Network and Subject Identification in Artificial Intelligence Industry Technical Standard:Based on Social Network Analysis and TOPSIS Entropy Weight Method. Science and Technology Management Research **42** (2022), 06, 143-152.

[10] WEI Ruibin. An Empirical Study of Keywords Network Analysis Using Social Network Analysis. Journal of Intelligence **28** (2009), 09, 46-49.

[11] LIU Zheng;WANG Yun. Survey method of product design based on knowledge measurement. Computer Integrated Manufacturing Systems **26** (2020), 10, 2690-2702.

[12] Liao Liefa,Le Fugang,Zhu Yalan. The Application of LDA Model in Patent Text Classification. Journal of Modern Information **37** (2017), 03, 35-39.

[13] TAN Chun-hui,XIONG Meng-yuan.Contrastive Analysis at Home and Abroad on the Evolution of Hot Topics in the Field of Data Mining Based on the LDA Model. Information Science **39** (2021), 04, 174-185.

[14] ZHAO Kai,WANG Hongyuan. Research on the Optimal Topic Number Selection Method for LDA: A Case Study Based on CNKI Literature. Statistics & Decision **36** (2020), 16, 175-179.

[15] Zhai Jianpeng. Research on Acquisition and Analysis of Product Design Requirement Based on Patent Knowledge Mining. Hebei University of Technology, 2019.

Design Studies and Intelligence Engineering
L.C. Jain et al. (Eds.)
© 2024 The Authors.
doi:10.3233/FAIA231427

Sustainable Material Innovation Design for Building Construction: Exploring Bio-Based Alternatives

Benyu YANG[a] and Qun WANG[b,1] and Siu Shing MAN[a]

[a] *South China University of Technology, China*
[b] *Guangdong University of Petrochemical Technology, China*
ORCiD ID: Benyu Yang https://orcid.org/0009-0007-3380-9454

Abstract. Modern architecture stands at the convergence of innovation and sustainability, urging a reevaluation of construction materials. This paper explores the transformative potential of biomaterials in reshaping the ecological and aesthetic landscape of the built environment. By scrutinizing conventional materials' limitations, we introduce bio-based alternatives. Examining bamboo, hemp concrete, mycelium composites, and Bio-plastics reveals their unique attributes and life cycle assessments. Comparative analyses demonstrate bio-based materials' superiority in terms of carbon footprint, energy consumption, and waste generation. The innovative design strategy of bio-based materials is proposed, and the possible problems in implementation are summarized and the corresponding solutions are put forward.

Keywords. Biomaterials, sustainable construction, architectural innovation

1. Introduction

The construction industry has historically relied on traditional materials such as concrete and steel, which have proven effective in building structures but have serious environmental consequences. The construction industry is a highly active sector all over the world [1]. It is responsible for a high rate of energy consumption, environmental impact, and resource depletion[2]. Buildings have a direct impact on the environment, ranging from the use of raw materials during construction, maintenance, and renovation to the emission of harmful substances throughout the building's life cycle[3]. Resource-intensive production processes, high energy consumption and the emissions associated with these materials have led to a growing focus on their long-term sustainability. As the international community recognizes the urgency of addressing climate change and resource depletion[4], there is an urgent need to reassess building practices and explore greener alternatives[5]. As the impact of traditional building materials on the environment increases, its shortcomings become more and more obvious. Buildings consume substantial amounts of available raw materials, especially non-renewable raw materials, and produce large amounts of waste during extraction, transformation, construction, and demolition[6]. The current trajectory of construction is not sustainable. In order to minimize the environmental impact of the industry, the use of sustainable building materials has become a major focus of research and development to achieve the

---

[1] Corresponding Author: Qun Wang, weeqee@163.com

goals of sustainable construction and minimize the impact on the environment, while maintaining structural integrity and performance[7].

This paper aims to address these challenges by investigating the potential of bio-based materials as sustainable alternatives in building construction. Bio-based materials from renewable resources such as bamboo, hemp, mycelium composites, and Bio-plastics offer a promising pathway to reduce carbon footprint, conserve resources and promote eco-friendly building practices. The main objective of this study is to explore the characteristics, advantages and feasibility of incorporating bio-based materials into construction projects. By doing so, we seek to contribute to the advancement of sustainable building practices and support the transition to a more resilient and environmentally conscious built environment.

2. Conventional building materials and bio-based materials

Traditional building materials, such as concrete and steel, have long been the backbone of the built environment. However, their widespread use comes with a series of serious environmental deficiencies. Carbon emissions are alleged as a major contributor to anthropogenic climate change[8]. Buildings worldwide consume 40% of energy and contribute 33% of carbon emissions[9]. In addition, the extraction and processing of raw materials such as aggregate and iron ore consumes limited resources and destroys ecosystems[10]. Energy-intensive manufacturing processes further exacerbate the environmental impact, resulting in a significant consumption of non-renewable energy sources. As the consequences of these practices become more apparent, the urgency of transitioning to more sustainable alternatives increases.

Bio-based materials, including bamboo, hemp, mycelium composites, and Bio-plastics, have brought a promising shift towards sustainable building practices. Some of these building materials have been used for centuries, only beginning to be replaced by concrete in the 20th[11]. These materials come from renewable resources and harness nature's regenerative potential. Bamboo, for example, has impressive tensile strength while being a rapidly renewable resource. Hempcrete consists of hemp fibers and lime-based binders with excellent insulating properties and low embodied energy. Mycelium composites grown from fungi exhibit extraordinary versatility and customization potential. Bio-plastics are derived from bio-sources and provide a moldable and biodegradable alternative to traditional plastics. Bio-based materials emphasize their renewable nature and have the potential to significantly reduce dependence on fossil fuels and non-renewable resources.

In addition, bio-based materials align with circular economy principles by facilitating a cradle-to-cradle design approach. Unlike traditional materials, which often end up as waste in landfills, bio-based materials can be biodegradable or recycled, closing the loop and minimizing environmental impact. By reducing the need for resource extraction and limiting production-related emissions, these materials provide a pathway for a more regenerative construction industry.

3. Selection and performance of bio-based materials

A key aspect of exploring bio-based alternatives is understanding the unique properties and benefits that each material brings. Known for its rapid growth and superior tensile strength, bamboo offers a sustainable solution for structural components. Its inherent flexibility and elasticity make it ideal for a range of applications, from beams to floors. Architect PT Bambu has built a green school out of bamboo in Bali, Indonesia, demonstrating the versatility and strength of bamboo in architectural applications. Hemp concrete is made from hemp fibers combined with a lime binder, providing an environmentally friendly solution for insulation needs. Its porous structure regulates moisture and thermal conductivity, contributing to energy-efficient buildings. "Hemponair" in Switzerland is a private residence that uses hemp concrete as its walls. The mycelium composite originates from fungal growth and exhibits extraordinary versatility in form and function. In Brooklyn, New York, architect David Benjamin (founder of The Living Architecture Studio) has created "Mushroom Farm", an innovative architectural project that demonstrates the use of mycelium composites as a sustainable bio-based building material. These materials can be molded into a variety of shapes, providing opportunities for intricate details and innovative designs. Bio-plastics from organic sources have plasticity similar to conventional plastics while being biodegradable, thus solving the common challenge of plastic waste.

The adoption of any building material depends on its mechanical properties and durability. Extensive analysis of the mechanical properties of bio-based materials is essential to ensure their suitability for a wide range of structural elements. Bamboo's high-strength-to-weight ratio and excellent flexibility contribute to its load-bearing capacity. Although the density of hemp concrete is lower than that of conventional concrete, it exhibits remarkable insulating properties and long-term durability. Mycelium composites have inherent strength and adaptability, allowing them to withstand a wide range of loads and conditions. The mechanical properties of Bio-plastics vary by composition, offering a range of possibilities for design and function.

The performance of biobased materials on key indicators is also compared, and the performance of biobased materials is scored based on the common sense and typical characteristics of these materials as well as empirical data. The performance of biobased materials in terms of tensile strength, insulation properties, environmental impact, life cycle assessment, energy consumption, resource consumption, carbon footprint, and contained energy was compared and each material was assigned a score for each attribute on a scale of 1 to 10, with higher scores indicating better performance. See figure 1 to 4.

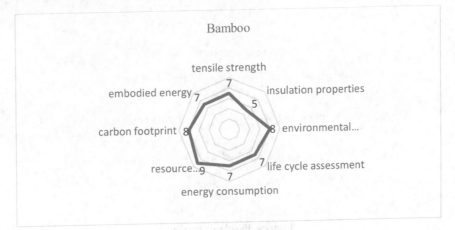

Figure 1. Bamboo fraction.

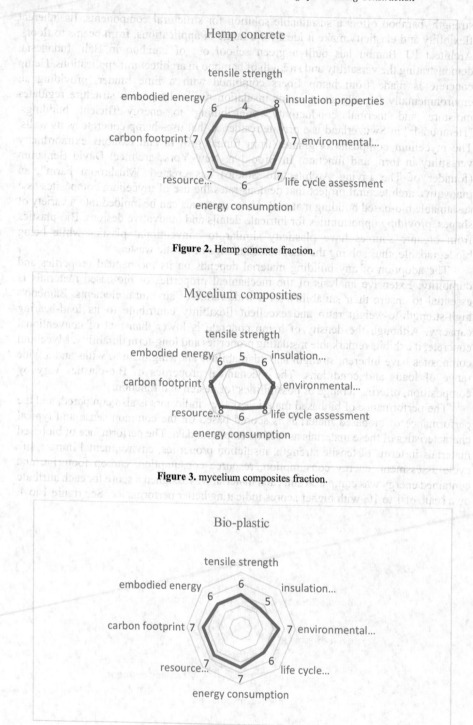

Figure 2. Hemp concrete fraction.

Figure 3. mycelium composites fraction.

Figure 4. Bio-plastic fraction.

4. . Innovative design strategies

Biomaterials have unique intrinsic qualities that offer architects new possibilities to design flexible and uniquely attractive buildings. These materials, such as bamboo, hemp concrete, mycelial composites, and Bio-plastics, introduce a fresh departure from traditional building materials and promote innovation in architectural design. Here's how the intrinsic properties of biomaterials can enhance the flexibility and uniqueness of buildings:

4.1. Organic aesthetics, sustainability and visual appeals

Biomaterials are valued for their organic textures, patterns, and colors that resonate with nature. This organic aesthetic is not just an aesthetic choice; It is closely related to sustainability. Biomaterials enhance architectural design by creating a harmonious connection between the built environment and the surrounding natural landscape. This inner beauty adds a layer of visual interest and realism to the space. The use of biomaterials is often an environmentally conscious statement that aligns with the Sustainable Development Goals and resonates with occupants who value eco-friendly living.

4.2. Customization, adaptability and formability

One of the main advantages of biomaterials is their versatility. They allow architects to customize the design according to the unique context of each project. Biomaterials are malleable and flexible during manufacturing and assembly, making them ideal for creating custom designs. Their adaptability simplifies the implementation of complex custom structures that are difficult to achieve with traditional materials.

4.3. Ecological and cultural significance

Biomaterials transcend their physical properties. They contribute to a deeper connection between the building and the environment. Embracing biophilic design principles, biomaterials emphasize the connection between humans and nature. Elements inspired by the natural world enhance the well-being and comfort of the occupants. In addition to ecology, biomaterials can also carry cultural significance through the use of indigenous materials that reflect local traditions. The integration of culture and environment into the architectural design results in buildings that represent the unique character of the region.

4.4. Tactile experiences and mixed material applications

Biomaterials provide a multi-sensory experience through their inherent texture and tactile properties. These qualities attract occupants and promote a deeper connection and interaction with the built environment. Spaces enriched with biological materials become more inviting and memorable. In addition, biomaterials seamlessly integrate with traditional materials, allowing architects to explore innovative hybrid solutions. This mixture of materials allows for structural integrity while achieving a unique aesthetic that balances tradition and innovation.

5. Implementation challenges and solutions

While bio-based materials hold great promise, they also present unique technical challenges during construction. The transition from traditional materials to bio-based alternatives may require adjustments to construction techniques, compatibility with existing systems, and careful material handling. Meeting these challenges is critical to ensuring seamless integration.

5.1. Strength and structure

Biomaterials often have different mechanical properties than traditional building materials such as concrete and steel. Ensuring that biomaterials meet the required strength and structural integrity standards is challenging.

Solution: Material characterization: Thorough characterization of the mechanical properties of biomaterials through testing, including tensile, compressive and bending strength. Mixing systems: Combining biological materials with conventional materials in a mixing system, taking advantage of their respective advantages. This approach can help achieve the desired structural properties while taking advantage of the advantages of biomaterials.

5.2. Durability

Biomaterials are prone to degradation, moisture absorption and biological attack, affecting their long-term durability.

Solution: Handling and protection: Apply appropriate treatments, coatings or sealants to enhance the resistance of biomaterials to environmental factors. Design considerations: Design load-bearing elements to minimize exposure to moisture and potential degradation sources, thereby extending the life of biomaterials.

5.3. Standards and specifications

Compared to traditional materials, biomaterials may lack established standards and specifications, leading to uncertainty in the design and approval process.

Solution: Conduct thorough research and testing to develop empirical data that can support the development of biomaterials design guidelines and standards. Work with regulators: Work with regulators to develop clear guidelines and specifications covering the use of biomaterials in load-bearing applications.

5.4. Construction techniques

The use of biomaterials may require specialized construction techniques that differ from traditional methods.

Solution: Conduct thorough research and testing to develop empirical data that can support the development of biomaterials design guidelines and standards. Work with regulators: Work with regulators to develop clear guidelines and specifications covering the use of biomaterials in load-bearing applications.

5.5. Dimensional change

Biomaterials, such as woody materials, also change in size due to changes in moisture content.

Solution: Proper drying and conditioning: Ensure that the biomaterial is properly dried and conditioned before being incorporated into the load-bearing element to minimize dimensional variation. Motion design: Incorporate design strategies that consider potential dimensional changes, such as allowing joints to be moved.

6. Conclusion

Through the lens of bio-based alternatives in building construction, a comprehensive exploration of sustainable material innovation begins. By delving into the environmental impacts, properties, challenges and practical applications of bio-based materials, a range of insights has been uncovered, revealing their potential to revolutionize the construction industry. Observe how these materials have the ability to reduce carbon emissions, conserve resources and improve the indoor environment, ultimately contributing to a more sustainable and resilient built environment.

It resonates deeply in the field of sustainable building practices. Bio-based materials provide a way to align buildings with ecological integrity and regenerative design principles. The feasibility of transitioning from traditional materials to bio-based alternatives without compromising structural integrity or design innovation was highlighted. Exploring bio-based alternatives is a positive step towards a more sustainable future, while ensuring the viability and longevity of the built infrastructure.

References

[1] Du Plessis, Chrisna. Action for sustainability: preparing an African plan for sustainable building and construction. Building Research & Information 33 (2005), 5, 405-415.

[2] Khasreen, Mohamad Monkiz, Phillip FG Banfill, and Gillian F. Menzies. Life-cycle assessment and the environmental impact of buildings: a review. Sustainability 1 (2009), 3, 674-701.

[3] Balaras, Constantinos A., et al. Heating energy consumption and resulting environmental impact of European apartment buildings. Energy and buildings 37 (2005), 5, 429-442.

[4] Vefago, Luiz H. Maccarini, and Jaume Avellaneda. Recycling concepts and the index of recyclability for building materials." Resources, conservation and recycling 72 (2013): 127-135.

[5] Van der Lugt, P., A. A. J. F. Van den Dobbelsteen, and J. J. A. Janssen. "An environmental, economic and practical assessment of bamboo as a building material for supporting structures." Construction and building materials 20 (2006), 9, 648-656.

[6] Berge, Bjorn. The ecology of building materials. Routledge, 2009.

[7] Ding, Grace KC. Life cycle assessment (LCA) of sustainable building materials: an overview. Eco-efficient construction and building materials 30 (2014), 2, 38-62.

[8] Pan, Wei, Kaijian Li, and Yue Teng. Rethinking system boundaries of the life cycle carbon emissions of buildings. Renewable and Sustainable Energy Reviews 90 (2018), 379-390.

[9] Sbci, U. N. E. P. Buildings and climate change: Summary for decision-makers. United Nations Environmental Programme, Sustainable Buildings and Climate Initiative, Paris 1 (2009): 62.

[10] Melià, Paco, et al. Environmental impacts of natural and conventional building materials: a case study on earth plasters. Journal of cleaner production 80 (2014), 179-186.

[11] Arrigoni, Alessandro, et al. Life cycle assessment of natural building materials: the role of carbonation, mixture components and transport in the environmental impacts of hempcrete blocks. Journal of Cleaner Production 149 (2017), 1051-1061.

Design Studies and Intelligence Engineering
L.C. Jain et al. (Eds.)
© *2024 The Authors.*
This article is published online with Open Access by IOS Press and distributed under the terms
of the Creative Commons Attribution Non-Commercial License 4.0 (CC BY-NC 4.0).
doi:10.3233/FAIA231428

Design of a Supernumerary Robotic Limb Based on Hybrid Control of Motion Imagination and Object Detection

Zhichuan TANG[a], Hang WANG[a], Zhixuan CUI[a], Jun DING[a,1], Lingtao ZHANG[a]

[a] *School of Design and Architecture, Zhejiang University of Technology, China.*

Abstract. Upper limb moto disorders are the main symptoms of stroke patients. Based on deep learning algorithms and object detection technology, we developed a brain-controlled supernumerary robotic limb system for upper-limb motion assistance. The system makes use of the motor imagery electroencephalogram (MI EEG) recognition model with graph convolutional network (GCN) and gated recurrent unit network (GRU) to obtain the patient's motion intentions and control the supernumerary robotic limb to move. The object detection technology can compensate for the disadvantages when using MI EEG alone like fewer control instructions and lower control efficiency. We also validated the feasibility and effectiveness of the system by designing model training experiment and target object grasping experiment. The results showed that the highest EEG classification accuracy using GCN+GRU algorithm achieved 92.32%, and the average success rate of grasping tasks achieved 88.67±3.77%.

Keywords. Stroke patients, Supernumerary robotic limb, Motor imagery, Object detection

1. Introduction

While the aging population continues to increase, the incidence rate of stroke and related diseases is also rising [1]. Patients with upper limb motor disorder caused by diseases such as amyotrophic lateral sclerosis (ALS), Parkinson's disease, progressive muscular atrophy (PMA), stroke, and spinal cord injury generally have limited mobility and daily activities [2]. These issues have already affected their daily activities, reduced the happiness of patients' lives, and brought enormous mental pressure to patients [3].

Supernumerary robotic limb, as wearable robot devices, can assist patients with motor disorder in various daily tasks [4]. Currently, the design and research of Supernumerary robotic limb remains an important challenge [5]. Most existing control methods use healthy limb to control the movement of the supernumerary robotic limb, which has problems such as high training time cost, high operational difficulty, and low overall coordination [6]. Therefore, many scholars have conducted in-depth application research on supernumerary robotic limb based on different physiological structures and application functions. Ciullo [7] propose a robotic supernumerary limb, the Soft-Hand X

---

[1] Corresponding author, School of Design and Architecture, Zhejiang University of Technology, 310023, China; E-mail: dingunun@163.com

(SHX) to re-enable hand use, and providing a degree of functionality and motivating against learned non-use. Charles[6] designed a robotic leg for assisting patients in walking with supernumerary limb assistance. Its more comfortable human-computer interaction mode makes it easier for patients to adapt to the inertial impact caused by the movement of supernumerary limb mechanical legs. Federico[8] designed a wearable supernumerary robotic limb that can provide support for the wearer with fixed objects around it, enabling it to complete corresponding tasks safely and stably.

Brain Computer Interface (BCI) as a system for human brain intention to interact with external devices [9], it can be used to identify the limb motion intentions of patients with upper-limb motor disorder, quickly transmit control commands, and manipulate external devices to complete daily life tasks [10]. Patients with upper limb motor disorder can use the motor imagination paradigm to imagine their own limb movements and output EEG signals to control external devices [11]. This approach allows patients to interact more naturally with external devices, enhancing or replacing the damaged physical functions of disabled individuals[12]. However, due to the low signal-to-noise ratio of EEG signals during motor imagery （MI）, the decoding accuracy of EEG is low [13]. Some recent studies have used some feature selection related algorithms [14], such as the Common Space Pattern (CSP) based on L1 Norm and Dempster Shafer theory [15], to find reliable features and improve the motor imagery classification performance [16]. Other studies have obtained deep features that can describe different MI classification through deep learning methods such as Deep Belief Networks (DBN)[17], and Long Short Term Memory (LSTM) networks[18]. Convolutional Neural Networks (CNN) [19] can be directly used for feature automatic extraction of raw input signals, and can obtain deeper and more differentiated feature information for EEG signal recognition [20,21]. However, traditional CNN methods do not consider the topological relationship and structural information of EEG electrodes, so they cannot grasp the topology relationship and structural information of EEG electrodes. Graph Convolutional Network (GCN) provides an effective way to describe the internal relationships between different nodes in a graph [22]. It is suitable for topological feature extraction of discrete spatial EEG signals, and combined with the temporal feature grasp by Gated Recurrent Unit network, it can fully extract the temporal and spatial feature information of EEG. However, due to the limitations of EEG decoding performance, it is still difficult to control external devices with multiple degrees of freedom to accurately reach and grasp the desired target in complex three-dimensional (3D) space through methods such as MI classification. Target detection as an auxiliary control method can solve the problem of insufficient control dimensions caused by brain computer interface control of supernumerary robotic limb.

Object detection technology can extract 2D or 3D information from images or videos, and use this information to recognize and locate target objects, thereby achieving auxiliary control for robots to grasp specific objects [23]. In this study, when the robotic arm enters an unfamiliar environment, the camera detects the measurement data of the target, obtains the corresponding environmental information and target features, guiding the robotic arm to carry out targeted movements, and helping the robotic arm determine and move its own position.

In this paper, we designed and developed a brain controlled supernumerary robotic limb system that meets the needs of patients with upper limb motor disorder. The system obtains the patient's motion intention through MI EEG signal recognition model based on graph convolutional neural network and gate loop unit network, achieving left and right motion control of the supernumerary robotic limb, and combines object detection technology to quickly grasp the target object, compensate for the limited control dimensions of MI control strategy while improving the control accuracy of the robotic arm.

2. External robot arm system

2.1. System framework

The supernumerary robotic limb system we have designed and developed is divided into software and hardware parts. Among them, the software part has two modules, including an MI recognition module and an object detection module. The MI recognition module is mainly used for obtaining EEG data and identifying motion intentions during patients engage in MI, then converting it into control signal and output. The object detection module is used to find, mark target objects, and calculate the grasping path. Combined with the control program, achieve the grasping and releasing function of the robotic limb. The hardware part includes a functional clothing, a robotic limb module, and a drive control module. The functional clothing is used to carry the robotic arm and related hardware, and the robotic arm module serves as a moving component to achieve grasping action. The workflow of the entire supernumerary robotic limb system is shown in Figure 1.

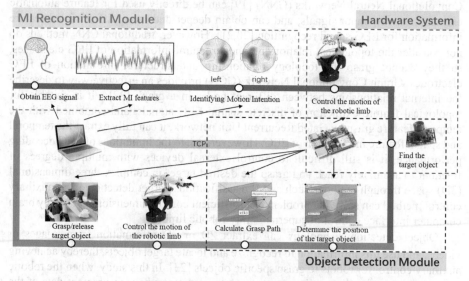

Figure 1. System framework diagram.

2.2. Hardware system

The hardware part of the supernumerary robotic limb we designed and developed is shown in Figure 2. The entire hardware system consists of a biomimetic robotic limb, a bionic hand, a camera, a functional clothing, a fixed base, a control backpack, and an EEG cap. The control backpack is embedded with hardware modules such as an electric motor drive board, a lithium battery, and a Raspberry Pi microcomputer. The entire robotic limb is fixed to the right shoulder of the functional clothing through a base, the control backpack is fixed to the back of the functional clothing, and the hardware part of the entire supernumerary robotic limb is fixed to the patient's upper torso through two elastic bands of the functional clothing. Both the robotic limb and the robotic finger control the servo motor drive through the drive board, and the camera is located at the end of the robotic limb to detect the target object in real-time, and cooperate with the robotic finger to achieve grasping action.

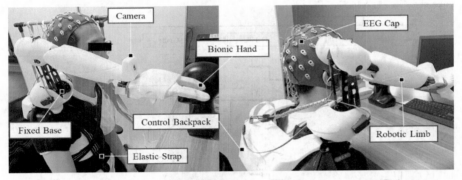

Figure 2. Hardware system.

2.3. Software System

The supernumerary robotic limb software we have developed and designed includes two parts: an MI recognition module and an object detection module, which are used to obtain and recognize the patient's motion intention and convert it into a robotic limb control signal. Combined with the object detection module, the supernumerary robotic limb grasping action is achieved.

2.3.1. MI recognition module

The MI recognition model we have developed and designed includes a feature extraction section and a classification section, specific framework as shown in Figure 3. Firstly, the collected EEG data is filtered across 11 frequency bands, and the EEG data from each frequency band is separately input into the MI recognition model. The data is divided into several time periods using the overlapping window method, and then reconstructed into graph data to extract spatial topology features into the GCN model. In the GCN model, each EEG channel corresponds to a node in the graph data, and the connection between two different nodes corresponds to the edges of the graph. Among them, the operation of graph convolution can be represented as

$$H^{(l+1)} = f(L^{sym}H^lW^l) \qquad (2\text{-}1)$$

where H^l and $H^{(l+1)}$ are the 1 th graph convolutional layer and the l+1 th graph convolutional layer, $f(\cdot)$ is the ReLU activation function, W^l is the weight matrix of the lth graph convolutional layer, and L^{sym} is the symmetric normalized Laplace matrix.

The time series data learned from the GCN model is then input into the GRU model for temporal feature extraction. There are update gates in the GRU model z_t and reset door r_t. There are two types of gates, whose operations can be represented as

$$z_t = \sigma(W_{xz}x_t + W_{hz}h_{t-1} + b_z) \qquad (2\text{-}2)$$

$$r_t = \sigma(W_{xr}x_t + W_{hr}h_{t-1} + b_z) \qquad (2\text{-}3)$$

Where σ represents the sigmoid function, W is the weight matrix and b is the deviation.

The Y value output by the GRU model will be sequentially transmitted to the fully connected layer, SoftMax layer, and classification output layer to generate category labels (left or right) for predicting MI motion intention. Finally, the best MI recognition model for the affected patient will be selected by comparing the best classification results of different EEG frequency bands.

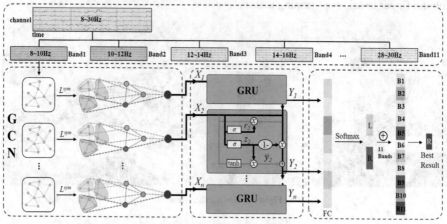

Figure 3. Framework diagram of MI recognition model.

2.3.2. Object detection and control module

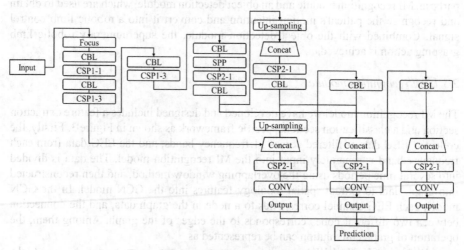

Figure 4. Framework diagram of the YOLO model.

The object detection module we have developed and designed is used to identify different target objects within the target area and provide position information of the object to further accurately control the motion of the robotic limb. Among them, we chose the more concise and faster YOLO [24] framework as the algorithm for the object detection module. The basic process includes two processes: pre-setting anchor boxes to locate the target and identifying the located target. The framework of the YOLO model is shown in Figure 4.

3. Experiment

3.1. Experimental Procedure

For our designed supernumerary robotic limb system, we conducted validation experiments on the MI recognition model and overall functionality, to evaluate the accuracy of the model and the grasping and collaboration capabilities of the supernumerary robotic limb. Firstly, we selected 10 subjects and trained them with MI models, obtaining MI models for each subject in different EEG frequency bands. Based on the model training results, we selected the model with the highest recognition accuracy in different frequency bands as the final model for this subject. Afterwards, the subject wears a 64 channel EEG cap and fixed the robotic limb to the right shoulder using two elastic bands. Each subject is required to conduct 25 grasping experiments on each target object, totaling 75 grasping experiments. They grasped different objects (paper cups, cloth bags, or plates), and the experimental scene is shown in Figure 5. The success rate of grasping is defined as the percentage of times the subject successfully grasp the target object.

Figure 5. Experimental Scenarios for Grasping Three Types of Objects.

3.2. Results of Experiment

In the MI model training experiment, we obtained MI recognition models of different subjects in different EEG frequency bands, and the model recognition accuracy is shown in Table 1. We found that the accuracy of the models trained by the same subject in different frequency bands was different. For example, subject 1 had the lowest MI classification accuracy (78.19%) in the 26-28Hz frequency band, and the highest MI classification accuracy (91.28%) in the 18-20Hz frequency band. The highest MI classification accuracy corresponding to each subject is shown in Figure 6. We selected MI recognition models from different subjects within the frequency band with the highest MI classification accuracy as the optimal model for each subject in the grasping experiment. To ensure the optimal results can be obtained in the grasping experiment. In the grasping experiment, the subject controlled the supernumerary robotic limb to perform grasping tests on three types of objects, achieving high target object recognition accuracy. The success rate of identifying and grasping three types of items by each subject is shown in Table 2. The results showed that the average success rate of grasping the cloth bag task was the highest, at 87.2 ± 3.60%. The average success rates of grasping the paper cup task and the plate task were 80.4 ± 3.67% and 81.6 ± 2.15%, respectively. Figure 7 shows the average success rate of each subject in three types of grasping tasks. The results showed that subject 10 had the highest average grasp success rate, which was 88.67 ± 3.77%, while subject 5 had the lowest average grasp success rate, which was 78.00 ± 3.27%.

Table 1. MI classification accuracy across EEG frequency bands for all subjects

Brands	Subject 1	Subject 2	Subject 3	Subject 4	Subject 5	Subject 6	Subject 7	Subject 8	Subject 9	Subject 10
8-10 Hz	0.8836	0.7847	0.9005	0.8108	0.8937	0.8747	0.8864	0.7765	0.7894	0.7861
10-12 Hz	0.7891	0.7409	0.9011	0.8306	0.8463	0.8629	0.8672	0.7895	0.8037	0.7971
12-14 Hz	0.8906	0.7761	0.9164	0.8557	0.871	0.8341	0.8903	0.8147	0.7686	0.9232
14-16 Hz	0.9122	0.7849	0.8896	0.8893	0.8977	0.8334	0.9011	0.8904	0.8064	0.9011
16-18 Hz	0.8902	0.8428	0.8548	0.8766	0.9026	0.8016	0.9047	0.8874	0.8791	0.8962
18-20 Hz	0.9128	0.8133	0.8247	0.8679	0.9032	0.7983	0.8945	0.8659	0.8447	0.8871
20-22 Hz	0.8439	0.8569	0.9017	0.7908	0.8907	0.7769	0.7839	0.8744	0.8806	0.7891
22-24 Hz	0.8017	0.8667	0.8948	0.7984	0.8528	0.6981	0.8896	0.8537	0.9148	0.8833
24-26 Hz	0.8022	0.8436	0.8961	0.8458	0.7837	0.7832	0.8738	0.8647	0.8904	0.7886
26-28 Hz	0.7819	0.8111	0.9018	0.8573	0.7739	0.7468	0.8457	0.8328	0.8746	0.775
28-30 Hz	0.7871	0.8005	0.8761	0.8366	0.7814	0.7233	0.8168	0.7906	0.8622	0.7351

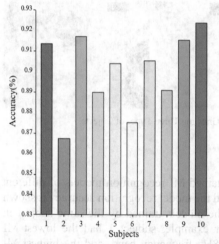

Figure 6. Maximum MI classification accuracy for each subject

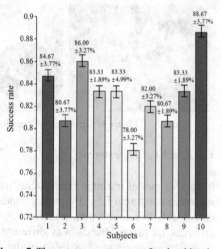

Figure 7. The average success rate of each subject in three types of crawling tasks.

Table 2 The success rate of each subject's three types of the grasping experiment

subject	paper cup	cloth bag	Ceramic plates
1	82.00%	90.00%	82.00%
2	78.00%	86.00%	78.00%
3	86.00%	90.00%	82.00%
4	82.00%	86.00%	82.00%
5	78.00%	90.00%	82.00%
6	74.00%	82.00%	78.00%
7	78.00%	86.00%	82.00%
8	78.00%	82.00%	82.00%
9	82.00%	86.00%	82.00%
10	86.00%	94.00%	86.00%
Average±std	80.4±3.67%	87.2±3.60%	81.6±2.15%

4. Conclusion and future work

This article designs a supernumerary robotic limb system based on BCI and object detection technology to assist patients with upper-limb motor disorder in completing daily grasping tasks. The MI recognition model and overall functional feasibility of the system are experimentally verified, providing a reference for solving the problems of high training cost and high operational difficulty of supernumerary robotic limb. Among them, the hybrid control strategy designed based on GCN+GRU network model and combined with object detection technology has made some preliminary theoretical contributions to improving the overall coordination and accurate recognition and transformation of motion intentions of Supernumerary robotic limb.

References

[1] I. Miyai, A. D. Blau, M. Reding, and B. T. Volpe, Patients with Stroke Confined to Basal Ganglia Have Diminished Response to Rehabilitation Efforts, Neurology **48** (1997), 1, 95–101.

[2] P. Raghavan, "Upper Limb Motor Impairment After Stroke, Physical Medicine and Rehabilitation Clinics of North America **26** (2015), 4, 599–610.

[3] R.-R. Lu et al., "Motor imagery-based brain-computer interface control of continuous passive motion for wrist extension recovery in chronic stroke patients," Neuroscience Letters **718** (2020), 134727.

[4] H. Xie, Z. Ding, S. Yoshida, T. Chong, T. Torii, and T. Fukusato, Augmenting Human with Compact Supernumerary Robotic Limbs, in 13th Augmented Human International Conference, Winnipeg MB Canada: ACM, May 2022, pp. 1–4.

[5] P. Maciejasz, J. Eschweiler, K. Gerlach-Hahn, A. Jansen-Troy, and S. Leonhardt, A survey on robotic devices for upper limb rehabilitation, J NeuroEngineering Rehabil **11** (2014), 1, 3.

[6] C. Khazoom, P. Caillouette, A. Girard, and J.-S. Plante, A Supernumerary Robotic Leg Powered by Magnetorheological Actuators to Assist Human Locomotion, IEEE Robot. Autom. Lett. **5** (2020), 4, 5143–5150.

[7] F. Parietti and H. Asada, Supernumerary Robotic Limbs for Human Body Support, IEEE Trans. Robot., 32 (2016), 2, 301–311.

[8] L. F. Nicolas-Alonso and J. Gomez-Gil, Brain Computer Interfaces, a Review, Sensors **12** (2012), 2, 1211–1279.

[9] A. Remsik et al., A review of the progression and future implications of brain-computer interface therapies for restoration of distal upper extremity motor function after stroke, Expert Review of Medical Devices, **13** (2016), 5, 445–454.

[10] M. A. Khan, R. Das, H. K. Iversen, and S. Puthusserypady, "Review on motor imagery based BCI systems for upper limb post-stroke neurorehabilitation: From designing to application," Computers in Biology and Medicine, vol. 123, p. 103843, Aug. 2020.

[11] F. Lotte, M. Congedo, A. Lécuyer, F. Lamarche, and B. Arnaldi, "A review of classification algorithms for EEG-based brain–computer interfaces," J. Neural Eng. **4** (2007), 2, R1–R13.

[12] S. R. Soekadar et al., "Hybrid EEG/EOG-based brain/neural hand exoskeleton restores fully independent daily living activities after quadriplegia," Sci. Robot., **1** (2016), 1, 3296.

[13] J. Jin, R. Xiao, I. Daly, Y. Miao, X. Wang, and A. Cichocki, "Internal Feature Selection Method of CSP Based on L1-Norm and Dempster–Shafer Theory," IEEE Trans. Neural Netw. Learning Syst. 32 (2021), 11, 4814–4825.

[14] J. Jin, Y. Miao, I. Daly, C. Zuo, D. Hu, and A. Cichocki, Correlation-based channel selection and regularized feature optimization for MI-based BCI, Neural Networks 118 (2019), 262–270.

[15] B. Sun, X. Zhao, H. Zhang, R. Bai, and T. Li, EEG Motor Imagery Classification With Sparse Spectrotemporal Decomposition and Deep Learning, IEEE Trans. Automat. Sci. Eng., 18 (2021), 2, 541–551.

[16] Z. Tang, C. Li, and S. Sun, Single-trial EEG classification of motor imagery using deep convolutional neural networks, Optik **130** (2017), 11–18.

[17] Y. Chu, X. Zhao, Y. Zou, W. Xu, J. Han, and Y. Zhao, A Decoding Scheme for Incomplete Motor Imagery EEG With Deep Belief Network," Front. Neurosci., **12** (2018), 680.

[18] G. Dai, J. Zhou, J. Huang, and N. Wang, HS-CNN: a CNN with hybrid convolution scale for EEG motor imagery classification, J. Neural Eng. **17** (2020), 1, 016025.

[19] B. Xu et al., Wavelet Transform Time-Frequency Image and Convolutional Network-Based Motor Imagery EEG Classification, IEEE Access, 7 (2019), 6084–6093.

[20] Y. Hou et al., Deep Feature Mining via Attention-based BiLSTM-GCN for Human Motor Imagery Recognition. arXiv, Dec. 02, 2021. Accessed: Aug. 08, 2023. [Online].

[21] R. Ying, R. He, K. Chen, P. Eksombatchai, W. L. Hamilton, and J. Leskovec, Graph Convolutional Neural Networks for Web-Scale Recommender Systems, in Proceedings of the 24th ACM SIGKDD International Conference on Knowledge Discovery & Data Mining, London United Kingdom: ACM, Jul. 2018, pp. 974–983.

[22] J. Qi et al., An improved YOLOv5 model based on visual attention mechanism: Application to recognition of tomato virus disease, Computers and Electronics in Agriculture, vol. 194, p. 106780, Mar. 2022.

[23] Redmon J, Farhadi A. YOLOv3: An Incremental Improvement. arXiv: April. 08, 2018. Accessed: August 8, 2023. [Online].

Design Studies and Intelligence Engineering
L.C. Jain et al. (Eds.)

97

doi:10.3233/FAIA231429

Measurement and Optimization of Navigation Bar Icon Design in Mental Health Apps

Zihan WEI[a], Yuxiang KUANG[a], Zhanhui GAO[b, 1]

[a] *Jiangxi University of Finance and Economics, Academy of Arts*
[b] *Foshan PERFECTID Industrial Design Co. Ltd.*

Abstracts. Iconic symbols in the digital age, as an important part of app design, play a central role in transmitting information between the app and the visitor. To optimize the design of mental health app navigation bar icons and improve the user experience of mental health apps. The design features are summarized by analyzing the current design status of existing mental health app navigation bar icons; the hierarchical analysis method is used to determine the evaluation index system of the navigation bar icon of the mental health app, the fuzzy judgment matrix is determined through the expert survey and the SPSS software is used to calculate the weight value of each evaluation element; redesigning mental health app navigation bar icons by refining design elements through icon recognition experiments and user preference surveys; evaluation and analysis of the program using fuzzy comprehensive evaluation to demonstrate the feasibility of this design solution. The evaluation results show that the scheme achieves the effective integration of recognizability, interactivity and aesthetics. In conclusion, a method for designing and evaluating the navigation bar icon of mental health apps based on fuzzy hierarchical analysis is proposed, and the feasibility of the method is verified through a specific design scheme.

Keywords. Mental health app, icon design, iconography, fuzzy hierarchical analysis, icon recognition

1.Introduction

Icons are not only used to beautify and decorate the application to bring the user the most direct visual experience of the interface components, but also to facilitate the user to understand and guide the user to operate the application functions of the important hub. The word "icon" is derived from the Greek word "eikon", which means image. In computer science, an icon is a graphical symbol displayed on the screen that guides or indicates a program, command, data file, window, option, or concept [1]. Usually, the icon used is related to the function of the project it needs to perform, in which the navigation bar icon mainly plays a role in connecting different contents or interfaces and is mainly used to guide the user how to go to the next target page or access the next target content, and when the user clicks on icon, the current interface will jump.

---

1 Corresponding Author: Zhanhui Gao, Foshan PERFECTID Industrial Design Co.Ld, 1501, Block 3, South Zone, Bikguiyuan City Garden, Chancheng District, Foshan City, Guangdong Province, P.R. China; E-mail: 379869619@qq.com.

There are many research results on icon design, from the perspective of icon cognition, Chun-Ching Chen investigates the icon design of applications for different mobile operating systems by designing icon identification experiments based on the key components of icons, to understand the recognition performance and user preference of different icon types [2]. Romain Collaud et al, developed icon design principles of aesthetics, complexity, and concreteness [3]. Provide a reliable reference source for navigation bar icon design evaluation metrics. Weili Li et al. proposed a fuzzy hierarchical analysis based on the underground station name graphic symbol design and evaluation method to validate the feasibility of this method through specific through specific case design, to improve the visual recognition of the name of the underground station. The visual recognition of subway station names is improved [4]. The above study provides a design research methodology for mental health app navigation bar icon design.

The research on navigation bar icon design of mental health apps is mostly summarized in the interface design research, and there are few specific studies on navigation bar icon design of mental health apps. Although the design of icons is included in the overall design of the interface, it also has its unique design thinking and design rules, based on mental health app design features, the fuzzy hierarchical analysis method is used to establish an evaluation index system for the design of icons in the navigation bar of mental health apps, and the design elements are extracted through icon recognition tests and preference surveys, so as to optimize the design of the navigation icons of mental health apps and verify their feasibility, so as to increase the efficiency of the use of the mental health apps.

2. Mental Health App Navigation Bar Icon Design Feature Analysis

2.1 Mental health app navigation bar icon design expression analysis

On the app application platform, the search was conducted by entering the keywords mental health and emotion, and 10 apps with distinctive navigation bar icon features were selected from the top 20 apps with a platform app (iOS system) rating higher than 4.7 and ranked in the top 20 apps to be analyzed.

Icons are mainly in the form of linear icons, faceted icons or line-face combination icons, and different styles of icon styles are formed by giving different design details.

Table 1. Mental health app navigation bar icon design expressions.

Form of expression	Hidden Meaning	Icon Classification
Linear Icons	Graphics are visually represented through lines, creating a variety of design styles through the thickness of the line, the color of the line, and whether or not the line segments are notched.	
Faceted Icons	Relative to the linear icon has a larger visual area, more can attract the attention of the user, so set often appear in the first screen of the home page function of the entrance area, or the bottom of the navigation of the selected state.	
Line-face Combination Icons	Based on the line thickness, color pattern, etc. of the linear icon, the area size and color variation of the surface icon, we can design the line and surface icon that combines with each other, outline the outer shape of the line, fill in the inner shape, or add the bottom shape outside of the line, and other design methods.	

2.2 Morphosyntactic analysis of navigation bar icon design for mental health apps

At the beginning of the twentieth century, the American semiotician Peirce put forward his famous trichotomy of symbols, which are icon, index, and symbol [5]. The trichotomy lays a good theoretical foundation for later generations to sort out all kinds of symbolic phenomena. According to the conceptual description, the navigation bar icons of mental health apps are categorized, to avoid subjectivity, five professionals engaged in UI interface design are invited to collaborate in the division, and the results are shown in the figure below.

Table 2(left). Semantics of mental health app navigation bar icon design image.

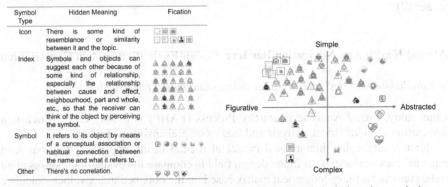

Symbol Type	Hidden Meaning	Fication
Icon	There is some kind of resemblance or similarity between it and the topic.	
Index	Symbols and objects can suggest each other because of some kind of relationship, especially the relationship between cause and effect, neighbourhood, part and whole, etc., so that the receiver can think of the object by perceiving the symbol.	
Symbol	It refers to its object by means of a conceptual association or habitual connection between the name and what it refers to.	
Other	There's no correlation.	

Figure 1(right). Mental health app navigation bar icon design morphological quadrant analysis.

Pierce's symbol trichotomy has some guidance for the classification of icons, but cannot accurately categories all icons, quite a lot of symbols are mixed with these three components, and even some do not have any relevance to the meaning, so it is not possible to determine the type of a particular symbol belongs to, so far there is no specific standard for the division of the icon's image degree, and most of the scholars adopt the scale to assess the user's perception of the image of the icon. Most scholars use a scale to assess the degree of users' perception of icon image [6].

To further understand the morphosyntax of icons and explore the relationship between symbol semantics and the morphological composition of symbols, the different types of symbols in table 2 are marked differently, with the square box representing the Icon, the triangular symbols representing the Index, the circular symbols representing the Symbols, and the heart symbols representing the Other. According to Pierce's semantics of symbols, the synthesis of the division of the opinions of several designers, the establishment of the four quadrants, according to the table 2 icon body pattern of the form of the division, horizontally by the image to the abstract, vertically by the simple to the complex, in which the image of the icon can be simply understood as the icon with a specific semantics, the abstract icon, that is, without any semantics of the icon, simplicity means that the combination of point, line and surface elements of an icon is simple in composition, and vice versa for complexity.

It can be observed from figure 1 that most of the icon forms of mental health navigation bar icons Icon and Index are simple and graphic, and the symbols are strongly related to the topics. The icon forms of Symbol and Other are mostly complex and abstract, and the relevance of the symbols to the topic is weak.

2.3 Analysis of mental health app icon design interaction form

The interaction process is the process of input to the computer and output to the user. Icon interaction is also a "relationship" between the viewer, the icon itself, and the web page [2]. According to the survey analysis, the interaction mode of mental health bar app navigation bar icon is mainly clicking, but the form of operation expression is different, and can be divided into two forms of expression: static and dynamic.

The use of interactive icons makes the user an active participant rather than a passive recipient, which improves the efficiency of icon use. Icons with good interactivity will help to complete the in-depth communication between the interface and the user [7].

3.Mental Health App Navigation Bar Icon Design Evaluation System Construction

3.1 Establishment of design evaluation indexes and model construction

In this study, Fuzzy Analytic Hierarchy Process (FAHP) is mainly used, which is a combination of hierarchical analysis and fuzzy comprehensive evaluation.

Firstly, establish a hierarchical model of mental health app navigation bar icon design indexes, invite experts in the design field to compare the evaluation indexes at all levels, construct a fuzzy judgement matrix based on the obtained index values, calculate the weight values of the indexes at all levels and carry out the ranking, according to the ranking of the weight values and at the same time combining with the icon recognition experiments and user preference surveys to guide the design practice, and finally carry out a fuzzy comprehensive evaluation of the design scheme for the navigation bar icons of health apps.

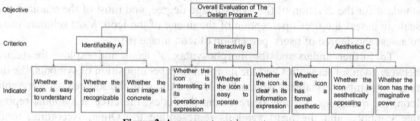

Figure 2. Assessment metrics system.

Through the literature reading to collect the indicators that affect the icon design, to screen out the most influential indicators, through the questionnaire survey, to collect the opinions of professionals engaged in the design, a total of 15 questionnaires were issued and 15 valid data were retrieved. According to the results of the questionnaire survey, interactivity > recognizability > design aesthetics > artistry (in order of importance) was selected as the first level indicators, and the top three second level indicators were also selected. Merge design aesthetics and artistry into aesthetics and then filter.

As shown in figure 2, according to the results of the questionnaire, based on the theories of cognitive psychology and semiotics, combined with the relevant icon design methods, the icon design indicators of the navigation bar icon design of mental health apps are divided into three levels: the overall evaluation of the design scheme Z is the Objective; recognizability A, interactivity B, and aesthetics C are the first-level indicators, i.e. the Criterion; and nine second-level indicators are divided into the Indicator based on the indicators of the Criterion. The details are as follows.

(1) Recognizability A includes the following indicators: a1 whether the icon is easy to understand; a2 whether the icon is recognizable; a3 whether the icon image is concrete.

(2) Interactivity B includes the following indicators: b1 whether the icon is interesting in its operational expression; b2 whether the icon is easy to operate; b3 whether the icon is clear in its information expression.

(3) Aesthetics C includes the following indicators: c1 whether the icon has the form of aesthetics, i.e., the way of expression, which is the way of experience of obtaining aesthetics in the form of visual elements; c2 whether the icon has the aesthetic attraction, i.e., whether it produces visual attraction; c3 whether the icon has the imaginative power.

3.2 Judgement matrix construction and weight determination

Adopting the 1-9 scale method, 1-9 scale values and meanings are shown in table 3 six experts in the field of design were invited to make a two-by-two comparison of the evaluation indexes of the navigation bar icon design of mental health apps, and the scale numerically embodies the level of importance between the two indexes.

Table 3. Scoring Scale weights of indicators of the evaluation system.

Factor i Over Factor j	Quantitative Value
equal importance	1
slightly important	3
more important	5
high priority	7
extremely important	9
the median of two neighboring judgments	2, 4, 6, 8
inverse comparison	1, 1/2, ..., 1/9

Table 4. weights of indicators of the evaluation system.

	AHP Hierarchical Analysis Results				Summary of Results of Consistency Tests			
Items	Eigenvector	Weight Value	Maximum Eigenvalue		CI	RI	CR	Consistency Test Results
			Z					
Identifiability A	2. 121	70. 706%						
Interactivity B	0. 604	20. 141%	3. 096		0. 048	0. 520	0. 092	pass
Aesthetics C	0. 275	9. 153%						
			A					
Ease of understanding a1	1. 668	55. 593%						
Discriminatory or not a2	1. 061	35. 372%	3. 054		0. 027	0. 520	0. 052	pass
Is the icon image specific a3	0. 271	9. 035%						
			B					
Is the icon manipulation presentation interesting b1	0. 814	27. 137%						
Ease of use of icons b2	1. 702	56. 731%	3. 029		0. 015	0. 520	0. 028	pass
Clarity of presentation of icon information b3	0. 484	16. 132%						
			C					
Whether the icon has formal beauty c1	1. 645	55. 593%						
Whether the icon is aesthetically appealing c2	0. 723	24. 091%	3. 018		0. 009	0. 520	0. 018	pass
Is the icon imaginative c3	0. 632	21. 061%						

Comprehensive six experts of the scoring value, remove the maximum value and the minimum value, take the average value, through the SPSSAU platform for online analysis, the software uses the sum product method of calculation, the number of orders of the judgement matrix for the third order, the analysis of the weight value of the indicators, and at the same time to carry out consistency tests in order to illustrate that the judgement matrix use as well as to get the weights are reasonable, scientific, usually the smaller the CR value, the better the judgement matrix is. Usually the smaller the CR value, the better the consistency of the judgement matrix, generally the CR value is less than 0.1, the judgement matrix to meet the consistency test. As shown in table 4.

From the weight value of each indicator, it can be obtained that the importance of each element in the mental health navigation bar icon design is ranked, which provides a reference for the mental health app navigation bar icon design. According to the weight value of each indicator, it is concluded that the recognizability indicator of mental health app navigation bar icon design is the most important, and the weight ratio of the ease of understanding of the icon is the largest among the secondary indicators, followed by the interactivity indicator, and the weight ratio of the ease of operation of the icon is the largest among the secondary indicators, and lastly, the aesthetics indicator, and the weight ratio of whether the icon has a formal aesthetic is the largest among the secondary indicators. Therefore, when designing icons, it is necessary to improve the comprehensibility of icons to improve the recognizable features of icons, and at the same time improve the operability of icons, enhance the interactive experience, and make them have formal aesthetics, to make the icons of the navigation bar of mental health apps practical and aesthetically pleasing.

4.Mental Health App Navigation Bar Icon Design Element Extraction

4.1 Mental health app navigation bar icon information content classification

All the mental health app navigation bar icons in table 1 were categorized according to the textual explanations accompanying their icons and the information content of the page to which they belonged, there are 8 modules, but not all apps had these modules.

To ensure the accuracy of the recognition test, the study did not categorize them in a general way. Mental health apps have their own functional characteristics, and most of the information architecture is common, among which the heart, online answers, and community have social attributes in their page information content, and most of the apps in this part of the psychological course are categorized in the home page. Due to the different focuses of the apps, the elaboration is also different, which results in the display of icons in the navigation bar of the apps as well as the setting of content boards are all different.

4.2 Experimental design of navigation bar icons for mental health apps

The experiment is divided into two parts, the identification experiment, and the preference survey, where the identification experiment contains an accuracy experiment and a discrimination experiment.

4.2.1 Objective

The recognition experiment is to analyze the most recognizable navigation bar icon design features to provide reference for mental health app navigation bar icon design. The preference survey is to extract more design elements that meet the evaluation indexes and achieve design diversification.

4.2.2 Participants

A total of 20 (10 male and 10 female, all aged 20-30) smartphone users were invited to take part in the experiment, and each participant was proficient in operating a smartphone and had used more than five apps.

4.2.3 Implementation

The experiments were conducted in the PS software on the same computer, all on a white background, the size of the icon in each test in accordance with the current iOS system app navigation bar design specifications size unity in 44 * 44px, icon line width is maintained at about 15-17px, the icon color unity in black, which line surface icon unity of black and grey.

4.2.4 Process

Accuracy experiment, all the icons are disrupted and distributed irregularly in the upper half of the A4 white background page, the testers take turns to conduct the test, select the icons and drag them into the table below to classify them, in order to ensure the irregularity of the distribution of the icons, the distribution of the icons seen by each tester in a different location, at the same time the testers will be given the answers to the checking after the test, and answer the questions, Q1 the reason you classified them incorrectly is; Q2 the reason you classified it correctly is. As in figure 3 there is no time limit for this experiment until all the icons are classified.

Figure 3. Accuracy experimental design (left) and discriminative experimental design(right).

Discriminative experiments, the icons with the correct rate below 40% were excluded through accuracy experiments, and the trials were reset. The same icon attributes and other interfering icons were arranged in a 5*5 arrangement in the page, as in fig 3 and the position of the icon arrangement as well as the interfering icons in the experimental diagram of the test looked at by each person was different, to ensure that the test icons were arranged in an irregular manner. The textual explanation of the icons was given before the experiment, and the experimental subjects were asked to select the category icons they belonged to from the experimental diagram, and to point their fingers until they reached the icons, and a person in charge of the experiment recorded the first selected icon of each tester.

The preference survey mainly set questions around the design image of mental health app icons, icon operation and interaction forms, icon colors and design opinions. The questionnaire was designed by Questionnaire Star and distributed to the testers to fill in.

4.2.5 Measurements

Data from three experiments were recorded and statistically analyzed.

- Accuracy Experiment- The correctness of the classification of each icon was derived from the results of each person's icon classification, while the responses to questions Q1 and Q2 were analyzed using word frequency software.
- Discriminative experiment- Sorting and analyzing the target icons according to the number of times they were selected in the experimental graph.
- Preference Survey- The questionnaire data was analyzed.

4.3 Analysis of results and discussion

4.3.1 Accuracy experiments

As shown in table 5 combined with the quadrant diagram (figure 1), it was found that most of the icons with more than 80 per cent correctness were in quadrants one and two, and the icons were highly figurative, i.e., they had concrete figurative semantics. Most of the icons with less than 20 percent correct are in quadrants two and three, where the icons are abstract, i.e., they do not have concrete image semantics.

Table 5. Results of the accuracy experiment analysis (left) and discriminatory experimental analyses (right).

Accuracy Experiments		Discriminatory Experiment	
Correct Rate	Icon	Icon Glyphs	Icon Selection Rate Sorting
80%-100%	⌂▣▢◉◉◉◉◉ ♟♟▢◉♟♟♟	Home Page	▣>◈>◱> ◉
		Heartfelt Wishes	\
60%-80%	◉▣◉◉◯	Online Q&A	◈=◉>◯
40%-60%	◉▣◈▣▢◯▣	Community	▣>◈
20%-40%	◉♡◉◉▣◯◉◉ ▢♡	Consult	◉>▣>▣
		Messages	▢>▲=▢>◯>◯=◯
0%-20%	◉▣◈◉◉▣◉◕ ◉▣▣	My Home Page	♣>♟>♟=◉=◯>♟=◯=◯
		Psychology Program	\

According to the results of word frequency analysis, the reasons for wrongly classifying icons can be roughly categorized into these points: abstract icons, which do not match the meaning of the words; similar meanings expressed by the icon images, multiple meanings of one picture, and confusion in classification; unfamiliarity with the icons, which is not understood; conflict with one's own understanding, and ambiguity in the meaning of the words. The reasons for correctly classifying icons can be categorized as follows: the icon is easier to understand than the image; the icon is familiar and often used; it matches the meaning of the word and has a high degree of similarity.

4.3.2 Discriminatory tests

As shown in table 5 combined with the results of the accuracy experiments, the icons in the categories of heartfelt and psychological courses were excluded because the lexical images were too close to each other resulting in a low accuracy rate of the icons belonging to these two categories. The analysis results show that the icons with high selection rate are in quadrant 1 and 3 respectively, with high icon image and more specific semantics, and at the same time, it is found that the one with more complex icon structure in the same category of icons is easier to identify.

4.3.3 Preference survey test

From the survey results show that 60% of the people prefer to use the face icon, 100% of the people choose to click as the operation method, 80% of the people prefer the dynamic form of interaction, the icon color is more inclined to the blue, green, most of the people in the design opinion hope that the mental health app icon design image is vivid and warm healing.

4.4 Discussion

It can be proved through the experiment that the higher the image degree, the easier it is to identify the icon, and the complexity of the icon composition has less impact on the recognition of icons, generally the more specific the icon is, the more complex the composition is and the easier it is to recognize it. At the same time, the experiment indirectly clarifies the classification of the information content board of mental health apps, which can be divided into homepage, community, counselling, news, and my, and these categories of icons have a small error rate and a high degree of familiarity. The preference survey provides a more comprehensive design reference for mental health navigation bar icons.

5 Mental Health App Navigation Bar Icon Design Options and Evaluation

5.1 Mental health app navigation bar icon design solution

According to the experimental results, the icon design of the mental health app is expressed in the form of face-shaped icons, the color is blue-green, and the interaction form of the icon has a dynamic effect, and the operation method is clicking. Home page, community, consult, messages, personal homepage as the icon text meaning, through the transformation of the icon form with high recognition rate in the experiment to establish the navigation bar icon image with the exclusive characteristics of mental health apps, modelling the use of the heart shape in the original icon form on the basis of the fusion of innovation, the overall design of the unity and aesthetics, specific as follows.

Table 6. Design proposal.

Icon Glyphs	Operating Method	Operation Expression (before – after clicking)
Home page	Click	
Community	Click	
Consult	Click	
Messages	Click	
Personal homepage	Click	

5.2 Mental health app navigation bar icon design solution recognition test

The design icon was unified in black and gray, with the same specification as the test icon in the recognition experiment, and 10 people (5 men, 5 women, who had not participated in the recognition experiment before) were arranged to perform the design icon recognition test according to the same steps of the recognition experiment in the previous section. The results showed that in the accuracy experiment, the correct rate of the design icons of this group were all above 90%, and in the discrimination experiment, the rate of the design icons of this group being selected were all above 80%. The results of the recognition test proved that the recognizability of the navigation bar icons of this group of mental health apps is high, and the design solutions have achieved the expected effect in terms of application guidance.

5.3 Evaluation of mental health app navigation bar icon design program

The design scheme is evaluated by comprehensive fuzzy evaluation method, and the evaluation set V= {unsatisfied, generally, satisfied} is established for the mental health app icon design scheme, and assigned the values of 0, 0.5 and 1 to form a quantitative evaluation set: V= {0, 0.5, 1}. The questionnaire is set up and data are collected based on "Questionnaire Star", which is published on WeChat, with real-name login and each respondent is allowed to answer only once. The sample consisted of designers with UI design experience, design students who are skilled in using various apps, and a random sample of people who have used psychological apps. The survey was conducted from 5th August 2023 to 7th August 2023, and a total of 96 valid questionnaires were returned, and the data of the questionnaire on the satisfaction with the design scheme are shown in table 7.

Table 7. Data from the questionnaire on satisfaction with the design program.

Title	Option	Options (unit: votes)		
		Unsatisfied	Generally	Satisfied
Identifiability A	Icons easy to understand a1	4(4.17%)	12(12.5%)	80(83.33%)
	Icons are recognizable a2	7(7.29%)	26(27.08%)	63(65.63%)
	Icons are graphic and concrete a3	7(7.29%)	20(20.83%)	69(71.88%)
Interactivity B	Icon manipulation presentation interesting b1	3(3.13%)	7(7.29%)	86(89.58%)
	Icons are easy to manipulate b2	4(4.17%)	27(28.13%)	65(67.71%)
	Icon information is clearly expressed b3	4(4.17%)	16(16.67%)	76(79.17%)
Aesthetics C	Icons have formal beauty c1	4(4.17%)	17(17.71%)	75(78.13%)
	Icons have aesthetic appealc2	5(5.21%)	19(19.79%)	72(75%)
	Icons are imaginative c3	5(5.21%)	18(18.75%)	73(76.04%)

Using online SPSS analysis software, the fuzzy comprehensive evaluation is carried out for 9 indicators and 3 comment sets, and the M (., +) operator for the study. Calculate the affiliation function of the design solution M (. , +), i.e:

First, establish the evaluation index weight vector matrix A, and construct the 9x3 weight judgment matrix R, and finally analyze the weight value of 3 comment sets, respectively: 0.048, 0.188, 0.764. From table 8, we can see that the weight value of satisfaction is the highest in the 3 comment sets (0.764), and combined with the law of maximum subordination, we can see that the result of the comprehensive evaluation is "satisfied".

Table 8. Results of weighting calculations.

Results of Weighting Calculations			
	Unsatisfied	Generally	Satisfied
Degree of Affiliation (Statistics)	0.048	0.188	0.764
Normalized Degree of Affiliation [Weight]	0.048	0.188	0.764

Online SPSS analysis software in the fuzzy comprehensive evaluation, will be based on the calculation of the weight value, as well as the score of each indicator item, to get the comprehensive score value, the principle of its calculation is the indicator item score and the weight value multiplied by the cumulative. The comprehensive score is shown in Table 9, and the overall satisfaction of the design solution is 85.8%, Illustrates that the design solution establishes a good human-application interaction while realizing the functional basis of recognizability of the mental health app navigation bar icons, at the same time, to meet the aesthetics of the design of the navigation bar icons.

Table 9. Overall evaluation of the design program.

Objective	Aggregate Score	Criterion	Aggregate Score	Indicator	Aggregate Score
				Icons easy to understand a1	0.9
		Identifiability A	0.84	Icons easy to understand a1	0.79
				Icons are graphic and concrete a3	0.82
Overall Evaluation of The Design Program Z	0.858			Icon manipulation presentation interesting b1	0.93
		Interactivity B	0.88	Icons are easy to manipulate b2	0.82
				Icons are easy to manipulate b2	0.88
				Icons have formal beauty c1	0.87
		Aesthetics C	0.86	Icons have aesthetic appeal c2	0.85
				Icons are imaginative c3	0.85

6. Conclusion

To make the navigation bar icon of mental health app really play the role of navigation and improve the efficiency of application use. The design method of mental health app navigation bar icon based on fuzzy hierarchical analysis, analyses domestic and international app icon design methods, summarizes the design law of mental health app navigation bar icon, proposes the design process of mental health app navigation bar icon based on fuzzy hierarchical analysis, and designs a complete set of mental health app navigation bar icon. The evaluation results show that the scheme better reflects the identifiability, interactivity, and aesthetics of mental health apps, verifies the reasonableness and feasibility of the fuzzy hierarchical analysis-based mental health app navigation bar icon design method, it is of great practical significance to improve the user experience of mental health apps and increase the willingness of users to continue to use the app. This design scheme can provide methodological reference for future mental health app navigation bar icon design.

References

[1] U.S. BenShneiderman, Translators: Zhang Guoyin, Li Jianzhao, etc., Designing the User Interface, Electronic Industry Press; 2005, p.135.

[2] Taipei, Taiwan. Chun-Ching Chen, User Recognition and Preference of App Icon Stylization Design on the Smartphone, International Conference on Human-Computer Interaction, HCI International 2015 - Posters' Extended Abstracts (2015), 9-15.

[3] Switzerland, U.K. Romain Collaud a, Irene Reppa, etc., Design standards for icons: The independent role of aesthetics, visual complexity and concreteness in icon design and icon understanding, Display 74 (2022), 102290.

[4] C.N. Weili Li, Yunhao Sun, etc., Design of graphic symbols for subway station names based on fuzzy hierarchical analysis method, Packaging Engineering 42 (2021), 14.

[5] C.N. Lingxuan Pei, Yang Liu, Interpreting Nanjing's Urban Imagery from Peirce's Semiotic Perspective, The Grand View of Fine Arts (2020), 07.

[6] C.N. Yunzhi Yan, A Study of Cognitive Processing of Icon Design Elements and Their Interactions, Guangdong University of Technology, 2013.

[7] U.S. Alan Cooper, The Inmates Are Running the Asylum: Why High-Tech Products Drive Us Crazy and How to Restore the Sanity, Beijing: Electronic Industry Press; 2006, p. 67.

Design Studies and Intelligence Engineering
L.C. Jain et al. (Eds.)
© 2024 The Authors.
This article is published online with Open Access by IOS Press and distributed under the terms
of the Creative Commons Attribution Non-Commercial License 4.0 (CC BY-NC 4.0).
doi:10.3233/FAIA231430

Research on the Application of Traditional Culture in Product Innovation Design

Jian HAN[a,1] and Xinran YU[b]

[a] *college of fine arts, Jiangxi Normal University, Nanchang, China*
[b] *college of fine arts, Jiangxi Normal University, Nanchang, China*

Abstract. Purpose: By analyzing the development status of traditional culture in my country, to explore the problems and difficulties encountered in product design of traditional culture in our country, to propose that traditional culture needs to be innovated and reformed, and to discuss the principles to be followed in the innovative application of traditional culture today gist. Methods: Through literature analysis, case comparison and other research methods to understand the social environment at home and abroad, to analyze the literature of traditional cultural product design innovation, and to summarize excellent design cases. Conclusion: The traditional innovative design of traditional culture needs balanced development, focusing on the regional and contemporary nature of products.

Keywords. traditional culture, product design, innovation

1. Overview of traditional culture

1.1. Concept

The word "culture" existed in ancient China. The original meaning of "wen" refers to the interlaced textures of various colors. The original meaning of "hua" is change, generation, good fortune. But today's "culture" broadly refers to the way of life of human society and the value system based on it. It is the sum of material wealth and spiritual wealth created by human beings in the process of social and historical development. Now refers directly to knowledge. Traditional culture refers to the national culture that reflects the characteristics and features of a nation through the evolution of a certain civilization and is the overall representation of various ideological cultures and ideological forms in the history of a nation. It includes a nation's values, epistemology, method system, way of life, thinking habits, etc. passed down from generation to generation. It is a relatively complete spiritual system. Chinese traditional culture is based on the three traditional cultural thoughts of Confucianism, Buddhism and Taoism. The three are interdependent, interpenetrating and influencing each other to build the whole of Chinese traditional culture. Traditional culture is diverse and broad, including ancient prose, poetry, music, folk music, drama, and national costumes, living customs [1-3].

---

[1] Jian Han.: Jiangxi Normal University, Vocational Title: Professor, Position: Department Director, Research direction: product innovation design, E-mail: 46335546qg.com.

1.2. Necessity

Traditional culture has its inevitability and importance, it has a profound impact on the individual, the society, and the country:

From the perspective of culture and identity, traditional culture is the spiritual pillar of the society, which embodies the history, value, and identity of the society. In a diversified society, people can understand their own cultural environment and improve their cultural identity through traditional culture. In addition to these, there is a sense of values, a code of ethics, and a code of conduct that is passed down from generation to generation. This value concept plays an important role in guiding people's behavior, cultivating people's moral quality, maintaining social harmony, and maintaining social stability. Because traditional culture is the witness of human history, only by inheriting and developing it, can human understanding and experience of history be passed on from generation to generation, and can human culture be enduring. This will prevent cultural heritage from being forgotten. The creation of many arts and cultures is also inspired by traditional culture. Traditional culture can stimulate people's creativity and promote new artistic creation and innovation.

Traditional culture not only occupies a place in the country, but also plays the role of a bridge in the world. In this process, the mutual understanding and mutual promotion between countries and nations, thus promoting cultural exchanges and cooperation among countries. People experience and inherit traditional culture together, which can strengthen social cohesion and unity, and thus promote the stable development of society. Therefore, as an important cultural resource, traditional culture attracts people to experience and understand. It plays a positive role in promoting regional economy, increasing employment, and improving regional image.

In general, traditional culture plays a huge role in maintaining individual identity, promoting cultural inheritance, promoting innovation, and enhancing social cohesion, and has irreplaceable value for the sustainable development of a society and a country [4].

2. Status of traditional culture

However, today, traditional culture is facing many practical problems and challenges. The following are some concrete examples to illustrate these problems:

The first is the loss and lack of culture, and the development of traditional agriculture and handicrafts in many villages in China has tended to stall. For example, many young people do not want to continue working in village but seek other opportunities in the city. This resulted in the loss of traditional agricultural production techniques and knowledge, which had a certain impact on the inheritance of rural culture. Second, commercialization and superficializing make traditional festivals and celebrations lose their deep cultural connotation in the process of commercialization; Taking the Chinese Spring Festival as an example, due to the influence of market competition, some places only pay attention to the publicity of firecrackers, shopping, and other aspects, while ignoring the cultural traditions behind the festival and the values related to family reunion. Third, the reform of education system, which is being carried out in many countries, is likely to weaken traditional culture. In some places, due to the emphasis on scientific and technological education, the inculcation of traditional culture may not be enough. For example, in our country, some schools attach much more importance to modern curriculum than to traditional cultural activities. Fourth, cultural collision: In the context of economic globalization, some traditional cultures are likely to suffer from the impact of different cultures. For example, in some parts of the developing nation, thanks to the popularity of Western popular culture, young people are more likely to accept foreign values than to pay attention to their own traditional culture. Fifth, the impact of the digital society. The rise of the digital society makes teenagers more addicted to the Internet, while ignoring the learning and experience of traditional culture. For example, many young people spend more time on network socializing and online games, but seldom participate in traditional cultural activities. Young people's participation is not enough: some young people do not have enough interest in traditional culture, and the enthusiasm to participate is not high. Some traditional festivals or rituals have fewer opportunities for young people to participate, which affects the inheritance of traditional culture among young people. Taking these examples together, traditional culture is facing a series of problems such as loss, commercialization, educational reform, cultural collision, digital impact, etc. These problems may have an impact on the inheritance and development of traditional culture and need to be solved by the joint efforts of all sectors of society [5-7].

Based on the plight of traditional culture in the context of The Times, traditional culture also faces similar and more complex problems in product design, mainly involving commercial distortion and innovation.

Commercial orientation distortion: In the business environment, some companies will use traditional cultural elements to design products, but due to excessive commercial considerations, cultural elements will be distorted. Commodities only attach some traditional cultural patterns on the appearance, but there is no real understanding of the cultural implications, which causes the emptiness of commodities. For example, the cultural and creative products of many museums on the market are printed directly on daily products with the patterns of artworks. For example, some products only pay attention to their appearances, but ignore the complex implications. This will cause people to have a wrong understanding and prejudice of traditional culture. For example, simply using a cultural symbol without understanding the deeper meaning raises questions about cultural sensitivity. In addition, there is the risk of cultural consumerization, that is, traditional cultural elements are consumerized and become a commodity rather than a true cultural inheritance. For example, some cultural souvenirs sold in scenic spots will become a kind of rampant commodities, thus losing their original cultural connotation [8].

Lack of creativity the design of some products relies too much on traditional cultural elements and lacks creativity; This will result in a stereotypical product design, which is difficult to appeal to young people. For example, the traditional pattern is directly applied to the product design, but it cannot integrate new elements and new ideas, resulting in the product is not novel enough. At the same time, because commodities are global, they inevitably face consumers from different cultures. When trying to apply traditional cultural factors to the design, special attention should be paid to avoid cultural collision and misunderstanding. For example, a symbol in one culture may have a different meaning in another.

Based on the above development status, to better understand the real problems faced by the innovation and inheritance of traditional culture in real life, as well as people's attitudes and expectations for traditional cultural inheritance, the author conducts research in the form of a questionnaire. From Table 1, both men and women have a simple understanding of traditional culture; However, both believe that the innovative inheritance of traditional culture is very important. However, there is still debate about how traditional culture needs to innovate. Moreover, most participants believe that the lack of young people's interest, the incompatibility of products with modern life, and the excessive similarity of products are the main problems faced by the current traditional cultural innovation and reform (as shown in Table 2), as can be seen from Table 3, the main factors for this are due to insufficient recognition and participation of the public.

Table 1. Results of the intersection (chi-square) analysis of women's and men's understanding of traditional culture and the importance of innovation

Topic	Options	Gender(%)		Total	x^2	p
		Female	Male			
How much do you know about traditional culture?	Learn a little	55(79.71)	15(48.39)	70(70.00)		
	Very little is understood	5(7.25)	5(16.13)	10(10.00)	11.560	0.009**
	Almost do not understand	1(1.45)	0(0.00)	1(1.00)		
	Well understood	8(11.59)	11(35.48)	19(19.00)		
	Total	69	31	100		
How important do you think is the innovation and inheritance of traditional culture?	In general, innovation can be carried out appropriately	3(4.35)	3(9.68)	6(6.00)		
	It is important and requires a continuous legacy of innovation	40(57.97)	10(32,26)	5050.00)	5.861	0.053
	Important, but need to maintain the traditional core	26(37.68)	18(58.06)	44(44.00)		
	Total	69	31	100		

*p<0.05** p<0.01

Table 2. Traditional cultural innovation faces major problems

In short, in product design, traditional culture has problems such as commoditization distortion, stereotypes of cultural symbols, collisions and challenges between different cultures, and insufficient creativity. In the process of integrating traditional culture, it is necessary to have a deep understanding of its connotation, pay attention to creativity, not be too commercial, and retain its own value and significance.

Table 3.   The main contributing factors to the problem

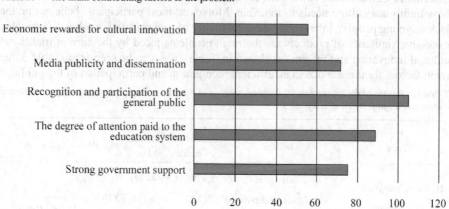

3. Key Issues and Measures of Traditional Culture Innovation and Inheritance

Although the protection of traditional culture and the innovation and inheritance of traditional culture have become the main theme of today's society, we are also working hard to explore, innovate and solve, through the above data analysis and investigation research, extract the following three problems facing the most prominent innovation and inheritance of China's traditional culture in product design, and propose corresponding improvement measures through in-depth secondary research and interviews [9-10].

3.1.   Unbalanced development—all-round development

Since traditional culture can be divided into material culture and non-material culture, compared to the two, material culture is more likely to receive people's attention and protection because it is real and visible. It is also divided into orthodox classic culture and folk culture. The former is the soul of the nation and the spiritual nourishment of society. After the protection and inheritance of the rulers, the precipitation of history, the assignment of material and status, it has been collected, learned, and inherited by the world; and the latter lacks a systematic protection awareness and mechanism, and its material and status are relatively low, so its value is seriously underestimated. Underestimated, except for direct inheritors, it is rarely widely known by the world. For example, in the same traditional culture, the Forbidden City and the Great Wall in Beijing can be preserved as completely as possible, but non-material cultures such as paper-cutting, shadow puppetry, and Peking opera may gradually become extinct as the number of inheritors decreases. It is also a traditional building, the Forbidden City can be completely preserved, and can be repaired periodically; however, residential buildings are rarely preserved, and are rebuilt or demolished with the times.

The power of public opinion is powerful, just like the current popular "national trend", which will strongly drive economic consumption, stimulate design innovation, and thus attract attention to traditional culture. From a positive point of view, once a traditional culture is developed, other traditional cultures will also be affected by "ripples", whether it is from the economic point of view of the businessmen or the psychology of consumers to catch up with the trend. It can be said that "let some cultures get rich first". At present, we have achieved partial development, and now we need to develop in an all-round way. Comprehensive development can be carried out in two ways. One is top-down, where the state and relevant departments issue laws and regulations to advocate the protection of traditional folk culture; the other is bottom-up, where designers pay attention to traditional folk culture and design a more diversified traditional culture product.

3.2.   The products are similar and lack regional characteristics—regional characteristics

Our current products are too homogeneous, and differentiation has become a kind of scarcity. The number of products to choose from continues to increase, and the proportion of truly meaningful products is declining. The first way to defeat homogenization is to increase the regional characteristics of products. For example, refrigerators, in our impression, seem to have the same function of keeping fresh and freezing ingredients. In some parts of Africa, in addition to the most basic fresh-keeping and freezing functions, refrigerators also need to have anti-theft functions. This is due to the relatively backward economic conditions in some parts of Africa, and after families with better conditions have refrigerators, they have added functions to prevent domestic servants from moving food without permission. Then our south is humid, and the temperature is high; the north is dry and the temperature is low, which will also form obvious regional differences. Using this regional difference, we can create unique regional products. Although the sales of regional products will be narrowed in general products, they will have an overwhelming advantage in products with strong regional characteristics, making their products more competitive in a market with serious homogeneity.

To enhance the regional characteristics of products, it is necessary to focus on the local regional culture itself. Take the tomb of Marquis Haihun in Nanchang, Jiangxi as an example. This is the tomb of Liu He, Marquis of Haihun in the Western Han Dynasty. This "Mountain of Money" is made up of five-baht coins, about 2 million pieces, weighing more than 10 tons. Its value is equivalent to 50 kilograms of gold today. In addition, it is famous for its goldware, including 285 gold cakes, each weighing about 250 grams. There are 20 gold plates, each of which weighs 1 kg. This is its unique feature. Then when promoting and designing, we can highlight the "golden" feature. In product design, whether using golden tones in terms of color or metal decoration in terms of materials, we can well promote the characteristics of Haihunhou, rather than stereotyped Museum design for bookmarks, silk scarves, badges. Only when the design has unique innovation points will people have memory points, so that it will no longer become a "homogeneous" product.

3.3.   Products do not fit modern life—modern products

Traditional culture is the product of people's historical life in the past. Every era has a different living environment and way of life, so it has its own different needs, and the market will provide and produce corresponding material and cultural products. Whether it is material or spiritual products, they are all adapted to people's needs. The core of my country's traditional thinking of using things is practicality. The reason why many traditional cultures have not been passed down is largely because it does not meet the needs of the later times. This requires contemporary traditional culture inheritors and designers to pay attention to the changes and development of traditional culture in the current social environment when they perceive social changes and think about inheriting traditions and innovative development and carry out "redesign" on this basis. It cannot and should not be forced to accept things that people do not need and cannot be produced for the purpose of inheriting traditional culture.

The inheritance and development of seal cutting seals is a positive case that can be used for reference. In ancient times, the seal was a token to show someone's identity and issue a certain order, and it was also a carrier for literati to express their hearts. In modern times, due to the popularization of fountain pens and simplified Chinese characters, signatures have become more convenient. Hand-carved signature seals have become a hobby of people who have leisure, elegance, and high life pursuits, but the seals have not disappeared from our lives because of this. A special chemical synthetic material invented by Japan in the early 1990s. The photosensitive stamp is made of a special equipment that instantly emits strong light radiation to cause photooxidation and thermal crosslinking on the surface of the material. It can be printed once oiled. More than 1000 times and can be refilled repeatedly. In addition, the personalized seal design makes the seal more widely used, such as company official seal, personal handwritten signature, children's fun seal... The integration of new materials and new needs in the modern era has made the seal continue to develop.

4. Case analysis of traditional culture integration

Although the innovative design of our country's traditional culture still has a lot of shortcomings, there are always some products that can stand out in the vortex of serious product homogeneity.

As the representative of Chinese traditional culture and the leader of Chinese museums, the Forbidden City has launched many cultural and creative products that we can learn from. Figure 1 shows the "everything goes well" office cup sold by the Palace Museum. This product is derived from Zhu Jianshen's "Auspicious Omens of Years" in the collection of the Forbidden City. Ripe persimmons are put into the vessel, and the lid is patterned with persimmon stems, implying that everything goes well, and you are always satisfied. There is an ear-shaped handle on one side. When using it, the index finger and middle finger are hooked and fit snugly with the small ear. It is easy and effortless to hold the cup with one hand; the cup body is coated with red lacquer glaze, and the handle is painted with gold by hand, which can easily distinguish and identify functions; At the same time, the outside of the cup has a matte texture, which increases friction and reduces the probability of hand slipping and breaking. The inside of the cup is made of smooth ceramic material, which is easy to clean.

From the product in Figure 2, we can see that in terms of name, it uses the homonym of "persimmon" in traditional Chinese characters to carry a beautiful meaning and endow the product with rich emotional value; in terms of shape: two persimmons The superposition of the shape becomes the mug that we often use in our daily life; in terms of color, it adopts the brick red of the red wall of the Forbidden City. When a product gives people the first impression that it is a product of traditional Chinese culture, then it is a successful cultural and creative product. Secondly, we look at its emotional value and its own meaning, whether it really combines traditional culture and modern products. Fusion, not blunt splicing.

Figure 1. "Everything goes well" cup   **Figure 2.** Y Chair.

Any form and symbol of beauty can be used as a design element in the design. The purpose of adding design elements in product design is to eliminate the strangeness of the product and convey accurate product information to users. Just like this chair, users can easily see that it is a Ming Dynasty armchair with Chinese tradition, but the difference can be seen if you look closely. First, the back of the chair adopts a "Y" character instead of the traditional curved backboard; secondly, the traditional Ming-style armchair is connected by tube feet, which are raised successively from front to back, which is a step-by- step style. Although this Y Chair also adopts a step-by-step shape, But the height has been increased a lot, and it mainly plays the role of supporting the chair, ignoring the function of the foot. This is a very Chinese-style Y Chair designed by Danish designer Hans Wegner based on Ming-style furniture. The application of Chinese elements in design is doomed to design with Chinese taste, which has nothing to do with the nationality of the designer. But one thing we need to think about is, why is it not the Chinese who have been familiar with it since childhood, but friends of other nationalities who have made our country's traditional culture so wonderful? Perhaps it is because we have been in this environment for a long time that we are too accustomed to traditional culture, and regard it as a normal life, so it is difficult to discover its wonderfulness. Sometimes we need to jump out of the usual thinking paradigm when designing, "Stand far away "To observe life, to observe things.

5. Epilogue

We should face up to the impact and impact of Western design concepts on Chinese contemporary products and designs, take the essence and discard the dross, creatively apply Chinese traditional culture to product design, endow Chinese traditional culture with infinite ductility, and create a new path. It belongs to the Chinese people's own road to the development of contemporary product design. After thousands of years of tempering, traditional culture has formed immeasurable aesthetic value, artistic value, and cultural value, making it feasible to infiltrate product design and even design. As long as it is applied properly, it will definitely enhance the appreciation of the product at the same time, it gives the product more cultural connotation, arouses the emotional resonance of users, and then better inherits and develops the traditional culture of the nation.

Supported by Humanities and Social Science Research Project of Jiangxi Province, project number: YS19115(Research on the Design of Xinyu China grass Embroidery Cultural and Creative Products from the Perspective of Intangible Cultural Heritage Living Inheritance)

References

[1] Zhang Lili, Zhu Yiyun. Inheritance and Innovative Design of Intangible Cultural Heritage under the Background of National Trends. Decoration **10** (2021), 30-35.

[2] Li Yanzu. The Contemporaneity and Regionality of Traditional Arts and Crafts – – Revisiting the Protection and Development of Traditional Arts and Crafts. Journal of Nanjing University of the Arts (Art and Design Edition) **1** (2008), 5-9.

[3] Chen Jun. Cultural Inheritance of Traditional Handicrafts and Contemporary "Redesign". Literature and Art Research, **5** (2012),137-139.

[4] Wang Weiwei, Hu Yukun, Jin Xin, etc. Research and Application of Extraction Model of Traditional Cultural Design Elements. Packaging Engineering **35** (2014), 06, 73- 76+81

[5] Bi Fengxia. Application of Traditional Cultural Elements in Modern Packaging Design. Packaging Engineering **31** (2010), 18, 69-72.

[6] Wu Handong. On the Legal Protection of Traditional Culture – Taking Intangible Cultural Heritage and Traditional Cultural Expressions as Objects. Chinese Law **1** (2010), 50-62.

[7] Zhang Yuan. The Application of Chinese Traditional Cultural and Art Elements in Modern Graphic Design [J]. Packaging Engineering **8** (2008), 156-158+216.

[8] Sang Lin. The Dilemma and Embarrassment of the Modern Transformation of Chinese Traditional Cultural Resources-Taking Henan Huaiyang Muni Dog as an Example. Decoration **2** (2011), 122-124.

[9] Li Zonggui. On the Connotation of Chinese Excellent Traditional Culture. Academic Research **11** (2013), 35-39.

[10] Zhang Lihao. Research on the application of Chinese traditional culture in design under the background of the digital age. Tomorrow Fashion **18** (2020), 58-59.

Design Studies and Intelligence Engineering
L.C. Jain et al. (Eds.)
© 2024 The Authors.
doi:10.3233/FAIA231431

117

Research on Sustainable Development of Intangible Cultural Handicraft from the Perspective of Social Innovation Design

Jian HAN [a,1] and Weimeng XU [a]

[a] *College of arts, Jiangxi Normal University, Nanchang, China*

Abstract. This paper first expounds the definition and development of social innovative design and sorts out several characteristics of social innovative design. Secondly, by analyzing the difficulties and problems encountered by intangible cultural heritage handicraft in contemporary inheritance and innovation, combined with the analysis and induction of cases of intangible cultural heritage handicraft in social innovation design, the experience and prospect of sustainable development of intangible cultural heritage handicraft under social innovation design are summarized.

Keywords. Social innovation design, Intangible cultural heritage handicraft, Sustainable development

1. Social Innovation Design

China is entering a period of social transformation, with better goals, and will also face many unprecedented opportunities and challenges. The World Economic Forum divides the world economic development into three types: factor-driven, efficiency-driven, and innovation-driven. China's economic achievements now mainly rely on factor-driven and efficiency-driven. In order to enhance global competitiveness and improve development efficiency, China is accelerating the transformation to an innovation-driven ecological economy [1].Our country has put forward a new development strategy, which has determined the development strategy of ecological civilization, and taken the "Rural Revitalization Strategy" as the carrier of "building ecological civilization", transforming the industrial development mode into the ecological and sustainable development mode from the perspective of development strategy. Moreover, the principal contradiction in Chinese society has become the contradiction between people's growing needs for a better life and unbalanced and inadequate development. In the context of social transformation and the goal of a better life, social innovation design can well contribute to social transformation and sustainable development, and effectively promote the realization of the goal.

---

[1] Jian Han,Unit: Jiangxi Normal University, Vocational Title: Professor, Position:Department Director,Research direction: product innovation design,E-mail:46335546qg.com..

[2] Weimeng Xu. Unit: Jiangxi Normal University, Master Candidate Design, product design direction.

1.1. Social Innovation Design Definition

Social innovation design is a design behavior from the perspective of social innovation. The concept of social innovation was first proposed by Peter F. Drucker, an American management scholar. Then The Young Foundation in the UK defined "social innovation" as: "social innovation is an innovative activity and service mode, aiming to meet social needs and create new ideas of new social relations or cooperation models [2]."

Italian pioneer scholar Ezio Manzini defined "social innovation" as: "social innovation is a process of change, which originates from the creative reorganization of existing assets, with the purpose of achieving the goals recognized by human society in a new way" [3]. The concept of "social innovation" has increasingly become the mainstream of society based on China's current characteristic economic, social environment and historical and cultural background, and has a huge positive impact. At present, in China, the social problems caused by social transformation are gradually complicated, and the government's governance mode needs to be transformed [4]. Under such characteristics of the times, China's social innovation theory has formed its special connotation: "social innovation is transforming from an innovation theory into a social action with wide participation [5]." It is necessary to pay attention to the close combination with China's reality, creatively integrate and use social resources, and build a social innovation model, new value and new path with Chinese characteristics [6]. In short, social innovation is an innovative behavior based on complex social problems and meeting social needs.

Design under social innovation is closely linked. Social innovation design takes social innovation as the goal, while social innovation takes design as an important means and driving force. Ezio Manzini created the discipline research field of "social innovation design" and set the definition: all activities that professional design can implement in order to activate, maintain and guide society towards sustainable development [7]. Social innovation is a breakthrough innovation, a form of innovation for social change; social innovation design is a design activity to realize this new form of innovation, a non-supplementary activity, which brings about innovative solutions based on new social forms and new economic models [6]. In general, social innovation design maintains an ultimate goal of promoting society to develop better in a new direction. Social innovation design promotes society to play the advantages of the design profession towards a sustainable society like an ecosystem.

1.2. Characteristics of Social Innovation Design

Based on the above analysis, the author sorts out the following important characteristics of social innovation design. Firstly, the design object is diversified. The design object is no longer a single party, but stakeholders in all aspects of the problem are included in the design process. This characteristic fits the goal of social innovation because society itself is a complex and changeable overall system, and solving problems only considering a single aspect will not promote the solution of the problem; secondly, the design process tends to multi-party collaboration. The diversification of the design object leads to the design process is no longer a single link, and the consideration of the needs of multiple objects requires the collaborative participation of all parties in the design process.

Whether during the design research or in the subsequent update of the design, the joint participation of all parties will make the solution of the problem more perfect; thirdly, the design method tends to systematization, localization, and networking. The continuous update of the design object and the design process leads to the change of the selection of the design method. In the design behavior for social innovation, since the complexity and intractability of social problems need to be responded to in an innovative way, it requires the design behavior to have a systematic concept of the whole problem. At the same time, problems come from real social situations, and innovative methods should be able to be practically implemented. In the process of design activities, localization awareness is required, and real and effective responses to problems can be made relying on the ecological nature and human economy of the region. The design method from the perspective of social innovation focuses on the constructive exploration of the network to generate sharing and value connection, focusing on participatory, collaborative design, co-creation, crowd wisdom, etc. [6].

2. Contemporary dilemmas and problems of intangible cultural heritage handicrafts

Intangible cultural heritage handicrafts are born and grown in traditional society, invented, and created by people in the region where traditional handicrafts are located. Traditional craftsmen produce important materials for economic circulation, and the manufacturing skills and products of crafts have gradually become important cultural memories and genes in the evolution of time. Intangible cultural heritage handicrafts have continued to exist in society and history, not only as the inheritance of skills, but also as a carrier of the relationship between people and economy, society and culture. Nowadays, society has begun to step into the process of modernization from tradition. In the social transformation with new goals, the sustainable development of intangible cultural heritage handicrafts will face a series of problems and dilemmas.

Table 1. Composition of four types of floating population (%)

	The year of 2000	The year of 2005	The year of 2010	The year of 2015	The year of 2020
Rural-urban mobility	52.2	61.4	63.2	48.9	66.3
City - city mobility	20.8	21.2	21.2	37.9	21.8
Rural to rural mobility	18.6	13.7	12.7	7.1	10.3
Urban-rural mobility	8.4	3.7	2.9	6.1	1.6

Data source: Editorial Board and editorial staff of China Census Yearbook 2020, China Census Yearbook 2020 Wang Pingping, Editor-in-Chief, China Census Yearbook, China Statistics Press,2020,4, Yearbook. DOI: 10.44303 / y.c nki. Yzgqp. 2022.000001.

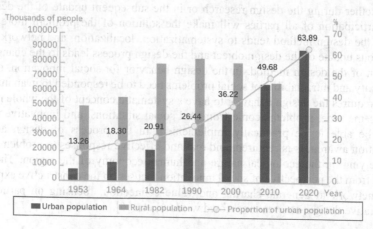

Figure 1. Every census of urban and rural population[2]

The inheritance group of intangible cultural heritage handicrafts is currently facing a critical situation. Intangible cultural heritage handicrafts are produced by specific regional communities, and any changes in these regions can significantly impact the sustainable development of such crafts. Based on data from the China Population Census Yearbook 2020 regarding four types of floating population (Table 1), it is evident that the migration patterns between rural and urban areas experienced substantial shifts between 2000 and 2020. The flow from rural to urban areas consistently increased during this period, with only a minor decline observed in 2015; moreover, it constituted the largest proportion among all four types of floating population. Conversely, the proportion of individuals migrating from urban to rural areas steadily decreased over time (except for 2015) and represented the smallest share among these four categories. This analysis indicates an ongoing trend where more people migrate from rural to urban areas, resulting in significant outflows from rural regions. Consequently, there has been a continuous rise in the proportion of urban populations due to rapid urbanization driving social modernization processes (Figure 1); however, numerous young talents possessing skills related to intangible cultural heritage handicraft inheritance have been compelled to leave their hometowns due to various factors. As a result, there has been an outflow of young talents while fewer craftsmen remain within these regions.

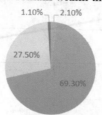

Figure 2. Age Distribution of Intangible Cultural Heritage Inheritor

Data source: China Intangible Cultural Heritage Network (https://www.ihchina.cn/)

---

[2]Bulletin of the Seventh National Population Census (No. 7) -- Urban and Rural population and Floating population [J]. China Statistics,2021(05):13.

At the same time, the loss of talents accelerates the shrinking and aging of the inheritance group. The "aging" of the intangible cultural heritage inheritors is hindering the sustainable development of intangible cultural heritage handicrafts. As of November 2022, 69.3% of the 1,882 known age intangible cultural heritage inheritors are aged 70 to 100, accounting for the largest proportion and serious aging（Figure 2）. People are the key factors for sustainable development, and the loss of population and the aging of inheritors are important dilemmas for the inheritance and innovation of intangible cultural heritage handicrafts.

The economic plight of intangible cultural heritage handicrafts needs to be activated. Regional brain drain makes the economy lack of power and self-renewal capacity. Intangible cultural heritage handicrafts are local creations made by people combining realistic needs and natural factors. The loss of regional population leads to the decline of regional economy, so the demand for handicrafts will decline. Gradually, when the economic cycle approaches to stop, a lifestyle and industrial form represented by handicrafts will lose vitality. The most regrettable result is that they will be like animal and plant specimens in the museum window, which we can only imagine their once vivid existence through the glass showcase. Lack of economic vitality and self-renewal capacity are problems that cannot be ignored in contemporary intangible cultural heritage handicrafts.

Balanced development of culture and economy is the key factor for sustainable development. Intangible cultural heritage handicrafts form our lifestyle and cultural memory from eating, clothing, housing and transportation, and weave excellent traditional Chinese culture. But in the process of globalization dominated by industrialization and Western aesthetics, traditional skills cannot compete with the fast and efficient pace of life, and are gradually marginalized, making it difficult to produce dynamic economic power. This leads to the continuous decline of people's cultural identity of intangible cultural heritage handicrafts, which sets obstacles to the development of excellent traditional culture and skills at the level of consciousness, causing difficulties. In the changes of population, economy and culture, the social living space of intangible cultural heritage handicrafts is constantly squeezed. Social innovation design needs to give full play to its strengths and create new living space for the sustainable development of intangible cultural heritage handicrafts.

Balanced development of culture and economy is the key factor for sustainable development. Intangible cultural heritage handicrafts form our lifestyle and cultural memory from eating, clothing, housing and transportation, and weave excellent traditional Chinese culture. But in the process of globalization dominated by industrialization and Western aesthetics, traditional skills cannot compete with the fast and efficient pace of life, and are gradually marginalized, making it difficult to produce dynamic economic power. This leads to the continuous decline of people's cultural identity of intangible cultural heritage handicrafts, which sets obstacles to the development of excellent traditional culture and skills at the level of consciousness, causing difficulties. In the changes of population, economy and culture, the social living space of intangible cultural heritage handicrafts is constantly squeezed. Social innovation design needs to give full play to its strengths and create new living space for the sustainable development of intangible cultural heritage handicrafts.

3. Contemporary Sustainable Development of Intangible Cultural Heritage Crafts from the Perspective of Social Innovation Design

3.1. Analysis of Practical Cases

Although the development and application of social innovation design in China has not been long, some domestic scholars have carried out some practical exploration on traditional handicrafts from the perspective of social innovation design. The author selected four representative cases in the case study to analyze the current situation of social innovation design in the sustainable development of intangible cultural heritage handicrafts（Table 2）.

Table 2. Representative design practice of traditional handicraft from the perspective of social innovation design

Year	Team	Project name
2016	Zhang Duoduo and Ji Tietuan of the Xintongdao · Huayao Flower Project Hunan University	
2017	Zhang Jianping's team of Chongqing University of Posts and Telecommunications	the Ya'an Social Innovation Design of the Porcelain Making Device
2022	Li Yanxin of Yunnan Academy of Arts	the practice of Zharan handicrafts in Dali Zhoucheng
2023	Xu Shanshan's team of Hefei University	the Social Innovation Design Research on the Living Inheritance of Hui Carving Skills

They are the Xintongdao · Huayao Flower Project in 2016, which was responsible for by Zhang Duoduo and Ji Tietuan of Hunan University; the Ya'an Social Innovation Design of the Porcelain Making Device in 2017, which was responsible for by Zhang Jianping's team of Chongqing University of Posts and Telecommunications; the practice of Zharan handicrafts in Dali Zhoucheng in 2022, which was completed by Li Yanxin of Yunnan Academy of Arts; and the Social Innovation Design Research on the Living Inheritance of Hui Carving Skills in 2023, which was responsible for by Xu Shanshan's team of Hefei University.

From the perspective of social innovation design, the four groups of teams all took handicrafts as nodes, respectively designed unique platform projects, and built new social interaction relationships. The Hui carve team created a social collaboration co-creation mode of lively art. This mode makes full use of the advantages of online and offline and relies on modern technology to create a platform for digital services. The main goal is to promote Hui carve art and related culture, strengthen the connection between stakeholders, and realize the full life cycle development of Hui carve art. At the same time, this mode emphasizes the role of human in the process of the inheritance of the lively art. Specifically, the digital service system promotes the interconnection of stakeholders through the spread of Hui carve art and related culture, and realizes the full life cycle development; while the practical experience activities are mainly committed to promoting the collaborative co-creation relationship among stakeholders, so as to promote the sustainable development of Hui carve art [8]. From the discovery of Hui carve, the exploration of Hui carve, to the co-creation of Hui carve, the platform carries out the connection and service of the whole link, injecting strong vitality into the activation of the art. The tie-dye team in Zhoucheng, Dali, established a platform for the construction of community culture in Zhoucheng, taking the traditional tie-dye handicraft as a new social relationship intermediary. Since the establishment of the Blue Heritage Platform, more than 20 young people from the village have joined the Blue Heritage family full-time, which is extremely rare in other dyehouses in Zhoucheng. The participation of new forces is the key to the inheritance and development of a traditional craft and a traditional culture. On the one hand, they can bring new ideas and concepts to traditional crafts and traditional culture, and on the other hand, they can influence the peers around to feel the charm, thus enhancing cultural identity and cultural confidence [9]. The Ya'an team carried out a social innovation project for the social reconstruction after the disaster. The Ya'an post-disaster reconstruction project is a social innovation practice to solve the poverty alleviation and employment, industrial renaissance, social relationship reconstruction and many other social problems caused by the Ya'an earthquake. With the support of the Mango V Fund of Hunan TV, the design force of the School of Design of Hunan University, the School of Fine Arts of Tsinghua University and the Sichuan Academy of Fine Arts, taking the Ya'an sand instrument as the object of the renaissance of the local traditional handicraft, through the cooperation with the government, mass organizations, representative enterprises, workshops, local craftsmen and The Ya'an post-disaster reconstruction project is a social innovation practice to solve the poverty alleviation and employment, industrial renaissance, social relationship reconstruction and many other social problems caused by the Ya'an earthquake. With the support of the Mango V Fund of Hunan TV, the design force of the School of Design of Hunan University, the School of Fine Arts of Tsinghua University and the Sichuan Academy of Fine Arts, taking the Ya'an sand instrument as the object of the renaissance of the local traditional handicraft, through the cooperation with the government, mass organizations, representative enterprises, workshops, local craftsmen and interdisciplinary experts, jointly build a network-based information display platform, spread local knowledge while introducing local craftsmen and workers into the whole industry, so as to gradually build a sand instrument innovation design service platform of "design, collection, cooperative production and brand promotion" [10]. The team in Hunan launched the "Huayao Flower" project for the minority Huayao in the poor mountainous areas of Longhui County, Hunan Province. The project is a typical case of "touching" the renaissance of the traditional community through the collaborative design method of social innovation based on the local intangible cultural heritage and other characteristic traditional culture and natural resources. The three-year "Huayao Flower" project has received strong support from the Ministry of Education, local government, social enterprises, and local residents. The project team has established an interdisciplinary joint design and social innovation network with the Hong Kong Polytechnic University, Queen Mary University of London, Milan Polytechnic University, Sichuan Fine Arts Institute, Tsinghua University Fine Arts Institute, Xinjiang Normal University, and other institutions [11].

The project has built a local knowledge platform to help the sustainable development of handicraft knowledge andThe project team has established an interdisciplinary joint design and social innovation network with the Hong Kong Polytechnic University, Queen Mary University of London, Milan Polytechnic University, Sichuan Fine Arts

Institute, Tsinghua University Fine Arts Institute, Xinjiang Normal University, and other institutions [11]. The project has built a local knowledge platform to help the sustainable development of handicraft knowledge and culture. The local brand created by the project helps the sustainable development of handicraft resources in terms of economy.

Integrating multiple active subjects into social innovation design is an important factor for the sustainable development of handicrafts. The four groups of cases actively link all parties involved in the design process and innovate and activate the social relations of handicrafts. Hui sculpture team analyzed the stakeholder structure of Hui sculpture culture, listed artists and craftsmen, the public, cultural and creative tourism enterprises, universities, government and cultural departments; tie-dye team took designers as a link to drive the linkage between craftsmen and local residents and tourists; Ya'an team mainly through the design force of colleges and universities, unite the government, enterprises, workshops, local craftsmen, cross-field experts, and cooperate to build an innovative design service platform; in the process of the project, scholars and designers solved problems with the internal vision of cultural holders, and then formed effective interaction with community residents, combined with the power of the government, universities, enterprises and the public, to activate the endogenous power of the traditional handicraft community.

3.2. Summary and Prospect of Sustainable Development

The sustainable development of intangible cultural heritage handicraft from the perspective of social innovation takes handicraft as a positive node, and accordingly compiles an innovative social relationship network. In the practice process, design skills such as collaborative design, participatory design and service design in the design concept are used to meet the demand for innovation in social transformation.

There is an idea called the capability approach, which rather than seeing people as objects with needs waiting to be met (by someone or something), sees them as active subjects, capable of actively pursuing their own happiness. [7] From this perspective, it can be considered that intangible cultural heritage handicraft itself is a member of social innovation. It does not limit the subjective initiative of intangible cultural heritage handicraft in self-development, allows it to become a part of modern lifestyle, and actively establishes intangible cultural heritage handicraft as an active party in modern life.In the design practice, intangible crafts are used as nodes to actively build a network of relations between stakeholders. Although designers cannot stipulate people's positive attention to intangible crafts, a close social network can help people form close connections with intangible crafts. Professor Mancini proposed in the book Design in the Age of Design by Everyone that social innovative design is the answer to these questions, which affects the "empowering ecosystem" at different levels in a timely manner through various interventions. The same goal of all interventions is to create a new infrastructure: a complex, structured platform that provides support for various independent and related projects. In the author's opinion, the compilation of an innovative social network of relations for intangible crafts in modern society is like the important condition of "infrastructure". An infrastructure, like a railway or the Internet, is not to be reinvented every time (new things), but to "infiltrate" into other social material structures. By introducing the traditional concept of infrastructure into the design process, we can make design go beyond the concept of "design project" and become an open long-term process where all parties can innovate together [7].

The term infrastructure was first coined by Leigh Srear and further developed by Pelle Ehn and his Faculty of Arts and Media at the University of Malmo. In Ehn's words, "an infrastructure, like a railroad track or the Internet, is not reinvented every time, but" seeps "into other social material structures." We bring the traditional concept of infrastructure into the design process, allowing us to move design beyond the concept of "design projects" and into an open, long-term process where people can innovate together. For Professor Mancini, the concept of "infrastructure" illustrates the nature of design processes that aim to make social projects and collaborative organizations more conditional. In fact, it requires a series of design actions [7].

As the author thinks that in the future, the sustainable development of intangible cultural heritage handicrafts under social innovative design should build a carrying infrastructure for development. It is necessary to improve different types of digital platforms, not only the existing webpage and mobile phone program platform, but also the digital platforms such as meta universe and digital twin. Create comfortable and convenient physical space to provide participants with face-to-face communication. Establish developed logistics services to pave the way for the circulation of handicrafts. Provide information services, establish a rich experience base, and dig more tacit knowledge of intangible cultural heritage craftsmen. Establish perfect evaluation services. At present, the innovation results of intangible cultural heritage handicrafts lack a set of achievement evaluation mechanism, which makes it difficult to respond in time to adjust in design activities. Activate cultural resources with design, link the development of industry and life, build a new meaning of traditional culture for modern life, and make intangible cultural heritage handicrafts form a sustainable development cycle in social innovation activities.

Acknowledgement

Supported by Humanities and Social Science Research Project of Jiangxi Province, project number: YS19115(Research on the Design of Xinyu China Grass Embroidery Cultural and Creative Products from the Perspective of Intangible Cultural Heritage Living Inheritance)

References

[1] Pan Zhaoyang, Tang Changqiao. Design Change under the socioecological transformation: Opportunities, challenges and approaches for social innovative design. Art and design (theory) **2** (2023), 3, 25-29.
[2] MURRAY R, CAULIER G J. MULGAN G. The open book of social innovation. London: Nesta, 2010.
[3] MANZINI E.Making things happen: Social innovation and design. Design issues, **30** (2014), 1, 57-66.
[4] Zhang Jian. Social Innovation in Contemporary China: Principles of Civil Society Transformation and State Incubation. Journal of Humanities 6 (2009), 10-15.
[5] Ji Guangxin, Liu Xiaojing. Review of domestic research on social innovation. Journal of China University of Petroleum: Social Science Edition **30** (2014), 6, 41-46.
[6] XU Zhidiankui, Bao Yixi. Research on design development trend from the perspective of social innovation. Packaging Engineering, 1-16
[7] MANZINI E. Design when everybody designs: An introduction to design for social innovation. MIT press, 2015.
[8] XU Shanshan, Liu Shiyu, Liu Ruiqi, et al. Research on Social innovation design of living inheritance of emblem carving technique. Hebei Pictorial, **7** (2023), 16-18,214.

[9] Li Yanxin. Research on Dali Zhoucheng Tie-dye handicraft Community Practice from the perspective of Social Innovation design [D]. Yunnan Arts University,2022.
[10] Zhang Jianping, Wang Liduan, Luo Xianyi. Yoann social innovation in the design of curium porcelain making machine. Journal of packaging engineering **12** (2017), 37-42.
[11] ZHANG Duoduo, Ji Tie. Collaborative Design "Touches" the revival of traditional communities: A case study of the intangible cultural heritage research and innovation practice of "New Channel · Huayaohua" project. Decoration, **12** (2016), 26-29.

Design Studies and Intelligence Engineering
L.C. Jain et al. (Eds.)
© 2024 The Authors.
This article is published online with Open Access by IOS Press and distributed under the terms
of the Creative Commons Attribution Non-Commercial License 4.0 (CC BY-NC 4.0).
doi:10.3233/FAIA231432

Third-Person Pain Experience Exploration Based on Multimodal Physiological Features Analysis

Baixi XING [a,1], Yuehan SHI [b], Kaiqi WANG [b], Xinjie SONG [b], and
Yanhong PAN [b]

[a] *Industrial Design Institute, Zhejiang University of Technology,*
Hangzhou, China
[b] *College of Design and Architecture, Zhejiang University of*
Technology, Hangzhou, China

Abstract. Third-person pain is an interesting empathy phenomenon that human has the ability to infer characters of other sufferers' pain by observing their behavior. In the literature, existing studies suggesting that first- person and third-person pain share common features of neuroimage, which indicates that pain behavior will cause influence on both sufferer and the observer. Consequently, it is significant to explore the third-person effects upon the observer. In this study, the evaluation and recognition of third-person pain experience was studied based on user physiological signal analysis. We built a third-person pain multimodal physiological features dataset and applied machine learning methods to explore a third-person pain experience recognition model. A classification accuracy of 95.83% was obtained in third-person pain degree recognition, which demonstrates the effectiveness of our approach. The proposed study shed light on the guiding future exploration of determinants of third-person pain process and empathy intelligence.

Keywords. Third-person pain, physiology signal, machine learning

1. Introduction

At present, user's perception need in artificial industry is becoming more and more prominent. Currently, affective and cognition intelligence are combined in AI systems. However it has some essential shortcomings that AI understands users' status based on massive data analysis, and AI could not truly understand users' emotion and give suitable responses. And artificial system's empathy ability could hardly meet users' requirement.

In order to study the problems of empathy intelligence limitations in AI system, we tried to find a research entry point for this question. Third-person pain is an interesting perception phenomenon that has a nature of empathy character, thus the recognition of third-person pain can provide a new perspective for empathy intelligence development in AI industry. Consequently, we attempt to find a method to detect and evaluate users' third-person pain experience.

Pain experience types vary with respect to the subjective and objective perception. First-person pain is a clear and subjective perception, which is also an obvious signal of

---

[1] Corresponding Author: Baixi Xing

threat and hurt. While third-person pain is an internal experience affected by observing suffers' behaviors or first-person pain response [1]. In this study, the intelligent evaluation of third-person pain can help us understand empathy mechanism and build computational model to predict the level of pain intensity.

We held experiment to investigate the physiological responses of third-person pain. We explored recognition model of third-person pain based on physiological features by machine learning algorithms. Specifically, we collected 18 video clips as third-person pain stimuli. A total of 24 participants were invited to view the stimuli videos and their physiology features were recorded to form the dataset. Several machine-learning algorithms were applied to find the optimal model of third-person pain recognition model. A 10-fold cross validation was conducted in the modeling experiment. The model results indicated that the classification accuracy is 95.83% in the best model performance based on RandomForest algorithm, which proved the effectiveness of the proposed method. The research paradigm of third-person pain model exploration is illustrated in Figure 1.

The main contribution of this work can be concluded in two aspects: (1) A novel physiology features fusion dataset of third-person pain was built; (2) An optimal model for third-person pain recognition was obtained by machine learning method.

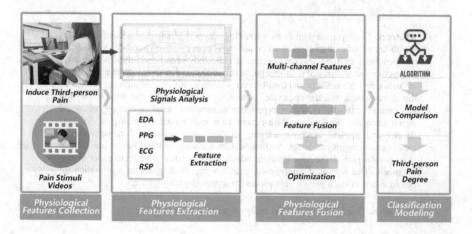

Figure 1. The research roadmap of third-person pain recognition model exploration.

This paper is organized as follows: section 2 presented the related works of third-person pain studies and existing avenues; section 3 introduces methods of different algorithms applied in the modeling experiment; section 4 shows the experiment of third-person pain stimulation and building physiology features dataset; section 5 compares the model performance of different algorithms for third-person pain recognition and discusses the experimental results; section 6 concludes with the future research directions.

2. Related Work

Recently, research interest in the phenomenon of third-person pain has steadily increased [2][3]. The advancement of AI intelligence and conceptual empathy models has accelerated this process. How socially transmitted information about an individual's internal experience is perceived by others? How can we measure the intense of third-person pain? Finding novel approaches to examine the explicit behavioral changes induced by watching suffering in others, as well as their consequences for the sufferer, should be a research goal [4]. Nowadays, technological and methodology developments have contributed to the study of the rising interest.

Researchers arranged the steps in the pain information transmission pathway from nociceptive input to social interpretation via nonverbal facial expression. According to Rosenthal's paradigm, an internal experience must first be stored in expressive behavior before pain communication may take place. Kaseweter explored the nature of the relationship and to explore the potential moderating influence of both third-person pain perception and situational factors [5]. Her findings indicated that individual differences in affective processing may moderate the relationship between empathy and social behavior, which is potentially contributing to difference in the cure of pain. The pain communication model proposed by Hajistavropoulos emphasizes that an observer may not perceive the message, perceive it appropriately, or misinterpret it, resulting in an overestimation or underestimating of the sufferer's painful state [6].

In the study of subjective pain detection aspect, studies have repeatedly shown that activation of brain regions characterized as the "pain matrix" can be triggered by the perception of painful facial expressions [7]. Whitmarsh et al. found that observation of the hand and feet in non-painful status will cause significant suppression of mu and beta oscillations over visual and sensorimotor regions. They found that viewing others' painful status compared to neutral stimuli engages both sensorimotor areas and visual areas [8]. Hein et al. examined skin conductance responses and self-reported emotion during painful electric shock exposure individuals' perception of the other's pain were positively connected with their skin conductance responses while they watched them appear to get shocks. This correlation also indicated that individuals were more likely to choose the personally costly alternative of tolerating the other's pain. It is quite interesting that the likelihood of costly aiding increased when the participant's skin conductance reactions during the observation of suffering in the other person matched their own responses [9].

3. Methodologies

In this study, we used Python to build the algorithm models with 10-folds cross-validation. In the experiment, five algorithms were implemented for the classification of third-person pain degree, including LibSVM, LibLinear, RBFNetwork, RandomTree and RandomForest. A brief introduction of these algorithms is presented below.

3.1. LibSVM

LibSVM is developed based on Support Vector Machine for solving the problems of classification and regression. Support Vector Machine (SVM) conducts classification via supervised learning method. The maximum-margin hyperplane is the decision boundary for learning approach. There are a number of extended SVM algorithms, including multi-class classification, least-square SVM, support vector regression, and semi-supervised SVM. SVM and the ensemble models that combine SVM are widely applied in artificial learning and multimedia exploration. It is outstanding in its effectiveness and superior performance in small-sample problems.

3.2. LibLinear

LibLinear is a linear classifier, which is efficient in classification of large amount of data or multiple dimensions of attributes. It is developed with classifiers of linear regression and support vector machine. Thus it has several optional classifiers, including L2-regularized classifiers, L2-loss linear SVM, and logistic regression, L1-regularized classifiers, L2-loss linear SVM and logistic regression, L2-regularized support vector regression, and L2-loss linear SVR and L1-loss linear SVR. For a sample data of (x_i , y_i), this methods can compute optimization issues without constrains:

$$\min_{\varphi} \frac{1}{2} \varphi^T \varphi + \gamma \sum_{i=1}^{k} \beta(\varphi; x_i, y_i) \qquad (1)$$

where $\gamma > 0$ is defined as a penalty value, while $\beta(\varphi; x_i, y_i)$ is the loss function. It is widely used in the classification and regression of large data sets.

3.3. RBFNetwork

RBFNetwork, the radial basis function network, is a typical neural network with three layers, including an input layer, a hidden layer and an output layer. It applies radial basis function for activation. RBFNetwork can be described as:

$$h(x) = Output(\sum_{n=1}^{N} \beta_n RBF(x, \varphi_n)) \qquad (2)$$

where φ_n is the n th center, and β_n is the corresponding weights. The functions of output can be selected according to different goal. The kernel selection of RBFNetwork is crucial in this method. This method can solve various problems of approximation, prediction, classification and regression.

3.4. RandomTree

RandomTree is a learning algorithm with a fast decision tree. It utilizes information gain/variance to construct a decision or regression tree, and it is using reduced-error pruning with backfitting approach. This method can decrease the decision tree complexity. For the given variables M and N of $\{m_1,...,m_i\}$ and $\{n_1,...,n_i\}$, so that the entropy and conditional entropy of N is described as:

$$E(N) = -\sum_{i=1}^{n} K(N = n_i) \log K(N = n_i) \qquad (3)$$

$$E(N|M) = -\sum_{i=1}^{t} K(M = m_i) \log K(N \mid M = m_i) \quad (4)$$

And the gain of variable M is presented by:

$$\theta(N; M) = E(N) - E(N \mid M) \qquad (5)$$

The pruning process includes pre-pruning and post-pruning. The expansion of the tree will be terminated when the gain is not recognized due to division.

3.5. RandomForest

RandomForest is a classifier that contains multiple decision trees, and its output categories are determined by the mode of the categories output by individual trees. RandomForest method has great performance in various tasks. Its advantages can be concluded in these aspects: 1) For many types of data, it can generate high accuracy classifiers; 2) It can handle a large number of input variables; 3) It can evaluate the importance of variables when determining categories; 4) For imbalanced classification datasets, it can balance errors; 5) It has great efficiency in learning.

4. Experiment

4.1. Third-person pain stimuli

In this experiment, we collected 18 video clips (each lasts for 60 second in MPEG-4 format with a resolution of 1280*1024 dpi) to construct a third-person pain video stimuli dataset. The illustration of the screenshots of the stimuli videos are presented in Figure 2. The video clips were collected and divided into three categories according to the induced third-person pain degrees, including Pain Degree I (mild pain, score 1~3), Pain Degree II (moderate pain, score 4~6) and Pain Degree III (severe pain, score 7~10).

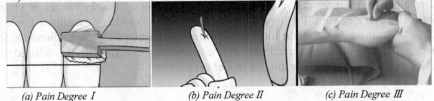

| (a) Pain Degree I | (b) Pain Degree II | (c) Pain Degree III |

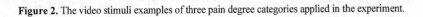

Figure 2. The video stimuli examples of three pain degree categories applied in the experiment.

4.2. Experiment participant

Specifically, 5 college students from Digital Media Design major were invited for the video selection and classification session of the stimuli videos. Then a total of 24 participants (aged from 19 to 39, 12 males and 12 females) were invited for video viewing experiment. Each participant was asked to watch 18 video clips of different pain levels. At last, a total of 432 signal records were collected, and only 384 valid physiology signal records were obtained in the experiment. Figure 3 shows that the participant is watch video clips in the pain stimuli experiment. The participant was situated in a separate experiment room with a constant lighting environment, seated in front of a laptop computer, and the stimuli video was shown on the screen. The participant wore multi-channel sensors of EDA (electrodermal activity), PPG (photoplethysmography), RSP (respiration) and ECG (electrocardiograms), see Figure 3.

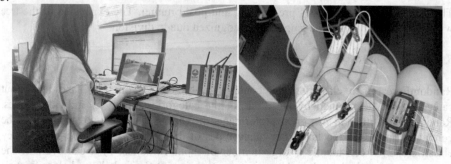

Figure 3. The participant is watch video clips in the third-person pain stimuli experiment with multi-channel sensors placed on the participant's chest and hand.

4.3. Third-person pain labeling

The most commonly evaluated index of clinical pain is its sensory intensity. There are multiple existing methods for evaluating pain intensity, including categorical scales (such as mild, moderate, and severe), numerical rating scales (NRS), visual analog scales (VAS), and validated verbal descriptive scales with excellent statistical characteristics. Due to its feasibility of scoring, NRS is the most commonly used method in clinical settings. Researchers concluded that NRS has higher usability than VAS [10][11]. Consequently, the experiment participants were asked to score the perceived pain degree in a NRS (Number Range Scare) scale of 0~10 for each video after viewing, see Figure 4.

In the scoring session, a total of 320 data samples' score results are consistent with the original pain degree classification. Inconsistent labeling mainly occurs in videos with high degree of pain. Participants reported that they could not empathize the high degree of pain while watching the videos. Since the participants' annotations are the direct reflection of their perception, in the modeling experiment, we utilized the participants' scores as the labeling for model exploration.

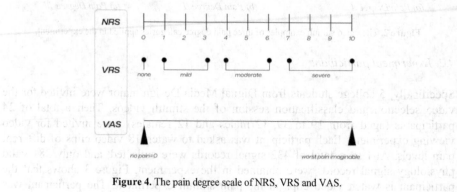

Figure 4. The pain degree scale of NRS, VRS and VAS.

4.4. Multimodal physiological features analysis

Multimodal physiological signals were collected in the experiment, including EDA, PPG, RSP and ECG, see Figure 5 of the physiological signals recorded in a video stimuli session.

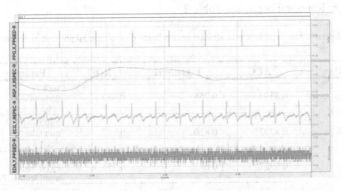

Figure 5. Multi-channel physiological signals were collected in pain stimuli experiment.

Then, the statistical features of multimodal physiology signals were applied for further modeling. The values of Average, Max, Min, Mean, Median, VAR (variance), STD (standard deviation) of the original signals were obtained to form the physiological feature dataset. Features were analyzed by CfsSubsetEvaluation method, which evaluates the worth of a subset of attributes by considering the individual predictive ability of each feature along with the degree of redundancy between them. The experiment result shows that Min value of ECG, Average value of EDA, Median value of EDA and STD of EDA were the best features for predicting modeling. The detailed features are introduced in Table 1.

Table 1. Statistical features of the physiological signals

Feature	Description
EDA	the statistical values of
ECG	Average, Max, Min, Mean, ,Median, VAR, STD of the
PPG	original signal
RSP	

5. Results and Discussion

Others' pain will strike a chord in the observers' mind, and the affective response can be detected via physiology cues. In this study, we transformed the third-person pain learning question into the exploration of physiology feature analysis and modeling. Machine learning methods were applied to recognize different level of third-person pain experience based on multi-modal physiology features fusion.

5.1. Experiment results

LibSVM, RBFNetwork, LibLinear, RandomTree and RandomForest were applied to explore the model. In the results comparison, Random Forest has the best performance. According to this experiment, the third-person pain experience can be recognized efficiently by RandomForest, see Table 2.

Table 2. Third-person pain experience recognition results based on multimodal physiology features dataset

Algorithm	ACC	F-Measure	ROC	Parameters setting
LibSVM	0.8594	0.756	0.852	cost 9, gamma 2, seed 1,
RBFNetwork	0.8203	0.820	0.897	minStdDev 2, numClusters 10, Seed 1
LibLinear	0.6927	0.682	0.751	cost 1, eps 0.001, numDecimalPlaces 2
RandomTree	0.625	0.627	0.757	minNum 5, numDecimalPlaces 1, maxDepth 0, seed 1.
RandomForest	**0.9583**	**0.958**	**0.995**	Numiterations 100, bagSizePercent 100, seed =1

In the best model exploration, we compared LibSVM, RBFNetwork, LibLinear, RandomTree and RandomForest algorithms to develop the third-person pain recognition modeling. Among all the methods, Random Forest achieved an accuracy of 95.83% for the best performance, which indicated the great potential of this method.

5.2. Discussion

In this study, we investigated the possibility of third-person pain sensing utilizing multimodal physiology features fusion. The experimental results have indicated that RandomForest is effective in the third-person pain recognition modeling based on human physiology signals. This study offers possible avenue of developing computer the empathy ability of sensing the communication of pain between sufferers and the observer. And it could also provide insight for human empathy characters in social scene. In the experiment, 24 participants were invited in third-person pain stimulation and pain level labeling work. The model performance is satisfied based on the dataset of 384 third-person pain experience samples, which manifests the effectiveness of the proposed approach.

6. Conclusion and Future Work

Third-person pain was triggered by the transfer of cognition first-person pain. Sufferers' pain can be communicated to others by their facial expression, behaviors and voice. We considered that third-person pain is important socialization ability, and it can be investigated as a starting point for empathy ability mechanism.

In this study, we present a third-person pain learning model based on multimodal physiology feature analysis. A novel third-person pain physiology feature database of 384 samples was built in the experiment. Physiology features of EDA, ECG, PPG and RSP were extracted for pattern exploration. Several machine-learning approaches were utilized in the exploration of modeling, including LibSVM, LibLinear, RBFNetwork, RandomTree and RandomForest. Finally, RandomForest method achieved the best result among all the models, with a classification accuracy of 95.83%. The results of modeling experiment suggested that it is promising to develop computer empathizing pain-aware ability.

In the further study, we will conduct the third-person pain experiments and pattern exploration in several aspects. Firstly, a third-person pain aware system can be developed to verify the model. Secondly, a larger database of third-person pain physiology features will be built for method optimization. Finally, the discovery will be examined with interdisciplinary methods and extent the study to AI-empathy intelligence research as a broader scope.

7. Acknowledgments

This study is partly supported by Fundamental Research Funds for the Provincial Universities of Zhejiang (GB202003008).

References

[1] Gisèle Pickering, Stephen Gibson.Pain, Emotion and Cognition-A complex Nexus, Springer, 2016.
[2] R. T. Azevedo, E. Macaluso, A. Avenanti, et al. Their pain is not our pain: Brain and autonomic correlates of empathic resonance with the pain of same and different race individuals. Human Brain Mapping, 2013.
[3] Galang, Michael Obhi, S. Sukhvinder. Exploring the effects of visual perspective on the ERP components of empathy for pain. Social neuroscience 15 (1a2) (2020).
[4] Giulia, Bucchioni, Carlotta, et al. Empathy or Ownership? Evidence from Corticospinal Excitability during Pain Observation. Journal of Cognitive Neuroscience, 2016.
[5] K. Kaseweter. Defining the line: examining the role of empathy in the prosocial treatment of pain, Dotoral Thesis. University of British Columbia - Okanagan, 2020.
[6] T. Hadjistavropoulos, K. D. Craig, S. Duck, A. Cano, L. Goubert, P. L. Jackson, J. S. Mogil, P. Rainville, M. J. L. Sullivan, A.C.de C Williams, T. Vervoort, T. D. Fitzgerald. A biopsychosocial formulation of pain communication, Psychol Bull 137(2011b),910-939.
[7] M. Botvinick, A. P. Jha, L. M. Bylsma, S. A. Fabian, P. E. Solomon, K. M. Prkachin. Viewing facial expressions of pain engages cortical areas involved in the direct experience of pain, Neuroimage 25 (1) (2005), 312-319.
[8] S. Whitmarsh. Sensory-motor rhythms are modulated in response to perception of pain in others. Science, 2023.

[9]   G. Hein, C. Lamm, C. Brodbeck, T. Singer. Skin conductance response to the pain of others predicts later costly helping, PLoS One **6**(8) (2011), e22759.

[10]   I. McDowell. Measuring health: a guide to rating scales and questionnaires, 3rd edn. Oxford University Press, New York, 2006.

[11]   M. J. Hjermstad, P. M. Fayers, D. F. Haugen, A. Caraceni, G. W. Hanks, J. H. Loge, R. Fainsinger, N. Aass, S. Kaasa. European Palliative Care Research C. Studies comparing Numerical Rating Scales, Verbal Rating Scales, and Visual Analogue Scales for assessment of pain intensity in adults: a systematic literature review. Pain Symptom Manage **41** (2011), 1073–1093.

Design Studies and Intelligence Engineering
L.C. Jain et al. (Eds.)
© 2024 The Authors.
doi:10.3233/FAIA231433

Development and Application of Offshore Trade Authenticity Verification Platform Based on Blockchain

Hai-Feng CHEN [a], Lv ZHANG[b], Shuai WANG[b], Shan-Shan SHI [b]

[a] *(Unicom Cloud Data Co., LTD, Beijing100080, China)*
[b] *(Unicom Internet of Things Co., LTD, Nanjing 210006, China)*

Abstract. Offshore trade is a widely used business model in international trade, but because of its opaque capital flow, transaction information is not open, offshore trade has certain risks. In order to guarantee the national economic security and trade interests, the authenticity verification of offshore trade has become an important issue. This paper designs and implements the offshore trade authenticity verification platform based on blockchain technology through the mapping relationship between the user demand analysis of offshore trade authenticity verification and platform functions. The application test of the constructed digital platform is carried out, and the test results show that it also has stable average response time and efficient TPS performance advantages under the premise of meeting daily business needs. This platform can actively promote regional trade facilitation, stimulate financial institutions' demand for industry exhibition, and achieve digital empowerment for the development of background offshore trade.

Keywords. Offshore Trade, Authenticity Verification, Demand analysis, Blockchain

1. Introduction

At present, the internal and external environment and conditions faced by China's opening up have undergone significant changes, and foreign trade has become more dependent on innovation-driven development. Fostering offshore trade is an important part of promoting the innovative development of foreign trade and exploring and developing new trade modes. Although offshore trade has some practical experience in China, it has not been fully developed because of the particularity of its trade form. The core of offshore trade development is to form an appropriate institutional environment, and the difficulty of offshore trade development is how to strike a balance between openness and security. From the overall plan of China's respective trade pilot zones, Shanghai, Guangdong, Liaoning, Zhejiang, Henan, Tianjin, Hainan, Hunan and Guangxi have all proposed the development of offshore trade business needs, Shanghai Free trade Zone has taken the lead in launching the pilot whitelist of new offshore international trade, and Tianjin has created a new type of trade in the real economy "Binhai model". Each trade zone is trying to explore the innovative development of offshore trade business in accordance with local conditions [1-4].

Blockchain technology is one of the areas of innovation in the digital transformation of business and society today. It has the characteristics of decentralization, non-tampering, information transparency, traceability and other technical advantages. In the field of trade finance, blockchain is mainly used in letters of credit, supply chain finance and cross-border payment credit enhancement to simplify financial financing procedures; In the field of logistics, the application of blockchain can simplify the exchange of information in the supply chain and enable digitization. Therefore, the application of blockchain technology has important practical significance for the systematic research on the innovation and development of offshore trade in the pilot free trade zone [5], which can promote the simplification of offshore trade financing lending process, establish cross-border transaction verification and provide risk control mechanism, etc., and enable the creation of new models in the field of digital trade [6].

2. Basic concepts and pain points of offshore trade

2.1. Offshore trade

Offshore trade refers to the trade of goods conducted by traders within a country/region, delivered directly from upstream producers outside the border/customs to downstream customers, without passing through the trader's own country/region. As a new type of trade mode, the most significant feature of offshore trade compared with traditional trade mode is the "three-flow separation" of order flow, goods flow and capital flow [7]. That is, the trade related fund settlement and document circulation processing activities occur in China, while the actual goods transportation activities occur outside China.

Offshore trade is the inevitable result of the continuous refinement of international trade division of labor, the inevitable product of economic globalization, and one of the important means for countries to control and master the global resource elements. The development of offshore trade in the China Pilot Free Trade Zone is conducive to smooth the domestic and international economic cycle, accelerate the construction of a new system of high-level open economy, deepen market-oriented reform, and create a business environment governed by law, internationalization and facilitation.

2.2. Pain points of offshore trade

1)There are regulatory risks in the authenticity verification of offshore trade.

At present, under the domestic demand for the convenience of offshore trade settlement, financial institutions and foreign exchange management approval standards put forward higher requirements for the authenticity verification of offshore trade. At present, the certification requirements for trade authenticity verification are customs declaration, bill of lading, record list and other materials that can reflect the actual flow of goods, as well as commercial documents reflecting the transfer of goods rights such as contracts, invoices and receipt and payment vouchers, so as to achieve superficial compliance verification of the authenticity of the overall trading business [9].

However, there are still some risks, which make it difficult for banks and regulators to grasp whether there is a real trade background in the transaction, and the certificate of goods rights cannot be verified by the third-party platform. If enterprises cooperate with overseas sale order companies, they collude with each other to forge contracts and fabricate bills of lading, which can realize fund transfer or arbitrage in disguise.

2) Lack of digital means for authenticity verification of offshore trade.

At present, banks rely on manual participation in the statistics of offshore trade balance data for post-tracking. For example, for the payment of goods in advance and the payment of goods in advance, the bank staff need to manually register the account and regularly contact the enterprise to understand the customs declaration information. This kind of manual work process has a large workload, passive management and high error rate, and there is a certain lag, which is difficult to timely reflect the situation of new entities and business types in the current period, and the regulatory body can not track the business situation in a timely manner. From the perspective of enterprises, in order to cooperate with the bank's verification management, it is necessary to submit various certification materials repeatedly, which is tedious and time-consuming.

3)The authenticity verification of offshore trade lacks credible data support.

At the same time, as the most important part of the authenticity verification of offshore trade business, that is, to verify the existence and circulation of goods. Because shipping has the advantages of large carrying capacity, can provide transportation services adapted to different types of goods, and developed global port network, the transfer of goods in offshore trade business often chooses shipping transportation mode. The shipping trade has a large number of participants, with shipping routes all over the world, and numerous organizational units for trading and transportation design, such as shipping companies, shipping port companies, terminal operators, ports, etc. Besides, the business systems of each organization are relatively discrete, and data information among organizations cannot be interconnected, resulting in data islands. As a result, users cannot obtain standardized and reliable data support with comprehensive scenarios, clear links, and reliable data.

3. Offshore trade authenticity verification platform functional demand analysis

1) Demand analysis of trading enterprises.

In the process of business transformation and industrial upgrading at this stage, enterprises need to further strive for the improvement of settlement financing efficiency.

2) Demand analysis of financial institutions.

The development of offshore trade business of financial institutions has been faced with compliance problems for a long time, so it is necessary to collect multi-dimensional verification data for cross-verification, improve the management efficiency of trade verification, and innovate the financial service model.

3) Demand analysis of government departments.

Although the policy level has clearly supported the development of offshore trade, the regulatory authorities have been faced with the problem of difficult supervision and compliance of offshore trade for a long time, and it is necessary to establish effective digital means to carry out risk control on the trading behaviors of overseas counterparties and access enterprises, so as to ensure the positive development of offshore business.

According to the user's business requirements, it is mapped into the platform function requirements, and then the correlation analysis of user requirements and platform functions can be carried out to prioritize the function development and construction. The mapping table of user requirements and platform functions is shown in **Table 1**.

Table 1. Mapping table of user requirements and platform capabilities

User demand	Function
W_1 Multi-dimensional verification data cross validation	R_1 Gateway
W_2 The innovation of financial service model	R_2 Trade verification inquiry
W_3 Trade verification management efficiency improved	R_3 Data inquiry
W_4 Effective digital means of offshore trade regulation	R_4 Report management
W_5 Improving the efficiency of offshore trade settlement financing	R_5 Abnormal risk monitoring
W_6 Foreign counterparty risk control	R_6 Statistical analysis of business development
W_7 Risk control of access enterprises	R_7 Blacklist management
	R_8 Message management
	R_9 Policy news display
	R_{10} Dynamic sharing
	R_{11} User message

In this paper, the score of user needs and functional needs is given by the expert group, and the degree of function meeting user needs is recorded as 5 points, 3 points, 1 points and 0 points from high to low, indicating strong correlation, medium correlation, weak correlation and no correlation. Calculate the absolute weight value for each function requirement as follows:

$$H_i = \sum_{i=1}^{n} W_i R_j \ (j = 0,1,2,\ldots, m) \tag{1}$$

H_i represents the absolute weight value of the function i, and R_{ij} represents the correlation degree value of the function i and the user demand j. According to the publicity, the weight value of each platform function is calculated and sorted, as shown in **Table 2**.

Table 2. Relationship matrix between user requirements and platform functions

User demand	Importance Degree	R1	R2	R3	R4	R5	R6	R7	R8	R9	R10	R11
W1	6.98	1	5	5	0	0	0	0	0	0	0	0
W2	5.53	3	0	0	3	0	3	0	1	3	1	3
W3	6.24	0	5	5	0	5	0	0	0	0	0	0
W4	6.35	5	0	3	5	0	5	0	3	0	0	0
W5	5.69	0	0	1	0	0	3	0	0	0	0	0
W6	6.76	0	3	0	1	5	0	3	0	0	0	0
W7	6.69	0	0	0	1	5	0	3	0	0	0	0
Weight H		55	86	91	62	98	65	40	25	17	6	17
Rank		6	3	2	5	1	4	7	8	9	11	9

According to the weight ranking of functional requirements, trade verification, data query, risk monitoring, and business development statistics will be the key content of the design of the offshore trade authenticity verification platform based on blockchain.

4. Architecture design of offshore trade authenticity verification platform based on blockchain

4.1. Platform design concept

The blockchain-based offshore trade authenticity verification platform is a service platform for enterprises, banks and government regulators with the ultimate purpose of offshore trade authenticity verification and compliance assurance. By integrating external data resources, using blockchain rights confirmation and encryption as data trust and security guarantee, using artificial intelligence technologies such as risk identification and behavior judgment as capabilities, tracking and cross-verifying information of transaction-related commercial documents and logistics links, and assessing enterprises and transaction information with credit risks according to preset standards, risk management and control are implemented. It provides strong data support for the authenticity verification of enterprises' offshore trade background and business supervision [8-10].

4.2. Platform function structure

Due to the business function requirements of efficient offshore trade authenticity verification, logistics data query, and risk control management service capabilities, the blockchain-based offshore trade authenticity verification platform is mainly summarized as "1+1+1", an integrated service management system, an application management system, and a background management system, as shown in **Figure 1**. The application management system is composed of five functional subsystems, which mainly include: trade registration intelligent evaluation system, data query auxiliary management system, risk monitoring dynamic early warning system, business development statistical analysis system, and business visual display system [11-14].

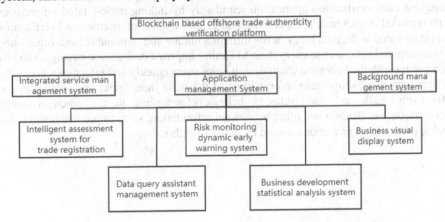

Figure 1. Function structure of Offshore trade authenticity verification platform.

4.3. Overall platform architecture

The offshore trade authenticity verification platform is composed of database (SQL), blockchain platform (Hyperledger Fabric), etc., and the running environment is Microsoft Windows Server 2008 and above. According to the development principles of system completeness, reliability, maintainability and expansibility, follow the information security guarantee service standards, and ensure the development specifications and operation safety of information systems. The system data logic structure is divided into five levels: infrastructure layer, data service layer, application support layer, application layer, and display layer. The overall framework of the offshore trade authenticity verification platform, which is supported by the dual systems of IT system standards and specifications and system maintenance and information security.

4.4. Blockchain network security architecture

Blockchain itself is a tamper-proof, decentralized distributed digital transaction record, which is jointly maintained by multiple parties, uses cryptography to ensure the privacy and security of transmission and access, and can achieve consistent data storage and difficult to tamper with the accounting technology [8]. Blockchain relies on a peer-to-peer network that no one party controls, and authentication of network transactions (transactional authentication) is achieved through cryptographic means and mathematical consensus protocols that define rules for updating the ledger and allow participants who have no specific trust in each other to collaborate, rather than relying on a single trusted third party.

The platform designs the blockchain network security architecture based on the alliance chain. As shown in **Figure 2**, decentralized ledger nodes are established in the alliance chain to ensure that each node is open, flat, equal and highly autonomous, and there is no mandatory control function between nodes and the data is open and transparent. It is composed of ledger nodes. Data information such as logistics, capital flow, business flow and enterprise behavior information of offshore trade are accessed and stored in each ledger node of the overall network through the Fabric SDK. Establish smart contracts covering secure encryption algorithms and authorized access mechanisms between various user roles, enabling key players in the organization to complete each verification application seamlessly by linking trade-related information data recorded in each node's ledger in real time. Each update information and verification report is stored to the data block in the form of a unique and immutable hash value using timestamp and asymmetric encryption to further improve data source management. By comparing with the historical chain data, it helps users quickly and effectively verify the authenticity of offshore trade information. At the same time, banks and regulators can effectively track and trace relevant behaviors according to the on-chain query, verification, verification and other behavioral information, so as to prevent information leakage and illegal operations caused by abuse of rights.

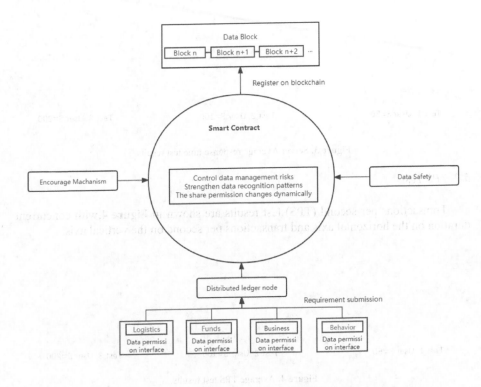

Figure 2. Blockchain network security architecture.

5. Application and test analysis of offshore trade authenticity verification platform based on blockchain

In this paper, the automated load test tool (Jmeter) was used to deploy the execution script in the Alibaba Cloud test environment, simulate the functional applications of various related systems to establish the test cluster environment, and respectively set up the stress test under the application scenario that the number of users applied for trade verification service is 50, 100, and 200, and the server is concurrent for 5 minutes. Focus on detecting host resource usage, including average server response times and transactions per second (TPS).

5.1. Response Time Test

The test results of the average response time of the server are shown in **Figure 3**. The horizontal axis is the concurrent duration, and the vertical axis is the response time.

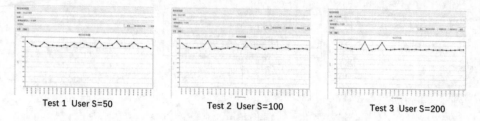

Test 1 User S=50   Test 2 User S=100   Test 3 User S=200

Figure 3. Server Average response time test results.

5.2. TPS Test

Transactions per second (TPS) test results are shown in **Figure 4**, with concurrent duration on the horizontal axis and transactions per second on the vertical axis.

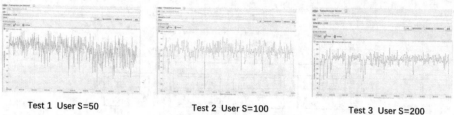

Test 1 User S=50   Test 2 User S=100   Test 3 User S=200

Figure 4. Average TPS test results.

5.3. Analysis of stress test results

The above stress test results are summarized as shown in **Figure 5**, and the following conclusions are reached:

(1) When the number of simulated concurrent users S=50, the average response time is 170ms and the tps is 310.3 per second, and the system performance is satisfactory;

(2) When the number of concurrent simulated users S=100, the average response time increases slightly to 337ms, and the TPS fluctuates slightly to 307.9 per second, indicating that the system performance is still good;

(3) Under the high load of simulating the number of concurrent users S=200, when processing more user requests, the average response time is slightly slowed down due to the limitation of server resources, but it can still ensure that 95% of the online transaction response time is less than 1s, although the TPS is reduced to 293.5 per second, no abnormal situation of requests being blocked or rejected is generated.

According to the pressure test results, the overall platform has no performance bottleneck, and the average response time is within 1 second, the exception rate is 0, meeting 99% availability, and verifying the performance advantage under the premise of meeting the daily business needs.

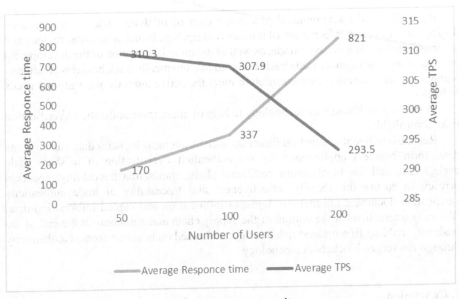

Figure 5. Pressure test results.

6. Platform design innovation

1) Integrate multiple third-party data sources, provide multi-dimensional and reliable verification data, and cross-verify to ensure efficient and authentic verification.

Integrate mature data providers in the market for multi-dimensional data analysis and trade verification. In the form of data call on demand, it provides effective evidence for offshore trade information, reduces the risk of fraud, and provides data support for banks to handle offshore trade. Achieve a more targeted whitelist review process by government agencies and regulatory authorities to reduce potential risks to customers.

2) Joint banks share key peer data, customize verification rules, break data silos, and improve risk control.

Cooperate with major banks that carry out offshore trade business, use blockchain technology to securely access the historical business inspection and processing data of shared banks, and set access rights. After obtaining authorization, different banks can retrieve the key fields of documents and obtain the processing results of documents in other banks, for example, they can know that under the same trade background, Whether the logistics document of the enterprise has been reused by other banks, or whether the document business has been rejected by other banks, but it does not show more business details.

In addition, unified risk control rules can be customized, such as requiring consistent information between trade, logistics and customs data, and preventing multiple buyers or sellers from repeating under the same logistics document. The system background automatically carries out information matching verification and returns results without manual intervention, so as to further improve the efficiency and accuracy of risk control.

3) Use big data to automate statistical analysis, improve business management initiative, and eliminate manual errors.

By updating the accumulated processing data of offshore trade, it can instantly display various report information of business enterprises, banks, industries, regions and other aspects based on offshore trade, as well as dynamic information of the development process of specific offshore trade businesses, and automatically track business conditions without regular manual communication to meet the active analysis and statistics needs of banks.

4) Relying on blockchain technology to help offshore trade authenticity verification risks controllable.

Realize intelligent acquisition functions such as overseas logistics data and customs data, form business applications for the authenticity verification of offshore trade background, and use blockchain's certificate chain, transaction traceability, and data privacy to ensure the security, effectiveness and traceability of trade authenticity verification document information, logistics information and capital information data. Objectify interactions at the bottom of the supply chain and autonomy at the end of the business, enabling fine-grained risk management based on business context authenticity through converged blockchain technology.

7. Conclusion

Trade digitalization is an inevitable trend in the development of cross-border trade. Blockchain has the ability to provide trusted data in the virtual world, and can share trusted data across the world. By building an offshore trade platform based on blockchain technology, it can actively enhance the coordination ability of the industrial chain and supply chain of banks and enterprises, and promote the supervision efficiency of offshore trade to a large extent.

The offshore trade authenticity verification platform proposed in this paper is representative in terms of system functions, innovative and diversified in terms of application services, which greatly improves the level of trade facilitation and enables digital enablement to promote the development of offshore trade in the background. Moreover, stress tests are carried out based on the platform's own performance, and the results are satisfactory. The overall platform is conducive to strengthening the convergence of key enterprises and industrial chain scenes and ecological docking, stimulating the exhibition needs of financial institutions, accelerating local governments to promote the construction of advanced manufacturing and new infrastructure, continuously optimizing the business environment, and enhancing the competitiveness of the open economy, which is a kind of technology platform worth promoting.

References

[1] Yan H Z, Zheng S, Huang S H, et al. Experience Drawn from the Development of International Offshore Financial Markets for Shanghai Foreign Trade Zone. Shanghai Journal of Economics, 2014 (10):7.

[2] Baldwin R, Okubo T. International Trade, Offshoring and Heterogeneous Firms. NBER Working Papers **22** (201), 1, 59-72.

[3] Kecheng, Yang, Ming, et al. China's Offshore Financial Development in Free Trade Zones.2018.

[4] Zhan Lianke, Xia Feng. Research on offshore trade development of Hainan Free Trade Port under the new pattern of domestic and international double circulation. Economics and Management Review **1037** (2019), 3, 136-147.

[5] Prithviraj, David, William, et al. Blockchain Technology in International Commodity Trading. Journal of Private Enterprise 2020,35(2): 23-46.

[6] Shuchih Ernest Chang,Yi-Chian Chen,Tzu-Ching Wu. Exploring blockchain technology in international trade. Industrial Management & Data Systems **119** (2019), 8, 1712-1733.

[7] Han Yapin, Yin Zhengping. Further consolidate the foundation of China's offshore trade development. International Economic Cooperation, 2021.

[8] Zhang B. Digital innovation of cross-border trade under the background of blockchain. Statistical Theory and Practice, 2020. (in Chinese)

[9] Xu Jinsong, Ma Xinlu. Thoughts on Further Monitoring and Verification of offshore resale business. Northern Finance, 2016.

[10] Jiang Feng, Zhu Yunyi, Qian Sisi. Discussion on innovating the authenticity Review method of Trade in Goods. Hainan Finance, 2020.

[11] Cui Di. Exploration of methods for verifying the authenticity of trade in Goods. Theoretical Observation, 2020.

[12] Huang Bingzhi, Liu Zongyuan. Development of new international trade formats and institutional bottlenecks under the emergence of new technologies: A case study of the development of foreign trade integrated service platform. Science Development, 2022.

[13] Liu Xianliang, Zhou Zhidan, Ji Fujian. Construction and development countermeasures of Ningbo Foreign Trade Integrated Service Platform -- taking Shimaotong as an example. Journal of Zhejiang Wanli University **34** (2021), 1, 27-32.

[14] Gu Bin, Lu Meihua. Research on digital trade regulation based on blockchain technology. China Economic & Trade Guide (Middle) **1** (2020), 12-14.

Design Studies and Intelligence Engineering
L.C. Jain et al. (Eds.)
© 2024 The Authors.
This article is published online with Open Access by IOS Press and distributed under the terms
of the Creative Commons Attribution Non-Commercial License 4.0 (CC BY-NC 4.0).
doi:10.3233/FAIA231434

Design of Children's Artistic Creation Products Integrating AR and Tangible Interactions

Jiarui LIU[a,1] and Lingyan ZHANG[b,c]

[a] *School of Industrial Design, China Academy of Art Hangzhou, China, 310001*
[b] *Design Innovation Centre, China Academy of Art Hangzhou, China, 310001*
[c] *Design-AI Lab, China Academy of Art, Hangzhou, China, 310001*

Abstract. To enhance the aesthetic and creative development of children aged 7 to 12, the research aims to create interactive children's artistic creation products that are better suited for their learning and experience growth. This research proposes a method based on Interface interaction hierarchy Design and gesture interactions within an augmented reality (AR) spatial environment. Taking children as the research subjects, this study aims to reshape the contemporary methods of artistic creation for children. Firstly, a questionnaire survey was conducted to comprehend their attitudes, opinions, and experiences regarding children's artistic creation products that integrate AR and tangible interactions. Secondly, an A/B comparative user experience test was conducted, involving the participation of 40 children who used children's artistic creation products integrating AR and tangible interactions. Their usage processes and outcomes related to visual interfaces and spatial interactions were documented. The results confirm that the purity and intensity of colors, and the dynamic effects of images will attract children. A single-level interactive interface is better suited for children to navigate and execute commands. And regarding spatial gesture interactions, employing familiar hand-held actions based on everyday intuitive gestures (such as grabbing for movement, zooming, rotating, etc.) makes it easier for children to naturally interact and successfully engage in artistic creations. Within the process steps of combining software and hardware operations, triggering software interface commands through the recognition of the physical product's form and the hand's grip style offers increased simplicity and usability. This study contributes to the artistic creation field within future virtual reality environments like AR, by providing a more intricate approach to behavior design, centered around children's capabilities. It offers refined methods for integrated hardware and software interaction, immersive creative experiences, and design decisions for interactive interfaces. In conclusion, this study concludes in a design practice based on the research findings. It affirms that the proposed method for designing children's artistic creation product contributes significantly to enhancing children's artistic expression and fostering creativity. This research provides a new perspective and methodology for the future development of children's artistic creation product designs.

Keywords. Augmented Reality, Artistic Creation, Space Interaction, Tangible Interaction, Children Gesture Design

---

[1] Corresponding Author , School of Industrial Design, China Academy of Art ,Building 18,No.352 Xiangshan Rd,Xihu District, Hangzhou, Zhejiang, P.R.China; E-mail:lnfxljr@126.com.

1. Introduction

The emergence of digital media and new technologies has immersed us in a media-centric society that evolves alongside technological progress. These progressions have reshaped how we connect, create, access, and use information, as well as in the mediums through which we engage in these activities. [1] With the intervention of digital technology, contemporary children's artistic creation is gradually undergoing a shift towards digitalization. The incorporation of technologies such as Augmented Reality (AR), Virtual Reality (VR), and Artificial Intelligence (AI) has expanded the realm of artistic creation, providing greater possibilities for creative expression. The medium for artistic creation is no longer restricted to paper, gradually extending into virtual spaces.

Based on research into interactive children's product design that incorporates audiovisual associations, it has been observed that children aged 7 to 12, during this stage of artistic development, become more discerning about their creations. And the structured sequence for depicting objects no longer satisfies them. While frameworks are still used for drawing, they are more intricate than the ones used in earlier stages. Overlapping becomes visible, and there's a heightened sense of spatial relationships [2]. Furthermore, by emphasizing art-based and multimodal practices, not only does it describe children's knowledge and comprehension of the surrounding world, but also various symbolic representations such as auditory cues, gestures, language, spatial relationships, and visual patterns can be employed to elucidate essential content and concepts. This approach uncovers children's creativity and facilitates effective communication methods [3]. Hence, we have chosen to target the age range of 7-12 years, a pivotal period for enhancing aesthetics and creativity. During this stage, children have moved beyond the unstructured scribbles of their early years and entered a phase characterized by a deeper understanding of concepts and divergent thinking. Exposure to artistic creation products during this stage can nurture children's artistic perception and creativity, allowing them to explore their interests, values, and sense of identity. This contributes to the development of their individual expression and self-concept.

Therefore, this paper presents a method based on interface hierarchy design within an AR spatial environment and gesture interactions. The study centers on children as research subjects, aiming to reshape contemporary approaches to children's artistic creation. Employing questionnaire surveys and A/B comparative experimental tests, the study engaged 40 children aged 7-12 years in a series of tests encompassing visual colors, animations, software interaction hierarchies, spatial gesture interactions, and methods of triggering operational functions. This research endeavors to offer a new perspective and methodology for the future development of children's art education.

2. Literature review

2.1. The Status of Research on Children's Artistic Creations

Children's artistic creation plays a significant role in their growth and development. Artistic creation serves as a means not only for expressing personality and emotions but also for nurturing children's creativity, imagination, and expressive abilities. By engaging in artistic creation, children can exhibit their inner worlds, discover themselves, and enhance their self-confidence.

Existing children's artistic creation products also encompass various interaction modes, primarily categorized into tangible interaction and virtual interaction. The majority of commonly seen products are based on tangible interaction, where children can use physical tools such as brushes, handles, and other tangible instruments for creation. They directly engage in drawing, doodling, coloring, and other forms of artistic expression on physical surfaces like paper or clay. With the advancement of technology, virtual interaction is also gaining prominence. Some products support gesture interaction, allowing children to control the shape, size, and color of brushes using gestures. This enhances the interactivity and enjoyment of the creative process [4]. For example, Tracy's research substantiated that incorporating digital artistic creation tools as supplements is highly useful for learning traditional paper-based artistic creation forms and enhancing overall learning [5]. Various projects in children's art education from different countries, a series of experimental art projects initiated by Google Creative Lab, and virtual reality interactive art exhibitions held worldwide by the Japanese new media art collective TeamLab are successful examples of applying generative art to contemporary children's art education. Such as AI shadow puppetry and VR art learning courses. These artistic creation products break down the boundaries between art and technology, sparking children's active engagement in artistic creation [6].

These interaction modes aim to stimulate children's creativity and imagination, and foster their interest and learning in art. Additionally, certain products integrate both tangible interaction and virtual reality technologies, allowing children to interact with virtual artworks, thereby enhancing the sense of immersion and engagement in the creative process.

2.2. Application and development of AR technology and tangible interaction in children's artistic creation

Some studies suggest that technology can significantly enhance children's learning experiences across various subjects [7]. tangible interaction technology refers to the technology that involves interacting with physical objects. Research on tangible interaction is inspired by various disciplines, including psychology, sociology, engineering, and human-computer interaction [8]. The combination of tangible interaction technology and AR technology allows children to immerse themselves more effectively in artistic creation. In recent years, the utilization of AR technology and tangible interaction has gained increasing prominence in children's artistic creation. The use of augmented reality systems enhances students' engagement in visual art learning [9]. There are already numerous examples of using AR technology for artistic creation. For instance, by leveraging sensor technology and tangible interaction devices, children can interact with digital artworks through gestures, language, sound, and other means. This enhances their sense of engagement during artistic creation, thereby increasing their interest and curiosity in artistic exploration [10]. Through the combination of AR technology and tangible interaction, children can interact with virtual artworks, enhancing their understanding and appreciation of art pieces. The integration of new technology not only provides children with novel artistic experiences but also enriches the content and format of children's art education. It helps expand their horizons and stimulates their creativity.

In conclusion, the design of children's art creation products that integrate AR and tangible interaction requires following specific design methods and processes. To ensure the quality and effectiveness of these products, this paper employs questionnaire surveys, experimental design research methods, and AB comparison tests. Placing children's needs and experiences at the forefront, the study conducts research on children's requirements and collects user feedback. By assessing factors such as children's preferences for visual interfaces, the intuitiveness of visual operations, and the natural comfort of spatial gesture interactions, the study aims to better understand their expectations and needs. This approach helps cater to the children's requirements and assess the effectiveness and sustainability of their artistic learning experiences in an AR environment.

3. Method

3.1. Questionnaire Design

To explore the usage needs of the target users for art creation products, this study surveyed the form of a questionnaire. The survey was conducted for both children and educators to understand their attitudes, opinions, and experiences regarding children's art creation products that integrate AR and tangible interaction. Through quantitative and qualitative data analysis, the study aimed to gather insights into users' perspectives on the product as well as their suggestions for improvement.

Children are the primary subjects of this research, but the survey was distributed to parents of these children. Through the internet, a survey was disseminated to parents of children nationwide to collect user data. The purpose was to establish a more direct connection with parents and gain insights into the current developmental status of various abilities in their children. This also aimed to understand parents' perceptions of their children's capabilities and their expectations regarding art creation products. The collected data serves as a foundational reference for further case studies in this area[11]. The purpose of this survey is to utilize the gathered information and data to ascertain the psychological, behavioral, and needs aspects of children. It aims to acquire user preferences and explore opportunities that can guide design practices. Additionally, it serves as guidance for creating prototypes of art creation products and exploring methods to establish immersive experiences for children.

The questionnaire is divided into three sections. The first section aims to gather basic information about the survey participants. The second section focuses primarily on the practical usage of children's art creation products. The third section involves understanding the expectations of the target users regarding art creation products,to uncover potential opportunities for the design of children's art creation products. Certain questions in the survey employ the Likert 10-level scale, where users rate the provided content based on their real experiences and feelings, ranging from "Dislike Very Much" (1) to "Like Very Much" (10). The questionnaire statements are presented as shown in Table 1, comprising a total of 11 questions.

Table 1. Survey Questionnaire on Visual Brightness, Color, and Motion Effects in Children's Group

variate	Question
	Ages of Parents and Children
Basic Information	Gender of Children
	Age of Children
	Whether to contact children's art education
	What products or toys related to artistic creation have you used

	What kind of activities do children like to do?
	What tools do children use to draw and doodle?
	Brightness: Brighter colors can stimulate children's interest in using
Product Using condition	Dynamic effect: More dynamic effects can stimulate children's interest in using
	Color range: How many colors do you think are more suitable for children?

3.2. Interaction Interface Testing

The purpose of this experiment is to explore the influence of the design of icon hierarchy and icon distance in interactive interface on the operation of children aged 7-12 years old in an AR environment, and to produce the design scheme of Child-centered functional icon hierarchy and distance in AR environment by setting two experiments. The two experimental objectives are divided into two items: (1) In the AR interactive interface, which is more suitable for children's choice and operation of art functions, single-level and double-level function icons. (2) Whether the distance between icons in the AR interface affects children's tapping efficiency.

The two experimental designs primarily employed the AB comparison testing method and observational method for conducting research. A total of 40 children aged 7-12 were recruited for this testing, and an AR headset was prepared. For investigating the impact of icon hierarchy on children's interactions. A flow is designed that requires children to tap the functional steps and provides A/B single-level and double-level interfaces (Image 1).

By recording the completion times of children, a comparison can be made to determine which design approach enhances the efficiency of children's ability to quickly retrieve functions. Subsequently, through the creation of charts, a comparison can be made to identify which icon hierarchy better aligns with a child-centric design approach based on their abilities.

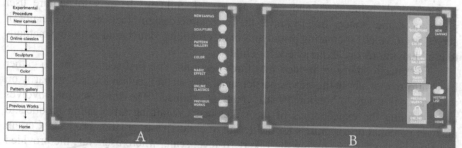

Image 1. Setting of action steps and A/B Icon Hierarchy interface

In testing the influence of icon distance on children's operation, as shown in Image 2, a process requiring children to open functional steps is designed, and an interface with different icon distance between A and B interface. The interval is 2PX and 1PX respectively. By recording the completion time of children, the interface in which the design scheme has a higher fault tolerance rate is compared, and it is helpful for children to quickly retrieve the function. Then the chart is drawn to compare which distance between icons is more consistent with the child-centered design.

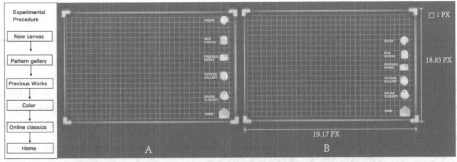

Image 2. Setting of action steps and A/B Icon distance style on the interface

3.3. Gesture and Spatial Interaction Testing

The purpose of this experiment is to explore the design of different gestures and spatial interactions in an AR environment. Three sets of gestures were designed to control the zooming, rotation, and movement of virtual objects. The testing objectives are divided into three parts: (1) In spatial interactions within the AR environment, which gesture is more suitable for children to zoom in on objects to achieve artistic shaping tasks? (2) In spatial interactions within the AR environment, which gesture is more suitable for children to rotate virtual objects? (3) In spatial interactions within the AR environment, which gesture is more suitable for children to move objects and graphics?

This experimental design primarily employed A/B testing and questionnaire surveys. As illustrated in Image 3, at the Gesture and Spatial Interaction Testing site, a total of 40 children aged 7 to 12 were gathered, and AR glasses were provided for them to wear. In the software, we design A and B different gestures to move, rotate and zoom virtual objects in the space. Subsequently, a questionnaire was distributed to the children for them to rate their experiences, as shown in Table 2. And a chart is drawn to compare which gesture command is more in line with the child-centered design and easier to operate and learn.

Image 3. Experiment site of gesture and space interaction test

Table 2. Test score table for zooming, moving, and rotating virtual objects in AR space.

Test content	Gesture category	Satisfaction rating (check)
Zoom object test	Gesture Test A	1 2 3 4 5 6 7 8 9 10
	Gesture Test B	1 2 3 4 5 6 7 8 9 10
Moving object test	Gesture Test A	1 2 3 4 5 6 7 8 9 10
	Gesture Test B	1 2 3 4 5 6 7 8 9 10
Rotating object test	Gesture Test A	1 2 3 4 5 6 7 8 9 10

	Gesture Test B	1 2 3 4 5 6 7 8 9 10
The test of ways to trigger the	Gesture Test A	1 2 3 4 5 6 7 8 9 10
function of artistic creation	Gesture Test B	1 2 3 4 5 6 7 8 9 10

In the AR spatial testing, as shown in Image 4, the AR software was designed to use gestures of single-handed palm expansion and contraction, as well as double-handed spreading and closing, to control the zooming of virtual objects. The purpose of this design was to assess which gesture was better suited for children to manipulate object zooming, and to enable children to achieve smoother transitions between objects during object sculpting.

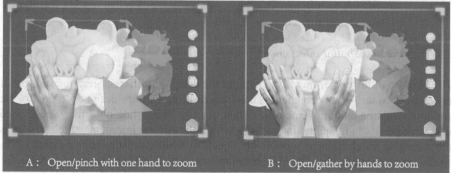

A : Open/pinch with one hand to zoom   B : Open/gather by hands to zoom

Image 4. A/B Different gestures control virtual object zoom.

In the AR space testing, as shown in Image 5, in the AR software design, different gestures are used to trigger the rotation of virtual objects, including swaying with a single hand palm facing left or right, and swaying with 2 or 3 fingers facing left or right. This aims to test which gesture is more suitable for children to control object rotation, enabling smoother and more convenient color selection or virtual object rotation during children's interactions.

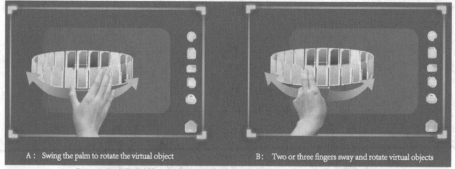

A : Swing the palm to rotate the virtual object   B: Two or three fingers sway and rotate virtual objects

Image 5. A/B Different Gestures for Controlling Virtual Object Rotation

In the AR testing environment, as shown in Image 6, within the AR software design, two different gestures are used to control the rotation of virtual objects: one is using a clenched fist for movement and the other is using an open hand for movement. The purpose of this testing is to determine which of these gestures is more suitable for children to manipulate object movement, aiming to provide a smoother and more natural experience for children when dragging objects or placing them in different positions within the virtual space.

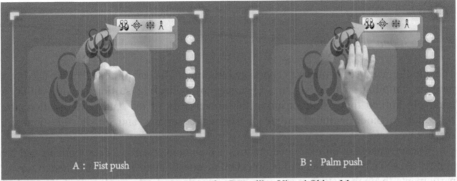

A : Fist push   B : Palm push

Image 6. A/B Different Gestures for Controlling Virtual Object Movement

3.4. Testing of Integrated Software and Hardware Trigger Functions

The objective of this experiment is to explore the methods of activating different functions in an AR environment through integrated interaction between handheld physical art tools and virtual interfaces. Explore which type of triggering method is more suitable for children.

This experiment is primarily designed using the AB testing method and questionnaire survey. A total of 40 children aged 7 to 12 are gathered, and an AR headset along with a physical handheld tool are prepared. The AR visual capabilities can recognize the appearance of the physical handheld tool and the grip of the hand. The methods to activate different creative functions are depicted in Image 7. They involve either recognizing the physical tool's appearance and hand grip through the interface or activating the functions by physically pressing the tool onto the functional icons.

And then, we administered a questionnaire (Table 2) to the children to gather their ratings, and then compared the results using graphical representations to contrast which method of activating artistic creation functions is more suitable for children.

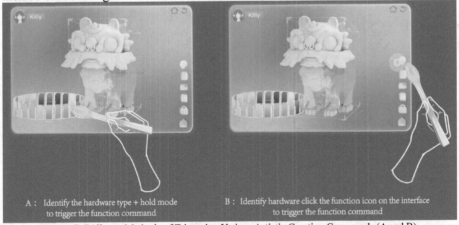

A : Identify the hardware type + hold mode to trigger the function command   B : Identify hardware click the function icon on the interface to trigger the function command

Image 7. Different Methods of Triggering Various Artistic Creation Commands (A and B)

4. Result

4.1. Questionnaire Results

The questionnaire collection was conducted in China. The sampling technique used was random sampling, which has the advantage of collecting sufficient data within a relatively limited time while ensuring the universality of the data. The questionnaire collection methods included online questionnaire surveys and on-site questionnaire surveys.

The advantage of online questionnaires is their convenience for respondents and the ability to reach a broader range of people. Online questionnaires are distributed to survey participants through instant messaging apps, emails, and other online tools. A total of 103 online questionnaires were collected. The sample characteristics are shown in Table 3, and the basic results of the questionnaire are shown in Figure 1.

Table 3 provides a comprehensive overview of the sample characteristics. Among the collected responses, male children accounted for 60.19%, while female children accounted for 39.81%. Children aged 5-7 constituted 22.33% of the sample, those aged 8-10 comprised 40.78%, and children aged 11-12 represented 36.89%. Notably, 80.58% of the children had been exposed to children's art education.

Table 3. Sample characteristics

trait	type	Frequency	Percentage
gender	Male	62	60.19%
	Female	41	39.81%
age	5-7	23	22.33%
	8-10	42	40.78%
	11-12	38	36.89%
whether to contact children's art education	yes	83	80.58%
	no	20	19.42%

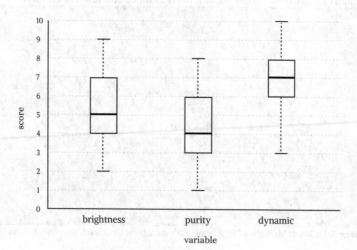

Figure 1. Questionnaire Results

The questionnaire results indicate that children are more sensitive to high-brightness colors, and most parents would choose to display 4-7 colors with high purity and brightness in a single interface for their children. Special effects feedback can attract children's immersive experiences. Their daily activities include drawing, playing musical instruments, basic programming, and dancing. The toys at home typically have both entertainment and educational aspects, such as early learning robots, electronic drawing boards, LEGO toys, and electronic pets. 83.24% of children use physical paper and pens as their drawing tools, while 16.76% of children use electronic devices such as tablets for drawing. Some children have also experienced virtual reality art creation systems in museums. In terms of interface, using graphical language instead of traditional text makes it easier for children to quickly understand functional attributes. Additionally, simplifying complex steps of an art experience can help children focus more on the entire process of art creation.

4.2. Experimental Test Results for Functional Icon Hierarchy and Distance in the Interaction Interface

The experimental conclusion reveals that during the testing of different interface designs for functional icon interaction hierarchy (Figure 2), 95% of the children completed the given selection process within the 20-60s time frame. However, within the same time frame, only 55% of the children completed the process in the dual-function option hierarchy design (Table 4). This indicates that the design with a single-function hierarchy results in shorter operation times for children. This experimental result highlights that simplifying unnecessary steps in interface design can lead to smoother interactions for children, and it also enhances the promptness of receiving feedback on functionality.

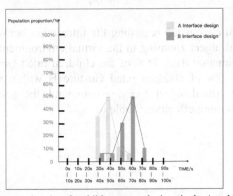

Figure 2. The reaction time for children to tap the icon in the A and B interface.

Table 4. Analysis Table for Two Different Functional Icon Hierarchy Levels, A and B

Type	A	B
20s-30s	0.0%	0.0%
20s-40s	35.0%	5.0%
20s-50s	85.0%	10.0%
20s-60s	95.0%	40.0%
20s-70s	100.0%	90.0%
20s-80s	100.0%	100.0%

In the test of different spacing designs between functional icons (Figure 3), for the design with icons spaced 1 pixel apart, 90% of the children completed the given selection process in the 10s—50s time range. In the same time range, 70% of the children completed the process in the design with icons spaced 2 pixels apart. This indicates that a tightly spaced design of icons with a distance of 1 pixel in the AR interface leads to shorter operational times for children, creating a smaller visual area and thus making it easier to locate the icons. (Table 5)

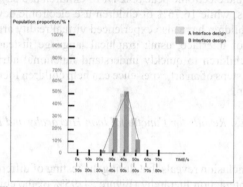

Figure 3. The reaction time for children to tap the icon in the A and B interface.

Table 5. Analysis Table for two different distance function icons (A and B)

Time/s \Type	A	B
10s-20s	0.0%	0.0%
10s-30s	0.0%	2.5%
10s-40s	20.0%	37.5%
10s-50s	70.0%	90.0%
10s-60s	100.0%	100.0%

The experimental conclusion regarding the interaction between different gestures and controlling virtual object zooming in the virtual environment (Figure 4), based on the analysis of experimental data, 75% of the children rated Gesture A between 7-10 points, whereas only 5% of children rated Gesture B within the same range. This indicates that for the virtual object zooming command, the gesture of single-handed opening and closing is more effective. (Table 6)

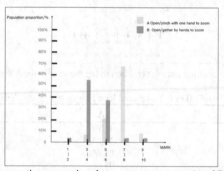

Figure 4. The proportion comparison between zoom gesture A and B in satisfaction

Table 6. Analysis of Questionnaire Ratings for A and B Gestures in Controlling Virtual Object Zooming

Mark / Type	A	B
1-2	0.0%	2.5%
3-4	5.0%	55.0%

5-6	20.0%	37.5%
7-8	67.5%	2.5%
9-10	7.5%	2.5%

In the testing of the interaction relationship for different gestures controlling the rotation of virtual objects in the interface (Figure 5), the analysis of experimental data indicates that 82.5% of children rated gesture A between 7 and 10 points, while only 10% of children rated gesture B in the same range. This clearly demonstrates that in the context of virtual object rotation commands, the interface's recognition of the left-right shaking gesture with the palm has a higher error tolerance and results in greater satisfaction among children (Table 7).

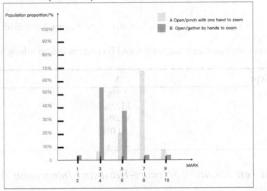

Figure 5. The proportion comparison between rotate gesture A and B in satisfaction

Table 7. Analysis of Questionnaire Ratings for A and B Gestures in Controlling Virtual Object Rotation

Mark \Type	A	B
1-2	0.0%	12.5%
3-4	0.0%	62.5%
5-6	17.5%	15.0%
7-8	75.0%	5.0%
9-10	7.5%	5.0%

In the testing of the interaction relationship for different gestures controlling the movement of virtual objects in the spatial environment (Figure 6), the analysis of experimental data indicates that 52.5% of children rated gesture A between 7 and 10 points, while 72.5% of children rated gesture B in the same range. This clearly shows that in the context of controlling virtual object movement commands, the use of the gesture B, involving palm pushing or pulling, leads to a more natural and convenient experience, resulting in higher satisfaction among children. (Table 8)

Therefore, in the AR environment, it is evident that children prefer using natural and instinctive gestures from daily life during the interaction process of controlling virtual object zooming, rotation, and movement. These gestures have a higher tolerance for errors, leading to better feedback and easier control in achieving the desired effects.

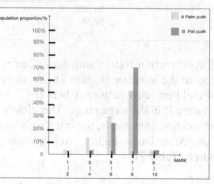

Figure 6. The proportion comparison between move gesture A and B in satisfaction

Table 8. The Analysis of Questionnaire Ratings for A and B Gestures in Controlling Virtual Object Movement

Mark / Type	A	B
1-2	2.5%	0.0%
3-4	15.0%	2.5%
5-6	30.0%	25.0%
7-8	50.0%	70.0%
9-10	2.5%	2.5%

4.3. Experimental Test Results of Software-Hardware Integration Triggered the Interface Functions

The experimental conclusions indicate that in testing the interactive relationship of triggering different functions through software-hardware integration (Figure 7), the analysis of experimental data reveals that children who gave a score between 7-10 for triggering functions through recognizing the physical model's form and hand grip posture accounted for 85%. Additionally, children who scored between 7-10 for triggering interface functions through physically tapping on icons in the interface accounted for 75%. Comparatively, Method A has a slight advantage. Therefore, when designing software-hardware interactive links, retaining both methods to trigger different creative function commands is advisable, allowing children to choose based on their personal preferences. (Table 9)

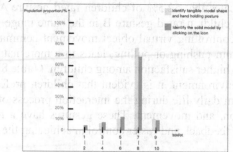

Figure 7. The proportion comparison between Trigger function mode A and B in satisfaction

Table 9. Questionnaire Rating Data Analysis for Triggering Different Functions through Two Different Methods (A and B)

Mark / Type	A	B
1-2	0.0%	5.0%

3-4	5.0%	7.5%
5-6	10.0%	12.5%
7-8	75.0%	67.5%
9-10	10.0%	7.5%

5. Design Practice

The practical results of this project's design have been implemented in the design that integrates AR visual interfaces with hardware (Image 8). The combined software and hardware product design has pioneered an innovative model for digital art education. Integrating art education with Augmented Reality (AR), this approach enables children to learn the creative processes of various traditional art disciplines through multimodal interactions.

In the field of digital art education, we have combined Augmented Reality (AR) technology to design three physical smart products with the children agency. Firstly, the AR system recognizes the distinct forms of the physical hardware and the way they are held. Subsequently, the digital interface automatically transitions between shape sculpting, painting coloring, and magical material effects functionalities. The innovative integration of the verified visual interface design, hardware tool design, and the interconnected design of gestures and virtual objects enhances the potential of digital art education to encompass a wide range of artistic disciplines in the future. This interactive design is adaptable to various forms of artistic learning. The entry point of toy design is to utilize associative experiences, which involve transitioning from one sensory experience to another, creating a fusion of sensory stimulation and psychological mapping. This approach allows users to gain richer experiences and achieve educational enlightenment goals [12].

Indeed, in the design practice, the incorporation of visual content (including 4-7 colors, animations, etc.) along with engaging and enjoyable behavior and process design aims to ignite children's artistic interests and creativity. This approach immerses children in the AR space, allowing them to perceive and shape their everyday reality anew, providing a sense of hope and anticipation through the product. The goal is to design and empower artistic education to seamlessly integrate into the artistic lives of the new generation.

Image 8. AR Visual Image of Integrated Software-Hardware Triggering Function

6. Conclusion

In summary, this study proposes a method that integrates AR with tangible interaction, with a focus on children as the research subjects, aiming to reshape contemporary art creation methods for children. The research employs a combination of questionnaire surveys and AB comparative experimental tests, involving 40 children aged 7 to 12 years. These tests cover various aspects including visual color, animation effects, software interaction hierarchy, spatial gesture interaction, and operational methods for triggering functionalities.

The results confirm the following findings: (1) Displaying 4-7 colors with high purity and brightness, along with special effects feedback, can engage children in an immersive experience within a single interface. (2) A single-level interactive interface is better suited for children to navigate and execute commands. Replacing traditional text with graphical language makes it easier for children to quickly understand functional attributes, and the spacing between icons within the interface affects children's operational efficiency, with relatively clustered areas being more suitable for children to locate items efficiently. (3) Regarding spatial gesture interactions, employing hand gestures that mimic familiar physical actions from everyday life (such as grabbing to move, zooming, rotating, etc.) makes it easier for children to naturally interact and successfully engage in artistic creations. (4) Within the process steps of combining software and hardware operations, triggering software interface commands through the recognition of the physical product's form and the hand's grip style offers increased simplicity and usability. This study contributes to the artistic creation field within future virtual reality environments like AR, by providing a more intricate approach to behavior design, centered around children's capabilities. It offers refined methods for integrated hardware and software interaction, immersive creative experiences, and design decisions for interactive interfaces.

This article aims to explore innovative interactive design for children's art education based on augmented reality technology. The goal is to enhance children's awareness and understanding of various art forms, while nurturing their artistic expression and creativity. However, this study has certain limitations, such as its focus on individual functional requirements in the conducted experimental tests, without conducting a comprehensive examination of the entire interaction process. Further investigation could delve into this aspect in future research. Nevertheless, the conclusions drawn from this study are valuable for enhancing children's comfort and proficiency in operating within the AR virtual reality environment, thereby fostering their artistic expression and creativity. This research provides new perspectives and approaches for the future development of children's art education, contributing positively to their holistic growth and the preservation of traditional culture.

Acknowledgements

This work was supported by Design Discipline Young Design Talent Cultivation Project of China Academy of Art.
This work was supported by Design-AI lab of China Academy of Art (CAADAI2022A001).

References

[1] Domínguez-Lloria, S., Martínez López de Castro, R., Fernández-Aguayo, S., Pino-Juste, M. Content Analysis of Mobile Device Applications for Artistic Creation for Children between 4 and 12 Years of Age. Appl. Sci. **11** (2021), 11327.
[2] Matt Fussell. The Stages of Artistic Development. The Virtual Instructor, 2022.
[3] Georgina Barton. Arts-based educational research in the early years. International Research in Early Childhood Education. **6** (2015), 62.
[4] Ferrés, J., Piscitelli, A. La competencia mediática: Propuesta articulada de dimensiones e indicadores. Comunicar **19** (2012), 75–82.
[5] Tracy Kwei-Liang Ho, Huann-Shyang Lin,A web-based painting tool for enhancing student attitudes toward learning art creation, Computers & Education **89** (2015), 32-41.
[6] Ramírez, H.; Ramírez, M.; Manrique, E.; Salgado, M. Digital education using apps for today's children. In Proceedings of the 13th Iberian Conference on Information Systems and Technologies (CISTI), Caceres, Spain, 13–16 June (2018), 1–6.
[7] D. Arrowood, T. Overall. Using technology to motivate children to write changing attitudes in children and preservice teachers R. Ferdig, et al. (Eds.), Proceedings of society for information technology & teacher education international conference (2004), pp. 4985-4987
[8] Van Den Hoven E, Frens J, Aliakseyeu D, et al. Design research & tangible interaction. In Proceedings of the 1st international conference on Tangible and embedded interaction. 2007: 109-115.
[9] A.D. Serio, M.B. Ibanez, C.D. Kloos. Impact of an augmented reality system on students' motivation for a visual art course Computers & Education **68** (2013), 586-596
[10] Hornecker E, Buur J. Getting a grip on tangible interaction: a framework on physical space and social interaction. In Proceedings of the SIGCHI conference on Human Factors in computing systems. 2006: 437-446.
[11] Young S., Eadie T., Suda L., Church A. LEARN: essential elements of museum education programs for young children. Curator: The Museum Journal **65** (2022):209–223.
[12] Bai Q. Research on the Design of Interactive Children's Vocal Enlightenment Toys Based on Audiovisual Association Experience. Occup Ther Int. 2022, 7686818.

Design Studies and Intelligence Engineering
L.C. Jain et al. (Eds.)
© *2024 The Authors.*
This article is published online with Open Access by IOS Press and distributed under the terms
of the Creative Commons Attribution Non-Commercial License 4.0 (CC BY-NC 4.0).
doi:10.3233/FAIA231435

Digital Baseball Sport Design Based on DMC Gamification Theory

Jiqing FU[a], Lingyan ZHANG [b,c,1], Xinyi ZHENG[b], Fang'er YANG[a] and Yongqi LIN[a]
[a] *School of Industrial Design, China Academy of Art, Hangzhou, China, 310001*
[b] *Design Innovation Center, China Academy of Art, Hangzhou, China, 310001*
[c] *Design-AI lab, China Academy of Art, Hangzhou, China, 310001*

Abstract. With the rapid advancement of digital technology, digitized sports have become a significant trend in the global sports industry. This study aims to explore how to combine gamification theory to achieve the digital transformation of baseball sports, enhancing the accessibility and popularity of baseball activities. This research delves into gamified digital baseball design by analyzing the characteristics and current status of baseball sports, along with the successful application of DMC gamification theory in the sports domain. It outlines user interviews and questionnaire surveys, and based on the research findings, proposes strategies for integrating gamified elements, enhancing interactive experiences, and providing typically motivational elements. These strategies infuse the concept of gamification into digital baseball design. Finally, this study engages in practical design, merging DMC gamification theory with baseball sports, aiming to provide users with novel and enriched baseball experiences, driving the dissemination and development of baseball. This research offers new insights and practical references for the development of baseball sports and the application of gamification theory in the sports domain.

Keywords. Gamification Theory, DMC Model, Digital Sport, Innovation Design

1.Introduction

With the progress of society and the improvement of people's living standards, the concept of national health has gradually become a focal point of social attention. The continuous development and application of digital technology will bring about more opportunities and challenges across various industries. As an integral part of social activities, sports equally benefit from the advancements in digital technology. Currently, new forms of digital sports have emerged, such as VR spectatorship, online fitness, and smart sports venues, marking digitization as a primary trend in the development of sports industries worldwide.

Among numerous ball sports, digital baseball gaming, as a popular type of sports game, contributes to physical well-being. Its exercise value and enjoyable nature attract a considerable number of sports enthusiasts. Baseball requires specialized training facilities and professional equipment, but the proliferation of digital sports introduces baseball to a broader audience, overcoming spatial limitations. However, for ordinary players unfamiliar with baseball, which is a sport rich in strategy and competition, there

---

[1] Corresponding Author. Lingyan Zhang; China Academy of Art, Hangzhou, China, 310001; E-mail: zhanglingyan@caa.edu.cn

exists a notable learning curve. Novices find it challenging to attain a satisfying sports experience, leading many to abandon the sport in the early stages of engagement.

n recent years, gamification theory, as a design concept that emphasizes engaging participation and enhancing experiences, has gradually garnered widespread attention in the realm of sports. Within this context, the integration of gamification theory with specific sports disciplines has become a forward-thinking and innovative research direction, aiming to explore the role of digital design in increasing engagement and enhancing experiences. Merging digital baseball with gamification theory allows players to gain a deeper understanding of the rules, techniques, and strategies of baseball, elevating the awareness and comprehension of the sport. Moreover, the gamified approach enables players to delve further into experiencing and understanding baseball, fostering a passion for the sport and propelling its development. As an emerging genre of digital gaming, digital baseball gaming offers new opportunities and challenges to the digital gaming industry, driving its transformation toward inclusivity, diversification, and innovation. By leveraging gamification theory, this research envisions a prospective and innovative approach to enhancing sports engagement and experiences through digital design, demonstrating the potential for advancing both the sports and gaming sectors.

Therefore, the integration of digital design and gamification theory to infuse new vitality into baseball has become a topic of great interest. By incorporating gamified elements into baseball, it not only sparks athletes' enthusiasm and drive but also enhances the engagement and entertainment value for spectators. This contributes not only to propelling the development of baseball but also provides a robust practical example for the application of digital design in the sports domain.

In summary, this study aims to delve into the digitized design of baseball based on gamification theory. Drawing from successful instances of gamification theory in other domains and considering the characteristics and needs of baseball, the exploration involves optimizing various aspects of baseball through digitized design. Through in-depth research and empirical analysis, we aim to uncover the potential effects of digitized design in enhancing participation and allure within baseball. Ultimately, this endeavor aims to offer users a more enriched and satisfactory experience, providing novel insights and references for the future digital development of sports.

2.Literature Research

2.1. Theory of Gamification

Gamification theory is a design approach that combines game design principles with non-game contexts, aimed at igniting participants' interests, enhancing learning outcomes, and elevating user experiences. Gamification, by introducing game elements such as challenges, achievements, rewards, etc., encourages active user participation and provides real-time feedback, thereby stimulating motivation and engagement. Gamification has been successfully applied in various domains including education, health, marketing, and has achieved remarkable results. It is suitable for behavior change, guiding users to cultivate positive habits. Kevin Werbach proposed that in the early stages of gamification, internal gamification, external gamification, and behavior change gamification are particularly prominent. Applying gamification to the field of sports and fitness can increase user engagement and effectively alter their habitual behavior patterns.

The term "Gamification," coined by Nick Pelling in 2003, refers to incorporating game design elements and principles into non-game contexts to provide an enjoyable experience akin to that of gamers[1][2]. By 2010, Jane McGonigal's TED talk "Game can make a better world" brought global awareness to the profound impact gamification could have on the world[3]. It was at this point that "Gamification" began to be widely adopted as a specific design method. Consequently, the popularity of the term "Gamification" has increased each year. Various theoretical models are associated with gamification design, such as the DMC hierarchical model, Mechanics-Dynamics-Aesthetics model (MDA) for gamified development, and the Octalysis Behavior Analysis Framework[4].

Among them, the DMC (Dynamics, Mechanics, Components) model is one of the key concepts in gamification theory, proposed by Kevin Werbach in his book [1]. The DMC model divides into three levels: D (Dynamics), M (Mechanics), and C (Components), and conducts a detailed analysis of mechanics and components[5]. This model analyzes the structure and operation of games through these three core elements, providing designers with an in-depth understanding of the framework of game systems. Dynamics: Dynamics refer to various interactions and events in the game, as well as how these events occur and evolve in the game. It encompasses elements such as rules, behaviors, and interactions in the game. Dynamics create the fundamental operational mechanisms of the game and determine the actions and choices players can make in the game. Mechanics: Mechanics refer to the rules, systems, and interactions in the game, as well as the basic processes that drive the progression of the game and how these elements interact to lead to specific outcomes. Mechanics define how players interact with the game world, covering specific gameplay and operations. Components: Components are surface elements that can be directly perceived by users. Components are the concrete manifestations of dynamics and mechanics and are the most fundamental elements of gamification.

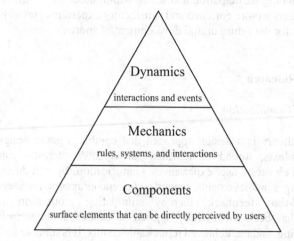

Figure 1. DMC theoretical model.

The core idea of the DMC model is that by gaining a deep understanding of the dynamics, mechanics, and goals of a game, designers can better create interesting and engaging gaming experiences. In gamification design, the DMC model is widely used to analyze systems and activities in non-gaming contexts, enabling the integration of gamified elements to enhance user engagement. In summary, the DMC model in gamification theory offers designers a systematic analytical approach to better comprehend and apply gamification principles, thereby optimizing experiences and engagement in non-gaming scenarios. In this study, we will explore how to apply the DMC model to the digitized design of baseball to enhance the experiences of both players and spectators.

2.2. Digital sports development status

The rapid development of digital technology has profoundly transformed the landscape of sports, bringing forth new experiences and opportunities for the masses. Particularly in the realm of baseball, the integration of digital technology is propelling the sport into a more modern and diverse phase. Virtual reality technology stands out as another remarkable domain within digital sports. In baseball, virtual reality technology can be employed to create highly realistic game experiences, making spectators feel as if they are on the field themselves. Furthermore, virtual reality can offer innovative training methods. For instance, athletes can engage in virtual confrontations with virtual pitchers to enhance their batting reaction time and decision-making within a virtual environment. Simultaneously, virtual reality provides coaches with better perspectives for analyzing and refining athletes' techniques. Multimodal interaction technology emerges as a crucial innovation within the digital sports domain. In baseball, multimodal interaction technology finds application in various facets. During training, athletes can don virtual reality headsets to immerse themselves in a lifelike batting experience, while simultaneously hearing authentic stadium sounds, thus better simulating actual game conditions. Additionally, coaches can utilize multimodal interaction technology to analyze athletes' movements and offer real-time feedback, aiding them in continual technique optimization. Digital sports also emphasize the importance of real-time data analysis and feedback.

In conclusion, the integration of multimodal interaction technology and virtual reality technology, alongside the introduction of real-time data analysis and feedback, continually enriches and expands the potential of baseball. These innovations not only enhance the quality of games and training but also provides a new path for the future development of baseball.

2.3. Gamification theory and digital sports

Gamification is considered both a collection of game elements and a process of creating gaming experiences to increase motivation for sustaining desired behaviors[6]. Numerous studies have integrated gamification theory with digital sports, and a wealth of literature attests to the positive impact of the DMC model on promoting exercise behaviors[7]. Áron Tóth, in his research, examines the effects of gamification in sports applications on individuals' exercise habits and performance. This offers a possibility for a broader user base to utilize motion tracking applications within gamified systems to monitor and analyze their performance, thereby maintaining users' engagement[8].

In virtual environments, athletes can safely experience their surroundings and interact with various objects even under controlled critical conditions[9]. Paula Bitrián's research findings indicate that interactions with achievement-related game elements within sports applications satisfy the needs for competence, autonomy, and relatedness[10].

In conclusion, gamification design offers a robust framework for digital sports, aiding designers in thorough analysis of various elements within sports. By employing gamification design models, the design and optimization of digital sports can be enhanced, providing athletes and players with richer and more immersive experiences.

3.Case Studies

This paper begins by analyzing existing cases of sports-related mobile applications, summarizing their commonalities and characteristics, and extracting design insights that can be applied. It then analyzes gamification elements that can be transferred to the digital baseball app. The digital sports app market offers a diverse array of choices, catering to both sports enthusiasts and casual players, ensuring that everyone can find an app suitable for their preferences. Currently, sports-themed games in the market have garnered immense popularity among the general public, prompting us to select five representative apps for analysis. The results are shown in Table 1.

Table 1. Sports APP case study

Application	Image	Introduction	Type	Advantages	Features
FIFA Mobile Soccer		Players can create and manage their own football clubs and participate in competitions and tournaments	Football simulation game	Officially authorized players, teams and modes of play; Diverse competitions and events; Social interaction features.	Live events, build and upgrade teams, online battle mode
NBA Live Mobile Basketball		Allows players to form their own NBA teams and participate in competitions	Basketball simulation game	Official NBA players and teams; Multiple game modes; Team management and training.	Live matchmaking, playoffs, league formation.
PES Club Manager		Players can play as the manager of a football club, managing the team and the game.	Football manager simulation game	In-depth manager simulation experience; Official players and teams; Strategic and tactical planning.	Player training, transfer market, tactical setup.

| Top Eleven | | Players can create their own football clubs, participate in competitions and compete | Football manager simulation game | A variety of tactical and strategic options; Multiplayer online battle; Social interaction function. | Real-time games, club management, training of players. |
| WGT Golf | | Various golf courses and game modes available. | Golf simulation game | Realistic golf experience; A variety of courses and game types; Social play. | Multiplayer online matches, real court simulations, challenges. |

By comparing these digital sports apps, several conclusions and perspectives can be drawn regarding the benefits of gamified sports apps in promoting user engagement and acceptance of a particular sport. For instance, (1) Enhancing Motivation and Engagement: Gamification elements such as achievements, leaderboards, and rewards can stimulate users' interest and motivation, making them more willing to participate in sports and use the app. (2) Creating Engaging Experiences: Gamified sports apps often introduce enjoyable challenges, interactions, and activities, offering users a more entertaining experience and increasing their desire to use the app. (3) Fostering Social Interaction: Many gamified sports apps allow users to compete, collaborate, and share achievements with others, creating a social interactive environment that encourages communal participation in sports. (4) Personalized Training Plans: Some apps can provide personalized training plans based on users' physical condition, goals, and interests, enabling users to tailor their exercise routines more effectively. (5) Overcoming Monotony: Sports can become mundane and repetitive, leading to loss of interest; however, gamified sports apps introduce new challenges and tasks to help users maintain their interest and motivation.

In this sense, with the growth of mobile gaming applications, gamified sports apps like Nike+, Strava, Fitbit, and Endomondo have significantly proliferated. Applying gamification principles, these apps incorporate various gaming elements such as challenges, medals, rankings, competitions, avatars, etc., to encourage and maintain habits related to physical exercise. Through this approach, they influence individuals to perceive exercise as a fun, enjoyable, and engaging activity, thereby boosting their motivation.

In conclusion, gamified sports apps, through a variety of engaging elements and features, can ignite users' interest, motivation, and engagement, leading them to participate more actively in a sport and continue using the app. This gamified approach can make exercise more enjoyable, challenging, and to some extent, enhance users' receptiveness to sports.

4.Methodology

Surveying and researching the target users is an indispensable part, and the selection of research methods in this paper is based on the user characteristics of sports apps. We determined the use of both questionnaire surveys and user interviews to comprehend user types and requirements. Table 2 outlines the research methods and survey objectives for different stages of the study. With the DMC model as the theoretical foundation, we conducted quantitative and qualitative analyses to uncover users' latent needs.

4.1. Procedure

This study employs a method based on the DMC model, combining in-depth interviews and questionnaire surveys. The process is shown in Table 2. Initially, through in-depth interviews, user pain points are preliminarily explored to understand their perspectives on existing digital sports games. This serves as a foundation for further defining the design of gamified digital baseball. Subsequently, an online questionnaire is utilized to broaden the research scope, targeting individuals with an interest in sports, in order to further uncover users' underlying needs.

Table 2. Research procedure.

Stage	Method	Users	Aim
step 1	in-depth interview	People with experience in using sports apps	Excavate users' pain points, understand users' experience in using sports apps on the existing market, and initially understand the common problems and functional requirements of users when using them
step 2	questionnaire survey	People who like sports	To further understand the psychological expectations of users and tap the potential needs of users

4.2. In-depth interview outline design

In this study, in-depth interviews and questionnaire surveys played a pivotal role in gaining a comprehensive understanding of individuals' attitudes, perspectives, and expectations toward gamified digital baseball design. In-depth interviews allowed for one-on-one in-depth discussions with respondents, enabling a more comprehensive grasp of their viewpoints, experiences, opinions, and actual experiences with gamified digital sports apps. This approach yielded rich detailed information, enabling insight into diverse attitudes and needs among different demographic groups, thereby incorporating greater diversity into the research. The in-depth interview protocol was designed to delve deeper into respondents' perspectives and opinions. Additional relevant questions were introduced based on respondents' answers to gather more detailed and comprehensive information. The interview process remained open-ended, allowing respondents to express their viewpoints while flexibly adapting the protocol to suit the actual interview circumstances.

User Interviews The user interview outline consists of two parts. The first part addresses questions related to the experience with gamified digital sports apps. The questions include: (1) Have you ever tried using a digital sports gaming mobile application? If yes, please share your experience of using it. (2) Do you believe that digital sports gaming apps can enhance your interest and engagement in the respective sport? Why? (3) What role do digital sports gaming apps play in enhancing your experience with the sport? (4) From your perspective, can digital sports gaming apps inject more fun and innovation into sports activities? (5) What are the strengths and weaknesses of the specific digital sports gaming app you have used?

User Interviews - Part 2 The second part pertains to attitudes towards gamified digital baseball design, with questions including: (1) What are your views on integrating gamified elements into digital baseball design? (2) Which gamified elements do you find most appealing and likely to keep you engaged and involved? (3) What distinctive features should be present in gamified digital baseball design? (4) In your opinion, which gamified features could most effectively encourage users to embrace and participate in baseball activities? (5) What expectations do you have for the future design of gamified digital baseball applications?

For this in-depth interview, a total of 6 participants were interviewed, including 4 males and 2 females. Each participant has experience using sports gaming apps and shared their insights on gamified digital baseball applications, discussing their usage experiences and impressions.

4.3. Questionnaire survey outline design

A questionnaire survey can gather a large number of responses, thereby providing a broader data foundation and reflecting the opinions of a larger population. Through a questionnaire survey, common trends and shared perspectives can be identified, revealing the general views of the public on gamified digital baseball design. Additionally, the results of the questionnaire survey can be used to validate or support viewpoints obtained from in-depth interviews. Therefore, following the in-depth interviews, a questionnaire survey was conducted to further investigate. By combining in-depth interviews and questionnaire surveys, subjective and objective data are comprehensively collected, leading to a more comprehensive understanding of participants' attitudes, opinions, and expectations. This approach provides stronger support for the conclusions drawn from the research. The questionnaire outline is presented in Table 3.

Table 3. Questionnaire outline.

variate	description	source
Dynamics	Do you think gamified digital baseball design can make the game of baseball more fun and engaging?	
	Are you willing to use gamified digital baseball design to enhance your baseball experience?	Hassan et al. [11]
	Do you think that incorporating gamification into digital baseball design will increase user engagement?	
Mechanics	Do you think adding more interaction to your game would improve the experience	
	Which of the following mechanisms do you find more appealing to you?	Chen[12]
	What features do you think the gamified digital baseball design should focus on?	

Components	Which of the following gamification elements do you think makes you more eager to explore?	Werbach & Hunter [13]

5.Result

5.1. Interview content sorting and summary

Excerpts from interview records are shown in Table 4. Summarizing the interview contents of the 6 participants reveals that they generally believe that integrating gamified elements into digital baseball design can enhance user engagement and interest. The majority of interviewees agreed that gamified digital baseball design can make the sport more enjoyable and appealing. Interviewees emphasized the positive impact of gamified elements on their baseball experience, citing increased interactivity and challenges. They highlighted the advantages of gamified digital baseball design, such as heightened interest, motivation, and real-time feedback. Some interviewees also pointed out certain drawbacks, including in-app purchases and potential excessive focus on virtual achievements. Regarding design features, interviewees suggested various gamification elements such as achievement systems, virtual reality experiences, and personalized training to enhance user experience and engagement.

Table 4. interview record.

Interviewee	Interview excerpts	Demand
A	I think the gamification element can make people more motivated to participate, because with the sense of achievement and the element of competition, they will be more willing to invest time and energy to play.	Dynamics
B	I used to play an app that had an achievement system where every time you play, you get some rewards, which makes me feel very accomplished, and it's fun to see where you are on the leaderboard and compete with your friends.	Dynamics Mechanics
C	Personally, I think it's a good idea, especially for people who don't know much about baseball. The gamification element can make the game more fun, not just sport, but also entertaining.	Components
D	I think gamified digital baseball design can encourage more people to try baseball, especially young people. Making baseball more accessible to them through gamification, and gradually developing interest, is also a good way to promote.	Dynamics
E	The gamification element can make training that would normally be boring fun, and I find myself more motivated to complete the training program. In addition, real-time feedback allows me to keep abreast of my progress and where I need to improve.	Dynamics
D	I think some apps will have some content that requires a lockout, which may deter some users. In addition, sometimes too much focus on virtual achievements can make people overlook the fun of the sport itself.	Mechanics

5.2. Analysis of questionnaire survey results

The survey was conducted using random sampling and distributed through online channels. A population screening question was added to the survey's homepage: "Do you have an interest in sports?" If a user answered negatively, they were directed to the end page, thereby filtering out the target users. Over the course of one week, a total of 83 responses were collected; after eliminating invalid responses, 57 valid responses remained. Among these, 61.3% were male and 38.7% were female. This survey was based on the DMC model and investigated from three dimensions: dynamics, mechanics, and components.

The results indicate that in terms of dynamics, gamified digital baseball design is more appealing to users (mean score=3.73). Integrating gamified elements into digital baseball design enhances user engagement (mean score=3.13). The majority of users expressed their willingness to try gamified digital baseball design to enhance their baseball experience (mean score=3.28).

From the mechanics perspective, increasing interaction within the game enhances the gaming experience (mean score=2.96). 72% of the respondents find the reward mechanism most appealing, followed by victory feedback, level progression, and competition mechanism. Moreover, more users believe that gamified digital baseball design should focus on increasing the enjoyment of baseball matches and providing personalized sports experiences.

At the component level, incorporating gamified elements increases players' desire for exploration. Here is the ranked selection of elements: achievement systems and rewards, virtual reality/augmented reality experiences, real-time leaderboards and competition, unlocking new stadiums and game modes, challenge tasks and special events, social sharing and interaction, personalized training, multiplayer online battle mode.

5.3. Game elements refining and design model building

Based on the aforementioned analysis, we summarize and distill the digital baseball design principles based on the DMC model, as depicted in Figure 2. First, at the motivation level, the core requirement lies in the integration of gamified elements. In this phase, various game modes and high-quality visual effects should be established to attract user participation and continued use. Some users mentioned during interviews that they would like to see the incorporation of virtual reality or augmented reality technology. Furthermore, based on the survey results, a majority of users also selected this option. Thus, in the design of digital baseball, we can divide it into virtual and physical components. The game interface can be set up in a virtual presentation, while physical components such as bats, baseball gloves, etc., can be integrated with interesting design methods to incorporate more gamified elements, driving user engagement.

Next, at the mechanics level, enhancing interactive experiences for users during usage is crucial. Establishing reward mechanisms, victory mechanisms, level progression mechanisms, competition mechanisms, etc., helps create a positive feedback system for users. Corresponding to specific processes, challenges, opportunities, competitions, collaborations, resource acquisition, rewards, transactions, turns, victory states, and other processes can be established.

Finally, at the component level, optimization of gamified elements is necessary. Achievement systems and rewards garner the most user attention. Therefore, throughout the game, dynamic feedback touchpoints should be set up to provide users with positive feedback in the form of dynamic elements such as achievements, points, badges, and leaderboards.

Figure 2. Digital baseball design principles based on DMC model.

6.Digital baseball game design based on DMC theory

Based on the design principles outlined above, this study embarked on the practical design of digital baseball. The design aims to offer users a novel and enriched baseball experience, thereby fostering the popularity and promotion of baseball sports. The design involves streamlining rules and operations while prioritizing user experience and entertainment value. This approach is intended to attract a wider audience to engage in baseball activities and to provide both baseball enthusiasts and the general public with a more engaging virtual experience platform.

6.1. Game flow design

The initial concept of the solution was to utilize Augmented Reality (AR) technology to present this design proposal. Our idea was to center the design around hitting the ball, focusing users' attention on the hitting action itself. By simplifying rules and operations, we aimed to allow users to quickly get into the game and experience the thrill of hitting. Incorporating the concept of "everything can be hit," users could interact with everyday objects, creating more vivid and engaging situational experiences. Through AR technology, real-life spherical objects could be transformed into virtual baseballs, enabling users to interact with the virtual world within their actual surroundings, thus presenting unforeseen impacts on the real world through virtual effects. Simultaneously, the design incorporated gamified scenes and visual presentations to provide users with an immersive experience. By combining visual and sound effects technology, we aimed to further enhance users' sense of engagement and the experience of hitting the baseball. The application of haptic feedback technology allowed users to more realistically sense the force and impact of hitting the ball, enhancing their perception of the moment of impact. Refer to Figures 3 and 4 for visuals.

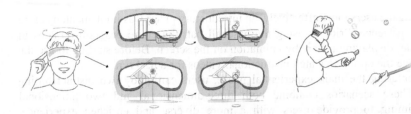

Figure 3. Idea of combining augmented reality.

Figure 4. Concept of everything can be hit.

Finally, considering that the original intention of the design was to enhance the accessibility of baseball, and the issue of high equipment costs and barriers to entry remained with AR glasses and digital baseball bats, we decided to eliminate the use of AR glasses. Instead, we opted for a digital screen to serve as the medium for the digital baseball experience, with third-party hardware providers fulfilling the screen's hardware requirements. This change ensured the realism of hitting while aligning with the goal of popularizing baseball, and it freed players from the constraints of AR glasses when experiencing digital baseball. Simultaneously, to maintain the concept of "everything can be hit" and to infuse a sense of daily life into "baseball," we ultimately settled on a variety of selectable game scenarios. Additionally, for a sports game with broad accessibility, the successful hitting detection range should be expanded. This approach is depicted in Figure 5.

Figure 5. Game start scene.

6.2. Virtual interaction design

In order to engage users more effectively, an introductory phase was implemented before the actual experience. Prior to using the baseball bat, the entire program remains in standby mode, displaying a standby animation on the screen. Before starting to use the bat, users have the option to watch instructional videos for a trial run.

Upon entering the main experiential phase, users can enjoy two distinct hitting scenarios. These scenarios combine both three-dimensional and two-dimensional elements, aiming to provide users with a more diverse and enriched experience. Additionally, to infuse vibrancy, interest, and immersion into this phase, we deliberately designed a cute yet slightly mischievous snow monster character to guide users through the experience. This character possesses its unique appearance and abilities, such as shooting fireballs, teleporting, and creating duplicates. Players engage with the snow monster by hitting baseballs to combat it. This interaction allows users to feel a more immersive experience during the hitting process. See Figures 6 for reference.

Figure 6. Game interactive interface.

6.3. Hardware interaction design

To ensure the sensory effects of the experience, we designed a baseball bat that utilizes smartphone gyroscope technology. By installing a mobile app on the user's phone and obtaining data permissions, the app gains access to the gyroscope information and vibration capabilities of the smartphone. The position information from the gyroscope determines the virtual baseball's hit range. When a successful hit is made, the smartphone provides vibration feedback to the user, completing the interactive experience. Beyond the fundamental functions of the digital bat, the content displayed on the foldable screen can provide users with various sensory experiences, including sound, light, and vibration. By altering materials and structure and enhancing the vibrational and tactile effects, users can achieve a more realistic and immersive sensation. During the actual experience, one phone needs to be affixed as the bat, with a replaceable themed top, catering to various players' individual preferences and distinguishing the digital bat from traditional ones. Refer to Figure 7 for illustration.

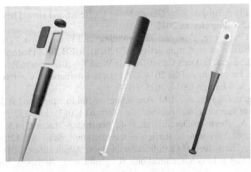

Figure 7. Physical baseball bat design.

7. Conclusion and prospect

This study is based on the discussion of gamified digital baseball design, aiming to provide a more enriched and immersive experience to promote the popularity and development of baseball. The research findings indicate that integrating gamification principles with baseball sports enhances the playability and entertainment value of baseball games. By carefully balancing aspects such as gameplay mechanics, realism, and entertainment, diverse game modes, and personalized gaming experiences, more players can enjoy the fun of digital baseball gaming. In future research, further exploration can be conducted on how gamification can facilitate baseball education and training. By designing engaging and interactive baseball learning games, players' understanding of baseball rules, skills, and strategies can be deepened. Designing well-structured reward mechanisms, social features, competitions, and viewing modes can enhance participation and popularization of baseball sports. Additionally, future research could consider utilizing technologies like virtual reality (VR) or augmented reality (AR) to further enhance the digital baseball gaming experience. These technologies can provide users with a more realistic and immersive feeling, intensifying their sense of participation and immersion in baseball sports.

In summary, a user-friendly approach to digital baseball game experience design requires a balanced consideration of gameplay mechanics, realism, and entertainment, along with diverse game modes and personalized gaming experiences. This approach aims to enhance the playability and entertainment value of the game, allowing a larger number of players to enjoy the pleasures of digital baseball gaming. Future research could further explore applications in baseball education and training, as well as the potential for enhancing the gaming experience using emerging technologies.

References

[1] WERBACH K, HUNTER D. Gamification Thinking: The New Power to Change the Future of Business[M]. ZHOU Kui, WANG Xiao-dan, Translated. Hangzhou: Zhejiang People's Publishing House, 2014.
[2] Hamari, J.; Koivisto, J.; Sarsa, H. Does Gamifification Work? —A Literature Review of Empirical Studies on Gamifification. In Proceedings of the 2014 47th Hawaii International Conference on System Sciences, Waikoloa, HI, USA, 6–9 January 2014, 3025–3034.

[3]   Jane McGonigal. Reality is Broken:Why Games Make Us Better and How They Can Change the World. Zhejiang People's Publishing House, 2012.

[4]   Yang, Pianpian; Xu, Ting; Feng, Yuanyue; Zhao, Yating; and Wang, Xijia, "The impact of gamification elements on the evaluation of marketing activities" (2018). ICEB 2018 Proceedings (Guilin, China). 35.

[5]   Hamari, J.; Koivisto, J.; Sarsa, H. Does Gamifification Work? —A Literature Review of Empirical Studies on Gamifification. In Proceedings of the 2014 47th Hawaii International Conference on System Sciences, Waikoloa, HI, USA, 6–9 January 2014, 3025–3034.

[6]   Abramovich, S.; Schunn, C.; Higashi, R.M. Are badges useful in education? It depends upon the type of badge and expertise of learner. *Educ. Technol. Res. Dev.* **61** (2013), 217–232

[7]   González-Fernández, A.; Revuelta-Domínguez, F.-I.; Fernández-Sánchez, M.R. Models of Instructional Design in Gamification: A Systematic Review of the Literature. *Educ. Sci.* **12**(2022), 44.

[8]   Á. Tóth and E. Lógó, The Effect of Gamification in Sport Applications, 2018 9th IEEE International Conference on Cognitive Infocommunications (CogInfoCom), Budapest, Hungary, 2018, 000069-000074.

[9]   F. Rebelo, P. Noriega, E. Duarte, and M. Soares, Using virtual reality to assess user experience, *Hum. Factors*, 54(2012) 964–982.

[10] Paula Bitrián, Buil I, Sara Catalán.Gamification in sport apps: the determinants of users' motivation. *European Journal of Management and Business Economics*, 2020.

[11] Hassan, L., Dias, A. and Hamari, J. How motivational feedback increases user's benefits and continued use: a study on gamification, quantified-self and social networking, *International Journal of Information Management*, 46(2019)151-162.

[12] Chen, Y. and Pu, P. Healthy together: exploring social incentives for mobile fitness applications, in Proceedings of Chinese CHI'14, Toronto, (2014), 25-34.

[13] Werbach, K., D. Hunter, For the Win: How Game Thinking Can Revolutionize Your Business. Philadelphia, PA: Wharton Digital Press, 2012.

Design Studies and Intelligent Engineering
L.C. Jain et al. (Eds.)
© 2024 The Authors.
doi:10.3233/FAIA231436

Power System Uncertainty Modeling Based on Gaussian Process

Tianze ZHANG

School of Computer Science and Technology, Xinjiang University, Urumqi, China

Abstract: In order to solve the problem of low accuracy of parameter estimation in expectation maximization algorithm, a modeling method based on Gaussian component number reduction is proposed. Taking the nonparametric kernel density estimation results as the base Gaussian mixture model, the Gaussian mixture model with any number of Gaussian components can be established by reducing the number of Gaussian components by using the density-preserving hierarchical expectation maximization algorithm, which overcomes the problem that the expectation maximization algorithm has low parameter estimation accuracy when there are many Gaussian components. In order to reduce the burden of modeling calculation under large samples, a hierarchical modeling method based on time scale is proposed. In order to solve the problem of Gaussian component number combination explosion of independent random variables, a hierarchical modeling method of "combination-reduction" is proposed. The proposed method is tested by using measured multidimensional wind speed data and load data with complex distribution characteristics. The experimental results show that the Pearson and Spearman correlation coefficients of GMM constructed based on this method are very close to the sample data. The absolute value of Pearson correlation coefficient error is 0.03739, and the root mean square value of error is 0.02388. The absolute value of Spearman correlation coefficient error is 0.11693, and the root mean square error is 0.05797. Conclusion: The accuracy of the proposed method is significantly better than that of Gaussian mixture model and Copula function method based on expectation maximization algorithm.

Keywords: uncertainty analysis; Gaussian mixture model; Electric power system; Multidimensional random variables; Relevance; Wind power

1. Introduction

At present, the development of power system operation control and dispatching depends on "empirical analysis" and "off-line design". The basic idea is to perceive the system situation and analyze the situation, and the dispatcher gives the operation control strategy according to his own knowledge, experience, and off-line strategy. It takes minutes for normal dispatchers to complete the above processes, so traditional manual operation can only solve the problems of system operation and scheduling. For problems that are too late to perceive, analyze and make decisions, such as equipment or system failures, it is necessary to adopt preset protection settings and stable control strategies to solve them. In the traditional power system, this kind of preset protection control depends on experience and deterministic criteria for setting, and its applicable scenarios are limited. With a large number of wind power, photovoltaic and electric vehicles connected to the power grid, the reform of the power market continues to advance, and the influence of the external environment on the power grid increases, the modern power system has strong uncertainty and complexity, and the system has many operation scenarios and strong coupling of protection and control, which leads to a decrease in the matching degree between the setting scheme and the operation scenarios and a decrease in the adaptability of the traditional methods [1-3].

In order to solve the above problems, on the one hand, it is necessary to develop a more robust protection control system, on the other hand, it is even more necessary to quickly adjust the system operation mode, so that the system operation state can be maintained within the applicable range of protection and stable control, so as to realize the system security and stability in the whole time process. However, the ability of ordinary dispatching operators to process information and analyze problems is limited. With the increasing complexity of modern power system, it is more difficult to ensure the safe and economic operation of power system. Therefore, it is the right way to solve this problem by studying the methods of big data, domain knowledge and artificial intelligence (AI) and developing an industrial artificial intelligence system suitable for power system to help dispatchers make decisions more efficiently, quickly, conveniently and accurately.

2. Literature review

The uncertainty and weak controllability of the output of new energy sources such as wind power increase the risk of transmission congestion in the system. The occurrence of transmission congestion will not only affect the realization of unit power dispatching plan and the utilization rate of new energy, but also pose a serious threat to the adequacy and reliability of the system. At present, most congestion management methods for power systems with new energy sources are from the planning level, mainly by improving the topology of medium and long-term transmission networks, improving the weak links and transmission capacity limits of the system. From the short-term operation level, the research on congestion scheduling management methods can be mainly divided into two categories.

The related research thinks that the uncertainty of wind power can be dealt with by increasing the positive and negative rotating reserve capacity, and the reserve capacity demand of the system is set to 20% of the predicted wind power output [4]. In addition, considering the distribution characteristics of new energy forecasting error and reserve constraints, combined with the forced outage rate of the unit, the required rotating reserve capacity is accurately quantified [5]. Shen and J divide the system into regions according to the similarity of transmission congestion distribution factors, define "congestion regions" and ensure the adequacy of spare capacity in each region, so as to reduce the congestion risk of lines in real-time operation [6]. Based on the risk optimization theory, Fan Fan, M put forward Dynamic Reserve at Risk,DRaR) and conditional reserve at risk (DCRAR) as evaluation indexes of system operation adequacy, and quantified the reserve demand level in each period to make the optimal decision-making scheme [7]. Zhang and F describe the uncertainty of wind power through multiple scenarios, and construct a two-stage stochastic planning and dispatching model, thus realizing the overall simulation of unit output planning and real-time power adjustment [8]. Tong, Z, based on the computing framework of SP, established a cooperative optimal scheduling model of source and load with the objective function of minimizing the expected total cost of the system. Because the optimal solution is closely related to the specific scenes generated, it is usually necessary to simulate a large number of scenes to ensure the accuracy of the optimal solution [9]. Therefore, it is proposed to simplify the original scene by scene reduction technology, and replace the original sample set with this subset for calculation [10].

This paper analyzes the problem that the parameter estimation accuracy of multidimensional Gaussian mixture model, GMM) based on expectation-maximization (EM) algorithm is not high. A GMM modeling method based on nonparametric kernel density estimation and density-preserving hierarchical expectation maximization (KDE-DPHEM) is proposed. Based on the results of multidimensional kernel density estimation, KDE), GMM modeling is realized by reducing the number of Gaussian components, and the accuracy of GMM is significantly improved by increasing the number of Gaussian components, which overcomes the problem that EM algorithm is difficult to obtain high-precision GMM when there are many Gaussian components. On this basis, in order to reduce the computational burden of probabilistic modeling under large samples, a hierarchical modeling method based on time scale is proposed. In order to solve the problem of Gaussian component number combination explosion after multiple independent random variables are combined, a hierarchical modeling method of "combination-reduction" is proposed. Based on KDE-DPHEM algorithm, this paper systematically puts forward the modeling method of power system probability model based on multi-dimensional GMM, and comprehensively tests the proposed method by using the actually collected multi-dimensional wind speed and multi-dimensional load data. The results verify the effectiveness and advantages of the proposed method.

3. Research methods

3.1. GMM method based on KDE-DPHEM algorithm

Using KDE method to model probability density function does not need prior information of random variable distribution type, and it can be used for arbitrary d Dimensional random variable x, based on n The joint probability density function estimated by KDE method is shown in Formula (1) [11-13].

$$f(x) = \frac{1}{n}\sum_{i=1}^{n} K_{\mathrm{H}}(x - x_i) \tag{1}$$

Where: f(x) for x Joint probability density function of; x_i for x DediiSamples; n Is the number of samples; KHIs a kernel function.

when K_{H} When it is a Gaussian kernel function, KDE obtains a special GMM with the number of Gaussian components equal to the number of samples, and takes this model as the base GMM, as shown in Formula (2).

$$f^{(b)}(\mathbf{x}) = \sum_{i=1}^{n} \frac{1}{n} \mathbf{N}(\mathbf{x} \mid \mathbf{x}_i, \mathbf{H}_i) = \sum_{i=1}^{K_b} \omega_i^{(b)} \mathbf{N}\left(\mathbf{x} \mid \mu_i^{(b)}, \Sigma_i^{(b)}\right) \tag{2}$$

Where: $f^{(b)}(x)$ Based on GMMx Joint probability density function of; K_b Is the number of Gaussian components of the base GMM, which is equal ton; $\omega_i^{(b)}$ Weidii The weight of a Gaussian component is equal to1/n; $\mu_i^{(b)}$ Weidii The mean vector of Gaussian components is equal to the first.i Samplex$_i$; $\Sigma_i^{(b)}$ Weidii The covariance matrix of Gaussian components is equal to the bandwidth matrix.H$_i$.

When the samples are sufficient and the bandwidth is appropriate, the base GMM based on KDE method is the most accurate GMM, and this model is often used as a benchmark model to evaluate the accuracy of parameter estimation methods. The Gaussian component number of base GMM is extremely large, which is not practical in the subsequent probabilistic uncertainty analysis of power system. Further, the basis GMM of the formula (2) is reduced to the basis GMM of the formula (3) $K_r(K_r < K_b)$The simplified GMM of Gaussian components adopts DPHEM algorithm in the reduction process.

$$f^{(r)}(x) = \sum_{j=1}^{K_r} \omega_j^{(r)} \mathbf{N}\left(x \mid \boldsymbol{\mu}_j^{(r)}, \boldsymbol{\Sigma}_j^{(r)}\right) \tag{3}$$

DPHEM algorithm transforms the reduction of base GMM into the following optimization problem: satisfy the base model for probability distribution $f^{(b)}(x)$ Virtual sample set based onX, begf$^{(b)}$(x) Parameters to simplify the model.$f^{(b)}(x)$ The expected value of log-likelihood function of is the largest, as shown in Equation (4).

$$\arg_{\left(\omega_j^{(n)}, \mu_j^{(p)}, \Sigma_j^{(r)}\right)} \max \mathbb{E}_{X \sim f^{(b)}(x)}\left[\ln f^{(r)}(X)\right] \tag{4}$$

Where: $f^{(r)}(x)$ To simplify GMMx Joint probability density function of; $\omega_j^{(r)}$ Weidij The weight of Gaussian components; $\mu_j^{(r)}$ Weidij Mean vector of Gaussian components; $\Sigma_j^{(r)}$ Weidij Covariance matrix of Gaussian components; K_r In order to simplify the Gaussian component number of GMM; Virtual sample setXbym Virtual samples {X$_1$,X$_2$,...,X$_m$} Composition, in the actual solution process does not need to really generate the sample; $\mathbb{E}$For expectation.

Equation (4) is solved by variational EM algorithm. The iterative steps of DPHEM algorithm are basically the same as those of conventional EM algorithm, which are divided into E-step and M-step, as shown in equations (5)-(9).

E-step:

$$E_{i,j} = \ln\left[\mathbf{N}\left(\mu_i^{(b)} \mid \mu_j^{(r)}, \Sigma_j^{(r)}\right)\right] - \frac{1}{2}\operatorname{tr}\left[\left(\Sigma_j^{(r)}\right)^{-1}\Sigma_i^{(b)}\right] \tag{5}$$

$$z_{ij} = \frac{\omega_j^{(r)}\exp\left(mE_{i,j}\right)}{\sum_{l=1}^{K_r}\omega_j^{(r)}\exp\left(mE_{i,l}\right)} \tag{6}$$

M-step:

$$\omega_j^{(r)} = \sum_{i=1}^{K_b} z_{ij}\omega_i^{(b)} \tag{7}$$

$$\mu_j^{(r)} = \frac{1}{\omega_j^{(r)}} \sum_{i=1}^{K_b} z_y \omega_i^{(b)} \mu_i^{(b)} \tag{8}$$

$$\Sigma_j^{(s)} = \frac{1}{\omega_j^{(r)}} \sum_{i=1}^{K_b} z_{ij} \omega_i^{(b)} \left[\Sigma_i^{(b)} + \left(\mu_i^{(b)} - \mu_j^{(r)} \right) \left(\mu_i^{(b)} - \mu_j^{(r)} \right)^T \right] \tag{9}$$

Where: Z_{ij} Is a variational parameter; subscripti $\in[1,K_b]$; subscriptl、 $j \in[1,K_r]$; tr Is the trace of the matrix; The number of virtual samples m is generally 10 times.K_b; Other symbols have the same meanings as Formula (2)-(4).

Because the basis GMM in this paper is obtained by KDE method, large numbersm Will lead to the formula (6) exp (m$E_{i,j}$)The numerical value overflows, and there is a numerical problem of 0/0. Based on equations (5) and (6), this paper proposes an improved E-step, as shown in equations (10)-(12). Compared with the Log-Sum-Exp technique.ln(z_{ij}) , and then calculate exp [ln(z_{ij})]The algorithm in this paper has higher computational efficiency and better numerical stability [14-15].

$$A_{i,j} = \frac{1}{2} tr\left[\left(\Sigma_j^{(r)} \right)^{-1} \Sigma_i^{(b)} \right] + \frac{1}{2} \ln \left| \Sigma_j^{(r)} \right| +$$
$$\frac{1}{2} \left(\mu_i^{(b)} - \mu_j^{(r)} \right)^T \left(\Sigma_j^{(r)} \right)^{-1} \left(\mu_i^{(b)} - \mu_j^{(r)} \right) \tag{10}$$

$$l_{i,\min} = \arg \min_l \left(\Lambda_{i,l} \right), l = 1, 2, \cdots, K_r \tag{11}$$

$$z_{ij} = \frac{\omega_j^{(r)} \exp\left[m\left(\Lambda_{i,l_{\min}} - \Lambda_{i,j} \right) \right]}{\sum_{l=1}^{K_1} \omega_l^{(r)} \exp\left[m\left(\Lambda_{i,l_{\min}} - \Lambda_{i,l} \right) \right]} \tag{12}$$

KDE and DPHEM constitute a two-stage KDEDPHEM algorithm, which can realize the modeling of any Gaussian component GMM and overcome the bottleneck problem of parameter estimation of EM algorithm for more Gaussian components GMM.

3.2. Hierarchical modeling of time scale for large samples

The sample size of power data is increasing. In order to reduce the computational burden of modeling, a hierarchical modeling method based on GMM model characteristics and DPHEM algorithm is further proposed. Taking the two time scales of month and year as an example, the monthly scale probability model is first constructed, and each monthly scale sample is the conditional probability sample of the annual scale sample. Further, the 12-month scale model is accumulated into the annual scale model with the proportion of the number of samples in each month as the weight. Fig. 1 is a schematic diagram of the modeling flow of a two-layer structure. Suppose a sample X The sample size of is n, according to the monthly scale samples. X be split into M Block, each sample is recorded asX_{b1}、 X_{b2}、 … 、 X_{bM} , the number of samples per block is: n_1、 n_2、 … 、 n_M. GMM is established for each sample by KDE-DPHEM algorithm, and the number of Gaussian components of GMM for each sample is as follows:K_{b1}, K_{b2}, ... , K_{bM}, the first M The joint probability density function of the blocks is shown in Formula (13). According to the total probability formula, X The joint probability density function of is composed of X_{b1}, X_{b2}, ... , X_{bM} The joint probability density function and the corresponding sample number ratio are accumulated as weight coefficients, and the annual scale based GMM model is shown in Formula (14). Gauss component number of formula (14) $K = Kb_1 + Kb_2 + \cdots + K_{bM}$; such as K If it is too large, further reduction is carried out by using DPHEM algorithm, and the annual scale simplified GMM shown in equation (15) is obtained. Consider that more general case, the sample X Divided into multiple layers according to the time scale, we only need to model the bottom time scale directly, and then aggregate from the bottom time scale layer by layer until the top time scale. The time scale layering method not only reduces the computational burden of large sample modeling, but also obtains multi-time scale probability models, and the modeling process can be parallelized [16-19].

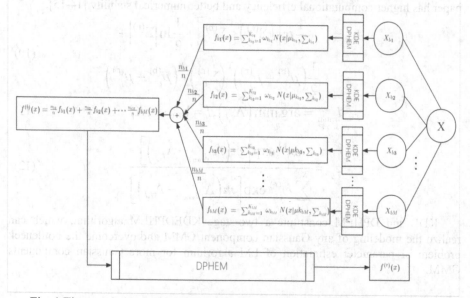

Fig. 1 Time-scale hierarchical modeling method for large samples

$$f_{bM}(\mathbf{x}) = \sum_{k_{bM}-1}^{K_{bM}} \omega_{k_{bM}} \mathsf{N}\left(\mathbf{x}\mid \mu_{k_{bM}}, \Sigma_{k_{bM}}\right) \tag{13}$$

$$f^{(b)}(\mathbf{x}) = \frac{n_1}{n} f_{b1}(\mathbf{x}) + \frac{n_2}{n} f_{b2}(\mathbf{x}) + \cdots \frac{n_M}{n} f_{bM}(\mathbf{x}) \tag{14}$$

$$f^{(r)}(\mathbf{x}) = \mathrm{DPHEM}\left[f^{(b)}(\mathbf{x})\right] \tag{15}$$

3.3. "Combination-Reduction" Hierarchical Modeling of Combination Explosion

In the actual power system, variables may be correlated or independent. Assume that the system has P Group multidimensional random variables $\xi^{(1)}$, $\xi^{(2)}$, ... , $\xi^{(P)}$ Groups are independent of each other, forming a multidimensional random variable. ξAs shown in formula (16) [20].

$$\xi = \left[\xi^{(1)\mathrm{T}}, \xi^{(2)\mathrm{T}}, \cdots, \xi^{(P)\mathrm{T}} \right]^{\mathrm{T}} \qquad (16)$$

Arbitrary firstp Group random variable $\xi^{(p)}$ The joint probability density function of is α_p The GMM model composed of 10 Gaussian components is shown in Formula (17).

$$f\left(\xi^{(p)}\right) = \sum_{k=1}^{\alpha_p} \omega_k^{(p)} \mathbf{N}\left(\xi^{(p)} \mid \boldsymbol{\mu}_k^{(p)}, \boldsymbol{\Sigma}_k^{(p)}\right) \qquad (17)$$

Where: $f\left(\xi^{(p)}\right)$ for $\xi^{(p)}$ Joint probability density function based on GMM; $\omega_k^{(p)}$ for $f\left(\xi^{(p)}\right)$ sequencek The weight of Gaussian components; $\boldsymbol{\mu}_k^{(p)}$ for $f\left(\xi^{(p)}\right)$ sequencek Mean vector of Gaussian components; $\boldsymbol{\Sigma}_k^{(p)}$ for $f\left(\xi^{(p)}\right)$ sequence k Covariance matrix of Gaussian components.

According to probability theory, ξThe joint probability density function of can be derived as shown in formula (18), and the number of Gaussian components is α. The corresponding Gaussian component parameters are shown in equations (19)-(21).

$$f(\xi) = \sum_{k=1}^{\alpha} \omega_k \, \mathbf{N}(\xi \mid \boldsymbol{\mu}_k, \boldsymbol{\Sigma}_k), \alpha = \prod_1^P \alpha_p \qquad (18)$$

$$\mu_{l_1 l_2 \cdots l_P} = \left[\mu_{l_1}^{(1)\mathrm{T}}, \mu_{l_2}^{(2)\mathrm{T}}, \cdots \mu_{l_P}^{(P)\mathrm{T}} \right]^{\mathrm{T}} \qquad (19)$$

$$\Sigma_{l_1 l_2 \cdots l_P} = \begin{bmatrix} \Sigma_{l_1}^{(1)} & 0 & 0 & 0 \\ 0 & \Sigma_{l_2}^{(2)} & 0 & 0 \\ 0 & 0 & \ddots & 0 \\ 0 & 0 & 0 & \Sigma_{l_P}^{(P)} \end{bmatrix} \qquad (20)$$

$$\omega_{l_1 l_2 \cdots l_P} = \omega_{l_1}^{(1)} \omega_{l_2}^{(2)} \cdots \omega_{l_P}^{(P)} \qquad (21)$$

Where: f(ξ) for ξ Joint probability density function based on GMM; ω_k for f(ξ) sequencek The weight of Gaussian components; $\boldsymbol{\mu}_k$ for f(ξ) sequence k Mean vector of Gaussian components; Σ_k for f(ξ) sequence k Covariance matrix of Gaussian components; lp $\in$[1, αp], p $\in$[1, P].

ξGaussian component number of α Will follow P Increasing the problem of combined explosion leads to a great amount of calculation in the analytical method of probability uncertainty analysis of power system. Taking the independent load of 10 nodes as an example, that is, the dimension of each group of random variables is 1, assuming that each load GMM model only uses 4 Gaussian components, the combination number of 410 will make the analytical method lose its efficiency advantage. In the scene with more complicated probability distribution and more nodes, the combined Gaussian components will be astronomical.

Aiming at the above-mentioned combined explosion problem, a hierarchical modeling method of "combination-reduction" is proposed based on GMM model characteristics and DPHEM algorithm. Only two groups of random variables are combined at a time: $f(\xi^{(1)})$ and $f(\xi^{(2)})$ Combine $f(\xi^{(1,2)})$; $f(\xi^{(3)})$ and $f(\xi^{(4)})$ Combine $f(\xi^{(3,4)})$; ...; $f(\xi^{(P-1)})$ and $f(\xi^{(P)})$ Combine $f(\xi^{(P-1,P)})$. After combination $f(\xi^{(1,2)})$, $f(\xi^{(3,4)})$, ...$f(\xi^{(P-1,P)})$ It is still a multi-dimensional GMM model and still independent of each other, and the above process can be further repeated. Before combining again, the last combination result is reduced by DPHEM algorithm, that is $f(\xi^{(1,2)})$, $f(\xi^{(3,4)})$, ...$f(\xi^{(P-1,P)})$ Reduce to $f^{(r)}(\xi^{(1,2)})$, $f^{(r)}(\xi^{(3,4)})$, ...$f^{(r)}(\xi^{(P-1,P)})$Then combine in pairs, so as to avoid combination explosion. For P groups of multidimensional random variables, the above method only needs P-1 "combination-reduction" operation, and the computational complexity is linear with P. The reduction step of the above method will produce a certain precision loss. The smaller the error between the joint cumulative probability of the obtained model and the original model, and the closer the Pearson correlation coefficient of any two groups of independent random variables is to zero, the smaller the precision loss is. The intermediate GMM in the reduction process and the Gaussian component number of the GMM finally obtained can be configured according to the accuracy requirements and computing power.

4. Result analysis

4.1. performance verification of GMM method based on KDE-DPHEM algorithm

The wind speed of NaselleRidge and Megler in BPA Power Bureau in January 2016 was taken as the test data, and the wind power output was converted from wind speed according to IEC Class II fan model. NaselleRidge and Megler are about 18km apart, and the wind speed has a significant correlation. The joint probability density functions of wind speed and wind power are modeled respectively, and the errors of GMM method based on EM algorithm, GMM method based on KDE-DPHEM algorithm and Copula function method are compared with the KDE results. GMM methods based on EM and KDE-DPHEM algorithms are tested by different Gaussian components. The Copula function method adopts Gaussian, T, Clayton, Frank, Gumbel and many kinds of mixed Copula respectively. The root-mean-square error, RMSE) of joint probability density function is used for comparison, and 40,000 sampling points are evenly divided into 200×200 grids in the defined domain, and the root-mean-square error is obtained by statistical calculation of each point error.

The optimal Copula is t-Frank-Gumbel mixed Copula. When the number of Gaussian components is less than 10, the GMM errors based on EM algorithm and KDE-DPHEM algorithm are greater than the optimal Copula function. When the number of Gaussian components is greater than 10, the GMM error based on EM algorithm decreases slowly with the increase of Gaussian components. When the number of Gaussian components is greater than 20, the error level of GMM based on EM algorithm has not been significantly improved. When the number of Gaussian components is greater than 20, the error of GMM based on KDE-DPHEM algorithm is obviously lower than that of EM algorithm, and the error is obviously reduced with the increase of Gaussian components. When the number of Gaussian components is greater than 40, the error is less than half of the optimal Copula function. When the number of

Gaussian components is increased to 100, the error is only 18.54% of the optimal Copula and 20.56% of the EM algorithm.

The joint probability density function of wind speed and wind power output obtained by different methods, the Gaussian component number of GMM is 100. In the GMM modeling of wind power output based on EM algorithm, the covariance matrix is ill-conditioned in the iterative process, and the GMM result based on EM algorithm is better before the ill-conditioned problem appears. The whole and details of GMM based on KDE-DPHEM algorithm are highly similar to those of KDE and histogram, and the density characteristics of each local area are described in detail. The outer contour of GMM results based on EM algorithm is similar to that of KDE, but the detail error is large. The high-density region of t-Frank-Gumbel mixed Copula is similar to that of KDE and histogram, but it also has the problems of overall similarity and large detail error. Compared with KDE and histogram, Gaussian Copula is quite different, which shows that Gaussian Copula is not suitable for describing the correlation structure of wind speed and wind power output in NaselleRidge and Megler. The above results show that GMM method based on KDE-DPHEM algorithm has the advantage of high accuracy, and the modeling accuracy is significantly better than GMM method based on EM algorithm and the optimal Copula function method.

4.2. Verification of Time Scale Hierarchical Modeling Method

The 5-minute wind speed of NaselleRidge and Megler wind stations from January 2015 to December 2017 is selected as the test data, and the joint probability distribution of wind power output of the two stations is taken as the modeling goal. The total sample is about 315,000 sets of two-dimensional data. The data are divided into 12 blocks by month, and each sample has an average of about 26,000 sets of data. The time-scale hierarchical method is used to model. Based on the results of KDE, the annual scale GMM obtained by time scale layering method is compared with the annual scale GMM obtained by direct modeling, and the k of annual scale GMM and monthly scale GMM are set to 100.

The error analysis of the joint probability density function obtained by modeling is shown in Table 1. The results obtained by time scale method have high similarity with KDE and histogram, but little difference with direct method. Table 1 shows that the error of the time-scale hierarchical method is in the same order of magnitude as that of the direct method, the calculation time required is 44.39% of that of the direct method, and the amount of data to be processed by the single DPHEM algorithm is about 1/12 of that of the direct method, and the calculation complexity is significantly reduced. The 12-month monthly scale probability model obtained by time scale stratification method and its aggregated annual scale basis GMM belong to the intermediate model of time scale stratification method. The monthly scale model can be used for the probability analysis of monthly scale; The error of annual scale basis GMM is about half of the final simplified GMM, which can be used when higher accuracy is required.

Table 1 Comparison of annual scale model errors and time consumption of different methods

way	Root Mean Square Error (RMSE)		Time /s
	probability density	cumulative probability	
YB model	3.17×10^{-2}	3.05×10^{-4}	239.41
YR model	6.39×10^{-2}	8.08×10^{-4}	233.02
YD model	8.56×10^{-2}	6.22×10^{-4}	482.17

4.3. High-dimensional correlation modeling verification

In order to further verify the high-dimensional modeling ability of the method proposed in this paper, all related random variables in IEEE33-node distribution network are modeled by multi-dimensional GMM. The correlation load data of 32 nodes connected with load in IEEE33-node distribution network consists of 192 residential loads superimposed in turn every 6 households, and scaled to the average value consistent with the original deterministic load; Four groups of wind turbines with rated power of 0.4MW are connected to four different nodes, and the relevant wind power output is obtained by converting the wind speed of four wind stations (Naselle Ridge, Megler, Troutdale and BiddleButte) of BPA Power Bureau according to the method in Section 4.1. Due to a large number of missing wind speed data in the first half of 2010, the load and wind power data are unified in the second half of 2010, with a data resolution of 10min, about 26,000 pieces, and a data dimension of 36 dimensions. Random variables in each dimension are recorded as x_1、 x_2、 ...、 x_{36}, x_1—x_{32} Corresponding to the active load of 2-33 nodes, x_{33}—x_{36} Corresponding to the active output of four groups of wind power, the data takes the load as positive and the output as negative.

The computer configuration used for modeling is Intel Core i7-10510UCPU and 16GB memory. The time scale layering method is adopted, and the Gaussian component number of the monthly scale GMM is set to 1000, and the Gaussian component number of the semi-annual scale GMM is set to 100. The total modeling time is 608.02s. Pearson and Spearman correlation coefficients of GMM constructed based on this method are very close to the sample data. The absolute value of Pearson correlation coefficient error is 0.03739, and the root mean square value of error is 0.02388. The maximum absolute error of Spearman correlation coefficient is 0.11693, and the root mean square error is 0.05797, which proves that the method proposed in this paper has good high-dimensional correlation modeling ability. In the actual larger-scale system, the correlation random variable has regional characteristics, and the correlation within the region is significant, but the correlation between regions is low. At this time, it can be modeled by regions, and then a higher-dimensional GMM model of the whole system can be formed by the "combination-reduction" method.

5. Conclusion

In this paper, based on KDE-DPHEM algorithm, the probabilistic modeling method of power system based on multidimensional GMM is systematically improved, and the effectiveness of the proposed method is verified by an example test. The main conclusions are as follows:

1) KDE-DPHEM algorithm can continuously improve the accuracy of GMM model with the increase of Gaussian components, which overcomes the bottleneck that the accuracy of EM algorithm is difficult to improve after the number of Gaussian components is greater than 10. By increasing the number of Gaussian components, GMM model approaching KDE results can be obtained, and the modeling accuracy is significantly higher than that of Copula function method and EM algorithm.

2) The hierarchical modeling method of time scale effectively reduces the computational burden of GMM modeling under large sample data and can obtain multi-time scale intermediate models.

3) The hierarchical modeling method of "combination-reduction" effectively solves the problem of Gaussian component number explosion after the combination of independent random variables.

4) The proposed method accurately describes the complex correlation structure of high-dimensional random variables, and the large-scale correlation coefficient matrix of the high-dimensional model is close to the actual value.

5) The proposed method studies the modeling method of GMM with a given number of Gaussian components. According to the experience of an example, setting the number of Gaussian components to 100 orders of magnitude can get a higher precision result. In the future, we will further study how to balance the number of Gaussian components and model accuracy and realize the adaptive configuration of Gaussian components.

References

[1] He, Y., Li, H., Wang, S., & Yao, X. (2021). Uncertainty analysis of wind power probability density forecasting based on cubic spline interpolation and support vector quantile regression. Neurocomputing, 430, 121-137.

[2] Gu, B., Zhang, T., Meng, H., & Zhang, J. (2021). Short-term forecasting and uncertainty analysis of wind power based on long short-term memory, cloud model and non-parametric kernel density estimation. Renewable Energy, 164, 687-708.

[3] Dall'Armi, C., Pivetta, D., & Taccani, R. (2022). Uncertainty analysis of the optimal health-conscious operation of a hybrid PEMFC coastal ferry. International Journal of Hydrogen Energy, 47(21), 11428-11440.

[4] Petkov, I., & Gabrielli, P. (2020). Power-to-hydrogen as seasonal energy storage: an uncertainty analysis for optimal design of low-carbon multi-energy systems. Applied Energy, 274, 115197.

[5] Zhao, X., Ge, C., Ji, F., & Liu, Y. (2021). Monte Carlo method and quantile regression for uncertainty analysis of wind power forecasting based on Chaos-LS-SVM. International Journal of Control, Automation and Systems, 19, 3731-3740.

[6] Tong, Z., Chen, X., Tong, S., & Yang, Q. (2022). Dense Residual LSTM-Attention Network for Boiler Steam Temperature Prediction with Uncertainty Analysis. ACS omega, 7(13), 11422-11429.

[7] Zhang, F., Wang, X., Wang, W., Zhang, J., Du, R., Li, B., & Liu, W. (2023). Uncertainty analysis of photovoltaic cells to determine probability of functional failure. Applied Energy, 332, 120495.

[8] Fan, M.,Li, Z., Ding, T., Huang, L., Dong, F., Ren, Z., & Liu, C. (2021). Uncertainty evaluation algorithm in power system dynamic analysis with correlated renewable energy sources. IEEE Transactions on Power Systems, 36(6), 5602-5611.

[9] Shen, J., ZWang, Q., Ma, Z., & He, Y. (2021). Nonlinear optimization strategy for state of power estimation of lithium-ion batteries: A systematical uncertainty analysis of key impact parameters. IEEE Transactions on Industrial Informatics, 18(10), 6680-6689.

[10] Hosseini, S. H. R., Allahham, A., Walker, S. L., & Taylor, P. (2021). Uncertainty analysis of the impact of increasing levels of gas and electricity network integration and storage on Techno-Economic-Environmental performance. Energy, 222, 119968.

[11] Medrano, M., Liu, R., Zhao, T., Webb, T., Politte, D. G., Whiting, B. R., ... & Williamson, J. F. (2022). Towards subpercentage uncertainty proton stopping - power mapping via dual - energy CT: Direct experimental validation and uncertainty analysis of a statistical iterative image reconstruction method. Medical physics, 49(3), 1599-1618.

[12] Dash, R. C., Sharma, N., Maiti, D. K., & Singh, B. N. (2022). Uncertainty analysis of galloping based piezoelectric energy harvester system using polynomial neural network. Journal of Intelligent Material Systems and Structures, 33(16), 2019-2032.

[13] Yin, T., Li, W. T., Li, K., & He, Z. Z. (2021). Multi-parameter optimization and uncertainty analysis of multi-stage thermoelectric generator with temperature-dependent materials. Energy Reports, 7, 7212-7223.

[14] Deng, H., Chen, W., Cao, D., Chen, J., & Hu, W. (2020). Uncertainty analysis and robust control of fuel delivery systems considering nitrogen crossover phenomenon. International Journal of Hydrogen Energy, 45(56), 32367-32387.

[15] Shen, X., Zhang, Y., Zhang, J., & Wu, X. (2022). An Interval Analysis Scheme Based on Empirical Error and MCMC to Quantify Uncertainty of Wind Speed. IEEE Transactions on Industry Applications, 58(6), 7754-7763.

[16] Zhang, H., Liu, Y., Yan, J., Han, S., Li, L., & Long, Q. (2020). Improved deep mixture density network for regional wind power probabilistic forecasting. IEEE Transactions on Power Systems, 35(4), 2549-2560.

[17] Petkov, I., & Gabrielli, P. (2020). Power-to-hydrogen as seasonal energy storage: an uncertainty analysis for optimal design of low-carbon multi-energy systems. Applied Energy, 274, 115197.

[18] Zhou, W., Zhao, Z., Nielsen, J. B., Fritsche, L. G., LeFaive, J., Gagliano Taliun, S. A., ... & Lee, S. (2020). Scalable generalized linear mixed model for region-based association tests in large biobanks and cohorts. Nature genetics, 52(6), 634-639.

[19] Abdar, M., Pourpanah, F., Hussain, S., Rezazadegan, D., Liu, L., Ghavamzadeh, M., ... & Nahavandi, S. (2021). A review of uncertainty quantification in deep learning: Techniques, applications and challenges. Information fusion, 76, 243-297.

[20] Schielzeth, H., Dingemanse, N. J., Nakagawa, S., Westneat, D. F., Allegue, H., Teplitsky, C., ... & Araya‐Ajoy, Y. G. (2020). Robustness of linear mixed‐effects models to violations of distributional assumptions. Methods in ecology and evolution, 11(9), 1141-1152.

Design Studies and Intelligence Engineering
L.C. Jain et al. (Eds.)
© 2024 The Authors.
This article is published online with Open Access by IOS Press and distributed under the terms
of the Creative Commons Attribution Non-Commercial License 4.0 (CC BY-NC 4.0).
doi:10.3233/FAIA231437

Digital Personality in the Voice Interaction Products Design

Lingyan ZHANG[a,b] and Yun WANG[b,c,1]

[a] *Design Innovation Center, China Academy of Art, Hangzhou, China, 310001*
[b] *Design-AI lab, China Academy of Art, Hangzhou, China, 310001*
[c] *School of Industrial Design, China Academy of Art, Hangzhou, China, 310001*

Abstract. The advent of the intelligent era has ushered in an evolution of user experience objectives, transforming human-machine interaction methods. As machines are endowed with digital personality, the interaction between humans and machines has fundamentally diverged from that with traditional hardware products. Voice interaction products on the market are also gradually moving towards a more personified direction. The personification of smart voice products narrows the psychological gap between humans and machines, representing a significant trend in current voice product development. However, the integration of digital personality introduces new challenges to human-machine interaction. People's preferences vary, and it remains to be seen whether individuals are willing to embrace digital personality that mirror their own personalities. Consequently, this study designed an experiment to evaluate the digital personality of a car-assistant in a driving scenario. By consistently presenting personified voice stimuli, we collected post-experiment data to observe changes in user psychology and behavior. The results of ANOVA showed that there were significant differences in driver preference under different personality similarity ($F=6.452$, $p<0.01$). The research findings indicate that the personality of voices does influence users' preference to a certain extent. Voices that closely match a user's personality can enhance preference, offering users a superior perceptual and experiential.

Keywords. Digital Personality, Voice Interaction, Human-Machine Interaction, Product Design, Technological Humanization

1. Introduction

Personification is defined as attributing human motivations, characteristics, or behaviors to inanimate objects, essentially transforming products that originally lacked human actions and emotions to possess them, imbuing products with personified traits to provide a personified interaction experience during their use. Digital personality is frequently utilized in product design and technological innovation with the aim of enhancing user experience and shaping user preferences [1]. The onset of the intelligent era has prompted an evolution in our experiential objectives, altering the ways humans interact with machines, pushing towards a more natural and emotionally rich direction. Nowadays, an increasing number of products are being endowed with personality. The

---

[1] Corresponding Author. Yun WANG, China Academy of Art, Hangzhou, China, 310001, E-mail: wy_james@126.com

introduction of digital personality to smart voice interaction products has substantially distinguished them from traditional hardware offerings.

Speech is one of the most quintessential hallmarks of humanity and serves as a primary means by which we gain social recognition [2]. Extensive research indicates that when machines are endowed with personified speech characteristics, the interaction between humans and machines feels as if one is interacting with another human being [3]. Altering voice attributes and spoken content can confer various digital personality upon machines, influencing user interaction, trust, and even purchasing intentions [4]. With technological advancements, voice interaction technology has become a ubiquitous presence in our lives. From smart home devices to smartphone voice assistants, voice interaction has seamlessly integrated into our daily routines. A critical catalyst behind this is the progression of artificial intelligence, making such interactions increasingly natural and human-like.

In recent years, voice interaction products on the market have been gradually leaning towards personification. Traditional voice interaction design, despite considerable technological advancements, still retains numerous limitations at the user experience level. For instance, most voice assistants come across as overly mechanical, devoid of genuine emotion and personality, potentially creating a sense of detachment for users. Moreover, faced with intricate and emotionally charged user demands, conventional design methods might fall short. Against this backdrop, the emergence of digital personality as a novel design methodology and philosophy is timely. Its central tenet is to make interactions with machines feel like conversing with a real person by endowing them with personality. This personification of smart voice products bridges the psychological gap between humans and machines, marking a pivotal developmental trajectory for voice products.

Hence, this paper aims to delve deeply into the application of digital personality in voice interaction product design, elucidating how digital personality reshapes our interaction experiences, while also forecasting their future development trends and potential.

2. Related Works

2.1. Digital Personality

According to Burger, personality can be defined as a consistent behavioral pattern and intrinsic process originating from within the individual. A consistent behavioral pattern implies that individuals exhibit similar behavior across different times and situations. Intrinsic processes refer to all the emotions, motivations, and cognitive processes occurring within us that impact our behavior and feelings [5]. Based on Ryckman's perspective, personality is defined as a set of dynamic, organized characteristics unique to an individual that distinctly influences their cognition, motivation, and behavior in various scenarios [6]. Different scholars hold varied views on the definition of personality, but they all underscore that personality is a unique characteristic that distinguishes an individual from others.

With the continuous evolution and deepening of artificial intelligence, particularly breakthroughs in natural language processing and machine learning, machine-human interactions have evolved beyond simple task execution and now strive for more intricate and human-centric experiences. In this context, the concept of a "digital persona" emerged. As the pursuit for a more optimized and human-like voice interaction experience intensified, this novel concept gradually gained widespread attention within the industry. This idea aims to enhance the depth and richness of human-machine interaction by simulating human personality traits and emotions.

Over the past several decades, there's been a surge of interest in personality theories and measurement methods, with various personality assessment techniques emerging. The Big Five Personality traits and the Myers‐Briggs Type Indicator (MBTI) are currently the most commonly employed personality assessment methods[7]. The Big Five Personality model, proposed by Goldberg, is grounded in personality structure theory and informed by practical experience, delineates five fundamental dimensions of personality: Openness, Conscientiousness, Extraversion, Agreeableness, and Neuroticism [8]. Each dimension possesses bipolar traits, and individuals exhibit varied tendencies across these five dimensions [9]. Numerous longitudinal studies affirm the sustained stability of these characteristics over time [10]. Thus, this study has chosen to utilize the Big Five Personality model as its research paradigm for personality.

2.2. Voice Interaction Product Design

Cognitive psychologist Donald Norman once posited that if a product can establish a connection with its users at a personality level, it can better foster positive emotions during its use, create pleasant memories, and consequently enhance user willingness, tolerance, and trust toward the product [11]. For designers, studying the personality of a product offers two key benefits: Firstly, a product's personality can influence the interaction between the user and the product. The personality of the product can help predict how users will interact with it [12]. Secondly, a product's personality might affect user preferences. People tend to prefer products that resonate with their own personalities, possibly because such products help them manifest and express their self-concept [13]. While the appearance of a product is its most direct representation of personality, other aspects of product design, such as sound, texture, and smell, can also convey personality traits [12]. With the proliferation of artificial intelligence, the modes of interaction between people and products have expanded, giving rise to voice interaction. Voice has been integrated into a variety of products, becoming a pivotal means of connecting humans and products.

In recent years, voice interaction technology has seen extensive application across various products and services, marking a significant shift in human-machine interaction paradigms. From basic command recognition to sophisticated natural language processing, advancements in voice interaction technology have rendered our communication with the digital realm more intuitive and natural. Currently, voice interaction products have three primary applications in our daily lives: The first category serves as intelligent assistants, such as Siri, Google Assistant, and Alexa, offering users a range of functionalities like weather updates, alarm settings, and information retrieval [14]. The second category functions as control hubs for smart homes, where users can voice-command lights, thermostats, or other intelligent devices. The third category encompasses in-car voice assistants. During driving, users can voice-command music playback, navigation, or phone calls, thereby mitigating the risks of distraction.

2.3.   Emergence of Digital Personalities in Voice Interactive Product Design

With the widespread adoption of voice interaction technology and increasingly profound research in artificial intelligence, digital personalities are emerging as a new trend in the design of voice interaction products. Applications of digital personalities in voice interaction products are vast, with the most emblematic being personalized voice assistants. Unlike traditional voice assistants, digital personalities allow users to customize their assistant's character, tone, and even sense of humor to align with personal preferences and emotional needs. Depending on a user's context and mood, digital personalities can provide more pertinent advice or feedback. For instance, when a user is feeling down, the system might proactively offer consolation or crack a joke to lighten the mood. Beyond this, they are also employed in educational and children's interactive products. Here, digital personalities can modify teaching methods based on a child's progress and emotional state, making learning more effective and engaging. These digital avatars can simulate friends for children, forging deep emotional bonds and enhancing their receptivity and interest in educational content.

Many scholars have embarked on extensive studies of voice personalization. For instance, research by Lee and colleagues found that interactions and atmospheres vary considerably between users and voice assistants with different personality traits [15]. Poushne, after comparing personality traits across seven voice assistants, discovered that personalized voice assistants offer consumers an enhanced user experience and heightened perceived control. Voice output, being a primary medium for human-machine interaction, can serve as a manifestation of robotic personality traits. Nass's research underscored that different vocal characteristics of computers can denote different personalities; for instance, a loud, high-pitched, fast voice might represent an extroverted personality, while the opposite can be suggestive of an introverted one [16]. Clearly, voice interaction is set to be a pivotal focus in the evolution of personality-infused smart products.

Propelled by digital personalities, voice interaction products are evolving beyond emotionless machines to become companions capable of forming emotional bonds with users. However, this also ushers in new challenges, like ensuring the authenticity and appropriateness of digital personalities, safeguarding user privacy, and ensuring these systems are not misused, all of which demand rigorous research and contemplation.

3. Digital Personality in In-Car Voice Assistant

3.1.   Influence of In-Car Voice Assistant Personality on Driving Behavior

With the rise in vehicle ownership domestically, the number of drivers unfamiliar with the roads is rapidly increasing. The need for consumers to reach their destinations safely and conveniently has become urgent, leading to a concomitant rise in the usage of navigation systems. These systems offer users a wealth of location information, meeting their travel information needs while profoundly influencing their driving behavior and travel habits. Vehicles serve as one of the most natural acoustic environments in people's lives [17], with a myriad of sounds always accompanying drivers throughout their journey. Substantial evidence suggests that using voice interaction in vehicles, as opposed to traditional visual or manual interactions, can enhance driver performance, reduce cognitive load and fatigue from passive tasks, and keep the driver's visual attention on the road [18]. Large et al. explored drivers' inclinations towards personalized voice navigation and found that even though the personality traits of navigation aren't directly tied to its functionality, drivers still adjust settings based on personal preferences and usage habits. Moreover, the voice of navigation can potentially influence how drivers utilize the provided information [18]. In studies examining factors affecting driving behavior, the element of personality is frequently delved into. Different drivers may have implicit demands concerning the personality of in-car voice assistant. Voices matching user needs can cater to drivers' emotional requirements, bridging the distance between drivers and vehicles, and facilitating interaction with in-car systems. However, personalized navigation voice content is more complex, and processing such voice information could increase drivers' cognitive load, potentially affecting driving safety [19].

Driving is an activity requiring intense focus. However, human attention is finite, incapable of processing large amounts of information concurrently. If one needs to manage multiple cognitive tasks simultaneously, the efficiency of each task diminishes. Introducing new information and communication technologies in vehicles, such as navigation systems, mobile phones, and in-car internet, might distract drivers, subsequently affecting their driving behavior and performance.

3.2.   Voice Personality Similarity of In-Car Voice Assistant

One determining factor of attraction between any two individuals is the degree of their personality similarity. Personality is defined based on scores derived from one or multiple individual difference measurements [20]. These studies often originate from the Similarity-Attraction Theory. The Similarity-Attraction Theory proposes that individuals are drawn to those with personalities similar to their own and prefer to interact with them [21]. This pattern has been corroborated by psychological studies. People also tend to favor and trust voices that match their own and prefer interacting with technologies that exhibit personality traits similar to theirs1. When in-car voice assistant possesses personalized characteristics, the displayed personality traits can differently impact individuals with varying personalities. The closer the voice's personality traits align with those of the driver, the greater the potential attention the voice can command, subsequently influencing the driver's behavior and performance.

Miyajima and colleagues contend that driving behavior varies among drivers, with each individual's unique driving style exerting influence on their behavior [22]. Jafarpour & Rahimi's research mentions that driving behavior is a multifaceted issue, influenced by numerous factors such as gender, age, driving experience, driver's personality type, temperament, emotions, and distractions from external or internal stimuli [23]. Some scholars attempt to explain the influence of voice features on driving behavior from a similarity-attraction perspective. For instance, Nass et al. in a study examining driver emotions (happy/sad) × car voice emotions (energetic/depressed) discovered that perceived voice emotions not only influenced drivers' attitudinal reactions but also impacted safe driving behaviors. When user emotions aligned with car voice emotions, drivers displayed a more positive attitude and drove more safely [24]. Jonsson and Nils embarked on similar research regarding driver interactions with in-car information systems, specifically focusing on the effects when driver personalities did not match car voice personalities. Through a study exploring driver (dominant/submissive) × car voice (dominant/submissive) dynamics, they found that when the navigation system emitted a dominant voice, drivers tended to follow instructions consistent with the voice's personality traits [25]. These studies offer perspectives pertinent to this research, exploring the connection between personalized voice navigation and driving behavior, affirming that drivers' behaviors are influenced by the similarity-attraction principle. Such phenomena may also manifest in scenarios where drivers use in-car voice assistant with personalized traits.

3.3.   User Preference for Personalized Navigation Speech

A comprehensive review of the literature reveals that safe and effective driving requires drivers to maintain cognitive alertness amidst continuously changing auditory backgrounds. If used correctly, in-car voice assistant can enhance driving enjoyment and safety. Conversely, improper use may result in severe consequences. However, the impact of personalized in-car voice assistant on a driver's behavior during the driving process has not been elucidated to date. Additionally, existing digital service providers have yet to establish a comprehensive recommendation mechanism. This research will primarily analyze the effects of personalized in-car voice assistant on driving behaviors with the goal of improving safety when drivers utilize such personalized in-car voice assistant.

This study will investigate the influence of navigation voice personality traits on driving behavior using an experimental research approach. Drawing from the Similarity-Attraction Theory, the study posits the following hypotheses: As the similarity between the in-car voice assistant's personality traits and the driver's personality traits increases, users will exhibit a greater preference for that voice.

4. Evaluation Experimental Design

4.1.   Experimental Variable

To examine the impact of a car voice assistant's digital personality on user preferences, this study designed an evaluative experiment. We began by preparing a set of experimental materials. By separately collecting users' own personality scores and the personality scores of the experimental materials, we aimed to investigate whether the similarity between the digital personality and the user's personality would affect their preferences. Through the experimental results, we sought to understand how the onboard voice assistant's digital personality influences the user's psychology. Based on these findings, we derived recommendations for a safe and reasonable digital personality for the onboard voice assistant, providing users with more references for choosing in-car voice assistant.

Independent Variable: The independent variable of this experiment is the degree of similarity between the navigation voice's personalized traits and the driver's personality traits. All participants filled out the BFI-2 personality test before the start of the experiment. The BFI-2 scale provides continuous trait values for each dimension, with 12 questions per dimension. A minimum score of 12 indicates an extremely low presence of the trait, while a maximum score of 60 suggests an extremely strong presence. After obtaining the voice personality score matrix and the driver personality score matrix, we calculated the Euclidean distance between them. Based on these scores, we mapped the similarity level of the navigation voice personality and the driver's personality onto three dimensions: high, medium, and low.

Dependent Variable: Collected using scales and interviews, we aimed to measure if the similarity in a car voice assistant's personality would modulate emotions and subsequently impact driving behavior. After the experiment, preference measurements were taken using a scale, with each item having a maximum score of 9.

4.2.   Preparation of Experimental Materials

4.2.1 Measuring Voice Personality
Cognitive science reveals that individuals form perceptions about others' traits in their minds in less than a second upon first encounter. Therefore, in this experiment, the assessment of voice personality leverages commonly used personality measurement scales, adopting a third-party evaluation method. This study opted for the BFI-10 scale to evaluate the personality of the experimental materials. The BFI-10 scale is relatively concise, consisting of 10 items, which can effectively streamline the assessment process. This scale has been extensively employed for evaluating voice personality.

4.2.2 Selection of in-car voice assistant's personality
Initially, 12 distinct voice characteristics were selected from an online voice synthesis platform. These 12 different voices were used to synthesize the same content, with the initial voice content uniformly set to "Ready to go, a total of 15 kilometers, expected arrival at 3:50." To eliminate the interference of gender factors, all voice samples for this experiment are in a female tone. A preliminary group of 20 users was invited to rate these 12 voice tones. The rating results can be seen in Tables 1.

Table 1.   scores of sound personality in five dimension characteristic

No.	Personality five dimension characteristic score				
	Extraversion	Agreeableness	Conscientiousness	Neuroticis	Openness
voice 1	**2.895**	1.053	1.421	−2.053	1.105
voice 2	−0.211	**2.474**	1.579	−1.579	0.158
voice 3	1.421	0.474	0.842	−0.842	0.474
voice 4	−1.211	1.105	1.579	−1.000	0.105
voice 5	1.632	0.579	0.579	−1.263	1.263
voice 6	−0.737	0.368	0.737	1.526	−1.368
voice 7	0.158	1.789	**2.737**	−1.105	−0.842
voice 8	1.842	−0.368	−0.895	−0.316	**2.211**
voice 9	−0.158	1.105	1.158	−1.526	0.158
voice 10	−1.368	−0.789	0.053	**2.211**	−1.105
voice 11	−0.368	1.684	1.579	−1.895	−0.368
voice 12	0.474	0.895	−0.368	−0.474	0.632

Note: The bolded values are the highest horizontal and vertical values.

Upon comparing the ratings for each voice, it was found that Voice 1 exhibited the best extroversion among the five personality dimensions and had the highest extroversion score out of all 12 voices. Hence, within these 12 voices, Voice 1 was determined to have the highest level of extroversion. The selection of voices for the other personality traits followed the same logic. Specifically, the voices with the strongest tendencies toward agreeableness, conscientiousness, neuroticism, and openness were chosen, corresponding to Voice 1, Voice 2, Voice 7, Voice 10, and Voice 8 respectively. These five voices were synthesized with the chosen content to form the final experimental materials.

4.3. Experimental Procedure

Participants who had not previously been exposed to the experimental materials were recruited. They were tasked with evaluating the voice tones within a simulated driving environment. The demographics of the participants can be found in Table 2. Each participant listened to five different sounds, and 31 participants completed 155 sets of experiments.

Table 2. Subject information (mean $\pm$ standard deviation) (n=31)

variable	information	
sex	male	female
population	11	20
Average age (years)	26.09 ± 5.11	24.65 ± 1.39

To immerse the participants more deeply into the experience, this study employed a driving simulator to set the experimental scene. Real-time navigation voice simulation was implemented using the Wizard of Oz method. The Wizard of Oz technique is a design approach used for rapid product development to enhance user experience, where users engage in voice dialogues with a computer. Unbeknownst to the user, another individual sits behind the computer, choosing which voice component to feedback. During the experiment, a tester, without the participant's knowledge, played the in-car assistant's voices, which were adjusted in real-time based on the participant's driving scenario. After the voice simulation was completed, participants were asked to complete a questionnaire to gather data.

5. Result

5.1 Similarity Calculation

5.1.1 Euclidean Distance Calculation
Given the personality scores of the five experimental voice materials, as well as the scores of 31 drivers, the drivers' personality scores were self-assessed. Based on the Euclidean distance calculation formula (Equation 1), where D_i represents the personality trait scores of the driver and Vi denotes the personality trait scores of the voice.

$$d(D,V) = \sqrt{\sum_{i=1}^{n}(D_i - V_i)^2} \qquad (1)$$

To accelerate the convergence speed of the K-means clustering and prevent data obliteration, as well as to reduce the sensitivity of the algorithm to outliers, normalization of the raw Euclidean distance data was required after computing the similarity between each driver's personality and the personalities of the five voices. This procedure rescales the calculated Euclidean distance to a range of 0-1. Post-normalization, the average iteration number decreases, and the potential clustering outcomes are reduced. Normalizing data can speed up the convergence of the K-means clustering algorithm, yielding better convergence results. The normalization calculation formula is shown in Equation 2, where $d*$ is the normalized standard distance. In this context, *max* represents the highest value in the scoring vector, and *min* stands for the lowest value.

$$d^* = \frac{d - d(min)}{d(max) - d(min)} \tag{2}$$

5.1.2 Similarity Level Division

In clustering techniques, the K-means algorithm stands out as one of the simplest, most effective, and commonly employed methods. Moreover, the K-means algorithm primarily utilizes the Euclidean distance metric for its operations, consistent with the methodology adopted in this study for computing personality similarities [27]. Therefore, this research employs the K-means clustering algorithm for partitioning similarity levels.

The fundamental principle behind the K-means clustering algorithm is the segmentation of data samples based on distance. Presuming similarity as a multi-dimensional dataset encompassing n data points, K-means clustering segments these data samples into K groups, i.e., K clusters ($C_1, C_2, \cdots, C_i, \cdots, C_j, \cdots, C_k$). Each cluster has a centroid, and clusters are mutually exclusive. The main objective of the K-means clustering algorithm is to minimize the sum of squared errors within these clusters [26]. The objective function of the K-means clustering algorithm can be defined as(Equation 3-5):

$$J(X,C) = \sum_{k=1}^{K} \sum_{x_i \in C_k} \left\| x_i - v_k \right\|^2 \tag{3}$$

$$C_k = \left\{ x_i \in X \middle| k = \arg\min_{j \in \{1,2,\dots, K\}} \left\| x_i - v_j \right\|^2 \right\} \tag{4}$$

$$v_k = \frac{\sum_{x_i \in Ck} x_i}{|c_i|} \tag{5}$$

Initially, the similarity between the voice persona and the driver's personality was categorized into three levels: high, medium, and low. Thus, three cluster centroids were defined, with the number of iterations set at ten. All normalized similarity scores were then assigned to the cluster whose centroid they were closest to. Once the cluster centroids converged, the clustering process was terminated. Following the application of the K-means clustering algorithm on similarity levels, the clustering results, as shown in table 3, delineated the 155 similarity levels from this study into three categories. The cluster centroids were 0.63, 0.45, and 0.28, respectively corresponding to low, medium, and high similarity levels. The numbers of cases in these clusters were 34, 52, and 69, respectively. Based on a significance level of $p<0.001$, the convergence of the three cluster centroids was deemed satisfactory, hence concluding the clustering process.

Table 3. Similarity level K-means clustering results.

Similarity level	center of cluster	Number of cluster	F	p
low	0.63	34		
medium	0.45	52	357.420	0.000
high	0.28	69		

5.2 Measurement of Preference

5.2.1 Homogeneity of Variance Test

Initially, an analysis for homogeneity of variance was conducted on the emotional measurements under different personality similarity levels, with the results detailed in Table 4. The outcomes indicate that the sample meets the assumption of homogeneity of variance, making it suitable for subsequent one-way ANOVA analysis.

Table 4. Chi-square test for mood measures with different personality similarities

variable	Levene	df 1	df 2	p
preference	0.458	2	152	0.633

5.2.2 One-way ANOVA Analysis

A one-way analysis of variance (ANOVA) was then performed on the emotional variables associated with varying degrees of personality similarity, with the results presented in Table 5. As per the findings, under the guidance of in-car voice assistant of different personality similarity levels, drivers' preference scores were as follows: low similarity voice (3.235) < medium similarity voice (4.872) < high similarity voice (6.135). This suggests that the more the navigation voice's personality aligns with the driver's personality traits, the higher the driver's preference for the navigation voice. Conversely, as similarity decreases, the preference for the navigation voice also diminishes. Furthermore, the ANOVA results indicated a significant difference in driver preference across different personality similarity levels ($F=6.452, p<0.01$).

Table 5. One-way ANOVA analysis of mood measures under different personality similarities

variable	low (n=34)		medium (n=52)		high (n=69)		ANOVA	
	M	SD	M	SD	M	SD	F	p
preference	3.235	3.737	4.872	3.979	6.135	3.885	6.452	0.002

5.2.3 Bonferroni Post-Hoc Comparison

Given that the results of the one-way ANOVA indicated significant differences in driver preferences across various personality similarity levels, a further Bonferroni post-hoc comparison was conducted on the dependent variable to examine the differences in effects between each pair of personality similarity levels. The results of the Bonferroni post-hoc comparison can be found in Table 6.

The findings revealed that in terms of preference, a significant difference exists only between voices of high personality similarity and those of low personality similarity. No significant differences were observed in other comparisons.

Table 6. Bonferroni post hoc comparison of pleasure and liking with different personality similarities

variable	(I)	(J)	Mean Difference (I–J)	standard deviation	significance	95%confidence interval	
						Lower limits	upper limits
preference	high	medium	1.263	0.714	0.236	−0.464	2.991
		low	2.900*	0.814	0.001	0.929	4.871
	medium	high	−1.263	0.714	0.236	−2.991	0.464
		low	1.637	0.857	0.174	−0.438	3.711
	low	high	−2.900*	0.814	0.001	−4.871	−0.929
		medium	−1.637	0.857	0.174	−3.711	0.438

5.2.4 Bonferroni Post-Hoc Comparison

In order to explore the influence of personality similarity on drivers' emotions, Pearson correlation analysis was carried out first. The results are shown in Table 7, and there is a significant correlation between liking degree and personality similarity degree.

Table 7. Pearson's Correlation between Personality Similarity and Emotion Measure

	index	preference
Similarity	Pearson correlation	0.279**
	Sig.(two tail)	0.000

Based on the correlation coefficient table, we propose conducting a regression analysis with preference as the dependent variable. Grouping in order based on the degree of similarity, the ordinal logistic regression variable assignments are as follows: low similarity = 1; medium similarity = 2; high similarity = 3. An ordinal logistic regression analysis will be conducted using a scale of standardized scores as the dependent variable. Firstly, a parallel lines test was conducted, and the p-value for preference was 0.685, which is greater than 0.05. This satisfies the conditions for conducting an ordinal logistic regression analysis, and hence an ordinal logistic regression analysis on preference was carried out.

Model fit information indicated a χ^2 of 12.575 with $p=0.002$, signifying a good model fit. The R^2 result showed a Cox and Snell R^2 coefficient of 0.078, which is less than 0.19, indicating a relatively weak explanatory power. Results of the ordered logistic test are detailed in Table 8. The impact of low-similarity voice on preference is -1.349 times that of high-similarity voice ($p<0.001$). The effect of medium-similarity voice on preference is -0.576 times that of the high-similarity voice ($p>0.05$).

Table 8. Results of ordered logistic regression analysis of preferences under different personality similarities

variable	level	β	S.E	Wald	p	95%CI
preference	low	−1.349	0.39	11.938	0.001	−2.114 ~ −0.584
	medium	−0.576	0.33	3.045	0.081	−1.223 ~ 0.071
	high(contrast)					

6. Discussion

Participants' compliance with the in-car voice assistant's instructions is closely tied to their level of preference. The more positive an individual's attitude towards a particular behavior, the more likely they are to engage in it. Hence, this study, through a designed assessment experiment, invited participants to gauge their preference for in-car voice assistants with different personalities. The results revealed a significant correlation between the participants' preference for the in-car voice assistant and the similarity of their own personalities. Even though participants were not informed about their own personality traits or the personality attributes of the in-car voice assistant prior to the experiment, qualitative feedback suggested that participants tended to be more attracted to, and displayed a higher preference for, in-car voice assistants that closely matched their own personalities. This finding supports the similarity-attraction theory, which posits that personality similarities play a crucial role in interpersonal communication and interactions. Previous research has also indicated the importance of personality matching in human-computer interaction; when there's a good match, users tend to have a more favorable perception [28].

In addition to the aforementioned quantitative analysis, we conducted interviews post the assessment experiment. Some participants mentioned that when the navigation voice was more aligned with their own personality, they felt more at ease, perceiving the voice navigation as playing a "friend" role in reminding them. However, when there was a low similarity between the in-car voice assistant's personality and their own, the voice navigation seemed more like a "stranger". When the in-car voice assistant issued reminders in such cases, participants often experienced feelings of "embarrassment" and lacked confidence in themselves. Furthermore, the study discovered that participants' psychological responses did not linearly change with the similarity of the voice's personality. But, from the qualitative data, it is evident that when the similarity was at its lowest, participants felt the least psychologically secure.

7. Conclusion

In summary, a digital persona is not merely a preset response pattern or algorithm but rather a virtual entity capable of simulating human emotions, thoughts, and behavior patterns. It can learn and adapt based on its interaction history with users, providing a more personalized service. While traditional AI possesses learning capabilities, digital personas emphasize adaptation to individual users. They continuously learn and optimize from interactions with specific users, placing a premium on emotional connection and communication experience. Overall, digital personas present new opportunities and challenges in the design of voice-interactive products.

With the advent of voice-interactive products, certain design principles for human-machine interaction emerged, such as emphasizing user-friendliness, making interaction flows as straightforward as possible. Feedback mechanisms are also necessary; when a device fails to understand a user's command, it typically provides feedback, asking if the user needs assistance or wishes to provide information again. However, despite technological advancements, many voice-interactive products still feel mechanical, devoid of emotion and lacking genuine humanization. This not only renders interactions tedious for users but also fosters distrust, like concerns over potential misuse of information collected by voice assistants or a lack of full trust in voice commands given by in-car systems. Moreover, preferences vary among individuals, and it remains to be verified whether people are willing to accept digital personas that resemble their personalities.

In light of this, our study, set within a driving context, designed an evaluation experiment for the digital persona of in-car assistants. By continuously presenting personalized voice auditory stimuli, multi-dimensional data was collected to observe changes in user psychology and behavior. The results indicate that the digital persona of in-car voice assistants can, to some extent, influence the psychological state of users. Voices that closely match a user's personality can enhance likability, providing a superior perceptual and experiential quality. This research focuses on the utilization of digital personas in voice-interactive products. By emulating human emotions and personalities, digital personas offer deeper, more human-centric interactive experiences, better meeting user needs. With the continuous evolution of digital personas in the future, voice assistants will better understand and respond to users, offering more natural and fluid interactions, becoming an increasingly commonplace and valuable part of our daily lives.

Acknowledgement

This work was supported by National Social Science Foundation of Arts Major Project (Grant Number: 20ZD09) and Design-AI lab of China Academy of Art (CAADAI2022A001).

References

[1] Choi, J. G., & KIM, M. S. Anthropomorphic Design: Projecting Human Characteristics to Product. *IASDR*. (2009), 22.
[2] Heath, S. *Image-music-text. Fontana*, London. 1977.
[3] Large, D. R., & Burnett, G. E. Drivers' preferences and emotional responses to satellite in-car voice assistant, *International Journal of Vehicle Noise and Vibration* 9(2013), 28-46.
[4] Nass, C. I. & Brave, S. Wired for speech: How voice activates and advances the human-computer relationship. 2005. MIT press Cambridge.
[5] Jerry M. B. *Personality (10th ed.)*. 2017. Boston, MA: Cengage Learning.
[6] Ryckman R.M., *Theories of Personality*. 2004. Thomson. Wadsworth.
[7] Furnham A. The big five versus the big four: the relationship between the Myers-Briggs Type Indicator (MBTI) and NEO-PI five factor model of personality. *Personality and individual differences* 21(1996), 303-307.
[8] Goldberg, L. R. The development of markers for the Big-Five factor structure. *Psychological Assessment* 4(1992) 26-42.
[9] Gosling S. D., Rentfrow P. J., & Swann W. B. A very brief measure of the Big-Five personality domains. *Journal of Research in Personality* 37(2003), 504-528.
[10] Costa P. T., & McCrae R. R. Personality in adulthood: a six-year longitudinal study of self-reports and spouse ratings on the NEO Personality Inventory. *Journal of personality and social psychology* 54(1988), 853.
[11] Norman & Donald A. The Design of Everyday Things. *Sveučilište u Splitu*, 2002.
[12] Janlert L. E., & Stolterman E. The character of things. *Design Studies* 18(1997), 297-314.
[13] Govers, P. & Schoormans, J. Product personality and its influence on consumer preference. *Journal of Consumer Marketing* 22(2005), 189-197.
[14] Poushneh A. Humanizing voice assistant: The impact of voice assistant personality on consumers' attitudes and behaviors. *Journal of Retailing and Consumer Services* 58 (2021), 102283.
[15] Lee S., Jaemyung L., & Lee K. P. Designing Intelligent Assistant through User Participations[C]// Conference on Designing Interactive Systems. ACM, 2017.
[16] Nass C., & Lee K. M. Does computer-generated speech manifest personality? an experimental test of similarity-attraction[C]// Sigchi Conference on Human Factors in Computing Systems. ACM, 2000.
[17] Li R., Chen Y. J. & Zhang L.H. Effect of Music Tempo on Long-Distance Driving: Which Tempo Is the Most Effective at Reducing Fatigue? *i-Perception* 10(2019).
[18] Large, D. R., Burnett, G., Antrobus, V., & Skrypchuk, L. Driven to Discussion: Engaging Drivers in Conversation with a Digital Assistant as a Countermeasure to Passive Task-Related Fatigue. *IET Intelligent Transport Systems*. 2018.
[19] Peelle J. E. Listening effort: How the cognitive consequences of acoustic challenge are reflected in brain and behavior. *Ear and Hearing* 39(2018), 204.

[20]   Byrne D., Griffitt W., & Stefaniak D. Attraction and similarity of personality characteristics. *Journal of Personality and social Psychology* 5(1967), 82.

[21]   Lee K. M., Peng W., & Jin S. A. Can robots manifest personality?: An empirical test of personality recognition, social responses, and social presence in human-robot interaction. *Journal of Communication* 56(2006), 754-772.

[22]   Miyajima C., Nishiwaki Y., & Ozawa K. Driver modeling based on driving behavior and its evaluation in driver identification. *Proceedings of the IEEE* 95(2007), 427-437.

[23]   Jafarpour S., & Rahimi-Movaghar V. Determinants of risky driving behavior: a narrative review. *Medical Journal of the Islamic Republic of Iran* 28(2014), 142.

[24]   Nass C., Jonsson I., Harris H., Reaves B., Endo J., Brave S., & Takayama L. Improving automotive safety by pairing driver emotion and car voice emotion[C]//CHI'05 extended abstracts on Human factors in computing systems. (2005)1973-1976.

[25]   Jonsson I. M., & Dahlbäck N. In-car information systems: Matching and mismatching personality of driver with personality of car voice[C]//International Conference on Human-Computer Interaction. Springer, Berlin, Heidelberg (2013)586-595.

[26]   Xiao Y., & Yu J. Partitive clustering (K - means family). Wiley Interdisciplinary Reviews: Data Mining and Knowledge Discovery 2(2012), 209-225.

[27]   Gupta M K. & Chandra P. Effects of similarity/distance metrics on k-means algorithm with respect to its applications in IoT and multimedia: a review. *Multimedia Tools and Applications* (2021) 1-26.

[28]   Dahlbäck, N., Swamy, S., Nass, C., Arvidsson, F., Skågeby, J.: Spoken Interaction with Computers in a Native or Non-native Language - Same or Different? In: Proceedings of INTERACT (2001)294-301.

Design Studies and Intelligence Engineering
L.C. Jain et al. (Eds.)
© *2024 The Authors.*
doi:10.3233/FAIA231438

Construction of Intermediate Knowledge in Design: A Case Study of Cultural and Creative Product Design

Lintao TANG [a,1] and Jianwei YIN [a]

[a] *Academy of Arts and Design, Tsinghua University, Beijing, China*

Abstract. Intermediate-level knowledge is conceptual knowledge that resides between design instances and theories. It supports designers in lateral thinking and facilitates the sharing and communication of specific domain design knowledge. This paper proposes a method for constructing intermediate knowledge to support team knowledge co-creation. We introduce the knowledge construction process through a case study in the context of creative cultural design. In this case study, eleven design patterns were extracted from a collection of 121 design instances. These patterns, serving as typical intermediate knowledge, were transformed into a card-based tool to support designers' creative ideation. Finally, we evaluated its efficiency and effectiveness in two student projects.

Keywords. Intermediate Knowledge, cultural and creative design, creative Ideation, card-based Tools

1. Introduction

The goal of design research is to systematically explore knowledge (Archer, 1981; 1995). Creative procedures, design methodologies, guidelines, principles, patterns, and heuristics are all design knowledge. This paper focuses on the intermediate-level knowledge in design, which resides between concrete instances and abstract theories. Starting from the standpoint that intermediate knowledge plays a pivotal role in the design of creative thinking, we put forth a method to construct intermediate knowledge. Through a case study, we will illustrate the constructing process of intermediate knowledge for cultural and creative products and assess its impact on novice designers during the ideation stage.

A critical skill possessed by the expert is to develop abstract conceptual knowledge through the accumulation of extensive design practice (Cross, 2004). Experts can identify underlying patterns, principles, and techniques, and apply them to new design contexts. Darke (1979) observed that professional architects often employ generative conceptual principles known as "Primary Generators" to aid in framing design problems and developing design solutions. However, novices, tend to focus more on the structure of the problem and lack domain-specific generative principles, which hinders their ability to co-evolve between problems and solutions (Dorst & Cross, 2001). Lawson (2004) suggested that the development of designers, progressing from novices to experts, relies

---

[1] Lintao Tang, Academy of Arts and Design, Tsinghua University, Beijing, China ; E-mail: tanglt@mail.tsinghua.edu.cn.

on continually acquiring patterns (schemas) and strategies (gambits) from accumulated design precedents. In other words, the development of a designer's professional knowledge largely depends on their ability to accumulate experiential knowledge such as strategies, principles, patterns, and techniques.

Hoök and Löwgren (2012) referred to this experiential knowledge as intermediate knowledge, which resides between design instances and theories. It is more abstract than specific instances but not as general as theories. The history of intermediate knowledge can be traced back to the pattern language in the field of architecture (Alexander et al., 1977). Later, "design patterns" in the field of software design (Gamma et al., 1995), "design heuristics" in product design (Yilmaz et al., 2011), and "strong concepts" in interaction design (Hoök & Löwgren, 2012) were successively proposed.

We argue that Intermediate knowledge can help designers engage in creative thinking, support their lateral thinking (de Bono, 1970), assist them in framing design problems (Schön, 1983), and generate more promising solutions. Numerous prior relevant studies indicated that intermediate knowledge can be constructed into design tools, especially card-based tools, to support design innovation. Lockton et al. (2013) developed the Design with Intent toolkit, and employed design patterns to help designers solve sustainable behavior problems. Zhuang and Leung (2015) employed the Interaction Tarot card-based tool to construct intermediary knowledge, assisting designers in creative ideas for interactive design. Hu et al. (2020) introduced a design heuristic tool named SDHC into classroom teaching to promote the dissemination of professional knowledge in service design. Chen and Ma (2022) employed grounded theory to extract GUI micro-interaction design techniques, providing references for designers' divergent thinking.

2. An Approach to Constructing Intermediate Knowledge

In this paper, we start from the position that "design knowledge resides in products themselves" (Cross, 1999). Design instances not only embody the knowledge of form and structure but also reflect the thinking, professional skills, and values of their designers. In other words, designers' knowledge is "embedded" within the works they create. Cross (1999) referred to this research as "Design Phenomenology".

Previous research on design instances has mainly focused on perspectives such as Design Precedents, Case Studies, Design by Analysis, and Everyday Design. Stolterman (2008) described it as "ultimate particulars," emphasizing the uniqueness of instances in the design space and the conceptual knowledge they contain; Eckert and Stacey (2000) argued that instances provide a language for designers to describe the context and possible new designs; Kim and Lee (2014) emphasized the interactive context reflected by instances in users' daily use, naming them "daily design", which can serve as a design resource to support designers' creative thinking. Whether as potential concepts, communication languages, or sources of inspiration, instances are a shared form of knowledge in the field of design. This paper will follow Lawson's suggestion to explore the schemas and gambits within design instances, which is the intermediate knowledge we refer to in this context. Then, how do we construct intermediate knowledge?

Knowledge construction involves discovering common patterns through the expression of designers' thoughts, skills, and values and subsequently forming explicit and communicable domain-specific knowledge. Just as Dieter Rams proposed "Ten Principles of Good Design" and Jakob Nielsen introduced "Usability Heuristics"

(Nielsen & Molich, 1990), accomplished designers can externalize their professional experience into various principles. This necessitates those producers of intermediate knowledge, including professional designers, design researchers, or design educators, to possess a certain level of expertise. They have the capability to abstract and generalize generative strategies, principles, patterns, and techniques from design instances. Moreover, they also need to employ specific methods to help them extract and express these pieces of knowledge.

In this context, the method of "Annotated Portfolios" (Gaver & Bowers, 2012) has been adapted to support collaborative knowledge production. This method was described as a means of explicating design thinking and communicating design outcomes (Gaver & Bowers, 2012). Designers annotate the instances in the portfolio to create textual descriptions. The text serves as a substitute for theory, establishing a relationship between the abstract and the concrete, as well as between indexing and being indexed. A single annotation holds specific significance for an individual instance and, when shared across the portfolio, attains generalized meaning. The shared annotations within the portfolio represent the "family resemblance" in design quality, which is also referred to as intermediary knowledge.

Gaver & Bowers' method involves initially annotating the first instance, then introducing a second instance to the collection and comparing their annotations. This process is repeated in subsequent instances. However, this method is more suitable for a smaller number of instances. When dealing with a larger set of instances, adaptations to the method are necessary.

The adapted method consists of three main stages: Building a Portfolio, Annotating Instances, and Comparing Annotations. Building a Portfolio involves collecting relevant instances. Annotating Instances involves understanding and expressing the creative strategies (Cross, 2006) inherent in the instances. Through the comparison of annotations, which essentially involves comparing and summarizing creative strategies, conceptual intermediate knowledge is obtained.

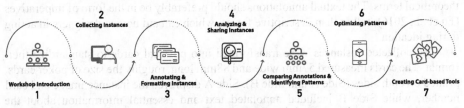

Figure 1. The process of intermediate knowledge construction.

3. A Case Study of Intermediate Knowledge Construction

In this case, we extracted creative strategies from typical cultural and creative design instances and then generalized them into design patterns. These design patterns, as a typical form of intermediate knowledge (Löwgren, 2013) were compiled into card-based tools to support the cultural and creative design practices of novice designers.

We employed a workshop for knowledge co-creation, by breaking down the process into 7 steps. The process is illustrated in Figure 1. The workshop engaged 23 second-year industrial design master's students (12 males and 11 females), with an average age of 23. These participants had systematic knowledge of design theory and practical experience in cultural and creative design. The workshop spanned three weeks and was led by two experienced teachers.

3.1. Workshop Introduction

Due to the diverse aesthetics, functionalities, and contexts inherent in design instances, combined with participants' varied motivations, experiences, and values, their attitudes towards instances reflect a wide range of multifaceted and heterogeneous characteristics (Gaver & Bowers, 2012). To ensure alignment of perspectives among all participants, the facilitator provided a comprehensive introduction to the workshop's objectives and the methodology for constructing it.

3.2. Collecting Instances

After obtaining a preliminary understanding of the subject, participants were asked to select 5 to 10 cultural and creative design instances based on their interests and preferences, thus forming a collection of instances. Granting designers freedom in collection ensured instances presented varying creative strategies or design heuristics. Given the workshop's time and efficiency constraints, the total number of instances was limited to around 150 to alleviate cognitive pressure during the annotation and comparison process.

3.3. Annotating & Formatting Instances

Participants were encouraged to adopt concise and prescriptive textual annotations to highlight the creative strategies within the instances. It should be noted that annotations involve a deep understanding of instances rather than superficial descriptions of phenomena. They can consist of open-ended and heuristic sentences rather than theoretical terms. The textual annotations should preferably be in the form of imperatives (Fu et al., 2016), rather than descriptive forms, which can aid novice designers in acting during ideation.

The collected instances were transformed into physical cards to standardize their format. The cards measured 57mm wide and 88mm long, roughly the size of poker cards, printed on both sides (Side A and Side B). Side A displayed the instance image and card number, while Side B included annotated text and essential information about the instance, such as design year, design description and the information about the designer or institution. (Figure 2)

3.4. Analyzing & Sharing Instances

Every designer shared the instances collected during the session and provided detailed explanations about their annotations. This can familiarize participants with all instances, understand how others annotate instances from different perspectives. The facilitator should guide participants to provide in-depth explanations about the instances, rather than evaluating the strengths and weaknesses of the instances and annotations. These cards would be revised based on the discussions during the session and multiple copies would be produced for use in the next stage.

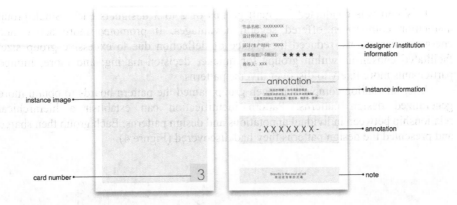

Figure 2. Instance card sample.

3.5. Comparing Annotations & Identifying Patterns

To identify patterns in creative strategies, all annotations were compared and categorized. The facilitators provided an A3-sized paper as the "Pattern Board" (Figure 3). The Pattern Board included sections for "Pattern Name," "Instance Placement Area," and "Pattern Board Guidelines." The tool used a concentric circles diagram to define affinities between annotated instances. The most representative instance, designated as the "Chief," was placed at the center to signify its typicality in terms of creative strategies. Other instances with related or similar strategies were positioned on different concentric circles based on their affinity relationships.

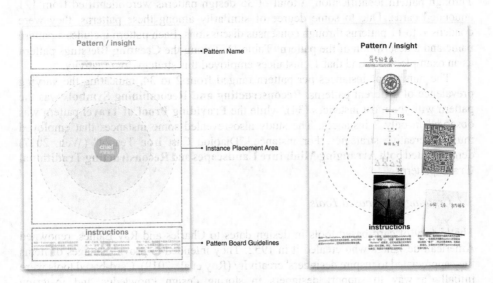

Figure 3. Pattern Board.

This step was conducted in small groups of 2 to 3 designers each. Small-group annotation comparison offered several advantages. It promoted more active and energetic discussions, reduced the chance of deflection due to excessive group size; facilitated consensus within groups for quicker decision-making; and more, limited participants more likely to discover diverse patterns.

After annotation comparison, each group named the pattern boards to obtain more generalized design patterns. Pattern identification can establish a hierarchical relationship between individual annotations and design patterns. Each group then shared and presented the design patterns they had discovered (Figure 4).

Figure 4. Design patterns sharing.

3.6. Optimizing Patterns

Through pattern identification, a total of 35 design patterns were identified from 121 annotated cards. Due to some degree of similarity among these patterns, they were condensed to 11 patterns through consensus discussions. Each pattern includes a pattern name and a description of the pattern (Table 1). Taking the **Creating Blessings** pattern as an example, we found that 11 instances employed this strategy for creativity.

The number of instances per pattern ranged from 2 to 34, indicating the varying prevalence of different patterns. **Reconstructing and Recombining Symbols** was the pattern with the most instances (34), while the **Providing Proof of Travel** pattern was observed in only 2 instances. The study also revealed some instances that employed multiple creative strategies. For instance, "Diaolou Cast Iron Teapot" (Wen, 2017) demonstrated both **Arranging Miniature Landscapes** and **Reconstructing Traditional Crafts** patterns.

3.7. Creating Card-based Tools

The history of card-based tools in design dates to Charles and Ray Eames, renowned American designers who created it in 1952. They intended to provide images of items they appreciated to inspire designers' creativity (Roy et al., 2019). Card-based tools were initially a way to support designers in storing design knowledge and fostering brainstorming. Lockton et al. (2013) found that designers, after using card tools, could spark concepts that hadn't emerged in traditional brainstorming sessions.

The 11 design patterns were presented in card format, as shown in Figure 5. The front side of each card includes the pattern name, pattern explanation, and a QR code for accessing more instances. The back side contains a representative instance and its information.

Table 1. Eleven design patterns were identified from 121 annotated cards.

Patterns	Descriptions	instances
Recreating Past Experiences	Enabling products to recreate past behaviors and experiences during usage, such as adapting cultural artifacts for new contexts using modification.	6
Enhancing User Engagement	Creating dynamic interactive effects for users during product usage, such as allowing the product to be in an incomplete state that users can complete through interaction.	14
Providing Proof of Travel	Enabling products to record visited locations and serve as a memento for sharing travel experiences.	2
Reconstructing & Recombining Symbols	Transforming cultural symbols or combining them to create a new product.	34
Arranging Miniature Landscape	Creating a sense of unfamiliarity by miniaturizing typical cultural heritage elements such as landscapes and sculptures.	11
Making symbols wearable	Viewing the body as a "display platform" and cultural symbols as "wearable exhibits."	16
Crafting Punning Allusions	Creating products using well-known " Punning Allusions" "idioms," or "catchphrases" can generate unexpected feelings.	5
Creating Blessings	Enabling users to experience the culture of blessings provided by the product.	11
Turning waste into treasure	Transforming seemingly useless local materials into commemorative items.	3
Reconstructing Traditional Crafts	Exploring the potential of incorporating traditional craftsmanship into new products' CMF.	6
Stimulating Sensory Experience	Initiating sensory exploration by engaging various sensory attributes such as visual, auditory, taste, smell, and touch to stimulate people's sensory experiences.	25

4. Empirical Evaluation of Intermediate Knowledge Cards

Through participatory observation, this study conducted two distinct cultural and creative practice projects to test the efficiency and effectiveness of intermediate knowledge cards in specific contexts.

4.1. Participant Observation

The experimental task is a virtual project for two senior students, namely the cultural and creative design of Shang and Zhou bronze culture and Beijing's central axis culture.

Before the experiments, the two designers conducted thorough investigations into Shang and Zhou Dynasty bronze culture and Beijing's central axis culture, respectively, and developed preliminary proposals. The proposals indicated that the first designer was constrained by the form and texture of bronze artifacts, while the second designer was fixated on the idea of a cultural map. This reflected that the two designers possessed varying degrees of design fixations (Jansson & Smith, 1991)

During the experiments, researchers presented the cards to designers one by one and allowed designers to browse the cards independently. Inspired by the cards, designers verbally reported the ideas they envisioned. If necessary, researchers could provide explanations for the cards but tried not to interrupt the designers' thought process. The experiment was recorded in audio format, transcribed into written notes, and used for analyzing the design activities. After the experiment, brief interviews were conducted regarding the opportunities and challenges presented by the intermediate knowledge cards. Designers were also asked to develop the solutions discussed during the session.

Figure 5. Intermediate knowledge card sample.

4.2. Results

Both designers were able to generate responses and reflections based on the intermediate knowledge cards. They generated many feasible creative ideas with specific patterns. The designers attempted to "bridge" the cultural information they had investigated with the intermediate knowledge, structuring their artifact knowledge into meaningful ideas. This "bridging" often triggered more potential ideas.

For instance, the pattern of **Reconstructing and Recombining Symbols** made designers realize that the evolution process of bronze artifacts could serve as the starting point. Another designer, in the report for the Central Axis buildings with pattern **Enhancing User Engagement**, presented various alternative ideas for users to "fill buildings with colored objects," "color it," and "use them as game pieces".

Beyond the inspiration effects of a single pattern, designers also engaged in conceptual bridging between two or more patterns. In the first experiment, the idea of "utilizing casting and welding rebuilt artifacts" was initially presented in the pattern **Enhancing User Engagement**. Inspired by **Reconstructing and Recombining Symbols**, an interesting combination emerged that went beyond rebuilding a specific bronze artifact, but also highlighted the different forms and craftsmanship across various eras. In the second experiment, the designer initially proposed the idea of "filling buildings with colored objects" in pattern **Enhancing User Engagement**. Later, Under the influence of **Stimulating Sensory Experience**, an interesting addition has been made to the idea, giving the filling a certain sense of smell. It indicates that the inspirational effect of the intermediate knowledge cards not only occurs within individual cards but also occurs between different cards. The combination of intermediate knowledge cards yields various alternative solutions in specific contexts.

Furthermore, Designers exhibited different levels of attention to the 11 cards, reflecting their varying interests. This study also indicates that not all patterns have equally strong inspirational effects across different projects. This could be attributed to two reasons. On one hand, it is indeed challenging for designers to bridge their existing knowledge of artifacts with certain intermediate knowledge. On the other hand, once designers find a satisfactory solution, their motivation to continue exploring other patterns diminishes. This could be explained by the principle of cognitive economy in the creative process.

4.3. Interviews

In the post-experiment interviews, both designers affirmed the significance of intermediate knowledge cards in their creative processes. The designer from the first experiment admitted, "I initially focused on collecting information about historical artifacts and existing cultural products..., but I only referred to their forms.... The **Reconstructing and Recombining Symbols** card inspired me significantly. I changed my perspective, and the different casting techniques in the Shang and Zhou cultures may be the idea I most want to develop....." This creative idea was realized in her final solution (Figure 6). She reported her work as follows: "By using a set of combined molds to cast soap, users experienced the casting process of bronze artifacts."

Although the design solution from another designer did not appear directly in the report, the pattern **Enhancing User Engagement** had an indirect impact on designers, and we have given an analysis of this in the results section. The designer's final design, the "Seed Ticket" for Beijing's central axis buildings (Figure 7), incorporated user engagement, and the hidden seeds inside the ticket allow users to plant it.

Figure 6. The proposal for Shang Dynasty bronze culture: Handmade Soap Series

Figure 7. The proposal for Beijing Central Axis culture: 'Seed Ticket' Series

5. Conclusions

The study of intermediate knowledge can be traced back to Alexander's pattern language and the tradition of design thinking by Cross and Lawson. It is the general characteristic of solutions, the design elements of potential design solutions, having a generative role that can be applied by designers to new problem contexts.

This study extracted 11 design patterns from 121 creative cultural instances through a process of knowledge co-creation. These patterns, serving as typical intermediate knowledge, transformed into a card-based tool to support creative ideation. The extracted design patterns do not exhaust all possible intermediary knowledge but reflect the shared interests of participants in the process of knowledge co-creation.

Through two experiments, this study indicates that intermediate knowledge does indeed have a potential inspirational effect during the ideation phase for novice designers. The findings suggest that designers consciously bridge their existing knowledge with intermediate knowledge. This deliberate bridging effectively enhances design solutions and alleviates design fixations. Additionally, it was found that designers tend to further develop their ideas from the previous pattern and create conceptual bridges between two or more patterns, which effectively promotes the deepening and iteration of the solution.

In conclusion, we believe that intermediate knowledge holds some potential academic contributions. First, it can integrate and structure design knowledge from specific domains. Second, it externalizes the implicit knowledge of expert designers, facilitating the transfer of design knowledge between experts and novices. Third, it can enhance the efficiency and effectiveness of designers in design practice, particularly for novice designers. Furthermore, it can also assist innovative teams, companies, and organizations in knowledge innovation, fostering a spiral of knowledge evolution within the organization.

References

[1] B. Archer, A View of the Nature of Design Research, *In: Jacques R, Powell J (eds): Design: Science: Method*. Westbury House, Guildford, 1981, 30-47.

[2] B. Archer, The Nature of Research, *Co-design* January (1995), 6-13.

[3] N. Cross, Expertise in design: An overview, *Design Studies* **25**:5 (2004), 427–441.

[4] J. Darke, The primary generator and the design process, *Design Studies* **1**:1 (1979), 36-44.

[5] K. Dorst & N. Cross, Creativity in the design process: co-evolution of problem–solution. *Design Studies* **22**:5 (2001), 425-437.

[6] B. Lawson, Schemata, gambits and precedent: Some factors in design expertise, *Design Studies* **25**:5 (2004), 443–457.

[7] K. Höök & J. Löwgren, Strong concepts: Intermediate-level knowledge in interaction Design research, *ACM Transactions on Computer-Human Interaction* **19**:3 (2012), 1-18.

[8] C. Alexander, *A Pattern Language: Towns, Buildings, Construction*, Oxford University Press, 1977.

[9] E. Gamma et al., *Design Patterns: Elements of Reusable Object-Oriented Software*, Addison-Wesley, 1994.

[10] S. Yilmaz & C. M. Seifert, Creativity through design heuristics: A case study of expert product design. *Design Studies* **32**:4 (2011), 384-415.

[11] E. de Bono, Lateral thinking: creativity step by step, Harper & Row, 1970.

[12] D. A. Schön, The Reflective Practitioner: How Professionals Think in Action, Ashgate, 1983.

[13] D. Lockton et al., Exploring Design Patterns for Sustainable Behaviour, *The Design Journal* **16**:4 (2013), 431-459.

[14] David W. Chung & Rung-Huei Liang, The Construction of Intermediate-Level Knowledge in Ideation with Interaction Tarot, *Journal of Design* **20**:3 (2015), 21-44.

[15] Y. Hu et al., Practice and Thinking of Classroom Teaching Mode Based on Heuristic Service Design, *Zhuangshi* **330** (2020), 76-79.

[16] Chun-Ching Chen & Jia Yang Ma, Use Grounded Theory to Explore the Design Tool of Microinteractions, *Journal of Design* **27**:2 (2022), 1-23.

[17] N. Cross, Design Research: A Disciplined Conversation. *Design Issues* **15**:2 (1999), 5-10.

[18] E. Stolterman & M. Wiberg, Concept-driven interaction design research, *Human-Computer Interaction*, **25**:2 (2010), 95–118.

[19] C. Eckert & M. Stacey, Sources of inspiration: a language of design. *Design Studies* **21** (2000), 523-538.

[20] H. Kim & W. Lee, Everyday design as a design resource. *International Journal of Design* **8**:1(2014), 1-13.

[21] J. Nielsen & R. Molich, Heuristic evaluation of user interfaces, *CHI '90: Proceedings of the SIGCHI Conference on Human Factors in Computing Systems* (1990), 249–256.

[22] B. Gaver & J. Bowers, Annotated Portfolios. *Interaction* **19**:4 (2012), 40–49.

[23] N. Cross, *Designerly Ways of Knowing*, Springer, London, 2006.

[24] J. Löwgren, Annotated Portfolios and Other Forms of Intermediate-Level Knowledge, *Interaction* **20**:1(2013), 30-34.

[25] K. K. Fu et al., Design principles: Literature review, analysis, and future directions. *Journal of Mechanical Design* **138**:10 (2016), 101103.

[26] R, Roy & J. P. Warren, Card-based design tools: A review and analysis of 155 card decks for designers and designing, *Design Studies* **63** (2019), 125–154.

[27] D. G. Jansson & S. M. Smith, Design fixation, *Design Studies* **12**:1 (1991), 3-11.

Design Studies and Intelligence Engineering
L.C. Jain et al. (Eds.)
© 2024 The Authors.
This article is published online with Open Access by IOS Press and distributed under the terms
of the Creative Commons Attribution Non-Commercial License 4.0 (CC BY-NC 4.0).
doi:10.3233/FAIA231439

AI-Driven Interactive Painting Synthesis System for Children's Art Education

Mengyue TANG[a], Baixi XING[a,1], Zhichuan TANG[a], Pan ZOU[b], Jiayin YU[a] and
Haojing ZHANG[a]
[a] *Zhejiang University of Technology, Hangzhou, China*
xingbaixi@zjut.edu.cn
[b] *Staatlichen Akademie der Bildenden Künste Stuttgart, Stuttgart, Germany*
panzou@gmx.de

Abstract. Art education is important to the overall development of children, and art training can start from improving children's art appreciation and perception. In this study, we built an interactive painting synthesis system for children's art education to let them know about world famous paintings and art history. The interactive learning systems can provide engaging ways of art education based on image synthesis, style transfer and animation generation technology. Specifically, an image dataset of famous paintings was established for painting synthesis and an application "ARTIST" was developed based on First Order Motion Method. The system "ARTIST" can attract children's active participation via interesting art creation interaction and enhance their learning motivation in their exploration.

Keywords. Art education, Painting synthesis, First order motion

1. Introduction

Art education helps children develop their language, social communication, decision-making, risk-taking, and invention skills. The artificial intelligence industry is booming over recent years, and the field of children's art education is undergoing tremendous change. The continuous development of digital technology provides children with varied learning experiences. Through interactive learning, children can be deeply involved in the learning process, which increases their interest of learning. Artistic learning, as a creative form of education, is also gradually emerging in the trend of digital children's education [1]. Digital media and applications enable children to appreciate and learn about works of art in a virtual environment, thus developing their aesthetic cognitive ability [2].

In this work, we applied image synthesis and animation generation techniques to develop a learning system "ARTIST" which guided children to learn about art appreciation and art history. Specifically, the system allows users to interact by clicking on image segments in the painting to explore detailed information about the artwork with an immersive experience. Additionally, the system ensures introduction of new and engaging activities, attracting children's active participation and enhancing their learning motivation. Besides, the system facilitates comprehensive online art

---

[1] Corresponding Author: Baixi Xing, xingbaixi@zjut.edu.cn.

history education, enriching children's knowledge. The research roadmap of this work is presented in Figure 1.

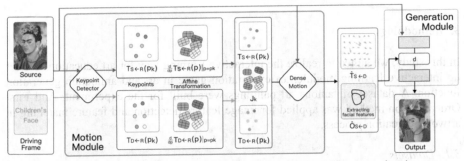

Figure 1. Research roadmap of painting synthesis exploration for children's art education.

The main contribution of this work can be concluded in two aspects: (1) A dataset of famous paintings with image segmentation was established; (2) An "ARTIST" application for children's art education was developed based on First Order Motion Method.

2. Related Work

2.1. Research and development of digital art exploration applications

Over the past few years, a number of interactive learning systems have emerged that aimed to provide more engaging ways of learning through AI technology [3]. For example, virtual museum applications can lead children to explore history and culture, and digital drawing tools can help children to create their own works of art [4]. In addition, some digital art applications were developed based on image generation and style transfer techniques that enabled users to blend their own photographs with famous paintings to create personalized art works [5].

2.2. Image synthesis and animation generation techniques

Various techniques can provide support on art style transfer and animation generation, including convolutional network, Generative Adversarial Network and Transformer model etc. [6].

First Order Motion has been widely utilized for dynamic generation and transformation of images and videos. This model, based on deep learning technology, can apply the motion and style of a source image or video to a target image or video, thereby achieving style transfer and animation generation [7]. In the existing research, this model is extensively employed in various domains, such as video animation generation, expression transformation, and artistic creation. It has remarkable capabilities of creating vivid effect in multimedia generation and transformation [8].

FFmpeg provides powerful support for digital art and animation as a multimedia processing tool. It can be used for tasks such as video compositing, format conversion and animation rendering. In our study, we applied FFmpeg to combine the generated animation effects with images of famous paintings to create smooth and vivid interactive scenes.

3. Methodology

In this study, we aimed to realize the interactive learning way for art education. We set up interactive learning module, art exploration game in art and animation generation function. A dataset of famous art paintings were built for the experiment. And First Order Motion method was applied for image feature detection and feature matching in artwork recreation process.

3.1. Datasets

We collected images of world famous paintings from various artists in different periods. These data were filtered, standardized and converted into a standardized .jpg format for processing by the system[9]. We acquired images of famous paintings from public art databases, museum websites and online art communities. Then we conducted image preprocessing, including noise reduction, contrast enhancement and color correction to ensure image quality and consistency [10]. The dataset is presented as a gallery in the system, in which users can browse through various famous paintings. The information of the artworks is shown in the labeling, including the artist, art period, and style.

3.2. Image segmentation

In the painting exploration function, users have the opportunity to engage with the detailed information of the painting segments, facilitating exploration of distinct sections. Thus, image segmentation was performed on the paintings to extract specific regions [11][12]. The applied method is shown as follows.

Algorithm 1 : Image Segmentation and Detail Extraction
(1)   *Initialization : import cv2 ,import numpy as np*
(2)   *def image_segmentation(image):* # *Perform image segmentation using OpenCV to extract detail regions* # *Return the segmented detail image pass* # *Read the painting image* *painting_image = cv2.imread('painting.jpg')* # *Perform image segmentation and detail* *extraction detail_image =* *image_segmentation(painting_image)*
(3)   *Output: cv2.imshow('Detail Image',* *detail_image),cv2.waitKey(0) ,cv2.destroyAllWindows()*

3.3. First Order Motion

To achieve the animation of famous paintings, the initial step involves faces detection in artworks. Subsequently, First Order Motion was employed to extract pre-recorded reference videos from the database [10][11]. Then, audio and video elements were integrated by FFmpeg.

In model training process, we used a diverse video dataset of the same object category. Our model learns to reconstruct training videos by merging a single frame with a learned motion latent representation [12]. It captures motion via keypoint shifts and local affine transformations in frame pairs from the same video. During model testing, our model applied learned motion to pairs of source image and created video frames.

This sequential program brought the characters depicted in the artwork to life and dynamically introduced themselves. The applied method is presented as follows.

Algorithm 2 : Paintings Motion Generation

---

(1)   **Initialization   :   import   cv2,import   imageio,from skimage.transform import resize,from demo import load_checkpoints, make_animation**

---

(2)   # Load pre-trained model
**generator, kp_detector =
load_checkpoints(config_path='config/vox-256.yaml',
checkpoint_path='vox-cpk.pth.tar')**

Read the painting detail image
painting_detail = cv2.imread('painting_detail.jpg')

Prepare user photo (can be your own photo)
**user_photo = cv2.imread('user_photo.jpg')
user_photo = resize(user_photo, (256, 256))[..., :3]**

Generate animation using the First Order Motion model
**predictions = make_animation(user_photo, painting_detail,
generator, kp_detector, relative=True)**

---

(3)   **Output: for frame in predictions: cv2.imshow('Animated
Painting', frame)
if cv2.waitKey(25) & 0xFF == ord('q'):
break,cv2.destroyAllWindows()**

3.4. "Picturesque" interactive experience

We hope to create an immersive "picturesque" artistic experience for children, making them feel like being in the scene of the artwork To implement the "Picturesque" experience, we blended painting features with users' portrait characters. The method is illustrated as follows [13].

Algorithm 3 : Picturesque
(1)   ***Initialization*** *: import imageio,from skimage.transform import resize,from demo import load_checkpoints, make_animation*
(2)   *# Load pre-trained model* ***generator, kp_detector =*** ***load_checkpoints(config_path='config/vox-256.yaml',*** ***checkpoint_path='vox-cpk.pth.tar')*** *# Read the painting detail image and user photo* ***painting_detail = cv2.imread('detail_image.jpg') user_photo*** *= cv2.imread('user_photo.jpg')* *# Resize user photo to match the painting detail* ***user_photo = resize(user_photo, (256, 256))[..., :3]*** *# Embed user photo using the First Order Motion model* ***predictions = make_animation(user_photo, painting_detail,*** ***generator, kp_detector, relative=True)***
(3)   ***Output:*** *imageio.mimsave('embedded_animation.gif',* *[img_as_ubyte(frame) for frame in predictions])*

4. Application

An art learning system "ARTIST" was developed based on the proposed method. It can guide children to learn about famous paintings through interactive games [14]. Users can access our "ARTIST" learning system through their mobile devices, and learn knowledge by clicking on the segments in the paintings to get dynamic interactive feedback. The system architecture and module design are shown in Figure 2.

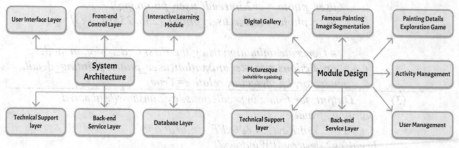

Figure 2. System architecture and module design.

4.1. Application modules

The main application modules of this system can be concluded in three aspects:

- The Interactive Learning Module is devised to enhance children's comprehension and learning of renowned artworks. The Interactive Learning mode of "Famous Paintings in Motion" predominantly enables individuals or objects within famous paintings to introduce themselves via the First Order Motion model, imparting the knowledge of famous paintings to children through a distinctive interactive approach.

- The Detail Exploration Game constitutes an inventive exploration module founded on image segmentation technology: participants are asked to uncover concealed intricacies within paintings, including objects and expressions of secondary characters, which can train children's ability of observation and analysis [15][16].

- The "Picturesque" function empowers users to integrate their personal photos into renowned artworks, fostering captivating interactive scenes. Users can select different paintings, and observe subsequent interactions with the characters in the artwork. This personalized interactive experience helps stimulate children's creativity and imagination [17].

4.2. User interface demonstration

The specific usage process of the system is as follows:

- Firstly, the homepage displays the introduction of online activities and present famous painting gallery of the day for users to enjoy and learn, see Figure 3.

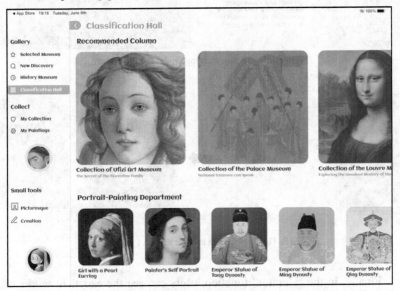

Figure 3. Homepage interface of the system.

- Secondly, users can also click on the resource library to view famous artistic paintings, with a detailed list of the artwork name, art period, artist's name, and exhibition museum of the paintings etc.

- Thirdly, each painting is set with interactive learning panels for further exploration. Specifically, story panels can provide introduction of the artwork, see Figure 4. And exploration panel presents interactive learning of the details of the paintings and artistic style transfer effect of user portrait image, see Figure 5.

Figure 4. Interactive learning module of the system.

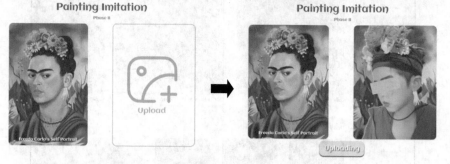

Figure 5. The artistic style transfer effect of user portrait.

- Finally, in the "Curator" function, users can see the excellent works of other people from previous events, while in the "Personal center", users can see their own generated artworks exhibition.

5. Conclusion

In this study, we constructed an interactive learning system for children's art education. The system allows children to learn about famous paintings through interaction, in order to provide a rich and diverse learning experience. Through this research, we created an engaging way of art learning for children, which increased the motivation and interest in their learning process.

In the future, we plan to further improve the learning experience of the system in the follow aspects:

- Collect more painting images to expand the dataset.

- Explore more innovative interactive learning modules, such as audio guidance and sentiment analysis, to create multidimensional sensory experience.

- Introduce intelligent recommendation algorithms to customize personalized learning plans and recommended content based on users' interests and learning history.

6. Acknowledgments

This study is partly supported by Fundamental Research Funds for the Provincial Universities of Zhejiang (GB202003008).

References

[1] R. Z. Cheng, "ArtMatch: Classifying Famous Paintings and Matching Them with Children's Artwork," in 2020 International Conference on Computational Science and Computational Intelligence (CSCI), Las Vegas, NV, USA: IEEE, Dec. 2020, pp. 1487–1490. doi: 10.1109/CSCI51800.2020.00275.

[2] K. Choi and H. Kim, "The Effect of Question-based Havruta Famous Painting Appreciation on Children's Painting Appreciation Ability and Painting Representation Ability," HSS21, vol. 11, no. 6, pp. 2665–2680, Dec. 2020, doi: 10.22143/HSS21.11.6.188.

[3] B. Wu, "Design and Implementation of Painting Style Rendering System Based on Deep Learning," in Frontier Computing, J. C. Hung, N. Y. Yen, and J.-W. Chang, Eds., in Lecture Notes in Electrical Engineering, vol. 1031. Singapore: Springer Nature Singapore, 2023, pp. 1779–1784. doi: 10.1007/978-981-99-1428-9_239.

[4] Y. Hong and J. Kim, "Art painting detection and identification based on deep learning and image local features," Multimed Tools Appl, vol. 78, no. 6, pp. 6513–6528, Mar. 2019, doi: 10.1007/s11042-018-6387-5.

[5] S. Yang, S. Yang, W. Yang, and J. Liu, "Automatic portrait oil painter: joint domain stylization for portrait images," Multimed Tools Appl, vol. 77, no. 13, pp. 16113–16130, Jul. 2018, doi: 10.1007/s11042-017-5190-z.

[6] M. K. Islam Zim, "OpenCV and Python for Emotion Analysis of Face Expressions," in 2023 3rd International Conference on Innovative Practices in Technology and Management (ICIPTM), Uttar Pradesh, India: IEEE, Feb. 2023, pp. 1–7. doi: 10.1109/ICIPTM57143.2023.10118007.

[7] H. Gupta and C. Sharma, "Face mask detection using transfer learning and OpenCV in live videos," in 2022 International Conference on Fourth Industrial Revolution Based Technology and Practices (ICFIRTP), Uttarakhand, India: IEEE, Nov. 2022, pp. 115–119. doi: 10.1109/ICFIRTP56122.2022.10059441.

[8] A. Siarohin, S. Lathuilière, S. Tulyakov, E. Ricci and N. Sebe, "Animating Arbitrary Objects via Deep Motion Transfer," 2019 IEEE/CVF Conference on Computer Vision and Pattern Recognition (CVPR), Long Beach, CA, USA, 2019, pp. 2372-2381, doi: 10.1109/CVPR.2019.00248.

[9] B. P. M and J. F. Daniel, "First Order Motion Model for Image Animation and Deep Fake Detection: Using Deep Learning," 2022 International Conference on Computer Communication and Informatics (ICCCI), Coimbatore, India, 2022, pp. 1-7, doi: 10.1109/ICCCI54379.2022.9740969.

[10] L. Bai, T. Zhao, and X. Xiu, "Exploration of computer vision and image processing technology based on OpenCV," in 2022 International Seminar on Computer Science and Engineering Technology (SCSET), Indianapolis, IN, USA: IEEE, Jan. 2022, pp. 145–147. doi: 10.1109/SCSET55041.2022.00042.

[11] A. Bhat, R. K. Jha, and V. Kedia, "Robust Face Detection and Recognition using Image Processing and OpenCV," in 2022 6th International Conference on Computing Methodologies and Communication (ICCMC), Erode, India: IEEE, Mar. 2022, pp. 1273–1278. doi: 10.1109/ICCMC53470.2022.9753792.

[12] A. Datta, O. K. Yadav, Y. Singh, S. S, K. M, and S. E, "Real-Time Face Swapping System using OpenCV," in 2021 Third International Conference on Inventive Research in Computing Applications (ICIRCA), Coimbatore, India: IEEE, Sep. 2021, pp. 1081–1086. doi: 10.1109/ICIRCA51532.2021.9545010.

[13] A. Alotaibi, "Deep Generative Adversarial Networks for Image-to-Image Translation: A Review," Symmetry, vol. 12, no. 10, p. 1705, Oct. 2020, doi: 10.3390/sym12101705.

[14] M. Konstantakis, E. Kalatha, and G. Caridakis, "Cultural Heritage, Serious Games and User Personas Based on Gardner's Theory of Multiple Intelligences: 'The Stolen Painting' Game," in Games and Learning Alliance, A. Liapis, G. N. Yannakakis, M. Gentile, and M. Ninaus, Eds., in Lecture Notes in Computer Science, vol. 11899. Cham: Springer International Publishing, 2019, pp. 490–500. doi: 10.1007/978-3-030-34350-7_47.

[15] A. Kumari Sirivarshitha, K. Sravani, K. S. Priya, and V. Bhavani, "An approach for Face Detection and Face Recognition using OpenCV and Face Recognition Libraries in Python," in 2023 9th International Conference on Advanced Computing and Communication Systems (ICACCS), Coimbatore, India: IEEE, Mar. 2023, pp. 1274–1278. doi: 10.1109/ICACCS57279.2023.10113066.

[16] P. Patel, P. Morreale, and G. Avirappattu, "Assessment of Static and Dynamic Image Presentation for User Cognition and Understanding," in HCI International 2022 - Late Breaking Papers. Design, User Experience and Interaction, M. Kurosu, S. Yamamoto, H. Mori, M. M. Soares, E. Rosenzweig, A. Marcus, P.-L. P. Rau, D. Harris, and W.-C. Li, Eds., in Lecture Notes in Computer Science, vol. 13516. Cham: Springer International Publishing, 2022, pp. 450–459. doi: 10.1007/978-3-031-17615-9_31.

[17] D. S.-M. Liu and N. Tu, "Video cloning for paintings via artistic style transfer," SIViP, vol. 15, no. 1, pp. 111–119, Feb. 2021, doi: 10.1007/s11760-020-01730-3.

Design Studies and Intelligence Engineering
L.C. Jain et al. (Eds.)
© 2024 The Authors.
This article is published online with Open Access by IOS Press and distributed under the terms
of the Creative Commons Attribution Non-Commercial License 4.0 (CC BY-NC 4.0).
doi:10.3233/FAIA231440

"Ask Aloud Protocol": Toward a Participant-Driven Question-Asking Design Research Method

Lintao TANG [a,1], Sihang WANG [b,2]

[a,b] *Academy of Arts & Design, Tsinghua University, Beijing,*
China

Abstract. In the field of problem formulation for design research, the conventional Think Aloud Protocol (TAP) has faced challenges in addressing complex problems such as Wicked Problems (WPs) over its two-decade history. Instead, the utilization of questions as a verbal tool has emerged as a more effective approach, producing insightful outcomes for intricate design challenges. Moreover, the largely untapped potential of participant-generated questions in design research holds promise for reducing subjective biases in designer-driven problem formulations and strengthening the role of participants. This study presents the Participant-Driven Ask Aloud Protocol (AAP) and employs it in spatial planning experiments at both QILI South Urban Village and the China World Mall's Transit-Oriented Development (TOD) in Beijing, China. The analysis highlights AAP's effectiveness in broadening the scope of generative design possibilities and facilitating a more precise and efficient identification of WPs in the design process.

Keywords. Think Aloud Protocol, Ask Aloud Protocol, Question-Asking, Participatory Design, Spatial Experiment

1. Introduction

As a problem-intensive process, design activities stimulate deeper questioning compared to reading comprehension and classroom learning within intellectually interactive environments [1]. Researchers have suggested that design should primarily focus on solving problems to reach a final solution [2]. However, the introduction of the conceptions such as "Wicked Problem" [3] and "Ill-Structured Problem" [4] revealed that many modern design issues are intricate, lacking clear definitions, and have open-ended characteristics. These problems involve complex connections that are hard to clarify and often lack sufficient information for resolution [5]. Complex issues that were once considered straightforward within the design domain are yielding unforeseen downstream complexities over time [3]. Conventional methods of problem identification and definition are no longer adequate in today's intricate design landscape. One such typical method, the established "Think Aloud Protocol" technique, originally proposed by Lawson [6], is often used to delve into participants' perspectives. This method underscores the validity of insights generated from verbal data for cognitive exploration. However, even within participatory frameworks, designers often retain primary influence, framing participants' thinking within predefined parameters, for instance,

---

[1] Corresponding Author: Tanglt@mail.tsinghua.edu.cn
[2] Corresponding Author: wang-sh22@mails.tsinghua.edu.cn

"design a comfortable car" or "design a habitable building." These predefined objectives constrict the realm within which participants can contribute to the design quandary.

Therefore, the essential challenge lies in tackling designer subjectivity during the research phase. Additionally, effective identification and resolution of complex design problems demand innovative mediums and methods to amplify generative design capacity in participatory research.

2. Constraints in Designer Problem Identification and Participatory Design

2.1 Constraints Imposed by Designer-Defined Problems

When presenting a design problem, designers often demonstrate a preference for exploring potential solutions rather than preemptively articulating all facets of the problem [7][8]. Nevertheless, Cross [9] introduces a more nuanced approach that distinguishes between the practices of expert and novice designers, advocating for active problem construction as opposed to mere problem-solving. Cross further suggests that adept designers, in treating well-defined design challenges as if they were ill-defined [10][11], broaden the spectrum of conceivable problem-solving avenues. The significance of problem formulation is accentuated by its intrinsic link to idea generation. Notably, scholars Dorse and Cross [12], in their endeavor to unravel the enigma of the "creative leap"[12], ascertain that devoting more time to comprehending and defining the problem is connected to yielding more creative outcomes.

The initial concept models of design thinking, originating in the 1980s, primarily directed researchers' attention towards investigating the "designer's cognitive approach" [9][13]. Within this phase, design was comprehended through the lens of the designer's role in defining problems, shaping the evolution of the design domain, and functioning as the generator of creativity. However, this framework had an inherent deficiency: it disregarded the considerable influence of one's cultural perspectives, values, and biases on the veiled realm of creativity [8][14]. The designer's framing of the problem space unavoidably bears such personal perceptions, thereby engendering subjective limitations. This phenomenon interconnects with design "Fixation" [15], a concept describing the inappropriate application of preconceived knowledge to novel contexts. It delineates a cognitive process where individuals adhere to a consistent mental framework, often unconsciously. In this regard, designers' cognitive processes can also be restricted in specific directions [16].

Therefore, in the realm where problem formulation significantly impacts design creativity, the conventional designer-centric authority over problem identification and formulation necessitates a reconsideration. This prompts a shift, advocating a diluted designer-driven influence during problem definition. Addressing this, Buchanan [16] suggests that design problems don't necessarily stem from specific issues; rather, they arise from a "Quasi-subject Matter" [16], involving the creation of a problem domain without predetermined constraints. Researchers also note that depending on problems initiated solely by designers often results in conventional designs rather than groundbreaking ones, achievable only by a few exceptional design talents [17]. However, relying on chance is not a viable solution. To confront this challenge, contemporary discourse revolves around reducing the dominance of the "expert" while concurrently enhancing the role of design stakeholders [18].

2.2 Constraints in Designer-Led Participatory Design

The popularity of "Participatory Design" [19][20] is grounded in the notion that participants frequently possess experiential and cognitive insights beyond those of designers, thereby fostering diversity through a range of cognitive styles. Schön [21] contends that the boundary between the designer's unique realm, the Design World, and its integration within the broader design community remains an evolving question warranting continual re-evaluation in each design endeavor. In this context, the domain of cognitive participatory design converges with fields such as "User Psychology" [22] and "Distributed Cognition" [23]. However, even in design meetings attended by participants, the discourse often adheres to the designer's guidance, characterized by prescribed dialogues and structured inquiries (e.g., Questionnaire and Focus Group Method [24]). Consequently, debates concerning the subjectivity of design persist. Within the pre-problem definition phase of design, much remains to be explored regarding participant perceptions. Yet, an absence of suitable mediating methods currently inhibits such investigations.

3. Participant-Driven "Ask Aloud Protocol" and Case Overview

3.1 Participant-Driven "Ask Aloud Protocol"

The Think Aloud Protocol (TAP) method for design cognitive research is widely recognized as a central technique for probing thought processes [25][26][27]. It requires participants to explicitly articulate their actions and reflections while undertaking tasks, thereby revealing feelings of contentment, perplexity, or frustration with interface elements [28]. This process enables observers to gain insights into cognitive processes. Description and information acquired using methods as such significantly shape how designers approach conceptualization, influencing both the process and outcome. This affects idea generation and processing [29][30]. TAP produces various forms of spoken content, with the majority being Statements. Statements are not highly specific when the essence of the question domain is unknown. In contrast, the discourse form of questions shows promise in uncovering design potential, as the act of formulating questions often implies the generation of additional design opportunities [31].

During the trajectory of design impact thinking, questioning plays a crucial role in scrutinizing design discourse [31][32]. Moreover, the act of questioning itself is deemed indicative, for the questions themselves can offer substantial information and knowledge [33]. Questioning triggers the questioner's pre-existing knowledge, facilitating a more profound examination of complicated problems. It requires them to engage in higher-level reflective cognitive operations that access multifaceted dimensions of individuality. Therefore, questioning not only constitutes a commonplace cognitive activity in human lives but also possesses an exceptional aspect [34]. However, question-asking is a universal propensity, not limited solely to designers. Notably, participants engage in questioning in their daily lives, with their queries often arising from their own life experiences, typically differing from the questions curated by designers within the framework of a design project.

According to the above discussion, this study introduces a novel design research approach, the Participant-Driven Ask Aloud Protocol (AAP). It suggests that, when the designer's guidance is reduced, compared to the conventional TPA method, the AAP method is expected to enhance the quantity and quality of design generative possibilities, foster creativity in preliminary investigations, and counter design "Fixation". Additionally, the new method can be more effective in identifying and tackling design issues such as the WPs. The subsequent section of the paper has two objectives: examining existing instances of using "question-asking" in design and validating the efficacy of the AAP method through a comparison of two spatial planning and design experiments in Beijing, China.

3.2 Case Overview of Question-Asking Research in Design

Within this section, the aim is to identify research gaps in the application of participant questioning within design practices. To achieve this, the paper utilizes Eris' [31] question taxonomy as a framework to summarize and analyze classic experimental instances. A total of six cases are categorized into three classes based on the questioning subjects: "question initiated by designers," "question initiated by design educators and students," and "question initiated by participants and users." These tripartite case types are examined across three primary dimensions: "expert (designers, engineers) guidance," " design objectives," and "research findings."

3.2.1 Assessment Method: Question Taxonomy

Eris [31] refined and extended Graesser and McMahen's [35] question taxonomy of Low-Level Questions (LLQ) and Deep-level Reasoning Questions (DRQ), and introduced a category typical to design activities, termed Generative Questions (GDQ). GDQs encompass divergent thinking, as questioners deviate from mere facts and explore potentialities emerged from various prompts [31]. Both LLQs and GDQs share a common expectation of acquiring specific answers or sets of answers. LLQs and GDQs primarily focus on discerning facts and comprehending them, whereas generative questions prioritize envisioning possibilities [36].

When dealing with LLQs, designers might position themselves as solution executors, which means producing specific outputs aligned with client needs without extensive contribution to the problem domain. Design creativity aligns more cohesively with GDQs, premised on the idea that multiple known alternatives and unknown answers coexist, irrespective of their veracity. In essence, GDQs aim to reveal alternatives to established answers and generate unanticipated possibilities [2]. Hence, an increasing influx of questions corresponds to an expanding spectrum of design possibilities. Eris [31] provides examples such as DRQ: "Why does the moon rise at night?" In contrast, a GDQ example is "How does a person get to the moon?" In the latter, the questioner explores potential methods for reaching the moon, prioritizing potential answers over their factual correctness. This highlights the generative question's ability to expand exploration.

3.2.2 Design Expert Initiated Question-Asking Scenarios (Table 1)

Eris [31] showcased examples of three distinct design scenarios, wherein audio-visual and transcript data of questions posed by designers and engineers were extracted and analyzed. These scenarios encompass: a global design team focusing on passenger cars and light trucks in the United States; a project involving paper bicycle prototyping by four mechanical engineering design graduates; and the creation of a prototype device for measuring body contours' length by three mechanical engineering students. Notably, these research scenarios center on designers' design processes, with the questioners being the designers themselves. Importantly, these scenarios lack engagement of design participants or users, and their design objectives are limited to specific object forms.

Similarly, a study by Aurisicchio, et al. [37] observed product reasoning activities within an engineering design department over a nine-week period. Through verbal protocol analyses, the researchers assisted engineering designers in formulating design questions, aiming to aid the development of new products as well as process and strategy refinement, with a clear focus on problem-solving. For instance, "How can a front roller bearing (FRB) be adequately lubricated and cooled at low cost?" was posed. The core of this practice revolves around experts (engineering designers) seeking cost-effective solutions for lubrication and cooling, rather than solely the act of posing the question itself.

In both cases, design participants and users were absent, and the design goals were explicitly oriented toward solving specific design problems. These goals significantly shaped the problem-solving process and limited the exploration of various possibilities, a limitation that this paper seeks to investigate. In these cases, the questions posed were primarily LLQs and DRQs, with a notably lower occurrence of GDQs compared to the previous scenarios. Notably, only 15.4 percent of the questions in Eris' [31] study were identified as GDQs, indicating a relatively small proportion.

Table 1. Overview of Design Cases Involving "Question-Asking".

Researcher	Question Initiator	Expert Guidance	Design Objective	Findings
Eris, 2003 [31]	Designer	Yes	Develop vehicles, paper bicycle prototypes and equipment prototypes	Proposed a new design question classification-GDQ.
Aurisicchio, et al., 2007 [37]	Designer	Yes	Develop Engineering Products	Provided guidance to novice designers on essential questions to ask.
Cardoso, et al., 2014 [38]	Design Student & Teacher	Yes	No	Recommended teachers, design reviews to ask student LLQs and provide instructions for students.
Sonalkar, et al., 2016 [39]	Design Education Reviewer	Yes	No	Highlighted the importance of student participation in articulating PV in design reviews.
Cardoso, et al., 2016 [2]	Design Student	Yes	Design a 21st Century Birthday Celebration	Captured Inflections in design discourse and the impact of rare Inflections to resist design fixation.
Kato, 1986 [34]	Computer User	Yes	Improve computer user manual	Offered insights for computer manual design and revision.

3.2.3 Design Question-Asking in Educational Scenarios (Table 1)

Cardoso et al. [38] analyzed design comments (transcripts) from undergraduate industrial designers, instructors, and clients during review sessions. The study concluded that design instructors and reviewers should emphasize the use of LLQs and provide guidance to students. Teachers and clients collectively posed more questions than students did, including a higher number of GDQs. For instance, an instructor suggested, "Can you do something in this area between this surface and that surface? Maybe, create a shelf?" In such conversations, experts and clients take the lead. Importantly, LLQs were more prevalent than DRQs and GDQs in this study, regardless of whether they were asked by students, teachers, or clients. However, the questions posed by clients, who represent design participants, were not specifically examined. The essence of the research lies in fostering synergy across various facets of design education, rather than focusing on generative design problems.

Sonalkar et al. [39] examined video and audio material from reviews presented at a design research symposium. These reviews encompassed Industrial Design and Mechanical Engineering projects conducted by design students. The objective was to visualize student interactions with the reviewing Professional Vision (PV), emphasize the importance of student engagement in articulating PV. Through verbal content analysis, this study found that most of the content consisted of declarative discourses, with questions predominantly falling into the LLQ category, such as "Is the Washer and Dryer two different things?" or "Is this on the Wall?" Only a limited number of DRQs and GDQs were present. Fundamentally, the research focused on problem-solving and improving design education, with both the design reviewer and the student acting as experts.

Cardoso et al. [2] investigated the impact of new media on the creative process, using data derived from collaboration between an American greeting card company and researchers at Midwestern University. A multidisciplinary team of seven students undertook the task of designing a 21st-century birthday celebration, operating within a restricted design goal. The study examined rare inflection points in design discourse, indicating that these points tend to arise during intensive idea generation phases. The team, playing the role of designers, did not incorporate greeting card users. The study summarized the average occurrence (per hour) of LLQ, DRQ, and GDQ, with LLQs significantly outweighing DRQs and GDQs.

All three research cases are related to the development of design education, primarily involving design experts or students. The shift from "questioning" to "obtaining answers" characterizes iterative processes of knowledge acquisition in these contexts, signifying the central aim of improving knowledge acquisition among design students. These cases emphasize the significance of the answers, rather than the design generative potentials, of the questions themselves.

3.2.4 User Initiated Question-Asking Scenarios (Table 1)

Takashi's [34] study centered on computer user interfaces during the 1980s, presenting the Question-Asking Protocol as an alternative to the conventional TAP. The aim was to elucidate users' expectations for interactive computer systems, specifically informing the development of new manuals and the enhancement of existing ones. Takashi's approach involved observing the actions of computer users guided by manuals and prompting them to pose questions when encountering unsatisfactory behavior. However, each user's question received an immediate response from a computer expert. For instance, "P: I want to restore that sentence. How do I do that? T: To return to the marker, move the cursor to a line and then move it to the right." This process essentially maintained an expert-led problem-solving dynamic, where participants primarily posed LLQs, promptly addressed by an expert in an instant.

The Question-Asking Protocol method shares similarities with the Participant-Driven AAP approach presented in this paper, as both derive from the traditional TAP framework and involve the verbal form of questions asked by design participants or users. However, there are fundamental distinctions between the two. Takashi's study does not involve users naturally posing questions based on their experiences while interacting with computerized products. Instead, it stipulates that participants should not need to possess any prior knowledge or direct experience of the computer system under investigation. The focus of his research heavily leans towards problem-solving aspects, overshadowing its generative nature. This restates the fundamental difference between his approach and the one proposed in this paper.

3.3 Design Aspects of the Four Protocol Forms in Relation to Generativity

Through the conceptual review and the case studies, a clear distinction emerges regarding the benefits of Statements, representing traditional TAP, and the three question categories in the context of design: LLQs contribute to advancing the design process and achieving solutions; DRQs facilitate designing for learning and comprehension; and GDQs have the capacity to expand design generativities. Within this framework, design generative opportunities are most significantly expanded by GDQs, followed by DRQs, LLQs, and Statements. The potential provided by declarative Statement discourse in traditional TAP aligns with that of LLQs, as both entail deterministic discourse and answers (*Figure 1*).

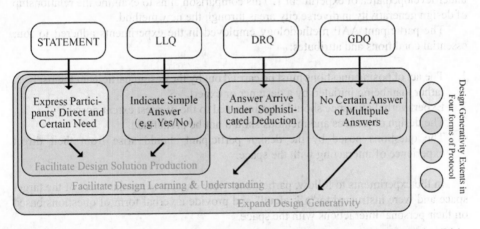

Figure 1 Diverse Aspects of Design Contribution From: Statement, LLQ, DRQ, and GDQ, Based on Eris' Question Taxonomy.

The analysis of the cases demonstrates that in traditional studies, designers and experts continue to be the main initiators of questioning. Within these studies, structures of guided and predetermined question-and-answer frameworks were established by designers. Such practices inherently restrict the creative potential of question-asking in design contexts. A research gap persists in the exploration of participant-driven questioning, unbounded by designers and predefined design objectives, thereby highlighting the significance of the innovative participant-driven AAP method. Building on these premises, two design experiments employing the AAP method were conducted.

Their objective was to further investigate the effectiveness of the method and its potential contributions.

4. Participant-Driven "Ask Aloud Protocol" Experiments

4.1 Experiment Objectives and Method

Spatial challenges, including categories such as planning and architectural design, exemplify instances of WPs. The complexity and uncertainty inherent to spatial problems, combined with their extensive implications, have historically posed challenges in problem definition. Additionally, designers often find themselves needing to manipulate entities within unfamiliar spatial contexts. In such situations, inquiries raised by space users can bring to light hidden facets for the designer, potentially revealing connections that even participants themselves are unable to acknowledge.

This paper presents two experiments conducted using the participant-driven AAP method in Beijing, China. Firstly, in an underdeveloped urban area, QILI South Urban Village, we analyzed verbal reports consisting of "Statements" and "Questions" from space users (residents) to examine whether AAP can enhance design generativity more effectively than TAP. Additionally, researcher investigated the potential correlation between AAP outcomes and WPs. The second experiment was conducted as a comparative study to experiment 1, exploring how the generative capacity of participant questioning in a well-developed city center (World Mall TOD) compares to the underdeveloped area of experiment 1. This comparison aims to examine the relationship of design generativity in diverse city areas through the new method.

The participant AAP methodology employed in the experiments adhered to four essential conditions and attributes:

1. The act of posing questions must be carried out by the design participant themselves, rather than being initiated by a designer or expert.
2. Expert verbal guidance should be minimized to the greatest extent possible.
3. The design objectives and methods should not be predefined.
4. The questions posed by the design participant should arise from their direct experience of interacting with the space.

In the experiments to follow, participants were chosen as regular users of the target space and were instructed to "ask aloud" and provide a verbal form of questions based on their personal interactions with the space.

4.2 Experiment 1——QILI South Urban Village, Beijing

4.2.1 Experiment Space

The QILI South Urban Village, situated between the 5th and 6th Ring Roads in northwestern Beijing, has remained in a partially demolished condition for several years. Adjacent to the recently developed Hi-Tech Zone, characterized by office towers hosting corporations such as Xiaomi, Wanda, and other entities, the village stands in stark contrast to its surroundings (*Figure 2*). The village's semi-demolished and deteriorated structures continue to house numerous residents, primarily consisting of individuals who were previously displaced, as well as construction workers, among others, within the vicinity. The village is contiguous with the QIYAN Road No.1 Estate, with most of its inhabitants having been relocated from the former QILI South Urban Village.

4.2.2 Participants

Four participants from the QIYAN Road No.1 estate were chosen to take part in the experiment. They were former residents of the QILI South Urban Village, with an average age exceeding 55 years.

4.2.3 Experiment Process

Printed photographs of the urban village were taken on the day, and research method manuals were prepared for the participants to assist them in their questioning process (Figure 2). To minimize guiding influence, researchers were introduced as spatial researcher rather than designers. Only two prompts were presented: "How do you reflect on your experience living in QILI South urban village?" and "How do you perceive and wish to articulate your thoughts about the surrounding environment?" These prompts were devoid of any value judgments, and they refrained from detailing design goals, methods, or elements. During a 30-minute session, participants were tasked with presenting their verbal Statements in the initial 15 minutes and formulating verbal Questions in the subsequent time frame. This structure enabled participants to exercise their "Think Aloud" capabilities while delivering Statements, concurrently facilitating the advancement of the AAP process.

Figure 2. Photos of QILI South Urban Village, the developed Hi-Teck area and QIYAN Road No.1 Estate (left 4); Experiment process photos (right 3).

4.2.4 Results from Experiment 1

Within the designated 30-minute timeframe, the four ex-residents of the urban village collectively presented 9 Statements and raised a total of 22 Questions. These Questions were subsequently classified into LLQs, DRQs, and GDQs based on Eris' [31] question taxonomy, resulting in 5 LLQs, 9 DRQs, and 8 GDQs (*Table 2*). This distribution highlights a notably greater prevalence of DRQs and GDQs compared to Statements and LLQs. This disparity potentially suggests that the challenges encountered by space users, especially within the context of WPs, often encompass questioning of relatively higher-level complexities.

Table 2. AAP results collected from villagers in the experiment.

LLQ	DRQ	GDQ
What is this bundle of wires made from? Is it for telephone communications?	Why don't they dry their quilt upstairs (with upstairs windows half demolished)?	Have any of the village roadside stalls now become centralized?
Is this a motorbike?	What about travelling problems, after these many years of road repairs?	There are no big parks around here for the elderly to exercise, what can we do about it?
We have waste segregation equipment in QIYAN Road No.1 Estate, but does the village have it?	Why are some of the rooms in the village are air-conditioned and some are not?	Why are there no cemeteries here? Everyone dies, and faraway cemeteries are unaffordable for average families.
Isn't it very unsafe for people to still live in urban villages?	When will it be demolished?	Why don't they demolish the village and why don't they redesign thses buildings?
Isn't this wire dangerous, and isn't it dangerous for someone to stay down there?	Why are there Buidings of four, three and two floors in the village?	The village was half demolished into a mess, why don't they tidy it up?
	Are people afraid to go inside the village during the night?	If the village is demolished, where will the stranded villagers and workers live?
	Why does this building have a brick wall on this side and a cement wall on the other side?	We were living in nice, villa-like houses. Why did they demolish our house in the first place?
	Why do people go to the village for lamb kebabs?	Who is going to do the demolition, developers or someone else? Can we choose?
	Why are there some nice cars parked here?	

Subsequently, the paper extracts segments from the four classifications that accentuate design prospects: 3 instances in the Statement category, none in LLQ expressions, 3 instances in DRQ, and 7 instances in GDQ. It was observed that LLQ expressions in this experiment did not prominently manifest attributes closely tied to design generativity.

- Within the "Statement" category (*not shown in Table 2*), three instances bear relevance to design possibilities, as follows: "The ground in a proper neighborhood will never be covered with dirt as in the urban village, and the policy regarding this problem has been in place for many years," "The south side of the area was built higher than the village ground level and we now live in a pit," "There's no collective heating in the village, the north parlor was too cold in winter, and residents always had to wear a cotton jacket". These three statements clearly express the needs of participants and address direct design solutions or engineering modifications. For instance, the second statement proposes a solution of reconstructing the floor to level the area.

- Three questions within the DRQ category can yield valuable design solutions. When contemplating the answers to these questions, various design possibilities can be discerned. For instance, consider the question, "What about travelling problems, after these many years of road repairs?" This question suggests multiple design possibilities, such as designing temporary roads to aid villagers' travel during the repair period or optimizing the engineering design to expedite the project.
- GDQs exhibited the highest count of questions, totaling seven. These questions were most relevant to design and showcased the highest value in terms of design generativity. For instance, consider the question, "There are no big parks around here for the elderly to exercise, what can we do about it?" This question doesn't possess a standardized answer, instead, it offers numerous potential avenues like "transform QILI urban village into a park," "identify suitable areas in the area for park design," "implement decentralized parks within smaller zones," "formulate park spaces between various neighborhoods," "create a gym or fitness area for the elderly within the vicinity," and more. Another inspiring query is, "Why are there no cemeteries here?" Responses to this question could encompass design concepts such as "transforming a portion of QILI urban village into an urban cemetery," "innovating new forms of urban cemeteries to engage young individuals and children in the difficult topic of Death," "developing spatially efficient cemeteries," and "establishing decentralized cemeteries as an integral aspect of every forthcoming development plot," and more.

4.3 Experiment 2——China World Mall TOD, Beijing

4.3.1 Experiment Space

The second experiment was conducted in the lower ground area of the China World Mall, situated in the eastern section of Beijing's 3rd ring road. The mall occupies a central position within the renowned Central Business District (CBD), showcasing the city's modernity and prosperity. The lower ground circular space of the mall is intricately interconnected with various amenities, including underground stations, shops, restaurants, cinemas, and more. This lower ground network creates a complex environment that may potentially cause confusion for users who are unfamiliar with the layout. For this study, a connecting space in the lower ground was selected, it functions as a public resting area and links the hotel, underground station, and other facilities.

4.3.2 Participants

Experiment 2 involved the random selection of 15 participants who are frequent users of the space. Upon conducting interviews, their professional backgrounds were summarized as follows: 7 individuals were professionals in finance and investment industries; 3 were employed in fashion design and luxury industry; 2 were working within exhibition and interior design fields; 2 worked in the education industry; and 1 worked in the energy industry. The participants' average age ranged from 25 to 30 years old.

4.3.3 Experiment Process

Participants were instructed to "ask aloud" and pose approximately 10 questions concerning any aspect of the space. The researchers refrained from presenting themselves as designers, instead requiring participants to "express any thoughts you have about the space in the form of a question." The same participant manual from Experiment 1 was provided, along with a small incentive, to encourage participation (*Figure 3*).

Figure 3. Experiment 2 location and process.

4.3.4 Results from Experiments 2

A total of 123 questions were gathered from the pool of 15 participants. In *Table 3*, participants were assigned codes P1 to P15. The categorical examination reveals that, on average, each participant posed approximately 1.9 LLQs, 3.8 DRQs, and 2.5 GDQs. While variations existed among individuals, the average count for DRQs and GDQs exceeded that of the other two types, with LLQs showing the lowest occurrence. The subsequent arguments delve into the analysis of Experiment 2 and its comparative assessment with Experiment 1:

- Based on the data analysis, the distribution of outcome questions in this experiment leans towards DRQs, diverging from Experiment 1, which favored GDQs. However, both experiments displayed a minimal frequency of LLQs. Therefore, it can be inferred that the Participant-Driven AAP approach continues to yield significant design possibilities in Experiment 2. In context, Experiment 1 is situated on the urban periphery, marked by distinctive planning and construction limitations. Conversely, Experiment 2 is positioned at the city's core, characterized by pioneering planning and construction. This suggests that in urban areas marked by comprehensive planning, the design generativity stemming from Participant-Driven AAP might be less pronounced than in urban spaces facing substantial planning challenges.
- In terms of the highest occurrence of DRQ questions, participants demonstrated a keen interest in spatial understanding. For instance, questions about details such as "why is the floor divided like this" and "what led to the choice of this color for the floor tiles" were posed by a significant number of participants, totaling nine. Moreover, inquiries related to facility and design elements were evident, including "What is the rationale behind the circular layout of the entire space?" (Participant 4, fashion designer) and "What distinct characteristics define the lighting design in this area?" (Participant 5, luxury industry employee), among others. These questions transcend conventional urban planning concerns to enrich the spatial experience. Notably, despite their frequent use of the space, participants exhibit

limited familiarity with the environment, yet express an eagerness to acquire spatial knowledge.

- In terms of GDQ content, it's noteworthy that certain DRQ questions possess the potential for expansion into GDQ questions. For instance, in relation to the floor design inquiry mentioned earlier, P4 asked, "Why is the floor in the shopping mall covered with tiles rather than rubber like at the airport?" In this instance, P4's thought process evolved from a simple inquiry for understanding to a generative exercise involving the proposal of potential design options.
- While the number of GDQs is not the highest, their value is primarily associated with the dimension of design possibilities. For instance, "All the shops feature floor-to-ceiling windows; how can we infuse them with distinct character?" "What led to the circular design of the ceiling? Could there be a curtain-like feature that descends?" and so forth. All of which, from designer perspectives, demonstrate the most creative leads in generating unconventional designs.

Table 3. Participant-Driven AAP verbal result data analysis based on 3 question categories.

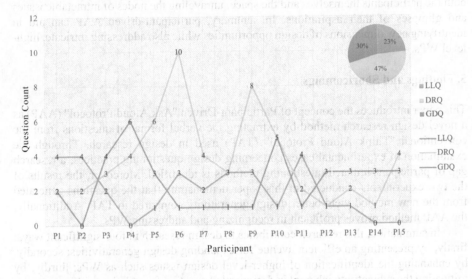

4.4 Discussion

Comparing the frequencies of verbal Statements and questions in Experiment 1 reveals that diverse living conditions prompt participants to ask more questions than make Statements. DRQs and GDQs consistently surpass LLQs in both experiments, highlighting Participant-Driven AAP's influence on spatial design generativity. Statements usually convey direct needs, with designers as executors. Conversely, questioning, particularly GDQs, reveals intricate dynamics. The new method yields more GDQs, thereby expanding the design potential of participatory practices. The scarcity of LLQs might result from residents' daily experiences and interactions with the space, leading them to focus on complex, higher-level issues. The traditional designer-led question approach could differ, potentially fostering more LLQs due to designers' unfamiliarity with the space, which can be limiting to design generative potential.

The comparative analysis of Experiments 1 and 2 indicates a focus on DRQs and GDQs, respectively. Influenced by distinct spatial attributes (developed vs. developing) and user relationships with the space (residence vs. workplace), these experiments demonstrate that well-planned urban spaces exhibit lower generativity than those facing severe planning challenges. This underscores the potential of the Participant-Driven AAP approach, along with Eris' problem taxonomy, in evaluating spatial design complexity. That is to say, when using Participant-Driven AAP to investigate a space, a high occurrence of GDQs signifies higher-level problems (WPs) requiring immediate attention. Experiment 2's DRQ content suggests participants seek to learn extra spatial information, highlighting that city-center workspaces, while functionally efficient, might not fully resonate with their users. Furthermore, these DRQs possess the potential to evolve into GDQs.

In essence, Participant-Driven AAP significantly enhances design generative potential compared to traditional TAP and serves as a valuable tool for evaluating spatial complexities. Furthermore, the participants' questions unveiled substantial insights into both the participants themselves and the space, unraveling the nodes of intractable issues and glimpses of their aspirations. In summary, participant-driven AAP can aid in identifying new dimensions of design opportunities while also addressing intricate, high-level WPs.

5. Findings and Shortcomings

This paper introduces the concept of Participant-Driven "Ask Aloud Protocol" (AAP) as a novel design research method by extracting the verbal format of questions from the conventional "Think Aloud Protocol" (TAP) used in design research. Through the examination of experimental cases concerning design questioning practices, a research gap of participant-initiated questioning methods is identified. Moreover, the results of the two experiments conducted in this paper demonstrate that the questions generated from the new method yield better design generativity compared to TAP. Additionally, the AAP method proves proficient in recognizing and addressing WPs.

In summation, this research contributes to design research in four significant ways: firstly, by presenting an efficient avenue for expanding design generativities; secondly, by enhancing the identification of higher-level design issues such as WPs; thirdly, by mitigating the subjectivity inherent in designer-led question formulation within the realm of design problems; and fourthly, by surpassing the constraints of the traditional TAP method in terms of efficiency, accuracy, and the number of design opportunities. Several limitations of this study warrant deeper exploration in subsequent experiments. For instance, while this paper's method expands the spectrum of design possibilities in terms of problem discovery, it prompts inquiry into how designers should further navigate the question-answer domain when generating designs. Also, the applicability of the AAP approach beyond the confines of planning and urban spatial design poses an intriguing question. These inquiries merit further studies by design researchers operating within this domain.

In the rapid evolution of Artificial Intelligence (AI), it has come to light that Large Language Models, typified by ChatGPT, hinge upon the participatory involvement of each user to facilitate iterative refinement [40]. Herein, the art of posing questions assumes paramount significance. Questions are fashioned to encapsulate the intended breadth of responses, akin to designers soliciting specific outcomes through participant inquiries, within circumscribed contextual boundaries. Much like designers, ChatGPTs' responses are constrained by their knowledge repository and algorithmic architecture, akin to a designer's cognitive modality. Overcoming these confines necessitates collaborative research endeavors and profound contemplation concerning the question-formulation facet. By harnessing the integration of diverse experiential insights and perceptual nuances, this pathway of research holds promise for delineating novel trajectories in design evolution.

References

[1]   Özgür E. Perceiving, Comprehending and Measuring Design Activity through the Questions Asked while Designing [Ph.D. Dissertation]. [Stanford University]; 2002.

[2]   Cardoso C, Badke-Schaub P, Eris O. Inflection moments in design discourse: How questions drive problem framing during idea generation. Design Studies. 2016 Sep; 46:59–78. DOI: 10.1016/j.destud.2016.07.002

[3]   Rittel HWJ, Webber MM. Dilemmas in a general theory of planning. Policy Sciences. 1973 Jun;4(2):155–69. DOI: 10.1007/bf01405730

[4]   Simon HA. The structure of ill structured problems. Artificial Intelligence. 1973;4(3-4):181–201. DOI: 10.1016/0004-3702(73)90011-8

[5]   Xun G, Land SM. A conceptual framework for scaffolding III-structured problem-solving processes using question prompts and peer interactions. Educational Technology Research and Development. 2004 Jun;52(2):5–22. DOI: 10.1007/bf02504836

[6]   Lloyd P, Lawson B, Scott P. Can concurrent verbalization reveal design cognition? Design Studies. 1995 Apr;16(2):237–59. DOI: 10.1016/0142-694x(94)00011-2

[7]   CRISMOND DP, ADAMS RS. The Informed Design Teaching and Learning Matrix. Journal of Engineering Education. 2012 Oct;101(4):738–97. DOI: 10.1002/j.2168-9830.2012.tb01127.x

[8]   Silk EM, Rechkemmer AE, Daly SR, Jablokow KW, McKilligan S. Problem framing and cognitive style: Impacts on design ideation perceptions. Design Studies. 2021 May; 74:101015. DOI: 10.1016/j.destud.2021.101015

[9]   Cross N. Designerly Ways of Knowing: Design Discipline Versus Design Science. Design Issues. 2001 Jul;17(3):49–55. DOI: 10.1162/074793601750357196

[10] Thomas JC, Carroll JM. The psychological study of design. Design Studies. 1979 Jul;1(1):5–11. DOI: 10.1016/0142-694x(79)90020-6

[11] Ball LJ, Christensen BT. Advancing an understanding of design cognition and design metacognition: Progress and prospects. Design Studies. 2019 Nov; 65:35–59. DOI: 10.1016/j.destud.2019.10.003

[12] Dorst K, Cross N. Creativity in the design process: co-evolution of problem–solution. Design Studies. 2001 Sep;22(5):425–37. DOI: 10.1016/s0142-694x(01)00009-6

[13] Oxman R. Thinking difference: Theories and models of parametric design thinking. Design Studies. 2017 Sep;52:4–39. DOI: 10.1016/j.destud.2017.06.001

[14] Puccio GJ, Chimento MD. Implicit Theories of Creativity: Laypersons' Perceptions of the Creativity of Adaptors and Innovators. Perceptual and Motor Skills. 2001 Jun;92(3):675–81. DOI: 10.2466/pms.2001.92.3.675

[15] Jansson DG, Smith SM. Design fixation. Design Studies. 1991 Jan;12(1):3–11. DOI: 10.1016/0142-694x(91)90003-f

[16] Buchanan R. Wicked Problems in Design Thinking. Design Issues. 1992;8(2):5–21. DOI: 10.2307/1511637

[17] Björk BC. A conceptual model of spaces, space boundaries and enclosing structures. Automation in Construction. 1992 Dec;1(3):193–214. DOI: 10.1016/0926-5805(92)90013-a

[18] Harder MK, Burford G, Hoover E. What Is Participation? Design Leads the Way to a Cross-Disciplinary Framework. Design Issues. 2013 Oct;29(4):41–57. DOI: 10.1162/desi_a_00229

[19] Cross N. Design Participation. London: Academy Editions; 1972.

[20] Bjögvinsson E, Ehn P, Hillgren PA. Design Things and Design Thinking: Contemporary Participatory Design Challenges. Design Issues. 2012 Jul;28(3):101–16. DOI: 10.1162/desi_a_00165

[21] Schön DA. Designing as reflective conversation with the materials of a design situation. Knowledge-Based Systems. 1992 Mar;5(1):3–14. DOI: 10.1016/0950-7051(92)90020-g

[22] Moran TP. Guest Editor's Introduction: An Applied Psychology of the User. ACM Computing Surveys. 1981 Mar;13(1):1–11. DOI: 10.1145/356835.356836

[23] Busby JS. Error and distributed cognition in design. Design Studies. 2001 May;22(3):233–54. DOI: 10.1016/s0142-694x(00)00028-4

[24] Hanington B, Martin B. Universal Methods Of Design. S.L.: Rockport Publishers; 2019.

[25] Crutcher RJ. Telling What We Know: The Use of Verbal Report Methodologies in Psychological Research. Psychological Science. 1994 Sep;5(5):241–1. DOI: 10.1111/j.1467-9280.1994.tb00619.x

[26] Payne JW. Thinking Aloud: Insights Into Information Processing. Psychological Science. 1994 Sep;5(5):241–8. DOI: 10.1111/j.1467-9280.1994.tb00620.x

[27] Ericsson KA, Simon HA. How to Study Thinking in Everyday Life: Contrasting Think-Aloud Protocols With Descriptions and Explanations of Thinking. Mind, Culture, and Activity. 1998 Jul;5(3):178–86. DOI: 10.1207/s15327884mca0503_3

[28] Newell A, Simon A.H. Human problem solving. Englewood Cliffs: NJ: Prentice Hall; 1972.

[29] Murray JK, Studer JA, Daly SR, McKilligan S, Seifert CM. Design by taking perspectives: How engineers explore problems. Journal of Engineering Education. 2019 Apr;108(2):248–75. DOI: 10.1002/jee.20263

[30] Silk EM, Daly SR, Jablokow KW, Yilmaz S, Rosenberg M. Interventions for Ideation Impact of Framing, Teaming, and Tools on High School Students' Design Fixation. Proc of the 2014 Annual Meeting of the American Educational Research Association (AERA). 2014.

[31] Ozgur Eris. ASKING GENERATIVE DESIGN QUESTIONS: A FUNDAMENTAL COGNITIVE MECHANISM IN DESIGN THINKING. DS 31: Proceedings of ICED 03, the 14th International Conference on Engineering Design, Stockholm. 2003 Jan 1.

[32] Ozgur Eris, Leifer L. Facilitating Product Development Knowledge Acquisition: Interaction between the Expert and the Team*. International Journal of Engineering Education. 2003 Jan 1;19(1).

[33] Flammer A. Towards a theory of question asking. Psychological Research. 1981 Dec;43(4):407–20. DOI: 10.1007/bf00309225

[34] Kato T. What "question-asking protocols" can say about the user interface. International Journal of Man-Machine Studies. 1986 Dec;25(6):659–73. DOI: 10.1016/s0020-7373(86)80080-3

[35] Graesser AC, McMahen CL. Anomalous information triggers questions when adults solve quantitative problems and comprehend stories. Journal of Educational Psychology. 1993;85(1):136–51. DOI: 10.1037/0022-0663.85.1.136

[36] Cash P, Dekoninck EA, Ahmed-Kristensen S. Supporting the development of shared understanding in distributed design teams. Journal of Engineering Design. 2017 Jan 4;28(3):147–70. DOI: 10.1080/09544828.2016.1274719

[37] Aurisicchio M, Bracewell R, Wallace K. Characterising Design Questions That Involve Reasoning. Guidelines for a Decision Support Method Adapted to NPD Processes. 2007 Aug 31.

[38] Cardoso C, Ozgur Eris, Badke-Schaub P, Aurisicchio M. Question asking in design reviews: how does inquiry facilitate the learning interaction? 2014 Jan 1; DOI: 10.5703/1288284315941

[39] Sonalkar N, Mabogunje A, Leifer L, Roth B. Visualising professional vision interactions in design reviews. CoDesign. 2016 Feb;12(1-2):73–92. DOI: 10.1080/15710882.2015.1135245

[40] Rospigliosi P 'asher'. Artificial intelligence in teaching and learning: what questions should we ask of ChatGPT? Interactive Learning Environments. 2023 Jan 2;31(1):1–3. DOI: 10.1080/10494820.2023.2180191

Design Studies and Intelligence Engineering
L.C. Jain et al. (Eds.)
241
doi:10.3233/FAIA231441

An Interactive Application for Hand Muscle Fatigue Relief Based on Gesture Recognition

Siyu PANG[a], Baixi XING[a,1], Zhichuan TANG[a], Pan ZOU[b], Zhepeng XU[a] and
Hailong ZHANG[a]

[a] *Zhejiang University of Technology, Hangzhou, China*
xingbaixi@zjut.edu.cn
[b] *Staatlichen Akademie der Bildenden Künste Stuttgart, Stuttgart, Germany*
panzou@gmx.de

Abstract. Prolonged use of a keyboard or mouse can lead to continuous bending and twisting of the wrist, which can lead to muscle fatigue and pain. Finger exercises can reduce the hand muscle fatigue effectively. However, the repetitive exercises will bring boring and tedious experience. In this paper, we developed a hand rehabilitation exercise system based on gesture recognition technology and gamification design, which provides a more enjoyable, personalized and effective rehabilitation experience. The hand fatigue relief system was designed with the fusion of game elements and gesture interaction, which can enhance users' engagement and their rehabilitation motivation.

Keywords. Muscle fatigue, Finger exercises, Gamification design, Gesture recognition technology

1. Introduction

The rapid information technology development has completely changed individuals' lifestyles and work methods, elevating computers as the important tool in people's workplace, and elevating mobile phones as seemingly ubiquitous "third affiliates" [1]. About half of employees are often surrounded by electronic devices, and they may encounter health problems related to wrist and finger joints. This concern is particularly evident among technical personnel engaged in computer-centered tasks, which are often characterized by prolonged sitting and immobility. A few people actively choose to rest, while over 30% of people choose activities such as computer games or mobile phone use during their break [2]. However, prolonged keyboard input, mouse clicks, and screen interaction often lead to various hand diseases, including arthritis, tendinitis, and synovitis. The main manifestations are discomfort in the wrist, decreased wrist flexibility, numbness, and finger stiffness. It is undeniable that these issues have affected personal quality of life and professional efficiency [3]. In order to reduce hand fatigue, some games and applications have been developed specifically for this purpose. However, existing solutions often lack fun, and users do not practice on their own, resulting in no significant improvement, making it difficult to continue attracting users' attention and interest, and achieving the goal of reducing fatigue and preventing hand diseases. How to combine advanced gesture recognition technology to design a more

---

[1] Corresponding Author: Baixi Xing, xingbaixi@zjut.edu.cn.

comprehensive, interesting, and practical hand fatigue relief game has become an important direction of current research.

Based on the above content, this study attempts to study the construction of an enhanced interactive game framework for alleviating hand fatigue. This objective is achieved through the methods of established Openpose-based gesture recognition, machine learning methodologies, and gamification design model. This study aims to enhance the effectiveness of alleviating hand fatigue by promoting dynamic and sustained user engagement through engaging gaming experiences and astute mitigation strategies. The proposed system delves into the technical field by utilizing gesture recognition technology for real-time posture monitoring and adjustment. In addition, it also explores the integration of gamified design in the field of rehabilitation application. The overall research roadmap of this article is shown in Fig. 1.

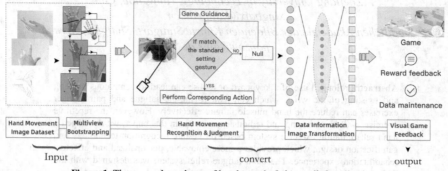

Figure 1. The research roadmap of hand muscle fatigue relief application study.

2. Related Works

2.1. Gesture recognition in human-computer interaction

Gestures can convey information and express users' intuitive intentions. At present, gesture recognition technology is being widely applied and developed as a new human-computer interaction mode. By analyzing user gestures and actions, more intelligent and smooth interface operations can be achieved, thereby alleviating hand muscle tension and reducing the occurrence of hand fatigue. In addition, gesture recognition has shown great potential in replacing traditional control methods, promoting human-machine collaboration, translating sign language, satisfying physical and virtual reality experiences, and helping to improve and guide standardized actions [4].

Visual based gesture recognition is a widely applied technology in human computer interaction that uses cameras to capture scenes containing gestures, and then deploys computer algorithms to recognize, extract, and classify gesture features present in images. In a broad sense, developing a comprehensive mechanism for gesture interaction in a visual based gesture recognition system includes three basic stages: data collection, data processing, and gesture representation [5]. For visual based gesture recognition sensing devices, the popular universal RGB cameras on the market fully meet these requirements. Given the inherent robustness and speed of camera-based gesture recognition methods, this technology has been widely applied in various fields, such as virtual reality (VR), augmented reality (AR), and education. For instance, Zixin Zhou developed an auxiliary system for Gu Zheng fingering practice that leverages gesture recognition to provide user feedback assistance, and the comparative experiments have revealed a significant enhancement of novice self-directed practice abilities [6].

2.2. Hand rehabilitation movements

Hand rehabilitation training plays a crucial role in alleviating hand fatigue and promoting muscle recovery. Through carefully customized rehabilitation exercises, targeted exercises can be carried out to solve different problems in hand muscle tissue, thereby stimulating muscle activity and enhancing blood circulation. Healthcare professionals typically provide advice on exercise for patients during treatment [7]. It is studied that hand manipulation exercises can promote local motor enhancement, effectively enhancing muscle strength, flexibility, and coordination, while reducing discomfort related to prolonged use of electronic devices. In an existing study, Shuo Jiang demonstrated that repetitive exercise is the best strategy for restoring muscle activation, enhancing muscle strength, and avoiding hand fatigue [8].

When choosing hand rehabilitation exercises, it is necessary to attach great importance to the fatigue relief of specific areas, especially for areas such as finger joints or wrist muscles. This selection process must take into account the actions that ordinary people can easily master for learning and imitation purposes, as well as the differences in user needs and abilities. Therefore, exercise selection should be based on the user's perspective, ensuring its practical effectiveness in promoting rehabilitation progress and improving user satisfaction.

2.3. Rehabilitation guidance based on gesture recognition

Gesture recognition technology provides a new approach for rehabilitation guidance; by real-time monitoring of user gestures, the system can accurately recognize the accuracy of user actions, providing more targeted guidance [9]. Researchers generally believe that specific hand rehabilitation systems using computer vision technology exhibit higher correlation and interactivity, helping to enhance hand flexibility and reduce discomfort. For instance, empirical findings by Farnaz Farahanipad revealed that nearly all participants rated games with gesture recognition as moderately to highly effective and engaging [10]. This technology can significantly help users understand the correct rehabilitation actions. In addition, gesture recognition technology can record users' rehabilitation progress and process, providing valuable data for rehabilitation experts to design more effective personalized rehabilitation plans [11].

2.4. Gamification design principles

Repetitive exercise therapy strives to cultivate effective motor learning and neural plasticity by creating games that are consistent with corresponding training actions, thereby making the rehabilitation process more systematic, professional, informative, and enjoyable [12]. However, scholars emphasize that the effect of repeated practice is not always positive, as continuous repetition often leads to monotony and decreased motivation [13]. Therefore, the integration of gamified design principles is crucial. This requires attracting users' different senses through goals, rules, feedback, and voluntary participation activities in the game. Integrating gamified elements into repetitive behavior can become a key driving force for improving user engagement and emotional satisfaction, making the experience enjoyable and promoting sustained behavioral persistence. Gamification design uses game elements to motivate positive behavior and enhance motivation and participation in specific tasks [14]. In addition, gamified design facilitates real-time feedback and result display, providing users with a sense of achievement and fatigue, thereby improving satisfaction and willingness to continue using.

Yu-Kai Chou created the Octagonal Behavioral Analysis Framework after proposing a theory of gamification analysis, also known as the Octalysis Framework for analyzing and designing gamified experiences, see Fig. 2. He found that human behavior is driven by the driving factors behind it, while successful games are supported by multiple driving factors [15].

In the conceptualization of games, users have a clear need to alleviate their hands in this area, so providing challenging tasks in the game to give users a certain sense of mission will make the game more attractive to them. And design relevant reward mechanisms, such as points and medal collection. Encouraged by a sense of achievement driven mechanism, users feel a sense of achievement and are willing to continue participating, enhancing participation and continuity.

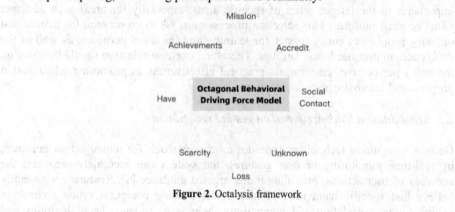

Figure 2. Octalysis framework

3. Methodology

3.1. Openpose working mechanism

By leveraging the hand's symmetry and the flexibility attributes of the fingers, coupled with existing finger exercise movements aimed at alleviating hand fatigue, finger exercises and real-time interactive games for the hand are synergistically integrated through techniques like gesture recognition and machine learning. Consequently, this system necessitates the gathering of data, its subsequent analysis, and the presentation of visual feedback within the gaming context to enhance guidance efficacy.

The data acquisition layer comprises an annotation approach involving the selection of 21 key hand points alongside corresponding gesture categories. This approach is adopted to accommodate complex gestures and enhance recognition accuracy. These 21 hand points encompass pivotal hand and joint areas, their annotation encapsulating the entirety of hand motion patterns. A representation of the annotation process is provided in Figure 4. For data annotation, the 21 key hand points in conjunction with gesture labels are utilized to annotate gesture images. Each key point incorporates both observable and latent attributes [16]. The gesture labels encompass gesture classification, the gender of the data collector, the side of the hand (left or right), the orientation of the gesture (front or back), the environment of acquisition, camera orientation, gesture rotation angle, and other pertinent aspects.

The gesture model, derived from visual imagery extracted from gesture labels and employing parametric modeling methodologies, is an abstract construct. This model is essentially categorized into two modalities: a 2D gesture model predicated on visual features and a 3D gesture model founded on skeletal attributes [17]. By employing the pertinent data pertaining to gesture acquisition and labeling, judgments regarding the correctness of the current gesture are made in accordance with stipulated criteria. Ultimately, the evaluated gesture is directly presented on the interactive interface to ensure the precision and comprehensiveness of the fatigue alleviation request.

3.2. Workflow of Openpose

Initially, a limited set of annotated image datasets containing human hand keypoints is employed to train a Convolutional Pose Machines (CPM) network, which is similar to methods used for human pose keypoints. This training process yields an initial estimation of hand keypoints. A total of thirty-one high-definition (HD) cameras were deployed to capture diverse viewpoints of the human hand, as depicted in Fig. 3.

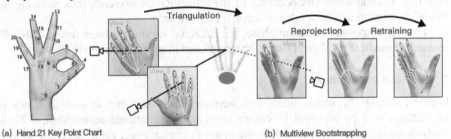

(a) Hand 21 Key Point Chart   (b) Multiview Bootstrapping

Figure 3. The Hand recognition technology is (a) Hand 21 key point chart and (b) Multiview Bootstrapping

The captured images are input into the hand keypoint detector to yield preliminary keypoint detections. Once the keypoints from varying viewpoints of the same hand are available, a process of keypoint triangulation is undertaken to deduce the three-dimensional (3D) positions of these keypoints.

The 3D positions of the keypoints are projected back from their 3D space onto each 2D image corresponding to different viewpoints. Subsequently, the network is subjected to further training using these 2D images and their associated keypoints, enabling the prediction of hand keypoint locations. This approach proves particularly effective for scenarios where keypoint predictions are challenging. Notably, a more accurate hand keypoint detector can be attained through a limited number of training iterations.

The efficacy of gesture recognition techniques was identified when employing conventional RGB cameras. By utilizing multi view bootstrapping, a rich training dataset can be constructed to improve the quantity and quality of annotations. Building a large number of annotated datasets is often an important bottleneck in various machine learning and computer vision tasks. To address this issue, multi perspective geometry is used as an external source of supervision to enhance weakly supervised learning [18].

3.3. System architecture and module design

3.3.1. Standard setting and database construction for rehabilitation

Establishing standards is a key mechanism to ensure consistency and data consistency in rehabilitation training. In our system, the selection of rehabilitation training and the conceptualization of gamified design constitute two crucial design elements that require meticulous and rigorous standardization. Firstly, the standardization of rehabilitation actions is a key factor in ensuring the effectiveness and safety of rehabilitation training. Secondly, the gamification design concept includes incorporating game elements and principles into rehabilitation exercises to enhance user engagement and motivation.

In the process of selecting rehabilitation actions, drawing on existing literature and consulting rehabilitation experts and doctors can help improve the accuracy and rationality of the selected actions. A standardised approach to data preparation in rehabilitation requires important considerations such as the integration of physiological and rehabilitative principles such as muscle strength and joint co-ordination suggested by rehabilitation specialists, followed by the complexity of the postures and movements, which need to be simple and easy to understand for the user to ensure a high rate of completion and accuracy of the rehabilitation exercise, thus reducing the risk of discomfort and injury due to incorrect movements.

During the posture selection phase, we collected various postures from a carefully researched medical validated posture library related to manual therapy [19].

3.3.2. System architecture

Initially, during the initial interaction between users and the system, a series of interactions will be arranged to ensure continuous operational sustainability. These interactions include elements such as the system's startup page, game selection options, personal information configuration, and progress indicator display. Subsequently, the system takes on the task of capturing the posture and movements of the user's hand, which is then converted into understandable data for processing by the system. This specific functional layer can include various hardware components, including gesture sensors, cameras, and gesture recognition algorithms. The subsequent level involves the integration of gamified design principles, including the game's contextual framework, progress level, task allocation, and mechanisms to reward user participation. This layer closely integrates gamification elements with the goals of muscle relief plans, ensuring the coherence and purposefulness of gamification principles (Shown in Fig.4).

Figure 4. Gesture Recognition Capture Map

When users run the system, integrated technical support provides real-time feedback on rehabilitation actions and guides users in correctly executing rehabilitation actions. The game has designed a reward mechanism to motivate users to complete tasks and achieve rehabilitation goals, providing them with an interesting interactive experience while guiding them towards liberation. Finally, in order to maintain the long-term stability of the system, it is necessary to regularly update and maintain the data standard library and incorporates the latest medical research and rehabilitation theories to maintain the standardization of rehabilitation exercises. The function for gesture-controlled games to relieve hand fatigue is shown below.

Function : Hand Gesture Controlled Game for Hand fatigue relief

---

1)   **Get user gesture :** *//handGesture = getHandGesture() // Use OpenPose to recognize the user's hand posture and movement*

Complete the game with gestures :

2)   *//rehabPlan = designRehabPlan(handGesture) // The user chooses a relief plan based on the condition of the hand*
//gameElements = integrateGameElements(rehabPlan) // Integrate the rehabilitation plan with the gamified elements
//Hand fatigue relief games playGame(gameElements) // Users play hand fatigue relief games and perform rehabilitation actions and tasks
//Real-time feedback and personalized adjustment feedback = provideRealtimeFeedback(handGesture, rehabPlan) // Provides real-time feedback according to the user's rehabilitation progress
//if(gameIsCompleted(rehabPlan)){user.isplaying = false // If (gameiscompleted (rehabplan)){user.isplaying = false // If the user has completed the game, then decide whether to continue the game}}
//Data analysis and personalized Adjustment analyzeDataAndAdjustPlan(user, handGesture, feedback) // Collect and analyze user rehabilitation data and adjust rehabilitation plans and game tasks

---

3)   **Game over:**///DisplayResultsAndFeedback (user) / / display saveGameData rehabilitation results and feedback of user information (user) / / save the user's data recovery and game record return user}

---

4. Application

4.1. Application operation process and modular design

This hand rehabilitation exercise system uses gesture recognition technology and gamified design to help users reduce hand muscle fatigue. By integrating game elements and gesture interaction, it provides an enjoyable, personalized, and efficient rehabilitation experience that motivates users to exercise.

1) User interface and interaction module: Provide a user-friendly interface, including start page, game level selection, personal information settings, etc. The interaction module is responsible for responding to user gestures and achieving interaction with the game.

2) Gesture recognition module: Use gesture recognition technology to monitor user gestures and convert them into game actions. This module needs to be highly accurate and real-time to ensure that user gestures can be accurately captured and converted into

in-game actions.

3) Gamification design module: This is the core module of the game, responsible for designing interesting game scenes, levels, tasks, and reward mechanisms. The gamified design module should develop game tasks related to rehabilitation goals based on rehabilitation plans and user situations.

4) Real time feedback and achievement module: Provides real-time feedback on rehabilitation actions, guiding users to correctly execute rehabilitation actions. At the same time, a reward mechanism has been designed to encourage users to complete tasks and achieve rehabilitation goals, in order to increase their sense of achievement and sustained engagement.

5) Data analysis and personalized adjustment module: Collect and analyze rehabilitation data of users to understand their progress and performance. Based on the analysis results, the system can adjust the difficulty and content of the rehabilitation plan to maintain the effectiveness of rehabilitation.

6) Data storage management module: stores user personal information, rehabilitation data, progress records, and other information. At the same time, ensure data security and privacy protection.

7) User feedback and support module: Provides user feedback and support channels to help users solve problems and receive rehabilitation advice.

4.2. Main interface and function introduction

The main user interfaces of the application "TUJI's Adventure" are shown in Figure 5. The gesture-based hand fatigue relief game has the following key functions:

● Personalized fatigue relief strategy: Using collected data, the system provides personalized suggestions and strategies to alleviate hand fatigue. It suggests appropriate exercise, relaxation techniques, and pauses based on the user's fatigue level to promote a balanced and safe gaming experience.

● Gesture based rehabilitation exercises: The game design integrates a series of gesture-based rehabilitation exercises aimed at alleviating hand fatigue, improving hand flexibility and strength. Users can use therapeutic gestures and actions to counteract the effects of prolonged gaming.

● Interactive and captivating games: Game design provides an interactive and captivating gaming experience, inspiring users to participate in activities that alleviate fatigue. Users can follow the prompts to engage in pleasant hand movements, which can help users to relax their hands.

5. Conclusion and future work

The aim of this work is to develop a hand rehabilitation system that utilizes gesture recognition technology and gamification design principles to solve hand fatigue problems. Gesture recognition and gamification techniques were applied in the system establishment. This process helps to identify key attributes for connecting gesture recognition and fatigue relief, thus developing a game model centered on gesture interaction. Subsequently, based on the research results, an application was designed to provide a more enjoyable and effective rehabilitation experience. This work is of benefit in improving hand muscle fatigue, maintaining overall physical health.

In the next stage, we plan to combine multimodal interactions to enhance the naturalness of rehabilitation interactions. In addition, we are exploring ways to extend gamified rehabilitation systems to mobile platforms, so that users can easily take rehabilitation training at any time and place. Our efforts include integrating social interaction and competition into a gamified framework, transforming the mitigation process into an engaging multiplayer interactive experience.

Gesture recognition and guidance

Gesture control and game feedback

Figure 5. User interface of the application "TUJI's Adventure" and the user interaction mechanism.

Acknowledgments

This study is partly supported by Fundamental Research Funds for the Provincial Universities of Zhejiang (GB202003008).

References

[1] F. Guo, L. Li, and M. M. Li, et al. Mobile game operating mode of the effect of visual and muscle fatigue study [J]. Journal of industrial engineering and management, 2020, 25(5): 1-7. doi: 10.19495 / j.carol carroll nki. 1007-5429.2020.05.001.

[2] 2021 CBNData.2021.white-collar health map. https://new.qq.com/rain/a/20210413A06EJ300

[3] J. M. Daniels, E. G. Zook and J. M. Lynch, "Hand and Wrist Injuries Part I. Nonemergent Evaluation", American Family Physician, vol. 69, no. 8, Apr. 2004.

[4] J. Tian, W.l. Zhang, T. Zhang, et al. Research Status of Gesture Recognition Based on Vision: A Review[J]. IOP Conference Series: Earth and Environmental Science, 2021, 632(4).

[5] N. Mohamed, M. B. Mustafa and N. Jomhari, "A Review of the Hand Gesture Recognition System: Current Progress and Future Directions," IEEE Access, vol. 9, pp. 157422-157436, 2021, doi: 10.1109/ACCESS.2021.3129650.

[6] G. Kai, J. X. Lu, C. Liu, H. B. Yang, Development, Research, Optimization and Experiment of Exoskeleton Robot for Hand Rehabilitation Training. Appl. Sci. 2022, 12, 10580. https://doi.org/10.3390/app122010580

[7] S. Jiang, P. q. Kang, X.Y Song, Benny P.L. Lo, Peter B. Shull, "Emerging Wearable Interfaces and Algorithms for Hand Gesture Recognition: A Survey", IEEE Reviews in Biomedical Engineering, vol.15, pp.85-102, 2022.

[8] M. Zabri Abu Bakar, R. Samad, D. Pebrianti, M. Mustafa and N. R. H. Abdullah, "Computer vision-based hand deviation exercise for rehabilitation," 2015 IEEE International Conference on Control System, Computing and Engineering (ICCSCE), Penang, Malaysia, 2015, pp. 389-394, doi: 10.1109/ICCSCE.2015.7482217.

[9]] Farahanipad, F., Nambiappan, H.R., Jaiswal, A., Kyrarini, M., & Makedon, F. (2020). HAND-REHA: dynamic hand gesture recognition for game-based wrist rehabilitation. Proceedings of the 13th ACM International Conference on PErvasive Technologies Related to Assistive Environments.

[10] F. Zhang, X. Wang, Y. Yang, Y. Fu and S. Wang, "A human-machine interface software based on android system for hand rehabilitation robot," 2015 IEEE International Conference on Information and Automation, Lijiang, China, 2015, pp. 625-630, doi: 10.1109/ICInfA.2015.7279362.

[11] D. Rand, T. Schejter-Margalit, I. Dudkiewicz, R. Kizony, G. Zeilig and R. Kizony, "The use of the iPad for poststroke hand rehabilitation; A pilot study," 2013 International Conference on Virtual Rehabilitation (ICVR), Philadelphia, PA, USA, 2013, pp. 109-113, doi: 10.1109/ICVR.2013.6662068.

[12] X. H. Hong, L. Y. Duan, S. Y. Mao and W. L .Qiu. "Research on the Design of Hand Rehabilitation Training Instrument Based on Self-Efficacy of the Elderly." DSIE (2022).

[13] C. A. Y. Mei, Y. H .Pang, K. H. Wee, et al. Hand Gesture Controlled Game for Hand Rehabilitation[P]. International Conference on Computer, Information Technology and Intelligent Computing (CITIC 2022),2022.

[14] E. A. Fedechen, D. P. Junior, and R. Pereira (2022). Gamification in Open Design: Supporting the Choice of Context-Appropriate Gamification Elements. Proceedings of the XVIII Brazilian Symposium on Information Systems.

[15] K. Li, Z. G. Hong and M. Y. Shi, "Research on the Application of Gamification Design Methods in IoP-Based System," 2019 IEEE/ACIS 18th International Conference on Computer and Information Science (ICIS), Beijing, China, 2019, pp. 274-278, doi: 10.1109/ICIS46139.2019.8940314.

[16] B. X. Chen, L. X. Yu, X. Meng, et al. Visual gesture recognition based on hand key points[J]. Journal of Physics: Conference Series, 2021.

[17] H. J. Cui and Y. X. Wang, "Research on Gesture Recognition Method Based on Computer Vision Technology," 2020 International Conference on Computer Information and Big Data Applications (CIBDA), Guiyang, China, 2020, pp. 358-362, doi: 10.1109/CIBDA50819.2020.00087.

[18] T. Simon, H. Joo, I. Matthews and Y. Sheikh, "Hand Keypoint Detection in Single Images Using Multiview Bootstrapping," 2017 IEEE Conference on Computer Vision and Pattern Recognition (CVPR), Honolulu, HI, USA, 2017, pp. 4645-4653, doi: 10.1109/CVPR.2017.494.

[19] Harvard Health Publishing, 2019. 5 exercises to improve hand mobility. https://www.health.harvard.edu/pain/5-exercises-to-improve-hand-mobility5-exercises-to-improve-hand-mobility

Design Studies and Intelligence Engineering
L.C. Jain et al. (Eds.)
© 2024 The Authors.
This article is published online with Open Access by IOS Press and distributed under the terms
of the Creative Commons Attribution Non-Commercial License 4.0 (CC BY-NC 4.0).
doi:10.3233/FAIA231442

Residential Spatial Layout Design Using Advanced Optimization Techniques

Yalong MAO[a], Zhe LAI[b,1], Zitong CHEN[c], Shaojie WANG[d], and
Lukui HUANG[e]

[a] *Architectural Design & Research Institute, South China University of Technology, China*
[b] *Senior Engineer, Ph.D., South China University of Technology, Guangzhou, China*
[c] *B.E, Zhongkai University of Agriculture and Engineering, Guangzhou, China*
[d] *Department of Architecture, Ph.D., South China University of Technology, Guangzhou, China*
[e] *Guangxi University of Finance and Economics, Nanning, China*

Abstract: Spatial layout design profoundly influences architectural development, yet traditional manual approaches suffer from limited solutions due to human cognitive constraints and cost-effectiveness consideration. This study explores selected advanced optimization algorithms—Simulated Annealing Algorithm, Dijkstra Algorithm, Frei Otto's Woolthread Model, Slime Mould Algorithm, and Genetic Algorithms—to enhance residential spatial layouts design. Prototypical cases of common residential planning and design challenges were utilized for the simulated experiments. Comparative analysis highlights Dijkstra's Algorithm and the Genetic Algorithm as optimal choices for path optimization and visual adjustments, contributing to the research on residential spatial layouts.

Key words: minimal path, design layout, optimization algorithms, residential planning

1. Introduction

Design layout serves as a foundational element for architectural development. Traditional manual layouts are labor-intensive and tend to yield limited solutions due to cognitive constraints [1]. Automated computational methods, such as optimization algorithms, offer a more efficient and diverse exploration of layouts, mitigating time and cost constraints. However, challenges persist in developing effective computational solutions due to complex site conditions and engineering constraints [2].

The overall floor plan, as an important spatial carrier, often requires cumbersome and repetitive adjustments during the design process. Modern architects turn to residential layout automation for more cost-effective solution to this issue. In this paper, we introduce and compare a series of advanced optimization algorithms which are particularly applicable for optimizing spatial distribution problems in residential planning and layout design. The selected optimization algorithms for automated residential layouts include Simulated Annealing Algorithm, Dijkstra Algorithm, Frei Otto' Woolthread Model, Slime Mould Algorithm, and Genetic Algorithm.

---

[1] Corresponding author: Zhe Lai; Email: 269442001@qq.com

1.1 Introduction to the selected optimization algorithms

1.1.1 Simulated Annealing Algorithm

Simulated annealing, introduced by Kirkpatrick et al. in 1983[3] as a modification of the Metropolis-Hastings algorithm, is a probabilistic approach for globally optimizing a cost function with multiple local optima. The simulated annealing algorithm has been applied in a wide range of optimization problems in areas such as engineering [4-6] and renewable energy[7]. In urban planning and architecture, Hong (2011) developed a model using simulated annealing for accurate traffic flow forecasting [8]. Sonmez (2008) optimized structural designs for lightweight and high-performance [9]. AlHalawani et al. (2013) generated procedural facade layouts with simulated annealing [10]. Yeh (2006) solved facility layout problems in hospital design by generating optimized floorplans [11] and Michalek et al. (2002) arranged house rooms using a similar technique [12].

1.1.2 Dijkstra's Shortest Path Algorithm

Dijkstra's algorithm, proposed by Edsger Dijkstra in 1959, efficiently finds the shortest path from a source node to all others in a weighted graph. Dijkstra's algorithm has been widely used in areas like network routing [13], transportation[14-15], robotics[16], and video games [17]. In urban planning, Zhong et al. (2022) combined Dijkstra's algorithm with geographic information systems for eco-commuting route recommendations [18]. Within architecture, Sharmeen et al. (2022) optimized evacuation route planning in buildings using Dijkstra's algorithm [19].

1.1.3 Frei Otto' Woolthread Model

Developed by German architect and engineer Frei Otto in the 1970s-1990s, the woolthread model, created at the Institute for Lightweight Structures (ILEK) in Stuttgart, serves as an analog model for optimizing path networks [20-21]. Pioneering the woolthread model's application for generating urban layouts, street networks, and settlement patterns, Otto demonstrated that organic complexity could exhibit inherent optimality and logic. The model challenges the conventional notion of orderly, high-performing, and optimized urban patterns in contrast to modernist grids [22].

1.1.4 Slime Mould Algorithm

The Slime Mould Algorithm, introduced in 2020 [23], has gained considerable attention for its simplicity, strong optimization capabilities, and reliable convergence in addressing diverse real-world problems. Its applications span areas such as traffic prediction [24], path optimization in mobile robots [25], and resource allocation [26].

1.1.5 Genetic Algorithm

Genetic Algorithm (GA) is a special kind of stochastic search algorithm that depicts the biological evolution as the problem-solving technique. GA can be applied for nonlinear programming like traveling salesman problem, minimum spanning tree, scheduling problem. Multiple studies also applied GA to solve complex problems urban design [27-30].

1.2 Project Objective

In the early stages of residential development, layout design involves individual units, regional planning, and road networks. This paper addresses common challenges in residential planning by comparing the performance of the wool-thread model, slime mould algorithm, and Dijkstra's algorithm for on-site building layout. Simulated annealing and genetic algorithms are assessed for view deviation. Using advanced optimization algorithms, we aim to identify optimal strategies for generating residential layouts, translating design concepts into mathematical parameters to drive a generative layout system (Figure 1).

1.3 Optimization methods

This paper adopts the essentials of the optimization algorithms as the solution approach:

    a) Clear definition of an objective function for measurement
    b) Traverse the variable space to find the optimal value of the objective function
    c) Use mathematical or heuristic techniques to accelerate the optimization process
    d) Termination conditions to judge whether a satisfactory solution is found

Hence, the prototype problems in residential planning and design to be solved include:

    a) Use Voronoi division to determine the basic functions of building objects
    b) Traverse these functions using Python
    c) Optimize using genetic algorithms, Dijkstra's algorithm, slime mould algorithm, and wool-thread model.
    d) Compare the above algorithms and attempt to propose corresponding optimal strategies and methods (Figure 1).

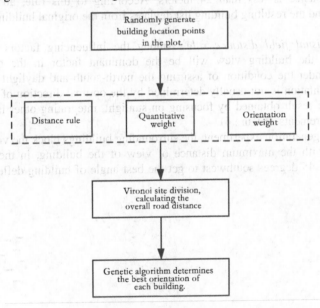

Fig. 1 Illustration of Program Workflow

2. Experiment in Settlement Generation Design

2.1 Distribution of housing units

In urban residential design, individual unit placement is influenced by factors like sunlight, landscape orientation, terrain, and building clusters. Grasshopper generates random building points constrained by Python for proximity checks. Models are evaluated through weighted calculations considering building count, view quality, and distance from exits. Genetic algorithms determine the optimal combination of random seeds and rotation angles for the highest scores, followed by computing the optimal view angle for each building.

Distance greater than 24m

```
for pt in pts:
    distances = rs.Distance(pt,pts)
    distances.sort()
    if distances[1] < 24:
        pts.remove(pt)
    else:
        pass
```

Figure 2 Schematic diagram of distance rules

2.1.1 Distance rule. The distribution of residence monomers is mainly based on the distance between the monomers. First of all, it is necessary to maintain the minimum distance between residential buildings. In order to simplify the experiment, the minimum distance of the experiment is set to 24 meters. Secondly, random coordinates points are generated in the red building line by the popular geometry component. Thirdly, in Python, the minimum distance from the central point of every building to the other buildings is traversed. The building shall be removed when the nearest building distance is less than 24 meters. According to this rule, all buildings are traversed, and the resulting building list deviates from the original building set number.

2.1.2 Visual field distance rule. Among the influencing factors of residential orientation, the building view will be the dominant factor in the distribution of buildings under the condition of assuring the north-south and daylight distance. The house's orientation is not usually determined by the optimal direction of sunlight but a compromise result obtained by focusing on sunlight, integrating other landscapes and vision requirements. (Figure 4)

In this generation experiment, the surrounding buildings block the view of the site, combined with the maximum distance of view of the building, in the southeast 45 degrees and 45 degrees southwest to get the best angle of building deflection. (Figure 3)

Fig. 3 Sketch map of visual range rules   **Fig. 4** Sketch map of orientation rules   **Figure 5** Multi-agent calculation result

2.2. Site division

The integrated factors for residential building design include land use uniformity and convenience. In residential building design, common methods of residential land planning include multi-agent plots design, and environmental zoning. Among them, the Environment of the subdivision is a classic prototype of polygon subdivision in architectural design. It is a continuous polygonal structure that is made up of two parallel bisecting curves. The space between any polygon and other equals that between any point in the polygon and other polygons. The geometry adheres to non-orthogonal building requirements, ensuring uniformity in each building's location. The polygonal grid creates small plot areas with geometric rationality and random beauty. (Figure 5).

2.3. Path optimization and generation

Road planning in residential areas considers hierarchy and convenience. Hierarchy involves primary roads at the residential level, secondary roads at the neighborhood level, and access roads to houses. Road forms are evaluated based on pedestrian flow rates during generative design. Connectivity is crucial, requiring roads to link residence units, neighborhood exits, and key nodes through the shortest paths. Site layout performance is compared using Dijkstra's algorithm (Figure 6), slime mold algorithm (Figure 7), and wool-thread model (Figure 8).

Figure 6 Minimal path using   **Figure 7** Minimal path using   **Figure 8** Minimal path using
Dijkstra's algorithm   slime mould algorithm   wool-thread model

Comparing three algorithms, Dijkstra's method proves optimal for the minimal path strategy. It addresses the shortest path problem in a weighted graph, calculating a unique shortest path between starting and ending points in a road grid. Evaluating road network throughput and hierarchy involves overlaying the number of shortest paths across segments. Regional planning and path generation are intertwined in residential areas, where experiments assess flow line smoothness along land boundaries. Overlaying road traffic reveals route hierarchy. Figures 7 and 8 show that the slime mold and wool-thread algorithms have higher hierarchical levels and point-to-point overlays than Dijkstra's. Consequently, Dijkstra's is the optimal strategy for shortest path challenges in residential planning and land use integration.

2.4. View Deviation and Generation

To investigate the view deviation, we calculated the total distance of the shortest path from each building to the site entranceand combined with certain weighted building views and number of buildings to evaluate the random building points generated by the Populate Geometry component. By comparing the optimal strategies of the genetic algorithm and simulated annealing algorithm, the optimal strategy for generating random building points is determined.

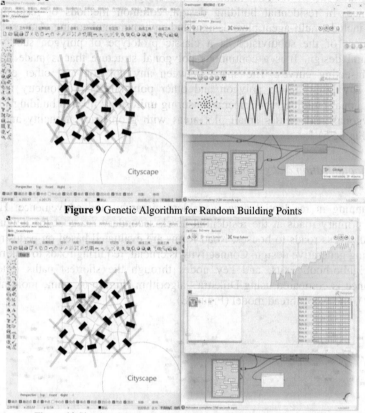

Figure 9 Genetic Algorithm for Random Building Points

Figure 10 Simulated Annealing Algorithm for Random Building Points

The combined evaluation metrics of the number of buildings, building views, and total distance from buildings to the entrance are 0.643 and 0.677 for genetic algorithm and simulated annealing algorithm respectively (random seed of the Populate Geometry component equals 95). Although the score for simulated annealing algorithm is slightly higher, its computation time is relatively long. Moreover, the optimal solution generated is essentially a fuzzy, approximate range. Therefore, for view deviation, the genetic algorithm is selected as the optimal strategy (Figures 11 and 12).

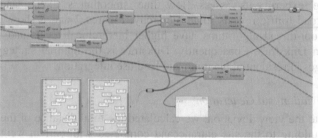

Figure 11 Result of Genetic Algorithm

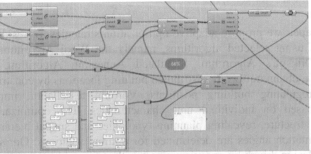

Figure 12 Result of Simulated Annealing Algorithm

2.5 Assessment of Building View Deviation

Among the factors influencing residential orientation, building views are the dominant determinants in building layout, provided that approximate north-south alignment and sunlight distances between buildings can be ensured. Residential orientation is often not determined by the optimal sunlight direction, but a balance between sunlight, other landscape, and view requirements (Figure 12).

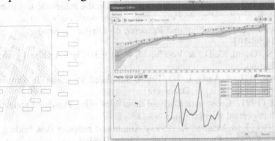

Figure 13 Result of Simulated Annealing Algorithm

In this generative experiment, surrounding buildings obstructed site views. The optimal angle for building deviation, considering maximum visible distance, ranged from 45° southeast to 45° southwest. Facade widths were sampled, and distances to nearest obstacles directly in front were overlaid and weighted. This value, combined with building views and count, assessed random building points from Populate Geometry (Figure 13). Larger values indicated better views. Genetic algorithms then determined optimal deviation angles for each building, achieving the best combination for the entire site.

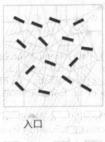

Figure 14 Result of Simulated Annealing Algorithm

3. Conclusion

In this paper, we propose adaptive optimization strategies for residential building design issues using selected algorithms, namely the Wool Algorithm, Slime Mold Algorithm, Dijkstra's Algorithm, Simulated Annealing Algorithm, and Genetic Algorithm. We obtain uniformly distributed building locations by constraining random points and regulating building positions. Voronoi tessellation improves spatial distribution based on individual unit characteristics. The optimization algorithm analyzes site structure, revealing planning typologies and spatial hierarchy divisions. Building orientation angles are determined for optimal solutions. Our study provides insights into design driven by optimization algorithms in residential areas. Performance comparison of five algorithms identifies Dijkstra's and Genetic Algorithm as optimal for path optimization and visual perspective adjustment in residential design.

References

[1] Zhang Baizhou; Li Biao; Exploration on Architectural Space Layout Based on Multi-agent and Dijkstra Algorithm——A Case of the Residence Generative Design. *Urbanism and Architecture* 2020,17(27):7-10+20

[2] Research on the influence of topographic regularity in the automatic layout of industrial parks based on genetic algorithms. *Digital technology - the whole building life cycle——Proceedings of the 2018 National Symposium on Teaching and Research on Digital Technology in Architecture for Architecture Faculties.*,2018:98-103.

[3] Kirkpatrick, S., Gelatt, C. D., & Vecchi, M. P. (1983). Optimization by simulated annealing. science, 220(4598), 671-680.

[4] Van Laarhoven, P. J., & Aarts, E. H. (1987). Simulated annealing. In Simulated annealing: Theory and applications (pp. 7-15). Springer, Dordrecht.

[5] Abramson, D. (1991). Constructing school timetables using simulated annealing: sequential and parallel algorithms. Management science, 37(1), 98-113.

[6] Tracey, N., Clark, J., & Mander, K. (1998). Automated program flaw finding using simulated annealing. *ACM SIGSOFT Software Engineering Notes*, 23(2), 73-81.

[7] Ekren, O., & Ekren, B. Y. (2010). Size optimization of a PV/wind hybrid energy conversion system with battery storage using simulated annealing. *Applied energy*, 87(2), 592-598.

[8] Hong, W. C. (2011). Traffic flow forecasting by seasonal SVR with chaotic simulated annealing algorithm. *Neurocomputing*, 74(12-13), 2096-2107.

[9] Sonmez, F. O. (2008). Optimum design of composite structures with simulated annealing. *Composite Structures*, 86(1-3), 69-82.

[10] AlHalawani, S., Yang, Y. L., Liu, H., & Mitra, N. J. (2013). Interactive facades analysis and synthesis of semi-regular facades. In Computer Graphics Forum (Vol. 32, No. 2pt3, pp. 215-224).

[11] Yeh, I. C. (2006). Architectural layout optimization using annealed neural network. *Automation in Construction*, 15(4), 531-539.

[12] Michalek, J. J., Choudhary, R., & Papalambros, P. Y. (2002). Architectural layout design optimization. *Engineering optimization*, 34(5), 461-484.

[13] Huang, R. H., Chen, Y. P., Tsai, H. W., & Shen, C. C. (2011). Gbps: a new energy efficient routing protocol for wireless sensor networks. *Journal of Information Hiding and Multimedia Signal Processing*, 2(2), 173-182.

[14] Boryczka, U., & Ciura, G. (2015). Path planning for UAV performing detection using Dijkstra algorithm. *Journal of Theoretical & Applied Mechanics*, 53(2).

[15] Wang, K. C., & Chi, Y. C. (1998). A revised Dijkstra's algorithm for the path planning of a cooperative carrying robot system. In Proceedings of IEEE International Conference on Robotics and Automation (Vol. 3, pp. 2611-2616).

[16] Krajnik, T., Nitsche, M., Pedre, S., Preucil, L., & Mejail, M. (2018). The best of both worlds: Making robot navigation in virtual environments more efficient by leveraging state information. In 2018 European Conference on Mobile Robots (ECMR) (pp. 1-6).

Design Studies and Intelligence Engineering
L.C. Jain et al. (Eds.)
© 2024 The Authors.
doi:10.3233/FAIA231443

A Review on Vascular Biometrics for Finger Vein Authentication System

D Jude HEMANTH[1] and Nisha Joy THOMAS
Department of ECE, Karunya Institute of Technology & Sciences,
Coimbatore, India Corresponding

Abstract. In the area of biometric authentication, vascular biometrics has been highlighted off late due to its much-appreciated list of advantages which promotes more efficient person identification and authentication. Finger Vein Recognition Systems (FVRS) is an emerging biometric technology gaining much attention throughout the world especially in the banking sector, cashless/ cardless money transfer, ATM systems and soon. Finger vein authentication systems have the threat of spoof attacks or presentation attacks (PA) which affects the security measures in a serious manner. Since vascular biometrics is receiving more attention in the field of financial transfer, being aware of the possible security attacks is a necessity. This paper presents a review of selected literature on presentation attacks in finger vein authentication systems. Also listing the pros and cons of the presentation attack detection methods and certain ways to prevent PA. The pros and challenges of dealing with FVRS have also been listed here.

Keywords. vascular biometrics, finger vein authentication, presentation attack, fake vein attack, biometric security, spoofing.

1. Introduction

Identity identification is now a big part of how people live their lives. Logging into computers or online accounts, using ATMs, and getting permission to enter a bank or a certain area are just some of the most common times when name verification is needed. There are many ways to find out who someone is. Most people use passwords, but they are becoming less common because biometrics seem to be the best way to identify a person [8].

A biometric authentication system measures specific physical characteristics or behaviors in real-time to verify a person's identity. As a result, algorithms used in biometric authentication systems may be used to identify or validate the person by comparing the data to other biometric records in the database. [1]. Finger vein biometrics, also called vascular biometrics is coined as such because of the authentication performed by verifying the unique pattern of blood vessels (veins) under the skin in the fingertips. This physical trait is different for every human being on earth. Compared to other biometric modalities like fingerprint, face recognition, iris recognition etc., vascular biometrics stands out with the greater number of benefits such as:

- difficult to forge compared to other biometric modalities.

---

[1] Corresponding Author: judehemanth@karunya.edu

- contactless authentication.
- this pattern of veins seems not to evolve with time and contains enough discriminant information to be used as a person recognition method [4] .
- multiple fingers can be used to acquire sufficient vein information for finger vein recognition, and finger vein capture devices are smaller in volume [21].
- in addition, customers can register one of their fingers as a "stress finger" to use when under stress. For instance, if a criminal makes an individual to take out currency, the customer's stress finger can be detected by the bank, which can then implement an automatic countermeasure, such as closing the ATM and displaying an "out of service" notification [27].
- finger vein recognition is a major biometric method that is thought to be safer, reliable, and on the rise [3].
- less time-consuming and simpler to use for the end user [10] . Only roughly 400 bytes of data need to be sent, so the user's name can be validated in a few seconds [27].

Identification and verification are the two main ways that biometric security systems work. In the recognition mode, the data that is put in can be compared to all the patterns that are already in the database. Using this method, it is possible to find out if this person is in the database. In verification mode, biometric data is matched to the unique pattern of a single person. If they aren't the same individual, it stops many people from using the same name [2]

Despite the advantages mentioned above, finger vein recognition system has challenges associated with it as well, since the effects of environmental illumination, ambient temperature, and scattering of light during the acquisition of finger vein images can lead the vein patterns to be confusing and incoherent [6]. A further consideration is that extremely cold and 'dead' fingers (such as those of individuals with Raynaud's syndrome) are difficult to read using finger vein pattern recognition [10]. Information about the person's health issues can be leaked [13].

Late strange of applications using vascular biometrics [28]:

- Application of pay-by-finger in retail industry.
- Finger Vein Authentication using visible light smartphone cameras. Infrared light is usually used for the sensor to acquire the vein image.
- Public Biometrics Infrastructure (PBI) technology also allows the utilization of electronic data with digital signatures in lieu of traditionally signed paper transaction docs. It allows branches to conduct processes electronically, thus boosting the productivity of banking work (paperless procedures).
- At present, finger vein recognition technology is mostly used for identity authentication, financial transactions, and information security. It is expected to be used in other sectors soon. In the smart healthcare sector, finger vein recognition can enhance patient identity identification and medical data access control, enhancing security and privacy. Finger vein recognition technology can be used in smart transport to authenticate drivers and improve traffic safety by allowing only authorized drivers to drive vehicles.

Mr. Takeyuki Mayumi who is currently engaged in the facilitation of biometrics authentication deployment at Hitachi, says that " The global need for biometric authentication has experienced a significant increase" [11].Certain countries including

Japan, China, South Korea has implemented finger vein systems in ATM systems and other countries like UAE, India, Brazil is exploring the use of this technology in ATM systems and banking sector. However, there are attacks that could weaken the level of protection provided by finger vein biometric systems [2].

Hence it is extremely important to be aware of the possible security threats, to prevent possible attacks. There is still a great deal of unknown territory in the field of presentation attacks (PA), studies of vulnerability, and attack detection, according to the published research content on biometric vein recognition [17].

1.1. Outline

The rest of this paper is organized as follows: Section 2 points out the motivation and problem statement. The different types of attacks in FVRS are mentioned in Section 3, focusing on the presentation attack. A review on certain chosen papers of presentation attacks is portrayed along with possible preventive measures. Section 4 gives an outline of the datasets used for FVRS and PA. Section 5 shows the parameters which justify the algorithms. Towards the end of the paper, section 6 gives the conclusion.

2. Motivation and Problem Statement

The main motivation is the threat to security in person authentication. Biometric protection gets more important as technology and electronic payment methods become more widely used [27]. Since vascular biometrics have been used in the banking sector for financial transfers and many other person authentication areas, vulnerability of PA to the FVRS is a major concern and PAD algorithms need to be tried and tested with various datasets to increase the features to withstand PA.

3. Different types of Attacks in FVRS

Finger vein pattern detection systems can be attacked in several different ways:

1. Direct Attack: A presentation attack refers to the deliberate action of an individual impersonating another person with the intention of gaining unauthorized entry into a system [17]. This kind of attack that belongs to the category of direct attacks[5] or physical attack. In this type of attack, the attacker shows the recognition system a captured biometric trait of the victim, like a picture of a finger vein, to make it think they are the victim. In a physical attack, a synthetic master vein image is used to make a real thing called a Presentation Attack Instrument (PAI) [25]. The PAI is then used to attack the recognition system with a presentation attack. [7]

2. Logical Attack: That means using a Trojan horse or another type of malware and virus to attack the parts of the biometric system, channel interception, replay attacks. Direct attacks on biometric systems are more interesting because the attacker doesn't need to know anything about the system being attacked. This kind of attack takes advantage of the flaws in the matching process [24].

In this paper, we focus only on presentation attacks. Presentation attacks, commonly referred to as spoofing, encompass the act of acquiring the biometric data of an individual through various means. This may involve capturing a high-quality image of the person's face, fingertip, or iris, or recording their voice. Subsequently, this acquired data is utilized to generate a replica image, either in two-dimensional or three-dimensional form. Such a replica can then be transformed into a mask or overlay, enabling an imposter to assume the identity of the victim [9]

3.1. Presentation Attack

The authors of [7] are evaluating the vulnerability of finger vein recognition (FVR) systems to master vein attacks. In these attacks, a manipulated image resembling a vein is used to match fraudulently with multiple identities. The findings highlight the significance of instituting increased security measures in FVR systems [7]. The authors explain two techniques for generating master veins in finger vein recognition systems. This method employs a pre-trained generative model and an evolutionary algorithm. The utilized generative model combines 2-VAE and WGAN-GP models. Typically, the LVE algorithm is used to generate master biometric samples; in this instance, it is used to generate master veins. This method employs an adversarial machine learning (AdvM) attack to target a robust CNN-based surrogate recognition system. The attack involves the creation of an image resembling a vein that can be used to impersonate multiple enrolled identities.

The researchers in [12] suggest a PAD [24] approach for a near-infrared (NIR) camera-based finger vein recognition system that uses a convolutional neural network (CNN) to improve the ability of handcrafted techniques to find veins. For dimensionality reduction and classification, they also employ principal component analysis (PCA) and support vector machine (SVM). The experimental results show that their proposed method is superior to other techniques for determining finger-vein images associated with presentation attacks.

The work in [14] talks about the security problems with biometric systems, such as presentation attacks (PAs), in which fake biometric features or presentation attack tools are used to pretend to be someone else. The authors suggest a new method for detecting fingerprint presentation attacks (PAD) that uses a device that can take pictures in the short-wave infrared (SWIR) range. They test the method on a collection of more than 4,700 samples and show a low detection equal error rate (D-EER) of 1.35 percent, even in a situation where attacks are unknown.

The paper [15] talks about how fake finger vein pictures can be used to find presentation attacks. In this method, the pictures are broken down, the information is encoded, and a cascaded support vector machine model is used to classify the images. Experiments have shown that the proposed method works better than ways that are already in use. The paper talks about how important biometric techniques are in different situations, but it also says that they can be attacked by "presentation attacks."

The main goal of the study in [16] is to figure out how dangerous vein attack databases are in the field of biometrics for finger and hand veins. The study looks at how well different vein recognition methods can find attack specimens from a public database of attacks and a private database of dorsal hand veins. The goal is to figure out the Impostor Attack Presentation Match Rate, which is the number of attacks that were accepted when they shouldn't have been. The study also suggests a fusion method that detects presentation attacks by putting together comparison scores from different classification schemes.

Table 1. Highlights of the above review.

Ref.	Strengths	Limitations
[7]	Miura's system is readily corrupted by non-vein-appearing	CNN based FVRS could fool LVE method

	samples produced by a WGAN- GP model with vein-like. characteristics.[18][19]	
[12]	Employing a CNN-based approach, a suitable image feature extractor is found. Creates an extremely high degree of detection precision when compared to earlier techniques.	Needs an enormous number of computations and is more complicated than former techniques.
[14]	Use of SWIR images in combination with state-of-the-art CNNs offers a reliable and efficient solution to the threat posed by presentation attacks.	Unpredictable about the efficiency in attacks evolved in future
[15]	This is the first time that the amount of blurriness and the way noise is spread out in real and fake pictures are looked at as two different things.	Is applicable to large difference between real and forged images
[16]	Keypoint strategy SIFT is typically, highly resistant to PLUS, attacks.	The texture-based procedures LBP and CNN are typically. vulnerable to IDIAP and SCUT attack samples only.

3.2. Possible preventive measures

Presentation attacks can be stopped and made less dangerous in finger vein pattern recognition systems by using some of the countermeasures.

Here are some ways to approach the problem:

1. Liveness Detection: Using methods for liveness detection can help figure out if the finger vein pattern shown is from a real person or a fake one [25]. To make sure the picture is real, this can mean looking at things like blood flow or specific movements. [20]

2. Multimodal biometrics: Adding finger vein pattern recognition to other biometric methods, like fingerprint or iris recognition, can make the system more secure overall. When multiple biological traits are used together, it becomes harder for attackers to fool the system.[7][23]

3. Quality Assessment: Using quality assessment algorithms [26] can help find pictures of finger veins that look suspicious or aren't very good. By looking at things like picture resolution, focus, and noise levels, the system can get rid of images that don't meet the quality standards. This makes it less likely that a presentation attack will work.

4. Finger vein Datasets

1. Shandong University made the SDUMLA-HMT database, which is a biometrics library with many kinds of information. The finger vein database constitutes a

component of the SDUMLA-HMT collection. It has pictures of the veins in 6 fingers from 106 people. The index, middle, and ring fingers on both hands constitute the 6 fingers. The SDUMLA-HMT archive has six pictures for each finger of every individual[29].

2. Finger vein recognition and finger vein presentation assault detection (anti-spoofing) are both supported by the VERA Finger Vein dataset. The dataset includes 440 NIR bona fide photos from 110 clients that were taken using an open sensor. Additionally, the set of images comprises presentation assaults (spoofing attacks) on the same 440 images that can be studied to determine the vein identification systems' susceptibility as well as to create presentation attack detection methods [31][32].

3. The pictures in the archive, FV-USM came from 123 students and faculty at Universiti Sains Malaysia, 83 of whom were men and 40 of whom were women. Each subject gave four fingers: the index finger on the left, the middle finger on the left, the index finger on the right, and the middle finger on the right. This gave a total of 492 finger classes [33].

4. The Finger Image Archive at HongKong Polytechnic University is made up of images of finger veins and finger surface textures taken at the same time from both male and female subjects. There are 6264 images from 156 people in the database [34].

5. The UTFVP Finger vein Database has 1440 pictures from 60 clients that can be used to recognize finger veins. The University of Twente in the Netherlands made this collection[36].

6. THU-FVFDT (Tsinghua University Finger Vein and Finger Dorsal Texture Database) is a collection that includes raw photos of 220 different subjects' finger veins and dorsal textures. Raw images have a resolution of 720 x 576 pixels [37].

5. Parameters for Evaluation

Shown below is a table displaying the parameters used for evaluating the efficiency of FVRS and PAD.

Ref.	Purpose	Parameters
[38][39]	FVRS	Equal Error Rate (EER), (True Acceptance Rate
		(TAR), False acceptance rate (FAR), False
		recognition rate (FRR)
[12][14][15][16]	PAD	Attack Presentation Classification Error Rate
		(APCER) Bona Fide Presentation
		Classification Error Rate
		(BPCER) SpoofFalse
		Acceptance Rate (SFAR)
		Average classification error
		rate (ACER)

6. Conclusion

In this paper, the advantages of vascular biometrics along with the challenges have been listed. The applications of vascular biometrics in various fields also have been portrayed. There are attacks that can affect the performance of FVRS like the presentation attacks. Selected work on PA & PAD has been highlighted in a table. Also, some preventive measures that can be adopted have been mentioned. Certain available databases for FVRS and PA have also been listed out along with the parameters that decide the efficiency of the purpose.

References

[1] I. Boucherit et al., Finger vein identification using deeply-fused Convolutional Neural Network Journal *of King Saud University - Computer and Information Sciences* **34** (2022) 646-656.

[2] Finger Vein Recognition Using Deep Learning Technique Wasit Journal of Computer and Mathematic Science

[3] S. Shakilet al. An optimal method for identification of finger vein using supervised learning, *Measurement: Sensors* **25** (2023)

[4] Alexandre Sierro, Pierre Ferrez, Pierre Roduit, Contact-less Palm/Finger Vein Biometrics

[5] Pedro Tome and S´ebastien Marcel, On the Vulnerability of Palm Vein Recognition to Spoofing Attacks

[6] Kashif Shaheed et al., A Systematic Review of Finger Vein Recognition Techniques, *Information* **9** (2018)

[7] Huy H. Nguyen, Analysis of Master Vein Attacks on Finger Vein Recognition Systems, *IEEE* (2023)

[8] Shazeeda Shazeeda, Bakhtiar Affendi Rosdi, Finger vein recognition using mutual sparse representation classification, *IET Biom., The Institution of Engineering and Technology* (2018), Vol. 8 Iss. 1, pp. 49-58.

[9] A. Morales et al., Chapter 6, Introduction to Iris Presentation Attack Detection, *Handbook of Biometric Anti-Spoofing*, 2019.

[10] https://www.recogtech.com/en/knowledge-base/5-common-biometric-techniques-compared

[11] https://social-innovation.hitachi/en/article/pbi/

[12] Dat Tien Nguyen et al., Spoof Detection for Finger-Vein Recognition System Using NIR Camera, *Sensors,* 2017.

[13] A. Krishnan, T. Thomas, Finger Vein Recognition Based on Anatomical Features of Vein Patterns, IEEE

[14] Ruben Tolosana et al., Biometric Presentation Attack Detection: Beyond the Visible Spectrum IEEE TRANSACTIONS ON INFORMATION FORENSICS AND SECURITY, VOL. 15, 2020.

[15] Xinwei Qiu et al., Finger Vein Presentation Attack Detection Using Total Variation Decomposition

[16] Johannes Schuiki et al., Extensive Threat Analysis of Vein Attack Databases and Attack Detection by Fusion of Comparison Scores.

[17] A. Anjos etal. Chapter 18, An Introduction to Vein Presentation, Attacks and Detection, Handbook of Biometric Anti-Spoofing pg.419

[18] Naoto Miura, Akio Nagasaka, and Takafumi Miyatake. Feature extraction of finger-vein patterns based on repeated line tracking and its application to personal identification. Machine Vision and Applications, 15(4):194-203, 2004.

[19] K. Shaheed et al., Recent advancements in finger vein recognition technology: Methodology, challenges and opportunities, Information Fusion 79 (2022), 84- 109

[20] KEVIN W. BOWYER, Presentation Attack Detection for Iris Recognition: An Assessment of the State of-the-Art ADAM CZAJKA, Research and Academic Computer Network (NASK),

[21] S. Dong, J. Yang, Y. Chen, C. Wang, X. Zhan, et al., Finger Vein Recognition Based on Multi-Orientation Weighted Symmetric Local Graph structure, KSII Trans. Internet Inf. Syst. 9 (10) (2015)

[22] https://social-innovation.hitachi/en/article/touchless-finger-vein/

[23] Ryszard S. Choras, Chapter Multimodal Biometrics for Person Authentication, *Security and Privacy from a Legal, Ethical, and Technical Perspective,* IntechOpen.

[24] R. Raghavendra, Presentation Attack Detection Algorithms for Finger Vein Biometrics: A Comprehensive Study, International Conference on Signal-Image Technology & Internet-Based Systems (2015)

[25] J. Galbally et al., Handbook of Biometric Anti-Spoofing: Trusted Biometrics Under Spoofing Attacks. Springer Publishing Company, Incorporated, 2014, page 4.

[26] Huafeng Qin et al., Quality Assessment of Finger-vein Image, IEEE Transactions on Information Forensics and Security

[27] https://social-innovation.hitachi/en-eu/case_studies/why-the-future-lies-in-fingerveinid/

[28] Zhou, L. (2023). Finger Vein Recognition Technology: Principles, Applications, and Future Prospects. International Journal of Biology and Life Sciences, 3(2), 45-48.

[29] Yilong Yin, Lili Liu, and Xiwei Sun. Sdumla-hmt: a multimodal biometric database. In Chinese Conference on Biometric Recognition, pages 260-268. Springer, 2011.

[30] K. Syazana-Itqan, A Review of Finger-Vein Biometrics Identification Approaches, Indian Journal of Science and Technology, Vol 9(32)

[31] Vanoni, Matthias, Tome, Pedro, & Marcel, Sébastien. (2014). VERA FingerVein [Data set]. https://doi.org/10.34777/8pkt-6z66

[32] Pedro Tome, Ramachandra Raghavendra, Christoph Busch, Santosh Tirunagari, Norman Poh, B. H. Shekar, Diego Gragnaniello, Carlo Sansone, Luisa Verdoliva and Sébastien Marcel: "The 1st Competition on Counter Measures to Finger Vein Spoofing Attacks", in Proceedings of the 8th IAPR International Conference on Biometrics (ICB), 2015

[33] Mohd Shahrimie Mohd Asaari, Shahrel A. Suandi, BakhtiarAffendi Rosdi, *Fusion of Band Limited Phase Only Correlation and Width Centroid Contour Distance for finger based biometrics*, Expert Systems with Applications, Volume 41, Issue 7, 1 June 2014, Pages 3367-3382, ISSN 0957- 4174, http://dx.doi.org/10.1016/j.eswa.2013.11.033.

[34] Ajay Kumar and Yingbo Zhou, "Human Identification using Finger Images", IEEE Trans. Image Processing, vol. 21, pp. 2228-2244, April 2012

[35] Ton, B. T., & Veldhuis, R. N. J. (2013). A high-quality finger vascular pattern dataset collected using a custom designed capturing device. In *Proceedings of the 2013 International Conference on Biometrics (ICB)* (pp. 1-5). (Proceedings International Conference on Biometrics (ICB); Vol. 2013). IEEE.

[36] Tome et al., On the Vulnerability of Finger Vein Recognition to Spoofing, IEEE International Conference of the Biometrics Special Interest Group, (2014)

[37] Yang W et al. Comparative competitive coding for personal identification by using finger vein and finger dorsal texture fusion. Information Sciences. 2014; 268:20–32

[38] Luo et al. FVCT: Finger Vein Authentication Based on the Combination of CNN and Transforme

[39] Kashif Shaheed et al., A Systematic Review of Finger Vein Recognition Techniques (2018)

© 2024 The Authors.
This article is published online with Open Access by IOS Press and distributed under the terms
of the Creative Commons Attribution Non-Commercial License 4.0 (CC BY-NC 4.0).
doi:10.3233/FAIA231444

Research on Improving the Quality of Japanese Chinese Machine Translation Based on Deep Learning

Jialing LU [a] and Fengxian YIN [a]

[a]Shenyang Aerospace University

Abstract: In order to improve the quality of Japanese-Chinese machine translation, the research on improving the quality of Japanese-Chinese machine translation based on deep learning is put forward. The maximum entropy model is used to effectively classify Japanese possible states and passive states, and then the features of Japanese possible states and passive states are effectively integrated into the log-linear model to improve the translation model, so as to improve the accuracy of selecting possible states and passive states in translation rules. The experimental results show that this method can effectively improve the translation quality of Japanese possible sentences and passive sentences. On large-scale Japanese Chinese materials, the maximum translation BLEU value can be increased from 41.50 to 42.01, and the overall intelligibility of translation results has been improved by 2.71% in manual evaluation. Conclusion: This method can improve the accuracy of rule selection.

Keywords: passive; Possible state; Statistical machine translation; Maximum entropy model

1 Introduction

In recent years, with the gradual popularization of the Internet, the amount of information and data has increased dramatically, and international communication has become increasingly close, and the language barrier has become one of the main reasons that restrict the development of globalization. Countries have invested a lot of manpower and material resources in translation, but manual translation can no longer meet the demand, while machine translation can effectively reduce the communication cost of human beings, so it has broad application space in social, commercial, educational, and other fields. At present, machine translation cannot completely replace manual translation, but it can assist translators, improve communication efficiency, and effectively save time and labor costs. On the other hand, language differences will also affect the political, economic, cultural, and military exchanges between countries. In recent years, the contacts between China and Japan have become more and more frequent and close, and doing a good job in Japanese translation has an important impact on the exchanges between the two countries [1-4].

As early as the 1840s, machine translation was put forward by researchers, and its development has experienced ups and downs. Early machine translation used dictionary matching, and then developed a rule-based method, relying on the rules formulated by language experts to carry out translation work. In the early 1990s, IBM researchers put forward a statistical machine translation model based on the noise channel model, and based on this model, put forward a statistical machine translation model based on words. However, due to the limitations of poor computing power and long running time of statistical methods at that time, the research on statistical machine translation methods once stagnated. In recent years, with the development of computers and the enrichment of Internet corpus, the factors restricting statistical methods have been improved, and more researchers have begun to devote themselves to statistical machine translation, which has become a research hotspot again. At present, the application of neural network-based methods in machine translation has been further concerned and explored by researchers, and the method of deep learning has made great progress [5-8].

2 Literature review

Since the birth of machine translation, its research methods have been advancing in the alternation of rationalism and empiricism. Rationalism refers to the manual compilation of translation rules and dictionaries by linguists based on linguistic theories, and RBMT is a typical example. Empirical method is based on information theory and mathematical statistics, driven by large-scale corpus, and automatically acquires translation knowledge through machine learning cardinality. This method is also called corpus-based machine translation (CBMT) or data-driven machine translation [9-11].

Looking at the development trend and technical status quo of machine translation research, the following research directions or problems may become the bastions that machine translation must overcome in the future: the optimization of end-to-end neural network machine translation: there are still many shortcomings in end-to-end machine translation, such as poor interpretability leading to untraceable translation errors, high computational complexity leading to efficient training only by GPU servers, and simple network structure leading to difficulty in incorporating prior information [12-13] . Therefore, enhancing the interpretability of the model, reducing the computational complexity of the neural network (which means that it can be trained efficiently on the CPU) and designing a more reasonable coding and decoding network are all widely concerned research issues in the future. Machine translation for small data: At present, machine translation relies on a large number of parallel texts as training data, but many language pairs containing small languages or languages in specific application fields often do not have enough bilingual parallel corpus. This problem makes it difficult to achieve good results in machine translation at present. How to solve the problem of machine translation of small data by semi-supervised or weakly supervised methods based on the powerful feature representation ability of deep learning will also become a hot research direction in the future. Machine translation of nonstandard texts: The Internet is the place where the most language texts are produced, but most of the language texts used on the Internet are nonstandard, with many spoken words, new words and even many of them not conforming to standard grammar. At present, machine translation systems are almost all developed on the basis of normative texts, and their ability to deal with these spoken words, new words and all kinds of memes produced in the new era is weak [14-18] . Caruso, T. et al. [19] trained a model that combined the probability of language model with syntactic and semantic features of the output translation. Deng, J, et al. [20] put forward an automatic evaluation index learned from manual evaluation and pseudo-reference translation, which is generated by other machine translation systems and does not need high translation quality. Ekhosuehi, V.U. et al. [21] selected the information of phrase boundary words to construct the maximum entropy model and applied it to phrase ranking. Yang, X. et al. [22] established a maximum entropy rule selection model by using the boundary word information of non-terminators. Zhang, T. et al. [23] used the maximum entropy model to integrate lexicalization features such as location information into the hierarchical phrase model. Shirani, K. et al. [24] use the number and types of non-terminators to classify hierarchical phrase rules and solve the problem of rule selection. Using classification model to fuse the missing contextual information in hierarchical phrase model can effectively improve the translation quality, but the disadvantage of this method is that lexicalized information still lacks the constraints of linguistics and syntax.

On the basis of summarizing the above methods, this paper puts forward a method to integrate the possible state and passive dynamic features of Japanese into the translation model. Firstly, the corpus is divided into passive, possible and other voices, and the corresponding syntactic features are extracted to construct a maximum entropy classification model, and it is effectively classified. Then the voice features are extracted synchronously when extracting hierarchical phrase rules, and the voice features are integrated into the translation model by using the maximum entropy model. Finally, possible and passive translation models are constructed to improve the translation accuracy of these two voices. This method not only uses the maximum entropy model to fuse rich contextual information, but also introduces the linguistic constraint of voice to guide the decoder to choose appropriate rules according to different voices. Experiments show that this method improves the BLEU value of 0.1~0.5, and the overall intelligibility of translation results is also improved by 2.71% in manual evaluation.

3 Research Methods

3.1 hierarchical phrase model

Hierarchical Phrase Based model can automatically extract formal grammar from double sentence pairs without linguistic labeling and assumptions, and it is one of the best statistical machine translation systems at present.

3.1.1 Rule Extraction

The hierarchical phrase model uses context-free grammar (SCFG) rules for translation, and its rule form is shown in Formula (1).

$$X \to \langle \alpha, \gamma, \sim \rangle \tag{1}$$

Among them, X Non-terminal, α and γ They are the source language and target language end of the rule, including terminators and non-terminators, and the corresponding relationship of non-terminators is represented by "~".

The extraction process of hierarchical phrase rules is as follows: based on the word alignment information of bilingual corpus, phrase rules are extracted from left to right. After that, the phrasal rules are replaced by sub-phrases, thus the formal syntactic relationship is obtained. Although this syntactic relationship simplifies modeling and decoding, the rules do not retain contextual information in the process of generalization, which leads to the fact that sub-phrases can match any syntactic components and often lead to errors in translation.

3.1.2 Translation model

The translation process of hierarchical phrase translation system can be described as for a given source language sentence.fFrom all possible translation results.eFind the translation result with the highest score. Hierarchical phrase translation system uses logarithmic linear model in the translation process, which combines multiple features. Every time the log-linear model is transformed, the sum of the scores of the previous steps will be calculated. Equation (2) is the conversion score in the logarithmic linear model, which is usually expressed in logarithmic form, as shown in Equation (3).

$$P(d) = \prod_i^M \varphi_i(d)^{\lambda_i}, \tag{2}$$

$$score\ (d) = \log P(d) = \log \prod_i^M \varphi_i(d)^{\lambda_i} = \sum_i^M \lambda_i \log \varphi_i(d) \tag{3}$$

among φ_i Is the characteristic function, λ_i Is the corresponding feature weight,dRepresents each step of the translation process. The following features are used in the hierarchical phrase translation model: forward and backward translation probability, P(e|f) and P(f|e) , positive and negative lexicalization weights,P_w(e|f)andP_w(f|e), n metalanguage model,P_{lw}(f), regular quantity punishment, exp(-1), length punishment,exp(|f|). The decoder combines the above features with the log-linear model, and uses the algorithm of CYK form to translate the sentences in the test set by using the extracted hierarchical phrase rules.

3.2 Translation model with maximum entropy feature
3.2.1 Translation System Structure

In this paper, voices are divided into passive, possible and other voices, and the voice information is integrated into the translation model through the maximum entropy model.

Firstly, the corpus is classified, and the passive and possible sentences in the corpus are manually extracted and screened out, and the remaining sentences are classified into other voices; Then the training corpus is analyzed syntactically, and the features of different voices are extracted to train the maximum entropy model. In the process of rule extraction, the corresponding features are extracted, and the voice features are fused into the rule table through the maximum entropy model to generate translation models with different voices. Finally, in the process of translation, the voice of the input sentence is first judged, and the corresponding translation model is selected according to the voice, so that the rules are automatically filtered in the decoding process.

This paper mainly discusses the hierarchical phrase rule classification based on maximum entropy model, the selection of classification features and the integration of maximum entropy model and translation model, and only briefly describes the translation process.

3.2.2 Maximum entropy rule classification

Maximum Entropy model can satisfy all known constraints, make no assumptions about unknown information, and can easily integrate various contextual information as voice features, so this paper chooses the maximum entropy model as the classification model. Suppose there is a sample set. $T = \{(x_1, V_1), (x_2, V_2), \cdots, (x_n, V_n)\}$, in which$x_i(1 \leq i \leq n)$Is the context of a sentence,$V_i(1 \leq i \leq n)$Represents the voice category of a sentence. The constraint of maximum entropy is realized by the characteristic function, and the definition of sentence voice classification is shown in Formula (4).

$$f(x, V) = \begin{cases} 1(= \text{ word}) \wedge (= \text{ sentence voice category}) \\ 0 \text{ Other} \end{cases} \qquad (4)$$

The maximum entropy model of voice is established as shown in Formula (5).

$$P = \text{argmax}_{p \subseteq C} \ H(P) \qquad (5)$$

among $H(P)$ It's a model P Entropy of, C Is a set of models that meet the constraints. Given the text set and related constraints, there is a unique probability model. P^*, its entropy value is the largest, as shown in formula (6) and (7).

$$P(V \mid x)^* = Z(x)\exp \left(\sum_i \lambda_i f_i(x, V) \right) \qquad (6)$$

$$Z(x) = \frac{1}{\sum_V \exp \left(\sum_i \lambda_i f_i(x, V) \right)} \qquad (7)$$

Among them, $Z(x)$ Is a normalized constant, f_i That is, the model features, λ_i Is the parameter of the model, that is, the weight of the characteristic function. By studying on the training set, it can be concluded that λ_i The specific value of.

Equation (7) describes the maximum entropy probability model of a sentence. For each hierarchical phrase rule containing core verbs $< \alpha, \gamma >$, the following maximum entropy voice classification model can be constructed, as shown in Formula (8) and Formula (9).

$$P\big(V \mid \alpha, \gamma, f(X_k)\big)$$
$$= Z(x)\exp \left[\sum_i \lambda_i f_i\big(V(\alpha), f(X_k)\big) \right] \qquad (8)$$

$$Z(x) = \frac{1}{\sum_{\gamma'} \exp \left[\sum_i \lambda_i f_i\big(V(\alpha), f(X_k)\big) \right]} \qquad (9)$$

Among them, α As the source language end of the rule, γ For the target language end, V Is the voice category corresponding to the rule. X_k Represents the non-terminal contained in it. A rule may contain multiple non-terminators, k Is the number corresponding to the non-terminator. Nonterminal X_k The source language sub-phrase in is $f(X_k)$, $V(\alpha)$ Voice information representing the context in the source language phrase, $f_i\big(V(\alpha), f(X_k)\big)$ Is a binary characteristic function, λ_i Is the characteristic weight of the function.

3.2.3 Feature Selection and Rule Extraction

The selection of feature function directly affects the classification performance. A relatively complete Japanese case frame library is constructed by using a large number of network resources and applied to syntactic analysis. Extract lattice frame features from large-scale corpus to complete the task of transforming dynamic sentences into main dynamics. Among them, the accuracy of dynamic sentence recognition is very high, which shows that lattice framework can effectively distinguish the voice of sentences. For the above-mentioned maximum entropy rule classification model, the following characteristics are specified:

The central structural word feature F1 of a sentence. Predicate verbs and suffixes in Japanese sentences, that is, the root node information of parsing tree.

The main structural feature F2 of the sentence is the lattice frame information of the central predicate, which is the first node of the parsing tree at the source language end.

The predicates of passive and possible sentences are different from the deformation of other voices, but the passive and possible forms of many verbs have the same form, so it is necessary to introduce the structural characteristics of sentences to distinguish them.

It is illustrated by the example of "underground money, private money, hatred, theft in Dorobou" (my wallet was stolen by a hateful thief on the subway).

Firstly, syntactic analysis and annotation are carried out before extraction. The sentence features extracted according to the labeling results are shown in Table 1.

Table 1 Feature Extraction in Example Sentences

Feature type	eigenvalue
F1	Steal the money.
F2	Underground shopping center, Dorobou.

Taking phrases in sentences as examples, when extracting hierarchical phrase rules, the corresponding maximum entropy features are also extracted. Firstly, the following three phrase rules are extracted from the word alignment relationship:

$$X \rightarrow \ <れ, Bei>$$

$$X \rightarrow \ < Dorobou, thief >$$

$$X \rightarrow \ < Dorobou stole it, was stolen by a thief >$$

From the above rules, a hierarchical phrase rule with two non-terminators can be obtained:

$$X \rightarrow \ <X1 \ steals \ 走 \ X2, X2X1 \ steals >$$

The generalized part of the rule contains the root node, that is, the predicate verb or suffix information, so it is necessary to extract the features of the rule, that is, extract its complete root node information (including rules, non-terminators and boundary words) and sentence structure information in non-terminators. 3.2.4 Translation Model Fusion

The maximum entropy features of the extracted rules are classified by using the maximum entropy model, and the maximum entropy probability values of the three voices are obtained.$P(V_1)$, $P(V_2)$, $P(V_3)$, corresponding to passive, possible and other voices respectively. There is also a class of rules that do not contain voice information in the rule table, including rules without non-terminators (that is, phrase rules) and rules without sentence center nodes in non-terminators. In the experiment, such rules are classified into other voice categories, namely$P(V_1) = 0$, $P(V_2) = 0$, $P(V_3) = 1$. Then voice features are added to the translation models introduced in the previous section, and finally three translation models are generated. For example, will be$P(V_1)$Add a rule table to generate a passive rule table, and similarly, add it separately.$P(V_2)$、 $P(V_3)$Generate a rule table of possible voices and other voices. Finally, each individual translation model contains the following characteristics: forward and backward translation probability, forward and backward lexicalization weight, N-gram language model, rule number punishment, length punishment, and voice characteristics.$P(V)$. The new features have the same status as the original features, and their weights can be adjusted at the stage of weight optimization. By directly adding features to the translation model, the original features of the hierarchical phrase model are retained, and the voice features of new rules are also incorporated without increasing the complexity of the decoding algorithm. In the decoding stage, firstly, the input sentences are classified by voice, and different translation models are selected for translation according to the classification results.

4 Result analysis

4.1 Experiment and Tool Preparation

The data in this paper comes from 500,000 sentences of Japanese-Chinese daily conversation information extracted from web pages, and the passive sentences and possible sentences are manually classified and extracted. The relevant information of the corpus is shown in Table 2.

Table 2 Information of materials used in the experiment

category	Training set	Development set	Test set
Be dynamic	8294	491	514
Possible state	41239	507	509
Other statements	473943	503	501
All data sets	523474	1499	1522

In this paper, Juman and KNP are used as tools for Japanese word segmentation and syntactic analysis, and stanford-chinese-segmenter is used to segment Chinese sentences. Use Dr. Zhang Le's Maximum Entropy Toolkit as a classification tool. Word alignment information is obtained by GIZA++, and a five-element language model is trained on the target sentence by using the SRI language model tool. Based on the NiuTrans statistical machine translation system of Northeastern University, the hierarchical rules were extracted and decoded, and the evaluation index of translation quality was BLEU-4. Finally, five students manually evaluated the translation results.

4.2 Test Set Sentence Classification

Firstly, the voice classification effect of the maximum entropy model is tested. Because the test set needs voice recognition and classification before translation, the classification accuracy of maximum entropy model directly affects the translation effect. The training corpus uses 500,000 sentences of Japanese-Chinese daily conversation corpus from the translation training set. 1500 sentences are extracted from the translation development set and the test set as the classified test set, of which 500 sentences are passive sentences, 500 sentences are possible sentences, and the remaining 500 sentences are other voices. After syntactic analysis of the training set and the test set, the central structure word F1 and the main structure F2 of the sentence are extracted to train and test the maximum entropy model. Use the accuracy to evaluate the recognition of voice. Because F2 is an auxiliary feature, the recognition efficiency is very low only by adding F2, so no comparison is made. The experimental results are shown in Table 5. The results show that the passive and possible states can be effectively identified by adding the features of the trunk structure and the head word of the sentence.

4.3 Translation experiment results

In the experiment, the classified test set is used for translation, which can eliminate the influence of wrongly classified sentences on the translation results and better analyze the system performance. The experimental results of BLEU are shown in Figure 1.

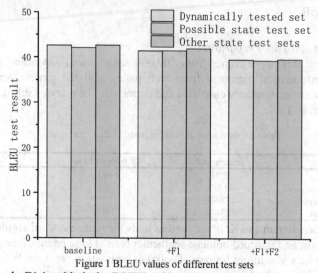

Figure 1 BLEU values of different test sets

When only F1 is added, the BLEU values of passive and other voices are slightly lower than those of baseline system, and the BLEU values of possible States are increased, but the change range is very small. Compared with the translation results with all features, some ambiguity problems have not been improved when only F1 is added. The reason is that only adding the head word can't effectively distinguish between passive and possible predicate verbs with the same deformation.

Because the BLEU value can't fully reflect the translation effect of voice information, this paper evaluates the translation results of the test set after adding all the features based on the manual evaluation standard in the Outline of Machine Translation Evaluation. The sentence score varies from 0.0 to 5.0 according to the intelligibility, and can contain one decimal place. The final score is the arithmetic average of all the scores. Finally, formula (10) is used to convert the evaluation results with a percentage system.

Total intelligibility

$$= \text{sum of all sentence scores/total number of sentences} \quad (10)$$
$$/5 \times 100\%.$$

In this paper, only the best results with all features are evaluated manually, and the evaluation results are shown in Table 3.

Table 3 Manual evaluation of different test sets

translate	Dynamically tested set	Possible state test set	Other voice test sets	All test sets
Baseline/%	69.80	71.02	67.39	69.37
+Maxent Feature/%	72.45	74.13	69.69	72.08

The experimental results show that, compared with the hierarchical phrase model, the BLEU value of this method is increased by 0.09 on the passive test set and 0.51 on the possible test set, and the translation of other voices is not affected. Because BLEU adopts the complete matching of N-gram, the processing of voice has little effect on BLEU value. By analyzing the results of manual evaluation, it can be seen that the intelligibility of this method is improved by 2.29%~3.11% compared with the baseline system in the passive, possible and other voice test sets, and it is better than the baseline system in intelligibility.

4.4 Analysis of experimental results

The comparative experimental results show that compared with the traditional hierarchical phrase translation model, the translation model with voice features eliminates the ambiguity of some phrases in rule selection during translation. The example sentences shown in Table 4 are possible states. In the decoding process, the rules of possible states are selected for translation, and lexical information is not lost, and better translation results are obtained compared with the baseline system.

Table 4 Translation Results of Possible Sentences

Original sentence	Right side のがりかどに [see えます] 1 .
reference translation	At the right corner [visible] 1 .
Baseline	There is a turn at the corner on the right.
+MaxentFeature	Turn right and there is [visible] at the corner 1 .

By analyzing the experimental results, it is found that the reference translations of Japanese passive sentences have different word orders. Some reference translations of Japanese passive sentences are passive sentences or ba sentences, while others are active sentences. Example sentences shown in Table 5 are passive in Japanese, but the corresponding reference translation is not passive. Compared with the translation of "continuous documentaries are broadcast live at 7 o'clock every day", the use of active sentences here is more in line with language habits, and the BLEU value is higher when there is no voice information. In the translation model with voice features, it is impossible to judge and classify different dynamic expressions, which is the main reason why the BLEU value of the dynamic test set has not been significantly improved in the experiment.

Table 5 Translation Results of Dynamic Sentences

Original sentence	Play it at seven o'clock in a row.
reference translation	The documentary is shown at seven o'clock every night.
Baseline	The documentary series is broadcast live at seven o'clock every day.
+MaxentFeature	The documentary series is broadcast live at seven o'clock every day.

5 Conclusions

This paper puts forward a method to improve the possibility and passivity of Japanese Chinese statistical machine translation, which can improve the accuracy of rule selection. Firstly, a classification model is constructed for sentences with dynamic and possible states, and the voice features of sentences are integrated into the hierarchical phrase translation model by using the maximum entropy model, so that different voice rules can be automatically filtered in the decoding process. Finally, the experimental results show that the proposed method can effectively improve the translation quality. The future work mainly includes: how to effectively solve the imbalance of learning data and improve classification accuracy and translation performance; Try to integrate the translation methods of possible state and passive state into other statistical translation models, such as tree-to-string model; Secondly, the syntactic structure, global features and bilingual features of sentences are added to the model to improve the translation accuracy; Thirdly, try to integrate neural network language model to improve translation accuracy.

References

[1]   Bharadiya, J. (2023). A Comprehensive Survey of Deep Learning Techniques Natural Language Processing. European Journal of Technology, 7(1), 58-66.

[2]   Zhang, L., & Komachi, M. (2021). Using sub-character level information for neural machine translation of logographic languages. Transactions on Asian and Low-Resource Language Information Processing, 20(2), 1-15.

[3]   Harada, S., & Watanabe, T. (2022). Neural machine translation with synchronous latent phrase structure. Journal of Natural Language Processing, 29(2), 587-610.

[4]   Fan, A., Bhosale, S., Schwenk, H., Ma, Z., El-Kishky, A., Goyal, S., ... & Joulin, A. (2021). Beyond english-centric multilingual machine translation. The Journal of Machine Learning Research, 22(1), 4839-4886.

[5]   Mao, Z., Chu, C., & Kurohashi, S. (2022). Linguistically driven multi-task pre-training for low-resource neural machine translation. Transactions on Asian and Low-Resource Language Information Processing, 21(4), 1-29.

[6]   Bashir, M. F., Javed, A. R., Arshad, M. U., Gadekallu, T. R., Shahzad, W., & Beg, M. O. (2023). Context-aware Emotion Detection from Low-resource Urdu Language Using Deep Neural Network. ACM Transactions on Asian and Low-Resource Language Information Processing, 22(5), 1-30.

[7]   Kim, Y., Ra, D., & Lim, S. (2021). Zero‑anaphora resolution in Korean based on deep language representation model: BERT. ETRI Journal, 43(2), 299-312.

[8]   Su, X., Zhu, D., Ren, J., & Rätsch, M. (2021). Automatic identification of focus personage in multi-lingual news images. Multimedia Tools and Applications, 80, 11015-11030.

[9]   Rivera-Trigueros, I. (2022). Machine translation systems and quality assessment: a systematic review. Language Resources and Evaluation, 56(2), 593-619.

[10]   Abidin, Z., Permata, P., & Ariyani, F. (2021). Translation of the Lampung Language Text Dialect of Nyo into the Indonesian Language with DMT and SMT Approach. INTENSIF: Jurnal Ilmiah Penelitian Dan Penerapan Teknologi Sistem Informasi, 5(1), 58-71.

[11]   Lee, S. M., & Briggs, N. (2021). Effects of using machine translation to mediate the revision process of Korean university students' academic writing. ReCALL, 33(1), 18-33.

[12]   Farooq, U., Rahim, M. S. M., Sabir, N., Hussain, A., & Abid, A. (2021). Advances in machine translation for sign language: approaches, limitations, and challenges. Neural Computing and Applications, 33(21), 14357-14399.

[13]   Natarajan, B., Elakkiya, R., & Prasad, M. L. (2023). Sentence2signgesture: a hybrid neural machine translation network for sign language video generation. Journal of Ambient Intelligence and Humanized Computing, 14(8), 9807-9821.

[14]   Pham, M., Crego, J. M., & Yvon, F. (2021). Revisiting multi-domain machine translation. Transactions of the Association for Computational Linguistics, 9, 17-35.

[15]   Haddow, B., Bawden, R., Barone, A. V. M., Helcl, J., & Birch, A. (2022). Survey of low-resource machine translation. Computational Linguistics, 48(3), 673-732.

[16]   Luo, Y., Tang, N., Li, G., Tang, J., Chai, C., & Qin, X. (2021). Natural language to visualization by neural machine translation. IEEE Transactions on Visualization and Computer Graphics, 28(1), 217-226.

[17]   Jalal, A., Ahmed, A., Rafique, A. A., & Kim, K. (2021). Scene Semantic recognition based on modified Fuzzy c-mean and maximum entropy using object-to-object relations. IEEE Access, 9, 27758-27772.

[18]   Bajgiran, A. H., Mardikoraem, M., & Soofi, E. S. (2021). Maximum entropy distributions with quantile information. European journal of operational research, 290(1), 196-209.

[19]   Caruso, T., Clemente, G. V., Rillig, M. C., & Garlaschelli, D. (2022). Fluctuating ecological networks: A synthesis of maximum‑entropy approaches for pattern detection and process inference. Methods in Ecology and Evolution, 13(11), 2306-2317.

[20]   Deng, J., & Deng, Y. (2022). Maximum entropy of random permutation set. Soft Computing, 26(21), 11265-11275.

[21]   Ekhosuehi, V. U. (2021). On the stable Gani-type attainability problem controlled by promotion at maximum entropy. Journal of the Operations Research Society of China, 9(3), 673-690.

[22]   Yang, X., Li, Y. P., & Huang, G. H. (2022). A maximum entropy copula-based frequency analysis method for assessing bivariate drought risk: a case study of the Kaidu River Basin. Journal of Water and Climate Change, 13(1), 175-189.

[23]   Zhang, T., Shen, H., Xia, X., Wang, L., Mao, F., Yuan, Q., ... & Gong, W. (2023). Himawari-8 High Temporal Resolution AOD Products Recovery: Nested Bayesian Maximum Entropy Fusion Blending GEO With SSO Satellite Observations. IEEE Transactions on Geoscience and Remote Sensing, 61, 1-15.

[24] Shirani, K., & Naderi Samani, R. (2022). Prioritization of effective parameters and landslide susceptibility zonation using maximum entropy and dempster shafer in Doab Samsami, Chaharmahal Bakhtiyari. Journal of Range and Watershed Managment, 75(1), 51-72.

[25] Fathi, F., Chen, L., & de Borst, R. (2021). X‑IGALME: Isogeometric analysis extended with local maximum entropy for fracture analysis. International Journal for Numerical Methods in Engineering, 122(21), 6103-6125.

Design Studies and Intelligence Engineering
L.C. Jain et al. (Eds.)
© *2024 The Authors.*

doi:10.3233/FAIA231445

Computer-Aided Putonghua Test: Problems and Strategies

Yuhan SONG[a,b,1]

[1]*School of Literature and Journalism, Sichuan University.*
[2]*The Engineering & Technical College of Chengdu University of Technology*

Abstract. The implementation of mandarin test is one of the most important measures to popularize Putonghua in China. With the rapid development of modern information technology, especially the effective integration of computer, network and speech recognition technology, the model of computer-aided Putonghua proficiency test was born in a new form, which provides a good opportunity to promote the standardization and modernization of Putonghua proficiency test. Based on a brief introduction of the advantages of computer-aided Putonghua test, this paper mainly discusses the typical problems in the process of Putonghua test, and then puts forward the corresponding solutions in order to better promote the development of this test.

Key words. computer-aided Putonghua test, problems, strategies

1. Introduction

Since computers appeared, they have been contributed a lot to the whole world and have been applied to different research domains such as reading skill teaching [1], mechanic studies [2], climate changes [3], manual evaluation [4], implant surgery [5] and their combination with 3D etc. [6].

Besides, computer-aided technology has also been used in language teaching and learning as well as language test, so does in Computer-aided Putonghua Proficiency Test (CAPT). CAPT refers to the intelligent testing system of Putonghua proficiency in China, which aims to let the examinees take the Putonghua test on a computer by means of machine instead of human. This process mainly consists of three steps: digital information collection, computer aided network evaluation and evaluation process by network monitoring. In a certain period, the examinee must complete the voice intelligence test. Compared with the traditional scoring mode by human, CAPT technically solves the problem of low efficiency of manual test and embodies the scientific and fair evaluation of test results to a certain extent. Therefore, it gradually replaced the traditional universal testing mode, and has been welcomed and adopted by more and more universities and testing institutions.

---

[1] Corresponding Author.

Table 1. Putonghua Test Proficiency

Level	Quantity of words	Listening	Reading	Writing
1	150	Yes	Yes	No
2	300	Yes	Yes	No
3	600	Yes	Yes	Yes
4	1200	Yes	Yes	Yes
5	2500	Yes	Yes	Yes
6	5000+	Yes	Yes	Yes

2. The benefits of CAPT

Compared with the previous manual test, CAPT has made a great breakthrough in terms of the number of examinees as well as its testing scale, efficiency, and cost. It has brought a revolution in the phonetic test of mandarin and has also become the inevitable trend of Putonghua proficiency test to be scientific and standardized. Xu Yanli [7] believes that CAPT has the following advantages[7]:

· It technically solves the problems of high cost and low efficiency of manual test;
· It eliminates the influence of human factors from the angle of the management;
· The evaluation is more objective and the test results are fair and reasonable;
· It realizes the purpose of informatization of CAPT by means of advanced modern technology.

As a matter of fact, CAPT also has another big advantage, that is, the fast information retrieval. As is known to all, the computer-aided system has a complete database system, which records much test-related information, such as the time and place of the test, the examinee's name, gender, identification number, photo, telephone number and so on. In previous Putonghua tests, the above information was recorded manually with the potential result that information retrieval was not only troublesome but also easy to lose.

The biggest concern is that once a candidate loses his or her certificate, it will be difficult to have another one. On the contrary, all the information of the examinee can be stored in a powerful data management system via CAPT; therefore, if it happens, candidates can easily find their testing scores at the testing agency and get a new certificate. In terms of the information management of candidates, the use of the database also makes it very simple. In the Internet era, the test candidates only need to fill in their own information (such as name, gender, ID number, etc.) through the Internet at a specified time, and the computer terminal will automatically collect such information. Compared with the traditional manual way of collecting examinee data, the use of computer database greatly simplifies this process and improves the work efficiency. Especially in the era of COVID-19, security has been greatly enhanced by such kind of telecommunication.

Table 2. Levels of Putonghua Test Proficiency

Levels	Name	Description
Level I	Beginner	Learners who have just started learning Chinese
Level II	Elementary	Learners who have a basic understanding of Chinese

Level III	Intermediate-Low	Learners with a good grasp of Chinese vocabulary and grammar
Level IV	Intermediate-High	Learners with solid understanding of Chinese grammar and vocabulary
Level V	Advanced-Low	Learners with a near native level understanding of Chinese vocabulary and grammar
Level VI	Advanced-High	Learners with native-level grasp of Chinese vocabulary and grammar

3. The Problems of CAPT

3.1. Poor Compatibility of Hardware

As far as the current CAPT is concerned, there is a common fault, that is, the standard of the testing software is too high for the hardware. To some extent, it has hindered the popularization of CAPT. As is known to all, the establishment of a standard machine-testing room requires high configuration of some computer equipment and related voice equipment, which needs a lot of money. However, the testing agencies or universities don't have enough money to buy such high-quality test hardware as computers, sound cards, headsets, etc. However, in the testing process, the test software is not compatible with the above speech sampling equipment, which causes abnormal speech recognition and background evaluation, and ultimately affects the test efficiency and test results.

3.2. Insufficient Basic Conditions of CAPT

It is common knowledge that Putonghua test is a large-scale national test with many participants, which puts forward higher requirements for the basic conditions to testing institutions or colleges. These basic conditions include:

· Advanced computer-assisted testing software system;

· Sufficient hardware facilities and related auxiliary equipment required for the computer-assisted test as well as a fixed test site;

· Professional Putonghua testers and specialized personnel for computer operation management and equipment maintenance;

· Strict operation and management standards of computer-assisted test [8].

As far as the current situation is concerned, although CAPT has been carried out for many years, the testing system of many institutions is still far from the advanced standard. For instance, some universities even have no Putonghua testing institutions, so their students must go to provincial Putonghua testing centers to take the test, which actually brings a lot of trouble for them. Even in some universities that have obtained the qualification of computer testing, professional Mandarin testers, computer testing administrators and equipment maintenance personnel are also not enough to hold such a massive test. In addition, some colleges or universities have not established a special machine-aided testing room; therefore, it is likely that they will use a computer classroom as a testing room. At the same time, the hardware and software facilities of different universities are not of the same standard while the size of the machine room and the configuration of the machine are also different, so many factors will have a great influence on the test effects and bring some uncertainty to the accuracy of the score.

3.3. Unsatisfied Phonetic Judgment

In the process of computer-aided test, it is found that the computer test score is not enough to show the intonation and co-articulation phenomenon [9]. As is known to all, Chinese tone values are relative, and Chinese intonation is not a simple stack of syllables and tones. When the examinee is reading the material or speaking according to a certain material, he or she should pay attention to not only the pitch but also the pause, the sound strength, and the length of the sound. In acoustics, intonation is closely related to pitch, length and strength, and its main factors are also different in various contexts. In actual communication, many intonations are used to distinguish the meaning of language and examinees' different pronunciation will cause a variety of intonations, which has nothing to do with the sound quality itself. And the machine-assisted test mode happens not to be able to recognize this phenomenon. In addition, phonemes in the speech environment are affected by the speech before and after them, which reflects the effects of co-articulation. Therefore, acoustic, and physiological parameters will change. Co-articulation is not only reflected between syllables and syllables as well as words and words, which is also unable to be achieved by computer-aided software.

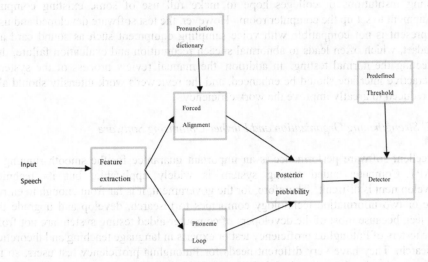

Fig 1. Pronunciation error detection

3.4. Difficult Test Supervision

The computer-assisted test of Putonghua not only gives students more freedom, but also greatly increases the difficulty of test supervision. Since there is no face-to-face tester supervision in the testing process, it is difficult for candidates to completely self-control their behavior in a relatively independent space. Some candidates will try every means to cheat, for instance, taking the test for others, taking some prepared materials into the testing room, reciting the brought materials and even repeating the given material at times. At present, the typical cheating behavior is that some students will take out their mobile phones to read the content stored on the mobile phone when they complete the fourth task of speaking according to the given material. Once cheating occurs, if the test administrator stops it in public, it will certainly affect other candidates. Therefore, CAPT also brings some challenges to invigilator.

4. Strategies of CAPT improvement

4.1. Improving the Hardware of the Testing System

As can be seen from the above, the adaptability of the current testing software system to hardware must be strengthened, and the testing cost should be substantially reduced. Although the current computer-aided test system has gone through many modifications and improvements, and its stability has also been improved; there are many areas that need further improvement. One of the most important points is to change the software system's over-dependence on certain hardware. Generally speaking, based on building a standard computer-aided testing room, if other new and high-grade equipment are also installed, it will be a dream to have CAPT since it will cost a huge amount of money whether to colleges or testing agencies. Moreover, the maintenance of computer electronic equipment is very short, and the replacement is fast. Therefore, the testing institutions or colleges hope to make full use of some existing computer equipment to set up the computer room. However, the test software developed and used at present is not compatible with voice sampling equipment such as sound card and headset, which often leads to abnormal speech recognition and evaluation failure, thus affecting the normal testing. In addition, the manual review process of the system's interactive interface should be enhanced, and the reviewer's work intensity should also be reduced to greatly improve the work efficiency.

4.2. Strengthening Organization and Further Optimizing Software

Excellent software performance is an important guarantee for the smooth running of CAPT. Computer aided testing system is widely applicable, but its technical development is difficult. Therefore, for the government, it is far from enough to entrust one or two information technology companies to research, develop and upgrade this project, because most of the developers of computer-aided testing system are not front-line testers of Putonghua proficiency test or experts in language teaching and theoretical research. They have very different needs for Putonghua proficiency test users, so the software that has been developed will naturally be unreasonable in practice [10]. For such an important scientific and technological research project, it should be led by the national authority to organize the top experts and research institutions in speech-processing technology nationwide in collaboration with linguistic experts, including the backbone professionals who have been engaged in the teaching and testing of Putonghua for a long time. It is necessary to employ some interdisciplinary talents who are familiar with both computer technology and Putonghua theory and testing, so as to further optimize the adaptability of the system to hardware and the accuracy of software system testing, and to modernize Putonghua testing from management, testing, training to research [11].

4.3. Enhancing the Phonetic Evaluation

The evaluation model of pronunciation in computer-aided test should be enhanced and the objectivity of the analysis report should be strengthened. At present, there is a unified reference standard for Putonghua proficiency test all around China, that is, *Putonghua Proficiency Test Outline* [9], which develops a complete set of scoring criteria in detail. Both the examinee and the academic research institution can check the examinee's completion of each test according to the scoring rules and summarize the pronunciation problems, to understand the details of the tester's scoring. At present, the testing software delivered to all regions is designed according to the requirements of the *outline* in theory, but the actual scoring process is not implemented according to the scoring rules. Therefore, in the actual testing process, the testing agencies should gradually improve the scoring criteria of computer evaluation, including such aspects as the addition and omission of Chinese characters, reading passage with wrong pronunciation, the process of natural fluency, intonation, pause and rhythm etc., so that the computer test can gradually replace manual test in a humanized and scientific way.

4.4. Establishing the Scientific Examination Management System

It is particularly important to establish and perfect the relevant rules and regulations of CAPT to strengthen the administration of Putonghua test. In view of the situation that some students take advantage of the machine-assisted test in a cheating way, a perfect supervision system should be established as soon as possible, so that the examination management can follow the rules. Specifically, it is mainly reflected in the following aspects:

· Before the test, students' registration and information entry check should be well prepared in a systematic and scientific way. On the one hand, students need to be familiar with the examination process and objects in advance; On the other hand, supervisors need to be familiar with the handling of emergencies and accidents.

· In the test, the management of the test process should be standardized, for example, standardizing the job responsibilities of supervisors, standardizing the examinee test process, and standardizing the test environment etc.

· After the test, the test agency should standardize the result evaluation, the certificate management, and the test file management etc. At the same time, the testing institutions should reflect on the various problems in the test, analyze the causes of them and find solutions to avoid similar accidents next time. Meanwhile, the testing agency should further clarify the work responsibilities of supervisors in each step so that the examination work can be standardized and institutionalized.

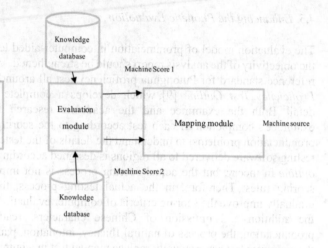

Fig 2. CAPT Structure

5. Conclusion

Although the implementation and application of CAPT is not too long, it is a change and challenge of Putonghua proficiency test, the result of the rapid development of computer and network technology and is also the need of long-distance communication in the new era. In the application process, the computer-aided Putonghua proficiency testing system presents various problems and deficiencies, but its advantages and benefits are also obvious. It is believed that this epoch-making testing method will be improved in the process of implementation and will have better application and broad prospects.

References

[1] Razak Abdul Norizan et al. Innovation Attributes of F2F Computer-Assisted Cooperative Learning in Teaching Reading Skills. *International Journal of Web - Based Learning and Teaching Technologies,* (17) 2021, 1-17.

[2] Goguta Luciana et al. Selective Laser Sintering ve rsus Selective Laser Melting and Computer Aided Design-Computer Aided Manufacturing in Double Crowns Retention. *Journal of Prosthodontic Research,* (65) 2021, 371-378.

[3] Das Usha et al. Developing Knowledge Tool Using Computer Aided Personal Interview Technique for Assessing the Climate Knowledge of Farmers of Odisha. *Journal of Community Mobilization and Sustainable Development,* (15) 2021, 661-667.

[4] Saloniemi Mikko, Lehtinen Valtteri, Snäll Johanna. Computer-Aided Fracture Size Measurement in Orbital Fractures-An Alternative to Manual Evaluation. *Craniomaxillofacial Trauma & Reconstruction,* (14) 2021, 209-217.

[5] Han YenTing et al. Comparison of Dental Surface Image Registration and Fiducial Marker Registration: An In Vivo Accuracy Study of Static Computer-Assisted Implant Surgery. *Journal of Clinical Medicine,* (10) 2021, 4183-4183.

[6] Bianchi Giuseppe et al. Computer Assisted Surgery and 3D Printing in Orthopedic Oncology: A Lesson Learned by Cranio-Maxillo-Facial Surgery. *Applied Sciences,* (11) 2021, 8584-8584.

[7] Xu Yanli. Comparison between Computer-aided Test and Manual Test. *Journal of Changzhou Normal University,* (28) 2012, 57-60.

[8] Ye Jun, Wang Yijia, et al. Research on the Implementation of Computer-aided Putonghua Proficiency

Test. *Language and Character Applications*, (2) 2007, 142-147.

[9] Song Xinqiao. Differences in Scoring of Putonghua Proficiency Test. *Language Planning*, (9) 1998, 12-14.

[10] Lei Jun. Problems and Technical Countermeasures of Computer-aided Mandarin Testing. *Journal of Wuhan university of technology*, (32) 2010, 160-163.

[11] Zou Yueliang. Practice and Thinking of Computer-aided Putonghua Proficiency Test in Colleges. *Science and Technology Information*, (28) 2009, 595-596.

Design Studies and Intelligence Engineering
L.C. Jain et al. (Eds.)
© 2024 The Authors.

doi:10.3233/FAIA231446

Research on Factors Influencing User Experience in H5 Interactive Advertising Based on Flow Theory

Biao GAO [a,b,1] and Yi HU [b]

[a] *Jiangxi Publishing & Media Group CO., LTD., Nanchang 330038, China*
[b] *Jiangxi University of Finance and Economics, Nanchang 330013, China*

Abstract. With the advancement of HTML5 technology, mobile web interactive advertisements based on HTML5 have offered users a superior experience. Drawing from Flow Theory, we constructed a research framework to elucidate how 'flow' influences user acceptance and sharing intentions towards H5 interactive advertisements. Furthermore, we aimed to identify factors influencing the flow experience of users. Given the Person-Artifact-Task (PAT) model, which frames the precursors to flow around three dimensions: person, tool, and task, this paper employs a model centered around the person, tool, and task. We categorized factors impacting flow experience into user factors and ad design factors. Adopting a quantitative research approach, we surveyed users of H5 interactive ads in China. Regression analysis was conducted using SPSS (version 26.0). Findings indicate: (1) Within user factors, Entertainment and Perceived Control, and within design factors, Interface Design Quality and Interactive Narrative, have a positive influence on flow. (2) Flow positively affects the acceptance and sharing willingness of users towards H5 interactive advertisements.

Keywords. H5 Interactive Advertising, Flow Theory, User Experience, PAT Model

1. Introduction

In an era where internet information technology and digital media are flourishing, the rise of the mobile internet industry has paved the way for a new trend in media convergence. As mobile social interaction becomes increasingly dominant in China, investments in digital and mobile technologies for online advertising channels have steadily risen year by year. HTML5, being accessible on mobile devices, harnesses various social platforms to enhance interaction and dissemination. Although there's been an increase in interactive modalities within H5 interactive advertisements, there's still a depth lacking in research on interactive effectiveness and the emotional experiences users encounter during interaction. Flow theory is among the most applied concepts within experience theories. It offers fresh insights into understanding mental perceptions and unlocking human potential. Currently, it stands as a critical guiding thought increasingly applied across multiple design disciplines.

---

[1] Corresponding author: Biao Gao, E-mail: biaogao.edu@outlook.com

Hence, this study aims to explore the influence and role of flow theory in H5 interactive advertising. Building on flow theory, we establish a research framework elucidating how flow impacts user acceptance and sharing intentions towards H5 interactive ads. We also analyze the factors influencing the flow experience within H5 interactive advertising, and integrating the PAT model, categorize these factors into user-related and ad design-related components.

2. Literature Review

2.1. H5 Interactive Advertising

HTML, an acronym for Hyper Text Markup Language, was born in 1990. It consists of descriptive text formed by HTML commands, which can denote text, graphics, animations, sounds, tables, links, and more. HTML5 operates seamlessly on both web and mobile platforms. Users can also access and view content anytime, without restrictions based on device or location[1]. In the context of this study, H5 interactive advertising refers to ads presented using HTML5 technology as a medium, wherein users are either permitted or autonomously interact with the content[2]. These advertisements are created by product designers using instantly participatory and modifiable digital interactive mediums that include transaction and payment functionalities, allowing user feedback on conveyed product information, user services, or viewpoints. Given the measurability, precision, customization, personalization, and easy localization of H5 interactive advertising[3], interactive digital marketing can arguably be considered one of the most potent tools available to advertisers.

2.2. Flow Theory

Numerous researchers have delved into the study of the flow experience, exploring various aspects of flow, such as its antecedent variables, dimensions, and outcomes. Csikszentmihalyi[4] defined flow as the holistic sensation people feel when they are completely immersed in an activity. Hoffman & Novak[5] posited that flow is a cognitive state experienced during an activity. This cognitive state is described as an intrinsically pleasurable optimal experience. While there are significant individual variations based on factors such as gender, age, cultural background, and social class, when individuals describe their experienced state of flow, they often allude to commonalities.

Over the subsequent decades, researchers have further discussed and refined the characteristics of flow, progressively categorizing them into stages of antecedents to flow, the flow experience itself, and outcomes from flow. The PAT model (Person-Artifact-Task Model) constructed by Finneran & Zhang[6] posits that factors influencing the flow experience primarily arise from three dimensions: the person (P), the tool or artifact (A), and the task (T). The "person" refers to the user, who, as the main operator of mobile networks, can achieve goals through the "artifact" or medium. Flow experience can emerge when there is alignment between the goal and the medium itself. Research indicates that, within the model of advertising research, flow is a crucial predictor in user acceptance and purchase intention in interactive advertisements.

3. Research Model and Hypotheses

3.1. Selection and Definition of Research Variables

Drawing from the theory of flow, the PAT model, characteristics of H5 interactive advertisements, and user experience, we constructed a research model in two stages. First, we categorized factors influencing the flow experience into user factors and advertisement design factors. We then investigated how elements in the user factors of H5 interactive advertisements, namely Entertainment, Informativeness, and Perceived Control, and elements in the design factors, namely Interface Design Quality, Aesthetics, and Interactive Narrative, influence the users' perception of flow. In the second stage, we positioned flow as a mediating variable to explore its influence on advertisement acceptance and the willingness to share within the user experience.

3.1.1. User Factors

Given that the PAT model delineates the precursors to the flow experience into three dimensions: person, tool, and task, this study adopts a model framework centered on the individual (user), the tool (H5 interactive advertisement design), and the task. Within this structure, and considering the characteristics of interactive advertisements, the factors influencing the flow experience are divided into user factors and advertisement design factors. The individual, or user, is the primary entity experiencing flow. Moreover, the concept of the user has always been pivotal in marketing. Thus, within the context of H5 interactive advertisements, user factors are analyzed in terms of user needs and the appeal to the user. Informativeness refers to the breadth and depth of details conveyed in the advertisement about a product or service, facilitating more informed decision-making by the user in online advertisements[7].

At the same time, Ducoffe[8] identified informativeness and entertainment as antecedents to users' attitudes towards advertisements. The entertainment value of an ad can fulfill a user's desire for escapism, aesthetic appreciation, and emotional expression. This enhances the flow experience, thereby fostering a positive attitude towards the advertisement[9]. In line with this, the present study references the dimensions of informativeness and entertainment from Ducoffe's[8] model of online ad value and posits the following hypotheses:

H1: Entertainment has a positive influence on Flow.

H2: Informativeness has a positive influence on Flow.

Within flow theory, perceived control is defined as one's sense of mastery over their environment and actions[10]. In the digital landscape, the abundance of information and products leads to a growing demand among consumers for greater control, reduced effort, and higher efficiency when viewing ads. Thus, in the context of H5 interactive advertising, whether a user can effortlessly and swiftly access information becomes a critical determinant of user experience. Drawing on the research of Ghani et al.[11] and Taylor & Todd[12], this study incorporates three measurement items to gauge perceived control, leading to the hypothesis:

H3: Perceived Control positively influences Flow.

3.1.2. Ad Design Factors

Within the PAT model, tools (or artifacts) serve as essential conduits for facilitating the flow experience and also act as mediums for users to gather information. In H5 interactive advertising, the quality of interface design is linked with factors like the ad's duration, size, color scheme, musical effects, animations, and the smoothness of its loading − all of which influence an ad's efficacy[13]. Superior interface design fosters an enhanced user experience, immersing users more deeply[14]. Some scholars have observed that a user's evaluation of an ad's interface design quality can impact their sense of immersion, satisfaction, and purchase intent[15]. Guided by the research on mobile interactive ad video quality assessment by GuChao et al.[16], we propose the following hypothesis:

H4: The quality of Interface design has a positive effect on Flow.

Aesthetic design aids designers in maintaining a consistent artistic style for the ad, offering inherent aesthetic value, which can shape a user's ad experience and, to an extent, satiate their aesthetic demands in H5 interactive advertising. Salen & Zimmerman[17] explored the impact of aesthetic design on flow and game experience. We aim to investigate whether the aesthetic design in ads influences users' sharing and forwarding experiences and propose:

H5: Aesthetic design positively influences Flow.

Interactive narratives offer a storytelling approach where the audience can influence, choose, and alter the plot[18][19]. Such interactivity can foster a connection between the audience and the ad's story, heightening their sense of engagement. The more users are satisfied with an ad's interactive narrative, the greater resonance they feel with the ad's designers. Past research indicates that interactive narratives in ad design exert a discernible influence on user experience. Hence, we suggest:

H6: Interactive Narrative exerts a positive impact on Flow.

3.1.3. The Impact of Flow on Ad Acceptance and Willingness to Share

Concentration is a crucial component of the flow experience. Users in a state of flow are wholly engrossed in their present activity[20][21]. If users are juggling multiple tasks at once, their ability to achieve this state of flow is compromised. Thus, if users focus their attention solely on the H5 interactive advertisement, they are more likely to enter this flow state. This, in turn, may influence their acceptance of the advertisement and their inclination to share it. Consequently, we posit the following hypotheses:

H7: Flow has a positive impact on Ad acceptance.

H8: Flow positively influences the Willingness to share.

Drawing upon the analyses presented, this study proposes a theoretical model for how H5 interactive advertisements influence user experience, as depicted in Figure 1.

4. Research Methods

This study utilized a survey method to test the hypotheses previously outlined, and used the QuestionnaireStar platform to create the electronic survey. The questionnaire was then divided into two main sections to evaluate our theoretical model. The first part pertained to demographic questions concerning the respondents and their engagement

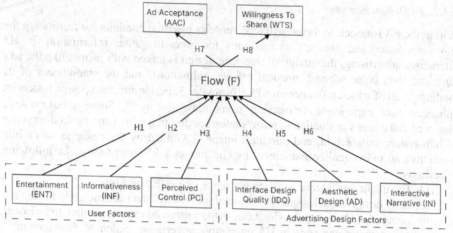

Figure 1. Theoretical model

with H5 interactive advertisements. The second part revolved around descriptive statistics and internal consistency analysis. Responses for each item corresponding to a construct were gauged using a 5-point Likert scale, with 1 signifying "strongly disagree" and 5 indicating "strongly agree." After filtering out duplicate or patterned responses, we successfully collected 556 valid responses. The data from these questionnaires were then analyzed using SPSS software (Version 26.0).

5. Data Analysis

5.1. Demographic Analysis of the Sample

Based on the data from the returned questionnaires, it's evident that among those who have either browsed or expressed interest in browsing H5 interactive advertisements, females are more prevalent, accounting for 65.3% of the sample. In terms of age, the 18-25 age bracket is the most represented, making up 46.4%. Within the sample, 79.5% have watched an H5 interactive advertisement. Regarding the platforms on which they viewed these ads, WeChat leads with 61.3%, followed by Douyin (TikTok) at 41.7%, and then Xiaohongshu and Weibo at 39.4% and 31.3%, respectively.

5.2. Descriptive Statistics and Internal Consistency Analysis

5.2.1. Descriptive Statistics

Descriptive statistics are utilized to characterize the features of data. In our study, we employed four standard measures for evaluation: mean, standard deviation, skewness, and kurtosis. From the questionnaire data, we can observe that the means and standard deviations for each item are within reasonable ranges. Additionally, all means are above 2.5, suggesting that respondents generally hold positive attitudes toward the statements or behaviors in the items. In terms of skewness and kurtosis, all items have absolute skewness values of less than 1 and absolute kurtosis values of less than 7, which indicates they conform to univariate normality.

5.2.2. Internal Consistency Analysis

Cronbach's alpha is widely used in academia to assess the reliability of scales. For a scale to be considered reliable, its Cronbach's alpha value should exceed 0.70. In this study, the Cronbach's alpha values for all items ranged from 0.806 to 0.903, surpassing the recommended threshold. This indicates that each item on the scale possesses a high degree of reliability.

5.3. Correlation Analysis

The correlation coefficient is a statistical measure used to reflect the degree of relationship between variables. For this study, we employed the Pearson coefficient. According to Table 1, the association among the nine variables in the study all demonstrate a moderate to strong correlation. Specifically, the correlation coefficients between the variables 'Flow' and 'Ad acceptance' with the other seven variables (excluding 'Aesthetic design') are greater than 0.70, indicating a strong correlation.

Table 1. Item Correlation Matrix

Constructs	ENT	INF	PC	IDQ	AD	IN	F	AAC	WTS
ENT	1								
INF	0.807**	1							
PC	0.702**	0.688**	1						
IDQ	0.776**	0.787**	0.681**	1					
AD	0.452**	0.471**	0.492**	0.467**	1				
IN	0.744**	0.776**	0.662**	0.813**	0.516**	1			
F	0.737**	0.720**	0.711**	0.733**	0.485**	0.749**	1		
AAC	0.759**	0.733**	0.725**	0.748**	0.525**	0.756**	0.825**	1	
WTS	0.683**	0.672**	0.647**	0.677**	0.428**	0.660**	0.730**	0.805**	1

5.4. Path Analysis

In this study, the Durbin-Watson values for the three regression sets are around 2, and R^2 is greater than 0.50. This indicates that the data has an established independence, and the independent variables have a relatively high explanatory power over the dependent variables. The influence of the independent variables (ENT, PC, IDQ, IN) on the dependent variable (F) is significant, and the impact of the independent variable (F) on the dependent variables (AAC, WTS) is also significant, supporting the hypotheses. However, the influence of the independent variables (INF, AD) on the dependent variable (F) is not significant, meaning those hypotheses are not supported.

5.5. Hypothesis Testing

From the path analysis, we can deduce that there are effective paths from the independent variables (ENT, PC, IDQ, IN) to the mediator variable (F). The significance levels of each path are below 0.05. This suggests that within the user factors of H5 interactive ads, ENT and PC, and design factors of IDQ and IN have a positive correlation with Flow. An effective path exists between the mediator variable (F) and dependent variables (AAC, WTS), with each path having a significance level below 0.001. This indicates that Flow also has a positive correlation with user experience factors such as Ad acceptance and Willingness to share. Results of the hypothesis testing for path coefficients and their significance can be found in Table 2, and the diagram of the path analysis model is illustrated in Figure 2. In conclusion, out of the eight hypotheses presented, six are supported by the data.

Table 2. Results of Hypothesis Testing

Hypothesis	Path coefficient	P value	Result
H1 ENT->F	0.209	P<0.001***	YES
H2 INF->F	0.080	P>0.05	NO
H3 PC->F	0.243	P<0.001***	YES
H4 IDQ->F	0.134	P<0.05*	YES
H5 AD->F	0.045	P>0.05	NO
H6 IN->F	0.281	P<0.001***	YES
H7 F->AAC	0.768	P<0.001***	YES
H8 F->WTS	0.773	P<0.001***	YES

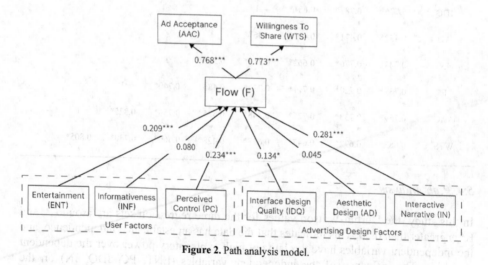

Figure 2. Path analysis model.

6. Discussion

In this study, we utilized the Flow Theory to discuss the factors influencing user experience in H5 interactive advertisements. Through data analysis, we verified our hypotheses, illuminating the relationships between variables. Among the eight hypotheses, H1-H6 aimed to elucidate the relationships between user factors, design elements, and Flow in H5 interactive ads. All hypotheses, with the exception of H2 and H5, were supported by the data. The most significant influencing factor was Interactive Narrative (β =0.281, p<0.001), followed by Perceived Control (β =0.243, p<0.001), Entertainment (β =0.209, p<0.001), and Interface Design Quality (β =0.134, p<0.05). Each of these factors positively affected Flow, consistent with the findings of Ducoffe[8], Katifori et al.[10], and Shin[14].

However, H2's hypothesis regarding the impact of Informativeness on Flow did not meet expectations, contrasting with Ducoffe's[8] conclusions. This discrepancy might be attributed to the greater emphasis on entertainment and interactivity in H5 ads, which possibly overshadowed the visibility or quantity of product or service information. For example, popular forms of H5 interactive ads, such as video, game-based, composite, data-driven, and tech-focused ads, prioritize user engagement over presenting product or service details.

In H5, the effect of Aesthetic Design on Flow also didn't align with expectations, conflicting with the findings of Salen & Zimmerman[17]. Two potential reasons can explain this result. Firstly, the survey might not have adequately differentiated between the measurement items of aesthetic design and those of interface design quality. Secondly, users may prioritize the overall quality of H5 interactive ads over mere aesthetic requirements.

Lastly, H7-H8 highlighted the relationship between Flow and the user experience of H5 interactive ads. The study indicates that Flow (β =0.768, p<0.001) positively impacts User Ad Acceptance, and similarly, Flow (β =0.773, p<0.001) has a positive influence on the User's Willingness to Share. These findings are in line with the research of Koufaris[20] and Novak et al.[21].

7. Conclusion

This research, leveraging the Flow Theory, successfully constructed a specialized framework focused on examining how Flow influences the user experience in H5 interactive advertisements. This innovative framework not only presents a fresh perspective on the application of Flow Theory in advertising research but also serves as a potential reference for other fields of study. Importantly, for the first time, we integrated the PAT Model explicitly categorizing the factors influencing the Flow experience into "User Factors" and "Ad Design Factors." This clear categorization undoubtedly paves a lucid path for future research endeavors. Delving deeper, our understanding of the relationship between Informativeness, Entertainment, and Perceived Control with the Flow experience has been significantly clarified under the "User Factors" section. Meanwhile, in terms of ad design, we affirmed the pivotal roles of Interface Design Quality, Aesthetic Design, and Interactive Narrative in shaping the core of the Flow experience. These profound findings considerably deepen our understanding of the application of the Flow Theory within the advertising domain.

From a practical standpoint, by optimizing these core elements of advertisements, one can not only enhance the user's Flow experience but also amplify the ad's acceptance and intent to share. For advertising platforms and brands, gaining a profound understanding of these Flow-influencing factors and applying them in practice can undoubtedly boost the overall efficacy of advertisements and enhance the return on investment.

Acknowledgments

This work was supported by Jiangxi Provincial University Humanities and Social Sciences Research Project [Grant Number GL22223]. This work was also supported by the Science and Technology Research Project of the Jiangxi Provincial Department of Education [Grant Number GJJ2200517].

References

[1]   Zhu, X., Chen, D., Chen, Y., & Chen, H, A resource integration approach for HTML5 mobile applications, *Information Technology and Management* 14 (2013), 169-181.
[2]   Stewart, D.W, The new face of interactive advertising: it's time to rethink traditional ad research strategy, *Marketing Research* 16 (2004), 10–15.
[3]   Trappey, R. J., & Woodside, A. G, Consumer responses to interactive advertising campaigns coupling short-message-service direct marketing and TV commercials, *Journal of Advertising Research* 45 (2005), 382-401.
[4]   Csikszentmihalyi, M., Play and intrinsic rewards, *Journal of Humanistic Psychology* 15 (1975), 41-63.
[5]   Hoffman, D. L., & Novak, T. P, Marketing in hypermedia computer-mediated environments: Conceptual foundations, *Journal of marketing* 60 (1996), 50-68.
[6]   Finneran, C. M., & Zhang, P, A person–artefact–task (PAT) model of flow antecedents in computer-mediated environments, *International Journal of Human-Computer Studies* 59 (2003), 475-496.
[7]   Schlosser, A. E., Shavitt, S., & Kanfer, A, Survey of Internet users' attitudes toward Internet advertising, *Journal of interactive marketing* 13 (1999), 34-54.
[8]   Ducoffe, R. H, Advertising value and advertising on the web, *Journal of advertising research* 36 (1996), 21-21.
[9]   McQuail, D., *McQuail's mass communication theory,* Sage publications, (2010), 632p.
[10] Marios Koufaris, Applying the Technology Acceptance Model and Flow Theory to Online Consumer Behavior, *Information Systems Research* 13 (2002), 205-223.
[11] Ghani, J. A. , Supnick, R. , & Rooney, P., The Experience Of Flow In Computer-Mediated And In Face-To-Face Groups, *Proceedings of the International Conference on Information Systems,* 1991 December 16-18; New York, NY, USA. University of Minnesota, (1991), 229-237.
[12] Taylor, S., & Todd, P. A, Understanding information technology usage: A test of competing models, *Information systems research* 6 (1995), 144-176.
[13] Martins, J., Costa, C., Oliveira, T., Gonçalves, R., & Branco, F, How smartphone advertising influences consumers' purchase intention, *Journal of Business Research* 94 (2019), 378-387.
[14] Shin, D, How does immersion work in augmented reality games? A user-centric view of immersion and engagement, *Information, Communication & Society* 22 (2019), 1212-1229.
[15] Zarei G, Asgarnezhad Nuri B, Noroozi N, The effect of Internet service quality on consumers' purchase behavior: The role of satisfaction, attitude, and purchase intention, *Journal of Internet Commerce* 18 (2019), 197-220.
[16] Gu, C., Lin, S., Sun, J., Yang, C., Chen, J., Jiang, Q., ... & Wei, W, What do users care about? Research on user behavior of mobile interactive video advertising, *Heliyon* 8 (2022), 1-20.
[17] Salen, K. , & Zimmerman, E., The Game Design Reader: A Rules of Play Anthology, *The MIT Press* (2006), 954.
[18] Baldwin, S., & Ching, Y. H, Interactive storytelling: Opportunities for online course design, *TechTrends* 61 (2017), 179-186.
[19] Meadows, M. S., Pause & effect: the art of interactive narrative, *Pearson Education* (2002), 272.
[20] Koufaris, M, Applying the technology acceptance model and flow theory to online consumer behavior, *Information systems research* 13 (2002), 205-223.
[21] Novak, T. P., Hoffman, D. L., & Yung, Y. F, Measuring the customer experience in online environments: A structural modeling approach. *Marketing science* 19 (2000), 22-42.

Design Studies and Intelligence Engineering
L.C. Jain et al. (Eds.)
© 2024 The Authors.
This article is published online with Open Access by IOS Press and distributed under the terms
of the Creative Commons Attribution Non-Commercial License 4.0 (CC BY-NC 4.0).
doi:10.3233/FAIA231447

Research on Automotive Front Face Styling Based on Shape Grammar

Lingling LIU[a], Biao MA[a], Mengyuan PAN[a,1], Zhen CHEN[a], Zeyu YANG[a], and Xinyao HE[a]

[a] *Guilin University of Technology of Art and Design*

Abstract. Automotive front face styling design needs to satisfy both innovative aesthetics and the recognition of brand identity. Under the dual drivers and constraints, this research focuses on the design method for inheriting brand identity in automotive front face styling. A design process combining shape grammar and product family DNA is proposed. The Audi sedan series front face is selected as the research object. Firstly, the dominant styling features and implicit design intentions of the brand DNA are extracted, and a mapping is established between the two. Then, the initial shape is determined based on user expectations and constraints. Finally, suitable grammar rules are selected based on shape grammar theory to derive and generate design solutions. The automotive front face styling designed through this method exhibits excellent brand recognition and matches the users' design intentions. This design process can effectively reduce deviations between conceptual design and final products in the early stage of automotive front face styling design, minimize repetitive design, and thus shorten the development cycle, reduce costs, and enhance market competitiveness.

Keywords. Shape grammar; Product family DNA; Automotive front face; Styling design

1. Introduction

Consumers place a much higher emphasis on styling when purchasing cars compared to other products, and this tendency is gradually increasing. With the development of diversified consumer behavior, consumers have a greater aesthetic perception and attention to automotive styling. They pay more attention to the image and symbolism of luxury, craftsmanship, and contemporaneity conveyed by automotive styling. Currently, scholars both domestically and internationally have explored automotive styling design and proposed innovative practical methods. For example, Lu Zhaolin et al. [1] studied the thinking mechanism of automotive designers in the fuzzy early design stage through verbal report experiments and mathematical statistical analysis, and summarized corresponding patterns. Zhao Jing et al. [2] applied shape grammar theory and derivation rules to existing brand styling features, generating new electric vehicle styling that meets brand inheritance requirements. However, automotive styling design needs to consider multiple factors, including brand DNA, user demands, and feature innovation. Therefore, this paper proposes a method that combines shape grammar with product family DNA for research on automotive front face styling design. When determining the constraints

---

[1] Corresponding author:Pan Mengyuan;Postal address: Guilin University of Technology of Art and Design,Guilin,China,541000;Email address: 2199294637@qq.com

of shape grammar, product family DNA is introduced to determine genetic constraints and guide the design process.

2. Research methods

2.1. Overview of shape grammar

Shape Grammar (SG) is a shape manipulation theory proposed by George Stiny and James Gips in the early 1970s. It is based on previous research and has been innovated upon [3]. Deoxyribonucleic Acid (DNA) was originally a concept in molecular biology used to store genetic information [4]. In the field of industrial design, DNA is metaphorically used to refer to the design genes that represent the brand inheritance of a product, indicating the design features that have been retained after multiple iterations of innovation. Shape Grammar, as a formalized method in the stage of conceptual design, can effectively inherit existing features and evolve from prototypes, generating a large number of innovative designs.

2.2. The law of use of shape grammar

The core idea of shape grammar in design practice is to combine the design subject with design elements. Basic element styles are extracted from existing products and design elements and generalized into geometric shapes. Then, these geometric shapes are derived according to the rules of shape grammar to generate a series of new patterns. Finally, these new patterns are recombined and assembled to form new design styles and structural forms. The definition of shape grammar can be represented as SG = (S, L, R, I), where S is a finite set of derived shapes that are generated according to the rules R after being symbolically labeled. L is a finite set of symbols for derivation rules, R is a finite set of rules for derivation, and I is the initial shape for derivation [5].

2.3. Design and research process

The research on automotive front-end styling design based on shape grammar can be roughly divided into five stages: product form analysis, extraction of brand styling genes, determination of constraints, selection of grammar rules, and generation and selection of design solutions [6].

In Stage 1, the product form analysis stage, the elements of automotive front-end styling design are identified through literature research. In Stage 2, a specific automotive brand is selected, and its styling genes are collected to establish a gene library. In Stage 3, constraints are determined based on factors such as user needs and brand positioning. In Stage 4, suitable derivation rules are selected from a set of shape grammar rules to guide the design process. In Stage 5, the front-end styling solutions derived in the previous stage are evaluated using the 5-stage SD method through a questionnaire. The solution with the highest score is considered the optimal solution. The research process for automotive front-end styling design is illustrated in Figure 1.

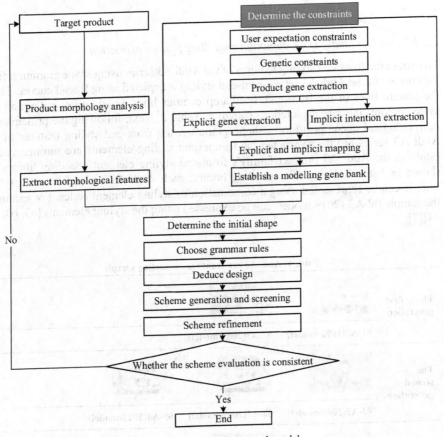

Figure 1. Shape grammar research model

3. Case verification

The Audi A3 is a flagship model under the Audi brand. Since its introduction in 1996, it has undergone three generations of updates and has launched more than 20 different models. As a luxury car brand from Germany, the Audi A3 has enjoyed great popularity in both domestic and international markets, making it one of the most representative models of the Audi brand. This makes the Audi A3 an ideal choice for research purposes. Detailed information about the research samples can be found in Table 1.

3.1. Product morphology analysis

The styling features of passenger cars mainly include overall vehicle design, front-end styling, body waistline, interior CMF (color, material, finish), and rear-end styling. Among them, the front-end styling is the most representative design element that reflects the brand characteristics, making it the key focus of shape grammar-based morphological extraction. When designing the front-end of a car, it is typically divided into four parts: front headlamp assembly, hood curve, grille, and fog lamps. Shape grammar is applied to extract and evolve these parts individually.

3.2.   Brand modelling gene extraction

3.2.1.   Product family DNA dominant modelling feature extraction

To extract the front-end styling features of the Audi A3 series using shape grammar, first, the contour of the Audi A3 series front-end styling is depicted using Bessel curves. Then, the feature lines of the front-end, headlamp contour lines, hood curve, grille, and fog lamp contour lines are depicted, as shown in Table 2. Next, following the principles of morphological decomposition in shape grammar, the front-end styling features of the Audi A3 series are deconstructed, and important styling elements are summarized to establish the Audi A3 product family's front-end styling element encoding library, as shown in Table 3. Using this encoding library, each Audi A3 series front-end styling sample can be represented using a combination of styling element codes. For example, the sample 09-A3 (2019 model) can be expressed using the styling elements [a3, b3, c2, d3][7].

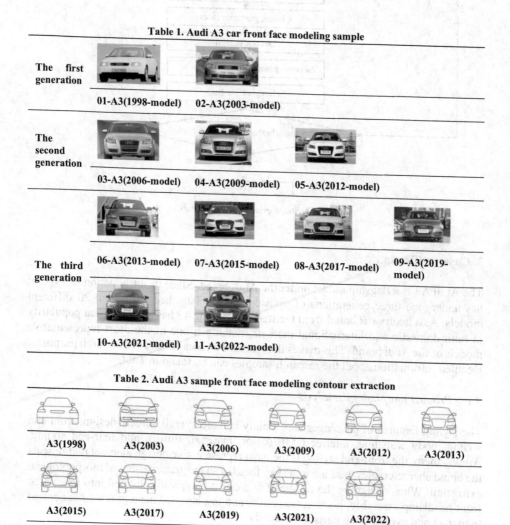

Table 1. Audi A3 car front face modeling sample

The first generation	01-A3(1998-model)	02-A3(2003-model)	
The second generation	03-A3(2006-model)	04-A3(2009-model)	05-A3(2012-model)
The third generation	06-A3(2013-model) 07-A3(2015-model) 08-A3(2017-model) 09-A3(2019-model)		
	10-A3(2021-model) 11-A3(2022-model)		

Table 2. Audi A3 sample front face modeling contour extraction

A3(1998)	A3(2003)	A3(2006)	A3(2009)	A3(2012)	A3(2013)
A3(2015)	A3(2017)	A3(2019)	A3(2021)	A3(2022)	

Table 3. The main modelling elements of the front face of Audi A3 series product family coding library

Styling features	Styling elements			
X_1:Headlight group	A_{11}:Simple geometry	A_{12}:Simple and irregular shape	A_{13}:Complex and irregular shape	
X_2:Enter the style gate	A_{21}:Flattening	A_{22}:Rounded trapezoid	A_{23}:Hexagon	A_{24}:Flat hexagonal
X_3:Hood curves	A_{31}:Outer convex arc	A_{32}:Inner concave arc	A_{33}:Short straight arc	A_{34}:Long straight arc
X_4:Fog lamp	A_{41}:Class parallelograms	A_{42}:Inverted trapezoid	A_{43}:Regular trapezoid	A_{44}:Irregular pentagon

3.2.2. Product family DNA recessive modelling intention extraction

From a perceptual perspective, the semantic differential method was used to select styling intention vocabulary [8], the Richter scale method was used to rate the intention vocabulary, and the Delphi method was used to statistically analyze the ratings, as shown in Figure 2.

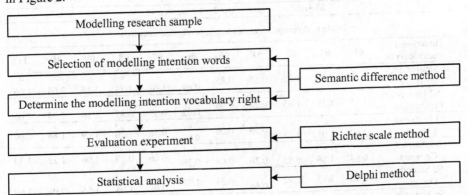

Figure 2. Implicit modelling intention extraction model

By referring to Audi's brand-related materials, core feature terminologies were extracted. At the same time, a large amount of imagery vocabulary related to car styling was collected through various means such as literature, interviews, and questionnaires. Through expert interviews, vocabulary that had similar meanings or was not suitable for evaluating car styling was eliminated. Following the principles of the semantic differential method, opposite-meaning words were paired, resulting in a final selection of 60 sets of styling imagery vocabulary. These imagery words were combined with the primary styling element encoding library of the Audi A3 product family's front-end styling to create a survey questionnaire. Ten professional car styling designers and 20 design professionals, including teachers and students, were invited to participate in the questionnaire survey. Based on the frequency of selection of the imagery vocabulary, the top six sets of vocabulary were chosen as representative styling imagery for the Audi A3 front-end samples. The specific results are shown in Table 4.

Table 4. Six groups of modelling intention vocabulary

Modelling intention vocabulary		
S1 Straight line - Short line	S2 Heavy - Lightweight	S3 High end - Low end
S4 Ample - Compact	S5 Smooth - Dynamic	S6 Majestic - Shabby

Using an imagery vocabulary combined with a coding library of the main styling elements of the Audi A3 series front face, a 7-level imagery vocabulary SD scale was created, with scores of 3, 2, 1, 0, -1, -2, -3, as shown in Table 5. The Delphi method was employed to invite 10 automotive design experts to rate the SD scale. Positive values were used to represent the imagery vocabulary on the left side, while negative values represented the imagery vocabulary on the right side. The absolute value of the score indicates the strength of the imagery represented by the sample. A total of 10 valid survey responses were collected. The SPSS software was used to obtain the mean values for each group of imagery vocabulary for each sample vehicle. The specific results are shown in Table 6.

Table 5. Example of Audi A3 front face modelling SD intention vocabulary table

Sample model	Intentional vocabulary	Corresponding score	Intentional vocabulary
	Straight line	3、2、1、0、-1、-2、-3	Short line
	Heavy	3、2、1、0、-1、-2、-3	Lightweight
	High end	3、2、1、0、-1、-2、-3	Low end
	Ample	3、2、1、0、-1、-2、-3	Compact
	Smooth	3、2、1、0、-1、-2、-3	Dynamic
	Majestic	3、2、1、0、-1、-2、-3	Shabby

Table 6. Average score of sample perceptual intention

Intentional vocabulary	01	02	03	04	05	06	07	08	09	10	11
S1 Straight line-Short line	2.33	1.75	1.86	0.56	0.85	0.69	1.02	1.53	1.86	2.05	1.96
S2 Heavy-Lightweight	1.75	1.58	1.65	0.25	0.96	0.02	0.53	0.87	1.86	2.23	2.06
S3 High end-Low end	2.02	1.05	1.25	0.59	0.26	0.05	0.58	1.28	1.69	1.88	2.06
S4 Ample-Compact	0.58	1.56	0.85	0.26	0.64	0.26	0.06	0.59	1.06	1.28	1.59
S5 Smooth-Dynamic	2.05	1.85	1.92	0.65	0.74	1.05	0.06	1.05	1.56	2.05	1.69
S6 Majestic-Shabby	1.05	0.74	0.58	0.68	0.55	0.85	1.06	1.28	1.69	2.26	2.56

3.2.3. Mapping analysis between modelling features and modelling intentions

Based on the extraction of explicit styling features and evaluation of implicit styling imagery from samples of the Audi A3 car's front face, it is determined that the styling imagery depends on the external styling features of the product. Therefore, the genetic makeup of the product family's styling is formed by the mapping relationship between the explicit styling features and implicit styling imagery of the product family.

Subsequently, a joint analysis of the Audi A3 car's front face styling features and styling imagery is conducted to construct a mapping model between the product family's styling features and styling imagery evaluations.

Multiple regression analysis was conducted using SPSS 26.0 software [9]. The explicit styling elements were set as independent variables, and the implicit styling imagery was set as the dependent variable. A linear regression analysis equation was established to analyze the partial correlation coefficients between the various feature elements of the car's front face and the imagery vocabulary. Taking the example of the "S3 high-end to low-end" imagery vocabulary, the results of the partial correlation coefficients are shown in Table 7.

Table 7. Analyse results of 'High end - Low end'

Model	Unstandardized coefficients		Standardized coefficients	t	Significance	Collinearity statistics	
	B	Standard error	Beta			Allowance	VIF
(Constant)	-4.041	0.992		-4.075	0.007		
Headlight group	1.600	0.534	0.797	2.995	0.024	0.447	2.237
Enter the style gate	-0.068	0.252	-0.060	-0.269	0.797	0.646	1.547
Hood curves	0.232	0.413	0.159	0.562	0.594	0.398	2.511
Fog lamp	0.093	0.155	0.112	0.605	0.568	0.928	1.078

The influence of various design elements in the front face of a car on the aesthetic perception is related to the magnitude of the partial correlation coefficient. A larger partial correlation coefficient indicates a stronger impact of the design element on the aesthetic perception. The partial correlation coefficient can be positive or negative, with positive values indicating a positive influence and negative values indicating a negative influence. Based on the research findings, it is possible to identify the design elements with larger absolute values of the partial correlation coefficient as the key design genes in the front face design of automobiles.

3.3. Determine the constraints

The design of the front face of a car needs to consider both brand genes and user expectations. For the Audi A3, which targets young people, the body shape needs to highlight a sense of fashion and high-end. User expectations include factors such as social trends and consumer aesthetic psychology, establishing constraints and associations between constraints and perceptual images. User expectation images are obtained through sensory engineering methods, and 60 sets of adjective pairs describing car images were collected through data collection and expert evaluations. The adjective pairs were rated using a Likert scale, with scores ranging from 3 to -3. Adjectives with an average score above 1.5 were extracted as user expectation images. These adjectives, ranked from highest to lowest score, are: high-end (2.12), technological (2.08), elegant (1.99), open (1.93), flowing (1.68), and individual (1.56).

In summary, considering both brand genes and user expectations, we have determined the final intended vocabulary as "high-end" and "imposing". Based on the mapping relationship between the design features and the desired image, we can determine that the larger the values of the four prominent features: front headlights A13, grille A24, hood curve A33, and fog lights A43, the more the front face of the car will exhibit the characteristics of "high-end" and "imposing". In particular, the front headlights A13 (with a partial regression coefficient of 1.600) have a significant impact on the "high-end vs low-end" desired image. Based on this information, we can determine the initial shape, as shown in Table 8.

Table 8. Initial shape

Headlight group	Enter the style gate	Hood curves	Fog lamp

3.4. Scheme generation

Based on the previous constraints, suitable grammar rules were selected to deduce the confirmed initial shape. The deduced solutions are shown in Table 9. A 5-point SD method was used to evaluate 81 new solutions through a questionnaire. The evaluation results showed that the new solutions scored above average for the "high-end" and "imposing" image words, indicating that the new solutions performed well in these image aspects. Solution 21 had the highest score, indicating that this method can effectively continue the brand features and meet user needs.

Table 9. 81 preliminary front face design proposals for cars

| 64 | 65 | 66 | 67 | 68 | 69 | 70 | 71 | 72 |

| 73 | 74 | 75 | 76 | 77 | 78 | 79 | 80 | 81 |

4. Conclusions

This study takes the design of the front face of the Audi A3 as an example and explores the application of shape grammar guided by product DNA in automotive front face design. By quantifying the design variables of explicit design features and implicit design intentions, and applying them to solution deducing and optimization, the feasibility of the proposed design method has been validated. However, automotive design is a complex integrated design process, and when applying this method to design cars, it must be based on a unified overall style. In future research, it is necessary to combine the front face design with other genetic factors in automotive design, improve the establishment of the genetic library for automotive product families, and integrate shape grammar to form a comprehensive and systematic analysis and design method.

References

[1] Lu Z, Frenkler F. Research on Styling Design of New Energy Vehicles Based on Product Semantic Analysis. Mechanical Design, 2017, 34(03): 111-116.

[2] Zhao J, Zhang L. Brand Inheritance Design Method for Electric Vehicles Based on Shape Grammar. Packaging Engineering, 2018, 39(22): 151-156.

[3] Fu L, Wang N, Zhu K, et al. Research on Innovative Design of Ming-style Stools Based on Shape Grammar Perspective. Mechanical Design, 2022, 39(S2): 227-234.

[4] Stiny G. Introduction to Shape and Shape Grammar. Environment and Planning B: Planning and Design, 1980, 7(3): 343-351.

[5] Wu Q, Lv J, Pan W, Liu D. Research on Case-based Cultural Creative Product Design Method. Journal of Engineering Design, 2017, 24(02): 121-133.

[6] Wei Y. Product Form Design Method Based on Shape Grammar and Genetic Constraints. Mechanical and Electronics, 2016, 34(12): 11-15.

[7] Fu Y, Luo S. Exterior Shape Genetic Design of Product Family Based on Styling Image. Computer Integrated Manufacturing Systems, 2012, 18(03): 449-457.

[8] Li L, Lu J, Zhang J. Sensory Image Design Based on Product Genes. Journal of Nanjing University of Technology (Natural Science Edition), 2019, 41(01): 71-78+88.

[9] Cheng Y, Xu X. Research on Front Face Styling Genes of Automotive Brands Based on Product Family DNA. Mechanical Design and Manufacturing, 2022, No.381(11): 37-43.

Design Studies and Intelligence Engineering
L.C. Jain et al. (Eds.)
© 2024 The Authors.
This article is published online with Open Access by IOS Press and distributed under the terms
of the Creative Commons Attribution Non-Commercial License 4.0 (CC BY-NC 4.0).
doi:10.3233/FAIA231448

An Overview of Deepfake Methods in Medical Image Processing for Health Care Applications

Dhanya LAKSHMI and D Jude HEMANTH[1]
Department of ECE Karunya Institute of technology and science, Coimbatore, India

Abstract. AI has become a part and parcel of the medical industry. Especially machine learning-based deep learning models with their ability to handle large amount of data continuously made significant contributions to the healthcare industry. One of the most promising technological developments in the field of deep learning is "deepfake". Deepfake is a method of synthesizing fake images, audio, or video through deep learning models. Deepfake medical image processing is used in different applications like medical image synthesizing, modality transfer, data augmentation, dataset expansion, resolution enhancement, denoising, and reconstruction of medical images. Therefore, its wide range of applications provided a new realm of opportunity for the medical professional for quick, easy, and accurate diagnosis of dis-ease. This study provides an overview of deepfake implementation in the field of medical image processing. This paper is focused on providing clarity for the research questions (RQs), What are deepfake? What are the most common methods to generate a medical deepfake? What are the major applications of deepfake in the medical field? What is the need for deepfake detection? These research questions may help the researchers and academicians to understand the domain specified.

Keywords. medical image processing, deepfake, computer-aided diagnosis, deepfake medical image.

1. Introduction

A wide range of business enterprises, including the financial service and banking sector, educational department, media and entertainment, marketing, e-commerce, and healthcare, have benefited from the massive development and advancement of artificial intelligence (AI) to various degrees and in different forms. AI accompanied by deep learning has been a key facilitator for several innovative commercial breakthroughs in the digital world. Web search engines like Google targeted advertising includes online advertising on YouTube, content and product suggestions on Netflix and Amazon, and self-driving cars like Tesla are some examples of AI breakthroughs. The Development of intelligence systems assist people even in day-to-day lifestyle like email spam filters, face unlocks on smartphones, based on consumers' prior purchases and browsing patterns Amazon utilizes this manmade intelligence to suggest products to their customers, smartwatches are good enough to differentiate between routine tasks and aerobic exercise, AI-powered chatbots are available around the clock to help customers with their queries in online shopping, online banking and more.

---

[1] Corresponding Author.

Life expectancy has increased globally due to significant advancements in medical technology, but as people live longer, healthcare systems must contend with expanding patient demand, rising expenditures, as well as a workforce meeting the demands of patients. Healthcare is about to undergo a major revolution, thanks to artificial intelligence. A rapid increase in healthcare data in recent times shows that AI is applied increasingly in the healthcare industry. Here are some applications of AI in the medical field,

- Aid healthcare professionals,
- Patient care,
- Personalized disease treatment,
- Aid in medical imaging,
- Deepening doctor-patient engagement,
- Accelerated drug development,
- Sharpening disease detection and diagnosis,
- Aid administrative procedures,

The rest of the paper is mainly to address the following research question (RQs)
Deepfake: What are deepfake?
Generation of medical deepfake: What are the most common methods to generate a medical deepfake?
Deepfake in modality transformation of medical images, Deep Fake in medical data augmentation: What are the major applications of deepfake in the medical field?
Exploitation of medical deepfake: What is the need for deepfake detection?
The question is framed to perform a detailed survey of deepfake in the field of medicine. The rest of the survey paper is based on the above four RQs.

1.1 Deepfake

Deepfake is a specific type of tampering method where pictures, videos, and audio are created, modified, synthesized, or altered, using deep-learning models. Computer- generated deepfake is extremely challenging to distinguish as they give the impression of being authentic and convincing. The phenomenal growth in computer vision systems together with deep learning models allowed the creation of Deepfakes at a faster pace and lower cost. Photo editing or manipulation is age-old, but the effortless making and the realistic nature of synthetic media is an exciting feature of today's technological development. The technological advancement in Generative adversarial networks GAN[1] and variational autoencoder VAE[2] play a considerable contribution in the generation of deepfake. The creation, sharing, and editing of videos and photographs are now more widely available than ever because of the rising popularity of internet-based communication like Facebook, Twitter, and YouTube and the availability of cellphones with impressive camera quality[3]. There are several benefits of using deepfake in various fields, some of them are:

- Entertainment
- Education
- Social media
- Healthcare
- Film production

• Forensic science and more.

1.2   Deepfake in medical image analysis

Deep learning models perform extremely well in pattern matching and feature extraction in images. As a result, they are used to detect various types of cancer present in the Computed Tomography (CT) scan, classify different types of disease in Magnetic Resonance Imaging (MRI), and predict abnormalities in X-rays[4]. To accurately perform these tasks deep learning algorithms, need a large amount of data. But due to privacy issues in handling medical data, researchers were not able to access the available medical images. To handle this challenge GAN models were introduced into the medical image application to generate synthetic medical images that are not real but seem to be as original as possible. This will help to expand the data set to the required numbers. Studies have been done on how data quality and quantity affect the performance of deep learning models in the medical field[7]. deepfake model comparatively shows better performance in data augmentation specifically in data expansion by synthesizing or reconstructing medical images.

Each medical imaging technique like CT, MRI, X-ray, and more has its own pros and cons [5]. For example, details about internal organs and structures like blood veins, muscles, fat, and bones are provided through a CT scan, which even assists to inspect internal bleeding, diagnosing tumors, or assessing any other internal damage or injuries. But, ionizing radiation is used in CT scans, which has the potential to harm DNA and increase the chance of developing cancer. There are a few types of cancers that are virtually undetectable or extremely difficult to spot on a CT scan namely, liver cancer, uterine, and prostate cancer where MRI shines. MRI provides valuable insights in diagnosing a variety of non-cancer applications, such as soft tissue or joint injuries, in addition to this injuries or dysfunction of internal systems were also provided by MRI. However, the patient must remain motionless for 20 to 40 minutes during an MRI Scanning which may not be possible for a few patients.

As per the need of medical practitioners for ensuring accurate diagnosis of disease appropriate imaging techniques were chosen. It is extremely difficult to interpret and evaluate the vast number of clinical data because each patient frequently takes several numbers of scans. To help clinicians for providing appropriate treatment intelligent healthcare is a crucial study area. Deep learning models play a crucial role in providing intelligent healthcare. Specifically, deepfakes are applied in medical image processing for reconstructing and denoising medical images, to give both patients and physicians a visual dissipation about what their surgery is all about. synthetic patient data were produced by deepfake technology, without incurring the cost of involving actual patients[6]. Deepfake models would create virtual patients from the information they already own to enhance data protection and privacy among medical specialists. Similarly, Multi-domain medical image generation was also possible in deepfake methods where MRI is generated through CT [8].

2   Generation of medical deepfake

The two promising tools for deepfake generation are GAN and VAE models. Both models are designed and employed for the same application called image and video generation, but procedures are quite different. Many studies have taken place to illustrate the deep learning model (GAN and VAE) capability of learning important attributes from the image data to achieve the desired objective. In this section, the application of GAN and VAE in generating various medical deepfake is discussed.

2.1   GAN applied to medical deepfake.

Since 2014 GAN are used in deep learning models and since 2016 GAN is applied to medical image analysis [9]. There are various types of GAN used for medical deepfake generation namely, Original GAN, (DCGAN)Deep Convolutional Generative Adversarial Networks, (CGAN) conditional generative adversarial network, Pulse2pulse GAN, WaveGAN, progressive growing GANs (PGGAN), (Tripartite-GAN) Tripartite Generative Adversarial Network, cycleGAN, multi-CycleGAN, (M-GAN) multi- channel generative adversarial networks, (TGAN) Temporal GAN, (LAPGAN) Laplacian Pyramid of Adversarial Networks, (WGAN)Wasserstein GAN, (catGAN) categorical generative adversarial networks, (ACGAN) Auxiliary Classifier Generative Adversarial Network, StyleGAN. Table 1 summarizes the different types of GAN used in medical deepfake and their application in the medical field was also discussed.

Table 1. Different types of GAN models used in medical deepfake and their applications

Ref no	Type of GAN	Application
[10]	(DCGAN)Deep Convolutional Generative Adversarial Networks,	They used DCGAN for generating deepfake chest X-rays.
[11]	(CGAN) conditional generative adversaria l network,	They used CGAN for generating 3D lung nodules in different scales.
[12]	Pulse2pulse GAN,	They are used to generate deepfake ECG
[12]	WaveGAN,	They are used to generate deepfake ECG
[13]	progressive growing GANs (PGGAN),	They are used to generate 256 x 256 deepfake medical images.
[14]	(Tripartite-GAN) Tripartite Generative Adversarial Network,	They used tripartite-GAN instead of contrast agent injection by synthesizing CEMRI for the detection of liver tumors.
[15]	cycleGAN,	They used cycle GAN medical image modality transformation.
[16]	multi-CycleGAN,	They used multi-CycleGAN for MRI to CT modality transfer.
[17]	(M-GAN) multi-channel generative adversarial networks,	M-GAN is used to synthesize PET images from CT.
[18]	(LAPGAN) Laplacian Pyramid of Adversarial Networks,	They used DCGAN and LAPGAN to generate deepfake realistic images of skin lesions.
[19]	(WGAN)Wasserstein GAN,	They use WGAN and DCGAN to generate deepfake MR images.
[20]	(catGAN) categorical generative adversarial networks,	able to produce a real-world dermoscopic image.

[21]	StyleGAN.	used to increase the accuracy of retinal diagnostics.

Despite the extensive usage of GANs in various fields, there is a significant impact on the medical domain, where the study is performed. GAN utilizes its computational capability and the availability of massive healthcare records to generate, manipulate, and evaluate medical data. In traditional data augmentation image cropping, inverting, copying, and alignment is possible whereas generating an entirely new image is not possible which can be performed by GAN.

In [22] the author used one-dimensional noise as input to generate a brain MRI using the GAN model. More Realistic high-resolution fake/synthetic brain MRI images were generated through this method and image denoising was achieved despite using the dataset containing only 528 images for training the network. In [19] the author proposed a method to generate synthetic brain MRI images with a resolution of 128x128. In [23]data augmentation is carried out by implementing GAN to increase the CNN performance during liver lesion classification. GAN is used for the generation of deepfake prostate lesions in MRI images[24]. Fig 1 shows the real and deepfake based generated synthetic images used and generated in various papers [8],[25],[26].

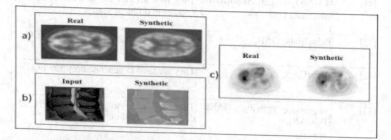

Fig. 1. Shows a) Real and Synthetic PET images of a normal patient [25] b) Input MRI and Synthetic CT [8]c) Real and synthetic PET images [26].

2.2   VAE applied to medical deepfake

VAE comprises an encoder that encodes the incoming input data and a decoder is used to reconstruct the data. Both the encoder and the decoder are separate convolutional neural networks (CNN) combined to perform the learning process [2]. The VAE is used to generate new synthetic images whereas, in the field of medicine, VAE is usually applied for segmentation and disease diagnosis.

To handle insufficient and unbalanced medical image data VAE is utilized together with StyleGAN to generate deepfake cell images to classify white blood cells. This method shows a light for easy and accurate diagnosis by doctors [27]. VAE is used to enhance the act of risk assessment to treat HCC patients by detailing normal tissue conditions, for subsequent cancer therapy with SBRT[28]. A hybrid model is proposed with the combination of VAE-GAN to detect abnormalities in chest radiography by neglecting the usage of lesion labels and abnormal images for training the network [29].

The survey shows that comparatively GAN is more widely used in medical deepfake applications than VAE.

3   Deepfake in modality transformation of medical images

Magnetic Resonance Imaging (MRI) and Computed Tomography (CT) are the most extensively used medical imaging techniques. The researchers predominantly work on these two fields in modality transformation. As we have discussed in section 1.2 MRI performs better than CT, but it may be difficult for some patients to remain motionless for nearly half an hour. Whereas, regarding CT the patients are exposed to strong ionizing radiation which may cause cancer. So, in some cases, CT scanning is convenient for the patients to whom MRI scanning is suggested and vise-versa. So, using deepfake models modality transformation is performed like CT to MRI, MRI to CT, CT to PET, PET-CT, and so on.

Using MRI images as input deepfake CT images of the lumbar spine are generated using pseudo-3D Cycle GAN architecture. The author concludes that CT images of the lumbar spine generated using pseudo-3D Cycle GAN architecture are performing better than the single-slice Cycle GAN model [8]. Similarly, in [16] multi- CycleGAN is employed for the unpaired head and neck MRI images to deepfake CT image generation through modality transfer. The cross-modality transfer is performed to generate 3-D deepfake CT images from 2D X-ray images addingto this, deepfake 2D X- ray image is also generated in the processes of 3D-CT image synthesis [30]. Table. 2 shows the data set used for medical deepfake synthesis.

Table 2. shows the dataset used for medical deepfake synthesis

Sl.NO	DATASET	Deepfake output	Anatomic site
1	DRIVE[31]–[33]	Fundus or retinal Image	Eye, vessels
2	ADNI[34], [35]	CT	Brain
3	SPACE[36]	ultrasound image	Fetal profile
4	STARE [29]	neuronal image	Neuro
6	HRF [29]	neuronal image	Neuro
7	SRC[37]	Chest image	Lungs
8	LIDC-IDRI[38]	CT	Lungs
9	NeuB1[29]	neuronal image	Neuro

Most of the medical image analyses are performed using private datasets because it is very difficult to collect the medical image data as only a minimal number of patients particularly affected by the specific disorder are available to take the scan which must be labeled by a medical professional is a time-consuming process. The other main reason is it's quite expensive because we need to pay to access those data. So, few of them collect data directly from a medical institution.

4   Deep Fake in medical data augmentation

To improve the quality and performance of deep learning model in the generation, classifications, and segmentation tasks data augmentation techniques   like dataset expansion, denoising, resolution enhancement, and regeneration of medical images is carried out in many studies using computer-aided deepfake technology. MRI is widely used in medical imagining techniques, but the major challenge is a decline in the quality of images even due to the slight shifting caused by involuntary activities like breathing and heartbeat because of the slow acquisition of data samples accumulated in the k-space instead of image space which may lead to interference in spatial frequency data. The deepfake-based regeneration process helps in regaining the reduced quality. As we discussed in section 3 collecting medical data is quite complicated and expensive but for the better performance of deep neural networks, we need a huge volume of data to train the network in that case, deepfake helps in dataset expansion through data augmentation which includes both the new medical image generation and alteration.

5   Exploitation of medical deepfake

Even though there is a massive progressive growth in deepfake implementation in the medical field they are used for malicious purposes. Medical images can be edited to inject or eliminate signs of health complications for the purpose of committing insurance scams, ruining ongoing research work, for some terrorist attacks, taking revenge on others, or for the purpose of committing murders. The attackers with access to medical image data can alter the image for example by injecting or removing cancer in a 3D scan which may lead to the wrong diagnosis. In [39] the author gives an idea of the possibility to inject and remove lung cancer from a 3D CT scan. These deepfake - generated images are not easy to differentiate and it has become comparatively simpler to generate fake content. These kinds of attacks can cause a huge impact on the life of innocent people. There is a chance of losing life through misdiagnosis. So, there needs to generate an efficient method to detect deepfake. The study shows that 98% of the research work is deepfake-based medical image generation, and the remaining 2% of the research work is only based on medical image tampering or deepfake detection. As there is a huge gap between the generation and detection of medical deepfake there is a need for researchers to perform intensive studies in medical deepfake detection.

6   Conclusion

The paper summarizes the major application of deepfake in the field of medical imaging and gives an overview of the most used approaches like GAN and VAE for deepfake medical image generation. The study shows that the GAN model is the most popular model among the other existing models. Especially DCGAN, PGGAN, and CGAN are the most frequently used frameworks. The datasets used for generating deepfake medical images were discussed. The research also highlights an emerging threat in the field of healthcare due to the fast-growing pace of deep learning model-based deepfake framework. This study may contribute to the researchers in the understanding of the key role of synthetically developed deepfake medical images in easy, and accurate diagnosis of medical abnormalities.

References

[1] "Ivan Mehta. 2019. A new study says nearly 96 of deepfake videos are porn. https://thenextweb.com/apps/2019/10/07/a-new-study-says-nearly-96-ofdeepfake-   videos-are-porn. Accessed: 2020-02-11.".

[2] S. Zavrak and M. Iskefiyeli, "Anomaly-Based Intrusion Detection from Net-work Flow Features Using Variational Autoencoder," IEEE Access, vol. 8, pp. 108346–108358, 2020, doi: 10.1109/ACCESS.2020.3001350.

[3] A. Ismail, M. Elpeltagy, M. S. Zaki, and K. Eldahshan, "A new deep learn-ing-based methodology for video deepfake detection using xgboost," Sen-sors, vol. 21, no. 16, Aug. 2021, doi: 10.3390/s21165413.

[4] M. Puttagunta and S. Ravi, "Medical image analysis based on deep learning approach," Multimed Tools Appl, vol. 80, no. 16, pp. 24365–24398, Jul. 2021, doi: 10.1007/s11042-021-10707-4.

[5] S. Liu et al., "Deep Learning in Medical Ultrasound Analysis: A Review," Engineering, vol. 5, no. 2. Elsevier Ltd, pp. 261–275, Apr. 01, 2019. doi: 10.1016/j.eng.2018.11.020.

[6] S. Neethirajan, "Is Seeing Still Believing? Leveraging Deepfake Technology for Livestock Farming," Frontiers in Veterinary Science, vol. 8. Frontiers Media S.A., Nov. 23, 2021. doi: 10.3389/fvets.2021.740253.

[7] A. M. Barragán-Montero et al., "Deep learning dose prediction for IMRT of esophageal cancer: The effect of data quality and quantity on model perfor-mance," Physica Medica, vol. 83, pp. 52–63, Mar. 2021, doi: 10.1016/j.ejmp.2021.02.026.

[8] R. Oulbacha and S. Kadoury, "MRIto CT Synthesis of the Lumbar Spine from a Pseudo-3D Cycle GAN," in Proceedings - International Symposium on Biomedical Imaging, Apr. 2020, vol. 2020-April, pp. 1784–1787. doi: 10.1109/ISBI45749.2020.9098421.

[9] X. Li, Y. Jiang, J. J. Rodriguez-Andina, H. Luo, S. Yin, and O. Kaynak, "When medical images meet generative adversarial network: recent devel-opment and research opportunities," Discover Artificial Intelligence, vol. 1, no. 1, Dec. 2021, doi: 10.1007/s44163-021-00006-0.

[10] H. Salehinejad, S. Valaee, T. Dowdell, E. Colak, and J. Barfett, "Generaliza-tion of Deep Neural Networks for Chest Pathology Classification in X-Rays Using Generative Adversarial Networks," in ICASSP, IEEE International Conference on Acoustics, Speech and Signal Processing - Proceedings, Sep. 2018, vol. 2018-April, pp. 990–994. doi: 10.1109/ICASSP.2018.8461430.

[11] T. Bu, Z. Yang, S. Jiang, G. Zhang, H. Zhang, and L. Wei, "3D conditional generative adversarial network-based synthetic medical image augmentation for lung nodule detection," Int J Imaging Syst Technol, vol. 31, no. 2, pp. 670–681, Jun. 2021, doi: 10.1002/ima.22511.

[12] V. Thambawita et al., "DeepFake electrocardiograms: the key for open sci-ence for artificial intelligence in medicine", doi: 10.1101/2021.04.27.21256189.

[13] C. Han et al., "Combining noise-to-image and image-to-image GANs: Brain MR image augmentation for tumor detection," IEEE Access, vol. 7, pp. 156966–156977, 2019, doi: 10.1109/ACCESS.2019.2947606.

[14] J. Zhao et al., "Tripartite-GAN: Synthesizing liver contrast-enhanced MRI to improve tumor detection," Med Image Anal, vol. 63, Jul. 2020, doi: 10.1016/j.media.2020.101667.

[15] A. Chartsias, T. Joyce, R. Dharmakumar, and S. A. Tsaftaris, "Adversarial Image Synthesis for Unpaired Multi-Modal Cardiac Data."

[16] Y. Liu et al., "CT synthesis from MRI using multi-cycle GAN for head-and-neck radiation therapy," Computerized Medical Imaging and Graphics, vol. 91, Jul. 2021, doi: 10.1016/j.compmedimag.2021.101953.

[17] L. Bi, J. Kim, A. Kumar, D. Feng, and M. Fulham, "Synthesis of Positron Emission Tomography (PET) Images via Multi-channel Generative Adver-sarial

Design Studies and Intelligence Engineering
L.C. Jain et al. (Eds.)
© 2024 The Authors.
This article is published online with Open Access by IOS Press and distributed under the terms
of the Creative Commons Attribution Non-Commercial License 4.0 (CC BY-NC 4.0).
doi:10.3233/FAIA231449

Optimization Analysis of Product Design Process Based on Reinforcement Learning Algorithm

Yuping HU[a] and Qian LI[b]

a. Academy of art and design, Shaoyang Unigersity, Shaoyang
422099, Hunan, China
b. School of Jewelry and Art Design, Wuzhou Unigersity, Wuzhou
543003, Guangxi, China

Abstract: In order to reduce therework iteration in the product development process, the optimization analysis of product design process based on reinforcement learning (multi-objective process optimization genetic algorithm based on design structure matrix (DSM) theory) is proposed. By optimizing the task execution sequence, therework in the product development process can be reduced to compress the progress and reduce the cost. The optimization algorithm is an improved genetic (GA) algorithm, in which time and cost are considered in the fitness function. In the selection, crossover and mutation operators, the strategy of maintaining optimal solution is adopted. The simulation results show that the optimization algorithm can reduce the development time by 30% ~ 40% and the cost by 7% ~ 20% for product development projects with high task coupling. Conclusion: The optimization algorithm can effectively reduce therework iteration in the project development process, thus shortening the product development time and saving the development cost.

Keywords: process optimization; Genetic algorithm; Simulation; Design structure matrix

1 Introduction

In today's era when innovation is the main theme, R&D plays a decisive role for a country and an enterprise, and successful R&D project management is the basis to ensure the success of the project. The 18th National Congress of the Communist Party of China put forward the strategy of "innovation-driven development", and the core of innovation lies in separating the independent innovation ability of enterprises. However, the management level of Chinese enterprises is backward, especially the management ability of large-scale complex R&D projects is weaker, which seriously affects the independent innovation ability of China enterprises. The survey shows that 70% of China's current R&D projects are beyond the estimated time schedule, with an average of 20% to 50% exceeding the planned delivery time. More than 90% of R&D projects are over the budget, and the higher the complexity of the projects, the more they exceed the project plan. Therefore, it is of great theoretical and practical significance to systematically study the efficient management methods and models of R&D projects that adapt to China's national conditions, and to enhance the independent innovation ability and management ability of enterprises.

This means that the project manager must improve the design and management ability of complex systems, which is closely related to the tools adopted. In recent years, Design Structure Matrix, DSM) based on process management and Quality Function Deployment, QFD) based on meeting customers' needs have been widely used in the process management of complex product design and R&D [2]. QFD, as a quality management technology and method with the idea of source management, is a method of planning and systematic analysis in advance by identifying and analyzing the "customer voice" and transforming it into engineering and management measures, which enables managers to identify the engineering and manufacturing problems in the early stage of the project life cycle and facilitate the development of preventive strategies. DSM provides a better method for designing, analyzing, and organizing complex systems. It can visually analyze complex R&D projects. The "Multi-domain Matrix" (MDM) is the latest development of DSM, which is used to analyze the dependencies between cross- domain elements.

2 Literature review

Understanding the influencing factors of R&D process is the first premise to formulate optimization scheme and carry out implementation activities, and it is also one of the key contents in the theoretical research of R&D process optimization. Different researchers focus on different aspects of the factors that affect the new product development process. Some scholars have expounded the influence of R&D department on new product R&D from the perspective of organizational setting. Sharma, A. and others found through the survey data of 243 R&D departments that an influential R&D department is more likely to achieve high-level R&D performance, and the R&D department can improve its influence in the organization by improving the degree of innovation and customer relationship [4]. Khan, M.I.H. and others empirically tested the effects of variables related to organizational flexibility of R&D departments on habit and behavior innovation and management efficiency in enterprise R&D process by studying 112 companies [5]. There are also some scholars who think that new product development is a collective activity, and the ability of R&D personnel and the communication between R&D personnel have a positive impact on the performance of R&D activities. Yang, W. and others linked the strategic decision of R&D department from 2009 to 2013 with the financial health of the company, and pointed out that in order to improve the financial performance, managers of enterprises (especially small and medium-sized enterprises) should participate more in research activities, and should pay attention to using more structural and functional R&D methods in the allocation of R&D strategic decisions [6]. Arboretti, R. and others analyze that the education, experience, age, and gender of R&D personnel have great influence on new product development from the demographic dimension [7]. There are also a few scholars who extend the research perspective from the inside of the R&D department to the outside and consider the importance of external factors in the product development process. Panzer, M. et al. put forward that the participation of suppliers is the key coordination process of product design and process design, and integrating material suppliers into the process of new product development can improve product quality, reduce the cost of new products, and promote the smooth launch of new products [8]. According to the product life cycle theory, Diao, Y and others divide the process optimization into six stages, namely, finding the optimization project, finding the optimization goal, diagnosing the process problems, redesigning the process, integrating the process and evaluating the optimization results [9].

In this paper, considering both time and cost, the multi-objective process optimization of product development is studied, and an intelligent algorithm for optimizing product development process based on the priority rule of process execution is designed.

3 Research methods

3.1 Parallel product development model
3.1.1 Basic assumptions and problem description
The premise assumptions of the concurrent product development model are as follows:
1) The product development project can be decomposed into multiple tasks, and the completion time and cost of each task obey certain statistical laws; The relationship between tasks can be expressed by Boolean information flow matrix.
2) After the completion of the project, information will be output to other tasks, which will lead to the start or rework of other tasks. Therework probability and rework impact can be estimated in advance, which are expressed by rework probability matrix and rework impact matrix respectively, and do not change with time [10,11].
3) Each task has a maximum number of rework times. When the number of rework times of a task exceeds the specified value, even if other tasks provide it with information, the task will not be reworked (this assumption is to avoid the situation that the project cannot be completed due to endless rework).
4) There are sufficient resources in the project execution process, and multiple projects can be executed in parallel, so there is no resource bottleneck.
In the process of product development, there may be information circulation between tasks. If all the upstream processes for which a task has information input have been completed, the task can be executed [12]. When a task is completed, it will output information to the downstream task, so that the downstream task can start work. At the sametime, it may also provide feedback information to the upstream task, so that the upstream task can correct its work with a certain probability, that is, rework; In addition, when the results of downstream tasks fail to meet the specified requirements, it will also cause rework of upstream processes. The rework of one task may lead to therework of other tasks, thus making the whole project form a complex network structure.

3.1.2 Modeling of complex product development process
Due to the problem of rework in the process of project development, the relationship between the overall project duration and cost and the duration and cost of each task is difficult to be obtained by analytical method, and only approximate solutions can be obtained by simulation. The simulation model is a discrete event simulation model, and the trigger event is that one or more tasks are completed at a certain point; The status includes three aspects: the unfinished quantity of each task, the executable status of each task and the rework times of each task. Given the task execution priority sequence, the product development simulation process is as follows:
Step1: Traverse all tasks. If a task does not depend on other upstream tasks, or if all the upstream tasks on which it depends have been completed, and the task has not yet been completed, it is an executable task, which means that the task can be started at the current time [13,14]. Find all executable tasks, and set the shortest completed task time among the tasks as the current simulation time slice according to the execution time and unfinished quantity of these tasks. dt, and add it to the accumulated time tt. dt. The calculation formula of is the following formula (1):

$$dt = \min_{E_{it} \neq 0} \{V_{it} \cdot T_i\}. \tag{1}$$

Step2: For each executable taski, atdt. The amount of work completed in time isdt / T_i , the execution cost is$C_i^* dt / T_i$. Among them: T_i For the taski The execution time, C_i For the taski The execution cost of. Accumulate the cost into the total cost TC, ift Time taski The original remaining workload is set tok_{jt} %, then after time. dt After that, the remaining workload becomes k_{jt} % − dt /T_i . For a certain item in dt Tasks completed in timei If the task outputs information to the task.j , andj At this time has been partially completed, theni The completion of may lead to a partially completed task.j Rework [15]. When the taskj When therework times of are less than the maximum rework times (nj < M_{rw}) to generate random numbers.r. ifr ≤ R_{ij} (R For rework probability matrix), thenj Need to rework. j Add 1 to the rework times, and according to the rework impact matrixP Re - calculationj The unfinished workload is as follows (2):

$$k_{jt}\% + (1 - k_{jt}\%) \times P_{ij}. \tag{2}$$

ifr > R_{ij} , do notrework. Set the executable status of tasks with a remaining workload of 0 to 0.

Step3: Find and execute all executable tasks again until all tasks are completed.

Because the rework process is random, the project cost and project duration obtained by each simulation are a random value. If the following equation (3) is satisfied after such simulation is performed for many times:

$$\begin{cases} \dfrac{\left|\frac{1}{L}\sum_{l=1}^{L} TT_l - \frac{1}{L+1}\sum_{l=1}^{L+1} TT_l\right|}{\frac{1}{L}\sum_{l=1}^{L} TT_l} < 0.005, \\ \dfrac{\left|\frac{1}{L}\sum_{l=1}^{L} TC_l - \frac{1}{L+1}\sum_{l=1}^{L+1} TC_l\right|}{\frac{1}{L}\sum_{l=1}^{L} TC_l} < 0.005, \end{cases} \tag{3}$$

It shows that the simulation results tend to be stable, and the simulation program is stopped. Among them: TT_l andTC_l Respectively the firstl The project duration and project cost obtained from the second simulation, L Is the total number of simulations.

According to the task parameters and task execution sequence of the project, the distribution of completion time and cost of the project can be obtained through multiple simulations, so as to carryout risk analysis and determine the probability that the development project can be completed under the specified time and cost requirements. The formula for calculating the probability that a product development project can be completed as required is the following formula (4):

$$P(T_E, C_E) = 1 - F(T < T_E, C < C_E). \tag{4}$$

3.2 product development process optimization algorithm

According to the correspondence between task execution priority sequence and project time cost, this paper designs an improved genetic algorithm to find the approximate optimal task execution sequence [16]. In the design of fitness function, both time and cost are considered, and in the design of genetic operator, a variety of optimal solution keeping strategies are used, so that the algorithm can converge quickly, but it can breakthrough the local optimal solution. The goal of this algorithm is to reduce unnecessary rework iterations in product development through reasonable project development process design, thus reducing development costs and shortening development time.

The necessity of genetic algorithm struggle for existence often exists among natural creatures, and only those with strong adaptability can survive in the fierce struggle for existence and pass on their excellent genes from generation to generation. The evolution process of natural organisms is consistent, from low to high, simple to complex [17]. Moreover, it is in the genetic process of this generation that the population gradually evolves into individuals who are more adaptable to environmental variability, so that the biological population can continue to develop and improve. With this kind of natural evolution law of survival of the fittest and survival of the fittest, today's genetic algorithm (GA) has been abstractly developed. The optimization algorithm of design structure matrix belongs to sorting combination optimization, so the order of design activities essentially determines the optimal solution of objective function. For sorting combinations, the difference between the sub-optimal solution and the optimal solution is often very small, and the sub-optimal solution retains most of the excellent genes of the optimal solution (that is, the design activity order). For product development activities, the process of finding the optimal product component development sequence is very similar to the process of natural organisms evolving from weak to strong, so genetic algorithm is chosen as the optimization algorithm in this paper.

DSM scheduling strategy is embedded into DSM simulation program, and DSM simulation outputs the value of fitness function corresponding to each chromosome on the premise of satisfying the constraints of optimization problem, thus overcoming the problem that there are many uncertain factors in optimization problem, and it is difficult to provide genetic algorithm with fitness function expressed in analytical form. For each chromosome obtained, DSM simulation is called to obtain the average project duration and cost corresponding to the chromosome, and then the subsequent genetic operation is returned and executed [18]. In each iteration of the algorithm, DSM simulation is used to obtain the fitness function, and the chromosomes are sorted non-dominantly. Through many iterations, the population keeps approaching the Pareto optimal set. The overall framework of the algorithm is shown in Figure 1.

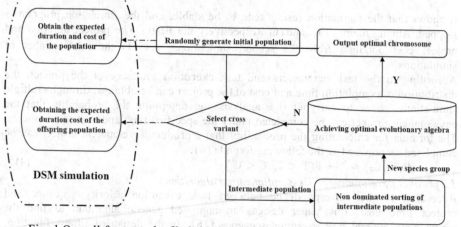

Fig. 1 Overall framework of hybrid algorithm based on simulation and genetic algorithm

3.2. 1 Chromosome coding scheme

This paper adopts task coding method. Individual Id. It's a task sequence Id = $\{i^1, i^2, \ldots, i^n\}$ A that represents the priority of task execution, and each Id Corresponding to a schedule planning scheme. The decoding process is based on the task priority sequenceId. And determine the execution order of each task, the total project completion time and completion cost.

3.2. 2 Fitness function

The shorter the project time and the lower the cost, the greater the individual's adaptability. The importance weight of time and cost can be determined by expert scoring or investigation and interview [19]. Because of the randomness of the simulation process, it is impossible to get the maximum and minimum values of the project time and cost, and it is impossible to standardize the project time and cost. In order to eliminate the influence of dimension, taking the average execution time and cost of the project in the initial situation as the standard, the fitness function can be defined as the following formula (5):

$$Ft(Seq) = \cfrac{1}{w_T \cfrac{\frac{1}{L}\sum_{j=1}^{L} TT_j(Seq)}{TT_j(Seq0)} + wc \cfrac{\frac{1}{L}\sum_{j=1}^{L} TC_j(Seq)\cdot}{TC_j(Seq0)}} \tag{5}$$

Among them: Seq Execute a priority sequence for the task; TT_j (Seq) and TC_j (Seq) According to the priority sequence Seq In the first j The total time and cost of the project obtained in the second simulation; Seq0 Is an initial task priority sequence; L Is the number of simulations; w_T and wc They are the importance weights of time and cost respectively, including $w_T + wc = 1$。

3.2.3 Genetic Operator and Termination Strategy

Assume that the number of individuals in the initial population is M, it is randomly generated. M A 1 ~ n Randomly arranged integer sequences, each sequence is a task execution sequence, corresponding to an individual. In order to realize the optimization of the whole population, individuals with strong vitality are selected from the population to produce a new population. In this paper, the proportional selection operator (roulette selection operator) is adopted, that is, the probability that an individual is selected and passed on to the next generation population is directly proportional to the fitness of the individual.

The crossover algorithm adopts single-point crossover. On the issue of intersection selection, this paper has made some improvements to the traditional intersection method. For two parents i and j, its fitness is respectively Ft (i) and Ft(j), the calculation formula of the intersection is the following formula (6):

$$X = Floor(\frac{Ft(i)}{Ft(i) + Ft(j)} * N) + 1. \tag{6}$$

Among them: N Is the chromosome length, that is, the number of project tasks; Floor () is an integer function. DaughterId' Chromosome part 1 (front X Gene values) were taken from the parent in sequence. i In front of X Genes, part 2 N − X Three genes were taken from the father. j. Slave parent j The first gene of begins to be selected sequentially. If a gene value is duplicated with the gene in the first part, the parent is selected instead of the duplicated gene value. j The next gene value of until the parent is selected. j Dedi X Genes. The cross- generated offspring has the parent. i The gene ratio of is listed as the following formula (7):

$$\frac{Ft(i)}{Ft(i) + Ft(j)}, \tag{7}$$

Have a father j. The gene proportion of is the following formula (8):

$$\frac{Ft(j)}{Ft(i) + Ft(j)} \tag{8}$$

Through this method, the parent with higher fitness will have more genes to pass on to the next generation, so as to better realize the survival of the fittest. The newly generated individuals are used to replace the individuals with low fitness in the population.

The mutation algorithm in this paper is: if the chromosome length isN, randomly generate two 1 ~ N Integer betweeni andj , the individuali Bit sumj The gene values at positions are mutually reversed. Randomly select a certain proportion of individuals in the population with probabilityP_m Perform mutation operation to replace individuals with low fitness in the population with newly generated individuals. When the average fitness change of the upper and lower generations is very small, it can be considered that the algorithm has converged and stopped. The judgment formula is as follows (9):

$$\left| \frac{\sum_{i=1}^{M} Ft(Id_{ki}) - \sum_{i=1}^{M} Ft(Id_{(k+1)i})}{\sum_{i=1}^{M} Ft(Id_{ki})} \right| < 0.005. \tag{9}$$

Among them: k Represents genetic algebra, Id_{ki} Express the first k Daididii An individual, M Represents the population size. Find out the individual with the greatest fitness from the last generation population, decode the gene of the individual and get the optimal solution. Population size P_s , crossover probability P_c , mutation probability P_m , reproductive algebra G_n Etc. can be estimated according to experience, or determined by many experimental comparisons.

4 Result analysis

A simple example is given to illustrate the application of this model in a chip research and development project, which can be roughly divided intoA ~ I These nine development tasks. The completion time of these tasks obeys the normal distribution, and the expected execution time is {30, 40, 35, 39, 52, 55, 62, 29,39} respectively, and the variance is {3.4, 4.2, 3.9, 3.8, 4.6, 4.8, 3.9. The cost per unit time of each task is {2, 3, 2,1, 4, 3, 2, 4, 3} respectively, and the maximum rework times of each task is 5. The relationship between these tasks is shown in Figure 2.

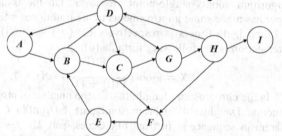

Figure 2 Chip Design Information Flow Diagram

Therework probability matrix and rework impact matrix of this project is shown in Table 1 respectively. Ifthere is norework, the sum of the completion costs of all tasks is 1 019.

Table 1 Project Task Duration and DSM Influence Matrix

task	A	B	C	D	E	F	G	H	I
A	-	0.8(0.9)	-	-	-	-	-	-	-
B	-	-	0.6(0.7)	0.7(0.6)	-	-	-	-	-
C	-	-	-	-	-	0.7(0.6)	0.9(0.8)	-	-
D	0.6(0.8)	-	0.7(0.8)	-	-	-	0.7(0.7)	-	-

E	-	0.8(0.9)	-	-	-	-	-	-
F	-	-	-	-	0.8(0.7)	-	-	-
G	-	-	-	-	-	-	0.8(0.8)	-
H	-	-	0.7(0.8)	-	0.9(0.7)	-	-	0.9(0.8)
I	-	-	-	-	-	-	-	-

Note: The number before parentheses is the rework probability. R_{ij}, the number in brackets is rework impact rate. P_{ij} 。

The Monte Carlo simulation program is compiled on the platform of Mat lab 7. 0, and the distribution of the completion time and cost of the development project is calculated. The simulation results show that the average value of the simulation results tends to be stable when the number of simulations exceeds 200. In fact, when the simulation process reaches 172 times, the simulation stop condition is reached [20]. When the tasks in this project are executed in the priority order of {A, B, C, D, E, F, G, H, I}, the average completion time of the project is about 588. 0, and the variance is 117. 7. The completion cost is 3 487. 7 and the variance is 710. 4. Set the number of simulations to 300.

Due to the correlation between tasks, the project has been reworked many times during the execution, which greatly increases the construction period and cost. If the project completion time is required to be within 500 and the cost is within 3 500, the probability that the project can be completed as required is only 19. 3%.

An improved genetic algorithm optimization program is written on the platform of Mat lab 7. 0 to find the approximate optimal project development process. The parameter is set to population number. M= 50, the number of individuals in each iteration is 20, the crossover probability is 0. 8, and the mutation probability is 0. 1. In order to facilitate observation, the fitness function value is expanded by 10 times, so that it is between 1 and 10. Due to different market conditions, the importance of time and cost to the success of the project will be different. This case only investigates the task execution optimization under the following two special circumstances.

1) There is no requirement for development time, and only the cost is considered, namely $w_C = 1$, $w_T = 0$. At this time, the change of population average fitness is shown in Figure 3. When the genetic algorithm program runs to about 40 generations, the average fitness function of the population tends to be stable. The approximate optimal project execution priority order is {G, C, D, H, B, E, F,A, I}; The average project execution time is 414. 0, and the variance is 100. 7. The average execution cost is 2 808. 0, and the variance is 543. 6. Compared with the original scheme, the time is saved by 29. 6% and the cost is saved by 19. 4%. Under this arrangement of project execution sequence, the probability of project completion time within 500 and completion cost within 3 500 can reach 75. 7%.

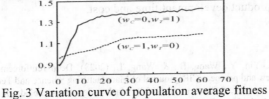

Fig. 3 Variation curve of population average fitness

2) only consider the time, regardless of the development costs, namely $w_C = 0$, $w_T = 1$. At this time, the simulation optimization results are shown in Figure 5. When the genetic algorithm program runs to about 20 generations, the average fitness of the

population tends to be stable. The approximate optimal project execution priority order is {G, C, D, B, E, F, H,A, I}. The average project execution time is 370. 1, and the variance is 70. 2. The average execution cost is 3 249. 8, and the variance is 474. 1. Compared with the original scheme, the time is saved by 37. 1% and the cost is saved by 6. 8%. Under this project execution sequence arrangement, the probability that the project completion time is within 500 and the completion cost is within 3 500 can reach 73. 3%.

By comparing the above simulation results, it can be found that the project execution time is also optimized while optimizing the cost; While optimizing the project, the cost situation has also been improved. Under different weights, the focus of optimization is different. In any case, the probability that the project can be successfully completed under the dual requirements of time and cost is greatly improved. In order to verify the stability of the above optimization results, the optimization program is run again, and the optimization sequences obtained are {g, c, d, h, b, I, e, f, a}, {g, c, d, b, e, f, h, i, a} respectively. Under the above two execution priority sequences, the completion time of software development projects is 418. 7 and 378. 6, and the completion cost is 2 888. 5 and 3 187. 5, respectively, and the data changes are not more than 5%.

The simulation results show that different optimization processes can be obtained according to the preference of managers for schedule and cost. For highly coupled product development projects, this algorithm can effectively reduce the rework iteration in the product development process. In this case, the compression range of development time is between 30% and 40%; The cost reduction range is between 7% and 20%, and the effect is remarkable.

5 Conclusion

Aiming at the problems of task coupling and rework iteration in parallel product development, this paper proposes a multi-objective process optimization algorithm based on genetic algorithm. The algorithm can get different priority sequences of project execution by giving different weights to the project duration and cost. The example analysis shows that the optimization algorithm can effectively reduce the rework iteration in the project development process, thus shortening the product development time and saving the development cost.

Because this paper does not consider the resource constraints in the process of project development, it is not applicable to development projects with strict resource constraints. In addition, this model assumes that therework probability and rework impact are known, which can be estimated by expert experience or historical data. This assumption is usually not valid for small companies lacking historical data and development experience, which is also a limitation of this paper. Future research can further explore the impact of the changes of rework probability matrix and rework impact matrix on product development time and cost.

References

[1] Li, C., Zheng, P., Yin, Y., Wang, B., & Wang, L. (2023). Deep reinforcement learning in smart manufacturing: A review and prospectsCIRP Journal of Manufacturing Science and Technology, 40, 75- 101.
[2] Dabbagh, S. R., Ozcan, O., & Tasoglu, S. (2022). Machine learning-enabled optimization of extrusion-based 3D printing. Methods, 206, 27-40.
[3] Vinitha, N., Vasudevan, J., & Gopinath, K. P. (2023). Bioethanol production optimization through machine learning algorithm approach: biomass characteristics, saccharification, and fermentation conditions for enzymatic hydrolysis. Biomass Conversion and Biorefinery, 13(8), 7287-7299.

[4] Sharma, A., Mukhopadhyay, T., Rangappa, S. M., Siengchin, S., & Kushvaha, V. (2022). Advances in computational intelligence of polymer composite materials: machine learning assisted modeling, analysis and design. Archives of Computational Methods in Engineering, 29(5), 3341-3385.

[5] Khan, M. I. H., Sablani, S. S., Nayak, R., & Gu, Y. (2022). Machine learning-based modeling in food processing applications: State of the art. Comprehensive reviews in food science and food safety, 21(2), 1409- 1438.

[6] Yang, W., Xiang, W., Yang, Y., & Cheng, P. (2022). Optimizing federated learning with deep reinforcement learning for digital twin empowered industrial IoT. IEEE Transactions on Industrial Informatics, 19(2), 1884- 1893.

[7] Arboretti, R., Ceccato, R., Pegoraro, L., & Salmaso, L. (2022). Design of Experiments and machine learning for product innovation: A systematic literature review. Quality and Reliability Engineering International, 38(2), 1131- 1156.

[8] Panzer, M., & Bender, B. (2022). Deep reinforcement learning in production systems: a systematic literature review. International Journal of Production Research, 60(13), 4316-4341.

[9] Diao, Y., Yan, L., & Gao, K. (2022). A strategy assisted machine learning to process multi-objective optimization for improving mechanical properties of carbon steels. Journal of Materials Science & Technology, 109, 86-93.

[10] Haq, Z. U., Ullah, H., Khan, M. N. A., Naqvi, S. R., & Ahsan, M. (2022). Hydrogen production optimization from sewage sludge supercritical gasification process using machine learning methods integrated with genetic algorithm. Chemical Engineering Research and Design, 184, 614-626.

[11] Lee, S., Zhang, Z., & Gu, G. X. (2022). Generative machine learning algorithm for lattice structures with superior mechanical properties. Materials Horizons, 9(3), 952-960.

[12]Mahajan, S., Abualigah, L., Pandit, A. K., & Altalhi, M. (2022). Hybrid Aquila optimizer with arithmetic optimization algorithm for global optimization tasks. Soft Computing, 26(10), 4863-4881.

[13] Sohail, A. (2023). Genetic algorithms in the fields of artificial intelligence and data sciences. Annals ofData Science, 10(4), 1007- 1018.

[14] Deng, W., Zhang, X., Zhou, Y., Liu, Y., Zhou, X., Chen, H., & Zhao, H. (2022). An enhanced fast non-dominated solution sorting genetic algorithm for multi-objective problems. Information Sciences, 585, 441-453.

[15] Muneer, S. M., Alvi, M. B., & Rasool, M. A. (2022). Genetic algorithm based intelligent system for estate value estimation. International Journal of Computational and Innovative Sciences, 1(1), 28-38.

[16] Ji, Y., Liu, S., Zhou, M., Zhao, Z., Guo, X., & Qi, L. (2022). A machine learning and genetic algorithm-based method for predicting width deviation of hot-rolled strip in steel production systems. Information Sciences, 589, 360-375.

[17] Xia, X., Qiu, H., Xu, X., & Zhang, Y. (2022). Multi-objective workflow scheduling based on genetic algorithm in cloud environment. Information Sciences, 606, 38-59.

[18]Abdollahi, J., & Nouri-Moghaddam,B. (2022). Hybrid stacked ensemble combined with genetic algorithms for diabetes prediction. Iran Journal of Computer Science, 5(3), 205-220.

[19] Zhou, J., Huang, S., Zhou, T., Armaghani, D. J., & Qiu, Y. (2022). Employing a genetic algorithm and grey wolf optimizer for optimizing RF models to evaluate soil liquefaction potential. Artificial Intelligence Review, 55(7), 5673-5705.

[20] Shehadeh, A., Alshboul, O., Tatari, O., Alzubaidi, M. A., & Salama, A. H. E. S. (2022). Selection of heavy machinery for earthwork activities: A multi-objective optimization approach using a genetic algorithm. Alexandria Engineering Journal, 61(10), 7555-7569.

Design Studies and Intelligence Engineering
L.C. Jain et al. (Eds.)
© *2024 The Authors.*
This article is published online with Open Access by IOS Press and distributed under the terms
of the Creative Commons Attribution Non-Commercial License 4.0 (CC BY-NC 4.0).
doi:10.3233/FAIA231450

Product Design Process Based on GANs Model

Yuping Hu[a] and Danfeng CHEN [b, 1]
aAcademy of art and design, Shaoyang University,
bSchool of Jewelry and Art Design, Wuzhou University

Abstract: In order to solve the difficulties and shortcomings when users use images to describe their requirements, a product design process based on GANs model is proposed. Build a generation countermeasure network and train an intelligent image generation model, so that the computer can quickly generate design cases, and can artificially control the generation results to realize the establishment of case base and the adjustment of image content. In addition, an image artistic style similarity measurement model is proposed to calculate the style differences between images. The results show that the measurement results of this method are consistent with the subjective evaluation of designers. The statistical results of 30 groups of data show that the probability that this method is consistent with the designer's evaluation results is 90%. So far, in the above performance evaluation experiments, the similarity measurement results of the same/different style works are obviously different, which conforms to the rules of style similarity. In the task of ranking style similarity, this model is 90% consistent with the ranking results of designers. Conclusion: The model is effective in performance evaluation experiments, which lays a foundation for developing style-based design case retrieval and recommendation.

Keywords: demand description; Design images; Generating a countermeasure network; product design

1 Introduction

The possibility of artificial intelligence simulating human thinking process includes not only passive tasks (target recognition), reactive tasks (automatic driving), but also creative tasks (writing music, image generation, etc.). An important method for artificial intelligence to achieve creative tasks is realized by the DeepNeural Network (DNN) in Artificial Neural Network (ANN). Generative Adversarial Networks (GANs) is a deep neural network model. GANs includes two models: Generative Model (G for short), which takes random noise as input and tries to generate sample data; Discriminative Model (D for short) takes real data or generated data as input and tries to predict whether the current input is real data or generated data [1]. Both the generating model and the discriminant model try their best to optimize their networks until they reach a dynamic equilibrium, that is, Nash equilibrium, which forces the generated data to be almost indistinguishable from the real data statistically, thus

---

[1] Corresponding Author.

generating data that cannot be distinguished from the real data. There are more than 500 varieties of GANs, which are widely used, including image generation, audio generation, image conversion, image synthesis, image generation through words, image restoration and so on [2]. Using GANs for product design means that GANs can learn good intermediate features from the known large- scale unmarked images or videos of a product and create images that can express the characteristics and forms of the product in the computer vision environment to generate new product design. Among them, Deep Convolution Generative Adversarial Networks (hereinafter referred to as DCGANs) is an important variant of GANs, and DCGANS is more controllable and stable in machine training than GANS [3]. The generation model and discriminant model of DCGANs can learn rich hierarchical expressions in both the object individual and the scene and can realize the generation of images that meet the characteristics of product design.

2 Literature review

In actual training, GAN will have some problems such as unstable training, disappearing gradient and insufficient diversity of generated samples. Therefore, later studies put forward improvement measures around these problems in theory. In generating countermeasure network, it is necessary to choose appropriate indicators to measure the distance between the generated distribution and the real distribution. The conventional GAN uses JS divergence. In order to make it more general, Schleich, B. et al. proposed to use a general F divergence to measure the distance between them, where F is a user-defined convex function, and different F can derive different divergence expressions, which can be said to be the unification of a series of loss functions used to generate countermeasures [4]. Yan, K. and others put forward Wasserstein distance to generate a confrontation network (WGAN). Firstly, the reasons for the gradient disappearance of GAN were analyzed theoretically, and then the difference between the generated distribution and the real distribution was calculated by using Wasserstein distance instead of the original JS divergence, which basically solved the problem of the gradient disappearance of GAN in theory. In addition, WGAN also theoretically analyzes the reasons why the samples generated by GAN are concentrated in a few categories and carries out experiments to show the superiority of WGAN in this respect [5]. In order to alleviate the problem of mode collapse of GAN, Pan, T. and others put forward a new design: UnrolledGAN, which believes that the reason of mode collapse of GAN is that the generator only considers the optimal solution of the current state when updating parameters. In this regard, the UnrolledGAN generator not only considers the current state of the generator, but also takes the current state as the starting point and the state of the discriminator after many updates! Combining these two kinds of information to make the optimal solution, so as to avoid short-sighted behavior [6]. Li, W. et al. introduced a new generative countermeasure network: Energy-BasedGAN(EBGAN), which regarded the discriminator as an energy function, so as to use a wider loss function for training. Samples near the real distribution area will be given low energy, and those far away from the real distribution area will be given high energy. The goal of the generator is to make the generated samples tend to the lowest energy as much as possible. The author gives an experimental case. Let the discriminator use an automatic encoder structure, which outputs the difference between the reconstructed data encoded and decoded in the discriminator and the original input data instead of the classifier. At this time, the model training is more stable than GAN [7]. Liu, Q. et al. put forward information generation countermeasure network

(InfoGAN) on the basis of CGAN. The input of its generator is divided into two parts, one is random noise, and the other is implicit coding corresponding to different characteristics of generated data, which makes the implicit coding interpretable for generated data. InfoGAN expands the information theory of GAN, and its goal is to maximize the information between implicit coding and generation distribution [8].

This paper mainly focuses on the adjustment of case layout and style, and the technical realization of design case retrieval function based on style similarity. According to the technical research of GAN, case base and case adjustment can be realized by training the image generation model and intervening in the image generation process. The key to achieve style-based recommendation or retrieval is to find an effective measurement method of style similarity. Therefore, the content of this paper includes the construction and training of image intelligent generation model, and the establishment and evaluation of image style similarity measurement model.

3 Research methods

Generating countermeasure network is the most favorable method to deal with the problem of image generation at present. It can learn its feature distribution from excellent design cases, and then generate results similar to the input samples. In this paper, the composition, principle, development and application of GAN are described in detail, and the quality of images generated by GAN is guaranteed [9,10], and the degree of customization of image generation content is continuously improved. According to the functions put forward in the third chapter of this paper, this section will realize the establishment of interior design case base based on GAN training image intelligent generation model and meet the adjustment and customization of design case function layout and decoration style. The technical realization route is shown in Figure 1:

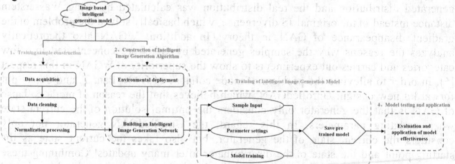

Fig. 1 Roadmap of Intelligent Generation Technology for Basic Images

Firstly, training samples are constructed to provide a good database for machine learning. Secondly, building a reasonable generation countermeasure network model is the core to realize image generation and adjust the generation results [11]. Then configure the training environment, set the training parameters and train the model. Finally, the pre-training model is saved, and the generated results of the model are tested and evaluated.

3.1 Training sample construction

With the rapid development of information technology and database technology, people can obtain and share a large amount of data from the network very conveniently and cheaply, and the scale of data sets used for machine learning is growing exponentially.

As the basis of machine learning, the correct processing and cleaning of training data is particularly important. It is a big challenge to process huge data with different attributes into training samples for machine learning. A high-quality training data set should have the following characteristics: a. With the increase of image complexity, only when the data of training set reaches a corresponding number can it achieve better generation results [12]. B. The training samples should be as rich as possible, so as to avoid the generated design scheme being extremely similar and lacking in diversity. C. The accuracy of training samples is an important factor affecting the accuracy of generated data! Low-precision samples should be presented as far as possible. D interference factors in training data should be reduced as much as possible, and the less interference factors, the better the generation effect.

(1) sample acquisition

Because there are many types of interior design cases according to space, and the contents of each space are quite different, in order to reduce the difficulty of model training, atypical interior space-bedroom design case is selected as the training model. At the sametime, in order to ensure the quantity and quality of input samples, a total of 63,055 bedroom design prints and real shots were saved from domestic and foreign design websites Petals, E-Net, Developer Design Bar and Pinterest, which ensured the unity of the quantity, quality and types of samples [13].

(2) sample cleaning

According to the characteristics of an excellent data set, the ideal training data set should have a reasonable shooting range and angle and contain indoor information as completely as possible. However, because the pictures are stored in batches, they contain many interference factors and the quality is uneven. Excluding the data with non-bedroom scenes, small shooting range and resolution lower than 512*512px, 5671 effective training samples were finally retained.

3) sample processing

Because the original data obtained are quite different in size, format and naming, it is not conducive to batch reading and operation by machines. Therefore, using the image processing libraries Opencv2, OS and Pillow of Pvthon, all the pictures are converted into the. pg format of three color channels and renamed uniformly from the number 0001. Then, the short side of the image is taken as the target size, and the image is cut into a square in the center. Finally, based on local pixel resampling, the image size is processed to 256*256px.

3.2 Generation of countermeasures network construction

(1) Model building environment

The programming of this model is based on Python language and TensorFlow, a deep learning framework. TensorFlow is an open source software library developed and maintained by GoogleBrain, a Google artificial intelligence team. It supports a variety of programming languages, and contains various tools, libraries and resources needed for programming, so that developers can build and deploy machine learning applications conveniently and efficiently [14]. Tensorflow can well support multi-threading, queuing and asynchronous operations, and can reasonably allocate computing tasks to different devices, thus improving the speed and efficiency of training. This model uses deep neural network, and because the task target is complex, the training process needs to consume huge computational power. Therefore, this paper chooses local computer for programming and testing, and uses supercomputer for model training. The main parameters of the local computer are as follows: GPU is NVIDIA RTX2080 8GB memory, CPU is Inteli7-7700, memory is 16GB, and hard disk is 1162GB. The main parameters of the supercomputer are as follows: 4 NVIDIA RIX 2080 Ti GPUs with 32 G video memory.

(2) Conditional Generation Model I -StyleGAN

Many varieties and applications of GAN. Among them, the progressive training method of PGGAN solves the problem of generating high-resolution images. StyleGAN is a new conditional generation model proposed by NVIDIA on the basis of PGGAN. The decoupling of image features is realized by adding a feature Mapping Network to the input part of the generator. The mapping network consists of eight fully connected layers, and its goal is to encode the input vector into an intermediate vector w, and then input it into the generator for training, so as to obtain the feature control vectors of different resolution levels of the image [15]. The lower the resolution level, the rougher the image features it controls, and the finer the image features it affects. For example, when training the face generation model, the low-level control vectors affect the rough features such as posture, hairstyle and facial contour, while the high- level control vectors affect the microscopic features such as the colors of eyes, hair and skin. Because the training cost increases with the improvement of the resolution of the generated image, in order to control the training cost, this paper sets the target generation size as 256*256px, that is, the generator only selects the seven resolution levels of StyleGAN for training. The training process of each resolution level takes 8*8 resolution as an example. The main network of the generator consists of an up-sampling layer, two AdaIN modules and a convolution layer. The function of the upsampling layer is to upsample the network output (4*4 images) of the previous layer to 8*8 resolution, and use it as the input of the network of this layer to speedup the training of the model. The up-sampled image, feature vector and noise are input into the pattern module AdaIN, which can be simplified as weighted summation of the feature vector and the up-sampled image input, thus realizing the control of the image generation style. The introduction of noise is to add some random changes to the image and enrich the image generation results [16]. After one convolution and one AdaIN, the image with 8*8 resolution is output.

Subsequently, the image generated by the generator and the 8*8 image downsampled by the real sample are input into the discriminator at the 8*8 resolution level to calculate the loss. Repeatedly repeating the above process, the optimization goal of the generator is to update the network parameters so that the loss value is as small as possible. The optimization goal of the discriminator is to update the network parameters, so that the smaller the loss value of the real sample, the better, and the greater the loss of the generated sample. After the current resolution level training is completed, the network output is passed to the next resolution level for training until the 256*256 resolution level training is completed.

(3) Sample input and training parameter setting

The image samples are respectively down-sampled to 256*256, 128 * 128 * 4 * 4 resolutions and stored in the. tfrecords data format dedicated to TensorFlow, which is convenient for data reading. Adam optimizer is selected as the optimization method of head training, and the whole network is set to be trained iteratively for 11,726,000 times, which is measured by the number of real images input into the network for training [17]. Because two feature vectors are added to each resolution level for style control, 14 feature control vectors are generated in this model.

3.3 Model training and effect demonstration

The model training takes 4 days, 15 hours, 11 minutes and 37 seconds. During the training process, Tensorboard, a visual tool library that comes with TensorFlow, is used to check the training effect of the model. Save the pre-trained model for model testing and observe the effect of sample generation, as shown below.

(1) Model training results

With the increase of iteration times, the effect of the image generated by the generator is continuously improved, and the performance of the discriminator to distinguish the generated image from the real image is also continuously improved [18]. In Figure 2, the horizontal axis represents the training process, and the vertical axis represents the score Loss/scores/real, which is the score curve of the real sample, and Loss/scores/fake shows the score curve of the generated sample. With the training, the score of the real image is higher and higher, while the score of the generated image is lower and lower, which shows that the ability of the discriminator to distinguish the real sample and generate the sample is constantly improved, and the training result is good. For the generator, although the target loss value can measure the performance of the generator to a certain extent, it does not explain whether the quality and diversity of image generation are enough. In this paper, FID (Frechet InceptionDistance) is selected as an index to measure the performance of the generator. Image features are extracted by depth neural network, and then the distance of feature distribution between real samples and generated samples is calculated by using mean and covariance matrix. The smaller the FID, the closer the feature distribution of the generated sample is to the real sample, that is, the better the diversity of the generated sample, and the higher the quality [19]. It is observed from Figure 2 that with the training, FID is gradually reduced and finally maintained at a low stable value, which shows that the model training is stable without violent shock and the effect is good.

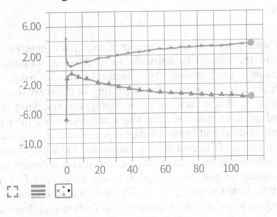

Matches (2)

★ Loss/scores/real (.)

▲ Loss/scores/fake (.)

Fig. 2 Model training effect

(2) Image generation effect

According to the function analysis of the system, the design assistant system should have the function of design case base and case customization. The model can generate a large number of design cases quickly with an image generation efficiency of 7.2s/100 sheets, dynamically update the case base, and provide users with many choices. It is almost difficult to distinguish the generated sample from the real sample under thumbnail preview, and the generated model fits the distribution of the real sample well. The enlarged detail map of the generated sample shows the wall, floor, ceiling, color, fabric and decorations completely, but it is only vague in the local decorative details such as edge lines, fabric folds, carpet patterns, decorative painting patterns and lighting, which can better express the spatial layout and decorative information on the whole.Image generation control According to the network model built above, 14 control variables were generated in the training process of the generator. Low-dimensional control variables mainly affect coarse-grained image features such as spatial layout, window style, wardrobe or not, while high-dimensional control variables mainly affect fine-grained image features such as lamp style, background wall pattern, color, and texture. According to the needs of interior design and decoration customers to adjust the functional layout and decoration style of design cases, only three adjustment options are provided for users in actual product development: coarse-grained functional layout adjustment, medium-grained pattern style adjustment and fine-grained color texture adjustment. Among them, the coarse-grained adjustment changes the control variables of the [0.4] layer for the same bedroom design picture, and the overall functional layout has changed differently.

The control variable of the [4.8] layer is selected for the medium granularity adjustment, which mainly affects the characteristics of the background wall, lighting, bed, and window style of the design case. Finally, the [8.14] layer control variable is used to adjust the details of image generation, which mainly affects the details of image such as color and texture.

4 Result analysis

The core idea of style similarity measurement is to extract the style features of images, and then calculate the similarity between features as a standard to measure style similarity. Commonly used image style features include color, texture, light and shadow, brush strokes, lines, layout, etc. According to different features, corresponding distance calculation methods such as color histogram matching and image gradient calculation are adopted. In painting, the characteristics other than the picture content such as color, line, texture and brush strokes represent the style of this image, which is also called painting style. Different from painting art, the style of interior design works is not obviously influenced by a single factor, and it is a complex modeling process to establish a relationship between its design style and some specific representations [20]. Based on the style transfer based on GAN, this paper proposes a style similarity measurement method based on multi-dimensional feature distribution. When extracting image features, the influence of different dimensions of features (such as low-dimensional color, texture, lines and high-dimensional local details, curve shapes, etc.) on the image style is comprehensively considered, and the distribution of these features is used to reflect the style, rather than the extracted features themselves. For example, European style and French style all have complicated curve decoration and pattern hook edge. However, the carved decoration in French style is mostly used for colonnades and bent legs, while the crochet in European style is mostly found in the hook edge of gypsum line.

4.1 Image Multi-dimensional Feature Extraction Based on CNN
Based on the principle of image feature extraction by convolutional neural network (CNN), different feature information is extracted by setting different convolution kernels to do inner product with each pixel of the image. The higher the number of convolution kernels and convolution layers, the more and more complex the feature

information can be extracted. Low-level convolution outputs low-dimensional features such as colors and boundaries, while high-level convolution outputs high-dimensional features such as shapes and details.

4.2 Image Style Representation Based on Gram Matrix

According to the definition of Gram matrix, the diagonal elements in the matrix represent the vectors themselves, while the other elements in the matrix represent the relationships between the vectors. In the task of style transfer, image features are taken as image content, and the gleim matrix of these feature vectors is used to represent the image style, thus realizing the separation and reorganization of image content and style. The Gram matrix of features can represent the distribution of features, for example, the feature circle usually appears at the same time as the feature red, and there is usually no curve where the right angle appears, and this feature correlation is regarded as the style in the sense [21]. In this paper, the idea is used for reference, and the style similarity of two pictures is equal to the similarity of their feature distribution. The closer the image feature distribution is, the more similar the style is.

4.3 Style similarity measurement model design

The evaluation of design style similarity is subjective and depends on the designer's cognition of the degree, so it is difficult to describe it with unified standards (such as high similarity, medium similarity, low similarity or 70% similarity, etc.). In order to facilitate the comparison of styles by machines, the model proposed in this study can be realized. Multi-dimensional feature extraction can be carried out for any two input pictures, and the difference of feature distribution in different dimensions can be calculated, and finally the difference of styles can be output.

The specific parameters of the model are set as follows:

(1) According to the characteristics that the higher the convolution level, the more complex the extracted image features are, and the features extracted from the high convolution level tend to the image content. Therefore, in this study, only the first five convolution layers of VGG19 are selected to output the feature map.

(2) Calculate the distribution relation of image features to describe the image style. Gleim matrix operation is performed on the image features extracted from each convolution layer, and five matrices describing the distribution of image features are output.

(3) Calculate the mean square error (MSE) of the feature distribution on the five convolution layers of the two images, and then sum the five differences as the style difference of the images. The greater the MSE value, the lower the similarity of styles between the two pictures. On the contrary, the closer the styles are.

4.4 Model performance verification

Because the similarity of styles is relative, it is generally believed that the similarity between works of the same style is greater than that of different styles, and the similarity between works can be compared. In order to verify the effectiveness of this model in the similarity evaluation of interior design styles, 20 graduate students majoring in design were selected to classify and rank the interior design styles, and whether the model output of this study is consistent with the subjective evaluation of designers was compared. The selection of experimental images follows the following principles: 1) The contents of images are consistent, and all of them choose bedroom design images; 2) Standardize the image with the same size, clarity and proportion.

(1) consistency experiment of subjective and objective evaluation of different/similar style differences. Seven design websites at home and abroad were investigated, and

eight styles, American, Chinese, European, industrial, Japanese, Mediterranean, modern and Southeast Asia, appeared in the classification of interior design styles at the sametime [22]. Taking these eight styles as the goal, the experiment retrieved 127 pictures of bedroom design, and the designers reclassified the pictures respectively, and finally only retained the results of more than half of the designers' classification as the classification results. Because designers have achieved high consistency in the classification of Chinese style, European style and Mediterranean style, nine images are selected from each of these three styles to objectively measure the similarity of styles. See Table 1 for the statistics of experimental data.

Table 1 Designers' Image Style Classification Results

	Amer ian	Chine se- style	europ eanis m	Indust rial wind	Japa nese	The Mediterran e an Sea	mode rn times	Southe ast Asia	Oth err
Search results	12	28	24	15	9	12	14	13	0
Classificati on result	5	18	14	6	6	9	4	6	54
experime nt al data	0	9	9	0	0	9	0	0	0

Using this model to calculate the style gap between similar works, it is counted aspa__ lable$_1$__lable$_2$ The style gap between heterogeneous works is recorded asCr__lable$_1$__ lable$_2$, lableIs the style to which the data belongs. The box diagram of data is established by SPSS, and the style differences of different/similar works are analyzed. As shown in Figure 3, the light-colored block represents the similarity gap between the two design style groups, and its corresponding dark-colored block describes the similarity gap between the two design style groups. The results show that the style differences between groups are scattered, and the median and upper and lower quartiles are higher than those within groups.

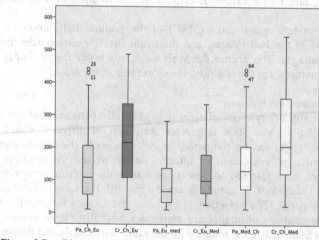

Figure 3 Box Diagram of Style Difference of Works with Different/Similar Styles

The data range, average, standard deviation and variance are selected as the benchmarks for evaluating the performance of the method. As shown in Table 2, in the objective evaluation of the similarity of different/similar styles among the six groups, the range, average, standard deviation and variance of style differences among the groups are higher than those within the group. All the above results show that the style difference between different works calculated by this algorithm is obvious, and it is higher than similar works, which conforms to the objective law of style similarity.

Table 2 Distribution of Style Difference of Different/Similar Design Works

data type	Number of cases	range	average value	standard deviation	variance
Pa _ Ch _ Eu	72	430.4224	139.542357	109.419877	11972.709
Cr _ Ch _ Eu	72	478.026	222.159053	131.1405312	17197.838
Pa _ Eu _ Med	72	218.4538	89.9334164	62.5112324	3907.654
Cr _ Eu _ Med	72	300.4666	133.138343	83.1728165	6917.717
Pa _ Ch _ Med	72	428.4227	154.346048	102.0648985	10417.245
Cr _ Ch _ Med	72	521.7923	243.339199	143.1871511	20502.56

(2) Consistency experiment of subjective and objective evaluation of style similarity ranking. According to the designer's classification results, three different pictures from the same style were selected and divided into one group, with a total of 30 groups. Choose one picture in each group as the target, marked as So. In the form of electronic questionnaire, please ask the designer to compare the other two pictures with So Style similarity, in which a more similar image is marked asS i, and the other is marked asDi. Taking the ranking results of most designers as the final ranking results, that is, thinking that Sia nd SoThe style difference between them should be less than Di and So. According to the ranking results of designers, the method of this paper is used to analyze 30 groups of cases respectively Si, Di and So. The similarity between them is calculated.

5. Conclusions

In this paper, the image intelligent generation model is built and trained based on Style GAN. The loss curve of the discriminator and the FID index of the generator show that the training effect of the generator and the discriminator is good. The generated image has a high similarity with the input training samples, and the image generation effect can display the image information completely, which lays the foundation for establishing the   design case base based on this model in the following. At the same time, the function layout of coarse-grained   image, the local style of medium-grained image and the style details of fine-grained image are adjusted and controlled, which satisfies the customization of design cases by users. Secondly, the image style is described by the multi-dimensional feature distribution of the image, and a measurement model of image style similarity is established, and an experiment of subjective and objective evaluation consistency is designed to verify the effectiveness of the model in the calculation of style similarity, which provides a basis for the subsequent   recommendation of interior design reference drawings based on style similarity based on the model.

References

[1] Zhou, X., Hu, Y., Wu, J., Liang, W., Ma, J., & Jin, Q. (2022). Distribution bias aware collaborative generative adversarial network for imbalanced deep learning in industrial IoT. IEEE Transactions on Industrial Informatics, 19(1), 570-580.

[2] Yuan, L., Yu, S., Yang, Z., Duan, M., & Li, K. (2023). A data balancing approach based on generative adversarial network. Future Generation Computer Systems, 141, 768-776.

[3] Zhang, Y., Wang, Y., Jiang, Z., Liao, F., Zheng, L., Tan, D., ... & Lu, J. (2022). Diversifying tire-defect image generation based on generative adversarial network. IEEE Transactions on Instrumentation and Measurement, 71, 1-12.

[4] Schleich, B., Qie, Y., Wartzack, S., & Anwer, N. (2022). Generative adversarial networks for tolerance analysis. CIRP Annals, 71(1), 133- 136.

[5] Yan, K., Chen, X., Zhou, X., Yan, Z., & Ma, J. (2022). Physical model informed fault detection and diagnosis of air handling units based on transformer generative adversarial network. IEEE Transactions on Industrial Informatics, 19(2), 2192-2199.

[6] Pan, T., Chen, J., Zhang, T., Liu, S., He, S., & Lv, H. (2022). Generative adversarial network in mechanical fault diagnosis under small sample: A systematic review on applications and future perspectives. ISA transactions, 128, 1-10.

[7] Li, W., Chen, J., Cao, J., Ma, C., Wang, J., Cui, X., & Chen, P. (2022). EID-GAN: Generative adversarial nets for extremely imbalanced data augmentation. IEEE Transactions on Industrial Informatics, 19(3), 3208-3218.

[8] Liu, Q., Meng, X., Shao, F., & Li, S. (2022). PSTAF-GAN: Progressive spatio-temporal attention fusion method based on generative adversarial network. IEEE Transactions on Geoscience and Remote Sensing, 60, 1- 13.

[9] Yang, Y., You, Q., Jin, Z., Zuo, Z., & Zhang, Y. (2022). Construction of surface air temperature over the Tibetan Plateau based on generative adversarial networks. International Journal of Climatology, 42(16), 10107-10125

[10] Feldkamp, N., Bergmann, S., Conrad, F., & Strassburger, S. (2022). A Method Using Generative Adversarial Networks for Robustness Optimization. ACM Transactions on Modeling and Computer Simulation (TOMACS), 32(2), 1-22.

[11] Zhu, L., Baolin, D., Xiaomeng, Z., Shaoliang, F., Zhen, C., Junjie, Z., & Shumin, C. (2022). Surface defect detection method based on improved semisupervised multitask generative adversarial network. Scientific Programming, 2022, 1- 17.

[12] Tang, L., Deng, Y., Ma, Y., Huang, J., & Ma, J. (2022). SuperFusion: A versatile image registration and fusion network with semantic awareness. IEEE/CAA Journal ofAutomatica Sinica, 9(12), 2121-2137.

[13] Kammoun, A., Slama, R., Tabia, H., Ouni, T., & Abid, M. (2022). Generative Adversarial Networks for face generation: A survey. ACM Computing Surveys, 55(5), 1-37.

[14] Huang, J., Cui, K., Guan, D., Xiao, A., Zhan, F., Lu, S., ... & Xing, E. (2022). Masked generative adversarial networks are data-efficient generation learners. Advances in Neural Information Processing Systems, 35, 2154-2167.

[15] Zhou, H., Hou, J., Zhang, Y., Ma, J., & Ling, H. (2022). Unified gradient-and intensity-discriminator generative adversarial network for image fusion. Information Fusion, 88, 184-201.

[16] AlAmir, M., & AlGhamdi, M. (2022). The Role of generative adversarial network in medical image analysis: An in-depth survey. ACM Computing Surveys, 55(5), 1-36.

[17] You, A., Kim, J. K., Ryu, I. H., & Yoo, T. K. (2022). Application of generative adversarial networks (GAN) for ophthalmology image domains: a survey. Eye and Vision, 9(1), 1- 19.

[18] Brophy, E., Wang, Z., She, Q., & Ward, T. (2023). Generative adversarial networks in time series: A systematic literature review. ACM Computing Surveys, 55(10), 1-31.

[19] Sajeeda, A., & Hossain, B. M. (2022). Exploring generative adversarial networks and adversarial training. International Journal of Cognitive Computing in Engineering, 3, 78-89.

[20] Zhang, Z., Liu, Y., Han, C., Guo, T., Yao, T., & Mei, T. (2022). Generalized One-shot Domain Adaptation of Generative Adversarial Networks. Advances in Neural Information Processing Systems, 35, 13718- 13730.

[21] Güemes, A., Sanmiguel Vila, C., & Discetti, S. (2022). Super-resolution generative adversarial networks of randomly-seeded fields. Nature Machine Intelligence, 4(12), 1165- 1173.

[22] Lu, X., Liao, W., Zhang, Y., & Huang, Y. (2022). Intelligent structural design of shear wall residence using physics -enhanced generative adversarial networks. Earthquake Engineering & Structural Dynamics, 51(7), 1657-1676.

Design Studies and Intelligence Engineering
L.C. Jain et al. (Eds.)
© 2024 The Authors.
This article is published online with Open Access by IOS Press and distributed under the terms
of the Creative Commons Attribution Non-Commercial License 4.0 (CC BY-NC 4.0).
doi:10.3233/FAIA231451

333

Explainable Artificial Intelligence (XAI) for Air Quality Assessment

Sayan CHAKRABORTY[1], Bitan MISRA[2], Nilanjan DEY[3]

[1,2,3]*Department of Computer Science and Engineering*
Techno International New Town, West Bengal, India

Abstract- Accurate air quality analysis is essential for comprehending the reasons for and consequences of air pollution, which is a serious environmental concern. Understanding the underlying causes contributing to pollution levels is challenging when using traditional methodologies for air quality analysis since they frequently lack transparency and interpretability. This work examines the integration of XAI with deep learning to enhance air quality prediction. Explainable AI provides a solution by illuminating the ways in which AI models make decisions. It emphasizes the requirement for clear and understandable AI models to win stakeholders' trust and adoption. Utilizing explainable AI makes it feasible to improve the readability and transparency of air quality studies, allowing stakeholders to comprehend and verify the predictions and suggestions made by AI systems. Rough woodland. To classify the data, XGBoost and KNN are used. SHAP and LIME are then applied to discover the major characteristics and variables that affect air quality predictions. These findings can help to improve decision-making and the creation of efficient plans for the management and mitigation of air quality.

Keywords: Explainable artificial intelligence (XAI), Artificial intelligence (AI), Air quality analysis, SHAP, LIME

1. Introduction

The practice of predicting the amount of air pollution in a certain place or region at a specific future time is known as air quality prediction. It entails analyzing and interpreting data pertaining to air pollutants, meteorological conditions, pollutant emission sources, and other pertinent elements using various models and approaches. The process of predicting air quality often entails gathering historical or real-time information on pollutant concentrations, weather factors (such as temperature, humidity, wind speed, and direction), emissions inventories, and other pertinent variables. To predict future air quality levels, these data are then examined using mathematical models and statistical techniques [1-3]. The evaluation and administration of the effects of air pollution on public health, the ecosystem, and different industries, such as agriculture, transportation, and manufacturing, depend heavily on-air quality forecasts. Authorities and politicians can protect the public's health by making decisions based on accurate air quality predictions, putting suitable mitigation measures in place, and issuing alerts or warnings. Depending on the requirements and capabilities of the system, air quality prediction systems can offer short-term forecasts (a few hours to a few days ahead) or longer-term projections (weeks to months ahead). To illustrate these projections to the public and convey the degree of air pollution and related health hazards, color-coded maps or air quality indices can be used. It is crucial to remember that the geography, local infrastructure, and specific activities taking place can all affect the causes and severity of air pollution [2, 3].

Depending on the situation and the specific classification scheme being employed, the major air contaminants can change. However, several contaminants are widely acknowledged as being significant air pollution culprits. These "criteria air pollutants" have been determined to be threatening for both public health and the ecosystem. Particulate matter (PM) is used to describe the suspension of liquid droplets and solid particles in air. There are two size fractions that can be distinguished: PM 10 (particles with diameters of 10 micrometers or less) and PM 2.5 (particles with diameters of 2.5 micrometers or less). PM can come from a number of sources, including combustion, industrial emissions, automobile exhaust, and environmental dust and pollen. Sulfur-containing fossil fuels in particular release sulfur dioxide as a gas when they are burned. In the presence of sunshine, nitrogen oxides (NOx) and volatile organic compounds (VOCs) mix to form ground-level ozone. Vehicle emissions, industrial activities, and chemical reactions involving VOCs are the main sources. Specifically, in cars and power plants, the burning of fossil fuels produces nitrogen dioxide [2-4]. The negative health impacts of exposure to air pollution can be both temporary and permanent. Vulnerable groups that are particularly at risk include children, elderly individuals, and persons with preexisting respiratory or cardiovascular problems.

This research analyses the most significant pollutant utilizing explainable artificial intelligence (XAI) [5, 6] to overcome the aforementioned issues. To combat the black-box aspect of artificial intelligence (AI) models, XAI strategies attempt to offer insights into the decision-making process and the underlying variables that affect predictions. These discoveries can be used to create prediction models that are more precise, to pinpoint the variables that have the greatest influence on air quality and to guide the processes used to decide on air pollution reduction tactics. It is possible to obtain deep learning architectures with improved credibility and accuracy for predicting air quality. As a result, its practical use is improved. This paper's contributions can be summarized as follows.

1. To predict air quality, the random forest, XGBoost, and K-nearest neighbor (KNN) models are employed.

2. Using the SHapley Additive exPlanations (SHAP) and local interpretable model-agnostic explanations (LIME) techniques, the impact of air pollutant parameters on air quality prediction is highlighted, which helps to increase the precision of air quality prediction.

The article's remaining sections are structured as follows. In Section 2, a discussion of the relevant literature is offered. Section 3 provides a description of the dataset and methodology applied in this study. In Section 4, the outcome of the air quality prediction is analyzed, and the SHAP and LIME techniques are used to assess the explainability of the deep learning architectures. Section 5 contains the article's conclusion.

2. Literature review

To improve the understanding of AI models employed for air quality analysis, researchers have investigated various machine learning interpretation techniques. To identify the variables affecting air quality predictions, methodologies such as feature significance analysis, rule-based designs, and local explanatory techniques are being used. Deep learning approaches are employed for a variety of big data forecasting issues. Long short-term memory (LSTM) networks are used in a deep learning model for predicting future air quality values in smart cities [4]. To calculate the air quality index, a thorough examination [7] of the effectiveness of various machine learning models, including linear regression, decision tree, random forest, artificial neural network, and support vector machine models, is conducted. Article [8] discusses a thorough examination of studies that have been done on air pollution forecasting using machine learning algorithms that use sensor data. One can draw the conclusion from this study [8] that the authors currently use complex and advanced methodologies rather than straightforward machine learning methods. In addition, the primary prediction goal was PM 2.5, and China accounted for the majority of the case studies. In the Jing-Jin-Ji region, which has the worst air pollution in China, a neural network with a temporal sliding long short-term memory extended model [9] is used to forecast the following 24 hours' average PM2.5 concentration. A multidisciplinary approach is used in the research on explainable AI for accurate air quality analysis, combining knowledge from areas including air quality research, machine learning, and meteorology [10]. Article [11] presents a visual analytics method to assist specialists in validating and confirming the learning of the ML model with their domain knowledge. The system consists of numerous coordinated views that may be used to display the impact of input characteristics at different degrees of aggregation in both the temporal and geographic dimensions. Additionally, it presents an analysis of the efficacy of ML and traditional architectures in terms of accuracy and geographic map effectiveness, as well as an animation of the raw wind trajectory data for the input time. User engagement can help with exploration, while data visualizations can offer overviews of various parts of the data [12]. Article [12] presents a visual analytics platform for building unique interactive visual analytics dashboards with clearly defined components that are connected to one another. In article [13], scientists provide a new architecture that incorporates a highly stacked 1-dimensional CNN with a residual connection and attention mechanism that provides state-of-the-art results in PM 2.5 and PM 10 prediction through extensive tests using Seoul air pollution data and public benchmarks. From the literature review, it is identified that different air pollutants have different amounts of effect in different areas. Hence, it is important to identify the pollutant that contributes the most to air pollution in that area so that necessary steps can be taken. Our study aims to bridge this gap by applying explainable AI to identify the pollutant that has the highest contribution in determining air quality.

3. Proposed Method

The current framework analyzed the dataset and performed preprocessing to clean the data, as there were many null and redundant data. Following preprocessing, the data are further analyzed using three popular supervised learning models: random forest, KNN and XGBoost. The key reason behind choosing these models is their distinct advantages. High prediction accuracy and scalability are provided by XGBoost, nonlinear decision boundaries are a strength of KNN's classification jobs, and high-dimensional data are successfully handled by random forest's robustness against overfitting. The dataset is split into an 80-10-10 ratio in training-testing-validation data. Then, each of the machine learning architectures is applied to the data.

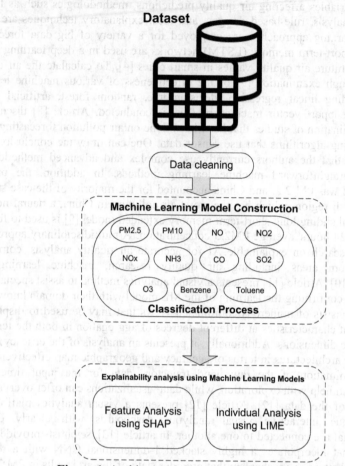

Figure 1. Architectural diagram of the proposed method

The proposed approach's block diagram, as detailed in the section, is shown in Figure 1. Two popular methods for analyzing machine learning architectures are LIME and SHAP, as depicted in the diagram. They are used with machine learning models to offer an understanding of the predictions made by the model and the significance of various characteristics. Tools for model interpretation and explainability include LIME and SHAP. They can assist in debugging models, gaining confidence in forecasts, understanding how machine learning models make decisions, and spotting bias or unfairness in predictions. These techniques are frequently applied in a variety of fields, such as healthcare, finance, and natural language processing, where the capacity to comprehend data is essential for making decisions and adhering to regulations. Machine learning models are given interpretability and explainability using LIME and SHAP. They aid in understanding the reasons behind the predictions made by models as well as the features that influence those forecasts the most. Stakeholders may enhance the transparency and accountability of machine learning models by employing these strategies to acquire insights into how they make decisions.

4. Results and Discussion

In this work, machine learning frameworks such as random forest, KNN and XGBoost were applied using the Python environment in the Windows 10 operating system. The work was tested on an Intel i3 8th generation-based computer system. The dataset (https://www.kaggle.com/datasets/rohanrao/air-quality-data-in-india?resource=download) contains data on the AQI (air quality index) at hourly and daily rates from a large number of sites dispersed throughout various Indian cities. For the current framework, data from 2015 to 2020 were examined. The metric used to assess classification accuracy is accuracy. Accuracy is typically a key component of accurate forecasting. The aspect of successful forecasts that characterizes good predictions is precision. The portion of the total number of already retrieved real-world samples is called recall. The F1 score is a suitable metric for profiting from the occasion. For viewing the F1 score, an analogy between precision and recall is discovered, although there is still a jagged class propagation. The obtained results of the classification models are presented in Table 1.

Table 1. Comparative analysis of the results using the random forest, KNN and XGBoost models

Methods	Precision	Recall	F1-score	Accuracy
Random Forest	0.81	0.81	0.81	0.81
KNN	0.8	0.8	0.8	0.80
XGBoost	0.84	0.83	0.84	0.83

Table 1 shows that the XGBoost-based framework outperformed the random forest and KNN-based classification models in terms of accuracy. High performance and accuracy are hallmarks of XGBoost. To construct a strong learner, XGBoost combines the predictions of several weak learners (decision trees). It builds the ensemble of trees iteratively while using a gradient descent optimization algorithm to optimize a certain objective function. Random Forest is a similar ensemble learning technique that aggregates the predictions of various decision trees. However, unlike XGBoost, random forest creates every decision tree on its own. KNN is a nonparametric method that categorizes fresh data points in accordance with the training data's k nearest neighbors' dominant class. KNN can function well when the decision boundary is nonlinear and is straightforward to construct. Although XGBoost is known for its great prediction performance and accuracy, tuning and parameter optimization may be more difficult for XGBoost than for random forest and KNN. Conversely, random forest is frequently chosen when interpretability and feature relevance are crucial.

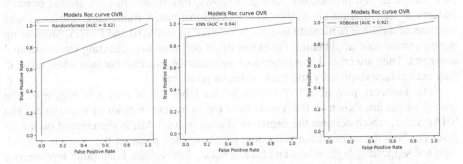

Figure 2. RoC Curves of the Random Forest-, KNN- and XGBoost-based Frameworks

The RoC curves for the random forest-, KNN-, and XGBoost-driven architectures are shown in Figure 2. The RoC and AUC score provide an indication of the model's efficacy. The model performs better at differentiating between positive and negative classifications with a higher AUC. The performance of two or more diagnostic tests was compared using the RoC curve to evaluate a test's overall diagnostic performance. It is also used to establish the proper cutoff value for determining whether a possibility even exists. The KNN algorithm, bases its predictions on the majority class of its nearest neighbors. KNN was able to acquire a higher AUC score since the dataset had a clear structure or clusters. KNN is a distance-based algorithm that depends on feature value similarity. Features in the dataset were quite pertinent. As a result, KNN has excelled and received a higher AUC rating. In further processing, the XGBoost-based framework was chosen due to its higher accuracy in classification compared to KNN- and random forest-based models.

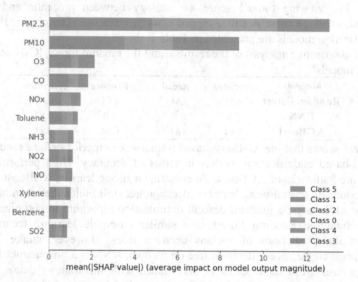

Figure 3. XGBoost-based SHAP summary plot

Figure 3 depicts a SHAP summary plot that gives a machine learning model's feature importance a visual representation. The top features are displayed in order of relevance, along with the matching SHAP values, which demonstrate the influence each feature has on predictions. As Fig. 3 shows, PM 10 and PM 2.5 are the primary features in determining air quality in the XGBoost-based framework. Different size fractions of airborne particulate matter are referred to as PM10 and PM2.5. Monitoring these particles aids in obtaining the extent of air pollution and directing environmental strategies. They are crucial components of air quality evaluation because when inhaled, they may induce respiratory and cardiovascular problems.

The summary plot of SHAP values for the label "0" is shown in Figure 4. The feature names are shown on the Y-axis from top to bottom in order of importance. The SHAP value, which denotes the degree of change in log odds, is represented on the X-axis. To show the value of the associated property, each point on the graph is colored, with red suggesting high values and blue denoting low values. Each point represents a row of data from the original dataset.

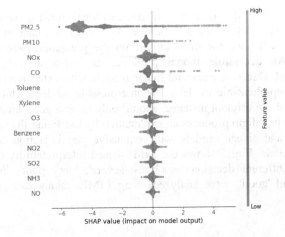

Figure 4. XGBoost-based SHAP summary plot for label 0.

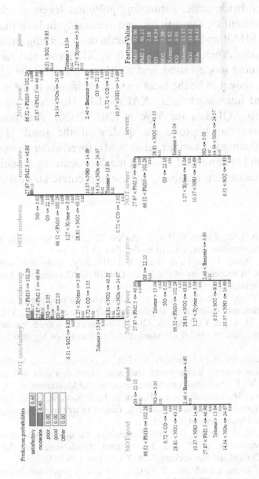

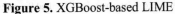

Figure 5. XGBoost-based LIME

The output of LIME is a list of justifications showing how each attribute contributed to the prediction of a data sample. As a result, it is easy to determine which feature changes will have the most impact on the prediction, which provides local interpretation. An accessible model produces an explanation by localizing the underlying model. Decision trees and linear models with extensive regularization are examples of comprehensible models. The interpretable models, which are trained on few alterations of the original instance, should only offer a good local approximation. An interpretable paradigm produces an explanation by localizing the underlying model. Decision trees and linear models with extensive regularization are examples of interpretable models. Fig. 5 shows the LIME-based interpretability of the XGBoost-based model. Different decisions, such as 'severe', 'very poor', 'poor', 'moderate', 'satisfactory', and 'good', were analyzed using LIME, taking different features into consideration.

5. Conclusions

Researchers from all across the world are working to resolve the problem of air pollution on a worldwide scale. Estimating pollution levels is inherently challenging due to the data's instability, dynamicity, and variability in both place and time. In this study, we use the SHAP and LIME explainable deep learning methods to demonstrate how air contaminants affect air quality. KNN, XGBoost, and random forest are the three machine learning models used, and XGBoost provides the highest accuracy. PM 10 and PM 2.5 are shown to be the most significant factors in determining air quality in the XGBoost-based framework using XAI models. However, the dataset used in this study only contains AQI data for 5 years (2015-2020). Additional features of XAI model incorporation can improve the quality of the result. Future research will concentrate on analyzing the various reliable ML forecasting techniques. This makes it easier to analyze and comprehend in-depth the deep learning models used to predict air quality, and it increases their reliability for use in accurate air quality prediction.

References

[1]   Kang, G. K., Gao, J. Z., Chiao, S., Lu, S., & Xie, G. (2018). Air quality prediction: Big data and machine learning approaches. Int. J. Environ. Sci. Dev, 9(1), 8-16.
[2]   Yi, X., Zhang, J., Wang, Z., Li, T., & Zheng, Y. (2018, July). Deep distributed fusion network for air quality prediction. In Proceedings of the 24th ACM SIGKDD international conference on knowledge discovery & data mining (pp. 965-973).
[3]   Zhu, D., Cai, C., Yang, T., & Zhou, X. (2018). A machine learning approach for air quality prediction: Model regularization and optimization. Big data and cognitive computing, 2(1), 5.
[4]   Kök, İ., Şimşek, M. U., & Özdemir, S. (2017, December). A deep learning model for air quality prediction in smart cities. In 2017 IEEE international conference on big data (big data) (pp. 1983-1990). IEEE.
[5]   Kamal, M. S., Northcote, A., Chowdhury, L., Dey, N., Crespo, R. G., & Herrera-Viedma, E. (2021). Alzheimer's patient analysis using image and gene expression data and explainable-AI to present associated genes. IEEE Transactions on Instrumentation and Measurement, 70, 1-7.
[6]   Kamal, M. S., Dey, N., Chowdhury, L., Hasan, S. I., & Santosh, K. C. (2022). Explainable AI for glaucoma prediction analysis to understand risk factors in treatment planning. IEEE Transactions on Instrumentation and Measurement, 71, 1-9.
[7]   Madan, T., Sagar, S., & Virmani, D. (2020, December). Air quality prediction using machine learning algorithms–a review. In 2020 2nd International Conference on Advances in Computing, Communication Control and Networking (ICACCCN) (pp. 140-145). IEEE.
[8]   Iskandaryan, D., Ramos, F., &Trilles, S. (2020). Air quality prediction in smart cities using machine learning technologies based on sensor data: a review. Applied Sciences, 10(7), 2401.

[9] Mao, W., Wang, W., Jiao, L., Zhao, S., & Liu, A. (2021). Modeling air quality prediction using a deep learning approach: Method optimization and evaluation. Sustainable Cities and Society, 65, 102567.

[10] Yang, Y., Mei, G., & Izzo, S. (2022). Revealing influence of meteorological conditions on air quality prediction using explainable deep learning. IEEE Access, 10, 50755-50773.

[11] Palaniyappan Velumani, R., Xia, M., Han, J., Wang, C., LAU, A. K., & Qu, H. (2022, March). AQX: Explaining Air Quality Forecast for Verifying Domain Knowledge using Feature Importance Visualization. In 27th International Conference on Intelligent User Interfaces (pp. 720-733).

[12] Kalamaras, I., Xygonakis, I., Glykos, K., Akselsen, S., Munch-Ellingsen, A., Nguyen, H. T., ... &Tzovaras, D. (2019, November). Visual analytics for exploring air quality data in an AI-enhanced IoT environment. In Proceedings of the 11th international conference on management of Digital EcoSystems (pp. 103-110).

[13] Choi, J., Kim, J., & Jung, K. (2021, January). Air quality prediction with 1-dimensional convolution and attention on multimodal features. In 2021 IEEE International Conference on Big Data and Smart Computing (BigComp) (pp. 196-202). IEEE.

Design Studies and Intelligence Engineering
L.C. Jain et al. (Eds.)
© 2024 The Authors.
This article is published online with Open Access by IOS Press and distributed under the terms
of the Creative Commons Attribution Non-Commercial License 4.0 (CC BY-NC 4.0).
doi:10.3233/FAIA231452

Construction of the Place Spirit of Qianmen Street in Beijing: Historical Performance and User Needs

Zuqun ZHANG [a,1] and Chenggang LU [a], Haotian ZHAO [a], Qi CHEN [a], Qiuyu WU [a], and Tingting HE [a]

[a]*School of Design and Art, Beijing Institute of Technology*

Abstract. Objective Qianmen Street is an important historical and cultural district and commercial space in Beijing. It interweaves with the needs of users to form the spirit of place. **Method** Using two analysis methods of diachrony and synchronicity, this paper divides Qianmen Street into four historical change stages: the period of formation, the period of throes, the period of transformation and the period of future, and analyzes the basic elements of place composition in each period. Taking the language landscape as the starting point, this paper analyzes the cultural memory of the language landscape of Qianmen Street by using the semiotic theory. At the same time, the interaction design method was used for analyzed the place object's demands intention based on the synchronic subject's requirements. **Result** This paper puts forward the theoretical framework of the three elements of place spirit and the realistic needs of place subjects. **Discuss** It is speculated that the fourth stage construction of Qianmen Street will focus on the balance of economy and culture.

Keywords. Qianmen Street; Spirit of place: historical performance; user demand

1. Introduction

Historical and cultural block is a dynamic display of the historical details of a city. By using natural elements to superimpose man-made objects of human activities to present rational characteristics and cultural heritage, it creates a sensual atmosphere of materiality and spirituality of its place to the "other".

At the local scale, the most intuitive material carriers of culture are written records such as local histories, house signs, and account books, which constitute a kind of linguistic and cultural landscape. Jan Assmann thinks that writing skills are preservation, communication and translation. In a certain time and space, people can write and store history through words. And share with other regions. And exchange its connotation(Assmann, 1994). At the same time, the memory of words also provides the basis for the formation of collective cultural memory. Jan Assmann argues that the key to the production of cultural memory is the official classicization and abstraction of

---

[1] Corresponding Author, School of Design and Art, Beijing Institute of Technology, No. 5 Zhongguancun South Street, Haidian District, Beijing, 100081, China; E-mail: zhangzuqun@126.com.

texts(Xiaobing, 2007). This approval from official authority gives cultural memory a sacredness and uniqueness.

In Landry & Bourhis's theory, there is a symbolic carrier of language and characters, which has the function of information display and symbolic function, namely "language landscape"(Guowen & Shouhui, 2014). In the physical scene in the historical block, there are two main types of linguistic and cultural landscapes: officially empowered public linguistic and cultural landscapes for private use, empowered by individual business practices. No matter public or private, it is enough to constitute the externalization and manifestation of cultural memory.

Christian Norberg-Schulz used the form of phenomenology to redefine the spirit of place. It is pointed out that poetic dwelling is a meaningful way of human existence. But only when people truly identify with the place of living can human poetic dwelling gain meaning (Norberg-Schulz, 1979). Therefore, the acquisition of the spirit of place needs to depend on the identity of the subject population. Cultural memory is an important source of residents' sense of identity. Cultural memory is precious for the spirit of place, cognitive measurement, maintenance, and so on. The formation of the spirit of place depends on the internal maintenance of cultural memory. The cultural sacrifice is externally reflected by the classical language landscape.

Since the middle of the 20th-century Scholars generally believe that the built environment can be explained by semiotics theory(Jenks & Baird, 1969). For example, in the exploration of architectural theory, many scholars(Chang, 2017; Huybrechts, 2018; Ke, Zhongtao, Jing, & Yalin, 2021, etc.) have analyzed the multi-value of landmark building evolution by analyzing the evolution of urban landmark symbols. However, as far as the results are concerned, there are few studies that focus on semiotic theory to deduce the causes, processes and mechanisms of the formation of the spirit of place. Taking the linguistic landscape as the starting point, the semiotics of place was introduced as a tool to analyze the causes and processes of the formation of linguistic and cultural symbols in the Qianmen Street historical district from the perspective of diachrony. At the same time, stand at the synchronic angle. The interaction design method is used to obtain the user demand intention of Qianmen Street. To reveal the formation mechanism of the spirit of place in the historic district. It is expected to establish a theoretical framework for the analysis of place and spirit.

2. Research location and methodology

2.1. Research location

Qianmen Street is a famous historical and cultural district in Beijing, carrying more than 700 years of history, which contains the historical and cultural genes and the spirit of the place to this day. Beijing Dashilar historical and cultural block is one of the first batches of Chinese historical and cultural blocks announced in 2015. Qianmen Street was selected as one of the first batches of 12 "Beijing Municipal Tourism and leisure blocks" in Beijing in 2021. After multiple destruction and reconstruction, the site can initially cover four types of artificial places. This form-rich artificial place and the pervasive spirit of place are ideal objects for research.

Since the place is a continuous function in time, its analysis should also take time as a clue, the time course of Qianmen Street through five renovations was outlined by the history of Beijing's urban construction. However, there is no academic consensus on the starting point of when the second, third and fourth of these transformations occurred, while the first transformation (caused by the great earthquake in Kangxi years) and the fifth transformation (to meet the 2008 Olympic Games) are not much controversial. Based on the influence of man-made transformation on Qianmen Street, the article agrees that the second transformation took place after the fire of the " The Gengzi Incident ", the third transformation was the "three great reconstructions" in the early days of the founding of the people's Republic of China, which nationalized all the shops along the street.The fourth transformation took place in the 1980s when there were many skyscrapers, which completely broke the old urban pattern(Shujiao, 2019).

According to semantics, the place spirit stages of Qianmen Street are coded as follows: in which G represents the times of transformation, while the first letter of the elements is represented by the first letter of "field" Pinyin, and the second, third and fourth letters represent the stages, times of transformation and place elements in alphabetical order. The article dismantles the assessment elements of the spirit of place theory and divides them into three components: natural places, artificial places, and place objects. Natural places only play a fundamental role in the formation of the original places, The artificial places, on the other hand, have undergone several changes and present a huge range of changes. Especially, the latter three transformations have changed the landscape more, presenting an important externalization of the spirit of place (Table 1). The place object gradually evolves from the bottom of society to ordinary residents and tourists, and especially in the fifth transformation the change of the place object causes more sociological controversies.

Table 1. code of spiritual transformation formation in Qianmen Street

Stage	Transformation	Factor	Content
Stage I	G1 Earthquake	Natural places (Caca)	/
		Artificial places (Cacb)	Scene repair
		Place object (Caac)	Merchants, dramatists, prostitutes, commoners, scholars
	G2 Conflagration	Natural places (Caca)	/
		Artificial places (Cabb)	Zhengyang Gate was destroyed and many shops were burned down and rebuilt
		Place object (Cabc)	Merchants, dramatists, prostitutes, commoners, scholars
Stage II	G3 Three great reconstruction	Natural places (Cbca)	/
		Artificial places (Cbcb)	Unified style, time-honored brand merger
		Place object (Cbcc)	Merchants, civilians
	G4 Reform and opening-up	Natural places (Cbda)	The river channel is covered by pavement
		Artificial places (Cbdb)	New Western buildings poured into Qianmen Avenue
		Place object (Cbdc)	Merchants, residents, out-of-town residents
	G5 2008 Olympic Games	Natural places (Cbea)	/
		Artificial places (Cbeb)	Commercial pedestrian street, tourist attractions, livable
		Place object (Cbec)	Merchants, locals, out-of-town residents, tourists

		Natural places (Ccea)	/
Stage III	After G5	Artificial places (Cceb)	Commercial pedestrian street, tourist attractions, livable
		Place object (Ccec)	Merchants, locals, out-of-town residents, tourists
Stage IV	After G5	Natural places (Cdea)	Natural landscapes increase
		Artificial places (Cdeb)	Pedestrian street, tourist attractions, livability, ecology
		Place object (Cdec)	Fewer tourists and more functions of life

2.2. Methodology

The article focuses on the development history of Qianmen Street. By analyzing the characteristics of place spirit in each period, the trajectory of change of place spirit is sorted out; the core elements of place spirit (i.e., locality) of Qianmen Street are refined through the dual comparison of history and the present, so that whether the core of place spirit is transformed can be judged. By analyzing the interconnection between the three elements of natural places, artificial places and place objects, the key kernel of place spirit contained in them could be found. Although linguistic the landscape is a product of artificial places, it is directly related to the formation of place spirit because it is the representation of cultural memory and the intuitive embodiment of place identity, so it needs to be analyzed and understood independently.

According to the analysis of the article, the judgment criteria for three elements of the spirit of place was formed by deconstructing the linguistic landscape from perspective of the symbolic theory of place, and by quantifying the cultural elements of place and linguistic landscape features separately through symbolic coding analysis, the spiritual characteristics of the place in the historical dimension are therefore got. Then, through the user needs analysis method to dismantle the reality dimension, evaluate and judge the loss or not of the spirit of today's place from the perspective of the experience highlights the rationality. And the qualities of the current spirit of place are obtained, presenting the diversity of local cultural ecology. With the transformation of these two qualities by the theory of placeness, the place spirit of Qianmen Street becomes the same object that can be compared and transferred. Then the transformation or not of the place spirit of Qianmen Street emerges.

Christian Norberg Schulz believes that the characteristics of place are the function of time(Norberg-Schulz, 2010a), and time is the key perspective of place spirit, which is essential to explore the interactive relationship between place and people. Generally speaking, place refers to the two-dimensional synthesis of natural space and cultural character. The cultural character can be further divided into two elements: artificial place and place object. Therefore, the emergence of place spirit is inseparable from the interaction of natural place, artificial place, and place object. Norbert Schutz divides artificial places into four types: romantic, cosmic, classical, and compound(Norberg-Schulz, 2010b). He believes that romantic places are more land friendly; The cosmic place is the orderly embodiment of the horizontal and vertical lines; Classical places have the care for Humanistic residence, taking into account the dual attributes of place and nature. It is also a compromise between romantic and cosmic places, which is an ideal state; Compound places are the combination of any of the above landscapes.

The theory of placeness: similar to the spirit of place, the field of cultural geography has analyzed the concept of "placeness " for a long time, pointing more to residents' identification with regional culture(Crang, 2003). As Mike crang mentioned: The understanding of geography should be divorced from the level of high culture. Embrace a more broad, more basic and more universal category. His judgment of " placeness " is that: Placeness is the unique nature of a region after it has established an internal connection with the external others. Its essence is to mark the presence of the specificity of the area (Kong Xiang, Hongyan, & Shangyi, 2011).

Place Semiotics: Scollon first proposed place semiotics, focusing on the social connotation of signs and words in physical space. He believes that language slogans and symbols in any place can convey a certain social meaning(Scollon & Scollon, 2003). Place semiotics is mainly composed of three logical structures: Code preference, instruction and placement. Code orientation refers to the spatial relationship of language materials, which is used to show the social relationship of language; Word carving is a way to present the meaning of landscape, involving theoretical composition, materials, and changes; Placement is the spatial location of the landscape, and the meaning of placement in different places will be different. This paper hopes to make a quantitative evaluation of the language landscape of Qianmen Street in the transitional period, to expand the use boundary of place semiotics.

Dual coding theory: Allan Urho Paivio believes that there are two processing systems in the brain, verbal and nonverbal, which process character and image information respectively. Through the joint action of these two kinds of information, people can obtain a stable cultural memory(Yulong & Chaoyun, 2007). This paper transforms the place information of Qianmen Street into understandable codes, which can be used as a symbolic analysis tool to help refine the spirit of place.

User demand analysis: interaction design is a method to regulate and guide user behavior by analyzing the characteristics of people and things. Using persona and user journey maps, this paper can well evaluate the internal feelings of the subject of the place, and infer the spiritual orientation of the place in the next stage of Qianmen Street through the needs of the subject. Among them, persona usually includes contact points, behavior, emotional experience, pain points, opportunity points and user needs; User journey map is a visual way to tell the user's experience by setting the persona.

This paper hopes to determine the theoretical framework through the dual analysis of the history and reality of Qianmen Street. This paper uses the combination of qualitative and quantitative methods to analyze and code the place elements of Qianmen Street, make a statistical analysis of the language landscape in three periods, and classify it by using the framework of place semiotics, so as to obtain the quantitative expression of language and cultural landscape. Finally, the user needs analysis tool is used to explore the needs of the character portrait. Based on the integration dimension of historical performance and user needs, a theoretical framework of dual dimensions of history and reality is formed to predict the trend of place spirit in the next stage.

3. Historical performance of place spirit in Qianmen Street

The historical exhibition is composed of two parts: the exhibition of place elements and the exhibition of linguistic landscape, in which the place elements actually assemble the place spirit, and the historical review of them can clarify the changes of the spirit of the place in different periods. The linguistic landscape is actually contained within the artificial place, and the cultural memory originates from the officially recognized text, and the communal linguistic landscape has exactly this characteristic, so the linguistic landscape is explained and analyzed separately. The spirit of place is established or not by the collective "identity" of residents and visitors.

By reviewing the transformation of Qianmen Street in the historical field, the development of the spirit of the place is roughly divided into three stages: the period of formation (before 1949), the period of throes (1949-2009), the period of transformation (2009-2021) and the period of future (after 2021), different place spirit could be summarized from each stage. The artificial place is an important part of place character, its evolutionary trajectory in the spirit of place evolves from a romantic landscape to a composite landscape composed of cosmic and romantic types, and after the transformation stage, the current stage presents a composite landscape composed of cosmic and classical in appearance form. (figure1).

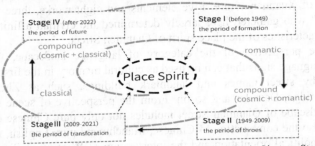

Figure 1. Schematic diagram of artificial place transformation in Qianmen Street

3.1. The period of Formation (before 1949)

The natural environment is the basic element of the formation of the place's spirit. By analyzing the characteristics of natural elements, the reasons for the formation of artificial places could be acquired. According to the history of the Ming Dynasty records, there was a Sanli river outside the old capital, and residents lived by the river(Tingyu, 1974). By the end of the Ming Dynasty, it had become "the old way of the Sanli River taken the land as the basis for governance"(Tong & Yizheng, 2001). It can be seen that the Sanli river had disappeared by the end of the Ming Dynasty. However, Sanli river has had an important impact on the life of residents and the formation of market culture in Qianmen area. Due to the irregularity of the river, the planning and construction of the street also conforms to the irregular and disordered characteristics, leaving a special urban texture.

Based on the natural geography and landform of natural places, romantic artificial places had gradually evolved. Qianmen commercial space was originated from the opening of the Beijing Hangzhou Grand Canal in the Yuan Dynasty. An endless stream of Southern businessmen came to the capital for business transactions, and some businessmen settled in Qianmen area(Baoping, 2006a). During the prosperity of the Ming Dynasty, there were 1078 commercial stores on Qianmen Street(Bang, 1980), and "The residents had been here for a long time", a fixed place for business convergency and settlement has formed in Qianmen Street(Changyuan, 1983). With the "drive Han movement" of the Qing Dynasty, the Han people continued to move from the inner city to the outer city of Beijing, and gathered in Qianmen to become the second-generation commercial service center of Beijing.The settled residents created, acquired and continued the spirit of place which seen commerce as the core and intersecting with life. In the late Qing Dynasty and the early Republic of China, Gengzi incident was incurred. Qianmen area was set on fire by the Boxers and the old buildings were destroyed, which also provided a new opportunity for the post-war reform and reconstruction of the area.The national capitalists who grew up in the wave of patriotism constantly promoted the commercial development of Qianmen Street, and a new (Chinese style) bank with a completely westernized appearance appeared(Baoping, 2006b). During this period, the most stable image of Qianmen Street of old Beijingers was formed. For a long time after the founding of new China, influenced by the regional natural and geographical characteristics and cultural habits, the streets and alleys present the architectural characteristics of free arrangement, and the place buildings of Qianmen Street maintained a strong romance.

The early objects of Qianmen Street can be divided into five categories (businessmen, scholars, actors, prostitutes and civilians) who was representing the typical roles of Xuannanculture."Five elements and eight works, three teachings and nine streams" who gathered here largely determined the civilian affinity and bottom business characteristics of the place spirit of Qianmen Street.

From the perspective of the category of language landscape, there are few exemplary language signs that can be used as cultural memory in the first stage, mainly represented by street names and landmark buildings, such as Zhengyang gate, Zhengyang bridge, Dashilar and so on. From the perspective of scene semiotics, the language landscape of Qianmen Street includes not only pure Chinese of Zhengyang bridge, but also the combination of Chinese, Manchu and pure English, which reflects the Manchu political orientation and the intervention of Western civilization in China after the entry of the Qing Dynasty.In terms of lettering, there were few materials available in this period, mainly wood and stone, and the location was usually in the most prominent place of the building. The national integration revealed by the Manchu Chinese double language logo and the political situation of China's poverty and weakness revealed by the pure English logo are the externalization of the change of the spirit of the place. The place space and national political events have an internal relationship, shaping a special local memory.

Figure 2. typical common language landscape during the formation of place spirit (author's reform)

It can be seen from the above that the natural places in the formation period reflect the initial location characteristics of Qianmen Street, while the artificial places in this period laid the initial commercial and living characteristics of Qianmen Street. The civilians and grass roots constitute the main body of the site objects of Qianmen Street. The inclusive language landscape of Qianmen Street has shaped the characteristics of commercialization, daily life, popularization and diversification for the locality.

3.2. The period of throes (1949-2009)
From the founding of new China to entering the new century in 2009, Qianmen Street had been experienced several historical periods of new-democracy, public-private

partnership, the decade of the "Cultural Revolution": , three great reconstructions and reform and opening up. Given there is huge differences among the events above, the spirit of place shows the characteristics of stage differences. During this painful period, the natural places generally continued the location pattern of the previous period. In particular,In the 1970s, the moat was transformed by government into an asphalt road, the original river was covered under the road, and therefore the Zhengyang bridge was hard to find.

Figure 3. Comparison of Zhengyang bridge today and night (author's reform)

The founding of new China could be considered as the start point of artifical place's great change. Socialist transformation of "public-private partnership" was first envent, which has reshaped the business style of time-honored brands to a certain extent.The original 55 stores in Dashilan street were reduced to 34 due to the intervention of the government. Some time-honored stores were forcibly merged into large shops or commercial groups controlled by the government(Zhan, 2011). Many time-honored brands have lost their original spatial pattern and business essence, leaving only empty material shells(Ran, 2008). With the intervention of external forces, people's original cultural identity has gradually declined. The people think that the time-honored brands have "changed" and lost their original flavor. The commercial spirit of the place has been reduced to a certain extent.

In the first three decades of reform and opening up, due to the strong rise of modern commercial centers such as Xidan and Wangfujing, the status of Qianmen Street commercial center gradually declined to a secondary one(Shuyue & Baoxiu, 2011).The commercial center pattern of Beijing's three pillars (Xidan, Wangfujing and Qianmen) has evolved into a single central business district (Xidan) and a multi-level commercial center. Qianmen is a second level high-level commercial center (city level), juxtaposed with Wangfujing, Dongqiao bridge, Cuiwei Road, Beijiao, Haidian, and mwangyuan (Yang Wuyang, 1994) .The Research Report of the Beijing Academy of Social Sciences once pointed out that the Qianmen Street area struggles with high population density and poverty,which makes it become an urban slum(Wei, 2005). Due to the lack of fine management, Qianmen Street grow effectively in the vertical angle because of Beijing's urban planning, and grow savagely in the back street in the horizontal angle. Moreover, there was a trend of antique style in time-honored brand and all of which adopted glazed tiles and double evade roofs, which actually made their their original diversified characteristics lost(Jiafang, 1999). Therefore, the artificial places in this period have typical compound characteristics, which not only has the affinity to the earth in the romantic period, but also has the coexistence of cosmic type and romantic type, showing the coexistence of overall disorder and local high order.

Because only businessmen and civilians were left in the public-private partnership stage, diversified occupations and practitioners in history were disappeared. According to the original census report of Xuanwu District of Beijing at the beginning of the new century: In the early stage of reform and opening up, the residents in Qianmen area showed the characteristics of high population density, high degree of population aging, low education level, low income level, and high proportion of temporary residents(Yihan, 2004). The special complex place objects and the painful background of the times influence and shape each other, and construct the place spirit characteristics of the special times.

At this stage, the phased characteristics of the language landscape of Qianmen Street are obvious. (1) In the early days of the founding of the People's Republic of China, there was no significant difference between the public language landscape of Qianmen Street and that of the Republic of China. However, in the period of public-private partnership, due to the characteristics of socialist public ownership and the general lack of people's material life, time-honored brands with the characteristics of national capitalism were nationalized, and the original private language landscape was officially corrected and became a part of public cultural memory. The language landscape of this period showed a unified and monotonous visual image, which was expressed in the left-right arrangement of Chinese characters, with white or gray background and red characters, and strong ideological legacy and insufficient supply of productive forces could be found on the landscapes. That is to say, the cultural memory of language landscape in the period of public-private partnership focuses on collectivity and identity. (2) In the period of reform and opening up, the language landscape had been become more diversified with the rise of market economy and the awakening of commodity consciousness. Although its material, structure and color still bear the shadow of the joint venture period, it presents a diversified and mixed style on the whole. Qianmen Street, as an old commercial street, was no longer a fixed format in the placement space, but were arranged on the facade or interior of the building according to the needs of the merchants themselves; Many iron and plastic products had been added to the material, and the color has also broken through the monotonous color matching in the past and adopted diversified and rich colors. The main street of Qianmen began to settle in foreign brands such as KFC. Not only has the code orientation of Chinese English bilingual, but also the English brand is bigger than the Chinese brand. At this stage, residents' psychological perception of private language landscape is higher than that of public cultural landscape, and cultural memory presents a generalized form. Chaotic slogan advertisements make Qianmen Street continued the impression of "dirty, messy and poor", which become one of the sources of people's common memories of Qianmen Street. Due to the disorderly entry of major foreign brands, the placeness itself had been impacted. Although it enhances the commercial content, it also reduces the locality to a certain extent.

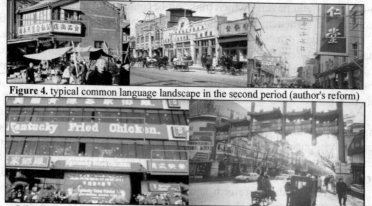

Figure 4. typical common language landscape in the second period (author's reform)

Figure 5. language landscape of Qianmen Street before and after the new century (by the author)

During the pain period, the changes of artificial places and place objects in Qianmen Street reflect the ups and downs of commercial characteristics. From the unification of "public-private joint ventures" leading to the loss of diversified commercial forms, to the disorderly entry of various stores and the mixing of good and bad places after the reform and opening up, leading to excessive and disordered commercialization. The change of language landscape in this period is consistent with the change trend of artificial places, which reflects the transition of "pluralism unity pluralism disorder" of cultural memory.

3.3 The period of transformation (2009-2021)

After many argumentations, Qianmen Street has carried out the largest and most "thorough" urban reconstruction in history since 2009. The original environmental art design was to strive for innovation under multiple limited conditions, trying to meet four conditions at the same time: 1. Respected the original urban texture and restored the alley space; 2. Application of new materials and technologies were necessary; 3. Coordination with preserved buildingsshoulde be considered; 4. Effective integration of commercial space and cultural space. Finally, based on the restoration of the architectural style in the late Qing Dynasty and the early Republic of China, danger removal, relocation and repair operations were carried out with great momentum. The author interviewed a number of tourist samples from the perspective of sociology, and they said that "Qianmen can never return to the past".

During the transformation period, the transformation of the language landscape pattern of Qianmen Street has been relatively stable, and a considerable number of site elements have begun to be reconstructed. Time honored brands have sought new ways. Among them, the art experience mode represented by traditional cultural immersive experience is the mainstream mode, and the new language landscape is reshaped. The cultural identity based on the "local attachment" of Qianmen Street is also gradually restored.

- Artistic experience

The operator of Qianmen Street had also experienced the change from Tianjie Real Estate Development Co., Ltd. with government background to SOHO China. SOHO China claimed to highly integrate Chinese culture with world brands, build "Beijing's Champs Elysees" and become the gathering place of world famous brands. Some traditional time-honored brands began to be distributed on both sides of the street. In the east of the road, there are mainly Quanjude roast duck shop, cheap square roast duck shop, huixianju fried liver shop, yongantang medicine shop, black monkey hat shop, DuyiShaomai restaurant, zhengyanglou restaurant, ruishengxiang, jiulongzhai fresh fruit shop, tongsanyi dried fruit sea flavor shop, zhengmingzhai pastry shop, etc.There are yongzenghe bank, ruijuxiang silk shop, tianhuizhai snuff shop, Tongrentang medicine shop, Liubiju sauce vegetable garden, Yilong mutton restaurant, uncle Jia's stew and so on in Luxi and Xili streets. They are found in all walks of life.The government tried to restore the bustling scene of old Beijing's "watching things on the Tianqiao, shopping to the Dashilar" and "Ma Juyuan on top of the head, stepping on the NeiLianSheng, wearing eight kind of Yang clothes and four Heng around the waist".Some fast fashion brands H&M, Zara and UNIQLO had also begun to settle in. From the transformation of Qianmen, this historical and traditional commercial street was at the crossroads of the "conflict" between eastern and Western cultures. After this groping forward and repeated setbacks, Beijing TianjieYingshi Business Management Co., Ltd., a joint venture of Tianjie group, Beijing Yingshi and Xinglong company, began to attract large-scale investment in 2013, in terms of environmental design, Qianmen Street was divided into three, created "North cultural tourism experience area", "middle cultural creativity experience area" and "south urban life experience area". China seal cutting art museum, Zhu Bingren bronze carving, jicuiyuan (exhibition and sale of intangible cultural heritage products), the appearance of Peking Opera and intangible cultural heritage experience center had opened the prelude to the intangible cultural heritage experience. Some cultural experience projects such as cultural brand experience stores with labels and Madame Tussauds Wax Museum had also sprung up. So far, the whole street was "hot in the north and cold in the South". Xianyukou and Dashilar near Zhengyangmen arrow tower were popular because of the existence of many old Beijing delicacies, while the south section was much deserted.

Takes tianparadise (Beijing Opera Museum), located in the southwest of the intersection of Qianmen Street East Road and Xianyukou street, Dongcheng District, Beijing, as an example. It is known as the world's first quintessence Beijing Opera experience Museum. The long-standing tianparadise theater was built in 1785, with a total area of nearly 5000 square meters. MeiLanfang, a master of Peking Opera, performed here at the age of 17. Cheng Yanqiu's performance career originated here. Han Shichang, the king of Kunqu Opera, became popular here. It is an absolutely authentic resort for (Ningchun&Fujia, 2018) Peking opera play and experience. Based on the 237 years old historical buildings, it combines traditional Peking Opera with fashion, cultural and creative technology, and carries out a variety of visitor experience and participation programs. the cultural roots inherited by The Peking Opera Museum and it is also expected to become a new landmark of Beijing culture.

Make up the experience: Visitors have the opportunity to watch the actors put on makeup backstage. The staff will explain every step of Peking Opera makeup. Of course, visitors can also experience the feeling of simplifying their own makeup.

Wearing experience: Understand the traditional costumes and props, understand the historical materials related to Peking Opera, wear the traditional costumes and props to maintain the best sense of reality. On the basis of retaining the traditional costume style and integrating the modern costume aesthetic design, the improved fashion aesthetic design clothing is also welcomed by young people.

Peking opera stage experience: After video popularization and live lectures on the small stage of the theater, visitors can act out a Peking Opera program and characters.

Small production experience: you can make handicrafts such as Peking Opera Face book, rabbit doll, paper cutting and decal on site.

Purchase experience: develop secondary derivatives of cultural innovation, from small mask key chains to large improved versions of clothing; From the traditional handbag, bellyband handkerchief, postcard, and picture book decoration, to the trendy pillow, mobile phone case, mouse pand ad, and mug. There are practical pillows, bowls and chopsticks, cards, and picture frames, as well as collectible PekingOpera-style clothes, commemorative coins, CD records, historical relics... These cultural derivatives are worth collecting.

In the field survey of Qianmen Street in March 15, 2021 and October 2022 led by the author, it was observed that there were not many visitors to the Museum of Peking Opera. Tourists have not fully recognized the diversified experience and consumption of Peking Opera. As the quintessence of Chinese culture, Peking Opera is a kind of comprehensive artistic aesthetic combining the elegant aesthetics of highbrow solemnnes and the popular literature or art. Peking opera itself is also the product of historical development and artistic grafting. In the context of today's changing times, how does Beijing Opera carry out modern integration and innovation on the basis of inheriting tradition? The author thinks: Will originally to "singing, music, chanting, dancing" give priority to, the audience and actors perform binary fragmented system, through aesthetic boundaries, make the people and roles, let visitors in Qianmen street on stage "appearance", true zero distance contact form, the participation, and appreciation, understanding, and crossing of history and experience, role-playing, they gradually comprehensive aesthetic feeling of Peking Opera. In the context of today's changing times, how does Beijing Opera carry out modern integration and innovation on the basis of inheriting tradition? The author thinks: Will originally to "sing - read - do -" give priority to, the audience and actors perform binary fragmented system, through aesthetic boundaries, make the people and roles, let visitors in Qianmen street on stage "appearance", true zero distance contact form, the participation, and appreciation, understanding, and crossing of history and experience, role-playing, they gradually comprehensive aesthetic feeling of Peking Opera.

The landscape design of Qianmen Street shows the tendency of hard assimilation, and the appearance can recover the architectural appearance of a certain era in the past to a certain extent, but it just can not retain the soul of Qianmen Street, lost the spirit of the place. The transformation of historical and cultural blocks is essentially a kind of comprehensive environmental art centering on the restoration of spiritual space. After experiencing large-scale real estate, the strong impact of e-commerce, and the re-empowerment of new retail, the physical business environment is far worse than the non-store business form, and the planning of the business district presents chaos and disorderly competition. Under the premise of high rents and high human resource costs, a large number of physical stores in Qianmen can only survive by raising the prices of products and services sold, and some cultural and creative stores even rely on charging tickets to subsidize the high costs. Due to the impact of the COVID-19 pandemic, the flow of tourists and people from outside the city has fallen sharply and fluctuated. Content and experience have become the standard way for business circles to save themselves, but the new consumption mode with the aesthetic value of the new era and new fashion is trying to change the old business operation in a larger sense. Many non-body examinations, fashion fusions, and other projects are more gimmicks but do not bring the local cultural identity to the community people and foreign tourists. Intangible cultural heritage itself is a very traditional production and life matter, which belongs to the category of secondary and tertiary cultural creation derivative cultural experience project. Its gathering and development here cover the academic boundary between non-genetic inheritance and cultural creation.

● Language landscape sample

The evolution of the elements of the character of the place eventually aroused widespread doubts from all walks of life, and the public generally believed that this kind of improper intervention destroyed the appearance and style of Qianmen Street. This bottom-up subjective judgment of the public need objective and comprehensive evidence. As a symbol landscape, language landscape is an important part of space construction. Therefore, it is relatively persuasive to judge the attenuation of cultural memory from the perspective of public cultural language landscape. According to the detailed data obtained from the field investigation of the author's team and using quantitative analysis (table 2), the Chinese code appeared 235 times, accounting for 63.34% of the total sample; English codes appeared 136 times, accounting for 36.64% of the total sample. Among them, the location name signs are marked with Chinese code. For the guidance signs and information signs, more consideration is given to the needs of foreign tourists, and the interpretation is made by the combination of Chinese and English code and text.

Table 2. statistical analysis of common language code types and quantities in Qianmen Street

The type of code	Quantity	proportion
Chinese	235	63.34%
English	136	36.64%

There is further analysis of quantitative for common language landscape code types (table 3). Among the 236 public language landscapes in Qianmen Street, there are 100 monolingual public landscapes, accounting for 42.37% of the total sample; There are 136 bilingual public landscapes, accounting for 57.63% of the total sample. It can be found that there is only one kind of monolingual public landscape in Chinese, and the form of expression is relatively single.

Table 3. Statistics of common language landscape types of Qianmen Street

Common language landscape classification（236）	The type of code combination	Quantity	proportion
Monolingual	Chinese monolingual	100	42.37%
Bilingual	Bilingual in Chinese and English	86	36.44%
	Bilingual in Chinese and phoneticize	50	21.19%

According to the field investigation of the author's team, the functions of public language landscape can be divided into six types: Name signs, Inscriptions, warning signs, information boards, slogans and guidance signs. In terms of materials and material performance, there are six kinds of paper materials, advertising cloth materials, plastic materials, metal materials, stone materials and wood materials (table 4), of which the first letter adopts the phoneticize initial of "identification";The second letter uses A and B to indicate the difference between monolingual and bilingual; The third letter indicates the difference of materials in alphabetical order; The fourth letter indicates the different identification functions in alphabetical order. Statistics show that the public language landscape in Qianmen area has the international paradigm of bilingual code, which is more in line with the use of modernization. This is because Qianmen Street has assumed the function of cultural display window after the recent transformation, and the main object of regional sign is foreign tourists. Through the functional connection between tourists and the outside world, the placeness of Qianmen Street has been reactivated.

Table 4. common language landscape use function and material data code of Qianmen Street

	Functional classification	Quantity	material	The type of code	Quantity	Specific name
Qianmen Street Communal language landscape (236)	Name signs	11	wood	monolingual(Baaa)	3	Zhengyang Gate Archway, Guanghe Building, LangfangErtiao Hutong
			cloth	bilingual (Bbba)	1	Police booth
			paper	monolingual(Baea)	2	Duty Guard Platform、Sky Street Ice
			metal	monolingual(Baca)	3	Qianmen sign, XianYuKou sign, Dashilar sign
				bilingual (Bbca)	1	Dongcheng District Qianmen Fire

						Rescue Station
		plastic	monolingual(Bada)	1		Qianmen Chao Market
Inscriptions	6	stone	monolingual(Bafb)	4		Temple Street City project introduction、Vermilion Bird、Black Tortoise
		metal	monolingual(Bacb)	2		Tang Bohu、Wang Xizhi
Warning signs	8	paper	monolingual(Baec)	3		Do not climb, pay attention to safety、Please do not play on the cartoon duck to avoid falling, thank you
			bilingual(Bbec)	2		Climbing is prohibited、Be careful with the steps
		plastic	bilingual(Bbdc)	1		Repairing
		metal	bilingual(Bbcc)	2		It is forbidden to use it, so please detour it
		paper	monolingual (Baed)	5		List of disinfection situations, warm tips, etc
Information boards	50	metal	monolingual(Bacd)	20		National Intangible Cultural Heritage、China's time-honored brand、Beijing Quality Service Store、Bell Car license plate、Street and Hutong environmental
			bilingual(Bbcd)	24		Qianmen Street strong electric information board, China time-honored shop information board, shop information board, business hours information board, etc
		glass	bilingual(Bbgd)	1		Tax Refund Shop
Slogan	53	cloth	monolingual(Babe)	5		Folk culture、Prosperity, strength, civilization and harmony、Green
		paper	monolingual(Baee)	45		Socialist core value、State ideology、The political form of the state、A model of the times、Civilized

Guide signs	108	paper			table, healthy you and me、Top 10 Annual List Figures
			bilingual (Bbee)	3	"China Everbright Bank"Flyers、Qianmen Street publicity
			monolingual(Baef)	2	Railway Line 7, Metro Line 8、Shijia Hutong
		metal	monolingual(Bacf)	9	Evacuation routes、Bathroom sign
			bilingual (Bbcf)	94	Qianmen Street building sign、Bathroom sign
		plastic	monolingual(Badf)	3	Wangpi Hutong、Intelligent garbage sorting experience station、Shijia Hutong

Atistics show that Beijing Qianmen Street, as a tourist commercial block with antique style and modern fashion elements, is characterized by the gathering of traditional commerce, history and culture, attracting Chinese and foreign tourists who are interested in traditional Chinese culture. Its public language landscape has the international paradigm of dual code, which is more in line with the trend of modern and global international communication. After the recent cultural transformation, Qianmen Street gradually began to assume the function of international communication and cultural exhibition window. Through the public language landscape, the identity characteristics of traditional Beijing are displayed, so that tourists can form functional connections with the outside world, and emphasize their social groups and cultural identities. In this way, the common cultural identity is constructed in the modern context and the special cultural memory is reconstructed in Qianmen Street.

● Social tear

According to Christian Norberg-Schulz's theory of place spirit, whether to locale object's identity and the places of artificial and natural sites, as well as the influence of the artificial objects and places of natural double change will inevitably change habitat to place objects, even destruction, an important influence on the location, object identification and even tear. The transformation of Qianmen Street is a typical case of forced change of local identity. Therefore, further discrimination is needed: the psychological change of the place object after the artificial place change. In order to reshape the urban marginal line and to explore the cultural root, especially the Olympic Games in Beijing, the fifth transformation for Qianmen Street had been started. Since the completion of a new round of reconstruction in 2009, 76% of the buildings have recovered the appearance of the Republic of China, and more than 20 foreign well-known brands have been introduced(Qiao, 2008). The livability of the residents on the back of the commercial street is considered in the plan; the status of intermixing of commerce and residence and diversified commerce construction has been restored, forming a classical artificial place.

Has been limited by the positioning is not clear, Qianmen Street has a "day street" said, but the latest old city transformation far from reaching the "Oriental Champs-Elysees famous street" expectations. In this transition period, its positioning has changed repeatedly, from "high-end shopping street" at the beginning, to "cultural experience street" announced in 2013, and then to the introduction of intangible cultural heritage stores in 2018 to find a way out. The official data by the end of 2016 and the research data of the author's research group in November 2021: the stores on Qianmen Street are mainly divided into time-honored brands, cultural experience-based brands, international first-line brands and low-end tourist souvenirs, but lack of leisure and entertainment, health industries and other business forms, and the commercial atmosphere has not been fully explored. Both international famous brands and domestic modern commercial brands have not maintained a consistent style in the unique field of Qianmen Street. Based on the ancient typical reconstruction of Qianmen Street is faced with the challenge of combining Chinese and Western styles and mixing styles, the forced restoration of Qianmen Street style shows the embarrassment of its positioning disorder. The uncoordinated development of artificial sites has not achieved the purpose of returning the "Beijing flavor" to old Beijing. The new renovation of artificial sites in Qianmen Street should be treated in two ways: on the one hand, the appearance of the city and the quality of residents' living environment should be improved, and the unique local cultural traditions should be restored to a certain extent. But on the other hand, Qianmen Street is only reduced to a mixed window of various cultures, not to show the most authentic old Beijing culture. As for the objects of the site, two-thirds of the original residents were forced to move out, while tourists flooded in. The decrease of settlers and sense of identity will inevitably lead to the decrease of local attachment to Qianmen Street and the atrophy of local place spirit.

The forcibly restored style of Qianmen Street shows its disordered positioning and the uncoordinated development of artificial places did not achieve the goal of returning the flavor of old Beijing. The new transformation of artificial places in Qianmen Street should be treated in two ways: on the one hand, the appearance of the city and the quality of residents' living environment's improvement does restored the local unique cultural tradition to a certain extent; but on the other hand, Qianmen Street has only become a window of cultural stacking, which does not show the purest Beijing culture. For the object of the place, two-thirds of the original residents were forced to move out, and tourists poured in. The decrease of settlers and identity will inevitably lead to the shrinkage of place spirit.

Time honored brands are the first feature and soul foundation of Qianmen Street, and Qianmen Street is also the home of time-honored brands. The orientation of "cultural experience consumption block" and "national intangible cultural heritage Street" is fullen of cultural paradoxes. Can all cultures be experienced? Is the ultimate purpose of cultural experience to guide consumption? How to find "cultural mosaic" original starting points? "Cultural puzzle" formed from Eastern and Western business is cultural integration or cultural tearing? As many tourists commented: the Qianmen Street has evolved from "the Qianmen Street of old Beijingers" to "the Qianmen Street of outsiders". This makes the region evolved from a spatial field of cultural heritage to a cultural label with sociological tearing characteristics and cultural conflict, and also makes the region become an experimental field for multidisciplinary interpretation with cultural heritage as the core.

From the dimension of historical development, the functions and roles of Qianmen Street in the three periods are invariably related to the needs of the times, from its initial role as a canal marketplace during the Ming and Qing dynasties, to its transformation from a primary to a secondary commercial centre after the founding of the People's Republic, and finally to the diverse forms of artistic experience and commercial agglomeration after the transformation of the old city, Qianmen Street generates a coupling between cultural centripetal and centrifugal forces. The difference in the spirit of place in each time period also determines the direction of change in the spirit of place. In terms of the elements of artificial and natural places, in the first period, the natural places gave the artificial places the basic conditions of the Cao Yun market, which contributed to the creation of a romantic landscape on Qianmen Street; in the second period, the intervention of modernization caused the artificial places on Qianmen Street to lose their romantic character, presenting a composite (cosmic + romantic) landscape and transforming it into an archaic type; in the third period, Qianmen Street turned to assume In the third period, Qianmen Street turns to a large number of diverse cultural functions, making this period the completion of the archaic landscape. In the future, the trend will be towards a composite landscape with a cosmopolitan and archaic form of Qianmen Street.

4. User needs of Qianmen Street place spirit

User journey diagram is a design tool in service design, which is used to explore and analyze the points of contact of users in the service process, so as to analyze the different needs of different contacts. The specific operation is that with the placing the persona who already created in a service process, all contact points can be obtained and customer needs can be analyzed also.

Firstly, there is demand for persona creating. According to the attention of the word "Qianmen", people aged 19-24 account for 12%, and the ratio of men to women is 100:1; The proportion of 25-34 years old is 44%, and the ratio of men to women is 56:44; The population aged 34-49 accounts for 44%, and the ratio of men to women is 50:50.

The place objects of Qianmen Street can be divided as passengers and residents. According to the "settlement" characteristics, residents are suitable sample for persona's construction. According to the age and sex ratio, residents are roughly divided into three categories: office workers, housewives and shops. Since residents aged 35-49 belong to the core owner of social discourse power, and Commercial attributes are attributes that have always existed in the historical context and reality of Qianmen Street's development, and eventually identified shopkeepers as objects for user profiling.

Finally, six needs are detected in the user's main behavior: attracting tourists, selling and communicating, expressing local consciousness, communicating feelings as resident and obtaining empathy (figure 6).The above six needs can extract two common points: cultural exchange and economic benefits. This suggests that the presentation of regional culture and regional economic development are still the two main themes involved in the spirit of place on Qianmen Street. The harmony between commerciality and culture is the key for the sustainable development of Qianmen Street. Judging from current research and demand trends, Qianmen Street is not yet sufficiently prominent to become a classic symbol of the highest level of Chinese elements, but it is still important to use the old Beijing cultural gathering space as a classic symbol of the second level of Chinese elements. Qianmen Street still needs to further explore the profitability of the cultural-economic integration of its user groups and commercial formats, with the second tier of classic Chinese culture as its core selling point.

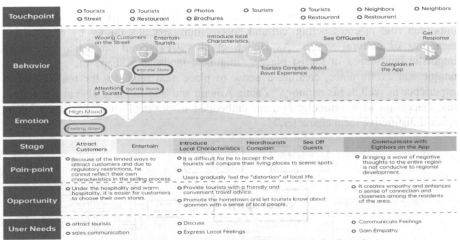

Figure 6. user journey map of Qianmen Street (self-made by the author)

5. Discussion and Conclusions

5.1. How does the language landscape construct the locality

In the course of historical development, linguistic landscapes have had different roles at each stage. There is an interactive relationship between linguistic landscapes and cultural spaces: on the one hand, the shaping of linguistic landscapes is governed by the type of cultural space and cultural attributes, for example, there is a clear difference in linguistic diversity between the linguistic landscapes of governmental authorities and those of tourist attractions. The former usually use a single official language or national lingua franca, while the latter are predominantly multilingual landscapes for reasons such as the provision of language services to foreign tourists. On the other hand, linguistic landscapes not only have an informative function in reflecting the characteristics of cultural spaces, but also play an important role in constructing 'cultural spaces' into 'spatial cultures' by constructing meanings of cultural spaces. As Heller. et al. (2014) point out when discussing linguistic landscapes in tourist places, "linguistic landscapes shape the space into a unique and exotic place, creating a 'sense of place' that regulates the tourist's social experience as well as his memory." Zhang Aiheng and Sun Jiuxia (2019) also point out that "language as a symbolic system, embedded in physical signs, gives the 'plain' space a distinctive local character."

5.2. Theoretical framework of place spirit

Therefore, there is synchronic in the course of historical development, linguistic landscapes have had different roles at each stage. There is an interactive relationship between linguistic landscapes and cultural spaces: on the one hand, the shaping of linguistic landscapes is governed by the type of cultural space and cultural attributes, for example, there is a clear difference in linguistic diversity between the linguistic landscapes of governmental authorities and those of tourist attractions. The former usually use a single official language or national lingua franca, while the latter are predominantly multilingual landscapes for reasons such as the provision of language services to foreign tourists. On the other hand, linguistic landscapes not only have an informative function in reflecting the characteristics of cultural spaces, but also play an important role in constructing 'cultural spaces' into 'spatial cultures' by constructing meanings of cultural spaces. As Heller. et al. (2014) point out when discussing linguistic landscapes in tourist places, "linguistic landscapes shape the space into a unique and exotic place, creating a 'sense of place' that regulates the tourist's social experience as well as his memory." Zhang Aiheng and Sun Jiuxia (2019) also point out that "language as a symbolic system, embedded in physical signs, gives the 'plain' space a distinctive local character."

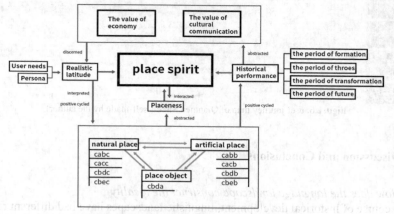

Figure 7. mental framework of Qianmen Street

5.3. Theoretical demonstration

In the analysis of the spirit of place theory and the case study of Qianmen Street, the translation of the symbols from "cultural space" to "spatial culture" shows the characteristics of "locality". In the first period, the natural geographical basis of the natural places and the geomorphological features deterlemined the basic spatial texture of Qianmen Street, and the artificial places formed in this spatial field conformed to the romantic pro-local character; In the second period, due to the multiple fluctuations of social ideology, artificial places also evolved complex characteristics, showing a staggered disorder of cosmic and romantic. Compared with the artificial place, the place object has undergone a structural iteration in the third stage. The original place object is composed of settled residents, who was gradually replaced by a large number of floating population and non-indigenous people. For the reason above, the quantitative translocation of the population subject was also completed. At this stage, the place spirit's change or not has a lot of Sociological Controversies. However, from the perspective of cultural geography, even Qianmen Street swings in giving consideration to the balance of regional culture and economy, the commercial and civilian attributes have not qualitatively changed also, its original "local" character is still preserved in the depths of its historical development. Therefore, the theory of place spirit in the case of Qianmen Street has been confirmed. As for the future direction of Qianmen Street, there is a speculation that the sustainable development of Qianmen Street mainly depends on whether to continue the " placeness" of the place and give consideration to the balance between cultural value and economic value.

Acknowledgments

This study is one of the achievements of the Beijing Social Science Foundation's planned project "Beijing Ancient Capital Art Space Factor Excavation and Heritage Protection" (project number 21YTB020)、The Humanities Quality Education Curriculum Construction Project of Beijing University of Technology: "Ancient Capital and Culture (Heritage)" and "World Heritage Appreciation".

References

[1] Assmann, J. *Lesende und nichtlesende Gesellschaften. Zur Entwicklung der Notation von Gedächtnisinhalten,* Forschung&Lehre, Deutscher Hochschulverband, Berlin, 1994.

[2] Xiaobing, W., Writing, Ritual & Cultural Memory, *Jiangxi Social Sciences* **02** (2007), 237-244.

[3] Guowen, S., & Shouhui, Z., Linguistic landscape studies: Perspective, *theories and approaches* **46** (2014), 214-223.

[4] Norberg-Schulz, C., *Toward A Phenomenology of Architecture*, Rizzoli, New York, 1979.

[5] Jenks, C., & Baird, G., *Meaning in Architecture*, London,1969.

[6] Chang, Q., A Chinese Approach to Urban Heritage Conservation and Inheritance: Focus on the Contemporary Changes of Shanghai's Historic Spaces, *Built Heritage* **1**(2017), 13-33.

[7] Huybrechts, E, The Historic Urban Landscape and the Metropolis, *Built Heritage* **2** (2018), 20-30.

[8] Ke, C., Zhongtao, H., Jing, X., &Yalin, Y., Study on the Civic Cultural Value Evolution Process of Shanghai Urban Landmarks through the Perspective of Semiotics, *Shanghai Urban Planning Review* **1** (2021), 103-109.

[9] Shujiao, W., The functional changes and contemporary remodeling of urban cultural space ——— A case study of Qianmen in Beijing, *Governance Modernization Studies* **1** (2019), 61-66.

[10] Norberg-Schulz, C., *Towards a Phenomenology of Architecture*, Huazhong University of Science and Technology Press, Wuhan, 2010a.

[11] Norberg-Schulz, C., *Towards a Phenomenology of Architecture*, Huazhong University of Science and Technology Press, Wuhan, 2010b.

[12] Crang, M., *Cultural Geography*, Nanjing University Press, Nanjing, 2003.

[13] Kong Xiang, Hongyan, Y., &Shangyi, Z., *Structuralism and Humanism Analysis of Locality Formation Mechanism——Take the role of 798 and M50 art districts in the shaping of urban locality as examples*, Geographical Research **30** (2011), 1566-1576.

[14] Scollon, R., &Scollon, S. W., *Discourses in place: Language in the material world*, Routledge, London, 2003.

[15] Yulong, L., &Chaoyun, W., Theory and Application of Knowledge Visualization, *Modern Educational Technology* **06** (2007), 18-20.

[16] Tingyu, Z., *History of Ming*, Zhonghua Book Company, Shanghai, 1974.

[17] Tong, L., &Yizheng, Y., *Di Jing Jing Wu Lue*, Shanghai Ancient Books Publishing House, 2001.

[18] Bang, S., *Wan Shu Za Ji*, Beijing Ancient Books Publishing House, Beijing,1980.

[19] Changyuan, W., *Chen Yuan Shi Lue*, Beijing Ancient Books Publishing House, Beijing, 1983.

[20] Baoping, L., *Qianmen · Dashilar*, Beijing Press. Beijing,2006.

[21] Zhan, S., Adjustment of Beijing Urban Commercial Network in the 1950s, *BEIJING DANGSHI* **04** (2011), 53-54.

[22] Ran, S., The fleeting years of Laoqianmen, *China Newsweek* **30** (2008),64-69.

[23] Shuyue, B., &Baoxiu, Z., The role of the transformation of traditional commercial blocks in the protection of historical and cultural cities: an example of Dashilan Commercial Street in Qianmen, *Beijing Planning Review* 03(2011),30-33.

[24] Wei, W., Renovation of Dashilan Encounters Difficulty, *Urban and Rural Development* **08** (2005), 22-24.

[25] Jiafang, Y., What does Dashilar look forward to in the confusion? *Business Culture* **01** (1999), 44-46.

[26] Yihan, G., *Tentative Study On the Preservation and Small-Scale Transformation of the Dashilar Area in Beijing* (master), Tsinghua University, Beijing, 2004. *Times of Economy &Trade* **10** (2018), 14-29.

[27] Ningchun, H., &Fujia, L., Research on the Development and Industrial Improvement of Qianmen Commercial District in Beijing,

[28] Qiao, X., Beijing Qianmen Street regains 600-year-old memory of the capital, *Relations Across Taiwan Straits* 08 (2008), 61-62.

[29] Jiuxia, S., &Aiheng, Z., A Study on the Changes of Yangshuo West Street Language Landscape from the Perspective of Sociolinguistics, *Tourism Tribune* **36** (2021), 39-48.

362

Design Studies and Intelligence Engineering
L.C. Jain et al. (Eds.)
© 2024 The Authors.
This article is published online with Open Access by IOS Press and distributed under the terms
of the Creative Commons Attribution Non-Commercial License 4.0 (CC BY-NC 4.0).
doi:10.3233/FAIA231453

Design of Intelligent Wheelchair for the Disabled Elderly of Mild and Moderate Type

Chuan-xin SHENG [a], Wei-liang LI [b], Lian-xin HU [c,1] , and Ze-feng WANG [d]

[a]School of Art, Huzhou University, Huzhou Zhejiang 313000, China
[b]Zhongshan Youyu Industrial Design Co., Ltd, Zhongshan Guangdong 528400, China
[c,d]School of Information Engineering, Huzhou University, Huzhou Zhejiang 313000, China

Abstract. In order to improve the current problem of poor usability, comfort, and low user motivation in traditional wheelchairs. The physiological status, psychological emotions, and lifestyle of elderly people with mild to moderate disability and caregivers was analyzed through the method of user observation, user interviews and literature research, so as to clarify the multi-level and diverse needs of users and the design positioning. Three usage modes of sitting and driving, reclining and lying flat, and the intelligent control mode of assistant path planning, intelligent obstacle avoidance has been conceived, and the main dimensions and structure have been optimized according to the design positioning. In conclusion, from the perspective of the needs of users and caregivers, an intelligent wheelchair solution that combines aesthetic appearance and ease using functions, nursing burden reducing, and positive emotions enhancing of users' can be obtained, which providing a certain reference for the design of intelligent products for disability assistance.

Keywords. product design, intelligent wheelchair, disabled elderly of mild and moderate type, caregivers, user requirement.

1. Introduction

Modern design emphasizes design ethics and humanistic care for vulnerable groups [1]. The "14th Five-Year Plan for Healthy Aging" proposes to promote the sustainable development of the elderly health industry and support the age-appropriateness of intelligent products for the elderly, including enhancing assistive products for the elderly with disabilities. Currently, many scholars have conducted research on the modular application of functional modules and human-computer comfort of smart wheelchairs [2-3]. Zhang Hang [4], from a modular perspective, designed a multimodal control smart wheelchair. Zhao Yufei [5] conducted research on the mechanical structure of wheelchairs based on ergonomics and designed a flexible and fully functional smart wheelchair. Yang Kaisi [6] built the overall hardware framework and control system for a smart wheelchair bed using SolidWorks and Matlab/Simulink software. However, the above studies have paid less attention to user segmentation among the elderly with

---

[1] Corresponding Author. HU Lian-xin (1989-), lecture, Ph.D . His main research interests cover AI algorithm, computer vision, etc. E-mail：lianxin.hu@zjhu.edu.cn.

disabilities, with a focus on intelligent control design, virtual simulation validation, and human-computer relationship optimization. Meanwhile, traditional wheelchair products in the market lack aesthetics, have poor usability, and fall short in enhancing users' motivation and preserving their dignity, and they also pay little attention to the health, emotions, and feelings of caregivers.

This article focuses on the sub-group of mildly to moderately disabled elderly individuals, employing user research methods [7] to understand the physiological conditions, psychological emotions, and lifestyles of disabled elderly individuals and caregivers. This approach allows for insights into the diverse needs of users, leading to the key design principles of smart wheelchairs. Throughout the design process, there is a strong emphasis on intelligent technology that better aligns with product functionality and caters to the emotional needs of disabled elderly individuals. The result is a smart wheelchair that combines aesthetic appeal, user-friendly features, and the ability to enhance the positive emotions of users.

2. User Analysis

In this paper, the primary focus is on elderly individuals with mild to moderate disabilities who have upper limb weakness for manual wheelchair operation, lower limb functional impairments, and limited mobility [8-9]. The physiological and psychological characteristics of caregivers were also analyzed. The research indicates that the caregiving burden has a direct impact on the quality of life of disabled elderly individuals. It emphasizes that only by fully considering the feelings of each individual during the research process can valuable and genuine needs for the design phase be obtained [10].

2.1. Physiological Condition Analysis

In this study, the behavior habits of several disabled elderly individuals using wheelchairs were observed. A total of 20 elderly individuals aged 65 and above with mild to moderate disabilities, as well as 13 caregivers from the northern Zhejiang region, were selected as research samples. Through home interviews lasting 25-30 minutes, their physiological conditions, including physical muscle strength, medical conditions, cognitive abilities, and perceptual capabilities, were analyzed. The conditions are summarized in Table 1. Therefore, the design of the smart wheelchair should consider the following factors: (1) reducing accidents that may occur during travel or caregiving processes, (2) minimizing the physiological injuries resulting from prolonged sitting or lying for disabled elderly individuals, (3) reducing the physical burden on caregivers, and (4) addressing the cognitive decline and diminished judgment of disabled elderly individuals by improving product usability, reducing operational steps, enriching product semantics, and making the operation methods more obvious and user-friendly[11].

Table 1. Results of the analysis of physiological condition

	Disabled elderly in mild and moderate type	Caregiving staff
Body muscle function	Muscle strength decreased obviously	Mostly female, less physically powerful

Disease status	Complications, eczema and lumbar injury	Severe muscle and bone strain, waist injury, back injury, excessive fatigue caused poor immunity
Thinking ability	Memory deterioration, poor judgment	--
Sensory ability	Basic senses gradually decline	--

2.2 Psychological and Emotional Aspects Analysis

(1) Analysis of Psychological Characteristics of Mild to Moderate Disabled Elderly Individuals: Mild to moderate disabled elderly individuals often experience psychological conditions such as loneliness, insecurity, anxiety, and a sense of diminished self-esteem due to the decline in physical muscle strength and changes in their living environment [12]. Some of them lack self-confidence when it comes to mobility and are hesitant to use mobility aids like wheelchairs in public places. Others may experience caregiving conflicts due to dissatisfaction with the care they receive. Therefore, in the design, emphasis should be placed on enhancing the positive and optimistic emotions of users, boosting their acceptance and confidence in using smart wheelchairs, improving emotional trust between disabled elderly individuals and caregivers, and reducing the occurrence of caregiving conflicts.

(2) Analysis of Psychological Characteristics of Caregivers: Prolonged and demanding caregiving tasks often lead caregivers to experience depressive emotions, which have negative effects on both the caregivers and the elderly individuals they care for [13]. Caregivers also carry a heavy psychological burden due to concerns about neglect or mistakes leading to secondary injuries for disabled elderly individuals. Therefore, product improvements should be implemented to assist caregivers in performing heavy tasks, such as helping mildly to moderately disabled elderly individuals get in and out of bed or use the restroom. Functional safety design can also be employed to prevent caregiving accidents, thereby alleviating the psychological burden on caregivers.

2.3 Lifestyle Analysis

Compared to severely disabled elderly individuals, those with mild to moderate disabilities have greater mobility and some social needs. They also maintain a strong sense of belonging to society. The paper delves into the lifestyle of mild to moderately disabled elderly individuals from aspects such as daily routines, modes of transportation, typical behaviors, social interactions, and their personal and societal relationships, to fully understand the characteristics of their lifestyle (Table 2). Based on these characteristics, the conclusion is drawn that not only should efforts be made to enhance their self-care abilities, but also to develop features that promote independent mobility and interactive experiences. This would assist these individuals in venturing out actively and gracefully, expanding their social circles, and increasing avenues for emotional communication. Additionally, it is crucial to address the need for cost-effective caregiving.

Table 2. Description of lifestyle and stylistic characteristics

Lifestyle	Description of type characteristics
Work and rest habit	Regular work and rest, indoor and outdoor fixed place activities, due to the deterioration of body muscle can lead to toilet, up and down, go out becomes more difficult
Travel mode	Travel alone with crutches, a wheelchair or with the assistance of a caregiver
Typical behavior	Pay attention to rehabilitation exercise, short outdoor travel, willing to accept rehabilitation technology products
Communication mode	Focus on personal image development and be willing to communicate with children, caregivers and peers
Social contact	Gradually withdraw from the original social circle, desire to participate in more social activities, and receive more emotional support from relatives and communities
Value consumption view	Advocating frugality, feel that the cost of care is expensive, do not want children to bear too much

3. User Requirements Refinement and Design Positioning

By using a card-sorting method, common requirements between mild to moderately disabled elderly individuals and caregivers were organized to determine the design positioning of the product (Table 3).

Table 3. Requirement mining and functional positioning

User Requirements	Design positioning
Security requirements to prevent accidents	Reduce the product volume, save the use of space, not easy to roll over the stable structure, a key start SOS function design
Reduce the need to sit and wait for physical harm	Wheelchair posture adjustable design to achieve different rest modes
Easy-to-use functionality required	The integrated and simplified design of the components reduces the cognitive load, and the operation interface is intuitive and easy to understand
Reduce the physical and mental burden of caregivers, reduce nursing conflicts, and reduce nursing costs	Help with self-care, help go to bed and toilet, save the caregiver's energy and time
Enhance the self-care ability of activities, the need to go out actively and gracefully	Intelligent travel function to assist independent driving, increase the product endurance, obstacle sensing ability, travel direction change
Intelligent interaction needs	Control fun, enjoyable intelligent interactive experiences
Improve the user's positive emotions, improve the user's acceptance of the wheelchair, and improve the user's travel confidence	Light and compact, simple, stylish, a certain sense of sports appearance

Based on the summarized findings, the design of the smart wheelchair should take into consideration the following aspects: (1) Functional Design: Design safe and user-friendly features, provide multiple rest modes, and support the ability of mild to moderately disabled elderly individuals to enhance self-care and travel independently. This not only saves the energy and time of caregivers but also aims to improve the physical and mental health of both parties, reduce negative emotions, prevent caregiving conflicts, and lower caregiving costs. (2) Structural Design: Consider stability and practicality in the design of the structure. (3) Interaction Experience: Design an intuitive and comprehensible interface with satisfying smart interactive experiences and autonomous driving enjoyment. (4) Exterior Design: Focus on lightweight and compact aesthetics that save space, with a minimalistic, fashionable design that exudes a sense of sportiness.

4. Smart Wheelchair Design

4.1 Conceptual design

4.1.1 Function Design

In order to conceive a solution that reduces caregiving burdens, the paper analyzed the main factors affecting the quality of care: long caregiving hours, physical effort required to move elderly individuals, lowered caregiving trust due to conflicts, and a lack of dignity. Based on these factors, a new smart wheelchair design concept was formulated, as shown in Figure 1. The structure of the smart wheelchair was optimized using a clever folding mechanism that allows the backrest, seat, and legrest to maintain the same level after adjustment. Additionally, the armrests can be folded downward to reduce obstacles and distance hindrances when mildly to moderately disabled elderly individuals are transferring to and from the bed or the restroom. This design not only reduces the risk of accidental falls during the process of moving elderly individuals but also minimizes the risk of musculoskeletal injuries for caregivers due to prolonged lifting.

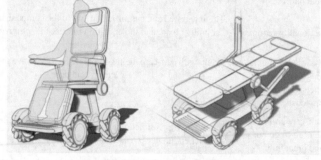

Fig. 1 Sketch of concept idea

Furthermore, three usage modes were designed: sitting and driving, reclining, and lying flat, as illustrated in Figure 2. These flexible functional modes provide comfortable driving and resting experiences for mild to moderately disabled elderly individuals, preventing issues such as body tension reflex and inadequate compensatory control abilities that can arise from maintaining the same posture for extended periods[11]. The integration of a one-key startup feature enables this innovative usage mode to transition from the bed to the wheelchair without the assistance of a caregiver[14], empowering disabled elderly individuals to develop self-care skills, reduce caregiving time, and alleviate negative emotions.

Fig. 2 Schematic diagram of three usage modes

In the design, addressing the issue of aesthetics in traditional wheelchairs, the paper focused on a design positioning that emphasizes lightweight, simplicity, and fashion. Figure 3 showcases the utilization of chassis space to conceal various exposed components typically found in traditional wheelchairs, including shock absorbers, lift systems, batteries, and cruise sensing systems. This integration results in a streamlined exterior appearance that exudes a sense of solidity and stability. The seat, lumbar support, and backrest are fixed by backrest supports and back connecting rods, with the elongated back connecting rods emphasizing a lightweight visual feature. The left and right armrests can be folded downward through the armrest pivot axis. The drive wheels are positioned at the front of the wheelchair for maneuverability both indoors and outdoors, while the auxiliary wheels are located at the rear of the driven wheels, providing balance support when users are lying flat for rest. The overall design layout breaks away from the loose structure of traditional wheelchairs, providing the foundational framework for creating a modern, sleek, and integrated intelligent mobility aid.

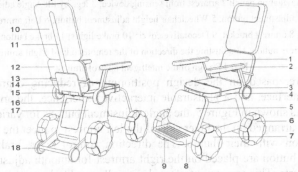

1 left armrest; 2 Right armrest; 3 handrail rotating shaft; 4 seats; 5 leg leans; 6 driving wheels; 7 driven wheel; 8 foot pedal; 9 Cruise sensing system; 10 Lean back; 11 back connecting rod; 12 lumbar support; 13 Seat belt; 14 backrest bracket; 15 Connecting shaft; 16 battery; 17 chassis; 18 training wheels
Fig. 3 Design of the key part

4.1.2 Smart control system design

A smart wheelchair should consist of three main modules: wireless communication, wheelchair propulsion, and intelligent detection, to enhance its safety, intelligence, and convenience[15]. This design adopts a simplified and integrated approach, and after multiple design tests, it was determined to integrate the intelligent module into the armrest position. The main purpose of this integration is to make it convenient for disabled elderly individuals to perform relevant operations within easy reach.

As shown in Figure 4, the intelligent control armrest design includes integrated modules in both the left and right armrests. The left armrest integrates the central control navigation wireless communication module and the drive module for adjusting the legrest and backrest tilt angles. The right armrest integrates drive modules for adjusting the direction control lever, emergency calls, brakes, and wheelchair height adjustment to accommodate various operations during driving. The front and rear side of both left and right armrests feature built-in object sensing modules, which promptly detect pedestrians or objects approaching the wheelchair, allowing for automatic evasion or stopping to prevent collisions. The central control navigation wireless communication module is positioned at the front of the left armrest, primarily assisting users with navigation and communication functions. It records the locations where elderly individuals frequently use the wheelchair, plans the most commonly used routes, and thereby enhances travel efficiency [16-17]. The control lever module is located at the front of the right armrest, with a visually intuitive and understandable design that aligns with user cognitive experience and operating habits, helping users better control the wheelchair's direction.

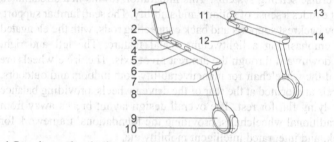

1 Central control navigation panel; 2 armrest front sensing device; 3 legs by tilt Angle adjustment button; 4 backrest tilt Angle adjustment button; 5 Wheelchair height adjustment button; 6 Left armrest; 7 armrest rear induction device; 8 armrest bracket; 9 Decorative cover; 10 brake lights; 11 brake button; 12 Emergency distress button; 13 adjusting the direction of the remote rod; 14 Right armrest

Fig. 4 Design of the intelligent control armrest

Furthermore, based on the design positioning of reducing cognitive load, an intuitive user interface, and a pleasurable interactive experience, the armrest interface was designed. As shown in Figure 5, the angle adjustment buttons for various wheelchair components are arranged on the inner side of the left armrest to meet the user's need for flexible operation with their thumb. The direction control lever, brake button, and emergency call button are placed on the right armrest for smooth adjustment of travel direction and alerts. This armrest interface design allows elderly users to quickly enjoy the smart control fun brought by one-key startup, even with reduced assistance from caregivers. This, in turn, stimulates a joyful driving experience and enhances the user's attachment to the smart wheelchair.

Fig. 5 Interface design of the armrest

4.2 Three-Dimensional Design

(1) Exterior Design. To further increase the acceptance of the smart wheelchair among disabled elderly individuals, an overall design was created that is harmonious, simple, and conveys a sense of motion. As shown in Figure 6, the bottom chassis of the smart wheelchair and the top seat form an aesthetic visual contrast: the large-volume chassis features bold edges and a cool dark color, enhancing driving stability while conveying a sense of motion and technology. The seat part incorporates rounded lines and a light beige color tone, adding softness and warmth to the overall design. The slightly concave seat surface in the middle and the shock-absorbing mechanism effectively cushion vibrations from the ground, improving the product's support and comfort. The inclusion of safety buckles prevents users from tilting to the side, increasing the product's sense of security. The design of the handles follows a smooth and rounded cross-sectional shape that is flat on the top and bottom, providing an ergonomic grip.

Fig. 6 Design scheme of intelligent wheelchair

The stylish and sporty appearance imparts an elegant outdoor travel experience, not only enhancing the user's affinity for the smart wheelchair but also boosting their confidence and dignity during travel. Importantly, it helps disabled elderly individuals actively integrate into outdoor activities and gain more emotional support from the outside world. An outdoor usage scenario is depicted in Figure 7.

Fig. 7 Scenario diagram of outdoor usage

(2) Overall Dimension Design. Based on the design positioning of space-saving and reducing overall volume, size parameters were determined using Chinese elderly size models and biomechanical parameters [18], considering various postures adopted by disabled elderly individuals during wheelchair use. As shown in Figure 8, the main dimensions of the wheelchair are: length 1210mm, width 770mm, height 1100mm, seat height 460mm, armrest height 210mm, and central control screen height 170mm. When in the expanded state, the wheelchair's length dimension is 1780mm, meeting the usage needs of most disabled elderly individuals. The seat dimensions are: width 450mm, depth 460mm. Additionally, three reclining positions were determined through three-dimensional virtual simulation experiments: sitting at 100 degree, reclining for a short rest at 112 degree, and lying down at 175 degree, allowing disabled elderly individuals to achieve various relaxation positions.

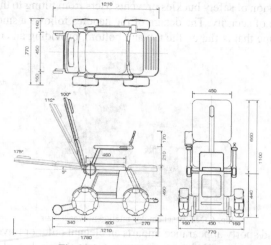

Fig. 8 Diagram of dimensional design

4.3 Structural Design

(1) Backrest Adjustment Structure Design. Multiple degrees of freedom adjustment for the backrest are achieved using direct-drive control technology. As shown in Figure 9, the core components consist of a die-cast aluminum backrest frame and an electric motor. The die-cast aluminum backrest frame is fixed to the back of the lumbar support, while the motor is fixed inside the seat. The motor drives a worm gear transmission

device, which in turn drives the rotating gear to maintain a constant speed of operation, thereby moving the backrest frame. The backrest linkage rod serves to connect the lumbar support and the backrest. Users can easily adjust the reclining position of the wheelchair by pressing the backrest angle adjustment button on the inside of the left armrest. Compared to traditional hydraulic adjustment methods, electric power-driven control provides better positioning accuracy and flexibility, allowing users to achieve the desired backrest adjustment angles.

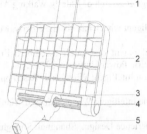

1 back connecting rod; 2 backrest bracket; 3 Turboworm transmission device; 4 rotation gear; 5 Motor

Fig. 9 Structure design of electric drive

(2) Height Adjustment Structure Design. The wheelchair's height adjustment is achieved using a lift platform height adjustment structure to reduce height differences during body movement for disabled elderly individuals. As shown in Figure 10, an electric motor drives a worm gear transmission device to rotate. This rotation drives the lead screw in synchronization, which, in turn, moves the movable rollers forward and backward [19]. Support bars connect to the seat fixed bracket, and a rotating axis serves to connect the two support bars, enabling relative movement of the movable rollers to achieve the lifting and lowering function of the seat.

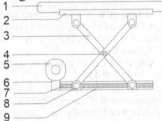

1 seat surface; 2 seat surface fixed bracket; 3 support rod; 4 axis of rotation; 5 Motor; 6 Turbo worm transmission device; 7 screw rod; 8 Activity roller; 9 Baseplate

Fig. 10 Structure design of height adjustment

5. Conclusion

This design proposal, with its thoughtful humanistic care, satisfaction of emotional needs for mildly and moderately disabled elderly individuals, and effective reduction of caregiving costs, was awarded the 2022 Red Dot Design Award in Germany. The approach primarily involved user research methods to understand the common needs of disabled elderly individuals and caregivers, leading to a well-defined design positioning.

Significant improvements were made to the main functions, external aesthetics, dimensions, and core structure of the smart wheelchair. The resulting design offers three resting modes and a novel smart control experience. It is characterized by low caregiving burden and excellent driving experience. It not only effectively reduces the physical and mental burden on caregivers but also helps disabled elderly individuals build confidence and dignity in their mobility. This design provides valuable insights for the development of intelligent assistive devices for vulnerable groups.

References

[1] Victor Papanek. Design for the Real World. Translated by Zhou Bo. Beijing: CITIC Publishing House, 2022.

[2] Zhang Lu, Li Ting. Modular Design Research of Elderly Walking Aids Based on User Needs. Think Tank Era, 2020, 50(12): 294-297.

[3] Li Xuelian. Design study on intelligent wheelchair for the elderly. Mechanical Design, 2014, 31(04): 100-104.

[4] Zhan Hang. Research and Development of Module-assembled Emg-assiited Rehabilitation Intelligent Wheelchair. Jilin: Northeast Electric Power University, 2022.

[5] Zhao Yufei. Design and Research on Intelligent Wheelchair Based on Ergonomics. Hefei: Hefei University of Technology, 2016.

[6] Yang Kaisi. Research of Detachable Intelligent Wheelchair Bed. Tianjin: Tianjin University of Technology, 2019.

[7] Han Ting. User Research and Experience Design. Shanghai: Shanghai Jiao Tong University Press, 2021.

[8] Luo Yimin. Study on Intelligent Elderly Functional Electric Wheelchair and Disabled Elderly Life Reconstruction. Standard Science, 2019, (01): 108-111.

[9] Ge Hongyan. Research on the Design of Mobile Assistant Products with Limited Light and Moderate Activities. Chengdu: Southwest Jiaotong University, 2019.

[10] Zhong Yulan. Design Research of Life Care Assistive Device for Elders with Disabilities in Inclusive Design [D]. Wuhan: Wuhan University of Technology, 2018.

[11] Xiong Jian, Huang Qun. Elderly Walker Navigation Folding Electric Car Design and Research. Science and Technology & Innovation, 2015(11): 89-90.

[12] Li Yuejie. Design and research of daily travel substitutefor the elderly with mild disability. Jinan: Shandong University of Art and Design, 2020.

[13] Xia Jing, Wang Xiuhong, Li Fang, et al.The Correlation between Self-efficacy of the Elderly with Mild or Moderate Disability at Home and Depression of Family Caregivers. Journal of Guizhou Medical University, 2019(08): 927-935.

[14] Cheng Shen, Qiuping Bi, Huanzhi Lou, et al. A new designed intelligent wheelchair with elevating lazyback. 16th IEEE Conference on Industrial Electronics and Applications, 2021(01): 136-141.

[15] Li Jiadong, Zou Cunzhi, Sun Yuanao, et al. Multifunctional Service Smart Elderly Wheelchair. Scientific and Technological Innovation, 2020, (16): 10-11.

[16] Zhong Guangming, Liu Jieping, Xing Haolin, et al. Innovative design of elderly electric rehabilitation wheelchair. Mechanical Design, 2023(03): 149-154.

[17] Jian Kong, Peng Li. Path planning of a multifunctional elderly intelligent wheelchair based on the sensor and fuzzy Bayesian network algorithm. Journal of Sensors, 2022(09): 1-13.

[18] Zhou Hui. Structure Design and Research on Motor-Driven Chair of The Old Man. Hangzhou: Zhejiang University of Technology, 2015.

[19] Wang Haibo, Liu Yu, Li Yingfu, et al. The Design and Realization of UG Based Auxiliary Wheelchair Assisting the Elderly to Sit and Rise. Modern Manufacturing Technology and Equipment, 2021, 57(08): 40-42.

Design Studies and Intelligence Engineering
L.C. Jain et al. (Eds.)

doi:10.3233/FAIA231454

Deep Subspace K-Means Clustering for Syringe Defect Detection Without Defective Samples

Fei YAN[a] , Xiaodong WANG[a], Longfu HONG[a], Zhiyao XIE[a]
[a] *College of Computer and Information Engineering, Xiamen University of Technology,*
Xiamen, China

Abstract. Modern clustering techniques are becoming more popular, but traditional clustering methods often heavily rely on artificial feature extraction, costing too much human labor resources. This task is especially important when it comes to finding surface defects on medical syringes. To solve this problem, our study comes up with a new way to detect syringe defects without defective samples using deep fuzzy subspace clustering in a smooth way. In particular, our method combines conventional fuzzy c-means and deep autoencoder into a joint framework. During the clustering process, the autoencoder part automatically extract features from dataset itself and generates the representative feature embeddings. After the feature extraction, the fuzzy clustering is performed to find the optimal data structure. This "feature learning, fuzzy clustering" process is iteratively performed until the objective function converges. This new method improves the accuracy and reliability of clustering by a lot, which makes it a great choice for finding scale defects on medical syringes. The efficacy of our method is evaluated on four publicly accessible datasets and one medical syringe dataset. The results demonstrate its potential to revolutionize the field of surface defect detection in this critical domain.

Keywords. Defect detection, medical syringe, clustering, autoencoder

1. Introduction

In real-world syringe production lines, scale defect detection is a critical step to control syringe quality. However, due to the variability in syringe materials and uncertainty of regarding the types of defects, it is hard to collect sufficient training samples in a supervised manner. In this case, recent studies commonly employ clustering to accomplish this task. Clustering is a fundamental data processing approach that involves the organization of data into separate clusters. This process is guided by the idea that entities exhibiting similarities tend to stay together. Generally, clustering approaches aim to enable a significant level of similarity within individual clusters while simultaneously reducing the similarity across samples originating from different clusters. Over the course of time, there has been significant research conducted on clustering algorithms, achieving lots of successes in many domains such as data mining [1], pattern recognition [2], and defect detection [3].

The K-means (KM) algorithm is well recognized as a prominent clustering technique because of its straightforwardness and minimal processing burden. However, KM works in a "hard" membership assignment manner, which can be easily affected by noise and may confront degraded clustering performance. To address these limitations, some researchers have proposed "soft" clustering approaches, which allows each data point to be assigned to multiple clusters. For example, Bezdek [4] proposed a fuzzy c-means (FCM) clustering, which relaxes the hard membership assignment constraint to a soft one. Additionally, Xu et al. [5] imposes a robust loss function to deal with data with noise. However, these methods work in the original high-dimensional feature space, which usually contains redundant features and noisy features. These features may impact the performance of the clustering algorithms and lead to suboptimal results. To cope with this issue, many researchers proposed to reduce the feature dimension by transforming the original data into low-dimensional feature space. For example, Wang et al. [6] integrated feature selection into graph clustering, which can remove the noisy features among data while improving clustering performance. However, the above subspace clustering methods heavily rely on the handcrafted features, which require time-consuming feature engineering and domain-dependent knowledge. To deeply analyze the useful information among data, recent studies tend to integrate the deep learning techniques into the clustering procedure. For instance, Shaham et al. [7] transformed conventional spectral clustering into a deep learning framework using a Siamese network. However, these deep clustering methods highly depend on the Laplacian matrix, which consumes too much computation and memory resources. In contrast, some other methods perform clustering without the help of the Laplacian matrix. For example, Xie et al. [8] proposed a deep autoencoder-based clustering framework, where the feature encoding and clustering modules are jointly performed to boost each other's performance. However, these methods are "hard" type clustering methods and suffer from slow convergence in model optimization, which may be hard to meet the demand for real-world applications. To overcome this problem, Zhang et al. [9] proposed an adaptive deep fuzzy clustering framework, which employs an entropy regularization to reduce the influence of noisy samples. Nevertheless, this method contains too many hyperparameters, which is impractical for real-world applications.

To tackle the foregoing challenges, this paper provides a deep fuzzy clustering strategy for syringe defect detection. Finding that in real-world industrial defect detection area it is hard to collect enough defective samples, we add deep a feature encoding strategy into the fuzzy c-means clustering procedure, making it can automatically learn the relevant features from data and groups data at the same time. The effectiveness of our method is verified with several commonly-used clustering methods on four publicly available datasets. In addition, we propose a blob-similarity-based unsupervised clustering method. This method first segments the syringe scales using non-defective samples and extracts the scale blocks to reduce feature dimension and filter out noise. We test our method on one real-world syringe dataset. Experimental findings verify the effectiveness of our method.

2. Methodology

In this section, we provide a detailed overview of the proposed framework for identifying medical syringe defects. Our method contains two main steps, that is, clustering phase and scale extraction phrase. In the clustering phase, we feed the input data into deep autoencoder to obtain the feature embeddings. After that, the fuzzy c-means clustering is performed with these feature embeddings in a joint framework. Finally, to cope with the defect detection issue for syringe scale, we propose a blob-similarity-based approach to extract the semantic information among scales, which is beneficial for scale defect detection.

2.1. Fuzzy C-means with Deep Feature Encoding

Given a dataset $\mathbf{X} = [x_1, x_2, \cdots, x_N] \in R^{D \times N}$ containing n data points with D features, the goal of KM type clustering methods is to partition $\mathbf{X}$ into groups, so that samples within the same cluster exhibit a higher degree of similarity, while samples between different clusters exhibit a lower degree of similarity. Let $\mathbf{V} = [v_1, v_2, \cdots, v_C] \in R^{D \times C}$ represent the cluster center matrix and v_i represent the center for the ith cluster, where C is the total number of clusters. Let $\mathbf{Y} = [y_1, y_2, \cdots, y_N]^T \in \{0,1\}^{N \times C}$ be the cluster indicator matrix for $\mathbf{X}$. $y_{ij} = 1$ if the ith sample is a member of the jth cluster, $y_{ij} = 0$ otherwise. Subsequently, the objective function of FCM can be stated as:

$$\min_{\mathbf{Y}\mathbf{1}_C = \mathbf{1}_N, \mathbf{Y} > 0, v_j} \sum_{i=1}^{N} \sum_{j=1}^{C} y_{ij}^m \|x_i - v_j\|_2^2, \tag{1}$$

where $\mathbf{Y} > 0$ indicates that all of the elements in $\mathbf{Y}$ are strictly greater than zero. m is the fuzzifier parameter (ranging from $[1, \infty]$), which plays a crucial role in determining the degree to which each data point is associated with a specific cluster. A larger value of fuzzifier parameter m signifies an increased level of fuzziness inside the clusters. This implies that data points possess membership degrees that are distributed over numerous clusters, leading to more flexible boundaries between clusters. On the other hand, a smaller value of m will result in more distinct boundaries between clusters, as data points will exhibit stronger membership in a single cluster. The inherent flexibility of the FCM framework enables its applicability to a diverse array of datasets.

Our method aims to utilize the power of feature encoding ability of deep learning technique for fuzzy c-means clustering. Following previous works [9], we impose the deep feature autoencoder (AE) model to automatically learn the underlying semantic information among data. This AE model contains $L + 1$ layer (L is an even number), where the first $\frac{L}{2}$ layers form an encoder to reduce the dimensionality of the input data, the last $\frac{L}{2}$ layers form a decoder to reconstruct the data. After each hidden layer, we use a tanh activation function, that is, $f_{tanh}(\cdot)$ to explore the nonlinear information within the input data. Guided by the squared error loss function, the proposed method can be formulated as:

$$\min_{\mathbf{W}^{(l)}, \mathbf{b}^{(l)}, \mathbf{Y}, \mathbf{V}} \sum_{i=1}^{N} \left\| h_i^{(L)} - x_i \right\|_F^2$$

$$+ \lambda_1 \sum_{i=1}^{N} \sum_{j=1}^{C} y_{ij}^m \left\| h_i^{\left(\frac{L}{2}\right)} - v_j \right\|_2^2 + \lambda_2 \sum_{l=1}^{L} \left(\left\| \mathbf{W}^{(l)} \right\|_F^2 + \left\| \mathbf{b}^{(l)} \right\|_2^2 \right), \tag{2}$$

where $\mathbf{W}^{(l)}$ and $\mathbf{b}^{(l)}$ are the weight matrix and bias of the lth layer, respectively. $h_i^{(l)}$ is the input of the lth layer. λ_1 and λ_2 are two user-defined parameters.

2.2. Optimization

Our objective function in Eq. (2) contains four kinds of hyperparameters, that is, $\mathbf{W}^{(l)}$, $\mathbf{b}^{(l)}$, $\mathbf{Y}$, and $\mathbf{V}$. In this section, we utilize the coordinate blocking technique to optimize it:

1) **Firstly, update $\mathbf{W}^{(l)}$ and $\mathbf{b}^{(l)}$ by fixing $\mathbf{Y}$ and $\mathbf{V}$.** According to the definition of $h_i^{(l)}$ and the SGD algorithm, we can update $\mathbf{W}^{(l)}$ and $\mathbf{b}^{(l)}$ as follows:

$$\begin{cases} \mathbf{W}^{(l)} = \mathbf{W}^{(l)} - \gamma \nabla_{\mathbf{W}^{(l)}} \mathcal{F} \\ \mathbf{b}^{(l)} = \mathbf{b}^{(l)} - \gamma \nabla_{\mathbf{b}^{(l)}} \mathcal{F}, \end{cases} \tag{3}$$

where γ is the learning rate. $\nabla_{\mathbf{W}^{(l)}} \mathcal{F}$ and $\nabla_{\mathbf{b}^{(l)}} \mathcal{F}$ are defined as:

$$\begin{cases} \nabla_{\mathbf{W}^{(l)}} \mathcal{F} = \delta_i^{(l)} h_i^{(l-1)^T} + \lambda_2 \mathbf{W}^{(l)} \\ \nabla_{\mathbf{b}^{(l)}} \mathcal{F} = \delta_i^{(l)} + \lambda_2 \mathbf{b}^{(l)}, \end{cases} \tag{4}$$

where $\delta_i^{(l)}$ is defined as

$$\delta_i^{(l)} = \begin{cases} \left(\mathbf{W}^{(l+1)} \delta_i^{(l+1)} + \lambda_1 \Lambda_i^{(l)} \right) \odot f_{tanh}'\left(z_i^{(l)}\right) & l \neq L \\ \left(\mathbf{h}^{(l)} - \mathbf{h}_i^{(0)} \right) \odot f_{tanh}'\left(z_i^{(l)}\right), & l = L \end{cases} \tag{5}$$

where $\Lambda_i^{(l)}$ is defined as

$$\Lambda_i^{(l)} = \begin{cases} \left(\mathbf{h}_i^{(l)} \mathbf{1}^T - \mathbf{V} \right) y_i & l = \dfrac{L}{2} \\ 0, & l \neq \dfrac{L}{2} \end{cases} \tag{6}$$

where $z_i^{(l)}$ is the input of lth layer and $\odot$ is the element-wise multiplication.

2) **Secondly, update $\mathbf{V}$ by fixing $\mathbf{W}^{(l)}$ and $\mathbf{b}^{(l)}$, and $\mathbf{Y}$.** By taking the derivative of Eq. (2) with respective to v_j and set it to 0, we have:

$$v_j = \frac{\sum_{i=1}^N y_{ij}^m h_i^{\left(\frac{L}{2}\right)}}{\sum_{i=1}^N y_{ij}^m}. \tag{7}$$

3) **Finally, update $\mathbf{Y}$ by fixing $\mathbf{W}^{(l)}$ and $\mathbf{b}^{(l)}$, and $\mathbf{V}$.** By letting $d_{ij} = \left\| h_i^{\frac{L}{2}} - v_j \right\|_2^2$ and following the optimization procedure of FCM [4], we have:

$$y_{ij} = \frac{d_{ij}^{-\frac{2}{m-1}}}{\sum_{j=1}^C d_{ij}^{-\frac{2}{m-1}}}. \tag{8}$$

According to the above optimization steps, we can iteratively update $\mathbf{W}^{(l)}$, $\mathbf{b}^{(l)}$, $\mathbf{Y}$, and $\mathbf{V}$ until the model converges.

2.3. Unsupervised Syringe Scale Defect Detection

In real-world syringe production lines, syringe scale defects are one of the most commonly encountered defects on syringes. Despite defective items being relatively rare, when such an occurrence does happen, it can have significant consequences for humans, such as infections and injuries. Therefore, it is highly motivated to ensure the quality and safety of syringe products to avoid such consequences. However, there are several challenges for the syringe scale defect detection task: 1) Owing to the complexity of syringe production line, syringe scale defects vary dynamically; 2) Due to the fast production speed and low defect rate, it is hard to collect enough detective syringe samples. In this case, it is impractical to finish this task in a supervised manner. To cope with these challenges, based on our deep fuzzy clustering framework above, we propose a blob-similarity type syringe scale defect detection method. The flowchart of this method is shown in Fig.1. The detailed procedures of the proposed method are listed as follows:

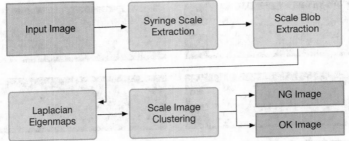

Figure 1. The flowchart of our syringe defect detection.

Scale Extraction. We first extract the individual scales or regions of interest (ROIs) from the syringe images using the deep segmentation model in [3], only utilizing the non-defective syringe images, which can be easily collected.

Blob Extraction. After extracting scales, we utilize image processing techniques to detect scale blobs within each scale. Concretely, we use connected components with 8-connectivity to locate the scale blobs. Then, the attributes of these blobs, including location and area, are identified to represent each scale.

Laplacian Eigenmaps Extraction. To further learn the high-level semantic information among each blob, we construct a similarity matrix on blobs extracted above and apply Laplacian Eigenmaps to reduce the dimensionality of the feature space while retaining essential information about the relationships between blobs.

Scale Image Clustering. Finally, we apply our deep fuzzy clustering to cluster the image data into two groups, namely, the normal group and the defective group.

3. Experiments

3.1. Datasets and Compared Methods

Four publicly available datasets, that is, UMIST [2], JAFFE [10], YALE [11] and ORL [12] are used to validate our proposed method and the other compared methods. Besides, one real-world syringe dataset (SYRINGE) collected from the actual production line of medical syringes is also used to verify the effectiveness of our method. This syringe dataset captured by industrial cameras consists of 590 normal images and 567 defective images. Following [3], these defective images are artificially generated from normal images with various kinds of defects, including "broken", "length abnormal", "excessive", "width abnormal", "missing", and "other". Some typical syringe images are shown in Fig. 2. A detailed description of these datasets is exhibited in Table 1. Six popular clustering methods are chosen for comparison. These methods are briefly described as follows.

1) **KM.** It is a classic hard clustering method that is simple and efficient.

Table 1. Detailed description of the selected datasets.

Name	Size	Dimensionality	Class
ORL	400	1024	40
YALE	165	1024	15
JAFFE	213	1024	10
UMIST	575	1024	20
SYRINGE	1157	13440	2

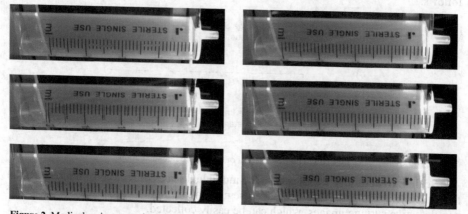

Figure 2. Medical syringe samples with defects (the first column) and without defects (the second column).

2) RSFKM [5]. It utilizes the group sparse technique to improve the robustness of its loss function over outliers.

3) FCM [4]. It imposes a fuzziness parameter to allow each data point to attach to multiple clusters. FCM is suitable for many applications where the "hard" clustering methods (such as KM) fail.

4) AE [13]. It is a two-step deep clustering method that first applies AE to obtain the feature embedding from the data and then utilizes other clustering methods to get the final clustering results.

5) DEC [8]. Unlike AE, it combines AE and clustering into a unified framework.

6) DFKM [9]. It is a deep fuzzy K-means clustering method, which imposes an adaptive loss function and robust entropy regularization.

3.2. Experimental Settings

We implement our method using Pytorch and train it for M epochs with a batch size of 16 on an NVIDIA GeForce GTX 2080 Ti GPU using the Adam algorithm. Table 2 shows the detailed experimental settings of our method for different datasets. Three evaluation criteria, namely, Accuracy (ACC), Purity, and Normalized Mutual Information (NMI), are chosen in this paper. Detailed definitions of these evaluation criteria can be found in [9,14]. For the compared methods, we chose their best hyperparameters following the strategy in [9]. Our method has five hyperparameters, that is, λ_1, λ_2, γ, M, and m. We set $\gamma = 0.001$ and $m = 1.2$. For λ_1 and λ_2, we tune them from {0.001, 0.01, 0.1, 1, 10, 100, 1000}. All the compared methods are run 10 times, and the average results along with the standard deviation, are reported.

Table 2. Parameter Settings for Five Selected Datasets.

Datasets	λ_1	λ_2	lr	M	m	Struct
ORL	1	0.01	1×10^{-3}	50	1.2	1024-512-200-512-1024
YALE	1	0.01	1×10^{-3}	50	1.2	1024-512-300-512-1024
JAFFE	1	0.01	1×10^{-3}	50	1.2	1024-512-200-512-1024
UMIST	1	0.01	1×10^{-3}	50	1.2	1024-512-300-512-1024
SYRINGE	1	0.01	1×10^{-3}	50	1.2	50-32-10-32-50

Table 3. Clustering performance (ACC%) of different methods on four public datasets.

Datasets	KM	FCM	RSFKM	AE	DEC	DFKM	Ours
ORL	58.75±3.03	60.15±1.38	25.62±2.51	51.87±2.32	27.45±8.56	**61.43±1.64**	**62.33±0.02**
YALE	38.36±4.57	47.39±2.81	30.36±3.99	40.24±3.45	42.30±1.45	**51.43±1.73**	**49.12±0.04**
JAFFE	88.52±5.60	89.91±5.56	58.92±6.49	84.79±4.77	62.95±8.66	**90.83±5.18**	**91.23±0.76**
UMIST	41.90±3.07	43.66±1.78	29.46±3.73	42.61±1.81	36.47±3.36	**45.57±1.08**	**45.97±0.01**

Table 4. Clustering performance (NMI%) of different methods on four public datasets.

Datasets	KM	FCM	RSFKM	AE	DEC	DFKM	Ours
ORL	77.58±1.08	76.97±0.69	53.19±2.32	72.80±1.05	55.22±7.99	**81.13±0.97**	**79.54±0.05**
YALE	48.17±2.89	**53.04±1.54**	35.74±3.06	46.93±2.22	48.71±1.49	**55.92±1.61**	52.36±0.07
JAFFE	89.41±3.51	90.85±4.32	68.23±3.35	85.41±2.57	82.83±2.75	**92.01±3.07**	**94.13±0.11**
UMIST	64.86±1.51	65.63±0.97	44.52±4.62	63.77±1.73	56.96±5.79	**67.04±1.45**	**65.71±0.03**

3.3. Performance Comparison on Public Datasets

Table 3-5 present the clustering performance of all the compared methods on four public datasets, where the top two results are bolded. From these results, we can see that in most cases, the fuzzy type clustering methods, that is, FCM, DFKM, and our method, outperform the KM type clustering methods. This indicates that imposing the soft membership assignment is beneficial for clustering. Besides, the deep fuzzy clustering methods, that is, DFKM and our method, are superior to the other methods, indicating the importance of the deep feature encoding module for clustering. Lastly, our method achieves competitive results with DFKM. It should be noted that our method has fewer hyperparameters compared to DFKM, making it more efficient in model deployment for real-world applications.

3.4. Performance Analysis on the SYRINGE Dataset

We apply our method to one real-world syringe dataset. In this experiment, we follow the scale extraction steps in Section 2.3 to obtain the Laplacian Eigenmaps and perform our deep learning clustering method on them. It should be noted that during the similarity matrix construction process, we utilize a fully-connected similarity graph with an Euclidean distance metric. Besides, the dimension of Laplacian Eigenmaps is set to 50. Detailed clustering results are shown in Table 6, where BK refers to "broken", LA refers to "length abnormal", WA refers to "width abnormal", EX refers to "excessive", MIS refers to "missing", OT refers to "other", and OK refers to the normal image. We can see that our method can better identify defective syringes. Concretely, our method only misclassifies 10 samples out of 567 samples, achieving 98.24% average ACC. This demonstrates that our method is practical for real-world applications. Besides, the highest misclassified samples occurred in "broken" category. To better understand how our method works, we illustrate some of the misclassified sample in Fig. 3. In this figure,

Table 5. Clustering performance (Purity%) of different methods on four public datasets.

Datasets	KM	FCM	RSFKM	AE	DEC	DFKM	Ours
ORL	63.90±2.12	64.42±1.02	26.98±2.57	57.22±1.63	28.93±10.08	**68.35±1.12**	65.50±0.01
YALE	42.42±3.27	48.12±2.68	41.33±3.41	42.06±2.22	43.52±1.24	**52.73±1.68**	49.49±0.02
JAFFE	88.16±4.92	88.22±7.07	61.31±5.85	85.26±3.43	**95.21±2.38**	91.25±4.23	92.20±0.87
UMIST	50.43±1.80	51.57±1.72	32.09±4.25	49.18±1.76	42.61±5.54	53.67±1.15	**54.17±0.03**

Table 6. Detection Results on the SYRINGE dataset.

Metric	BK	LA	WA	EX	MIS	OT	OK
ACC (%)	91.00	100.00	98.90	100	100	100	71.99
Numbers	100	88	91	94	109	85	590

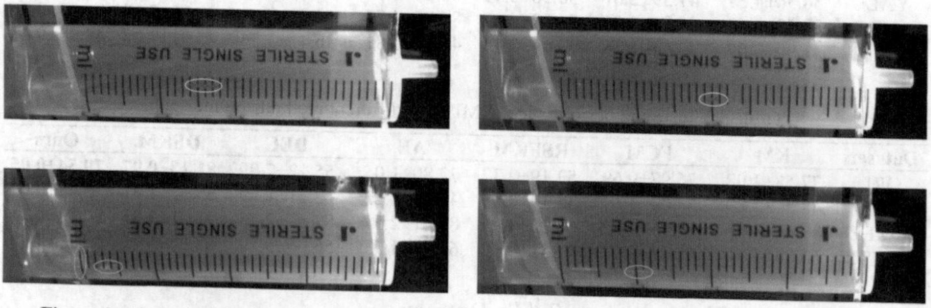

Figure 3. Medical syringe samples with defects (the first row) and without defects (the second row).

the first row shows the "broken" samples, while the second row presents the normal samples. We can see that these misclassified "Broken" samples contain some quite small defects (marked by green circles), which are hard to identify. In addition, we can see that the normal samples in the second row contain some light streaks produced on the surface of the syringe due to the illumination of the lighting. These light streaks are quite similar to defects, making them hard to identify.

4. Conclusion and Future Work

This paper addresses the challenges associated with traditional clustering methods, which heavily rely on artificial feature extraction and thus consume significant human labor resources. Concretely, we have introduced a novel approach that detects scale defects on medical syringes without requiring defective samples. Our method employs deep fuzzy subspace clustering, which combines fuzzy c-means with a deep autoencoder in a unified framework. Our method significantly enhances the accuracy and reliability of clustering, positioning it as an excellent choice for surface defect detection on medical syringes. Extensive experimental results on four publicly available datasets, as well as a real-world medical syringe dataset, clearly demonstrate the effectiveness of our method.

5. Acknowledgments

This paper was supported by National Natural Science Foundation of China (Grant No. U1805264), National Natural Science Foundation of Fujian Province (Grant Nos.

2023J011428, 2021J011186, 2022J011236), Program of XMUT for High-level Talents Introduction Plan (Grant No. YKJ20016R), Scientific Research Fund of Fujian Provincial Education Department (Grant Nos. JAT200486, JAT200478), University Industry Research Fund of Xiamen (Grant Nos. 2023CXY0413, 2022CXY0416).

References

[1] Chenhui Gao, Wenzhi Chen, Feiping Nie, Weizhong Yu, and Feihu Yan. Subspace clustering by directly solving discriminative k-means. Knowledge-Based Systems, 252:109452, 2022.

[2] Chenping Hou, Feiping Nie, Xuelong Li, Dongyun Yi, and Yi Wu. Joint embedding learning and sparse regression: A framework for unsupervised feature selection. IEEE Trans. Cybern., 44(6):793–804, 2014.

[3] Xiaodong Wang, Xianwei Xu, Yanli Wang, Pengtao Wu, Fei Yan, and Zhiqiang Zeng. A robust defect detection method for syringe scale without positive samples. The Visual Computer, 2022.

[4] James C. Bezdek. A convergence theorem for the fuzzy isodata clustering algorithms. IEEE Transactions on Pattern Analysis and Machine Intelligence, PAMI-2(1):1–8, 1980.

[5] Jinglin Xu, Junwei Han, Kai Xiong, and Feiping Nie. Robust and sparse fuzzy k-means clustering. In Proceedings of the Twenty-Fifth International Joint Conference on Artificial Intelligence, page 2224–2230. AAAI Press, 2016.

[6] Xiaodong Wang, Pengtao Wu, Qinghua Xu, Zhiqiang Zeng, and Yong Xie. Joint image clustering and feature selection with auto-adjoined learning for high-dimensional data. Knowledge-Based Systems, 232:107443, 2021.

[7] Uri Shaham, Kelly P. Stanton, Henry Li, Ronen Basri, Boaz Nadler, and Yuval Kluger. Spectralnet: Spectral clustering using deep neural networks. In 6th International Conference on Learning Representations, ICLR 2018, Vancouver, BC, Canada, April 30 - May 3, 2018, Conference Track Proceedings, 2018.

[8] Junyuan Xie, Ross B. Girshick, and Ali Farhadi. Unsupervised deep embedding for clustering analysis. In Proceedings of the 33nd International Conference on Machine Learning, ICML 2016, New York City, NY, USA, June 19-24, 2016, volume 48 of JMLR Workshop and Conference Proceedings, pages 478–487, 2016.

[9] Rui Zhang, Xuelong Li, Hongyuan Zhang, and Feiping Nie. Deep fuzzy k-means with adaptive loss and entropy regularization. IEEE Trans. Fuzzy Syst., 28(11):2814–2824, 2020.

[10] Michael J. Lyons, Julien Budynek, and Shigeru Akamatsu. Automatic classification of single facial images. IEEE Trans. Pattern Anal. Mach. Intell., 21(12):1357–1362, 1999.

[11] Athinodoros S. Georghiades, Peter N. Belhumeur, and David J. Kriegman. From few to many: Illumination cone models for face recognition under variable lighting and pose. IEEE Trans. Pattern Anal. Mach. Intell., 23(6):643–660, 2001.

[12] Deng Cai, Chiyuan Zhang, and Xiaofei He. Unsupervised feature selection for multi-cluster data. In Proceedings of the 16th ACM SIGKDD International Conference on Knowledge Discovery and Data Mining, Washington, DC, USA, pages 333–342. ACM, 2010.

[13] G. E. Hinton and R. R. Salakhutdinov. Reducing the dimensionality of data with neural networks. Science, 313(5786):504–507, 2006.

[14] Xiao-dong Wang, Rung-ching Chen, Fei Yan. High-dimensional Data Clustering Using K-means Subspace Feature Selection. Journal of Network Intelligence, 4(3):80-87, 2019

Design Studies and Intelligence Engineering
L.C. Jain et al. (Eds.)
© *2024 The Authors.*
This article is published online with Open Access by IOS Press and distributed under the terms
of the Creative Commons Attribution Non-Commercial License 4.0 (CC BY-NC 4.0).
doi:10.3233/FAIA231455

The Promotion of Cultural Heritage Protection Driven by Artificial Intelligence in the Context of Hemei Rural Construction

Min MA[1]

Department of Media, College of Arts, Hunan Women's University

Abstract: In order to use digital technology to protect intangible cultural heritage and regional culture, the innovative digital design of intangible cultural heritage is put forward from the perspective of Internet. This paper puts forward a collaborative innovative design method of "root carving technology+digitalization". Taking "Zhu Zhanghui's lecture" in Yuelu Academy as the representative, this paper explores the innovative methods of developing scene-based root carving products by regional culture. The results show that the acceptance of using light-cured resin as the accessory of root carving is not high, and the proportion of people in the industry who appreciate or accept it is only 71.3%. Developing the design around the basic model is conducive to improving production efficiency, ensuring the improvement of efficiency while retaining the uniqueness of hand made. The whole root carving product has a certain artistic conception and can appreciate the connection with the concept of time, but the specific story can be strengthened. Conclusion: Integrating the situational story method into the root carving design of Hunan School can enhance the overall atmosphere and story of the root carving works, enhance the story of the root carving cultural and creative products of Yuelu Academy, and be conducive to the promotion and dissemination of regional root carving culture and academy culture.

Keywords: root carving; Digitization of intangible heritage; Digital design; collaborative design

1. Introduction

The trend of the combination of culture and industrial manufacturing in China puts forward the actual demand for creative design, that is, to study the common key technologies based on China style, take cultural heritage (especially intangible cultural heritage) as a typical sample, study the cultural ecology, cultural forms and expression methods of China's historical development, as well as regional cultural differences and cultural values, comprehensively analyze the design elements of China's aesthetic characteristics, construct a framework model of China style, and realize the development of Chinese style design to intelligence and high-end. Intangible cultural heritage preserves national individuality and national aesthetic habits in a "living" state, and contains the unique spiritual value, thinking mode, imagination and cultural consciousness of the Chinese nation, which is the basic basis of China's design style and the classic cultural elements and prototype [1]. Because of its intangible, dynamic,

---

[1] Corresponding Author.

spatio-temporal characteristics, the increasing and accelerating globalization and modernization process have led to great changes in domestic cultural ecology, and the protection and development of intangible cultural heritage with sound, image and skills as the means of expression has encountered great challenges. In recent years, through database construction, digital application and big data analysis, digital technology provides a technical platform for the recording, preservation and dissemination of intangible cultural heritage in China, and also provides a new way for the inheritance, innovation and development of intangible cultural heritage. At the same time, many problems still exist, such as: (1) the research topics of intangible digital protection are relatively scattered, and there is no scientific protection model for the whole life cycle management of intangible digital information from the overall view of intangible resources; (2) Pay attention to presenting intangible cultural forms, and lack the display of intangible cultural structure and significance to explore the internal mechanism of non-genetic inheritance and innovation; (3) It is difficult to show the vitality of intangible cultural heritage and reflect the cultural creativity of inheritors [2]. In order to inherit and develop intangible cultural heritage, realize the activation and creative utilization of intangible cultural heritage, the concepts of participatory digital protection and productive protection came into being, which supported giving inheritors and owners the right to participate in digital protection, fully exploring the potential social and economic value of intangible cultural resources, and promoting the development of cultural industries through the transformation of creativity, creativity and innovation [3].

2. Literature review

Due to historical reasons in Italy, many intangible cultural heritages are scattered in private and church hands, which leads to many difficulties in practical protection. In order to solve this problem, Xu, Z. and others set up a society to manage and strengthen the sharing of these resources. The main work is registration, sorting and other control work, which makes further protection more convenient. For example, the "Internet Cultural Heritage Project" was established to provide people with resources that can be queried online. The system can integrate the resources of libraries and other related cultural institutions, and facilitate people and other institutions to obtain digital resources of intangible cultural heritage through online platforms and other channels [4].

The digital protection of French intangible cultural heritage in its national library has developed well. In 2003, the digital project Gallica completed the historical introduction of thousands of illustrations and related documents, nearly 10 million books and hundreds of thousands of still images. Król, K. and others started "Digitization of Cultural, Scientific and Educational Contents", which belongs to the project of "Investing in the Future" and planned digital cultural skills, mainly in the fields of books, music and images [5].

The research on intangible cultural heritage in China started late, starting in 2003, when the UNESCO Committee of the National People's Congress drafted the Draft Law on the Protection of Traditional Ethnic and Folk Cultures in People's Republic of China (PRC), which was later renamed the Law on the Protection of Intangible Cultural Heritage in People's Republic of China (PRC) (draft). In 2004, China became the sixth country to join the Convention for the Protection of Intangible Cultural Heritage, and it was not until recently in 2011 that the People's Republic of China (PRC) Intangible

Cultural Heritage Law was formally implemented. As people pay more and more attention to intangible cultural heritage, relevant theoretical works on intangible cultural heritage are also emerging one after another. Xie, R. and others have expressed their opinions. For example, The Paradox and New Path of the Protection of Intangible Cultural Heritage, The Origin, Current Situation and Related Issues of the Concept of Intangible Cultural Heritage, and Intangible Cultural Heritage Towards the Concept of Discipline have all sorted out and understood the definition and concept of intangible cultural heritage. For example, Protection and Utilization of Intangible Cultural Heritage, Re-understanding of the Characteristics and Protection of Intangible Cultural Heritage have made their own interpretations on how to protect intangible heritage [6]. The research on intangible cultural heritage abroad started earlier than that in China. Nikolakopoulou, V. and others first put forward the concept of "intangible cultural wealth" and promulgated the Law on the Protection of Cultural Property to define its category [7]. Cui, C. and others also promulgated relevant laws in 1962 to regulate their country's cultural property. It was not until the adoption of the Convention for the Protection of the World Cultural and Natural Heritage in 1972 that the worldwide protection activities officially began. In this Convention, the proposal on intangible cultural heritage was put forward for the first time. Although the proposal was rejected at that time, with the development of time, the concept of intangible cultural heritage was put forward and put on the agenda again with the attention of relevant government departments. It was not until 2003 that UNESCO promulgated and adopted the Convention for the Protection of Intangible Cultural Heritage, in which the connotation of intangible cultural heritage was clearly defined [8].

The main purposes of this product survey are: to understand the acceptance of "Zhu Zhang Zhi Hui" in the root carving industry; Discover the shortcomings of the product; Find the part with high user recognition and analyze the competitive advantage of the product. In this digital scene root carving design, the design method is quite different from traditional root carving products, and there is some innovation in the application of materials with scene root carving products. It is very important to investigate the market acceptance of innovative products.

3. Research methods

3.1 sketch design

Sketch is a key link in the initial stage of design, and it is an informal form used to describe the general idea of design. Based on the investigation, analysis and derivation process mentioned above, the project team will fully imagine and associate with the user perception model and product positioning and complete the preliminary modeling design of root carving products with full conceptual sketch design.

3.1.1 Concept sketch scheme

In the design process, the design requirements are often put forward in the form of keyword description and oral communication, or by collecting excellent similar designs to form an image version [9]. Designers need to use fragmented information and elements to guide the direction of subsequent design, and at the same time, they need to decompose and integrate the fragmented information elements semantically to form a complete design scheme.

The purpose of conceptual sketch scheme design is twofold. First, the important innovation of this root carving design is the application and integration of resin materials, which need to be integrated in conceptual design [10]. Secondly, the focus of the scene-based root carving is to make the theme of the story clear, and the conceptual design should be carried out under the principle of ensuring cultural identity and recognition, reflecting the core spirit of Zhu Zhanghui's speech. There are two basic types of root carving suitable for the theme of Zhu Zhanghui's lecture: ring type and tree type. It is necessary to complete the conceptual modeling design by constantly updating, iterating and trying the sketches around the two basic types and related design elements.

The design elements mainly focus on the relevant intention extraction of Zhu Zhanghui. In the story told by Zhu Zhanghui, in the category of humanistic elements, there are two people, Zhu Zhanger and the audience, and the architectural elements include lecture hall and Hexi platform. There are many text elements in inscriptions and poems. Among the natural elements, there are ginkgo leaves in the autumn of Yuelu Mountain, which contain the meaning of time and study; There is Ziyang Cinnamomum camphora planted by Zhu Xi for Meiji learning ambition; White horses led by people who drink horses [11,12]. By following the above design principles and using elements reasonably, we can design related scene root carving products around the story.

According to the images related to Zhu Zhanghui's lecture, the relevant elements were extracted and iterated, and three preliminary conceptual sketch schemes were formed through the design of elements and root carvings.

Conceptual sketch scheme 1 mainly revolves around the concept of "applying the practice". This design hopes to integrate the concept of "thousand-year inheritance and applying the practice" mentioned by Zhu Zhanghui into the works, which tells the story of the Millennium changes of an academy after Zhu Zhanghui's speech. The basic form of the whole modeling uses a ring shape, hoping to create an atmosphere that crosses just visiting. Looking back at the past years through the traces of old trees, after thousands of years, the spirit will last forever [13]. The works mainly embody three elements, namely, Ginkgo biloba, Ziyang camphor and Zhu Zhang, all of which are associated with the event of "Zhu Zhang will speak".

The second concept sketch scheme is to reproduce the core scenes of speaking. This scheme takes Zhu and Zhang as the core design elements, adds simplified elements that can reflect the school scenes, uses tree-shaped modeling as the basic form, and restores the speaking scenes with minimalist language. I hope to restore the scene told by Zhu Zhanghui simply and directly. The past events turned white and remained in my memory, and the old trees at that time stood here and made people forget history.

The inspiration of the concept sketch scheme 3 is the influence on the generations of the academy after the lecture. This scheme hopes to depict the passage of time after Zhu Zhanghui's lecture in a more subtle way, but the spirit of the lecture will last forever. The white horse symbolizes that time passes like a white horse, and it is also the unprecedented grand occasion of drinking horse pond in front of the academy when Zhu Zhanghui speaks.

3.1.2 Concept sketch scheme evaluation

After the above conceptual sketches were evaluated and reviewed by the project team, the first creative scheme was finally chosen, that is, the design around the concept of "practical application".

The members of the project team believe that the design of the first scheme can intuitively express the theme of Zhu Zhanghui, and the elements used are also familiar to the target audience. The whole scene has a certain sense of time travel, the composition is more creative than the second scheme, and the story is clearer than the third scheme. Although the story of the second scheme is clear, the overall design language is too straightforward, and the craftsmanship of the root carving part is not as good as other schemes. The overall artistic conception of the third scheme is good, but the white pony is used to show the grand occasion of many horse drinkers when Zhu Zhanghui speaks, and it implies the concept of time passing, which has certain connotation, but the story is obscure, which does not highlight the advantages of situational root carving in telling stories, and the story is too weak for readers to watch. To sum up, the first concept is the design direction of this root carving design.

Deepen the connotation and form design of the elements in Scheme 1, and the specific meanings of the elements used are:

- Ginkgo biloba in the Academy: When Zhu Zhanghui talked about it, it was in the autumn of Lushan, and ginkgo was in full bloom. At the same time, Ginkgo biloba means "eternal", and it is an eternal witness when the essence of traditional culture is scattered and passed down from generation to generation [14].
- Ziyang camphor tree: Zhu Xi planted a camphor tree behind the school after Zhu Zhanghui's lecture. After thousands of years, it has become a towering tree. It happens that this material is a hollow old camphor tree. Both of them have the meaning of growth, development and inheritance. The material and story are very appropriate. Moreover, Zhu Xi once planted camphor trees in his hometown and became famous. The element of camphor trees bears Zhu Xi's spirit of constantly pursuing and surpassing himself in academics, and it is also a response to his parents' expectations, which is integrated with the spirit of an academy in a Millennium university.
- Zhu and Zhang: Zhu and Zhang are the soul figures of this story and the founders of the academy's thousand-year history. Characters are the core part of the scene root carving, so it is necessary to restore the posture that Zhu and Zhang can speak as much as possible.

Through the deepening process of element connotation and form design, the preliminary design scheme is obtained. The elements used are Ginkgo biloba leaves, Zhu Zhang and Ziyang Cinnamomum camphora in an academy, and the root carving style adopted is ring-shaped.

3.2 root carving renderings design

Rendering design is a common design display method in the early stage of design, which can transform conceptual design into concrete and visible visual expression and help designers express and spread their own design ideas. The ultimate goal of renderings design is to transform the conceptual design into the final product according to the realization of renderings [15]. The cost of trial and error can be effectively reduced by designing the renderings for root carving products. According to the evaluation results of the conceptual sketch scheme, the project team took the deepened design scheme as the prototype and designed the renderings after shooting the physical drawings of the root wood. The environment of the renderings is set in a scene that reflects certain soothing emotions, and the overall color is warm, highlighting the wooden texture and natural softness of root carving products.

According to the design of the sketch of the creative idea, the selected ring root material is measured to facilitate the fitting of the size and proportion in the subsequent application of related elements. The production of 3D digital model will be divided into two parts, which are modeled and rendered by digital technology on the computer respectively.

Image source: The first part of the author's self-drawing is the rough root mould showing the overall product space structure, and the rough root mould is modeled on the computer with C4D software. The main purpose of making a rough heel model is to facilitate the subsequent adjustment of the proportion, collocation and size of different elements, and to find the most suitable spatial structure of the root carving product.

The second part is to make printable models of some characters or elements and integrate them into the scene root carving products as innovative elements in the root carving products. The model that can be printed is different from the rough model, so it needs to be made into a high-precision model, which is called high-precision model for short. The model must be a complete solid model with wall thickness, and the accuracy requirement is relatively high. There are three elements involved in the work: Zhu and Zhang, Ginkgo biloba in the Academy and Cinnamomum camphora in Ziyang. In this innovative design method, the resin material model is combined with root carving products, and the rough model of the above three elements in the material library of an academy built in the previous article can be used, and then further fine-tuning and adaptation can be carried out. Among them, Zhu Zhang and Xueyuan Ginkgo need to print, so they need to make a high mold. Ziyang Cinnamomum camphora is realized by traditional carving, and the final effect is uncertain with the materials. Therefore, the model only needs to be used to make the overall effect diagram of the product, because it needs to be refined and modified on the basis of the rough mold in the material library.

The combination and construction of ginkgo leaves were carried out. Firstly, the preliminary modeling is completed by C4D software. Because of the need for 3D printing in the future, it is necessary to refine the model to ensure that the ginkgo leaf is a model with solid and wall thickness, and the thickness should not be too thin. Secondly, because the leaves have a certain thickness, they need to be combined and deleted on the computer in advance, and the shape needs to be matched reasonably. After many combinations and adjustments, the design of the whole ginkgo leaf shape has been completed [16]. Finally, because the Ginkgo biloba leaves are thin and small in size, there is no need to hollow out the model, and after the combination of the models, you can wait for the subsequent printing and effect presentation.

The rough models of Zhu and Zhang were extracted from the material database of the project team, and the model was modeled by reverse engineering in the preliminary research of the "Virtual Academy" project. After model refinement, reduction and combination adjustment, and hollowing out, the model design of Zhu and Zhang was completed. Finally, the rough model of root material modeling is combined with the model of material, and the three-dimensional structure effect of the whole scheme is obtained.

3.3 Product physical display

After the completion of the work, the product display map is photographed, and the whole photographic environment conforms to the characteristics of the product. The key words of product positioning are soothing, culture, creativity, Zen, academy stories, wood and so on. As a whole, a warm yellow tone is adopted, and traditional cultures such as root carving products and tea culture can be well integrated, and integrated with the whole environment of log tone, creating a peaceful and quiet Zen.

3.4 Dynamic interactive display process

After the design of dynamic interactive program is completed, the pictures and model materials that need to be used should be integrated to present better visual effects. The key words of product positioning are soothing, culture, creativity, Zen, academy stories, wood, etc. Combined with the final effect of product positioning, the warm yellow color tone is adopted in the design of the whole interactive process, and the photographed product physical map is put into the environmental effect map which conforms to the characteristics of the product. In the process of interaction, we should add some dynamic graphic display elements in visual design. Through the addition of dynamic graphics, the positioning of root carving products can be strengthened, giving the whole quiet, warm and soothing mood, so as to enhance the emotional experience of users. In terms of interaction, the function needs to be as simple as possible, mainly showing the appearance and function of the product clearly. Based on the above analysis, it is designed that the "Zhu Zhang Zhi Hui" dynamic interaction is the emotional version of visual design.

Combining the product positioning of "Zhu Zhang Zhi Hui" with the user's use scene, the background picture of the scene used in this dynamic interactive exhibition and the decorative elements used are made in photoshop software through partial shooting and partial drawing.

The static frame of the dynamic interaction process finally output by the computer display program is divided into the following processes:

- After loading, enter the cover page and click the "Learn More" button to enter the subsequent physical display section.
- The user is prompted with the function of the product's incense burner by words, and the user moves the sandalwood on the desktop to the incense mouth at the top of the root carving product and lights the backflow sandalwood.
- After the user lights sandalwood, the smoke slowly floats out with time.
- Smoke wafts out and gradually becomes rich. At this time, users can view the three-dimensional model of the product from multiple angles through text prompts, and users can enter the viewing screen of the three-dimensional model by rotating the model.
- After entering the model display screen, the user can rotate and watch the 3D model within a limited angle by zooming in, zooming out and rotating. After 10 seconds, the prompt button "Return to Home Page" appears.

Through this dynamic display process, users can appreciate the details of the product, and at the same time, they can understand the product functions more intuitively and feel the usage scene of the product.

4 Result analysis

4.1 User feedback survey

4.1.1 User product feedback

The main positioning of this product is nature, Zen and leisure, and the user groups are mainly tourists, traditional culture lovers and root carving product lovers. According to the theory of usability testing, it takes 15 test users to find out all the existing problems in the product testing. According to this theory, 15 young tourists, fans of Hanfu, Chinese studies and tea culture were invited as typical representatives of user groups to experience products and interactive programs.

The user's experience process is divided into two parts, the first part is the experience of interactive programs, and the second part is the evaluation and suggestion of the final works. Summarize the suggestions given by users as follows:

- Some details of digital sculpture design are not enough, and the reduction degree of characters can be further improved. As a root carving product, there are few hand-carved parts, so the craftsmanship of the details can be stronger [17].

- In the animation part of the function demonstration, the incense is put into the incense mouth and automatically ignited, which can increase the link of user's own ignition, and design the matching ignition tool to improve the whole experience process.

- The operation of the interactive program is slightly stuck, which is not smooth and natural enough, and the smoke effect produced in the animation is not realistic enough, which affects the overall atmosphere and sense of substitution. Collect and sort out the feedback data of 15 users, and get the user feedback table in Figure 1.

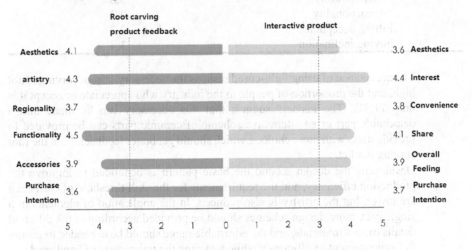

Figure 1 User experience feedback

4.1.2 Root carving industry feedback survey

At the same time of design innovation, it may cause destructive innovation, and it is impossible to gain the sense of identity of specific culture-related enthusiasts, practitioners and inheritors. The attitude of craftsmen towards technical intervention and the sense of innovation are an important part of the collaborative innovation process of handicrafts and digital technology [18]. In the design of root carving products in this innovative scene, the materials and design flow are quite different from other root carving products, and there will be many new performances in the final presentation effect. Therefore, it is necessary to visit people in the root carving industry for evaluation and suggestions for subsequent improvement and creation.

Use questionnaires and face-to-face interviews to conduct a comprehensive return visit survey. Firstly, in the form of questionnaire, a survey questionnaire was distributed to 80 root carving craftsmen, root carving market merchants and root carving collectors, with a recovery rate of 100% and an effective rate of 100%. Because of the innovative application of resin materials in this paper, the acceptance of traditional root carving art practitioners is highly uncertain, so it is evaluated and the acceptance table of resin/nylon and other 3D printing materials by root carving industry practitioners is obtained [19]. Synthesize the contents of other investigations related to this root carving product, sort out and analyze the data, and get the basic identification degree, artistic evaluation, commodity evaluation and other data of this product as shown in Table 1. Evaluation scoreS_iCalculate according to the following formula (1):

$$S_i = \frac{\sum_{i=1}^{80} s_i}{80 \times 5} \tag{1}$$

Among them,s_iRepresents the score of an evaluation index. According to the results, several practitioners with very different views were selected for further follow-up interviews. The representative evaluations and suggestions obtained are as follows:

Table 1 Feedback data of root carving industry insiders on "Zhu Zhangzhihui"

evaluating indicator	score
Aesthetics	4.1
artistry	4.0
territoriality	3.6
functionality	4.2
Fitting acceptance	3.7
buying inclination	3.4

- The acceptance of using light-cured resin as the accessory of root carving is not high, and the proportion of people in the industry who appreciate or accept it is only 71.3%. The insiders suggest that this accessory can be made into a detachable part or an alternative scheme of ceramic parts can be provided to provide users with more choices, which should get better feedback from the root carving market.

- Developing the design around the basic pattern is beneficial to improve the production efficiency, and the requirements for the skill threshold of craftsmen are lower, but the artistry is also reduced. In the application of elements in a single part, more design schemes should be provided according to the different details of root materials, and the adjustable range should be expanded to ensure the improvement of efficiency while retaining the uniqueness of hand-made.

- The whole root carving product has a certain artistic conception, and can realize the connection with the concept of time, but the specific story can be strengthened.

4.2 Outlook: "Handicraft+Digitalization" Collaborative Innovation to Build a Regional Cultural Ecology

The so-called regional cultural ecology is a system that integrates many internal and external factors that constitute the regional cultural system and the interaction between them. The value of studying and constructing regional cultural ecology lies in that the intangible cultural heritage can be developed and passed down naturally and healthily through production and lifestyle, which is more dynamic and open than the independent inheritance of culture. Therefore, constructing regional cultural ecology is an effective method to revitalize regional culture at present [20].

Taking the root carving in Hunan as an example, digital technology has been incorporated into the traditional technological process, and the communication efficiency in the design demand stage can be improved by quickly drawing conceptual sketches; Through real-time collaborative design, the direction of the conception and deepening stage is ensured to be accurate, and the cost in the modification process is correspondingly reduced; Through digital technology, the types of root carving materials, artistic forms and display methods are improved in the design and implementation stage.

In the future development, through the similar collaborative innovation design method of "handicraft+digitalization" in this paper, digital technology can be more deeply involved in the design and production process of handicrafts, further enrich and improve the cultural ecological construction of different regional cultures, attract more human and material resources to invest in it, produce a more perfect design and production process, and produce more products with the unique ingenuity of traditional handicrafts and the aesthetic and value orientation of modern people.

5 Conclusion

(1) "Handicraft+Digitalization" collaborative innovation design

This paper summarizes the problems existing in the current root carving industry, analyzes the feasibility and advantages of digital design involved in root carving product design, and puts forward the method of "root carving technology+digitalization" to jointly build the regional cultural ecology of Huxiang. Taking "Zhu Zhanghui's lecture" in an academy as a representative, this paper explores the innovative methods of developing scene-based root carving products in Huxiang regional culture. At the same time, three-dimensional printing products are innovatively added to the root carving design, which enriches the expression forms of products.

(2) The situational story method is applied to the root carving design of an academy.

Integrating the situational story method into the root carving design of an academy enhances the overall atmosphere and story of the root carving works, which can enhance the story of the root carving cultural and creative products of an academy and provide reference for the development of other products. At the same time, the style of root carving in Hunan is used in the products, which is conducive to the promotion and dissemination of root carving culture in Hunan and the culture of an academy.

(3) Study on the basic type of root carving.

Through market visits and online surveys, the characteristics of root wood suitable for the scene were found, the characteristics of several basic types were summarized, and the method of integrating design elements and product functions into the basic types was put forward to ensure the batch production of root carving products while maintaining the ingenuity and natural beauty.

(4) Interactive program design for handicraft exhibition.

The dynamic interactive display design of handicraft product function and shape is carried out, and the interactive program is built by TouchDesigner. Through the dynamic display process, users can appreciate the details of handicraft products, and at the same time, they can understand the product functions more intuitively and feel the usage scene of the products.

References

[1]   Hou, Y., Kenderdine, S., Picca, D., Egloff, M., & Adamou, A. (2022). Digitizing intangible cultural heritage embodied: State of the art. *Journal on Computing and Cultural Heritage (JOCCH)*, *15*(3), 1-20.

[2]   Yue, M., Wang, G., & Li, Z. (2022). The Digital Protection and Inheritance of Intangible Cultural Heritage:--Taking the Qing Dynasty horse-face skirt as an Example. *Highlights in Art and Design*, *1*(3), 83-87.

[3]   Liu, Y. (2022). Application of digital technology in intangible cultural heritage protection. *Mobile Information Systems*, *2022*, 1-8.

[4]   Xu, Z., & Zou, D. (2022). Big data analysis research on the deep integration of intangible cultural heritage inheritance and art design education in colleges and universities. *Mobile Information Systems*, *2022*, 1-12.

[5]   Król, K. (2021). Digital cultural heritage of rural tourism facilities in Poland. *Journal of Cultural Heritage Management and Sustainable Development*, *11*(4), 488-498.

[6]   Xie, R. (2021). Intangible cultural heritage high-definition digital mobile display technology based on vr virtual visualization. *Mobile Information Systems*, *2021*, 1-11.

[7]   Nikolakopoulou, V., Printezis, P., Maniatis, V., Kontizas, D., Vosinakis, S., Chatzigrigoriou, P., & Koutsabasis, P. (2022). Conveying Intangible Cultural Heritage in Museums with Interactive Storytelling and Projection Mapping: The Case of the Mastic Villages. *Heritage*, *5*(2), 1024-1049.

[8]   Cui, C., Zhao, Y., & Wang, L. (2021). Protection and dissemination of Chinese intangible cultural heritage based on digital games. *International Communication of Chinese Culture*, *8*, 483-491.

[9]   Chatzigrigoriou, P., Nikolakopoulou, V., Vakkas, T., Vosinakis, S., & Koutsabasis, P. (2021). Is architecture connected with intangible cultural heritage? reflections from architectural digital documentation and interactive application design in three aegean islands. *Heritage*, *4*(2), 664-689.

[10] Aljaberi, S. M., & Al-Ogaili, A. S. (2021). Integration of cultural digital form and material carrier form of traditional handicraft intangible cultural heritage. *vol*, *5*, 21-30.

[11] Turillazzi, B., Leoni, G., Gaspari, J., Massari, M., & Boulanger, S. O. M. (2021). Cultural heritage and digital tools: The ROCK interoperable platform. *International Journal of Environmental Impacts*, *4*(3), 276-288.

[12] Skublewska-Paszkowska, M., Milosz, M., Powroznik, P., & Lukasik, E. (2022). 3D technologies for intangible cultural heritage preservation—literature review for selected databases. *Heritage Science*, *10*(1), 1-24.

[13] Wu, C., & Wu, X. (2021). The Art-Craft Boundary in Contemporary Central China: The Case of Root Carving. The Journal of Modern Craft, 14(2), 141-154.

[14] Wang, B. (2021). Digital design of smart museum based on artificial intelligence. Mobile Information Systems, 2021, 1-13.

[15] Meron, Y. (2021). Terminology and design capital: examining the pedagogic status of graphic design through its practitioners' perceptions of their job titles. International Journal of Art & Design Education, 40(2), 374-388.

[16] Huda, A., Azhar, N., Almasri, A., Wulansari, R. E., Mubai, A., Sakti, R. H., ... & Hartanto, S. (2021). Augmented Reality Technology as a Complement on Graphic Design to Face Revolution Industry 4.0 Learning and Competence: The Development and Validity. Int. J. Interact. Mob. Technol., 15(5), 116-126.

[17] Chen, L., Tong, T, W., Tang, S., & Han, N. (2022). Governance and design of digital platforms: A review and future research directions on a meta-organization. Journal of Management, 48(1), 147-184.

[18] Marion, T. J., & Fixson, S. K. (2021). The transformation of the innovation process: How digital tools are changing work, collaboration, and organizations in new product development. Journal of Product Innovation Management, 38(1), 192-215.

[19] Zhang, Y., Meina, A., Lin, X., Zhang, K., & Xu, Z. (2021). Digital twin in computational design and robotic construction of wooden architecture. Advances in Civil Engineering, 2021, 1-14.

[20] Ng, M. S., Graser, K., & Hall, D. M. (2023). Digital fabrication, BIM and early contractor involvement in design in construction projects: A comparative case study. Architectural Engineering and Design Management, 19(1), 39-55.

Design Studies and Intelligence Engineering 393
L.C. Jain et al. (Eds.)
© 2024 The Authors.
This article is published online with Open Access by IOS Press and distributed under the terms
of the Creative Commons Attribution Non-Commercial License 4.0 (CC BY-NC 4.0).
doi:10.3233/FAIA231456

An Analysis and Modeling Method for Design Information Based on User Generated Reviews Mining and Extenics

Jin-juan DUAN [a], Feng ZHANG [b], Zhe-wen BAI [c] and Gaofeng LI[d,1]

a School of Wedding Culture & Media Arts, Beijing College of Social Administration
(Training Center of Ministry of Civil Affairs), Beijing 102600, China
b Department of Design Science, Kookmin University, Seoul 02707, Korea
c College of Architecture & Design, Tongmyong University, Busan 48520, Korea
d School of Rehabilitation Engineering, Beijing College of Social Administration
(Training Center of Ministry of Civil Affairs), Beijing 102600, China

Abstract. To address the inapplicability of data classification results in industrial design, and the lack of theoretical research on design information analysis methods, a design information analysis method based on user experience data was proposed. User experience positive and negative user experience datasets were established through user experience data mining and applying text classification algorithms to perform initial processing of the data. Design features are obtained by extracting effective information from the data, and a design feature analysis is established by combining with the extension class element theory model. Effective information about users and products in the data is classified and analyzed; a conjugate relation between user information and product information is studied, and a design information correlation transformation model is established based on the extension compound theory. Finally, user and product information correlation analyses are combined to obtain an effective product design strategy. The effectiveness of this method is verified by taking electric scooters used by the elderly as an example.

Keywords. User experience; data mining; text classification; extension model

1. Introduction

E-commerce websites serve as a bridge for communication between users, and between users via enterprises. User generated reviews (UGR) has become an important strategic resource for current enterprises, and methods for obtaining useful information from UGR generated online are a hotspot in current research [1].

UGR is mostly composed of plain text, and its structure is diverse and vague, requiring tremendous efforts to extract relevant detailed information[2] . In the front-end analysis for design, it is necessary to extract effective information from the data, and analyze the data in combination with design theory. Current researches on the analysis of data generated by users online mainly focused on sentiment quantification [3], sentiment analysis [4], feature extraction [5], and user Kansei image extraction[6].

---

[1] *Corresponding Author: LI Gao-feng, professor of Beijing College of Social Administration (Training Center of Ministry of Civil Affairs), Beijing 102600, China. E-mail: chicotli@126.com.*

The combination of Kansei engineering and UGR mining can help extract users' emotional requirements efficiently; however, when the subsequent data are applied to design procession, it is difficult to achieve the user information and product information fully to dominate the later product design and development planning effectively. In response to these problems, many related methods from the perspective of user data feature extraction were explored. For example, Zhou et al. [7] proposed an enhanced feature model based on emotional features and rough set methods, mining user preferences from user comment data related to specific product features and improving the quality and efficiency of product line planning to a certain extent. Guang-yao et al. [8] proposed a data conversion method by combining rough set theory and quality function deployment (QFD). By integrating Linguistics, Kansei engineering, and computers, Jiao Y et al. [9] proposed a method of Kansei knowledge extraction from UGR, and a relational extraction method to generate the relationship of product design features and user perceptual evaluation.

However, there is not enough attention on how to classify these product features and demand information, and how to guide the final product improvement, optimization and innovation. Product features were effectively correlated, and design problems were transformed to devise product design strategies to satisfy user requirements. Taking electric scooters used by the elderly as an example, the specific test and analysis procedure of the design information analysis method proposed in this paper were demonstrated.

Most current studies mainly focused on English. There is a significant difference between English and the dominant languages spoken in China. The techniques and methods used for English comments cannot be directly applied to Chinese comments [3]. research on mining UGR information in Chinese is imperative. Therefore, we developed a design information analysis and modeling method based on the extenics theory suitable for extracting user experience information from Chinese reviews.

2. Extenics theory

2.1. Extension elements and extension class elements

Extension elements include object elements, feature elements and relation elements. They are the logical cells of extenics and are collectively called elements. Extension element theory can help designers effectively and clearly express the relation among user requirements, functions, and the environments in the design process.

To describe a class of objects, the concept of class elements are defined in the extension element theory [10]. Given an object $\{O\}$, if for any$\{O\}$, regarding the feature c_i $(i = 1,2,...,n)$, $v_i = c_i(O) \in V_i$, then $\{B\}$ is expressed in Eq.(1):

$$\{B\} = \begin{bmatrix} \{O\}, & c_1, & v_1 \\ & c_2, & v_2 \\ & \vdots & \vdots \\ & c_n, & v_n \end{bmatrix} = (\{O\}, C, V) \tag{1}$$

Here, V_i is the value of feature C_i, and B is the class elements.

2.2. Extension analysis method

The extension analysis method is the basis of creativity generation in extension science, including two categories: extension analysis method and conjugate analysis method [11].

The extension analysis method is a formal method to expand elements and obtain multiple innovation paths or ideas for solving contradictory problems, including divergence tree method, correlation network method, implication system method, and split-combination chain method. In the analysis process of design problems in front-end design, how to define the interrelations between problems and determine the correlation between various factors are bottlenecks faced by designers.

The conjugate analysis method divides objects into four different sets in terms of its materiality, systematicness, dynamicity, and opposition: imaginary, real, and intermediate parts; soft, hard, and intermediate parts; latent, visible, and intermediate parts; and positive, negative, and intermediate parts, respectively, thus totaling four groups of eight pairs of conjugate parts [12].

3. Data *min*ing experiment

3.1. Experimental process

Electric scooter used by the elderly are taken as an example to mine the user experience data of the product from Jingdong E-mall (www.jd.com).

●   The requests library in the Python programming language was used in the form of a lightweight web crawler, and a total of 4,523 pieces of data were crawled. After deleting invalid data, 2,042 pieces of data were obtained for analysis

●   The small amount of noise was cleaned up and invalid characters and punctuations were removed; Jieba library was applied to obtain segmented data.

●   In the stage of calculating the word vector, the Word2Vec word vector training model [13] was used to calculate the word vector for word segmentation.

●   In the data classification stage, the Bi-LSTM algorithm [14] was used for text classification. Based on the emotional polarity, the UGR data were divided into positive data and negative data. And both positive and negative user UGR datasets were established.

3.2. Results of data classification

After data classification, a total of 1,800 positive UGR data and 246 negative UGR data were obtained, as shown in Table 1.

Table 1. Positive and negative UGR dataset

Positive user experience data
I bought it for grandpa. It is inconvenient for old people to commute in. Yes, I like it very much. The scooter is small, easy to assemble, easy to operate, and smooth to drive. Recommend!
...
Negative user experience data
Except for the lack of battery volume, everything is OK. The seat is not high enough, so I have to adjust it to the highest Position.
...

Through the analyzing of Table 1, it is found that the data obtained through the data classification algorithm are relatively formless and hard to be applied to design analysis and practice directly. The data contain many types of effective information related to product design, and further effective information should be extracted. Effective design information is mainly concentrated in negative user data [15].

4. Methodology

4.1. Design information and feature extraction

Python was applied to segment the negative data content. And data statistics was performed on the part of speech and word frequency of each word obtained.

Initial data statistics shows that UGR cover users (elderly, etc.), products (battery, seat, charger, wheels, etc.), behavior (traveling, shopping, ordering, etc.), performance (slow, speed, braking, workmanship, etc.), service (attitude, after-sales service, poor, etc.), and other related information, which will be specifically classified in subsequent research.

By analyzing the content of negative data, relevant user and problem descriptions are obtained, as shown in Table 2.

Table 2. User descriptions and problem descriptions

Negative UGR data	User description	Problem description
Power display on the dashboard needs improving, difficult to recognize for the elderly.	Decreased vision	Small instrument panel display
There is no speed gear; there is only one speed; ; the old man responds slowly.	Slow response	There is no speed gear
...	...	...

Based on Table 2, the hidden design information was extracted and classified, as shown in Table 3.

Table 3. Design feature extraction

Design information	Feature attribute	Feature classification
safety and stability	psychological	User Feature
tire material, scooter body material, chassis material	material	Product Feature
...	...	...

4.2. Design feature classification

From the design feature extraction results reported in Section 4.1, the design features can be divided into user features and product features. The former includes physiological features, psychological features, demand features, and behavior features. The latter includes internal and external features. Internal features refer to the information about each component of the product, including structure, material, and function; external features refer to the information that reflects the interaction between users and products, and between products and the environment.

4.3. Extension design information analysis and modeling

To efficiently obtain, identify, sort, and classify the useful and meaningful design information data of different dimensions from UGR, an extension design information analysis method based on the extension element theory, conjugate analysis method, extension composite element theory, and extension transformation theory was proposed. The method was shown in Fig. 1.

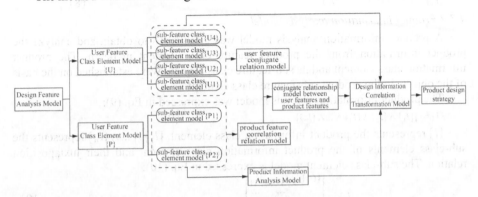

Figure 1. Extension design information analysis

4.3.1 Design feature analysis model

A design feature analysis model is constructed based on the extension class element theory, including a user feature class element model and a product feature class element model. The user feature class element model is expressed in Eq. (2):

$$\{U\} \Rightarrow \{U_1\} \wedge \{U_2\} \wedge \{U_3\} \wedge \{U_4\} \tag{2}$$

$\{U\}$ represents the user feature class element: user physiology feature class element, user psychology feature class element, user demand feature class element, and user behavior feature class element; "$\wedge$" represents the juxtaposition relations of the four sub-feature class elements.

$$\{U_1\} = \begin{bmatrix} \{O_1\}, & C_{11}, & V_{11} \\ \cdots & \cdots \\ \{O_n\}, & C_{ij}, & V_{ij} \\ \cdots & \cdots \end{bmatrix} \tag{3}$$

where $\{O\}$ represents the object of the sub-feature element, C represents the feature, V represents the value of the object O about the feature C, $n \geq 1$, $i \geq 1$, and $j \geq 1$. And the mutual influence relation between the sub-feature class elements is described:

$$mid_U = \{U_1\} \otimes \{U_2\} \otimes \{U_3\} \otimes \{U_4\} \tag{4}$$

The product feature class element model is expressed in Eq. (5):

$$\{P\} \Rightarrow \{P_1\} \wedge \{P_2\} \tag{5}$$

$\{P\}$ represents the product feature class element, and $\{P_1\} \wedge \{P_2\}$ represents the juxtaposition relation between the product internal feature class element $\{P_1\}$ and the product external feature class element $\{P_2\}$. $\{P_1\}$ is expressed in Eq. (6):

$$\{P_1\} = \begin{bmatrix} \{O_1\}, & C_{11}, & V_{11} \\ \cdots & \cdots \\ \{O_n\}, & C_{ij}, & V_{ij} \\ \cdots & \cdots \end{bmatrix} \tag{6}$$

where $\{O\}$, C, and V respectively represent the object, the feature of the object and the value of $\{O\}$ about the feature, $n \geq 1$, $i \geq 1$, and $j \geq 1$.

There are interrelations within the product feature class elements and within each sub-feature class element. The correlation net method [23] is used to describe this interrelated relation, as expressed in Eq. (7):

$$\{P_1\}(O_1 \wedge ... \wedge O_n) \sim \{P_2\}(O_1 \wedge ... \wedge O_n) \tag{7}$$

The correlation among each sub-feature class element is expressed in Eq. (8):

$$\{P_1\} \sim (O_1 \sim O_2 \sim \cdots \sim O_n) \tag{8}$$

4.3.2 Product information analysis model

A product information analysis model was established to obtain and analyze the product information from the product feature class element in depth. The product information class element and its sub-feature class element were established on the basis of the objects in the product sub-feature class element.

The product information analysis model was expressed in Eq. (9):

$$\{I\} \Rightarrow [\{I_1\} \wedge \{I_2\} \wedge \{I_3\} \wedge ... \wedge \{I_n\}] \tag{9}$$

$\{I\}$ represents the product information class element, $\{I_1\} \wedge ... \wedge \{I_n\}$ represents the sub-class elements of the product information class element and their juxtaposition relation. The sub-class element model is expressed in Eq. (10):

$$\{I_1\} = \begin{bmatrix} \{O_1\}, & C_{11}, & V_{11} \\ & ... & ... \\ \{O_n\}, & C_{ij}, & V_{ij} \\ & ... & \end{bmatrix} \tag{10}$$

where $\{O\}$, C, and V represent the object, the feature of the object, and the value of $\{O\}$ about the character respectively, $n \geq 1$, $i \geq 1$, and $j \geq 1$.

4.3.3 Design information correlation transformation model

During the design analyzing and problem solving, there is often a conjugate relation between user information and product information, as expressed in Eq. (11):

$$mid_{U-P} = \{U\} \otimes \{P\} = A \tag{11}$$

Therefore, it is necessary to perform a correlation analysis on the extracted and classified information based on their conjugate and correlation relations, as shown in Fig. 2

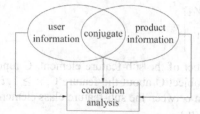

Figure 2. Conjugate analysis chart of user information and product information

The design information correlation transformation model was established on the basis of the extension compound theory of the matter and affair elements. We supposed A taken multiple user feature class elements with conjugate relations as the product function element, as expressed in Eq. (12):

$$A(\{U_1\} \wedge ... \wedge \{U_n\}) = \begin{bmatrix} U_1\{O_1\} \wedge ... \wedge U_n\{O_n\}, & AC_1, & AV_1 \\ & ... & ... \\ & AC_n, & AV_n \\ & C_{DA}, & V_{DA} \\ & ... & ... \end{bmatrix} \rightarrow TA = \begin{bmatrix} U_1\{O_1\} \wedge ... \wedge U_n\{O_n\}, & C'_{DA}, & V'_{DA} \\ & ... & ... \end{bmatrix}$$

$$\tag{12}$$

Here, the model takes multiple sub-feature class elements in the user feature class elements as objects $U_1\{O_1\} \wedge ... \wedge U_n\{O_n\}$; AC is the feature value related to the multiple sub-feature class elements in the user feature class element; AV is the value of AC, and C_{DA} is the design feature analyzed from the object $U_1\{O_1\} \wedge ... \wedge U_n\{O_n\}$; V_{DA} is the value of C_{DA}; TA represents the new product function element obtained by transformation, that is, the new product design strategies. The feature C'_{DA} is the optimization direction of TA, and V'_{DA} is the value of C'_{DA}.

5. Deduction of the new product strategies

5.1. Design feature analysis model

5.1.1 User feature analysis model

Using Eqs. (2) and (3) to analyze the user feature and combining with the data listed in Table 1, the user feature of the electric scooter was obtained. The users are elderly people over 60; the user physiological feature $\{U_1\}$ were expressed as Eq. (13):

$$\{U_1\} = \begin{bmatrix} \text{vision loss,} & \text{Affecting the distinction of things,} & \text{Simplification of manipulation the display} \\ & & \text{The bright color of the font} \\ & & \text{Enhancing text recognition} \\ \text{memory decay,} & \text{Affecting product operation,} & \text{Simplification of control settings} \\ \text{slow response,} & \text{Affecting judgment} & \text{Simplification of driving control} \\ & \text{of driving obstacles,} & \text{Intelligent auxiliary speed regulation} \\ \text{reduced mobility,} & \text{Weak control,} & \text{Simplification of operation} \\ & & \text{Intelligent aided emergency control} \end{bmatrix}$$

(13)

Similarly, the user psychological feature $\{U_2\}$, user demand feature $\{U_3\}$, and user behavior feature class element $\{U_4\}$ were obtained, and a user feature analysis model is constructed.

5.1.2 Product feature analysis model

The product features were analyzed according to Eqs. (5) and (6.) The product features of the electric scooter are divided into internal feature class element $\{P_1\}$ and external feature class element $\{P_2\}$, where $\{P_1\}$ includes three objects, namely the $\{O_1\}$ structure, $\{O_2\}$ material, and $\{O_3\}$ function, and $\{P_2\}$ includes two objects, namely the $\{O_1\}$ interactivity and $\{O_2\}$ environment. Hence, the model of the product feature class element, part of which was shown in Table 4.

Table 4. Product feature class element model

Product feature class element $\{P\}$	Object $\{O\}$	Feature value C	Amount-value V
Product internal feature class element $\{P_1\}$	$P_1\{O_1\}$ Structure	P_1C_{11} Chassis	P_1V_{111} Low chassis
		P_1C_{12} Absorb shock	P_1V_{121} Lack of shock absorbable function
		...	...
Product external feature class element $\{P_2\}$	$P_2\{O_1\}$ Interactivity	P_2C_{11} Seat	P_2V_{111} Low seat P_2V_{112} Unadjustable height seat P_2V_{113} Too narrow seat
		...	...
...	...	...	...

5.2. Product information analysis model

Based on the above analysis of the product features, the objects in the internal and external features of the product were extracted, and an independent analysis was carried out using Eqs.(9) and (10) to determine the problems in the product. Table 5 presents part of the product information analysis model.

Table 5. Product information analysis model

Product information class element $\{I\}$	Object $\{O\}$	Feature value C	Amount-value V
Structure $\{I_1\}$	$I_1\{O_1\}$ Scooter assembly	I_1C_{11} Assembly	I_1V_{111} Difficult assembly
	$I_1\{O_2\}$ Chassis	I_1C_{21} Chassis	I_1V_{211} Low chassis/thick chassis/small wheels
	...	...	...
Material $\{I_2\}$	$I_2\{O_1\}$ Scooter body	I_2C_{11} Plastic	I_2V_{111} Poor seismic and compressive resistance
	...	...	...
...	...	...	...

5.3. Establishing conjugate relation and correlation criterion

5.3.1 Conjugate relation criterion

It was found that there is a conjugate relation between user features as well as between user and product features. Therefore, the following conjugate relation criterion was established:

- In the same class elements, the features or values of objects belonging to different subclass elements have conjugate relations of the same factors. For example, there are similar value related to the speed factor of U_1V_{312} (Lack of speed regulation), U_2V_{151} (Lack of speed regulation), and U_4V_{211} (low speed), which are values of different sub-class element all belongs to user class element.

- The objects belonging to different class elements have conjugated relations of the same feature or values. For example, the feature value of $\{O_1\}$ (safety) of the object $\{U_2\}$ belonging to the user psychological features has the same factor (speed) as the feature of $\{O_3\}$ (function) of the object $\{P_1\}$ belonging to the internal features of the product.

5.3.2 Correlation criterion

There is a correlation between the values of different objects within product features. For example, there is a correlation between the value P_1V_{121} (Lack of shock absorbable function) and the value P_2V_{221} (bump road conditions), which are of different objects .

5.4. Design information correlation and transformation

Through the analysis of the user features, product features, and product information, the existing product design problems are integrated from the user perspective are integrated. It is necessary to establish a design information correlation transformation model based on user features based on the conjugate relation and correlation between each feature class element.

Based on the conjugate relation criterion, we divided the conjugate relation in the user features into the following three groups:

- User physiological feature $\{U_1\}$ "slow response,", user psychological feature $\{U_2\}$ "safety", and user behavior feature $\{U_4\}$ "short distance travel" have conjugate relations, as expressed in Eq. (14):

$$mid_{Ua} = \{U_1\}(\text{slow response}) \otimes \{U_2\}(\text{safety}) \otimes \{U_4\}(\text{short distance travel}) \tag{14}$$

- "reduced mobility" and "memory decay" of $\{U_1\}$, and user demand feature $\{U_3\}$ "convenience" have conjugate relations, as expressed in Eq. (15):

$$mid_{Ub} = \{U_1\}(\text{reduced mobility}) \otimes \{U_1\}(\text{memory decay}) \otimes \{U_3\}(\text{convenience}) \tag{15}$$

- "stability" of $\{U_2\}$ and "comfort" of $\{U_3\}$, and "shopping" of $\{U_4\}$ have conjugate relations, as expressed in Eq. (16):

$$mid_{Uc} = \{U_2\}(\text{stability}) \otimes \{U_3\}(\text{comfort}) \otimes \{U_4\}(\text{shopping}) \tag{16}$$

- We group the object user physiological feature $\{U_1\}$ "visual loss" separately based on the correlation criterion, as expressed in Eq. (17):

$$\text{vision loss} \sim (\text{environment} \wedge \text{structure} \wedge \text{interactivity}) \tag{17}$$

The design information correlation transformation model was established based on the above conjugate relations, part of which was shown in Table 6 .

Table 6. The design information correlation transformation model

Product function affair element $A(\{U_1\} \wedge ... \wedge \{U_n\})$	Object $U_1\{O_1\} \wedge ... \wedge U_n\{O_n\}$	Feature AC/C_{DA}	Value AV/V_{DA}
$A_1\left(\begin{array}{c}\{U_1\} \wedge \{U_2\} \wedge \\ \{U_4\}\end{array}\right)$	slow response∧safety∧ short distance travel	product features	function, interactivity, structure, material, environment
		be affected objects	speed, speed regulation, brake, use environment, operating mode, chassis height, tire material, wheel size, battery life
		design analysis	Nonconformity between theoretical and actual speeds/low efficiency of motor power utilization;
			...

New product function affair element	Object	Feature value	Amount-value
TA_1	slow response∧safety∧ short distance travel	optimization direction	1. Improving motor power and utilization efficiency;
			...

5.5. Product design strategies

According to the analyses reported in Sections 5.1–5.3, based on the design feature analysis model, the product information analysis model, and the correlation transformation analysis model of the electric scooter, the design strategies of new products were deduced, which can be divided into four parts, as shown in Table 7.

Table 7. Product design strategies

product	product feature	product design strategies
electricscooter used by the elderly	function	1. Increasing power and utilization efficiency; 2. Adding anti-backward tilting device and shock absorber; 3. Adding speed regulation gear; 4. Optimizing battery life and increasing battery waterproof, anti-theft, and anti-leakage functions; 5. Adding smart auxiliary speed adjust and control function to treat sloping road, adding smart braking control function. 6. Adding GPS positioning function; 7. Adding voice auxiliary operation.
	material	1. Optimizing the tire material to avoid slipping; 2. Optimizing the material of scooter body and increasing the strength of scooter body.
	structure	1. Increasing control display area; 2. Optimizing product structure design and connection mode to facilitate assembly; 3. Improving product structure and materials to reduce product weight; 4. Optimizing structural design of the seat to enhance the stability; 5. Increasing the wheel size and raise the chassis height.
	Interactivity	1. Separating the brake and accelerator operation; 2. Adding voice controlled emergency electronic brake; 3. Optimizing the product display area/Optimizing the font size design, and making the color more pleasing; 4. Optimizing the ergonomic design of the seat (in terms of the length, width, height, and the rotation angle); 5. Increasing the length of the scooter body, improving its stability, and expanding the loading space.

6. Conclusions

In the era of big data, applying big data analysis technology to the field of industrial design can help designers solve these problems and enable an efficient data-led design practice. Although UGR are of great value to industrial design, the efficiency of data conversion and application for practical purposes needs further improvement.

To solve the insufficient data conversion and application efficiency in data application, a user experience data design information analysis method for industrial design was proposed, which is combined with the extension theory to establish an extension design information analysis method. Through a case analysis of scooters intended for the elderly, it is proved that this method can improve the conversion and application efficiency of user experience data, providing a new theoretical method for product design based on UGR. However, the proposed extension design information analysis method is currently in the stage of theoretical research. In the future, research on intelligent design information extraction and analysis will be conducted with this method.

Acknowledgment

The paper is funded by Central University Basic Research Funding, grant number JBKYZD2023–1.

References

[1] Liu H, Cui T, He M. Product optimization design based on online review and orthogonal experiment under the background of big data. Proceedings of the Institution of Mechanical Engineers, Part E: Journal of Process Mechanical Engineering, 2021, 235(1):52-65.

[2] Wang W M, Wang J W, Li Z, et al. Multiple affective attribute classification of online customer product reviews: A heuristic deep learning method for supporting Kansei engineering. Engineering Applications of Artificial Intelligence, 2019, 85:33-45.

[3] Yang YP, Chen DK, Gu R.Consumers' Kansei Needs Clustering Method for Product Emotional Design Based on Numerical Design Structure Matrix and Genetic Algorithms. Computational Intelligence and Neuroscience.2016.1687-5265.

[4] Kim Wonjoon , Ko Taehoon , Rhiu Ilsun . Mining affective experience for a kansei design study on a recliner. APPLIED ERGONOMICS,2018.0003-6870.

[5] Abdi A Shamsuddin S M, Hasan S, et al. Deep learning-based sentiment classification of evaluative text based on Multi-feature fusion. Information Processing & Management, 2019, 56(4):1245-1259.

[6] Yeh CT, Chen MC. Applying Kansei Engineering and data mining to design door-to-door delivery service. COMPUTERS & INDUSTRIAL ENGINEERING,2018.0360-8352.

[7] Zhou Feng, Jiao Jianxin Roger, Yang Xi Jessie. Augmenting feature model through customer prefere-nce mining by hybrid sentiment analysis. Expert Systems with Applications, 2017. 0957-4174.

[8] Guang-Yao S I, Wang K, Wen-Qiang L I. et al. Research on product demand analysis method based on Big Data and rough set. Chinese journal of engineering design, 2016.

[9]J iao Y, Qu Q X. A proposal for Kansei knowledge extraction method based on natural language processing technology and online product reviews. Computers in Industry, 2019, 108:1-11.

[10] YANG Chun-yan, CAI Wen. Study on Extension Engineering. Strategic Study of CAE,2000,2(12):90-96.

[11] CAI Wen, YANG Chun-yan. Basic theory and methodology on Extenics. Chinese Science Bulletin,2013,58(13):1190-1199.

[12] YANG Chun-yan, CAI Wen. Extenics. Beijing: Science Press, 2014.

[13] Wei, L.; Wang, L.; Liu, F.; Qian, Z. Clustering Analysis of Wind Turbine Alarm Sequences Based on Domain Knowledge-Fused Word2vec. Appl. Sci. 2023, 13, 10114.

[14] Shobana J, Murali M. An Improved Self Attention Mechanism Based on Optimized BERT-BiLSTM Model for Accurate Polarity Prediction. The Computer Journal, 2022(5):5.

[15] Jin J, Ji P, Gu R. Identifying comparative customer requirements from product online reviews for competitor analysis. Engineering Applications of Artificial Intelligence, 2016, 49(Mar.):61-73.

Design Studies and Intelligence Engineering
L.C. Jain et al. (Eds.)
© 2024 The Authors.
This article is published online with Open Access by IOS Press and distributed under the terms
of the Creative Commons Attribution Non-Commercial License 4.0 (CC BY-NC 4.0).
doi:10.3233/FAIA231457

The Application of the "Feitian" Element from the Yungang Grottoes in Jewelry Design

Jinwei LU[a], Shuwei YU[a,1], Feiyang LIU[a], Jiongzhou WENG[a],
Hao HUO[a], Xiaojiang ZHOU[a], Jinhong HU[a], Ming ZHANG[a],
and Yue WU[a]

[a] *China Jiliang University, College Art and Communication*

Abstract. This article employs Principal Component Analysis (PCA) to investigate the perceptual characteristics of Feitian figures in the Yungang Grottoes. It analyzes participants' ranked preferences for these figures' perceptual imagery, extracting three pairs of representative characteristics. Building upon this analysis, the article explores design elements and spiritual communication, presenting a jewelry design methodology that concurrently considers the perceptual, representational, and spiritual aspects of Yungang Feitian figures. The study evaluates three design approaches: traditional, hybrid (traditional and AI-assisted), and pure AI-assisted jewelry design. The objective is to innovate design methodologies, summarize new approaches, and skillfully integrate traditional culture with modern design.

Key words. Yungang Grottoes, Feitian Element, Jewelry Design, Northern Wei Feitian, Sensory Characteristics, AIGC

1. Introduction

Yungang Grottoes embody the fusion of Buddhist art and Chinese culture. Notably distinct in architecture, cultural background, and spiritual attributes, they differ from other Chinese grottoes. Despite extensive research on aspects like architecture and aesthetics, there is a notable gap in exploring product design inspired by the Feitian sculptures in the Yungang Grottoes. This paper employs a research methodology combining quantitative and qualitative analysis. It applies sensory engineering and Principal Component Analysis (PCA) to assess the perceptual tendencies of the Feitian figures. The study analyzes the compositional significance of elements in the Feitian sculptures and interprets their design elements, as well as their underlying spiritual essence. By integrating cultural connotations with contemporary design philosophies, the paper establishes a jewelry design methodology. This methodology is then applied in modern jewelry product design, creating products that encompass both cultural heritage and contemporary aesthetics.

---

[1] Corresponding Author. 1545675175@163.com

2. Overview of the Distinctive Features of the Flying Celestial Beings in the Yungang Grottoes

Spanning 65 years from 460 to 525 AD, the Yungang Grottoes, commissioned by the Northern Wei imperial family, house over 51,000 statues, including an abundance of flying celestial beings (Feitian) sculptures. Through on-site investigation and research, over 50 locations with more than 2,300 Feitian figures have been identified [1]. The Buddhist statues in the grottoes can be categorized into three distinct periods based on their portrayal of Feitian figures [2].

During the initial phase under the "Central Asian Model," the Yungang Grottoes, then known as the "Five Caves of Marvelous Brilliance," were constructed in reverse order, from Cave 20 to Cave 16. In this phase, both male and female Feitian figures were present, characterized by robust physiques and rugged facial features, emanating a pronounced Central Asian Gandhara influence [3]

In the middle phase under the "Yungang Model," influenced by Han culture [4], the Yungang Grottoes' construction combined Central Asian and Han styles. Delicate facial expressions and a celestial landscape emerged, distinguishing this period. This marked a fusion of the "Central Asian Style" and "Han Cultural Style."

In Figure 1, robust "Central Asian Style" Feitian figures stand alongside more graceful "Han Cultural Style" counterparts. They're positioned together beneath the pagoda in Cave 6 [5].

Figure 1. The Flying Celestial Being on the Lower Part of the Pagoda Wall in Cave 6

In the "Longmen Model" phase, after Emperor Xiaowen relocated the capital, the Longmen Grottoes emerged. However, it didn't surpass the Yungang Grottoes in importance to Chinese Buddhism. The Yungang Grottoes still relied on devotees' offerings for expansion. With rulers' attention diverted, commoners and officials could contribute. This led to diverse Feitian representations in Caves 4, 15, 22, 23, 27, and 28. Feitian figures evolved towards delicacy and slenderness, influenced by Han culture [6]. Drapery became more intricate. With Northern Wei stability and increased cultural exchange, southern influence grew. This laid the aesthetic groundwork for refined Feitian figures in the Sui and Tang dynasties.

3. A Study on the Sensory Imagery and Element Extraction of 'Feitian' Figures in the Yungang Grottoes

The 'Feitian' sculptures in the Yungang Grottoes exhibit a wide range of styles, from bold and lively to subtle and introverted. Assessing their overall style is challenging due to their diverse and intricate elements. This poses a significant challenge for heritage preservation and redesign.

This section employs statistical principles and methods to determine key sensory imageries representing the 'Feitian' figures in the Yungang Grottoes. This ranking of sensory tendencies supports subsequent design concepts and practices.

3.1 Establishing a sample set of Yungang Feitian images

The Yungang Grottoes house over 2300 Feitian sculptures. Due to their sheer number, individual experiments are impractical. The author curated a representative sample set of 38 figures, encompassing diverse historical periods, cultural influences, sculptural styles, and design elements.

Following expert consultations and group deliberations, a refined selection of 12 well-preserved images with distinct attire and facial expressions was chosen as a reference sample set, shown in Figure 2 [7] [8], to represent the characteristic "Feitian" figures of the Yungang Grottoes. This refined sample set, denoted as Y, was established for subsequent research.

$$Y= \{y_1, \ y_2, \ y_3, \ ..., \ y_{12}\} \hspace{2cm} (1)$$

Figure 2. Streamlined Representation of "Feitian" Figures in Yungang Grottoes.

3.2 Establishing a set of evaluation criteria for Yungang Feitian images

After confirming research samples, it's vital to establish evaluation criteria for Feitian imagery in Yungang. The "2H" analysis method proposed here focuses on expressive presentation and spiritual essence, involving "How" (presentation) and "How much" (expansion), as depicted in Figure 3.

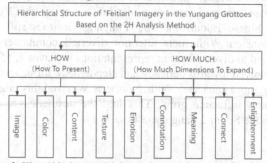

Figure 3. Hierarchical Analysis of the Yungang Grottoe "Feitian" Imagery

The current study on the sensory imagery of Feitian figure samples uses the 2H analysis method. In the "How" stage, four dimensions—form, color, content, and texture—are considered. This is combined with adjectives from scholars' regional cultural creative product design library and relevant literature. This results in the sensory imagery collection of the characteristic "Feitian" figures in the Yungang Grottoes, referred to as set A (see Figure 4) [9].

$$A= \{A_1,\ A_2,\ A_3,\ ...,\ A_{12}\} \tag{2}$$

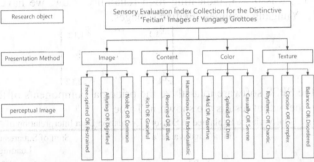

Figure 4. The Distinctive Sensory Imagery Collection of "Feitian" Images in the Yungang Grottoes

Twelve sensory descriptor sets for assessing "Feitian" figures in Yungang Grottoes were obtained through categorization. While some maintain semantic associations, further reduction through subjective judgment is impractical.

Principal component analysis[i] condenses variables without significant information loss. The next step involves summarizing the descriptors through surveys and this analysis to identify the most typical sensory characteristics of the "Feitian" figures.

3.3 Data Collection and Analysis

Participants used the semantic differential method to rate the correspondence between 12 selected "Feitian" image samples and sensory evaluations on a scale of -3 to 3 [10] [11]. A total of 162 questionnaires were collected, with 149 considered valid. The average scores for each "Feitian" image sample in the Yungang Grottoes, along with their correspondence with each pair of sensory adjectives, were computed (see Table 1):

Table 1. Average Scores for the Consistency between "Feitian" Image Samples and Sensory Evaluation

Sample	Sensory Imagery Indicators											
	A1	A2	A3	A4	A5	A6	A7	A8	A9	A10	A11	A12
y1	1.85	2.1	.51	1.05	.07	.39	0.17	.73	1.15	1.85	2.1	.51
y2	.73	.25	.61	.71	.13	.07	2.07	.52	.93	.73	.25	.61
y3	.9	.7	.83	.25	1.82	2.35	2.34	.27	0.02	.9	.7	.83
y4	.51	2.05	.31	.07	1.02	.92	.62	.1	.01	.51	2.05	.31
y5	.72	.72	.97	.52	.03	.13	1.74	.79	.72	.72	.72	.97
y6	.05	.52	.83	.73	2.15	.72	.83	.07	.83	.05	.52	.83
y7	.15	.83	2.01	.85	.37	1.9	2.03	.31	.41	.15	.83	2.01
y8	.98	.07	.47	0.27	2.12	.24	0.72	.28	.62	.98	.07	.47
y9	.1	2.15	.52	.05	.97	.82	.51	0.13	.7	.1	2.15	.52
y10	.83	.93	1.93	.72	1.83	2.02	0.7	.97	.82	.83	.93	1.93
y11	1.21	1.45	.07	2	.94	.75	.97	0.5	.15	1.21	1.45	.07

y	1	2	-	1	-	-	-	1	0	1	2	-
12	.7	.44	1.22	.37	0.25	2.18	1.89	.27	.73	.7	.44	1.22

The experimental data was validated using SPSS software. The Cronbach's Alpha coefficient [12] was 0.755, indicating high reliability. Now, we have the mean data matrix for the Yungang Grottoes "Feitian" images.

$$\begin{bmatrix} \bar{x}_{1,1} & \cdots & \bar{x}_{1,12} \\ \vdots & \ddots & \vdots \\ \bar{x}_{1,12} & \cdots & \bar{x}_{12,12} \end{bmatrix} \quad (3)$$

Using the SPSS software to analyze the principal components of the mean data in equation (3), the output results are shown in Table 2:

Table 2. Total Variance Explained in Sensory Evaluation Data Interpretation of "Feitian" Images

Constituent	Initial Eigenvalue 'a			Sum of Squares of the Extraction Loadings		
	Total	Variance Percentage	Cumulative	Total	Variance Percentage	Cumulative
1	4.958	41.319	41.319	4.958	41.319	41.319
2	2.334	19.451	60.770	2.334	19.451	60.770
3	1.435	11.958	72.728	1.435	11.958	72.728
4	1.041	8.673	81.401	1.041	8.673	81.401
5	0.877	7.308	88.709	-	-	-
6	0.696	5.797	94.506	-	-	-
7	0.300	2.500	97.006	-	-	-
8	0.204	1.697	98.703	-	-	-
9	0.101	0.838	99.541	-	-	-
10	0.050	0.415	99.956	-	-	-
11	0.005	0.044	100.000	-	-	-
12	3.537E-17	2.947E-16	100.000	-	-	-

Table 2 displays "Initial Eigenvalues," representing the contribution of each component. This percentage signifies its significance. When the cumulative percentage exceeds 80%, it's considered acceptable. For Components 1 to 4, the cumulative variance reaches 81.401%, surpassing the standard. Therefore, selecting Principal Components I to IV effectively captures and summarizes the data relationships. The variance percentages for these components are V_{ar1}=41.319%, V_{ar2}=19.451%, V_{ar3}=11.958%, and V_{ar4}=8.673%.

Table 3. Principal Component Loadings for the Sensory Evaluation Indicators of "Feitian"

Evaluation Criteria	Principal Component			
	I	II	III	IV
1	0.864	0.195	0.156	0.199
2	0.831	-0.143	-0.263	0.186
3	-0.736	0.506	-0.253	0.216
4	0.737	0.509	0.262	0.038
5	-0.432	-0.106	0.699	0.078

6	-0.745	0.603	0.084	0.181
7	-0.523	0.547	-0.016	-0.496
8	0.738	0.239	-0.141	-0.119
9	0.524	0.245	0.559	0.338
10	-0.681	-0.081	0.324	0.321
11	-0.064	-0.764	0.415	-0.399
12	-0.37	-0.615	-0.323	0.494

Table 3 lists the factor loadings, which indicate the correlation between evaluation indicators and principal components. Larger absolute values imply stronger correlation. Dividing these values by the square root of the corresponding initial eigenvalue gives the scoring coefficient matrix for Principal Components I to IV.

$$\begin{bmatrix} a_{1,1} & \cdots & a_{1,4} \\ \vdots & \ddots & \vdots \\ a_{12,1} & \cdots & a_{12,4} \end{bmatrix} \tag{4}$$

The weighted average of the coefficients of the affective indicators in these two principal component linear combinations yields the model for the weight coefficients of affective evaluation indicators.

$$v_{ai} = \frac{a_{i1}Var_1 + a_{i2}Var_2 + a_{i3}Var_3 + a_{i4}Var_4}{Var_1 + Var_2 + Var_3 + Var_4}, \quad i=1, 2, \ldots, 12 \tag{5}$$

Utilizing equation (5), the coefficients of the comprehensive score model for each evaluation indicator are computed. The variables v_{a1} to v_{a12} are normalized to obtain the weights wa1 to wa12 for the sensory evaluation indicators.

$$w_{ai} = \frac{v_{ai}}{\sum_{i=1}^{12} v_{ai}}, \quad i=1, 2, \ldots, 12 \tag{6}$$

This results in the weight data for the twelve sensory evaluation indicators, as shown in Table 4.

Table 4. Weighted Sensory Evaluation Indicators for "Feitian" in the Yungang Grottoes

Evaluation Criteria	Composite Score Coefficients	Evaluation Criterion Weights
1	$v_{a1}=0.267$	$w_{a1}=0.150$
2	$v_{a2}=0.154$	$w_{a2}=0.086$
3	$v_{a3}=0.097$	$w_{a3}=0.054$
4	$v_{a4}=0.283$	$w_{a4}=0.159$
5	$v_{a5}=0.021$	$w_{a5}=0.012$
6	$v_{a6}=0.046$	$w_{a6}=0.026$
7	$v_{a7}=0.087$	$w_{a7}=0.049$
8	$v_{a8}=0.175$	$w_{a8}=0.099$
9	$v_{a9}=0.261$	$w_{a9}=0.147$
10	$v_{a10}=0.094$	$w_{a10}=0.053$
11	$v_{a11}=0.125$	$w_{a11}=0.070$
12	$v_{a12}=0.168$	$w_{a12}=0.095$

The evaluation indicators are ranked as follows: w_{a4}, w_{a1}, w_{a9}, w_{a8}, w_{a12}, w_{a2}, w_{a3}, w_{a10}, w_{a7}, w_{a6}, w_{a5}. The top three pairs of sensory features with the highest weights suggest that the "Feitian" images in the Yungang Grottoes evoke a sense of richness, freedom, and relaxation. This diversity in emotional and sensory characteristics is a key factor in the cherished status of Feitian culture in the Yungang Grottoes as a precious cultural heritage in China.

4.   Jewelry Design Practice Based on the Sensory Image of "Feitian" Elements in the Yungang Grottoes

Three sets of affective preference adjectives were derived through principal component analysis. Now, we aim to apply these representative Yungang Feitian imageries in concrete design. First, abstract imagery adjectives will be translated into specific Yungang heritage elements. Then, these cultural design elements will be integrated, emphasizing a core cultural essence. Through various design methods, we'll achieve a unified design expressing the product's spiritual, affective, and representational features.

4.1   The analysis and translation of affective imageries

"Rich" implies density and intensity in attributes like texture, taste, and fragrance. It artistically denotes vibrant colors, refined design, profound spiritual expression, and meticulous attention to detail.

In the Yungang Grottoes, intricate decorative patterns play a vital role in creating a sense of opulence. The widely used honeysuckle pattern embodies regularity and unity, providing a magnificent visual impact and symbolizing orderly governance. This precise, finely carved style with minimal empty spaces became a distinctive feature of the Yungang sculptures.

The honeysuckle pattern is of significant importance in both the visual and spiritual aspects of Yungang art, serving as a crucial reference for subsequent designs.

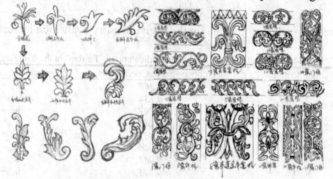

Figure 5. Excerpt from the Draft of Extracting Honeysuckle Decorative Element[ii]

"Free-spirited" suggests being carefree and transcendent, evoking a sense of flowing like clouds and water. This perception of the Yungang Feitian is easily understood when examining their distinctive characteristics.

The Yungang Feitian exude lightness, freedom, and exuberance in their graceful figures and billowing garments, conveying a palpable sense of freedom. Symbolically, they represent beings capable of transcending the earthly realm, evoking a spirit of carefree freedom.

In some artistic works, the Yungang Feitian assume poses reminiscent of dance. Through dynamic and graceful forms, they convey an atmosphere of unrestrained freedom and emotional expression, resonating with viewers' sense of carefree emotions.

Figure 6. Excerpt from the Draft of Extracting Feitian Figurative Elements [13]

The Yungang Feitian emanate ease and joy for two main reasons. Firstly, their light and graceful postures naturally instill a feeling of relaxation and comfort in viewers. Secondly, their primary duty is to entertain the Buddha through joyful dances and music, becoming their most significant form of existence. Whether holding musical instruments or engaging in song and dance, the Yungang Feitian create a relaxed and lively entertainment scene, providing viewers with a serene viewing experience.

The pipa, introduced from the Western Regions during the Qin Dynasty [14], became beloved by the imperial court's nobility. It was a fixture at royal banquets. In the Wei and Jin periods, male musicians gained prominence, including court musicians, literati, and scholars. The pipa's association with relaxation aligns perfectly with its representation [15].

Figure 7. Excerpt from the Manuscript Analyzing Artworks Related to the Pipa Element[iii][iv]

4.2 The extraction of the core spiritual essence

Modern product design increasingly emphasizes promoting traditional Chinese virtues and aesthetics. Traditional culture is a vital source of inspiration for artists, enriching their creativity. However, translating it into design often fixates on formal structures, potentially leading to a skewed understanding of its underlying traits. This results in a characteristic feature: a simplistic juxtaposition of traditional elements with modern art, often straying from the original cultural essence.

For jewelry inspired by the Yungang Grottoes' "Feitian" culture, it's crucial to go beyond surface resemblances. Delving into the spiritual characteristics is paramount. This involves exploring the fusion of Hu and Han cultures, gaining insight, and expressing the artistic essence of the Yungang's "Feitian." This approach should be woven throughout the jewelry design process.

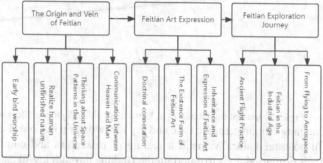

Figure 8. Extraction and Essence of the Yungang Flying Celestial Spirit

Chinese dance is often described as an "art of drawing circles [16]," creating a cyclical rhythm. This reflects a pursuit of balance and rotation, symbolizing the harmonious relationship between humanity and nature, and humanity and the universe. Dance postures are linked to the Chinese Tai Chi diagram, illustrating principles of uniform motion, yin and yang interplay, and the ever-changing nature of all things.

Furthermore, Chinese music and dance express the harmonious spirit of Tai Chi through body movement and attire. Feitian's formal features truly capture the essence of harmony and motion.

4.3   Design expression methods

Generative AI is revolutionizing product design. The era of AI brings intelligent tool platforms, optimizing different design stages. Technologies like 5G boost sales, but with heightened competition, analyzing practical cases with emerging design tools is a prevailing trend.

Integrating intelligent tech expands design thinking, diversifies approaches, cuts costs, and uncovers user needs, leading to more competitive products. The author combines traditional and AI-assisted techniques, showcasing a fusion of conventional and cutting-edge design approaches.

Figure 9. AI-Assisted Design Imagery Generation Illustration

4.4   Design case expression

The concept of "圆融" (Harmony) originates from Chinese Han Buddhism. "圆" signifies completeness and comprehensiveness, while "融" denotes integration and harmony, implying the attainment of perfect integration by eliminating delusional attachments.

In this artwork, "圆融" encompasses the fusion of Feitian imagery - integrating the pipa and honeysuckle symbolizing music and rules, and the lotus and ribbons representing regeneration and spiritual vitality. It also embodies the wearer's fusion with the millennium-old Yungang Feitian dance. The intertwining of the central jewelry piece with Feitian imagery on the packaging creates an interactive experience, immersing the wearer in a celestial realm, deepening the spiritual connection. The flowing ribbons, frozen in time, capture the essence of their graceful and lively dance.

Figure 10. Illustration for the Packaging Design of "Harmony of the Feitian"

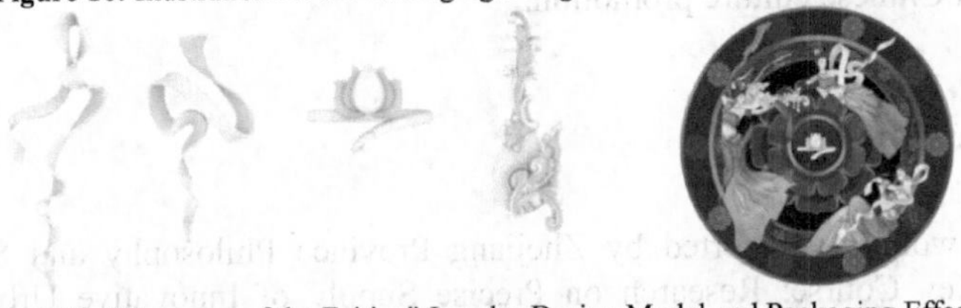

Figure 11. "Harmony of the Feitian" Jewelry Design Model and Packaging Effect

The AIGC (Artificial Intelligence in Graphic Communication) design technique is executed as follows: Hand-drawn line drafts are first colorized using the Stable Diffusion tool. Various keywords guide the creation of different textures and color combinations, offering a range of options for later selection.

Figure 12. "Harmony of the Feitian" Jewelry Design AIGC Coloring Sketch (AI-assisted completion)

Next, select the design products that align with cultural imagery, design specifications, and technical requirements, and proceed with further detailed refinement:

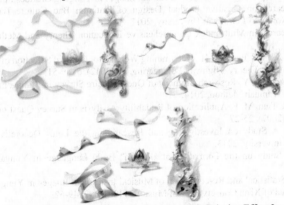

Figure 13. "Fusion of the Celestial Being" Jewelry Design AIGC Coloring Effect Image (AI-assisted completion)

5.   Conclusion

This study aims to fuse contemporary design methods with a focus on artistic representation of traditional Chinese culture. By combining mathematics and aesthetics, it offers a clearer organization of key design elements. Additionally, the paper works on refining the AI-assisted design workflow in the context of AIGC development, contributing to both commercial and societal advancements in design modernization and traditional Chinese culture promotion.

Acknowledgments

This work is supported by Zhejiang Province Philosophy and Social Sciences Annual Key Course: Research on Precise Supply of Innovative Urban Community Elderly Care Services in Standardized Format (Project Number: 22NDJC020Z), and Project supported by the Zhejiang Province Ideological and Political Education Research Project (Project Number: 220141)

References

[1] Su, B. A Study on the Staging of Yungang Grottoes. Archaeology Journal, 01 (1978), 25-38.
[2] Yungang Research Institute. (n.d.). A Century of Research on Yungang Grottoes
[3] Gong, Z. Tracing Gandhāra Art. Beijing: People's Fine Arts Publishing House., 2006
[4] Zhang, J. The Evolution of "Feitian" from Han Dynasty "Feathered Man" to Yungang Grottoes. Shandong University., 2018
[5] Wang, Y. Preliminary Exploration of Flying Deities and Heavenly Music in Kizil Murals. Soochow University, 2012
[6] Ma, Y. The Origin and Stylistic Evolution of "Feitian". Lanzhou University., 2013
[7] Chen, Y. The Reconstruction of Feitian Sculptures in Dazu Rock Carvings and the Contemporary Image of Feitian Dance. Chongqing University, 2014
[8] Liu, X. Preliminary Study of Musical Instrument Images in Yungang Grottoes.Shanxi University, 2007
[9] Liu, Z. Research on Creative Product Design of Platinum Bao Culture Based on Image Symbol Transformation.Northeast Petroleum University, 2017
[10] Su, W. Research on Multi-index Comprehensive Evaluation Theory and Method. Xiamen University, 2000
[11] Pan, L., Liu, X. P., & Feng, X. H. Determining Weights for Optimal Selection of Deep Excavation Based on Fuzzy Mathematics Theory. Highway Engineering, 37 (2012), 5, 49-51.
[12] Luo, S. Q., & Jiang, Y. Research Methods of Questionnaire Survey in Management Science. Chongqing University Press: Wanjuan Method, 2014.
[13] Zhang, H., & Tian, M. F. Application of Reliability Analysis in Survey Questionnaire Design. Statistics and Decision 21 (2007), 25-27.
[14] Wen, L. L. A Study on Investigating and Researching the Lotus Decorative Patterns of Yungang Grottoes.Shanxi University, 2013.
[15] Sun, L. T. Study on the Formation of "Feitian" Body Language in Yungang Grottoes. Shandong University, 2019.
[16] Wu, Q. Y. Statistical and Re-correction of Musical Instrument Images in Yungang Grottoes in Datong. Symphony (Journal of Xi'an Conservatory of Music) 34 (2015), 2, 49-62.

Design Studies and Intelligence Engineering
L.C. Jain et al. (Eds.)
© 2024 The Authors.
This article is published online with Open Access by IOS Press and distributed under the terms
of the Creative Commons Attribution Non-Commercial License 4.0 (CC BY-NC 4.0).
doi:10.3233/FAIA231458

Behavior-Oriented Low-Carbon Campus Mobile Interface Design Research

Yunjia CHEN[a,b,1] and Ruiyun FENG[a]

[a] *China Academy of Art, Hangzhou, China, 310001*
[b] *Design-AI lab, Hangzhou, China, 310001*

Abstract. Using the Fogg behavior model as the theoretical basis of behavior analysis, the generation and guidance of low-carbon behavior on campus are investigated from the perspectives of behavioral motivation, behavioral ability and triggering factors. At the same time, a relationship analysis was carried out on the needs of low-carbon campus construction and the design of a low-carbon campus user interface, and a research method characterized by a low-carbon campus and with the interface system as the intrinsic factor was proposed. The design inferences resulted in the quantification of low-carbon behavior and the design of low-carbon behavior. The interaction and low-carbon behaviors inspired the three interface function modules, and the feasibility of the method application was validated through design practice and experiments. This study provides new thinking and direction for interdisciplinary theoretical exploration, and its practical experience also provides new vision and support for the popularization and promotion of low-carbon development.

Keywords. behavioral design, Fogg behavioral model, low-carbon campus, interface design

1. Introduction

At the United Nations Conference on Human Environment in 1972, the discussions triggered by international environmental issues had a major impact on the path of sustainable development of mankind in the future[1]. As a part of society, schools and the education department have also begun to pay attention to environmental protection and sustainable development. In 2005, the United Nations Ten-year Education Sustainable Development Plan issued by UNESCO pointed out that education is a key factor in achieving sustainable development, and schools should become an important carrier in promoting sustainable development[2]. At the beginning of the 20th century, the United Kingdom proposed the concept of "low-carbon economy" in the energy white paper "Our Energy Future - Creating a Low-Carbon Economy" [3]. Based on the above,, the concept of a low-carbon campus emerged, which aims to reduce the negative impact of campuses on the environment through energy management, reduction of resource consumption, waste reduction, and improvement of environmental awareness. On campus, the daily behavior of teachers and students directly affects the energy consumption and carbon dioxide emissions of the campus. The bottom-up construction

---
[1] Corresponding Author. Yunjia CHEN; China Academy of Art, Hangzhou, China, 310001; E-mail: chenyunjia@caa.edu.cn

path practiced by Harvard University has effectively promoted the construction of sustainable development, which proves the important significance of the participation of teachers and students in the governance of campus environments[4]. The "Green Microaction Manual" released by the United Nations Environmental Planning Department provides a green campus framework and 40 low-carbon microaction examples that can be adopted by universities and can effectively help each construction plan guide user behavior[5]. How to motivate teachers and students to implement low-carbon behavior and guide a low-carbon lifestyle is the top priority of low-carbon campus construction. This study takes the low-carbon campus application of China Academy of Art (CAA) as the research object to carry out research and practice on low-carbon behavior-oriented mobile interface design.

2. Research methods

2.1. Fogg behavior model

B.J. Fogg, founder of the Behavioral Design Laboratory at Stanford University, established a theoretical model that is widely used in user behavior research—Fogg Behavioral Model. Fogg believes that the occurrence of personal behavior is determined by three factors: behavioral motivation, behavioral ability and triggering factors[6]. Fogg behavior model has been widely applied across various fields, including product design research aiming to improve user behavior and sustainable development goals. Mota et al. extended the Fogg Behavior Model to develop the Ubiquitous Model for Persuasive Behavior Change Systems and applied it in a case study to reduce electricity consumption[7]. Akmal et al., combining the Fogg Behavior Model with User-Centered Design, created an application to decrease household food waste[8]. Motivation includes three subcategories: feelings, expectations, and sense of belonging. Ability contains six subcategories: time, money, physical power, mental power, social acceptance, and habits. Ability here does not refer to allowing people to acquire new skills but to lower the learning barrier for products. Triggers include some kind of incentive to enhance motivation, some kind of guidance to enhance ability, and some kind of reminder. In addition, the Fogg behavior table is a supplementary tool of the Fogg behavior model, which is used to help designers and researchers better understand and classify different types of target behaviors. The table describes 15 behavior types, and each type of behavior uses different psychological strategies and persuasive techniques[9].

Based on the Fogg behavior model, in the interface design of low-carbon campus applications, we can improve the low-carbon awareness of teachers and students and promote the development of low-carbon behavior by the comprehensive effect of enhancing user motivation, improving user capabilities, and increasing trigger factors. Form a good low-carbon campus atmosphere.

Table 1. Three elements of the Fogg behavior model

Elements	Motivation	Ability	Trigger
Contents	Sensation	Time	Spark
	Pleasure/Pain	Money	
	Anticipation	Physical Effort	Facilitator
	Hope/Fear	Brain Cycles	

	Belonging	Social Deviance	Signal
	Social Acceptance/Rejection	Non-Routine	
Attributes	Intrinsic attributes	External attributes	External stimulus

2.2. User interface design

The user interface is the medium of interaction and information exchange between the system and users. User interface design is a design field that focuses on the interaction process between users and products. It involves visual interface design and user experience design for digital products such as websites, software, and mobile applications. The main goal of user interface design is to make users feel comfortable during the operation process and easy to understand and control while achieving the core functions and goals of the product. It is classified according to the workflow of user interface design and includes three parts: user research, interaction design, and interface design.

- **User research**

Before user interface design, the research on user needs through communication, questionnaire, etc., to understand the daily process, environment and usage habits of interface target users, unearth the potential needs of users, and complete the interface design from the perspective of users and implementation. The design of the interface should take the user as the starting point to improve the usability and ease of use of the interface design and make the designed products easier to accept and use. The end point of interface design should be returned to the users. After the product is released, we should continue to conduct user research to collect feedback from users and simplify and optimize unreasonable interaction design and interface aesthetics so that the interface quality will be constantly improved based on user needs and opinions.

- **Interaction design**

This refers to the interaction engineering between humans and systems, which defines the content and structure of the interaction between humans and computer systems to achieve the purpose of information exchange. The job content of an interaction designer is to design the interaction process of the entire user interface, including defining information architecture and operation processes, organizing interface elements, and using interactive design tools for prototyping. The purpose of interaction design is to improve the usability of products so that users can perform corresponding operations quickly and accurately.

- **Interface design**

Refers to the "shape" design of a software product, whose main content is to design an aesthetic and convenient user interface based on the needs of users and the interaction design framework, using aesthetics and user psychology. User research reports and interaction design results need to be used as input in interface design so that interface design remains true to the original intention of the product, improves the practicability of the product. Jakob Nielsen elaborated on how to conduct usability testing to improve interface design, and also proposed the "Ten Usability Principles" to help designers identify and fix interface problems[10].

3. Low-carbon behavior-oriented user interface

3.1. Analysis of the low-carbon behavior of users

Our survey found that in the scenes involved on campus, although there are various types of low-carbon behaviors in which teachers and students can directly or indirectly participate, they basically include the following aspects. In the dormitory and teaching of teachers and students, the measures include the use of energy-saving equipment, reasonable arrangement of indoor temperature, reduction of the standby time of electrical appliances, and the turning off of lights for one hour. Green transportation and green travel include cycling, walking, and taking public transportation. Water conservation includes the reuse of wastewater, the conservation of water for greening and the use of water-saving equipment. In terms of waste recycling, we include waste sorting, the use of green packaging, the use of renewable resources, and secondhand trading. In terms of a green diet, the empty plate campaign, the reduction of the use of disposable tableware, the reduction of the number of take-out orders, and the encouragement of vegetarianism are included. In terms of environmental protection education, the group organized environmental protection themed activities, promoted green courses, and held low-carbon lectures. In terms of low-carbon academic research, we include deepening the concept of a low-carbon campus, studying energy-saving technologies, and developing renewable energy. In terms of campus environment, we organized tree planting activities and optimized the greening layout.

According to the contents of the Fogg behavior model table, all low-carbon behaviors can be divided into 15 different types, and the characteristics of the behavior types are analyzed according to the characteristics of the behavior types to derive the low-carbon behaviors suitable for application in low-carbon campus products.

First, in terms of green behavior, green behavior refers to newly understood and attempted behaviors. This type of low-carbon behavior requires higher learning costs, and it is difficult for teachers and students to be satisfied in terms of behavioral ability and behavioral motivation. Therefore, guiding this type of behavior requires higher cost input, so this type of behavior is not selected for initial behavior guidance, but it can be shared as a challenge goal with users with behavioral ability and motivation.

In terms of blue behavior, blue behavior refers to the performance of familiar behaviors, such as daily eating and living, which is a routine behavior. For routine behaviors, users generally have the ability to perform these behaviors. Therefore, behavioral motivation becomes a greater determining factor. In blue behavior, single-point behavior can best meet the guidance of behavioral motivation, and the difficulty should gradually increase in guiding users to participate. The low-carbon transformation of daily behavior should also start from a single behavior. If users are required to change their daily behavior continuously or every day, they will be hindered by the user's daily behavior inertia, thereby reducing behavioral motivation. Therefore, among the blue behaviors, single-point behaviors are chosen for preliminary guidance; for example, teachers and students empty plate for lunch that day, and there is no extravagance.

In terms of purple behavior, purple behavior is a practice of continuously increasing behavioral density and behavioral intensity, which requires strong behavioral motivation. However, carrying out this type of low-carbon behavior only once cannot produce obvious low-carbon benefits, and it is also very likely to generate excess carbon emissions. In addition, purple radial behavior is too difficult to achieve, requiring high behavioral motivation and ability to achieve. Therefore, for purple behaviors, we should choose intermittent behaviors to try and choose low-carbon behaviors that do not easily generate associated carbon emissions to guide.

In terms of gray behavior, gray behavior refers to the practice of reducing the density and intensity of behaviors. This behavior type actively lowers the standards of behavioral ability and behavioral motivation, making it easier for users to perform. However, it is difficult for a single engagement of gray behavior to help cultivate users' low-carbon habits, and its low-carbon benefit is not high. In addition, radial gray behavior requires users to have certain perseverance and determination, which requires higher physical and mental strength, as well as better result expectations. As a result, it is expected that it is more difficult to judge and user behavior is more difficult to maintain. Therefore, gray discontinuous behavior was chosen as a guide; for example, a student reduced his weekly or monthly electricity consumption in the dormitory.

Black behavior refers to the cessation of a certain behavior. The low-carbon benefit of this behavior type in a single point of behavior is not large, and the impact on teachers and students in the formation of low-carbon behavior habits is also relatively small. In addition, the behavioral motivation and ability required for this type of low-carbon behavior are low, and the possibility of forming radial behavior is high. The behaviors can be started from simple, conventional low-carbon behaviors, such as stopping the use of paper receipts and paying electronically. In daily life, it is common to replace paper tickets with electronic tickets, and it is easier to implement this low-carbon behavior.

Table 2. Table of Fogg's Behaviors for Low-Carbon behaviors

	Green Behavior	Blue Behavior	Purple Behavior	Gray Behavior	Black Behavior
Dot Behavior	Use energy-saving products	Empty plate	Campus tree planting	Reduce use of express packaging	No electronic products today
Span Behavior	Learn low-carbon knowledge for one month	Continue to use reusable bags for shopping	Subway travel replaces taxis	Reduce electricity consumption in dormitories	No heating in winter
Path Behavior	Become an Environmentalist Now	Garbage sorting every day	Buy green products	Reduce the use of disposable tableware	Stop using paper tickets

3.2. Interface interaction function module

As a representative part, the low-carbon campus represents the characteristics of the low-carbon concept and sustainable development and is involved in the dissemination of low-carbon concepts, the improvement of teacher-student participation, the optimization of resource allocation, and low-carbon operation and management. The motivation of low-carbon behavior, the ability of low-carbon behavior, the trigger of low-carbon behavior, etc., are reflected in the interface function module.

The motivation for engaging in low-carbon behavior is composed of feelings, expectations and a sense of belonging. Low-carbon behavior itself is a kind of benevolent behavior. Before users engage in low-carbon behavior, if they can perform the expected evaluation of the results and let them clearly know the effects of the behavior, it will help to improve the users' positive psychology. Therefore, in the interface interaction, the low-carbon behavior of the teachers and students can be calculated and quantified, and the data results can be visualized through the carbon footprint and carbon integral, giving the behavior an objective calculation standard and evaluation standard. The quantification of low-carbon behavior is also a precondition for all functions. Only by quantifying behavior can we give relevant feedback on other functions from an objective perspective.

Low-carbon behavioral capacity includes time, money, physical power, mental power, social acceptance and irregularity. In terms of time and money, users can be allowed to independently arrange how and when they generate low-carbon behaviors, which can lower the participation threshold and improve the efficiency of interface operation. In terms of physical and mental strength, interesting and gamified functions such as low-carbon activities, low-carbon games and low-carbon tasks can be combined to give users more levels of participation experience. In terms of social acceptance, users need to have a certain degree of environmental awareness and the concept of sustainable development. Therefore, in the interface interaction, the concept of a low-carbon campus is communicated as much as possible through clear and concise information, and the popularization of low-carbon knowledge helps users to practice low-carbon behavior awareness and corresponding abilities. In terms of unconventional aspects, to develop a low-carbon lifestyle, it is necessary to turn low-carbon behavior into a daily habit. Therefore, you can design content interaction that combines low-carbon behavior with daily campus behavior. While promoting the carbon campus culture, you can also experience the fun of practicing low-carbon behavior, thereby enhancing user stickiness and promoting the development of low-carbon behavior.

In Fogg behavioral model, a trigger is an external stimulus that generates target behavior. For example, when performing low-carbon behavior, the use of external stimuli that motivate, assist, and signal is used to make users easier and more willing to engage in low-carbon behavior. In the interaction design of a low-carbon campus interface, user feedback can be enhanced, and reward and incentive mechanisms can be designed to help stimulate user needs; through the establishment of low-carbon groups and communities, the sharing of relevant stories and cases of others can help enhance users' sense of identity and sense of belonging.

Table 3. Behavior-oriented low-carbon campus interface functional modules

Functional module	Quantifying low-carbon behavior	Motivation
	Behavior quantification, data visualization, carbon accounts, carbon footprint	
	Low carbon behavior interaction	**Ability**
	Activities, gamification, fun, enhanced experience	
	Low carbon behavior incentives	**Trigger**
	Low carbon rights exchange, shopping mall, welfare, etc.	

4. Interface design experiment

4.1. Experiment purpose and objects

To guide power-saving behavior in the dormitory area, an interface design experiment was conducted. The experimental subjects were mainly dormitory students at the Xiangshan campus of CAA. The purpose of the experiment is to prove that this study uses the method of combining the Fogg behavior model with the interface design workflow to optimize the interactive experience of low-carbon campus products and achieve effective and quantifiable carbon reduction results. The electricity consumption data provided by the campus construction office of CAA were used in the experiment as the basis for evaluating the results.

4.2. Analysis of Power Saving Behavior

First, behavior analysis was performed on the electricity use behavior of students in the dormitory. Based on the judgment of the behavior type of reducing electricity consumption in the dormitory area, this behavior belongs to the gray intermittent behavior type, which is characterized by persistence and weakening behavior intensity. According to the three-element analysis of the Fogg behavior model, the analysis of the power-saving behavior of the student dormitories started from the three main factors: behavioral motivation, behavioral ability and triggers. From the motivation of students to save electricity, electricity saving is to reduce the use of electricity. In some cases, it may cause a decrease in the user's electricity experience, such as reducing the time that the lights are on and the length of use of air conditioners. brings negative feelings to the physiological or psychological experience of the user. The behavior of saving electricity is directly related to the electricity bills paid, and there is a certain purpose of saving electricity. Therefore, when users engage in this behavior, they have a high opinion of the results, thus promoting continuous power-saving behavior. At the same time, power-saving behavior is a behavior with high acceptance in society and is generally accepted, which can have a positive effect on user behavior.

In terms of behavioral ability, the continuous power-saving behavior requires the user to continue to perform and memorize the corresponding actions for a certain period of time, which putsplaces higher demands on ability in terms of time, physical strength, and mental strength; however, power saving electricity can reduce the corresponding actions. Electricity bills belong to the basic ethical norms of society, so it is easier to meet the ability standard in terms of money and social acceptance. In addition, the electricity -saving behavior may be an unconventional behavior when it is implemented for the first time, and it takes a certain amount of time and effort to turn it into a routine behavior.

The low-carbon behavior of electricity saving may be slightly insufficient in behavioral motivation, so it needs to be compensated for in terms of time, mental, physical and unconventional behavioral capabilities. Excitation-extrinsic motivation can be used to stimulate users to perform power-saving behavior to compensate for the lack of behavioral motivation; support-directional guidance can be used to let users understand and learn low-carbon skills and solve the lack of time, mental, and physical resources; and signaling—timely information transmission—can be used to remind users to perform power-saving behavior to maintain this behavior and gradually develop it into a habit.

4.3. Interface design requirements

In terms of functional requirements, according to the previous description of the functional modules of the low-carbon campus interface design, it is first necessary to quantify low-carbon electricity-saving behavior and provide evaluation criteria for electricity-saving behavior. Therefore, according to the IPCC carbon footprint calculation method, clear personal electricity-saving behavior can be obtained by multiplying electricity savings by the average carbon dioxide emission factor of China's regional grid and dividing by the number of electricity users in the dormitory (the dormitory types are divided into four-bed rooms and sixteen-bed rooms). the contributed emission reductions.

To address the lack of motivation for electricity-saving behavior, an electricity consumption ranking list was set up to stimulate users' behavioral motivation through competition among electricity-saving rankings in the same building. At the same time, the carbon emission reduction caused by power saving is converted based on the fact that the emission reduction amount per gram of carbon dioxide is equal to one carbon credit, and the generated carbon credits are awarded to users with power-saving behavior, thus further motivating users to engage in power-saving behavior.

In response to the lack of electricity-saving behavior ability and to reduce the physical, mental, and time consumption of users, a smart electricity bill is designed and provided, where the electricity consumption data are clearly displayed on the interactive interface, and at the same time, the target electricity savings can be set to make up for it. The user's power-saving behavior ability is insufficient. At the same time, it is supported by a small low-carbon skill function module to give users corresponding low-carbon skills and more conveniently indicate the direction and method of power-saving behavior.

According to the function of the daily bill push, the issuance of carbon credits is used as a positive message reminder to remind users when they check their daily bills or use products, and the information related to power-saving behavior is transmitted to be triggered to implement power-saving behavior.

4.4. Interface prototype design

The prototype of the dormitory electricity-saving interface mainly takes electricity billing as the core function, the quantification of electricity-saving behavior and the electricity-saving ranking list as secondary functions, and the small low-carbon skills as auxiliary functions. As a prerequisite for guidance on electricity usage behavior, the quantification of user power-saving behavior also belongs to the first-level information level. Therefore, it is preferentially displayed on the page to provide users with decision criteria (Figure 1).

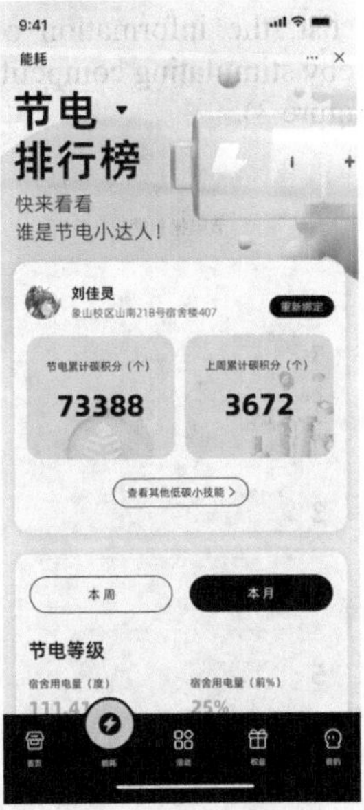

Figure 1. Quantification of electrical behavior

In the electricity bill part, the detailed information on electricity consumption is mainly displayed in the form of the electricity saving level, electricity consumption comparison of similar dormitories, and electricity consumption curve. At the same time, the weekly electricity consumption and the monthly electricity consumption can be switched. In the electricity consumption level, the four levels were divided according to the amount of electricity consumption, and emotional expressions such as smiling face and crying face were used as displays to guide users to engage in power-saving behavior (Figure 2).

Figure 2. Electricity bill

On the power-saving ranking list, the information of the top three dormitories is prioritized and highlighted, thereby stimulating competition among users and promoting more power-saving behavior (Figure 3).

Figure 3. Power saving ranking list

Finally, as an auxiliary function of small low-carbon skills, it provides users with low-carbon and power-saving tips in all aspects in the form of card messages to assist and guide users in power-saving behavior and provides users with behavioral practices and directions (Figure 4).

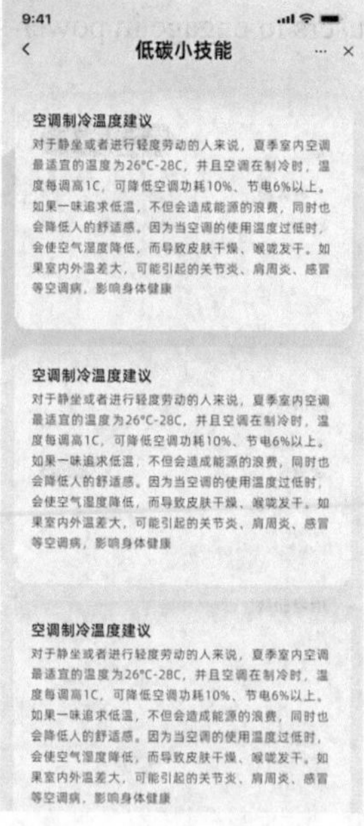

Figure 4. Small low-carbon skills

4.5. Experimental results

After two weeks of trial operation of the power-saving behavior-related interface design application, based on the data feedback provided by the campus construction office of Xiangshan Campus of CAA, the average savings of electricity in the four-person dormitory within three weeks was 38 kWh, and the maximum savings was 119 kWh. The daily average saving of electricity is 1.8 kWh; the average saving of electricity in the sixteen-person dormitory is 101 kWh within three weeks, the maximum is 472 kWh, and the daily average saving is 4.8 kWh; the student dormitory can earn carbon credits up to 42,640 points for electricity saving, which is the cumulative reduction of carbon dioxide. The emission volume was 42.64 kg.

According to the feedback of the experiment results, the students have implemented the corresponding electricity usage behavior and obtained the corresponding electricity saving results. The low-carbon campus interface design experiment guided by electricity-saving behavior obtained positive results, which can prove the effectiveness of the design method. This method can be applied to other behavior-guided low-carbon campus interface designs. It should be noted that the feedback data on the subjective needs of users were not provided in the experimental process. The interface was mainly used according to the objective requirements and the overall needs of the low-carbon campus interface design. The accuracy of the results needs further verification.

5. Design Practice

5.1. Interface function architecture

The low-carbon campus mobile interface functional modules are mainly composed of home page, energy consumption, activities, rights and interests, carbon treasure map game and personal carbon account sections. Among them, energy consumption is the main core functional module, and personal carbon accounting is the prerequisite for all functional modules. Activities, rights and interests, and the carbon treasure map game are functional modules to enhance user experience. In terms of the overall structure, energy consumption is the first level of information, activities, rights and interests, and personal carbon accounts are the second level of information, and the carbon treasure map game is the third level of information. The rest of the assistive functions were at level four and above.

5.2. Interface visual architecture

Graphic visual design mainly revolves around color and graphics. The overall low-carbon campus interface style needs to satisfy the requirements of light weight, youthful vitality, digital technology, and the campus cultural characteristics of CAA.

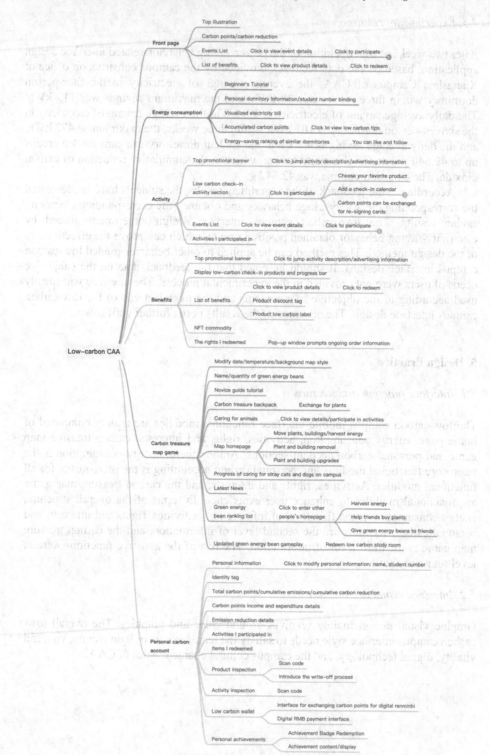

Figure 5. Interface functional framework

- **Digital technology**

This product uses the dual-carbon technology algorithm in energy consumption management, carbon account management and carbon footprint calculation. Digital intelligence is the powerful technical support for the product, and this element should be displayed at the visual level to enhance the sense of digital technology in the user experience. A digital sense usually involves the use of modern design elements and technologies, including the use of flat design language on graphics and buttons to make them briefer and clearer. In the main graphic design, the design form of the combination of 3D elements and two-dimensional elements is used to reflect the modern characteristics. In color matching, bright main colors and bright auxiliary colors are used. On the material, adding transparency effects, such as translucent elements, layers, and interface effects, can enhance the modern and technological sense.

- **Gome characteristics**

The campus of CAA has the poetic quality of "humanistic landscape, spiritual home". In the article "The Prospect of the University: On the Construction and the Spirit of the 'University'", Prof. Xu Jiang, former president of CAA, proposed the ideal of "the Prospect" of the construction of Chinese universities: the Prosperity of the University is the relationship between mountains and rivers on the university campus. The environment of youth also refers to the environment of spiritual shaping facing the historical fork, values, and spiritual quality in youth, and at the same time, it is the soil for the continuous deepening of the academic spirit of a university. He believes that the construction of universities should be people-oriented, pay attention to humanistic care and emotional experience, focus on the construction of the spiritual level, be inclusive and diverse, and have a sense of social responsibility. Prof. Xu Jiang compared the natural environment of the university campus to green hills, and he created the campus landscape from reality to the spiritual level, using the green to nourish creation and to cultivate personality and mind.

Based on the above style characteristics, in color matching, bright and breezy main colors are used, with clear introduction auxiliary colors. The main colors are light grass green (Hex: 99ED73), which represents youthful vitality, green and low carbon, and blue (Hex: 62ECE6), which represents digital technology. As auxiliary colors, black and white with a clear brief introduction and blue–gray (Hex: E0E6E6) were used with the background.

Hex: 99ED73   Hex: 62ECE6   Hex: 000000   Hex: FFFFFF   Hex: E0E6E6

Figure 6. Interface color selection

In the main color matching, a large number of gradients from light grass green (Hex: 99ED73) to cyan blue (Hex: 62ECE6) are used to blend the main colors to create the characteristics of a green landscape. At the same time, the use of gradient colors has been a trend in recent years. The design trend can better fit the aesthetics of the young group.

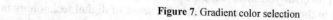

Figure 7. Gradient color selection

In terms of graphic design, a large number of rich and active 3D graphic designs were used, supplemented by the characteristic display of different sections and the characteristics of various activities, which can enhance the characteristics of technology and modernization while adding interest. In 3D graphics, transparent materials and overlay effects are often used to enhance the lightweight and digital characteristics of the products.

Figure 8. 3D pattern design

While performing 3D graphic design, the design language of plane buttons and other graphics followed the design language based on the introduction, with the main use of black and white color matching. Some buttons representing low-carbon activities and low-carbon rights and interests used brighter colors and had various shapes. The rounded corner design is used to enhance the intimacy of the product.

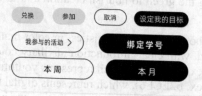

Figure 9. Flat button design

5.3. Resonance of low-carbon behavior

Low-carbon behavior guidance works from the three aspects of behavior quantification, behavior interaction and behavior incentives and finally generates behavioral resonance on the campus to enhance the low-carbon cultural atmosphere and establish a consensus on low-carbon development, thus circularly and positively promoting the construction of low-carbon campuses. The realization of this process mainly depends on the activities section. In the activity list, users can choose to participate in low-carbon activities such as subway riding, empty plate campaign, and electronic bills. Users only need to upload the vouchers, which will be verified by the background database. After the verification is passed, the system will automatically update the cumulative amount of carbon reduction to the user's carbon reduction data, and the user's carbon account will also be rewarded with corresponding carbon points.

At the same time, a "low-carbon clock-in" is set up in the interactive mechanism to encourage users to continue to participate in low-carbon activities. Once the cumulative number of clock-in days reaches the target value, users can receive extra desired rights and interests while earning carbon points.

Figure 10. Flat button design

5.4. Interface usability testing

After the interface design of the low-carbon campus mini program is completed, we need to conduct a usability test of relevant functions and apply it in different scenarios. First, the usability, ease of use, effectiveness, error frequency, and satisfaction degree of each function of the mini program were the main aims. By inviting users to participate in the experiment, based on the process of users performing relevant operations and given tasks, the problems in the product are discovered and understood to correct and optimize the overall experience of the product.

5.4.1. Usability testing

Purpose of testing: To provide an interactive prototype, to discover design deficiencies and to develop optimization strategies based on the feedback of testers in specific scenarios.

Test subjects: Ten student users from the Xiangshan Campus of CAA were invited to conduct the test.

Test task: The main test tasks are proposed based on the functional modules of the product. The task types mainly include personal, energy consumption, activity, equity, and carbon treasure map games. The specific tasks are shown in the following table:

Table 4. Usability testing task content

Number	Task type	Task content
1	Personal	View the total amount of carbon credits and the cumulative emission reductions
2		View carbon credit balance details and emission reduction details
3	Energy consumption	Enter the energy consumption page to bind your student ID number
4		View the electricity consumption level and electricity consumption in the dormitory
5		Check the energy-saving leaderboard and find "My Dormitory"
6		View "Small low-carbon skills"
7	Activities	View the details of any event
8		View "Example" on the event details page
9		Participate in and complete any activity
10		Reupload event picture
11		View "My Activities"
12	Equity	View any product details
13		Redeem any benefit product
14		View the "Redemption Details" of the product
15	Carbon treasure map	Enter the carbon treasure map game
16		Enter the Carbon Treasure Mall to purchase any treasure
17		Check the backpack and plant the purchased treasures
18		Collect Green Energy Beans on the map
19		Recycle any treasure on the map
20		Go to "My Achievements" to redeem any badge
21		Check the ranking of friends and collect the green energy beans from any friend
22		Ask any friend for Green Energy Beans
23		Distribute green energy beans to a friend based on the news dynamics

5.4.2. Test results and optimization strategy

According to the proposed task goal, the feedback of each user participating in the test was observed, and the time spent by the user and the contents that hindered the operation were recorded to obtain the experience feedback of each functional section.

Table 5. Usability testing task evaluation form

Task number	Task time/s										Average/s
1	8	5	10	7	9	6	11	9	12	7	8.4
2	54	47	60	56	51	50	58	49	55	45	52.5
3	23	27	20	25	24	21	22	18	26	20	22.6

4	29	32	35	26	28	31	27	34	30	33	30.5
5	11	15	13	9	12	10	14	12	8	11	11.5
6	11	9	8	14	12	10	7	13	11	9	10.4
7	39	32	42	36	37	40	44	35	38	41	38.4
8	10	5	12	13	9	11	8	6	7	10	9.1
9	16	11	19	20	17	15	14	18	17	16	16.3
10	6	8	2	4	5	7	9	3	5	4	5.3
11	10	12	7	15	9	11	8	13	6	14	10.5
12	25	27	22	31	29	26	23	24	28	27	26.2
13	10	14	13	11	12	9	7	11	13	8	10.8
14	17	20	16	14	19	18	15	12	14	20	16.5
15	3	7	5	1	4	2	6	5	3	4	4
16	16	18	12	20	14	17	15	19	16	13	16
17	5	3	9	7	6	8	4	7	6	5	6
18	3	6	5	8	7	4	2	1	6	5	4.7
19	17	15	19	18	20	16	14	13	18	12	16.2
20	9	7	12	6	8	10	11	8	7	9	8.7
21	10	12	8	13	11	9	7	14	12	10	10.6
22	12	10	15	11	13	14	13	11	10	14	12.3
23	14	20	12	16	15	13	17	11	16	18	15.2
Test user	**U1**	**U2**	**U3**	**U4**	**U5**	**U6**	**U7**	**U8**	**U9**	**U10**	/

The test results showed that in the personal section, users could clearly view the total number of personal carbon credits and quickly view the carbon credit revenue and expenditure details and emission reduction details. The usability of the personal carbon account was verified, and the interaction logic and framework were simple. Easy to understand. However, some details need to be modified in use. Half of the users had to try multiple times when clicking the "Back" button. This is due to the small click range of this button, and the click range needs to be enlarged to improve the page switching experience.

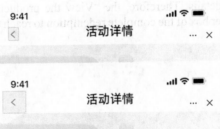

Figure 11. "Back" button click range

In the energy consumption section, users can quickly bind and view the power-saving ranking without obvious obstacles in the operation process. However, users are not clear about the usage of each function of this functional block, and they need to explain the usage of the functions on the electricity bill, such as the electricity saving level, electricity saving carbon points, electricity usage comparison, and electricity usage ranking list. Therefore, based on this result, a complete novice guidance tutorial for the energy consumption section was designed. When using this section for the first time, the operation logic and usage method of each function were explained based on the novice tutorial so that users could better understand how to participate.

Figure 12. "Beginner's guidance for the energy consumption sector

In the event section, users spend more time viewing the event details and clarifying the event information. Currently, most event information can only be presented in text form. Therefore, through the hierarchical design of the text information, users can better read content. At the same time, after users understand the activity information, the operation process is simple and efficient, and they encounter no obvious obstacles in the process of participating in the activity.

In the rights and interests section, users did not encounter obvious blocking factors and could clearly and quickly redeem products based on existing carbon points. However, some users hesitated to check the "exchange details". This is because the information level of the product details is relatively deep, and multiple interactions are required to open the redemption details. Therefore, the "View the products I have redeemed" is designed in the reminder box of the complete redemption to reach the "redemption details" page faster.

Figure 13. Reminder box of successful redemption

In the carbon treasure map game section, there are many operable tasks, some of which are complicated, and the intention is not clear. Therefore, based on the carbon treasure map experience process, the corresponding novice guidance tutorial is designed to help users understand the basic operation of the game more quickly. In other game experience operations, the user did not encounter obvious obstacles; the process is clear, providing a simple and easy-to-understand user experience.

Figure 14. Carbon treasure map novice guide

Based on the above test results, the users evaluated and scored the usability of the current prototype using a 10-point scale. The specific scores are shown in the following table:

Table 6. Table of prototype usability scores

Assessment object	U1	U2	U3	U4	U5	U6	U7	U8	U9	U10
Score	7	6	8	7	7	6	8	9	6	7
Average score	7.1									

Based on usability testing and the optimization strategy of each functional area, the product underwent preliminary iterations. However, the number of users participating in the testing was relatively small, which would have a certain impact on the usability results. After the product is launched, based on more user experience feedback, more product experience data can be collected to discover experience problems in the product and make improvements and optimizations.

6. Conclusion

Using the Xiangshan campus of China Academy of Art as a case, this study proposes a research construction method characterized by a low-carbon campus with an intrinsic interface system to investigate low-carbon behavior on campus from the perspective of low-carbon behavior motivation, low-carbon behavior ability and low-carbon trigger factors. The generation and guidance of the method were conducted, and the feasibility of the method application was verified through design practice and experiments. In terms of theoretical research, this study provides new thinking and directions for interdisciplinary theoretical exploration; in a practical sense, the practical experience of this study also provides new vision and support for the popularization and promotion of low-carbon development. In addition, in terms of user behavior guidance, the Fogg behavior model itself has certain deficiencies. In the future, we can refer to and use theoretical models in other disciplines for more research. At the same time, short-term research has a certain effectiveness, and the practical results may be affected by various factors. In the future, we should continue to focus on sustainable and long-term practice processes to contribute to global low-carbon development.

Acknowledgements

This work was supposed by the "Study and practice of integrated science and art low-carbon campus construction strategy", a major bidding project of China Academy of Art in 2022 (Grant No.ZB2022008), and Art Key Grant Project of National Social Science Foundation of China (Grant No.20ZD09).

References

[1] United Nations. Report of United Nations on the Human Environment. 1973. A/CONF.48/14/Rev.1.
[2] United Nations Educational, Scientific and Cultural Organization (UNESCO). United Nations Decade of Education for Sustainable Development (2005-2014): International Implementation Scheme. Paris: UNESCO, 2005.
[3] Department of Trade and Industry. Our energy future–creating a low carbon economy. The Stationery Office, 2003.
[4] Xu J. Research on the Governance Structure and Operation Mechanism of Sustainable Development University Construction: A Case Study of Harvard University. *Journal of Tongji University (Social Science Edition)*, **28** (2017), 85-93.
[5] United Nations Environment Programme, GRID Arendal and Behavioural Insights Team. The Little Book of Green Nudges: 40 Nudges to Spark Sustainable Behaviour on Campus. Nairobi and Arendal: UNEP and GRID-Arendal, 2020.
[6] Fogg B J. A behavior model for persuasive design. Proceedings of the 4th international conference on Persuasive Technology, 2009.

[7] Mota F P, Primo T T, Botelho S S C. Ubiquitous Model for Persuasive Behavior Change Systems: A Case Study on Energy Efficiency. *IFAC-PapersOnLine*, **53** (2020): 17487-17492.

[8] Akmal M, Niwanputri G S. Spoonful: Mobile Application for Reducing Household Food Waste using Fogg Behavior Model (FBM). 2021 International Conference on Data and Software Engineering (ICoDSE). IEEE, 2021.

[9] Fogg B J. The behavior grid: 35 ways behavior can change. Proceedings of the 4th international Conference on Persuasive Technology. 2009.

[10] Nielsen J. Usability engineering. Morgan Kaufmann, 1994.

Design Studies and Intelligence Engineering
L.C. Jain et al. (Eds.)
© *2024 The Authors.*
This article is published online with Open Access by IOS Press and distributed under the terms
of the Creative Commons Attribution Non-Commercial License 4.0 (CC BY-NC 4.0).
doi:10.3233/FAIA231459

Interface Design of College Life Circle APP Based on Improved KJ Method-Entropy Power Method

Xiaofei LU[a,1] and Shouwang LI[b]

[a] *School of Art, Xi'an University of Science and Technology, Xi'an.*
[b] *School of Art, Xi'an University of Science and Technology, Xi'an.*

Abstract. With the expansion of the size of the city and university groups and the diversification of user demand services, the map APP design needs to consider the relationship between urban development and user demand. Therefore, to improve the users' demand and enhance the users' use of neighborhood services, an APP based on the university life circle, "U-Tour", is designed. Firstly, the improved KJ method and entropy weight method are used to obtain the user demand and weight, and the existing living circle demand and weight; secondly, the comprehensive weight and ranking are obtained; and then the two types of variables are verified through correlation analysis, and the design of "U-Tour" APP is carried out based on the comprehensive weight and ranking after the verification is passed. It is found that the weights of traffic and access service, accommodation service and catering and shopping service are higher in the comprehensive demand, which are 0.252, 0.232 and 0.152 respectively, which proves that the APP design based on university life circle needs to focus on the navigation design and service design. The study points out that college map-based APP design needs to be measured to the factors of city life and user needs.

Keywords. University, Life Circle, App interface design, Improved KJ method, Entropy weight method, Correlation analysis

1. Introduction

Accompanied by the change of people's travelling mode and living needs, the living area as a planning method gradually affects people's production and life through the connection of facilities and needs, space and behavior [1]. In recent years, in Chinese cities, the number of infrastructures, trade places and cultural consumption service centres built around the special group of college students has been increasing, while at the same time, the enrolment scale and area of colleges and universities have been expanding, which has led to the creation of college living circles [2]. Taking the school as the starting point and the surrounding POI as the destination, the college life circle has become an important factor influencing the development of the city. However, there are still some problems with college life or college life circle, such as Chai Zonggang [3] mentioned that the backward concept of college campus planning in China and the

---
[1] Corresponding Author: Li Shouwang, lishouwang155@163.com. ORCiD ID: Li Shouwang https://orcid.org/0009-0009-7546-0216

phenomenon of human-vehicle conflict in colleges and universities need to be based on the theory of life circle to update the concept of college campus planning. In his study, Sun Yingnan[4] also found that there are irrationally placed service facilities in the living circle of colleges and universities. These studies reflect that the university community has difficulties in travelling and the university life circle cannot meet the needs of people well.

This study aims to use the improved KJ method to explore the needs of university users, and also extract the needs of the existing university life circle through the entropy power method, so as to better address the needs of users through the different functional interfaces of the APP design. This study proposes for the first time the improved KJ method-entropy weight method: that is, adding user assignment in the KJ method to carry out the calculation of user needs, and on this basis, weighting the results of the improved KJ method and entropy weight method to obtain the final demand weights.

The rest of this study is as follows: Chapter 2 reviews the research on college life circle and related APP design, traditional KJ method-entropy weight method, and improved KJ-entropy weight method, to illustrate the reasonableness and feasibility of the study; Chapter 3 conducts experiments using the improved KJ method-entropy weight method and verifies the results of the experiments, which proves the validity of the present study; Chapter 4 develops a specific design practice based on the results of the study, and designs a college life circle and related APP. Based on the results of the study, Chapter 4 develops a concrete design practice, designing the interface of the college life circle APP-"U-Tour".

2. Theoretical Background

2.1. College Life Circle and Its Related APP Design

Accessibility is used in urban planning and plays an important role in urban transport sustainability and environmental sustainability. Measurements of accessibility can be broadly classified into two categories: place-centred and person-centred, where life circle as a place-centred accessibility analysis takes into account the importance of the time dimension[5]. In traditional life circle analysis, the origin (starting point) is given and points of interest (POIs) in its vicinity are displayed based on that point, showing different travelling times through points, lines, or areas. Location-centred accessibility spatio-temporal analysis not only enriches the spatio-temporal data of urban space, but also provides pre-design information for urban design. The study of life circle in urban space focuses on the driving time around certain types of locations in the city centre, for example, Wu Guohao et al.[6] analysed the isochronous circle of the fire station in Nanjing, analysed the spatial accessibility of the fire station through its spatial distribution pattern and coverage, and put forward reasonable development suggestions for the layout of fire fighting resources. Another example is the study by Wu, Chao-Yu and Zhou, Xiang[7] on the distribution of educational facilities, which found that the "isochronous circle" approach based on the actual travelling distance and population size can better provide educational facility services for mountainous cities. These studies demonstrate that analyses of life circles can be used to identify the problems and needs of life circles in certain types of locations.

For the college life circle research focuses on student travel behaviour, daily needs, service mode, such as Li Xuefeng[8] through the student daily life circle, for the student campus public facilities configuration and campus planning to provide solutions to the problems that arise. Zhang Jing and He Tian[9] explore the value of the campus WeChat service platform for the design of college life circle in Changzhou, which shows that online service is valuable for perfecting the user experience and improving the college life circle, and lays a theoretical foundation for this study. The map APPs designed for college groups in China are mainly divided into two types: navigation and information service, such as "My University" APP, which has the functions of campus guide, campus socialisation and study assistant, and is a more mature map APP at present. There are more information service APPs in the theoretical research, such as the campus errand APP designed by Bao Wenxia[10] based on the Axure platform, which digs deeper into the user requirements to drive the digital campus environment. He Runxin and Tang Xuelian[11] designed the "Zhixiao" APP for college staff, which provides the staff with services such as financial enquiry, campus food ordering, student list enquiry, etc. It provides a specialised service platform for college staff.

From the above studies, it is easy to find that there are many APP designs based on certain types of services or groups in colleges and universities, with more specific functions and focusing on services within the campus, while there are fewer studies on APP designs targeting the needs of the periphery of the campus. College life circle APP design is committed to the use of POI around the campus, through the navigation guide, provide information and other ways to drive the campus internal and external services, so as to meet the needs of different groups.

2.2. Traditional and Improved KJ Method - Entropy Weight Method

The KJ method, also known as the affinity diagram method, was proposed by Professor Jiro Kawakita of Tokyo Institute of Technology in 1964 as a method of investigation and analysis from the product itself. The traditional KJ method collects the needs of user groups through questionnaires and other forms, and then gradedly summarises and collates them according to their interrelationships, lists the list of indicators, and finally forms a clear first-level indicator of the content of the needs[12]. While entropy in entropy weight method is a measure of the degree of disorder of the system, you can use the entropy value to judge the degree of dispersion of a certain indicator, and analysis based on the premise of objective data is the basis of entropy weight method[13].

In the known design research, the KJ method is often used in the improvement of design research, in addition to the combination of different methods for innovative design[14], such as W Ding and YM Zhou[15] KJ technology and AHP (Hierarchical Analysis) combined with the elderly wheelchair design, from the point of view of the designer and the elderly to explore the needs of the power wheelchair and then carry out the design of the entity, the method of the user's real ideas and needs for in-depth excavation, which provides a certain theoretical basis for the study of the user's needs in this paper. This method provides a certain theoretical basis for this paper to study the user's needs by digging deeper into the user's real ideas and needs. Another example is He Yongliang[16], who extracts the functional requirements of the gun and ammunition cabinet from the traditional KJ method, and then uses the KANO model to carry out data statistics and analysis for the functional design, which converts the requirements into actual real-world functions. From the above papers, we can see that the traditional KJ method can get the required design elements from the user in the case of vague design requirements, and then carry out innovative design. However, as far as the KJ method itself is concerned, the traditional KJ method only obtains the elements of requirements through the card processing editor, which have an explanatory role, but cannot derive the specific weights of these elements.

Therefore, this study adopts the improved KJ method in the research methodology, and the flow is shown in Fig. 1. The improved KJ method retains the research process (Step 1) of the traditional KJ method, such as respondent selection, grouping of textual information, and creation of function cards, etc., but it adds users' subjective assignments of textual information in the research in order to compute the weights of the indicators at different levels in Step 2. At the same time, add the calculation of the weight of the function card, that is, in step 3, let the users choose the indicators that they think are the most important, and determine the weight of each indicator through the weight of the most important indicators chosen by different users. Finally, the results in step 2 and step 3 are superimposed to obtain the final user requirement weights and ranking.

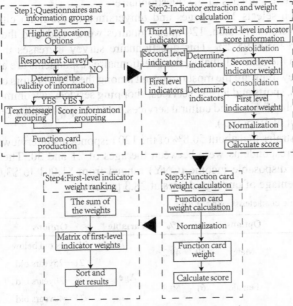

Figure 1. Improved KJ method research flow chart.

In addition to this, the entropy weight method, which is based on objective data analysis, is added to analyse the requirements, considering that the improved KJ method only considers user requirements. Entropy weight method has been widely used in design research to combine with other models to enhance the objectivity of design requirements. For example, Wang Weiwei et al.[17] determine the weights of evaluation indexes through F-AHP, and extract the key Chinese Spring Festival cultural design factors through entropy weighting method in the design, and then Yang Yuling et al.[18] firstly AHP and entropy weighting method respectively on the pre-determined indexes to calculate the weights, and then use the combination of AHP-entropy weighting method to get the comprehensive ordering of the design scheme, and select the optimal ASD child intervention APP navigation interface design. programme. The above study shows that the entropy weight method is feasible to be combined with other models and that this method can help designers to select the optimal design solution or design factors.

Compared with the traditional KJ-entropy weighting method, the improved KJ-entropy weighting method starts from the user demand and the objective reality demand,

and takes the similar or the same index data as the premise to derive the specific weights of the above two types of variables, and then weights the weights to get the final demand and ranking results, i.e., the comprehensive demand and ranking results. In addition, in order to measure whether the final results are credible, the method will analyse the correlation between the two types of variables, and the final results will be credible when the two types of variables are correlated.

3. Experiments and Results

3.1. User Requirements Analysis

- Descriptive statistics of the questionnaire

This research selects 16 colleges and universities in the main city of Xi'an, 126 questionnaires were distributed, 120 questionnaires were valid, and the validity rate of the questionnaires was 95.2%. This questionnaire survey increases the choice of the college group on the demand, that is, the questionnaire respondents are allowed to select the indicators they think are the most important among the 11 indicators of living services, catering services, sports and leisure services, shopping services, accommodation services, scientific and technological and cultural services, and transport facility services, and give them a score (out of 10 points).

Table 1 illustrates that about 50.8% of the 120 respondents interviewed were female, and 70% of the respondents were between the ages of 21 and 30. The group with the highest monthly disposable income (CNY) ranged from $1,001 to $3,000 per month, with a high percentage of undergraduates at 28.3 per cent.

Table 1. Demographic characteristics(n = 120).

Variable	Options	n	%	Variable	Options	n	%
Gender	Male	59	49.2	Age	21years old below	19	15.8
					21—25years old	84	70
	Female	61	50.8		26—30years old	6	5
					31—40years old	3	2.5
Monthly disposable income (CNY)	<500	22	18.3		40years old above	28	7.1
	501-1000	19	15.8	Career	Undergraduate	34	28.3
	1001-3000	42	35		Postgraduates	17	14.2
	3001-5000	12	10		PhD and above	9	7.5
	5001-7000	17	14.2		Teaching staff	21	17.5
	>7000	8	6.7		Other staff	39	32.5

- User Requirements Indicators and Weights

Screening respondents' specific needs as tertiary indicators, including demand for commercial complexes, demand for snack abundance, demand for beverage merchants, etc. POI coding classification can more objectively reflect the city's data characteristics[19], so these specific demand indicators are categorised according to the degree of similarity of POIs, which can basically be classified into 11 categories of secondary demand indicators. Finally, the weights of the second-level indicators are merged and processed according to the Golder POI coding table, resulting in six categories of first-level indicator demand weights. User Requirements indicators merging and weights are shown in Figure 2.

It is found that accommodation services, catering and shopping services, and transport services occupy the first three places in the needs of the university community, with weights of 0.267, 0.232, and 0.171 respectively, followed by sports, science, education and culture services, medical and health services, and social work services, with weights of 0.149, 0.105, and 0.076 respectively.

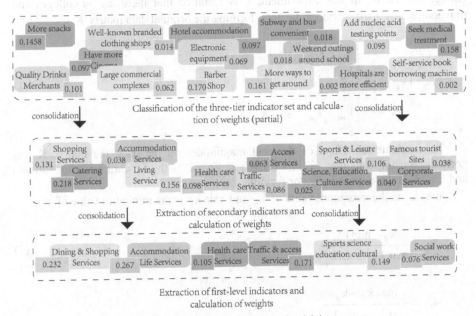

Figure 2. Indicator extraction and weighting.

3.2. Demand Analysis of Existing Life Circle

- Data sampler

The data were taken from the points of interest (POIs) in the four main districts of Xi'an, Beilin District, Lianhu District, Yanta District and Xincheng District in the 2021 Gaode map, and four colleges and universities were selected in each district. Firstly, the locomotive collector was used to crawl the latitude and longitude coordinates, categories and names of 4000 POIs, and the POIs were sorted according to the POI classification and coding table provided by Gaode Map, with a total of 18 categories (only the major categories were counted); secondly, the current situation of college Life Circle in Xi'an's main urban areas was analysed by using the 30-minute walking isochronous circle, and the interval of the isochronous circle was 5 minutes. Secondly, the 30-minute walking "isochronous circle" was used to analyse the current situation of university life circle in the main city of Xi'an, and the isochronous circle interval was 5 minutes. Based on the OSM data and the Open Route Service of the OGC standard Open LS interface, we analyse the walking isochronous circle range of the major colleges and universities in the four districts, and obtain the isochronous circle set from the centre to the edge; once again, the latitude/longitude coordinates of the 4,000 POIs extracted from the first step are substituted into the Arc GIS software, and we finally obtain the number of college

Life Circle and the related POIs in Xian, and the specific number of samples is the number of POIs. The number of specific samples is the pre-data calculated by entropy weight method.

- Entropy weighting method for calculating life circle demand

The study can calculate the weight of each POI indicator in the existing life circle according to the information entropy to derive the objective demand hierarchy of the college life circle. In this experiment, it is assumed that there are m colleges and universities and n evaluation indicators, forming the original data matrix K:

$$
K = \left(k_{ij} \right)_{m \times n} = \begin{bmatrix} k_{11} & k_{12} & \cdots & k_{1n} \\ k_{21} & k_{22} & \cdots & k_{2n} \\ \vdots & \vdots & \ddots & \vdots \\ k_{m1} & k_{m2} & \cdots & k_{mn} \end{bmatrix} \tag{1}
$$

To eliminate the effect of different magnitudes on the data, the matrix K was normalised using equations (2) and (3). Where Eq. (2) is the forward indicator formula and Eq. (3) is the reverse indicator formula.

$\max k_{ij}$ is the maximum value of k_{ij} and $\min k_{ij}$ is the minimum value of k_{ij}.

$$
k'_{ij} = \frac{k_{ij} - \min k_{ij}}{\max k_{ij} - \min k_{ij}} \tag{2}
$$

$$
k'_{ij} = \frac{\max k_{ij} - k_{ij}}{\max k_{ij} - \min k_{ij}} \tag{3}
$$

Calculate the characteristic weight of the evaluation value of the i school under the j evaluation indicator, i.e. the value of the indicator weight of the j evaluation indicator in the i school:

$$
f_{ij} = \frac{K'_{ij}}{\sum_{j=1}^{n} K_{ij}} \tag{4}
$$

Entropy value calculation. Calculate the first value of the j indicator:

$$
E_j = -\frac{1}{\ln m} \sum_{j=1}^{n} p_{ij} \ln f_{ij} \, , \, 0 \le E_j \le 1 \tag{5}
$$

Determine the weights of the evaluation indicators W_j.

$$W_j = \frac{1-E_j}{\sum\limits_{j=1}^{m} E_j}, 0 \le W_j \le 1, \sum\limits_{j=1}^{m} W_j = 1 \tag{6}$$

$$W_j = \begin{bmatrix} 0.2163 & 0.0843 & 0.0757 & 0.0669 & 0.0552 & \cdots & 0.0293 \end{bmatrix} \tag{7}$$

The 18 indicators in equation (7) are ranked in a weight hierarchy, in which the first three indicators with higher weights are road ancillary facilities, public facilities, and transport facility services, with weights of 0.216, 0.084, and 0.076, respectively.

3.3. Design Requirements Results

The 6 user requirements indicators and 18 life circle requirements indicators are combined with the indicators, and the merger refers to the classification table of GODE POI codes), and seven indicators are obtained for catering and shopping services, accommodation and life services, traffic and access services, medical and health services, sports, science, education and culture services, social work services, and public and governmental departments.

Secondly, the combined weights W are calculated using equation (8), where W_i and W_j are the user requirements weights and life circle requirements weights, respectively.

$$W = 0.5W_i + 0.5W_j \tag{8}$$

Table 2. Demand calculation and sequencing.

Variant	Indicators	weights	Consolidation of indicators	Combined weights	Rank
User Requirements	Catering & Shopping Services	0.232	0.232		
	Residential Life Services	0.267	0.267	Catering & Shopping Services	3
	Traffic Access Service	0.171	0.171		
	Health Services	0.105	0.105		
	Sports Science Education and Cultural Services	0.149	0.149	Residential Life Services	2
	Social Work Services	0.076	0.076		
Life Circle Requirements	Living Services	0.032	0.032		
	Catering Services	0.044	0.044		
	Sports and Leisure Services	0.036	0.036		
	Shopping Services	0.029	0.029	Traffic Access Service	1
	Accommodation Services	0.038	0.038		
	Science, Education and Culture Services	0.051	0.051		
	Scenic Spots	0.076	0.076		
	Corporate	0.030	0.030	Health Services	7
	Traffic Facilities	0.076	0.076		

Government Institutions and Social Organisations	0.048	0.048	Sports Science Education and Cultural Services	4
Healthcare Services	0.033	0.033		
Roads	0.216	0.216		
Financial and Insurance Services	0.038	0.038	Social Work Services	5
Residential	0.036	0.036		
Name and address information	0.047	0.047		
Access Facilities	0.041	0.041	Public and Government Sector	6
Public Facilities	0.084	0.084		
Car Service	0.055	0.055		

Table 2 comprehensive ranking results show that the importance of transport services, accommodation and living services, catering and shopping services occupy the first three and the weight is significantly higher than the other items of demand, the weight of the first three were: 0.252, 0.232, 0.152, the last four were sports, science, education and cultural services: 0.117, social work services: 0.090, public and government departments: 0.089, Medical and health services: 0.068.

3.4. Correlation Analysis Validation of Variables

If there is a correlation between the two variables and the correlation is significant, it can verify the rationality of the final demand ordering method, in which case the priority order of the final demand obtained has a certain basis and significance.

Table 3 shows that through Pearson correlation coefficient analysis, it can be known that the correlation coefficient between user requirements and life circle requirements is 0.546, which is significantly correlated at the level of 0.05, i.e., there is a significant strong positive correlation between user requirements and life circle requirements. Therefore, the final comprehensive weights and ranking obtained in this study are reasonable and can be designed based on this.

Table 3. Correlation analysis between user requirements and life circle requirements.Note:* Indicates significant correlation at the $P < 0.05$ level.

	Mean	Std.	User requirements	Life circle needs
User requirements	5.5611	3.82917	1	
Life circle needs	5.6111	4.31698	0.546*	1

4. Innovative Design of Life Circle APP for Xi'an Colleges and Universities

Based on the results, the APP interface design is carried out, and the correspondence between the design strategy, service groups, and design panels is shown in Table 4.The university groups served by this APP design can be divided into staff groups, school production staff, catering-related staff, and student groups. The definitions and weightings of each group are shown in Figure 3, and the design strategy is described in the following:

Strategy 1: Build a clear travelling mode and navigation path. The determination of travelling mode and the selection of navigation path are the core of college life circle APP design, and also the demand of traffic access service.

Strategy 2: Demonstrate the content of commercial services of different systems. the APP contains two categories of catering and shopping and accommodation life services, and the design can visualise and indicate the distance, passage distance and time of these information, so that the college user group can retrieve them more easily when using them, and promote the accessibility and utilisation of this type of POIs in the college life circle.

Strategy 3: Provide users with richer guidance on activity facilities. Convenient and rich activity facilities guidance can help university groups to quickly obtain the location, which is consistent with the characteristics of the map app itself. The design helps users to quickly collect locations by displaying the locations of medical and health services, sports, science, education and cultural services, social work services, public and governmental departments in the vicinity of the school, which improves the efficiency of users' navigation in the future.

Table 4. Correspondence between design strategy, service groups, and design boards.

Design strategy	Supporting services	Type of target group	Design board
Strategy 1	Traffic Access Service	All tertiary groups	Navigation Interface
Strategy 2	Catering & Shopping Services	All tertiary groups	Services Interface
	Residential Life Services	Faculty, staff and university students mainly	
Strategy 3	Health Services	All tertiary groups	Convenience Interface
	Sports Science Education and Cultural Services	High school students mainly	
	Social Work Services	Work production staff, faculty and staff mainly	
	Public and Government Sector	Work production staff, faculty and staff mainly	

The overall design of "U-Tour" APP is divided into four sections, namely, navigation, services, university convenience points, and my page, see Figure 4. The navigation interface includes three modules, namely, starting point setting, starting navigation, and access information.

A: Navigation interface, including the starting point settings, start navigation, access information three modules. The starting point setting module and the start navigation module can help users to quickly obtain the location, so as to build a clear navigation path; the access information includes four pieces of information: access distance, access speed, access time, and access service points, of which the access service points can reflect the existing POI data in the college life circle, help users to more quickly obtain all kinds of services around the school, and also meet the user's needs in the navigation process. B: The service interface adds the information of different services.

B: The service interface increases the display of different service types, and the order of display is catering services, shopping services, accommodation services, living services, and the order of display refers to the final comprehensive weighting, and the display form is mainly based on the label classification and modularity.

C: The interface of the convenient location of the university mainly presents the accurate locations of medical and health services, sports, science, education and cultural services, social work services, public and government departments, and users can collect the locations.

D: "Home" summarises the user's collection information, navigation history and browsing history, helping users to find the POI locations they are interested in conveniently and efficiently.

5. Conclusion and Limitations

The study shows that the demand of college life circle app design mainly focuses on three aspects: traffic and access service, accommodation and life service, and catering and shopping service. In addition, this study also proves that the improved KJ method can get the user requirements and weights by increasing the user assignment, and the improved KJ method-entropy weight method is also feasible to analyse the requirements. In terms of design practice, the user and urban space perspectives can be analysed to determine the functions required for the design of map-based apps. However, this paper only calculates the demand for life circle through the number of POIs of the existing life circle, and does not measure other factors affecting the demand for life circle, so other factors can be added or changed in the future to make the research results more accurate and comprehensive.

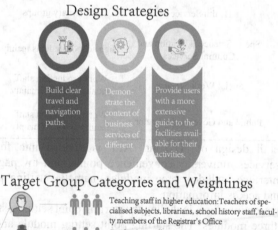

Figure 3. APP design strategy, user group classification and weighting.

A:Navigation Interface B:Services Interface

C:Convenience Interface   D:Home

Figure 4. "U-Tour" interface design demonstration.

References

[1]   Liu, T.; Chai, Y., Daily life circle reconstruction: A scheme for sustainable development in urban China. Habitat International 2015, 50, 250-260.doi:10.1016/j.habitatint.2015.08.038

[2]   Fu, Y.; Sun, Y. In Research on the daily life circle of college students in Shenyang based on the time and space behavior of College Students, 2020 Chinese Control And Decision Conference (CCDC), 2020; IEEE: 2020; pp 2587-2594.doi:10.1109/CCDC49329.2020.9164347.

[3]   Zonggang, C., Life-circle based human-vehicle conflict and solution model of Lanzhou university campus. Journal of Lanzhou Jiaotong University 2022, 41, (03), 19-26.doi:10.3969/j.issn.1001-4373.2022.03.004

[4]   Yingnan, S. Study on the Configuration of Service Facilities in the Living Circle of Higher Education Concentration   Areas.   bachelor's   degree,   Northeastern   University, 2019.doi:10.27007/d.cnki.gdbeu.2019.001107

[5]   Wang, C.; Zhao, S.-j.; Ren, Z.-q.; Long, Q., Place-Centered Bus Accessibility Time Series Classification with Floating Car Data: An Actual Isochrone and Dynamic Time Warping Distance-Based k-Medoids Method. ISPRS International Journal of Geo-Information 2023, 12, (7), 285.doi:10.3390/ijgi12070285

[6]   Guohao, W.; Yuehong, C.; Chunwei, S.; Zekun, X.; Mingruo, Y., Spatial Accessibility Analysis of Fire Stations with the Support of Isochronous Circle Models--Taking Nanjing as an Example. Geography and Geographic Information Science 2023, 39, (02), 17-24,

[7]   Chaoyu, W.; Xiang, Z., From Concentric Circle to Isochronous Circle——Exploration of Dynamic Simulation Evaluation of Educational Facilities in Mountainous Cities. Chongqing Architecture 2019, 18, (07), 5-9.doi:10.3969/j.issn.1671-9107.2019.07.05

[8]   Xuefeng, L. An analysis of university campus accessibility modelling based on an individual's daily life circle. bachelor's degree, Kunming University of Science and Technology, 2016,

[9]   Jing, Z.; Tian, H., Reflections on the Design of Changzhou College Life Circle Based on WeChat Marketing Approach. The Practice of Economics and Trade 2015, (14), 177,

[10] Wenxia, B.; Zi'en, W.; Baoyi, Z., Prototype Design of the Campus Legwork APP Based on Axure Platform. Office Self 2022, 27, (08), 15-18.doi:10.3969/j.issn.1007-001X.2022.08.005.

[11] Runxin, H.; Xuelian, T., Application and Practice of Campus APP for Higher Education Staff--Taking "Zhixiao" APP as an Example. Modern Information Technology 2020, 4, (04), 155-157.doi:10.19850/j.cnki.2096-4706.2020.04.045

[12] Ohiwa, H.; Takeda, N.; Kawai, K.; Shiomi, A., KJ editor: a card-handling tool for creative work support. Knowledge-Based Systems 1997, 10, (1), 43-50.doi:10.1016/S0950-7051（97）00015-4

[13] Zhu, Y.; Tian, D.; Yan, F., Effectiveness of entropy weight method in decision-making. Mathematical Problems in Engineering 2020, 2020, 1-5.doi:10.1155/2020/3564835

[14] Yan, J.; Lijuan, S.; Lujun, L., Application of KJ method in improved design. Art Des 2015, 9, 95-97,

[15] Ding, W.; Zhou, Y. M. In Design of Elderly Assisted Wheelchair Based on KJ-Technique and Analytic Hierarchy Process (AHP), International Conference on Human-Computer Interaction, 2023; Springer: 2023; pp 433-441.doi:10.1007/978-3-031-35992-7_59

[16] Yongliang, H., Functional Design of Gun & Ammunition Cabinet Based on KJ Method and KANO Model. Packaging Engineering Art Edition 2022, 43, (14), 82-89.doi:10.19554/j.cnki.1001-3563.2022.14.009

[17] Weiwei, W.; Wang, S.; Ting, W.; Wang, Y.; Chen, J., Extraction and Application of Chinese New Year Cultural Design Factors Based on F-AHP and Entropy Weight Method. Packaging Engineering Art Edition 2022, 43, (16), 198-208,

[18] Bingchen, Z.; Yuling, Y.; Yang, W. Y.; Fuxu, S., Interactive Design of Intervention APP Based on Needs Analysis of ASD Children. Packaging Engineering Art Edition 2022, 43, (18), 122-135.doi:10.19554/j.cnki.1001-3563.2022.18.016

[19] Hu, J.; Li, J. Y., Experimental Design of Spatial Data Acquisition Based on Gaode Map. Frontiers of Modern Education 2021, 2, (3), 45-50.doi:10.19554/j.cnki.1001-3563.2022.18.016

Design Studies and Intelligence Engineering
L.C. Jain et al. (Eds.)
© 2024 The Authors.
This article is published online with Open Access by IOS Press and distributed under the terms
of the Creative Commons Attribution Non-Commercial License 4.0 (CC BY-NC 4.0).
doi:10.3233/FAIA231460

449

Research on Rural Aged Outdoor Seating Based on Fusion Design Concept

Zhixian ZHANG[a]
[a] Ginkgo College of Hospitality Management

Abstract. To improve the quality of life of the rural elderly and help them adapt to the rural environment, a design method of outdoor seating that can be widely used in rural public Spaces is explored. Firstly, key words representing the characteristics of outdoor seating in rural public space were identified through literature research and user interviews, and the results obtained were basically consistent with the conclusions of literature research, to establish the main characteristics of seating. Then, based on the Analytical Hierarchy Process (AHP), the key words are constructed into the integrated design index system of rural public space outdoor seating, and the weight of each index is calculated. Finally, based on the analysis results and the construction of index system, the design method of outdoor seat integrated design concept is discussed, and the design analysis, standard formulation, scheme design and comprehensive evaluation of an outdoor seat are verified in practice. This design process increases the objectivity of decision making in the design process. The research results show that the comprehensive application of qualitative analysis and quantitative evaluation can implement the concept into the design practice, so that the design scheme of rural public space outdoor seating for aging can play a role in the fusion of people, things and space, and provide innovative ideas for aging design.

Keywords. Fusion design, The country, Senility, Innovative design of outdoor seating.

1. Introduction

With the intensification of population aging and the implementation of the rural revitalization strategy, the number of middle-aged and elderly people in rural areas has gradually increased. The elderly are an important part of rural communities. To improve their quality of life and help them adapt to the rural environment, rural public spaces need facilities and services suitable for the elderly. As one of the important facilities of rural public space, outdoor seating has an important impact on the comfort, safety, and social needs of the elderly. However, the existing outdoor seating design often only considers the needs of the general population, ignoring the special needs of the elderly. Or to show that they have made a suitable design for the elderly, simply and roughly set up prominent signs and eye-catching facilities on the outdoor seats, so that the elderly feel that they have received special design care in the process of use. The purpose of this research is to design an outdoor seat in rural public space that is suitable for the rest of the elderly, considers the users of all ages, and conforms to the public aesthetic [1-3].

2. Aging design theory and demand analysis of rural public seats

2.1. Age-appropriate design theory and its connotation

Age-friendly Design, also known as age-friendly design or age-adaptive design, is a design method that focuses on meeting the needs of the elderly and improving the quality of life of the elderly. It mainly refers to the special needs and use habits of the elderly in product design, environmental design, service design, etc., so that the elderly can still carry out various activities conveniently, freely, and independently in daily life. This design approach recognizes the possible changes in the physical abilities, vision, hearing, cognitive abilities of the elderly, and therefore takes these needs into account as much as possible in the design of products, environments, services, and so on. Aging design mainly includes furniture that is easy to enter and move, comfortable space layout, safety facilities and measures, easy to operate and understand, and in line with ergonomic principles. In general, the goal of age-appropriate design is to provide a safe, comfortable, convenient, and meaningful living environment for the elderly.

2.2. Fusion design connotation

Fusion design was proposed by Lu Ji in the book "Barrier-free Fusion Design and Application" in 2021. Fusion design is a revolutionary barrier-free design idea, which can bring new ideas and methods to barrier-free design. First, as a conscious design behavior, the idea of fusion and unity design is based on the idea of harmony. Secondly, integrated design is barrier-free design. Then, fusion design is also a universal design methodology; Finally, fusion design is future-oriented design.

Fusion design attaches importance to the user's feelings, makes it clear that the purpose of design is people, and "no one can be left behind", focusing on the observation and analysis of human behavior [4-5].

2.3. Demand and aging design trend of rural public seats

2.3.1 The demand for seats in rural public space
Rural public space is usually a place for residents' activities and leisure. To allow people to have a comfortable place to rest and relax, it is necessary to set an appropriate number of seats. This can allow residents to have a suitable rest place in outdoor activities and increase the comfort of residents' activities.

2.3.2 The design trend of age-appropriate outdoor seating
Wang Shanshan proposed that outdoor public seats should be suitable for the communication needs, behavior habits and comfort needs of the elderly; Sun Cuicui found through the survey that the elderly have a greater demand for seat armrests, backrests and waist rests. Tian Mi found that there are some problems such as the seat size is not suitable for the elderly group, and the seat modeling color is single. In addition, in view of the widespread sedentary problem of the elderly, Gong Yibing believe that the difficulty of the elderly standing up is the focus of research. Therefore, to provide the elderly with safe, comfortable, and can support the body of the seat, and reduce the psychological barrier of the elderly, is the trend of aging outdoor seat design [6-7].

3. Discussion on the integrated design method of rural outdoor seating for aging

3.1. The embodiment of fusion design in the design of rural outdoor seating

Fusion design mainly discusses three fusion dimensions of human-object-space in the design of rural outdoor seating for aging. It should not only emphasize the special needs and physiological characteristics of the elderly, but also use appropriate design language and techniques to highlight respect for users of other ages. Reflecting the humanistic care of "no one can be left behind" and emphasizing the appropriate fusion of multiple functions in outdoor seats to meet the different needs of different people. In order to reduce the existence of special objects, it is also necessary to achieve harmony without difference in the fusion design of the concept of great harmony and realize fusion and play in different public Spaces in rural areas according to local conditions, reflecting the fusion of products and environment [8-9].

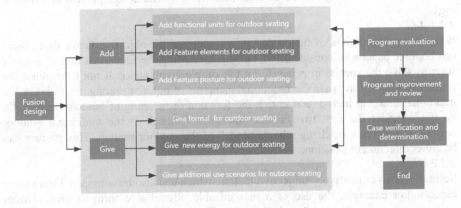

Figure 1. Fusion design process of rural outdoor seating

3.1.1 Fusion of human and object in rural outdoor seating design
The elderly and people of other ages are the users of rural public Spaces, so people and the environment represent the two ends of the design elements of rural age-friendly outdoor seating. Therefore, the seat should provide basic functions such as rest and space for socialization. For the elderly, it is important to ensure that the elderly can reduce their physical burden when sitting and give adequate support when standing. The primary concern for children is safety, not getting bumped. For users of other ages, they pay more attention to the comfort of the seat, in short, reflecting the user-centered design idea at the physiological and psychological level.

3.1.2 Fusion of human and space in rural outdoor seating design
The natural environment of rural public space is different in different regions. The space range is large and small, and the shape is different. When designing outdoor seating, it is necessary to consider the needs of the elderly and other age groups, such as being able to better appreciate and enjoy the natural beauty and the social needs of people to communicate and interact. Through reasonable layout and design, to create a comfortable, safe and pleasant outdoor activity space, so that people can better enjoy the beauty of nature.

3.1.3 Fusion of objects and space in rural outdoor seating design
Integrated design is not only reflected in the universal applicability of users "no one

can be left behind", but also reflected in the appearance design of outdoor seats and the fusion of nature. The seats echo the surrounding natural landscape, echo the rural style, and use the appropriate formal beauty rules, the use of appropriate materials, shapes, colors, etc., so that the outdoor seats meet the aesthetic of most users.

3.2.   Fusion design method of rural outdoor seating

Fusion design, as the name implies, is to put different elements together, and at the same time, it must be integrated into a whole through certain means. Different from the design method of general products, the fusion design of rural public space outdoor seating should first be concerned about what is the object of fusion. The objects of fusion can be divided into two categories: physical image (defined as "Add") and mental image (defined as "Give"). "Add" refers to adding one or more objective factors, while "Give" refers to more subjective factors. These factors may not be used all the time, but the design is started from these factors. The design process is shown in Fig1.

3.2.1 Add

When using the method of fusion design, we increase the objective factor first , there can be three aspects of consideration, such as increasing the functional unit of outdoor seats to solve the special in general, but the simple combination is not to increase the functional unit. Or increase the functional elements of outdoor seating, try to break the traditional thinking inertia, and enrich the function or meaning of outdoor seating. Or do not consider the first two factors, retain the "shape" of the traditional outdoor seating, but increase or change the "attitude" of the outdoor seating. This posture can be either direction or position.

3.2.2 Give

Secondly, it gives relatively subjective factors, which can also be considered from three aspects. For example, the use of a recognizable, identifiable form to give outdoor seating more recognition and aesthetic value. The form here can also be color. To give new energy to outdoor seating, it can be the use of waste materials to transform into seats, or it can be the re-excavation of forms. Giving outdoor seating additional use scenarios does not have to be related to the function, but it can add value to the functional space and attract more people to use it [10-11].

4. Application of the fusion method of rural outdoor seating

4.1.   Based on literature analysis and interview, integrated design analysis of rural outdoor seating for the elderly

Fusion design needs to find accurate objective factors and subjective factors, and then seek the optimal solution of the design problem. The key words in the fusion criteria of rural age-appropriate outdoor seating design are rural public space, age-appropriate design, and outdoor seating. Therefore, the design scheme should reflect the fusion with the rural public space and the fusion with the aging design. To verify the matching degree between the keywords obtained from the analysis of existing literature and the needs of rural elderly people for outdoor seating, 50 rural elderly people were invited to accept interviews. The outline of the interview focuses on the needs of users, outdoor seating, and rural public space. The sorted documents are analyzed by keyword word frequency. In the analysis of the needs of people in the aging design of outdoor seating, the keywords such as "comfortable", "safe", "durable", "multi-functional", "support", "armrest", "non-slip" and "easy to identify" have the highest word frequency. In the analysis of the interview results on the fusion demand of outdoor seating and rural public space, the keywords such as "comfortable", "safe", "beautiful", "multi-functional" and "easy to clean" have the highest frequency of words. In the statistics of the key features of people's needs in rural public space, "social", "entertainment", "leisure", "convenience", "service" and "activity" are high-frequency requirements for space, which are highly consistent in meaning with the keywords summarized in literature analysis. The key features of the integrated design of rural aged outdoor seats obtained from literature analysis are indirectly verified. The unification of the two provides a clear direction for the design issues such as key functions, positioning, and style of seats, and provides solid theoretical support for design practice.

4.2. Based on AHP, the integrated design index system of rural outdoor seating was constructed

Analytical Hierarchy Process (AHP) can stratify design ideas based on goals, criteria, and schemes, to decompose design tasks systematically and from top to bottom. It is often used in design decision-making and is one of the mainstream methods for weighting all elements of design system.

After the verification of the interview results, the characteristics of the rural age-appropriate outdoor seat based on the integrated design can be summarized as " comfortable " , " safe", "durable", "multi-functional", "easy to identify", "beautiful", "social", "leisure", "harmonious" and "symbiosis".

The design index system of rural outdoor seating based on fusion design is constructed by combining the keywords of the key features of rural outdoor seating with 6 fusion dimensions belonging to 3 target layers: user (fusion of user and seat, fusion of user and space), seat (fusion of seat and space, fusion of seat and user) and space (fusion of space and user, fusion of space and seat).

To further realize the quantitative role of the design index system in scheme evaluation, a judgment matrix of 3 target level demand analysis, 6 first-level criterion level and 10 second-level scheme level index is established according to AHP. An expert group composed of 5 design practitioners and 5 university teachers used Saaty 9-point scaling method (Table 2) to score the weights of indicators at all levels, and finally calculated the weights of primary and secondary indicators through SPSSAU (Table 3-8), normalized the weights of indicators at both levels, and added the final weights to Table 1.

Through weight calculation, it can be seen that the importance ranking of indicators in the integrated design criteria level of rural public space elderly outdoor seating is as follows: fusion of user and seat (0.3086) > fusion of seat and user (0.2442) > fusion of user and space (0.2063) > fusion of seat and space(0.1223) > fusion of space and user (0.0593) = fusion of space and seat (0.0593).The design indicators of the scheme level were normalized, and their weights were ranked as follows: comfort (0.21) > rest (0.14) > durability (0.13) > multi-function (0.11) > Safety (0.10) > Social (0.07) = beautiful(0.07) > Harmony (0.06) = symbiosis (0.06) > easy identification (0.05).The two indexes of comfort and leisure of outdoor seating occupy the top two places of importance, which reflects the characteristics of users' demand for outdoor seating in rural space.

Table 1. Integrated design index system of rural elderly outdoor seating.

S/N	Target level requirement analysis	Criterion level firstId	Scenario level secondId	Indicator specification	weight
1		fusion of user and seat A (0.3086)	Comfort a1 (0.6667)	User feel comfortable, relaxed and happy	0.21
2			Safety a2 (0.333 3)	User's body is protected from harm	0.10
3	User:no one can be left behind	fusion of user and space B (0.2063)	Social b1 (0.333 3)	Promote communication among users	0.07
4			Rest b2 (0.6667)	Users get rest	0.14
5		fusion of seat and space C (0.2442)	Durability c1 (0.5396)	Not easy to damage and deformation	0.13
6			Multi-function c2 (0.4604)	Provides other additional functions	0.11
7	Seat: unity of function and form	fusion of seat and use D (0.1223)	Easy identification d1 (0.4416)	The appearance has easily recognizable features	0.05
8			Beautiful d2 (0.5584)	Attractive, pleasant and harmonious in appearance	0.07
9	Space: Harmonious coexistence	fusion of space and user E (0.0593)	Harmony e1 (1)	A state of balance and harmony is formed between space and people	0.06
10		fusion of space and seat F (0.0593)	Symbiosis f1 (1)	Space and people are interdependent	0.06

Table 2. Saaty's 9-point scale

scale	implication
1	Both elements g are equally important than i
3	Compared to the two factors, factor g is slightly more important than factor i
5	Comparing the two factors, factor g is significantly more important than factor i
7	Comparing the two factors, factor g is more important than factor i
9	Comparing the two factors, factor g is more important than factor i
2、4、6、8	The middle of the above two adjacent scales
Count backwards	Judgment of comparison between element g and i fg,
	Then the judgment of the comparison between the elements i and g fgi=1/fy

Table 3. Judgment matrix and results of the primary index

firstId	A	B	C	D	E	F	weight	Consistency check
A	1	3	2	5	6	6	0.3086	
B	1/3	1	1/2	1/3	4	4	0.2063	
C	1/2	2	1	3	5	5	0.2442	CR=0.003<0.1
D	1/5	1/4	1/3	1	2	2	0.1223	
E	1/6	1/4	1/5	1/2	1	1	0.0593	
F	1/6	1/4	1/5	1/2	1	1	0.0593	

Table 4. Judgment matrix and results of the secondary index a

firstId	a1	a2	weight	Consistency check
a1	1	4	0.21	CR=0.007<0.1
a2	1/4	1	0.10	

Table 5. Judgment matrix and results of the secondary index b

firstId	b1	b2	weight	Consistency check
b1	1	1/4	0.07	CR=0.008<0.1
b2	1/4	1	0.14	

Table 6. Judgment matrix and results of the secondary index c

firstId	c1	c2	weight	Consistency check
c1	1	1/2	0.13	CR=0.003＜0.1
c2	2	1	0.11	

Table 7. Judgment matrix and results of the secondary index d

firstId	d1	d2	weight	Consistency check
d1	1	3	0.05	CR=0.006＜0.1
d2	1/3	1	0.07	

Table 8. Judgment matrix and results of the secondary index e and f

firstId	e1	weight	Consistency check	firstId	f1	weight	Consistency check
e1	1	0.06	null	f1	1	0.06	null

4.3. Seating scheme design and evaluation

4.3.1 Seating scheme design

Rural elderly outdoor seating mainly reflects the fusion between User-seat-space, therefore, will not be affixed with the label of "chair for the elderly", but will reflect the appearance of young and fashionable. However, considering that the elderly need certain support after sitting for a long time, a backrest with armrest shape is specially designed. The design of the sitting surface mainly uses the shape of circular sitting, creating a relaxed and pleasant rest atmosphere that can talk to each other. The sitting surface uses environmentally friendly recycled new concrete materials, which are durable, retain the texture of the material, and integrate close to nature and rural natural scenery. The seat leg armrests are made of dark stainless steel support material to isolate the ground moisture and keep the seat dry and comfortable (Figure 2).

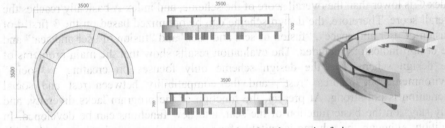

Figure 2. Preliminary design of rural outdoor seating fusion

4.3.2 Fuzzy comprehensive evaluation of design scheme

In order to verify the matching degree of the design scheme between the rural residents and the evaluation index, an evaluation team consisting of 10 members who participated in the formulation of the design index was invited again to evaluate the design scheme. Each index of the design scheme is scored by four grades: excellent, good, medium and poor. The membership degree was calculated based on the weight of the corresponding index by counting the number of evaluation times corresponding to the 4 levels of each index and its proportion in the total number of evaluations. The results are shown in Table 9.

10 members rated 6 primary and 10 secondary indicators of the design scheme. Among them: the molecules in each score represent the number of people who evaluate each index of the design scheme as each level; The denominator is the total number of

people participating in the evaluation (10).Through the comprehensive weight calculation, the four first-level indexes of the design scheme and the membership degree of the whole population in the four levels can be obtained. By assigning 10, 8, 6 and 4 points respectively to the four grades of excellent, good, medium and poor, the overall score of the design scheme can be calculated as S=9.18.Similarly, the scores of the four first-level indicators can be calculated and converted into a 10-point scale with 2 decimal places, so as to obtain SA=9.07, SB=8.52, SC=8.35, SD=9.51,SE=9.43, SF=9.24.

Table 9. Detailed evaluation on design scheme

Evaluation index	Index weight	Membership degree of each design index to each level			
		excellent	good	medium	poor
a1	0.21	4/10	5/10	1/10	0
a2	0.10	7/10	3/10	0	0
firstId A	0.3086	0.1697	0.1235	0.0154	0
b1	0.07	9/10	1/10	0	0
b2	0.14	4/10	2/10	3/10	1/10
firstId B	0.2063	0.1341	0.0309	0.0309	0.0104
c1	0.13	7/10	2/10	1/10	0
c2	0.11	3/10	3/10	3/10	1/10
firstId C	0.2442	0.1221	0.0611	0.0488	0.0122
d1	0.21	6/10	3/10	1/10	0
d2	0.10	6/10	4/10	0	0
firstId D	0.1223	0.0734	0.0428	0.0061	0
e1	0.06	5/10	4/10	1/10	0
firstId E	0.0593	0.0297	0.0237	0.0059	0
f1	0.06	5/10	4/10	1/10	0
firstId F	0.0593	0.0297	0.0237	0.0059	0

4.3.3 Design scheme improvement

According to the evaluation results, the score of the design scheme in index B and index C is lower than the overall score of the scheme, and index A basically reaches the overall score. Therefore, the design scheme can be optimized based on the 3 firstId of "fusion of user and space", "fusion of seat and user" and "fusion of user and seat" and the design indicators included. The evaluation results show that the main problems of the design scheme are the design scheme only focuses on creating a "social" environment, but ignores "rest", and the compatibility between rest and social interaction is not strong. At present, the function of the program lacks diversity, and only stays on the basic function of the seat, and new functions can be developed. In addition, although the scheme is suitable for most people to use but not comfortable enough, it can also be designed from the perspective of ergonomics.

Designers focus on improving design solutions around issues.

- Designers focus on the problem to improve the design scheme. The design has changed from a ring to a rectangular single module design, which can be used in combination with a single module or a group of repeating seat modules. The flexible use of different site Spaces can meet the rest function of rural residents, facilitate the movement and assembly of seats, and realize the creation of social scenes.
- Designed as a simple and intelligent modular system, it consists of one or more seat modules made of recycled concrete material. Can also add green plant module, charging module, etc. (Figure 3)

- The design of the sitting surface mainly adopts organic streamline shape, ergonomic sitting position, and depth, forming smooth and convex curves. The legs of the seat use dark stainless steel support material to isolate the ground moisture and keep the seat dry and comfortable.

Figure 3. Combination of Seat Module, Green Plant Module, and Charging Module

4.3.4 Determination of design scheme

After improvement, the design scheme has been thoroughly designed (Figure 4).Based on the design intent diagram , 10 judges were invited to review the design proposal, and the results showed that S'A=9.63, S'B=9.46, S'C=9.67, S'D=9.51, S'E=9.36, S'F=9.48.It can be seen that the overall improvement of the design scheme has been achieved through improvements in three aspects: "fusion of user and space", "fusion of seat and user" and "fusion of user and seat" .The design scheme fully expresses the fusion of multiple dimensions of rural elderly friendly outdoor seat design, fully reflects respect for the elderly, improves the quality of life of rural residents, and realizes the harmonious coexistence of human-object-space in the integrated design concept.

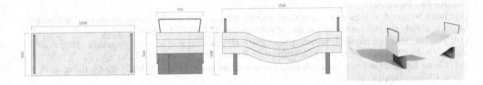

Figure4. Improved Rural Elderly Adaptability Outdoor Seating Fusion Design Scheme

5. Peroration

Introducing the concept of fusion design into the design and research of aging friendly outdoor seats is a more systematic solution to the aging needs of rural public spaces. This helps to build an outdoor environment where "human-object-space" coexist harmoniously. A design index system that "fusion of user and seat" "fusion of seat and user", "fusion of user and space" "fusion of seat and space", " fusion of space and user " fusion of space and seat". It has also provided sufficient guidance for specific outdoor seat design, achieving a complete closed-loop from theoretical research to design innovation.

The design case is based on the fusion of "human-object-space "in rural public space environment. However, there is a lack of more comprehensive thinking on the production and processing costs that may be involved in the later stages of the product, as well as the new problems that may be faced in the actual use process. A complete design practice approach should include a broader exploration of the product lifecycle. For example, in the process of product design iteration and update, factors such as engineering and cost are included in the design standards to guide the design scheme. Future research can further improve the design scheme of aging outdoor seats and conduct practical applications and evaluations to make it more feasible.

Acknowledgments

This work is supported by 2023 Sichuan Key Social Science Research Base (Expansion) National Park Research Center Project (PN: GJGY2023-YB014); 2023 Sichuan Provincial Department of Education Humanities and Social Sciences Key Research Base Research Center of Industry Design Industry Project (PN: GYSJ2023-26); 2023 Sichuan Key Social Science Research Base Li Bing Research Center Project (PN: LBYJ2023-015).

References

[1] LU J. Barrier-free Fusion Design and Application. Liaoning People's Publishing House, 2021
[2] Wang Jiangping. Planning and Design of living environment for the elderly. China Electric Power Press, 2009.
[3] Architectural Society of Japan, Ed. New concise barrier-free architectural design data fusion. China Building Industry Press.2005
[4] Yu Yunying. Psychology and Behavior of the Elderly. Beijing Normal University Press,2015.
[5] Liu Shaoshuai. Research on rural aging space based on Maslow's Demand Theory. Shanxi Architecture, 2017
[6] Takahashi Yingzhi Group. Environmental Behavior and Space Design. China Building and Architecture Press, 2006
[7] Song Chenxu. Study on the suitability of outdoor public space in rural areas of Handan. Hebei University of Engineering, 2020.
[8] Wang Jiangping. Planning and design of living environment for the elderly. Beijing: China Architecture and Building Press, 2009.
[9] Chen Chongxian, A meta-analysis of studies on the effects of natural landscape on physical and mental health of elderly people. Journal of Landscape Architecture 27 (2019), 11, 90-95.
[10] Yan Lin, Study on physical characteristics of 60 ~ 69 years old people in the context.of aging: A case study of Anhui Province. Journal of Shijiazhuang University 21 (2019), 3, 117-123.
[11] Chang Xiaofei, Lai Feng. Research progress on outdoor environment of elderly residential areas in China. Chinese Garden

Design Studies and Intelligence Engineering
L.C. Jain et al. (Eds.)
© 2024 The Authors.
doi:10.3233/FAIA231461

Effect of Music Therapy on the Rehabilitation of Elderly People with Dementia

Zhenyu Liu[a,1], Cheng Yao[a] and Fangtian Ying[b]

[a] *College of Computer Science and Technology, Zhejiang University*
[b] *School of Industrial Design, Hubei University of Technology*

Abstract. Objective: Evaluating the Effectiveness of Music Therapy on the Rehabilitation of Elderly People with Dementia. Methods: Twenty-four Elderly People with Dementia were selected and randomly divided into the Experimental and the Control Groups, with twelve people in each group. In the Control Group, Elderly People with Dementia were given regular care and treatment; In the Experimental Group, they were given extra twenty sessions of group music therapy. In the Experimental Part, The Mini-Mental State Examination(MMSE) and the Cornell Scale for Depression in Dementia(CSDD) were used to score and compare the twenty-four elderly People to verify their validity. Results: After treatment, the experimental group showed better MMSE and CSDD scores than the control group ($P<0.05$). Conclusion: The result showed that music therapy combined with regular care and treatment could improve the cognitive function and emotional states of elderly people with dementia, alleviating their autistic symptoms and promoting rehabilitation

Keywords. Music Therapy, Dementia, Rehabilitation

1. Introduction

Dementia is a global societal challenge, affecting over 55 million people worldwide. As the population ages, the number of individuals living with dementia is expected to rise significantly. Currently, no pharmacological treatment is available to stop the progression of dementia, despite ongoing advancements in clinical trials.

However, there is growing interest and research in non-pharmacological interventions, such as music therapy, to improve the well-being and quality of life of individuals with dementia[1]. Music therapy utilizes the power of music to stimulate various cognitive processes, evoke emotions, and elicit memories. It is a person-centered approach that recognizes the individual's preferences, experiences, and cultural background.

Studies have shown that music therapy can positively impact individuals with dementia. It has been found to reduce agitation and anxiety, improve mood, enhance communication, and facilitate social interaction[2]. Music therapy sessions often involve listening to familiar music, singing, playing musical instruments, and engaging in rhythmic activities. The therapeutic benefits of music therapy in dementia care extend

---

[1] Corresponding Author.

beyond mere enjoyment. Music uniquely activates multiple areas of the brain, even in individuals with advanced dementia[3]. It can tap into preserved neural pathways, allowing for emotional and cognitive connections that may otherwise be inaccessible.

As the field of music therapy continues to evolve, ongoing research is being conducted to understand its mechanisms of action better and to refine therapeutic approaches. By incorporating music therapy into comprehensive dementia care plans, healthcare professionals, caregivers, and families can provide meaningful interventions and support for individuals with dementia[4].

Inspired by this, the purpose of this study is to investigate the effect of music therapy on the rehabilitation of elderly people with dementia (see Figure 1).

Figure 1. An illustration showing elderly people with dementia receiving music therapy.

2. Related Work

2.1. Music Therapy and Cognitive Function

There have been many studies showing that music can effectively stimulate and enhance the memory of elderly patients with dementia[5, 6]. Therefore, music therapy is often used to awaken the memory and emotions of dementia patients, stimulating both long-term and short-term memory. When elderly dementia patients listen to music that has left a deep impression on their lives, it can strongly evoke their memories of past life experiences. Through storytelling and discussions about their past experiences, their thinking abilities, language expression, and cognitive abilities can be improved in all aspects[7]. Furthermore, music can also stimulate the thinking abilities and problem-solving skills of elderly dementia patients. Studies have shown that music can inspire creative thinking and inspiration in the brain[8]. When elderly dementia patients engage in music activities, they can exercise and improve their thinking abilities by collaborating, thinking, and solving problems with music[9]. This is crucial for enhancing the cognitive abilities and quality of life of elderly dementia patients.

2.2. Music Therapy and Emotional States

Depression, agitation, and wandering are common behaviors associated with dementia and frequently observed among nursing home residents. Even with pharmacological treatment, behaviors often persist, hindering the quality of life for elders, their families, and caregivers.

People with dementia need to be provided with a creative outlet for expression, especially during times of distress, dysfunction, and deflated mood that often occur due to the diagnosis. For people with dementia, music therapy leads to positive self-esteem, increases competence and independence, and diminishes feelings of social isolation[10]. Ashida used music therapy techniques such as reminiscence with familiar songs for people diagnosed with dementia who had symptoms of depression and found, in a pre-post test analysis, that after five sessions of small group music therapy, symptoms of depression were significantly reduced[11].

3. Method

3.1. Participants

This study selected Twenty-four elderly dementia patients who resided in a charitable nursing home in Hangzhou, China, from October 2021 to June 2023. Those elderly dementia patients were randomly allocated to an experimental or a control group, giving 12 in each condition (see Table 1).

They met the classification and diagnosis criteria for mental disorders in China, supported by head CT or MRI scans, and had been receiving stable doses of medication for at least three months. The initial score on the Mini-Mental State Examination (MMSE) was ≥ 10, and the initial score on the Cornell Scale for Depression in Dementia (CSDD) was ≥ 6. No statistically significant difference in general information between the control and experimental groups ($P>0.05$) made them comparable. All participating members signed an informed consent form, and this study was conducted with the consent of the relevant person in charge of the nursing home and the elderly patients' families.

Table 1. Comparison of general data between two groups ($\bar{x} \pm s$)

Group		Experimental group	Control group
Number (n)		12	12
Gender (n)	Male	6	6
	Female	6	6
Average age (years)	Male	68.78±3.4	70.13±4.1
	Female	70.12±2.8	69.24±3.6
Level of education (n)	Under junior high school education	3	2

	Above junior high school education	9	10
The average length of stay in the nursing home (months)		23.4±4.3	21.8±3.9

4. Study design

4.1. Control group

The control group adopted conventional nursing and treatment methods to provide comprehensive care and support.

First, understanding the patient's medical history is crucial in assessing and developing personalized nursing plans. By understanding the patient's medical history, symptoms, and disease progression, nursing staff can better understand the patient's needs and priorities. Personal care is another important aspect, including supporting diet, personal hygiene, daily activities, and social interaction. Proper dietary arrangements and food choices help maintain the patient's nutritional status and provide the necessary energy and nutrients.

In addition, safety care is also essential. Due to cognitive impairments in elderly dementia patients, they may face risks such as falls, accidental injuries, and getting lost. Therefore, nursing staff must take appropriate safety measures, such as providing a safe living environment, appropriate assistive devices, supervising walking activities, and conducting regular safety assessments and inspections. Conventional medication treatment is essential in managing symptoms and behavioral problems in elderly dementia patients. Using drugs that improve a patient's cognitive function or anti-psychotic drugs is a common treatment strategy. These medications can help alleviate the patient's cognitive decline and improve attention and memory.

4.2. Experimental group

The experimental group received 20 additional music therapy sessions with the assistance of a music therapist in addition to routine nursing and treatment, which were the same as those obtained by the control group. Each session took place once a week and lasted for 40 minutes.

Each therapy session was divided into seven sessions: Session 1: Prior to each music therapy session, the music therapist evaluated the results of the previous session's music activities and observed the physical and mental condition of the patients in order to determine an appropriate treatment plan ; Session 2: Instruments such as triangles, clappers, maracas, handbells, and tambourines were used to engage the patients in music-playing activities, stimulating their music perception and motor skills ; Session 3: Therapeutic singing activities were conducted, where familiar songs were selected for the patients to sing along to, utilizing fill-in-the-blank lyrics to facilitate memory recall and participation ; Session 4: Music appreciation was encouraged by exposing the patients to different types of music, enhancing their emotional experience and aesthetic sense[12] ; Session 5: Color sound bell, hand function, and attention rehabilitation activities were conducted, with the music therapist encouraging patients to vocalize a color out loud and then press the corresponding colored bell, promoting cognitive and hand-eye coordination abilities ; Session 6: Traditional festival music was incorporated, encouraging patients to accompany the music briefly with an instrument to showcase their sense of celebration and engagement[13] ; Session 7: Each participant was given the opportunity to choose an instrument that represented themselves and take turns initiating a group improvisation, fostering individual expression and collaboration[1].

5. Measurement

5.1. Cognitive Function

We measured the effect of music therapy on cognitive function in elderly patients with dementia using the Mini-Mental State Examination (MMSE) for scoring.

The Mini-Mental State Examination (MMSE) is a widely used screening tool to assess cognitive function in individuals[14]. It consists of questions and tasks that measure various cognitive domains such as orientation, memory, attention, language, and visual-spatial abilities. The total score on the MMSE ranges from 0 to 30, with lower scores indicating poorer cognitive function[15]. The MMSE is commonly used in clinical settings to aid in diagnosing cognitive impairment and dementia.

5.2. Emotional States

We measured the effect of music therapy on Emotional States in elderly patients with dementia using the Cornell Scale for Depression in Dementia(CSDD) for scoring.

The Cornell Scale for Depression in Dementia (CSDD) is a widely used assessment tool to evaluate emotional states in individuals with dementia[16]. It consists of 19 items that assess various depressive symptoms, including mood, behavior, physical signs, and self-esteem. Each item is rated on a scale from 0 to 2(0 = None, 1 = Mild or Intermittent, 2 = Severe), with higher scores indicating more severe depressive symptoms[17]. The CSDD is commonly used in research and clinical settings to aid in diagnosing and monitoring depression in individuals with dementia[18].

5.3. Data Processing

Data were analyzed, and information was measured using SPSS 22.0. t-test for paired samples was used for intra-group comparisons. n(%) was used for numerical calculations, and $P < 0.05$ for comparison between groups.

6. Results

6.1. Comparison of the scores of the Mini-Mental State Examination (MMSE) before and after the treatment between the two groups of Elderly People with Dementia

According to the provided data, the MMSE scores of the experimental group showed changes before and after treatment at different time points. Before treatment, the MMSE scores of the experimental group were similar to those of the control group. However, at ten weeks and twenty weeks after treatment, the MMSE scores of the experimental group significantly improved, indicating a positive impact of the treatment on cognitive function. The treatment effect of the experimental group was notably better than that of the control group (see Figure 2).

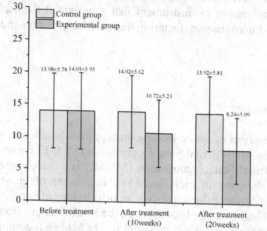

Figure 2. Comparison of the scores of the Mini-Mental State Examination before and after the treatment between the two groups.

6.2. Comparison of the scores of the Cornell Scale for Depression in Dementia(CSDD) before and after the treatment between the two groups of Elderly People with Dementia

According to the provided data, the CSDD scores of the experimental group showed changes before and after treatment at different time points. Before treatment, the CSDD scores of the experimental group were slightly lower than those of the control group. However, at ten weeks and twenty weeks after treatment, the CSDD scores of the experimental group significantly decreased, indicating a positive effect on the relief of depressive symptoms. The treatment effect of the experimental group was notably better than that of the control group (see Figure 3).

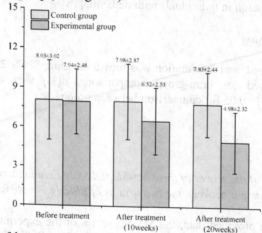

Figure 3. Comparison of the scores of the Cornell Scale for Depression in Dementia before and after the treatment between the two groups.

7. Discussion and Conclusion

This study assessed the effectiveness of music therapy in rehabilitating elderly people with dementia. The experimental group, who received twenty sessions of group music therapy in addition to regular care and treatment, showed significant improvements in MMSE and CSDD scores compared to the control group. These findings align with previous research highlighting the positive effects of music therapy on cognitive function and emotional well-being in individuals with dementia. These findings emphasise the potential of music therapy as a non-pharmacological approach to promote rehabilitation in individuals with dementia. Further research is needed to explore this population's long-term effects and optimal duration of music therapy interventions.

8. Acknowledgment

This research was supported by the Fundamental Research Funds for the Central Universities (Grant No. 226-2023-00086), Research Center of Computer Aided Product Innovation Design, Ministry of Education, National Natural Science Foundation of China (Grant No. 52075478), and National Social Science Foundation of China (Grant No. 21AZD056).

References

[1]   Raglio A, Filippi S, Bellandi D, Stramba-Badiale M. Global music approach to persons with dementia: evidence and practice. Clinical Interventions in Aging. 2014 Oct:1669.

[2]   Vink A, Hanser S. Music-Based Therapeutic Interventions for People with Dementia: A Mini-Review. Medicines. 2018;5(4):109.

[3]   Wall M, Duffy A. The effects of music therapy for older people with dementia. British Journal of Nursing. 2010;19(2):108–113.

[4]   Ray KD, Götell E. The Use of Music and Music Therapy in Ameliorating Depression Symptoms and Improving Well-Being in Nursing Home Residents With Dementia. Frontiers in Medicine. 2018;5:287.

[5]   Fusar-Poli L, Bieleninik Ł, Brondino N, Chen X-J, Gold C. The effect of music therapy on cognitive functions in patients with dementia: a systematic review and meta-analysis. Aging & Mental Health. 2018;22(9):1103–1112.

[6]   Lyu J, Zhang J, Mu H, Li W, Champ M, Xiong Q, Gao T, Xie L, Jin W, Yang W, et al. The Effects of Music Therapy on Cognition, Psychiatric Symptoms, and Activities of Daily Living in Patients with Alzheimer's Disease Yu J-T, editor. Journal of Alzheimer's Disease. 2018;64(4):1347–1358.

[7]   Brotons M, Koger SM. The Impact of Music Therapy on Language Functioning in Dementia. Journal of Music Therapy. 2000;37(3):183–195.

[8]   Gómez Gallego M, Gómez García J. Music therapy and Alzheimer's disease: Cognitive, psychological, and behavioural effects. Neurología (English Edition). 2017;32(5):300–308.

[9]   Zhang Y, Cai J, An L, Hui F, Ren T, Ma H, Zhao Q. Does music therapy enhance behavioral and cognitive function in elderly dementia patients? A systematic review and meta-analysis. Ageing Research Reviews. 2017;35:1–11.

[10] Matthews S. Dementia and the Power of Music Therapy: Dementia and the Power of Music Therapy. Bioethics. 2015;29(8):573–579.

[11] Guétin S, Portet F, Picot MC, Pommié C, Messaoudi M, Djabelkir L, Olsen AL, Cano MM, Lecourt E, Touchon J. Effect of Music Therapy on Anxiety and Depression in Patients with Alzheimer's Type Dementia: Randomised, Controlled Study. Dementia and Geriatric Cognitive Disorders. 2009;28(1):36–46.

[12] Tsoi KKF, Chan JYC, Ng Y-M, Lee MMY, Kwok TCY, Wong SYS. Receptive Music Therapy Is More Effective than Interactive Music Therapy to Relieve Behavioral and Psychological Symptoms of Dementia: A Systematic Review and Meta-Analysis. Journal of the American Medical Directors Association. 2018;19(7):568-576.e3.

[13] Belgrave M. The Effect of Expressive and Instrumental Touch on The Behavior States of Older Adults with Late-Stage Dementia of The Alzheimer's Type and on Music Therapist's Perceived Rapport. Journal of Music Therapy. 2009;46(2):132–146.

[14] Dick JP, Guiloff RJ, Stewart A, Blackstock J, Bielawska C, Paul EA, Marsden CD. Mini-mental state examination in neurological patients. Journal of Neurology, Neurosurgery & Psychiatry. 1984;47(5):496–499.

[15] Kukull WA, Larson EB, Teri L, Bowen J, McCormick W, Pfanschmidt ML. The mini-mental state examination score and the clinical diagnosis of dementia. Journal of Clinical Epidemiology. 1994;47(9):1061–1067.

[16] Williams JR, Marsh L. Validity of the Cornell scale for depression in dementia in Parkinson's disease with and without cognitive impairment: Cornell Depression Scale in Parkinson's Disease. Movement Disorders. 2009;24(3):433–437.

[17] Alexopoulos GS, Abrams RC, Young RC, Shamoian CA. Cornell Scale for Depression in Dementia. BIOL PSYCHIATRY.

[18] Kørner A, Lauritzen L, Abelskov K, Gulmann N, Marie Brodersen A, Wedervang-Jensen T, Marie Kjeldgaard K. The Geriatric Depression Scale and the Cornell Scale for Depression in Dementia. A validity study. Nordic Journal of Psychiatry. 2006;60(5):360–364.

Design Studies and Intelligence Engineering
L.C. Jain et al. (Eds.)
© 2024 The Authors.
This article is published online with Open Access by IOS Press and distributed under the terms
of the Creative Commons Attribution Non-Commercial License 4.0 (CC BY-NC 4.0).
doi:10.3233/FAIA231462

467

Research on Intelligent Shoe Washing Machine Design and Evaluation Method Based on AHP-DEMATEL

Feiyang LIU[a], Shuwei YU[a,1], Jiongzhou WENG[a], Jinwei LU[a], Ming ZHANG[a], Jinhong HU[a], Xiaojiang ZHOU[a]

[a] *College of Arts and Communication, China Jiliang University, Zhejiang, China*

Abstract. This study aims to improve user satisfaction in designing intelligent shoe washing machines using the AHP-DEMATEL method. Beginning with the collection and categorization of basic user data, AHP constructs a hierarchical analysis model of user requirements. DEMATEL is then integrated to identify and analyze comprehensive impact relationships among requirements. Weighted calculations determine the influence degrees between user demand data, resulting in composite factors based on AHP-DEMATEL. The intelligent shoe washing machine is designed based on composite user demand data, and outcomes are evaluated to establish a reliable product design scheme. Design, conducted using the AHP-DEMATEL composite method, is followed by satisfaction assessment using demand indicators, resulting in a completed scheme. Applying AHP-DEMATEL effectively addresses unclear user demand indicators during product development, significantly enhancing the user experience. This study provides valuable reference for similar product user demand research.

Keywords. Intelligent shoe washing machine, AHP, DEMATEL, evaluation method

1. Introduction

Shoe washing machines, as niche household appliances, have gained market recognition and experienced rapid demand growth this year, forming a potential market of billions. However, existing shoe washing machines are primarily modified versions of early washing machines, with working principles that do not align well with the needs of shoe cleaning, often resulting in shoe damage. Research shows that developers of shoe washing machines often underestimate the importance of acquiring user demand information and fail to properly process demand data, directly leading to products falling short of user expectations[1]. Therefore, reconsidering how to approach shoe washing machine product design, extracting and processing user demands in a scientifically rational manner, and evaluating the final design scheme are key factors in the success of development[2]. In response to these challenges, this paper proposes a research model for intelligent shoe washing machine design based on the AHP-DEMATEL method. It explores user preferences for attributes in intelligent shoe washing machine design,

---

[1] Corresponding Author: Shuwei YU, College of Arts and Communication, China Jiliang University, Zhejiang, China; E-mail: 553561524@qq.com.

gathers reliable user demand data, and ultimately creates a design scheme for evaluation, resulting in a user-satisfying product.

2. Current State and Significance of Shoe Washing Machine Design Research

2.1. Current State and Existing Problems

The shoe washing machine industry is undergoing a period of innovation and change, with the success of product design directly influencing marketability. Based on 2022 consumer data, shoe washing machine products are mainly categorized into semi-automatic and fully automatic types, utilizing internal brushes and friction to clean shoe surfaces. Some brands have added features such as air drying and drying to enhance the product experience. Considering industry development and product life cycle theory, these products are currently in the growth stage of their industry life cycle. The industry has not yet established standardized production specifications, and designs still adhere to washing machine principles and appearances, resulting in low cleaning efficiency, significant shoe damage, and inability to meet the demanding cleaning requirements of high-end branded shoes. Both industry development and user demand call for innovative solutions for such products. Several scholars have conducted research in this area. Wang Yinbin et al.[3] designed a shoe washing machine that uses ultrasonic waves for cleaning, reducing shoe damage to some extent but not resolving the efficiency issue. Xu Guanghong et al.[4] improved the entire shoe washing machine, designing a new type that combines cleaning, drying, and disinfection, achieving positive results. These examples indicate that while technological integration is a promising approach, deeper analysis of user demands is necessary for effective problem-solving.

2.2. Issues Addressed by the AHP-DEMATEL Method and Approach

The Analytic Hierarchy Process (AHP) is a scientific method that combines qualitative and quantitative analyses[5]. This approach breaks down factors related to the research object into multiple levels, calculating weights for each indicator to guide optimal method selection[6][7]. The Decision Making Trial and Evaluation Laboratory (DEMATEL) method is applicable to studying interrelationships among target factors. Its essence lies in utilizing graph theory and matrix tools to establish logical structural relationships among factors, identifying key elements within the system, and resolving complex problems[8].

In practice, many scholars have explored these methods, but individually, AHP and DEMATEL cannot fully address product design challenges. AHP overlooks cross-factor relationships, where one factor can be influenced by multiple higher-level indicators simultaneously, and it lacks clarity in analyzing interdependencies among factors at the same level. DEMATEL relies on expert rankings based solely on cause-and-effect relationships without considering factor weights or factors like user satisfaction as decision criteria. However, combining both methods effectively overcomes these limitations[9]. Initial indicator weights are determined using AHP, followed by DEMATEL adjustments to enhance accuracy and objectivity. This results in an evaluable design scheme. This paper primarily describes the AHP-DEMATEL combined method for product design and evaluation, using the intelligent shoe washing machine as a case study to formulate a design strategy.

3. Construction of User Demand Model for Intelligent Shoe Washing Machine Based on AHP-DEMATEL Method

The user demand model for intelligent shoe washing machines is constructed using the AHP-DEMATEL method. Initially, the AHP is employed to calculate the initial weights. of various indicators. Subsequently, the DEMATEL method is utilized to refine these weights, thereby effectively enhancing the accuracy and objectivity of weight assignments. During the process of deriving design solutions, the proposed design

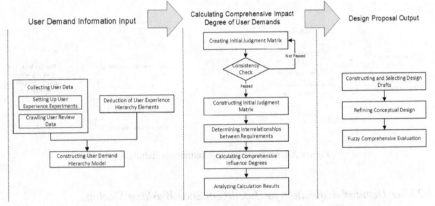

Figure 1. Design Process Flowchart Based on AHP-DEMATEL.

scheme is subjected to evaluation. Through comprehensive technological integration, the AHP-DEMATEL design and evaluation method is established. The specific method construction and workflow are depicted in **Figure 1**.

3.1. Constructing the Hierarchy Model of User Experience Requirements for Intelligent Shoe Washing Machine

3.1.1 Deriving User Experience Hierarchy Elements from Maslow's Theory

User experience spans the entire lifecycle of a product and is pivotal to realizing its commercial value[10]. Building upon Maslow's five levels of human needs, Luo Shijian [11]proposed five user experience requirements. Chen Wei[12] expanded upon this foundation by integrating the characteristics of industrial products and emphasized both material and spiritual attributes of products, resulting in six user experience hierarchy levels for design. Based on these levels of user experience design requirements and taking into consideration the user demands of intelligent shoe washing machine products, a re-analysis of these user experience elements and hierarchy levels can be conducted. These can be categorized into functional needs of practicality, intelligence, and efficiency; sensory needs of visual, tactile, and auditory experiences; emotional interaction needs of usability, communication, and preference; and self-needs of personalization and self-worth. This categorization effectively caters to diverse user demands, allowing for data extraction and analysis based on these hierarchy levels. The deduced relationships between user experience requirements are depicted in **Figure 2**.

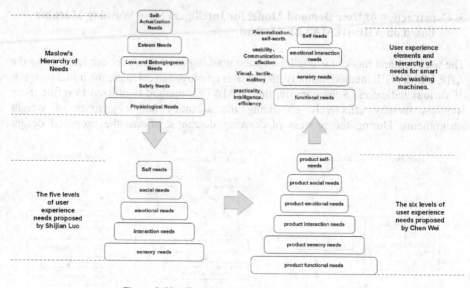

Figure 2. User Experience Requirement Hierarchy Diagram

3.1.2 User Demand Acquisition for Intelligent Shoe Washing Machine

Building upon the established user experience elements and hierarchy for the intelligent shoe washing machine, user experiments were conducted to assess the machine and collect feedback from ten university students. The experiment involved using everyday shoes, including canvas shoes, basketball shoes, and running shoes. Each pair of shoes was divided, with one allocated to the experimental group and the other to the control group. Participants followed the proper procedure for using the shoe washing machine to wash one shoe, two shoes, and four shoes simultaneously. Their actions were observed, and feedback was recorded, with consistent control variables such as washing program, duration, detergent type and quantity, and water temperature maintained throughout the experiments.

Following multiple rounds of experimental testing and the analysis of feedback from the ten participants, three main issues were identified:

1) Water Flow Impact: When cleaning a small number of shoes, the washing machine drum's size relative to the volume of shoes resulted in significant water flow interference, leading to insufficient contact with the brushes during cleaning. Conversely, cleaning four pairs of shoes at once led to crowding within the drum, resulting in suboptimal cleaning results.

2) Installation and Size Constraints: The use of the shoe washing machine necessitated the installation of water inflow and outflow pipes, restricting the experience to a fixed location. Furthermore, the machine's large size proved to be unsuitable for use in limited spaces.

3) Adhesive Separation Concerns: The shoe cleaning process, which takes 40 minutes, involves the shoes remaining submerged, making them susceptible to adhesive separation.

Based on the results of these user experience tests, it became evident that the tested shoe washing machine achieved a certain level of cleanliness but exhibited poor user experience, indicating the need for further optimization. Leveraging the feedback from these experiments, a web scraping technique was employed to search for and extract evaluation data related to shoe washing machines from e-commerce platforms such as JD and Taobao, using the keyword "洗鞋机" (shoe washing machine).This process yielded a dataset comprising 10,633 usable entries, which included usernames, evaluation content, and publication dates. After data preprocessing, involving the removal of duplicates and obviously illogical entries, an analysis and synthesis of word frequencies, user sentiment, and other factors within the evaluation content were carried out to identify user demands. By integrating the outcomes of the user experience tests and utilizing the user experience design hierarchy elements as an organizational framework, 20 key demand keywords were determined through additions, deletions, and further segmentation. This ultimately led to the creation of the Intelligent Shoe Washing Machine User Experience Demand Hierarchy Model, as illustrated in **Figure 3**.

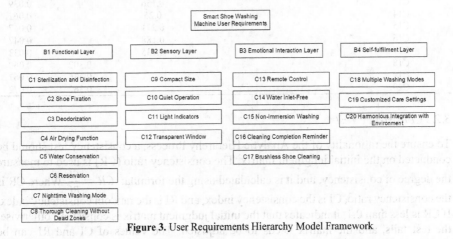

Figure 3. User Requirements Hierarchy Model Framework

3.2. Calculating Initial Weights and Consistency Check

3.2.1 Calculating Initial Weights

Based on the previously constructed hierarchy model for user experience requirements of the smart shoe washing machine, inviting a total of 30 participants, including expert users and regular users, to conduct pairwise comparisons for various factors using a 1-9 scale method, and establishing the initial judgment matrix Z. According to the fundamental principles of AHP , using a more precise geometric mean method to calculate the initial weight values W for the user experience requirements of the smart shoe washing machine, as shown in **Table 1**.

Table 1. Initial Weights of Intelligent Shoe Washing Machine User Demands

Second-level Indicators \ First-level Indicators	B1 Functional Requirements	B2 Sensory Requirements	B3 Emotional Interaction Requirements	B4 Self-fulfillment Requirements	Initial Weight Values W
	0.344	0.211	0.248	0.198	
C1	0.083				0.029
C2	0.191				0.066
C3	0.102				0.035
C4	0.105				0.036
C5	0.193				0.066
C6	0.103				0.035
C7	0.122				0.042
C8	0.101				0.035
C9		0.236			0.050
C10		0.328			0.069
C11		0.175			0.037
C12		0.261			0.055
C13			0.156		0.039
C14			0.25		0.062
C15			0.271		0.067
C16			0.188		0.047
C17			0.135		0.033
C18				0.302	0.060
C19				0.336	0.067
C20				0.362	0.072

3.2.2 Consistency Test

To ensure the rationality of the Analytic Hierarchy Process, a consistency test should be conducted on the initial judgment matrix. The consistency ratio (CR) is used to measure the degree of consistency, and it is calculated using the formula: $CR = \frac{CI}{RI}$. Where CR is the consistency ratio, CI is the consistency index, and RI is the random consistency index. If CR is less than 0.1, it indicates that the initial judgment matrix is consistent; otherwise, the test fails, and the matrix needs to be adjusted. The values of CI and RI can be calculated using formulas $CI = \frac{\lambda_{max}-n}{n-1}$ and $\lambda_{max} = \sum_{i=1}^{n} \frac{(ZW)_i}{nW_i}$. Where λ_{max} is the maximum eigenvalue of the matrix and n is the number of criteria. Based on the formulas mentioned above, the consistency ratio CR for the judgment matrix composed of the first-level criteria is calculated to be 0.004, which is less than 0.1. Similarly, the CR values for the other judgment matrices are also less than 0.1, indicating onsistency.

3.3. Determining the Interrelationships of User Requirements for Smart Shoe Washing Machine

To assess the impact relationships between user requirements, an additional 30 expert users were invited to complete a DEMATEL questionnaire. They used a 0-4 scale to score a 16x16 matrix created from 16 specific requirements, thereby constructing the direct impact matrix Y for pairwise comparisons of requirements. The normalized direct impact matrix N was obtained using formulas $N = \frac{Y}{s}$ and $s = \max_{1 \leq i \leq n} \sum_{j=1}^{n} y_{ij}$. The comprehensive impact matrix T was then calculated using formula $T = N(I - N)^{-1}$. Where I is the identity matrix. Based on matrix T, the comprehensive impact relationships for each requirement were determined, including influence degree (D), being influenced degree (R), centrality (D+R), and reason degree (D-R), as defined in **Table 2**. Using these definitions, the comprehensive impact relationships for the smart shoe washer's requirements were calculated, and the results are presented in **Table 3**.

Table 2. Comprehensive Impact Relationship Definitions

Comprehensive Impact Relationship	Definition
Influence Degree (D)	The sum of each row in matrix T, indicating the overall influence of a specific factor on other factors.
Being Influenced Degree (R)	The sum of each column in matrix T, indicating the cumulative influence received by a specific factor from other factors.
Centrality (D+R)	Represents the magnitude of a specific factor's role within the system, with larger values indicating higher importance.
reason degree (D-R)	Reflects how a specific factor affects other factors. A positive value implies significant influence on other factors, classifying it as a causal factor. Conversely, a negative value suggests being heavily influenced by other factors, categorizing it as a result-oriented factor.

Table 3. Table of Comprehensive Impact Relationship for Smart Shoe Washing Machine Requirements

C_i	D	R	D+R	D-R	C_i	D	R	D+R	D-R
C1	0.638	1.566	2.204	-0.927	C11	0.276	1.558	1.833	-1.282
C2	1.918	0.75	2.669	1.168	C12	0.203	1.485	1.687	-1.282
C3	0.738	1.242	1.98	-0.504	C13	1.462	0.002	1.464	1.46
C4	1.591	0.988	2.579	0.602	C14	1.861	0.559	2.419	1.302
C5	0.132	1.138	1.27	-1.006	C15	0.935	1.765	2.7	-0.83
C6	1.892	0.821	2.713	1.071	C16	0.875	1.232	2.107	-0.357
C7	0.797	1.643	2.44	-0.846	C17	0.675	0.875	1.55	-0.2
C8	2.213	1.452	3.665	0.761	C18	1.632	1.063	2.695	0.569
C9	2.031	1.574	3.605	0.457	C19	0.681	0.558	1.239	0.122
C10	0.109	0.491	0.6	-0.381	C20	1.425	1.001	2.426	0.424

3.4. Calculating Comprehensive Impact Factor

Using a single method can lead to one-sided results in calculations, therefore it is necessary to weight the initial weights of each requirement with their centrality[13], constructing a comprehensive impact factor $X_i = W_i M_i / \sum_{j=1}^{n} W_j M_j$, as shown in **Table 4**.

Table 4. Comprehensive Impact Degree of Each Requirement

C_i	W_i	D+R	$W_i*(D+R)$	X_i	C_i	W_i	D+R	$W_i*(D+R)$	X_i
C1	0.029	2.204	0.064	0.030	C11	0.037	1.833	0.068	0.032
C2	0.066	2.669	0.176	0.082	C12	0.055	1.687	0.093	0.043
C3	0.035	1.980	0.069	0.032	C13	0.039	1.464	0.057	0.027
C4	0.036	2.579	0.093	0.043	C14	0.062	2.419	0.150	0.070
C5	0.066	1.270	0.084	0.039	C15	0.067	2.700	0.181	0.084
C6	0.035	2.713	0.095	0.044	C16	0.047	2.107	0.099	0.046
C7	0.042	2.440	0.102	0.048	C17	0.033	1.550	0.051	0.024
C8	0.035	3.665	0.128	0.060	C18	0.060	2.695	0.162	0.075
C9	0.050	3.605	0.180	0.084	C19	0.067	1.239	0.083	0.039
C10	0.069	0.600	0.041	0.019	C20	0.072	2.426	0.175	0.081

3.5. Analysis of Calculation Results

When comparing the rankings of comprehensive impact factors with the initial weights obtained solely through AHP, it becomes evident that the ranking based on comprehensive impact factors is more accurate. For instance, C9 although initially ranked lower when using AHP alone, holds a higher centrality ranking, indicating its significant influence on other factors. Given controlled costs and mature technology, it may be prudent to prioritize upgrading and iterating this element.

C5 initially assigned a higher weight, overlooked interrelationships among factors. After considering comprehensive impact relationships, this element is categorized as a result factor, influenced by other factors. Enhancing this function would require improvements to its source factors, potentially increasing development costs. Hence, practical development may require an adjustment of the development sequence accordingly.

Furthermore, C15 holds the highest ranking in terms of comprehensive impact factors, making it a top priority. Its centrality and causality also indicate that optimizing this factor can not only enhance product competitiveness but also significantly improve related factors. Addressing user feedback on suboptimal shoe cleaning effects by implementing C15 could lead to higher user satisfaction.

C10 initially had a relatively high weight and attractiveness, but its centrality is comparatively lower, considering it a result factor influenced by other factors. While it does impact user satisfaction and deserves attention, reducing noise falls under technical issues and faces challenges due to industry homogenization. Therefore, its development should be considered within the broader context of technical and cost considerations.

Based on the rankings of comprehensive impact factors, the top eight elements for prioritized implementation, considering development costs and technological capabilities, are C15, C9, C2, C20, C18, C14, C8, and C7.

4. Design Application of Smart Shoe Washing Machine Based on AHP-DEMATEL Method

4.1. Construction and Selection of Design Proposal Based on AHP-DEMATEL Method

Based on the aforementioned method, the weighted ranking results were obtained, and an AI-generated product concept map was created. Multiple user experience requirements were input as keywords into the Midjourney software, and after extensive. data training, three intelligent shoe washing machine design concepts were generated as shown in the **figure 4**. To achieve the most optimal design outcome and align with user requirements, a fuzzy comprehensive evaluation method was employed to assess the three design concepts. Ten experts are invited to use the primary indicators from the user experience requirement hierarchy as evaluation criteria, utilizing four levels of assessment: "Excellent," "Good," "Qualified," and "Unqualified." Scores above 90 are

Design Concept 1   Design Concept 2   Design Concept 3

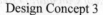

Figure 4. Design Proposal

classified as "Excellent," scores between 80 and 90 as "Good," scores between 60 and 80 as "Qualified," and scores below 60 as "Unqualified." Through the calculation of the fuzzy evaluation results, Proposal 1 receives a score of 80.46, Proposal 2 scores 73.39, and Proposal 3 scores 74.87. Based on the results of the user requirement analysis, Proposal 1 is selected as the final design proposal for further development.

4.2. Design Solution Based on AHP-DEMATEL Method

Using the results of the comprehensive impact analysis, design solutions are developed. Visual representations of the effects can be seen in **Figures 5**.

1) Optimized Core Functions: The shoe washing compartment focuses on washing and drying, while the care compartment offers functions like sterilization, drying, and deodorization. The modular design ensures it's compact and lightweight, allowing users to customize combinations and configurations.

2) Improved Cleaning Method: Inside the shoe washing compartment, a stainless-steel frame holds shoes in place, and 35 high-pressure water jets clean the shoe surfaces from all angles, avoiding brush use that might harm the shoes. This fixation prevents prolonged soaking and related issues like adhesive separation. The compartment includes a 5-liter water tank for cleaning and wastewater collection, eliminating the need for hoses and improving the user experience.

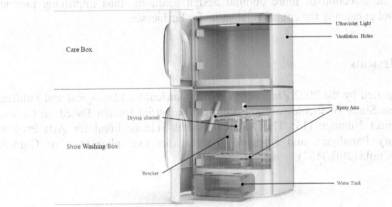

Figure 5. Functional Analysis Diagram of Smart Shoe Washing Machine

4.3. Design Proposal Evaluation Based on AHP-DEMATEL Method

To validate the feasibility of the design concepts, a comparison is made with three popular brands of shoe washing machines available on the Taobao platform, considering their sales volume and high ratings. Twenty expert users, including homemakers, design professionals, and frequent users of shoe washing machines, are invited to assess the four options using the fuzzy comprehensive evaluation method. The computed results are presented in **Table 5**.

Table 5. Comprehensive Scores of Four Shoe Washing Machines

product	Comprehensive Score
AHP-DEMATEL Smart Shoe Washing Machine	87.53
Changhong Fully Automatic Shoe Washing Machine	71.21
Audley Drum-Type Shoe Washing Machine	76.21
Midea Fully Automatic Shoe Washing Machine	74.33

5. Conclusion

This study focused on the intelligent shoe washing machine and employed a combined model that integrates AHP and DEMATEL to assess various factors comprehensively and establish a comprehensive ranking. The research findings highlight two key points. First, when compared to traditional design methods, the use of the AHP-DEMATEL approach effectively eliminates the influence of subjective factors in prioritizing product requirements. It also addresses the limitations stemming from the neglect of interrelationships between elements in the Analytic Hierarchy Process, enabling the accurate identification and resolution of design challenges to enhance user experience and product satisfaction. Second, applying this method to evaluate product proposals allows for the selection of more optimal design solutions, thus improving product suitability and enhancing the commercial value for businesses.

Acknowledgments

Project supported by the 2022 Zhejiang Province Curriculum Ideological and Political Project: Case Study of Ideological and Political Industrial Design Based on Correct Values, Project Number 113; The National Social Science Fund for Arts Project: Contemporary Paradigms and Standard Systems for the Inheritance of Chinese Traditional Crafts (20BG137).

References

[1] Yu, S., Lu, J., & Lu, T. Evaluation Method of Assembly Design for Electric Energy Metering Box Based on DFA Theory. Packaging Engineering 43 (2022), S1, 36-41.
[2] Geng, X., Xu, S., & Ye, C. Optimization Design of Product Functional Requirements Considering Quantitative KANO Analysis. Computer Integrated Manufacturing Systems 22 (2016), 07, 1645-1653.
[3] Wang, Y., Wang, Y., Ji, H., & Ding, Z. Design of a New Multifunctional Shoe Washing Machine Based on Ultrasonic Principle. Industry and Technology Forum, 17 (2018), 13, 53-54.
[4] Xu, G., Chen, B., Yang, L., & Zhang, Z. Development and Finite Element Analysis of a New Multifunctional Shoe Washing Machine. Machinery Design & Manufacture 10 (2016), 236-239.
[5] Deng, W., & Zhu, H. Design Evaluation of Children's Smart Watch Based on Analytic Hierarchy Process. Packaging Engineering 39 (2018), 8, 121-125.
[6] Xu, X., Liu, J., Yan, Y., & Yang, J. Development and Theoretical Trends of Intelligent Design Methods. Packaging Engineering 41 (2020), 4, 10-19.
[7] Hou, J., Zhang, Y., & Wu, L. Research on Design of Smart Baby Stroller Based on AHP Analytic Hierarchy Process. Packaging Engineering 43 (2022), 2, 50-55.

[8]   Qin, X., & Lu, X.   Research on Factors Affecting the Ecological Security System of Coastal Cities Based on BP-DEMATEL Model. Management Review **27** (2015), 5, 48-58.

[9]   Zhang, H., & Ye, S. Research on the Mutual Relationship of Key Success Factors of PPP Projects Based on AHP-DEMATEL Method. Science and Technology Management Research **36** (2016), 22, 203-207.

[10] Luo, S., Zhu, S., & Ying, F. Context-Based User Experience Design in Mobile Interface. Computer Integrated Manufacturing Systems **16** (2010), 2, 239-248.

[11] Luo, S., & Zhu, S. User Experience and Product Innovation Design. Beijing: China Machine Press, 2010.

[12] Chen, W. Application of User Experience Design Elements in Product Design. Packaging Engineering **32** (2011), 10, 26-29+39.

[13] Liu, C., & Wu, Z. Study on Commercialization Factors of Renewable Energy Technology Based on AHP and DEMATEL. Science and Technology Management Research **35** (2015), 1, 107-112+116.

Design Studies and Intelligence Engineering
L.C. Jain et al. (Eds.)
© 2024 The Authors.
doi:10.3233/FAIA231463

Jiangxi NanFeng Nuo's Cultural and Creative Product Design Research

Xin LIU[a] and Lei CHEN[b]
a Nanchang Vocational University
b Nanchang Institute of Technology

Abstract. Nanfeng Nuo culture and blind box combine to attract young groups of Nanfeng Nuo cultural concerns, enhance the inheritance of Nanfeng Nuo culture, and improve the activity. Main conclusions: First, the release of the questionnaire to determine the target consumer groups; second, through the hierarchical analysis method to build the relevant evaluation system; and finally, according to the evaluation system algorithm to derive the weighted ranking of the design program for the evolution of the design program to derive the Nanfeng Nuo Native Cultural and Creative Products final design program and application of the practice. Innovation: the use of hierarchical analysis in Nanfeng Nuo culture and blind box design to protect the applicability of the design method to avoid extracting user needs and preferences when the subjective one-sidedness clears Nanfeng Nuo's creative design elements and design goals.

Keywords. Nuo Cultural; Culture and creative Products; Blind box; Analytic Hierarchy

1.NanFeng Nuo cultural profile target group positioning

1.1 Nanfeng Nuo cultural profile

Nuo culture is known as a living fossil of Huaxia culture, and Gan Nuo culture has a profound accumulation, Retained numerous, with a complete system. Among them, Nanfeng County in Jiangxi is one of the 100 counties and cities in Jiangxi, with the wealthiest and most significant number of Nuo cultural groups; it is known as the "hometown of Chinese Nuo dance."[1] In May 2006, The State Council announced the first batch of national intangible cultural heritage lists; in Nanfeng, the Nuo mask symbolizes Nuo culture. Nuo masks are props that must be used in Nuo dance and Nuo opera, their role as a vehicle for god. It was many ordinary people's spiritual support and solace in ancient times.

At present, the dissemination channels of Nanfeng Nuo culture are mainly in aspects such as Nuo dance performances, book promotion[2], development of related products, and sales. Most of the design plane retains the original "earth flavor" with no playability or fun. As Nanfeng Nuo culture of existing derivatives of less variety and lack of personality, not with the contemporary young groups of aesthetic interest, life scenes, and experience to maintain synchronization, the hearts of modern consumers are prone to leave too old-fashioned and rigid impressions.

1.2 Target Group Positioning

In order to effectively develop cultural and creative products in line with Nanfeng Nuo culture, the questionnaire from the gender of tourists, age group, understanding of Nanfeng Nuo culture, love, purchase intention, and other aspects of statistics, and ultimately determine the Nanfeng Nuo cultural target groups[3]. Most of the users of this questionnaire are mainly in the age groups of 20-25 years old and 25-30 years old, which are 26.5% and 19.9%, respectively. Occupations are predominantly student-oriented. According to the questionnaire data, all survey respondents know the Nanfeng Nuo culture, a total 83.4%, of which 49.7% of people know Nanfeng Nuo culture, but do not understand, 16.6% said that Nanfeng Nuo culture is extraordinary e.g.: Figure 1. This author believes that the development of Nanfeng Nuo's cultural and creative design work is essential.

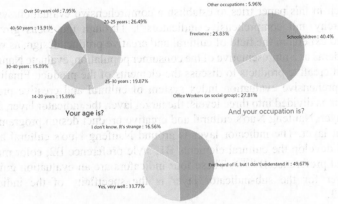

Figure 1.questionnaire 1 (e.g. survey)

e.g.:Figure 2 shows that 31.1% of the survey respondents are interested in Nanfeng Nuo's cultural development of creative products, followed by "a little bit of interest" of the survey respondents, accounting for 49.7%. Finally, 19.2% of the survey respondents said Nanfeng Nuo's cultural development of creative products could be more enjoyable. According to the questionnaire survey re "your favorite cultural and creative categories are" data feedback, the highest-ranked blind box hand puppet category, canvas bags, and cell phone cases, followed by the author in the design of the practice will use this data to select the design of Nanfeng Nuo cultural categories.

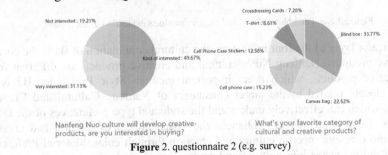

Figure 2. questionnaire 2 (e.g. survey)

Through the analysis of the results of the questionnaire above, we will use Nanfeng Nuo cultural and creative products consumer positioning, 20-25 years young consumer groups; these consumer groups generally have a strong interest in regional culture and have a high degree of acceptance of new things and tolerance, is the main force of cultural and creative products market consumption. Attractive designs easily attract these consumers; therefore, because of the habits of this type of consumer group, storytelling, fun, and creativity are the three main aspects to be considered in the design of cultural and creative products.

2.Modeling of Hierarchical Analysis Approach Comprehensive Evaluation System

2.1 Integrated evaluation system

The research in this paper tries to establish a comprehensive evaluation system with a clear hierarchy and comprehensive indicators[4]. Through the focus group research method, two experts in the field of cultural and creative product design, as well as three college students as a representative of the consumer population, evaluate Nangfeng Nuo's cultural and creative products to discuss the elements of the product. Finalize Nanfeng Nuo's comprehensive evaluation index system of cultural and creative products. The index system is divided into three levels: the target layer, the indicator layer, and the sub-indicator layer. Nanfeng Nuo's cultural and creative product design program evaluation is the target layer. The indicator layer is around Nanfeng Nuo's cultural and creative products to develop the cultural elements B1, style preference B2, color matching B3, and material preference B4[5][6]. These four indicators are an evaluation guideline. The bottom layer for the sub-indicator layer is the specificity of the indicator layer. e.g.:Figure 3.

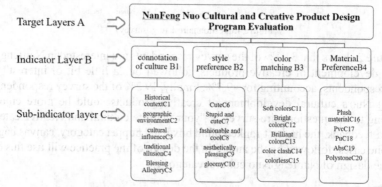

Figure 3.Nan Feng Nuo cultural and creative products evaluation index system

In the indicator layer of the four indicators, the cultural connotation of B1 is the core of the creative products. Nanfeng Nuo's cultural and creative products are different from other creative products, which is an important method. Style Preference B2 is an indicator closely related to the target consumers of Nanfeng Cultural and Creative Industries, which can effectively understand the style and type preferences of the target consumers. Color matching B3 enhances the visual appeal of cultural and creative products and conveys specific culture and emotion through color. Material Preference B4 injects unique tastes into cultural and creative products to meet target consumers' diversified and diverse pursuits for the texture of cultural and creative products.

2.2 Integrated Evaluation System Algorithm

First, the hierarchical model is constructed, which will be set as the target, indicator, and sub-indicator layers. After constructing the model, the judgment matrix is applied, and the two factors between the layers are compared. The details can be referred e.g.:Table 1.

Table 1. Reference to quantitative values between indicators

Ratio of factor I to factor J	Quantitative values
Equally important	1
Slightly important	3
More important	5
Overriding important	7
Extremely important	9
The median of two adjacent judgments	2, 4, 6, 8
Reciprocal	$a_{ij}=1/a_{ji}$

The first step is the scale to determine and construct the judgment matrix; this step is the source of the original data (judgment matrix), such as the example of the use of a 1-9 points scale (the lowest for 1 point, the highest for 9 points); and combined with the three experts to score the final judgment matrix form. See Table 2.

Table 2. Indicator judgment matrix

Program Evaluation A	connotation of culture B1	style preference B2	color matching B3	Material PreferenceB4	Wi
connotation of culture B1	1	1	2	4	0. 3701
style preference B2	1	1	2	3	0. 3452
color matching B3	1/2	1/2	1	2	0. 1850
Material PreferenceB4	1/4	1/3	1/2	1	0. 0997

Step 2: Calculate the corresponding weights of each element; if the weights need to be calculated, the largest (CI) must be calculated first, which is used for the consistency test in the next step. The algorithm uses YAAHP version 12.3, and the judgment matrix is normalized according to columns. See Table 3, Table 4.

Table 3. Sub Indicator judgment matrix

connotation of cultureB1	Historical contextC1	geographic environmentC2	cultural influenceC3	traditional allusionC4	Blessing AllegoryC5	Wi
Historical contextC1	1	2	1	1/2	1/3	0. 1367
geographic environmentC2	1/2	1	1/2	1/3	1/4	0. 0791
cultural influenceC3	1	2	1	1/2	1/3	0. 1367
traditional allusionC4	2	3	2	1	1/2	0. 2444
Blessing AllegoryC5	3	4	3	2	1	0. 4030

Table 4. Sub Indicator judgment matrix

connotation of cultureB1	Historical contextC1	geographic environmentC2	cultural influenceC3	traditional allusionC4	Blessing AllegoryC5	W i
Historical contextC1	1	1. 4990	0. 9129	0. 5261	0. 4000	0. 1396
geographic environmentC2	0. 6671	1	0. 6090	0. 3510	0. 2668	0. 0931
cultural influenceC3	1. 0955	1. 6421	1	0. 5764	0. 4381	0. 1529
traditional allusionC4	1. 9006	2. 8491	1. 7350	1	0. 7602	0. 2653
Blessing AllegoryC5	2. 5002	3. 7479	2. 2823	1. 3155	1	0. 3490

The third step is consistency test analysis; in constructing the judgment matrix, there may be logical errors, such as A is more important than B, B is more important than C, but C is more important than A. Therefore, it is necessary to use the consistency test to determine whether there is a problem; the consistency test uses the CR value to analyze. a CR value less than 0.1 means that through the consistency test, and vice versa, it did not pass the consistency test. Refer to Figure 4, Table 5.

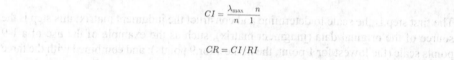

$$CI = \frac{\lambda_{max} - n}{n - 1}$$

$$CR = CI/RI$$

Figure 4. Randomized one-time test arithmetic equations

Table 5. Table of RI coefficients

Randomized Consistency RI Tables									
Nth order	3	4	5	6	7	8	9	10	11
Ri value	0.52	0.89	1.12	1.26	1.36	1.41	1.46	1.49	1.51

Step 4: Analyze the conclusion. If the weights have been calculated, and the judgment matrix satisfies the consistency test, the weight factors are calculated and ranked. See Table 6[7].

Table 6. Nanfeng Nuo cultural and creative product design comprehensive weighted ranking

Goals	Dindicators II	Weights	Dindicators III	Weights	Arrange
Nanfeng Nuo Cultural and Creative Design Index system	connotation of cultureB1	0. 3581	Historical contextC1	0. 05	8
			geographic environmentC2	0. 0333	12
			cultural influenceC3	0. 0548	7
			traditional allusionC4	0. 095	3
			Blessing AllegoryC5	0. 125	1
	style preference B2	0. 3328	CuteC6	0. 0818	4
			Stupid and cuteC7	0. 1232	2
			fashionable and coolC8	0. 0415	11
			aesthetically pleasingC9	0. 0558	6
			gloomyC10	0. 0305	13
	color matching B3	0. 2012	Soft colorsC11	0. 03	15
			Bright colorsC12	0. 0428	10
			Brilliant colorsC13	0. 0305	13
			color clashC14	0. 078	5
			colorlessC15	0. 0199	17
	Material PreferenceB4	0. 1079	Plush materialC16	0. 0087	20
			PvcC17	0. 0471	9
			PuC18	0. 0203	16
			AbsC19	0. 015	19
			PolystoneC20	0. 0168	18

2.3 Analysis of results

A comprehensive evaluation system in ranking indicators gives a particular Nuo Nanfeng Nuo cultural and creative design guidance, which should be emphasized in the design process[8]. The first in the ranking is Blessing Allegory C5, which indicates that consumers attach more importance to the feelings brought by cultural and creative products from the spiritual level and emphasize the core connotation of the cultural and creative products to convey to the consumers, and need to control the refinement of the cultural elements in the overall design process. Sort the second is stupid moe C7, the appearance of creative products is the most direct first impression of consumers in the purchase, clear consumer preferences on the style of Nanfeng Nuo creative products to help the excellent development of cultural and creative products; Traditional allusions C4 ranked third, is the entire design of the first phase of the cultural elements of the screening process of the most important indicators, in the cultural connotation of the B1 indicator composition accounted for more significant weight, but also one of the cores of Nanfeng Nuo cultural and creative products[9]. See Figure 5.

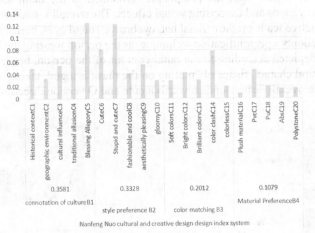

Figure 5. Degree of preference for user needs

3.Design Applications

According to the data collected by the questionnaire, it is based on Nanfeng Nuo's cultural and creative products target group of 20-25-year-old young people. The design style is preferred for cute, creativity, and storytelling[10]. Then, according to the AHP method, the user needs sorting to build a hierarchical analysis matrix and calculation to get Nanfeng Nuo's cultural factors of the importance of sorting, the final design of the case according to the hierarchical analysis of the influence of the factors for continuous modification. Six thematic stories were selected, and the characters, appearance, and cultural meanings of the stories were extracted. The six stories in the Nuo Face are Open the Mountain, Paper Money, Zhong Kui, Big Ghosts, Tiny Ghosts, Guan Gong, Lei Gong, Nuo Gong, and Nuo Women. The names of Nuo dance programs are all named after mask characters. In ancient times, the fundamental purpose of Nuo dance was to expel evil diseases, but in modern times, it gradually evolved into a performance that entertained people and gods. Zhong Kui Drunken "is a performance with rich entertainment meanings. Zhong Kui performs together with big and small ghosts, and the drunken Zhong Kui is subjected to a series of teasing by big and small ghosts, which has a dramatic effect. The opening performance of "Kaishan" is generally one of the essential programs, where the performer who plays the role of Kaishan wields an axe and chops around to achieve the effect of dispelling ghosts, as well as the meaning of dispelling disasters and avoiding evil spirits. The performers of 'Paper Money' will dance with a rope wrapped in paper money at both ends, which carries the meaning of widespread wealth. The 'Thunder Lord' performers wield chisels and axes with a fast rhythm and a passionate atmosphere, which also means dispelling evil and receiving blessings. Nuo Gong Nuo Po "tells the story of a person who gets a child at an ancient age. In ancient times, Nuo Gong Nuo Po was a reproductive worship of people, symbolizing multiple sons and blessings and yearning for a better life. The famous red-faced Guan Gong in "Guan Gong" overcame difficulties and killed six generals in the Three Kingdoms.

Nanfeng Nuo's cultural and creative IP image gives the feeling of cute people who want to get close to, in line with the pro-people, grounded in the main idea, effectively weakening the vicious and exorcising visual effects. The overall visualization retains the original distinctive features: the official hat, eyebrows, round eyes, horns, and fangs. The image effect adopts a personification technique, as the person wearing the Nuo mask, the body part is depicted according to the outer contour of the person, better reflecting the Nanfeng cultural characteristics of "putting on the mask is a god, taking off the mask is a person." The overall design tends towards a cute and Q version direction.

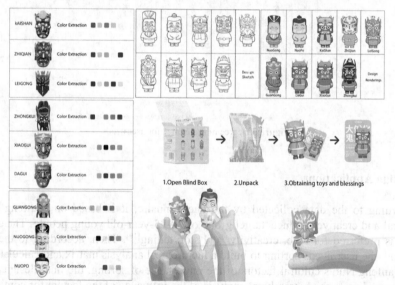

Figure 6. Nanfeng Nuo's cultural and creative product design program

4. Conclusion

This paper is based on a hierarchical analysis of Nanfeng Nuo culture and blind box in the combination of exploration and research, mainly through questionnaires, demand analysis, weighting, and other processes, to determine the target consumer groups, to complete the Nanfeng Nuo culture and blind box of innovative integration. Preliminary construction of an evaluation system model applicable to the development of Nanfeng Nuo creative products effectively helps designers to grasp the core connotation of Nanfeng Nuo creative products, to avoid subjective initiative leads to the deviation of the design direction, to ensure that the objective evaluation of the design program and accurate selection of the best. The design practice provides a scientific and practical guide to design in line with the contemporary aesthetic and cultural connotations of Nanfeng Nuo's cultural and creative products.

References

[1] Zeng Gong. Jiangxi Nanfeng Nuo Culture. Jiang Xi: Jiangxi Peoples Publishing House, 2005:740.
[2] Shu Si Qiang. Study on the inheritance and protection of Nanfeng exorcism dance from the view of intangible cultural heritage. Northwest Minzu University,2017.
[3] A Ruo Yao. Series of Cultural Creation Design on IP Figure of Dragon Boat Culture in Daling Village. Guangzhou University,2022.
[4] Zhu Yun Feng.Design of Gold Foil Cultural and Creative Products Based on Fuzzy Analytic Hierarchy Process. Packaging Engineering,2022,43(22):341–349.
[5] XU Zhan min, LI Yang. Application of Extraction Model of Product Design Factors of Floral Culture. Journal of Graphics,2017,38(01):45-51.
[6] WANG Jian-hua, GUI Ya-xin. Modern Furniture Design with Dong Architectural Culture. Packaging Engineering,2021,42(22):157-164.
[7] Zhou Qi, Niu Yan Na, Bi Wei Long. Product Design of Shadow Puppet Game Based on Analytic Hierarchy Process.PackingEngineering,2021,42(22): 157-164.
[8] Yang Xian Ying, Li Wei Zhan. The Mechanism of Traditional Culture in Product Design. Design,2019,32(05):92–93.
[9] Xiong Jia Hui, Yang Mei. The Application of Qingdao Folk Culture Factors Research in Tourist Souvenirs. Design,2020,33(16):120-123.
[10] Liu liang. Establishment and application of design factor extraction model based on qiangs' traditional dancing, culture.PackagingEngineerpng,2021,42(06):327-335

Design Studies and Intelligence Engineering
L.C. Jain et al. (Eds.)
© 2024 The Authors.
This article is published online with Open Access by IOS Press and distributed under the terms
of the Creative Commons Attribution Non-Commercial License 4.0 (CC BY-NC 4.0).
doi:10.3233/FAIA231464

How to Use Self-Attention Mechanism Model to Improve Driving Interface Design and Evaluation Research

ZHANG Ming[a,1], YU Shuwei[a1]
Jinhong HU[a], Yue WU[a], Feiyang LIU[a], Jinwei LU[a] Jiongzhou, WENG[a] Hao, HUO
[a], Cheng LI[b], Xiaojiang ZHOU[a] and Dongfang PAN[a]
[a]*China Jiliang University, College Art and Communication*
[b]*Suzhou Art&Design Technology Institute*

Abstract. The core of the paper is to enhance the handling of the car's central control interface through the Self-Attention mechanism in the Transform model, especially for specific driving groups, which vary greatly between groups, this study targets female drivers, aiming to solve the unique problems faced by women in central control interaction, and will add other groups such as men, the elderly, people with specific diseases, etc. in subsequent research plans. The main process of the study involves analyzing handling data from existing interfaces, using self-attention mechanisms to understand the characteristics of female drivers, and predicting user satisfaction. Studies have shown that improving the design based on the self-attention mechanism is beneficial to interface designers to improve the design, improve the efficiency and safety of female drivers, and ultimately improve the driving experience of specific groups.

Keywords. Self-Attention Mechanism, Model Central, Control, Interface Female, Driving, Interaction Design

The automotive on-board central control is an important interaction hub for new energy vehicles, which directly affects driving comfort and ease of use. Since the current stage of automobile design often draws on the experience of traditional fuel vehicle central control design, cannot meet the driving experience in the field of new energy vehicles, in the driving process of female drivers and male drivers experience is quite different, how to meet women's needs for central control interaction comfort and ease of use, has become a key issue in the design of vehicle central control interactive interface. Therefore, from the perspective of women's psychology and physiology, it is increasingly important to design better interaction ease of use, which is also the key to this research.

To solve the above problems, it is not only necessary to study the psychological and physiological characteristics of women, but also to use AI algorithm tools to better meet women's higher requirements for central control interaction design. Therefore, this paper plans to combine the Self-Attention Mechanism in the latest Transformer model to form a data algorithm by studying the psychological and physiological preferences of female users with driving satisfaction, and then design an interaction design scheme to finally design a vehicle central control interaction system that users are satisfied with.

---

[1] Corresponding Author: YU Shuwei E-mail : frunner@qq.com

1. Theoretical background

1.1. Comparison of the Self-Attention Mechanism and Recurrent Neural Network

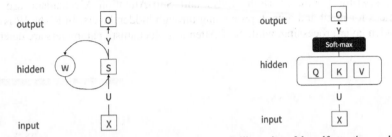

Figure 1. Recurrent neural network (RNN) diagram.   **Figure 2.** Illustration of the self-attention mechanism.

The Transformer model is a powerful neural network architecture for natural language processing and other sequential data tasks. It was first proposed by researchers at Google in 2017[1] and excels in a variety of NLP tasks, such as translation, text generation, and sentiment analysis.

Traditional sequence models (such as Rerrent Neural Network, RNN) face some problems when processing long text, such as long-term dependencies that are difficult to capture, resulting in information loss. The Transformer solves these problems, making it better able to handle long sequences.

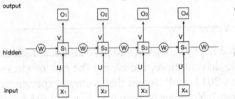

Figure 3. Recurrent neural networks (RNNs) unfold   **Figure 4.** Self-Attention Computational Graph.
the graph by time.

Figure 1 shows a basic Recurrent Neural Network (RNN) with input (X), output (O), hidden layer (S), and weight matrix (W) connections (Figure 2). The hidden layer depends on both current and past input (S). RNN struggles with long time series, limiting its ability to capture complex correlations. This limitation is evident when studying intricate female central control behavior, challenging RNN's capabilities.

The Transformer model's core idea is Self-Attention Mechanism, shown in Figure 3. It processes inputs (X1 to X4) to calculate the hidden layer's output (O) by considering all input data. Figure 4 illustrates the model's calculations, including data vectors, Query,

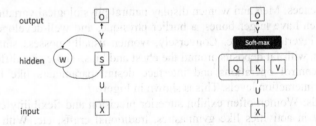

Figure 5. Recurrent neural networks (RNNs) versus Self-Attention patterns1.

Key, Value vectors, weight calculation (α), and final output generation. This allows the model to grasp context across the input sequence simultaneously and maintain positional information through an attention coding mechanism.

Comparing Figure 5: Both RNNs and Self-Attention Mechanism use vector sequences for input and output, processing through hidden layers. In RNN, W is reused for hidden layer processing, while Self-Attention Mechanism parameters are determined

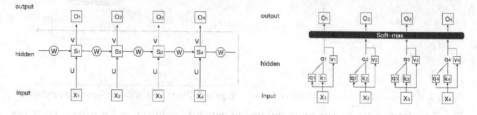

Figure 6. Recurrent neural networks (RNNs) versus Self-Attention patterns2.

through input decoding before output.

Figure 6 shows the difference. In RNN, outputs depend on previous input, but this connection weakens with longer sequences, causing information loss. Self-Attention Mechanism efficiently computes and maintains correlations between input values.

1.2. Behavioral characteristics of the target group

1.2.1. Psychological characteristics of the target group

Female and male driving behaviors differ due to physiological and psychological factors[4]. Emotions, particularly stress, affect female drivers more, increasing the risk of stress-related issues and accidents[5]. Guo Shuang's 2014 study found that women experienced higher anger and nervousness levels than men[6]. Younger women tend to avoid risks[7] and are more conservative regarding violations[8]. Both genders use roads differently, with women preferring lower-grade roads, having a more detailed memory of branch line details[9].

Female drivers and male drivers have a large difference in the hazard seeking index, women have higher sensitivity to danger[10], and the hazard seeking index is closely related to their own driving behavior[11], which reflects why the dangerous behavior of female drivers is much lower than that of men. At the same time, women's risk perception levels are much higher than men's[12].

1.2.2. Physiological characteristics of the target group

Physical Differences: Men and women display natural physiological variations in body shape. Men often have larger bones, a burlier physique, and well-developed muscles, resembling an inverted triangle. Conversely, women usually possess smaller bones, slimmer figures, with fat deposits around the chest and hips. These size differences can affect central control operations and interface design parameters like button size, placement, and interaction levels. This is shown in Figure 7

Motor Skills: Women often exhibit superior precision and flexibility compared to men, especially in activities like gymnastics, traditional crafts, etc. With the rise of intelligent central control screens, the reliance on physical buttons has decreased, and women adapt well to multi-function displays.

Visual Abilities: Studies show women may have slightly lower visual acuity than men, possibly due to their higher education levels and differences in field of vision[13]. This influences driving behaviors and offers insights for interaction design[14].

Spatial Skills: Drivers rely on senses to assess objects, location, and object speed. Women tend to have weaker spatial skills than men during driving.

Figure 7. Diagram of physiological differences between men and women

1.2.3. Research process of target group driving interaction based on Self-Attention mechanism

Female drivers prioritize safety, which affects car central control design. Using the Self-Attention Mechanism and female driver psychology, a model (Figure 8) evaluates existing solutions via user satisfaction and collects user data for input. After encoding, it computes Q, K, V matrices, calculates attention scores with Soft-max, and derives an output matrix O with operation information. This informs a new design compared to the original through user satisfaction assessments.

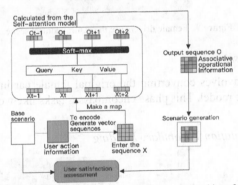

Figure 8. Framework diagram of the interaction of female driving control interface based on self-attention

2. Interaction design method of female central control interface based on Self-Attention Mechanism model

This paper explores vehicle-machine interaction layout design for female users, considering the Self-Attention Mechanism in the Transformer model and female interaction behavior.

Collect female users' interaction data, establish function correlations based on usage order, and optimize the central control interface design within the vehicle screen. Determine function placements based on their associations and conclude the optimized design through data analysis.

2.1. The Self-Attention model fits the target group interaction data

2.1.1. Analysis of the psychological characteristics of the target group

Female drivers, although more safety-conscious and risk-averse than men, often find themselves navigating complex road conditions on lower-level roads. This contradiction between psychological traits and driving behavior poses safety risks. Women can become nervous and make incorrect decisions in intricate road situations.

Figure 9 illustrates the sequential actions of female drivers using the central control screen: starting music, selecting playlists, activating air conditioning, and navigating. We collected interaction data from female drivers, spanning 13 provinces, primarily involving Tesla Model 3 central control interactions. This data, from 136 questionnaires, provides insights into female drivers' habits and experiences. After filtering, we retained 128 valid datasets for analysis.

Figure 9. Female drivers use the central control scene

2.1.2. Data Preprocessing

Data preprocessing involves converting the original female car interaction data into a format suitable for the model. This phase encompasses tasks like word segmentation and encoding.

2.1.2.1. Word Segmentation/Vocabulary Building

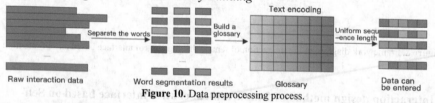

Figure 10. Data preprocessing process.

Word segmentation divides text into sequences of words or phrase, creating discrete tokens. For example, "navigate to downtown" becomes ["navigate", "to", "downtown"] based on questionnaire data.

A vocabulary is established using all text data in the dataset. This vocabulary comprises all possible words or phrase, each assigned a unique integer.

2.1.2.2. Text Encoding

Text encoding transforms segmented text into a format accepted by the model. Typically, we employ vocabulary indices to represent words. For instance, ["Navigation", "To",

"Downtown"] might be encoded as [10, 56, 102], where 10, 56, and 102 correspond to vocabulary word indices. Here's the text encoding based on questionnaire outcomes.

Table 1. Text encoding

function	encode
Defogging of car windows	[8.27, 71, 37, 22, 6, 0, 0, 0]
air conditioning	[7.56, 36, 38, 38, 16, 6, 2, 0]
Music	[6.97, 21, 29, 38, 28, 15, 4, 1]
Car status	[5.9, 4, 17, 24, 36, 34, 13, 8]
Phone pairing	[4.9, 1, 9, 9, 24, 44, 30, 10]
Front passenger seat adjustment	[3.56, 3, 4, 3, 13, 15, 40, 24]
Main driver seat adjustment	[2.63, 0, 0, 2, 8, 13, 25, 33]
navigation	[1.65, 0, 2, 0, 3, 6, 16, 15]
volume	[0.94, 0, 0, 0, 2, 3, 6, 10]

2.1.3. Application of Self-Attention Mechanism in interface interaction data analysis

The female interaction data input sequence can be obtained by 2.1, assuming a length of N: $X=[x1,x2,x3,...,xi,...,xn]$, where each xi represents the encoding of a word or phrase.

2.1.4. Calculate Q, K, V matrices

First, the input sequence X is passed through a linear map (usually called the embedding layer) to obtain three sets of vectors, representing the query (Q), key (K), and value (V)

$$Q = W^q X \tag{1.}$$
$$K = W^K X \tag{2}$$
$$V = W^V X \tag{3}$$

2.1.5. Calculate attention score

Calculate the dot product between the query vector and the key vector to obtain the attention score (attention weight) A

$$A = softmax\left(\frac{K^T Q}{\sqrt{d_k}}\right) \tag{4}$$

2.1.6. Calculate the output matrix O

Using the weighted sum value of the attention score A weight, the context vector O is obtained:

$$O = VA \tag{5}$$

The Self-Attention Mechanism calculation process, shown above, involves the softmax function, query, key, and value computation. It establishes meaningful correlations between input sequence locations based on content, aiding in processing women's interaction data.

2.2. Design fitting feedback and female central control interaction design scheme generation

Shih showed the impact of car central control interface layout on user visual retrieval efficiency during driving15 .Taking Tesla as an example, as shown in Figure 11, the central screen size of Model 3 is 15 inches, 1920 x 1200, and the entire interface can be divided into three areas, the driving information area on the left, the content switching area on the right, and the shortcut menu area at the bottom for switching different menus. Driving information area: 508 x 1020, content switching area: 1340 x 1020, shortcut menu area: 1920 x 120.

Designing car screens for women should consider their physiological and psychological characteristics. Women generally have a smaller interpupillary distance (53mm ~ 68mm) compared to men (60mm ~ 73mm), potentially affecting their depth perception. Due to body size differences, female drivers might find the right side of the screen less accessible. Therefore, placing buttons in the middle and left of the screen is advisable. Soft colors should be used to avoid creating a sense of depression. To prevent driver nervousness, concentrate the shortcut menu area at the bottom during driving.

2.2.1. Self-Attention Mechanism data output

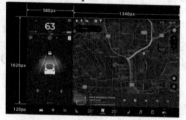

Figure 11. Original interface

Through the analysis of the output results of the Self-Attention Mechanism to guide the generation of design schemes, due to the complex interactive functions of the vehicle-machine central control interface and the large number of layers, this study selects the air conditioning module with the highest frequency of user use as an example for analysis and research. Figure 9 code calculates the sub-attention weight matrix of the relevant air conditioning module.

This study utilizes Self-Attention Mechanism output for design scheme guidance. Given interface complexity and layers, we analyze the frequently used air conditioning module.

The sub-attention weight matrix of the relevant air conditioning module is calculated by the following code: Attention weights for air conditioning:
tensor([0.8839, -10.3928, 32.2866, 25.0024, 8.0664, -8.0448, -27.3606,-17.2605, 7.5087, 31.3909, -7.4695, 0.6751, -15.3708, 13.1083,-10.0089, 20.4724])

Calculation results: Window defogging, main driver's seat adjustment, passenger seat adjustment, and navigation have negative weights, suggesting occasional single-function use. Music, car status, mobile phone pairing, and volume exhibit positive weights, indicating a strong correlation with air conditioning, especially music and car status.

2.2.2. Interface layout optimization

According to the analysis results of attention weight, the interface layout is optimized. Setting the high-attention section to a more prominent and easy-to-navigate location ensures that users can quickly find and use important features and options. Use attention weight analysis to find out the most important features and options in a particular task. In the air conditioning interface design, these features can be highlighted with a larger, more eye-catching style to direct the user's attention.

The analysis of attention weight optimizes the interface layout, prioritizing high-attention sections for user accessibility. This approach highlights crucial features and options in the air conditioning interface design, making them more prominent and user-friendly.

Based on attention weight analysis, the interface layout is optimized by highlighting high-attention sections for quick and easy access to important features. These significant features in the air conditioning interface design can be emphasized with a larger, more eye-catching style to direct user attention

Figure 12. scheme 1   **Figure 13.** Scheme 2

Conclusions drawn from data prompted interface logic adjustments. Figure 11 shows the original interface, with female user data indicating a strong air conditioning and music module correlation. To accommodate this, the music module was placed near the air conditioning module. Modules for car status, mobile phone pairing, and volume were also positioned nearby for easier access.

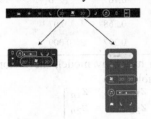

Figure 14. Schematic diagram of functional location adjustments   **Figure 15.**.Illustration of how to adjust the use of the air conditioner

Figure 14 illustrates the relocation of the car air conditioner module based on usage frequency. In scheme 1, the air conditioner was moved to the lower left corner of the screen, facilitating convenient access for female drivers. Scheme 2 positioned the air conditioning module in the center of the driver's line of sight. Additionally, as figure 15 the interaction method was adjusted to include left-right and up-down scrolling with color gradients to guide users.

Music and volume control, highly relevant to the air conditioning module, were streamlined in scheme 1, placing them above the air conditioning module for a more compact layout. Scheme 2 adopted a similar approach for intuitive volume adjustment.

3. Design satisfaction evaluation of the target group's vehicle central control interface generated by the self-attention mechanism

3.1. The target group car central control uses the satisfaction evaluation level construction

In order to obtain the satisfaction evaluation of the in-vehicle central control from the perspective of female users, the following seven indicators were determined by questionnaire method and expert interview method to establish the satisfaction evaluation model, as shown in Figure 16.

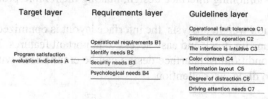

Figure 16. Program satisfaction evaluation indicators

3.2. Satisfaction level weight calculation

Table 2. Benchmark layer weights

Guidelines layer	Original scenario	Scheme1	Scheme2	CR	Consistency check
Operation compatibility C1	0.157	0.594	0.249	0.051	Pass
Operational simplicity C2	0.2	0.6	0.2	0	Pass
Interface intuitiveness C3	0.136	0.625	0.238	0.017	Pass
Color contrast ratio C4	0.167	0.667	0.167	0	Pass
Information layout C5	0.105	0.637	0.258	0.037	Pass
Distraction C6	0.614	0.117	0.268	0.07	Pass
Driving attention requirement C7	0.54	0.163	0.297	0.009	Pass

By constructing a good satisfaction evaluation hierarchy model, the factors in it are compared in pairs, and a judgment matrix is established:

$$Z = \left(z_{ij}\right)_{m\times n} = \begin{bmatrix} z_{11} & z_{12} & \cdots & z_{1n} \\ z_{21} & z_{22} & \cdots & z_{2n} \\ \cdots & \cdots & \cdots & \cdots \\ z_{m1} & z_{m2} & \cdots & z_{mn} \end{bmatrix} \tag{6}$$

where z_{ij} represents the relative importance of factor i to factor j, satisfying $z_{ij} = \frac{1}{z_{ji}}$. Using the above judgment matrix, according to the basic principles of analytic hierarchy method, the square root method is used to calculate the weight value of the criterion layer of the new scheme generated by the Self-Attention Mechanism in this study, as shown in Table 2.

3.3. Scheme selection and determination

Based on the scenario summary results, the ranking of the three scenarios is obtained. Option 1 scored the highest in the analysis, with a quantitative score of 2.143, so this study was based on Scenario 1 for in-depth design.

Through comparative analysis, the functional scores of air conditioning, music, window defogging and main driver seat adjustment are relatively high, and through design optimization, users have higher recognition of the optimized interactive interface, while the functions of car status, passenger seat adjustment and navigation have lower scores. This may mean that when designing a central control interface, focus on those features that score low to improve the user experience.

3.4. Evaluation results and design satisfaction evaluation

Table 3. Comparison of old and new solutions

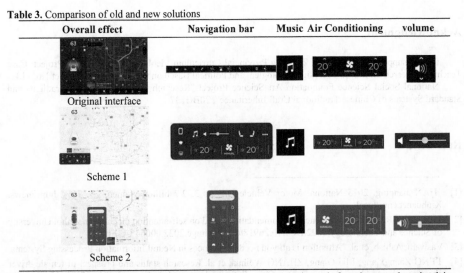

| Overall effect | Navigation bar | Music Air Conditioning | volume |

Data analysis indicates that air conditioning, music, window defogging, and main driver seat adjustment have higher functional scores post-optimization. Conversely, car status, passenger seat adjustment, and navigation received lower scores, highlighting the need for focused design improvement. Table 4 compares the three scenarios.

The Transformer model's Self-Attention Mechanism improvement enhances female-centric vehicle central control interface design. It assesses user behavior to uncover vital methods for intelligent interaction design, enhancing female user satisfaction. This informs user-centric central control interaction system design.

4. Conclusion

This research aims to improve car central control interactions for female drivers by enhancing the Transformer model's Self-Attention mechanism. It involves analyzing driving interface data, predicting user satisfaction, and creating new interfaces based on feedback from female users to address gender-specific attention differences.

The results indicate that the Self-Attention mechanism improvement method in the Transformer model offers crucial techniques for automotive interaction designers, enabling intelligent generation and interaction design. Additionally, our research enhances the overall driving experience for female drivers in terms of central control interface efficiency and safety. This not only innovates automotive interface design but also provides valuable insights into addressing gender-related impacts on interaction design.

Due to the conditions, there are many details that have not yet been perfected. The target group of this study is female drivers, and in the follow-up research, other groups will be used as the target groups such as men, the elderly, and groups with special diseases, etc., through the research methods and paths explored in this study, to improve the driving experience for other groups and solve the problems that may be encountered in the use of the central control platform. In future research, it is hoped that interested scholars can conduct detailed research according to these directions.

Acknowledgment

Project supported by the 2022 Zhejiang Provincial Curriculum Ideological and Political Project: Case Teaching Research on Industrial Design Ideological and Political Based on Correct Values, Project No. 113.

National Social Science Foundation Art Science Project "Research on Contemporary Paradigms and Standard Systems of Chinese Traditional Craft Inheritance", 20BG137

Reference

[1]   HAN Jianping. 2015 National Motor Vehicle Drivers 3. 2.7 billion women, 25. 71%. http://news. Xinhuanet.com/local/

[2] NING Yulin. Research on sequence recommendation based on self-attention mechanism.Anhui University of Science and Technology,2022.DOI:10.26918/d.cnki.ghngc.2022.000645.

[3] Vaswani, Ashish, et al. "Attention is all you need. "Advances in Neural Information Processing Systems.

[4]   FENG Zhongxiang, LIU Qiang, ZHANG Weihua, et al. Research status and prospect of female driver characteristics and behavior mechanism.China Safety Science and Technology,2016,12(04):124-130.)

[5]   Orit T B A, Mario M, Omri G. The multidimensional driving style inventory – scale construct and validation. Accident Analysis and Prevention,2004,36(3) : 323 − 332.

[6]   GUO Shuang, SUN Long, CHANG Ruo song. Compilation of Driver Emotional State Scale. China Journal of Health Psychology, 2014,22(6) :893 - 894.

[7]   SHI Jing,TAO Li, BAI Yun. Analysis of "driving rush" behavior and factors of motor vehicle drivers in Beijing. China Safety Science Journal,2010,20 (8): 30 - 39.

[8]   West R,Hall J. The role of personality and attitudes in traffic accident risk. Applied Psychology,1997,46(3) : 253 − 264.

[9]   REN Yijing: HUANG Chun xiao. Research on female driving behavior characteristics based on the current urban road system. A case study of Nanjing central urban area. Shanghai Urban Planning Journal, 2018(05):107-112.

[10] Boholm A. Comparative studies of risk perception: a review of twenty years of research. Journal of Risk Research,1998,1 (2) : 135 – 163.

[11] XieXiaofei. Journal of Peking University (Natural Science Edition), 2001(06): 859-868.

[12] Tova R, Amit S, Avi E, et al. Risk perception of driving as a function of advanced training aimed at recognizing and handling risks in demanding driving situations. Nuclear Instruments and Methods in Physics Research,2008,40(2) : 697 -703.

[13] HU Min,LI Qianling,LIANG Xizheng. Investigation on visual acuity status of driver center in Zhongshan City, 2012-2013[J]. Preventive Medicine Forum, 2014, 20 (11), 818 - 819.

[14] LI Zuomin. Traffic engineering. Beijing: China Communications Press,2000.

[15]   Wenlong. Research on position evaluation of automotive HMI central control screen based on touch interaction and visual interaction. Jilin University, 2023.

Design Studies and Intelligence Engineering
L.C. Jain et al. (Eds.)
© 2024 The Authors.
This article is published online with Open Access by IOS Press and distributed under the terms
of the Creative Commons Attribution Non-Commercial License 4.0 (CC BY-NC 4.0).
doi:10.3233/FAIA231465

Research on the Interactive Narrative Design of Jiangnan Sizhu Based on the Perception of Cultural Symbols

Jiang YAO [a,1] and Bing FENG [b]

[a] Institute of Art and Design, Nanjing Institute of Technology
[b] School of Art, Nanjing Vocational University of Industry Technology

Abstract. The inheritance and dissemination of folk culture in the context of new media has become a key research topic in the current academic community. This article summarizes the relationship between the perception of folk cultural symbols, audience attitudes, and interactive narrative design. By collecting relevant data and establishing hypothesis models, it explores the role and influence of interactive narrative design between the perception of folk cultural symbols and audience attitudes. Based on this, an interactive narrative model for the perception of Jiangnan Sizhu cultural symbols is constructed from the perspectives of text structure, formal structure, and interactive structure. To exploring the ways and methods of interactive narrative design to better promote the dynamic inheritance and dissemination of Jiangnan Sizhu, so as to present characteristics that are in line with the cultural ecology of the new era and reflect its dynamic value. The research results show that as a representative of intangible cultural heritage and folk customs in the performing arts category, the inheritance and development of Jiangnan Sizhu inevitably need to keep up with the times. Interactive narrative can be an effective means to enable the audience to achieve a conscious experience of aesthetic culture and value identification through its cultural imagery, endowing Jiangnan Sizhu with more cultural connotations, value space, and dissemination channels. At the same time, it provides reference directions and paths for interactive narrative design in the inheritance of other intangible cultural heritage customs.

Keywords. Symbol Perception; Cultural Imagery; Interactive Narrative Design. Jiangnan Sizhu

1. Introduction

The perception of cultural symbols from a sociological perspective views culture as a diverse synthesis. The basic starting point of the Tartu school's research on "cultural memory" is to view culture as a symbolic system, creating, and forgetting information in cultural memory, elucidate the characteristics of different types of cultural memory, and search for the most suitable symbol elements to assume the responsibility of cultural memory [1]. The perception of cultural symbols from the perspective of design studies focuses on the characteristics and meanings of cultural symbols, studying how to construct multiple meanings of cultural symbols through design and continuously acquire new meanings in order to be better perceived by people [2]. Among them, how

[1] Corresponding author, Institute of Art and Design, Product design, Nanjing Institute of Technology, Nanjing211167, China; yjdesign@njit.edu.cn;

to transform intangible, vague, and abstract cultural symbols into perceptible experience models through design has become a research difficulty. The process of transforming abstract symbols into artistic symbols emphasizes the intentionality of symbol expression and people's perception of symbols [3]. Therefore, symbols can be used to express people's emotions and thoughts and are also important elements in cultural construction. Modern hermeneutics believes that the emotional centered meaning contained, metaphorical, and symbolic in a text constitutes the meaning of cultural symbols [4]. From this, the design and construction of cultural symbols can be based on "form" and generate multiple connotation systems with infinite meaning.

Folk customs are not only one of social ideologies, but also a cultural heritage with a long history [5]. From the perspective of musicology, research on Jiangnan Sizhu mostly focuses on repertoire, musical forms, instruments, and music systems; From the perspective of folklore, it focuses on inheritors, improvement of musical instruments, and innovation in performance forms [6]. Therefore, the study of Jiangnan Sizhu has interdisciplinary and diverse characteristics. This study using interactive narrative design to excavate its deep cultural symbols through the artistic representation of Jiangnan Sizhu, promote group cognition, and promote the inheritance and dissemination of Jiangnan Sizhu.

2. Literature review

2.1. Sign Theory and Cultural Sign Perception

Modern semiotics regards symbols as meaningful media that convey certain information in a certain context. Chiyoshihiko believes that the meaning of symbols changes with cultural and social contexts [7]. Saussure believed that symbols are composed of the signifier and the signified [8].Peirce believed that symbols are composed of representative items, symbolic media, and explanatory items, and their relationship determines the essence of the process of symbolization. Through the analysis of the process of symbolic meaning can be contextualized to generate infinite meaning. Susan Langer believing that art is a symbol that objectifies human emotional activities and needs to be studied from an aesthetic perspective [9]. People's perception of cultural symbols is related to human experience. Therefore, the symbolic meaning of cultural symbols needs to be jointly recognized by a group to have universal significance.

2.2 Narrative Theory and Interactive Narrative Design

Interactive narrative through interaction and explores immersive experiences from different perspectives of narrative. Foreign research mainly focuses on game design, film and television animation, computer technology, literary and artistic research, and other fields. Galylean and Tinsley Azariah extended the research field of interactive narrative to the field of video production[10]; Stacey Hand and Duane Varan validated through experimental data that incorporating interactive elements in game design can continuously improve the audience's emotional experience[11]; Marie Laure Ryan believes that through interaction, narrative experiences can be continued[12]; Chris Crawford believes that interactive narrative can achieve different sensory experiences by selecting different narrative plots[13]. Domestic research mainly focuses on new media narrative, virtual interaction technology, user experience design, and other fields. Hong.W. and Suren.L. believe that interactive narrative integrated with culture can deepen the audience experience [14]; Vrettakis, E. proposed the design method and implementation approach of interactive narrative from the perspective of cognitive psychology [15]; Dzedzickis, A. studied user emotional needs in interactive narratives from a new media perspective, and explored design methods for interactive narratives[16].

2.3 Jiangnan Sizhu and Its Contemporary Development Issues

Jiangnan Sizhu has a long history and profound traditions. The performers cooperate with each other according to the repertoire and improvise, fully leveraging their subjective initiative and teamwork[17].From the perspective of Intangible Cultural Heritage Inheritance, although the government's guidance to the public and cultural infiltration have played a positive role in the inheritance of Jiangnan Sizhu, Jiangnan Sizhu lacks its own social ecology and cultural form of inheritance, and the audience's recognition of Jiangnan Sizhu is not high, coupled with the impact of global cultural convergence, which makes it face more severe development challenges. The fundamental reason lies in the artistic form and language construction of Jiangnan Sizhu, and then there is a deviation in the propagation path.

2.4 research hypothesis

After clarifying the relevant concepts and their relationships, this study proposes five hypotheses, namely (Figure 1):

Hypothesis 1: There are three levels of perception of folk culture: folk cultural imagery, symbolic cultural imagery, and connotative cultural imagery;

Hypothesis 2: Three levels of audience attitude: audience cognition, audience emotions, and audience behavior;

Hypothesis 3: The relationship between the three levels of audience attitude;

Hypothesis 4: The perception of folk culture and the attitude of the audience interact through interactive narrative design.

Hypothesis 5: The relationship between folk cultural perception and audience attitudes.

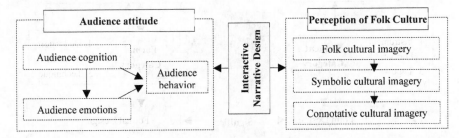

Figure 1. Hypothesis Model(This study)

3. Research Design

3.1. Research Method

This study is based on the "cultural image theory". Image is interpreted as a state of mind in the field of psychology. It is the intermediary of thinking activities and the basis of psychological activities [18]. Cultural images form connotative cultural symbols through inherent and unique cultural meanings, reflecting historical culture, social consciousness, national spirit, as well as people's impression, cognition and emotion of perceptible cultural entities [19]. This study takes Jiangnan Sizhu as the research object, analyzes its atmosphere folk custom image, symbol image and connotation image according to the cultural image theory, and constructs the relationship model among Jiangnan Sizhu cultural perception, interactive narrative design and audience attitude [20].

An analysis of the folk cultural image of Jiangnan Sizhu (Figure 2): Jiangnan Sizhu is an indispensable folk form in Jiangnan region, such as festivals and wedding customs, and is the product of emotional cognition, aesthetic context and value standards [21].

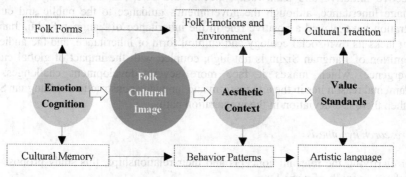

Figure 2. Folk cultural image of Jiangnan Sizhu(This study)

Analysis of the symbolic cultural image of Jiangnan Sizhu(Figure 3): Jiangnan Sizhu is a complex of cultural symbols such as musical instrument shape culture, performance form culture, and skill culture. As a medium, symbols reflect people's subjective consciousness and play the role of cognition, communication, and dissemination[22].

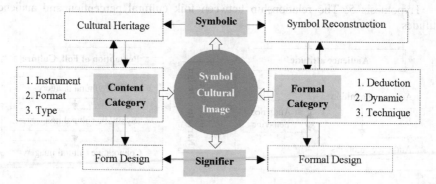

Figure 3. Symbol cultural image of Jiangnan Sizhu(This study)

An analysis of the connotative cultural image of Jiangnan Sizhu(Figure 4): the taste of Jiangnan Sizhu is all between the harmonious tunes, which coincides with the connotation of Chinese traditional Confucian culture[23]. The Confucian thought of the unity of heaven and man is the highest realm of the golden mean [24].

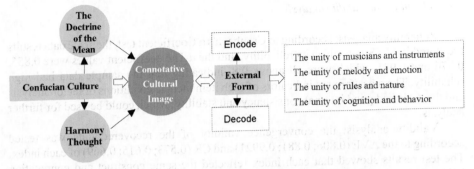

Figure 4. Connotation cultural image of Jiangnan Sizhu(This study)

3.2. Scale design

Taking "the perception of cultural symbols of silk and bamboo in the south of the Yangtze River" as the research object, the questionnaire is designed based on some existing questionnaires, including three parts: the first part is the research introduction, which explains the basic situation of silk and bamboo in the south of the Yangtze River; The second part is the basic information of the respondents; The third part quantifies the cultural symbols of southern silk and bamboo, and collects and sorts out the indicators of concern through semi-structured interviews. This study summarizes some evaluation indicators on the basis of the existing ones. In the pre survey stage, throughthe analysis of the data, part of the data that has no obvious correlation with the potential variables to be measured is deleted, and the sentences of the items are modified according to the feedback of the investigators, forming the final questionnaire.

According to the scale, according to the three levels of folk culture perception set above, six measurement items are designed, and the items refer to Mthrabian & Epstien (1972); According to the three levels of the audience's attitude, six measurement items are designed. The items refer to levs.Vygotsky (1930); According to the relationship between the perception of folk culture and the audience's attitude, three measurement items are designed, and the items refer to Westbrook (1980). And it is refined according to the visual, perceptual and memory of interactive narrative experience. The likert 5 subscale is used for the measurement scale, "1" means very disagree, "2" means disagree, "3" means average, "4" means agree, "5" means very agree.

3.3. Data collection

The questionnaire selected some people in southern Jiangsu, Shanghai, Zhejiang and other regions, as well as tourists as the research object, and collected research data through questionnaire stars, wechat circle of friends, interviews and other forms. After 2-3 weeks of intensive collection and interviews, 248 questionnaires were collected. After deleting the invalid questionnaires, 213 questionnaires were finally counted, with an effective rate of 86%. According to the statistical data analysis, the respondents' attitudes towards the interactive narrative experience of the folk culture of silk and bamboo in the south of the Yangtze River are visual (62.3%), perceptual (41.8%), and perceptual (32.2%).

3.4. Reliability and validity analysis

Reliability analysis: according to Cronbach's α Coefficient test, the scale data results are stored in SPSS to analyze its reliability, and the α The coefficient values were 0.855, 0.876 and 0.921, which were all above 0.8, indicating that the sample data had high reliability. The measurement indicators of each item met the conditions of factor analysis, and the scale had good internal consistency and stability, which could be used for further analysis.

Validity analysis: the convergence validity of the recovered data was tested according to the AVE (0.806; 0.881; 0.9921) and CR (0.573; 0.615; 0.669) of each index. The test results showed that each index reflected the same construct and connotation index, indicating that the convergence validity index of the scale data met the requirements; the standard load system of the scale was obtained through data detection. Except that F1, F2 and F4 items were greater than 0.6 and less than 0.7, the rest items were greater than 0.7. The reason was that the respondents were affected bythe description clarity and experience degree of interactive narrative design. The mean variance extracted AVE value and combined reliability CR index were verified again, and the test results showed that the scale data had good aggregate validity. See Table 1 for detailed data.

Table 1. Reliability and Validity

Dimension	Index	Standard load	T value	AVE	CR	Alpha
Perception of Folk Culture	F1: I have gained a basic understanding of Jiangnan Sizhu through explanation	0.63		0.806	0.573	0.855
	F2: Gain a deeper understanding of Jiangnan Sizhu through video media	0.65	13.074			
	F3: The interactive form made me actively understand the Jiangnan Sizhu culture	0.72	12.426			
	F4: The narrative technique made me empathize with Jiangnan Sizhu	0.67	11.708			
	F5: Virtual experience is more conducive to the dissemination of folk culture	0.70	12.149			
	F6: Folk culture is an important component of traditional Chinese culture	0.82	16.879			
Audience attitude	A1: Jiangnan Sizhu reminds me of the regional characteristics of Jiangnan	0.82		0.881	0.615	0.876
	A2: Jiangnan Sizhu reminds me of special people and things	0.83	17.076			
	A3: Jiangnan Sizhu have aroused my interest in folk culture	0.81	16.889			
	A4: I am willing to recommend Jiangnan Sizhu Culture to my family and friends	0.75	14.148			
	A5: I am willing to participate in the experience in specific scenarios	0.83	16.912			
	A6: Jiangnan Sizhu make me feel the charm of Chinese folk music	0.86	18.325			
	D1: Interactive Narration Makes Jiangnan Sizhu Easy to Understand	0.81		0.921	0.669	0.921

Interactive Narrative Design	D2: Interactive narration is beneficial for the popularization and inheritance of Jiangnan Sizhu	0.82	19.854
	D3: Interactive narrative design benefits cultural identity of Jiangnan Sizhu	0.77	17.774

3.5 Hypothesis model validation

The model was estimated, and the test showed that the main fitting indexes under the hypothetical conditions were greater than 0.9, indicating that the fitting indexes were good, and the overall hypothetical model was up to standard. Hypothesis model validation results show that interactive narrative design has a significant impact on the perception of folk cultural symbols of silk and bamboo in the south of the Yangtze River; Interactive narrative design has a significant positive impact on the audience's attitude; Audience cognition has a significant positive impact on audience emotion; Audience cognition and audience emotion have significant positive effects on audience behavior (see Table 2).

Tab.2 Results of supposed test

Assumption Path	Beta value	T value	P value	Inspection results
Interactive Narrative Design → Perception of Jiangnan Sizhu Folk Culture Symbols	0.195	2.116	*	establish
Interactive Narrative Design → Audience Attitude	0.687	8.825	***	establish
Audience cognition → Audience emotions	0.145	3.676	***	establish
Audience cognition → Audience behavior	0.134	2.566	*	establish
Audience emotions → Audience behavior	0.164	2.633	**	establish

Note: * * * indicates $P<0.001$ and is significantly correlated.

4. Architecture of Interactive Narrative Design Model for Jiangnan Sizhu

4.1. A study of narrative generation

First, the space-time generation of narration. The modern narrative discourse of Jiangnan Sizhu is constructed by time. The multiple narrative dimensions of Jiangnan Sizhu are constructed in space. Second, the scene generation of narrative. Through the field, the narrative generation has a formal meaning, so that the experiencer has more ways to interpret Jiangnan Sizhu[25]. Establish the communication between the audience and the perception of Jiangnan Sizhu cultural symbols through the situation, so as to achieve the unity of things and me. Third, the media generation of narrative. Through the interleaving of words and images, it is easy for the audience to understand and accept. At the same time, the continuous updating of narrative media has brought more plasticity to the communication form of Jiangnan Sizhu. The design method of narration can transform the cultural information of Jiangnan Sizhu into a language that can be recognized. (Figure 5).

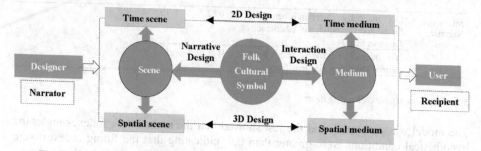

Figure 5. Interactive narrative generation structure of cultural images in Jiangnan Sizhu(This study)

4.2. A study of Interactive narrative architecture

From the above data, it can be seen that interactive narrative can be used as an effective research way to put the folk image, symbol image and connotation image of Jiangnan Sizhu in the narrative system, so that the audience can reconstruct the historical and cultural memory and emotional experience, and realize the conscious experience of aesthetic culture and value identification(Figure 6).

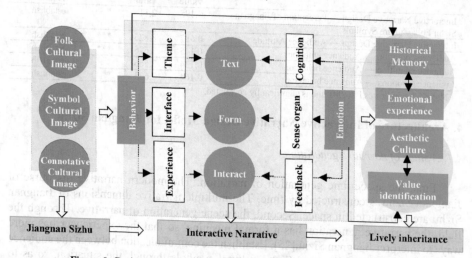

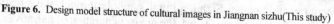

Figure 6. Design model structure of cultural images in Jiangnan sizhu(This study)

5. Conclusion

The results show that interactive narrative design has a significant impact on the perception of folk cultural symbols of silk and bamboo in the south of the Yangtze River; Interactive narrative design has a significant positive impact on the audience's attitude; Audience cognition has a significant positive impact on audience emotion; Audience cognition and audience emotion have significant positive effects on audience behavior. This provides important enlightenment for the design of folk culture inheritance and dissemination. Based on the theory of cultural image, this paper analyzes the folk cultural image, symbolic cultural image and connotative cultural image of Jiangnan Sizhu, and puts forward four elements of the narrative generation of Jiangnan Sizhu cultural image, on which the design content and ideas of interactive narrative of Jiangnan Sizhu cultural symbol perception are constructed. Interactive narrative can enhance the value expression of Jiangnan Sizhu in the context of the new era through diversified, multi-channel and multi-path design. At the same time, the research of interactive narrative design has a richer innovation path worthy of further exploration.Through the design model and analysis of this study, the effectiveness of interactive narrative design in the field of folk cultural symbol perception and communication is verified. Whether the model is reliable in the inheritance and dissemination of folk culture in other countries and regions needs further verification.

Acknowledgments

This research was funded by the General Projects of Jiangsu Province Social Science Foundation Program, grant number No. 20YSB010; Nanjing University of Engineering School Research Fund Project Grants, grant number No. YKJ202233.

References

[1] Tamm, M. Introduction: Juri Lotman's semiotic theory of history and cultural memory. *Essays in Cultural Semiotics* (2019), 1-26.

[2] Zhang, X. The application of ethnic cultural symbols in modern visual communication design. *Scientific and Social Research* (2021), 3(1).

[3] Feldman, C. F. *Intentionality and interpretation*. Psychology Press, 2023.

[4] Aprillyanto, M. A. Analysis of the Meaning of Local Cultural Symbols in the" Kuku Bima Ener-G North Sumatra Version" Advertisement on Television (Roland Barthes Semiotics Analysis). *Journal of Social Science and Humanities* (2022), 1(2), 35-44.

[5] Holtorf, C., & Högberg, A. (Eds.). *Cultural heritage and the future*. Routledge, 2020.

[6] Wong, J. Y. Chinese musical culture in the global context–modernization and internationalization of traditional Chinese music in twenty-first century. *Chinese Culture in the 21st Century and its Global Dimensions: Comparative and Interdisciplinary Perspectives* (2020), 105-122.

[7] Mingyu, W. A. N. G. A Review of Linguistic Semiotics. *Contemporary Foreign Languages Studies* (2023), 23(2), 5.

[8] Rudrakumar, S., & Venkatraman, R. A semiotic analysis of Saussure and Barthes's theories under the purview of print advertisements. *Journal of Language & Linguistics Studies* (2022), 18(1).

[9] Makkreel, R. Cassirer, Langer, and Dilthey on the Distinctive Kinds of Symbolism in the Arts. *Journal of Transcendental Philosophy* (2021), 2(1), 7-20.

[10] Pizzo, Antonio, Vincenzo Lombardo, and Rossana Damiano. *Interactive storytelling: a cross-media approach to writing, producing and editing with AI*. Taylor & Francis, 2023.

[11] Ryan M L. From narrative games to playable stories: Toward a poetics of interactive narrative. *StoryWorlds: a journal of narrative studies* (2009), 1: 43-59.

[12] Chen, J., Ryan, M. L. Storyworld, transmedia storytelling, and contemporary narrative theory: An interview with Marie-Laure Ryan. *Frontiers of Narrative Studies* (2022), 7(2), 147-155.

[13] Crawford, C. Interactive storytelling. In The video game theory reader. *Routledge*, 2013.

[14] Hong,W., Suren,L. Immersion and Narration: Research on Museum Culture Immersive Experience Design under New Media Imaging Technology. *Hundred Artists* (2018), 34 (4), 161-169.

[15] Vrettakis, E., Kourtis, V. Narralive–Creating and experiencing mobile digital storytelling in cultural heritage. *Digital Applications in Archaeology and Cultural Heritage* (2019), 15.

[16] Witzleben, J. L. Jiangnan Sizhu music clubs in Shanghai: context, concept and identity. *Ethnomusicology* (1987), 240-260.

[17] Chow-Morris, K. L. Improvising hegemony, exploring disjuncture: The music and cultures of Jiangnan sizhu (China), 2004.

[18] Leppert, R. Art and the committed eye: The cultural functions of imagery. *Routledge*.2019.

[19] Jackson, J. C., Watts, J., Henry, T. R. etc. Emotion semantics show both cultural variation and universal structure. *Science* (2019), 366(6472), 1517-1522.

[20] Han, J., Forbes, H., & Schaefer, D. An exploration of how creativity, functionality, and aesthetics are related in design. *Research in Engineering Design* (2021), 32(3), 289-307.

[21] Kubat, U., & Swaminathan, V. Crossing the cultural divide through bilingual advertising: The moderating role of brand cultural symbolism. *International Journal of Research in Marketing* (2015), 32(4), 354-362.

[22] Yoon, J. Searching for an image conveying connotative meanings: An exploratory cross-cultural study. *Library & Information Science Research* (2008), 30(4), 312-318.

[23] Baifan, T., Shengyu, H. The Strategy and Implications of Space Narrative Used in the User Experience Design for Mixed Reality Marketing Scene, 2023.

[24] Loschky, L. C., Larson, A. M., Smith, T. J. The scene perception & event comprehension theory (SPECT) applied to visual narratives. *Topics in cognitive science* (2020), 12(1), 311-351.

[25] Nigrini, Tian. Narrative spatial architecture as a model for the creation of non-linear narrativity in carnivalesque storyworlds. *North-West University (South Africa)*, 2023.

Design Studies and Intelligence Engineering
L.C. Jain et al. (Eds.)
© 2024 The Authors.
doi:10.3233/FAIA231466

Construction of User Portrait System for Online Shopping of Cultural and Tourism Products Based on Generalized Regression Neural Network

Yue XU [a], Xuyan HU [a], and Jiande ZHANG [b]

[a] (School of art and design, Nanjing Institute of Technology, Nanjing 211167, China)
[b] (School of computer Engineering, Nanjing Institute of Technology, Nanjing 211167, China)

Abstract. In response to the development dilemma of product similarity and singularity in the cultural and tourism market, the system constructs a user portrait system which is based on Generalized Regression Neural Network (GRNN). It aims to improve the accuracy of user portrait for online shopping of cultural and tourism products, and make judgments on the visualization, intelligence, digitization, and development trends of cultural and tourism network services. The study summaries four types of user demand elements through traditional questionnaires and AHP analytic hierarchy process. It forms a hierarchical model for user portrait system analysis. The study integrates user online shopping process data into the design and analysis process, and combines GRNN to intelligently analyze the target users, makes the analysis results of the software more objective and reasonable. It provides reference and decision-making for the cultural and tourism market, platform, product development, and service optimization.

Keywords. Generalized Regression Neural Network (GRNN), Online shopping users, Cultural and Tourism Products, User profile, Analytic Hierarchy Process

1. Introduction

With the rapid recovery of the tourism industry, the continuous improvement of the network economy, e-commerce, and Internet of Things technology, the cultural and tourism product market has begun to expand from traditional markets to internet platforms, serving the local cultural industries, agricultural products, surrounding and characteristic product markets. However, the singularity and similarity of cultural and tourism products have put the further development of cultural and tourism products and surrounding markets into difficulties. The design of the user portrait analysis system for online shopping cultural and tourism products aims to integrate user shopping behavior and perspectives into the design process. Based on the characteristics of cultural and tourism products and its user's data, the system is determined by the Analytic Hierarchy Process (AHP). In the construction of the cultural and tourism product user portrait system, intelligent data analysis and mining are used to achieve intuitive portrayal of cultural and tourism product users, providing cultural and tourism products prediction of the current status and development trends of online platforms and services.

2. Research Status

2.1. Related research and objective

Cooper proposed User Portrait, which aims to highly extract user information and summarize user features by assigning tags (Cooper, 2004). Currently, user portrait technology is relatively mature, but research topics and application scenarios still need to be expanded (Zhang Haitao, 2019). The application scenarios of user portrait vary, and their construction dimensions are also different. Online health community user portraits aimed to identify user emotional expression features (Wang Shuai, 2022); The portrait of a collaborative innovation research team is constructed through a team performance evaluation system, reflecting the collaborative innovation ability (Liu Xingbing, 2021).

With the high-quality development of cultural and tourism industry, the cultural and tourism product market is more prosperity in China. People are enthusiastic about purchasing cultural tourism products offline during the tourism process, but the widespread application of digital technologies such as artificial intelligence, virtual reality, and augmented reality has accelerated the development of online and digital cultural tourism products. The dissemination and resource sharing of cultural products are more convenient, and more tourists use online shopping to purchase, mail, and share characteristic products during or after tourism. Online services usually use this type of data for user preference and demand analysis. Compared to other online products, the number of online shopping users for cultural and tourism products is relatively small. It is hard to accurately depict user characteristics due to insufficient information (Zhang Tao, 2020). The offline purchase is the main channel because of the characteristics of the tourism products. As an extension of the experience and promotion channel, if the online purchase path lacks timely user preferences and shopping feedback, it cannot assist in improving the online shopping experience, platform and products, and providing personalized services. The research aims to construct a user portrait system, providing visual analysis results and predictions for different stakeholders.

2.2. Application of GRNN

The judgment of user portrait should be based on Generalized Regression Neural Network (GRNN), quantifying the input and output of subjective feelings. Traditional user research and design processes can provide algorithm design teams with a sensory to rational process experience. It helps models apply to user experiments and achieve more objective and comprehensive portrait results. GRNN plays an important role in the analysis systems for cultural and tourism products. It is a form of data analysis model through the intelligent analysis application process.

2.3. The Purpose of Applying AHP Analytic Hierarchy Process

With the arrival of the digital and intelligent era, more tourism groups, including the elderly, are able to independently order online cultural and tourism products. Departments and groups related to the cultural and tourism industry need to pay immediate attention to the trend of cultural and tourism consumptions. They also concern the current status of cultural and creative consumption. They need to evaluate feedback on ordering channels and the preferences for using digital ordering platforms. The user portrait system is also an analysis and comparison system for consumers. It is designed to summarize, analyze, and compare information data, behavioral data, user preference data, and user transaction data from different consumer groups. However, the result is not good due to the small amount of data information and the particularity of the products. The Analytic Hierarchy Process (AHP) is introduced to classify and extract the demand element based on research. By distinguishing the weight of elements and combining with GRNN, it provides objective feedback on the characteristics, preferences, consumption trends, and digital cultural and tourism status of the consumptions.

3. Methodology and Research Framework

Based on the target online users, it formed the construction method of the cultural and tourism product user portrait system. The research proposes to extract elements from the user's behavior. It conducts hierarchical analysis of different elements, mining user preferences, and generating user portrait based on user's preferences. It aims to apply the constructed portrait to personalized recommendations or improve the services through comparison. The system can also solve problems such as homogenization of the cultural and tourism product market, lack of big data support, and lack of relevant analysis support for development. The study combines objective descriptions of online shopping behavior with a summary of the characteristics and preferences of the consumers. It provides a basis for design researchers to deeply develop the cultural and tourism market and products. Based on cultural and tourism questionnaire surveys and the methods of AHP, a more accurate analysis element model is constructed to refine element weights. The model also addresses the objective constraints of limited data information and difficulty in precise characterization. It promotes the development of digital cultural and tourism products and the construction of online service. The research framework is shown in figure 1. Based on the demand model, it collects uses relevant elements. The data processing is uniformly through input and correction of information variables. The portrait data is based on GRNN, and features are extracted from the data. Based on user sequences, user tags are constructed to analyze and compare the user portraits.

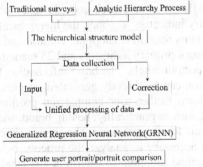

Figure 1. The research framework

4. Methodology and research framework

Firstly, the research analyzes the purpose of establishing user portraits, and combines traditional research to structure a conceptual model based on data. It includes basic information, behavior, preferences, and transactions. Secondly, it needs to determine the main label attributes of the target user group. Finally, the research combined with the AHP to further analyze the weights of different labels, in order to more comprehensively express different user characteristics and provide comparative analysis modules. Element research shows that the user group exhibits significant differences in gender, age, purchasing influence, online shopping activity, and cultural and creative interest themes.

4.1. Demand Research and Element Indicator Analysis

At the theoretical level, the core content of user portrait construction is the label indicator system. In existing research, user portrait indicators are generally summarized into seven categories of characteristics: user basic information, emotions, psychology, behavior, social interaction, consumption ability, and preferences. This study mainly focuses on tourists in the Jiangsu region, conducting a questionnaire survey and interview on the online shopping needs of cultural and tourism product audiences. 412 valid questionnaires and 17 in-depth interview records were collected. The basic information of the survey shows that tourists have a wide geographical distribution, but local short distance travel users from Anhui, Zhejiang, and Jiangsu account for 76% of the surveyed population. The proportion of women is 58%, slightly higher than men. The travel groups mainly consist of couples, family members, and middle-aged and elderly people. The occupational distribution is relatively broad, with retirees, students, enterprises and institutions, and study tour ranking in the top five. The demand for cultural and tourism products shows that although most tourists purchase items during their travels, a considerable number of people still choose to repurchase or search for similar tourism products online after the trip. It is used for sharing, giving, and enjoying in the future. Age has a significant impact on users' online shopping activities. Middle-aged and elderly users over 55 years old have a stronger willingness to repurchase and share, but they are not proficient in operating online platforms and will repurchase through WeChat groups, contact shopping guides online, etc.

Based on research, feature extraction is carried out. The key feature requirements are the basic value of cultural and tourism products, network security, service experience, and sharing needs. Based on research records and correlation analysis, filter out meaningless secondary indicators to obtain the hierarchical structure of target audience portrait feature indicators for online shopping cultural and tourism products (See Table 3 for details), including 4 primary indicators and 25 secondary indicators. This indicator is used to construct portrait labels. The basic information features such as age, region, gender, and occupation can be directly generated, or classified and discussed through algorithm paths to form further user comparison profiles. Other indicators of basic information features, such as practicality, health, brand, and price, reflect the real needs of users for cultural and tourism products. The service experience reflects the themes of users' attention. It is necessary to analyze the process, behavior, results, and feedback generated by users' online shopping to determine the label attributes. Security features are the foundation of user online shopping behavior, and label attributes need to be processed and determined. By combining sharing needs to reveal users' confidence, enthusiasm, activity, and influence in online shopping, it is also necessary to process the text to obtain user profile label attributes.

4.2. Weight of User Profile Elements

4.2.1 Building a hierarchical model

AHP is a decision-making method proposed by Saaty in the 1970s, which systematically and hierarchically analyzes complex problems (T. L. Saaty, 1980). The study combines the above research and AHP hierarchical analysis of the hierarchical weights of user portrait elements to construct a hierarchical model for analyzing system of cultural and tourism products. Among them, the audience's online shopping needs are the target A layer, and the basic value (B1), security (B2), sharing (B3), and online shopping experience needs (B4) are the first level indicators B layer. Then, the second level indicators below each B layer are the element C layer. Unlike other online cultural and tourism product user analysis, as shown in Table 2, the study developed a hierarchical structure model based on AHP.

4.2.2 Constructing a judgment matrix

To be more objective, it is compared the importance of corresponding indicator elements with the previous indicators. The secondary indicators are compared with a scale of number from one to nine, as shown in Table 1. After taking the scale values, each element is assigned a value to form a comparison matrix for secondary indicators.

$$A = [a_{ij}] = \begin{bmatrix} a_{11} & a_{12} & \cdots & a_{1n} \\ a_{21} & a_{22} & \cdots & a_{2n} \\ \vdots & \vdots & \ddots & \vdots \\ a_{n1} & a_{n2} & \cdots & a_{nn} \end{bmatrix} \tag{1}$$

Table1. Definition of Importance Level Scale

Scale a_{ij}	Implication
1	Indicates that i and j are equally important compared to each other
3	Compared the factors i and j, the former is slightly more important than the latter
5	Compared the factors i and j, the former is more important than the latter
7	Compared the factors i and j, the former is much more important than the latter
9	Compared the factors i and j, the former is extremely important compared to the latter
2,4,6,8	Represents the intermediate value of the adjacent judgments mentioned above

4.2.3 Hierarchy sorting and consistency testing

It aims to solve the maximum eigenvalues and eigenvectors of the matrix corresponding to user needs and normalize them.

$$\lambda_{max} = \sum_{i=1}^{n} \frac{[B_1 W]_i}{n w_i} \tag{2}$$

$$w_i = \frac{1}{n} \sum_{j=1}^{n} \frac{a_{ij}}{\sum_{k=1}^{n} a_{kj}} \tag{3}$$

$$CI = \frac{\lambda_{max} - n}{n - 1} \tag{4}$$

The maximum eigenvalue of the judgment matrix B₁ is determined by formula (2). W represents the weight of each element in the primary and secondary indicator.

Perform consistency check on the matrix, with CR=CI/RI. RI refers to the average random consistency indicator. When CR<0.1, it is considered that the judgment matrix meets the consistency condition, otherwise it needs to be corrected. According to the solving process, the CR of the judgment matrix B_1 is 0.0037<0.1. The consistency of corresponding indicators under other target layers is also less than 0.1. These indicate a low degree of deviation of the matrix and good consistency in the solution results.

4.2.4 Constructing a weight analysis system for feature indicators

Solve the weight of the target user's online shopping needs, and take the comprehensive weight to compare the results. According to the weight of the two levels indicators (Table 2), the importance order of online shopping needs of tourism product users is: B1 basic needs, B4 network service needs, B2 security needs, and B3 sharing needs. According to the weight values of the secondary indicators, it can be seen that users have a high demand for elements such as cultural connotations and regional characteristics, packaging, applicability to special groups, reliable sharing link, convenient sharing, mode of payment, clear browsing information and authenticity, reliable online shopping touchpoints, and after-sales guarantee. Users have a relatively low demand for low prices, brands, personal information security, uniqueness and promotional activities, collectible or additional purchases (temporarily not purchased) and transportation safety indicators.

Table 2. Hierarchy of user profile feature indicators

Target layer	Primary indicators	Weight	Secondary indicators	Weight	Comprehensive weight
the demand for online shopping of cultural and tourism product	B1 basic value requirement	0.385	C1 low price	0.0710	0.0273
			C2 health	0.2500	0.0963
			C3 cultural connotation/regional characteristics	0.2976	0.1146
			C4 package	0.3241	0.1248
			C5 brand	0.0357	0.0137
			C6 practicality (taste, purpose, etc.)	0.1429	0.0550
			C7 suitable for special groups (children/pregnant women/elderly)	0.2727	0.1050
	B2 security requirements	0.230	C8 personal information security	0.4000	0.0920
			C9 comment Area Privacy	0.1000	0.0230
			C10 share link source reliability	0.5000	0.1150
	B3 sharing needs	0.077	C11 convenient sharing	0.3737	0.2877
			C12 cost-effective	0.2727	0.0210
			C13 regional cultural characteristics	0.1818	0.0140
			C14 promotional activities	0.0909	0.0070
			C15 uniqueness	0.0909	0.0070
	B4 service experience requirements	0.308	C16 platform reliability	0.0882	0.0272
			C17 transport Safety	0.0588	0.0181
			C18 convenient search	0.0882	0.0272
			C19 display product	0.0882	0.0272

popularity and reviews		
C20 can be collected/added for purchase (temporarily not purchased)	0.0294	0.0091
C21 mode of payment	0.1471	0.0453
C22 clear display information/ authenticity	0.2059	0.0634
C23 reliable online shopping contacts	0.1176	0.0362
C24 after sales guarantee	0.1764	0.0543

4.3. Intelligent User Portrait Analysis Solution

After constructing an indicator hierarchy based on the AHP method, it can be used for intelligent analysis software design, digital processing of data, and visual output. The user portrait analysis system combines demand weighting to intelligently translate behavioral and characteristic indicators of users. It analyzes and compares the cultural and tourism products consumers. The system could input, modify, intelligently analyze and compare different data, including behavior data, user preference data, and user transaction data. It aims to analyze the characteristics of cultural and tourism product consumer groups more accurately based on limited data, optimize the cultural and tourism industry and digital media services. The system can also combine user ordering, evaluation, and feedback to provide cultural and creative consumption suggestions for users, achieve more intelligent data processing, enhance user experience and sharing needs. At the same time, it also provides solutions such as data storage, viewing historical data, parameter correction, generating portrait, comparing user portraits, and generating profile charts.

The user portrait system interface is mainly divided into four parts: parameter selection and setting area, parameter control correction area, portrait generation area, and comparison parameter setting and portrait generation area.

Parameter selection and setting area: Various parameters can be selected to generate personalized user portraits, and parameters can also be added through the "Other" option.

Parameter control correction area: Based on the actual guiding significance of the data, set parameter control correction areas to facilitate data improvement, refinement, and parameter adjustment based on the development of cultural and tourism.

Portrait generation area: As shown in Figure 2, it can generate user images and intelligently analyze results.

Comparison parameter setting and image generation area: The comparison parameter setting interface allows for the selection of various parameter indicators and provides a "Comparison parameter summary" box for parameter addition, deletion, and confirmation, as well as the generation of comparison images.

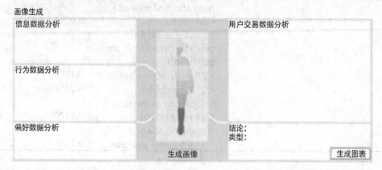

Figure 2. The Portrait Generation Module for the Conceptual Model of User Portrait System

5. Building an Intelligent User Portrait Model Based on GRNN

When constructing an intelligent user portrait model, a large amount of user data is analyzed. The model is applied to analyze the demand, interest, and feature information of consumer groups for cultural and tourism products. The general steps for building an intelligent user portrait model include six steps: data collection, data processing, intelligent algorithm selection, model training and optimization, user portrait generation and analysis, and model evaluation and improvement. Intelligent models can help the cultural and tourism market better understand target users, provide personalized recommendations, personalized services, and precise marketing.

5.1. The Application of GRNN Neural Network Model

Generalized Regression Neural Network (GRNN) is a highly parallel oriented basis network with fast learning speed and strong nonlinear mapping ability. Its structure is shown in Figure 3, consisting of four layers of network: input layer, pattern layer, summation layer, and output layer. In response to the issues of user information data, user behavior data, user preference data, and user transaction data in this study, such as the large number of detail variables, the high correlation of internal detail factors in each type of data, and the complex relationship between user portrait and various input factors, a generalized regression neural network is used to construct user portrait. For example, in user information data, user age, occupation, online shopping platform, gender, education level, type of cultural and tourism product browsing, etc. are used as inputs. In user behavior data, browsing frequency, duration, whether to add a purchase, external contacts, comment content and so on are used as inputs. In user preference data, product type, brand preference, sharing frequency, login method, and geographical location of the product are used as inputs, The user transaction data uses correlation rate, promotion conversion rate, churn rate and so on as input data. Respectively corresponding to $X_1, X_2, \cdots X_n$, after neural network model training, its output is $Y = [Y_1, Y_2, \cdots, Y_n]^T$, displayed as a portrait model.

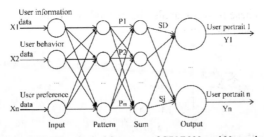

Figure 3. The Topological Structure of GRNN Neural Networks

5.2. GRNN Neural Network Algorithm

GRNN is a feedforward neural network in which each layer is assigned to a specific computational function for nonlinear regression during data processing.

The first layer is the input layer. It is responsible for receiving information. It directly transfers the data to the pattern layer when the input layer receives the input vector X. The second layer is the pattern layer. After inputting the data to the pattern layer, the pattern layer neurons recombine and process the data. It stores the connection weight of the i-th neuron in the i-th Gaussian function P_m, the neuron transfer function used by this stored procedure is as follows:

$$P_i = exp\left[-\frac{(X-X_i)^T(X-X_i)}{2\sigma^2}\right], i = 1,2,\cdots m \tag{5}$$

In the formula, X is the network input variable; X_i is the training vector corresponding to the i-th neuron in the pattern layer; σ is the smoothing factor.

The third layer is the summation layer. The neurons in the pattern layer generate an output vector P_m, and feedback the results to the third layer summation layer. In the summation layer, perform arithmetic summation and weighted summation on the output vectors of each neuron in the pattern layer, as follows:

(1) Simple arithmetic summation

$$S_D = \sum_{i=1}^m P_i \tag{6}$$

(2) Weighted summation

$$S_j = \sum_{i=1}^m y_{ij}P_i, j = 1,2,\cdots n \tag{7}$$

In the equation, y_{ij} is the j-th element in the i-th output sample.

The fourth layer is the output layer. The network output y_i is equal to the quotient of S_j divided by S_D. The formula is as follows:

$$y_i = \frac{S_j}{S_D}, j = 1,2,\cdots n \tag{8}$$

5.3. Display of User Portrait System

After analyzing and processing user data through intelligent algorithms, the user portrait is output, as shown in Figure 4. The obtained user portrait information is displayed in a visual and easy way to help the cultural and tourism market better know the target audience, formulate precise strategies and decisions, better meet user needs and improve user experience. These results can also be expanded and modified according to different data sources and analysis purposes.

User portrait

Age:60-65
Proportion:34%(man) ,66%(women)
Education:29%(high),5%(bachelor or above degree)

The top three professions:
public institution,
state-owned enterprise,
civil servant...

Preference:
food,
souvenirs,
drink,
children's toys...

Shopping Route:
28%(online ordering),
72%(offline purchase)

Platform browsing time:
97%(30-60min)

Associated purchase rate:
33.3%

Collection rate:37%

Online shopping demand:

Basic value
Other
Security
Service experience
Share

Figure 4. User portrait

6. Conclusion

The cultural and tourism product portrait system based on GRNN aims to build a visual and intelligent platform. Its results reflect the effectiveness, service quality, and attractiveness of cultural and tourism product information. It constructs intelligent data analysis on different groups. The user portrait system uses labels, motivation, and online shopping behavior of different descriptions of crowd roles to provide reference for different stakeholders. It can also perform relatively efficient intelligent analysis on the limited data of the target audience. The system could effectively assist in the development of cultural and tourism products, the improvement of network services, and the sustainable development of building the cultural and tourism market.

Acknowledgments

Support. 2021, the Humanities and Social Sciences Research Project of the Ministry of Education: A Study on the aging of digital media in the Yangtze River Delta Economic Zone cultural and creative industries in rural China (No. 21YJC760092); The Ministry of Education's Industry School Cooperation Collaborative Education Project: Intelligent Manufacturing New National Standard Teacher Training(202102571006)

References

[1] Cooper A, the inmates are running the asylum: why high-tech products drive us crazy and how to restore the sanity, 2nd Ed. New York: Sam Publishing, 2004.

[2] Zhang H, Xu H, etc. Research Status and Prospects of User Portraits in Library and Information Field at Home and Abroad, Library and Information Service **23** (2019), 7, 8.

[3] Wang S. Research on Emotional Expression Characteristics Based on User Portrait in Online Health Community. Information Studies: Theory & Application **45** (2022), 6, 179-187.

[4] Liu X B, Zhai Y C, etc. Construction of Collaborative Innovation Scientific Research Team Portrait Based on AHP Model. Science and Technology Management Research **41** (2021), 19, 136-140.

[5] Zhang T, Weng K N, etc. Building user profiles in niche field based on web browsing behavior. Beijing: Systems Engineering-Theory & Practice **40** (2020), 3, 641-652.

[6] Saaty T L. The analytic hierarchy process: planning, priority setting, resource allocation. New York: McGraw-Hill, 1980.

Design Studies and Intelligence Engineering
L.C. Jain et al. (Eds.)
© 2024 The Authors.
This article is published online with Open Access by IOS Press and distributed under the terms
of the Creative Commons Attribution Non-Commercial License 4.0 (CC BY-NC 4.0).
doi:10.3233/FAIA231467

Research and Design of Wearable Olfactory Displays

Hongfang TANG, Weibin DING, and Xi ZHU
Shanghai Institute of Visual Arts

Abstract. Olfaction is considered an important sensory modality in the next generation of Virtual Reality (VR) systems. As devices that control the generation and delivery of odors, olfactory displays enable people to smell real scents in virtual environments. Current challenges faced by olfactory displays include a lack of previous research, the bulk and weight of equipment, demands of wearing invasive devices, and limited varieties of scents storage, etc. This study focuses on making olfactory displays more wearable and on increasing the variety of scents stored in them. The prototype of such device has been built and to evaluate the performance and user experience of it, relevant tests were conducted. The results indicate that the convenient wearable olfactory display developed by the team can provide olfactory perception in virtual environments and satisfies users' requirements on both wearing comfort and olfactory experience.

Keywords. Olfactory Display, Wearable, Multi-sensory, User experience

1. Introduction

With the continuous advancement of technology in the metaverse ecosystem, applications based on visual experiences such as VR, AR, and MR are becoming increasingly popular. As the enhancement of immersion will require not just audiovisual stimulation, integration of multimodal perception will be the challenge and focus for the next generation of immersive virtual reality interactions. Developing virtual olfactory technology and devices help intensify the multidimensional and multimodal interaction in reproducing a real-world experience. Application of this technology has tremendous market potential and socioeconomic value in fields such as education, healthcare, entertainment, art, etc. However, compared to the rest four senses (vision, hearing, touch, and taste), interactive perception research on olfaction is still in its early stage, with many challenges and technological bottlenecks ahead. Consequently, the research and design of olfactory display devices may provide reference and tools for future research, offering insights into the interaction mechanisms and relationships among multiple senses in the field of multimodal design.

2. Background and design value

Multisensory design, which goes beyond visual perception, aims to engage multiple senses, including vision, hearing, taste, smell, and touch, to conduct effective stimulation on users, so as to increase their consumer desire and to impress them with pleasant design experiences. The major focus of it is on user experiences, exploring the interrelationships between the two key design elements—humans and objects. Through paying attention to specific sensory needs of individuals, multisensory design upgrades the product, injecting vitality and novelty into it.

Among the five senses, olfaction is second only to vision in terms of perceptual ability. The olfactory system primarily relies on the olfactory organ, nose, to receive external stimuli, which are then processed by the brain to generate sensations and trigger corresponding reactions. Olfaction is the most sensitive and immediate sense, which could set off a wide range of reactions even involving the occurrence or cessation of other senses. Each scent is like a unique identity card, carrying its own special memories and information.

Scholars Barfield et al., first defined the virtual olfactory display: "A collection of hardware, software, and chemicals that can be used to present olfactory information to the virtual environment participant." [1] Virtual olfaction refers to the ability of users to smell real odors in human-computer interaction under a virtual environment. As a hardware device for odor generation, transmission, diffusion, and interaction, the olfactory display is becoming a research hotspot. Increasing evidence suggests that virtual olfaction can greatly enhance the perceptual, immersive, interactive, and imaginative aspects of virtual reality systems [2], and it can be widely applied in various fields such as industry, medicine, education, entertainment, military, etc. Research on virtual olfaction technology will become a frontier in the field of virtual reality, and the innovation and development of olfactory displays will undoubtedly become a research focus.

3. Research status and pain-point problems

3.1. Research status of olfactory display

The olfactory display is an indispensable research instrument in the study of virtual olfaction systems, especially for the virtual olfactory reproduction technology. Domestic or abroad, experts and researchers have done quite a number of research on the development of olfactory displays, resulting in many types such devices with different functionalities.

In 2013, Haruka Matsukura et al. proposed an olfactory display based on airflow vaporization [3], known as the "olfactory screen system." Users would perceive the scent as if it were emitted from some specific virtual source on the screen, which may be relocated as is willed. The olfactory screen system relies on four DC fans to control the odor distribution. And U-shaped hoods are installed on each side of the LCD screen, with a pair of axial fans mounted at the top and bottom ends. When users approach the screen, they can capture the flow of odor from the U-shaped hoods.

Another representative device is a burden-free air-gun-based olfactory display developed by Yasuyuki et al. [4] The prototype consists of a nose tracker, an air gun platform, an air gun, and an odor generator. This olfactory display system integrates the visual-based facial tracking technology to the nose tracking functionality, thus eliminating the need of wearing any devices or glasses, while the scent can only be perceived in a limited space and period of time.

Wearable olfactory displays refer to olfactory displays that can be worn by users and are designed for use in large spaces, including outdoor environments. As such devices are smaller, lighter, and more wearable than traditional ones, users may freely move around while wearing them. Tomoya et al. developed the prototype of a wearable olfactory presenter for outdoor use [5-6], where scents are delivered to the user's nose through tubes. Intensity of the scent in outdoor environment can be controlled based on the distance between scent sources and the user's position. However, this olfactory display may block part of the user's face and require the additional burden of wearing some devices.

In olfactory display systems, the mechanical performance of odor generation and transmission is crucial. Generally, to ensure a good variety of odors and their delivery to the user's nose within a short period, the entire system tends to be constructed as complex, bulky, and noisy, as a result of which, it can only be used in specific situations, leading to poor user interaction experience. This answers why few olfactory displays are available for commercial applications. Wearable olfactory displays may serve as a possible path for improving the user experience of virtual olfaction. The research and design of wearable olfactory displays enables the application of virtual olfaction technology in more scenarios through achieving better human-computer interaction.

3.2. Existing pain point problems

None of the current olfactory displays has accomplished commercial success. In fact, these devices are often expensive, complex, cumbersome, or very limited in the quantity and variety of scents that can be stored and generated. For instance, olfactory display devices "meta cookie+" developed by Takuji Narumi et al. [7] and "odor field" by Yamada, T. et al. [8] were able to provide a certain number of scents, nonetheless, they are cumbersome and uncomfortable to wear and are also very susceptible to the external environment, such as airflow, etc. Some other devices have difficulties in controlling or switching scents quickly[9]. For these reasons, it is necessary to develop new device and system that provides a compact, non-cumbersome, and unexpensive olfactory display device that contains multiple odors.

Based on the above-mentioned concept, in 2015, Ding Weibin and his team developed a lightweight and low-cost wearable olfactory display at the Politecnico di Milano and successfully applied it in an experiment testing fatigue resistance during car driving [10]. The prototype is based on the ultrasonic atomization method (in which fine particles from a liquid are generated by using ultrasonic energy) and air cannons that generate and deliver odors. In each air cannon is placed a small cylindrical of porous cotton functioning as a container for diluted water-soluble commercial scents. The cylinder of porous cotton is drenched with the scented water, and driven by the ultrasonic energy, a scented mist is generated and released in the air.

This wearable olfactory display device provides a design solution that is acceptable to the user's body. Nevertheless, there are still some defects remained in it:

Limited number of odors: It can only accommodate four types of odors.

Limited use of scent materials: It is not suitable for high-viscosity essence.

Inaccurate delivery: It is not accessible to all users, and the scents couldn't reach the nose effectively.

Inability to control the intensity of smell: For example, the generated odors can't be effectively delivered to the participant's nose, and it is challenging to control the quantity of odor materials.

These are the pain points of the wearable olfactory displays, which demands us to develop a more advanced and user-friendly wearable olfactory displays.

4. Design and Development of a New Wearable Olfactory Display

4.1. Ideas and Design

The new wearable olfactory display prototype was developed in the Politecnico di Milano, based on the air-flow technique for fragrance transmission. The main components of it include an Arduino board, a head-mounted frame, air pumps and a compact cartridge with a scent generator. Our primary aim is to relieve the cumbersomeness of wearing devices on the face or body, for which we implement a suitable frame shaped like a headset microphone where the olfactory display is integrated, so the user can wear it on his/her head. Next, we focused on solving the problem of how to store the fragrances within a very narrow space. We designed a compact cartridge to store the fragrances for the purpose. A porous material soaked with an oily fragrance is contained into a small device that delivers the scented air to the user' s nose as shown in Figure 1.

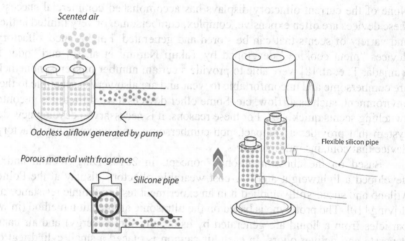

Figure 1. Structure of the cartridge for storing fragrances.

This olfactory display is integrated into a frame the user can wear on the body. A porous material soaked with an oily fragrance is contained into a small device that delivers the fragrance to the user' s nose. The delivery process is achieved by means of a small pump that blows air through the pipe and eventually through the porous material. And the selection of fragrance is done through an app that controls the olfactory display via an Arduino board, as is demonstrated in figure 2. Current version of the olfactory display includes two small devices on each side, allowing the delivery of maximum 8 different fragrances.

4.2. User experience evaluation

To assess the parameters and user experience of wearing this new olfactory display, the team conducted research on how to ensure users a stable delivery of scented air and wearing comfort.

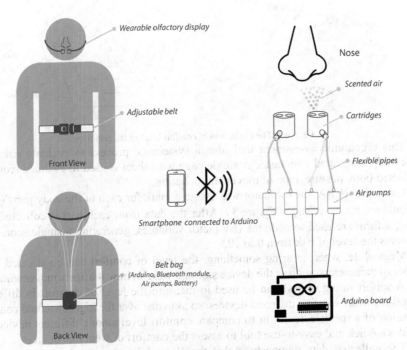

Figure 2. The schematic of the olfactory display

Meanwhile, ergonomic test and parameter test were carried out on the prototype., where participants were required to wear the device which had a cartridge placed 3cm from their noses. After the experiment, subjects had to fill a questionnaire and score each question from "0" to "10" for Rapid Entire Body Assessment, and "1" to "20" for Comfort Rating Scales, as can be seen in Table 1.

Table 1. Level of effect of the different scales for the wearability of a system

| | Metric | Units | Level of Effect | | | | |
			Low	Moderate	Large	Very Large	Extreme
Energy cost	Relative perceived exertion	Borg CR-10 score	0–1	2–3	4–5	6–7	8–10
Biomechanical	Posture	REBA score + body map	1	2–3	4–7	8–10	11–15
	Localised pain and discomfort	Borg CR-10 score	0–1	2–3	4–5	6–7	8–10
Comfort	General wearable	CRS score	0–4	5–8	9–12	13–16	17–20

Level of Effect	Wearability Level	Outcome
Low	WL1	System is wearable
Moderate	WL2	System is wearable, but changes may be necessary, further investigation is needed
Large	WL3	System is wearable, but changes are advised. Uncomfortable
Very Large	WL4	System is not wearable, fatiguing, very uncomfortable
Extreme	WPL5	System is not wearable, extremely stressful and potential harmful

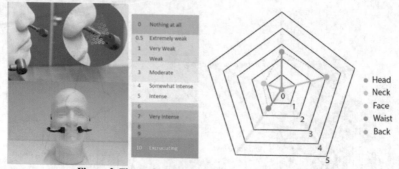

Figure 3. The evaluation of comfort level of the prototype

This ergonomic assessment tool uses a systematic process to evaluate risks for whole body associated with tasks. A single page worksheet is used to evaluate required or selected body posture, type of movement or action.

Using the REBA, the evaluator will assign a mark for each of the body parts (such as shoulders, neck, wrists). (Figure 3) After the data from each part is collected and scored, a form are used to code the risk factor variables, generating a single score that represents the level of risk from 0 to 10.

Meanwhile, when wearing something, the level of comfort can be affected by a number of parameters, such as the device size and weight, how it affects movement. The CRS (comfort rating scales) can be used to measure the level of comfort in different dimensions while wearing different devices, so as to discover the highest-scored comfort dimension of a specific device or to compare comfort level among different devices. It provides a quick and easy-to-use tool to assess the comfort of wearable devices.

The collected data demonstrate that the Wearability Level of this prototype is "WL1", which means that the novel olfactory display is comfortable to wear.

4.3. Results analysis

To evaluate the wearable performance of the Wearable Olfactory Display, we recruited 42 undergraduate students majoring in design for this test. Among them, there were 18 male students and 24 female students, with an average age of 21.6 years. The following is our test plan and experimental description.

Firstly, we will provide each participant with a wearable olfactory display device and ensure it fits properly on their body. We will assess the comfort, adaptability, and stability of the device and record participants' feedback.

Secondly, we will design a series of sensory tasks for participants to perform while wearing the device. These tasks may include distinguishing different scents, perceiving scent intensity, and locating the source of scent, etc. We will record participants' accuracy and response times in completing these tasks, as well as their feedback on the wearable device.

Finally, we will gather participants' subjective feedback. Through questionnaires or face-to-face interviews, we will inquire about their opinions and suggestions regarding the comfort, usability, and sensory experience of the device.

Through these tests, we will be able to evaluate the wearable performance of the wearable olfactory display and obtain participants' overall feedback on the technology, acquiring guidance for further improvements and optimizations.

5. Conclusion

This research has developed an unburdened wearable olfactory display system and presented an innovative configuration of an olfactory display that does not require the user to wear any invasive equipment on the face and while providing a milder wearing experience.

Wearable olfactory display, as an emerging technology, combines olfactory display with wearable devices to provide users with personalized scent experiences. With the growing demand for personalization and augmented reality experiences, wearable olfactory display holds huge potential in the field of sensory interaction and smart devices.

However, wearable olfactory display technology still faces some challenges. Firstly, achieving miniaturization and portability is a key issue. Since wearable devices are typically worn on the body, factors such as device size, weight, and comfort need to be considered. Secondly, achieving diverse and personalized scent choices is also a challenge. Different individuals have different preferences and responses to different scents, so providing a wide range of scent options and customized experiences deserves much consideration.

Looking to the future, our next work will focus on accomplishing techniques for blending multiple scents and achieving controllable release concentrations. We will also conduct user experience testing with respect to different types of scents and concentration environments. With advancements and innovations of technology, the related devises will have a wider development prospect.

In conclusion, wearable olfactory display, as an emerging technology, has shown great potential in various fields. Despite many foreseen challenges ahead, we can expect wearable olfactory display to bring more personalized, immersive, and intelligent sensory experiences, driving the development of sensory interaction and smart device fields.

References

[1] Woodrow Barfield, Eric Danas. Comments on the Use of Olfactory Displays for Virtual Environments. Presence Teleoperators and Virtual Environments (S0924-1868), 1995, 5(1): 109-121.

[2] Wu Xinli, Yang Wenzhen, Yu Ling et al. Virtual smells the research progress of generating unit. Journal of system simulation, 2014, 26 (9): 1882-1888.

[3] Haruka Matsukura, Tatsuhiro Yoneda, Hiroshi Ishida. Smelling Screen: Technique to Present a Virtual Odor Source at an Arbitrary Position on a Screen. IEEE Virtual Reality. USA: IEEE, 2012: 127-130.

[4]Y Yanagida, H Noma, N Tetsutani, A Tomono. An Unencumbering, Localized Olfactory Display. CHI EA'03 CHI'03 Extended Abstracts on Human Factors in Computing Systems Proceeding. USA: ACM, 2003: 988-989.

[5] Tomoya Y Tanikawa, Hirota Hirose. Wearable olfactory display: Using Odor in Outdoor Environment. VR2006 Proceeding. USA: IEEE, 2006.

[6]Yamada, T., Yokoyama, S., Tanikawa, T., Hirota, K., Hirose, M., "Wearable Olfactory Display: Using Odor in Outdoor Environment", IEEE Virtual Reality 2006.

[7]Augmented Reality Flavors: Gustatory Display Based on Edible Marker and Cross-Modal Interaction, Takuji Narumi, Shinya Nishizaka, Takashi Kajinami, Tomohiro Tanikawa and Michitaka Hirose, CHI 2011 • Session: Olfaction, Breath & Biofeedback May 7–12, 2011 • Vancouver, BC, Canada

[8]Yamada, T., Yokoyama, S., Tanikawa, T., Hirota, K., Hirose, M., "Wearable Olfactory Display: Using Odour in Outdoor Environment", IEEE Virtual Reality 2006.

[9]D. W. Kim, D. W. Lee, M. Miura, K. Nishimoto, Y. Kawakami, S. Kunifuji, "Aroma-Chip based Olfactory Display, " KICSS 2007, The Second International Conference, Nov. 2007.

[10] M. Carulli, M. Bordegoni, U. Cugini, D. Weibin, A methodology for the analysis of the influence of odours on the users' evaluation of industrial products, Springer 2015, 1CoRD '15_Research into Design Acros Boundaries

Design Studies and Intelligence Engineering
L.C. Jain et al. (Eds.)
© 2024 The Authors.
This article is published online with Open Access by IOS Press and distributed under the terms
of the Creative Commons Attribution Non-Commercial License 4.0 (CC BY-NC 4.0).
doi:10.3233/FAIA231468

Research of Irrational User Model on Subway Emergency Product Design

Xiaofan SUN[a], Meidan DENG[a], Hongbin JIANG[b,1]

[a]*Department of Art and Design, Beijing City University, Beijing, China*
[b]*Academy of Art & Design, Tsinghua University, Beijing, China*

Abstract. Based on the existing user research methods, this paper explores how to apply the irrational user model as a guide to the specific emergency product design research process. Through qualitative and quantitative user research tools, it develops a user model of subway users in emergency situations. It is expected that the research in this paper can provide a kind of idea and perspective for the research and development of emergency products, so that emergency products can really become a reliable guaranteed link of public safety.

Keywords. Irrational user model, user research, emergency products, mental model, task model

1. Introduction

With the development of urbanization, we are living in an environment that has reached the stage of a "risk society". Various factors in society constrain each other, intricate and complex, and all kinds of accidents occur frequently. Urban rail transportation has had a profound impact on the mobility of residents. The area centered on the subway station forms a highly dense public space gathering node. Due to the mechanism of large linkage, subway safety and security is extremely important. Emergency products are at the end of the overall emergency response system. In all kinds of man-made accidents and natural disasters, how to use emergency products in extreme scenarios has always been the focus of ordinary users. In many cases, we often see that the existing products do not play a role in the accident and danger. It fails to match the user's psychology and behavior, and often misplaced and ineffective in extreme events. In the design of emergency products, more attention should be paid to the study of the psychology, thinking and behavior of ordinary users, and it is possible to get more in-depth and practical design results by starting from this direction.

2. Frameworks of irrational user Model

Professor Li Leshan of Xi'an Jiaotong University proposed the framework of irrational user model on the basis of Norman's user-centered theoretical research. In his book Human-Computer Interface Design, he clearly elaborated the concept of irrational user.

---

[1] Corresponding Author, Academy of Art & Design, Tsinghua University, Beijing, China; E-mail: jhblwjhb@vip.sina.com

He argues that existing user research is based on the theoretically normal thinking and actions of users. It ignores the situation when people are irrational and their behavioral thoughts are no longer bound by rules. Based on the complexity of users, he proposed that the connotation of irrational user model includes four aspects: "the task model and cognitive model of users' normal operation, the user's action and cognitive characteristics of non-normal environments, the user's wrongness, and the user's learning characteristics." Li Leshan proposed the framework of irrational user model (Figure 1) in Industrial Design Psychology, the user model should include two aspects: "Mental Model and Task Model". In both of them, the interrelationships of users, products and environment should be fully considered, and the factors related to non-normal environment and non-normal state users should also be taken into account.

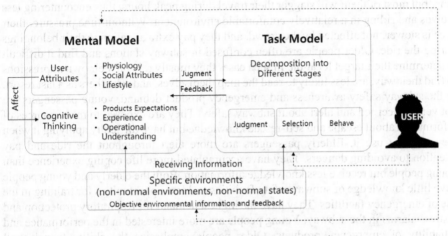

Figure 1. Irrational User Model Framework

3. Frameworks of irrational user Model

Exploring the construction of user models of subway users in emergency situations through existing qualitative and quantitative user research methods is one of the research focuses of this paper. Through the methods of questionnaire research and deep interviews with typical users, the user persona is established. In this way, the mental Model of subway users is organized to understand user characteristics. In order to be closest to the real fire environment, the decision-making behavior of subway users in the subway environment is deeply observed through simulation experiments and case studies. This provides the basis for constructing a task model of subway users.

3.1. Mental Model of Subway Emergency Escape Users

Through qualitative research and quantitative research, the mental Model of subway escape users is summarized according to two typical population classifications. Young passengers are mainly survival-oriented, with the best period of physical function and energy and stamina. Relatively speaking, they are more agile in thinking and more likely to receive all kinds of new information. While the elderly group is mainly life-oriented, with declining eyesight and physical strength in body functions. They are slow to react and easily fatigued. After experiencing many events in their lives, they are relatively gentle and calm in their personality traits, however, they are slower to accept new things. In mobility and commuting habits, young passengers generally commute to work. They commuting in the morning and evening peaks on weekdays, and the subway environment they encounter is heavily congested, with a high density of people and a poor ride experience. Due to the time pressure walking speed is faster, they closely follow the speed of the crowd. As the lines are relatively fixed, they are quite familiar with the station space and rely mainly on their sense of direction for way finding. When occasionally confused they find their way through self-reading maps. Middle-aged and elderly passengers, on the other hand, travel by subway for more casual purposes, mainly for shopping, meeting friends and other affairs. They do not have a fixed commuting time, but most of them will stagger their travel during peak hours, thus encountering less crowds and riding in a relatively comfortable environment. Without time pressure, their pace is slower, not affected by the crowd, and they pay extra attention to their belongings during the ride. Older people are often confused in subway stations and find it difficult to determine their target location. In such cases they mostly rely on their own impressions to find their way, are less likely to read the map themselves, and ask others as a last resort. In the subway safety awareness and emergency product demand, young passengers are not very concerned and alert about subway safety. They are exposed to many sources of information about escape and self-rescue knowledge but have difficulty applying it when they actually use it. Elderly passengers are more alert throughout the ride and pay attention to avoiding dangers. They have accumulated more life coping experience than young people but receive less knowledge information. Both the elderly and young people have little knowledge of subway safety facilities and few opportunities for training in the use of emergency facilities. They have the highest demand for respiratory protection and distress alarms in the subway. Young people are more interested in the performance and reliability of emergency products. Older people emphasize the ability to solve all problems with the simplest operations, as well as seeking psychological comfort during emergencies.

After realizing the danger, the first physiological instinctive reaction of all users is more or less the same: the heart rate and breathing rate are accelerated, the hands and feet are sweaty and cold, or there will be shrieking and panic. People experience psychological reactions of nervousness, anxiety, fear, and anger. Decreased comprehension of images and increased sensitivity to odors and sounds in a fire. Will choose to follow the crowd when there is little valid information. Young users will be relatively aggressive in their behavior or appear to be courage inspired. Whereas older users are relatively slow and difficult to think, so they are dependent on others and behave in a way that is mostly avoidance and self-preservation.

3.2. Task Model of Subway Emergency Escape Users

Due to the special environment of the subway and the contingency of emergency events, it is difficult to conduct a real live experiment to observe the users. Therefore, through simulation experiments, the viewing environment in the actual emergency escape is simulated in order to gain insight into how subway users make behavioral choices in the subway environment, and to provide valuable first-hand information for the establishment of the user model.

The experimental process is mainly divided into the following steps:

- Step1, before entering the subway, the test subjects were prepared in a simulation. Some data show that when the light reduction factor is greater than 0.5/m in an irritating smoke environment, the pedestrian's speed is reduced to 0.3 m/s, which is equivalent to walking blindfolded." To try to resemble a real initial fire scenario, subjects were made to wear sunglasses with low light transmission to simulate visual conditions. They were made to wear masks to increase breathing resistance to simulate a smoke environment with breathing difficulties. At the same time, the simulated noises, distress calls, alarms and footsteps during the escape were played on a loop in the headphones to increase the realism of the environment and create a tense atmosphere.

- Step 2, after riding the subway, the subjects were asked not to use any elevator carriers such as straight elevators or escalators during the participation period. Before arriving at the Haidian Huangzhuang Station, the subjects were told that there was a fire and that they needed to go to the Haidian Huangzhuang Station for a quick escape, and that they could not complete the task until they returned to the wide outdoor ground. Observers were required to pay attention to the subjects' reactions and states throughout the whole process, especially observing the subjects' behavioral actions at each turning node (carriage, platform, passageway, staircase, ticket hall, gate, exit, and other connecting points), as well as speculating on the motivation of the subjects' decision-making. At the same time the observer used a stopwatch to record the length of time spent at each node.

- Step3, after the task is completed, the observer and the subject return to the starting point of the escape together, recalling the process that has just taken place. They deeply communicated with the subjects about the mental process and the basis of behavioral choices at that time, and recorded the interviews.

- Step4, the results of the experiment were structured, from which a task model of the escapee was constructed.

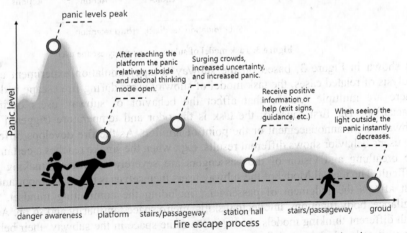

Figure 2. Schematic diagram of the psychological change of passengers' panic

As shown in Figure 2, when the realization of danger occurs, the first reaction is an instinctive stress reaction, the unknown state brings great pressure, at this time the lowest sense of security, the most disordered. After the subway stops to the platform, the panic of the passengers is relatively relieved, and they gradually open the rational thinking mode to find the evacuation path. In the process of evacuation, encountering bottlenecks such as staircases and aisles with narrow space and large crowds, people's psychological panic increases and their sense of security decreases. When seeing the green emergency exit sign or relevant evacuation help information, passengers' psychological panic recovered and became more rational. When passengers see the outdoor light, panic instantly decrease and gradually regain calm.

When passengers just realized that the fire occurred, the first reaction was to quickly escape, and the escape posture was mostly upright running. As the panic, panic stress response recedes, the spread of the fire leads to the spread of smoke, the escape posture will gradually choose to bend forward, in order to reduce the inhalation of harmful gases. Due to the large number of people, out of the instinct to protect themselves, passengers will gradually choose to escape along the walls, staircase handrails, railings and other solid dependence on the position, to avoid being rammed by the crowd. Due to the blockage of vision caused by smoke in the event of fire, passengers have an obvious orientation to light when choosing escape routes, and green escape signs and the light of subway station entrances and exits are important bases for judgment. At the turning points of different spaces (e.g. staircases between platforms and station halls, and selective exits in station halls), which are the places where the most confusion occurs, it is easy to get stranded.

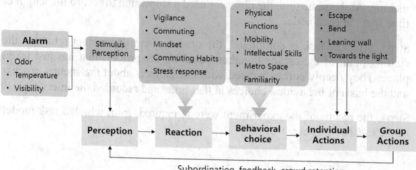

Figure 3. Task model of subway emergency escape users

As shown in Figure 3, based on the subway escape simulation experiment and the analysis of related cases, the task model of subway users during fire escape is derived. There are multiple reasons that affect the behavior of subway users during fire evacuation. The first cause of the task is the odor and temperature triggered by the subway alarm announcement or the point of ignition. As the fire develops differently, the user's behavior shows different results, e.g., when the smoke reaches a certain level, the breathing and vision of the passengers are severely obstructed, making escape difficult. The mental Model of the subway users themselves is the most important factor that affects the judgment of passengers, including the commuting mindset, habits, vigilance, body functions, intellectual skills, metro space familiarity and so on. As users with different thinking models cluster in the same space in the subway, their behaviors show disordered characteristics, and individually they are characterized by behaviors such as fleeing, bending over, leaning against the wall, and turning toward the light. The limitations of individual users' information mastery led to mutual influence, and it is easy to appear herd behavior, and group behavior has a great effect on individual users.

4. Conclusion

This paper explains in detail the theoretical concept of irrational user Model and the content framework included in irrational user Model. Most of the user research is based on the user's cognitive thinking and action logic is normal, while in relatively extreme environmental conditions, when human behavioral thinking is no longer constrained by the rules, the user model and design research is less involved. The irrationality model provides a path for research, especially for user studies on the design of emergency safety and security products in disasters.

The purpose of irrational user Model is to better understand users in product development and apply it to actual design practice. Through the existing qualitative and quantitative user research methods, exploring the construction of user models for metro users in emergency situations is the focus of this paper. This paper practices and verifies the operability and guidance of the irrationality model. The design orientation and design principles proposed on top of this research can only form a targeted solution for subway escape product design.

References

[1] Li Leshan. *Human-computer interface design*. Science Press, 2004.

[2] Li Leshan. *Industrial Design Psychology*. Higher Education Press, 2004.

[3] Fan Shengxi. *Behavioral and Cognitive Design: Humanization of Design*. China Electric Power Press, 2009.

[4] Cheng, Jianxin, Meiyu Zhou, and Junnan Ye. The Study of Modern Emergency Products under the Direction of New Ergonomics. *Cross-Cultural Design. Methods, Practice, and Case Studies*. Springer Berlin Heidelberg, 2013. 31-40.

[5] Xiaoli Wu, Feng Zhou, Yanli Chen, *Design Cognition: Design Psychology and User Research*, Nanjing : Southeast University Press, 2013.

[6] Fang Xing, Huang Peiqing, Huo Liangan. A Review of Research on Emergency Behavior of Crowds in Large Events. *Chinese Journal of Safety Science* 21.11 (2011): 22-28.

[7] Yuan Huan, Rao Rui, and Ji Haijuan. Analyzing the design direction of disaster prevention, mitigation and safety assistance products from the perspective of design psychology. *China Science and Technology* 008 (2010): 205-205.

[8] Liu Yongxiang, Ma Quanming. Establishment of irrational user model and safety design principle - Reliability consideration of user model in product design. Proceedings of the Sixth National Academic Conference on Human-Machine-Environment Systems Engineering. 2003.

[9] Xue Shengjian. Japanese Disaster Culture Concept Advocacy and the Application of Home Emergency Shelter Product Design. *Decoration* 6 (2014): 104-106.

[10] Zhu Jianfei. Industrial design countermeasures for urban rail vehicles against passengers' irrational behavior. *Electric locomotives and urban rail vehicles* 34.2 (2011): 52-54.

[11] Li Leshan. *The foundation of industrial design thinking*. China Architecture Industry Press, 2007.

[12] Dai Linong. Designing to meet the needs of users at different levels - A study of the Shanghai Metro - A user "needs-hierarchy" model." *Art & Design (Theory)* 6 (2007): 001.

[13] Su Yu, Zhao Dongfu. A study on pedestrian flow and wayfinding characteristics in integrated rail transit hubs. *Urban Rail Transportation Research* 17.8 (2014): 40-44.

[14] Herbert A. Simon. *The Cornerstone of Modern Decision Theory: The Finite Rationality Statement*. Beijing Institute of Economics Press, 1989.

Design Studies and Intelligence Engineering
L.C. Jain et al. (Eds.)
© *2024 The Authors.*
This article is published online with Open Access by IOS Press and distributed under the terms
of the Creative Commons Attribution Non-Commercial License 4.0 (CC BY-NC 4.0).
doi:10.3233/FAIA231469

Research on Sustainable Reconstruction of Rural Idle Primary Schools Based on Light Intervention: A Case Study of Nanqiang Primary School in Kaiping Tangkou Town

Zheng LI[a,1] and Xiaoya HOU[a]

[a] *South China University of Technology, Guangzhou, Guangdong, 510000, China*

Abstract. With the development of China's urbanization and the loss of rural population, the problem of insufficient students in rural primary schools has become more and more serious. The country adjusts the pattern of rural education and implements the policy of "withdrawal and integration", and the phenomenon of idle primary school space has also emerged one after another, resulting in a lot of waste of resources. Rural revitalization and development is facing the problems of insufficient capital and talents, fragile ecology and hollowing out of villages. From the Angle of "light intervention", this paper cuts into the transformation of "rural idle primary school", and takes Tangkou Nanqiang Primary School as an example to explore the research background, transformation principles and transformation strategies of Kaiping's "rural idle primary School" sustainable transformation.

Keywords. Light intervention, rural idle primary schools, Sustainable

1. Research background

1.1. Policy Orientation

1.1.1. Rural resource stock updating

China's development has entered a new period, and the development mode has changed from incremental development to stock renewal. Develop rural characteristic industries and build a beautiful countryside that is suitable for living and working. In 2019, the Ministry of Agriculture and Rural Affairs issued a notice on actively and steadily carrying out the utilization of idle rural residential land and idle residential land. On February 11, 2022, the Guangdong Provincial Department of Natural Resources held the annual provincial natural resources online work report meeting, emphasizing that "in order to better implement the rural revitalization strategy, it is necessary to further flexible use of rural land policy" and promote the integration and revitalization of rural stock resources.

---

[1] Corresponding author, Guangzhou, Address: South China University of Technology, University City, Panyu District, Guangzhou, Guangdong Province, China; Email: 15641025@qq.com.

1.1.2. The policy of "withdrawal and integration of rural primary schools"

With the deepening of the construction of small towns in China, a large number of young labor forces have migrated to cities to work. After the labor forces have obtained stable income and jobs in the cities, the population outflow mode has changed from the outflow of a single labor force to the outflow of the whole family. The hollowing out of rural areas has intensified, and the number of school-age children in rural areas has declined. In response to this phenomenon, the state adjusted the distribution of rural education from "one village, one school" to "withdraw and merge schools". A large number of primary school buildings were left idle, resulting in a serious waste of resources.

1.1.3. Policies for activating the utilization of "idle primary schools in rural areas"

In light of actual conditions, all localities made comprehensive use of idle school buildings. Xi 'an, Shaanxi Province issued the Opinions on the Disposal of Idle School Buildings in Rural Primary and Secondary Schools, organized centralized investigation of idle school buildings in primary and secondary schools, and each district and county investigated and identified the quantity, quality, floor area, construction area, land, housing ownership and use rights of all idle school buildings in their jurisdiction, so as to ensure that a school has one file and a special store[1].(Table 1)

Table 1. Policy documents related to "Rural Idle Primary Schools"

Time	Policy document name
2010	<Opinions of the Ministry of Education on Strengthening School Capital Construction Planning during>
2011	<Implementation Plan to support the Central and Western Regions in Using idle rural school buildings to rebuild kindergartens>
2015	<Guideline of The General Office of the State Council on Promoting the Construction of Comprehensive Cultural Service Centers at Grassroots Level>
2016	<Several Opinions of The State Council on Comprehensively Promoting the Reform and Development of Integrated Urban and Rural Compulsory Education in Counties>
2017	<Opinions of The General Office of the State Council on Stimulating Investment Vitality in the Social Sector through Progress>

1.2 Existing Difficulties

1.2.1. Rural material resources are abundant

With the rapid development of urbanization and the solidification of urban-rural dual structure, the development of urban and rural education, economy and human resources is uneven. This is followed by the hollowing out of villages, and a large number of material resources of great historical and cultural value in the countryside are left idle, including houses, schools, archways, shrines, ancient trees and so on. For example, a large number of school buildings in rural areas are idle due to the adjustment of the layout of primary and secondary schools and the hollowing out of villages. As of 2018, Kaiping City in Jiangmen had 188 idle school buildings, of which 40 were vacant schools[2].Idle material resources have a negative impact on social and economic development, quality of life and ecological environment in rural areas[3]. Idle material resources, as the most direct and realistic resources in rural areas, are the key to rural revitalization[4].

1.2.2. Rural revitalization capital and talents are insufficient, and the rate of return is low

Rural revitalization and development face the problems of insufficient capital and talents, low rate of return and hollowing out of villages. First, the rural land is owned by the collective, and it is difficult for villagers to benefit from the transfer of material resources. However, material resources are the most important resources in the countryside, and their value in introducing social capital has not been fully brought into play. Second, the financial foundation of rural areas is weak, the scale of enterprises is small, and the financing of enterprises is difficult. Third, the society has insufficient understanding of the emerging industries in rural areas, and cannot promote the introduction of rural talents and industrial upgrading. The lack of attention to folk culture, leisure tourism service industry and other models with high economic benefits and sustainable development has weakened the profitability of rural revitalization industry. In general, the single rural development mode has a lower rate of return compared with urban business, resulting in a one-way flow of production factors from rural to urban[5].

1.2.3.Rural ecology is fragile

There are a large number of ecologically fragile areas across China, covering more than 60 percent of the country. The spatial fragmentation and sparseness of There are a large number of ecologically fragile areas across China, covering more than 60 percent of the country. The spatial fragmentation and sparseness of rural settlements have increased the difficulty of rural construction and ecological protection. At the same time, rural socio-economic construction, large-scale infrastructure projects and long-term uncoordinated human development activities have intensified the ecological challenges in rural areas, resulting in ecological fragility becoming a more common situation in rural areas[6].Based on this background, more and more researches related to sustainable development focus on "rural sustainable development", mostly studying the rural sustainable development model from a macro perspective, lacking a micro perspective to explore the "adaptive optimization" transformation model of existing rural buildings.

2. The principle of light intervention in the sustainable reconstruction of idle rural primary schools

2.1. Integration of old buildings and new environment

2.1.1. Coordination

Coordination is a technique associated with contrast, in harmony with each other, in relation to each other, showing a complete, unified effect[7].First of all, the overall height and volume are harmonized. The new inserted space should form a dialogue with the old building and the original site environment, and create a harmonious, unified and complete space environment. For example, through the courtyard layout, each space is divided and harmonized, easy to use, and conducive to the construction of communication space; Secondly, local details are coordinated, some symbols of the old building are appropriately simplified and used in the new space, so that the spatial form, technique and style of the new space are consistent with the old building, and the continuity of the new and old space texture is realized. Based on this, the old building can be well protected and utilized, and transformed into a new environment that is not only suitable for contemporary aesthetic views and life needs, but also carries profound historical deposits; Materials and colors are in harmony. In the transformation, materials and colors are the main expressive elements of the building skin, which truly reflects the interaction between the new and old skin. In the new environment, colors coordinated with the surrounding environment are used to convey the language information of the old building, and the principle of "integrating the old into the new and the new into the old" is implemented.

2.1.2. Contrast

Contrast techniques can increase the change and interest of the old building and the new environment, and form a rich and diverse space sequence through the expression of volume, virtual and solid, size, color, material, etc, to create different spatial feelings [8].Combining time, place and the surrounding space environment, the technique based on contrast can produce a good harmonic effect and realize the symbiosis between the old building and the new environment.

2.1.3.Retention

Mr. Yu Kongjian once said that "the best way to create a good and meaningful environment is to preserve the legacy of the past." [9] Retention is one of the more common methods to deal with old and new buildings, emphasizing the local preservation of old buildings, old environment or old things.

The first is the preservation of building materials. The materials in the old buildings show a sense of dilapidated and rough texture, which endows the materials with traces of time and unique aesthetic charm. In the reconstruction of old buildings, materials with heavy texture should be retained and the decorative role of materials should be fully brought into play. Through the comparison technique mentioned above, the rough texture of the old building materials can be strengthened. At the same time, the reuse of old materials can realize the needs of sustainable development of old buildings, and continue the context and historical evolution of the original site.

Secondly, the preservation of the village's history and cultural connotation. Because the idle primary school is located in the center of the village, it has rich historical and cultural connotation. Through the preservation of the old buildings, it gives new connotation to the architecture and environment. Realize the dialogue between the new and the old, and continue the historical memory of the countryside.

2.2. Meet the diversified needs of users

The historical and cultural information in the space should be extracted and retained, and the original architectural space should be scientifically and reasonably deconstructed in combination with the new functional requirements and characteristics, so that the old space can be flexibly and reasonably utilized by different users. The large space can be divided into several subspaces by "space splitting" to adapt to the new functional requirements, so as to meet the diversified needs of users. The spatial splitting is mainly through "horizontal splitting" and "vertical splitting". "Horizontal split" that is, according to the needs of users, split the functional partition, and then according to the space within each functional partition for detailed splitting. "Vertical splitting" means to define the space vertically, adjust the spatial scale to enhance the comfort of the space, enrich the interest and vitality of the space, improve the utilization rate of the old space, increase the space density and building use area, and bring maximum economic benefits to the investors.

2.3. Reuse of the original site resources

A large amount of construction waste will be generated in the reconstruction process of rural idle primary schools, and most of it will be used as building materials, which can effectively reduce energy consumption and save a lot of reconstruction costs and resources, so as to realize the sustainable transformation of rural idle primary schools. The reuse of old building materials is mainly divided into direct utilization and reuse. Due to the relatively complex indirect recycling procedure, direct recycling materials are mainly used now. For example, the stone cage wall transformed with waste brick forms a new facade, forming a new facade enclosing form in space, while retaining the spiritual context of the original place.

2.4. Place historical spiritual context preservation

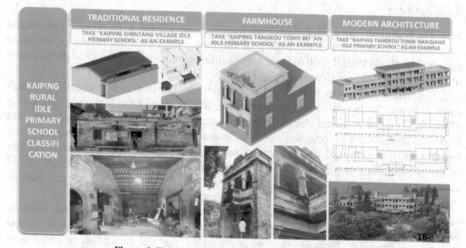

Figure 1. Kaiping rural idle primary school classification

Many unused primary schools in the countryside have a long history, reflecting the level and style of architecture at that time. For example, Kaiping rural idle primary schools can be divided into traditional houses, cottage houses and modern buildings, reflecting the historical evolution and continuity of the countryside (Figure 1). The active reuse of rural idle primary schools can effectively protect the rural historical context, respect regional culture, and reflect the sustainable design principle in the historical inheritance. Based on this, the reuse of idle rural primary schools not only needs to be repaired and arranged, but also needs to increase the emotional value needs of users on the basis of protecting the memory of the place. As mentioned above, through the reuse of construction waste and the retention of the old space interface, the scene of The Times can be reproduced and people can be brought back to the past memory.

3. Strategies for sustainable reconstruction of idle rural primary schools: a case study of Nanqiang primary School in Tangkou Town

3.1. Background information of Nanqiang Primary School in Tangkou Town

Figure 2. Tangkou Nanqiang primary School location

Figure 3. Agricultural resources and characteristic villages around Tangkou Nanqiang Primary School

Nanqiang Primary School of Tangkou Town, founded in 1929, has been adhering to the teaching concept of combining system and humanities from beginning to end, and has cultivated various outstanding talents for Tangkou Town for nearly a hundred years, but it is now idle. The site is rich in original vegetation, such as mango tree, ficus microleaf, ficus interfolius, Ligustrum, etc. (Figure 4). Kaiping Tangkou Nanqiang Primary School

Figure 4. Tangkou Nanqiang Primary School original natural vegetation

is located close to Tangkou Expressway entrance, with convenient transportation. (Figure 2) The surrounding characteristic villages are rich in agricultural resources, tourism resources and intangible cultural heritage resources (Figure 3). The tourist resources include Diaolou Group in Zili Village and Qingchuang Town in Tangkou. Zicun Diaolou Group is one of the world cultural Heritage sites; Tangkou Qingchuang Town is the Tangkou Old Ruins. The former government seat of Tangkou Town has now housed some well-known brands, young creative teams and design works. There are Bookstore Avant-Garde, Tangkou Space, Tangkou Qingchuang Space, Zuzhai Village Tourist toilet, etc. The intangible cultural heritage of Kaiping includes Pancun Lantern Fair, Kaiping Gray carving, Golden Sound lion drum making technique, Chikan tofu corner, Tangkou glutinous rice making technique, etc.

3.2. Transformation strategy of internal and external environment and green ecology

The overall strategy of internal and external environment and green ecology is mainly composed of three aspects: climate adaptation guidance, material reuse strategy and public participation in construction mode. (Figure 5)

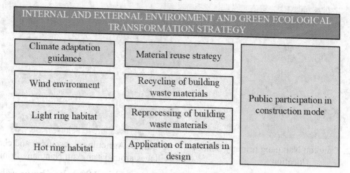

Figure 5. Internal and external environment and green ecological transformation strategy

Climate adaptability guidance refers to the study of wind, light and thermal environment of each type of representative rural idle primary school, to provide quantitative basis for the internal and external environment and green ecological transformation of rural idle primary school by means of low cost, low energy consumption, energy saving and emission reduction, and to provide design logic for the transformation. The material reuse strategy is divided into three steps, namely, recycling of building waste materials, reprocessing of building waste materials and application of materials in design. The recycling of building materials through the combination of manual and mechanical demolition, the maximum benefit of the material recovery. And based on the aesthetic characteristics of different properties of materials, through contrast, reconstruction and other methods to achieve the harmony of new and old materials. For example, the use of waste bricks and tiles with its unique texture, color and texture, recombination and arrangement, decorate the plane or facade, form a rich and human visual effect, that is, save natural resources and respond to the context of the site; Through the public participation in the construction mode to coordinate the interests of multiple parties, by the designer to solicit the village committee's transformation opinions and requirements, and put forward the design plan, solicit the opinions of the villagers representatives to adjust the draft plan, and then through the villagers' meeting to determine the final plan.

3.3. Sustainable space construction based on culture and economy

Integrate the resources of Nanqiang primary School in Tangkou Town, and jointly establish a village research base with the government, enterprises and universities. The establishment of rural college research base, based on the carrier of idle space, combines the campus curriculum content with the rural revitalization strategy, has significant economic value and far-reaching social value.

On the one hand, the countryside is rich in natural resources and cultural resources, which provide rich material and cultural resources for scientific research in colleges and universities. The unused rural space is used to provide research places and practice bases for college students, and the professional knowledge learned in classes is applied to rural practice to enrich the practical experience of college students. On the other hand, the "university research base" is an important measure to promote the integration of university resources, the integration of production and education, and the enhancement of the overall school-running characteristics and social influence[10]. Colleges and universities are a collection of all kinds of cutting-edge scientific and technological knowledge, innovative research experimental fields and knowledgeable talents. After years of accumulation and precipitation, colleges and universities have formed their own unique and perfect curriculum system, most of which are equipped with powerful supporting resources, perfect teaching staff structure and rich curriculum results[11]. By integrating the advantages of colleges and universities, they set up high-quality research teams, carry out distinctive research and education activities, and rely on university platforms to expand the influence and appeal of practical activities[12]. For example, activities such as "College Art Construction Festival" and "Land Art and Culture Festival" are carried out to publicize the characteristic culture of residential settlements and villages, so as to promote the active utilization of resources, heritage protection and inheritance of Nanqiang Primary School in Tangkou Town, and finally realize the self-confidence of rural culture. (Figure 6)

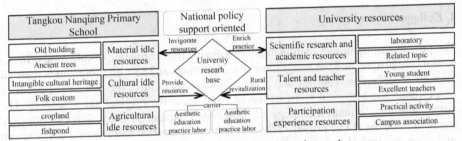

Figure 6. Sustainable space construction based on culture and economy

3.4. Narrative node space based on material and construction

Retain the spirit and context of the site, retain the unique historical characteristics and context spirit of the site, and use it as the main narrative element of the renovation design of rural idle primary school. Remove part of the wall and the abandoned toilet of Kai ping Tangkou school, and use the abandoned brick material for the design of each node. The narrative node space is formed by combining emotion and time. (Figure 7) The narrative elements that need to be preserved in Nanqiang Primary School in Tangkou Town include slides, teaching buildings, world maps, protection boundaries, broken walls, and some vegetation. Combined with the existing retained elements, the special functions are inserted, such as intangible cultural heritage experience, Kaiping characteristic food, and the functions of rural countryside, connecting emotions and space, and evoking the spirit of the place with the taste of words. Considering the hot summer climate in Guangdong, different activities are given to the venue at different times according to the light, and time and space are combined.

Figure 7. Nanqiang Primary School narrative elements retention and material reuse

4. Epilogue

The principle of light intervention in the sustainable transformation of idle rural primary schools is clarified, and the integration of old buildings and new environment is realized through coordination, contrast and preservation, so as to meet the diversified needs of users, retain the historical spirit of the site and reuse the original site resources. The sustainable transformation strategy of Tangkou Nanqiang Primary School with light intervention in rural idle primary school is formed by internal and external environment and green ecological transformation strategy, cultural and economic sustainable space construction and narrative node space construction. The space situation of the scattered rural idle primary schools is not limited to Kaiping, each region's general situation, context and customs, idle space characteristics are completely different. The case study of rural idle primary schools in Kaiping, taking Nanqiang Primary School in Kaiping Tangkou as an example, provides a feasible reference scheme for the same type of idle primary schools. In line with the local specific analysis, supplement the local cases, in order to change the existing rural primary school deactivation state for the rejuvenation of rural culture efforts, has a certain practical significance.

Acknowledgments

Funding Information: This paper represents the interim outcomes of the 2022 Characteristic Innovation Project for Ordinary Higher Education Institutions in Guangdong Province (Project No: 2022WTSCX001).This paper also represents the interim outcomes of the National Social Science Fund's Unconventional and Outstanding Discipline Team Project (Project No: 21VJXT011).

References

[1] Ministry of Education of the People's Republic of China, *Letter of reply to Proposal No. 4071 (Education Category No. 417) of the Fifth Session of the 12th National Committee of the CPPCC*, Beijing, 2023.

[2] Kaiping Municipal People's Government, *Notice of Kaiping Municipal People's Government Office on printing and distributing "Kaiping City Idle School Disposal Measures"*, Kaiping, 2023.

[3] Robert J.S. Beeton. A. Jasmyn J. Lynch, Most of nature: A framework to resolve the twin dilemmas of the decline of nature and rural communities, *Environmental Science & Policy* 23 (2012), 45–56.

[4] Zhou et al, Some parameterized inequalities by meansof fractional integrals with exponential kernels and their applications, *Journal of Inequalities and Applications* (2020), 163–175.

[5] Dai Xinling , We will open up channels for social capital to help rural revitalization, *People's Tribune*29(2019), 82–83.

[6] Jingbo Yin, Dongyan Wang, Hong Li, Spatial optimization of rural settlements in ecologically fragile regions: Insights from a social-ecological system, *Habitat International* **138** (2023), 82–83.

[7] Liu Xiaofeng, Hong Cheng, Searching for Harmony Between the New and Old Environments for the Public Construction Proiects-Andlvsis on How to Balance Between Remodeling and Exoanding the Old Environment for the Public Con.struction Projects, *Huazhong Architecture* **06** (2004), 107–108.

[8] Feng LiSa, Searching for harmony between the new and old environments for the public, *China Science and Technology Information* **14** (2005), 104.

[9] Yu Kongjian, The Culture that Has Been lgnored-Qijiang Park in Zhongshan City, The Beauty of Weeds, *New Architecture* **05** (2001), 17-20.

[10] Zhou Hua, Huang Yin, Lin Xiaoyin, Research on the construction of practical education system of "university + research" under the background of "double reduction"-taking Liuzhou City Vocational College as an example, *University 32* (2022), 50-53.

[11] Jia Junhua, Li Lijun, On the Function of University Resources from the Perspective of Research Practice of Primary and Secondary School Students, *Journal of Baotou Vocational & Technical College* 21 (2020), 18-21.

[12] Guo Xiuping, Wang Jingwen, Liu Shua, Analysis for Highe Vocation Colleges Participating in the Construction of "Rural Revitalization" Research and Practice Education-Based on the Development Perspective of "All-round Revitalization and All-round Revitalization" in Jilin Province, *Vocational and Technical Education* 14 (2021), 6-10.

Design Studies and Intelligence Engineering
L.C. Jain et al. (Eds.)
© 2024 The Authors.
This article is published online with Open Access by IOS Press and distributed under the terms
of the Creative Commons Attribution Non-Commercial License 4.0 (CC BY-NC 4.0).
doi:10.3233/FAIA231470

Application Research of Waterborne Plastic Waste Recycling Device Based on Green Design Principles

Zheng LI [a,1] and Biao LI [a]
[a] *South China University of Technology, Guangzhou, Guangdong, 510000, China*

Abstract. In light of the severe plastic pollution in water bodies, this paper designs a plastic waste recycling device based on the "green design principles" to address the issue of plastic debris in inland waterways. This approach aims to tackle the problem of plastic waste entering the oceans at its source. The overall structure of the device incorporates an environmental recognition system, a green product system, and an interactive system. These systems encompass regional environmental awareness, integrated product design awareness, modularization awareness, and more to adhere to the "3R" principles of green design, effectively addressing the problem of plastic pollution in water bodies.

Keywords. Green design, plastic waste, device design, recycling system

1.Introduction

The economic development and convenience brought about by plastic production are widely recognized. However, certain literature extensively discusses the impacts of plastic production and its lifecycle on human growth, endocrine disruption, and immune-related cancers [1]. Furthermore, the recycling and reuse of plastic waste have garnered increasing attention. Currently, plastic waste is primarily disposed of in landfills and eventually finds its way into the environment, flowing into rivers and oceans, posing a severe threat to marine ecosystems [2]. This is an urgent problem that needs to be addressed.

Existing research has summarized various methods for plastic waste recycling, including optional sorting, density separation, flotation, and Tribo-electrostatic separation [3]. In practical terms, there are mechanical recycling methods such as the floating salvage vessel developed by the Shanghai Municipal Waste Disposal Company and the Seabin marine garbage bin in Australia, which have proven effective in recovering plastic waste from water bodies [4]. However, these devices often suffer from issues such as high energy consumption, unsuitability for use in inland waterways or fast-flowing rivers where they may struggle to efficiently capture surface plastic waste.

In light of these challenges, this paper employs the "green design principles" to develop an innovative solution for plastic waste retrieval in inland waterways, akin to the capillary-like network of blood vessels. The objective is to reduce the volume of plastic waste entering the sea at its source.

---

[1] Corresponding Author. Guangzhou, Address: South China University of Technology, University City, Panyu District, Guangzhou, Guangdong Province, China; Email: 15641025@qq.com.

2. Understanding Green Design

"Green" products or services possess several key characteristics. For instance, they emphasize factors such as reducing energy consumption, reusing resources, and protecting the ecological environment during the product design phase, all while ensuring the functionality of the product is maintained as a paramount goal [5] . In today's green economy , the ease of disassembly in a product significantly influences its overall value and sustainability[6]. Partial disassembly, based on cost-effectiveness, can lead to the recovery of discarded components. This approach aligns with a systems theory perspective where resources become a basis for competition in businesses. Ghisellini P and others propose that future considerations should balance the interaction between environmental and economic systems, focusing on aspects such as recycled materials, reuse, and technological integration [7].

Scholars introduce environmental awareness into product modular analysis by considering eight environmental factor criteria. They utilize a fully hierarchical analysis method to determine the priority of these criteria, establishing a semi-quantitative environmental factor modular analysis model [8]. Furthermore, LI Zhongkai emphasize that modular design should meet product functionality, enhance the green performance of modular products, and prioritize considerations such as downsizing, reusability, and recyclability [9]. Based on these principles, the overall structural design is derived.

3. Overall Structural Design and Working Principles

3.1 Overall Structural Design

The core of green design is environmental consciousness. In green design, the system's overall structure incorporates an environmental recognition system, which encompasses awareness of the specific usage environment of the device; a green product system, which includes integrated product design awareness, modularization awareness, and awareness of using green materials; and an application system, which ensures the effective transmission of environmental awareness, low learning and usage costs, and clear recognition of the device's value.

3.2 Working Principles

3.2.1 Environmental Recognition System: Regional Environmental Awareness

In green design, environmental awareness is crucial, and it requires a deep understanding of the product's lifecycle and its relationship with the surrounding environment [10]. When it comes to plastic waste entering the ocean, it initially accumulates in small waterways within densely populated areas and areas with dense river networks. Approximately 90% of marine plastic pollution originates from rivers [11]. To enhance collection and recycling rates, the challenge is to optimize collection and transportation methods. Therefore, it is essential to have a thorough understanding of the conditions in the regional waterways and strategically place interception points.

In this section, existing GIS (Geographic Information System) technology can be employed. GIS's core functionality is to integrate various datasets and perform location-based analysis, storage, and display in the form of maps. This approach enables a comprehensive understanding of the characteristics of population distribution and river density in the region.

In November 2017, hydrogeologist Christian Schmidt conducted research on plastic waste carried by the Pearl River Basin in the Guangzhou region of China, ranking it 7th

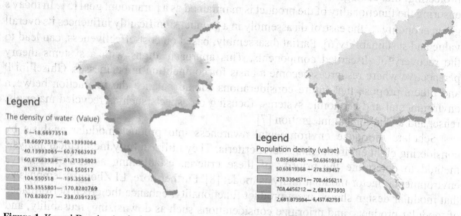

Legend

The density of water (Value)

☐ 0 — 18.66973518
☐ 18.66973518 — 40.13993064
☐ 40.13993065 — 60.67663933
☐ 60.67663934 — 81.21334803
☐ 81.21334804 — 104.550517
☐ 104.550518 — 135.35558
☐ 135.3555801 — 170.8280769
☐ 170.828077 — 238.0391235

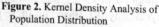

Legend
Population density (value)

☐ 0.035468485 — 50.63619367
☐ 50.63619368 — 278.339457
☐ 278.3394571 — 708.4456211
☐ 708.4456212 — 2,681.873903
☐ 2,681.873904 — 6,457.62793

Figure 1. Kernel Density Analysis of River Quantity

Figure 2. Kernel Density Analysis of Population Distribution

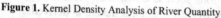

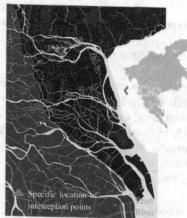

Specific location of interception points   Pearl River

Figure 3. Analysis of Regional Interception Points   **Figure 4.** Analysis of Specific Interception Points

in terms of plastic waste load among global rivers[12]. Therefore, this paper selects Guangzhou as the environmental research area. It uses ArcGIS kernel density analysis to analyze relevant population and river distribution data (as shown in Figures 1 and 2). Kernel density analysis is a vital data visualization technique that reveals the density distribution of data in a region through varying colors. Based on the density overlay of river quantity and population distribution maps, interception points (A, B, C, and D in Figure 3) are selected.

Points A, B, and C are located in areas with high population density in the city center, coinciding with high river density regions. Point D represents the primary waterway where the Pearl River flows into the sea. Intercept points are strategically placed based on regional environmental data to minimize environmental impact and enhance collection rates. Further specific interception points are determined based on this analysis (as seen in Figure 4 red triangle). Identifying hotspots with a significant source of plastic waste is key to addressing the plastic waste problem and is the first step in planning interception points. Plastic waste tends to accumulate in specific areas due to urbanization and population density factors. Utilizing existing data helps guide future actions effectively.

3.2.2 Green Product System

(1) Integrated Product Design Awareness
Integrated product design awareness consists of three interconnected modes: power integration, collection integration, and transportation integration (as shown in Figure 5).
Power Integration: This mode focuses primarily on reducing material and energy

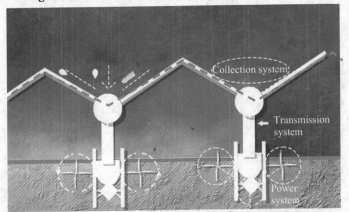

Figure 5. Analysis of Integrated Design Awareness

consumption. It utilizes the resources available in the waterway environment where the device is located, harnessing tidal energy, hydropower, and solar energy as the primary sources of power for the device. It enhances interactive features to engage the public in the device's energy generation process. To adapt to varying water currents and tidal energy intensities in different rivers, multiple compact gears are placed within the device, allowing turbines to generate power under different water flow conditions. Solar panels on the device's surface absorb additional power for daily needs. A part of the electricity also comes from public interaction through kinetic energy, as demonstrated at point E with exercise bikes (At the red dashed line in Figure 6). These bikes are equipped with power-generating mechanisms, encouraging the public to participate in plastic waste recycling activities.

Collection Integration: This mode leverages the characteristics of water flow to collect plastic waste efficiently. It uses a cascading baffle system configured in a "V" shape to align with the water's direction and guide plastic waste towards collection points. The angle between the baffles can be adjusted based on the width of the waterway to accommodate potential navigational requirements. The baffles can also be interconnected to enhance their barrier effect, especially in situations like heavy rain when increased land-based plastic waste might enter the waterway. In such cases, the baffles can be connected to create a barrier between the land and the river, preventing plastic waste from flowing into the waterway, as illustrated in the collection system in the plan view (At the red fold line in Figure 5).

Transportation Integration: In the transportation integration mode, the design optimizes the use of potential energy and the movement of the paddle conveyor to enhance plastic waste transportation efficiency. As the paddle conveyor moves, it generates a flow of water from point F to point B. This movement increases the suction force at point B, further attracting water from around the device to converge along the "V-shaped baffles." This, in turn, propels more plastic waste in the water to filter towards the collection point. Below point D, there is a perforated aluminum plate with dense circular holes of 3-5mm in diameter. This plate serves to separate plastic waste from the

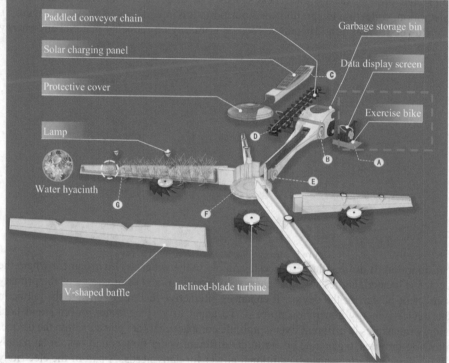

Figure 6. Design Explosion Analysis Diagram

water source. The water flows back into the river, while the plastic waste is lifted by the paddles and directed upwards into the storage compartment located above. These three integrated modes collectively achieve the low consumption of materials and energy within the collection device.

(2) Modularization Awareness

Modularization awareness in the design of the plastic waste collection device involves creating components that can be easily assembled and disassembled. This approach reduces the design and manufacturing cycle of the collection device and promotes resource efficiency through modular and standardized designs. Universal design of components increases their versatility and utilization, simplifies the production process, reduces product recycling and maintenance costs, and minimizes repetitive labor.

In this study, modularized structural components were investigated. For example, to

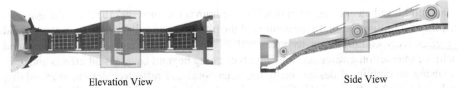

Elevation View   Side View

Figure 7. Connection Structure Diagram

accommodate variations in the slope of different riverbanks, a rod-like connecting mechanism was employed to allow the continuous extension of the paddle conveyor in the central part of the device,(At the blue box section in Figure 7), preventing it from getting stuck.

Furthermore, the "V-shaped baffles" inside the device are constructed using individual square wooden grids. (See blue box in Figure 7). These grids serve to adapt to the required length of the river to be intercepted and provide habitats for seabirds. The length of the baffles is determined based on the curvature of the coastline. If the coastline is straight and long, a single wooden grid is used to form a long and straight baffle. If the coastline is curved, modular wooden grids are combined to create a more flexible, segmented baffle that conforms to the curve of the coastline.

Small birds box
Large birds box
Hole drain
Floating body

Emergent plant

Submerged plant

Ecological floating bed

Floating plant

Figure 8

Moreover, the spatial layout of the modular wooden grids on the baffles can accommodate the resting needs of seabirds. Each individual bird nesting box is designed to accommodate different bird species with varying sizes of holes, and drainage holes are provided for excreta and tidal water drainage. Additionally, 500mm by 500mm individual ecological floating beds are connected for water purification through floating, water retention, and submerged plants. These floating beds purify the water quality by growing plants, providing shelter, food, and breeding spaces away from human activity for seabirds through a combination of three types of plants. (At Figure 8).

(3) Green Material Awareness

Due to the device's prolonged exposure to water, material selection prioritizes wood to avoid the generation of microplastics resulting from prolonged water contact. In this regard, researchers in relevant fields have explored the synthesis of organic silicon polymers and the use of materials like linseed oil-based emulsions to enhance the waterproof properties of wood [13-14].

3.2.3 Application System: Green Value Perception Transmission

Marshall McLuhan once asserted that "the medium is the message" to reveal the essential nature of communication. In the context of the plastic waste collection device, it is crucial to effectively communicate its green values to the public, convert information, and achieve interaction awareness. This involves going beyond basic visual effects and focusing on emotional design, including behavioral and reflective design, emphasizing values beyond aesthetics [15]. Green design should release additional value beyond the product itself, emphasizing the way information is conveyed. This approach ensures that the device's purpose of plastic recycling garners more support and enhances its intrinsic value. Utilizing various interactive branches and detailed experiences, the product tells the story of reducing plastic pollution, aiming to achieve green psychological goals.

In the nearshore part of the device, specifically at point E, (At the red dashed line in Figure 6), an exercise bike mechanism is installed. This serves the dual purpose of allowing exercisers to convert kinetic energy into electrical power for the device while providing an interactive display screen on the bike. The screen conveys ecological information stories, recording data such as energy supply, calorie consumption, and exercise duration, transforming them into personal data records. This approach turns plastic waste collection into a data-driven topic in personal social networks. By simplifying the learning and operation costs for the audience and facilitating the transition from individual to societal awareness, it fosters the formation of an

Figure 9. Interactive Information Chart

environmentally friendly social network. (At Figure 9). The device establishes an implicit interactive field of green environmental values, enhancing recognition of the device's value within society.

4. Conclusion

This design is specifically tailored to address the issue of plastic waste pollution in waterways, considering the current state of plastic pollution in water sources. Throughout the entire process, the design adheres to the "3R" principle of green design, incorporating environmental awareness, integrated design, modular design, green materials awareness, and information interaction awareness to form a systematic approach to green design for tackling plastic waste collection in specific regions.

The analysis of the unique characteristics of the distribution density of waterways and population density in the Guangzhou region was conducted to strategically select interception points along the rivers, enhancing the efficiency of plastic waste collection in the Pearl River. The design of the device fully reflects the diversity of river conditions, employing modular and integrated approaches, and utilizing green materials to minimize the potential for secondary pollution from the equipment.

Additionally, the device facilitates the transmission of green value information through interaction with users, increasing public awareness and engagement in green actions. This, in turn, expands its influence and enhances the devices efficiency in addressing plastic pollution.

Acknowledgments

This paper represents the interim outcomes of the 2022 Characteristic Innovation Project for Ordinary Higher Education Institutions in Guangdong Province (Project No: 2022WTSCX001). This paper also represents the interim outcomes of the National Social Science Funds Unconventional and Outstanding Discipline Team Project (Project No: 21VJXT011).

References

[1] United Nations Environment Programme, *Turning off the Tap: How the world can end plastic pollution and create a circular economy*, Nairobi, 2023.
[2] Prajapati, Ravindra, et al, Recovery and recycling of polymeric and plastic materials, *Recent Developments in Plastic Recycling* (2021), 15–41.
[3] Wu, Guiqing, Jia Li, and Zhenming Xu, Triboelectrostatic separation for granular plastic waste recycling: A review, *Waste management* **33** (2013), 585-597.
[4] PATELS, Utilization and development of marine energy, *Shanghai Electric Power* **1** (2009), 32-38.
[5] Lu Jia-yi, Jin Xiao-yi, Zhu Tian-bao, et al, Research on AGV path based on improved A* algorithm, *Mechanical Design and Research* **36** (2020), 49-52.
[6] Shi, H., Peng, S.Z., Liu, Y., Zhong, P, Barriers to the implementation of cleaner production in Chinese SMEs: government, industry and expert stakeholders' perspectives, *Journal of Cleaner Production* **16** (2008), 842-852.
[7] Ghisellini, Patrizia, Catia Cialani, and Sergio Ulgiati, A review on circular economy: the expected transition to a balanced interplay of environmental and economic systems, Journal *of Cleaner Production* **114** (2016), 11-32.
[8] Qian, Xueqing, and Hong C. Zhang, Design for environment: an environmentally conscious analysis model for modular design, *IEEE Transactions on Electronics Packaging Manufacturing* **32** (2009), 164-175.
[9] Li Zhongkai, Qian Hongtao, A method for environmental conscious modular product architecture design optimization. *Journal of Computer-Aided Design &. Computer Graphic*, **27** (2015), 166-174.
[10] Leng Yi-hu, Research on modular design of modern large bamboo furniture, Furniture and Interior Decoration, **29** (2022), 22-25.

[11] Lynch, Seán, OpenLitterMap. com–open data on plastic pollution with blockchain rewards (littercoin), *Open Geospatial Data, Software and Standards* **3** (2018), 1-10.

[12] Christian Schmidt, Tobias Krauth, and Stephan Wagner, Export of plastic debris by rivers into the sea, *Environmental Science & Technology*, 51 (2017), 12246-12253.

[13] Fu Xiao-hui, Synthesis of organosilicon polymers and their application in waterproof modification of wood, Beijing Forestry University, 2021.

[14] Chen Jin-yu. Preparation of linseed oil-based emulsion and its waterproof and moisture-proof modification of wood, Beijing Forestry University, 2021.

[15] Norman, D. A, Design Psychology 3: Emotional Design, CITIC Publishing House, Beijing, 2015.

Design Studies and Intelligence Engineering
L.C. Jain et al. (Eds.)
© 2024 The Authors.
doi:10.3233/FAIA231471

Research on the Design of Diet Management System for Sub-Obese People Based on FBM Behavior Model

Xiaolu LIU [a], Fangying LI [a,1], and Yingying HUANG [a]

[a] *Fuzhou University*

Abstract: Objective To provide a diet management system scheme for sub-obese people and improve their self-efficacy cognition and self-behavior ability in diet management. Methods According to the FBM behavior analysis framework, the diet management behavior of sub-obese people was divided into three stages. From the generation of diet management consciousness, the generation of diet management behavior and the maintenance of diet management behavior, we can gain insight into the behavioral pain points and specific needs of sub-obese people. Then, from three aspects: enhancing users' motivation, improving users' ability and increasing trigger mechanism, the framework of diet management persuasion strategy for sub-obese people is constructed, and on this basis, the system design scheme is put forward. Conclusion The dietary management behavior based on persuasion theory, through introducing the dietary management product system, is beneficial to improve the cognition of self-dietary management of sub-obese groups and guide them to realize the benign transformation of dietary behavior.

Keywords: FBM behavior model; Persuasion theory; Sub-obese people; Diet management system.

1. Introduction

Sub-obese people refer to overweight people who exceed the standard weight but have not yet reached the obesity standard. The World Health Organization defines sub-obesity as BMI body fat index greater than or equal to 25 less than 30. According to the latest data of the report on nutrition and chronic diseases of Chinese residents [1], more than 1 / 2 of adults in China are in the state of sub-obesity or obesity, and the rates of sub-obesity and obesity are 34.3 % and 16.4 %, respectively.Among them, the sub-obesity group is the most prominent group with unreasonable diet structure, unstable living habits and lack of exercise. With the change of people 's lifestyle and consumption concept, diet, as one of the main and controllable factors causing obesity, has been paid more and more attention. People begin to pay attention to their own diet health, and all kinds of diet health products emerge as the times require. Designers also begin to focus on the guidance of people 's healthy lifestyle and try to realize the transformation of sub-obese users ' benign living habits through the intervention of persuasion theory.

---

[1] Corresponding Author: LiFangying, 852 Ligong Road, Jimei District, Xiamen City, Fujian Province; E-mail: 2238862959@qq.com; ORCiD ID: Li Fangying https://orcid.org/0009-0008-7265-4560

2.Research theoretical basis and model introduction

The FBM behavior model is an insightful model of human behavior proposed by Stanford University 's behavioral science professor Fogg. The model includes three elements: behavioral motivation, behavioral ability, and trigger mechanism [2]. The absence of any of these three elements cannot produce behavior. Only when the motivation and ability achieve the ideal balance, the behavior will be actively generated in the state of the trigger mechanism, and the behavior sender can obtain a high-quality experience. Therefore, the FBM behavior model can be used to analyze the reasons why users do not produce behavior and their behavioral needs, and then to understand the methods and means to drive users to complete the task of target behavior and create a better user experience.

In the diet management system of sub-obese people, the FBM behavior model changes the user 's behavior through effective communication and guidance and pays attention to the user 's personal initiative and self-decision-making, helps sub-obese users to realize the impact of their bad eating behavior on health, and provides effective strategies to change their behavior. The main behavior of users in the diet management product system is to manage their own diet. Under the guidance of the FBM model theory, in the behavior of ' diet management ', the reason for prompting users to manage their diet and continue can be regarded as ' user motivation '. The physical and mental strength paid by users in diet management can be regarded as ' user ability '. The reminders, guidance and rewards provided by the product belong to the ' trigger mechanism '. The user will implement the behavior of adhering to diet management and develop scientific and healthy eating habits in the process. Therefore, the diet management product system for sub-obese people needs to create positive motivation for users, enhance users ' self-management behavior ability, increase the trigger mechanism for users ' use experience, and encourage users to improve their diet management ability and maintain their behavior.

3.Behavioral insights and needs analysis

3.1Behavior stage division and problem insight

Sub-obese users will experience different stages of development in diet management. The behavior of diet management can be divided into three stages: the generation of diet management awareness, the generation of diet management behavior, and the maintenance of diet management behavior. The user 's diet management level also fluctuates in this process. By analyzing the different behaviors and emotions of sub-obese users in the process of using diet management products, we can gain insight into the user 's diet management level and the pain points and needs of using diet management (Figure 1).

In the generation stage of diet management awareness, due to the lack of timely trigger mechanism of products, the loss of users with diet management motivation can not arouse the enthusiasm of sub-obese users for diet management. At the same time, most of the current diet management products are recipe recommendation, weight calculation and other functions, and the homogenization is more serious. It is difficult for users to select products in a targeted manner.

In the generation stage of diet management behavior, the complexity of the product easily leads to the loss of users. At present, most of the products require users to use complex steps to provide diet data, and the product itself is difficult to exert subjective initiative to make users tired of operation. Diet management-related knowledge is complex and diverse. For people who lack nutrition and health knowledge, it is easy to cause negative emotions due to insufficient cognitive ability, and it is difficult to adhere to the use behavior.

In the maintenance stage of diet management behavior, because sub-obese users are more sensitive than ordinary users, their lack of sense of achievement, satisfaction and honor in the use process will also lead to the lack of motivation for the next use behavior; at the same time, most of the current products belong to the guiding function of diet recommendation in terms of service content. They lack supervision mechanism and social interaction. The product content is boring and lack of interaction. It is difficult to give users a high-quality interactive experience, and it is easy for users to have negative emotions and terminate their behavior.

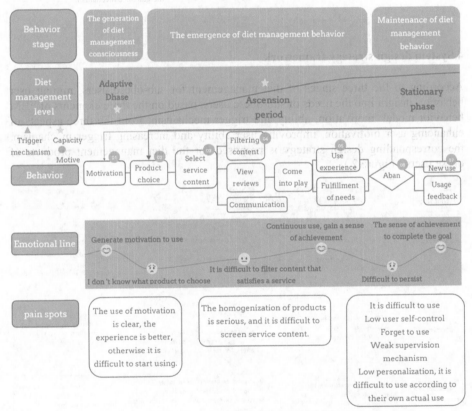

Figure 1. Behavioral journey map of each stage of diet management

3.2 Analysis of dietary management behavior elements and needs

Through the analysis of the behavior of sub-obese users in the process of using diet management products, the user 's behavior pain points are excavated, and the user pain points are classified from the three elements of the FMB behavior model, so as to gain insight into the potential needs of sub-obese users (Table 1).

Table 1. User needs of diet management products under FBM behavior elements

FBM elements	User behavior pain points	user requirements
Motive	The homogenization of existing products is serious. Lack of motivation. No sense of achievement. Lack of self-control. Lack of supervision, low execution.	Functional uniqueness. Auxiliary target determination. Social interaction. Strengthen the supervision mechanism.
Capacity	Diet management targeted weak. The effect of diet management is weak. Difficult to insist. The operation is complex and difficult.	Targeted development plan. Provide a comprehensive service mechanism . Improve product feedback efficiency. Improve professionalism.
Trigger Mechanism	Lack of guidance. Poor initiative Forget to use it. Poor implementation force.	Take appropriate incentives. Add appropriate use reminders. Strengthen the guidance mechanism

4.System design strategy framework

According to the three stages of diet management for sub-obese users, mining user behavior, insight into the needs of sub-obese users, based on the three elements of FBM behavior model: motivation, ability and trigger mechanism, from the three aspects of enhancing user motivation, improving user ability and increasing trigger mechanism, the corresponding design strategy is proposed for the diet management products of obese users (Figure 2).

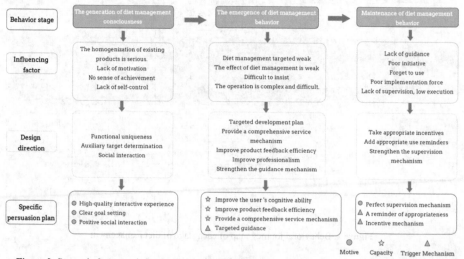

Figure 2. Strategic framework for the design of diet management system for sub-obese population under FBM model

4.1 Enhance user motivation

When designing diet management products for sub-obese users, it is necessary to enhance the user 's motivation. Only when the motivation is improved, the user will have enough enthusiasm to achieve the goal. The ways to enhance motivation mainly include attracting users with high-quality interactive experience, clear goal setting, perfect supervision mechanism and positive social interaction.

4.1.1 High-quality interactive experience

In the generation stage of diet management awareness, high-quality interactive experience can stimulate users ' motivation. The current diet management products are mainly in the form of software. The form is mainly based on the software side to provide information support. It is difficult to monitor the user's execution level and effect. Therefore, it is necessary to adopt high-quality interactive experience .Through the application of intelligent technology, the combination of hardware and software is adopted to provide a comprehensive diet management service system. For example, the use of sensors and other technologies to monitor the user 's diet, through intelligent assistance and management, to strengthen the connection between users and products, while the addition of new features is also conducive to enhancing the user 's motivation through personalized product features.

4.1.2 Clear goal setting

In the generation stage of diet management consciousness, clear goals can guide users to strengthen their own diet management. According to FBM model theory, the clearer and more detailed the goal, the stronger the personal motivation and the greater the possibility of achieving the goal behavior. Therefore, when designing diet management products, we should set targeted goals for sub-obese users according to their personal characteristics.

4.1.3 Positive social interaction

In the generation stage of diet management consciousness, providing positive social interaction can enhance users' behavioral motivation. Users can gain a sense of belonging by joining groups with common goals through social interaction, and at the same time, they can stimulate the challenge psychology, build a healthy competition cycle in the group, and then enhance the enthusiasm of users to achieve their goals.

4.1.4 Perfect supervision mechanism

In the maintenance stage of diet management behavior, because the self-regulation ability of sub-obese people is weak, it is difficult for products lacking supervision mechanisms to keep users motivated. Due to the influence of external stimuli, it is difficult for users to control their diet and maintain a healthy lifestyle. Therefore, an effective supervision mechanism can positively encourage users to maintain motivation, and at the same time regularly monitor users' progress, find problems in time, and put forward suggestions and adjustment plans.

4.2 Enhance user capabilities

The user stickiness of diet management products is largely determined by the user's own behavior ability. The main purpose of improving the user's ability to use is to enable users to continue to use behavior. The the same user will have different behavior abilities in different behavior scenarios, so it is necessary to implement corresponding and effective behavior design strategies according to the scenarios, so that users can have behaviors and pleasant experiences in the usage scenarios.

4.2.1 Improve users' cognitive ability

In the generation stage of diet management behavior, the difficulty of information provided by diet management products will affect the user's use status. When the information content received by users exceeds their ability, there will be a psychological gap, which will lead to the loss of use motivation. As far as diet control is concerned, users need to have certain knowledge of diet and calculation ability. The expected effect is not achieved because of a lack of professional guidance. Therefore, we should pay attention to cultivating users' intake of professional knowledge in order to improve users' cognitive ability, and at the same time, we can recommend appropriate diet management methods for users according to their behavior ability, and dynamically adjust the content according to the changes of users' ability.

4.2.2 Improve the feedback efficiency of products

In the generation stage of diet management behavior, the improvement of product feedback efficiency is beneficial for users to adjust the wrong diet management behavior in time, which will play a certain role in the development of users' ability. Feedback is an important part of the user's product experience, just like a medium, and it is essential for human-computer communication [3]. For food management products, we must have a good feedback mechanism to guide users to complete their behaviors through product feedback. For users' wrong operations, products must help users to correct them in a friendly way and encourage users to continue to maintain them. For users' correct operations, we should give appropriate encouragement. For example, users can continue to achieve the next goal through incentives.

4.2.3 Provide a comprehensive service mechanism

In the generation stage of diet management behavior, comprehensive service mechanism can encourage users to improve their ability of sustainable behavior. In view of the weak self-regulation ability of sub-obese people, it is difficult to maintain users' use of products by a single service. The comprehensive service mechanism includes a system of combining software and hardware, and combining products and services, which can guide sub-obese people in many aspects and improve their diet management ability.

4.3 Increase the trigger mechanism

Based on the FBM behavior model, food management products need to attract users to use them on time and in a certain way at the right time, that is, the trigger mechanism of user behavior, which needs to be set according to the strength of user motivation and ability.4.3.1 Targeted guidance

4.3.1 Targeted guidance

In the generation stage of diet management behavior, the user's use of stickiness can be maintained through targeted guidance. Users have enough behavioral motivation and ability, but diet management itself can easily make users feel anxious, which also makes it difficult for users to maintain their behavior. These need to be guided by purposeful guidance to guide users' psychology and behavior, to encourage users to have sustained behavior.

4.3.2 Appropriate reminder

In the maintenance stage of diet management behavior, users already have high motivation and ability to use, and currently, high-frequency use feedback and reminders are easy to arouse users' resistance. Their self-awareness is strong, and most of them are sensitive to their figure and weight. Repeated reminders are easy to cause users' anxiety; Too few reminders will also cause users to forget because of insufficient reminders, so it is necessary to display them appropriately in the appropriate position to urge users to always keep the concept of diet management.

4.3.3 Incentive mechanism

In the maintenance stage of diet management behavior, users can be stimulated to achieve their goals continuously through incentives. In terms of incentives, it includes interest value incentives, emotional incentives, and product incentives. At the level of interest value, users can be given certain benefits from their identity level and medal of honor. Emotional motivation includes social motivation, emotional interaction, etc., which can create a diet management exchange community and motivate users' initiative through praise and attention. From the perspective of product incentives, users can be attracted by punching in rewards, such as giving away lunch boxes for 20 days.

5. Diet management system design scheme

Under the guidance of the FBM behavior model, relying on the above product design strategy, this paper aims at the main group of sub-obese people--20-35 years old working people, according to the daily diet tableware and lunch box of the target population as the carrier, through the combination of software and hardware, products, and services. The form provides users with a scientific diet management plan and persuades users to improve their eating behavior from three aspects: improving user motivation, improving user ability, and increasing trigger mechanism, to promote the development of users ' healthy eating habits and improve sub-obesity from the diet mechanism.

The sub-obesity diet management service system is mainly composed of two parts: software and hardware smart meal boxes (Figure 3). The hardware part is based on the daily utensils of the target population boxes as the carrier. Through intelligent applications, equipped with sensors and other technologies to achieve food weighing, calorie calculation, food heating, eating supervision, and other functions. The design of the intelligent display screen with the camera can use image capture to calculate food calories and can also capture the user's chewing movements when the user eats. Through the analysis of chewing frequency and eating speed, the user's eating speed is regulated to prevent the gastric nerve reflex caused by too fast eating from failing to report the brain, resulting in excessive eating and aggravating obesity. The lunch box can heat the food through the front-end heating button, providing physical conditions for the user's diet management.

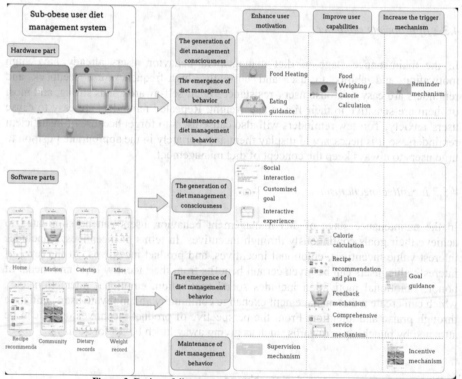

Figure 3. Design of diet management system for sub-obese people

The software part is mainly divided into four parts: diet matching, diet and exercise, ordering, and me. In the diet matching module, users can view the diet calorie data and nutrient composition data transmitted from the hardware side; and can view customized recipes and different food calories nutrition analysis and other professional knowledge; in the motion module, the user's chewing speed captured in the hardware end can be analyzed and feedback evaluation can be given to promote the establishment of feedback and incentive mechanism. The user can project the chewing operation in the software to the hardware end so that the user can follow the practice during the eating process, alleviating the current situation of indigestion caused by eating while brushing the electronic equipment; The ordering module can order meals through the software. The system recommends a variety of meal combinations suitable for users based on user data. Users can choose their own combinations to increase the user's dominance. After the user takes the meal, he places it in the lunch box to keep it warm; in addition to the basic functions, my module also sets up a collection area for the user's weight data and diet data. The user can view his own phased changes and formulate new plans based on this. goals: community functions can stimulate users to complete goals through likes, comments, etc.

Due to the complexity and long periodicity of the diet management process, the construction of a sub-obese diet management service system can comprehensively enhance the motivation of sub-obese users, enhance the ability of sub-obese users, and increase the trigger mechanism of the system. It is mainly divided into two parts: hardware module and software module to establish the system service system (Figure 4).

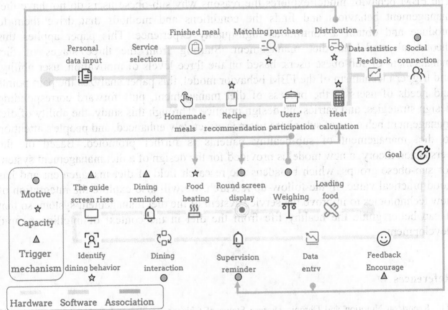

Figure4. Food management system use process

In terms of enhancing user motivation, the product interaction is optimized, the original software-led model is changed, and the combination of software and hardware is adopted. Through the lunch box, the user's eating behavior is supervised, so that the user has an intuitive understanding of their behavioral activities and can find problems in time and make suggestions and adjustment plans. On the software side, the system sets a clear target mechanism according to the physical characteristics of different users, to stimulate the user experience interest; at the same time, it is equipped with community functions. Users can share meals, and punch cards, encourage users 'initiative, and enhance users' motivation through social means such as likes, comments, and attention.

In terms of improving the user's ability, on the software side, recipe recommendation, and diet plan customization are carried out according to the user's characteristics, which reduces the difficulty of the user's screening. The guidance of scientific methods helps to improve the user's cognitive ability; with the finished meal function, the user's error behavior is reduced, and the overall system of software and hardware combination, product and service combination is formed to improve the user's behavior ability.

In terms of increasing the trigger mechanism, a circular display screen is designed in the lunch box to carry the mealtime-reminder and the food calorie display function; through the user's weight record and diet record, the software end gives the user targeted guidance in a timely manner; the community function and the daily card mechanism stimulate users to achieve their goals through incentives.

6. Conclusion

The FBM behavior model explores the reasons why sub-obese users do not have diet management behaviors and finds the conditions and methods that drive them to produce and obtain a continuous high-quality experience. This paper applies this theoretical model to diet management. Starting from the three stages of diet management of sub-obese users, based on the three levels of motivation, user ability, and trigger mechanism of the FBM behavior model, this paper analyzes the pain points and needs of users in the process of diet management, puts forward corresponding design strategies, and carries out design practice. Through this study, the ability of diet management behavior of sub-obese users is effectively enhanced, and people's attention to diet management of sub-healthy patients is further promoted. Based on the persuasion theory, a new model is provided for the design of a diet management system for sub-obese groups, which broadens the research field of diet management and has good practical value. In the follow-up research, we will also explore the integration of new technologies to improve the service system of the diet management system, so that it can better guide the healthy life from the diet in the context of intelligent rapid development.

References

[1] Report on Nutrition and Chronic Disease Status of Chinese Residents. Acta Nutrimenta Sinica **42** (2020), 06, 521.
[2] FOGG,B.J.A.Behavior Model for Persuasive Design. France: Proceedings of the 4th International Conference on Persuasive Technology, 2009.
[3] Wang Lin, Jiang Xiao.Research on the application of feedback mechanism in mobile Internet product design. Packaging Engineering, **34** (2013), 16, 75-78.
[4] Fang Xing, Wang Yufei. Research hotspots and development trends of persuasion design. packaging engineering: 1-14.
[5] Wang Shaofeng.Summarization of Persuasive Design Research. Packing Engineering **43** (2022), 22, 32-46.

[6] Cheng Sumei. Ethical Review of Persuasive Technology. Journal of East China Normal University (Philosophy and Social Sciences Edition) **55** (2023), 02, 61-69 + 174.

[7] ZHU Xingrong. A Review of Foreign Research on Persuasive Design. Design **36** (2023), 04, 70-73.

[8] Zhang Xuedong, Gao Leitao.Integrated framework and intervention measures of behavior design. Journal of Zhengzhou University of Light Industry (Social Science Edition) **24** (2023), 01, 89-97 + 110.

[9] Wang Xiangnan, Zhang Lin.Research on the design of persuasive children 's intelligent reading products. Design **36** (2023), 1, 121-124.

[10] Tan and Jiang.Research on the interaction design of online learning platform based on FBM behavior model. Packing Engineering **41** (2020), 4, 189-194.

560

Design Studies and Intelligence Engineering
L.C. Jain et al. (Eds.)
© 2024 The Authors.
This article is published online with Open Access by IOS Press and distributed under the terms
of the Creative Commons Attribution Non-Commercial License 4.0 (CC BY-NC 4.0).
doi:10.3233/FAIA231472

KYPHOTONE: Wearable Hunchback Corrector for Women

Yousheng YAO [ab,*], Yuan XIE [a,*], Fangtian YING [b,1], Zhihao HUANG [a], E TANG [a], Xiqin PAN [a], Junpeng ZHENG [a], Junqi ZHAN [a], Jin PENG [a], and Haoteng CHEN [a]

[a] *Zhongkai University of Agriculture and Engineering*
[b] *Macau University of Science and Technology*

Abstract. In human-computer interaction, there is a close relationship between "beauty" and empowerment. Aesthetics in human-computer interaction is not only about pursuing external beauty and visual appeal, but also about empowering users with better experience and functionality, and enhancing the capabilities of the interaction system, thereby improving user satisfaction and efficiency. In the real world, wearable testing systems are becoming increasingly popular for autonomous health testing. Hunchback is a problem that is detrimental to healthy growth and self-confidence. In this article, we introduce KYPHOTONE, an interactive system that can help hunchbacked women with their hunchback problems, designed for women. We analyze the materials, anthropometric measurements, and garment assembly of KYPHOTONE. KYPHOTONE consists of hardware and software programs. The hardware and software are utilized to provide real-time feedback based on the movements of women with hunchbacks during the wearing process, enabling real-time medical diagnosis, correction detection, and correction management. In addition, we conducted a preliminary user study of KYPHOTONE, which showed that women with hunchbacks are willing to wear it, which gives them more confidence in preventing hunchbacks.

Keywords. Sensor devices, hunchback correction, human-computer interaction, female design

1. Introduction

In human-computer interaction, aesthetic empowerment should not just be an empty pursuit of beauty, but is combined with the realization of functions. Through rational design and innovative interaction, aesthetics can make functions more intuitive and easy to use, providing a better user experience. Women are often excluded from the design process of wearable sensors due to the need for real-time biosignal detection systems. KYPHOTONE addresses the problem of atypical anthropometric measurements in the development and validation of current wearable technologies. This paper presents KYPHOTONE, a wearable female hunchback corrector based on sensing technology, including hardware and a software program with real-time feedback. When interacting with KYPHOTONE, the user determines whether she is hunchbacked or not through data

---

* The first two authors contributed equally to the article.

1 Corresponding author, Ying Fangtian, Macau University of Science and Technology, Avenida WaiLong, Taipa, 999078, Macau, 13067848819@163.com.

analysis and feedback from the hardware, and if she is hunchbacked, KYPHOTONE alerts the user through vibration. A three-step investigation was conducted through an iterative and innovative design process:

- Using current and past wearable devices for hunchback correction, we identified the unique design challenges associated with non-ideal models, this is especially relevant to women who have breast tissue to deal with.

- Following step 1, we identified design prototypes and iterations of design prototypes to determine optimization aspects of the hardware that have achieved accuracy in sensor data detection.

- A path forward for future research in this area is provided based on the results of design validation with four female participants.

2. Motivation and related work

2.1. hunchback corrector

The condition of hunchback is a habitual chronic disease, and body posture is an important factor in spinal health. As a result of prolonged poor posture, spinal morphology may change, lower back pain may develop, and musculoskeletal disorders may occur [1]. Known also as scoliosis, scoliosis is a lateral curvature of the spine in the shape of an S or C. When the spine is curved to one side more than 10 degrees is called scoliosis, and usually occurs at the age of 10 to 18 years old, If not treated in time, minor scoliosis generally does not have too many symptoms. However, if not treated in time, scoliosis may worsen. Severe scoliosis (more than 70 degrees) can lead to back pain and breathing difficulties. If scoliosis continues to worsen without treatment, severe scoliosis (more than 70 degrees) can lead to back pain, breathing difficulties, and compression of internal organs, affecting the patient's life and even becoming life-threatening[2]. With the continuous development of information technology, intelligent wearable device systems can be continuously enhanced and widely used in the fields of physical therapy health, and rehabilitation. Concepts such as telemedicine and telerehabilitation have emerged to assist patients in getting rehabilitation advice and physiotherapy information daily. This will also be one of the future directions of smart development in the field of treating female hunchbacks. There are various correction products on the market, such as Deng Yongcong proposed a utility model patent: a hunchback correction belt with intelligent reminder against strangulation [3]. Zhang Li proposed a utility model patent: a hunchback corrector with a detachable support structure, which provides a hunchback corrector with a detachable support structure to remind users to change their posture by vibration or sound, and the correction induction host and support structure can be easily detached and portable [4]. Luo Guanqiong invented a corrective apparatus for hunchback [5].

For women with a hunchback, a series of hunchback correction devices have been introduced in the market, mainly two categories of physical sitting posture correctors and intelligent hunchback correctors, as follows:

(1) Physical hunchback braces

Physical hunchback braces are inexpensive, mainly of human frame type, and are mandatory corrections. Often, when using such hunchback braces, the human body cannot operate other things, which generally have the defects of poor independence, inconvenient carrying, poor stability, low convenience of use, and no social attributes, and are not suitable for correction in daily life, and the correction effect is short and effective.

(2) Intelligent hunchback correction device

Smart hunchback corrector has a wearable, seat and writing pen, etc. It uses the principles of gyroscope, intelligent acoustic wave, and infrared ray, and adopts intelligent voice prompts, light prompts, or vibration prompts to urge correction of hunchback posture, which is more comfortable than physical sitting posture corrector, but it also lacks social attributes, and the hunchback corrector on the market often ignores anthropometric considerations of female body shape.

Smart clothing is an organic combination of many scientific fields such as traditional textile and clothing technology, fiber forming and processing technology, information sensing technology, communication technology, artificial intelligence, and biotechnology [6]. KYPHOTONE in this paper is a wearable smart clothing component that integrates advanced technology sensors into the garment and considers the female user's body structure in the design to achieve functionality and socialization.

2.2. Human structure design considerations

The failure to take into account anatomical differences between men and women has long plagued many industries. The term female is used to denote a female human (only for humans can it be called "female"), in contrast to a male human (i.e., male), who can produce egg cells in the body. The term female is used to denote a biological gender division or a cultural gender role. In contrast, the term "male" is defined as an individual who lacks the anthropometric characteristics associated with being female due to low or reduced levels of estrogen and progesterone. This definition is not limited to the gender of the individual but is also strictly limited to physical characteristics. Many garments are designed primarily for men and then modified for women. [7] This dissertation study aims to change this paradigm and suggests that female anthropometry and unique anthropometric differences be placed at the forefront of design.

3. Design Process

To design and develop KYPHOTONE, we first conducted design exploration sessions with experts. Here we described the design goals that emerged during the design process.

3.1. Design exploration with experts

We conducted a preliminary study with four spine specialists (2F, 2M, mean age = 38 years, P1, P2, P3, P4) from Guangzhou City, Guangdong Province, China, who had more than 5 years of experience and education in hunchback health care. Each design exploration lasted approximately 60 minutes and consisted of our initial ideas, a discussion session with experts who shared their previous experience in treating hunchbacks, and a semi-structured interview with their perceptions of the KYPHOTONE design prototype. They all agreed with our starting point "There is a real need for a wearable hunchback brace for women" and suggested the following: (1) P1 and P2 suggested that women's hunchbacks should be corrected in time to avoid further health problems. (2) P1 and P3 reveal that although many women are aware of the problem of their hunchback, it is difficult to correct it. (3) P2 and P4 suggested that we should provide timely feedback on women's hunchback problems and visualize the hunchback data.

3.2. Design Objectives

Based on our design exploration sessions with experts and related preliminary work, we synthesized the following key objectives for a wearable female hunchback orthosis: (1) Real-time feedback during exercises that allow users to demonstrate hunchback behavior. (2) To display female hunchback correction data and spinal development data in a visual way so that users can understand the data more clearly.

4. KYPHOTONE Design

4.1. System Description

Based on design discussions with experts, we developed a prototype of KYPHOTONE, which consists of hardware and software. The hardware is a module with clothing, a posture detection module, a vibration warning module, and an energy supply module. The software is an application that provides real-time data feedback. The software and hardware are connected through a WIFI, as shown in Figure 1. The application is divided into four parts. The first part is the home page, where other users and experts can share their hunchback problems and communicate with each other. the second one is Discover, in which you can share your situation; the third one is Insights, in which you have a dedicated doctor for health consultation; the fourth one is Profile, in which you can see your personal information such as your hunchback health test report. The interface design of some parts of the application part is shown in Figure 2(a), Figure 2(b), Figure 2(c), and Figure 2(d).

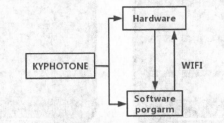

Figure 1. KYPHOTONE's conceptual framework.

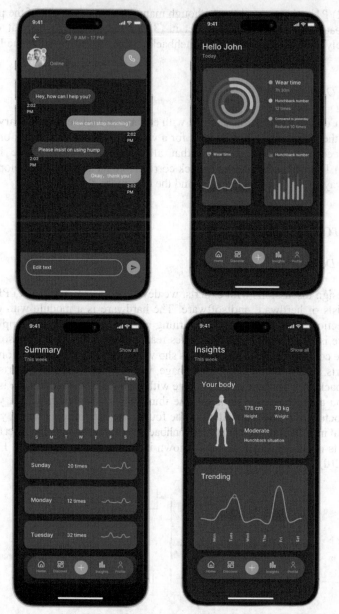

Figure 2. (a)User interface to ask questions to doctors (b)User Daily Camelback Data (c)User Weekly Camelback Data(d)User personal information interface

4.2. Requirements and User Experience

Researchers have made great strides in developing stylish, user-friendly systems where high-quality data detection is critical for hunchback identification and correction. The challenge for designers was to balance performance and form capabilities to make KYPHOTONE socially wearable. KYPHOTONE is a design solution for female-centric, real-time monitoring. When designing a wearable system for physiological signal collection, certain requirements of the overall system needed to be met in order to achieve a successful design that was both functional and aesthetically pleasing. When designing wearable systems for physiological signal collection, certain requirements of the overall system need to be met in order to achieve a successful design that is both functional and aesthetically pleasing [8]. These requirements are continuous data collection, unobtrusive design, easy data access and interaction, comfort, electronic durability, and reliability [9, 10, 11]. The challenges posed by these requirements are intuitive user interfaces, and privacy control and fit. During the development of KYPHOTONE, our main focus was on fit, signal quality, accessible electronics, and repeatability. Each aspect of the garment is specifically selected and validated to maximize each area of performance and create a total garment that meets the needs of the wearer. Our approach emphasizes the importance of innovative, iterative design methods to maximize performance in all areas. In developing effective women's undergarments, we identify areas of improvement that can be iterated upon, and these design iterations address the interface between the user and the sensor to meet the user's needs with the user's experience.

4.3. Sensors

The ten-axis posture sensor (Guangzhou Starwing Electronic Technology Co., Ltd.) used in KYPHOTONE is 1.5 cm square in size, as shown in Figure 3, and the posture sensor data test page is shown in Figure 4. This sensor integrates a three-axis angle, a three-axis gyroscope, a three-axis magnetometer, a three-axis acceleration, a quaternion, barometric pressure value, and a poster height expansion port, and the serial port directly outputs the posture angle, acceleration, angular velocity, magnetic field, barometric pressure and other data, easy to use.KYPHOTONE includes intelligent reminder hardware, said intelligent reminder hardware includes a motherboard, a key switch electrically connected to the input side of the motherboard and a USB external charging port, an angular sensing module electrically connected in both directions to the motherboard, a vibration reminder module, a charging module, and a WIFE transmission module, and through the posture sensing module promptly senses that the After the user produces a certain degree of inclination due to incorrect posture, the main board controls the vibration reminder module to remind the user to change the posture, and after restoring the normal state, the angle sensing module senses that the user is in the correct posture and stops the vibration reminder module vibration, so it can correct the wearer's irregular posture in a timely manner, and prevent the hunchback.

KYPHOTONE undershirt is designed to take into account the wearing comfort of women's compression garments as well as to take into account the maximum prevention of effects such as affecting the sensor data detection. The human body is not constantly in motion, it will submit to the requirements of the sensor system and user experience, requiring the ease of use, comfort, and localizability of the garment, the most comfortable and inconspicuous location of the sensor, and the accuracy of data detection is the center of the back.

Figure 3. Positive and negative side of the posture sensor

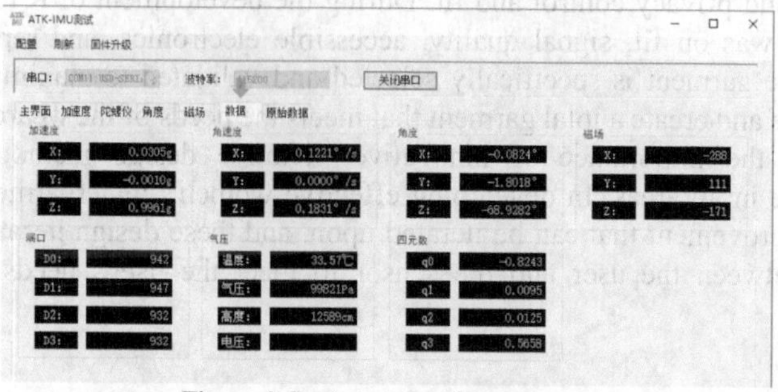

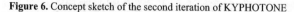

Figure 4. Posture sensor data test page

4.4. Wearing style

Traditional women's bras are worn from the overhead pull type, but considering that KYPHOTONE is required with sensors, the comfort of two closure methods (front zipper and front snap) was tested to prevent the overhead pull type from interfering with the sensor data detection. Initially, the front zipper was chosen as the closure method, as shown in Figure 5, which allows the user to put on and take off the undershirt by themselves, but it was found that the clothing with zipper comfort type was not high, as well as would interfere with the sensor signals. The second design iteration, shown in Figure 6, utilized a front snap closure, which was easier for the user to put on and take off on their own with less obstruction, and was a better design choice. The third iteration of the design, shown in Figure 7, is based on the second iteration of the design, with an additional adjustment strap to make the undershirt fit the body better and the sensors more stable.

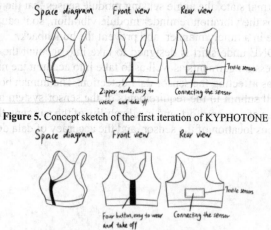

Figure 5. Concept sketch of the first iteration of KYPHOTONE

Figure 6. Concept sketch of the second iteration of KYPHOTONE

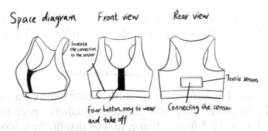

Figure 7. Concept sketch of the third iteration of KYPHOTONE

4.5. KYPHOTONE

In terms of the structure of the undershirt, the electronic components such as the smart correction component, control circuit board, and signal output module are designed as a template placed on the inside of the undershirt, and this module can be disassembled to facilitate later finishing such as washing and cleaning of the undershirt. While considering the aesthetics, we emphasize the comfort of the smart correction electronics in the design of the undershirt, and the undershirt meets the ergonomic requirements of women. The final KYPHOTON undershirt with integrated sensors, electronics, and closure mechanism is shown in Figure 8.

Figure 8. KYPHOTONE physical picture

5. Initial user research

To identify how women interact with KYPHOTONE and their perceptions of KYPHOTONE, we conducted a preliminary user study. We recruited 20 hunchbacked females (P1, P2, P3, P4,P5, P6, P7, P8,P9, P10, P11, P12,P13, P14, P15, P16, P17,P18, P19, P20) from the local community (mean age = 25 years). So the participants were taught how to use and introduce KYPHOTONE through our training, and the whole process was recorded with the participants' consent.

5.1. Procedures

The experiment was conducted in a classroom. First, the KYPHOTONE was briefly introduced and explained for use, and then participants were given 1 hour to use the KYPHOTONE for independent use. During this 1 hour, participants were observed. Upon completion, we encouraged participants to take the KYPHOTONE home and continue to use it for one week. After use, we explored participants' perceptions of the humpback corrector based on a questionnaire and conducted semi-structured interviews focusing on three questions:(1) Their interactions and problems with the back

KYPHOTONE. (2) Any suggestions for KYPHOTONE. (3) Differences between common back hump correctors on the market and KYPHOTONE.

5.2. Results

As shown in Table 1 Likert scale, all participants showed a high willingness to use KYPHOTONE. However, they had different opinions about female hunchbacks, for example, P4, who scored 5 in question c, told us that the hunchback detection can make us hunchback less often and make our female form and health better.P3, who scored 4 in question d, believed that it is more effective to not only make reminders, but also intervention behaviors when KYPHOTONE detects our hunchbacks. And all 20 participants pointed out that KYPHOTONE is helpful and a good experience and socialization for women with hunchback problems.

Table 1. Questionnaire results for hunchbacked women

Question	P1	P2	P3	P4	P5	P6	P7	P8	P9	P10	P11	P12	P13	P14	P15	P16	P17	P18	P19	P20	Avg
a. Would you like to use this KYPHOTONE Hunchback Corrector? (1: No - 5: Yes)	5	5	5	5	5	5	4	5	5	5	5	5	4	5	5	5	5	5	5	5	4.9
b.You can easily understand how to use this KYPHOTONE Hunchback Corrector? (1: Difficult - 5: Easy)	5	5	5	5	4	5	5	5	5	5	5	4	5	5	5	5	5	5	5	5	4.9
c. Does KYPHOTONE Hunchback Corrector help to correct hunchback in women? (1: Not useful -5: Useful)	5	4	4	5	5	5	4	5	5	5	4	4	5	5	5	5	5	4	5	5	4.7
d. Is it useful to remind KYPHOTON when you are hunched over? (1: Not useful - 5: Useful)	5	4	4	5	5	5	5	5	5	5	5	5	5	5	5	5	5	4	5	5	4.9
e. After using this KYPHOTON Hunchback Corrector, do you feel confident in correcting your hunchback? (1: no-5: yes)	5	4	5	5	5	5	4	5	5	5	4	5	5	5	5	5	4	5	5	5	4.8

When participants were asked about their opinions on the humpback corrector, P1 said, "I think the humpback corrector is particularly useful." and P10 said, "The humpback corrector reminds me every moment not to hump my back like it's my own doctor." P15 said, "The hunchback corrector lets me know when I hunch, how many times I hunch today, and makes me more aware of my physique." P1-10, P13, P15, and P17-20 all wished that the hunchback corrector would add more features.

6. Discussion and future work

6.1. Conduct other explorations

This undershirt can record the female user's humped back in real-time The concept proves that the human body is made up of many complex tissues, and the KYPHOTONE humped back corrector, to be adaptable to all people and used for daily testing, needs to be explored in more other ways, such as exploring the variability of human morphology and breast size in different groups to achieve the universality of KYPHOTONE.

6.2. Reflection

We found some shortcomings in the study. Firstly, affected by the epidemic, we only managed to have 4 experts as representatives of knowledge about women's hunchback health. If more experts had been included, we might have collected more relevant knowledge about women's humpback health. Secondly, the number of female users in the study is also low, as well as the lack of time for users to experience and the lack of long-term usage and feedback from users on the hunchback corrector.

7. Future Work

In the future, we will further improve the design of hardware and applications, expand the coverage of female hunchback health detection and prevention, optimize the performance and indicators of sensors, and apply more "micro feedback" to KYPHOTONE hunchback correctors, so that users can be more aware of their hunchback and the health condition of correction. Consider more functional components for the hunchback brace. Through the research in this paper, we hope to provide more resources to promote the development of wearable technology, designed more for women, to create a comfortable, socially acceptable, and effective wearable hunchback brace.

8. Conclusions

In this article, we introduce KYPHOTONE, an interactive system that helps women better correct their hunchbacks by providing real-time feedback and corrections based on the behavior of women with hunchbacks, allowing them to change their hunchback behavior while wearing KYPHOTONE. Our user studies have shown that women with hunchbacks can more effectively correct their hunchbacks and build self-confidence in correcting their hunchbacks by wearing the KYPHOTONE. The innovation of this paper is to improve the comfort and wearability of the garment-integrated electrodes and to achieve user testing, and this research opens the door to zero-distance communication between doctors and hunchback patients, reflecting "beauty" and empowerment in human-computer interaction.

9. Acknowledgements

We would like to thank all the experimenters and participants involved in this project, as well as the experts who told us and helped us in this process.In addition, this study was supported by the 2021 Guangdong Provincial Quality Engineering Modern Industrial College Project "Eco-design Industrial College", the Guangdong First-class Professional Construction Point: Product Design, the 2021 Guangdong Provincial Department of Science and Technology/Guangdong Provincial Bureau of Rural Revitalization "Guangdong Provincial Rural Science and Technology Specialists in Towns and Villages," stationed in Jiangdong Town, Chaoan District, Chaozhou City, Project No.: KTP20210374, 2021 Zhongkai College of Agricultural Engineering Quality Engineering Special Talent Cultivation Program Construction Project, "Excellence in Rural Revitalization Talent Design and Innovation Class"support.

References

[1] Han X. Study on risk factors associated with postural spine morphological changes in adolescents and children// *2018 Meeting of the Professional Committee of Exercise Physiology of the Chinese Physiological Society and Symposium on "Science and Technology Innovation and Exercise Physiology"*.

[2] Jiang Hui. Bending, hunching, sitting askew? *Scoliosis may be the cause of the problem Medical Food Reference*, 2022(1):1.

[3] Deng Yongcong. *A kind of hunchback correction belt with intelligent reminder:* CN213156764U. 2021.

[4] Zhang L. *A hunchback correction device with detachable support structure:* CN211270770U. 2020.

[5] Luo Guanqiong. *A corrective apparatus for treating hunchback:* 2021.

[6] DING Yongsheng, WU Yizhi, HAO Kuangrong.Theory and application of intelligent clothing.*Beijing: Science Press*, 2013.

[7] W Yu and J Zhou. 2016. Sports bras and breast kinetics. *In Advances in women's intimate apparel technology*. Elsevier, Amsterdam, The Netherlands, 135–146.

[8] Teresa Almeida, Rob Comber, and Madeline Balaam. 2016. HCI and Intimate Care as an Agenda for Change in Women's Health. *In Proceedings of the 2016 CHI Conference on Human Factors in Computing Systems*. (San Jose, California, USA).

[9] Genevieve Dion. 2013. Garment Device: Challenges to Fabrication of Wearable Technology. In Proceedings of the 8th International Conference on Body Area Networks (Boston, Massachusetts) (BodyNets '13). *ICST (Institute for Computer Sciences, Social-Informatics and Telecommunications Engineering)*, Brussels, BEL, 97–102.

[10] Vivian Genaro Motti and Kelly Caine. 2015. An Overview of Wearable Applica tions for Healthcare: Requirements and Challenges. In Adjunct Proceedings of the 2015 ACM International Joint Conference on Pervasive and Ubiquitous Computing and Proceedings of the 2015 ACM International Symposium on Wearable Computers (Osaka, Japan) (UbiComp/ISWC'15 Adjunct). *Association for Computing Machinery*, New York, NY, USA, 635–641.

[11] Norman RS Hollies, Anna G Custer, Catherine J Morin, and Marilyn E Howard. 1979. A human perception analysis approach to clothing comfort. *Textile Research Journal 49*, 10 (1979), 557–564.

Design Studies and Intelligence Engineering
L.C. Jain et al. (Eds.)
© 2024 The Authors.
This article is published online with Open Access by IOS Press and distributed under the terms
of the Creative Commons Attribution Non-Commercial License 4.0 (CC BY-NC 4.0).
doi:10.3233/FAIA231473

Map and Network Urban Analysis: A Case Study on Guangzhou Nanhuaxi Street Historic District's Urban Form

Hong LI[a, b, 1] and Xiaofeng WANG[c]

[a] *Guangdong Mechanical & Electrical Polytechnic, Guangzhou*
510515. lehon_1234@126.com
[b] *Fine Art and Design, Krirk University, Bangkok, 10220.*
lehon_1234@126.com
[c] *Fine Art and Design, Sunny Partnership Space Planning co., ltd, Guangzhou,*
510515.

Abstract. This study aims to explore the application of map and network urban analysis methods in urban form research, with a focus on the process and outcome of urban reorganization, using Guangzhou Nanhuaxi Street Historic District as a case study. By adopting map illustration and network urban analysis methods, this study reveals the characteristics and functions of the urban form of Guangzhou Nanhuaxi Historic District, in order to provide new perspectives and methods for urban planning and design. The study is analyzed in terms of the four elements of the network city: node connections, density, boundaries and accessibility. The form of development of this neighborhood in the form of three parcel clusters is analyzed in conjunction with historical documents. There is a positive relationship between the diversity of street types, the direction of pedestrian flow and the flow of goods and information, and the nodes in the system. The "fixed line" in the historical urban form determines the development and evolution of the urban form. This provides new perspectives and methods for urban planning and design. The results of the study help us to better understand the laws governing urban development and provide useful experiences and methods for future urban planning and design. Meanwhile, it offers new perspectives and insights for academic research and practical applications in the field of urban morphology.

Keywords. Map Analysis, Network Urban Analysis, Guangzhou Nanhuaxi Street Historic District's, Urban Form

1. Introduction

With the acceleration of urbanization, the traditional urban organization is undergoing a profound change, and urban spatial reconstruction has become a hot issue in current urban research. As a historical and cultural protected area in Guangzhou, the historical area of Nanhuaxi Street is also facing functional transformation and spatial reorganization in the process of urban change. Therefore, how to protect the historical lineage and at the same time carry out a reasonable update to achieve the community function enhancement and spatial optimization is the key issue facing of Nanhuaxi Street.

---

[1] Corresponding Author: Hong Li, lehon_1234@126.com

As an intuitive way to express urban form, map illustration can effectively present the evolution of urban space. Combined with the spatial analysis method of network theory, it can quantitatively analyze the correlation and structural characteristics of the elements in the city. The combination of the two methods applied to Nan Huaxi can reveal the urban organization of the region and provide theoretical support for its spatial reorganization. In this study, a combination of map illustration and network spatial analysis is used to analyze the urban morphology evolution process and potential spatial logic of Nanhuaxi neighborhood in Guangzhou, and to provide a theoretical basis for future functional renewal and spatial optimization on the basis of summarizing the historical evolution law of the area. The significance of this study is to enrich the application of graphical and network analysis in urban geography research, and to provide reference for the transformation of the old urban area of Guangzhou.

2. Literature Review

2.1. Map illustrations and networked cities

A city is a complex artificial construct, and this complexity can be seen as objects that influence each other being arranged in different ways on different levels. In order to analyze this complex urbanity in a simple and effective way, an effective way is to visualize its basic features and functions, and map illustration will show its power as an effective tool for expressing urban space. David Harvey calls a simple reproduction of reality a "model", and maps are one type of "model", which can be called map models. "When a model is developed to the point where it can be used to explain all relevant types of behavior, it becomes what can be called a theory." "To seek an explanation is to seek a theory. A theory is a system of representation who can be seen as a set of sentences expressed in specialized vocabulary, a language." (David Harvey, 1977) The coding of map symbols accomplishes such a task, as a language that can be articulated to seek an explanation. Thus the theoretical perspective of the "networked city" was born. This theory views the city as a network of nodes and connections, where each node is a carrier of urban functions and the connections represent the relationships and flows between these functions. Through this network perspective, we can understand the complexity of the city in a more systematic way, organize the seemingly chaotic urban phenomena into an orderly structure, and predict future trends. In addition, the theory of the "network city" emphasizes the interconnections and influences between and within cities, thus providing a new perspective to understand the internal dynamics and external relationships of cities.

Map illustration and web-based urban analysis methods are used in a variety of fields, including urban planning, social surveys, and environmental studies. Cartography is the art of making maps and has evolved with technology to help us understand our place in the world, analyze location relationships, and reflect on the impact of geography on our daily lives. Such methods include graphic ground maps, street maps, and Nolli type maps (Liu, X., Derudder, B., & Taylor, P, 2014) Thematic map visualization techniques are also used to derive insights from data, tell a powerful story, or to better understand the world around us. Dragica (2016) discusses the importance of having architectural dense complex networks in various scientific fields such as urban science and presents a methodology for quantifying road network complexity and determining building density using matrix pixel analysis and kernel distribution, using the city of Belgrade as an example. Agust Gudmundsson1 & Nahid Mohajeri2,3 (2013) focused on the orientation, length, density and network evolution of street networks in 41 cities in the United Kingdom, revealing the evolution and organization of the street network and highlighting the resilient and self-organizing structure of the street network.

2.2. Urban Reorganization of Historic Districts

Lu (2008) proposes a conceptual framework for understanding spatial change in Chinese cities, emphasizing the role of institutional frameworks, economic and urban policies, and structural shifts in the economy.Cheng (2017) examines the transformation of development zones into functionally sound cities in the Chinese context, emphasizing the processes of comprehensive urban planning and urban renewal.Shouhon (2003) analyzes the impact of urbanization and coexistence of suburbanization, emphasizing their impact on spatial change. Finally, Li (2023) explores the structure and restructuring of urban networks in Northeast China, emphasizing the need for collaborative urbanization. Li and Feng (2021) selected nine street offices (sub-districts), including 14 historic preservation districts in Old Liwan, and examined urban shrinkage through population growth rate, population aging, economic growth, and public life vitality, and explored the relationship between Old Liwan and changes in the city's development strategy, preservation policies, and urban renewal actions. Together, these papers provide insights into the urban reorganization of Guangzhou's South China West Street.

3. Methodologies

3.1. Take Guangzhou Nanhuaxi Historic District as an example

This study takes the Nanhuaxi historical district as a case study. When the focus of research is on contemporary phenomena, the case study method is deemed a method of choice. The Guangzhou Nanhua West Street historic district is situated in the important Chinese city of "Guangzhou". It was established during the Thirteen Factories era in the Qing Dynasty. The district has undergone the rise and decline of the merchants of the Thirteen Factories era, urban planning transformations during the Republican period, and industrialization in the early years of the People's Republic of China. These transitions have induced changes in its urban form, economic dynamics, and social structure, making it a compelling case for studying urban reorganization.

Early Qing Dynasty 1661 | Mid-Qing Dynasty 1776 | Mid-Qing Dynasty 1803 | Late Qing Dynasty 1890 | Republic of China Eia 1928 | After the Founding of the People's Republic of China

Figure 1. Morphological Evolution of the South China West Historic District.

The scope of Guangzhou's Nanhuaxi Street Historical and Cultural Protection Area is as follows: To the east, it reaches Baogang Avenue; to the west, it extends to Hongde Road. To the south, it is bordered by alleyways such as Qixing South, Longqing North, and Xinglong Lane, while to the north, it adjoins the Pearl River. The district stretches 950 meters from east to west and is 560 meters wide from north to south, covering a planned area of approximately 45.17 hectares. Nanhuaxi mainly adopts a neighborhood system, characterized by relatively low-rise buildings with high density, representing traditional residential forms. The northern side of Nanhuaxi Street belongs to the riverside residential area and integrated development zone. The buildings in this area face the Pearl River, with the Binjiang West Road and the Zhoutouzui area at its core, which is the traditional maritime business center of Guangzhou. Historically, the maritime industry of the Pearl River facilitated the commercial prosperity of this region.

Before starting the map diagramming work, it's essential to define the observation boundaries. This step incorporates the project boundaries as a part of the network, aiming to connect the system's interior with its exterior. Christopher Alexander believed that "a city is not a tree, but a network." Sifertis (1997) emphasized that urban systems shouldn't be hierarchically categorized; instead, they must be understood as networks with nodes.

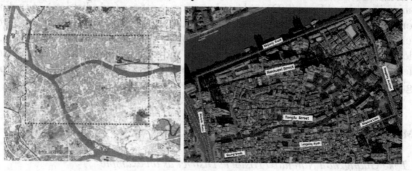

Figure 2. NanHuaxi Street Historic and Cultural District Area Boundary.

3.2. Data collection and methodology

This study primarily adopts archival research and visual documentation as the main methods of data collection. Archival materials include government planning reports, local literature, and vector map data. The vector map data provide quantitative data such as building floor counts, individual building area, facade length, and street dimensions. Site-specific characteristics are documented through field surveys using visual recording techniques, with photographs capturing features of the buildings, entrance locations, and other information. Table 1 summarizes the morphological elements and their data sources used in the study. Satellite maps are sourced from GOOGLEMAP, and vector maps are compiled by the Guangzhou Urban Planning and Design Survey Research Institute.

Table 1. Data sources for morphological elements

Element	Composition of data	Source of data
Nodes, connecting lines	Number of floors of the building Type of building	Vector map data
Density analysis	Number of floors of buildings street scale and their distribution	Vector map data

| Boundary analysis | Building monolithic form | Vector map data \ historical documentation |
| Accessibility Analysis | Building Street Scale\Building Functional Types | Map Data\Research Photos |

3.3. Data analysis methods

The methods of analyzing the data include map graphical analysis with node and connectivity analysis, density analysis, boundary analysis, and accessibility analysis.

3.3.1. Analysis of nodes and connecting lines

In the analysis of network structures, nodes, links, and boundaries of the system play a decisive role in shaping the network formation. Morphologically, nodes are defined by the overlap of residential areas and infrastructural zones, creating hubs of intense human and commodity concentration. Hence, nodes represent the flow of people, goods, and information. Links signify the movement of people, goods and information between two nodes. Nodes and links are two crucial factors influencing the network system.

In the following discussion, "system" serves as a metaphor for the Nanhuaxi historical district. Within this regional system, most are 2-3 story traditional residences (as shown in Figure 5), among which are structures from the late Qing Dynasty and the early Republic of China, including the mansion of the Thirteen Hong merchants from the Qing era, known as the "Pan Family Mansion," as well as villas owned by businessmen from the Republic period. Looking at the nodes and links within this system, the distribution of nodes is notably uneven. In the late Qing Dynasty and early Republic period, there was a bustling market near the Shuzhu Bridge (as shown in Figure 3). However, as the city developed, the Shuzhu Chong was covered and turned into an underground channel, causing the market to relocate. It moved south of Tongfu Road along the line of the Shuzhu Chong, becoming the area in Nanhuaxi with the highest concentration of business and information exchange. This area evolved into a primary node within the system. Secondary nodes of commerce and information exchange formed around the Nanwu Middle School and the Jinsu Garden area (as shown in Figure 6). Due to the "pavilion-style" high-rise residential building type in the system's living areas, there's essentially no provision for nodes of information or commercial exchange, resulting in the loss of links in the residential areas. If more nodes could be established in the residential areas west of the Shuzhu Chong, thus increasing the links between nodes, Nanhuaxi has the potential to form a comprehensive network structure. This could enhance people's overall spatial perception of Nanhuaxi and rejuvenate the vitality of this historic district.

Figure 3. Shu Zhu Chong on Maps and in Export Paintings

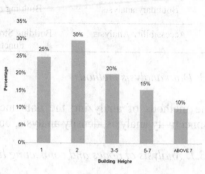

Figure 4. street and alley map   **Figure 5.** Statistical chart of the number of floors
                                                          in a building

Figure 6. Network Nodes and Connectivity

3.3.2. Density analysis

3.3.2.1. Particle density

In this context, 'grains' serve as a metaphor for architectural plots. The density of these grains can quickly and accurately manifest specific issues of a particular area at a designated location. The type of grains and the manner of their composition reveal the uniqueness of an area. However, the distinctiveness of a region is not static; it often changes with the evolution of time. On some level, it can reflect traces of characteristics that once existed, distinguishing them from other areas.

In the illustration below, lighter shades represent areas with low grain density, while darker shades represent areas with high grain density. Within the red circled area in the illustration, a 'pavilion-style' high-rise commercial residential zone emerges (as indicated by the red circle in Figure 7). It evidently disrupts the historical street and alley texture, resulting in heterogenous spaces that don't harmonize with the surrounding environment. Historical documentation reveals that to the left of this area was the bustling 'Shuzhu Bridge' from the mid-Qing Dynasty. However, today, due to the emergence of these heterogenous plots, the continuity of the plot texture is severed. This disruption is not only a destruction of the historical street fabric, but it also creates spaces that are out of sync with the surrounding environment. This area is close to Shuzhu Bridge and precisely where the entrance to the Wu Family Ancestral Hall is located. If one were to utilize mapping systems to analyze cities, adopting a perspective that respects cultural and historical continuity in urban development, designs that treat sites as mere blank slates would be avoided.

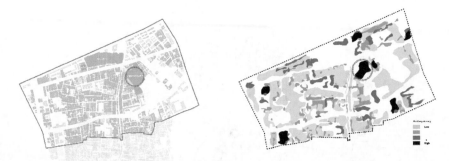

Figure 7. Particle density analysis

3.3.2.2. Degree of fragmentation

Fragmentation is intrinsically linked with coherence. When coherence shifts, fragmentation will inevitably change along with it. The greater the degree of fragmentation, the lesser the coherence. Here, 'fragments' metaphorically allude to the density of streets and alleys. The west side of Shuzhu Chong continued to develop on the basis of the Pan family's garden plot, forming the current street pattern. This plot has the highest degree of fragmentation, with a uniform distribution, weaker coherence, and smaller street scales. The numerous cul-de-sacs indicate a pedestrian-centric lifestyle of the time.

From Figure 8, Block A consists of buildings of smaller scale. This is mainly due to the decline of merchant families, the multiple divisions of the Pan family's garden, and the simple and unpretentious urban life during the late Qing Dynasty. The streets and alleys in the Shuzhu Chong area either run parallel or perpendicular to the water channels, signifying the influence of waterway transportation on the surrounding urban spaces at the time. Block B in the illustration was originally the garden of merchant Wu Bingjian during the Qing Dynasty's Thirteen Hongs period. Many dead-end streets have emerged in the Wu family's plot over the years. This pattern is primarily due to the emergence of enclosed small residential communities and high-rise commercial buildings. With the decline of the merchant class, by the late Qing period, the function of the Wu family's garden began to shift. During the early Republic, this plot was mainly used as a police station. In 1945, it served as an armory for the Guomindang and was bombed and later reconstructed. The plot now consists of diverse architectural types, including middle schools, elementary schools, police departments, and modern high-rise residential buildings. Block C in the diagram represents a vast enclosed area, primarily comprised of institutions like elementary schools, theaters, youth palaces, inspectors' offices, and temples.

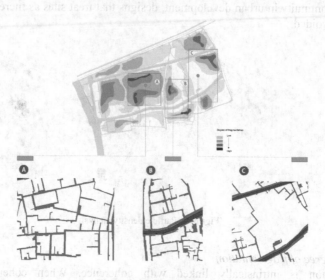

Figure 8. Degree of fragmentation.

From this, the degree of fragmentation evident in today's Nanhuaxi reveals two points:

Its development is primarily in clusters. The basic division of these clusters evolved from the original development of the Haitang Temple (Block C in Figure 8), the Pan merchant family (Block A in Figure 8), and the Wu merchant family (Block B in Figure 8).

The texture of streets and alleys within the system is intrinsically linked to the lifestyles of the time. For instance, the relationship between the water channels and the alleys hints at a lifestyle that was closely associated with this waterway. One can imagine how people's lives were deeply connected to this channel. It seems that these lifestyles were not considered by planners and designers during the planning process. However, in the analysis of the map diagram, they are clearly presented.

3.3.3. Boundary analysis

Regional boundaries serve as tools for defining, demarcating, arranging, and preserving areas, with urban systems comprising both regions and their respective boundaries. In the illustration below, streets and alleys together form the various boundaries within the Nanhuaxi area. These boundaries are clearly visible, connecting, separating, traversing, or penetrating different regions across all scales, thereby linking this area together. However, in reality, not all boundaries are always clearly visible. At times, they only exist on maps, showcasing the power and significance of cartography.

Figure 9. Boundary analysis

In Figure 9, all building textures are isolated, leaving only streets and alleys, revealing the traces of history on the map. Shuzhu Chong becomes clearly visible, and the boundaries of the Pan merchant family's ancestral hall, and the late Qing and early Republic commercial buildings also emerge one by one. The appearance of these boundary lines aligns with the theory of the "fixation line" proposed by Kevin Lynch. "A fixation line is a linearly characterized site that sometimes obstructs the development of settlements. Rivers and city walls often signify the fixed edge of traditional towns. During subsequent development of the settlement area, it forms a line between the inner fringe and the nearest outer fringe. Fixation lines can represent natural features like rivers, man-made features like railways, and even intangible boundaries such as those delineated by local authorities, parish boundaries, or land ownership."

The boundaries of the once-prosperous Haichaung Temple, the Pan family mansion, and the Pan family ancestral hall, as well as the boundaries of the late Qing and early Republic commercial buildings, are still clearly visible on the map, even beneath today's Tongfu Road. This situation can be explained using Kevin Lynch's (1984) "morphological framework" theory. He believes that the "morphological framework is a kind of prior planar feature, topographical contour, or a set of topographical contours, which exerts a morphological influence on subsequent development in terms of consistent planar layout, and often inherits certain features as inherited contours. The morphological framework forms the development pattern of the town's core area, often limiting future development trends. Thus, street and plot patterns have a morphological influence on subsequent development." All these relationships become even clearer with the separation and overlay of map layers.

3.3.4. Accessibility analysis

Accessibility is a critical feature for determining a place's advantage and can also serve as the primary criterion for differentiating entrance and exit roads and identifying suitable nodes. The level of accessibility in a particular location is mainly determined by opportunities for connections between different scales, including getting from one place to another, either quickly or slowly. The more diverse and numerous the road scales connected to a specific regional node, the higher its accessibility degree, and vice versa. Therefore, when a regional node is located on pathways of different scales, its accessibility index is relatively high.

In this topological depth difference map, roads are categorized into primary formal streets, inner streets, secondary inner streets, and alleys (as depicted in Figure 10). Formal streets represent those planned and funded by the government. They can accommodate vehicular traffic. Inner streets, formed due to the original river channel morphology, have reduced traffic capacity compared to formal streets, with a width of about 4-6 meters, and are directly connected to formal streets. Secondary inner streets have a width of 2-4 meters, while alleys are the narrowest channels, approximately 1-2 meters wide. Alleys connect to inner streets, have the weakest traffic capacity, and often lead to dead-ends. From the map, it's evident that along the Shuzhu Chong line (areas circled in black), due to connections to roads of various scales, several nodes emerge. These nodes are also the spots in the regional system with the highest foot traffic and the most goods and information exchange.

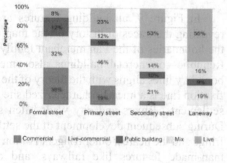

Figure 10. Accessibility analysis   Figure 11. Building Function Type Analysis

4. Research Results

If we refer to the objective phenomenon presented within a system as a "regional phenomenon", there must be various reasons influencing this phenomenon behind the scenes. The phenomenon presented by a specific region should be analyzed by synthesizing various cultural, political, and economic factors. The method of map interpretation aims to reveal hidden phenomena, apply geographical concepts, and connect these hidden phenomena with cultural, political, and economic elements. This enhances our understanding of cities and provides a foundation for their future development.

From the analysis of nodes and connections, it is evident that the phenomena presented by these network factors are influenced by elements like human interaction, goods exchange, and information flow. One could argue that the density of human interaction, goods, and information exchanges within a region will become a significant factor affecting its urban network characteristics. From the accessibility analysis, we observe that the main road nodes in Nanhuaxi are concentrated south of Nanhuaxi Road and south of Tongfu West Road, along the Shuzhu Chong line. These nodes are also where the density of human flow and goods exchange is the highest. It can be deduced that when a region is connected to more roads of diverse scales, its accessibility is higher, making it more likely to form nodes, preparing it for the city's future development.

From the boundary analysis within the region, it is clear that in the process of urbanization, Nanhuaxi's history has been forgotten. Its current state is merely an urban village with some preservation value or soon to be demolished. However, in the boundary interpretation, we can still see traces of Shuzhu Chong and merchant gardens in history, providing strong evidence for the inheritance of the city's regional context. From the density analysis, Nanhuaxi is primarily residential, with the spatial geographical structure developing into three clusters, each evolving from Hai Chuang Temple, Merchant Pan's family, and Merchant Wu's family. The spatial characteristics within these clusters are distinct, with the most communicative space being the Shuzhu Chong node. As a city with a network structure, overlaying today's network nodes with those from the Qing Dynasty's prosperous period reveals a lack of nodes in the Nanhuaxi system (as shown in Figure 12), resulting in a loose network structure, much like a fishing net with many holes. Commerce and information exchange are limited to Shuzhu Chong, Nanhuaxi Road, and Tongfu Road. Hence, for the sustainable development of historical and cultural districts, it's necessary to mend this city net based on its historical context, with the primary condition being the identification of nodes to connect the lines.

The power of map interpretation will provide the conditions and basis for further design and planning. The acquisition of these conditions and bases, that is, using the map as a tool for interpretation, reveals the subtle conditions within a city, recombines them, and thus presents a new world.

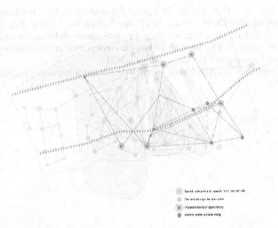

Figure 12. Overlay of present and past network nodes

5. Conclusion

From its inception to today, the development of urban space always follows a logical progression. If urban planners and designers can grasp this deductive logic, they can provide suitable new strategies for the transformation and development of urban spaces. This study aims to demonstrate that map interpretation and urban network, as research tools, can reveal hidden conditions within a city. In doing so, they help decipher the logic behind urban development, laying the groundwork for the city's future growth. Through the method of map interpretation, even if the urban morphology of a certain area gets disrupted during a developmental phase, one can still discern the culural structure revealed throughout the city's development.

During the map translation and interpretation process for Guangzhou's Nanhuaxi historical and cultural district, it was discovered that Nanhuaxi is a region with significant historical and cultural features. It bears the memories of Guangzhou's merchant golden age, once exhibiting the essence of life along its water alleys. However, in today's urbanization process, these historical continuities have been utterly disregarded, leading to the existence of numerous spatially heterogeneous areas today. Faced with these issues, the analytical mode of the mapping system can offer robust evidence and constructive strategies for the city's future direction and development.

References

[1] David Harvey. Explanation in Geography, The Commercial Press, p. 108.A.N. Author, Article title, *Journal Title* **66** (1993), 856–890.
[2] Liu, X., Derudder, B., & Taylor, P. mapping the evolution of hierarchical and regional tendencies in the world city network, 2000–2010. Computers Environment and Urban Systems **43** (2014), 51-66.
[3] Živković, D. Matrix pixel and kernel density analysis from the topographic maps. University Thought - Publication in Natural Sciences **6** (2016), 1, 39-43.
[4] Gudmundsson, A., Mohajeri, N. Entropy and order in urban streets networks. Scientific reports **3** (2013), 3324, 1-7.
[5] Kochan, D. Placing the Urban Village: A Spatial Perspective on the Development Process of Urban Villages in Contemporary China: Placing The Urban Village. Int. J. Urban Reg. **39** (2015), 927–947.
[6] Li, R. and Feng, J. historic conservation area policy and partial shrinkage in an expanding megacity in china: microscale study of 9 jiedao with 14 historic conservation areas in old liwan, guangzhou, china. Journal of Urban Planning and Development, 147, 2021
[7] Liu, Y. space reproduction in urban China: toward a theoretical framework of urban regeneration. Land **11** (2022), 10, 1704.

Design Studies and Intelligence Engineering
L.C. Jain et al. (Eds.)
© 2024 The Authors.
This article is published online with Open Access by IOS Press and distributed under the terms
of the Creative Commons Attribution Non-Commercial License 4.0 (CC BY-NC 4.0).
doi:10.3233/FAIA231474

Product Innovation Design Method Based on System Thinking

Dehui YE[a1], Lingxiao MENG[b2], and Ruikai ZHANG[c3]

ᵃGuilin University of Electronic Technology
ᵇSichuan University of Science & Engineering
ᶜCommunication University of China

Abstract. Aim To propose a product innovation design method based on system thinking. In the conceptual construction stage of product design, in view of the lack of integrity and innovation of design, we use product system thinking to build a combination of innovative design methods to stimulate the design ideas and inspiration of designers, and then better carry out product innovative design. Methods From the four dimensions of social, environmental, human and product in product system thinking, we constructed a combined innovation system of elements, concreted the design elements and substituted them into the combined innovation model, extracted the final design keywords through random shuffling and reorganization, and finally analyzed the acquired terms for design translation, so as to break through the design thinking pattern and establish the innovative design scheme. Results Based on the product system thinking, a new design innovation thinking method was constructed. The design scheme was highly innovative, the element positioning was clear and clear, the method was feasible, and it met the theoretical and practical needs. Conclusion The product innovative design method based on system thinking, taking the specific design practice as an example, has verified the effectiveness of this method, which makes the innovative scheme produce rapidly and have the design systematism at the same time, which opens up the design idea and improves the design originality and innovation.

Keywords. systematic thinking; product system thinking; design thinking; product innovation design method

1. Introduction

With the improvement and development of the design discipline, product design has shifted from only focusing on the design object itself to comprehensively considering the relationship between human behavior, usage scenarios, and technical factors[1]. In the fast-paced era, designers are required to shorten their design cycles while improving their level of design innovation [2]. The perspective of designers has shifted from objects to systems, and products also require systematic thinking to complete research and development [3]. Especially in the context of continuous iteration of artificial

1 Professor, School of Art and Design, Guilin University of Electronic Science and Technology;Guilin;E-mail: yager@sohu.com.

2 Corresponding Author. School of Mechanical Engineering, Sichuan University of Light Industry and Technology, Sichuan; E-mail: 937565608@qq.com.

3 School of Advertising, Communication University of China; Beijing.

intelligence technology, the emergence and development of "design+artificial intelligence" has improved the design efficiency of product system development and standardized the product design process. In the current practice of enterprise product design, on the one hand, enterprise designers are susceptible to the influence of mass-produced products and their own enterprise products; On the other hand, designers are limited by their own personal style and design habits, making it difficult for them to break through personal thinking patterns, making it difficult for enterprises to achieve breakthrough innovation in new product development. Based on this, an innovative design method guided by product system thinking is proposed to assist designers in quickly conducting innovative conceptual design thinking while considering the overall situation.

2. Overview of System Thinking

2.1. Systems and System Thinking

The term "system" comes from ancient Greek and means "set" or "group", referring to an interconnected whole composed of multiple parts. The founder of systems theory, biologist L. V. Beralanfy, believes that "a system is a complex of interconnected and interacting elements" [4]. System thinking is a way of thinking in which people use a system perspective to systematically understand the various aspects and structural functions of objects that are interconnected. Systematic thinking is a holistic approach with flexible and principled characteristics. Its core is the principle of integrity, which requires a global perspective to grasp and handle problems, and flexible disposal methods can be adopted while paying attention to overall benefits and results. The system is organic isomorphism rather than the sum of simple parts, with the characteristic of being greater than the sum of parts. From the perspective of system thinking, exploring the entire system and its constituent elements can better reflect the relevant aspects of system form and structure, and achieve the ideal state of 1+1>2.

2.2 Product Design Based on System Thinking

Systematization is an inevitable result of product design, and establishing a product system design is an inevitable trend in the development of product design. The product system consists of both internal and external systems of the product[5]. The external system of the product refers to the macro system of the product, while the internal system of the product refers to the micro system of the product. Macro system refers to the connection between the product itself and the external environment [6], consisting of social factors, environmental factors, user factors, and product factors; The product elements in the macro system are the micro system of the product, and the micro system refers to the product as a material entity with specific functions, and its internal elements and structures form an independent system[7], composed of the product's functions, structures, materials, colors, and other elements. The micro system and macro system are unified throughout the entire product lifecycle, as shown in Figure 1. The introduction of system thinking in product design is to comprehensively consider the internal and external factors of the product, in order to achieve the optimization of the entire product lifecycle.

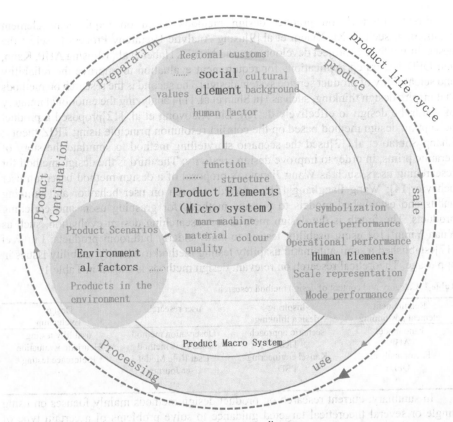

Figure 1. Product system diagram.

The commercial design of products is aimed at the economy, with a greater focus on the market, user research, and actual impact on the company. The conceptual design of products emphasizes the avant-garde nature of design, pursuing scientific and creative design concepts, breaking the constraints of existing materials and technology on design, and enabling product design to reach new heights[8]. For the divergence of design thinking, different combinations of system elements can be utilized based on the actual situation of the project to generate different system effects, in order to achieve innovation in product concepts.

3. Research on Product Design Methods

3.1. Research on Existing Product Design Methods

There are two main types of research on product design methods: design practice methods and design methodology research. The design practice methods mainly focus on specific methods such as biomimetic design, modular design, and combinatorial design. The research on design methodology mainly guides design with methodology theory. Through statistical analysis of the frequency of words related to HowNet, the research mainly includes four aspects:

Firstly, research on product design methods based on requirement element positioning: such as Xu Xiaoqi et al.[9]using Analytic Hierarchy Process to select the best solution for RV project development, and Nicolas Haber et al.[10]using AHP, Kano, and QFD integrated applications for requirement evaluation to improve the reliability and scientificity of product service system design; The second is the research on methods that inspire design thinking, such as Hu Shan et al. [11] analyzing the emotional imagery of wardrobe design to effectively design; Liu Xiaoyong et al. [12]proposed a product perception design method based on the conflict resolution principle using TRIZ theory; Zhang Shutao et al.[13]used the scenario storytelling method to simulate the story of ceramic prints, in order to improve design creativity; The third is the design method for researching users, such as Wang Jiangtao's proposal of a design method based on user behavior[14]; Wang Fangliang[15]conducted research on user behavior and thinking habits and established models to provide methods for grasping users and enriching products. The fourth is the design method for researching design evaluation, such as Yuan Yiran [16] using usability testing to study elderly bathroom products; Liu Wei [17]established a semi-automatic usability testing method to identify usability issues in app usage. Theoretical research on relevant design methods is shown in Table 1.

Table 1. Category and content of design method research

Requirement element positioning	Inspiring design thinking	user research	Design Evaluation
kano model	scenario approach	Observation method	usability testing
AHP	TRIZ	Interview method	Heuristic Evaluation
Factor analysis	Kansei engineering	User Role Model	Preference testing
QFD	PSD	User Journey	...
...	...	...	

In summary, current research on product design methods mainly focuses on using single or several theoretical targeted guidance to solve problems of a certain type of product. Micro systematic research on a specific product from a single dimension, or research on the relationship between users and products, results in limited innovation in product design and a lack of more macro thinking. By using systematic thinking to conduct design research from multiple dimensions, macro elements beyond the product can be included in the design category, making the design completer and more systematic. At the same time, the collision between various dimensional elements can generate new design language, leading to innovation in the design. Therefore, the research on design methods based on product system thinking is also the development and expansion of design thinking inspiration methods.

3.2. Product Design Based on System Thinking

Traditional product design often focuses on the micro system of the product as the research object, which focuses on the structure, materials, colors, textures, and other aspects of the product, lacking systematic design thinking; To present a brand-new situation for the product, it is necessary to start from the four dimensions of the product system. Based on system thinking in product design, designers are required to grasp the system and the whole, and consider the social, environmental, product, and user elements of the product. Based on the product system view, the characteristics of the four elements themselves and their interactions in the system are explored from different aspects, allowing the system to play a better role, thus achieving design breakthroughs and innovation.

The product innovation design method based on system thinking, by fully utilizing the product system, concretizes the macro system elements and micro system elements of the product, and establishes a product system entry library; By using computer software to shuffle and recombine the design entries of the term library, specific entries under each element of the product system are randomly extracted and combined to obtain sentences that break through conventional thinking; Through the interpretation and translation of sentences, an innovative conceptual solution for the product is ultimately obtained. The process architecture of product innovation design method based on system thinking is shown in Figure 2.

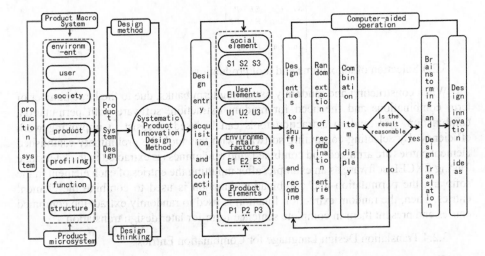

Figure.2 Framework of element combination innovation method based on system thinking

3.2.1 Design term description and collection

In the early stages of design, establish product system elements based on product system thinking and consider the logical relationships between system elements. By concretizing the content of social elements, environmental elements, product elements, and user elements in the product system, and considering the content of the four elements, specific term descriptions are provided to obtain keywords. At this stage, it is necessary to ensure the quantity and quality of specific entries. The number of key words obtained determines the number of entries to be combined in the later stage. The more element entries are obtained, the more direction they can provide for exploration. Only when the vocabulary is sufficiently concrete can innovative scenarios be combined, which in turn affects the quality of design language translation.

3.2.2 Construction of term bank and combination of term randomness extraction

The construction of a term bank is based on the acquisition of keywords, and through the acquisition of element keywords, the final generation of the element term bank is achieved. The element term library needs to classify and display the terms of the four elements of society, user, environment, and product within the product system, as shown in Table 2.

Table 2. Classified display of various elements

social element	User Elements	Environmental	Product
S1	U1	E1	P1
S2	U2	E2	P2
S3	U3	E3	P3
...	...	...	...
Sn	Un	En	Pn

$$total = \begin{bmatrix} S1 & U1 & E1 & P1 \\ S1 & U2 & E1 & P1 \\ S1 & U1 & E2 & P1 \\ S1 & U1 & E1 & P2 \\ S1 & U3 & E1 & P1 \\ S1 & U1 & E3 & P2 \\ ... & ... & ... & ... \\ Sn & Un & En & Pn \end{bmatrix} = Sn*Un*En*Pn$$

3.2.3 Selection of algorithms and tool production

When constructing and randomly extracting term banks, due to the large number of term combinations and the need for random extraction, software with permutation, combination, and random extraction tools can be used to assist in improving work efficiency. By selecting computing software with this tool, the preliminary established element entries are arranged and combined, and randomness is extracted in the later stage. Taking EXCEL software as an example, after inputting the entries of each element in the software, the permutation and combination function is used to combine the element entries. Then, the random extraction function is used to randomly extract the combined entries and present them in complete sentence form for later design translation.

3.2.4 Translation Design Language for Combination Entries

The complete sentences formed by different keyword combinations can be translated into design language, providing reference for design. Firstly, it is necessary to analyze and judge the rationality of the extracted statement; Secondly, from the perspective of design thinking, describe and express the design language of the usage environment, crowd characteristics, design points, and product functional elements. By comparing and evaluating multiple randomly extracted sentences, obtain reasonable innovative design points; Finally, feasibility analysis is conducted on the design points to evaluate the practicality of the design, and innovative design concepts are ultimately obtained.

3.2.5 Output of design innovation ideas

After obtaining a new design concept, the designer conducts a new design positioning based on the innovative concept and uses conventional product design assistance tools to design sketches, models, and product solutions.

4. Application of Product Innovation Design Method Based on System Thinking

4.1. Collection and display of product system element entries

This method is an innovative design method based on obtaining many product system element entries. Firstly, it is necessary to collect vocabulary descriptions for each element, which are generally nouns, such as "sharing economy", "elderly people", "seats", etc. The product system elements are divided into four elements: society, users, environment, and product. "Society" corresponds to social phenomena, "users" corresponds to user groups, "environment" corresponds to specific environments or scenarios, and "product" corresponds to different types of products. Through offline brainstorming, the four elements were transformed into specific vocabulary, and 36 vocabulary items were collected, including 9 vocabulary items for "social elements", 9 vocabulary items for "user elements", 9 various scenarios under "environmental elements", and 9 specific products under "product elements". Based on this, a vocabulary library was established and classified for display, as shown in Table 3.

Table.3 Classified display element library

Social	User	Environmental	Product
emission reduction	single women	Station	Seat
share economy	Office workers	kitchen	Storage
Two child policy	Delivery staff	Park	Tableware
be a vegetarian	Blind	scenic spot	fitness
single-parent family	Pupil	teaching building	Kitchenware
Double reduction policy	old people	Supermarket	Knapsack
Aging	college student	outdoors	Entertainment
Slimming	the disabled	Mall	Travel
COVID-19	left-behind children	hospital	mask

4.2. Design word combination display and random extraction

Based on the vocabulary of the term bank, classify, and organize vocabulary, and present data and arrange and combine the elements of the term, facilitating later brainstorming and design translation. Since the term library has 9 entries each under the four elements of "society", "user", "environment", and "product", totaling 36 entries. With the assistance of the permutation and combination function in Excel, the total number of combinations and all entries are displayed. Through the operation, a total of 6561 permutation and combination entries are obtained, which can be displayed in the software, as shown in Figure 3. Then, randomly extract 10 combined item data through a random extraction function, as shown in Table 4, and display Table 4 using design language to obtain 10 design statements, as shown in Table 5.

Figure.3 Schematic diagram of EXCEL auxiliary operation

Table.4 Random extraction combination

number	Combined results			
	Social	user	environment	products
1	Vegetarian background	Office workers	station	seat
2	Sharing Economy	university student	market	knapsack
3	COVID-19	pupil	teaching building	tableware
4	emission reduction	old people	kitchen	Storage
5	emission reduction	Disabled people	supermarket	entertainment
6	Second child policy	pupil	park	knapsack
7	COVID-19	Office workers	station	mask
8	emission reduction	Didi Driver	outdoors	body building
9	Weight loss background	blind	supermarket	tableware
10	Second child policy	pupil	supermarket	seat

Table.5 Design language display

number	Design statement
1	Seating products designed for office workers in a vegetarian setting for use at stations
2	Backpack products designed for college students in the context of the sharing economy and used in shopping malls
3	Tableware designed for primary school students in the context of the COVID-19 and used in the teaching building
4	Storage products designed for elderly people in the kitchen under the background of energy conservation and emission reduction
5	Entertainment products designed for disabled people in supermarkets under the background of energy conservation and emission reduction
6	Backpack products designed for primary school students in the context of the second child policy and used in parks
7	Respirator products designed for office workers and used in stations in the context of the COVID-19
8	A fitness product designed for Didi drivers to use outdoors in the context of energy conservation and emission reduction
9	Tableware products designed for blind people in the context of weight loss and used in supermarkets
10	Seat products designed for primary school students in the context of the second child policy and used in supermarkets

4.3. Design Analysis and Design Translation

Discuss and brainstorm design sentences based on random combinations, translate the sentences into design, and generate new product systems and design ideas. Since this method considers various aspects of the product from the perspective of system thinking, preliminary analysis is mainly conducted from three aspects: crowd characteristics, design points, and design priorities when designing and analyzing sentences. As shown in the first item of Table 5, "Seats designed for office workers to use at stations in a vegetarian context." Firstly, consider the characteristics of office workers who eat vegetarian food. This user may pay more attention to diet and a healthy lifestyle. To design seats for use at stations, it is possible to add health detection functions or time passing functions to public seats. Based on this, all ten items in Table 5 were analyzed and designed for translation, as shown in Table 6.

Table.6 Design Translation Table

| number | Design Analysis and Translation | | |
	Population Characteristics	Design points	Product Focus
1	Pay attention to diet and a healthy life	Passing time and taking a short break at the station	Health detection function, leisure and entertainment function
2	Pursuing trends and accepting new things	Shopping packaging and sharing products	Shared backpack, mall use
3	Curiosity, fun, and destructive	School is easy to use, not easy to break, and anti infection	Material not easily damaged, epidemic prevention function, safety and hygiene
4	Slow action and high forgetfulness	Health protection, food storage, environmental protection	Food storage reminder, health reminder, storage function
5	Neglecting people with disabilities	Supermarket population, supermarket imports and exports	Parent-child interaction, low-carbon products
6	Curiosity and fun	Daily backpack function, for two people to use	Dual use, growth function, entertainment function
7	Pursuing novelty and a healthy lifestyle	May be used at bus stops	Anti haze, anti mask makeup
8	Sitting for a long time, being alone, and making phone calls while cycling	Leisure, exercise, entertainment needs	Environmentally friendly and pollution-free, entertainment function
9	Population characteristics	Design points	Product Focus
10	Curiosity and fun	Import and export in supermarkets, entertainment needs	Dual use, entertainment function

Due to the randomness of the arrangement and combination, not every design statement produced is entirely reasonable. Taking the 10 randomly extracted statements mentioned above as an example, there are 2 completely unreasonable statements, such as "entertainment products designed for blind people in the kitchen in the context of a single parent family". "Single parents" and "blind people" are not closely related, and at the same time, kitchen entertainment products should be designed for them, although innovative, but not practical, Therefore, this sentence was discarded and re extracted. Some unreasonable statements, such as the fifth clause above: "The background of energy conservation and emission reduction is designed for disabled people and entertainment products used in supermarkets." Disabled people are not very reasonable in the combination, so they can be ignored, directly thinking about the entertainment products used in supermarkets, and reverse inference can be used to design entertainment products shared by multiple people. The total number of times the above extraction was 12, and 10 available data were obtained. Unreasonable statements accounted for 16% of the total extraction; A total of 2 unreasonable items account for 16% and can be temporarily retained. The process of collective brainstorming and design language analysis is shown in Figure 4.

Figure.4 Collective brainstorming and design language analysis

4.4. Design Analysis and Design Translation

Based on the 10 design directions of the above translation, select feasible design translation questions for design development. Through collective sketch deduction, starting from the fourth article "Designing storage products for elderly people in the kitchen under the background of energy conservation and emission reduction" that is suitable for design output, a conceptual design sketch for this topic is provided for elderly users, as shown in Figure 5.

Figure.5 Collective sketch deduction

Firstly, design and investigate the lifestyle habits, behavioral patterns, and psychological characteristics of elderly users: in terms of lifestyle habits, most elderly people live alone, and they often independently complete their shopping and cooking; In terms of behavioral patterns, the elderly are slow to move, forgetful, and advocate frugality; In terms of physical characteristics, various bodily functions decrease. According to research, elderly people often consume spoiled food due to improper storage or forgetting the shelf life of various types of food in the kitchen, which can lead to health hazards or poisoning. From this perspective, design an intelligent storage cabinet for the elderly to help them better store food.

Based on research and conceptualization, use design tools to establish a model to obtain the final design. In terms of design, modular design is adopted to increase space utilization, accurately frame disinfection and sterilization, and reduce energy consumption to achieve the goal of energy conservation and emission reduction; In terms of user behavior, considering the physical behavioral characteristics of the elderly, intelligent voice and lighting colors are used for reminders; The internal space is designed with different sized partitions to store different types of food. The final design rendering of the storage cabinet is shown in Figure 6; Detail diagram, see Figure 7; Use scenario diagram, as shown in Figure 8.

Figure.6 Design rendering of lockers

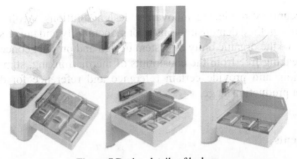

Figure.7 Design details of lockers

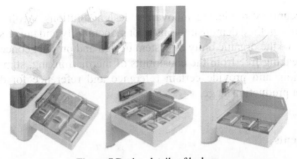

Figure.8 Use Scenarios of Lockers

5. Key points for method attention

By combining and innovating the description terms of product system elements, innovative conceptual designs can be obtained. However, in practical application, this method still has some uncontrollable factors that need further improvement. Firstly, when collecting description terms for element elements, the quality and quantity of terms will have an impact on later work. On the one hand, influenced by the descriptor's cognition, values, and design thinking, the subjective limitations on the quality of collected entries are strong, which will have a certain impact on later combination and translation. Therefore, in order to ensure the quality of entries, multiple people need to brainstorm and discuss to ensure the quality of the entries obtained in the early stage. On the other hand, the number of entries should not be too small to avoid having too few designable concepts points due to the small number of combined entries during random extraction and translation in the later stage; Secondly, the feasibility of the translated design items has only been preliminarily analyzed. If design output is to be carried out, further in-depth research is still needed on the combined items, fully investigating user characteristics and behavior patterns, user demand satisfaction, product technology and economy, and other aspects. Then, design output is carried out to ensure design quality.

6. Conclusion

In the process of product design, using only traditional methods for design practice can easily lead to innovation difficulties and incomplete product considerations. In this article, systematic thinking is used to innovate the combination of design elements, forming descriptive sentences that break through conventional ideas. This allows for multi-dimensional understanding of design objects, design thinking and research on products, making product design more systematic and more conducive to designers quickly and accurately producing innovative design solutions. At the same time, the application of this method demonstrates its strong operability and universal effectiveness, which can achieve the organic unity of system design and product concept output, assist designers in breaking free from the constraints of inertia thinking, stimulate innovative design inspiration, and provide certain reference and reference for designers in the product concept production stage.

Acknowledgments

Project No. JGY2021086 Project Name: Reform and Research on the Teaching Mode of the Art Master's Studio Connecting to the Second Classroom

References

[1] HUANG Yanqun, GAO Yige, SHENG Tianmeng, et al. X-ray instrument appearance design based on interactive system design theory. Mechanical Design, 2015, 32 (10): 126-128.
[2] DENG Weibin, WANG Tongtong, YE Hang. Product innovative design method based on parametric thinking. Packaging Engineering, 2022, 43 (08): 76-84.
[3] WANG Haoqi, LI Hao, WEN Xiaoyu, et al. Ontology-driven design information reuse framework for complex product systems. Computer Integrated Manufacturing System, 2021, 27 (06): 1662-1672.
[4] Francesco Tramonti, Franco Giorgi, Annibale Fanali. General system theory as a framework for biopsychosocial research and practice in mental health. Systems Research and Behavioral Science, 2019, 36(3); 332-341.
[5] ZHAO Hong, HUANG Bin. Object-oriented design method from the perspective of system theory. Journal of Systems Science, 2007 (02): 40-42.
[6] ZHANG Yuhong. Product system design [M]. Beijing: People's Post and Telecommunications Press, 2014.
[7] XIE Changyu. Design research and practice of AC charging pile based on product system thinking. Changsha: Hunan University, 2020.
[8] MENG Chuang. Research on sustainable design strategy in product conceptual design. Packaging Engineering, 2014, 35 (02): 81-83.
[9] XU Xiaoqi, CHENG Yongsheng, CHEN Guoqiang. Research on evaluation method and application of RV shape based on AHP method. Mechanical Design, 2020, 37 (06): 140-144.
[10] Nicolas Haber,Mario Fargnoli,Tomohiko Sakao.Integrating QFD for product-service systems with the Kano model and fuzzy AHP.Total Quality Management & Business Excellence,2020,31(9/10):929-954.
[11] HU Shan, FU Kaijie, JIANG Xu, et al. Wardrobe design based on perceptual engineering. Journal of Forestry Engineering, 2021, 6 (04): 176-183.
[12] LIU Xiaoyong, WU Xiaoling, LI Rongli, et al. Research on product perception design method based on TRIZ conflict resolution principle. Mechanical Design, 2021, 38 (10): 136-144.
[13] ZHANG Shutao, REN Zilin, SU Jianning, et al. Image design of ceramic printmaking based on scene story method. Packaging Engineering, 2019, 40(08): 28-33.
[14] WANG Jiangtao, HE renke. Research and application of smart home product design method based on user behavior[J]. Packaging Engineering, 2021, 42 (12): 142-148.
[15] WANG Fangliang, LI Liquan. Product design method based on user behavior habits. Journal of Nanjing Academy of Arts (Fine Arts and Design), 2016 (01): 205-209.
[16] YUAN Yiran. Usability test and design thinking for elderly bathroom products. Design, 2020,33 (05): 124-127.
[17] LIU Wei, LIU Zhengjie. A semi-automatic usability testing method for mobile APP. Packaging Engineering, 2022, 43(02): 122-131.

Design Studies and Intelligence Engineering
L.C. Jain et al. (Eds.)
© 2024 The Authors.
doi:10.3233/FAIA231475

595

Characteristics of Co-Design in the Context of Social Innovation

Zhi GUAN[a] and Yue QIU [a,1]

[a] *School of Design &Arts, Beijing Institute of Technology*

Abstract. The purpose of this study is to explore the characteristics of co-design methods in the context of design for social innovation, to expand the application scope of co-design methods and enrich their connotations. Using Citespace literature quantitative analysis tool to construct knowledge maps and summarizes the research hotspots of co-design in domestic and foreign. Dividing social innovation into 4 contexts: Local Culture, Community Construction, Public Welfare care, and Public Service. The Nvivo text grounded coding tool is used to extract the theme characteristics of the 4 contexts and commonly used co-deign methods. Ten application characteristics of co-deign in different contexts of social innovation are obtained, which deepens the theoretical basis of co-deign methods and provides a reference for co-deign research in social innovation and other fields.

Keywords. Co-design, Design for Social innovation, Knowledge map, Coding analysis, Characteristics

1. Introduction

Collaboration is not a new topic. Collaborative behavior is a genetic attribute of all social animals, which has always accompanied human existence and continues to evolve with the development of social, economic, technological, political systems and other factors [1]. Entering the post-industrial era, open digital platforms have broken through the limitations of physical dimensions, providing individuals with opportunities to actively participate in the design and production process. Design, as an intrinsic driving force in this historical transition period, its collaboration and participation are constantly being explored and stimulated, gradually developing co-design theory. In recent years, design research on social issues has become richer, and many emerging design directions have emerged. Among them, Design for Social Innovation (DSD has received growing attention in the design field. Co-design, as the core design strategy of DSl, runs through its en-tire development process. Meanwhile, the DSI also provides a platform for co-design to explore new directions and becomes a source of power for promoting the development of co-design. Therefore, exploring the application characteristics of co-design methods in the context of DSI helps us better understand the connotation of co-design and enriches the application category and theoretical system of this method. Characteristics of co-design methods in the context of DSI helps us better understand the

---
[1] Corresponding Author: Qiu Yue, School of Design and Art, Beijing Institute of Technology Number: 13701079091 Email: qiuyue@ bit.edu.cn Postal Code: 102488.

connotation of co-design and enriches the application category and theoretical system of this method.

2. Development of Co-design Theory

The concept of co-design originated in the Scandinavian region in the 1970s and rose in the field of computers. Initially called participatory design, which has a strong political color. Then it developed rapidly in the fields of business and management. Prahala[2] and others proposed that in emerging economies, the co-creation experience of consumers becomes the basis of value. Since then, the boundaries of co-design have been continuously expanded. Sanders[3] proposed the concept of fuzzy front end' from the perspective of co-design tools and methods: allowing participants to participate in the early exploration stage of innovation activities, thereby influencing the design that has not yet appeared. Manzini[4] defined co-design from the perspective of DSI as: a vast and multifaceted social dialogue between individuals and collectives, where participants initiate design actions at various nodes of their social networks.

By combing through the development process of co-design, it can be found that the depth and breadth in co-design gradually deepen and expand with the changes in social development, and penetrate into various fields of society at present, becoming one of the important method to resolve social contradictions and promote social development.

3. Hotspots and Frontier Trends of Co-design methods in Design field

3.1. Hotspots of Co-design in Design field

This study uses academic papers related to co-design in two Chinese journals, *Packaging Engineering* and *ZhuangShi*, and three foreign journals, *Design Studies*, *Design Issues*, and *CoDesign*, over the past decade as data sources, resulting in 255 valid domestic sample documents and 269 valid foreign sample documents. Using the information visualization tool CiteSpace, a keyword co-occurrence map of domestic and foreign co-design research literature is generated, resulting in 7 clustering nodes domestically and 9 clustering nodes abroad, as shown in Figure 1. The nodes of the keyword co-occurrence network are summarized and integrated to extract 6 main research hotspots.

Cluster 1: Design education.including thinking and methods.scholars combine co-design with the education system, using workshop discussions, interdisciplinary cooperation, and other methods to stimulate students' initiative and creativity, fostering a sense of collaboration in practice[5]. Cluster 2: Service Design, including public services and service systems. Co-design appears in the form of co-creation in service encounters, establishing a service system based on the interaction and collaboration between service providers and recipients[6]. Cluster 3: Architectural Design, including community design and urban planning. Co-design was widely applied in the fields of architecture and planning at the end of the 20th century. The community has become the most focused object, based on a group of people with similar values and high interaction, to carry out the design of community facilities, spaces, and services[7]. Cluster 4:

Interaction Design, including user experience and smart homes. The co-design of interactive design is a systematic project, which includes collaboration between users and design team, collaboration among information technologies, people with interaction methods[8]. Cluster5: Collaborative Innovation, including design management and school-enterprise cooperation. As a design management model and strategy, co-design integrates and allocates advantageous resources between enterprises and teams to build an ecosystem of collaborative innovation and improve the efficiency and success of enterprise [9]. Cluster 6:Design for Social Innovation (DSD, including clusters such as culture, community, and rural areas, this direction pays attention to changes in lifestyle, using co-design to creatively combine existing social resources, services, and knowledge to create new social relationships or lifestyle[10].

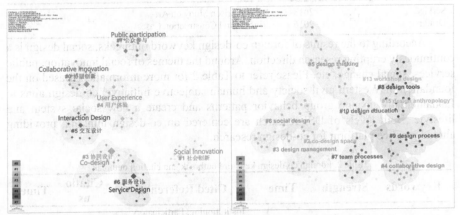

Figure 1. The cluster diagram of keywords in co-design research

Based on the content of the above clusters, there are two commonalities in the research of co-design at the theoretical level : (1) The coordination and integration features of co-design are reflected in different fields. (2) Most areas emphasise the cultivation of subjective initiative and collaborative consciousness for role participation. At the practical level, there are significant differences in the application of objects, tools of co-design in various fields. The form content is rich and diverse, and the relevance and commonality between various fields are not very clear.

3.2. Frontier Trends of Co-design in Design Field

Using Citespace's keyword outbreak detection and highly cited literature to explore the frontier trends of co-design research at domestic and foreign. DSI is a research direction that has been continuously erupting in co-design in recent years. The theme words revolve around rural areas, communities, intangible cultural heritage, service design, etc. Please refer to Table 1 for more information. Based on the political strategic background of Chinese poverty alleviation and people's livelihood construction, co-design has pro.posed innovative solutions to complex social problems such as rural revitalization and aging.

Table 1. Domestic co-design keyword outbreak and high-heat literature

Keywords	Strength	Time	Cited References	Citations	Time
Design for Social Innovation	2.82	2017-2022	Collaborative Design "Trigger" Revival of Traditional Community: Case Study on Design Research and Practice of "New Channel · HuaYaoHua" Project on Intangible Cultural Heritage	69	2016
Artificial Intelligence	2.10	2019-2020	Tacit Knowledge: The Microscopic Perspective of Design Innovation Research on Traditional Crafts	58	2015
Service Design	1.47	2013-2016	A Comparison Study on Art-driven Rural Construction Cases	54	2018

According to the results of foreign co-design keyword outbreaks, social design is a continuously erupting research direction. Around the themes of social innovation, public services, social change, etc. Please refer to Table 2 for more information. Based on the foundation of Western civil society and human subjective initiative, co-design aims to fundamentally change group behavior patterns and create a new social system and lifestyle. Both levels of DSI research are centered on co-design thinking, providing abroad practice platform for co-design research.

Table 2. Foreign co-design keyword outbreak and citation outbreak

Keywords	Strength	Time	Cited References	Citations	Time
Social design	2.19	2020-2022	Institutioning: Participatory Design, Co-Design and the public realm	3.38	2020-2023
Design method	1.92	2021-2022	Design, when everybody designs: An introduction to design for social innovation	2.99	2018-2019
Design anthropology	1.71	2021-2022	Democratic design experiments: between parliament and laboratory	1.88	2018-2019

4. Characteristics of Co-design in the Context of Design for Social Innovation

4.1 The Relationship between Design for Social Innovation and Co-design

Looking at the development process of DSI, it can be divided into three stages: (1) From the 1970s to the 1980s, design was used to meet the survival needs of the underprivileged. Papaneck[11]proposed design for the disadvantaged". (2) From the 1990s to the early 21st century, design provided public services for the middle class. Bovaird[12] emphasized the necessity, importance, and good practical effects of the public as end-users participating in public services. (3) From the 2010s to the present, design builds collaborative relationships for social transformation. Mancini[13] proposed that DSI is an activity in the co-design process aimed at changing society.

With the widespread application of information and communication technology, the social structure has shifted from traditional hierarchical to interconnected distributed. Co-design has become the research foundation and core means of DSI. At the same time.

DSI a comprehensive discipline that includes sociology, natural sciences, management design, and other fields. The research of this discipline can promote the reshaping of social structure and lifestyle. Its values and methodology are universal, which can guide the development direction of various disciplines from the source, and then stimulate the leapfrog development of co-design method research in various fields.

At present, research and practice on co-design in the context of DSI show a situation of small sample size, large dispersion, mixed application scenarios, and multiple methods. It has not yet formed a unified, systematic application characteristics and theoretical system.

Therefor, this study adopts a case study method, using the DSI case collection, DESIS network projects and relevant literature as sample sources. A total of 101 social innovation cases are collected. Based on factors such as project completeness, representativeness, and richness, 40 social innovation cases were selected as the research foundation. The NVIVO text grounded coding software is used to count the 269 instances of collaborative design methods in social innovation cases. Similar design methods are sorted and integrated based on semantic similarity and type, resulting in a total of 20 design tools and methods.Please refer to Figure 2 for more information.

According to the research classification of DSI cases by the DESIS network and the research hotspot classification of DSI literature by Jiang Yuhao[14], can be divided into 4 main themes: Local Culture, Community Construction, Public Welfare, and Public Service. 10 cases are selected for each theme, and data such as background, roles, and project structure are extracted to summarize the characteristics of each theme. A cross-matrix analysis is conducted on the correlation between theme characteristics and 20 co-design methods. The correlations between co-design methods and different theme characteristics are explored. Further, the application characteristics of co-design methods in different DSI contexts are defined.

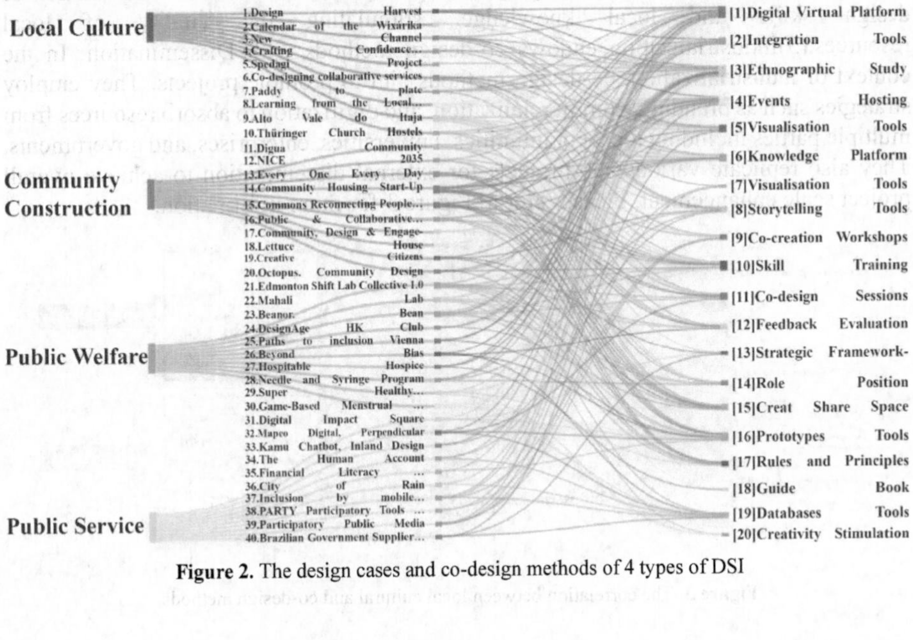

Figure 2. The design cases and co-design methods of 4 types of DSI

4.2. Characteristics of Co-design in Local Culture DSI Context

Local culture DSI cases often use traditional technology as resources to revitalize and revive traditional communities through co-design methods[15]. By encoding and analyzing cases 1-10, 3 high-frequency features of local culture cases are obtained: (1) Localization. Localization is based on the mutual integration between local cultural resources and non-local design teams, and carries out design practice activities. There are 8 types of main co-design methods, including participatory video, ethnographic study , storytelling, etc. (2) Activation. Activation. Activation combines professional design skills with local skills in an innovative way to enhance their value.There are 7 types of main co-design methods, including knowledge platform, skill training, co-creation workshop, etc. (3) Industrialization. Industrialization aims at introducing more local and non-local forces to promote the construction of a collaborative innovation network and achieve multi-party benefits[16]. There are 5 types of main co-design methods, including strategic framework, digital virtual platform, guide book, etc.

According to the correlation between the 3 local cultural context characteristics of "Localization", "Activation", "Industrialization" and the 20 co-design methods, 3 application characteristics of co-design methods can be derived: (1) Localization endows co-design methods with Experientiality: In the context of localization, co-design methods aim to integrate into the local culture, establish various participation channels, and experience and feel local culture from all aspects, helping designers discover problems from a local internal perspective. (2) Activation endows co-design methods with Interactivity: In the context of activation, the co-design method aims for knowledge exchange. It establishes an intercommunicating and integrating "knowledge community" between designers and local culture holders through forms such as visualization, gamification, and contextualization[17]. This promotes the innovative combination of design skills and local knowledge, stimulating the vitality of local resources.(3)Industrialization endows co-design methods with Dissemination: In the context of industrialization, co-design methods aim to promote projects. They employ strategies such as branding, commercialization, and digitization to absorb resources from multiple parties including local communities, universities, enterprises, and governments. They also replicate various sub-projects for external dissemination to achieve overall project scale enhancement. Please refer to Figure 3 for more information.

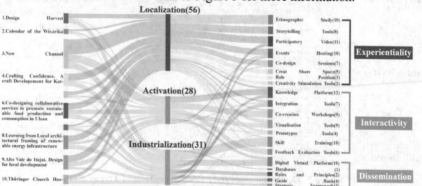

Figure 3. The correlation between local cultural and co-design methods

4.3. Characteristics of Co-design in Community Construction DSI Context

Community construction DSI cases often take urban communities as research objects, support community self-governance activities through co-design methods, and carry out community updates from aspects such as space, management, and services. By encoding and analyzing cases 10-20, 2 high-frequency features of community construction cases are obtained: (1) Sharing. Sharing aims to democratically collect individualized needs within the community. Through co-construction and co-creation, a solution for community resource sharing is coordinated and integrated, which address the complexity of community needs and the difficulty for government resources to cover comprehensively.There are 7 types of main co-design methods, including create share space, events hosting, integration tools, etc. (2) Self-governing. Self-governing aims to enhance the cohesion and self-organizational management capabilities of the community, form a structured organizational model, and achieve long-term sustainable operation of the community[18]. There are 10 types of main co-design methods, including rules and principles, skill training, feedback evaluation tools, etc.

According to the correlation between the 2 community construction context characteristics of "Sharing", "Self-governing" and the 20 co-design methods, 2 application characteristics of co-design methods can be derived: (1) Sharing endows co-design methods with Integrality:In the context of sharing, the co-design methods aim to meet diverse needs. Using idea cards, analogy cards, voting choices, and other methods to fairly screen and integrate a large number of ideas and creativity. It converges and focuses on a unified direction, and through joint deliberation, optimizes the best solution. (2) Self-governing endows co-design methods with Directionality: In the context of Self-governing, the co-design methods aim to cultivate the autonomous capabilities of community participants. Designers guide residents to independently formulate rules and regulations, agree on role division, and through regular seminars, community activities, service platforms, and other methods, help residents gradually break away from dependence on external teams and form a dynamic, flexible self-organizing management structure. Please refer to Figure 4 for more information.

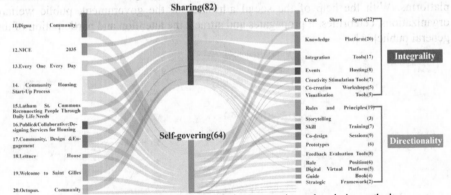

Figure 4. The correlation between community construction and co-design methods

4.4 Characteristics of Co-design in Public Welfare DSI Context

Public welfare DSI cases often take disadvantaged groups as research objects. Through the co-design method, they are transformed from passive recipients of social welfare into active participants, in order to form an equal and mutually beneficial service model[19]. By encoding and analyzing cases 21-30, 3 high-frequency features of community construction cases are obtained: (1) Humanization. Humanization aims to address the special psychological or physiological needs of disadvantaged groups. It establishes a trust relationship with these groups through empathetic, indirect, and inclusive forms of interaction. There are 6 types of main co-design methods, including storytelling, visualisation tools, events hosting,etc. (2) Equalization. Equalization aims to uncover the potential subject capabilities of disadvantaged groups, provide them with a platform and carrier for realization, and construct a service model of equal and mutually beneficial relationships[20]. There are 7 types of main co-design methods, including skill training, role position, rules and principles, etc. (3) Popularization. Popularization focuses on the reach of disadvantaged groups to the outside world, constructs a platform for the public to interact with them, and promotes the public's cognitive transformation towards disadvantaged groups.There are 7 types of main co-design methods, including digital virtual platform, guide book, prototypes, etc.

According to the correlation between the 3 community construction context characteristics of "Humanization", "Equalization","Popularization"and the 20 co-design methods, 3 application characteristics of co-design methods can be derived: (1) Humanization endows co-design methods with Perceptivity. In the context of humanization, the co-design methods aim at communication and understanding. In a shared scenario and through collaborative interaction, it enhances the trust of vulnerable groups in the outside world. This helps designers indirectly perceive and understand the characteristics and needs. (2) Equalization endows co-design methods with Empowerment. In the context of equalization, the co-design methods aim to unearth strengths and cultivate abilities. Through cooperative forms such as reward mechanisms and educational interactions, it stimulates the inherent potential of vulnerable groups. Moreover, it enhances the use value through design interventions, achieving self-creation of welfare. (3) Popularization endows co-design methods with Inspiration. In the context of popularization, the co-design method aims to call for dissemination. It strengthens the sense of public welfare experience and connection through online and offline interactive platforms. With the help of the social attributes of the government, public welfare organizations, celebrities, it propagates and attracts the attention and participation of the general public[21].

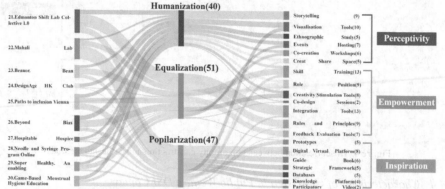

Figure 5. The correlation between public welfare and co-design methods

4.5 Characteristics of Co-design in Public Service DSI Context

Public service DSI cases are often initiated in a top-down manner, with co-design methods mainly intervening from the strategic and decision-making levels, providing timely, fair and effective social services for the public. By encoding and analyzing cases 31-40, 2 high-frequency features of community construction cases are obtained: (1) Networking. Networking aims to design and build a flexible, open, and comprehensive distributed network structure to cover a large area of the public. There are 9 types of main co-design methods, including strategic framework, rules and principles, databases, etc. (2) Diversifying. Diversifying aims to attract the government, the public, experts, news media,enterprises and institutions, social organizations, and other social subjects to participate in, consult and make decisions on public affairs together, so as to achieve continuous and healthy development of the relationship between the government and the public.and realize good governance of the society by the government[22]. There are 8 types of main co-design methods, including , digital virtual platform, knowledge platform, events hosting,etc.

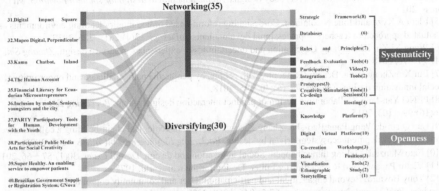

Figure 6. The correlation between public service and co-design methods

According to the correlation between the 2 community construction context characteristics of "Networking", "Diversification"and the 20 co-design methods, 2 application characteristics of co-design methods can be derived: (1) Networking endows co-design methods with Systematicity. In the context of networking, co-design methods aim to coordinate planning, through creative resource reorganization and global framework formulation, to expand the overall scale of the system and service range. (2) Diversifying endows co-design methods with openness. In a context of diversifying, co-design methods aim to expand and be compatible, using digital tools to promote the establishment of an open consultation platform for democratic dialogue. Through organizational patterns, they integrate and coordinate into a dynamic, balanced collective collaboration mechanism to achieve effective expression of individual will.

5. Conclusion

This study is based on the characteristics of four thematic contexts of DSI, using NVIVO text grounded coding software to analyze the application features of co-design in DSI cases, and summarizes 10 application features of co-design in the context of DSI: experientiality, interactivity, dissemination, integrality, directionality, perceptivity, empowerment, inspiration, systematicity and openness. It helps people to understand the research characteristics of co-design in the context of DSI from a more intuitive and systematic perspective in practice and methodology, and provides a systematic collaborative theoretical method for the discipline of DSI. These characteristics and research methods obtained above have certain universality and replicability, which expands the application category of co-design methods. It promotes the connection and communication between co-design and various disciplines, deepens the theoretical basis of co-design methods.

References

[1] Gary Alan Fine. Together: The rituals, pleasures, and politics of cooperation-about richard sennett, together: The rituals, pleasures, and politics of cooperation (new haven, yale university press, 2012). *European Journal of Sociology/Archives Europ´eennes de Sociologie*, 53(3):372 – 375, 2012.

[2] Coimbatore K Prahalad and Venkat Ramaswamy. Co-creating unique value with customers. *Strategy & leadership*, 32(3):4 – 9, 2004.

[3] Elizabeth B-N Sanders and Pieter Jan Stappers. Co-creation and the new landscapes of design. *Co-design*, 4(1):5 – 18, 2008.

[4] Ezio Manzini. Design, when everybody designs: *An introduction to design for social innovation*. MIT press, 2015.

[5] Eleni A Kyza and Iolie Nicolaidou. Co-designing reform-based online inquiry learning environments as a situated approach to teachers' professional development. *CoDesign*, 13(4):261 – 286, 2017.

[6] Wang Xi Xin Xiang-yang. Co-creation and uncertainties of experiences in service design. *Zhuang Shi*, (4):74 – 76, 2018.

[7] Liu Xin Zhong Fang. Design for people, with people, by people:the path, challenge and opportunity of social innovation design. *Zhuang Shi*, (5):40 – 45, 2018.

[8] PENG Yan-fang. Collaborative design of product interaction design system. *Packaging Engineering*, 36(16):99 – 103, 2015.

[9] Luo Quan-deWang Pang Bao-shu, Zhang Xiao-gang. Xiaomi. ecological chain-building a collaborative innovation development ecosystem driven by design. *Packaging Engineering*, 44(4):288 – 295, 2023.

[10] Ezio Manzini. Making things happen: Social innovation and design. *Design issues*, 30(1):57 – 66, 2014.

[11] Victor Papanek and R Buckminster Fuller. Design for the real world. 1972.

[12] Tony Bovaird. Beyond engagement and participation: User and community coproduction of public services. *Public administration review*, 67(5):846 – 860, 2007.

[13] Ezio Manzini and Francesca Rizzo. Small projects/large changes: Participatory design as an open participated process. *CoDesign*, 7(3-4):199 – 215, 2011.

[14] He Ren-ke Jiang Yu-hao, Chen Yong-kang. Analysis on the research progress of social innovation design. *Packaging Engineering*, 42(24):222 – 229, 2021.

[15] Zhang Duoduo Yang Yuanyuan, Ji Tie. Design and application of traditional culture in children's educational games:taking the logic huayao design practice as an example. *Zhuang Shi*, (12):78 – 81, 2018.

[16] YIN Ai-mu WANG Bao-sheng. A comparison study on art-driven rural construction cases. *Packaging Engineering*, 39(4):226 – 231, 2018.

[17] Zhang Duoduo and Ji Tie. Collaborative design "trigger" revival of traditional community: Case study on design research and practice of "new channel • huayaohua" project on intangible cultural heritage. *Zhuang Shi*, (12):26 – 29, 2016.

[18] Ezio Manzini Zhong Fang. Design for social innovation: A social systematic perspective. *Zhuang Shi*, (12):40 – 46, 2021.

[19] ZHANG Li GONG Miao-sen, LI Huan. Collaborative service design for intellectual disabled people. *Packaging Engineering*, 37(20):74 – 78, 2016.

[20] Joe Penny, Julia Slay, and Lucie Stephens. People powered health co-production catalogue. *Nesta, London*, 2012.

[21] Xiao Dong-juan Shao Ke. Co-design of public service for people with intellectual disabilities based on mec theory. *Design*, 36(3):57 – 61, 2016.

[22] James Tooze, Sharon Baurley, Robert Phillips, Paul Smith, Edwin Foote, and Sarah Silve. Open design: contributions, solutions, processes and projects. *The Design Journal*, 17(4):538 – 559, 2014.

Design Studies and Intelligence Engineering
L.C. Jain et al. (Eds.)
© 2024 The Authors.
doi:10.3233/FAIA231476

Study on Signage System Design for Fashion City Construction

Hong LIU[a,1] and Shanshan LU[a]

[a] *Beijing City University, China*

Abstract. Signage system is an important part of urban infrastructure. Excellent signage system design not only has humanized practical functions, but also helps to convey the city culture, and enhance the overall image. At the same time, signage system design has a certain role in promoting the construction of Hangzhou as a fashion capital. We summarize the positive effects of signage system on the construction of a fashion capital, study the application strategy of West Lake signage system in Hangzhou, and explore the future growing of signage system. With the development of 5G, AI and other new technologies, integrating them into the design of the signage system and building an intelligent signage system that meets the needs of the times and sustainable development is an important direction in the future.

Keywords. Signage System, Fashion Capital, Future Development

1. The role of signage design for a fashion city

1.1. Optimization of the urban environment

In commercial areas or parks, artistic signage is used to fill in the gaps in the landscape of the public space, and the signage system divides and manages the different environmental zones, making them standardized and unified. The city signage system allows people to gradually learn about the history, culture and development of the city, adds splendor to the urban environment, and naturally enhances the culture and fashion taste of the city.

1.2. Promotion of urban image

The city signage system is mainly reflected in functional use and environmental beautification. While conveying information, it is compatible with the user's habits and aesthetic needs. Signage system as a unique landmark into the daily life of residents, can reflect the city development status, traffic conditions and the cultural level of residents. It is not only an important embodiment of the city spirit, but also the accumulation of the city's image. The city signage system greatly enhances the reputation of urban environment and makes the city image more distinct. Nowadays, urban cultural image has become an important driving force.

---

[1] Corresponding Author: Hong LIU. E-mail: 260786426@qq.com.

1.3. Enhanced capacity of information transmission

In the future development, the city will continue to expand to the surrounding area, set up new areas and road sections, increase the demand for information, and accelerate the speed of information dissemination. The city signage system is an important center of urban development; enhancing the ability of signage system to transmit information is equivalent to enhancing urban vitality, and it is necessary to deliver the message truly effectively. The city signage system combines art and technology, which are applied to urban infrastructure to provide forward momentum for urban development.

2. Application for signage system design in Hangzhou West Lake

With the increasing maturity of industrial structure and production technology in China's signage system industry, "Internet of Things with New Technologies" into the industry has become a hot spot of concern. Signage system in the West Lake is oriented to build a signage system with humanized design that meets the needs of the times. It incorporates the concepts of "intelligence" and "humanization" to improve and supplement the guide function. With the rapid development of the network, people carry and use smart devices, thus the demand for the signage system is no longer just to find the route, but more interested in the interactive experience of smart devices and smart wayfinding facilities. The design boldly tries to adopt the AR virtual scene guidance system of information interaction, which can automatically lift the height of the signage, change the direction of the dynamic wayfinding signs and update the information dynamically on the screen. It not only meets the function of dividing different environments and areas, but also increases the artistic atmosphere of the scenic spot. The design enhances the convenience, interactivity and fun of the signage system, and also brings better guiding experience to the visitors.

2.1. Construct a five-level signage system and explore the design methodology

The design includes the whole process from data research, problem discovery, problem analysis, problem solving, planning and design, feedback, operation and maintenance. Detailed research is conducted on the history, architectural features, regional characteristics, development of Hangzhou West Lake, existing signage locations and characteristics of visitor groups, as well as the current status of the signage system. At the same time, based on the visitors' behavior and usage requirements, the design method of "vertical demand matching, horizontal system constructing" is created. Vertically, the content of the signage system is matched with the tourists' wayfinding behavior and information acquisition needs, and horizontally, a five-level signage system is constructed according to the hierarchy of tourists' wayfinding needs. In addition, it is also necessary to introduce elements such as intelligent wayfinding, information interaction and big data analysis to add intelligent functions to the design of the signage system.

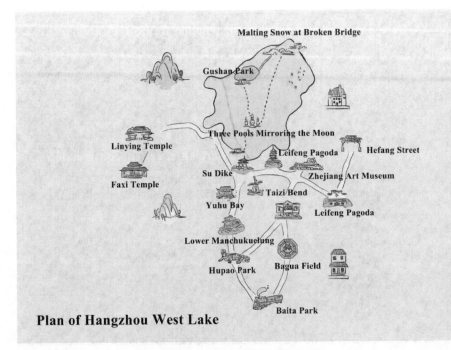

Figure 1. Plan of Hangzhou West Lake.

2.2. Integrate intelligent functions and concepts to show the new vitality of the city

Hangzhou West Lake signage system integrates intelligent functions and humanized concepts on the basis of traditional design to show the new vitality of Hangzhou. Through preliminary research and in-depth understanding of the current situation of the industry, the design incorporates real-time interactive information technology, big data analysis, virtual reality, AR display and voice interaction. The details are as follows:

A. The introduction of AR virtual reality and the screen guided by intelligent dynamic AI will enable travelers to find, inquire and view destinations in different directions

B. Visitors can interact with the signage system through the intelligent touch screen of the human-computer interaction AI and the virtual portrait intelligent voice interaction system. Users are able to release known information, satisfying the demand for personalized guidance, which in return lets the system collect information from tourists in a timely manner, providing raw data for big data analysis.

C. The humanized design concept is integrated into it, using text introduction and voice explanation in multiple languages to achieve multi-sensory cooperation. The guide sign adopts a telescopic function design, and for the disabled and children, it can automatically adjust the appropriate height for the convenience of tourists.

D. The design can share visitors' dynamic behavioral data, and carry out intelligent and comprehensive detection of water surface conditions, traffic, parking location, weather and resting locations available.

Design method and process construction frame diagram

Work flow	Data investigation	Problem analysis	Design planning	Supervision implementation	Evaluation feedback
	Composition of flow Mode of transportation Tourist flow Guide the status quo	Guide current situation problem analysis Marking service group division All kinds of people come to distribute Identification needs of different groups Primary and secondary road node analysis	Guide system construction Guide information architecture design Guide form and color design	Process guidance Effect control	Use effect tracking Follow-up service follow-up

Vertical matching requirements and horizontal system construction

Design method

Wayfinding behavior	Initial entry area	Intersection decision	Facility location	Cultural information acquisition	Auxiliary prompt
Information requirement	Primary node General situation of scenic spot Main road information Scenic spot layout Service facility location	Secondary node Scenic street layout Road bearing Target bearing Location of service facilities	Three-level node Subway station location Public toilet location Restaurant location	Four-level node Display information Cultural information	Five-level node Prompt information Service information
Guide matching	Primary node Scenic plan Main road information Guide Main attractions location guide Service facility location guide	Secondary node Scenic plan Destination direction guide Directions and distances of roads and facilities	Three-level node Service facility location information indication Target scenic spot location information indication	Four-level node Cultural introduction of scenic spot Tourist information	Five-level node Intelligent voice interaction Barrier free facilities Smoking area tips

Figure 2. Hangzhou West Lake Street road guide system design flow frame diagram.

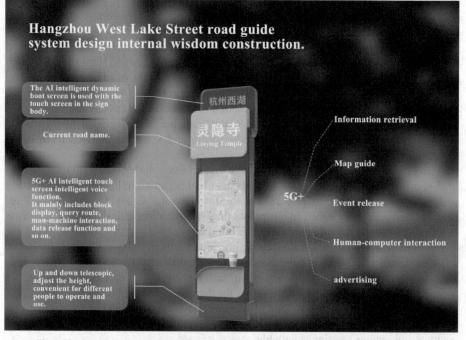

Figure 3. Hangzhou West Lake street road guide system design internal wisdom construction.

Aiming at aspects like the current Hangzhou, history of West Lake in Hangzhou and environmental protection, the design integrates tradition and fashion as well as nature and technology by collecting signage instruction information, sorting out a complete system and unifying the design style.

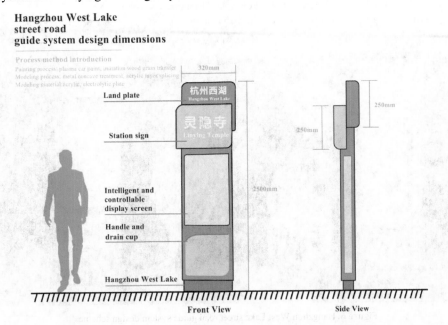

Figure 4. Hangzhou West Lake street road guide system design dimensions.

Figure 5. Hangzhou West Lake street road guide system design scheme.

Figure 6. Hangzhou West Lake street road guide system design scheme.

2.3. Introduce high-end technology and new materials to enhance the city's cultural identity

The signage system design of Hangzhou West Lake adopts new technology, new concept and new design, which is one of the directions of future signage system development. Taking the traditional signage system as the reference standard, from the perspective of design elements, core graphics, information architecture, establishment position, etc, the basic signage system is created to meet the needs of modern people; high-end technology and new materials are introduced to increase the intelligence of the system function. The signage system design focuses on the needs of pedestrians, motorists, and people with disabilities, and visualizes the surrounding environment. The design starts from finding the target location and route, and integrates intelligence, green new energy, big data cloud platform, visual design and other perspectives to create the first intelligent signage system in China. The design solution enhances the overall environment of the West Lake. The digital transformation contributes to the creation of Hangzhou as a fashion capital, the future development of scenic spots and the enhancement of the city's cultural identity.

2.4. Construct the beauty of the city with humanized and simple design

The design adopts a comfortable, simple and smooth design style, using bright colors, concise text and pictures, as well as smooth route guidance to establish a connection between people and West Lake, so that visitors can use the guidance system easily and pleasantly. The design optimizes the user interface, provides clear and easy-to-understand navigation icons and map information, and comprehensively considers the tourists' guiding needs and visual experience, which demonstrates the personality and quality, highlights the fashionable and technological style, and enhances the cultural identity.

3. Future development of signage system

The city signage system is the information carrier of fashion capitals, and the future development of city signage will be closely related to the development of information. The complexity of information needs to be communicated quickly and accurately to the audience. Nowadays, the design of city signage system is no longer simply to guide the direction and find the route, but also to consider the image of the city, regional characteristics and cultural background. Therefore, by combining the regional and cultural characteristics of a fashion capital, the scientific and humanized design can help to develop and improve the city's cultural image.

3.1. Regulation

Standardizing the design form is of great significance to enhance the function of signage system. At present, many designers are not clear about the function of signage, and they often treat it as artistic creation and like to show their own individual style on their works. But in real life, the practicality of signage is much more important than the beauty of the form, which can directly affect the operation of the city. Therefore, based on the complexity of the urban environment, the colors, fonts and graphic proportions of the signage must be researched and tested by professional departments, applying a unified visual language and establishing rigorous standard specifications. Population differences in different areas call for new rules based on norms. The future fashion capital signage system will make great strides in standardization, order and regulation.

3.2. Humanization

The humanized design of the signage system is to satisfy the common needs and at the same time, the humanistic care for the disadvantaged groups. In the design process, the visual height of wheelchair users and children is fully considered, and there are not many relevant design cases in China that take this into account. Different categories of barrier-free designs are subject to constant research and revision. Designers should not only consider the use and travel convenience of people with disabilities, but also concern about their mental health and emotional experience, highlighting the humanistic care for the disadvantaged groups. The design of signage system adopts diversified forms of expression and intelligent means such as AR and voice recognition technology to provide a more diversified and interesting way of information presentation, and to provide more convenient and efficient information service and interactive experience. Humanized design is strengthened in the design of the signage system, such as the supply of umbrellas, power banks, massage chairs to improve the user experience and satisfaction.

3.3. Personalization

Nowadays, people's demand for aesthetics is constantly rising, and personalization is also a major trend in the development of the future signage system on the basis of meeting the needs of use. After entering the era of diversified design, the use of color is one of the most important elements to reflect the personality in urban environment. Carolyn Bloomer, an American visual arts psychologist, said, "Color can evoke a variety of emotions, express feelings, and even affect our physiological feelings." Color in the signage system not only attracts visitors, but also complements the colors of the surrounding environment, thus increasing the sense of "presence". In addition to color, the future of personalized signage system provides more tailored and personalized navigation by identifying user needs and behavioral patterns, thus improving user experience and satisfaction. Phantom Imaging is used in display design to be able to project dynamic people into static backgrounds. Some window displays in France have already started to use Phantom Imaging technology to create dynamic business signs. It is believed that in the near future, it will also become the direction of signage system development in the city.

3.4. Intelligence

The city of the future is a "smart city" with 5G coverage and big data. Intelligent guide signs help to create a smart space. Based on 3D advanced rendering map and voice interaction, self-developed map and navigation technology as the core, taking into account the multimedia information dissemination system, the use of artificial intelligence with exquisite fidelity to restore the outdoor and indoor complex scenes and terrain, is the future direction of the signage system intelligent design development. Visitors are able to use location search, wayfinding guide, location finding, route planning, intelligent parking and other functions to help fashion capitals to improve service quality and play the value of offline traffic. VR panoramic guide utilizes the three-dimensional outdoor street on both sides of the map and virtual reality technology to restore the real scene, combined with the IP image as a navigation, comparable to the game level visual effect, bringing a new experience of immersive panoramic signage. Meanwhile, by scanning the QR code, with the help of AR rendering, artificial intelligence and real-time cell phone tracking and navigation, the guidelines such as straight ahead, turning and destination arrows are visually presented in the real-life image taken by the cell phone. Users can move forward according to the 3D arrow instructions, solving problems such as getting lost or not being able to read the map.

3.5. Environmental protection

The concept of nature, ecology and environmental protection occupies an important position in the design of signage system. The system advocates emission reduction, low carbon and recycling, and makes full use of wind, daylight and renewable resources to establish a recyclable ecosystem. The digital signage system, which makes it easier for users to access the information they need, helps reduce construction costs, resource energy consumption and environmental pollution. At the same time, the use of intelligent cooling technology, human body sensor technology and other technological means can improve efficiency and achieve the goal of sustainable development. Lengthening the life cycle of the signage system and making it easy to dismantle and recycle after use are key design considerations for the future.

4. Conclusion

As society progresses, signage system design plays a very important role for cities and their residents. It can show a city's overall development, planning and humanistic atmosphere. Hangzhou, as a specimen of a city exploring the field of fashion, signage system design can help it to build into a fashion capital. Signage system is also constantly changing and developing. In the future, intelligent signage system design will realize the interaction between the virtual and the real, and integrate the new Internet technology, which can bring different interactive experience for users and promote the construction of fashion capitals.

References

[1] Li Nan. How to show the cultural nature of urban guide system, Art Education Research, 2011.5.
[2] Tan Erbin. The application of new media art in urban environment guide system. China Newspaper Industry 2022(12): 20-22.
[3] Pan Yitian. Introduction to the function and value of guide system. Art Market, 2023(3): 94-95.
[4] Zhao Wei. Research on the innovative design and application of intelligent scenic area guide system in the new media era. Tianjin University of Technology, 2019.
[5] Li Jingyan. Principle and realistic application of AR augmented reality technology. Art Technology, 2018, 31(5):93.
[6] Feng Ji. Color design of urban guide system. Beijing: China Forestry Press, 2011.
[7] Ge Yihan. The interactive future of guidebook design. Architecture and Culture, 2021(7): 213-215.
[8] Gou Xiaoran &, Chen Limin. Analysis on the application of regional culture in the design of transportation guide system. Art Education Research, 2020(10):79-80.
[9] Fan Yue. Research on diversified design of urban guide system. Packaging Engineering, 2019(8): 276-279.
[10] Chen Zhiying, & Zhao Wei. Exploration on the design and development of "intelligent scenic spot" guide system based on new media technology. Packaging Engineering, 2018, 39(24): 60-63.

Design Studies and Intelligence Engineering
L.C. Jain et al. (Eds.)
© *2024 The Authors.*
This article is published online with Open Access by IOS Press and distributed under the terms
of the Creative Commons Attribution Non-Commercial License 4.0 (CC BY-NC 4.0).
doi:10.3233/FAIA231477

No Driver Is Alone: A Multicentered Human-Machine System Framework for Multitasking While Driving

Min LIN[a,c] , Mo CHEN[b], Yubo ZHANG[b], Xinying HE[a], and Fan YANG[a,1]
[a] *School of Industrial Design, Guangzhou Academy of Fine Arts, P. R. China*
[b] *School of Mechanical Engineering, Guangzhou City Univ. of Technology, P. R. China*
[c] *Guangdong Key Lab of ID Innovation and Applied Research, P. R. China*

Abstract. Driving is a multitasking process. With the advance of artificial intelligence and driver assistance systems, the tasks of driving go far beyond monitoring one's surroundings and turning the steering wheel. For example, using phones while driving is a common occurrence. However, past studies analyzing driving have only considered a single driver's view, based on the incorrect assumption that the driver is the only person who impacts road safety. This paper proposes a multi-centered human-machine system framework that takes more factors into account, including the drivers of surrounding vehicles and advances in driver assistance technology. An analysis of the scenario of phone calling while driving is performed using the proposed framework, followed by a preliminary evaluation with 18 beginner-level drivers. The results demonstrated the new framework's capability of identifying more approaches both theoretically and practically to better balance the driving and non-driving tasks, compared to the traditional framework. Future research topics with the multi-centered framework, including hierarchical analysis of treatments, collaborative driving support, and information interference are addressed.

Keywords. multitasking, multicentered, human-machine system, HCI, driving

1. Introduction

Intelligent vehicles are a clear trend in the automobile industry [1, 2]. Although autonomous driving has drawn constant attention from both academic and industrial domains [3-5], it still faces many challenges [6-8]. Its current situation is at a stage between full manual driving and complete self-driving: a stage of collaborative driving between human and vehicle. In such a human-vehicle collaboration mode, the driver assistance system (DAS) equipped in a vehicle has the capability of dealing with some driving tasks such as cruise control and forward collision warning (FCW) [9-11]. The application of DAS helps drivers release some cognitive resources used on driving tasks (DT) [12, 13], which to some degree promotes the attractiveness of non-driving tasks (NDT). Therefore, multitasking scenarios while driving will be increasingly common as DAS gets more popular and more powerful, bringing further challenges for human-

---

[1] Fan Yang, School of Industrial Design, GAFA, 168 Waihuan Xilu, Higher Education Mega Center, Panyu District, Guangzhou, Guangdong, P. R. China 51006; E-mail: fanyang@gzarts.edu.cn.

vehicle interaction.

Indeed, driving itself is a multitasking process [14, 15]. Drivers need to monitor the surroundings while controlling the steering wheel, as well as operating the brake and gas pedals. In every country, driving schools and drivers' license exams have the same purpose—preparing drivers to handle the multiple driving tasks with sufficient proficiency and reaction capacity. However, the addition of NDT makes the multitasking scenarios in driving more complex to analyze. Proficient driving alone becomes insufficient to simultaneously handle DT and NDT without reducing safety. Many earlier studies have shown that phone use while driving significantly increased the occurrence of road accidents [16-19].

Designing an effective human-vehicle interaction system to both provide a reasonable safety assurance and deliver a satisfactory user experience for multitasking driving scenarios is an important issue of the human-vehicle collaborative driving mode. Prohibiting NDT via mandatory regulations appears to be a simple solution for this issue yet proves impractical [19, 20]. Therefore, there is currently no widely accepted solution that would bolster NDT without significantly reducing road safety.

The following part is organized into three sections. In the first section, the driver-centered human-machine system (HMS) is discussed, and a new framework better suited for multitasking driving scenarios is proposed. In the second section, the classic scenario of calling while driving is then analyzed using the new framework, demonstrating the framework's capability of identifying more interested parties and generating more practical treatments, followed by a preliminary evaluation of some treatments. The last section lists three major research directions that need further investigation in the future.

2. Human-Machine System for Multitasking Driving Scenarios

A human-machine system is the combination of humans and the machines they interact with [21], either with intelligence or not. It is composed of three components: the human, the machine, and the surrounding environment. By analyzing the relations among these three components, one will be able to understand the information needed by each involving party and the possible actions based on this information, allowing the realization of appropriate solutions for human-machine interaction [22].

In terms of vehicle related solutions, safety is undoubtedly the most critical consideration. As the automobile industry advances and market competition intensifies, user experience has progressively attracted greater attention in vehicle designs, mostly regarding in-car comfort [23, 24] and user friendliness [25-27]. Nonetheless, HCI (Human-Computer Interaction) research directed at multitasking driving scenarios is still in its early stages, as HMS research nowadays investigates driving performance in multitasking scenarios instead of exploring solutions for better supports on DT and NDT.

2.1. Multitasking Driving Scenarios

Despite driving already being a multitasking process, the term "multitasking" here refers to the simultaneous performance of both driving tasks and non-driving tasks. Driving tasks refer to the activities directly related to car operation such as turning the steering wheel, braking, monitoring the rearview mirrors, changing gears, and route planning. Non-driving tasks refer to a driver's ongoing activities not related to driving, such as taking phone calls, adjusting the in-car air conditioner, changing the volume of the infotainment system, and chatting with other passengers in the car.

Performing NDT while driving is almost inevitable. For example, the pre-installed infotainment system in every car has very little to do with driving but rather serves to fight boredom through content like radio and music. Additionally, continued technological development has made NDT more complicated. In the past, driver interaction with NDT was mostly physical, such as pushing a button or turning a knob. Today, the list of NDT has expanded to include activities like reading and replying to text messages, watching short videos, and playing games. Moreover, they all require more visual attention and higher precision in operation [28, 29].

The main impact from NDT on DT is the competition for a driver's limited cognitive resources [15, 30]. When an NDT demands few resources, a driver will be able to accomplish DT with very little or even no negative influence. On the other hand, when the demand increases, a large impact on driving performance will appear, leading to risks such as lane departure, longer reaction times, or even road crashes [28, 31-33]. Therefore, NDT is not always a safety threat that requires strict regulation, but drivers cannot be given free rein to engage in NDT either. Neither banning NDT nor ignoring NDT is the best choice. Controlling the influences of NDT therefore becomes the logical solution that balances road safety and drivers' needs.

2.2. Driver-Centered HMS Framework

To deal with such a highly complicated scenario, a systematic approach like HMS is helpful in deconstructing and analyzing the issues encountered while multitasking while driving, and further developing an appropriate treatment. Oviedo-Trespalacios et al. (2016) [34] presented an HMS when reviewing the impact of phones on driving performance. The driver, car, phone, and road environment were the four components used for DT and NDT analysis. In this framework, DT included the human-car interface in the car, the human-car controls for the driver to operate, and the information presented by the environment, while NDT focused on the phone, involving the phone interface and the driver's actions on the phone (Figure 1).

The two components, the vehicle and phone, represent the two machines involved in DT and NDT, respectively. But no consideration was taken to identify the components on the human side in the human-machine system. Clearly, such a framework is based on one single person's view which has an implicit assumption that the driver is the only party capable of evaluating the scenario and taking actions. He/she is the center of the framework while the roles of machine and environment are constrained to providing information and receiving instructions. A decade ago, such an assumption was reasonable since the computing power and AI algorithms at that time were still insufficient. But as the situation changed, the driver-centered view became outdated. Both the machine and the environment nowadays can be intelligent. Considering them as two completely passive roles fails to accurately reflect their capabilities. As a result, the relationships among different parties in HMS become more complicated. It is necessary to re-examine each party's role to create a truly complete analysis of multitasking scenarios. Solutions that used to hide in the blind spot may now be discovered.

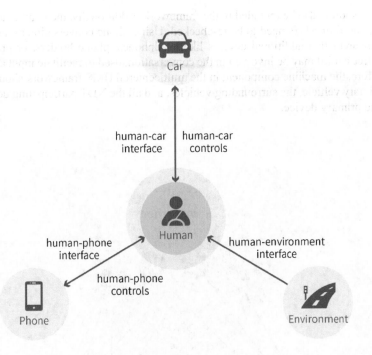

Figure 1. Driver-centered HMS Framework

2.3. Multicentered HMS Framework

When both the machine and environment become intelligent, they become capable of sensing, analyzing, decision-making, and action-taking just like humans. That is, the driver participating in the multitasking scenario is no longer the only center of the HMS. The human, machine, and environment are now multiple centers collaborating to seek best solution. Figure 2 illustrates the parties involved and the complex relations among them.

Firstly, only considering the driver themself is not enough. The result of DT does not solely depend on one single driver, but also the other surrounding drivers. Past studies tended to classify other drivers' behaviors into the environment component. At that time, they were treated more as troublesome obstacles rather than beneficial collaborators because there was little communication or collaboration between the primary driver and the surrounding drivers. But, when the impact of other drivers on road safe is realized, it becomes reasonable to move other drivers from the environment component to the human component. Beyond the driver and the surrounding drivers, there are still more be humans participating in an NDT, such as the other party of a phone call or text message. Therefore, the human component in the multicentered HMS framework should include the primary driver, the surrounding drivers, and the other NDT participants.

Secondly, the machine component is not limited to the primary driver's car and the device used for NDT. As mentioned before, the surrounding cars' performance will affect overall safety as well [35, 36]. In addition to the primary driver's vehicle, the surrounding vehicles should also be included in the framework. Additionally, the number and type of devices used in NDTs need to be re-checked. Using phone conversation as an example, it is apparent that additional devices like headphones, phone holders, or pre-installed handsfree car kit may be involved in the conversation, used to facilitate input and output. Therefore, the machine component in the multicentered HMS framework should include the primary vehicle, the surrounding vehicles, and all the NDT participating devices, not just the primary device.

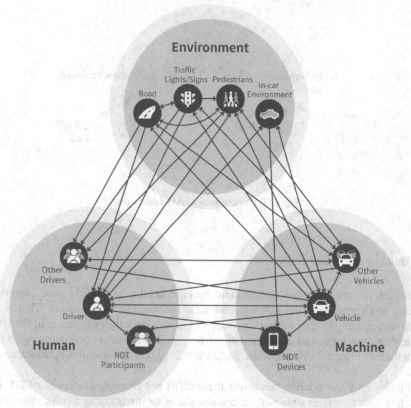

Figure 2. Multicentered HMS Framework

Lastly, the environment component needs expansion as well. Although intelligent roads have not been widely implemented, detailed classification of the road environment is helpful in the analysis of multitasking scenarios and the exploration of a future intelligent traffic system. In general, the road environment can be classified into three categories: pedestrians, the road, and traffic lights/signs. Pedestrians refer to the non-driver road users. They are not considered part of the human component because the separation of people and vehicles is the norm, and therefore pedestrians only have an accidental rather than routine appearance. While the road and traffic lights and signs provide different forms of interaction with road users, both convey traffic-related information to road users. The smarter they are, the more supports they can provide to drivers. In addition, the in-car environment, such as lighting and noise, might affect driving performance [37]. Therefore, the environment component in the multicentered HMS framework should include pedestrians, the road, traffic lights and signs, and in-car environment.

The relations among all these components are much more complicated than that of a driver-centered framework, thus providing greater space to understand the cognitive resource distribution between DT and NDT. An example of utilizing these relations to analyze and seek potential treatments is shown in the next section.

3. Analysis of Phone Calling while Driving

3.1. Relations and Treatments

Calling while driving is the multitasking driving scenario that had received much attention in driver related studies [38-41]. In the driver-centered HMS framework, the driver-phone relation appears to be the only relation that interferes with DT and therefore affects driving safety. Such a limited observation will probably lead to a one-sided conclusion that reducing the cognitive resources occupied by the phone is the only solution, which would then logically imply a policy of complete prohibition on phone use. Unfortunately, this is not true.

Table 1. The relations, treatments, and expected effects in the scenario of phone calling while driving.

Party	Relation Used	Treatment	Expected Effect
Primary Driver	Driver-Phone	Auto-filter nonurgent calls	Reduce phone calls
	Driver-Vehicle	Engage DAS automatically	Reduce driver error
	Vehicle-Road	Inform DAS status	Reduce driver error
	Vehicle-Traffic lights/signs	Use in-car indicators for traffic lights/signs	Reduce neglection of critical information
Caller	Caller-Phone	Wait for driver to call back	Reduce phone calls
	Caller-Vehicle	Receive traffic condition notice	Speed up conversation
	Caller-Driver	Receive "driving" notice	Speed up conversation
Other Drivers	Vehicle-Other vehicles	Receive DAS status	Manage expectation
	Vehicle-Other drivers	Receive "in-call' status	Manage expectation
Pedestrians	Pedestrians-Vehicle	Receive "in-call" status	Manage expectation

The mistake here is to throw the baby out with the bath water. The driver-phone relation is not the only relation that has potential impacts on DT and NDT. The driver is not alone. The other drivers, the other caller, and the pedestrians all impact road safety during the multitasking period. The multicentered HMS framework provides a map to follow different relations among these parties and look for reasonable supports from each of them. Some relations that can be used to develop possible treatments and their expected effects are listed in Table 1.

To the primary driver, there are at least four pairs of relations that can be utilized to lower the safety risk. The driver-phone relation may help filter nonurgent phone calls so that they can be dealt with later. This treatment may be implemented using an allowlist or some kind of negotiation process to pre-check the call's degree of urgency before passing the request to the driver. The driver-vehicle relation may enable DAS to apply certain restrictions on speed or lane changes to reduce driver error from distraction. If the road is smart, the vehicle-road relation can notify the road to help monitor and carry out these restrictions. Also, to ensure the driver notices critical traffic light and sign information (e.g. lane ending) in time, the vehicle-traffic lights/signs relation may suggest applying some kind of in-car indicators.

To the caller who participates in the NDT, earlier studies had shown that they tended to shorten the phone conversation if they were told the person they were talking with was driving [42-44]. Thus, it is reasonable to notify the caller of the driver's status of driving (via phone-caller relation) or facing a tough traffic condition (via vehicle-caller relation) so that the caller can set an accurate expectation of the conversation process.

For the other drivers surrounding the primary driver, they can benefit from knowing the primary driver's DAS status in an implicit way (via vehicle-other vehicles relation), and from knowing the "in-call" status in an explicit way (via vehicle-other drivers relation). Similar treatments apply for pedestrians (via vehicle-pedestrians relation) as well. By establishing an understandable expectation, the other drivers and the pedestrians can make decisions on how to react to the situation accordingly so their goals can be reached with little or no influence.

With the assistance from these treatments, the NDT devices may not have to redesign their user interface or interaction method dramatically. Some UI treatments such as driving mode can be help, but the collaborative adjustment of the in-car environment—such as muting radio or music via the vehicle-phone—and the vehicle-in-car environment relations may be more effective in reducing the negative impacts of NDT.

This example clearly demonstrates that the multicentered HMS framework can provide more detailed analysis of multitasking driving scenarios and formulate more possible treatments than the driver-centered HMS framework. The driver's limited cognitive resources can therefore be better distributed with the help of various relations among HMS components. More importantly, the new framework changes the relationship between DT and NDT from head-to-head competition into side-by-side collaboration. The research questions on multitasking driving scenarios are finally no longer all equivalent to a safety problem.

3.2. Preliminary Evaluation

Six treatments (Table 2) were carefully phrased to perform a preliminary evaluation. Eighteen Chinese participants (9 males and 9 females) were recruited. Male and female participants were separated into different groups to avoid potential conflicts of views between the genders. All participants were self-considered "newbies" in driving because they did not drive frequently, even those that held a driver's license for several years. Particularly, two screening criteria were applied. All participant must not have more than five years of driving experience, and must not have driven more than 15 days during the last month. Table 3 listed the demographic information of the participants. Beginner-level drivers were used for the evaluation to minimize potential bias—that is, experienced drivers may have preexisting driving habits which may bias their judgment of the proposed treatments.

Table 2. The treatments evaluated and the corresponding median scores.

No.	Treatment	Statement 1	Statement 2
1	Any incoming calls not from the persons in the allowlist will be ignored automatically if you are driving.	4	6.5
2	The caller will be informed automatically that you are driving after he/she makes the call.	7.5	8
3	If there is an incoming call when you are dealing with a complex road condition, the caller will be asked to wait.	8	7.5
4	When you are on the phone, any important information related to road safety will be presented in a more noticeable way than usual.	7.5	8
5	All the vehicles around you will be notified automatically that you are on the phone. (Assume there will be no legal consequences.)	7	6
6	When encountering complex road conditions, a phone conversation will be paused temporarily and resumed afterward automatically.	8	6

Table 3. The demographic information of the participants.

No.	Gender	Age	Experience (months)	No.	Gender	Age	Experience (months)
1	Male	26	48	10	Female	26	60
2	Male	26	45	11	Female	24	6
3	Male	25	60	12	Female	32	52
4	Male	27	6	13	Female	26	10
5	Male	22	19	14	Female	28	9
6	Male	25	32	15	Female	31	34
7	Male	24	39	16	Female	30	45
8	Male	24	52	17	Female	26	52
9	Male	24	9	18	Female	24	45

The treatments were presented one by one. Each treatment was explained verbally and presented in writing to every participant, who were then asked to independently express their viewpoint on two statements by selecting a score for each statement on a

11-point Likert scale. A score of 0 represented "completely disagree" and 10 represented "completely agree". Statement 1 was "I think the treatment will improve driving safety when I am on the phone". Statement 2 was "I would like to apply the treatment when I am on the phone while driving". The treatments and their resulting median scores are shown in Table 2.

Treatment 1, the allowlist treatment, was used as a baseline to examine the validity of the data. Namely, Treatment 1 attempted to wholly prevent the occurrence of multitasking scenarios, whereas the other treatments attempted to provide supports for multitasking. Interpreting the results of Treatment 1, it was therefore not surprising to observe a negative view for Statement 1, as well as a weak tendency in Statement 2 in favor of using it. Conversely, the other five treatments all received a score of 7 or more in Statement 1, indicating that the participants considered them effective in terms of improving driving safety. Such a finding implied the power of the multicentered HMS framework for generating potentially effective treatments, as all proposed treatments outscored Treatment 1. The interest of applying these treatments scored between 6 and 8. Interestingly, Treatment 5 and 6 both scored lower than Treatment 1 in this area, suggesting that the participants were more hesitant to use them despite agreeing that they were more effective. These scores may be due to unfamiliarity with or novelty of some proposed treatments, and such scores may improve when prototypes can be experienced comprehensively in a simulator. Overall, the data exhibited that beginner drivers view the proposed treatments as more effective at improving safety compared to traditional means of regulating NDT. Moreover, the participants showed a willingness to use these methods, indicating viability. Through this preliminary evaluation of the treatments distilled from the analysis based on the multicentered HMS framework, the potential of the proposed framework is not only justified theoretically, but demonstrated practically.

4. Future Research Questions

Driver behavior has been modeled with a three-level hierarchical structure [45, 46], which might be borrowed for classifying the various treatments generated from the multicentered HMS framework. For example, notifying all the involving parties about the primary driver's status, engaging DAS, and asking the caller to wait are on the strategic, tactical, and operational level respectively. The match between the treatments and the levels of control will help construct the policies of any intelligent DAS for multitasking driving scenarios. Therefore, identifying and sorting the various treatments hierarchically is a research question worth studying.

The cornerstone of the multicentered HMS framework is to consider more parties, including the surrounding vehicles, responsible for overall safety instead of blaming the primary driver for everything. According to this, the supports on information exchange and negotiation among vehicles will make the road system safer. Driving intentions, status, and needs are some of the main information that can be presented in more forms and through more channels. It is very likely to have a collaborative driving support system pre-installed in all future vehicles to utilize this information for better scenario sensing and decision-making. Therefore, collaborative driving support is another research question for the future.

Everything comes with pros and cons. When information exchange and decision-making activities involve more parties, the risk of potential interference increases. For example, when more than one vehicle is under multitasking driving conditions, communication among all vehicles involved may take longer, and the information presented in the same channel by different vehicles may interfere with each other. Therefore, how to reach a consensus effectively and in time, as well as how to pass it to all the parties effectively and in time, needs further investigation.

5. Conclusions

Safety is no doubt the most important concern while driving. Besides the primary driver, there are many components related to road safety in multitasking driving scenarios. The driver-centered HMS framework has failed to perform an effective analysis on the scenario and provide effective solutions. Therefore, the multicentered HMS framework is proposed as a better tool that takes into account not only the primary driver, but also the surrounding drivers, as well as the NDT participants and analyzes in detail the relations among humans, machines, and the environment. The treatments from the analysis aim to better support both DT and NDT and to synergize them to achieve the overarching goal of safety. Although the most common scenario is analyzed as a demonstration to show the power of the proposed framework, more studies are needed to make it applicable and valuable to all multitasking driving scenarios. Hierarchical analysis of treatments, collaborative driving support, and information interference are the three research questions for the future.

Acknowledgement

This work is supported by the HCI Research on Multitasking Driving project (23XSC09), GAFA. The authors thank Z. Jonathan Lin for his assistance in editing and proofreading the manuscript.

References

[1] Chai Z, Nie T, Becker J. The centennial automotive industry and the looming transformation. In: Chai Z, Nie T, Becker J. editors. Autonomous driving changes the future. Sringer Singapore; 2021. p. 1-15, doi: 10.1007/978-981-15-6728-5_1.

[2] Wang L, Liu Y. Analysis on different countries' intelligent connected vehicle industry policy. In: Striełkowski W, Black JM, Butterfield SA, Chang C, Cheng J, Dumanig FP, Al-Mabuk R, Scheper-Hughes N, Urban M, editors. Proceedings of the 6th Annual International Conference on Social Science and Contemporary Humanity Development (SSCHD 2020); 2020 Dec 18-19; Xi'an, Shanxi, China: Atlantis Press; c2021. p. 990-5, doi: 10.2991/assehr.k.210121.191.

[3] National Highway Traffic Safety Administration. Preliminary statement of policy concerning automated vehicles. Washington DC:NHTSA; 2013. (NHTSA's public docket; No. NHTSA-2012-0057).

[4] Society of Automotive Engineers(SAE). Taxonomy and definitions for terms related to driving automation systems for on-road motor vehicles. America: SAE International & ANSI; 2021. Standard No. J3016_202104.

[5] Standardization Administration of PRC(SAC). Taxonomy of driving automation for vehicles. China: SAMR & SAC; 2021. Standard No. GB/T 40429-2021.

[6] De La Torre G, Rad P, Choo KR. Driverless vehicle security: Challenges and future research opportunities. Future Generation Computer Systems. 2020 Jul;108:1092-111, doi:10.1016/j.future.2017.12.041.

[7] Thakurdesai HM, Aghav JV. Autonomous cars: technical challenges and a solution to blind spot. In:Gao

X, Tiwari S, Trivedi MC, Mishra KK, editors. Proceedings of the CICT 2019 Advances in Computational Intelligence and Communication Technology; Springer Singapore; c2021. p. 533-47, doi: 10.1007/978-981-15-1275-9_44.

[8]   Manglani T, Rani R, Kaushik R, et al. Recent trends and challenges of diverless vehicles in real world application. In: Proceedings of the 2022 International Conference on Sustainable Computing and Data Communication Systems (ICSCDS); 2022 Apr 7-9; Erode, India. IEEE; c2022. p. 803-6, doi: 10.1109/ICSCDS53736.2022.9760886.

[9]   Jumaa BA, Abdulhassan AM, Mousa-Abdulhass A. Advanced driver assistance system (ADAS): A review of systems and technologies. International Journal of Advanced Research in Computer Engineering & Technology (IJARCET). 2019;8(6):231-4.

[10] Li X, Lin KY, Meng M, et al. A survey of ADAS perceptions with development in china. IEEE Transactions on Intelligent Transportation Systems. 2022;23(9):14188-203, doi: 10.1109/TITS.2022.3149763.

[11] Murtaza M, Cheng CT, Fard M, et al. The importance of transparency in naming conventions, designs, and operations of safety features: from modern ADAS to fully autonomous driving functions. AI & SOCIETY. 2023;38(2):983-93, doi: 10.1007/s00146-022-01442-x.

[12] Eckstein L, Zlocki A. Safety potential of ADAS – combined methods for an effective evaluation. In: National Highway Traffic Safety Administration, editors. Proceedings of the 23rd International Technical Conference on the Enhanced Safety of Vehicles (ESV); 2013 May 27-30; Seoul, South Korea; c2013. p. 15-25.

[13] Benmimoun M. Effective evaluation of automated driving systems. SAE Technical Paper, 2017, doi: 10.4271/2017-01-0031.

[14] Aasman J, Michon JA. Multitasking in driving. Soar: A Cognitive Architecture in Perspective: A Tribute to Allen Newell. 1992:169-98, doi: 10.1007/978-94-011-2426-3.

[15] Salvucci DD, Taatgen NA. Threaded cognition: an integrated theory of concurrent multitasking. Psychological review. 2008;115(1):101-30, doi: 10.1037/0033-295X.115.1.101.

[16] Violanti JM, Marshall JR. Cellular phones and traffic accidents: An epidemiological approach. Accident Analysis & Prevention. 1996;28(2):265-70, doi: 10.1016/0001-4575(95)00070-4.

[17] Redelmeier DA, Tibshirani RJ. Association between cellular-telephone calls and motor vehicle collisions. N Engl J Med. 1997;336(7):453-8, doi: 10.1056/NEJM199702133360701.

[18] Seo DC, Torabi MR. The impact of in-vehicle cell-phone use on accidents or near-accidents among college students. Journal of American College Health. 2004;53(3):101-8, doi: 10.3200/JACH.53.3.101-108.

[19] McEvoy SP, Stevenson MR, McCartt AT, et al. Role of mobile phones in motor vehicle crashes resulting in hospital attendance: A case-crossover study. British Medical Journal. 2005;331(7514):428, doi: 10.1136/bmj.38537.397512.55.

[20] Rosenberger R. The phenomenological case for stricter regulation of cell phones and driving. Techné: Research in Philosophy & Technology. 2014;18(1/2):20-47, doi: 10.5840/techne201461717.

[21] Hastings D. The future of engineering systems: Development of engineering leaders. In: De Neufville R, De Weck O, Frey D, et al., editors. Proceedings of the Engineering Systems Symposium; 2004 Mar 29-31; Cambridge, Mass. p. 29-31.

[22] Wickens CD, Zhang K. An introduction to human factors engineering (2nd edition) . China: East China Normal University Press; 2007. p. 112-4.

[23] Hartwich F, Beggiato M, Krems JF. Driving comfort, enjoyment and acceptance of automated driving – effects of drivers' age and driving style familiarity. Ergonomics. 2018;61(8):1017-32, doi: 10.1080/00140139.2018.1441448.

[24] Guo YX, Sun QY, Su YQ, et al. Can driving condition prompt systems improve passenger comfort of intelligent vehicles? A driving simulator study. Transportation Research Part F: Traffic Psychology and Behaviour. 2021;8(2021):240-50, doi: 10.1016/j.trf.2021.06.007.

[25] Kun AL. Human-machine interaction for vehicles: Review and outlook. Foundations and Trends® in Human–Computer Interaction. 2018;11(4):201-93, doi: 10.1561/1100000069.

[26] Tan H, Sun JH, Wang WJ, et al. User exerience & usability of driving: A bibliometric analysis of 2000-2019. International Journal of Human–Computer Interaction. 2021;37(4):297-307, doi: 10.1080/10447318.2020.1860516.

[27] Tan ZY, Dai NY, Su YT, et al. Human–machine interaction in intelligent and connected vehicles: A review of status quo, issues, and opportunities. IEEE Transactions on Intelligent Transportation Systems. 2022;23(9):13954-75. doi: 10.1109/TITS.2021.3127217.

[28] Ge HM, Zheng MQ, Lyu NC, et al. Review on driving distraction. Journal of Traffic and Transportation Engineering 2021;21(2):38-55, doi: 10.19818/j.cnki.1671-1637.2021.02.004.

[29] Ebel P, Lingenfelder C, Vogelsang A. Multitasking while driving: How drivers self-regulate their interaction with in-vehicle touchscreens in automated driving. International Journal of Human–Computer

Interaction. 2023;39(16):3162-79, doi: 10.1080/10447318.2023.2215634.

[30] Anderson JR. Cognitive psychology and it's implications. China: People's Posts and Telecommunications Press; 2012. p. 68-92.

[31] Brown ID, Tickner AH, Simmonds DC. Interference between concurrent tasks of driving and telephoning. Journal of Applied Psychology. 1969;53(5):419-24, doi: 10.1037/h0028103.

[32] Horberry T, Anderson J, Regan MA, et al. Driver distraction: The effects of concurrent in-vehicle tasks, road environment complexity and age on driving performance. Accident Analysis & Prevention. 2006;38(1):185-91, doi: 10.1016/j.aap.2005.09.007.

[33] Li HT, Liu YY, Li WS. A review: Effects of cell phone use on driving performance. China Safety Science Journal. 2013;23(1):16-21, doi: 10.16265/j.cnki.issn1003-3033.2013.01.008.

[34] Oviedo-Trespalacios O, Haque MM, King M, et al. Understanding the impacts of mobile phone distraction on driving performance: A systematic review. Transportation Research Part C: Emerging Technologies. 2016;72:360-80, doi: 10.1016/j.trc.2016.10.006.

[35] Yu KP, Lin L, Alazab M, et al. Deep learning-based traffic safety solution for a mixture of autonomous and manual vehicles in a 5G-enabled intelligent transportation system. IEEE Transactions on Intelligent Transportation Systems. 2021;22(7):4337-47, doi: 10.1109/TITS.2020.3042504.

[36] Li T, Han X, Ma J, et al. Operational safety of automated and human driving in mixed traffic environments: A perspective of car-following behavior. In: Proceedings of the Institution of Mechanical Engineers, PartO: Journal of Risk and Reliability. 2023;237(2):355-66, doi: 10.1177/1748006x211050696.

[37] Braun M, Weber F, Alt F. Affective automotive user interfaces–reviewing the state of driver affect research and emotion regulation in the car. ACM Compuingt Surveys. 2021;54(7):1-26, doi: 10.1145/3460938.

[38] Fitch GM, Soccolich SA, Guo F, et al. The impact of hand-held and hands-free cell phone use on driving performance and safety-critical event risk. In: Virginia Polytechnic Institute and State University(Blacksburg), Virginia Tech Transportation Institute, et al., editors. Proceedings of the TRB Annual Meeting; 2013 May 9; Washington DC; p. 273.

[39] Wijayaratna KP, Cunningham ML, Regan MA, et al. Mobile phone conversation distraction: Understanding differences in impact between simulator and naturalistic driving studies. Accident Analysis & Prevention. 2019;129(2019):108-18, doi: 10.1016/j.aap.2019.04.017.

[40] Boboc RG, Voinea GD, Buzdugan ID, et al. Talking on the phone while driving: a literature review on driving simulator studies. International Journal of Environmental Research and Public Health. 2022;19(17):10554, doi: 10.3390/ijerph191710554.

[41] Benedetti MH, Lu B, Kinnear N, et al. The impact of Illinois' comprehensive handheld phone ban on talking on handheld and handsfree cellphones while driving. Journal of Safety Research. 2023;84:273-9, doi: 10.1016/j.jsr.2022.11.003.

[42] Crundall D, Bains M, Chapman P, et al. Regulating conversation during driving: A problem for mobile telephones? Transportation Research Part F: Traffic Psychology and Behaviour. 2005;8(3):197-211, doi: 10.1016/j.trf.2005.01.003.

[43] Bruyas MP, Brusque C, Debailleux S, et al. Does making a conversation asynchronous reduce the negative impact of phone call on driving? Transportation Research Part F: Traffic Psychology and Behaviour. 2009;12(1):12-20, doi: 10.1016/j.trf.2008.06.002.

[44] Maciej J, Nitsch M, Vollrath M. Conversing while driving: The importance of visual information for conversation modulation. Transportation Research Part F: Traffic Psychology and Behaviour. 2011;14(6):512-24, doi: 10.1016/j.trf.2011.05.001.

[45] Michon JA. A critical view of driver behavior models: What do we know, what should we do? In: L.Evans, R.Schwing, editors. Human Behavior and Traffic Safety. Boston, MA: Springer US; 1985. p. 485-524, doi: 10.1007/978-1-4613-2173-6_19.

[46] Van Der Molen HH, Botticher AMT. Risk models for traffic participants: A concerted effort for theoretical operationalizations. Road users and traffic safety. In: Van Ggorcum & Comp BV, editors. Proceedings of the TRB Annual Meeting; 1987; Assen Netherlands; p. 61-81.

Design Studies and Intelligence Engineering
L.C. Jain et al. (Eds.)
© 2024 The Authors.
This article is published online with Open Access by IOS Press and distributed under the terms
of the Creative Commons Attribution Non-Commercial License 4.0 (CC BY-NC 4.0).
doi:10.3233/FAIA231478

TIP CUP: An Interactive System to Promote Tea-Drinking Activities

Yousheng YAO [ab,*], Zhihao HUANG [a,*], Fangtian YING [b,1], Yuan XIE [a], E TANG [a],
Xiqin PAN [a], Fengping FENG [a], Junpeng ZHENG [a], Junqi ZHAN [a], Jin PENG [a], and
Haoteng CHEN [a]

[a] *Zhongkai University of Agriculture and Engineering*
[b] *Macau University of Science and Technology*

Abstract. Tea is a popular beverage and drinking it can be pleasant and promote health. Drinking the right amount of tea can bring refreshment and promote digestion, but quoting too much tea can be harmful to the human body. Brewing water with trace minerals can promote the taste and flavor of tea, and grasping the right brewing temperature can promote the precipitation of tea nutrients. In this article, we introduce Tip Cup, an interactive system that helps users obtain information about their tea through sensors and encourages beneficial tea brewing. Tip Cup consists of a hardware teacup and an application. During use, the tea cup and the application detect and record tea parameters for real-time feedback. The app guides the user to drink a good quality and appropriate amount of tea. We conducted a preliminary user study of the Tip Cup, evaluating four college students. The results show that Tip Cup has a high acceptance level and promotes users to brew quality tea.

Keywords. Tea, Detection, Sensing Technology, Internet of Things

1. Introduction

Tea is one of the most popular beverages in the world and from ancient times, people have had a good habit of drinking tea as it is considered to be health-promoting [1,2,3]. Factors such as water quality and temperature during the brewing process can determine the taste, flavor, and nutrient precipitation of tea, which can make brewing quality tea a challenging task, and excessive tea consumption can lead to insomnia and dental erosion [5].

As the healthiest beverage, moderate consumption of tea can prevent cancer and cardiovascular diseases, thanks to the antioxidants in tea [2,4]. The ratio of tea leaves to water, the temperature and time of brewing, and the number of cycles determines the precipitation of nutrients in tea [6], making it difficult to brew quality tea, and the brewing behavior of most people does not maximize the benefits of tea due to inexperience. Today's work culture has given rise to several unhealthy habits such as

---

* The first two authors contributed equally to the article.

1 Corresponding author,Ying Fangtian, Macau University of Science and Technology, Avenida WaiLong, Taipa, 999078,Macau,13067848819@163.com.

continuous, excessive consumption of tea to obtain a constant state of freshness, excessive consumption of tea can disrupt sleep, cause heart problems, erode teeth, and affect calcium absorption [5], and people can over-rely on the benefits of tea while ignoring the health problems caused by excessive tea consumption.

The technology of human-smart water cup interaction can provide more possibilities for human-computer interaction research, and Zhao Chongsen et al. [9] proposed a multifunctional smart water cup based on STM32, a water cup system that measures water temperature and water volume through sensors, aiming to help people develop good drinking habits and proved to be a good solution to people's drinking problems. Kang Yanping et al. [10] proposed a semiconductor cooling technology applied to a smart mug to realize the functions of the cooling, heating, and constant temperature of the mug, and exchanged data with a smartphone through a wireless communication module to understand various information such as water temperature and drinking habits in real-time, and demonstrated that the temperature-adjustable smart mug can be applied to different people who use it. Our work leverages the previous definition of a smart mug by combining it with step-by-step instruction and real-time feedback to support the user while tea brewing.

In this paper, we present Tip Cup, a sensor technology-based tea brewing system (Figure 1) that includes a hardware teacup and an app. When interacting with the Tip Cup, the tea cup detects the quality and temperature of the brewing water based on sensor signals to determine whether the user's brew is effective. the Tip Cup reminds the user of the timing of brewing and the best time to drink the tea through a signal light at the bottom, and the application records the user's drinking habits to remind the user to drink the tea in moderation.

To build Tip Cup, we conducted tea brewing exploration and developed a prototype with experts. To evaluate users' perception of Tip Cup, we conducted a user test. The results showed that users were willing to use Tip Cup during the tea brewing process and found the real-time prompts useful during the brewing process. Users were able to brew and drink good-tasting tea and establish healthy tea-drinking behaviors. The main contributions of our work are: (1) We designed an interactive system consisting of a hardware tea cup with sensors and an application that allows users to get real-time feedback on tea parameters while brewing and to make correct and effective brewing behaviors. (2) We propose a method to detect users' tea-drinking habits and guide them to drink tea rationally. (3) We further derive a support method for healthy tea drinking through user testing and semi-structured interviews.

Figure 1. Tip Cup system.

2. Related Work

2.1. Reasonable Tea Consumption Support

Previous work has confirmed that smartly detected water cup products can encourage users to establish healthy drinking habits [9,10]. High quality raw materials and rational brewing methods can further stimulate the sensory and nutrient precipitation of tea [6,8]. Due to this importance, many methods have been proposed to support the rational consumption of tea. For example, brewing tea with mountain spring water containing trace minerals can increase the precipitation of nutrients from the tea water. Increasing the number of brewings increases the precipitation of tea polyphenols from tea water. Ascorbic acid in tea water precipitates within 10 minutes of brewing, and the amount decreases after 10 minutes. tea water brewed at 90°C for 10 minutes can be full of aroma in taste, with a soft bitterness and high content of tea polyphenols, ascorbic acid and free amino acids. Inspired by this, this paper explores the possibility of user step-by-step prompts for brewing tea to support users to brew better quality and healthier tea.

2.2. Tea Detector

K. S. Abhijith et al. [7] proposed an immobilized tyrosinase biosensor for the detection of tea polyphenols and demonstrated that the sensor can rapidly and accurately analyze 80 samples with a single enzyme membrane [7]. Amruta Patil et al. [5] proposed the identification and classification of tea using sensory mechanisms and Arduino UNO, PH-based tea taste analysis, and classification of tea concentration in classes to promote healthy tea drinking. Zhong GuoYu et al. [8] used a TDS pen and sensory review to perform a rapid sensory review of tea water and demonstrated that brew length had a significant effect on tea broth concentration in the early stages. Previous work was done to test the coefficients of tea water in the laboratory and to suggest drinking strategies. Based on the previous work, we further the advantages of sensors and smart tea cups to provide step-by-step instruction and real-time feedback to brew quality tea instead of detecting poor quality tea to help users brew quality and healthy tea.

3. Design Process

To design the Tip Cup, we conducted design exploration sessions with experts. We described the design process and the resulting design goals.

3.1. Design Exploration With Experts

We conducted a preliminary study with three tea-making experts (2F, 1M, mean age = 42, P1, P2, and P3) from Chaozhou, Guangdong, China, who have more than 20 years of experience in tea making and tea brewing. Each exploratory session lasted approximately 60 minutes and consisted of a presentation of our preliminary ideas, discussion, and communication with the experts, sharing their previous experience with tea brewing and drinking habits, and semi-structured interviews to gather their insights on our prototype: (i) P1 and P3 suggested that users need real-time feedback on tea brewing and that ordinary users who are not professional tea brewers do not have professional tea brewing experience and skills, and that real-time temperature and ratio tips can help users identify the steps. (ii) P2 suggested that drinking tea could follow a sequence from lightly oxidized to heavily fermented, such as drinking green tea in the morning to feel refreshed and drinking black tea at night to promote metabolism. (iii) P3 suggests that the amount of tea consumed daily should not exceed 10 grams in general, and the temperature should be appropriate when drinking tea, as long-term consumption of overly hot tea can cause burns to the esophageal mucosa or even induce cancer.

3.2. Design Objectives

Based on our design exploration and preliminary work with experts, we synthesized the following key objectives for an interactive system that supports users in brewing tea: (1) Real-time feedback on the brewing process to avoid the user's subjective judgment from affecting the actual results. By physically displaying the parameters of the tea to help users judge the timing of brewing and the timing of drinking, it not only supports users to brew quality tea but also helps them to taste the tea and enhance the drinking experience. (2) Record users' drinking habits to prevent them from over-drinking tea. (3) Guiding users to establish healthy and scientific tea-drinking habits and helping users to make a scientific and reasonable tea-drinking plan, which helps tea become a healthy drink for users.

4. System Description

Based on previous work, we developed a prototype Tip Cup. The Tip Cup consists of hardware and software (Figure 2). The hardware is a teacup with weight detection, temperature detection, TDS detection, and an LED light display. The software is an application that provides step-by-step instructions and records drinking habits. The software is connected to the hardware via Wi-Fi.

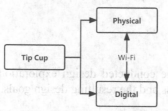

Figure 2. The conceptual framework of Tip Cup.

4.1. System Description

Users can use the application (APP) to view their tea drinking (Figure 3). In the app, users can enter their tea and water data, and the app will work with the hardware tea cup to guide the user through the brewing practice. The application collects data on the user's tea consumption, records the amount consumed, and provides early warning of excessive consumption. In addition, the app assists the user in making a tea-drinking schedule and shows the tea-drinking process through a calendar, and the app can instantly remind the user to drink tea through smartphone notification pop-ups.

Figure 3. Tip Cup APP interface.

4.2. Hardware

The hardware teacup of Tip Cup is made of ceramic, a conventional teacup material, and integrates different sensors and chip processors to handle multiple parts of the function

(Figure 4). We use Arduino UNO as a development board that can collect and transmit sensor data. Sending signals via Wi-Fi communication module.

Water quality TDS, temperature detection, to adapt to the high temperature and water immersion environment when brewing tea, we use the high-precision multi-parameter water quality sensor TFE-1, developed by Bit Atomic Technology Company from Shenzhen, Guangdong Province, China, with built-in TDS, EC, TEM detection function, working environment up to 220 °C, the material is 316 stainless steel and metal platinum, only 6mm in diameter, with waterproof function. We used the water quality detection chip BAT1U-M1 matched with the sensor, this chip is small, which can support the teacup for the solution of dissolved substances and temperature detection.

For tea weight detection, we use the HX711 load cell module, we put the weighing module at the bottom of the teacup, and when the user places the tea, the weighing module will collect the weight information and feedback to the user through the application.

LED light real-time feedback, we use the RGB-LED sensor module on the teacup to achieve real-time feedback, RGB-LED sensor placed at the bottom of the teacup, water quality TDS, temperature detection sensor collected data through the Arduino UNO transmission to the RGB-LED sensor module, RGB-LED sensor module issued different color lights feedback to the user tea dissolved substances and The data collected by the water quality TDS and temperature sensors are transmitted to the RGB-LED sensor module through the Arduino UNO.

4.3. Interaction And Principles

Based on the design exploration, we chose to develop three modes of tea brewing, tea monitoring and assisted drinking tea in the early prototype.

In the brewing tea mode, the user makes tea brewing. Placing the right amount, the tea user places the tea leaves in the strainer of the teacup, and the weighing module of the tea cup records the grams of tea leaves to determine whether the amount of tea brewed by the user is too much this time. The user can view the current tea weight in the application. To make a brew, remove the strainer that holds the tea leaves and pour boiling water into the teacup, the water quality detection module will detect the TDS value and temperature value of the water, and the TDS value and temperature value will be fed back to the user through the application. When the TDS detection module detects an increase in the value of dissolved substances in the tea water, it will think that the tea cup enters brewing mode, then the tea cup will record the brewing time, and when the brewed tea reaches the optimal drinking time and temperature, the RGB-LED module at the bottom of the teacup will again display a bright green light, prompting the user to drink the tea water immediately.

In addition to helping users brew quality tea, Tip Cup will record the tea data each time and send it to the application, which will record the daily tea consumption of users. In the application, users will enter their own height, weight, and age data to match the reasonable daily tea intake, and the application will use this as a warning for tea consumption to prompt users instantly, to prevent users from drinking too much tea and endangering their health. The application will be used as a warning for tea consumption and instantly alert the user to avoid overconsumption of tea, which is harmful to health.

The TDS detection module of the teacup can also detect the quality of drinking water to prevent users from drinking water with too many dissolved substances.

The application will push the relevant tea-drinking plan, to maximize the promotion of healthy tea-drinking, in the application

Users can make their own daily tea-drinking plan, and the app will match the type and amount of tea they drink daily. For special users, for example, women on their period, the app will push sugary tea for women on their period and warn them to avoid drinking tea with high concentration.

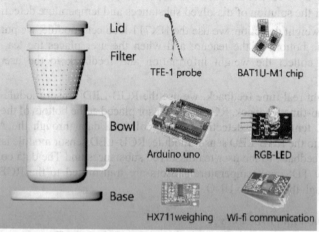

Figure 4. Tip Cup's hardware teacup and sensor.

5. Initial User Research

To identify how users interact with Tip Cup and what users think of Tip Cup, we developed a prototype that demonstrates the design concept (Figure 5). We conducted an initial user study. Influenced by the COVID-19 pandemic, we recruited four student users A, B, C, and D (2F, 2M, mean age 22.5) from a local university. All participants (PA, PB, PC, PD) had a daily tea-drinking habit, and the whole process was recorded with the participant's consent.

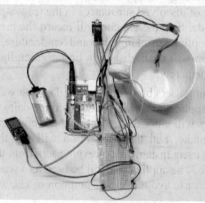

Figure 5. Prototype used in the study.

5.1. Related User Studies

The experiment was conducted in a classroom setting and began with a brief introduction to the prototype and how to use the system. Participants were then given 1 hour to use the Tip Cup independently. During this hour, we observed the participants. Upon completion, we encouraged participants to take the Tip Cup home and use it for 3 days. After use, we used a Likert scale questionnaire (Table 1) to collect participants' perceptions for a semi-structured interview. Three main questions were focused on: (i) The user's relationship with Tip Cup. (ii) Users' insights on the future development of Tip Cup. (iii) The difference between the daily way of drinking tea and the Tip Cup.

5.2. Results

As shown in Table 1, all participants showed a high willingness to use Tip Cup. PA and PD thought that real-time feedback would help them brew tea better, PB said that real-time feedback would prompt me to do it first, but if I missed the step, I would have to reheat the water and brew it again, and it would be better if Tip Cup could finish heating the water for me, PC thought that it was most important to finish brewing quickly. He did not want to keep watching Tip Cup's feedback.

When participants were asked about the Tip Cup's warning about overdosing on tea, PA said, "I think it makes sense to use this cup, I have a habit of drinking tea daily to stay awake, but I may drink too much, and the warning about overdosing makes me pay attention to healthy tea drinking." PB said, "I feel like it's like my tea-drinking butler, I can keep myself informed of my tea-drinking problems." PC hopes that future tea cups will be smart and lightweight.

Table 1. Results of participant survey

Question	PA	PB	PC	PD	Average
A. Are you willing to use Tip Cup in your daily tea-making activities? (1: No - 7: Yes)	7	7	6	7	6.75
B. You easily understand how to use Tip Cup? (1: Difficult - 5: Easy)	6	7	6	6	6.25
C.Tip Cup step-by-step tips for brewing tea helpful? (1: No help - 7: Yes help)	6	5	5	6	5.5
D.Tip Cup records your drinking habits and gives an early warning when you have an overdose, what is your opinion? (1: No help - 7: Yes help)	7	7	6	7	6.75
E. When you finish using Tip Cup, do you have confidence to establish a healthy tea-drinking habit? (1: No confidence - 7: Yes confidence)	7	6	6	7	6.5

6. Limitations And Future Work

We found certain limitations in our study. First, controlled by the epidemic, we only had four experts as knowledge and representatives of healthy tea drinking. With the inclusion of more experts, we may have collected other important factors. Second, the length of user experience is not enough, and we may lack long-term observation and feedback on Tip Cup.

In the future, we will further improve the system features and expand the coverage of Tip Cup's testing. In addition, we will optimize the workflow of Tip Cup to reduce user operation time so that Tip Cup can complete brewing tasks autonomously. We try to expand the hardware coverage of Tip Cup to expand reasonable and healthy tea drinking as a public service so that users can feel smarter and more convenient. Finally, we will also try to recruit more users.

7. Conclusion

In this article, we introduced Tip Cup, an interactive system that helps users brew quality tea and prevent overconsumption, providing real-time feedback and guidance based on their brewing behavior, allowing them to build sensible and healthy tea-drinking habits while brewing quality tea. Our user research shows that Tip Cup can guide users to brew quality tea and support them to establish sensible and healthy tea-drinking habits.

Acknowledgements

We would like to thank all the experimenters and participants involved in this project, as well as the experts who told us and helped us in this process.In addition, this study was supported by the 2021 Guangdong Provincial Quality Engineering Modern Industrial College Project "Eco-design Industrial College", the Guangdong First-class Professional Construction Point: Product Design, the 2021 Guangdong Provincial Department of Science and Technology/Guangdong Provincial Bureau of Rural Revitalization "Guangdong Provincial Rural Science and Technology Specialists in Towns and Villages," stationed in Jiangdong Town, Chaoan District, Chaozhou City, Project No.: KTP20210374, 2021 Zhongkai College of Agricultural Engineering Quality Engineering Special Talent Cultivation Program Construction Project, "Excellence in Rural Revitalization Talent Design and Innovation Class"support.

References

[1] V. R. Sinija,, and H. N. Mishra. "Green tea: Health benefits." Journal of Nutritional & Environmental Medicine 17.4 (2008): 232-242.
[2] S. I.Trevisanato, , and Y. I. Kim. "Tea and health." Nutrition Reviews 58.1 (2000): 1-10.
[3] N Khan, and H. Mukhtar. "Tea and health: studies in humans." Current pharmaceutical design 19.34 (2013): 6141-6147.
[4] D .L. McKay,, and J. B. Blumberg. "The role of tea in human health: an update." Journal of the American College of Nutrition 21.1 (2002): 1-13.
[5] Patil, M. Bachute, and K. Kotecha. "Identification and Classification of the Tea Samples by Using Sensory Mechanism and Arduino UNO." Inventions 6.4 (2021): 94.
[6] Hu Y F, HANG H." Effects OF TEA DRINKING METHODS ON THE CONTENT OF ACTIVE INGREDIENTS In TEA SOUP." SCIENCE AND TECHNOLOGY OF FOOD INDUSTRY.02(2002):27-29.
[7] K. S. Abhijith, et al. "Immobilised tyrosinase-based biosensor for the detection of tea polyphenols." Analytical and bioanalytical chemistry 389.7 (2007): 2227-2234.
[8] Zhong Guo-Yu, WU Cheng-jian,and Lin Yu-ling." Preliminary Study on the Concentration and Sensory Quality of Wuyi Shui-xian Tea Soup." China Tea 42.05(2020):39-41.
[9] Chongsen, Zhao, et al. "Intelligent Water Cup Based on STM32." Proceedings of the 2019 4th International Conference on Robotics, Control and Automation. 2019.
[10] Kang Yanping, Cheng Xiaohui,and Huang Peng." Intelligent water Cup Design using semiconductor refrigeration Technology." Journal of Guilin University of Technology 37.04(2017):707-712.

Design Studies and Intelligence Engineering
L.C. Jain et al. (Eds.)
© 2024 The Authors.
This article is published online with Open Access by IOS Press and distributed under the terms
of the Creative Commons Attribution Non-Commercial License 4.0 (CC BY-NC 4.0).
doi:10.3233/FAIA231479

A Brief Discussion on How Memetics Guides the User Experience Design of Cultural and Creative Products

Dingyu ZHU[a], Yuxiang KUANG[a], Yanqing YANG[a], and Zhanhui GAO[b, 1]

[a] *Jiangxi University of Finance and Economics, Academy of Arts*
[b] *Foshan PERFECTID Industrial Design Co.Ld.*

Abstract. The purpose of this paper is to explore the connection between memes and user experience from the perspective of memetics, and to correspond the three levels of culture with the three dimensions of user experience, so as to construct a new idea for the user experience design of cultural products. This paper takes the cultural and creative products of the Palace Museum as an example for analysis, and classifies the culture they convey. This paper argues that memetics can provide a new perspective and method for the user experience design of cultural and creative products, and help designers better understand and meet the needs of users in terms of senses, behavior and cognition, and create more valuable and attractive cultural and creative products.

Keywords. cultural and creative products; user experience; memetics

1.Introduction about memetics

Memetics is a new theory based on Darwin 's theory of evolution, proposed by British biologist Richard Dawkins in 1976 in his book The Selfish Gene, to explain the laws of cultural evolution. It refers to the ideas or notions that are imitated and spread among people in the cultural field, and are passed down from generation to generation. Meme (meme) uses a pronunciation similar to gene (gene), meaning similar due to the same gene, so meme refers to cultural gene.

Dawkins believes that memes are units of information that can be transmitted from one brain to another through various channels, and undergo evolutionary mechanisms such as variation, selection and inheritance in the process of transmission. Memes can be anything that can be copied, spread and preserved, such as language, customs, beliefs, art, technology, etc. Memes can be divided into three levels in the cultural level: material culture, behavioral culture and spiritual culture. Material culture refers to the manifestation of memes in material form, such as architecture, clothing, crafts, etc.;

---

[1] Corresponding Author.Zhanhui Gao, Foshan PERFECTID Industrial Design Co.Ld, 1501, Block 3, South Zone, Bikguiyuan City Garden, Chancheng District, Foshan City, Guangdong Province, P.R. China; E-mail: 379869619@qq.com.

behavioral culture refers to the manifestation of memes in human behavior, such as etiquette, habits, customs, etc.; spiritual culture refers to the manifestation of memes in human thought, such as beliefs, ideas, values, etc. There is a relationship of mutual influence and restriction between different levels of memes, forming a complex meme syste.

2.Introduction about user experience

User experience is the subjective impression that a product creates in the user during its use. This experience can be categorized into three areas: sensory, behavioral, and cognitive. The user's perception of product appearance, color, sound, smell, and other sensory factors, including aesthetics and comfort, form the basis of sensory experience. User's perception of product function, performance, operation, and other behavioral aspects make up behavioral experience. User's perception of product meaning, value, emotion, and other cognitive traits constitute cognitive experience.

User experience is a crucial factor impacting product satisfaction and loyalty, as well as a strong indicator of product quality and competitiveness. User experience design entails a user-centered approach, studying user needs, expectations, and behavior to design products that align with their psychology and emotions. The field of UX design spans several subject areas, including psychology, sociology, human- computer interaction, and industrial design. The objective is to enhance user satisfaction and product loyalty, boost interaction and communication between users and the product, ultimately generating greater value.

User experience design holds particular significance in the realm of cultural and creative product design, given that such products represent not solely material goods, but cultural symbols as well. Quality cultural and creative products prioritize the aesthetic and emotional needs of the user. Creative products should not only impart information and knowledge but also evoke emotions and values. Therefore, the use of scientific and effective methods to enhance the user experience design of cultural and creative products is a crucial concern for the cultural and creative industry.

3.The Connection between Memetics and User Experience Design of Cultural and Creative Products

The connection between memetics and user experience design of cultural and creative products is that both involve understanding how users perceive, interact with, and respond to the products, and how the products can influence the users' culture and vice versa.

So, how to connect memetics with user experience, how to guide user experience design with memetics. This section will explore the connection between memetics and user experience design from three aspects, namely material culture and sensory experience, behavioral culture and behavioral experience, and spiritual culture and cognitive experience. The relationship between them is shown in Figure 1.

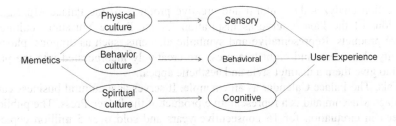

Figure 1. The relationship between memetics and user experience

Physical culture corresponds to sensory experience. It serves as the initial touchpoint for users to engage with cultural and creative products, providing the foundation for users to develop their sensory experiences. Designers of cultural and creative products should take into account users' sensory needs and preferences. Careful selection of appropriate materials, colors, shapes, and textures can elicit beautiful, comfortable, and pleasant experiences through sight, sound, smell, and touch. At the same time, it is important for cultural and creative product design to take into account the unique characteristics and connotations of culture, while carefully selecting representative and symbolic elements. This approach enables users to experience a sense of cultural resonance in their sensory encounters.

Moreover, behavioral culture is complementary to behavioral experience. Behavioral culture pertains to the expression of human behavior patterns when utilizing cultural and creative products, and is crucial in shaping users' behavioral experiences. To ensure positive experiences, the design of cultural and creative products must take into account users' behavioral needs and habits. This includes selecting appropriate functions, interaction methods, and other features to optimize the user experience. In the present era of rapid technological development, cultural and creative products should incorporate behavioral and cultural design to provide users with innovative experiences while also taking into account cultural heritage.

The cognitive experience corresponds to spiritual culture, which encompasses various modalities of human thought, including beliefs, concepts, and values. Spiritual culture serves as the foundation for users to comprehend and assess cultural and creative products. Additionally, it is a key area of focus for users to develop their cognitive experiences. The most significant aspect that should be conveyed to users through cultural and creative products is its underlying cultural significance. Users comprehend and perceive the cultural significance conveyed by a cultural and creative product during the cognitive experience. The cognitive experience is an integral part of the user experience and is interwoven throughout the entire process, similar to storytelling. A well-told story utilizes both sensory and behavioral experiences in tandem, expanding the sensory behavioral experience to a spiritual level through association.

4.User Experience Design Analysis of Cultural and Creative Products of the Palace Museum

This section analyzes the cultural and creative products of the Palace Museum. The collections of the Palace serve as inspiration for the Palace Museum's cultural and creative products. Representative and symbolic elements, such as dragons, phoenixes, longevity characters, and eight treasures, are creatively incorporated into the product design to give them a distinct style and aesthetic appeal.

Take The Palace Calendar as an example. It serves as a cultural business card for the Palace Museum and is a representative product of the Palace Press. The publication has been in circulation for 15 consecutive years and sold over 5 million copies. On September 14, 2023, The Palace Calendar: Book and Painting Edition - 2024 was officially released.

From a sensory perspective, The Palace Calendar offers a unique experience. Painting and Calligraphy Edition - 2024 showcases the intricate details and distinctive characteristics of traditional Chinese painting and calligraphy. The edition presents themes of flora, fauna, and nature that are representative of the four seasons including flowers, birds, grasses, insects, fish, and dragons, as well as vegetables, fruits, and beasts. Each theme is accompanied by distinctive traditional Chinese colors like Obi, Xueqing, Turmeric, and Yuhai Blue (refer to Figure 2) and unique fragrances, specifically tailored to each of the four seasons. The four characters on the cover of the Forbidden City Calendar feature the small seal script from the cover of the 1934 edition (refer to Figure. 3). The background features an auspicious cloud pattern, symbolizing good fortune and happiness in the coming year. This reflects respect for and a desire to inherit history. The antique paper used has a delicate texture and soft color that enhance the calligraphy and painting. The design of the Forbidden City Calendar adheres to these elements. Painting and Calligraphy Edition 2024 provides a visually engaging experience for users. The calendar allows for the appreciation of artistry through its carefully curated collection of paintings and calligraphy pieces. Its stimulating visuals promote a sense of comfort and pleasure as users interact with the calendar by seeing, touching, and turning its pages.

In terms of behavioral culture, The Forbidden City Calendar: Painting and Calligraphy Edition-2024 offers several interactive and educational features, including audio explanations, AR video animations (refer to Figure 4), and scent experiences. Painting and Calligraphy Edition-2024 includes extras such as a Fire Cloud Dragon Badge, bookmarks, and bookmarks, enabling users to appreciate the calendar and other cultural and creative products simultaneously. The 2024 Book and Painting Edition calendar aims to provide users with an enjoyable and engaging experience.

These features not only enhance users' understanding and appreciation of the calligraphy and painting works but also increase their interest in utilizing and collecting the calendar. The 2024 Painting and Calligraphy Edition expresses the spiritual and cultural values of traditional Chinese culture, including nature, harmony, beauty, and virtue. Thematic style designs for the paintings and calligraphy works, along with skillful interactive communication, convey these values to users. The Forbidden City Calendar provides a platform for this expression. Painting and Calligraphy Edition- 2024 selects Obi, Snowy Green, Turmeric, and Jade Hairpin Blue, which are traditional Chinese colors, to correlate with the four seasons theme. Additionally, the company tailors Plum Blossom Scent, Lotus Scent, Osmanthus Scent, and Pine and Cypress Scent to the various seasonal themes. These colors and scents can stimulate the user's visual and olfactory senses. With the assistance of emerging technologies, such as the Internet and AR, users may fully immerse themselves in the charms of Chinese culture.

The Forbidden City Calendar conveys elements of material culture. The 2024 Painting and Calligraphy Edition showcases small seal script, auspicious cloud patterns, traditional Chinese colors, and other patterns featuring birds, flowers, and animals. The conveyed behavioral culture includes painting, calligraphy, flower appreciation, and festive customs. The spiritual culture predominantly comprises Chinese concepts of festivals and family, as well as the Chinese people's appreciation for time, life, and aesthetics.

Figure 2   Figure 3   Figure4

5.Conclusion

This paper briefly discusses the connection between memetics and user experience design. User needs and motivations are the key factors that drive user experience design. The goal of user experience design for a cultural and creative product is to meet users' needs for appreciation and understanding of the culture carried by the product. Therefore, before designing a cultural and creative product, we need to conduct a comprehensive research and analysis of users ' needs for culture. And through the perspective of meme, we can use a new method to understand users' needs for cultural and creative products. The general idea is as described in this paper, to select cultural memes and apply them in the corresponding user experience design, to enhance users' experience in using cultural and creative products, and to achieve better cultural communication and inheritance. This paper also has many shortcomings, such as only proposing a design thinking of memetics guiding user experience design of cultural and creative products, which needs to be refined in terms of design methods. In addition, in the new era, the needs of ordinary people for cultural and creative products are changing, such as customization and personalization. How to solve these problems requires more in-depth and extensive research in the follow-up design theory and practice.

References

[1] DAWKINS R. The Selfish Gene. New York: Oxford University Press, 1976.

[2] Fu Yanxiang. Research on Xiangtan paper shadow cultural product design under the memetics. Packaging Engineering, 2020, 41(18):165-167

[3] Zhou Xian. Research on digital cultural and creative design based on user experience. Industrial Innovation Research, 2023(13):97-99.

[4] Zhong Linzhou. User experience design elements and their application in product design--Taking "Dunhuang Wall Story" as an example. Science and technology wind, 2019(15):248.

[5] Chen Huihui . Research on the Design Strategy of Non-legacy App from the Perspective of User Experience. Tomorrow's Style, 2021(22):110

[6] Deng Yu, Li Juan. Meme Theory and Its Application in Cultural and Creative Industries. Beijing: China Social Sciences Press, 2016.

[7] Wang Xiaojuan, Wang Xiaojuan. Application of Meme Theory in Cultural and Creative Product Design [M]. Beijing: China Academy of Art Press, 2018.

[8] Cheng Hui. An Overview of Domestic Cultural and Creative Product Design Methods. Beijing: Tsinghua University Press, 2021.

[9] Huang Guanghui, Chen Liang, Tang Shan. Macau Ruins of St. Paul 's Cultural and Creative Product Design Based on Meme Theory. Macau: Macau University of Science and Technology Press, 2016.

[10] Ge Lu. Mongolian Folklore Cultural and Creative Product Design Based on Morphological Matrix Method. Hohhot: Inner Mongolia University Press, 2019.

Design Studies and Intelligence Engineering
L.C. Jain et al. (Eds.)
© 2024 The Authors.
This article is published online with Open Access by IOS Press and distributed under the terms
of the Creative Commons Attribution Non-Commercial License 4.0 (CC BY-NC 4.0).
doi:10.3233/FAIA231480

641

MyCmp: Temporomandibular Joint Disorder Monitoring and Regulation System

Yousheng YAO[ab,*] , Xiqin PAN[a,*] , Fangtian YING[b,1] , E TANG[a] , Zhihao HUANG[a] ,
Yuan XIE[a] , BinAo HE[c] , Junpeng ZHENG[a] , Jin PENG[a] , Jiaqi ZHANG[a] , and
Haoteng CHEN[a]

[a] *Zhongkai University of Agriculture and Engineering, He Xiangning College of Art and Design, China*
[b] *Macau University of Science and Technology*
[c] *Hunan Agricultural University*

Abstract. Temporomandibular disorder (TMD) is a common musculoskeletal disease in the oral and maxillofacial regions. It is a complex syndrome mainly characterized by pain, popping, and abnormal joint movement in the temporomandibular joint area of the affected side. The masticatory muscle, temporomandibular joint, and related structures are involved. The pathogenesis of masticatory muscle, temporomandibular joint, and related structures is still unclear. As a wearable device with high social acceptance and widespread use, we designed a customized frame for glasses to monitor temporomandibular chewing movement data collection and generate a learning model. The temporomandibular joint disorder database was constructed to assist stomatologists in diagnosis and to help customize personalized precision treatment models for patients. We propose MyCmp to capture chewing signals and achieve accurate temporomandibular joint chewing data collection by combining piezoelectric sensors and motion sensors. We also propose a practical method that combines temporomandibular joint disorders with artificial intelligence, and we designed test experiments to evaluate the practical application of MyCmp. It is our hope that the development and use of MyCmp can benefit patients with TMJ disorders.

Keywords. Temporomandibular joint disorder, disorder detection, multi-modal, sensor, wearable device

1. Introduction

The temporomandibular joint (TMJ) consists of the mandibular head, the temporomandibular fossa, and the articular tuberosity. It is a joint between the left and right sides of the jaw, governing the opening and closing of the mouth and mastication. Temporomandibular disorders (TMD) are common musculoskeletal disorders of the oral and maxillofacial region, the pathogenesis of which is not yet fully understood. Clinical manifestations include pain in the joint area, joint popping during movement, and impaired jaw movement. This poses a significant challenge to clinicians in designing individualized treatment plans for patients with TMD[1].Currently, the diagnosis of TMJ

---

[*]The first two authors contributed equally to the article.

[1]Corresponding Author: Ying Fangtian, Macau University of Science and Technology, Avenida WaiLong, Taipa, 999078, Macau, 13067848819@163.com.

disorder relies on clinical assessment and magnetic resonance imaging (MRI). However, it has been found that there is wide variation in the agreement between the position of the articular disc on MRI and the clinical symptoms, ranging from 59% to 90%[2].This presents a substantial challenge to physicians in creating customized treatment plans for patients. Addressing how to provide accurate diagnosis and precise treatment for patients with TMJ disorders is the next question we will tackle.

At present, it is known that most diagnoses and treatments of TMD are based on conservative approaches, and the probability of therapeutic effectiveness remains unclear. Therefore, the diagnosis of TMD and the choice of a treatment plan are of paramount importance. Different TMD classifications require corresponding treatment plans, and combinations of different treatments can be considered[3]. To address these challenges, we conducted extensive research to develop a TMJ disorder monitoring and adjustment system. This system helps collect TMJ movement data for monitoring and adjusting masticatory habits. To broaden its applicability and practicality, the TMJ disorder monitoring and adjustment system must provide accurate monitoring while being energy-efficient in various environments. Through our research, we found that using glasses as a socially acceptable wearable device offers an effective solution. By attaching the monitoring system to glasses, we achieve precise monitoring. Placing the glasses close to the mouth is conducive to proper detection and identification of TMJ movements.

We have developed MyCmp (My Conditioning Monitoring Partner), a TMJ motion monitoring system attached to eyeglasses. Our development is divided into two parts: the first part involves MyCmp's use of two sensors to achieve accurate chewing signal capture, accomplished by combining piezoelectric sensors and accelerometers. The second part of our development is the direct attachment of these sensors to eyeglasses, eliminating the need for custom personalized frames.To ensure the reliability and evaluation of the MyCmp (My Conditioning Monitoring Partner) TMJ motion monitoring system we developed, we built a prototype and collected real data from users in real-world scenarios. The primary purpose of this data collection is to assess the system's accuracy and its adaptability in various scenarios. Over the course of a week, we collected TMJ movement trajectories from users throughout the day and accurately monitored the data. This data was then compared with MRI images to evaluate the MyCmp (My Conditioning Monitoring Partner) TMJ motion monitoring system we developed.The MyCmp (My Conditioning Monitoring Partner) temporomandibular joint motion monitoring system was designed to evaluate the system's rationality, accuracy, and applicability.

2. Background and Related Work

2.1. Diagnosis of temporomandibular joint disorder

Temporomandibular joint disorder (TMD) is one of the four most common diseases in the oromandibular system[4]. The clinical symptoms include pain, dyskinesia, joint popping/murmur, and headache, which are more common in young adults and significantly more common in women than men. Therefore, raising awareness of the disease among clinicians[6-7], and prompt diagnosis and treatment can reduce further damage.

Clinical symptoms of temporomandibular joint disorder (TMD) include TMJ pain, TMJ murmur, restricted mouth opening, occlusal distress, and joint popping. While these symptoms are not threatening, prolonged untreated symptoms can become more pronounced and affect the patient's psychological well-being and quality of life. The diagnosis is made clinically, in conjunction with MRI, which is one of the most complex parts of the body and is not as accurate as it could be.

With the increase in the attendance of such patients, accurate diagnosis is particularly important. Magnetic resonance imaging (MRI) is the imaging method of choice for diagnosing displaced articular discs. It is non-invasive, involves no exposure to ionizing radiation, and provides clear imaging of soft tissues[5]. However, it has been found that there is a wide variation in the agreement between the position of the articular disc shown in MRI and the diagnosis of clinical symptoms, ranging from 59% to 90%[2]. This also places significant pressure on clinicians to provide accurate diagnoses and develop treatment plans for patients.

2.2. Detection of temporomandibular joint disorder

Detection and diagnosis of temporomandibular joint disorder are currently based on clinical assessment using dental imaging, with two widely used modalities: the first involves X-ray radiographs, and computed tomography (CT) scans are commonly employed as auxiliary imaging tests for diagnosing TMD. However, CT diagnosis has faced criticism due to its limitations in observing soft tissues and intra-articular fluid around the TMJ.The second modality is magnetic resonance imaging (MRI), which has become increasingly popular with advances in imaging technology. MRI can effectively detect soft tissue structures around the TMJ and intra-articular effusion, but it may still fall short of providing dentists with the precise information needed to tailor treatment plans for individual patients.

Several studies[8-10]have explored the correlation between MRI manifestations and clinical symptoms in patients with TMD, primarily focusing on the relationship with. Koca et al.[8]evaluated clinical and MRI data from both bilateral joints in 350 individuals with TMD. They concluded that joint pain was associated with displacement of the articular disc, degenerative changes in the condylar bone, joint effusion, and deformation of the articular disc structure. Takahara et al[9].reported that increased ADDWoR (Additive of Anterior and Posterior Disc Displacement) and joint effusion were strongly linked to pain. HostGator et al.[10]also found that significant joint effusion was statistically associated with joint pain. Given this context, understanding the relationship between clinical symptom presentation and TMJ joint changes in patients with TMD is essential for accurately determining and preventing functional impairment resulting from abnormal changes. It is also crucial for developing appropriate treatment plans.

2.3. Treatment related to temporomandibular joint disorder

- TMD uses body posture therapy

In recent years, many researchers have suggested a correlation between TMD and body posture, making postural adjustment a new treatment modality for TMD patients. A two-month review revealed that the patient's masticatory muscles returned to their previous levels. This suggests that CPR therapy can effectively treat patients with TMJ disorder, but this method requires long-term self-adjustment of posture[11].

- TMD treated with an occlusal plate

Occlusal plates are currently a common treatment used in dentistry for patients with TMD. Patients wear a stabilized dental pad for several months to observe TMJ changes in patients with TMJ disorder. Some patients have reported improvements in clinical symptoms while wearing the occlusal plate. However, many patients find that the occlusal plates are not comfortable for long-term wear and do not fit all patients. They are not suitable for patients with existing temporomandibular problems or those undergoing orthodontic treatment with braces.

We developed MyCmp (My Conditioning Monitoring Partner), a TMJ movement monitoring system integrated with glasses. Our system serves two primary purposes:Firstly, it provides a comprehensive record of TMJ movement for patients experiencing TMJ disorder-related symptoms. It records biting patterns, oral opening and closing movements, and establishes an individualized medical history data collection, along with creating a digital model of the TMJ. We integrate artificial intelligence to learn from this model and generate a digital representation of the TMJ. This tool assists doctors in tailoring precise treatment plans for each patient.Secondly, the captured data will be linked to the app we plan to develop in the future. This app will serve as a reminder for patients to maintain correct chewing and biting postures. By improving their posture, we aim to treat TMJ disorder patients effectively.

3. Design Process

To establish the feasibility of implementing the MyCmp (My Conditioning Monitoring Partner) TMJ motion monitoring system, we first discussed its rationale with experts, then explored design options with our mentor, and finally presented the process and goals of our design.

3.1. Design Survey

We conducted a preliminary survey by consulting three individuals: one TMJ research specialist with over 10 years of experience, one specialist with more than 5 years of experience in the study of oral dental occlusion, and one patient diagnosed with TMJ disorder who has over 5 years of experience from Southern Medical University Dental Hospital in Guangdong Province, China. Our communication sessions involved a mean age of 40 (SD = 9.37) and were identified as K1, K2, and K3.The survey interviews lasted between 50 to 90 minutes, during which we presented our ideas on TMJ disorder detection, introduced the MyCmp (My Conditioning Monitoring Partner) TMJ motion monitoring system, engaged in discussions, and gathered their perspectives on our research topic.TMJ researchers believe that a real-time and accurate system for detecting TMJ motion trajectories would be highly beneficial for clinicians. Oral and dental occlusion experts emphasized the strong relationship between TMJ disorder patients and the muscular tissues around the temporomandibular joint. They identified one significant contributing factor as a long-term incorrect chewing pattern. They believe that MyCmp can autonomously guide patients to chew correctly, offering a valuable treatment option for TMJ patients.Patients diagnosed with TMJ disorder expressed their anticipation for MyCmp, stating, "It would be great to diagnose TMJ disorder without the need for surgery, and having a correct bite reminder is exactly what we need."Several recommendations emerged from these discussions:(i) K1 and K2 proposed the creation of a database of correct occlusions for various dental models to ensure accurate treatment.(ii) K3 suggested that MyCmp should be designed with the user's comfort in mind, considering the scenario in which it will be worn.

3.2. Design Objectives

After conducting preliminary research and discussing related work with psychologists, we identified key tasks that should be incorporated into an interactive system to guide the construction of the system:(1) The designed system should seamlessly integrate sensors with existing commercially available eyewear and should not be limited by specific materials and frame shapes.(2) The system should aim for an extended range to meet requirements while integrating low-power sensors.(3) Precise capture of TMJ motion signals is crucial for achieving accurate sensitivity.(4) The system's appearance should be adaptable to various scenarios and must prioritize comfort for wearers.

4. System Description

As part of our preliminary design research and discussions with experts, we developed a text model and conducted initial tests. Hardware refers to the integration of piezoelectric and accelerometer sensors on MyCmp, and we capture TMJ motion signals using the combination of these two sensors, as illustrated in Figure 1. The software design is connected to an app that reports the signals captured by the sensors, generating temporomandibular motion trajectory data throughout the day.

4.1. Hardware Design

The hardware refers to a combination of piezoelectric and accelerometer sensors on the MyCmp. We use this combination of sensors to capture the temporomandibular motion signal, as illustrated in Figure 1. The piezoelectric sensor is employed to detect temporomandibular and temporal muscle contractions during oral occlusion. This muscle contraction generates significant mechanical dynamic forces on the skin, making it more easily perceivable. For the piezoelectric sensor, we utilized a thin-film pressure sensor, as shown in Figure 2, which can make direct contact with the skin to obtain accurate sensing signals. We integrate the piezoelectric sensor with the glasses, ensuring natural contact with the skin to monitor the TMJ movement trajectory without causing user discomfort.

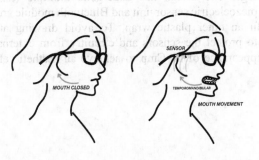

Figure 1. Temporomandibular motion trajectory signal capture.

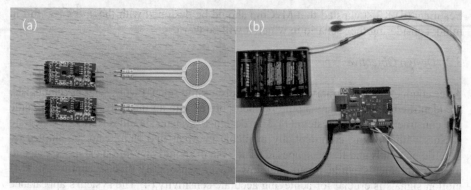

Figure 2. (a)Thin Film Pressure Sensors. (b)Sensor combination method.

4.2. Hardware construction and assembly

After completing the design, we integrated the piezoelectric sensors into the eyeglass frame for practical testing. To ensure user comfort without interference from other activities, we positioned the piezoelectric sensors on both sides of the eyeglass legs, close to the temporomandibular muscle occlusion point and near the upper zygomatic bone position. We also equipped the system with an ESP to provide sufficient computing power for running the deep learning model. Both wires were installed on either side of the eyeglass legs and connected to the ESP device, as illustrated in Figures 3 and 4.

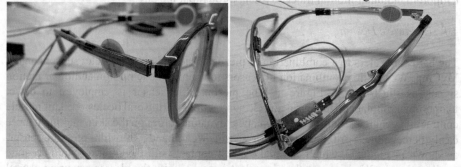

Figure 3 and Figure 4. Hardware construction and assembly method.

The piezoelectric sensor unit and the Bluetooth module are positioned on both sides of the glasses' legs. The design has undergone multiple tests to ensure accurate monitoring. The piezoelectric sensor unit and Bluetooth module are located on the inside of the legs, with an outer plastic wrap. To avoid drawing attention to the user's appearance and to protect the sensors and circuitry from external exposure, we have redesigned the appearance of MyCmp to achieve an aesthetic effect, as illustrated in Figure 5.

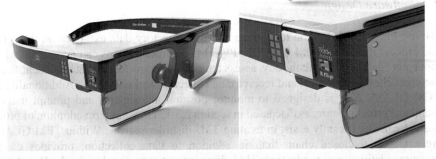

Figure 5. MyCmp exterior design.

4.3. Temporomandibular joint occlusion monitoring system design

We developed MyCmp (My Conditioning Monitoring Partner), a TMJ motion monitoring system, and designed the system framework of MyCmp, as depicted in Figure 6. For our hardware, we utilized a combination of piezoelectric sensors and accelerometers to collect various data points, including (i) the angle of mouth opening and closing, (ii) TMJ changes during food chewing, (iii) yawning and other scenarios requiring wide mouth opening that affect the TMJ and mandibular joint movements in occlusal posture.To process this data, we employed the ESP32 microcontroller for data preprocessing. The processed data is then transformed and relayed to the TEM GLASS APP via Python processing. We have designed a visualization page to present this data to TMJ disorder patients. These data are saved in real-time and utilized for AI learning. This AI learning process generates a dedicated personal database, accessible to physicians for tailoring treatments to individual patients.To prioritize user privacy, we ensure that raw data remains confidential and is not shared with external parties.

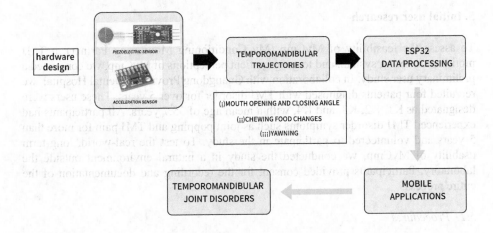

Figure 6. MyCmp's system framework.

4.4. Software Design

We use librosa with Python to analyze all TMJ trajectory data extracted on the server and process it into the TEM GLASS APP. TMJ disorder patients can review their TMJ movement data throughout the day, assess their bite patterns for correctness, identify any incorrect chewing patterns, and receive data collection and reminders. Additionally, the TEM GLASS APP is designed to monitor postural adjustments and prompt users to maintain correct posture, as discussed in section 2.3.1. The long-term adoption of proper posture can significantly assist in treating TMJ disorder patients.Within TEM GLASS, we establish a closed chain that, in addition to data collection, provides dietary recommendations for foods that TMJ disorder patients should avoid. The data is organized by individual, ranging from daily records to weekly, monthly, and annual data.

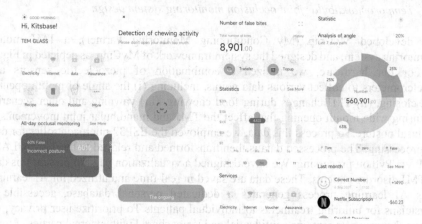

Figure 7. TEM GLASS APP design and data analysis.

5. Initial user research

To assess the feasibility of MyCmp (My Conditioning Monitoring Partner), a TMJ motion monitoring system, and to gauge patient perceptions of MyCmp, we conducted a preliminary user study. In collaboration with Guangdong Provincial Dental Hospital, we recruited four patients diagnosed with TMJ disorder for over 5 years. These users were designated as K1, K2, K3, and K4, with mean age of 35.7 years. All participants had experienced TMJ disorder symptoms such as joint popping and TMJ pain for more than 5 years and volunteered to participate in the study. To test the real-world, long-term usability of MyCmp, we conducted the study in a natural environment outside the laboratory. Participants provided consent for the recording and documentation of the entire process.

5.1. Procedures

The experiment was a 10-hour experience for four participants who chose to return the equipment and a week-long study for those who wished to continue. All four participants, including college students and office workers, were habitual eyeglass wearers. On the study day, participants arrived at the lab in the morning to collect their MyCmp glasses and downloaded the TEM GLASS app for a day of data collection. Throughout the morning, participants engaged in their usual daily activities. In the evening, they returned to the lab to return the equipment and participate in a semi-structured interview.

- How comfortable is it to wear MyCmp glasses?

- Is the TEM GLASS APP data self-perception accurate?

- Is the TEM GLASS APP effective in reminding the mouth opening function?

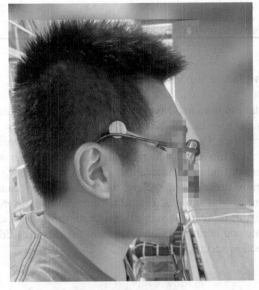

Figure 8. Participants try it on.

5.2. Results

In our formal interviews with the participants, K1 smiled and said, "The TEM GLASS APP's posture reminder feature subconsciously makes me pay attention to the angle of mouth opening and closing, and as a result, my joints pop much less throughout the day." K3 expressed, "Wearing it hasn't seemed to affect my daily activities, and I find the test data quite accurate personally. It even detected when I yawned and reminded me to be mindful of my mouth's movements." Both K1 and K3 have hopes for future improvements. They mentioned concerns about the current exposure of the sensor and wires, which could be problematic when exposed to water. They hope that, in the future, there will be a protective shell for the glasses, concealing the sensor and wires within.

Interestingly, an examination of K4's data revealed some undetected TMJ motion. When asked about the circumstances surrounding the false alarm, K4 responded, "I was wearing headphones, which might have caused them to come into physical contact with MyCmp, potentially affecting the monitoring system's detection data.

Overall, all participants expressed confidence in the usefulness of MyCmp glasses for treating TMJ disorder. My findings indicate that MyCmp glasses provide an effective means of collecting data and treating TMJ disorder patients.

Table 1. User Survey Results

Question	K1	K2	K3	K4	Average
1. Are you willing to wear MyCmp glasses for a long time? (1:willing - 6: unwilling)	5.7	6	6	5.8	5.9
2. Do you have confidence in the data detected by MyCmp glasses? (1: Yes - 6: No)	5.2	5.5	6	5.3	5.5
3. Do you think wearing MyCmp glasses has affected your normal life? (1: Yes - 6: No)	6	5.7	5.8	5.7	5.8
4. Has the reminder function of MyCmp glasses helped you to be actively aware of temporomandibular movements? (1: Yes - 6: No)	5.8	5.6	5.4	6	5.7

6. Limitations and future work

Firstly, it's important to note that MyCmp glasses may not be suitable for patients who are unwilling to wear glasses. Our research indicates that glasses are the most socially accepted wearable device. However, for users unaccustomed to wearing glasses, this may be a limitation of MyCmp. Often, the reluctance to wear glasses stems from not being accustomed to them or finding them unattractive. Nevertheless, we believe that as smart glasses become more prevalent in society, this situation may change.Secondly, in the initial development of MyCmp glasses, the sensors and wires were exposed. However, we plan to address this issue in the subsequent iterations of our design.

We will update and iterate MyCmp glasses in the future based on user feedback to improve data detection accuracy.

7. Conclusion

In this paper, we introduce MyCmp glasses, a data collection system that accurately detects TMJ trajectories in patients with TMJ disorder. It also incorporates a reminder function that combines Global Postural Reeducation (GPR) with real-time reminders to assist patients in regulating their posture and improving TMJ disorder. By integrating Global Postural Reeducation (GPR) into the real-time reminder function, we aim to enhance the treatment of TMJ disorder. The collected TMJ motion data can be provided to physicians to help customize treatment plans for individual patients. We have achieved accurate detection by combining piezoelectric sensors with accelerometers. User studies have demonstrated that MyCmp glasses, in conjunction with the TEM GLASS APP, facilitate data collection and analysis. We conducted real-world data collection from four patients outside the lab throughout the day, confirming the accuracy of our design in detecting TMJ motion.We believe that the MyCmp glasses we have developed can significantly benefit TMJ disorder patients and will be a valuable tool for their subsequent treatment.

8. Acknowledgements

Thank you to the members who participated in this project, as well as the experts who guided me in practice. In addition, this study was supported by the 2021 Guangdong

Provincial Quality Engineering Modern Industrial College Project "Eco-design Industrial College", the Guangdong First-class Professional Construction Point: Product Design, the 2021 Guangdong Provincial Department of Science and Technology/Guangdong Provincial Bureau of Rural Revitalization "Guangdong Provincial Rural Science and Technology Specialists in Towns and Villages," stationed in Jiangdong Town, Chaoan District, Chaozhou City, Project No.: KTP20210374, 2021 Zhongkai College of Agricultural Engineering Quality Engineering Special Talent Cultivation Program Construction Project, "Excellence in Rural Revitalization Talent Design and Innovation Class" support.

References

[1] Xu Chenxi, Cao Zemin, Xu Gangzhu. Research progress in the pathogenesis of temporomandibular joint disease. *Journal of Practical Hospital Clinics,* 2022,**19**(05):202–204.

[2] WANG Xinrui, WEN Baohong, QIAO Yongming, QIAO Yiqiang. The value of multilevel multidimensional MRI to assess temporomandibular joint disc position. *Guangdong Medicine*, 2022, 1–6.

[3] Liu Hongchen. Research and clinical progress of temporomandibular joint disease in China. Chinese Journal of Oral Journal of Chinese Stomatology, 2014, 49(7):385-389 Liu HC. Research and clinical progress of temporo-mandibular arthropathy in China[J]. *Chin J Stomatol,* 2014, **49**(7): 385-389.

[4] Dong M, Sun Q, Yu Q, et al. Determining the optimal magnetic resonance imaging sequences for the efficient diagnosis of tem-poromandibular joint disorders. *Quant Imaging Med Surg,*2021,**11**(4) : 1343–1353.

[5] Poluha RL, Cunha CO, Bonjardim LR, et al. Temporomandibular joint morphology does not influence the presence of arthralgia in patients with disk displacement with reduction: a magnetic reso- nance imaging – based study. *Oral Surg Oral Med Oral Pathol Oral Radiol,*2020,**129**(2) : 149–157.

[6] ROBERT L, GAUER, MICHAEL J, et al. Diagnosis and treatment of temporomandibular disorders. *Am Fam Physician,* 2015, **91**(6):378–386.

[7] Pei Yu-Wen, Zeng Chun-Guang, Yang Guang-Ming, et al. Diagnostic value of MRI in temporomandibular joint disorder syndrome. *Jiangxi Medicine*, 2020, **55**(10): 1522–1524.

[8] Guan Xiaohui,Ma Longbai. Advances in MRI studies of temporomandibular joint disorders. *Imaging Research and Medical Applications*, 2021, **5**(12):1–2.

[9] Zhao Erjun Zhang Dongmei. MRI imaging study of joint disc deformation in patients with unilateral joint pain TMD. *Imaging Research and Medical Applications*, 2018, **2**(18):30–32.

[10] Drace JE, Enzmann D R.Defining the normaltemporomandibularjointclosed-,partially open-,and open-mouth MR imaging ofasymptomatic subjects. *Radiology*, 1990, **177**(1):67–71.

[11] JIN Chunxiao, YANG Lin, LIU Yang, LI Xiaojing, YU Lixia, GAO Shanshan. Research progress on the correlation between temporomandibular joint disorder and body posture. *Dentistry*, 2022, **42**(04):368–372.

Design Studies and Intelligence Engineering
L.C. Jain et al. (Eds.)
© *2024 The Authors.*
This article is published online with Open Access by IOS Press and distributed under the terms
of the Creative Commons Attribution Non-Commercial License 4.0 (CC BY-NC 4.0).
doi:10.3233/FAIA231481

Feasibility Analysis on the Design of Elderly Volunteer Maintenance Service in Rural Cultural Facilities in Guangdong

Qi SONG[a,1], Yuxin LIANG[b], Bingjie SUN[b] and Riyang LI[b]

[a] *Guangdong University of Finance & Economics*
[b] *Guangdong University of Finance & Economics, Foshan University, Guangdong Polytechnic*

Abstract. In the context of rural community-based elderly care and rural cultural revitalization, with the maintenance system of rural cultural facilities in Guangdong as the foundation, this paper retrospects the status of "elderly volunteer service" at home and abroad and the service design theory involved in the maintenance system of rural cultural facilities, and introduces the theory and method of service design to demonstrate the feasibility of integrating "elderly volunteer service" and "the maintenance system of rural cultural facilities" through quantitative and qualitative research. Based on the findings of desktop research and field research, integrated the design principle of stakeholder-oriented, collaborative, real and holistic, this paper tries to put forward the guiding principles of the elderly volunteer maintenance service design of rural cultural facilities in Guangdong, including the principles of system construction, project management and content supply, and the corresponding design path and practical measures. This paper aims to improve the research system of community home-based care, and the level of social participation of rural elderly groups, practices a positive view of the elderly, and provides some theoretical and practical reference for the realization of "productive aging".

Keywords. Service design, Rural revitalization, Maintenance of cultural facilities, Elderly volunteer service

1. Introduction

According to the National Bureau of Statistics' 2021 "China Statistical Yearbook", as of 2020, the population aged 60 years and above in rural areas of China is approximately 121 million, accounting for 45.96% of the population aged 60 years and above in China. The "Rural Construction Action Implementation Plan" issued by the General Office of the CPC Central Committee and the General Office of the State Council in 2022 proposes to strengthen the construction of spiritual civilization, promote the construction of rural cultural facilities, and carry out in-depth rural spiritual civilization creation activities. Among them, the construction of rural cultural facilities is an important carrier to promote the high-quality development of rural spiritual civilization. However, rural areas lack accessible cultural services for the elderly currently, and rural cultural facilities generally have the problem of "emphasis on

---

[1] Corresponding Author: Qi Song, Deputy Dean, School of Art and Design, Guangdong University of Finance & Economics, 21 Luntou Road, Haizhu District, Guangzhou, China; Email: songqi@gdufe.edu.cn.

construction but neglect of maintenance". which seriously hinders the high-quality development of rural elderly care and rural cultural revitalization. Active aging, as defined by the World Health Organization in 2003, is a process of improving elderly individuals' quality of life by optimizing their health, social engagement, and ensuring opportunities as much as possible. Elderly volunteer is an important component of active aging. In the "Survey Report on the Living Conditions of the Elderly in Urban and Rural China" released by the China Research Center on Aging, 45.6% of the elderly nationwide expressed interest in volunteer services. However, rural communities in China face challenges in developing elderly volunteer services. Therefore, it is necessary to integrate elderly volunteer services into the maintenance system of rural cultural facilities, improve facility maintenance, ensure their sustainability, and promote rural spiritual development, aligning with active aging policies.

2. Comparative analysis of the current research status of elderly volunteer services at home and abroad

Foreign research on elderly volunteer services mainly focuses on the value dimensions of such services, with little attention given to the specific practical paths of elderly volunteer service. Wheeler believes that the elderly can significantly enhance their own happiness by participating in volunteer services. The elderly in good health are an important auxiliary human resource that can meet the service needs of some vulnerable elderly groups, disabled children and other vulnerable groups [1]. Van Willigen believes that longer involvement in volunteer service boosts life satisfaction and significantly contributes to maintaining psychological well-being among elderly volunteers [2]. Schwingel asserts that continual engagement of the elderly in volunteer services not only enhances social interaction and participation opportunities but also fortifies their psychological well-being [3]. Barron and others posit that the involvement the elderly in productive activities such as community-based volunteer services is an effective way to promote health [4]. Anderson contends that the participation of the elderly in volunteer services can alleviate symptoms of depression, enhance overall health, reduce functional limitations, and lower mortality rates [5].

Domestic research on elderly volunteer services primarily concentrates on macro-strategies for urban community elderly volunteer services, with little focus on rural communities where facing more severe aging challenges. Chen Ming and others believe that encouraging and supporting the elderly group to participate in volunteer services will help improve the effectiveness of human resources for the elderly group and facilitate a more reasonable allocation of social human resources [6]. Li Qin views participation in volunteer services as a crucial channel and pathway for the elderly to realize their life's societal value, experience joy, and be productive in old age [7]. Wu Jinjing and others emphasize the importance of recognizing the proactive role of the elderly in enhancing their own quality of life and creating more opportunities for them to unleash their potential [8]. Zhang Na believes that elderly volunteer services not only optimize the utilization of elderly human resources, addressing deficiencies in institutional and familial community care, but also boost elderly social engagement enthusiasm, enabling a form of "spiritual self-nourishment." [9]. Miao Qing contends that engaging in volunteer services plays a promoting role in the psychological well-being of vulnerable elderly populations. [10].

After reviewing the current status of research on elderly volunteer services both domestically and internationally, it is found that scholars have overlooked the role of elderly volunteering in rural communities. Consequently, there is a necessity to conduct an empirical research on the feasibility of integrating elderly volunteer services into the maintenance system of rural cultural facilities.

3. Empirical research

The subject research involves experimental settings focused on the maintenance system of rural cultural facilities in Guangdong and elderly volunteer services. A comprehensive approach is employed, combining qualitative and quantitative research methods, including desk research, quantitative analysis of survey questionnaires, and qualitative interviews with stakeholders. Centered around the maintenance system of rural cultural facilities in Guangdong, this paper starts with an exploration of the current cultural life of elderly populations in rural areas. It delves into the present status of elderly volunteer service participation, moving beyond surface observations to extract the essence of current pain points and demands of rural elderly volunteer services in Guangdong. The research aims to gain insights into the future trends of the integrated development of elderly volunteer services and the maintenance system of rural cultural facilities.

3.1. Scale design

Experiment 1 employed the structured framework of field research proposed by Robson and McCart [11]. Specific observation targets encompassed space, actors, activities, objects, behaviors, events, time, goals, and sensations. By combining firsthand data collected through field research, the obtained data was organized, filtered, and analyzed to derive the structured framework for field research of cultural facilities in Shancha Village.

Experiment 2 utilized the questionnaire model from the Fourth China Urban and Rural Elderly Living Situation Sampling Survey. Referencing the survey questionnaire structure and content related to the social participation of the elderly, a research questionnaire titled "Investigation on the Current Development of Elderly Volunteer Services in Rural Guangdong" was formulated. The questionnaire covers basic information about the elderly population, participation in elderly volunteer service activities, participation in elderly volunteer service organizations, and the demands for participating in elderly volunteer services.

3.2. Experimental process

Experiment 1 conducted a qualitative investigation on the maintenance system of rural cultural facilities in Guangdong. The field research took place on January 10, 2023, in Shancha Village, Qianshui Town, Wuchuan City, Zhanjiang City, Guangdong Province. During the field research, the author documented the current status of the maintenance system for public cultural facilities in Shancha Village. Two stakeholder interviews were conducted as part of experiment one, involving cadres of Shancha Village, villagers in Shancha Village, elderly villagers in Shancha Village, and staffs of Wuchuan Bureau of Economy and Information Technology (members of night-visiting group in Shancha Village). The focus was on in-depth communication with stakeholders, listening to and conveying their voices, aiming to understand the current state and demands of the rural cultural facility maintenance system in Guangdong.

Experiment 2 involved a quantitative survey on the current participation in elderly volunteer services in rural Guangdong. The online questionnaire survey took place from January 25, 2023, to February 5, 2023, targeting individuals aged 60 and above in rural areas of Guangdong Province. Tencent Questionnaire was the survey tool. Two hundred questionnaires were distributed to the target sample, with an expected return of 100 valid responses. Ultimately, 113 valid responses were received, covering 21 prefecture-level cities in Guangdong Province and reaching elderly populations with varying health conditions and cultural backgrounds. The goal was to identify pain points and needs in the current state of elderly volunteer services in rural Guangdong, gaining insights into the development status and future trends of elderly volunteer services in the region.

3.3. Subject information

A total of 113 pieces of sample data were effectively recovered in the experiment, covering rural areas in 21 prefecture-level cities in Guangdong Province, reaching elderly groups with different health conditions and educational levels. The gender ratio of the sample data is 63 males, accounting for 55.75%; 50 females, accounting for 44.75%. The age distribution of the sample data is 61 people aged 60-64, accounting for 53.98%; 29 people aged 65-69, accounting for 25.66%; 11 people aged 70-74, accounting for 9.74%; 6 people aged 75-79, accounting for 5.31 %; 4 people are 80-84 years old, accounting for 3.54%; 2 people are over 85 years old, accounting for 1.77%.

3.4. Data analysis

3.4.1. Experiment 1 Data Analysis

The maintenance system of rural cultural facilities in Guangdong lacks systematic management. According to the analysis of the field investigation and survey (Table 1), the talent structure of the maintenance system of rural cultural facilities in Guangdong is single and lacks dedicated management. It lacks scientific guidance and timely upgrading, has a single and scattered purpose, and is difficult to exert its due systematicity. Functions cannot meet the needs of villagers for organizing various cultural activities, resulting in cultural facilities in rural areas of Guangdong having a narrow scope of use, being old and outdated, with a high vacancy rate and a low degree of digitalization.

Table 1. Cadres of Shancha Village

Observation model	Data
Behavior	Carry out daily maintenance of cultural facilities in the village;
	Organize and carry out healthy and beneficial cultural and recreational activities;
	Organize and carry out volunteer services for civilized practice in the new era.
Touchpoint	Shancha Village Cultural Service Center;
	Shancha Village sports and cultural facilities;
	A new era civilization practice station.
Motivation	Implement CPC's principles and policies and actively advocate new trends in civilization
Preference	Organize regular cultural and entertainment activities;
	Organize volunteer services arranged by superiors.
Pain points	The utilization rate of cultural facilities in the village is low;
	Villagers' enthusiasm for participating in activities is low;

Need	The frequency of volunteering is low.
	Improve the use of cultural facilities in the village;
	Increase villagers' enthusiasm for participating in activities;
	Improve the spontaneity of volunteer service practice.

The maintenance system of rural cultural facilities in Guangdong lacks self-organized organizations. According to the analysis of field investigation and research (Table 2, Table 3), there is a severe homogenization of cultural content services in rural areas of Guangdong, particularly affecting the elderly population, who, as permanent residents, find their retirement lives monotonous and struggle to engage in appealing cultural activities. Simultaneously, the elderly express a desire to spontaneously organize cultural activities to continue realizing their intrinsic value. However, the cultural facility maintenance system lacks spontaneously organized professional outreach teams and avenues for participating in elderly volunteer services. This deficiency has resulted in a noticeable absence of philanthropic spirit in cultural facilities across rural Guangdong.

Table 2. Elderly villagers in Shancha Village

Observation model	Data
Behavior	Occasionally visit the rural library for reading, and assist in organizing and arranging books to maintain a clean environment in the library.
	Regularly engage in physical exercise at the village sports and cultural facilities. However, there is a lack of scientific methods for utilizing sports facilities, leading to occasional instances of improper exercise.
Touchpoint	Shancha Village Cultural Service Center;
	Rural library;
	Sports and cultural facilities.
Motivation	Meet spiritual needs after retirement;
	Exercise prevents chronic diseases in old age.
Preference	Teach cultural knowledge that younger generations like;
	Maintain environmental hygiene of cultural facilities.
Pain points	Community cultural activities are monotonous and it is difficult to arouse interest in participation;
	Retirement life is idle and boring, making it difficult to realize the elderly' self-worth.
Need	Enrich the content of services provided by cultural facilities;
	Build a mechanism for spontaneously organizing cultural activities;
	Increase the ways to realize the value of the elderly group.

Table 3. Villagers in Shancha Village

Observation model	Data
Behavior	Participate in cultural activities organized by the village committee;
	Participate in volunteer services carried out by the village committee.
Touchpoint	Shancha Village Cultural Service Center;
	A new era civilization practice station.
Motivation	Respond to the call of the village committee;
	Participate in public affairs in the village.
Preference	Help maintain order at cultural events;
	Guidance on the use of digital cultural facilities.
Pain points	Insufficient number of participants in cultural activities;
	Facilities struggle to meet event demand.
Need	Attract villagers to actively participate in cultural activities;
	Expand the usage scenarios of digital cultural facilities.

The rural cultural facilities maintenance system in Guangdong lacks a feedback mechanism. Based on the field research (Table 4), the analysis reveals a low level of digitization in the rural cultural facilities maintenance system in Guangdong. There is a lack of channels for timely feedback on villagers' cultural service needs. The Village Committee faces challenges in organizing and promoting cultural activities, with low accessibility and significant lag. Villagers exhibit a low enthusiasm for participating in cultural activities, resulting in a generally insufficient number of participants. Simultaneously, there is a singular feedback channel for the demand for elderly volunteer service projects, overlooking the largest demographic of elderly individuals in Guangdong's rural population. The absence of elderly volunteer service projects leads to a low frequency of cultural facilities engaging in volunteer services in rural Guangdong.

Table 4. Staff of Wuchuan Bureau of Economy and Information Technology

Observation model	Data
Behavior	Observe and listen to the social conditions and public opinions of the people in Shancha Village; Assist in resolving conflicts and disputes in Shancha Village.
Touchpoint	Shancha Village Committee; Shancha Villagers Community.
Motivation	Promote the CPC's policies and guidelines; Close to the grassroots masses.
Preference	Convey information about the cultural life needs of villagers in Shancha Village; Guide village committees to carry out spiritual civilization practices.
Pain points	There is an imbalance between the supply and demand of cultural services in Shancha Village; The quality of volunteer service practices in Shancha Village varies.
Need	Increase channels for feedback on villagers' cultural service needs; Increase the villagers' volunteer service system mechanism.

3.4.2. Experiment 2 data analysis

The younger age groups within the elderly population in rural Guangdong exhibit a higher proportion of participation in volunteer services, with varied preferences in service types across different age segments. Cross-analysis of sample data (Table 5) reveals that the age group of 60-64 has the highest participation rate in volunteer services. As the age increases, the proportion of elderly individuals engaging in volunteer services gradually decreases.

Table 5. Types of volunteer services participated by elderly groups of different ages in rural Guangdong

Unit: %

Age	Maintain Social Order	Mediate Disputes	Maintain Environment	Help Neighbors	Educating Generation	Participate in cultural activities	None
60-64	52.2	56.4	59.0	61.4	59.3	69.2	42.9
65-69	26.1	23.1	25.6	18.6	27.8	15.4	28.6
70-74	8.7	12.8	7.7	10.0	7.4	0	14.3
75-79	4.3	5.1	5.1	4.3	3.7	7.7	7.1
80-84	8.7	2.6	0	4.3	1.9	7.7	0
Over 85	0	0	2.6	1.4	0	0	7.1

The higher the educational level among the elderly in rural Guangdong, the higher the proportion of volunteer service participation. Elderly people with different educational levels focus on different types of volunteer services. Cross-analysis of sample data (Table 6) indicates that, among the elderly population in rural Guangdong who have never participated in volunteer services, 21.4% of the sample with no formal education, 50% with primary school education, and 7.1% each with education levels ranging from junior high school to university undergraduate and above.

Table 6. Types of volunteer services participated by elderly groups with different educational levels in rural Guangdong

Unit: %

Education level	Maintain Social Order	Mediate Disputes	Maintain Environment	Help Neighbors	Educating Generation	Participate in cultural activities	None
Uneducated	4.3	2.6	2.6	5.7	7.4	0	21.4
Primary	21.7	30.8	28.2	37.1	44.4	15.4	50.0
Junior	47.8	41.0	43.6	31.4	33.3	38.5	7.1
High	17.4	17.9	17.9	17.1	9.3	30.8	7.1
College	8.7	7.7	5.1	7.1	5.6	15.4	7.1
Bachelor	0	0	2.6	1.4	0	0	7.1

The proportion of elderly individuals participating in volunteer services in rural Guangdong increases with better health, and the preferences for volunteer service types vary among different health conditions. Cross-analysis of sample data (Table 7) reveals that, as health conditions decline, the proportion of elderly individuals in rural Guangdong participating in volunteer services gradually decreases, and the preferences in volunteer service types shifts from physical to mental tasks.

Table 7. Types of volunteer services participated by elderly groups with different health conditions in rural Guangdong

Unit: %

Health Status	Maintain Social Order	Mediate Disputes	Maintain Environment	Help Neighbors	Educating Generation	Participate in cultural activities	None
Very good	21.7	15.4	23.1	17.1	14.8	23.1	7.1
Better	39.1	33.3	48.7	40	42.6	46.2	50
Generally	30.4	46.2	28.2	38.6	37	30.8	28.6
Relatively Poor	4.3	5.1	0	4.3	5.6	0	7.1
Very bad	4.3	0	0	0	0	0	7.1

Most of the elderly groups in rural Guangdong have participated in volunteer service organizations, and their preference is cultural public welfare and mutual aid organizations. According to the sample data analysis, only 23 people in the sample data have never participated in volunteer service organizations for the elderly, accounting for 20.3%. The remaining 79.7% of the samples have participated in volunteer service organizations.

Most of the elderly groups in rural Guangdong have participated in activities organized by volunteer service organizations, and their preference is cultural and public welfare volunteer services. According to the sample data analysis, only 20 people in the sample data have never participated in activities organized by volunteer service organizations, accounting for 17.7%.

According to the analysis of sample data, the elderly population in rural Guangdong assigns varying levels of importance to volunteer service activities organized by community organizations. The ranked order of preferences from strong to weak demand is as follows: assisting disadvantaged elderly individuals, engaging in learning/entertainment activities, participating in intergenerational family activities, advocating for the rights of the elderly, participating in volunteer public welfare activities, and engaging in community public affairs and profit-oriented projects. This indicates that the elderly population in rural Guangdong expresses a preference for cultural and public welfare-oriented volunteer services.

4. Experimental results

- Service design combines elderly volunteer services to improve the maintenance system of rural cultural facilities. According to the results of the questionnaire survey, the elderly groups in rural Guangdong have the need to participate in volunteer services and prefer cultural and public welfare volunteer services. At the same time, the maintenance system of rural cultural facilities is deeply in line with the type of cultural public welfare volunteer services. According to the results of the field investigation, the maintenance system lacks systematic management, spontaneous organization and feedback mechanisms. The systematic principles of service design [12] can solve the pain points in rural cultural facilities maintenance systems by considering the holistic process of managing cultural facilities. Integrating elderly volunteer services within this framework helps meet the needs of stakeholders in the cultural facilities management system. Therefore, service design, when organically combined with elderly volunteer services, enhances the overall functionality of rural cultural facilities management systems.

- The service design concept meets the diverse needs of the elderly group in participating in volunteer services. According to the results of the questionnaire survey, the elderly groups in Guangdong's rural areas have different preferences for types of volunteer services due to different age groups, education levels and health conditions, and the main type of participation is cultural public welfare volunteer services. According to the results of the field survey, there is a phenomenon of lower participation enthusiasm than service supply and demand mismatch in elderly volunteer services in rural Guangdong. The user-centered principle of service design [12] can solve the pain points of carrying out elderly volunteer services, that is, considering the specific situation of elderly volunteer participants, focusing on the elderly group, and providing services that meet the needs of various users.

- The service design concept solves the systemic problems of the maintenance system of rural cultural facilities. According to the results of the field survey, cultural facilities in rural Guangdong lack villagers' spontaneous organization for maintenance, which is reflected in the lack of public welfare spirit and villagers are less involved in the maintenance of cultural facilities. According to the results of the questionnaire survey, the elderly groups in rural Guangdong have the need to participate in cultural public welfare volunteer services, but they lack the conditions for independent organization. The stakeholder co-creation principle of service design [12] can solve the pain points of the maintenance system of rural cultural facilities, that is, through co-creation between the elderly group and the stakeholders of the maintenance system of rural cultural facilities, the needs of the maintenance system of rural cultural facilities can be systematically met.

5. Conclusion

Based on the results of Experiments 1 and 2, this paper sorts out the problems of the maintenance system and elderly volunteer service firstly. Secondly, conducts a feasibility analysis on the design of the maintenance system. Finally, gains insight into the opportunities in the design of the maintenance system of rural cultural facilities , and proposes the guiding principles for designing the maintenance system.

5.1. Construction Principles of Elderly Volunteer Maintenance Service in Rural Cultural Facilities in Guangdong

- Consider the real needs of cultural facilities maintenance stakeholders as a whole. The specific method is to investigate the actual operating status of the maintenance system of rural cultural facilities in Guangdong, clarify the priorities of the needs of stakeholders, and propose systematic solutions that take into account the needs of all stakeholders.
- Provide continuous personalized and refined services centered on the elderly group. The specific method is to enrich the forms of the maintenance system of rural cultural facilities in Guangdong, clarify the tasks of the system, and match the difficulty of matching the preferences of older groups in different situations to participate in volunteer services.
- Establish a co-creation mechanism for feedback and iteration of cultural facilities maintenance services. The specific method is to optimize the digital feedback channel of the maintenance system of rural cultural facilities in Guangdong, synchronize the real-time work information of the maintenance system of rural cultural facilities in Guangdong, and introduce a gamified incentive tool for the maintenance system of rural cultural facilities.

5.2. Management Principles of Elderly Volunteer Maintenance Service in Rural Cultural Facilities in Guangdong

- Establish a volunteer maintenance service mechanism for rural elderly groups to spontaneously organize. The specific methods are to guide the elderly groups in rural Guangdong to establish volunteer science popularization groups, simplify the project establishment process of the maintenance system of rural cultural facilities in Guangdong, and guide the operation and maintenance.
- Establish a review mechanism for elderly volunteer service projects in rural cultural facilities. The specific methods are to evaluate the service capabilities of members participating in the volunteer maintenance of rural cultural facilities, select target types of elderly volunteer maintenance projects with correct value orientations, and simplify the review process for volunteer maintenance projects of rural cultural facilities in Guangdong.
- Establish an iteration mechanism for assistance units to guide volunteer service projects for the elderly. The specific method is to guide the target type of the elderly volunteer project in rural cultural facilities in Guangdong, check the practical quality of the elderly volunteer project, and review the iterative direction of the elderly volunteer project.

5.3. Content supply principles of Elderly Volunteer Maintenance Service in Rural Cultural Facilities in Guangdong

- Establish a recruitment mechanism for elderly volunteer caretakers of rural cultural facilities in Guangdong. The specific method is to strengthen pre-job training for volunteer maintenance projects of rural cultural facilities in Guangdong, accurately recommend projects that match the interests and abilities of the elderly groups in rural Guangdong, and effectively and reasonably allocate the scope of maintenance work for rural cultural facilities in Guangdong.

- Establish a coordination mechanism for the maintenance system of rural cultural facilities in Guangdong. Specific methods include setting up a work service manual for the maintenance system, setting up a work exit mechanism for elderly volunteers in cultural facilities to hand over, and setting up a work allocation mechanism that is consistent with the specific conditions of rural elderly groups.
- Establish a continuous supply mechanism for rural cultural facilities and services in Guangdong. The specific methods include setting up a UGC community for co-creation and sharing of Guangdong rural cultural facilities content, setting up a gamification achievement system, and setting up online communication channels linking cultural content of rural surrounding communities.

Acknowledgements

This study was supported by the grant of "Research on the Design of Elderly Volunteer Service in the Maintenance System of Rural Cultural Facilities" (Ref No. : GD23CYS19) from the 2023 Philosophy and social Science Planning Project of Guangdong province, the grant of "Reform and Practical Research on the Academic Evaluation Method of Ideological and Political Courses in Art Design" from 2021 Guangdong Province Undergraduate Higher Education Teaching Reform Project, and the grant of "Research on the Innovative Design of Foshan Intangible Cultural Heritage Products in the Context of the Humanities Bay Area" (Ref No. :2019GWQNCX076) from Guangdong Provincial Department of Education University Scientific Research Project-Youth Innovative Talent Project (Humanities and Social Sciences).

References

[1] Wheeler J A, Gorey K M, Greenblatt B. The beneficial effects of volunteering for older volunteers and the people they serve: A meta-analysis. The International Journal of Aging and Human Development, 1998, 47(1): 69-79.

[2] Van Willigen M. Differential benefits of volunteering across the life course. The Journals of Gerontology Series B: Psychological Sciences and Social Sciences, 2000, 55(5): S308-S318.

[3] Schwingel A, Niti M M, Tang C, et al. Continued work employment and volunteerism and mental well-being of older adults: Singapore longitudinal ageing studies. Age and ageing, 2009, 38(5): 531-537.

[4] Barron J S, Tan E J, Yu Q, et al. Potential for intensive volunteering to promote the health of older adults in fair health. Journal of Urban Health, 2009, 86: 641-653.

[5] Anderson N D, Damianakis T, Kröger E, et al. The benefits associated with volunteering among seniors: a critical review and recommendations for future research. Psychological bulletin, 2014, 140(6): 1505.

[6] Chen Ming, Lin Zhiwan. Theoretical thinking and empirical analysis of elderly volunteer activities. Journal of Demography, 2003(4):25-29.

[7] Li Qin. Research on volunteer services for the elderly in urban communities—taking Jinan as an example. Social Sciences, 2010(6):72-79.

[8] Wu Jinjing, Liang Bojiao and Zhang Xu. The impact of volunteer activities among urban elderly on their subjective well-being - based on a survey in Chaoyang District, Beijing. Southern Population, 2012, 27(5): 24-31.

[9] Zhang Na. Analysis of factors affecting the willingness to participate in volunteer services among the elderly in urban communities—taking Kaifeng City as an example. Northwest Population, 2015, 36(5):91-94+100.

[10] Miao Qing, Zhang Yu. Being productive and having fun in old age: the social compensation effect of public welfare participation. Journal of Zhejiang University (Humanities and Social Sciences Edition), 2017, 47(5):5-18.

[11] Robson Colin, McCartan Kieran. Real World Research. John Wiley& Sons, Inc., Hoboken, New Jersey, 2016.

[12] Ding Xiong, Du Junlin. Basic principles of service design: from user-centered to stakeholder-centered. Decoration, 2020, (3): 62-65.

Design Studies and Intelligence Engineering
L.C. Jain et al. (Eds.)
© 2024 The Authors.
This article is published online with Open Access by IOS Press and distributed under the terms
of the Creative Commons Attribution Non-Commercial License 4.0 (CC BY-NC 4.0).
doi:10.3233/FAIA231482

Evaluation and Application of Aging-Appropriate Bathing Facilities Design Based on Grounded Theory and Fuzzy Analytic Hierarchy Process

Xinhui, HONG[a,1] and Shunlan MEI[a]

[a]*Xiamen Academy of Arts and Design, Fuzhou University*

Abstract. Through field research on the home bathing scenes of assisted elderly people, grounded theory was used to code the original information of user interviews and bathing behaviors, and the various attribute needs of assisted elderly people for bathing behaviors were summarized. At the same time, the analysis was used as indicators in the analytic hierarchy process. The layer is being constructed; using this as the design index for aging-friendly bath products, experts are invited to evaluate and calculate the weight value of each index, and analyze the importance data of the indicators to design an aging-friendly bath product; finally, the fuzzy comprehensive evaluation method is used to test whether the plan is satisfactory. Degree, the study obtained the evaluation results of this program, proving the feasibility of combining grounded theory and fuzzy level analysis, making the theory and practice effectively connected and exerting practical significance. The combination of grounded theory and fuzzy level analysis can systematically carry out quantitative design and evaluation of products, reduce subjective influencing factors in the product design process, make the design more scientific, objective and rigorous, and provide effective program reference and optimization ideas for subsequent similar aging product design.

Keywords. bathing facilities, grounded theory, fuzzy analytic hierarchy process, Age-appropriate

1. Introduction

Actively responding to the aging of the population has been elevated to a national strategy. Bathroom space is a place where inconvenience and accidents are easy to occur in the daily life of the elderly, and the age-appropriate design and development of bathroom products is particularly important. The aging of the physical functions of the elderly makes it gradually difficult to take an independent bath, and various obstacles and safety hazards are prone to occur during the bathing process. Thomas M. Gill [1] et al. conducted experiments over a period of up to six years, showing that bathing has a higher probability of disability than other factors, suggesting the need for strategies to maintain and restore safe independent bathing in the elderly. William C. Mann [2] and

---

[a,1] Corresponding Author: Xinhui, Hong (1979-), associate professor, master. Her main research interests cover user research and experience innovation, industrial design and information interaction. E-mail: id_hxh@foxmail.com
[a] Second Author: Shunlan, Mei (1999-), female, master. His main research direction is the design of age-appropriate products. E-mail: 3211146803@qq.com

other studies analyzed whether the elderly need auxiliary bathing equipment and what type of auxiliary equipment is needed, including bathroom non-slip mats, handrails, bath stools, bath chairs and bath transfer benches, while analyzing the problems encountered by the elderly when using bathing equipment, calling on people to pay attention to their own needs when choosing assistive equipment. At present, there are two forms of design of aging bath equipment on the market, one is an integrated integral product, which combines the design of multi-functional bath equipment; The second is a split combination product, by adding auxiliary facilities to the existing bathing environment, such as adding different types of armrests, installing bath folding chairs, replacing showers that are easy to adjust height, etc. For the split combined elderly bath products, the existing product types are relatively rich; The development of integrated and integral elderly bath products is still relatively single.

Song Duanshu [3] et al. studied the toilet and bathing behaviors and action postures of the self-care elderly, walker elderly and wheelchair elderly through observation, and finally used the age-appropriate and intelligent design strategy of bathroom products to guide the design practice, and designed a bath equipment that combines bathing and toileting. Xuan Wei [4] proposed the principle of barrier-free design of elderly bathroom facilities by analyzing the existing problems of elderly bathroom facilities in China and considering the actual changes in the psychology and physiology of the elderly. Hu Hong et al. [5] combined the FBS theoretical model and the user research method of service design to design the service strategy of online and offline elderly bath products, and output the design scheme of the elderly bath chair. Zhang Jian [6] In view of the lagging standard of some assistive devices in China, because the degree of attention of bath chairs is not as good as that of walkers, toilet chairs and other products, there is currently no domestic standard, research takes bath chairs as an example, actively promote the transformation of general requirements standards for assistive device products for the disabled, so that China's assistive device product standard system is more perfect.

Hu Shan [7] et al. summarized the influencing factors that lead to the difficulty of elderly using smart phones through rooted theory, and based on this, they sorted out the key design elements of the mobile phone guide APP for the elderly to carry out design positioning. Wang zhiyuan[8] et al. conducted a scientific and reasonable evaluation of children's scooter design through FAHP, which provided a quantifiable reference for the selection and optimization of children's product design scheme. Yang mei [9] et al. evaluate the weight values of each criterion of elderly smart watches more objectively and reasonably through the FAHP method, effectively avoiding errors caused by subjective judgment during evaluation.

This paper combines the grounded theory with the fuzzy comprehensive evaluation method, systematically organizes the interviews and user behavior demonstrations through the grounding theory in the early stage of design, summarizes the user needs in the age-appropriate bath design, and uses this as the basis to make the criterion layer and index layer elements in the analytic hierarchy method. Through the design practice of the weight value evaluation of the elements, the fuzzy comprehensive evaluation of the scheme is carried out, and the evaluation results are obtained. The combined application of the two methods systematically analyzes the content of the survey, and scientifically verifies it in the practical part.

2. Related theories

2.1 Grounded theory

In the overall context of American sociological research in the 20th century, American scholars Barney Glaser and Anselm Strauss published "The Discovery of Grounded Theory: Strategies for Qualitative Research", which first proposed the theory of rooting [10]. In Grounded Theory, researchers do not focus on testing hypotheses from existing theoretical frameworks, but develop a new "theory" based on empirical data collected in the field [11]. Grounded theory refers to the process of researchers obtaining field data in in-depth interviews, field observations and other practical methods, and gradually conceptualizing and theorizing them, which ensures the connection between theoretical analysis and empirical practice in the early stage. The process consists of three steps, namely open coding, selection coding and theoretical coding, and first the original data is screened by keywords and collected and classified; Next, the research is concentrated and sorted out and the scope analysis of related connections is carried out, and gradually focused, integrated and compressed. Finally, create the required theory.

2.2 Fuzzy Analytic Hierarchy Process

The fuzzy analytic hierarchy method FAHP combines analytic hierarchy and fuzzy evaluation method. The Analytic Hierarchy Process (AHP)[12] is a practical multi-criteria decision-making method proposed by Professor Thomas L. Saaty of the University of Pittsburgh in the early 70s of the 20th century, which represents a complex decision-making problem as an ordered hierarchical hierarchy and gives the order of alternatives through people's subjective judgment and scientific calculation. The analytic hierarchy method generally combines some other decision-making methods to flexibly deal with some more complex decision-making problems; If combined with the fuzzy evaluation method, first establish the indicators at each level through the analytic hierarchy method, output the fuzzy comprehensive evaluation results through the evaluation data, and combine the application to quantitatively analyze the perceptual evaluation and rationally output the evaluation results.

3. Age-appropriate bath product design rooted in theory

3.1 Research object

In the "Code for Building Design of Elderly Care Facilities" [13], the elderly can be divided into self-care elderly, intermediary elderly and nursing elderly according to their physical conditions. These three types of people have different needs in bathing behavior. The self-care elderly will basically not have difficulties in the bathing process, but it is necessary to pay attention to the prevention of falls in the elderly, because once the elderly fall down, it is difficult for the elderly to recover physically; assisting the elderly relies on crutches, handrails, wheelchairs and other lifting designs Or the elderly with assisted living equipment; nursing elderly refers to the disabled or semi-disabled elderly, who mostly use artificial assistance or bathtub assistance for bathing.

Through field research, it is known that the physical function of the self-care elderly is relatively good. On the whole, it is safer and easier for the self-care elderly to complete the bathing than to assist and care for the elderly. As for Jiezhu elderly, there will be more needs in bathing. Generally, various handrails will be installed in the bathing area, and sitz baths will be chosen when taking a bath. It is necessary to optimize the design of bathing equipment, and it is also the development direction and trend of the elderly market.

3.2 Research content

When using grounded theoretical methods, it is necessary to analyze and select users of original data should be representative [14], taking Xiamen as an example, during the period, 40 users were interviewed and 16 in-depth visits were made; Among them, 13 best users were selected to investigate and analyze the target users, family members and caregivers. Of these, 54% were women and 46% were men; Age distribution varies from 63 to 94 years; In the distribution of physical conditions, there are wheelchair users and crutches, among which crutches include walking inconvenience caused by pathology, slow movement caused by old age, and visual impairment that requires crutches assistance.

3.3 Open coding for age-appropriate bath product design

After the above investigation is completed, the original recording is sorted into text to extract the representative sentences, and at the same time, the original sentences are conceptualized and classified, and finally the corresponding main categories are analyzed and sorted out, as shown in Table 1.

Table 1. Rooted in theoretical coding builds

Extraction of raw statement information	conceptualization	Main category
This hand is unconscious, and bathing is generally bathing with one hand, including dressing	Physical impairments make bathing more difficult	
When washing your feet, raise your legs to your knees, support the wall with one hand, and rub with the other	Physical stability in old age is not good	
Before bathing, I need to adjust the water temperature, move the bath stool to the bathroom, and ask me to assist in bathing when I am not in good health;	The assistance required in case of changes in physical condition varies	physical factors
The caregiver comes to help me take a bath, and I will help him take a bath when he is not in good health	Need help bathing	
Exhaust fan switch in the bathroom, with a label.	Poor memory	
The chair is low, sometimes propped up directly from the floor	The height of the chair was uncomfortable, and the old man could not get up strongly	Human-machine dimensions
A new shower holder is installed because the original one is too high	Lower the height of the bath equipment	
Install a handrail, sometimes hold up to get things when bathing	The armrest supports getting up to pick up the item	
Install handrails on the bathroom wall to help him walk in and out of the bathroom	Rely on support to avoid the risk of falls in and out of the bathroom	Ancillary needs
Before bathing, you need me to help him adjust the water temperature	Need help to adjust the water temperature	
The eyes cannot see clearly, and generally distinguish shampoo and shower gel by the shape of the bottle	Distinguish items by shape	

It is not convenient to put chairs in the bathroom, the rest of the family members are not convenient to bathe	The chair is placed in the bathing area	environmental factors
The previous renovation did not take into account the current physical condition, and the renovation was troublesome	The original bathing environment is difficult to change	
When the hand touches the switch by mistake, the water temperature becomes cold or hot	False touch switch poses a risk	Security needs
The corner of the partition between the bath and the toilet is easy to collide.	Corners are easy to bump	
The bath chair installed on the wall should be perforated, and the metal parts will corrode over time	Pay attention to the stability of the chair	
The stainless steel chair I specially bought for her, it is relatively stable and can be used for a long time,	Worry about the life of the product	
Place the towel on the seat surface while bathing	Poor seat comfort	
The non-slip toilet floor has a height difference, and wheelchairs and bath chairs will be slightly inclined when entering the bathing area	Ground height differences affect operation and safety	Usage requirements
I sit while taking a bath	Sitz bath	
When adjusting the water temperature, first adjust to the hottest effluent, and then adjust to the coldest effluent	Water temperature visualization is not provided	
After bathing, put a dry towel on the chair to prevent getting wet when dressing	The seat is wet after bathing, and it is difficult to sit and dress	
Towels are not placed in public places, there will be a smell when I am old, and I will put them back in my room	Fear of family dislike	Psychological factors
He loves to be clean and divides towels a lot	Pay attention to personal hygiene	
I feel that there is no trouble, there is no need to install handrails, it is not good to install on the wall	Disobedience to old age	
Fill the basin with water at the right temperature and wipe the body with a towel	Security psychology	

In the process of sorting out interview data and bathing operations, 26 representative original information were selected, and the information was conceptualized and primary coded, and 7 main categories with internal logical relationships were integrated, namely physical factors, man-machine size, auxiliary needs, environmental needs, safety needs, use needs, and psychological needs. In order to ensure the reliability of the research results, the three original interview materials reserved were coded and analyzed again, and no new categories were generated, and the verification theory was saturated.

4. Evaluation of bath products suitable for the elderly based on FAHP

4.1 Construct a judgment matrix and calculate the weights of each indicator

By analyzing the seven factors of the main category, among which many safety hazards are gradually becoming difficult due to the decline of physical functions in the elderly, the physical factors and safety needs are summarized as safety indicators in the analytic hierarchy method; Many elderly people have the psychology of disobeying the old and afraid of their children's dislike, and the installation of bath products suitable for the elderly they often feel that it is the "label" of the elderly, so they are unwilling to accept it, so they must take care of the psychological burden of the elderly, so as to reduce the size of man-machine and psychological factors to comfort needs; With the development of science and technology, it is relatively difficult for the elderly to operate the product, and the auxiliary facilities are the identification that distinguishes them from the young, thereby reducing the auxiliary needs and use needs to the ease of use indicators; Since the general family bathroom is a place shared by the family and is not easy to change, it is attributed to the inclusion index in the environmental factor; Some of these indicators are cross-subordinate. Finally, in the design evaluation index system of aging bath products, the criteria layer is divided into four elements: safety, inclusiveness and ease of use; There are 16 indicator layers under the benchmark layer, as shown in Table 2.

Table 2. Age-appropriate bath product design evaluation index system

Target layer	Corresponding encoding	Guidelines layer	Metrics layer
A Design evaluation index of aging bath products	2、8、9、15、16、17、19、21、26	B1 Security	B11 provides support facilities
			B12 Flat and non-slip ground
			B13 Shape is round and safe
			B14 The product structure is stable
			B15 Products have a long service life
	3、12、13、14、22、23、24	B2 Inclusiveness	B21 Has high versatility with family members
			B22 Device has a small footprint
			B23 The structure and technology need to match the original environment
			B24 High fault tolerance
	4、6、7、18、20、25	B3 comfort	B31 Added back flush function
			B32 The man-machine size is reasonable
			B33 Optimize the comfort needs of the sitz bath
			B34 Gentle and harmonious vision
	1、5、10、11	B4 ease of use	B41 Simple functionality
			B42 Convenient operation
			B43 The signs are eye-catching and easy to understand

In order to quantify the qualitative principle, the 1-9 proportional scale method compares between two elements, and evaluates the importance between the two elements of i and j, so as to form a numerical judgment matrix and calculate the weight value of each element. For the criterion layer B1, B2, B3 and B4, the importance of the two pairs was compared, and the weights between the elements of each criterion layer were determined. At the same time, the index layers B1, B12, B13, B21, B31, B41, and B42 are also compared with the importance of the size, and a certain value is assigned according to the importance, and the given value is marked as D_{ij}(i.j=1, 2..., n), and i and j represent the evaluation elements of the pair-by-two comparison; D_{ij} represents the important value of factors i and j relative to the target; n is the number of indicators, the constructed judgment matrix, ie

$$D = (D_{ij}) \; n \times n = \begin{cases} C11 \; C12...C1n \\ C21 \; C22...C2n \\ Cn1 \; Cn2...Cnn \end{cases} \tag{1}$$

The evaluation matrix of elderly bath products was constructed, a questionnaire survey was conducted, and two university professors and two corporate executives were invited to form an evaluation team to form a decision-maker, and the obtained evaluation values were calculated by Yaahp software. The calculation results show that safety has the greatest impact on the design of age-appropriate bath products in the criterion layer, with a weight value of (0.5872), followed by ease of use (0.2618), inclusiveness (0.0863), Comfort (0.0648); the importance of each indicator at the indicator layer is B14> B12>B11> B42> B41> B43> B13> B24>B32> B21>B15>B23> B33>B31> B21> B22> B34>B21, indicating that the four most important index elements in the design of bath products for the elderly are stable product structure, flat and non-slip ground, providing borrowing support, and convenient operation.

4.2 Age-appropriate bath product design practices

Design practices are developed through the importance data analysis of the above indicators, as shown in Figure 1. By optimizing the existing ordinary bath products, first, in the safety design, consider the safety control of temperature, round shape to reduce bumps, and add seats and auxiliary armrests; Second, in the design of ease of use, magnetic adsorption is used on the handrail for easy hanging and handling, and the function is simple; Third, in the inclusive design, consider the convenience of other family members, the bath chair is designed to be folded up and folded to reduce the obstruction to others, when the armrests on both sides are turned up and close to the wall, it is a magnetically attractive shower fixer; Fourth, in the consideration of comfort, reduce the height of the shower and gentle color vision.

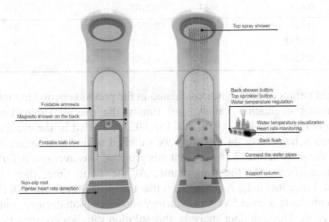

Figure 1. Rendering of age-appropriate bath products

4.3 Fuzzy comprehensive evaluation transformation matrix

According to the Likert scale survey questionnaire, the subjective feelings are transformed into quantifiable evaluations. Firstly, the design examples are set with five-point evaluation grades based on each index element, from very satisfied, satisfied, general, dissatisfied, and very dissatisfied. Scoring [15]. The experiment selected 20 consumers, ranging in age from 22 to 85, and collected 20 questionnaires, of which 19 were valid. The formula calculation is carried out through the questionnaire evaluation results and the weight values of each index, that is,

$$E = B \times R = \begin{cases} C11 \; C12 \ldots C1n \\ C21 \; C22 \ldots C2n \\ Cn1 \; Cn2 \ldots Cnn \end{cases} \qquad (2)$$

The results of the evaluation model are shown in Table 3.

Table 3.Evaluate the mode

Evaluation indicators R		5 Very satisfied with the proportion	4 Satisfaction percentage	3 Generally proportion	2 Dissatisfied proportion	1 Very dissatisfied with the proportion
B1	B11	0.3157	0.3684	0.3157	0	0
	B12	0.421	0.421	0.1578	0	0
	B13	0.3684	0.4736	0.1578	0	0
	B14	0.3684	0.3157	0.2631	0.0526	0
	B15	0.3157	0.2105	0.3157	0.1578	0
B2	B21	0.3157	0.3684	0.3157	0	0
	B22	0.421	0.2631	0.2105	0.1052	0
	B23	0.3684	0.421	0.2105	0	0
	B24	0.4736	0.421	0.1052	0	0
B3	B31	0.5263	0.3684	0.0526	0.0526	0
	B32	0.3157	0.4736	0.2105	0	0
	B33	0.3684	0.5263	0.1052	0	0
	B34	0.421	0.3684	0.2105	0	0
B4	B41	0.421	0.5263	0.0526	0	0
	B42	0.3157	0.5789	0.1052	0	0
	B43	0.5263	0.2631	0.5263	0	0

The weight values of each index calculated in the previous period are multiplied by the corresponding evaluation values, and finally the overall evaluation model is normalized to obtain E=(0.445, 0.459, 0.0715, 0.0232, 0), that is, the evaluation results of the designed scheme are: 44.5% are very satisfied with the scheme; 45.9% were satisfied with the programme; 7.1% felt that this program was average; A further 2.3 per cent were dissatisfied with the programme; At the same time, there is also 0% dissatisfaction. From this data, it can be seen that the overall evaluation of the program for aging bath products is level 5 very satisfactory and level 4 satisfactory, and the overall evaluation is good. Through data analysis, this solution satisfies consumers in terms of security and ease of use design; At the same time, it also shows that the installation of integrated bath products in the home bathroom environment has low adaptability, and consumers have concerns about integrated products; As for whether to add the back flushing function, different consumers will have different preferences. Finally, in terms of scheme optimization, strengthen the diversity of the back flushing function and provide the adjustability of the function; At the same time, the stability of the product is visually and structurally enhanced.

5. Conclusion

The "14th Five-Year Plan" National Planning for the Development of the Elderly Cause and the Elderly Service System proposes to strengthen the research and development and manufacturing of elderly products, focusing on the development of daily products such as age-appropriate home appliances, furniture, bath products, toilets, and auxiliary products such as smart wheelchairs for different life scenarios [16]. Due to the great differences in physical functions, psychological states and behavioral habits of the elderly population, bath products must combine the key tasks and specific behaviors of target users to optimize the "user experience" and refine the "age-appropriate elements", but the initiative and accuracy of elderly users to express their own needs are not high, and the purchase behavior is not limited to the elderly themselves. Therefore, this paper proposes a design demand insight method for aging bath products based on grounded theory and fuzzy hierarchy analysis, and encodes the information obtained from in-depth interviews step by step through grounding theory, constructs theory, and reduces demand omission. Then, the output design indicators are transformed, and industry experts are invited to rank the weight degree of design indicators to ensure the objectivity and rigor of the index model, and finally identify the variables and conditions of user perceived value and user tendency behavior to further guide design optimization. Its operation process and evaluation method can provide a reference for similar product demand analysis and design innovation.

Acknowledgments

The research supported by foundation items: The National Social Science Fund of China (21BGL067); Industry-university cooperative education projects sponsored by the Ministry of Education (220903569305027). And we would like to express our sincere gratitude to all the individuals involved in this research for their valuable contributions.

References

[1]   Gill, Thomas M., Zhenchao Guo, and Heather G. Allore. "The epidemiology of bathing disability in older persons." Journal of the American Geriatrics Society 54.10 (2006): 1524-1530.
[2]   Mann, William C., et al. "Use of assistive devices for bathing by elderly who are not institutionalized." The Occupational Therapy Journal of Research 16.4 (1996): 261-286.
[3]   Song Duanshu,Xu Yanqi,Cui Tianqi. Research on the Design of Age-Appropriate Intelligent Bathroom Products Based on User Behavior. Packaging Engineering,2020,41(18): 125-131.
[4]   Xuan Wei. Research on barrier-free design of elderly bathroom facilities. Packaging Engineering, 2012, 33(02): 39-42.
[5]   Hu Hong,Wang MingWei. Design of elderly bath products based on FBS model. Design, 2021, 34(23): 74-77.
[6]   Zhang Jian. Analysis of General Requirements Standards for Assistive Devices for the Disabled: A Case Study of Bath Chair Products. China Journal of Standardization, 2020(05): 165-169.
[7]   HU shan, Wang Kaihua, Wang JiangYu, et al. Design and Implementation of Mobile Phone Guide APP for the Elderly Based on Grounded Theory and SEM. Packaging Engineering, 2023, 44(02):137-147+224.
[8]   Wang ZhiYuan, Dai ZhiPeng. Design evaluation and improvement of children's scooter based on FDM and FAHP. Journal of Graphics, 2021, 42(05): 849-855.
[9]   YangMei, Cong YangFan, Li XueRui. Comprehensive evaluation and optimization method of age-appropriate products integrating FAHP and TOPSIS: A case study of elderly smart bracelet. Journal of Graphics, 2020, 41(03): 469-479.
[10] Wu Suran, Li Minghui. Sociological Research, 2020, 35(02): 75-98+243.
[11] Dunne C. The place of the literature review in grounded theory research. International journal of social research methodology, 2011, 14(2): 111-124.
[12] Zhang BingJiang, ed. Analytic hierarchy method and its application cases. Beijing:Publishing House of Electronics Industry, 2014.01.

[13] Guo Xu. Interpretation of the six key points of the "Code for the Design of Elderly Care Facilities Building". Engineering Construction Standardization, 2014(09):52-53.

[14] Kathy Charmaz. Practice Guide to Qualitative Research on Constructing Rooted Theory. Chongqing: Chongqing University Press, 2009.03.

[15] Qi Lainin. Statistical analysis and fuzzy comprehensive evaluation of Likert scale. Shandong Science, 2006(02): 18-23+28.

[16] State Council. "14th Five-Year Plan" National Planning for the Development of Elderly Undertakings and Old-age Service System, Guo Fa [2021] No. 35.

Design Studies and Intelligence Engineering
L.C. Jain et al. (Eds.)
© 2024 The Authors.
This article is published online with Open Access by IOS Press and distributed under the terms
of the Creative Commons Attribution Non-Commercial License 4.0 (CC BY-NC 4.0).
doi:10.3233/FAIA231483

Research on the Integration and Application of Design Thinking and Large Language Models in the Innovation Design of Fintech Products

Wenjing WANG [a,1] and Baixi XING [b]

[a] *Zhejiang University, Hangzhou, China*

[b] *Zhejiang University of Technology, Hangzhou, China*

Abstract. This study explores the integration and application of Design Thinking and Large Language Models (LLMs) in fintech product innovation design from the perspective of requirements management. Design thinking is human-centered, focusing on discovering and solving problems, integrating innovative solutions, and enhancing product value. By understanding and generating natural language, LLMs provide "on-demand" intelligent services through information retrieval, content creation, and human-like dialogue, meeting individualized needs. Through literature review and analysis, this paper reveals that the combination of the two can promote the full intelligence and continuous improvement of the innovation design process, enhancing the R&D efficiency and user experience of fintech products. This research aims to provide innovation design methods for the fintech field and promote its continuous innovation and development.

Keywords. Design Thinking; Large Language Models; Fintech; Product Innovation Design; Requirements Management

1. Introduction

With the rapid development of Fintech, the innovation research and development of fintech products are increasingly valued by banks and other financial institutions. Major banks have successively established fintech innovation departments or innovation R&D laboratories. Different from the information technology departments of banks, software centers, and fintech companies, such non-profit R&D innovation institutions directly established by the headquarters focus more on the top-level design of product innovation and the prototype research and development of new products, and focus on product research and development and requirements management in software engineering. When promoting specific innovation projects in the form of flexible teams, R&D personnel come from different functional backgrounds such as finance, IT, or management, and sometimes invite experts or users from other industries to participate. However, they often lack specialized knowledge in design and innovation management, and co-innovation faces the challenges of communication and collaboration as well as

---

[1] Corresponding Author.

knowledge integration, which makes it necessary to introduce advanced innovation design methods and tools.

Design thinking is a human-centered, iterative, experimental problem-solving method and a systematic collaborative method for creatively solving complex problems, playing an important role in the designs of various products and services [1]. LLMs have demonstrated excellent natural language understanding, generation, and knowledge integration capabilities by learning massive text data. However, there is very little research on the integration and application of the two. In order to explore the integration and application of design thinking and LLMs in the innovation design of fintech products, this paper will investigate from the perspective of improving the requirements management process of new product design.

This study mainly focuses on researching and analyzing more than 80 pieces of literature on the intersection of Design Thinking, AI, LLMs, Fintech, and Requirements Management (Requirements Engineering). We use Python programs to extract text from PDF files and perform word frequency analysis on the literature, as well as generate word frequency heat maps and word clouds based on country regions. The analysis reveals that China, India, Brazil, and Europe appear more frequently in these documents, indicating that emerging economies are very active in research in related fields.

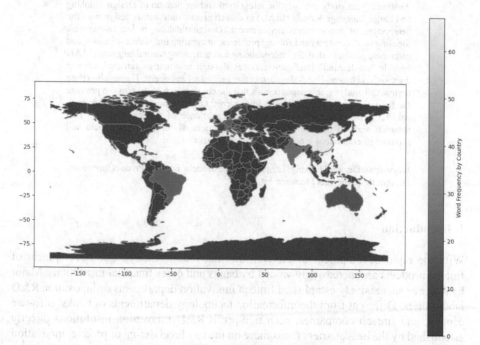

Figure 1. Word Frequency Heat Map by Country/Region

In this paper, we respectively describe the application of design thinking and LLMs in requirements management; and the positive impact of LLMs on fintech innovation; last but not least, we explore the possibility of integrating design thinking with LLMs and its potential value in fintech product innovation design.

2. Application of Design Thinking in Requirements Management

Design Thinking originates from Design Studies, an interdisciplinary study based on engineering, management, industrial design, anthropology, and information management. It emphasizes the concepts of mutual understanding, teamwork, and prototype experimentation, and encourages engineers to reduce the risk of innovation trial and error by practicing empathy, testing, and iterating to refine complex engineering requirements and solutions using Minimum Viable Product (MVP).

As early as 2013, design thinking was introduced into requirements engineering [2]. To date, a large amount of research has proven the potential of collaborative application of design thinking and requirements engineering, especially in the requirements elicitation phase [3, 4]. In requirements management, design thinking can provide deeper insights into user needs, create innovative solutions, and quickly validate and iterate prototypes. The introduction of design thinking has changed traditional requirements management methods, not only focusing on functional requirements but also prioritizing user experience [5]. Design thinking emphasizes acquiring requirements based on user experience. By deeply understanding customer scenarios and pain points, solutions beyond functional requirements can be proposed. Compared to traditional methods, design thinking in requirements management has shown unique advantages: focusing on process and results, emphasizing user experience, encouraging creativity, rapid prototype iteration, cross-functional team collaboration, etc. Case studies have shown that design thinking can effectively improve the quality of requirements definition and management, enhancing the final product's user experience and commercial value [5, 6].

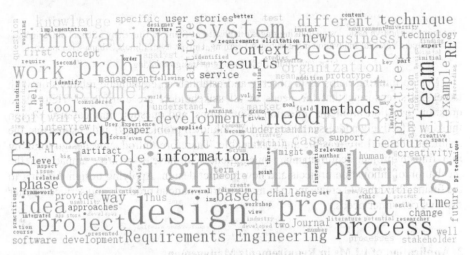

Figure 2. Word cloud extracted from 39 related papers

In recent years, the application of design thinking in New Product Development (NPD) and innovation has received increasing attention. As a user-centered methodology, it can effectively enhance the user experience and market competitiveness of products. Design thinking differs from traditional methods that rely on analytical thinking and logical reasoning to solve problems. It emphasizes empathy, collaboration, and experimentation, focusing on understanding the needs of people who will use the designed product or service. Design thinking also encourages collaboration among team members with different backgrounds and expertise to generate creative solutions and quickly understand what works and what doesn't through rapid prototype creation and idea testing [7]. Using design thinking is beneficial for generating new ideas based on user and stakeholder needs and can support software developers during the requirements acquisition process [8]. In the context of innovation with uncertainty and complexity, where all requirements are not assumed to be known at the outset but are learned and experimented with throughout the project lifecycle, traditional requirements management methods are no longer effective. Design thinking can help teams adapt to a constantly changing environment and improve project outcomes [6].

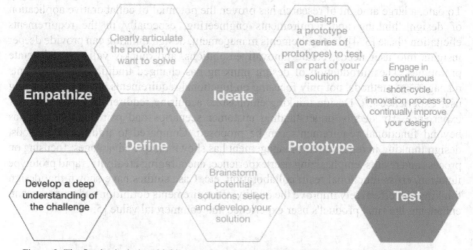

Figure 3. The five basic design thinking stages established by Stanford University's School of Design. Source: Center for Innovation in Teaching & Learning, University of Illinois Urbana-Champaign

https://citl.illinois.edu/paradigms/design-thinking

Design thinking helps us to observe and establish an empathetic relationship with target users, ensuring that the needs of all stakeholders are considered. Help us to question: question problems, question assumptions, and question implications. Design thinking effectively addresses ill-defined or unknown problems [9] and ensures that the solutions obtained are feasible and sustainable. Therefore, introducing design thinking into fintech project requirements management will have a positive impact on the incubation of innovation projects and new product design. Applying design thinking to the financial sector will create more human-centric financial products and services, better meeting consumer needs.

3. Application of LLMs in Requirements Management

LLMs refer to natural language processing models trained based on deep learning technology. They can capture rich knowledge from pre-trained data and can be regarded as experts in specific domains. Recent research has explored the use of LLMs to solve domain-specific tasks and assess their adaptability. The following briefly describes three typical emergent capabilities of large models: 1) Context learning, where GPT-3 generates the expected output of a test instance by completing a sequence of words from the input text; 2) Instruction adherence, whereby fine-tuning a multi-tasking dataset formatted with instructions, LLMs can perform new tasks without the use of explicit samples, perform well on tiny tasks, and improve generalization capabilities; 3) Progressive reasoning, through the chain-of-thinking reasoning strategy, LLMs can solve such tasks to arrive at a final answer by utilizing a prompt mechanism involving intermediate reasoning steps [10]. Although LLMs have the potential to solve general tasks, these abilities may not be manifested explicitly when performing specific tasks. Therefore, designing suitable task instructions or context-specific strategies, such as thought-chaining prompts, as well as instruction tuning for LLMs, are effective ways to stimulate these abilities and improve generalization to unseen tasks [11]. In requirements management, LLMs can be used to automate the processing of large amounts of user feedback and requirements data, extract key information, predict trends in user requirements, and even generate requirements documents [12, 13]. The application of LLMs will greatly improve the efficiency and granularity of requirements management, and the initial practice of LLMs has proved to be very positive in supporting requirements management [10]. LLMs have been proven to support demand management in a very positive way [10]. The application of LLMs will greatly improve the efficiency and refinement of requirements management.

Thanks to LLMs, artificial intelligence has evolved from perceiving and understanding the world to generating and creating it. Significant progress has been made in the field of Generative AI (AIGC). In a broad sense, AIGC can be seen as AI technology with human-like generative capabilities. It can autonomously generate and create new content and data based on training data and generative algorithm models, including initiating new scientific discoveries, creating new value and meaning, etc. AIGC emphasizes human-centricity and human-intelligence interaction. It is a digital content generation method in which humans and machines participate collaboratively, breaking the boundaries between humans, machines, and information resources and reshaping the paradigms of information resource generation and use [14]. AIGC is increasingly involved in the creative generation of digital content, releasing value in a human-machine collaborative manner, and becoming the foundational infrastructure for future internet content production [15]. AI becomes the main body of design, capable of "independently" completing certain tasks and ultimately deeply interacting and collaborating with designers to complete the design work [16].

LLMs can serve as a knowledge base providing expert knowledge and can be used to analyze and extract requirements from large amounts of unstructured data, such as customer feedback, social media posts, and user comments. LLMs can also be used to generate personas and conduct user interviews, generating information that can be used to understand user needs and develop solutions that meet these needs. They can promote collaboration among stakeholders by sharing context, generating requirement summaries, providing requirement feedback, and helping resolve conflicts. They can be used to conceive solutions and assess the feasibility and sustainability of these solutions.

Figure 4. Word cloud extracted from 38 related papers

The concept of Disruptive Technology was first proposed by American scholar Clayton M. Christensen in 1995 [17]. Compared to Sustaining Technology, which involves "incremental improvements to existing technology," Disruptive Technology refers to technologies that replace existing mainstream technologies in unexpected ways [18]. LLMs like GPT have the characteristics of general technologies, indicating that they may have significant economic, social, and policy impacts [19]. The extraordinary capabilities of LLMs show the potential of LLMs to build general artificial intelligence (AGI), but achieving AGI requires overcoming the limitations of existing models that are only suitable for specific tasks. Recently, researchers from Zhejiang University and Microsoft introduced the HuggingGPT framework, using LLMs to combine various AI models to solve more complex tasks [20]. This system, like a "project manager," can effectively manage and assign tasks to professional "engineers" (AI models). When receiving requirements, the system will analyze the requirements, assign tasks to the corresponding AI models for execution, and finally integrate the results to feedback to the user, showing the huge potential for intelligent implementation of project requirements management. LLMs can interact directly with users to obtain requirements and can also assist in evaluating the quality of requirement solutions. To some extent, LLMs are key to achieving automation in requirements management.

4. LLMs Empower Fintech Innovation

The World Bank and the International Monetary Fund (IMF) define "Financial Technology (Fintech)" as "technological innovation that transforms existing financial service methods, and develops new business models, applications, processes, and products" [21]. Generally speaking, fintech refers to innovative activities that use information technology to create and provide financial products and services for individuals and businesses, such as cashless payments, robo-advisors, and blockchain applications, etc.

Figure 5. Word cloud extracted from 12 related papers

At present, the financial industry is accelerating its digital and intelligent transformation, and the application of artificial intelligence technology is unstoppable. Bloomberg released a study [22] introducing its 50 billion parameter LLMs developed for the financial sector - BloombergGPT. This model underwent specialized training on various financial data to support various natural language processing (NLP) tasks in the financial industry, such as sentiment analysis, named entity recognition, news classification, and Q&A. The model is expected to be applied to actual work through more new methods to meet customer needs. Additionally, the open-source LLMs - FinGPT adopts a data-centric approach, providing researchers and practitioners with accessible and transparent resources to develop their FinLLMs [23]. FinGPT not only provides technical contributions but also nurtures an open-source FinLLMs ecosystem, collaborating through the AI4Finance community, aiming to increase transparency, and trust, promote innovation, and real-time adaptability in the financial sector [23].

Research shows that ChatGPT can significantly assist in idea generation and data recognition in financial research, improving research quality and efficiency. However, it faces difficulties in connecting multiple ideas, and domain knowledge and data scope are key to output quality [24]. LLMs have the potential to improve academic performance in economics and finance. A study using the case study method found that ChatGPT can significantly enhance the quality of academic research, especially in the fields of economics and finance [25]. Undoubtedly, future fintech innovation will rely on the support of LLMs.

5. Integration and Application of Design Thinking and LLMs

In exploring the integrated application of design thinking and Large Language Models (LLMs), we reviewed related research since 2013. These studies explored the possibility of combining the human-centric and innovative aspects of design thinking with the data processing capabilities of computational models [26]. Core principles of design creative thinking include accessibility and connectivity of ideas, both of which are assessed through computational models. The findings reveal the value of assessing new ideas based on these two principles, with the potential to transform current idea generation practices and research. With the emergence of LLMs, its large pre-trained corpus becomes a deeply promising source of knowledge capable of generating multiple ideas. The text generation mechanism of LLMs produces responses probabilistically and refines ideas or creativity through interaction with users, echoing early research on the integration of design and computational thinking.

Recently, LLMs have shown tremendous potential in simulating human behavior, opening up new possibilities for creating realistic, interactive artificial agents. The introduction of generative agents simulates coherent and realistic human behavior, offering new perspectives in areas like human-computer interaction and virtual worlds [27]. The key to generative agents lies in storing, integrating, and retrieving relevant memories to dynamically generate behaviors based on the environment and experience. This new type of interactive agent has broad application prospects but also brings ethical risks. Researchers have delved deeply into whether LLMs can understand language and the physical and social contexts it encodes in a human-like manner [28]. Some researchers have applied psychological tests to LLMs, finding that in some cases, LLMs exhibit human-like responses in the theory of mind tests [29, 30]. This suggests that LLMs have the potential to act as intelligent agents for specific tasks and be applied in daily work.

The Chain of Thought (CoT) offers LLMs a new way to demonstrate complex reasoning processes, significantly improving the model's performance in handling complex reasoning tasks. Scientists are exploring the workings behind CoT and how it unlocks the potential of LLMs [31]. The reasoning power of CoT reveals that models can not only imitate but also learn complex thinking patterns, paving the way for them to gain true design capabilities.

By using LLMs to simulate and study the process of design thinking, we can explore the accessibility and connectivity of ideas, providing quantitative analysis and guidance for design thinking. The integration of design thinking and LLMs has become a burgeoning interdisciplinary field full of endless possibilities, promising to deeply reveal the cognitive laws and process mechanisms of design creativity and inspire new design innovation ways.

Design thinking and LLMs each have their strengths, and their combined use in requirements management holds significant potential. Design thinking can guide LLMs to understand requirements from a human-centric perspective; LLMs can quickly process large-scale user data, supporting design thinking [16], and can also support the generation of requirement solutions [32]. The two complement each other, facilitating the comprehensive intelligent transformation of the requirements management process. Future research can continue to delve into the collaborative ways of design thinking and LLMs in requirements management, such as intelligent extraction, analysis, and re-expression of requirements information; intelligent generation of requirement solutions; rapid prototype creation, etc. The integration of methods is expected to further enhance the R&D efficiency and success rate of fintech products.

A preliminary envisioned integrated application model is where design thinking is responsible for defining the direction and principles of requirements management, ensuring a "human-centric" engineering ethic. Design thinking leads the insight and solution direction of requirements, LLMs quickly produce multiple requirement solutions for evaluation, design thinking is responsible for solution evaluation, providing qualitative input, and LLMs provide quantitative analysis. LLMs offer powerful language analysis and generation capabilities, achieving process automation. This leverages human wisdom as well as computational intelligence and a powerful knowledge base.

6. Conclusion and Outlook

Artificial Intelligence is ushering in a new round of explosive development, and the application of LLMs technology, represented by GPT, will have great value and impact in all walks of life, and profoundly change the way of production and life and the way of thinking of human beings. We should actively embrace technological innovation and fully consider the utilization of advanced tools in scientific research and work, while also facing the problems and risks of arithmetic bottleneck, commercial landing, and engineering ethics.

Design Thinking and LLMs have their specialties and show great potential in the field of requirements management. They not only help teams deepen their understanding of user requirements and innovate solutions but also improve the efficiency and accuracy of requirements management and promote the intelligent transformation of requirements management. However, at present, there are few cases of the integration of design thinking and LLMs applied to innovation design, and there is a lack of systematic and practical research. In the innovation design of cross-cutting fields, a macro-understanding of the involved fields becomes necessary, which includes understanding the mechanisms and modes of action of the main problems and, based on this, encapsulating the complex technologies and constructing a complete cognitive system of technological problems to more accurately identify and define the design problems [16]. In the future, it is necessary to further study the synergistic mechanism and key technologies of the two in demand management, especially how to realize the comprehensive intelligence and rapid iterative optimization of the demand management process. More empirical studies will also help to verify the effectiveness of the integration application, improve the efficiency and success rate of the development of financial technology products, and provide theoretical and practical references for researchers and developers in this field.

In the future, in-depth research on the integration and application of design thinking and LLMs will open up new ways for innovation and development in the field of financial technology. This integration is expected to promote the intelligent transformation of requirements management, shorten product development cycles, improve user satisfaction, and promote the prosperity of innovation design of fintech products.

References

[1] T. Brown, Design Thinking, 2008.
[2] V.C., B.W., U.F., P.C., From Palaces to Yurts: Why Requirements Engineering Needs Design Thinking, IEEE INTERNET COMPUTING 20 (2013), 91–94.
[3] H. Ferreira Martins, A. Carvalho De Oliveira Junior, E. Dias Canedo, R.A. Dias Kosloski, R. Ávila Paldês, E. Costa Oliveira, Design Thinking: Challenges for Software Requirements Elicitation, Series Design Thinking: Challenges for Software Requirements Elicitation 10, 2019.
[4] E. Kahan, A. Oliveros, M. Genero, A systematic mapping study on the application of design thinking in requirement engineering, Journal of Universal Computer Science 2021.

[5] R.G. Cooper, S.J. Edgett, E.J. Kleinschmidt, Benchmarking Best NPD Practices—II, RESEARCH-TECHNOLOGY MANAGEMENT 47 (2004), 50-59.

[6] S.B. Mahmoud-Jouini, C. Midler, P. Silberzahn, Contributions of Design Thinking to Project Management in an Innovation Context, Project Management Journal 47 (2016), 144-156.

[7] E. Gonen, Tim Brown, Change by Design: How Design Thinking Transforms Organizations and Inspires Innovation (2009), Markets, globalization & development review 10 (2019).

[8] E.D. Canedo, A.T.S. Calazans, G.R.S. Silva, P.H.T. Costa, R.P. De Mesquita, E.T.S. Masson, Creativity and Design Thinking as Facilitators in Requirements Elicitation, INTERNATIONAL JOURNAL OF SOFTWARE ENGINEERING AND KNOWLEDGE ENGINEERING 32 (2022), 1527-1558.

[9] I.D. Foundation, R.F. Dam, T.Y. Siang, What is design thinking and why is it so popular?, Interaction Design Foundation, 2021.

[10] J. Wei, X. Wang, D. Schuurmans, M. Bosma, B. Ichter, F. Xia, E. Chi, Q. Le, D. Zhou, Chain-of-Thought Prompting Elicits Reasoning in Large Language Models, 2023.

[11] W.X. Zhao, K. Zhou, J. Li, T. Tang, X. Wang, Y. Hou, Y. Min, B. Zhang, J. Zhang, Z. Dong, Y. Du, C. Yang, Y. Chen, Z. Chen, J. Jiang, R. Ren, Y. Li, X. Tang, Z. Liu, P. Liu, J. Nie, J. Wen, A Survey of Large Language Models, 2023.

[12] J. Devlin, M. Chang, K. Lee, K. Toutanova, Bert: Pre-training of deep bidirectional transformers for language understanding, arXiv preprint arXiv:1810.04805, 2018.

[13] A. Radford, J. Wu, R. Child, D. Luan, D. Amodei, I. Sutskever, Language models are unsupervised multitask learners, OpenAI blog 4 (2019).

[14] Li Baiyang, Bai Yun, Zhan Xini, Li Gang, Technical Characteristics and Evolutionary Trends of Artificial Intelligence Generated Content (AIGC), Library and Information Knowledge 23 (2023), 1-9.

[15] Tencent Research Institute, AIGC Development Trend Report 2023, 2023.

[16] Wu Qiong, Innovative Design Thinking in the Era of Artificial Intelligence, Decoration 19 (2019), 18-21.

[17] J.L. Bower, C.M. Christensen, Disruptive technologies: catching the wave, 1995.

[18] Li Jianping, Wu Dengsheng, Hao Jun, Research on Management Science and Engineering Driven by Technology, Chinese Management Science 22 (2022), 9-14.

[19] T. Eloundou, S. Manning, P. Mishkin, D. Rock, GPTs are GPTs: An Early Look at the Labor Market Impact Potential of Large Language Models, 2023.

[20] Y. Shen, K. Song, X. Tan, D. Li, W. Lu, Y. Zhuang, HuggingGPT: Solving AI Tasks with ChatGPT and its Friends in HuggingFace, 2023.

[21] H.M. Elsaid, A review of literature directions regarding the impact of fintech firms on the banking industry, Qualitative Research in financial Markets 13 (2021).

[22] S. Wu, O. Irsoy, S. Lu, V. Dabravolski, M. Dredze, S. Gehrmann, P. Kambadur, D. Rosenberg, G. Mann, BloombergGPT: A Large Language Model for Finance, 2023.

[23] H. Yang, X. Liu, C.D. Wang, FinGPT: Open-Source Financial Large Language Models, 2023.

[24] M. Dowling, B. Lucey, ChatGPT for (Finance) research: The Bananarama Conjecture, Finance Research Letters 23 (2023), 103662.

[25] L. Bard, G. AI, Exploring the role of artificial intelligence in enhancing academic performance: A case study of chatgpt, Artificial Intelligence in Education 23 (2023), 1-15.

[26] R. Sosa, J.S. Gero, The creative value of bad ideas: A computational model of creative ideologies, 2013.

[27] J.S. Park, J.C. O'Brien, C.J. Cai, M.R. Morris, P. Liang, M.S. Bernstein, Generative Agents: Interactive Simulacra of Human Behavior, 2023.

[28] M. Mitchell, D.C. Krakauer, The debate over understanding in AI's large language models, Proceedings of the National Academy of Sciences 23 (2023).

[29] B.A.U.E. Y Arcas, Do large language models understand us? DAEDALUS 22 (2022), 183-197.

[30] S. Trott, C. Jones, T. Chang, J. Michaelov, B. Bergen, Do Large Language Models know what humans know? 2023.

[31] G. Feng, B. Zhang, Y. Gu, H. Ye, Di He, L. Wang, Towards Revealing the Mystery behind Chain of Thought: A Theoretical Perspective, 2023.

[32] S.G. Bouschery, V. Blazevic, F.T. Piller, Augmenting human innovation teams with artificial intelligence: Exploring transformer-based language models, JOURNAL OF PRODUCT INNOVATION MANAGEMENT 23 (2023), 139-153.

Design Studies and Intelligence Engineering
L.C. Jain et al. (Eds.)
© 2024 The Authors.
This article is published online with Open Access by IOS Press and distributed under the terms
of the Creative Commons Attribution Non-Commercial License 4.0 (CC BY-NC 4.0).
doi:10.3233/FAIA231484

Mobile Agricultural Products Vending Vehicle with Autonomous Navigation Selling on Town Roads

Yousheng YAO [a,b,*], E TANG [a,*], Fangtian YING [b,1] , Xiqin PAN [a], Yuan XIE [a],
Zhihao HUANG [a], Junpeng ZHENG [a], Junqi ZHAN [a], Jin PENG [a],
Haoteng CHEN [a], and Wenjing FENG [a]

[a] *Zhongkai University of Agriculture and Engineering, He Xiangning College of Art and Design, China*
[b] *Macau University of Science and Technology, China*

Abstract. In the future, farmers may be able to enhance their agricultural sales by designing an efficient interaction space and sales model for mobile sales vehicles. The traditional mobile sales vehicle sales methodology is primarily based on offline spot sales. Offline fixed-point sales cannot guarantee consumer flow and variety quality, cannot be traced, and the price is rising due to logistics and operation costs. This article presents a mobile sales vehicle for farmers' direct sales operations that integrates agricultural products with live e-commerce for public sales and presentation. The combination of agricultural products presented in the mobile live program in the mobile sales vehicle, The utilization of a set flow path by an intelligent people flow system. The crowd flows heat map and the TD original display system are utilized for this purpose. User feedback is used to validate quantitative data. The results show that a mobile sales vehicle combined with live e-commerce is critical for farmers experiencing little or no sales growth.

Keywords. mobile sales vehicle, interactive place, live e-commerce broadcast, brand

1. Introduction

When compared to businesses, street vending vehicles, which evolved from tricycles carrying goods for sale, are more handy and versatile. Because of these qualities, street vending trucks are beginning to appear in neighborhoods such as pharmacy, book, and coffee businesses [1,2]. As science and technology advance, we must reevaluate our assumptions about the usefulness and aesthetics of mobile vending vehicles. Mobile vans, such as methadone vans, have proven to be effective in lowering HIV infection and transmission, as well as drug-related criminality. These medical vans provide for both safe drug administration and good publicity [3].

Mobile vending carts are an economical and handy way to sell products and are becoming increasingly popular among the general population. However, this sort of

---

* The first two authors contributed equally to the article.
[1] Corresponding Author: Fangtian,Ying, Macau University of Science and Technology, Avenida WaiLong, Taipa, 999078, Macau, E-mail:1290289579@qq.com.

vehicle has numerous disadvantages, including driver tiredness, wind and rain, damaged and rotting items, and so on. Street vending carts now have refrigerators to keep food fresh and well-presented.

Live e-commerce has grown in popularity in recent years, and with the emergence of the pandemic in recent years, sales of agricultural products have become increasingly depressed, prompting us to examine the present new mode of selling agricultural products. Agricultural products are also shifting from offline to online sales in this context, and the implementation of a collaborative multi-channel development approach for online and offline agricultural products can better help farmers expand sales channels, improve sales efficiency, and expand marketing reach.

The article explores user needs, creates a new sales scene, creates a new consumption scene of buying and selling, and provides users with a marketing and sales vehicle that combines online and offline sales by studying the opportunities and challenges facing traditional produce carts in today's e-commerce environment and applying marketing theory to analyze the problems of the sales model and consumer experience of traditional produce carts. Ceres is used to launch a transparent, full-color holographic display system[4], which allows for improved live streaming and interaction. Self-orientation and route planning in pre-planned locations are made possible by autonomous navigation.

In China, for example, Baidu Maps can detect population heat maps in real time and combine them with a mobile application for mobile sales.

2. Related work

Table 1 contains data regarding the products discussed in this article. It analyzes the sensors/features utilized by the for-sale autonomous vehicles, as well as measuring distances, etc. Sensors utilized in autonomous cars include millimeter wave sensors, laser sensors, ultrasonic radar, and image sensors, as illustrated in Table 1. Millimeter-wave radar sensors are quite expensive, have long sensing distances, and can operate in a wider range of situations, whereas image sensors are relatively inexpensive, rely on 3D information, provide visual effects [5], and are easier to install in self-driving vehicles.

Table 1. Information on unmanned dispensing vehicles.

Type	Sensors	Features	Test methods	Detection distance	Advantages
Unmanned dispensing vehicles	Unmanned dispensing vehicles	Electric waves	Measurement of distance, relative speed and direction as a function of the difference between the transmitting and receiving frequencies.	Long	Good reflectivity on metallic surfaces Can be used at night, against the light, in fog and in the rain
	Laser sensors (LiDAR) Waves of light		Distance measurement by time difference between emission and reflection of light 3DLiDAR direction and shape detection	Medium Long	Good reflectivity on non-metallic surfaces Can be used at night, in fog and in the rain
	Ultrasonic	Sound	Distance measurement	Short	Glass and water

radar	waves	by time difference between the transmitted wave and the return wave		surfaces also reflect
Display sensors	Camera	Image capture and target object identification	Long(stereo scopic camera) Medium(single-lens camera)	Identification of target objects, colours

Because there has been little research on mobile vending vehicles mixed with live streaming for sales, typical examples of vending vehicles paired with live streaming for analysis were not found. As a result, we examined the product's attributes independently. Recognizing the significance of self-driving cars on city streets, Jorge Enrique Caicedo Martinez et al.developed AutoNavi3AT, a software application that estimates and tracks self-driving automobiles on urban travel roadways using vanishing points from panoramic photos [5]. Lulu Tai, on the other hand, earned the Rising Star Anchor award in the 2021 Lazada Southeast Asia Cross Border live talent contest, which brings users closer together through the joy and variety of live-streaming with a vibrant image that can generate sales [6].

In this work, we demonstrate an interactive self-driving automobile called "Mobile Premium" that uses autonomous navigation and real-time live-streaming to attract followers during their leisure time. The "Mobile Premium" reduces costs by utilizing ultrasonic radar and laser sensors to enable autonomous driving and obstacle avoidance. We discovered that Ceres could assist us in broadcasting live offline by introducing a full-color holographic projection technology and building a small interactive interface for customers to buy and participate online.

3. Formal research

The lack of sales of agricultural products cultivated by farmers, the rise of China's grassroots economy, and the present wave of live goods transmission owing to the epidemic affecting the world economy all motivated the creation of this work. We investigated and researched sales carts, users, consumers, and live banding to find the true wants and pain areas of users. We grasp the farm produce vending consuming environment, the capabilities of live streaming short movies with items, the future development trend of vending carts, user research and particular analysis of vending carts, and so on. To pave the path for our design solution, we examine and summarize the pain and itch spots below.

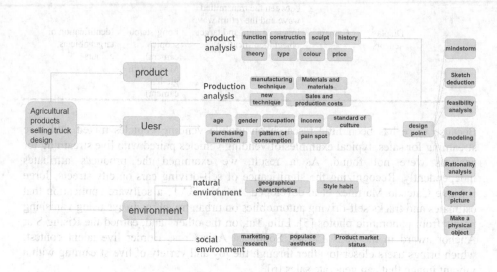

Fig. 1. Creating the vending cart research content.

3.1. Design survey

Produce vending vehicles must take into account the size of the vehicle and the user, leaving plenty of space for the user and consumer experience. The national standard GB T 13547-92 "Human dimensions of the working space" is employed as a data reference, taking into consideration the height and limb length of the 30-50-year-old business crowd I've positioned. The approximate height of the live cart space can be established by combining the condition of the scene in which both the user and the consumer are located, as indicated in the diagram below.

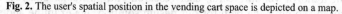

Fig. 2. The user's spatial position in the vending cart space is depicted on a map.

We combined theories of systematic design, digital design, interaction design, and brand design to design the spatial area of the vehicle in a unique way, investigating and analyzing the shape, color, structure, and materials of the mobile vending vehicle.

3.2. Design objectives

To address the issue of consumers' difficulty distinguishing between high quality and high price, we created a logo design for the branding of a mobile sales cart that would aid in the improvement of agricultural product brand image.

Mobile premium combined with the concept of mobile broadcast room to deliver high-quality agricultural products, deliver health and peace of mind

U-shaped language and quality products

Live camera and modeling language

Symbolizes speed and movement

Fig. 3. Ideas for vending vehicle branding.

We name it "Mobile Premium" because it combines live broadcasting with the distribution of excellent agricultural products and the provision of health and peace of mind, with the letter "U" representing for quality products and also as a design language for the entire vehicle. The brand image of the vehicle and the agricultural products it markets aims to increase consumer recognition and visibility of quality agricultural products so that they can be distinguished from other agricultural products on the market, as well as to promote agricultural product consumption and development by creating and transferring brand value.

To provide consumers with a good shopping experience, it is necessary to divide the sales area into several parts: driving area, display area, interaction area, and service area, which have different responsibilities in different areas and combine to form a complete shopping process that fits consumers' shopping habits. The shop's display section should be where customers spend the most time; this area should provide them adequate time to try out the products. The interactive area is used to draw traffic to the area; it is developed in tandem with the design of the live area, with the front of the live interactive area behind the section for the purchase of interactive design, to draw the consumer's attention in the shop to buy. The interaction and service areas are akin to what we term functional areas, and I have subdivided this. The seating in the driving area is designed to swivel $360°$ to allow for a swift transition between driving and selling; in some regions, due to the small size of the shop, it is divided into fewer zones, or the zones are connected in series to plan the consumer's movement.

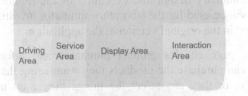

Driving Area   Service Area   Display Area   Interaction Area

Fig. 4. Area planning for agricultural produce-selling vehicles.

3.3. Question Mining

During our problem-solving session, we videotaped and studied the scenario with the produce truck. The main issue was the need for a more intuitive live vending model for mobile vending than the typical produce truck, as well as autopilot vending, which would ultimately alleviate most of the trouble, and a consumer-oriented foot traffic heat map.

Based on our findings and conversations, we have developed the following ten design requirements for our mobile vending vehicle:

- It's incredibly inconvenient not knowing where the traffic is.

- There was a large crowd gathered near the carts, and there was no order.

- The carts' appearance is not appealing enough, and many of them are over-decorated and do not seem nice.

- Vegetables and fruits, for example, are easily spoiled.

- The products offered by vending carts are all wholesale from many locations; it may be better to have a single brand, as in shops.

- The service provided to product customers has to be enhanced.

- When there are many people, one person can be quite busy...

- I'm hoping for genuine user input.

- Customers can place orders.

- My product is excellent; how can I communicate this to customers?

4. Design methods

This section discusses the "Mobile Premium" design and implementation, including functional and non-functional requirements, interface design, conceptual design, renderings, schematic testing, and test reports for the mobile vending trolley.

4.1. Design and implementation of the first mobile application

We explain the preliminary design and execution of the mobile application "Mobile Premium," which will be used for the laboratory simulator investigation. The following features are included in the original version of the application:

- The home page enables product purchases and information display. The customer can purchase the products they want using the search button on the home page, or they can select the things they want using the flowing tag recommendations and popular set recommendations. We may see the qualities of a certain product and a traceable photo of the pick-up location submitted by the farmer by clicking on a tag. This is really unusual.

- On the second screen, we can view the heat map distribution of the flow as well as the location of the mobile carts in real-time.

- The third page is a place for our users to provide comments and communicate about their purchases. Each user can take a picture of their purchase and share their status as an ins, allowing others to learn more about them.

- The final page is ours, where we can check information on our orders, logistics, preferred products, after-sales returns, and much more.

Fig. 5. Design of an interaction interface for sales vehicles.

Fig. 5 The interface design of the "Mobile Premium" is shown, and the application's implementation is backed by the UniAPP.

4.2. Hardware design

The following are the functional and non-functional needs of Mobile Premium, as well as the aforementioned working analysis:

- Configuration of ultrasonic and laser radar sensors and operation of the mobile dispenser vehicle; acquisition of images and corresponding panoramic images; road route planning; obstacle avoidance on the road by ultrasonic radar; live transmission on a continuous display; and servo control of the mobile dispenser vehicle for navigation.

- Non-functional requirements: The testing platform for the mobile delivery vehicle is a C51 development board; vision sensors include image sensors.

First, we used Rhino software to model and create the vending cart based on its functional needs, merging the general modeling structure with the U-shape and unifying the elements of the product modeling language. The effect was then rendered using Keyshot, which includes front, side, and top views, as well as a depiction of the vending cart scene.

Fig. 6. Diagram of the mobile product vending trolley.

Following that, we ran some important tests with the schematic machine, which can be seen in figure 7. We tested about 50 experiments, with the main ones being wireless control, ultrasonic obstacle avoidance, infrared tracking, ultrasonic tracking experiments, danger warning, ultrasonic distance measuring, and so on.

Fig. 7. Three different perspectives on the agriculture sales trolley.

4.3. Function and principle

The "Mobile Premium" is implemented in two parts: the first is the APP application on the Android device, and the second is the prototype's configuration, journey time, and route planning. The user can change the settings of the mobile vehicle, such as its speed, the fixed staging position, the control of the vehicle lights, the acquisition of image timings, and so on.

5. Initial user research

We did preliminary user research to establish that users could access the mobile cart movement and purchase things using the application. We put out an online appeal for experienced users, and we received many applications from people we dubbed K1, K2, K3, and K4 (with an average age of 31.6 years). All participants tested the application for three days in different settings, and the entire process was filmed with their permission. Table 1 shows the level of pleasure expressed by consumers after using the app.

Table 2. User survey results.

Questions	K1	K2	K3	K4	Media
1. Would you buy products over the air? (1: Yes - 6: No)	5.8	6	6	5.8	5.9

2. Do you find it easy to use the "Mobile Premium" application (1: easy - 6: not easy)?	5.3	5.5	6	5.4	5.55
3. Would you be willing to buy such products after experiencing the "Mobile Premium" application (1: Yes - 6: No)?	6	5.4	5.8	5.7	5.7

Due to the outbreak, we had a video conference with the experimenters after three days. First, we asked the users what they expected from a mobile vending cart, and the four experimenters watched the film with anticipation, since they were quite interested. "I used to buy fruit from the stalls because it was cheap," K1 answered when I asked him the question. It would be tempting for me to have software that could track the location of the vending carts at all times."K4 went on to say: "I would love to go to this mobile cart and experience it" . Both K2 and K3 are excited to see and experience it in person in the future, with K3 noting, "So I can buy gift boxes for people who are in a hurry and get them on the road" and K4 saying, "This mobile shop could win my heart more than a high-end branded shop."

5.1. Interview process

We basically questioned folks in the shape of friends during the interviews. Following that, we interviewed IT specialists to help us with our investigation. According to the experts, our concept was good, but it might not be perfect in terms of technical elements, and the needs of the users needed to be examined further. We are also encouraged by the experts' opinions because they will help us develop our mobile car.

5.2. Results and discussion

As seen in the table above, all members who participated in the experience showed a strong desire to try out this new mobile vending cart. In the future, the mobile live vending vehicle may offer various advantages:

- It It solves both the problem of not being able to leave the house, or rather leaving the house during an epidemic.

- It is more secure for the consumer to acquire.

- Protect the environment while conserving energy.
  Experimenting with a prototype was used to validate the functionality of the Mobile Premium. Our goal was to check all of the mobile shopping cart's functioning needs and improve it if any issues were discovered. Once these issues have been resolved, it will be feasible to test the functionality of the Mobile Premium in real-world situations.

6. Limitations and future work

The mobile shopping trolley is popular among consumers due to its low cost and versatility. It does, however, have limitations: product quality is not assured; it tends to break down over time; it is readily destroyed during transportation; and it has a limited distribution range. We focus on overcoming these restrictions and reimagining the classic mobile vending vehicle as a revolutionary self-directed, live-streaming mobile vending model in this work.

The study's disadvantage is that it was not experimentally tested in equal quantities, therefore our user data may be biased. We hope that it will be available on our city streets and on our mobile phones in the future. Meanwhile, we will focus on incorporating equiproportional physical testing into our future work so that we can better illustrate if it can solve the problems we are discussing.

7. Conclusions

This article explains the Mobile Premium application's interface design, functional design, appearance design, and user research. The software interface is the application that is utilized to give a shopping experience to the consumer. The program is supplemented with an applet to control the mobile shopping cart, which can be easily and swiftly controlled from the WeChat applet platform with a tiny memory. To obtain the greatest potential sales results, the applet instructs the mobile cart to go along a predetermined route and asks changes to the route plan based on a heat map of the crowd movement. The "Mobile Premium" live streaming function is based on a full-color holographic display device that is transparent [4]. We also plan the mobile car's purchase movements. For testing of the "Mobile Premium," we used a C51 microcontroller development board. Data processing for road obstacle avoidance, wireless networking, and user data collecting were the primary functional needs. Finally, the autopilot technology and live streaming format have increased the mobile vending vehicle's service channels, but there is still a lot of territory to cover for our technical services. This live mobile vending truck will surely increase agricultural product sales swiftly while also transporting regional farming culture to all parts of the world and making it a household name.

8. Acknowledgements

In addition, this study was supported by the 2021 Guangdong Provincial Quality Engineering Modern Industrial College Project "Eco-design Industrial College", the Guangdong First-class Professional Construction Point: Product Design, the 2021 Guangdong Provincial Department of Science and Technology/Guangdong Provincial Bureau of Rural Revitalization "Guangdong Provincial Rural Science and Technology Specialists in Towns and Villages," stationed in Jiangdong Town, Chaoan District, Chaozhou City, Project No.: KTP20210374, 2021 Zhongkai College of Agricultural Engineering Quality Engineering Special Talent Cultivation Program Construction Project, "Excellence in Rural Revitalization Talent Design and Innovation Class" support.

References

[1] CHEN Qiuying, XU Zhouhong, PAN Baobao. Design and application of a mobile cart for arthroscopic surgery items. China Rural Medicine,2022(3):35-35.

[2] Zhu Jing. The exploration and practice of introducing mobile carts in public libraries. Library theory and practice,2008(4):113-114.

[3] Lu Yaomei, Wu Junping, Guo Chunrong. Exploration of safety management of mobile methadone clinics. Chinese Journal of Drug Abuse Prevention and Control,2012(6):350-351.

[4] Ceres unveils full-colour transparent holographic display system for automobiles. Automotive Engineer, 2020

[5] Jorge Enrique Caicedo Martínez and Bladimir Bacca Cortes: "Autonavi3at software interface for autonomous navigation on urban roads Using Omnidirectional Vision and a Mobile Robot" Science and Engineering Neogranadina, 2022

[6] Guo Xixian". Internet broadcasting 'boosts' agricultural trade between China and ASEAN". China Today 71.09(2022):49-51.

[7] Shan Hu et al. Design of urban guide system based on PCA analysis Hu Shan, Zhou Mingyu, 2022

[8] Fang Rui and Dong Bin. "From form design to process design - From a digital perspective of "organicism" in contemporary design" Art Education, 2013

[9] Jan Kubasevich. "Interaction and Experience - Proceedings of the International Conference on Interaction Design: Designing for Communication and Interaction" Decoration, 2010

[10] Su Ran. "Bringing things back to their true nature: naturalism in the design of the brand "MUJI"" Fine Arts, 2014

Design Studies and Intelligence Engineering
L.C. Jain et al. (Eds.)
© 2024 The Authors.
This article is published online with Open Access by IOS Press and distributed under the terms
of the Creative Commons Attribution Non-Commercial License 4.0 (CC BY-NC 4.0).
doi:10.3233/FAIA231485

Effects of Growth Distributions on Tensile Properties of Palm Leaf Sheath Fibers

Xin LIU[a], Yanxin QI[a], Jianjun HOU[a], Zhihui WU[b1], and Jilei ZHANG[c]
[a]*Nanjing Institute of Technology, 211167, China*
[b]*College of Furniture and Industrial Design, Nanjing Forestry University, No.159
Longpan Road, Nanjing, Jiangsu 210037, China*
[c]*Department of Sustainable Bioproducts, Mississippi State University, Mississippi,
USA*

Abstract. Palm leaf sheath fibers (PLSFs), obtained from palm trees that are found in the southern part of China, has been used to make buffer and resilience products such as mattresses. After decomposition, it was found that the palm fibers wrap the tree trunks in three layers, by means of clockwise, counter-clockwise, and overlapping mechanisms. The length of the palm fibers measured between 200 and 350 mm, the weight between 0.002 and 0.006 g. It was also observed that PLSFs that were found at the middle and upper parts of the leaf sheath exhibited good tensile properties.

Keywords. Palm leaf sheath fibers; growth distribution; tensile properties

1. Introduction

Palm fibers (PFs) stripped from windmill palm trees growing in southern China are commonly used as raw materials for medical and weave products, etc. Windmill palm trees with a beautiful shape are tall and evergreen and are commonly used as ornamental trees. Windmill palm trees' trunks are straight and cylindrical shape with its lower part packed with leaf sheath fibers in a cross-mesh arrangement (Fig. 1). The majority of windmill palm trees' leaves grow on its tip portion with some leaves on the middle of the trunk.

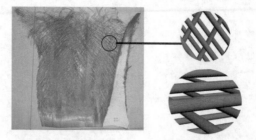

Figure 1. Cross-mesh arrangement of Windmill palm trees.

---

[1] Corresponding Author.

There are two types of PFs, palm leaf sheath fibers (PLSFs) (Fig. 2a) and palm petiole fibers (PPFs) (Fig.2b). PLSFs are extracted from leaf sheath sheets, while PPFs are from palm petioles. PLSFs have dark brown color, smooth and shiny surface, supple and elastic, feeling like human hairs; PLSFs do not contain any sugar and tannin components. PLSFs are more expensive if compared to PPFs because of their low annual yield about 2 kg per palm tree. PPFs have light brown color, rough surface like hay, and high yield. The high yield of PPFs leads to the processed PPFs being used to replace PLSFs. PPFs contain small amounts of sugar and tannin, which results in that mold can easily grow and bugs can reproduction on these fibers. In general, PFs has low cellulose content (36.85-44.78%), but high hemicellulose (20.2-26.24%) and lignin (15.07-15.15%) contents (Zhang et al. 2010). In addition, PFs have high contents of fat and wax (3.37-10.2%), increasing the softness of palm fibers (Zhang et al. 2010).

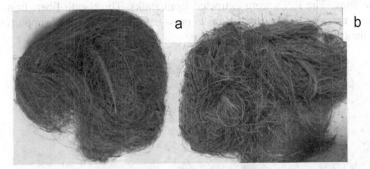

Figure 2. Two types of Palm fibers.

The fracture strength of PF leaves is normally high. As the fibers are long, their elongation is also large. There are some clear vertical stripes found lengthwise on the fibers, including many pores and nodes. Their cross-sections show an irregular dentate shape with a compact structure. The fibers sometimes have a layered structure, which is associated with gum impurity (Liu and Mao 2006).

Studies on chemical and physical properties of PFs (Zhai 2010) indicate that their tensile strength and Young's modulus decrease with the increase of their fiber bundle diameter. Li (2012) investigated the tensile-fracture and spring-back properties of PFs and concluded that the strength elongation of PFs is stable, with a good toughness.

Li (2013) and Guo (2014) have studied the combustion performance and tensile properties of PFs and concluded that heat treatment between 160 and 180℃ changed the tensile property of PFs dramatically. In another study, PLSFs were determined to be lighter, finer, and longer than PPFs, and that the tensile properties of PLSFs were better than those of PPFs (Liu et al.2017).

Palm fiber products suffer from complex external forces, such as tension, compression, bending, and twisting. Palm fibers are linear elastic material, fine and long. The main force on the fibers is longitudinal tension. The tensile properties of the fiber material obtained include the elastic modulus, elastic limit, elastic strain, tensile strength, and elongation after fracture.

2. Materials and methods

2.1. Materials

Generally, the growth years of a palm tree are from seven to eight years, and they grow approximately 1.2m high. A palm tree in the botanical garden of Nanjing Forestry University (China) was chosen for this study. As was shown in Fig. 3a, the tree stem used was straight, with a height of 1.3m and perimeter of approximately 0.6m. The tree trunk was wrapped by fibers, and the top part of the tree contained palm leaves. The trunk gradually shrank toward the apex of the stem of the tree and appeared as a pagoda shape.

As was shown in Fig.3b, the stalk was spirally arranged from the root of the brown stem to the apex. The PPFs were extracted from stalks. The sheath fiber, from which PLSFs were extracted, was found in a cross-mesh arrangement, supporting and protecting the trunk of the palm tree (Fig.3c).

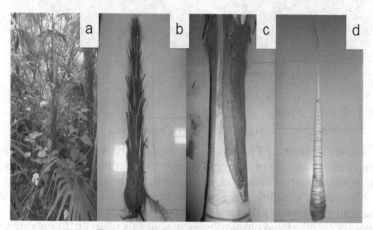

Figure 3. Anatomical process of palm trees.

After peeling off the sheath fiber, the stem of the palm was exposed, whose color was bright yellow and white, just like fresh bamboo shoots. There were altogether 47 pieces of leaf sheath after dissection, which were numbered from one to forty-seven. Sample No.1, No. 8, No.15, No.22, No.29, No.36, No.43, and No.47 are shown below (Fig. 4).

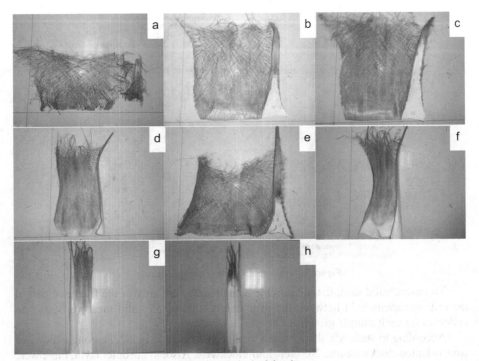

Figure 4. Palm leaf sheath.

During dissection, it was found that each layer of leaf sheath wrapped the stem of the trunk firmly, with the fibers crossed and overlapped. Leaf sheath fiber was the one found close to the old leaf sheath near the root, as was shown in Figs. 4a and 4b. The color of this fiber was dark brown. Because of a long exposure to air, the dark brown gradually turned black, but the fibers still had good robustness. The color of the middle part of the leaf sheath was nankeen, with fibers firmly interwoven (Figs. 4c, 3d, and 4e). At the bottom of the upper part of the leaf sheath was still lively, mature fiber bundles at the top of the fiber gradually separated as the peeling of parenchyma (Figs. 4f, 4g, and 4h).

2.2. Methods

Tensile testing was performed on a universal mechanical testing machine (Shimadzu AGS-X20KN, Kyoto, Japan, Fig. 5a). The length of the fiber specimen used was 50mm, and the speed of machine was set at 20min/min. Latex was used on the clamp surface to avoid slipping (Fig. 5b). During the test, the fiber specimens were fixed on the central line of the clamping device.

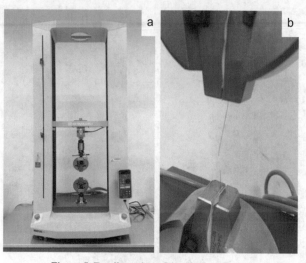

Figure 5. Tensile testing of the fiber specimens.

To ensure valid data, the measurements included were only of the fractured part of the test specimens held between the grippers. A total of 50 valid measurements was collected for each sample group.

According to statistics, there were a total of 483 fibers in No. 22, among which 205 were oriented clockwise and 205 were anti-clockwise. Also, in the outer layer, there were 201 fibers, while the middle layer contained 77 fibers and the inner layer had 205 fibers.

Length Distributions. The average length of the fibers was 326.66mm. The average length of clockwise oriented fibers was 336.77mm, and the average length of the anti-clockwise ones was 316.55mm. Also, the length of the outer layer fibers was 353.50mm on average, that for the middle fibers was 331.78mm, and that for the inner ones was 297.98 mm.

The length of a single PLSF was determined to be between 200and 350mm, accounting for 50.3% of the total specimens. Among this, most were 250 to 300mm, occupying 19.9%. According to Fig. 6a, the length distribution of PLSFs was marked by a wave crest, which gradually decreased.

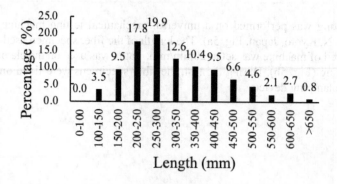

Figure 6a. The length distribution of PLSFs.

Weight Distributions. The average weight of a PLSF was approximately 0.0086g. The average weight in clockwise orientation was 0.0091g, and the average weight in anti-clockwise was 0.0082g. The average weight of the outer layer was 0.0086g, the middle layer 0.0186g, and inner layer 0.0048g.

According to Fig.6b, the weight of PLSF was concentrated between 0.002 and 0.006g, accounting for 49.5%, after which the average weight decreased.

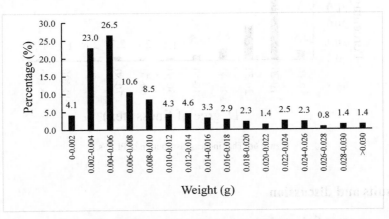

Figure 6b. The weight distribution of PLSFs.

Fineness Distribution. As a kind of natural fiber, the cross-section of the palm fiber is irregular, so the weight of fiber at a certain length or the length of fiber at a certain weight are often used to represent the fineness. According to an international rule, the gram number per 1000m long fiber is denoted as the tex number (T). The tex number is proportional to the fiber's thickness, that is to say, when the fiber is thicker, the tex number is larger.

$$T = \frac{m}{l} \times 1000 \tag{1}$$

where T refers to the tex number of the fiber, m(g) refers to the weight of the fiber, and l (m) denotes the length.

The measured average fineness of PLSFs was 26.56tex. The average fineness in clockwise orientation was 27.49tex, and that in anti-clockwise was 25.63tex. The fineness of the outer layer was 22.82tex on average, the middle layer was 64.18tex, and the inner layer measured 15.75tex. The middle layer turned out to be the thickest.

According to Fig.6c, the fineness of PLSFs was focused between 10 and 20tex for 52% of the fibers, while 20 to 30tex accounted for 20%, above which it substantially decreased.

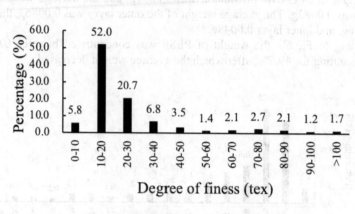

Figure 6c. The fineness distribution of PLSFs.

3. Results and discussion

3.1. Comparison of Tensile Properties of Fibers from Outer, Middle, and Inner Layers

After dissection, it was found that the PLSFs have three layers during the growth cycle. Ten fibers from each layer at the same position were chosen to obtain the tensile parameters, shown in Table 1. The elastic modulus and tensile strain of the middle layer were obviously greater than those of the outer layer and the inner layer, which suggested that the rigidity and elastic properties remained better. Table 2 shows the variance of the tensile parameters of various PLSF layers. The differences in the elastic modulus were noticeable, while other tensile properties were not obvious. Therefore, the tensile properties of the middle layer fibers appeared superior.

Table 1. Comparison of Tensile Properties of Fibers from Outer, Middle, and Inner Layers

Position	Elastic limit (MP)	COV (%)	Elastic strain (%)	COV (%)	Elastic modulus (MPa)	COV (%)	Tensile strength (MPa)	COV (%)	Elongation after fracture (%)	COV (%)
Outer layer	23.25	14.75	3.40	27.81	873.51	25.86	40.67	24.54	9.61	25.23
Middle layer	28.15	24.87	4.16	26.67	2115.47	28.85	42.33	32.29	5.33	27.68
Inner layer	40.52	34.46	2.84	33.05	1566.00	24.47	65.33	29.42	8.05	25.75

Table 2. ANOVA for Tensile Properties of Fibers from Outer, Middle, and Inner Layers

	Tensile properties				
	Elastic limit (MPa)	Elastic strain (%)	Elastic modulus (MPa)	Tensile strength (MPa)	Elongation after fracture (%)
P-value	0.159383257	0.490821407	0.0377831	0.192293128	0.405607111

Note: At the significance level of 5%, $p<0.05$ indicated that the influence of the factors on the index value was significant, and $p>0.05$ indicated that the impact of the factors on the index value was not significant.

3.2. Comparison of Tensile Properties of Fibers from Upper, Middle, and Inferior Parts

PLSFs grow from the smaller part of the tree to the upper part and are interwoven with each other. Ten fibers, collected from the upper, middle, and inferior parts of the tree growing in the same direction were chosen to obtain the tensile parameters. As is shown in Table 3, the tensile properties were uniform in various parts. The elastic modulus and elastic strain of the upper part were obviously greater than those of the middle and inferior parts. It can be seen from Table 4 that the differences in the elastic modulus were noticeable, while differences in other tensile property parameters were not obvious. Therefore, the upper fibers possessed the best tensile properties.

Table 3. Comparison of Tensile Properties of Fibers from Upper, Middle, and Inferior Parts

Position	Elastic limit (MPa)	COV (%)	Elastic strain (%)	COV (%)	Elastic modulus (MPa)	COV (%)	Tensile strength (MPa)	COV (%)	Elongation after fracture (%)	COV (%)
Upper part	39.17	26.86	5.78	25.05	2817.05	21.58	68.09	30.91	4.72	27.02
Middle part	23.25	30.80	3.40	21.07	1873.51	27.43	40.67	27.18	9.61	23.20
Inferior part	24.70	25.67	4.64	27.26	1315.22	28.28	44.82	26.25	7.94	26.25

Table 4. ANOVA for Upper, Middle, and Inferior Parts of Fibers

	Tensile property parameters				
	Elastic limit (MPa)	Elastic strain (%)	Elastic modulus (MPa)	Tensile strength (MPa)	Elongation after fracture (%)
P-value	0.73232922	0.30052417	0.017316927	0.515152484	0.348366328

Note: At the significance level of 5%, $p<0.05$ indicated that the influence of the factors on the index value was significant, and $p>0.05$ indicated that the impact of the factors on the index value was not significant.

3.3. Comparison of Tensile Properties of Fibers from Root, Middle, and Tip-End Parts

The PLSFs interweave with each other from the brown handle to the trunk. Ten fibers from the root, middle, and tip-end parts, respectively, were chosen for the tensile testing. It can be seen from Table 5 that the tensile properties of root, middle and tip-end parts were similar. According to Table 6, there was no obvious tensile property difference between root, middle, and tip-end parts.

Table 5. Comparison of Tensile Properties between Root, Middle, and Tip-End Parts

Position	Elastic limit (MPa)	COV (%)	Elastic strain (%)	COV (%)	Elastic modulus (MPa)	COV (%)	Tensile strength (MPa)	COV (%)	Elongation after fracture (%)	COV (%)
Root fiber	38.03	21.99	3.89	10.73	2128.31	23.58	60.82	16.86	6.62	23.50
Middle part	28.15	22.74	4.16	18.18	2115.47	27.42	42.33	29.55	5.33	28.82

Top-end part	16.90	34.51	3.45	22.29	1273.75	15.67	23.67	34.17	5.33	15.39

Table 6. ANOVA for Tensile Properties between Root, Middle, and Tip-End Parts of Fiber

	Tensile property parameters				
	Elastic limit (MPa)	Elastic strain (%)	Elastic modulus (MPa)	Tensile strength (MPa)	Elongation after fracture (%)
P-value	0.089948943	0.885675666	0.214933829	0.328798933	0.862484158

Note: at the significance level of 5%, $p<0.05$ indicated that the influence of the factors on the index value was significant, and $p>0.05$ indicated that the impact of the factors on the index value was not significant.

4. Conclusion

The measured length of a single PLSF fiber was approximately 200 to 350 mm, accounting for approximately 50.3% of the total, among which 19.9% of the fibers measured between 250 and 300 mm. The weight of a PLSF was from 0.002g to 0.006g, making up 49.5% of the total. The fineness of PLSFs was concentrated between 10 and 20 tex, occupying 52% of the total fibers. The middle layer had the best tensile properties. By testing the tensile properties from the upper, middle and inferior parts, it was found that the fibers from the upper part possessed the best tensile properties. There were no obvious tensile property differences between the root, middle, and tip-end parts of PLSFs.

Funding. Open access funding provided by Jiangsu University Philosophy and Social Science Research Project (No.: 2022SJYB0441), Qing Lan Project and Teaching reform and construction project of NJIT（No. JXGG2021014）

Declarations

Conflict of interest on behalf of all authors, the corresponding author states that there is no conflict of interest.

References

[1] Guo M. Structure and Mechanical Property Research of Palm Fiber. MS thesis, Southwest University, Chongqing, 2014.
[2] Guo JW. Cultivation of Palm Trees and Processing Technologies of Palm Sheet. Special Economic Animal and Plant **4** (1998), 31-32
[3] Li QY, Wei GJ and Zhu LJ. Basic research of palm fiber mattress. Furniture **34** (2013), 1, 21-28.
[4] Li, XL (2012) Research of basic property of palm fiber. MS thesis, Southwest University, Chongqing, 55.
[5] Liu X, Wu ZH, Zhang JL, Ge SS. Heated palm fiber strength. BioResources **12** (2017a), 1, 1335-1343.
[6] Liu X, Wu ZH, Zhang JL, Ge SS. Windmill palm fiber properties BioResources 12 (2017b), 2, 4342-4351.
[7] Liu XX, Mao S. Research of fiber of palm leaf. Shanghai Textile Technology **34** (2006), 9, 20-21
[8] Liu, XX, Wang ZY, Xu WL. Primarily investment into developing the palm leaf fiber. Journal of Textile Research **25** (2004), 3, 75
[9] Lu B, Zhang LW, Zeng JC. Natural Fiber Composites Material. Chemical Industry Press, 2005.
[10] Zhai SC. Structure, Chemical, and Physical Property of Palm Fiber. MS thesis, Nanjing Forestry University, Nanjing, 2010.
[11] Zhang TH, Li XL, Cheng L, Mao L. Property and its application status of palm fiber. Products Textiles **6** (2010),35-38.

Design Studies and Intelligence Engineering
L.C. Jain et al. (Eds.)
© 2024 The Authors.
This article is published online with Open Access by IOS Press and distributed under the terms
of the Creative Commons Attribution Non-Commercial License 4.0 (CC BY-NC 4.0).
doi:10.3233/FAIA231486

Research on Personalized Ceramic Bottle Design with Imagery and Neural Networks

Yong-xin GUO[a,1], Mimi LI[a], and Xiao-long CHEN[a]

[a]*Art Design College, Henan University of Urban Construction, Pingdingshan*

Abstract: In order to meet consumer demand for ceramic bottle design, the mapping relationship between user imagery needs and ceramic bottle product form design elements is established by analysing them. Firstly, the representative samples are screened by the Delphi method, and the stylistic features of ceramic bottles are summarised by using the principle of visual simplification, secondly, the elements of ceramic bottles are modularly deconstructed by using the morphological analysis method, and the importance of the product elements is calculated by the combination of the DEMATEL and the TODIM method, and the evaluative value of the pairs of imagery words is obtained by using the Likert scale method, and representative imagery words are determined by using the KJ method and the factor analysis method. Vocabulary. A BP neural network was used to construct the modelling imagery prediction model, and the model was trained with the weights of the sample modelling elements as the input layer, and the evaluation scores of the user's perceptual imagery as the output layer. According to the training and validation of the model, the optimal ceramic bottle shape with the best perceptual evaluation value can be predicted. This method solves the problem of designers not being able to grasp the needs of target users, improves the design efficiency of ceramic bottle products, and provides favourable support for the personalised design of ceramic bottle products.

Keywords. User Imagery; Product Design; BP Neural Network; Ceramic Bottle; TODIM Decision Making

1. Introduction

In the current society, the standard of living of all people and the concept of consumption has been greatly upgraded and changed. Products are no longer simply as the carrier of the use function, more and more people begin to pay attention to the spiritual level of feelings brought by the products, so it will become very important to satisfy the perceptual needs (e.g., identity, status, environment, etc.). Product modeling perceptual intention and BP neural network have been applied to product design related fields.

Literature 1 constructs quantitative relationship based on BP neural network, explores the connection between yacht styling features and consumers' perceptual intention, and realizes the evaluation of yacht styling features by combining the semantic difference method and so on. Literature 2 is based on BP neural network, develops feature training for BP neural network, establishes the evaluation system of perceptual intention features of goblet styling, and explores the intention evaluation of goblet styling

---

[1] Corresponding Author.GuoYongxin Research Direction: Product Design Strategy, Cultural Product Design.E-mail :719971622@ qq. Com Ministry of Education Humanities Science Project (No. 22YJC760131)

features. Literature 3 uses the semantic difference method to obtain relevant quantitative evaluation data, encodes the coffee table in modules, constructs a BP neural network-based linkage model between the user and multifunctional coffee table styling features, establishes relevant mapping relationships, and provides reference for the personalized design of the coffee table. Literature 4 explores the design method of vessel modeling based on BP neural network, and applies the multi-dimensional method to construct the mapping relationship between vessel modeling and users' perceptual intention, and tests its feasibility. Literature 5 combines the factor analysis method and morphological analysis method to explore and analyze the prosthetic bra, get the mapping relationship between the user's perceptual intention and the user's styling characteristics, and get the product styling personalized customization method based on BP neural network. Literature 6 and other electric forklift trucks as an example, to construct the BP neural network model of electric forklift truck styling elements and perceptual imagery, to find the maximum fit between engineering and design, and to explore the correlation between styling features and market perceptual cognition. From the existing literature can be found, BP neural network combined with related design methods can effectively tap the user's perceptual needs, has been widely used in industrial products, but for ceramic art products in the field of application is rare, so based on the BP neural network, to build the mapping relationship between the consumer's perceptual intention and ceramic styling features, for personalized customization of art ceramic products is very relevant research. The research is very urgent. This study is based on the theoretical basis of perceptual engineering, and combined with the characteristics of BP neural network simulation and prediction, to the user's perceptual needs as the center, to help designers design ceramic products to meet the consumer's imagery, to improve the effectiveness of ceramic product design.

2. Quantitative analysis of design elements and imagery vocabulary

The design process of personalized ceramic ware based on imagery and neural network, firstly, collects representative ceramic bottles, and cell phone users' imagery words through websites, ceramic books, museums, etc., and secondly, conducts morphological deconstruction of the representative samples, and calculates the weights and importance ordering of the styling elements as the input layer of the neural network as well as screens out the representative imagery words and evaluates them, and the normalized processing as the output layer of the neural network . And construct the BP neural network model, train and test it, form the mapping relationship related to ceramic modeling features and user's perceptual intention, in order to accurately locate the design direction of the porcelain bottle. Personalized customization of porcelain bottles. The research flow of this paper is shown in Fig. 1.

2.1 Sample Screening and Design Element Analysis

Sample collection through online websites, ceramic books, museums, award-winning works, etc., taking into account the similarity of the shooting angle of the ceramic bottles, the clarity of the picture and the similarity of the shape and other factors, a total of 120 samples were collected, and through the Delphi method, after the initial screening, 40 products were obtained, and the samples were re-modeled and rendered using the Rhinoceros software modeling to obtain the samples that are not affected by the material, color, and pattern influence sample images, as shown in Fig 2. In order to further enhance the saliency of the representative samples, using the principle of visual perception simplification proposed by Arnheim, the representative samples are drawn in wireframe diagrams to summarize the main styling features in ceramic bottles.

Morphological analysis was used to analyze the elemental structure of the ceramic bottle pairs, as shown in Fig. 3 and Fig.4, where the samples can be divided into four parts: the mouth, the neck, the abdomen and the base and coded for each of their elements. The variation of the mouth of the bottle is mainly related to the complexity of the mouth and the size of the opening, which can be divided into open mouth (P1), closed mouth (P2), flat mouth (P3) and deformed mouth (P4), etc., and the shape of the mouth of the bottle will change with the change of the bottle shape. Changes in the neck and shoulder are influenced by the shape of the mouth and the shape of the abdomen, and the main shapes are upper arc (J1), lower arc (J2), right angle (J3) and straight line (J4). Together with the belly, it constitutes the main variation in ceramic bottle form. The belly consists of a rounded (F1), diagonal (F2), concave (F3) and straight (F4) shape. The base consists of a right-angled footrim (D1), a beveled footrim (D2), a converging footrim (D3), and an inner foot (D4).

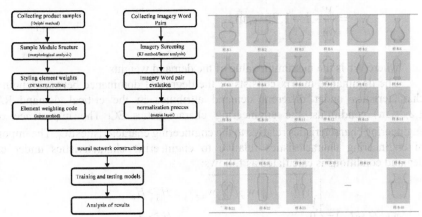

Figure 1. research process.

Figure 2. Sample of some ceramic bottles

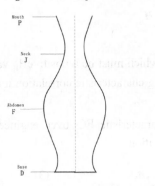

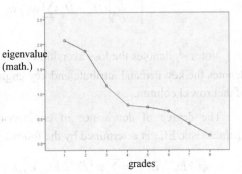

Figure 3. Product Deconstruction Schematic

Figure 4. Ingredient Factor Extraction Crushed Stone Chart

2.2 Weighting of design elements

When users evaluate ceramic bottle samples, the different modeling characteristics of ceramic bottle samples will be directly affected. Therefore, subjects and potential users are invited to judge the influence weights of different modeling elements. In this paper, a combination of DEMATEL and TODIM is used.

The DEMATEL method is an approach based on graph theory and matrix tools to analyze system elements in order to assess the interdependencies between complex factors. It analyzes the overall relationship between styling factors and demand indicators in order to obtain the influence relationship between the elements. Based on the weights of each key demand attribute, the key demand attribute importance is normalized to obtain the key demand attribute weights, the importance of each engineering characteristic relative to other engineering characteristics is calculated by taking advantage of TODIM's consideration of the psychological factors of the decision maker, and the ranking of engineering characteristics is determined by calculating the overall importance. Construct the element interaction matrix and rank its importance.

Ceramic Bottle Key Demand Attribute Weights The relative weights of can be calculated by the following formula:

$$w_{ir} = \frac{w_i}{w_r}, i = 1, 2, \ldots, m,$$ (1)

where Wr is the maximum value of the demand weights

The dominance matrix consists of the degree of dominance between engineering characteristics under different demand attributes in the critical demand $RA_i (i = 1, 2, \ldots m)$ conditions, the engineering characteristics EC_j The importance of the engineering characteristics relative to the engineering characteristics EC_u The importance of engineering characteristics relative to engineering characteristics under critical demand conditions is calculated as follows:

$$\varphi_i(EC_j, EC_u) = \begin{cases} \sqrt{(H_{ij} - H_{iu})w_{ir} \big/ \sum_{i=1}^{m} w_{ir}}, & H_{ij} > H_{iu} \\ 0, & H_{ij} > H_{iu} \\ -\frac{1}{\theta}\sqrt{(H_{iu} - H_{ij})\sum_{i=1}^{m} w_{ir} \big/ w_{ir}}, & H_{iu} > H_{ij} \end{cases}$$ (2)

Notes: θ denotes the loss aversion coefficient, which must be a positive H_{ij} value; denotes the key demand attribute and key engineering characteristic correlation matrix of thei rows j column.

The degree of dominance of engineering characteristic EC_j over engineering characteristic EC_u is determined by the following equation:

$$\varphi(EC_j, EC_u) = \sum_{i=1}^{m} \varphi_i(EC_j, EC_u), j, u = 1, 2, \ldots, n.$$ (3)

The overall dominance degree value of the engineering characteristic ECj with respect to other engineering characteristics can be calculated by using Equation (4):

$$\xi(ECj) = \cfrac{\displaystyle\sum_{u=1}^{n}\varphi(ECj, ECu) - \min_{1\leq j\leq n}\left\{\sum_{u=1}^{n}\varphi(EC_j, EC_u)\right\}}{\max_{1\leq j\leq n}\left\{\sum_{u=1}^{n}\varphi(EC_j, EC_u)\right\} - \min_{1\leq j\leq n}\left\{\sum_{u=1}^{n}\varphi(EC_j, EC_u)\right\}}, \tag{4}$$

where $j = 1,2,\ldots\ldots,n$

ξ (EC_j) The larger the value of the dominance degree, the more important the engineering characteristic ξ (EC_j) is more important.Overall value based on all engineering characteristics ξ (EC_j)(j=1,2,...,n),Individual engineering characteristics can be ranked, and key engineering characteristics for specific product development can be determined.According to the synthesized influence matrix, the weights of each key demand attribute are obtained, and the weight values of each individual element are synthesized, and the value advantage results ξ (EC_j) at all levels are as follows in Table 1.

Table 1. Critical Engineering Characteristics Dominance and Ranking Results

	EC_1	EC_2	EC_3	EC_4	ξ	Sort
EC_1	0.000	-5.280	-9.431	-0.570	0.400	3
EC_2	-2.371	0.000	-2.382	-0.331	0.491	2
EC_3	0.201	-2.871	0.000	-2.527	0.875	1
EC_4	-2.621	-6.256	-2.575	0.000	0.360	4

Critical Engineering Characteristics Dominance and Ranking Results:According to Table 2 Key Engineering Characteristics Advantage Degree, the 4 engineering characteristics sorting results are:

EC3>EC2>EC1>EC4.They are: ceramic vase belly (EC3), neck and shoulder (EC2), mouth (EC1), and base (EC4).

2.3 Imagery vocabulary screening

By reviewing books, magazines, newspapers, web pages, etc., 120 vocabularies from which adjectives reflecting consumer feelings as well as perceptual imagery of products were selected. The obtained adjectives and imagery vocabulary were located using the impression KJ method, and the collected imagery vocabulary was preliminarily ranked to remove the words with the least relevance as well as near-synonymous words, and the words with opposite meanings were paired, and the retained perceptual vocabulary was further screened. There are many ways to determine the perceptual imagery of the product, and in this study, the expert comprehensive evaluation method was used to obtain 8 pairs of imagery words that best reflect the ceramic bottles, which are fashionable-traditional, elegant-majestic, lightweight-bulky, soft-hard, coordinated-abrupt, slender-full, lightweight-heavy, and soft-heavy., lightweight-heavy, streamlined-hard.

The study used the Likert Scale method to conduct a perceptual imagery screening research on ceramic bottles in order to obtain words that could more accurately describe ceramic bottles. The perceptual imagery evaluation scores are represented by numbers 1, 2, 3, 4 and 5. For example, for the imagery word "harmonious - abrupt", 1 means very harmonious, 3 means no obvious bias, and 5 means very abrupt. Calculate the average of the perceptual imagery scores for each pair of imagery words for each ceramic vase, that is, the preference and score of the ceramic vase in terms of perceptual imagery.

A total of 70 questionnaires were distributed in this SD survey study, in which the ratio of men to women was at 1:1, and 20 professional ceramic masters and 40 ceramic consumers and 10 ceramics-related students were selected as the respondents, and 68 questionnaires were recovered, of which 65 were valid questionnaires. Cumulative statistical analysis of these questionnaires.

In order to accelerate the convergence speed of the subsequently built neural network during training degree, the results of the cumulative statistical analysis are normalized so that their values fall between 0 and 1. The method of normalization is shown below:

$$\overline{x}_1 = \frac{x_i - x_{min}}{x_{max} - x_{min}}$$

where is the normalized perceptual imagery score, is the current perceptual imagery score, the maximum of all perceptual imagery scores, and the minimum of all perceptual imagery scores.

The results after normalizing the perceptual imagery statistics are shown in Table 2.

Table 2. Perceptual evaluation value of the normalization process

brochure	tender-sturdy	slender-full	light-heavy	elegant-vigorous	stylish-traditional	lightweight-cumbersome	coordinated-abrupt	fairing-sturdy
1	0.34	0.59	0.63	0.54	0.46	0.38	0.61	0.69
2	0.32	0.45	0.39	0.38	0.69	0.54	0.35	0.49
3	0.42	0.67	0.31	0.52	0.32	0.2	0.42	0.43
4	0.63	0.35	0.61	0.56	0.39	0.53	0.56	0.32
5	0.2	0.42	0.32	0.6	0.42	0.41	0.61	0.59
...	...	...	...	...	...	...	...	...
40	0.61	0.69	0.42	0.52	0.63	0.58	0.36	0.42

As can be seen from the component factor extraction plot, see Figure 4, the eigenvalues greater than 1 in the plot are the first 3 component factors. The steepness of the connecting line between the rubble is high, so the first 3 factors are the main factors. The 8 sets of perceptual word pairs can be categorized into 3 classes. The extracted names of the main factors are: "light - thick", "soft - hard", "slender -fullness", which are used as the evaluation scale for the evaluation imagery words of ceramic bottle products. The rotated factor loading matrix is shown in Table 3.

Table 3 .Rotated component matrix

Imagery word pair	Ingredient		
	1	2	3
light–heavy	0.775	-0.386	-0.261
coordinated-abrupt	0.717	-0.279	0.182
stylish-traditional	0.652	0.007	-0.494
lightweight-cumbersome	0.429	0.408	-0.131
tender–sturdy	0.226	0.799	0.290
fairing-sturdy	0.058	0.681	-0.361
elegant–vigorous	0.152	-0.503	0.394
slender–full	0.527	0.335	0.655

3.Constructing BP Neural Networks

Matlab programming software platform is used to construct BP neural network, which includes three layers, including input layer, hidden layer and output layer, in which the hidden layer can be one layer or multiple layers , through the analysis of the data, the design elements of the ceramic bottle are coded to determine the input layer, and the evaluation value of the eight sets of perceptual imagery words is determined as the output layer (shown in Fig.5), and this is repeatedly trained until the target error is reached, to obtain the mapping relationship between the design elements and the imagery word pairs.

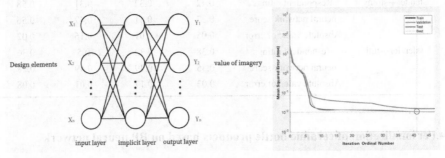

Figure 5. BP neural network model   **Figure 6.**Neural network training results

Because the product modeling feature elements in the input layer are abstract elements, it is necessary to encode each product feature into a computer-readable language. In this study, the switching nominal scale method is used to encode the design elements of ceramic bottle modeling, the coding number is composed of "1" and "0", the number of bits is consistent with the number of modeling feature elements, this paper extracts a total of 4×4 modeling elements, and therefore the code is 16 digits; According to the modeling classification for four categories, the code will be divided into four segments, the first segment for the first modeling element classification:, ceramic bottle mouth modeling a total of four elements, so the first segment has four digits, and so on.Take the first sample as an example, the modeling elements that make up the first sample are P3, J2, F1, and D3, so the first sample is coded 0 0 1 0 0 1 0 0 1 0 0 0 0 0 0 1 0.

The learning times of the ceramic bottle product neural network are set to be constrained within 10000 times, and the error between the actual target value and the predicted value is 0.001. The first 36 ceramic bottles are used as the training samples, and the target error value is 0.001, and the activation functions of the hidden layer and the output layer are Logsig and Purelin, respectively. and Trainlm is adopted to train the data, and the coded data and the imagery vocabulary evaluation value as the training dataset for ceramic bottle products. The data of the remaining four representative samples were used as the test set for the performance of the neural network. The training of ceramic production BP neural network is shown in Fig.6, and it reaches the training purpose when it reaches a total of 41 times.

In order to verify the reliability of the neural network, it is necessary to use the remaining sample data to test it, this study uses the last four sets of data , first of all, you need to import the samples into the input layer, and compare the results of the output layer with the results obtained from the questionnaire, the conclusion said that the two parts of the data relative error is very small (such as Table 4). Therefore, according to the test results, the constructed BP neural network prediction performance of ceramic products is better, the reliability of the data basically match.

Table 4. Test Network Results

Emotional lexicon	Measurement error	Sample 37	Sample38	Sample39	Sample40
light—heavy	Respondent ratings	0.46	0.40	0.78	0.63
	neural network score	0.44	0.53	0.77	0.69
	Absolute value of error	0.02	0.13	0.01	0.06
tende —sturdy	Respondent ratings	0.42	0.32	0.31	0.58
	neural network score	0.37	0.31	0.47	0.56
	Absolute value of error	0.05	0.01	0.16	0.02
slender—full	Respondent ratings	0.38	0.32	0.5	0.36
	neural network score	0.35	0.49	0.49	0.28
	Absolute value of error	0.03	0.17	0.01	0.08

4.Personalization of ceramic bottle products based on BP neural network

The main modeling elements of ceramic bottle products are divided into four parts: bottle mouth, neck and shoulder, abdomen, and foot, and the representative features of each part are combined in a matrix, which can be obtained as $4 \times 4 \times 4 \times 4 = 256$ combination methods, and all the combination methods are coded and then imported into the constructed BP neural network input layer of ceramic products, and then after the simulation operation, the evaluation codes of the different combination methods on the lightness-thickness, softness- "Therefore, these three sample ceramic bottle products are the optimal ceramic bottle products under the perceptual imagery vocabulary, and through the learning and training of the BP neural network, the user's needs and ceramic bottle products can be optimized. Through the learning and training of the neural network, the quantitative value of the combination of different design elements can be obtained. For example, the elements of a ceramic bottle product are P2, J2, F3 and D4, which are numbered 0100010000100001, and the numbering will be brought into the training of the neural network, which will result in the perceptual evaluation value of the modeling based on the five perceptual vocabularies as 2.547, 3.173, and 2.245 respectively, which can give the designer a clearer understanding about the perceptual imagery vocabulary. Can let the designer more clearly understand about the product modeling elements of the user's imagery weight value for the design of ceramic products to provide constructive guidance to increase the accuracy in the process of product development, so that the ceramic bottle modeling features to meet the user's perceptual needs, improve the efficiency of the design of ceramic bottle products.

5. Concluding remarks

This paper studies the mapping relationship between user imagery and ceramic bottle design elements, user imagery is converted to engineering thinking, the depth of the target user to participate in the design of the product, according to this method can be extended to other product design research, through a certain amount of research and summarization, the use of Spss software in factor analysis method to select "slender - full", "light - heavy", "soft - hard" three pairs of adjective pairs as an evaluation of the product appearance modeling evaluation scale, the ceramic bottle product deconstruction ", "light - heavy", "soft - hard" three pairs of adjectives as the evaluation of product appearance modeling evaluation scale, the ceramic bottle product deconstructed into four parts of the bottle mouth, neck, abdomen and base, the establishment of BP The BP neural network model is trained and the reliability of the neural network model is verified, so as to provide a more rational design basis for the designers to design the products, avoid the blind design of the enterprises, and clarify the perceptual needs of the market. It provides a strong theoretical basis for the future development trend of ceramic bottles and enhances the market competitiveness of the products.

References

[1] CHENG Yongsheng,XU Xiaoqi. Research on quantitative model of yacht styling imagery based on BP neural network. Furniture and Interior Decoration **29** (2022), 07, 74-79
[2] Fan Yuefei. Research on product imagery modelling design system based on perceptual engineering and neural network. Lanzhou: Lanzhou University of Science and Technology, 2011.
[3] SHUXIN CHEN, JINGYU LI, HONGBIN ZHANG et al. Research on the design of personalised multi-functional coffee table based on BP neural network. Packaging Engineering **43** (2022), 18, 247-254.
[4] XU Xiaoqi, Cheng Yongsheng. Research on modelling design of ceramic edible vessels based on BP neural network. Computer Simulation **39** (2022), 7, 466-470
[5] Yifei Chen, Chi Liu. Personalisation of prosthetic bra structure based on BP neural network. Wool Textile Technology **50** (2022), 7, 51-56
[6] YANG Jingjing, WANG Hanyou, LIANG Yusheng.Research on electric forklift styling design based on perceptual engineering and BP neural network. Industrial Design **01** (2013),158-160.
[7] Zhao Yanan. Research on the construction of perceptual imagery prediction model of office chair based on BP neural network. Furniture and Interior Decoration **09** (2021),118-122.
[8] YUAN Xueqing,CHEN Dengkai,YANG Yanpu et al. Imagery-associated product form bionic design method. Computer Engineering and Application **50** (2014), 8, 178-182.
[9] Qu Q. Xing. Research on the extraction method of emotional imagery and design elements of product appearance considering multi-dimensional design features. Liaoning: Northeastern University, 2014.
[10] Zabotto, Cristina Nardin, Sergio Luis da, Silva, Amaral, Daniel Capaldo, Janaina Mascarenhas Hornos, Costa, Benze, Benedito Galvo, Automatic digital mood boards to connect users and designers with kansei engineering. International Journal of Industrial Ergonomics. **74** (2019), 0, 102829.

[11] Guo, Fu1, Qu, Qing-Xing1, Nagamachi, Mitsuo, Duffy, Vincent G. A proposal of the event-related potential method to effectively identify kansei words for assessing product design features in kansei engineering research. International Journal of Industrial Ergonomics.2020 : 102940.
[12] ZHU Wentao,YIN Jun. Design research on constructing music "imagery schema" by factor analysis. Packaging Engineering,2022,43(24):159-166.

Design Studies and Intelligence Engineering
L.C. Jain et al. (Eds.)
© 2024 The Authors.
doi:10.3233/FAIA231487

713

Designing Cultural and Creative Products of Chinese Jingchu Patterns Based on Non-Finetuned Text-to-Image Systems

Yijin WANG[a,1]

ᵃ *China University of Geosciences School of Arts and Communication*

Abstract. Thanks to the massive data training and large base models, content generation based on artificial intelligence technology is booming. Text-to-image (T2I) systems have powerful semantic understanding and aesthetic perception capabilities, creating significant impacts on improving design efficiency and transforming design ecology. Although large-scale AI models already possess efficient multidimensional combination creation abilities, meeting most daily conceptual design requirements, there are still shortcomings when dealing with professional niche concepts, especially non-Western cultural elements. This paper takes Chinese Jingchu patterns as an example and points out the limitations of existing English-based T2I systems in describing sparse concepts and expressing non-Western cultures. Although re-adding large amounts of data and finetuning may solve some problems, the training skills and computing power required are generally not feasible for most designers. Therefore, this study aims to explore the application strategies of non-finetuned T2I systems in the design of Chinese Jingchu pattern cultural and creative products. We designed three methods: image caption-assisted text-to-image, multi-modal prompt, and text-to-image and image blending, and analyzed their characteristics in terms of Texture Fidelity, Product Accuracy, Image Aesthetics, Product Diversity, and Texture Diversity through user evaluation. Finally, we summarize the applicable scenarios and usage suggestions of the three methods.

Keywords. Text-to-image, Jingchu Pattern, Artificial Intelligence Generated Content, Computer Aided Design

1. Introduction

With the rapid development of artificial intelligence technology, we have seen significant advances in content generation based on big data training and base models in many fields. These advanced generation systems have already demonstrated their potential in the fields of natural language processing, computer vision, and human-computer interaction. In particular, the T2I systems (such as Midjourney, Stable Diffusion, etc.) have strong semantic understanding and aesthetic perception capabilities, which have positively impacted design efficiency and revolutionised design ecology.

However, current T2I systems still have shortcomings in handling the concepts of professional subdivisions, especially in recognizing and applying non-Western cultural elements. This is because professional concepts are extremely sparse compared to

---

[1] Corresponding Author.

popular culture in massive data sets. Partially mitigating this issue through retraining models or adjusting parameters requires further improvement in the quantity and quality of niche domain data and enhancing the learning efficiency of base model algorithms. Despite advancements made by methods such as Dreambooth[1] and Lora[2], challenges remain in fidelity and generalization. Even with parameter-efficient[3] techniques, finetuning a base model remains technically and computationally challenging for ordinary designers. Directly using unfinetuned T2I systems to achieve target concept generation without training is a highly challenging and potentially widely applicable technique.

Midjourney is one of the most successful T2I systems today with its simple and easy-to-use interactive chatroom approach, high-quality image generation and outstanding aesthetics. Midjourney provides several common features, such as image generation based on image prompts and text prompts, supporting image captioning, super-resolution, image blending, zoom-out inpainting, etc., offering designers great potential for recombination and serving as a reliable base T2I system.

This paper first takes Chinese Jingchu patterns as an example and points out the limitations of existing English-based T2I systems in describing sparse concepts and expressing non-Western cultures. We explore the application strategies of non-finetuned T2I systems in the design of Chinese Jingchu pattern cultural and creative products. We designed three methods: image caption-assisted text-to-image, multi-modal prompt, and text-to-image and image blending, and analyzed their characteristics in terms of Texture Fidelity, Product Accuracy, Image Aesthetics, Product Diversity, and Texture Diversity through user evaluations. This study is an exploration of T2I system application strategies in non-finetuned tasks, and the results are expected to promote innovation and development in the field, achieving better T2I system utilization.

The main contributions of this paper can be summarized as follows:

- **Constructing a professional dataset of Chinese Jingchu patterns**: Through digitizing textual data, we built a professional dataset of Chinese Jingchu patterns. Additionally, using image blending techniques, we generated various style-compliant Jingchu pattern images to provide rich materials for subsequent cultural and creative product design.

- **Designing three cultural and creative product generation methods**: Based on the Midjourney T2I system, we designed three methods for generating Chinese Jingchu pattern cultural and creative products and discussed their effects and characteristics in detail.

- **User research and improvement suggestions**: By surveying 20 users on their use of the baseline method and three proposed methods, we obtained usage suggestions for the three methods under different circumstances.

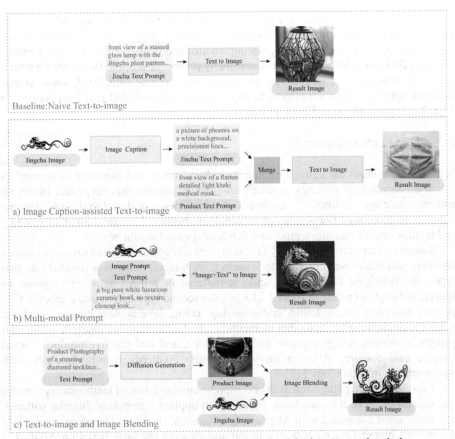

Figure 1. Schematic diagram of the baseline method and the three proposed methods

2. Related work

In this article, we discuss the related work in text-to-image systems, Jingchu pattern research, and text-to-image product design, as well as explore designing Chinese Jingchu pattern cultural and creative products based on AIGC T2I systems.

2.1. Text-to-Image Systems

In recent years, generative AI research has made explosive progress, with an increasing number of generative AI being applied to creative fields [4], especially in text-to-image systems. On January 5th, 2021, OpenAI released DALL-E[5], which generates images via text description. On April 10th, 2022, DALL-E-2[6] was launched, capable of generating images based on the "understanding" of themes, styles and color palettes, as well as re-creating images from original ones, signifying that AI generation technology has basically matured. On July 12th, 2022, Midjourney[7], the first AI-generated image platform open to the public, commenced its public test. Users generate images using text commands through a Discord bot, and the most remarkable advantage of Midjourney is its outstanding drawing effects. After Midjourney, several T2I products have been successively launched, such as Stable Diffusion[8] by StabilityAI on August 22nd, 2022, known for its controllability and adjustable parameters; DreamStudio released on August 23rd, 2022, offering users various painting palettes and materials; Bing Image Creator, based on DALL-E 2 by Microsoft, became freely accessible through Bing's image search feature on March 21st, 2023; Playground AI, released on June 29th, 2023, boasts unique dynamic lighting generation effects; finally, OpenAI released DALL-E 3 on September 21st, 2023, and integrated T2I into ChatGPT.

2.2. Jingchu Pattern Research

With the continuous enrichment of Jingchu cultural relics and literature discovered in recent archaeological findings, research on Jingchu patterns has deepened, involving pattern modeling features[9], aesthetic consciousness, and cultural connotations. Scholars from various fields, such as archaeology, history, Chuxue, history of clothing and textiles, and design, have produced rich academic achievements.

Jingchu pattern research mainly falls into three categories: targeted research, applied research, and atlas research. Targeted research on Jingchu patterns is divided into two types: the first type focuses on a specific material or artifact as an entry point for specialized study of patterns[10,11,12,13,14]; the second type delves into a specific Chu pattern, analyzing its modeling, craftsmanship, color, development history, symbolic meaning, aesthetic spirit, and other elements [15,16,17,18]. Applied research on Jingchu patterns combines design practice and involves cultural and creative products, brand images, and textiles. Atlas research on Jingchu patterns mainly emerges with advancements in technology [19].

Current Jingchu pattern research is comprehensive in terms of methodology, theory, and categories. However, academic literature on applied research of Jingchu patterns, especially those combined with AI generation research, is scarce. Therefore, we explore designing Chinese Jingchu pattern cultural and creative products based on AIGC T2I systems.

2.3. Text-to-image Product Design

The most widely used generative AI model is the text-to-image generation model, which has led to various AI art software[20-22], such as ELEAI, a generative AI design system for the packaging industry released by Xiaoxiang Zhihe on August 7th, 2023. More and more artists have expressed interest in text-to-image models on social media platforms. For example, former Rhode Island School of Design President John Maeda mentioned that text-to-image models could become a tool that actively creates art and changes the work paradigm of visual artists, even performing better than humans.

In recent years, text-to-image generation models have been applied with impressive results in game design, graphic design, and packaging design. In game design, for example, "Space Opera" created by Jason Allen using Midjourney won the digital category of the Colorado State Fair Art Competition in September 2022. In graphic design, NetEase's design team used Midjourney and Stable Diffusion to generate icons, live gift atmosphere effects images for CC business line, storyboard designs, scene designs, short video MCNs, AI character images, event main KV designs, font designs, event broadcast room designs, AR character attack effect concept images, AR stage effects, and proposal renderings for their competition business line in 2023. During the May Day holiday, Yili leveraged AI-generated holiday theme promotional posters for fan interactions; JD Inc. used AI-generated marketing posters for the first time during its 618 event, with emotionally appealing main visuals generated by Baidu Wenxin Yige. In packaging design in 2023, text-generation image models were mainly applied to beverage packaging design, for instance, FBIF food and beverage directly used Midjourney to generate bright-colored packaging designs that stimulate consumer appetite and conform to conventional yogurt packaging visuals.

3. Method

Our goal is to generate images of products decorated with Chinese Jingchu patterns without incurring additional training costs. First, we used text descriptions alone to generate images as a baseline method. This approach requires a high level of expertise with text prompts, and the generated product images may not fully conform to actual characteristics of Jingchu patterns. Therefore, based on the Midjourney T2I system, we designed three methods to achieve more accurate and less complex generation techniques. We experimented with bowls, masks, lamps, and jewelry with both baseline method and three proposed methods. In this section, we first introduce the method of constructing a Jingchu pattern image dataset, which originated from classics and was obtained through digitization and image blending, filtered and cleaned by Jingchu pattern experts. Then we discuss the design of these three methods.

3.1. Dataset Construction

We selected several representative patterns, including phoenix bird patterns, geometric patterns, plant patterns, and star patterns, we collected the patterns from both physical and digital books. Ultimately, we built a seed dataset of over 50 Jingchu patterns through digitization, covering common categories and features.

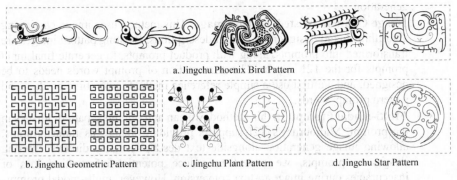

a. Jingchu Phoenix Bird Pattern

b. Jingchu Geometric Pattern   c. Jingchu Plant Pattern   d. Jingchu Star Pattern

Figure 2. Four Typical types of Jingchu Pattern

Since manually selecting images from digitized books is labor-intensive, we used image semantic blending technology to create more data that conforms to the distribution of Jingchu patterns, reducing dataset production costs. The blended images shown below demonstrate that their shape and semantic distribution are reasonably similar to real Jingchu patterns. With expert filtering, this method allows us to quickly obtain larger datasets, increasing the diversity of Jingchu pattern datasets.

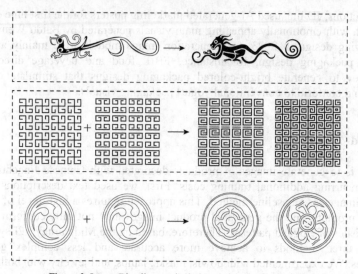

Figure 3. Image Blending to obtain larger datasets at low cost

3.2. Baseline Method and Three Pipelines

English-based T2I systems have significant limitations in describing sparse concepts and expressing non-European and American cultures. We tried various carefully selected text prompts for describing Jingchu patterns (as shown below), resulting in problems like misunderstanding the concept or inaccurate and confused pattern representations. Based on this issue and without training, we designed three methods for Jingchu pattern product design using the baseline method, as shown in Figure 1.

- **Naive Text-to-image as Baseline**: Designers describe Jingchu patterns directly using text prompts and combine them with product descriptions for T2I generation.

- **Image Caption-assisted Text-to-image**: This method uses image captioning algorithms to aid designers in textual descriptions. Existing pattern images are transformed into prompts, along with product prompts, to generate final input prompts for the T2I system. The combination of prompt words needs to be designed, and we first use a simple reference method to combine product and pattern prompt words.

- **Multi-modal Prompt**: In this method, we can add reference pattern images in the prompt. Midjourney's T2I supports providing images as input prompts, allowing image generation alongside text descriptions. By directly entering images as prompts, we expect to reduce potential information loss or inaccuracies during image-to-text conversion. However, multi-modal prompts place higher demands on the diffusion model's end-to-end output.

- **Text-to-image and Image Blending**: First, generate a product image that meets our expected style using product prompts. Then, use Midjourney's image blending function to blend pattern images into product images, achieving the final image generation with Jingchu patterns. This method aims to use two-stage image generation, separating product generation from pattern product generation.

4. Experiment Results and Analysis

To analyze and compare the characteristics of the baseline method and the three methods proposed, we collected evaluations from 32 different users aged between 20-35 on the images generated by these methods. There were five evaluation criteria: Texture Fidelity, Product Accuracy, Image Aesthetics, Product Diversity, and Texture Diversity. Users selected one of the five scores for each criterion: Extremely dissatisfied, Dissatisfied, Average, Satisfied, Excellent. The following is a brief introduction to the five criteria:

- **Texture Fidelity**: The degree of match between the output image and the pattern template. Users evaluate the pattern accuracy of single images produced by different methods.

- **Product Accuracy**: The degree of match between the output image and the product. Users evaluate product accuracy in single images produced by different methods.

- **Image Aesthetics**: The overall aesthetic quality of the output images. Users evaluate the aesthetics of single images produced by different methods.

- **Product Diversity**: Diversity of products in the output images. Users evaluate the diversity of multiple-image collections produced by different methods.

- **Texture Diversity**: Diversity of patterns in the output images. Users evaluate the diversity of multiple-image collections produced by different methods.

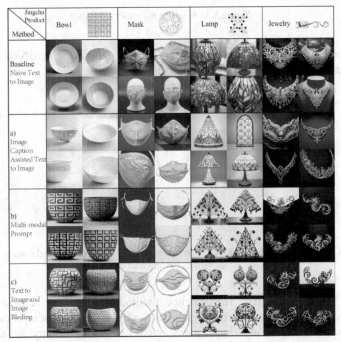

Figure 4. Different product and Jingchu pattern pairs generated results from baseline method and three proposed methods

We generated a total of 640 images using the baseline method and three proposed methods for four products (bowls, masks, lamps, jewelry) combined with ten pattern images. Each user evaluated 80 images. For texture accuracy and image aesthetics, we collected 2,560 image evaluation data points. For product diversity and texture diversity, we collected 128 method evaluation data points, as each user evaluated the four methods separately. To reduce potential biases, users were not informed of the specific methods used to generate the images they evaluated.

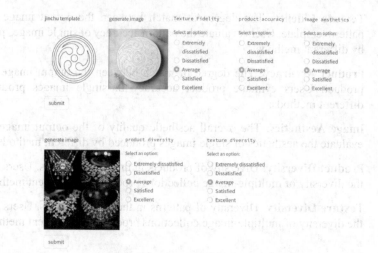

Figure 5. User Interface for user evaluation

Based on user feedback, we derived the following analysis results and recommendations for the three designed methods:

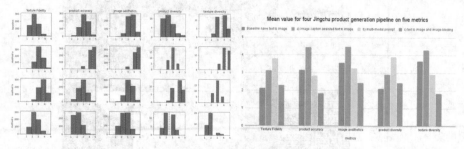

Figure 6. Left: User evaluation distribution on five metrics for four methods; Right: Mean value on five metrics for four methods

Texture Fidelity: The baseline method struggled to achieve satisfactory texture fidelity; the generated patterns had significant discrepancies from the reference patterns, and most users rated its texture fidelity as a score of 2 (dissatisfied). This confirms the limitations of existing English-based T2I systems in describing sparse concepts and expressing non-European and American cultures. All methods performed better than the baseline method in terms of texture fidelity, but image blending was only slightly superior. The multi-modal prompt method was significantly better than the other three methods; thus, for tasks requiring high texture fidelity, we recommend the multi-modal prompt method. The image caption-assisted text-to-image and multi-modal prompt methods achieved a good balance between texture fidelity and texture diversity (both ranking in the top two). If there is tolerance for texture fidelity and more texture diversity is desired, we recommend the image caption-assisted text-to-image method. None of the methods achieved an average texture fidelity score of more than 4, with the highest-scoring method-image caption-assisted text-to-image-being slightly better than average. This indicates that non-trained methods are somewhat effective for texture fidelity, but there is still considerable room for improvement.

Product Generation Quality: In terms of product accuracy, the image caption-assisted text-to-image method was clearly superior to the other three methods, possibly due to providing more accurate textual descriptions for T2I. In terms of product diversity, the multi-modal prompt method offered better options, which might be due to image + text being used directly as prompts, allowing the T2I model to generate a wider range of end-to-end combinations.

Image Aesthetics: In terms of image aesthetics, Image Caption-assisted Text-to-image and baseline methods achieve the best and second-best performance respectively. The results of the multi-modal prompt method and the image blending method are significantly worse than the good ones. We conjecture that using pure text prompts only is good for making aesthetic images while adding image prompts or using image blending might hurt the aesthetics in Midjourney.

Overall Evaluation of the Three Methods: Image blending ranked the lowest among all methods, although it has a low entry barrier because it directly blends two images. However, the blending effect has higher requirements for input images, such as size and position matching. Overall, this method is far from satisfactory in generating Jingchu products. Among all methods, the image caption-assisted text-to-image method ranked the highest overall, placing first in three criteria: product accuracy, image aesthetics, and texture diversity, and second in the remaining two criteria: texture fidelity and product diversity.

5. Conclusion

This paper uses Chinese Jingchu patterns as an example to highlight the limitations of existing English-based text-to-image (T2I) systems in describing sparse concepts and expressing non-European and American cultures. We first constructed a Jingchu pattern dataset and, based on the high-performing T2I system Midjourney, explored non-training strategies for designing cultural and creative products featuring Jingchu patterns. We proposed three strategies: image caption-assisted text-to-image, multi-modal prompt, and image blending. Through user evaluations of the generated images, we determined the effectiveness of these methods across five criteria: Texture Fidelity, Product Accuracy, Image Aesthetics, Product Diversity, and Texture Diversity. Although all methods outperformed the baseline method in terms of texture fidelity, there is still considerable room for improvement, even for the best-performing method, image caption-assisted text-to-image. Based on users' evaluation results, we summarized the usage recommendations for different methods.

References

[1] Ruiz, Nataniel, et al. "Dreambooth: Fine tuning text-to-image diffusion models for subject-driven generation." *Proceedings of the IEEE/CVF Conference on Computer Vision and Pattern Recognition.* 2023.

[2] Hu, Edward J., et al. "Lora: Low-rank adaptation of large language models." *arXiv preprint arXiv:2106.09685* (2021).

[3] Houlsby, Neil, et al. "Parameter-efficient transfer learning for NLP." *International Conference on Machine Learning.* PMLR, 2019.

[4] Shneiderman, Ben. *Human-centered AI.* Oxford University Press, 2022.

[5] Ramesh, Aditya, et al. "Zero-shot text-to-image generation." *International Conference on Machine Learning.* PMLR, 2021.

[6] Marcus, Gary, Ernest Davis, and Scott Aaronson. "A very preliminary analysis of DALL-E 2." *arXiv preprint arXiv:2204.13807* (2022).

[7] Borji, Ali. "Generated faces in the wild: Quantitative comparison of stable diffusion, midjourney and dall-e 2." *arXiv preprint arXiv:2210.00586* (2022).

[8] Rombach, Robin, et al. "High-resolution image synthesis with latent diffusion models." *Proceedings of the IEEE/CVF conference on computer vision and pattern recognition.* 2022.

[9] Cheng Yanping. "The Beauty of Chu Lacquer Furniture Decoration." *Art Hundreds* 6 (2008): 269-270.

[10] Liang Huiyin. "Research on the Value of Jingchu Art Han Embroidery." *Science and Education Wenhui* 24 (2008): 254-254.

[11] Gu Yi. "The Aesthetic World of Chu Costume Patterns." *Journal of Wuhan University of Science and Technology* 19.8 (2006): 14-17.

[12] Yu Lan, and Zhang Xiaoxia. "A study of phoenix and bird patterns on Chu silk during the Spring and Autumn Period and the Warring States Period from the perspective of semiotics." *Journal of Silk* 59.11 (2022).

[13] Xu Daosheng, and Li Ling. "Ambiguing Colors: Lacquerware, Bamboo Slips, Jade and Silk from Chu State." *(No Title).*

[14] Zhou Neng. "Dragon and Phoenix Patterns of Chu Warring States Period." *Southern Cultural Relics* 2 (2000): 21-26.

[15] Zhou Aimin, Ouyang Jinyan, and Chai Yingjie. "Analysis on the evolution and causes of Jingchu pattern themes." (2014).

[16] Bloomberg. *Research on the artistic form of Chu culture—Discussion on the artistic value of animal graphics.* MS thesis. Wuhan University of Technology, 2010.

[17] Zhou Aimin, Ouyang Jinyan, and Su Jianning. "Analysis on the evolution of geometric patterns in Jingchu." (2014).

[18] Li Li, and Zhang Yuxin. "Line Narration of Utensil Patterns—The Value and Significance of "Theme Narration" of Chu State Utensil Patterns during the Warring States Period." *Jiangxi Social Sciences* 4 (2011): 23-31.

[19] Yicheng Museum. "Chu Style and Han Rhythm: Display of Chu and Han cultural relics unearthed in Yicheng area." *(No Title)* (2011)

[20] WOMBO Inc. 2022. Dream by WOMBO. Retrieved October 5, 2022 from https://www.wombo.art

[21] Midjourney. 2022. Midjourney. Retrieved October 5, 2022 from https://www.midjourney.com

[22] Studio Morphogen. 2022. Artbreeder. Retrieved October 5, 2022 from https://www.artbreeder.com/

Design Studies and Intelligence Engineering
L.C. Jain et al. (Eds.)
doi:10.3233/FAIA231488

Operation Space Optimization Design of Mobile Chinese Food Cart Based on Ergonomics

Meidan DENG[a], Xiaofan SUN[a], Biyun ZHU[a], and Jinhua ZHANG[a1]

[a] *Department of Art and Design, Beijing City University, Beijing, China*

Abstract. Based on ergonomics and Chinese eating habits and taking ,this paper takes Beijing mobile food cart as the research object and analyzes mobile food cart workers' job duties and process as well as and the layout of the working space through field trips and interviews to deeply study how to reasonably plan the functional layout of the operation area in the limited space of the dining cart and improve work efficiency so as optimize the people-oriented operation space design of the mobile Chinese food cart. The study aims to give full play to the man-machine efficiency and design a multifunctional, clean and sanitary food cart for the operators of the mobile Chinese food cart, which will enhance the usability and comfort of mobile food carts and provide a valuable reference for other catering trailer' interior space layout design.

Keywords. Mobile Chinese food cart; Operating space; Ergonomics; User-friendly design

1. Introduction

In recent years, China has set up convenient catering trailers, buffet cabinets and other facilities at subway entrance and crowded streets, so that citizens can buy hot meals at any time, which makes people feel the warmth of urban fine management. But how to provide diversified meals to cater for the Chinese people's eating habits such as staple food with a balanced portion of vegetables and meat and make the catering cart easy and handy to use become a major concern.

With the Beijing mobile food cart as the research object, ergonomics as the theoretical basis, and through qualitative and quantitative data analysis, this paper will design the functional layout of the interior space of the cart and carry out further study on how to rationally plan the functional layout in the limited space to enhance its usability and comfort. Therefore, both cart staff and consumers can improve the operation and purchase efficiency, which is committed to promoting a user-friendly design of the operation space in the mobile Chinese food carts.

---

[1] Corresponding Author.

2. Research and Analysis of Mobile Carts

Mobile food carts are mobile kitchens set up on the street to prepare and sell food to passers-by. Taking those on the streets of Beijing as examples, there are three common styles (as shown in Figure 1): one is the food trailer, which generally stops near the subway entrance for a long time, mainly selling snacks such as drinks, biscuits, cooked food, etc., and occasionally selling hot food like boiled corns as the seasons change. This kind of food carts is generally operated legally, and the cart is semi-closed. The food sold is relatively sanitary and clean. Only the front part needs to be towed away if the food trailer needs to be repaired. The functional layout of the trailer can be divided into two parts: the sales area and the operation area. The sales area contains commodity display and cashier. There are devices like refrigerator, display rack. The operation area is mainly for machine processing, which is mainly equipped with operation table, microwave oven and so on. The division and functional layout of this kind of carts are unclear and unreasonable. The cart staff are often hurry-scurry and consumers have to queue up for their food.

Another type is a small food trailer, which only appears near the subway entrance or neighborhood during breakfast time. It is operated legally, but its space is limited, and the facility is crude. It does not have its own power and the gas tank is directly exposed outside the vehicle. There are serious security risks.

The third type is hand push food cart. Some vendors will also use tricycles. It is generally illegal, and its devices are poor. It mainly sells traditional and hot food, such as: pancake rolled with crisp fritter, Chinese hamburger, porridge and so on. It is generally all-open, with prepared food and semi-prepared food directly exposed outside. The sanitary conditions is worrying. Due to its illegal operation, the hand push food cart is more flexible and can be moved at any time in order to escape from the regulation enforcement by city inspectors.

Figure 1. Concession Food Trailer, Concession Food Trailer, Hand Push Food Cart.

The problems of the above three mobile catering carts (as shown in Table 1) will be solved and optimized one by one in terms of the spatial function layout and man-machine operation in the design process.

Table 1. Analysis of Status Quo of Existing Mobile Food Carts.

Name	Pros	Cons
Concession food trailer	• Semi-open, tidy&clean	• The spatial function layout is unreasonable. The sales and the meal pickup are in the same area. • The light source design is unreasonable. The light source area is set in the middle of the top of the cart, and the staff is in the shady area during operation. • The hanging cabinets is above the head of the staff, which is easy to cause a sense of depression; • There is no washing area and it is inconvenient to clean the items.
Small food trailer	• Less area occupation; • Food can be cooked on site.	• Small and cramped; • There is no electric box. It uses gas tank and is installed outside the cart, which have security risks. • It is an almost all open operating panel and food is exposed outside. The Food hygiene safety is a great problem. • There is no washing area and it is inconvenient to clean the items.
Hand push food cart	• Flexible and movable	• Poor equipment • The operating panel is all open and food is exposed outside. The Food hygiene safety is a great problem.

3. Design of Mobile Food Cart

3.1. Man-machine Size Design of facilities inside the Mobile Food Carts

According to the area of the open space near the subway entrance, the basic dimensions of the catering cart are: 5*2.4*2.5 meters. How to enable the staff to work effectively and comfortably in the interior limited space of mobile food cart, which requires that all the layout and equipment inside are analyzed and designed strictly according to ergonomics. Areas inside the cramped space that concerning the ergonomics are the operation area, sales area, food storage and display area.

• Operation Table Design
Ergonomic data show that the stand width of women is 66 cm, the male's is 70 cm. However, the basic spatial scope is not only limited by human size and their work area, but also influenced by their psychology. A space suitable for long working hours needs to consider the psychological scale on the basis of the physiological scale (as shown in Figure 2). Therefore, the optimization design of mobile food cart operation space

should take the psychological implication into consideration and enlarge the cramped space through appropriate space processing means and turn the depressed environment into a cheerful one. It is recommended to adjust the width of the operation table to 55cm (as shown in Figure3) given to the fact that the angle between the arms and the body is 5 degrees, so as to make the working environment more comfortable. The width of the washing area and the cooking area is set to 60 cm in consideration of the need to place the induction cooker, the mixing tank and the related tools on the operation table of the mobile food cart. The heating area and packing table, with less operation involved, are set to 36cm in size given to the width of the heating pot and cash register, which is to extend the walkway space for workers (as shown in Figure 4).

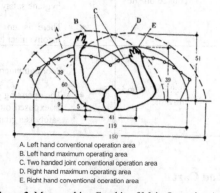

Figure 2. Human Engineering Mental Space Dimensions.

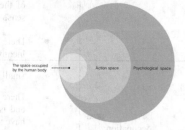

A. Left hand conventional operation area
B. Left hand maximum operating area
C. Two handed joint conventional operation area
D. Right hand maximum operating area
E. Right hand conventional operation area

Figure 3. Man-machine Graphic of Main Operation Area.

The height of the operation table and its size are also determined according to the size of the human body . When cutting vegetables and preparing food, people often need to bend over, which can easily lead to fatigue. At present, the height of operation table in some mobile food carts is about 75cm, which is similar to the height of a desk or a dining table, so it may be slightly short for a standing person. For example, if a person's height is 165cm, 75cm is the height from his arms to the table when his arms are straight. But it will be uncomfortable to work with the arms straight all the time while the body is upright. The study found that the upper arm and forearm need to maintain a proper angle when cutting vegetables, so as to give full play to the strength of the body and both hands can also cooperate to finish the task. The height data for most comfortable standing posture is shown in Table 2.

Table 2. Most Comfortable Operating Height (cm).

Height	150	153	155	158	160	164	165	169	170
Most comfortable height	80	81	82.5	84	85	86.9	87.6	89.1	90

Although the most comfortable height can be determined by heights according to the above chart, people of the same height can have differences in the height of their upper and lower bodies. Taking the height difference of 10 cm as an example, the most suitable height difference is usually about 5 cm according to the table. Therefore, the operating height of the mobile food cart takes into account the average height of Chinese male 173. 8cm and female 161cm and is set at 88.35cm (as shown in Figure 5).

- Display Case and Storage Cabinet Design

According to the previous research and analysis, the experience and comfort of taking items vary as the height of the storage cabinet is different. The most comfortable height is about 150 cm, followed by the less comfortable height is 175 cm to 180 cm. The thirld level is 65 cm to 120 cm. If the height is above 185 cm or below 65 cm, the view will be blocked and not very comfortable to operate (as shown in Table 3). Therefore, the food display area should be between 100cm to 175cm of the cabinet so that it is handy for the staff to take food. Area below 100 cm is a locker (as shown in Figure 6) that holds some spare food stock. The space of operation table below 88.35 cm are lockers for storage of inventory. The reason why the operation table and the display area below 100 cm are designed as storage cabinets is that the mobile food cart is a special place for selling food. A certain amount of food stock is bound to accumulate, so sufficient storage space must be ensured.

Table 3. Table of Visual Perception in Different Area.

Height above the ground	State and posture	Comfort	View
Less than 65cm	Squat down and reach out for something	Not very comfortable	Blocked
65-120cm	Stand up and reach out for something	Good	Clear
150cm	Stand up and reach out for something	Very good	Clear
175-180cm	Stand up and stretch the arm to take items	Good	Clear
More than 185cm	Stand up and take thing on a stool	Uncomfortable	Blocked

3.2. Mobile Food Cart Internal Space Functional Layout Design

The interior space of the mobile food car is narrow, so the features of its spatial function layout are mainly based on convenience, functional utility, comfort, and ventilation.

- Convenience

The main function of the mobile food cart is to make and sell food, and it needs to finish this process efficiently and quickly in the morning peak when the traffic volume is the largest, so the design of the operation table is very important. The layout of the mobile food cart operation table adopts a L-shape (as shown in Figure 4), and the cooking and washing areas that are most complicated to operate are arranged at the innermost part of the cart. There are separated from the walkway and does not interfere with each other. It make the operation table relatively independent. When several people work inside the cart at the same time, it can effectively prevent crowding and collision.

- Functional Utility

The main cooking area shall include the disinfection storage area, the washing area, the heating area and the cooking area. This functional area distribution is common in mobile food vehicles and is a compact arrangement of integral operating stations (as shown in Figure 4). From left to right, the worktop contains a washing area, a cooking area and a heating area. The washing area is located on the far left of the operator table, next to the refrigerator, to facilitate the continuity of the staff's whole working process. The general process is to take food ingredients from the refrigerator, wash them in the washing area, and then cook them in the cooking area. The cooking area is also provided with a mixing tank, which is used to collect the seasoning used in making meals, so that the operation table is neat, clean and regular.

The design of the washing area avoids the disadvantage that there is no washing function inside the existing mobile food cart. Since no water pipe is arranged at the parking position, a clean water bucket and a waste water bucket are arranged below the washing area of the operating table (as shown in Figure 5) . Just below the washing tank is the waste water tank. The waste water flows into the waste water tank after use by extracting the water from the clean water tank next to it. The two buckets are equipped with wheels underneath for easy towing to the washing room in the subway to store clean water and dump waste water to clean the waste water bucket. The water pipe connector on the bucket can be opened, and the diameter is 10cm. Generally, staff can put their arms into the bucket or use brushes to clean it. A small disinfection cabinet is arranged below the cooking area for disinfection, cleaning and storage of cooking utensils.

The heating area is mainly used for heating porridge, bean and stir-fried food. According to the survey, office workers are more inclined to choose Chinese breakfasts, such as porridge, steamed buns, steamed buns, soy milk, etc., while for lunch and dinner, they prefer hot food with meat and vegetables. Therefore, there are three heating pots in the heating area, which can be flexibly used according to the needs of three meals to meet the different tastes and nutritional combinations of customers. Below the heating table are two trash bins for collecting garbage. The garbage can is yellow, mainly to highlight its usage in the color, and the staff can see the garbage can at a glance when they need to throw garbage during the peak time, so as to improve work efficiency. There are two heating cabinets beside the heating pot, one for heating steamed buns and the other for heating baked sausages. The transparent glass cover used in both heating cabinets is easy to show food to consumers and enhance their desire to buy. The heating area is next to the sales area, and the 165cm wide sales window is mainly used for cash collection and food pickup, which can disperse the crowd and improve the purchasing efficiency (as shown in Figure 5).

Opposite the selling area is the storage area and the display area (as shown in Figure 6). From left to right, there are refrigerators, display cabinets and beverage display freezers, which has a large space for storing food.

- Comfort

In terms of comfort, apart from the problem of operation layout and dimensions as described above, the light source is also unreasonable because it is located in the middle of the top of the car. This lighting method can only play the basic role. The interior facilities and functional layout of the mobile food cart are set along the cart wall, which makes the light source located behind the operator's head. No matter which area the operator is in, he will stand on his own light. Furthermore, his shadow will be cast on the operation table and the whole operating process was performed in his own shadow. This indoor lighting environment is like reading and writing with your back to the light, which makes people feel very uncomfortable and affects the operation of the staff. Therefore, the optimized design of mobile food cart will make it more comfortable by setting the light belts in three area on the top of the cart (as shown in Figure 4). One is above the washing area and the cooking area. Another one is above the sales area and the commodity display area. These lighting area are all above the front of the staff, providing a comfortable and bright light source.

- Ventilation

Although there are windows in the existing mobile food cart, it is not well ventilated. The window at the head of the car is smaller. Basically, the sales window serves as the only one air vent, and the interior of the cart will be stuffy in bad weather. Besides, cooking food will also produce fumes. To solve this problem, one solution is to enlarge the size of the sales window. Another one is to install an exhaust fan and a ventilator in the middle of the cart top, which is also the main ventilation equipment (as shown in Figure 5).

4. Conclusion

With the development of the society, the utilization rate of the mobile food cart in the street is growing, and it requires a more reasonable layout of the mobile food cart's internal operation space and a user-friendly design. In the process of constructing the operation space, we should make full use of the theoretical research results of ergonomics and arrange the relevant equipment appropriately. This paper expects to finally get a functionally diverse, sanitary and convenient design of mobile food carts that optimizes the operation and purchase process from the spatial function layout. It also gives full play to the man-machine efficiency and provides a handy and cozy working environment for mobile food cart staff.

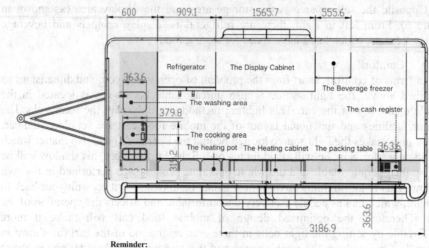

Reminder:
- The red area is the entire set of operating table.
- The yellow area is the light stripp

Figure 4. Dimension Figure of Operation Table inside the Mobile Food Cart.

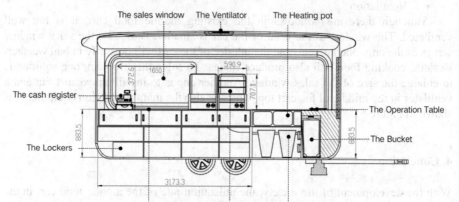

Figure 5. Mobile Food Cart Operation Table Height Figure.

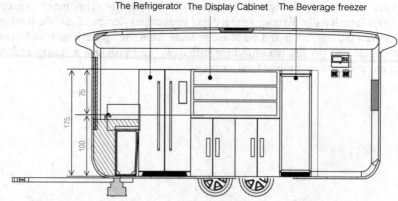

Figure 6. Mobile Food Cart Display Cabinet Dimension Figure.

References

[1] Long Shengzhao. Research Progress in Human, Machine, and Environment System Engineering (Volume 3). Beijing: Beijing Science and Technology Press, 1997.
[2] Ding Yulan. Ergonomics (Revised Edition), Beijing: Beijing Institute of Technology Press, 2000.
[3] Ji Yuna. The Rule of Distance in the Kitchen, Home Technology, 2006.
[4] Yang Yinghua. Research on the Application of Experience Design Methods in the Field of Automotive Design, Shenyang: Northeast University, 2006.
[5] Li Binbin. Design Psychology. China Light Industry Press. 2009.
[6] Liu Shenghuang. Ergonomics and Interior Design. China Construction Industry Press, 1997.
[7] Li Leshan. Industrial Design Psychology. Beijing: Higher Education Press, 2004.
[8] Ma Guangtao, Wu Xian. Preliminary Discussion on Humanized Design of Family Kitchen. Technological Innovation and Industrial Development (Volume A): Information Science and Engineering Technology, 2010:290.293.
[9] Liu Shuang. Kitchen Ergonomics. Art Exploration, 2002 (3): 71.72.
[10] Zhi Jinyi, Xu Bochu. Research on Ergonomics Based on Universal Design Concepts. Art and Design Forum, 2006 (53): 20-21.
[11] Alvin R. Tilly. Ergonomic Illustrations. Beijing: China Architecture, Ik Publishing House, 1998.
[12] Wang Jing. Analysis and Expansion of Humanized Furniture Design. Hefei University of Technology. 2006.
[13] Hu Jia. Research on RV Space Design. Huazhong University of Science and Technology. 2012.
[14] Yang Zhifa. Research on Size and Layout in Kitchen Furniture Design. Hefei University of Technology. 2010.
[15] Lu Yanping. Analysis and Countermeasure Research on China's RV Industry. Hunan University. 2014.
[16] https://baijiahao.baidu.com/s?id=1633155872590410446&wfr=spider&for=pc
[17] http://news.sohu.com/20120709/n347661215.shtml
[18] https://www.takefoto.cn/viewnews-177519.html

Design Studies and Intelligence Engineering
L.C. Jain et al. (Eds.)
© 2024 The Authors.
This article is published online with Open Access by IOS Press and distributed under the terms
of the Creative Commons Attribution Non-Commercial License 4.0 (CC BY-NC 4.0).
doi:10.3233/FAIA231489

Research on Emotional Experience Design of Cultural and Creative Products Based on User Needs

Donglin CHENG [a], Yuanyuan TAN [b,1] and Shi-le LEE[a]

[a] *Huanghe Jiaotong University, JiaoZuo 454950*
[b] *Guilin University of Electronic Science and Technology, China*

Abstract: Based on Maslow's hierarchy of needs theory, this paper explores the application of emotional design theory in the design of traditional cultural creative products from the perspective of user needs, and studies the design strategy of user emotional innovation for products created in the modern context. Methods: Based on the theory of user pyramid model, the design elements of museum cultural and creative products were extracted through user experience demand mining by non-contact research, and the elements of user demand were quantitatively transformed by QFD model. The framework of emotional experience design for cultural and creative products was constructed in the modern context. This design framework can effectively explain the support of current design elements for emotional design.

Key words: user demand; Cultural and creative products; Emotional design; Maslow's hierarchy of needs; Traditional handicrafts

1. Introduction

In 2021, The State Council issued the Opinions on Further Strengthening the Protection of Intangible Cultural Heritage [1], emphasizing that in the design and secondary development of intangible cultural heritage, cultural products that can integrate into modern life should be designed retaining cultural connotations and enhancing public cognition and cultural identity of intangible cultural heritage. Therefore, cultural and creative products are created to arouse more emotional resonance of users. Nowadays, the research results on the design of cultural and creative products are increasing year by year, and there is still a lack of certain theories to guide the emotional experience brought by products to users. Through the summarized research on design strategies of cultural and creative products, analyzing the existing practice cases of cultural and creative products, and explores the design methods of cultural and creative products based on classic emotional design theory from the perspective of users, so as to meet the needs of The Times and stimulate the vitality of traditional culture.

---

[1] Corresponding Author.Tan Yuan Yuan, Guangxi, doctor, associate professor, Guilin University of Electronic Science and Technology, Email: 22807593@qq.com

2. Theoretical Explanation and Analysis

With the advent of various social media tools, users' personal information content has become an important source for research and commercial use, and a large number of online comments often exist in an unstructured form in natural language. There is a need to establish a viable way to discover UX information from product reviews and integrate useful UX information to help designers inject insights into generating new design concepts.

Maslow's hierarchy of needs refers to a theory of demand structure proposed by Maslow in his Theory of Human Motivation in 1954 [2]. Functional requirements are that the appearance of the product has a certain attractiveness, and the product has the characteristics of ease of use and practicality [3]. Only by meeting the first two basic requirements can users achieve a physiological balance and pursue a higher level of experience. Experience and service demand demand is mainly based on the interactive behavior and operation service of cultural and creative products, while cultural demand is the ultimate goal of cultural and creative design. Users can cultivate their hearts and improve themselves in the process of use [4]. Its basic structure and contents are shown in Figure 1.

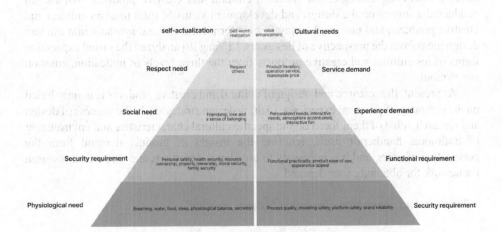

Figure 1. Maslow's classic demand pyramid and hierarchical analysis of cultural and creative products' needs

In view of the challenges in user experience analysis and the growing demand, with the increase of people's living standards and online shopping, the modern scientific text mining function is used to determine the user's emotions and explore the user experience from the user evaluation, and the scientific analysis tool is used to quantitatively transform the elements of user needs, combined with the emotion hierarchy theory. It can effectively measure the real needs of users and provide solutions.

3. Research Status of Cultural and Creative Products

3.1 Summary of Research on Cultural and Creative Product Design

At present, the research results on the design of museum cultural creative products are increasing year by year in the field of cultural and creative product design and humanities and history, but there are still problems such as high homogeneity of design products and insufficient breadth and depth of research. The development strategy of cultural and creative products is mainly developed from the perspective of designers, and there are few researches on the feedback and experience of users in the design of museum cultural creative products.

For example, Zhang Yue [5] and other researchers discussed the design strategy of cultural and creative products according to the current development status of cultural and creative products and combined with the characteristics of traditional Chinese culture elements. By studying the definition and essential features of cultural and creative products themselves, Wang Yaming [6] believes that non-legacy cultural and creative products should strengthen their design in the three key points of enhancing cultural sense, functionality and market effect. Chen Lu [7] uses the user-oriented 4C strategy to develop marketing strategies for museum cultural and creative products. Wu Jie [8] conducted a survey on the design and development status of rural tourism cultural and creative products, and proposed a way to transform rural cultural symbols into modern design ideas from the perspective of designers. Li Yang [9] analyzed the visual expression forms of his cultural and creative products from the three levels of indication, emotion and symbol.

At present, the research and design of cultural and creative products is mainly based on the summary of practical experience to draw design strategies. In the process of design and research, most of them focus on the specific cultural characteristics and environment of traditional handicraft itself, ignoring the insight of product demand from the perspective of users, and it is necessary to broaden the methods and theoretical research framework for obtaining user demand.

3.2 Online data acquisition of museum cultural creation

A number of "cultural creative products development projects and excellent enterprises with exemplary driving role" should be created, which provided comprehensive normative guidance for the development of cultural innovation business forms of museums [10]. Since then, museums have opened online purchase channels one after another. According to statistics, online product sales account for a large proportion. Users' comments obtained by means of online comment crawling can be rich and comprehensive, and can provide a relatively objective and comprehensive data analysis.

The research process as shown in Figure 2 was formed by combining relevant text emotion mining research ideas and user experience analysis methods. The first part uses the Octopus platform to obtain user review data, establish the online review corpus database of related museums, and screen out the more meaningful and effective review data. The second part is to conduct data analysis on the results of the first part. First, the review data is put into the KHCorder platform for text segmentation and word frequency statistics, and then the results of word segmentation are used as a thesaural for theme word cluster analysis [11]. The subject category analysis of user comments on museum cultural and creative products can obtain the relationship between the data and the evaluation theme. All demand points of users are sorted and refined by Maslow demand classification. The third part will summarize the user's demand index, use QFD house of quality analysis method to grade the obtained user demand and further parameterize it into design requirements.

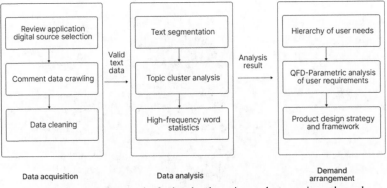

Figure 2. Research framework of cultural and creative product experience demand

In order to ensure the common influence of product personality on the analysis results, 26 cultural and creative products selected from the merchandise platform of Tmall were divided into four categories: home life, stationery, decorative crafts and practical crafts. During the collection process, the total amount of user comment data for each category of goods remained average. The collection date was May 2023. Finally, 14,606 valid user comments on museum cultural and creative products are collected, with a total corpus of 386,000 words.

3.3 Online data analysis of museum culture and creation

The author uses a Text Mining software called KHCoder developed by Japanese scholar Koichi Higuchi (2014). The software has powerful text data analysis function, with text segmentation, keyword extraction, co-occurrence analysis and visualization (such as cluster analysis tree) and other functions.

Firstly, the crawled user evaluation data is input into KHcoder software, and the data is divided into words, meaningless words are removed and similar words are combined for content screening. Then, the top 300 attractive high-frequency words are ranked, and the KHcorder scientific computing visualization software is first used to generate the network relationship diagram of highly attractive keywords, which can show the coocurrence relationship of word frequency of evaluation information. The largest node in the same color block is the central word of point degree. The crossed part between nodes represents the degree of connection between two nodes. The more intersecting parts, the more co-occurrence of the two words, and the stronger the correlation. From the figure, we can interpret the user evaluation information and clarify the user's product demand point and importance。

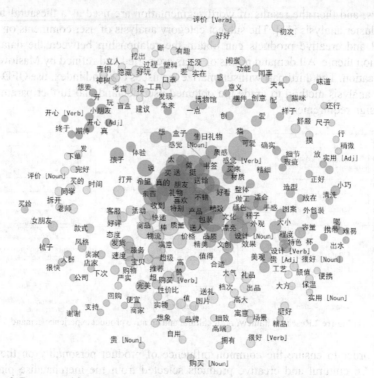

Figure 3. Feature word frequency clustering relation of user purchase attraction quadratic

Combined with the feature word cluster diagram and the five levels of product demand as guidance, the user experience theme categories attractive to users are divided. Product safety, product price, product style, packaging and exterior decoration, interactive experience, basic functions, product operation, delivery channels, cultural factors and brand image are the main themes that users pay attention to. "Product safety" refers to the current user's basic demand for product reliability; "Product style" is the pattern shape and external outline presented by the appearance surface that can represent its own characteristics; "Packaging exterior decoration" means the packaging appearance and packaging decoration of the product in the process of sale; "Interactive experience" refers to the interactive behavior produced by products and people, and the playability and interest generated; The functional "product operation" conveyed during the use of the "basic function" product covers the whole process of the product, including product publicity to user relationship maintenance; "Delivery path" includes the purpose of purchasing the product and the flow of users; "Cultural factor" including the legacy of ancient history and the new cultural inheritance of modern construction; The results of hierarchy division are shown in Table 1.

Table 1. User experience theme categories of user purchase attraction

Requirement classification	Main category	subcategory	Feature word（portion）
Security requirement	Product safety	Product quality	Quality 1665, fine 1158, worth 663, effect 578, quality 459

			189, detail 178, firm 174, defect 168, seal 167, workmanship 152, strong 145
	Product price	**Product price**	Price 720, expensive 648, value 324, cost performance 243, value 219, cheap 152
Functional requirement	**Product style**	**Color pattern**	Good-looking 3576, beautiful 2421, color 369, pattern 363, appearance level 246, pattern 187
		Shape modeling	Appearance 762, design 666, size 522, small 303, style 297, physical 273, shape
		Material texture	Feel 696, material 621, texture 612, comfortable 303, plastic 195, delicate 179,
	Outer Packaging	**Product packaging**	Packaging 2877, box 477, outer packaging 189, gift box 181, packaging box 179
Experience demand	**Interactive experience**	**Interactive mode**	Dig 597, open 426, Play 414, play 360, experience 336, Fun 198, Clean 180, open 171, dig 178, Carry 168, touch 154, dig 152
	Basic function	**Application function**	Cup 1170, bookmark 963, things 843, goods 598, capacity 514, blind box 221, decoration 382, mask 319, insulation 219, put in 205,
Service Demand	**Product operation**	**Operation content**	Details page 598, Evaluation 456, Series 509, Description 387, Event 345, Gift 327, Product introduction 289
	Other services	**Customer service**	Seller 605, service 489, attitude 378, customer service 366, picture 352, picture 264
		Consultation	
		Logistics service	Received 1002, Logistics 960, Express 654, delivery 639, speed 480, delivery 431, time 241, Soon 175, express 156, slow 149, delivery 146
Cultural needs		**Cultural factor**	Cat 660, Culture 618, Archaeology 291, implied 213, Sacred Tree 201, Craft 195

3.4 Induction of user experience design elements based on QFD analysis

The relationship between the core functions and key technologies of museum cultural and creative products can be intuitively seen by using the QFD House of Quality analysis method, so that more design energy and development resources can be invested in it, and the design efficiency can be improved while ensuring that the needs of users can be met to the maximum extent.

The user demand data investigated through the experiment is converted into the design elements required by the product design to form the first column of the House of Quality, the roof of the house of quality is generally used to analyze the interrelationship between the functions (but the technical functions described in this section are independent of each other and no obvious correlation has been found, so the roof can be temporarily vacant). The importance of design elements is derived from the word frequency analysis of user purchase attraction, and is divided into 1 to 10 points, with 1 point representing the least importance and 9 point representing the most important (take an integer). The main design style methods summarized by the above 26 kinds of cultural and creative products, "style transfer", "heterogeneous reconstruction", "digital technology", "essence restoration" and "intelligent voice", are added to the horizontal axis of QFD. According to the correlation degree between the method and the demand elements, "9 points" means very close correlation, 6 points means medium correlation, and 3 points means general correlation. A score of 0 means that there is no obvious correlation, so that the final score of the current function in the calculation forms the foundation of the House of Quality. The finished cultural and creative quality house designed around users is shown in Table 2.

Table 2. Schematic diagram of QFD Quality House created by Museum

	Design element	Degree of important	Style transfer	Heterogeneous reconstruction	Twin digit	Essential reduction	Personalized customization
User Requirements	Product safety	6			3	6	
	Product price	2	6		6	3	6
	Color pattern	7	6	6		6	3
Design Elements	Shape modeling	5	6		6		6
	Material texture	3	3	6		6	6
	Product packaging	4	3	3			3
	Interactive experience	4	3	6	9	3	6
	Basic function	7	9		3		3
	Product operation	3	3		3	6	6
	Promotion communication	2	3	3	3	3	3
	Cultural factor	3	3	6	3	3	
	Brand image	8	6	3	3	6	3
	Importance score		246	144	165	195	186
	Importance ranking		1	5	4	2	3

According to the score, designers can give priority to the method of style transfer when designing.Secondly, the design weight of essential restoration is second only to the style transfer method, indicating that users have a high degree of reflecting the cultural attributes of cultural and creative products, and it is necessary to refine its cultural factors and creatively integrate them into the product experience design during the design process. Due to the rise of the experience economy, personalized customization is also a strong demand for users to meet the interest and richness of products. At the same time, it can be seen that the two design functional methods of personality customization and style transfer have a certain positive correlation, so two parallel design methods can be adopted in the design process.

4.consumer demand combing and user experience demand level induction

The summarized theme categories will be corresponding to the user's experience process of purchasing museum cultural and creative products, and the user's sense of experience will be enhanced through the construction of experience link steps. Specifically, it can be divided into four stages, namely introduction, cognition, experience and empathy, and the corresponding relationship after division.

4.1 Introduction period - Create a "product label" to improve customer acquisition channels

When users browse to cultural and creative product information through information flow or search engines, brand characteristics and operation content are the main influencing factors. Cultural and creative products to attract users' attention, the first thing is to create a brand image with regional advantages, build a "product label", and enhance users' sensory recognition and trust.

Brand identity requires a deep understanding of the culture, history, traditions and characteristics of the location, including region-specific arts, crafts, styles, architecture, etc. Through the construction of logo attributes, folk stories and other elements to convey brand information, such as the Palace Museum because of the cat's "lazy" style and attract a large number of fans, so the launch of the "cute" blind box, Henan Museum launched the "ancient cultural relics" mining game blind box, the product is relatively more "hard core" and "realistic". Product operation mainly discusses the dissemination of product publicity content. In the era of convenient digitalization, the effective method is mainly to select suitable co-name objects in combination with the brand characteristics of cultural and creative products, so as to achieve the effect of expanding user objects and improving user experience. For example, the fusion of "Moutai" and "coffee", which are popular among young people, and the launch of "Maotai latte" are the needs of two types of users, business white-collar workers and elite men.

4.2 Cognitive stage - Create both "literature" and "things" to enhance cultural attributes

The cognitive experience of the product is the "strong" first impression of the product on the user when the user just comes into contact with the product, and the product style and packaging exterior are the main components. As cultural connotation is the core design element of cultural and creative products, product design should be supported by cultural connotation, so as to establish its own distinctive artistic image.

Product style refers to the three most direct physical aspects of product shape, color and material. Style design needs to modernize and regenerate based on the understanding of culture itself, and the cultural connotation is metaphorical in it [12]. The overall shape, appearance characteristics and structural design of the product, usually the external outline with a certain structural setting, usually determines the function of the product. In the appearance design of the product, the actual use needs and ergonomic principles of the product should be taken into account, and the appearance shape, curve and size of the product should be designed to make the product conform to the convenience of human body holding, operation and use; The original elements are generally shaped through scientific classification and subject matter, so as to integrate the original beauty as far as possible and emphasize the tactile feeling to the user.

4.3 Experience period – "practical" and "easy to use" to increase experience touch points

The product experience stage refers to the emotional experience users feel when using cultural and creative products, mainly including the functional characteristics of the product and the interactive experience between users and products. Under the background of user experience economy, the functional diversity of cultural and creative products is increasingly prominent, and the products are practical, easy to use and interesting, so as to fully mobilize the enthusiasm of users;

To improve the product experience, designers need to develop product experience links, and design ideas should be combined with their brands and product labels to meet user expectations and expectations. For example, the functional design of the product should meet the specific needs of the target users, or provide more users with the functional needs to choose from. In the process of product experience pay attention to user co-creation experience. Examples include designing components that can be adjusted, parts that can be assembled and spliced, or designs that participate in the creative process. You can use music, sound, texture, aroma and other elements to create an experience atmosphere, fully mobilize the user's multi-sensory experience. Once again broaden the new way of online experience, using virtual reality (VR) and augmented reality (AR) technology to provide users with immersive experience touch points.

4.4 Empathy - Dig deep into the power of "culture" and continue cultural inheritance

Cultural and creative products are not limited to the design of the product itself, but users pay more attention to the spiritual content brought by the product. The cultural empathy of the product mainly includes the "cultural factor" and "promotion and communication" of the product.

In the design of products, it is necessary to dig deep cultural connotations and link product design with specific cultural stories and traditions. Through stories and inheritance, products can be given deeper emotional resonance. The embodiment of the cultural characteristics of the final product requires the organic integration of cultural factors and cultural carriers. For constantly updating product design and experience content, such as launching limited edition products, regularly updating story content or designing new accessories. When consumers experience products, cultural sustainability means that users are willing to share products with other users and increase their self-value during the experience process, and then forming ecological user growth through building communities and other ways.

5.Conclusion

The analysis of the current theoretical research on cultural and creative products, finding that the lack of users' emotional needs in the design research of cultural and creative products, and the lack of a unified design theoretical framework to guide the design of cultural and creative products. Through mining users' evaluation of the existing practice cases of cultural and creative products, guided by the hierarchy of user needs, the elements of user needs are transformed into design elements of cultural and creative products by analyzing them, and the quantitative transformation is carried out by QFD model. The research finds that the research on emotional experience design of cultural and creative products requires practitioners in related fields to pay attention to the needs of user experience in practice, constantly improve and innovate, and provide more emotional resonance for users.

Acknowledgements

2023 Guangxi Higher Education Undergraduate Teaching Reform Project (2023JGB190)

References

[1]   The General Office of the CPC Central Committee and The General Office of the State Council issued the Opinions on Further Strengthening the Protection of Intangible Cultural Heritage,2021(24):14-17.
[2]   Guan Xiaolei. Research on the progressive trend of product demand based on Maslow's Hierarchy of Needs Theory.
[3]   Industrial Design,2018(09):41-43.
[4]   Gibson J J. The ecological approach to visual perception: classic edition. Psychology Press, 2014.
[5]   Donald A. Norman. NORMAN A D, The Design of Everyday Things: Norman A d, the Design of Everyday things: Revised and Expanded Edition . Beijing: China CITI Press, 2015.
[6]   Zhang Yue. The innovative research of Chinese traditional handicraft in the design of cultural creative products . Beijing University of Civil Engineering and Architecture,2017.
[7]   Wang Yaming, Wu Ping. Cultural heritage under the perspective of bamboo weaving technology, and product design . Journal of packaging engineering, 2020, 9 (20) : 24-29. DOI: 10.19554 / j.carol carroll nki. 1001-3563.2020.20.005.
[8]   Chen Lu. Recognition, Adaptation, Openness and Experience: The Development of Museum cultural and creative Products from the perspective of User Orientation . Media Observation, 2020, (11): 51-55.
[9]   Wu Jie. The context of modern rural tourism product design research . Journal of packaging engineering, 2023, 44 (14) : 419-428. The DOI: 10.19554 / j.carol carroll nki. 1001-3563.2023.14.047.
[10] Li Yang, Long Xin, Yang Longfei. For culture creative product design method of semantic expression research. Mechanical design and manufacturing: 1-5 [2023-09-30]. https://doi.org/10.19356/j.cnki.1001-3997.20230718.016.
[11] Hu Yao, Xiao Renbin, Zhang Wenxu. Product Review Data-driven Quality Function Development Customer Demand Mining. Computer Integrated Manufacturing Systems, 2022, 28(1): 184-196.
[12] Liu Jian, Huang Sai, Cao Jiagang, et al. Product service system design method based on User Generated Content . Packaging Engineering, 2020, 41(24): 118-125, 142.

Design Studies and Intelligence Engineering
L.C. Jain et al. (Eds.)
© *2024 The Authors.*
This article is published online with Open Access by IOS Press and distributed under the terms
of the Creative Commons Attribution Non-Commercial License 4.0 (CC BY-NC 4.0).
doi:10.3233/FAIA231490

Research on Renovation and Design of Urban Block Public Toilets Based on Service Design

Wei ZHANG[a,1], Yunjia QIAO[a], and Zijie ZHOU[a]

[a] *School of Art, Shandong Jianzhu University, P.R. China*

Abstract: This study focuses on urban block public toilets and explores their renovation and design through literature review, field research, and questionnaire surveys. Taking the block near Daming Lake Scenic Area in Lixia District, Jinan City as an example, this study applies service design concepts to analyze touchpoints, stakeholders' needs, and service processes of public toilets. It proposes renovation design principles and strategies aiming to enhance the service experience of public toilets and meet the diverse needs of different user groups.

Keywords: urban block, public toilets, service design, spatial renovation

1. Introduction

Public toilets are closely tied to urban services and serve as important indicators of a city's level of civilization and public service. However, the construction of public toilets has long been neglected in urban development, leading to the common sight of foul-smelling facilities that inconvenience urban residents. City block public toilets are an indispensable part of urban infrastructure and hold significant importance for residents and tourists. However, many current city block public toilets suffer from issues such as aging facilities and inconvenient services, which hinder the improvement of the quality of life for residents and visitors. Therefore, this study aims to utilize the concept of service design to transform and redesign city block public toilets, enhancing the service experience and meeting the needs of different user groups.

Extensive research on public toilet design has been conducted in Japan since the 19th century. In recent years, the "Tokyo Toilet" project, initiated by a Japanese charity organization, aimed to renovate and design the interior and exterior environments of public toilets in 17 locations in Shibuya, Tokyo. Renowned designers such as Shigeru Ban, Tadao Ando, and Kengo Kuma were invited to create innovative and aesthetically pleasing designs. [1]The facilities were equipped with user-friendly and accessible features, including multifunctional toilets, sound devices, emergency assistance devices, child-friendly toilets, and baby changing stations, catering to the needs of various user groups. The project also incorporated touchless toilets to challenge the common perception of public toilets being dirty and poorly maintained. This initiative provides

---

[1]Wei Zhang, School of Art, Shandong Jianzhu University, P.R.China, E-mail: 474562952@qq.com

valuable insights and references for the transformation and design of public toilets in China.Research on public toilets has also been conducted in Western countries. Clara Greed explored the significance of public toilets as an integral part of urban design in her book "Inclusive Urban Design: Public Toilets," addressing existing problems and emphasizing the importance of improving public toilets while proposing strategies and approaches for improvement.[2] Julie Hollen documented diverse toilet cultures in different regions during her travels, presenting the history of toilets in an entertaining manner and offering references for studying different toilet cultures. [3]The World Toilet Organization (WTO), founded in Singapore in 2001, is an international non-profit organization dedicated to promoting toilet and sanitation issues worldwide. They designated November 19th as World Toilet Day.

In recent years, Scholars in China have also paid attention to public toilets. Various works have been published, rigorously discussing toilet culture, psychological and physiological aspects of defecation, and the correlation between Eastern and Western civilizations. [4]These works humorously record anecdotes and highlight the necessity of a toilet revolution in China. They comprehensively discuss the design process and key points of public toilets and analyze the current status of domestic and international urban public toilets, providing detailed design methods from various perspectives.[5] Some researchers have focused on the problems of urban public toilet design, emphasizing the need to meet people's needs in the design of urban public toilets.[6] Others have analyzed the existing issues and proposed that solving the contradiction in urban environments requires scientific and effective strategies, as well as the participation and collective efforts of society as a whole. Research on urban public toilets covers various aspects such as hygiene, user satisfaction, environmental characteristics, technological innovation, and intelligent systems. These studies highlight the importance of cleanliness, accessibility, and user experience in public toilets, as well as the need for proper maintenance and management.[7] They also emphasize the role of technology in improving toilet facilities and addressing challenges related to pathogen transmission, odor control, and water usage. The research provides insights into improving hygiene, user satisfaction, and environmental conditions through innovative approaches and technologies, contributing to the understanding of the current challenges and potential solutions in providing clean, accessible, and user-friendly public toilets.

2. Application of Service Design Principles in City Block Public Toilets

The application of service design principles in city block public toilets includes touchpoint analysis, stakeholder needs analysis, and service process optimization. Touchpoint analysis involves analyzing and evaluating various touchpoints and interactions between users and public toilets. This can include the process of entering the toilet, the experience of using the facilities, and the perception after leaving the toilet. By understanding user needs and experiences at different touchpoints, targeted improvements and optimizations can be made to enhance user satisfaction.[8]

Stakeholder needs analysis focuses on understanding the needs of stakeholders related to public toilets, such as residents, tourists, and government departments. Different stakeholders may have different needs and expectations. For example, residents may prioritize the quantity and convenience of nearby public toilets, while government departments may focus on hygiene management and facility maintenance.[9] By comprehensively analyzing the needs of different stakeholders, more targeted and comprehensive strategies for public toilet services can be developed.Service process optimization involves evaluating and improving the service processes of public toilets to enhance efficiency and user experience. This includes optimizing processes from the moment users enter the toilet to using the facilities, cleaning and maintenance, and payment processes. Measures such as simplifying processes, optimizing facility layouts, and providing convenient payment methods can reduce user waiting time and cumbersome operations, thereby improving overall service effectiveness.

In practice, an example of applying service design principles to city block public toilets is the "Tokyo Toilet" project in Japan. The project invited renowned designers to transform and redesign public toilets in Shibuya, Tokyo, with innovative and aesthetic designs. The facilities were equipped with user-friendly features, such as multifunctional toilets, sound devices, emergency assistance devices, and facilities catering to specific user groups like children and mothers. The project also incorporated touchless technology, challenging the common perception of public toilets being dirty and poorly maintained. Through these improvements, the project aimed to enhance the service experience and meet the diverse needs of users. To sum up, the application of service design principles in city block public toilets includes touchpoint analysis, stakeholder needs analysis, and service process optimization. These approaches can help improve user experience, meet the needs of different stakeholders, and enhance overall service quality. The "Tokyo Toilet" project serves as an example of successfully applying these principles in practice.

3. Principles and Strategies for Renovation Design of City Block Public Toilets

When it comes to the renovation design of city block public toilets, there are several principles and strategies that can be considered. [10]

- Accessibility: Ensuring that the public toilets are easily accessible to all individuals, including people with disabilities, elderly individuals, and parents with young children. This can involve providing ramps, wider doorways, and suitable amenities.
- Hygiene and Sanitation: Prioritizing cleanliness and hygiene in public toilets through regular cleaning and maintenance. Incorporating features like touchless technology, automatic flushing systems, and hand sanitizer dispensers can help maintain a clean and safe environment.
- Privacy and Security: Designing public toilets to provide adequate privacy and security for users. This can include individual stalls with lockable doors, well-lit areas, and surveillance systems to ensure user safety.
- Sustainability: Implementing sustainable design practices in the renovation of public toilets, such as incorporating energy-efficient lighting, water-saving fixtures, and using eco-friendly materials. This helps reduce the environmental impact and promotes a more sustainable urban environment.
- Aesthetics: Enhancing the visual appeal of public toilets to create a pleasant and inviting atmosphere. This can involve incorporating artistic elements, vibrant colors, and landscaping around the facilities.
- User Experience: Considering the overall user experience when designing public toilets. This includes factors like adequate ventilation, comfortable

seating, clear signage, and provision of amenities like baby-changing stations and accessible facilities for different user groups.

- Community Engagement: Involving the local community in the design process and gathering feedback to ensure that the renovated public toilets meet their needs and preferences. This can be achieved through surveys, public consultations, and collaboration with local stakeholders.

By adhering to these principles and implementing appropriate strategies, the renovation design of city block public toilets can greatly improve the overall quality, accessibility, and user satisfaction of these essential urban facilities. Principles and strategies for the renovation design of city block public toilets include facility renovation principles, spatial layout strategies, and service function enhancement strategies.

Facility renovation principles refer to the principles to consider when renovating public toilet facilities. This includes providing a clean and hygienic environment, ensuring the reliability and durability of the facilities, and meeting users' basic needs, such as providing an adequate number of seating, handwashing facilities, and hygiene supplies. Additionally, the needs of different user groups, such as providing accessible facilities to meet the needs of individuals with disabilities, should also be taken into account.[11]

Spatial layout strategies involve considering appropriate spatial planning and layout in public toilet renovations. This includes determining the location of entrances and exits, the width of passageways, and the installation of partitions and dividers to provide privacy. [12]It also involves arranging the placement of facilities such as washbasins, toilets, and trash cans. By implementing a scientific spatial layout, a more comfortable, safe, and efficient usage environment can be provided. Service function enhancement strategies involve considering the addition of new service functions in public toilet renovations. [13]This can include adding facilities such as baby changing stations, nursing rooms, accessible facilities, and charging devices to meet the needs of different users. Additionally, the introduction of intelligent systems, such as automatic sensor devices, smart navigation, and information prompts, can enhance user experience and service effectiveness.

The renovation design of city block public toilets should adhere to facility renovation principles, rational spatial layout, and the consideration of adding new service functions. These principles and strategies can enhance the comfort, convenience, and user satisfaction of public toilets, providing better public services for urban residents and tourists.

4. Case Study: Renovation Design of Public Toilets in the Street Blocks near Daming Lake Scenic Area, Lixia District, Jinan City

Based on the interview survey data of users of the neighborhood public toilets(as shown in Fig. 1), it is evident that the main concerns of the users are focused on three aspects: hygiene conditions, facility conditions, and privacy conditions. Regarding hygiene conditions, 62.5% of the respondents selected "basically clean," 29.17% selected "not very clean," and 16.67% selected "poor cleanliness" inside the toilets. This indicates that the overall hygiene situation of the neighborhood public toilets is relatively good, but there are still some issues. The reasons can be analyzed from two aspects. On one hand, user behavior contributes to the problem, as some individuals engage in uncivilized behavior that affects the cleanliness of the toilets. It is necessary to increase publicity efforts on civilized use of public toilets and provide warning signs for guidance. On the other hand, inadequate supervision and cleaning by the management staff may result in an unclean environment inside the toilets. Therefore, stronger supervision is needed to ensure a clean and comfortable environment. Additionally, in order to provide a better service experience, a survey was conducted to analyze the other needs of the users regarding the neighborhood public toilets. Among them, 77.32% of the respondents hoped that the toilets could provide more services. Specifically, 63.64% of the respondents expressed a demand for charging stations, 77.27% expressed a demand for female hygiene products, and 63.63% expressed a demand for rest/waiting areas . Furthermore, during the interviews, some respondents also suggested the inclusion of caring services and assistance for the elderly.

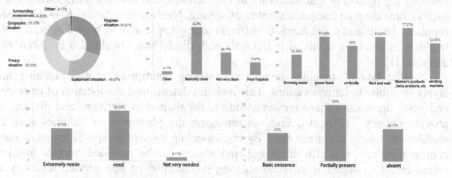

Fig. 1. Interview survey data on public toilets in the neighborhood

With the country officially entering an aging society, the scale and proportion of the elderly population in China have been consistently increasing over the past 30 years, with an accelerating growth rate. From 1990 to 2010, the total population of people aged 60 and above increased from 97 million to 178 million, with an average annual growth rate of approximately 3.06%. By the end of 2021, the national population of people aged 60 and above reached 267 million. According to statistics from the China Disabled Persons' Federation in 2022, the total number of disabled people in China has reached 85 million. The significant size of the elderly and disabled population poses higher requirements for the caring construction of neighborhood public toilets. Survey data shows that 58.33% of the respondents express a need for barrier-free facilities, and 37.5% strongly emphasize the need for barrier-free facilities(as shown in Fig. 2). This indicates a high demand for barrier-free facilities among users. At the same time, the survey also found that there is a lack of third restrooms in neighborhood public toilets, with only 25% of the respondents stating that most neighborhood public toilets are equipped with a third restroom. For the large population of the elderly and disabled, it is evident that their needs are not being met.

Through user interviews, targeted renovation designs can be implemented for the public toilets in the street blocks near Daming Lake Scenic Area, Lixia District, Jinan City. This will enhance the user experience, meet diverse user needs, and provide better public services for urban residents and tourists.Based on the diversity of the street block environment, a modular design approach is adopted to divide the public toilets in the street blocks into five modules. This includes Barrier-free module modules, gender free public restroom modules, workroom modules, men's urinal modules, and additional service modules.The design incorporates the shape and color of lotus leaves, which are characteristic elements of Jinan, and applies them to each module in conjunction with the surrounding environment. This enhances the indoor and outdoor environments of the public toilets in the street blocks, transforming them from ordinary facilities into urban public service spaces with regional characteristics, providing a better service experience for city dwellers.

To improve the public toilet search process, a user-friendly navigation interface is optimized. The application displays the user's current location, nearby public toilets, and available parking spots in real-time. It provides information on the status of public toilets and plans the best route for users. After selecting a specific toilet, real-time

Fig. 2. Block public toilet navigation interface design.

information on service scope, opening hours, available stalls, and facilities is displayed. The system updates information promptly and includes a feedback interface for users to share their experience(as shown in Fig. 2).

Fig. 3. Optimization of public restroom icons in the block.

The absence and confusion of wayfinding and indicator icons in the public restrooms of the block have brought difficulties to users.To address this issue, the design of wayfinding icons and indicator icons for street block public toilets has been created using simple lines combinations (as shown in Fig. 3),aims to clearly showcase the service functions provided by the street block public toilets.

The Barrier-free module is primarily designed for the elderly, mothers with infants, and disabled individuals. The overall space is set at 2.24 meters in length and 2.39 meters in width (as shown in Fig. 4). Considering that street block public toilets are mostly constructed on roadside locations with limited space, the accessibility facilities are integrated with the facilities for mothers and infants to create a comprehensive restroom space for special user groups (as shown in Fig.5). It is divided into a mother and infant area, a toilet area, and a cleaning area, with 1.5 meters of wheelchair activity space left in the middle to ensure easy access for wheelchair users.

Due to the different needs of different user groups, the height of the facilities within the space has been adjusted to accommodate them. Grab bars have been added

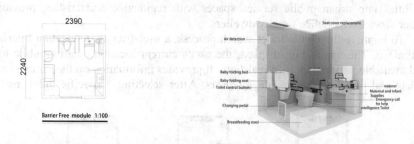

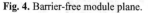

Fig. 4. Barrier-free module plane.   Fig. 5. Barrier-free module axonometric drawing.

to the washbasins, urinals, and toilets to provide support and protection for users during restroom use or cleaning. Considering the needs of the user group and the findings from preliminary research, smart toilets are used in the toilet area, and the operation buttons are placed on the side for integrated design (heating, flushing, etc.), providing clearer functional display and easier operation. Emergency call buttons are designed at low and high positions to ensure user safety. One of the main reasons for the rejection of toilet usage is hygiene concerns, so an induction device is installed on the side wall for automatic replacement of toilet seat covers by waving hands, ensuring the cleanliness of the toilet seat and improving user comfort (as shown in Fig. 6).

Fig. 6. Barrier-free module comparison effect diagram.

In terms of mother and infant facilities, considering the needs of parents going out with their children, additional facilities are provided. A breastfeeding seat is set on the left side upon entering, and other amenities such as a foldable baby bed, foldable chair, changing pedal, and hot water supply are included to assist with diaper changing, temporary care, and clothing changes for infants. During interviews with mothers and infants, many mothers expressed the inconvenience of carrying multiple items when going out with their children. Therefore, baby supplies will be provided in the cabinet beside the washbasin to reduce the burden of travel.

The workspace module serves as a space for managing the cleanliness and inspection of street block public toilets. The overall space is set at 1.72 meters wide and 1.48 meters long (as shown in Fig. 7). It is divided into a cleaning area and a workspace monitoring area (as shown in Fig. 8).

Workroom module 1:100

Fig. 7. Workroom module plane. **Fig. 8.** Workroom module drawing.

Through multiple surveys, it has been found that the management of street block

Fig. 9. Workroom module comparison effect diagram.

public toilets currently focuses on mechanized cleaning, with the workspace often left unattended and in a disorganized state. This lack of overall management can lead to usage issues. In the design of the workspace module, an intelligent monitoring screen is incorporated. The public toilet information system and management system are used to collect and analyze usage data from various modules. The indoor environment, air quality, and facility conditions are monitored. Managers can monitor and manage the various modules in real-time through the monitoring screen or mobile devices, ensuring their proper functioning. Considering the needs of the staff as stakeholders, provisions such as a refrigerator and microwave are added to one side, providing a better working environment for the staff (as shown in Fig. 9).

The original area of the public toilet at No.1 AnChasi Street is approximately 13.4m2, and the surrounding environmental area is about 225m2. It primarily includes gender-neutral toilets, a working area, and an accessible toilet (as shown in Fig. 10). However, a large amount of space around the public toilet remains unused, resulting in wasted environmental space. After the renovation, the north side of the public toilet's enclosing wall will be expanded, increasing the overall area to approximately 355m2. Each module will be incorporated within this expanded space, creating a relatively spacious environment. Based on the terrain, the working area module, men's urinals module, and accessible module will be located on the west side, while the gender-neutral toilet module and additional services module will be placed on the north side, forming a semi-enclosed arrangement (as shown in Fig. 11).

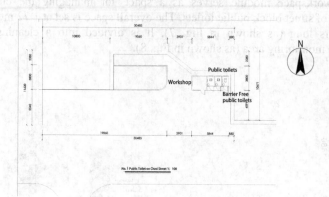

Fig. 10. The original plane graph of Public Toilet at No. 1 Anchasi Street

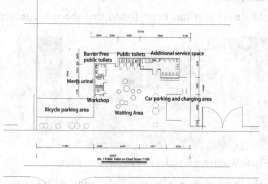

Fig. 11. Plan for Renovation of Public Toilet at No.1AnChasi Street

During on-site investigations, it was found that bicycles were often placed haphazardly, causing blockages at the entrance of the public toilet. To address this issue, the bicycle parking area is reorganized, and a canopy and flower beds are added to define the designated area and prevent bicycles from being placed randomly. Additionally, many taxi and ride-hail drivers stop in the area. Therefore, a temporary parking area for cars is planned, along with the installation of charging stations to meet the demand for electric vehicle charging. A canopy design is added based on the application of the modules. Based on lotus leaves as the basic structure.The canopy of the No. 1 Anchasi Street public toilet combines solid and void structures. The lotus leaf structure is placed within the overall design area, and the remaining parts are formed as void structures through spatial segmentation. The combination of solid and void structures, along with the addition of raindrop-inspired lotus leaf shapes, enhances the transparency and aesthetic appeal of the design. The bottom is supported by lotus leaf root structures, creating the final shape (as shown in Fig. 12.13).

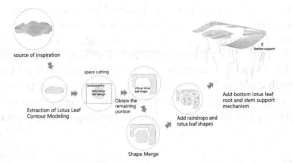

Fig. 12. Roof structure diagram of Public Toilet at No. 1 Anchasi Street.

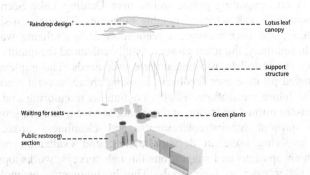

Fig. 13. Combination structure diagram of Public Toilet at No. 1 Anchasi Street.

And seats will be added in the front transition area of the area, featuring a lotus leaf shaped circular pattern, making it convenient for toilet users to temporarily wait or rest.

Fig. 14. Renderings show of public toilet at No. 1 Anchasi Street.

The final design of the renovated public toilets prioritized accessibility, hygiene, aesthetics, sustainability, and user comfort. Measures such as installing ramps, widening doorways, and providing signage ensured accessibility for all individuals, including those with disabilities. Regular cleaning schedules and adequate supplies of soap, toilet paper, and hand sanitizers maintained hygiene standards. The incorporation of touchless technology enhanced sanitation and minimized contact. Vibrant colors, artistic elements, and landscaping were used to create a visually appealing atmosphere (as shown in Fig. 14). Energy-efficient lighting, water-saving fixtures, and environmentally friendly materials promoted sustainability. User comfort was addressed through comfortable seating, well-ventilated spaces, temperature control, and amenities like baby-changing stations. Overall, the design aimed to provide a pleasant and inclusive experience for all users while minimizing environmental impact.

5. Conclusion

The research on renovating public toilets near Daming Lake Scenic Area in Lixia District, Jinan City, has achieved notable outcomes. Through on-site investigations, data collection, and user surveys, a renovation design scheme was developed and evaluated. In summary, the research successfully enhanced the quality and service level of the area's public toilets, meeting diverse user needs. The implemented renovation design garnered positive user feedback. Looking ahead, several recommendations are proposed for future renovations. Firstly, continuous monitoring and maintenance are crucial to ensure normal operation and ongoing service quality improvements. Regular inspections, prompt repairs/replacements, and cleanliness upkeep are essential. Secondly, involving users in decision-making and evaluation processes is vital. Gathering their opinions and suggestions through surveys, workshops, and suggestion boxes can better cater to their needs. Thirdly, innovative technologies like smart management systems, water-saving devices, and eco-friendly materials should be considered to enhance functionality and convenience. Lastly, sustainable development principles like energy conservation, emission reduction, and resource recycling should be prioritized. Well-planned layouts and facility selections can minimize environmental impact, while promoting sustainable management practices. In conclusion, significant progress has been made in renovating public toilets near Daming Lake Scenic Area. The findings offer valuable insights and recommendations for future designs, aiming to improve toilet quality and enhance user satisfaction.

Acknowledgment

Research Results of Social Science Planning Project in Shandong Province: Research on Public Toilet Renovation Strategies in Shandong Region from the Perspective of Urban Renewal(23CWYJ23).

References

[1] Qian Fengde, Shen Hang, Zheng Xiyang. Reflections on the "Tokyo Public Toilet" Plan and Its Impact on China's "Toilet Revolution". Meihe Times (Part 1), 2021 (08): 72-74
[2] Clara Glide Comprehensive Urban Design: Public Toilets. Beijing: Mechanical Industry Press, 2005
[3] Julie Holland Toilet God: The Civilization History of Toilets. First edition Shanghai: Century Publishing

Group Shanghai People's Publishing House, 2006

[4] Feng Suwei, Zhang Yiguo, Zhang Dongsu On the Culture of Toilets. First edition Shanghai: Tongji University Press, 2005

[5] Hao Jingtang, Zhang Hongying. The Toilet Revolution (Reportage). Beijing Literature, 2004 (8): 7-15

[6] Liu Bo. Optimization Design of Urban Public Toilets. Beijing: China Construction Industry Press, 2019: 125

[7] Li Ziwei, Chai Xiaoli General Theory of Public Toilet Design. First edition Shanghai: Tongji University Press, 2005

[8] Stickdorn, Marc. This is service design thinking:basics--tools--cases. BIS Publishers,2010.

[9] Xufang, M., & University, N. F. (2015). The survey and research on children toilet problems of city public place. Shanxi Architecture.

[10] Guangguang, D. & Jiaqing, O. U. (2017). Research on intelligent toilet based on internet of things. Journal of Guangxi Academy of Sciences.

[11] 石浦, 佑一, 沼田, 景三, 日垣, & 一男. (2015). Analysis of gaze under toilet activities in young healthy adults. 日本作業療法研究学会雑誌 = Japanese journal of occupational therapy research, 18.

[12] Gong, M., Li, K. , Tian, T. , Mao, X. , & Wang, C. . (2020). Research and analysis on the development of intelligent toilet. Journal of Physics: Conference Series, 1684(1), 012038 (5pp).

[13] Reynaert, E., Greenwood, E. E. , Ndwandwe, B. , Riechmann, M. E. , & Morgenroth, E. . (2020). Practical implementation of true on-site water recycling systems for hand washing and toilet flushing. Water Research X, 7.

Design Studies and Intelligence Engineering
L.C. Jain et al. (Eds.)
© 2024 The Authors.
This article is published online with Open Access by IOS Press and distributed under the terms
of the Creative Commons Attribution Non-Commercial License 4.0 (CC BY-NC 4.0).
doi:10.3233/FAIA231491

Exploring the Solutions of Sustainable Product Design: An ESG Perspective

Wei LI[a,1] and Jidong YANG[b]
ᵃ *Shanghai Publishing and Printing College*
ᵇ *Shanghai Tech University*

Abstract. In order to achieve "peak carbon emissions and carbon neutrality" in 2030 and 2060, every Chinese enterprise needs to take practical actions. However, for most manufacturing enterprises, the use of recyclable resources faces problems such as high costs, low acceptance, and information asymmetry, resulting in an unsatisfactory actual utilization rate. This article applies the perspective of ESG evaluation to explore how enterprises can develop sustainable development approaches that are in line with their own culture and current situation from three aspects. After comparing and summarizing different kinds of experiences of foreign and domestic companies, it is pointed out that Chinese enterprises cannot directly replicate foreign experience. Instead, they should explore a unique cooperative product design strategy by adopting modular design, building recyclable material data platforms, and constructing innovative usage scenarios.

Keywords. ESG sustainability innovation modularity information platform

1.Introduction

Since the global agreement on the United Nations Sustainable Development Goals (SDGs) in 2015, sustainable development has become a global consensus and a key demand of the international community. In the business field, the concept of sustainable development is summarized as more a specific ESG framework. Actually, the concept of ESG (Environment, Society, and Governance) was jointly proposed by the United Nations Environment Programme (UNEP) and Social Responsibility International (SRI) in 2005. It is an evaluation system that covers the comprehensive consideration of environmental protection, social responsibility, and corporate governance by enterprises[1]. In today's corporate development process, ESG involves not only ethical obligations for achieving sustainable development, but also key factors for investors, consumers, and regulatory agencies to evaluate company performance. The development of a company cannot be separated from the innovation of business models and core products, so ESG, as an evaluation system, also needs to revolve around these two factors. On the path of ESG implementation, due to differences in resource endowments, institutional policies, and cultural environment, and so on, there will be significant differences in the strategic positions and action plans of foreign and domestic companies in carrying out business models and product innovation design. Some companies prioritize environmental protection and use recyclable materials to reflect ESG, while others focus on social responsibility and collaborate with upstream and downstream enterprises to reflect ESG.

---

[1] Li Wei, PhD. Lecturer from Shanghai Publishing and Printing College; Email: hgzxliwei@126.com

Numerous scholars have gradually realized that ESG can play a very important role in mitigating corporate risks, enhancing reputations, and attracting a broader investment combination[2]. Notably, it also opens doors to innovative opportunities and a competitive edge in the market. Especially for Chinese enterprises in the transitioning period, they are facing many new challenges including cost factors, technical barriers, consumer culture, and supporting policies[3].Of course, challenges mean difficulties and also opportunities. In the overseas market, ESG has emerged as an evaluation system and a philosophy of growth based on public awareness and market consciousness, developing gradually from the grassroots level. Conversely, in the Chinese market, ESG, as an imported concept, has traversed the path from non-existence to establishment, representing a transformative force that has taken hold from the outside and is now influencing the inside. Initially, Chinese companies were compelled to adopt and respond to this concept in a passive manner. However, with the widening acceptance of ESG in the Chinese market, an increasing number of enterprises have begun to embrace it, implementing it while also reflecting on it. These companies have come to recognize the true value of ESG. Since the ESG ecosystem in China is still in the early stages of construction, for many Chinese companies, how to effectively integrate ESG into operations and explore commercial and social value from it is a challenge that lies ahead. Therefore, this article will explore the product design strategies which are the basic practices within the ESG framework by analyzing and comparing foreign and domestic experiences.

2.Product Design in the ESG Context

Product design methodology determines the underlying logic of enterprise product research and development. Traditional product design starts from meeting the needs of consumers in the market, but may neglect the public's demand when there is a conflict. In 1971, American designer Papanech published "Design for the Real World"[4], strongly criticizing design solely for commercial gain, advocating that designers abandon fancy, unsafe, immature, and useless products, save limited resources, and assume the responsibility of rational design. As a result, sustainability oriented design emerged and became a hot topic of debate in the field of product design. Over time, scholars such as Don Norman have further expanded the concept of sustainable design and proposed "ecological design"[5], emphasizing the importance of product life-cycle analysis and reducing resource consumption. It is pointed out that design should consider the entire life-cycle of the product, including the stages of manufacturing, use, and disposal, in order to minimize the impact on the environment as much as possible[6]. This laid the foundation for the rise of transition design. Transition design was first proposed by British design scholar Stuart Walker in the early 2010s. He elaborated how design can serve as a tool for gradually transition to a more sustainable approach[7] , with a particular emphasis on the cultural and social background of design, as well as the relationship between design and social values.

Although sustainable design, ecological design, and transition design may have slightly different approaches and objectives, they all share a common focus on the sustainability of enterprise and society. Often requiring interdisciplinary cooperation, these concepts span multiple fields and consider a range of influencing factors.In this trend, ESG has emerged as a global consensus in response to concerns about a range of sustainability challenges facing our planet. With the escalating urgency to address issues such as climate change, environmental degradation, and social inequality, ESG has become an integral framework for sustainable development and responsible investing. More importantly, ESG has evolved into the current important language system for international cooperation. As the demand for sustainable business practices grows, ESG has become a common denominator that enables businesses, governments, and other stakeholders to work together towards a more sustainable future. By incorporating ESG factors into decision-making processes, organizations can take a comprehensive approach to managing risks, improving reputation, and creating long-term value. With the globalization of ESG, it has also opened up new opportunities for cross-border cooperation and knowledge sharing. Therefore, it is essential for organizations to integrate ESG perspectives into their daily operations, strategic planning, business models and product design to stay relevant in today's fast-paced business environment. By embracing ESG, organizations can contribute to a more sustainable future while also mitigating risks, enhancing reputation, and creating long-term value for all stakeholders. In a country like China, with a large population and limited resources, these concepts are particularly important. ESG has emerged as a set of quantifiable evaluation indicators, particularly for listed companies, with over 60% of Fortune 500 companies releasing ESG reports each year. In this context, enterprises need to integrate ESG perspectives into the product design and development process not only to meet certain regulations but also to explore more immense markets.

3. Dilemma and chances in ESG context

At present, due to factors such as geopolitical, trade frictions, technological iteration, and evaluation standards, the concept of ESG itself has been discussed continuously, but its sustainable development proposition remains the core value of certainty. Moreover, in terms of capital, products, supply chain, technology, and other aspects, the characteristics of globalization are still significant, and an international perspective is the key to achieving long-term sustainable development for enterprises. Even for Chinese companies that have not been directly involved, their products, services, and solutions may still enter the global market through China's vast industrial manufacturing chain. Therefore, it is necessary for Chinese enterprises to consider the ESG value and direction of action from a global perspective. Currently, as China's development model is gradually shifting from one based on scale and speed to one based on quality and efficiency, the Chinese economy is entering a new stage of development. In this context, the core values of ESG—economic prosperity, environmental sustainability, and social equity—are highly aligned with important strategies such as high-quality development, common prosperity, and achieving the "Dual Carbon" goals (peak carbon emissions and carbon neutrality). With this trend, the development objectives of enterprises have also shifted from pursuing economic benefits alone to pursuing the co-development of both economic and social benefits[9].

At present, for Chinese A-share listed companies, the disclosure of ESG reports is not a mandatory task. However, in line with the mainstream requirements of the developing trends of domestic and international ESG, an increasing number of listed companies are preparing to release ESG information. It is often referred to as "Environmental, Social and Governance Report (ESG)", "Social Responsibility Report (CSR)", "Sustainable Development Report (SDR)" and the combination of relevant keywords when such information is disclosed. A total of 581 listed companies in A-shares have issued ESG reports, 947 listed companies have issued CSR reports, 82 Shanghai companies have issued SDRs, and 104 listed companies are named after keyword combinations such as "ESG", "social responsibility", and "sustainable development". according to the data from the "2022 ESG Action Report of Chinese Listed Companies" released by the International Research Institute of Green Finance at the Central University of Finance and Economics, 1455 out of all 4917 A-share listed companies have disclosed ESG or the related reports in 2022. Among these, 869 out of 2174 companies are from the Shanghai Stock Exchange and 586 out of 2743 companies are from the Shenzhen Stock Exchange.

Table 1. Disclosure of ESG Reports for All A-share Listed Companies in 2022

Stock Market	Disclosure Number	Disclosure Ratio
A-share listed companies	455	29.6%
Shanghai Stock Exchange	869	40.0%
Shenzhen Stock Exchange	586	21.4%

It seems that not all listed companies have yet paid attention to ESG, but the proportion of companies in the Shanghai and Shenzhen 300 that publish ESG reports is 86%. It can be seen that the actively traded and liquid corporate securities reflect the trend of ESG practice. Unfortunately, the information disclosed in existing ESG reports is still incomplete. In the 2023 ESG index of The Economist Intelligence Unit/EIU, China ranks 120th out of 150 countries/regions.

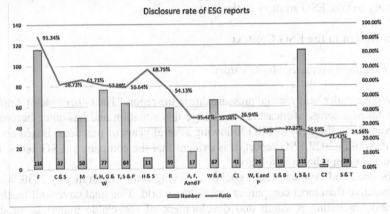

Figure 1. Disclosure rate of ESG reports for A-share listed companies
F:Finance.C&S:Culture&sports.M:Mining.E,H,G&W:Electricity,heat,gas&water.T,S&P:Transportation,storage&postal services. H&S:Health&social work. R:Real estate. A,F,A&F:Agriculture, forestry, animal husbandry&fishery. W&R:Wholesale & retail. C1:Construction. W,E&P:Water conservancy, environment & public facilities management. L&B:Leasing & business services. I,S&I:Information transmission, software & information technology services. C2:Comprehensive. S&T:Scientific research & technology services.

From the above figure, it can be seen that the top three industries in China with good ESG report disclosure are as follows: the finance industry, culture&sports industry, and mining industry. These data from the "2022 ESG Action Report of Chinese Listed Companies" shows the number and ratio of ESG reports released in China's fifteen major industries in 2022. The data of manufacturing industry isn't shown in the picture. Since 1005 manufacturing companies had released ESG related reports which was far higher than the other industries, but the disclosure ratio is only 28.86%. The low ratio may caused by the cost of using recyclable materials, technological limitations, market demand, and cultural factors[10]. Besides, ESG evaluation system may bring changes in corporate culture and management systems, as sustainable design requires comprehensive organizational adjustment and employee training. Furthermore, for listed companies, short-term market performance will be directly and quickly reflected in the company's market value. Therefore, many sustainable development projects that require long-term and large-scale investment will inevitably encounter many difficulties.

When ESG disclosure becomes mature, companies may fall into a dilemma of "business as usual". For companies, ESG reports are only a microcosm of ESG work, requiring rich practical cases and excellent performance data as support. If ESG report writing is regarded as the core or even the entire ESG work, and internal management and practical actions remain unchanged, the quality of ESG disclosure will be low and unable to meet the needs of stakeholders. For example, ESG reports lack quantitative and comparable data, and lack support from ESG cases, which makes it difficult for them to be recognized by investors and other stakeholders. In addition, with stricter regulation, the requirements for the quality of ESG disclosure and the credibility of disclosed information will become higher and higher. Therefore, more and more Chinese companies urgently need to improve the quality of ESG disclosure through internal ESG transformation and actual programs. Especially, the design of business model and the related products or services should be combined with the ESG factors to bring multiple user experiences, new opportunities and long-term competitiveness. In a word, it is hard but necessary to take ESG strategy as the lead.

4. Product Design in the ESG Context

4.1. ESG Paradigm overseas: Apple's story

Apple was once under heavy social pressure due to the report "The Other Side of Apple". But it has taken a series of measures to change this situation and has since become a leading example in the field of ESG following several years of practices. Based on the analysis of Apple's 2022 ESG report, it is evident that the company's ESG action is a systematic and comprehensive solution.

On the one hand, Apple has set a goal of achieving carbon neutrality by 2030, which is more proactive than most companies around the world. This goal covers all facets of the company, including research and development of recyclable materials, product design, supply chain management, product manufacturing, product logistics, product maintenance, energy usage, and the like. Apple is also promoting renewable energy in its global operations, such as through the use of solar and wind energy. As a company where over 80% of its total revenue is generated through hardware products, it needs to pay more attention on supply chain management, procurement of raw materials, product cycle management, as well as user privacy, data security, and so on. It reduces carbon emissions by carefully selecting materials, improving material utilization, and enhancing product energy efficiency. Additionally, it pursues various opportunities to improve energy efficiency and reduce energy consumption in its facilities and supply chain, including renovations. For example, Apple has gradually expanded the use of recycled aluminum in product material selection through research on aluminum metallurgy. Currently, according to Apple's ESG report, the casings of Apple's Apple Watch Series 7, MacBook Air, MacBook Pro, iPad, and other products are made of 100% recycled aluminum metal. Therefore, Apple will achieve its carbon neutrality goal by 2030 through the design and application of new technologies, flexible financing using innovative financial structures, and rapid deployment of renewable energy. Moreover, Apple places significant emphasis on data privacy and security. The company has implemented strict data protection measures globally to ensure the security and privacy of user data. Additionally, Apple actively engages in global data privacy standard development and regulatory activities, promoting the continuous improvement of data privacy and security levels across the industry.

On the other hand, Apple emphasizes economic inclusivity. The company supports small businesses and startups worldwide through investment and collaboration, with a focus on ethnic minorities and female entrepreneurs. Furthermore, Apple also helps people improve their skills and access to education. It has also formulated corresponding measures in terms of employee welfare and support for employee development. In its ESG report, it not only provides a detailed R&D process for sustainable materials but also elaborates on multiple training and support projects conducted by Apple around the world, fully reflecting the company's social responsibility and corporate governance level. The company has also implemented a range of practices to ensure pay equity at the intersection of race, ethnicity, and gender.To create a better work environment, Apple encourages open and honest communication among team members, managers, and leadership. The company also conducts regular surveys to gather feedback from employees, which serve as a valuable tool to assess how Apple is performing. In addition, Apple has built inclusion and diversity measures into its candidate assessment framework to promote a more inclusive workforce. In its report, Apple seems has done a lot of efforts to reflect its social responsibility and corporate governance.

In conclusion, Apple's practices have shown a standard ESG framework and set a model to other listed companies. Consequently, Apple's ESG report has received widespread recognition and praise in the financial market. Investors appreciate the company's sustainable development strategy and diversification plan, believing that these measures aid in improving the company's long-term value and performance. At the same time, consumers also acknowledge and support Apple's performance in environmental, social, and governance aspects. Generally speaking, Apple's path is a self-driven, self-defined standard path. It can establish guidelines to require relevant suppliers and partners to jointly achieve the sustainable goals that Apple has set. This may seem idealistic and difficult to achieve for many Chinese companies. Apple is unique and hard to replicate directly because its position in the global industry chain determines its voice in the system. It can view itself as an externally compatible system and incorporate the resources it needs to acquire into its system. Just like the "big pig" in the game of intelligent pigs. Apple has pricing power, initiative, and can determine the timing of action. It can construct system rules and transfer risks through the system to obtain systematic benefits. In this context, product design has been assigned a more prominent leadership role, empowered by social responsibility and supported by organizational structures, and the avenues that product design can explore are also more diverse. However, most Chinese enterprises have not yet gained such competitive advantages in the industrial chain, and are in a relatively loose and diverse supply chain system. It's hard to implement the above approaches not because the willing but because the context. On the contrary, the product design strategy of the environmentally friendly suitcase project jointly developed by companies in China has to some extent solved the problems faced by ordinary enterprises and can become a highlight of ESG information disclosure.

4.2. ESG Paradigm in China: Runmi's story

As the world's largest manufacturing economy and commodity exporter, Chinese listed companies occupy a significant position within these supply chains. To maintain their competitive edge in the export market, it is essential that they prioritize enhancing their ESG reporting and data transparency. However, the lack of specific implementation measures, especially a product or supply chain system that can reflect ESG factors, poses a significant challenge. In the process of Chinese path to modernization, ESG has enormous development potential. With the evolution and maturity of the ESG ecosystem, Chinese enterprises are gradually shifting from a "reactive" to a "proactive" mindset and moving beyond the "voluntary" disclosure phase. That's exactly the story of Runmi. Runmi Technology Ltd Company which is a Xiaomi Ecological Chain Company and produces high-tech tourism products. Its parent company is a listed company. As a leading e-commerce enterprise in the field of suitcases, Runmi is facing with a severe competitive environment and seeking market opportunities from different aspects persistently. Reducing costs and increasing efficiency is a common practice among Chinese enterprises such as Runmi. Using recyclable materials according to customary practices will inevitably lead to increased production costs and weakened market competitiveness. Runmi's designers solved this problem by sorting proper recyclable material, redefine the usage scenario and expand the application market of the material with the two other leading supplies. This process involves various stakeholders in the supply chain. For example, it needed to collaborate with upstream raw material suppliers such as Costron, one of the world's leading producers of high-quality polymers and their components. Moreover, it also required the cooperation of NONGFU Spring which is a packaging and drinking water & beverage enterprise in the upstream supply chain. Costron has the ability to purify the recyclable material to the new one. NONGFU Spring focuses on recycling the water barrels. In this default scenario, the cost of recyclable materials is likely to be higher than that of new materials. So in this way, whoever adopts the purified recyclable material will have a pressure of high material cost. So manufacturers' enthusiasm for using recyclable materials is bound to be low. However, Runmi finds a new market and a new usage for such materials. If there is a new definition and innovative application of the use of recyclable materials, the corresponding standards for recyclable materials will also change. Recyclable materials are only need to be suitable for new scenarios. The characterization of impurities can be a distinctive feature in product design, which can assist companies in developing new product styles and brand narratives without increasing the cost of cleanliness. In result, one blue ocean market is opened up.

Another crucial aspect of the process is the information flow. This collaborative process involves many companies, with each company's decisions and actions being influenced by the previous one. To enhance collaborative efficiency, it is imperative to establish a transparent and traceable recycling value chain jointly. In this process, it is essential for companies to collaborate seamlessly in terms of system, personnel, and communication. In particular, the project leaders, designers in this case, must play a pivotal role in clarifying material standards and synchronizing relevant data information to ensure the achievement of project goals. This is significantly distinct from Apple's global approach, as it fully embodies corporate social responsibility and demonstrates corporate governance by engaging with the local community.Additionally, further exploration and editorialization of the aforementioned information can elevate it to a prominent feature in the company's ESG report. As a result, Runmi utilized the material derived from the recycled water barrels of NONGFU Spring. Covestro transformed the recycled materials into the specific standards required by Runmi. On this basis, Runmi developed a range of low-carbon and environmentally friendly suitcases. This move is highly compatible with the travel and lifestyle of the new generation of consumers under the Runmi brand, enriching the brand image and helping Runmi open up new markets while garnering attention and profits in the capital market. This is not only a culmination of corporate brand enhancement, but also an illustration of companies fulfilling their social responsibility. If the seeds of utilizing recyclable materials can be sewn into consumer awareness through product iteration, it is also a means to implement environmental protection strategies.

Table 2. Tasks of each company during the innovation process

RUNMI	⟷ COVESTRO ⟷	NONGFU
Set material requirements	Process the material	Build recycling systems
Define product concept	Test material properties	Collect water barrels
Produce "ESG" suitcases	Provide related certificates	Transport recycled materials

By refining the design strategy of this suitcase with distinct ESG attributes (as illustrated in Figure 2), it was discovered that in this sustainable design endeavor, particularly the collaborative process, the modularity of product design thinking serves as the foundation. Designers can select materials based on distinct modules. For instance, although the performance of PC materials recycled by Costron from NONGFU Spring may not be as good as the original PC or PCR materials (such as cleanliness, particle size, and other standards), these "non-standard" features can also become a distinctive form of travel suitcases that caters to the novel and specific needs of its target customers. In this way the recycling approach itself is not the key problem.

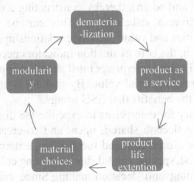

Figure 2. Design Strategy in ESG context

Furthermore, due to the significant risk of data loss in enterprise-to-enterprise information exchange, the establishment of digital industry frameworks and platforms holds paramount importance. Organizations need to leverage digital discourse structures and systems to achieve information transparency and efficient integration. When designers collaborate with diverse departments of different enterprises in research and development, they must be able to discern stakeholder requirements and offer innovative solutions to meet product design objectives in the ESG context. Ultimately, collaborations between companies also involve a clash and reconciliation of distinct governance structures, necessitating more standardized operational procedures. Hence, it is imperative for companies to recognize the importance of such cooperation and allocate the necessary resources to facilitate it. In particular, robust communication is essential to confirm comprehension and implementation of the standards. Especially designers need to integrate business strategies to achieve goals.

5. Conclusion

ESG is not just an evaluation system, but a set of thought tools. The core components of these are consistent, but the implementation approach varies, as there are many roads leading to Rome. According to the SCP theory of industrial economics, the industrial structure determines corporate behavior and corresponding performance. The paths taken by different enterprises in implementing ESG for their own product design and development depend on their respective backgrounds and structural locations. It is not advisable to blindly copy the so-called advanced experiences when implementing ESG. Instead, they need to carefully analyze their own situations and explore distinctive roads. As the environment rapidly changes for many Chinese companies, there are significant differences in industrial foundations. There are many obstacles to implementing the ESG concept and adopting the method of independently building closed systems. Therefore, taking the path of collaborative innovation with other enterprises is a worthwhile direction to explore.

Firstly, it is imperative to bridge the professional expertise of upstream and downstream participants and implement recycling strategies through essential knowledge and technological transactions. Additionally, the value-added aspirations of enterprise production activities must be seamlessly integrated with sustainable development objectives (such as environmental protection, social responsibility, and organizational governance, and so on), thereby constructing a mechanism and standard for the involvement of diverse stakeholders. This can be achieved by exploring sustainable value opportunities and value exchange relationships at various stages of the product life-cycle. In a word, the core evaluation indicators need to be unified. To truly unlock the potential of ESG value, enterprises must abandon opportunism, adhere to first principles, and focus on creating social value. By making continuous investments and refinements, they can reap the benefits that ESG brings.

Secondly, it is necessary for enterprises to expedite the digital transformation. The digitization of enterprises reflects a shared, open, and co-creative approach to digital thinking. By employing the aforementioned mechanism, enterprises can interface with digital platforms and establish specific digital sharing among collaborative organizations, facilitating consensus-building and decision-making.Since collaborative partners are interconnected, data from upstream companies directly affects product decisions in downstream companies. Especially in the consumer market, the agility and readiness of data platforms also determine an enterprise's accurate feedback to market information. Apart from physical information sharing, a fair and amicable cooperation atmosphere is necessary. In particular, data security is a concern since each company's data contains its own trade secrets. Therefore, a collaborative platform must ensure data fluidity while maintaining the most basic level of reliability and traceability.Establish an ESG digital management system within the enterprise. Besides, the application of ESG digital management system can improve the efficiency of enterprise ESG management, especially the smoothness and timeliness of ESG information and data flow within the enterprise, and high-quality ESG data is also a prerequisite for high-quality ESG reports. In this regard, ESG digitization can provide important support for the formulation, execution, supervision, optimization, and transparency of ESG strategies for enterprises.

Thirdly, modularity becomes the initial layout logic of the design. By dematerializing and modularizing the design, the standards for material selection, application scenarios, and traceability paths can be addressed at the source. However, it is worth noting that the level of granularity in modularity determines the efficiency of information flow between enterprises and the cost of management. This requires designers involved not only to have a product-oriented mindset but also to adopt a systemic, project-oriented mindset. They need to consider a product not only as a standalone product but also as a service system; and then explore a sustainable product design path that aligns with the company's actual situation and reflects the company's various values amidst complex information.While design may not be omnipotent, it can be transformed and enhanced through training. Especially in the age of AI, designers need to utilize tools to improve efficiency while continuously improving the self-awareness, expanding their boundaries and tapping into resources to drive enterprise innovation.

Currently, while ESG information disclosure remains a focal point for the majority of Chinese companies, an increasing number of Chinese enterprises are realizing that ESG information disclosure needs to be founded on high-quality ESG management and practice. Furthermore, outstanding ESG performance can assist companies in establishing competitive advantages in areas such as financial connectivity, market competition, talent attraction, and brand influence. This transformation arises from the company's deep understanding of the essence of ESG, as well as from learning from global best-practice cases. For the Chinese market, ESG is an imported concept that showcases global universality while also exhibiting discontinuities, such as environmental protection, low-carbon, circular economy, fairness, inclusiveness, data privacy, and corporate governance rationality. When ESG takes root and grows in China, it is necessary to fully consider China's unique cultural background and social foundation, as each country is at a different stage of development and attaches importance to different issues. Therefore, enterprises should consider both the global market and localization when implementing ESG practices.

Acknowledgment
This article is sponsored by the campus research initiation project of Shanghai Publishing and Printing College.

References
[1]Martina K.Linnenluecke. Environmental, social and governance (ESG) performance in the context of multinational business research. *Multinational Business Review*,(3) 2022(52-53) .

[2] Giulia Wally Scurati et al. Exploring the Use of Virtual Reality to Support Environmentally Sustainable Behavior: A Framework to Design Experiences. *Sustainability*, (13)2021(102-104).

[3] Sustainable manufacturing and industry 4.0: what we know and what we don' t. *Journal of Enterprise Information Management*, (4)2020(89-92) .

[4] Papanek, V. *Design for the Real World: Human Ecology and Social Change*, Thames & Hudson. 1971.

[5] Norman, D. A., & Verganti, R. Incremental and Radical Innovation: Design Research vs. Technology and Meaning Change. *Design Issues*, (30)2014(39-42).

[6] Shamraiz Ahmad et al. Sustainable product design and development: A review of tools, applications and research prospects. *Resources, Conservation and Recycling*, (132)2018(135-137).

[7] Irwin, T.The Emerging Transition Design Approach, *DRS International Conference* , 2018.

[8] Marita Sauerwein et al. Exploring the potential of additive manufacturing for product design in a circular economy. *Journal of Cleaner Production*, (226)2019(68-72).

[9] Zhao, J., & Li, Z. Implementing Sustainable Development Strategies in China: The Case of New Energy Vehicles. *International Journal of Sustainable Development & World Ecology*, (16)2009(88-90).

[10] Impact of lean Manufacturing Practices on Firms' Sustainable Performance: Lean Culture as a Moderator. *Sustainability*, (11)2019(60-65).

Design Studies and Intelligence Engineering
L.C. Jain et al. (Eds.)
© 2024 The Authors.
This article is published online with Open Access by IOS Press and distributed under the terms
of the Creative Commons Attribution Non-Commercial License 4.0 (CC BY-NC 4.0).
doi:10.3233/FAIA231492

The Preliminary Validation of PCMI in the Context of Museum Creativity

Hui CHENG [a, b, *] and Xiao QIU [a, c]

[a] *Zhejiang University of Finance and Economics Dongfang College*

[b] *University of Nottingham Ningbo China*

[c] *North China Electric Power University*

Abstract. This article aims to examine the findings from our previous research. Using the indicators from the PCMI model (Product Creativity Measurement Instrument) with the highest factor loading in each metric, six hypotheses have been proposed based on the previous conclusions, and an online survey was designed. One hundred seventy-four participants (43.10% males and 56.90% females, 51.15% consumers and 48.85% experts) across China were invited to assess the five Storm Bottles selected from the top museums worldwide. The result meets the criterion of reliability (Cronbach's α=0.95) and model fit. The result revealed that gender and expertise do not influence the perception of museum creativity. The data supported integrating Emotion, Attraction and Desire into the metric of Affect, and it is also proven that Affect rather than Novelty is the leading dimension impacting museum creativity. That Desire is a fast predictor for Creativity was supported by the result. Usefulness and Importance are found relevant, and positive relationships between Usefulness and Novelty, as well as Attraction, were witnessed.

Keywords. Product Design, Museum Creativity, Creativity Measurement, Metric Correlation, PCMI

1. Introduction

In the previous study, the authors of this paper found that the museum's creative industries are facing problems, and one of the dominant issues is the homogenization of the museum's creative products and the creativity deficiency in these kinds of products [1-9]. After reviewing the literature, we found no creativity measurement model designed for the museum's creativity. To fill the gap, we started the inquiry on the construction of a creativity measurement model for museum creativity. Before this paper, we conducted an online survey using five Storm Bottles from the top museums worldwide, and 224 participants were invited to rate the product samples independently (the overall Cronbach's α is 0.95) [10]. We analyzed the data in two steps and reported them in two papers. In the first paper of this serial, we analyzed the data by comparing the average scores of each dimension. We found: (1) Differences in gender and expertise may influence the measurement of creativity; (2) The products with high creativity share the same order of six metrics. Thus, there may be a "recipe" for improving product creativity; (3) Emotion is the leading dimension in high-creativity products. Therefore,

---

* Corresponding author: chenghui2050@163.com.

this dimension may be dominant in creativity assessment; (4) Novelty is not predominant in the sample assessment, and this phenomenon may happen in other museum's cultural and creative products; (5) Usefulness is easily influenced by other factors, which may include the preferences and interests of customers; (6) Importance ranks the last in all dimensions among all products, and this may be caused by the fact that we used products with the same function [10]. In the second paper, we put all the data in a line chart and found metrics correlations in the PCMI model. The findings of this paper include: (1) Emotion, Attraction, and Desire have positive relevance, and they can be bundled as Affect; (2) Affect dimension other than Novelty is the factor that impacts creativity assessment of museums' creativity positively dominantly, and significantly; (3) Importance has little impact on Overall creativity score, and this dimension may be ignored; however, it needs further validation; (4) Resolution has significant negative relevance with Novelty, while it has positive relevance with Attraction; (5) Desire may be a fast predictor for Creativity, but it has not been validated .

This paper aims to prove the reliability and validity of previous studies' results, find evidence through statistical analysis to support the findings and amend the conclusion if needed. We will analyze the results by Stata, SPSSPRO and SmartPLS.

The main findings from the two previous studies are summarized as follows: (1) Gender and experience may influence the perception of museum creativity; (2) Affect rather than Novelty is the leading dimension that impacts museum creativity; (3) Emotion, Attraction and Desire can be bundled into the dimension of Affect; (4) Usefulness is quickly impacted by other dimensions such as Novelty and Attraction; (5) Importance is relevant to Usefulness. Based on this, we proposed hypotheses as follows (See Table 1).

Table 1. Hypotheses from the Previous Studies

Hypotheses	Statements
H1	Gender and experience influence the perception of museum creativity.
H2	Emotion, Attraction and Desire can be bundled into the dimension of Affect.
H3	Affect rather than Novelty is the leading dimension that impacts museum creativity.
H4	Desire is a fast predictor of Creativity.
H5	Usefulness is negatively impacted by Novelty and positively influenced by Attraction.
H6	Importance is relevant to Usefulness.

2. Method

Following the instruments used in previous studies [10], we used the PCMI model for this assessment. The metrics include Novelty, Usefulness, Emotion, Attraction, Importance and Desire [11]. In Horn's model validation stage, they identified 41 pairs of adjectives and then categorized them into 6 metrics, each with several pairs. Lu and Luh [12] felt that using the PCMI model is time-consuming. To save time, they introduced a strategy by which any indicators whose factor loadings are below the threshold (they set >0.8) will be discarded. Following such a strategy, we chose the metrics with the highest factor loading. We selected the positive polar from the list. The indicators are Rare, Functional, Appealed, Favorable, Important, and Desire. We adjusted them in the style of 5-point Likert Scales (1 represents the lowest score, and 5 means the highest score). Correspondingly, the museum creative products we use are still "Strom Bottles" [10, 13], namely, Gayer-Anderson Cat, Anubis, Rosetta Stone, Qianli Jiangshan, and William the Hippopotamus.

Our target participants are experts in the design domain and general consumers of museum creativity. We adopted the criterion of experts following the tradition of creativity research, where experts are defined as anyone with domain knowledge of more than 8 years [14-16]. One hundred seventy-four participants across China were invited to participate in our survey to improve the data's diversity. Regarding the gender of participants, 43.10% of them are males, and 56.90% are females. Regarding group division, 51.15% are general consumers, and 48.85% are experts. Our previous report includes detailed demographics and descriptive statistics [10].

3. Result

3.1 Reliability and Validity Test

The Cronbach's α is 0.925, indicating the data are of high reliability. The KMO and Bartlett's p-values are 0.86 and 0, respectively, supporting the factor analysis. The AVE values of the metrics generated in the process of confirmatory factor analysis are 0.495 (Rare), 0.466 (Functional), 0.663 (Appealed), 0.584 (Favorable), 0.53 (Important), and 0.543 (Desirable), indicating metrics except for Rare and Functional are well extracted. Table 2 shows that only the AVE square roots of Rare and Functional are more significant than other metrics' Pearson correlations, suggesting only these two metrics have excellent discriminant validity. The model is of good fit because GFI=1 (>0.9), RMR=0 (<0.05), CFI=0.993 (>0.9), NFI=1 (>0.9), and NNFI=1.018 (>0.9).

Table 2. Discriminant Validity: Pearson Correlations and AVE Square Root

	Rare	Functional	Appealed	Favorable	Important	Desirable
Rare	0.704					
Functional	0.629	0.683				
Appealed	0.67	0.631	0.814			
Favorable	0.647	0.657	0.865	0.764		
Important	0.496	0.662	0.659	0.663	0.728	
Desirable	0.552	0.634	0.734	0.779	0.8	0.737

```
              | Attrac~n Useful~s  Novelty  Emotion Import~e   Desire Creati~y
 -------------+------------------------------------------------------------------
   Attraction |  1.0000

    Usefulness |  0.5543*  1.0000
               |  0.0000

       Novelty |  0.5456*  0.5236*  1.0000
               |  0.0000   0.0000

       Emotion |  0.7892*  0.5338*  0.5832*  1.0000
               |  0.0000   0.0000   0.0000

    Importance |  0.5943*  0.6088*  0.4631*  0.5554*  1.0000
               |  0.0000   0.0000   0.0000   0.0000

        Desire |  0.7387*  0.5537*  0.5068*  0.7048*  0.6812*  1.0000
               |  0.0000   0.0000   0.0000   0.0000   0.0000

    Creativity |  0.8653*  0.7693*  0.7410*  0.8555*  0.7974*  0.8574*  1.0000
               |  0.0000   0.0000   0.0000   0.0000   0.0000   0.0000
```

Figure 1. Pairwise Correlations Coefficients of the Metrics

We tested the correlations of each metric in Stata SE (V 17.0). In the process, we calculated the Correlation Matrix of the metrics, figured out the Pairwise Correlation Coefficients, and marked any value whose p-value is smaller than 0.001 with "*" (See Figure 1). As we can read from the report, the survey results are significant. The inner correlations of the six metrics and their relationship with Creativity are all superficially positive. The results follow what we got from confirmatory factor analysis.

3.2 The Moderating Effects of Gender and Expertise

Through average score comparison, the previous study revealed that gender and expertise may influence the rating of museum creativity [10]. We tested the moderating effects of these two factors in SmartPLS. It was found that no such moderating effects on Creativity. Thus, we rejected H1 (Gender and expertise influence the perception of museum creativity).

3.3 The Metrics of Affect in Creativity Measurement

● The Correlation of Emotion, Desire, and Attraction

From Figure 1, we found that the correlation of the metrics is all positive. Moreover, the results are significant and of high reliability since the p-values are 0. In addition, we found the values of Attraction-Creativity, Emotion-Creativity and Desire-Creativity are over 0.8; therefore, we concluded they are highly relevant. We conducted further confirmation using SmartPLS with the PLS-SEM algorithm and Bootstrapping. Before data analysis, we followed the strategy of average score calculation, which is also used in the most predominant creativity assessment models, including the CAT and CPSS models [17]. We calculated the Affect Score for each sample by the formula (1), and the final data analysis report is shown in Figure 2.

$$\text{Pleasure Score} = \frac{\text{Emotion Score} + \text{Attraction Score} + \text{Desire Score}}{3} \quad (1)$$

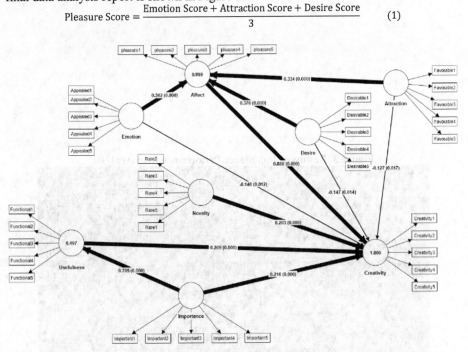

Figure 2. Path Coefficients and T values of the Metrics

In Figure 2, the values before the brackets along the path are Path Coefficients (β values), indicating the importance of the correlation between the Independent Variable and Dependent Variable (e.g. Novelty is vital to Creativity). The report revealed that the three β values (Emotion-Creativity, Desire-Creativity, and Attraction-Creativity) are negative. In comparison, the four β values (Affect-Creativity, Desire-Affect, Attraction-Affect, and Emotion-Affect) are positive. The paths are considered valid since the positive β values fall in the range of [0,1]. The values in brackets are p values, suggesting the significance of Independent Variables on the Dependent Variable. Also, we found the p values and β values (Emotion-Affect, Desire-Affect, and Attraction-Affect) are relatively high compared with that of Emotion-Creativity, Desire-Creativity, and Attraction-Creativity which strengthens the possibility of regarding them as a bundle. Furthermore, the R2 is 0.999, indicating the model has an excellent explanation. Regarding the role of Affect in Creativity assessment, we found that the β value of Affect-Creativity is far more significant than that of Novelty-Creativity.

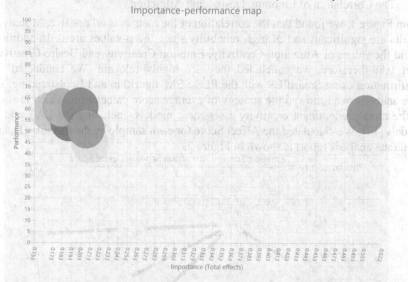

Figure 3. Results of Importance Performance Map Analysis

	Attrac~n	Useful~s	Novelty	Emotion	Import~e	Desire	Affect	Creati~y
Attraction	1.0000							
Usefulness	0.5543* 0.0000	1.0000						
Novelty	0.5456* 0.0000	0.5236* 0.0000	1.0000					
Emotion	0.7892* 0.0000	0.5338* 0.0000	0.5832* 0.0000	1.0000				
Importance	0.5943* 0.0000	0.6088* 0.0000	0.4631* 0.0000	0.5554* 0.0000	1.0000			
Desire	0.7387* 0.0000	0.5537* 0.0000	0.5068* 0.0000	0.7048* 0.0000	0.6812* 0.0000	1.0000		
Affect	0.9242* 0.0000	0.6007* 0.0000	0.5990* 0.0000	0.9145* 0.0000	0.6696* 0.0000	0.8935* 0.0000	1.0000	
Creativity	0.8653* 0.0000	0.7693* 0.0000	0.7410* 0.0000	0.8555* 0.0000	0.7974* 0.0000	0.8574* 0.0000	0.9436* 0.0000	1.0000

Figure 4. Pairwise Correlations Coefficients of the Metrics, Including the Affect Dimension

Following this analysis, we conducted Importance Performance Map Analysis (IPMA) in SmartPLS. It proved the role of the Affect in the creativity assessment for museum culture and creativity from another perspective. As we can see from the IPMA report (See Figure 3), the Affect has an extremely high value in the Importance Axis, suggesting the Affect rather than Novelty is the highest priority in creativity assessment.

Further, we validated the Affect dimension in Stata SE and discovered that the values of Affect-Creativity, Affect-Attraction, and Emotion-Affect are more significant than 0.9, and the value of Desire-Affect is near 0.9 (See Figure 4). These results indicate that the Affect dimension is highly relevant to Attraction, Emotion, and Desire. Moreover, the value of Affect-Creativity is more extensive than that of Novelty-Creativity, indicating Affect rather than Novelty is the leading dimension in museum creativity.

We noticed that the β values of Emotion-Creativity, Desire-Creativity, and Attraction-Creativity in Figure 2 are all negative. It may indicate that the Affect metric is a potential mediator. To confirm its role, we calculated the VAF value for each pair (Emotion-Affect-Creativity, Desire-Affect-Creativity, and Attraction-Affect-Creativity) by formula (1)-(3) and the corresponding VAF values are 176.9%, 179.6%, and 175.7%. Hair and Hult [15] pointed out that a VAF value greater than 80% can be considered "Full Mediation"; therefore, the Affect can be regarded as a mediator for Emotion, Attraction and Desire. Therefore, Emotion, Attraction and Desire can be bundled and even replaced by the Affect in creativity assessment for museum culture and creativity. Thus, we finally accepted hypotheses H2 (Emotion, Attraction and Desire can be bundled into the dimension of Affect) and H3 (Affect rather than Novelty is the leading dimension that impacts museum creativity).

● The Correlation of Desire and Creativity

Since the Desire and the Creativity Overall lines overlap, and the gaps are no more significant than 0.11 (See Table 3), we might use the score of the Desire aspect to fast predict the overall level of Creativity in museum culture and creativity.

Table 3. The Gaps between the Score of the Desire Dimension and the Overall Creativity

Product Sample	Desire	Creativity Overall Score	Absolute Gap Score
Gayer-Anderson Cat	3.33	3.32	0.01
Anubis	3.27	3.31	0.04
Rosetta Stone	3.24	3.24	0.00
Qianli Jiangshan	3.06	3.10	0.04
William the Hippopotamus	2.92	3.03	0.11

We analyzed the data with a t-test in Stata SE; the report is shown in Figure 5. From the result, we found the p values (0.1939, 0.3879, and 0.8061, respectively) are all larger than 0.05, supporting the hypothesis that Desire and Creativity are similar, and Desire can be used as a metric to fast predict the overall value of Creativity in museum cultural and creative products. Therefore, we accepted H4 (Desire is a fast predictor for Creativity).

```
Two-sample t test with equal variances
-----------------------------------------------------------------------------
Variable |      Obs        Mean    Std. err.   Std. dev.  [99.9% conf. interval]
---------+-------------------------------------------------------------------
  Desire | 1,110    3.157658   .0325646   1.084945    3.050216    3.265099
Creati~y | 1,110    3.193844   .0263612   .8782669     3.10687    3.280818
---------+-------------------------------------------------------------------
Combined | 2,220    3.175751   .0209474   .9869739    3.106731    3.244771
---------+-------------------------------------------------------------------
    diff |          -.0361862   .0418971              -.1742338    .1018614
-----------------------------------------------------------------------------
    diff = mean(Desire) - mean(Creativity)                    t =  -0.8637
H0: diff = 0                              Degrees of freedom =      2218

   Ha: diff < 0                  Ha: diff != 0                  Ha: diff > 0
Pr(T < t) = 0.1939        Pr(|T| > |t|) = 0.3879         Pr(T > t) = 0.8061
```

Figure 5. The t-test Result of Desire-Creativity

3.4 The Metrics of Usefulness and Importance in Creativity Measurement

As per Maslow's human need model, museum cultural and creative product does not belong to the category of daily necessity; thus, the importance of this category is low. Complaints about the Usefulness and function of the products are often witnessed in reports and surveys [18]. Based on this fact, we decided to examine the Usefulness metric closely.

- *The Correlation of Usefulness and Novelty*

Our previous study pointed out that the possible reason to explain this phenomenon is that Novelty and Attraction, besides Importance, impact Usefulness. We visually discovered that Novelty is a factor that may influence Usefulness negatively. However, the Pairwise Correlations Coefficient offered by Stata SE (value=0.5236, see Figure 1) in our research has not proven it. Moreover, the Linear Trend Test report (See Figure 6, Prob > F = 0.0000) confirms the positive correlation between Usefulness and Novelty.

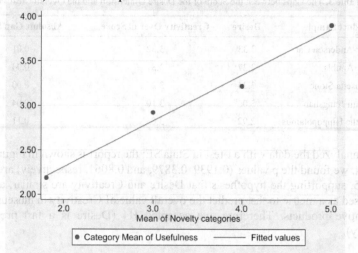

Figure 6. The Linear Trend Test Report for Usefulness and Novelty

- *The Correlation between Usefulness and Attraction*

As stated in our previous studies, apart from the impact of Novelty, Attraction may be another factor that positively impacts Usefulness. As the Pairwise Correlations Coefficient by Stata SE (value=0.5543, see Figure 1) and the Linear Trend Test report (See Figure 7, Prob > F = 0.0000) indicate, the correlation is confirmed as positive too.

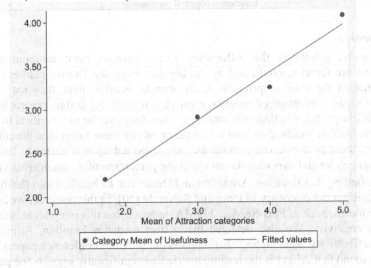

Figure 7. The Linear Trend Test Report for Usefulness and Attraction

- *The Correlation between Usefulness and Importance*

We found the line of Importance lies at the bottom of the chart and discovered the two Creativity Overall (one excludes Importance, and another includes) lines parallel on most occasions except causing a slight drop in the Overall score of Anubis. It seems that Importance has little influence on the Creativity Overall score except by pulling down the numeric value. However, it needs further confirmation. To confirm the role of Importance, we calculated the VAF value (Variance Accounted For) for Usefulness-Importance-Creativity. The VAF values of Usefulness and Importance are 40.5% and 42.1%, respectively, falling from 20% to 80%. Hair, Hult, Ringle, and Sarstedt (2014) pointed out that the VAF value between 20% and 80% can be considered "Partial Mediation", meaning Importance is a partial mediator in the correlation of Usefulness-Creativity.

In sum, H5 (Usefulness is negatively impacted by Novelty and positively influenced by Attraction) is only partially supported by the result because the impacts of Novelty and Attraction on Usefulness are proven all positive. Moreover, H6 (Importance is relevant to Usefulness) is accepted since we have found a mediating effect between Importance and Usefulness.

In sum, we obtained the decisions for the proposed hypotheses (See Table 4).

Table 4. Decisions of the Hypotheses

Hypotheses	Statements	Decisions
H1	Gender and experience influence the perception of museum creativity.	Rejected
H2	Emotion, Attraction and Desire can be bundled into the dimension of Affect.	Accepted

Hypotheses	Statements	Decisions
H3	Affect rather than Novelty is the leading dimension that impacts museum creativity.	Accepted
H4	Desire is a fast predictor of Creativity.	Accepted
H5	Usefulness is negatively impacted by Novelty and positively influenced by Attraction.	Partially Accepted
H6	Importance is relevant to Usefulness.	Accepted

4. Discussion

Theoretically, gender is the influencing factor because most museum creativity consumers are females, confirmed by the big data from the Taobao market [19]. The appearance of the creative products easily attracts females; thus, they may be more sensitive to the perception of museum creativity. Intuitively, design experts have seen more creative products in their surroundings. Thus, they may be more critical to museum creativity. In other words, they tend to rate the creativity score lower than the consumers. However, these preconceived notions are not supported by this research. Instead, we found that gender and expertise do not affect the perception of museum creativity.

The finding that Emotion, Attraction and Desire can be bundled into the dimension of Affect is per the discovery of Horn and Salvendy [20]. In this research, we have used multiple means, such as PLS-SEM and IPMA, to prove that this integration is reliable in museum creativity. We also detected that Affect mediates Emotion, Attraction and Desire in Creativity. This finding also supports our previous conference papers [10, 13]. We also found that Affect is the leading metric that significantly impacts the perception of Creativity, which corresponds with our previous in-depth investigation [13]. However, we are uncertain about the working mechanism of the Affect dimension on overall Creativity. Because Affect is usually evoked by other visual and olfactory factors of a product, including the shape, the texture, the color, or even the odor, these attributes can be labelled as Aesthetics and the Affect triggered is called Aesthetic Pleasure.

Our research supported the notion that Desire is a fast predictor of museum creativity. Horn and Salvendy [11] defined Desire as the product's desirability to a consumer. As we all know, product purchase balances the product's attributes, including appearance, function, uniqueness, and price. If the consumer desires to own the product eagerly, it may suggest it is satisfactory in almost all aspects. Otherwise, the consumer will not have any desire to purchase it. However, since few pieces of the literature revealed that Desire can fast predict Creativity, we decided to test this hypothesis further.

We discovered that Novelty and Attraction positively influence the perception of a product's functionality. Since we also proved that Importance is relevant to Usefulness, we may infer that Novelty and Attraction impact Usefulness and Importance. The reason for the influencing mechanism is that when consumers or their attentions perceive the uniqueness of a product, they may exaggerate the perception of the product's Importance and add extra values beyond the functionality.

We witnessed an imperfection in the process of confirmatory factor analysis where some indicators failed to meet the threshold of the statistical criteria. Since we reserve only one indicator with the highest factor loading for each metric, it is impossible to delete the unsatisfactory ones. Although the strategy introduced by Lu and Luh [12] did have at least more than two indicators for each metric, it is less rigorous to delete the indicators based on the factor loadings of the model inventors because the factor loadings are context-specific. In other words, the original PCMI model is tested in generic products, which is not the same context as museum creativity. Thus, transplanting the factor loadings of metrics into museum creativity faced unexpected challenges in the validity test.

5. Conclusion

This paper tested the findings concluded in our two previous conference papers. This research found that gender and expertise do not influence the perception of museum creativity. The data supported integrating Emotion, Attraction and Desire into the metric of Affect, and it is also proven that Affect rather than Novelty is the leading dimension impacting museum creativity. We also discovered that Desire is a fast predictor of Creativity. Although we can find the explanation in the product purchase process, we must further validate the hypothesis. Usefulness and Importance are found relevant, and positive relationships between Usefulness and Novelty, as well as Attraction, were witnessed. This research's main drawback is the indicators we used in the survey. Although the strategy of reducing indicators is from the literature, we faced unexpected indicators' validity issues in the validity test stage. The suggestion for validating the PCMI model in a new realm is to use the whole set of indicators rather than adopting some strategies to reduce the number of indicators.

Acknowledgments

This research is supported by the Provincial Fundamental and Commonweal Research Projects of Zhejiang (LGF22G030015).

References

[1] Bao, G. and W. Lu, *A Review of the Development of Cultural and Creative Products in Cultural Relics and Museums Institutions*. Art and Design (Theory) (艺术与设计(理论版)), 2019. **2**(12): p. 89-91.

[2] Cheng, H., *A Study on the Causes of the "Homogenisation" in Museum Creative Products*. Art and Design (Theory) (艺术与设计(理论版)), 2019. **2**(04): p. 95-97.

[3] Cheng, H., *Museum's Cultural and Creative Industry: Present Situation, Problem and Direction*. Packaging Engineering (包装工程), 2019. **40**(24): p. 65-71.

[4] Li, Y., *Design of Cultural and Creative Products of Traditional Festivals Based on Cultural Consumption*. Packaging Engineering (包装工程), 2019. **40**(14): p. 264-267.

[5] Zhao, Y., et al., *Research on the design strategy and application of cultural IP in museums: The example of Henan Provincial Museum*. Highlights in Art and Design, 2023. **2**(2): p. 89-93.

[6] Chakrabarti, A. and P. Khadilkar, *A measure for assessing product novelty*, in *International Conference on Engineering Design 2003 (ICED03)*. 2003: Stockholm. p. 159-160.

[7] Cheng, H., *Research of User-Centered Intelligent Technology in China's Cultural and Creative Product Design*, in *International Conference on Energy Resources and Sustainable Development 2020 (ICERSD2020)*, M. ANPO and F. Song, Editors. 2021, EDP Sciences: Harbin, China.

[8] Cheng, H., *Model Construction of Museum Culture and Creativity Industry with Society Governance Targeted*, in *International Conference on Economic Innovation and Low-carbon Development 2021 (EILCD2021)*, F. Wen and S.M. Ziaei, Editors. 2021, EDP Sciences: Qingdao, China. p. 03040 (5 pp.).

[9] Cheng, H., et al., *Exploring the Chinese Design Concepts That Shape China's Cultural and Creative Products for Museums*, in *International Symposium on Design Studies and Intelligence Engineering 2022 (DSIE2022)*, L.C. Jain, et al., Editors. 2023, IOS Press: Hangzhou, China. p. 1-12.

[10] Cheng, H., et al., *Insights on Metrics' Correlation of Creativity Assessment for Museum Cultural and Creative Product Design*, in *International Conference on Human-Computer Interaction 2023 (HCII2023)*, C. Stephanidis, et al., Editors. 2023, Springer, Cham: Copenhagen, Denmark. p. 376-384.

[11] Horn, D. and G. Salvendy, *Product creativity: conceptual model, measurement and characteristics*. Theoretical Issues in Ergonomics Science, 2006. **7**(4): p. 395-412.

[12] Lu, C.-C. and D.-B. Luh, *A Comparison of Assessment Methods and Raters in Product Creativity*. Creativity Research Journal, 2012. **24**(4): p. 331-337.

[13] Cheng, H., et al., *An In-depth Analysis of PCMI Dimensions for Museum Creativity*. Thinking Skills and Creativity, 2023. **50**: p. 101407.

[14] Björklund, T.A., *Initial mental representations of design problems: Differences between experts and novices.* Design Studies, 2013. **34**(2): p. 135-160.

[15] Chulvi, V., et al., *Assessment of the Relationships Among Design Methods, Design Activities, and Creativity.* Journal of Mechanical Design, 2012. **134**(11).

[16] Ahmed, S., K.M. Wallace, and L.T. Blessing, *Understanding the differences between how novice and experienced designers approach design tasks.* Research in Engineering Design, 2003. **14**(1): p. 1-11.

[17] Horn, D. and G. Salvendy, *Consumer-based assessment of product creativity: A review and reappraisal.* Human Factors and Ergonomics in Manufacturing & Service Industries, 2006. **16**(2): p. 155-175.

[18] Cheng, H., *Ways of Avoiding the Problem of Cultural Creative Products' Similarity, Basing on Haining.* Design, 2018. **298**(19): p. 96-99.

[19] Cheng, H., *Design Governance: Museum Cultural Creativity and Its Tool Design from a Perspective of Governance.* 2023, Hangzhou: Zhejiang University Press.

[20] Horn, D. and G. Salvendy, *Measuring consumer perception of product creativity: Impact on satisfaction and purchasability.* Human Factors and Ergonomics in Manufacturing & Service Industries, 2009. **19**(3): p. 223-240.

Design Studies and Intelligence Engineering 775
L.C. Jain et al. (Eds.)
© 2024 The Authors.
This article is published online with Open Access by IOS Press and distributed under the terms
of the Creative Commons Attribution Non-Commercial License 4.0 (CC BY-NC 4.0).
doi:10.3233/FAIA231493

Research on Parameterized Design of Urban Furniture in Wuyi Overseas Chinese Hometown from the Perspective of Digitalization and Localization

Liang CHEN [a,1], Zhenyi CHEN [a,2], Mingyuan Wu[b], and Ze LI[c]
a Wuyi University, Jiangmen, China
b Guangdong Jiangmen Vocational College of Traditional Chinese Medicine, Jiangmen, China
c City University of Macau, Macao Special Administrative Region, China

Abstract. "In the context of parametric design based on visual programming, this study explores an innovative approach combining digitization and localization. It applies a two-way progressive structural topology optimization algorithm to conduct research on innovative urban furniture design in the Wuyi Overseas Chinese Hometown. It utilizes digital media to connect with local cultural characteristics, taking the "qilou" architectural style in the Wuyi Overseas Chinese Hometown as a design prototype. Through the algorithm, the study progresses through initial design preparations, formative design, topology optimization design, and post-processing manufacturing to create urban furniture that embodies both local characteristics and aesthetically pleasing forms, as well as structurally sound and digitally ecological elements. It employs the power of design to address local and regional real-world issues, enhancing the daily experiences of local residents and out-of-town visitors. The design practice validates an innovative design pattern that combines parametric design with local cultural features, providing a novel generative tool and strategy for contemporary innovative furniture design in the Wuyi Overseas Chinese Hometown. Furthermore, it serves as a reference for applying this algorithmic model in other domains."

Keywords. Digitization, localization, Wuyi Overseas Chinese Hometown, urban furniture; Parametric

1. Existing Issues in Parametric Furniture Design

Compared to foreign counterparts, the development of parametric design in China started relatively late. The related research primarily concentrated in the field of architecture. In recent years, there has been a gradual increase in explorations within the field of furniture design. The main research direction focuses on investigating the feasibility of specific parametric software or design practices [1]. As an avant-garde

[1] Chen Liang, School of Art and Design, Wuyi University, Jiangmen, Guangdong, China; e-mail: 405037501@qq.com.
Funded Project: 2021 Guangdong Ordinary Colleges and Universities Young Innovative Talents Category Project (2021WQNCX077);2021 Guangdong Teaching Quality and Teaching Reform Project Construction Project (GDJX2021018).

design technology, parametric design possesses significant advantages, yet it still faces certain constraining factors [2].

"Through literature research and exhibition surveys, it has been observed that the application of parametric design in furniture design is continuously expanding. However, its primary practical application is somewhat weaker in the field of architectural design. Additionally, there are several issues identified:1) There is limited research on the theoretical basis of parametric design and the underlying logic in the formative stage.2) The majority of parametric design studies focus on algorithmic generation of complex furniture forms [3], lacking in-depth analysis of the relationship between parametric design, furniture products, and users.3) The core of parametric design lies in data analysis. Most designers primarily rely on their own experience or intuition to control and adjust parameters during the design process. Only parameters derived from objective data analysis experiments can lead to greater innovation on the functional and usage levels.4)In the practice of combining parametric technology with traditional culture, designers are more focused on how to transform traditional cultural symbols or elements for application in the appearance and surface decoration of furniture, thus downplaying critical factors in furniture design such as ergonomics, load-bearing forces, structural optimization, and material specifications. Based on the aforementioned issues, the following text will summarize the theoretical basis and development process of parametric design, distill existing parametric design method models, and utilize a bidirectional progressive structural optimization algorithm to generate urban furniture that embodies both local characteristics and digital ecology."

2.The scientific theoretical basis of parametric design

Parametric design does not refer to the limitation of using a specific software tool or modeling technique. It is a design thinking approach, a professional term widely applied in mathematics, design, and various fields [4]. The designer's design process no longer revolves around selecting a single final object, but rather, creating a group of designs that encompass all potential possibilities. This allows for an understanding of form through the analysis of the program's inherent logical patterns, and deliberate generation and modification of forms. This shift expands the designer's mindset from considering individual objects to contemplating a broad range of choices.

2.1. Theoretical Aspects of Parametric Design

Rivka Oxman considers parametric design as an entirely new 'design thinking' approach that has given rise to entirely new forms of design expression [5]. Philosopher Dennett refers to it as 'design Darwinism'. Complexity science theory provides the theoretical foundation for parametric design. The application of parametric design in product styling is influenced by the monad theory proposed by the German philosopher and mathematician Leibniz and the philosophical ideas put forth by the French postmodern philosopher Gilles Deleuze.

2.2. Complexity Science Theory

Chaos Theory: It is a method that combines qualitative thinking with quantitative analysis, and the 'butterfly effect' has become synonymous with chaos. The application of chaos theory in artistic form design began in the 1980s. The fractal theory in chaos theory proposes the beauty of fractals generated by self-similar forms, allowing for the existence of simple and orderly rules behind extremely complex phenomena [6]. Self-organization Theory: Originating from systems theory, it explores the forms of organizational evolution[7]. It is the process by which a system achieves ordered, complex structures through self-regulation within itself. In the practice of parametric design, the process involves the system self-adjusting to form ordered structures and complex forms of products. Nonlinear Theory: Since postmodernism, many architects have used computer-aided design as a tool to solve various issues of compound diversity. The techniques and concepts they employ, such as dislocation, twisting, confrontation, and mutation, have spontaneously incorporated the core ideas of nonlinear theory: architecture undergoes changes in a discontinuous and uneven state. Theoretically [8], it adheres to the principles of nonlinear complex scientific theory, and conceptually, it is based on the philosophy of nonlinearity in architecture.

2.3. Deleuzian Philosophical Theory

The philosophical ideas of the French postmodern philosopher Gilles Deleuze provide the conceptual foundation for parametric design. Deleuze's philosophical system is fundamentally based on the creation and generation of heterogeneous elements. His overarching philosophy emphasizes generativity and differentiation, gradually giving rise to concepts in post-structuralist philosophy aesthetics such as time crystals, folds, rhizomes, diagrams, and nomadism [9]. Deleuze's fold theory underscores an operation of 'more complex, supple, and heterogeneous forms', establishing a continuity of possibility [10]. Under the influence of fold theory, the development of nonlinear design has been propelled, leading designers to create many forms that challenge traditional concepts. Parametric design constructs parameter models through algorithms to generate designs encompassing all possibilities, and then refines specific models through the adjustment of relevant variables. This constitutes a dynamically generated design approach.

3.Visual Programming Parametric Design Method Model

3.1. Existing Parametric Design Methods

Common parametric design software includes CATIA, UGNX, Grasshopper, Pro/Engineer, SolidWorks, among others. Among them, Grasshopper is currently a popular and widely used parametric design software tool. Grasshopper is a plugin developed to address the drawbacks of difficult modeling, editing, and modification in Rhinoceros, as well as the need for remodelling for model adjustments. It possesses the following key features:

3.2. Furniture Visual Programming Parametric Design Method Model

In recent years, the most commonly used furniture visual programming parametric design in the field of design is based on the theory of parametric design. It employs parametric modeling generation technology to create a design by constructing a parameterized model group for furniture products. The matured 3D printing rapid prototyping technology is then utilized to materialize the product. The basic process can be summarized into four steps: Design Positioning: Analyze and summarize design requirements, extract defined parameters, and construct the system's physical architecture;   System Architecture and Functional Design: Human-computer parameter adjustment subsystem, modeling parameter adjustment subsystem, generate a large number of basic design proposals using relevant algorithms;   System Optimization: Optimize the design model structure and adjust the product form; Output Design Results: Conduct usability testing and subsequently manufacture, print, and assemble the actual product.

Throughout the entire process, there is a certain degree of disparity between the furniture model displayed in the Grasshopper plugin interface and the actual product model in terms of human-computer dimensions, perspective, and size proportions. Therefore, a rational and scientific parametric design for furniture necessitates the establishment of a personalized custom furniture design system physical architecture based on Rhino, Grasshopper, and Arduino. Initially, it is essential to employ a human-computer parameter acquisition device to gather relevant user anthropometric data in order to determine the pertinent dimensions of the seat. Subsequently, designers use the GH interface to adjust the seat's parametric model through relevant battery groups to meet aesthetic and mechanical elements. Then, the data is imported into sensors via Arduino, utilizing GH to construct an adjustable parametric model for the seat. Finally, the three-dimensional model is displayed and rendered in Rhinoceros.

Building upon the importation of sensor data, this method model requires further refinement of furniture functionality. Taking the seat as an example, the functional design primarily encompasses two adjustment subsystems: the human-computer parameter subsystem and the aesthetic parameter subsystem. Based on this, designers can fine-tune relevant parameters to generate a customized form of the seat that meets individualized requirements.

The aforementioned furniture visual programming parametric design method model is premised on personalized requirements. Utilizing anthropometric experimental data, it establishes a system for parametric furniture design, encompassing furniture shaping and functional parameter adjustments. This model is capable of generating furniture design proposals that align with ergonomic principles and individualized preferences. However, it also encounters challenges such as a complex process, user interface complexity, and variations in data testing. Additionally, factors related to furniture structure, load-bearing capacity, and materials are less emphasized.

The objective of this design project is to create urban furniture leisure chairs that embody both local cultural characteristics and digital ecology. In this process, particular attention is given to factors including furniture structure, load-bearing capacity, human-computer parameters, and material properties. Therefore, a bidirectional progressive structural optimization algorithm is chosen for the parametric design practice of the furniture.

4. Parametric Furniture Design Practice Based on Bidirectional Progressive Topological Optimization Algorithm in the Context of Digitalization and Localization Perspective

4.1. Bidirectional Progressive Structural Topology Optimization Algorithm

Today's designers, when using digital technology for form-finding, have shifted their focus from 'external form data' to 'structural data', prioritizing the safety and rationality of the form over its complex and diverse formative aspects. The Bidirectional Evolutionary Structural Optimization (BESO) algorithm possesses features that simulate natural forms and ensure sustainable performance. It was first proposed by Professor Yi-Min Xie in 1998 based on the foundation of the Evolutionary Structural Optimization (ESO) method. This algorithmic generation method represents a cutting-edge approach to structural optimization analysis and design. Its underlying principle follows a systematic design plan, providing multidimensional guided optimal structural outcomes, thus reducing costs and material waste. The main software packages capable of implementing progressive structural topology optimization currently include Abaqus, Karamba3D, and Ameba. Ameba, developed by Professor Yi-Min Xie's team in 2018, is a specialized plugin designed for the BESO algorithm. It boasts diverse grid processing capabilities and can handle data processing for both two-dimensional and three-dimensional topology optimization [11]. The design practice described in this paper is also based on Ameba for algorithmic generation experiments. The aim is to input data weights into the platform through this algorithm, allowing for form-finding. This process aims to achieve an optimization design result that is both aesthetically pleasing and rational, while also meeting the criteria of functional suitability, behavioral appropriateness, structural optimization, and material compatibility.

4.2. The Digitalization+Localization Integrated Parametric Furniture Algorithmic Generation Strategy

With the assistance of the Ameba software platform, the BESO algorithmic generation strategy can be implemented through a specific four-step process: Design Positioning, Initial Form Design, Topological Optimization Design, and Post-processing and Manufacturing. Firstly, Design Positioning requires clear definition of design objectives, design connotations, user requirements, and other considerations. Secondly, Initial Form Design primarily addresses the preliminary preset conditions of the model, which involves reading data on finite element grid division for the design area. The initial model can be categorized into target and non-target models. The target model involves constructing a geometric model for a real-world entity, while the non-target model utilizes the biomimetic modeling characteristic of the BESO algorithm to ensure structural rationality while achieving a design form rich in aesthetic features. Thirdly, Topological Optimization Design encompasses processes such as setting various load conditions, defining optimization parameters, material selection, preprocessing files before centralized data processing, and displaying iterative form-finding results. Fourthly, Post-processing and Manufacturing involves refining the serrated unit data results obtained from topological optimization to achieve a uniform and smooth effect. Finally, virtual results are interfaced with the equipment, and output data is read for size and material analysis, equipment operation analysis, and printing terminal analysis.

This is followed by actual operations using three-dimensional printing or data cutting on numerical control equipment, establishing an interconnected collaborative system (see Fig.1).

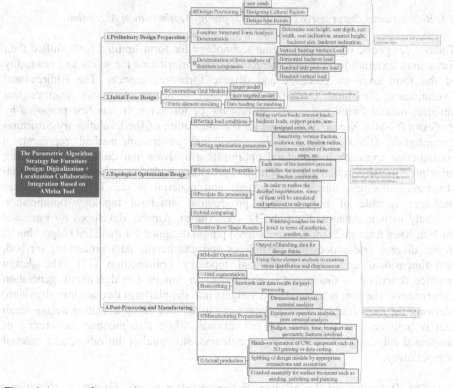

Figure 1. A strategy for generating parametric algorithms for furniture based on the Ameba tool for digital + in situ synergistic integration.

4.3. Parametric Design Practice of Urban Furniture in the context of Digitalization and Localization: A Case Study in Wuyi Overseas Chinese Hometown

4.3.1. Project Background

This design project aims to address the current issues in urban furniture in Jiangmen's Wuyi Overseas Chinese Hometown, which include a lack of diversity in furniture types, limited interactive experiences, weak spatial layout rationality, and a deficiency in showcasing the regional characteristics of the Overseas Chinese community. Starting from the perspective of 'Digitalization + Localization', we leverage the Ameba bidirectional progressive structural optimization algorithm to empower innovative and optimized design for urban furniture in the Overseas Chinese community. This involves integrating the local cultural characteristics of Wuyi Overseas Chinese Hometown with digital technology, resulting in a city furniture leisure chair that embodies both local features and digital ecological elements. This design endeavor aims to meet the urban development needs of Wuyi Overseas Chinese Hometown in the digital age, enhancing the daily experiences of local residents and out-of-town visitors.

4.3.2. Design Cultural Factor Positioning

The design takes the Jiangmen Xuding Street area's arcade-style buildings as its prototype, focusing on the theme of 'Digital Arcade'. Its aim is to conduct an experimental design collision between traditional culture and digital culture. From a design culture perspective, the Xuding Street area in Jiangmen is the birthplace of the city, with a history of over 700 years. An open market called 'Jiangmen Market' was established here by the ancestors of Jiangmen at the end of the Yuan Dynasty and the beginning of the Ming Dynasty. Due to its location at the highest point, it was named 'Xuding Street'. Additionally, because there are 33 levels of bluestone steps at Shuibu Head in the area, climbing them leads to Xuding Street, earning it the name 'Thirty-Three Market Street'.As an old commercial district of Jiangmen, the 'arcade' architecture here retains the charm of the past. The arcade is a type of corridor-style building, with a pedestrian walkway on the first floor facing the street, and the main building above the walkway, giving the appearance of the upper floors 'riding' on the first floor. This type of architecture was originally referred to locally as 'arcades with legs', later shortened to just 'arcades'. Chinese bas-reliefs and Manchu windows, along with Western elements like Roman columns and carvings, blend together, allowing cultural elements from different regions and eras to coexist harmoniously, forming a unique characteristic of the Overseas Chinese community. The top of the street is adorned with various types of decorative lights, while the exterior walls feature transformed European-style columns, window decorations, and Spanish-style balconies. At the same time, it is embellished with Chinese mountain flowers, Manchu windows, and stone inscriptions, making it akin to a 'Museum of International Architecture'.

Architectural decorative styles often bear a strong sense of their era. Against the backdrop of the modern fusion of Eastern and Western cultures in Jiangmen, arcades reflect a characteristic of cultural inclusivity. The decorative structures of arcades are diverse, with a particular emphasis on mountain flowers, windows and their frames, balcony railings, and columns [12]. Therefore, this design project inherits the open-mindedness, inclusiveness, and innovative spirit expressed by the arcades of Jiangmen in the context of cultural fusion between East and West in modern Jiangmen society. Taking the appearance of arcade architecture as the initial form, it integrates the wheat straw and persimmon vine patterns of the arcades. Utilizing the bidirectional progressive structural optimization algorithm, the project progresses through preliminary design preparations, initial form design, topological optimization design, and post-processing and manufacturing. This results in an urban furniture leisure chair that combines local characteristics with digital ecological elements. The design is then applied to actual street scenes.

4.3.3. Algorithm Generation Process

1. Initial Form Design: Constructing Geometric Entities and Grid Models
Taking the architectural appearance of the arcade as a prototype, the initial stage of form setting does not strictly require a replica simulation of the original arcade shape. Instead, it aims to simplify and refine, achieving a form that retains the charm of the arcade while also meeting the seating size requirements for easy topological optimization. In Rhino, the initial form of the leisure chair is established, and the initial model is linked to the 'Volume' battery. The AmebaMesh3D battery is selected to subdivide the model into 197,825 high-density meshes. The higher the mesh density,

the more refined the optimized model. Since the seating surface and backrest are the main force-bearing areas for armless leisure chairs, the 'Volume' is exploded using the battery command in GH. This extracts the surfaces that need to bear the load without affecting the geometric entity itself, determining that the seating surface and backrest surface are the key factors for load setting [13] (see Fig.2 and Fig.3).

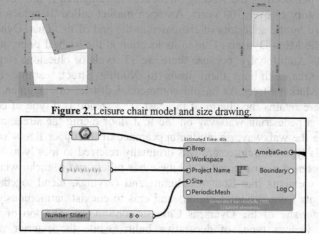

Figure 2. Leisure chair model and size drawing.

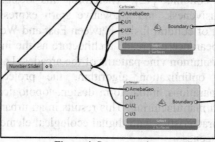

Figure 3. Build a grid model.

2. Topological Optimization Design

(1) Support Configuration

The typical load-bearing points of a regular seat are the four legs intersecting with the bottom surface. Therefore, in GH, the Support3D component is selected to import the seat support area, and the numerical value of support displacement is controlled. After multiple attempts, it was determined to control Ux and Uy within an absolute value range of 0.1, while Uz remains unchanged at 0, as shown in Fig. 4.

Figure 4. Support setting.

(2) Load Configuration

The stress on armless chairs primarily concentrates on the central and peripheral areas of the seat, the backrest, and the legs. With structural rationality as a premise, a uniformly distributed load is applied to the entire seat, as shown in Table 2. The corresponding load data is imported into the preprocessor through the NormallLoad3D component for logical editing, while simultaneously adjusting the slider to modify the area of force application, as shown in Fig. 5.

Tab 1. Leisure chair force analysis diagram.

Force Application Point	Center of the Seat	Backrest	Entire seat surface
Legend	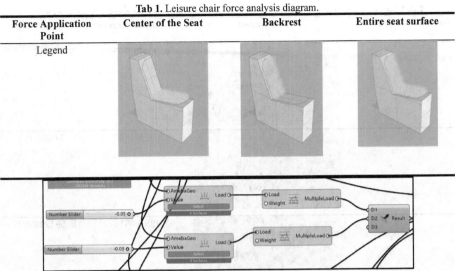		

Figure 5. Load setting

(3) Material Specification

In the bidirectional progressive structural optimization algorithm, material specification is achieved by parameterizing key performance parameters of the material, combined with the system's default material library. This enables the algorithm to search for the optimal material combination during the design process, with the goal of optimizing the structure. The optimization method can optimize the distribution of material combinations within a specified range and generate models with minimized weight and maximized structural performance. The system's default isotropic materials include ABS plastic, nylon, steel, aluminum, etc. Additionally, users can set parameters such as material density, Poisson's ratio, and elastic modulus. In this practice, ABS plastic was selected, and three different types of seats were used to compare the different structures generated by the algorithm.

(4) Optimization Parameter Configuration

In Ameba, the optimization parameters are set using the BESO OptParameters operator. One of the objectives of topological optimization is to minimize the use of material. Through multiple experimental operations, it was determined that when the constraint volume is set to 0.01 (vf), a more suitable optimization objective can be generated. The lower the purge rate value, the more precise the mesh optimization, typically set to 0.02 (ert). Sensitivity 'S' represents the density of stress (default is 1). For a model with a mesh subdivision value of 1.28 million, the filter radius needs to be set to double (rmin) (delete units below double) in order to compute the generation. Additionally, the default maximum iteration steps are applied.

(5) Iterative Form Generation

As shown in the table below, the topological optimization process is displayed for iterations ranging from 2 to 142. The structural morphology changes occur at intervals of 20, with a target volume fraction of 0.05 (vf) and a purge rate of 0.02 (ert) (to increase optimization time and enhance optimization precision). Throughout the iteration process, while satisfying the constraint of material volume fraction, the total strain energy gradually changes, and the flexibility curve eventually stabilizes to achieve a visually pleasing, efficient, and reasonable convergent result.

Tab 2. Stress cloud of evolutionary data and 3D topology optimisation results for leisure chairs

Number of Iterations	Illustration	Volume Fraction	Total Energy
2		0. 960402705	5. 899681
22		0. 641171668	6. 7355322
42		0. 428060814	8. 59480358
62		0. 285759485	11. 6855876
82		0. 190755767	16. 5284284
102		0. 127366737	23. 9552045
122		0. 09999677	31. 0344120
142		0. 100001546	31. 2132831

(6) Generated Form

The table below shows six different display modes of the optimized leisure chair. Based on the results below, it can be concluded that the maximum equivalent stress is 2.315 MPa, and the overall maximum displacement of the seat is 2.136 mm. The final algorithm-generated result shows a relatively uniform distribution of stress areas, meeting the requirements for the use of the leisure chair in terms of structural form.

Tab 3. Leisure chair optimization results display and illustration

Display Modes	Illustration	Maximum Value and Position
Mises		Maximum Equivalent Stress: 2.315MPA
Principal		Maximum Compression: 1.763MPA Minimum Tension: 1.763MPA
Displacement Uxyz		The maximum displacement of the entire seat is 2.136mm, located at the top and middle of the backrest.
Displacement Ux		The maximum displacement in the X-axis direction is 3.361mm, located at the top of the backrest.
Displacement Uy		The maximum displacement in the Y-axis direction is 1.157mm, located at the top of the backrest.
Displacement Uz		The maximum displacement in the Z-axis direction is 2.135mm, located at the top of the backrest.

3. Post-processing and Manufacturing
(1) Model Optimization

Because the bidirectional topology optimization method optimizes the seat by increasing or decreasing the mesh, the optimized model surface contains a large number of 'non-manifold edges,' also known as 'serrated' units. Therefore, post-processing is required to repair and smooth the model surface in order to obtain a smooth manifold surface, remove non-manifold edges, and meet the quality requirements of the product. The Mesh checker battery is used to detect the mesh. The original optimization result will have non-manifold edges. After adjusting the smoothness and reconstruction of the dangling edges and points, as shown in Fig. 6, the mesh model has been optimized. Finally, the QuadMesh battery is used to turn the mesh into a polygonal mesh. The model surface is more refined and can be directly placed in Rhino for rendering (see Fig. 7, 8, and 9 10).

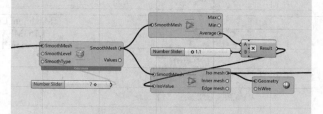

Figure 6. Mesh checker.

Figure 7. The model after the final reconstruction of the surface.

Figure 8. Render the renderings.

Utilizing the bidirectional topology optimization method, we altered the initial form and, considering functional usage, redefined the load and support parameters. Employing metallic materials, we generated two additional design proposals. To further validate the structural performance of the topology-optimized results, it is necessary to employ finite element analysis to examine the stress distribution and displacement of the seat, predict product performance, and identify potential weak points.

Figure 9. Scenario 2 Render the renderings.

(2) Scenario Simulation

Figure 10. Leisure chair use scene diagram.

(3) 3D Printed Physical Model

Utilizing additive manufacturing 3D printing technology, the mechanical structure of the seat is analyzed. Materials with sufficient strength and durability, such as nylon and engineering plastics like ABS, are chosen for the physical production of the seat. Throughout this process, considerations are made for budget, time, and geometric features involved in the design. The design model is divided and assembled using appropriate connecting methods. Finally, surface treatments such as polishing, painting, and coating are applied to showcase distinctive surface characteristics (see Fig.11).

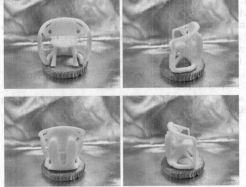

Figure 11. 3D printing model.

The BESO algorithm is currently one of the advanced topology optimization algorithms. It has not only found effective practical applications in STEM fields but is also gradually being explored in multidimensional approaches in art and design disciplines. This paper, based on the elucidation of the fundamental connotation, developmental history, related theories, design process, and current issues of visual programming parametric design, summarizes the advantages of the Bidirectional Evolutionary Structural Optimization (BESO) algorithm. It clarifies the algorithm's generation strategy and optimization method in furniture design, explores how digital technology can empower the reactivation of local culture. Taking the 'qilou' architecture in the Jiangmen Old Street, a traditional arcade-style building, as the design prototype, it conducts a collaborative algorithmic generative design practice. This provides opportunities for diverse choices in generating urban furniture design outcomes. However, since the BESO algorithm requires relevant data support in various aspects such as form, structure, material, and energy conservation, it is necessary to further validate the versatility of its application with more new tools and new design method systems. This will create more opportunities for sustainable design and creation in empowering the local cultural industry through digital algorithmic generation.

References

[1] Dai Qiqi, Research on Personalized Customization Design System of Seats Based on Parametric Design , China Academy of Art(2021),26-28.

[2] Jiang Feng,Application of Parametric Design in Public Buildings,Decoration (2019),110-113.

[3] Cui Qiang,Application Research of Parametric Design in Industrial Product Design,Beijing University of Technology(2018),16.

[4] Song Jie, Chen Qiming, Chen Li, et al, Research on Furniture Design Based on Parametric and Additive Manufacturing Technology, Forest Industry (2022),52-56.

[5] Oxman R, Thinking difference: Theories and models of parametric design thinking, Design studies(2017),4-39.

[6] Dong Xuan,Research on the Application of Chaos Theory in Morphological Design,Popular Literature and Art(2010),225.

[7] Liu Luchan, Sun Caiyun,Research on the Operation Mechanism of Virtual Teaching and Research Room in the "Intelligent+" Era of Colleges and Universities Based on Self-Organization Theory,Higher Education Research in Heilongjiang(2023), 122-127.

[8] Gong Xiaowen, Wang Xiaofan,Application of Nonlinear Theory in Architectural Design,Shanxi Architecture(2007),23-24.

[9] Liu Yang,Research on Contemporary Architectural Creation Thought Based on Deleuze's Philosophy,Harbin Institute of Technology(2013),28-30.

[10] Wu Shangbo,Research on the Influence of Deleuze's "Fold" Theory on Contemporary Architectural Creation Thought, Xi'an University of Architecture and Technology(2020),13-20.

[11] Pu Yang, Bao Dingwen,Research on Innovative Design Based on Bidirectional Progressive Structural Topology Optimization Algorithm,Packaging Engineering(2023),1-15.

[12] Zhang Chao,Analysis of the Decorative Style of Republic of China Arcades in Jiangmen, Guangdong, Journal of Yunnan Arts University(2016),74-77.

[13] Zhou Zhengya,Research on Topology Optimization Design of Leisure Chair Structure and Morphology,Central South University of Forestry and Technology(2021),34-35.

Design Studies and Intelligence Engineering
L.C. Jain et al. (Eds.)
© *2024 The Authors.*
This article is published online with Open Access by IOS Press and distributed under the terms
of the Creative Commons Attribution Non-Commercial License 4.0 (CC BY-NC 4.0).
doi:10.3233/FAIA231494

Does the Manufacturing Industry Also Need Gamification? - A Gamification Design Practice for CNC Machine Tool Skill Training

Tian-shu LI[a] and Min-yang LIU[a,1]

[a] *Beijing Information Science & Technology University, China*

Abstract. In CNC (Computer Numerical Control) vocational colleges, the current traditional pedagogy has become conflicting with the learning preferences of the "Generation Z", resulting in their low sense of competence, low learning autonomy, and insufficient recognition of industry identification. Thus, gamification design provides novel ideas for addressing these issues. Based on the theories of self-determination theory and motivational affordances, this study analyzes the sore points and study needs of students who are majoring in CNC technology at vocational colleges. Hence, according to the 12 dimensions of motivational affordances, the "needs-affordances-features" framework and the course content of CNC technology, a set of gamification design strategies for CNC machine tool skill training is proposed. Consequently, a smartphone-based interactive design practice is completed. Following this design practice, a user experience test is executed, and a positive result is obtained. Theoretically, this study explores the feasibility of modified gamification design processes that combine the motivational affordance model and the "needs-affordances-features" framework. Practically, the integration of gamification design into CNC machine tool skill training is not only a bold attempt to boost the learning motivation of students, but also a practical research foundation for the innovative development and transformation of CNC technology vocational education.

Keywords. gamification; interaction design; motivation affordance; CNC machine tool skill training; user experience; Generation Z

In recent years, "manufacturing power" has become a key focus of China's national strategy. The intelligent transformation and development of the manufacturing industry inevitably require the reserve and cultivation of more high-quality talents. This also puts forward higher requirements for CNC technology vocational colleges that cultivate talents for the manufacturing industry[1]. However, as "Generation Z" becomes the main body in vocational colleges, the shortcomings of traditional vocational education are revealed. The learning experience is dull and uninteresting, resulting in low initiative in students' learning and poor learning outcomes. Since researches have shown that gamification has a positive impact on enhancing educational effectiveness[2], this study will take CNC machine tool skill training as an example to conduct research on gamification interaction design to improve the students' learning experience.

---

[1] Corresponding Author: LIU Min-yang. E-mail: 1321530532@qq.com

1. Vocational Education of CNC Technology

1.1. National Encouragement for the Reform and Upgrade of Vocational Education

The manufacturing industry in China is in a period of comprehensive transformation and upgrading, aiming to achieve connectivity and integrated development through intelligent and innovative production methods. In order to carry out this strategic goal, the country is initiating to put much greater emphasis on vocational education, encouraging students to improve their skill levels, and injecting fresh power into enterprises. Vocational colleges as the main institutions for training front-line employees in the manufacturing industry, are also actively reforms and upgrades. It is exploring various teaching methods to cultivate versatile talents with excellent vocational skills, flexibility, creativity and continuous independent learning capabilities[3].

1.2. Technical Training for CNC Machine Tools

Nowadays, students in CNC technology vocational colleges generally belong to the "Generation Z", who refers to the generation born between 1995 to 2010, and grew up with the development of the internet[4]. They show significant differences from their parents in terms of thinking patterns and behavioral habits, forming distinct learning preferences. They display a strong interest-driven learning motivation. Simultaneously, they seek enjoyable learning experiences and immediate feedback, as well as attaching importance to the realization of personal value. These learning preferences are not easily satisfied within the traditional pedagogy of vocational colleges, which has led to a series of problems in the current CNC technology vocational education.

Firstly, CNC machine tool skill training involves monotonous and challenging course content, often requiring high levels of manual dexterity. This results in students lacking confidence in their abilities, leading to feelings of reluctance and decreased motivation to learn. Secondly, the cramming education is still the main teaching approach in the classes of CNC technology[5], which contradicts the learning preferences of the Generation Z, and limits their learning autonomy to a great extent. Thirdly, the content taught in schools may not align well with actual factory application scenarios. Students may lack a clear understanding of the practical value and future prospects of CNC machine tool skill, resulting in a lack of ideals and a sense of purpose[6]. This leads to a problem of insufficient recognition of industry identification.

1.3. Gamification in manufacturing skill training

The application of gamification in the field of manufacturing is still in its nascent stages but has shown promising trends[7]. Some studies apply gamification to manufacturing employee skill training. For example, Oliver Korn et al. gamified the process of mechanical assembly, making it easier for employees to perceive the accuracy and effectiveness of the assembly process[8]. Jessica Ulmer et al. designed a combined point and leveling VR-based gamification system for assembly training (as shown in Figure 1a)[9]. Furthermore, gamification can also be used to learn manufacturing-related software. For example, the gamified teaching system

"GamiCAD" helps guide new users of AutoCAD to become familiar with the operation of AutoCAD (as shown in Figure 1b)[10].

To address the aforementioned issues and respond to the national call for talent development in the manufacturing industry, it is of great research significance to explore a CNC machine tool skill training strategy that aligns with the learning preferences of the Generation Z, of which the design practice should adopt innovative teaching methods, such as gamification, to provide students with clear and appealing learning objectives, adding interest to what might otherwise be a monotonous mechanical learning experience.

a VR-based gamification system on assembly training   b GamiCAD

Figure 1. Gamification applications for manufacturing skill training

2. Gamification in theory

2.1. Gamification Concept and Applications

It has been recognized that gaming behaviors in the processes of production and daily life have driven human development and civilization. Therefore, people realize that the value of games is not only entertainment, and then put forward the concept of gamification. The term "gamification" was first coined in 2002 but gained widespread academic discussion after 2011. Sebastian Deterding et al. gave the first clear definition of gamification as "the use of game design elements in non-game contexts."[11]. Gamification related research aims to stimulate user motivation, enhance user experiences, and promote the achievement of expectations by combining various game elements[12]. Points, badges, and leaderboards, commonly referred to as PBL, exhibit distinct gaming characteristics and are frequently used game elements[13].

Self-determination theory (SDT) serves as the theoretical foundation for research related to gamified motivation. SDT categorizes motivation into three types, namely, intrinsic motivation, extrinsic motivation, and amotivation. It also defines the fundamental psychological needs of humans are defined as autonomy, competence, and relatedness. Meeting these needs can enhance intrinsic motivation[14] whereas individuals can also integrate experiences from their environment and gradually internalize them, resulting in the development of both intrinsic and extrinsic motivations.

2.2. Motivation Affordances in Gamification Design

"Affordance" refers to the available action possibilities. Donald Norman defined the subject of affordance as "the combination of the actual properties and perceived properties of an object"[15]. Building upon this, Zhang introduced the term "motivation affordance"[16], which refers to the properties of an object that determine whether and how it can support one's motivational needs. The theory of motivation affordance suggests that certain attributes of objects can serve to motivate users after meeting their needs. By controlling these attributes, motivation can be purposefully stimulated. Karahanna et al. proposed a comprehensive framework called "needs-affordances-features"[17], which enhances the practicality of the motivation affordance theory.

Gustavo Fortes Tondello et al. summarized 6 gamification design methods based on self-determination theory and motivation affordance theory, then proposed 12 dimensions of motivation affordance[18], classifying them into three major categories, namely intrinsic motivation affordance, extrinsic motivation affordance, and context-dependent motivation affordance (as shown in Figure 2).

Intrinsc Motivation affordance		Extrinsc Motivation affordance	Context-dependent Motivation affordance
Purpose and Meaning	Autonomy and Creativity	Ownership and Rewards	Feedback
Challenge and Competence	Relatedness	Scarcity	Unpredictability
Completeness and Mastery	Immersion	Loss Avoidance	Change and Disruption

Figure 2. 12 dimensions of motivation affordances by Tondello et al.

Intrinsic motivation affordances emphasize the enhancement of users intrinsic motivation through the fulfillment of three fundamental needs: competence, autonomy, and relatedness. Extrinsic motivation affordances serve as external incentives that can stimulate user behavioral motivation. Context-dependent motivation affordances will produce different motivation effects according to different situations. Intrinsic motivation affordances serve as motivators by satisfying needs, whereas extrinsic motivation affordances add further incentives, and context-dependent motivation affordances rely on the usage context to transform into either intrinsic or extrinsic. These three types of motivation affordances complement each other. In this study, the 12 dimensions of motivation affordances are used as a design guideline and integrated into the "needs-affordances-features" framework so as to conduct the design practice.

3. Gamification Design for CNC Machine Tool Skill Training

3.1. Needs Analysis of CNC Machine Tool Skill Training

Through a preliminary analysis, it is observed that students in CNC technology vocational colleges generally exhibit low sense of competence, low learning autonomy, and insufficient recognition of industry identification. In order to gather a further understanding of these three aspects, a questionnaire is made and distributed to students who are majoring in CNC machine tool discipline. 1026 respondents are retrieved and 84.72% of the total are students from higher vocational colleges. Due to the nature of the CNC discipline, approximately 90% of the respondents are male, and their ages ranged from 18 to 25 years.

The questionnaire is centered on two primary aspects: academic performance and future employment prospects. Identify the most pressing issues among students separately. Ultimately, the top four concerns in the academic performance section and one concern in the future employment section were chosen(as shown in Figure 3), resulting in a total of five key sore points. These sore points allow for a comprehensive assessment of the current learning experiences of students.

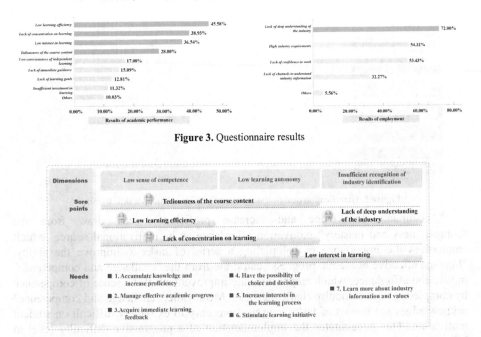

Figure 3. Questionnaire results

Figure 4. Needs analysis of CNC machine tool skill training

The analysis of the questionnaire is shown in Figure 4. After classifying the questionnaire results, 5 sore points are summarized and clustered into three problem dimensions as mentioned above. Some of the sore points can be triggered by multi-dimensional problems. For example, "the tediousness of the course content" can be mainly caused by the low sense of competence and low learning autonomy while "the lack of deep understanding of the industry" is more the result of insufficient recognition of the industry identification. Hence, in order to derive the solution to the problem in the later process, the sore points are transformed into the learning needs of students by the three problem dimensions and eventually 7 needs are proposed.

3.2. Gamification Design Framework for CNC Machine Tool Skill Training Based on Motivation Affordances

To fulfill the 7 needs clarified in the above analysis, a gamification design framework for CNC machine tool skill training was built (as shown in Figure 5), by adopting the well-known "needs-affordances-features" framework and utilizing the 12 dimensions of motivation affordances.

In this framework, suitable motivation affordances should be selected for each need, and then the design strategies are proposed with the features being clarified (as shown in Figure 5). Meanwhile, in order to ensure the rationality of the strategies and features, it was necessary to take the course contents as the guidelines. In this case, the curriculum of "CNC Machine Tool Operation and Programming" was chosen as the example, in which students were required to attain the knowledge of basic cognition of CNC machine tools, CNC machine tool processing operations, and CNC machine tool processing programming.

After the analysis according to the framework, this study obtains 5 design strategies and 13 features to guide the design practice.

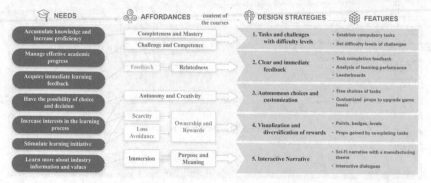

Figure 5. Gamification design framework of CNC machine tool skill training

"Accumulate knowledge and increase proficiency" can draw from the "completeness and mastery" motivation affordance as its motivational source, which emphasizes the importance of completing a series of tasks to improve the ability. "Manage effective academic progress" can draw from the "challenge and competence" motivation affordance, which emphasizes the improvement of the sense of competence by completing high-difficulty challenge tasks. Meanwhile, "challenge and competence" acknowledges the impact of tasks ranging from easy to extremely difficult on student motivation. This necessitates the implementation of a progressive difficulty level to boost student learning motivation. Both of these affordances underscore the importance of tasks completion. Consequently, "tasks and challenges with difficulty levels" design strategy is proposed. Its primary features include compulsory tasks facilitating students consolidation of knowledge, and challenges providing students with a gradual transition from easy to difficult learning experiences.

"Acquire immediate learning feedback" means that students expect feedback on learning results to gauge their level of skill development and achieve a sense of competence. Therefore, this study adopts the "feedback" motivation affordance as a motivational source and incorporates the "relatedness" motivation affordance within it. By feedback information, students subconsciously form competitive relationships, which encourage them and enhance their capabilities. As a result, the "clear and immediate feedback" design strategy is proposed. Students can clearly perceive their development and deficiencies based on learning feedback. The features of this strategy include task completion information, learning performance analysis and leaderboards.

"Have the possibility of choice and decision" means that students expect to have more autonomy, thereby strengthening their sense of independence in the learning process. To fulfill this, this study leverages the "autonomy and creativity" motivation affordance, emphasizing the importance of meeting students autonomy needs. Additionally, the mechanisms associated with "autonomy and creativity" offer high interactivity, thereby enhancing the enjoyment of activities and aligning with the goal of "increasing interests in the learning process." Ultimately, the "autonomous choices and customization" design strategy is proposed, which includes features like "free choices of tasks" and "customized props to upgrade game levels". These elements increase autonomy and interactivity during the learning process, alleviate learning pressure, and enhance interests in learning.

Task rewards can motivate students to engage actively in learning and experience enjoyment. Therefore, both "increase interests in the learning process" and "stimulate learning initiative" draw from the external motivation affordance as their motivational source, which encompasses "ownership and rewards", "scarcity" and "loss avoidance". "Scarcity" enhances motivation by making rewards harder to attain. "Loss avoidance" affordance requires that rewards be time-sensitive to improve learning efficiency and increase learning engagement. Hence, the "visualization and diversification of rewards" design strategy is proposed, incorporating features such as points, badges, levels and props to establish a system of learning incentives and penalties.

The "immersion" motivation affordance aims to create an immersive system to enhance user experience, with narrative mechanisms being a commonly used approach. "Learn more about industry information and values" can draw from the "immersion" motivation affordance as its motivational source by incorporating information about the CNC machine tool industry into the immersive system and presenting it using narrative mechanisms. Meanwhile, the "purpose and meaning" motivation affordance is further employed by setting meaningful task objectives to help students appreciate the values of the CNC machine tool industry. Consequently, the "interactive narrative" design strategy is proposed, which includes manufacturing-themed science fiction narratives and dialogue interactions to enhance user immersion.

4. Gamification Design for CNC Machine Tool Skill Training

This application is designed to assist students in consolidating and strengthening their knowledge in the course of CNC machine tool skill training. The main mechanism is to set question tasks so that students can practice exercises anytime and anywhere after class. This application is called "Divine Manufacturer Realm", which means to "create hope with machinery". The protagonist is designed with the image of a future mechanical engineer, and the interactive interface incorporates machinery and technology-related elements, which aims to enhance students' sense of involvement and engagement in continuous learning, thereby achieving the expected study goals, a set of the UI designs is shown in Figure 6.

Figure.6 UI design of "Divine Manufacturer Realm"

- "Tasks and challenges with difficulty levels"

In this application, students can obtain virtual mechanical parts by completing tasks. The tasks are divided into three categories, namely mainline tasks, daily tasks and challenge tasks. The mainline tasks are carried out in conjunction with the narrative, and the storyline corresponds to the course learning content. The daily tasks aim to maintain students practicing in this application regularly and continuously. Challenge tasks require higher accuracy in answering the questions.

All tasks are set with difficulty levels. Students can receive different rewards based on varying levels of correctness in answering the quiz. For example, daily tasks require students to achieve 60% accuracy to obtain mechanical parts while challenge tasks need to achieve 100% accuracy to have ultra-precision mechanical parts.

- "Clear and immediate feedback"

Feedback can inform students of their current game status, interaction results, and subsequent operations that need to be operated. For example, students can understand their performances compared with others through game levels, mission progress, rankings, gained props and rewards. Meanwhile, they can also view the analysis of personal capabilities and customized strategies in aspects of competence, endurance, exploration, concentration, and enthusiasm.

- "Autonomous choices and customization"

There are two types of choice mechanisms provided to meet students autonomous needs. The first type is that students are able to choose whatever tasks they desire to conduct and whenever they prefer to complete them.

The second type is the customization of props that students gain from the game. In this application, the main mission is to unlock a series of virtual CNC machine tools and to manufacture high-level mechanical parts with them so as to upgrade the game levels. Each of the CNC machine tools has a unique appearance and processing capabilities. Students can choose their preferred CNC machine tools and upgrade the components of spindles, cutters, workbenches and the CNC systems to improve the processing precision of the equipment so as to obtain more game rewards.

- "Visualization and diversification of rewards"

Visualization rewards allow students to receive positive feedback more intuitively, which motivates them to complete a greater number of tasks and alleviates the boringness of mechanical learning. This application includes four types of rewards, namely virtual mechanical parts, game energies, experience points and corresponding badges by completing tasks.

- "Interactive Narrative"

The background of this application's story involves a group of engineers who refuse to leave their homeland during doomsday. Instead, they attempt to save themselves by constructing a base, awaiting a new hope. Students can always grow up with the characters in the story and accumulate knowledge in the tasks as learners.

Students can also drive the plot forward by completing the interactive dialogues with the characters, which may enrich their learning experience and improve their learning motivation by creating an immersive sense of learning, playing, and working.

5. User experience test

To assess the applications ability to fulfill the educational needs of students and stimulate their learning motivation, a test is conducted. Six participants (males/females=4:2) are recruited to complete testing task and fill out a user experience questionnaire. The questionnaire utilized a 7-point Likert scale to rate 9 items, which are based on the Gameful Experience Questionnaire developed by HOGBERG J[19], and integrated with the content of the application.

The test is structured into three phases; 1) Familiarization with the application, where the experimental personnel provided an overview of the applications features and assigned tasks; 2) Completion of the primary tasks within the first part of the CNC machine tool recognition content, where participants are required to complete a minimum of two groups of daily tasks and challenge tasks, while other functions are explored at random intervals; and 3) Verification of task completion by the experimental personnel, followed by a demonstration of the personal information, honors, and rankings pages, and finally, completion of the user experience questionnaire. The results of this testing are presented in Table 1.

Table 1. The results of user experience test

Dimension/ Item	P1	P2	P3	P4	P5	P6	Average
Learning needs							**5.77**
I feel an increase in ability by completing tasks	6	5	7	7	6	6	6.17
Let me have a clear learning goal	4	3	6	7	4	5	4.83
Receive positive feedback on the completion of tasks	5	7	6	6	7	7	6.33
Learning autonomy							**6.00**
I want to strive to be better	5	6	5	7	7	6	6.00
Completing tasks without feeling forced	4	5	7	4	7	7	5.67
I feel like I could explore new something	7	5	7	6	7	6	6.33
learning experience							**5.89**
I have a deeper understanding of the value of CNC machine tool industry in the process of learning	5	6	5	7	6	5	5.67
I hope my role can bring more hope to mankind	7	5	4	7	4	6	5.50
I have an interesting learning experience	6	5	7	7	7	7	6.50

Upon conducting a preliminary analysis of the user experience questionnaire, positive feedback was received across all indicators (Average>4). The average score for each dimension was approximately 6.0. The test results indicate that the application is capable of effectively meeting the educational needs of vocational college students learning CNC machine tool skill courses and enhancing their overall learning experience. However, certain limitations were observed during the testing process. The scope of the test was limited to the relatively basic CNC machine tool recognition content, and the duration of the test was brief, with the participants lacking the opportunity to gain an in-depth understanding of the applications functionality through extended usage. Additionally, the sense of achievement was relatively low, resulting in lower scores for some indicators. During the testing process, the participants exhibited differing opinions regarding the same game mechanics, highlighting the need for further research to personalize the application in the future.

6. Conclusion

The students in CNC technology vocational colleges generally exhibit low sense of competence, low learning autonomy, and insufficient recognition of industry identification. Based on the motivation affordances, this study transforms sore points of students into design demands and then forms a set of gamification design strategies for CNC machine tools skill training in a smartphone-based application, which achieves relatively positive results in a user experience test. Accordingly, this study clarifies the feasibility of using motivation affordances in gamification design and fulfills the innovative exploration of gamification in the field of CNC machine tool skill training. Normally in the context of the manufacturing industry, the concept of gamification typically stands as an outlier. This anomaly can be primarily attributed to the industrys inherent conservatism and its adherence to rigid protocols. In an effort to challenge this status quo, this study goes beyond the conventional approach of employing standard gamification elements. Instead, it delves into the utilization of narrative as a gaming element, a less explored avenue in prior research, ultimately achieving improvements in both psychological and behavioral outcomes. This provides new design insights and lays a corresponding research foundation for the gamification development of CNC machine tool skill training.

Acknowledgments. This work was supported by Qin Xin Talents Cultivation Program, Beijing Information Science & Technology University (QXTCPC202103); Supply and Demand Matching Employment Program of Ministry of Education of the people's Republic of China ("Human Factors and Ergonomics Specialization", 2021); General Project of Beijing Municipal Commission of Education Research Plan (KM202011232013).

References

[1] HUANG Xiao-dong, Research on Talents Training of Vocational Education Facing the "Two Modernizations" of Mechanical Industry, *Education and Vocation* **11**(2022), 51-56.

[2] LUO Zhan-ni, Gamification for educational purposes: What are the factors contributing to varied effectiveness?, *Education and information technologies* **1**(2022), 27.

[3] WANG Zhi-ping, YANG Xiao-yong, Exploration of Training Path for Composite Technical Skills Talents in Intelligent Manufacturing, *Vocational Education for Mechanical Industry* **03**(2022), 28-31+49.

[4] AO Cheng-bing, Diversified Characteristics, Realistic Causes and Subcultural Significance of Generation Zs Consumption Concept, *China Youth Study* **06**(2021), 100-106.

[5] XU Ming, LI Zhi-jun, MENG Wu-zhou, Teaching Reform and Exploration of Metal Cutting Machine Tool Course in the Background of the new engineering department. *Journal of Anyang Institute of Technology* **19.06**(2020), 122-123.

[6] LI Pei-gen, Whats New for New Engineering Education, *Research in Higher Education of Engineering*, **04**(2017), 1-4+15.

[7] KEEPERS M, et al. Current state of research & outlook of gamification for manufacturing, *Journal of Manufacturing Systems* **64**(2022), 303-315.

[8] KORN O, FUNK M, SCHMIDT A, Design approaches for the gamification of production environments: a study focusing on acceptance, *ACM*, ACM, 2015.

[9] ULMER J, et al. Gamification of virtual reality assembly training: Effects of a combined point and level system on motivation and training results, *International Journal of Human-Computer Studies*, (2022), 165.

[10] WEI L, GROSSMAN T, FITZMAURICE G, GamiCAD: A gamified tutorial system for first time AutoCAD users, *Acm Symposium on User Interface Software & Technology*, ACM, 2012.

[11] DETERDUNG S, DAN D, KHALED R, et al. From Game Design Elements to Gamefulness: Defining "Gamification", *nternational Academic Mindtrek Conference: Envisioning Future Media Environments*, ACM, 2011.

[12] KOIVISTO J, HAMARI J, The rise of motivational information systems: A review of gamification research, *International Journal of Information Management* (2019).

[13] YANG Ming-heng, YAO Jie, XIAO Tao, An Empirical Study on PBL Gamification Design for Exercising Motivation, *Packaging Engineering* **42**(2021), 9.

[14] DECI E L, RYAN R M, Conceptualizations of Intrinsic Motivation and Self-Determination, 1985.

[15] NORMAN D A, *The Psychology of Everyday Things*, Basic Books, 1988.

[16] PING Z, Motivational Affordances: Fundamental Reasons for ICT Design and Use, *Communications of the ACM* **51.11**(2008), 145-147.

[17] KARAHANNA E, XU S X, XU Y, et al. The needs-affordances-features perspective for the use of social media, *MIS Quarterly* **42.3**(2018), 737-756.

[18] TONDELLO G F, DENNIS L K, MARIM G, et al. Gameful Design Heuristics: A Gamification Inspection Tool, *International Conference on Human-Computer Interaction* (2019), 224–244.

[19] HOGBERG J, HAMARI J, WASTLUND E, et al. Gameful Experience Questionnaire: an instrument for measuring the Perceived Gamefulness of System Use, *User Modeling and User-adapted Interaction***29**(2019), 619-660.

Design Studies and Intelligence Engineering
L.C. Jain et al. (Eds.)
© 2024 The Authors.
This article is published online with Open Access by IOS Press and distributed under the terms
of the Creative Commons Attribution Non-Commercial License 4.0 (CC BY-NC 4.0).
doi:10.3233/FAIA231495

799

Research on Multimodal Interaction Design Patterns for Visually Impaired People Under Sensory Compensation Theory

Wei ZHANG [a] and Cong AN [b,1]

[a] *Beijing Information Science and Technology University*
[b] *Associate Professor, Beijing Information Science and Technology University*

Abstract. Based on the theory of sensory compensation, this paper mainly applies the multimodal interaction design method to solve the difficulties and challenges faced by the visually impaired people watching the game as an application scenario, so as to provide a reference for the accessibility design. In terms of research ideas, the technical principles and applications of visual enhancement, auditory compensation, tactile compensation and olfactory compensation are investigated by combing the development of sensory compensation and the three realization methods of visual enhancement, visual substitution and visual replacement for visually impaired people. By dividing the game-viewing scene into five sub-scenes to gain insight into the specific needs of visually impaired people, combining the needs with the three forms of application of sensory compensation mentioned above, discussing their adaptive relationship with different scenes, and exploring the multimodal interaction design mode under the different needs of visually impaired people, in summary, this research come up with the design of the multimodal interaction system for the visually impaired people used to watch the game. The design example verifies that the multimodal interaction design mode based on sensory compensation design with intersecting and complementary senses of vision, audio, and tactility can help to improve the quality of spectator services and daily travel and life of the visually impaired people.

Keywords. Sensory compensation, visually impaired people, multimodal interaction design

In recent years, technology has been gradually integrated into the construction of spectator scenes and the design of facilities for the visually impaired, including tactile flooring, sound guidance systems, etc., which provide richer services for the visually impaired at the tournaments, however, there is still room for expanding and deepening the interaction mode. This paper will focus on the obstacles faced by the visually impaired in daily lives, and promote the research and application of product and service design that meets the needs of the visually impaired through the study of the theory of sensory substitution and sensory compensation to create a multimodal interaction system. The research aims to solve the problems of access to information, travel, object recognition and spatial perception for the visually impaired; To construct a journey scenario for the visually impaired to watch the game, design intelligent products and interface systems that optimize the output of information, ensure worry-free travel, and provide a multi-sensory game-viewing experience and multi-modal interaction.

---

[1] E-mail: ancong0506@163.com

1. Sensory compensation theory: mechanism underpinning sensory substitution

Since the 19th century, scholars suggested that the visual deficit could be compensated for by one of the remaining senses [1]. William Hanks Levy, a British educator and blind writer, first proposed the "five senses" as a systematic element of sensory compensation for the blind. According to this, the relationship between the human brain and the five senses of sight, hearing, touch, smell and taste is like the relationship between a battery and five wires; in the case of blindness, the total energy of the "battery" is distributed to only four "wires", resulting in the rest of the senses having a stronger ability to acquire information [2]. At that time, a number of scholars argued that sensory compensation for the blind was primarily based on hearing and touch, but most of these were based on empirical descriptions rather than on experimental studies.

Until the 1970s, Prof. Paul Bach-y-Rita, University of Wisconsin System, through experiments to prove the substitution relationship among the "five senses", not only proved the possibility of sensory compensation, but also clearly put forward the theory of sensory substitution. In the experiment, 400 matrix-arranged tactile stimulators mounted on the back of the chair were able to project images scanned by a camera onto the back of blind person, enabling the blind to accurately perceive and describe the layout, depth and placement of objects in space. This led him to propose the concept of "sensory substitution", one sensory modality (mainly tactile) is utilized to obtain environmental information for use by another sensory modality (mainly visual), which was published in Nature [3]. Subsequently Paul Bach-y-Rita and others developed the first sensory substitution system, arguing that visually impaired people can feel image information through their skin [4]. Following this pioneering experiment, researchers discovered that different skin regions of the body including abdomen, back, thighs, forehead or tongue can be used as sensory organs for visual input [5]. These studies have provided important references for the design of visual substitution devices, and scholars have successively investigated a number of auditory substitution programs for vision, such as the vOICe (the capitalized letters spelling "Oh, I see!") technology auditory device [6] and the prosthesis substituting vision with audition (PSVA) [7], both of which are based on the principle of utilizing a head-mounted video camera to capture visual frames in real time as it moves, and convert them into a set of corresponding sounds, so the testers can achieve visual recognition. Tactile and auditory sensory substitutes in effect convey only grayscale visual information, and while luminance is sufficient to accomplish the perceptions of shape recognition, object localization, and distance estimation, saturated color can enliven the picture. An early device that mapped the image to a specified color and then played a recording of that color could be considered a non-sensory assistive technology. For sensory substitution of smell, a unique type of perceptual processing, experiments have demonstrated that image perception can be generated through odors, especially after associative learning between perceived odors and their names [8].

There are still many unresolved issues in this research field, and the exploration of body parts in the theory of sensory substitution is continuing and expanding. In fact, in the process of perceiving and using products, people's senses such as vision, hearing, touch, taste and other senses do not simply play their own roles, but rather, they are integrated and shaped by each other, and when one of the human sensory organs is damaged and unable to play a normal role, as a kind of physiological compensation, certain other senses may have functions beyond the normal human being, so that as far as possible, the human being will be able to get the corresponding ability, and this is the phenomenon of sensory substitution.

2. Sensory compensatory design pathways and technical principles

Sensory compensation theory was applied to the design field at the beginning of the 21st century, especially with the development of barrier-free design and aging design, and has been widely adopted as a universal feature, mainly in human-computer interaction (HCI) research. Currently, there are three ways to help improve the lifestyles of the visually impaired, which can be categorized according to the utility: visual enhancement, visual substitution, and visual replacement. These are discussed in the following sections.

2.1. Visual Enhancement

A large proportion of visually impaired people are not completely blind and have some ability to see, they just don't see things clearly. Although the industry has long used color filters or contact lenses to help visually impaired people add brightness to restore some vision in certain situations, they are not adapted to all shades of color. In recent years, researchers have found that accurate spectral separation and acquisition of different frequency band image information can be achieved using multispectral imaging, and the imaging results can reflect the vision of normal people and color-blind people [9], which can help visually impaired to increase the brightness and color in order to restore part of their vision. Incorporating multispectral lenses into the product design allows visually impaired people to access spectral information for better object recognition.

2.2. Visual Substitution

Visual substitution is similar to visual enhancement, but the output is non-visual, as tactile, auditory or others. Since senses such as tactile have a much lower information capacity than vision, the information must be processed to a level that the user can handle.

- Auditory Compensation

Hearing is second only to vision in obtaining external information, has the most direct and rapid characteristics. The vibration of air molecules creates sound waves, and the auricles can pick up vibrations coming from any direction and transmit to the brain via the auditory nerve. It has been shown that auditory compensation for the blind is a spatial attention mechanism that is enhanced when the visual system is completely deprived, which contributes to the improvement of different auditory abilities such as sound discrimination, speech recognition or auditory spatial localization [10]. The use of auditory surrogates in design can give visually impaired assistance in avoiding obstacles in traveling, reading text, and exhibiting guides, e.g., by using cars with artificial voices to help visually impaired warn of the vehicles that are coming and going. Researchers have utilized the Google Vision API to convert images captured by a built-in camera into digital text and the TTS (Text to Speech) library to convert text into audio [11] to overcome dyslexia in visually impaired. In recent years, some museums have also implemented interactive technologies to automatically play audio guides and descriptions through infrared sensing technology to meet the visually impaired' needs when visiting museums.

- Tactile Compensation

Tactile compensation is a more prevalent form of compensation in current research. Physiologically, the sense of touch is a pattern of integrated information from receptors and nerve endings concerned with pressure, temperature, pain and movement. Tactile perception is primarily associated with the pressure sensation (from mechanoreceptors), not only the smoothness, roughness, size and shape of an object's surface, but also the spatial awareness sensed from the internal sensation of body position, movement and balance, so that tactile is a communicative sensation that is receptive, expressive, communicative, and empathic. Tactile compensation refers to the use of senses such as forehead, hands, feet, back and even tongue to help visually impaired people recognize the shape of objects and spatial perception in the form of touch or stimulation signals, which can be realized through material and texture. In mobility design, the combination of white cane and blind can assist visually impaired people to avoid obstacles, and German designer Jakob Kilian developed a sensory surrogate glove device that transmits the relative positions and distances of nearby objects as vibratory stimuli to the back of the hand, assisting blind people in navigational tasks such as object recognition and wayfinding [12]. The sense of tactility is more realistic and subtle than vision, and and a more genuine perception can be obtained through contact.

-    Olfactory and Gustatory Compensations

In human coordinates, smell is a sensory sensation that can be realized at a distance, while taste is a close sensation. Since the senses of olfaction and gustation are mainly formed by the accumulation of life experience, the design for olfaction and gustation is characterized by uncertainty and individual differences, which is more difficult to be realized in the sensory compensatory interaction design for the visually impaired group.

In addition to the visual enhancement and visual substitution, the use of non-sensory forms of visual replacement is one way to enhance the blind' vision. As it relates to scientific, technical and medical issues, this category will not be discussed in this article.

It can be seen that there is still a lot of space for the research on the development of sensory compensatory design theory, and the application in design is still improving. From a comprehensive point of view, the single-sensory alternative mode and its products can no longer satisfy the diversified living environments and needs of the visually impaired, so this paper is mainly based on the theory of sensory compensatory design, and researches on the multi-modal interaction design mode of multi-sensory interaction in different scenarios, to solve the obstacles of the visually impaired people's viewing problems, and to provide theoretical references to the accessibility design of the visually impaired people and the design of sensory compensatory design.

3. Multimodal interaction design for visually impaired people

3.1. Needs based on visually impaired people

Visually impaired people are those who have visual impairments, including visual field disorders, color vision disorders, etc. In fact, a large proportion of visually impaired people still have some visual function, but the things they see are not very clear. With reference to psychologist Maslow's hierarchy of needs, and taking into account the psychological and social characteristics of the visually impaired, they are categorized into three levels of needs. The first need of the visually impaired is the "safety need", which means that the user is safe and secure. The second demand is "interaction demand", which means that the visually impaired should maintain good interaction language and behavior, such as easy-to-understand language, simple operation process, and so on. The third need is the "spiritual need", which means that the visually impaired is treated with care and respect. Successful interaction design can help visually impaired use products more easily and improve their quality of life, so interaction needs are crucial in their life.

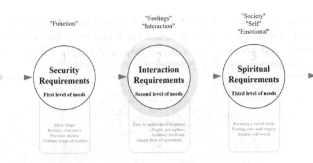

Figure 1. Hierarchy of needs of the visually impaired.

3.2. Multimodal interaction

The term "modality" means "senses", and multimodality means the fusion of two or more senses, which means human-computer interaction through multiple modes such as vision, hearing, smell, touch, environment, and so on, and is one of the channels through which human beings can obtain information through their experience and senses. It was first proposed by German physiologist Hermann von Helmholtz (1821-1894). Multi-sensory perception is able to provide complementary information from one sense to that from another compared to uni-sensory perception, and the combination of the obtained multi-sensory perceptual information enables more accurate estimation of information about an object in space, such as the enhancement of the perceptual experience of a touch screen button by combining visual and complementary audio/haptic feedback.

Any sensory information that peoples receive while interacting with a product that has been intentionally or unintentionally created can have an impact on the perception, cognition, experience and behavior of the product [13]. Since each sense can provide complementary information that is difficult to be captured by the other senses, multisensory experiences allow people to synthesize multisensory information more closely and deeply in order to understand their surrounding environments and situations, and in addition, multisensory compensation methods that combine multiple senses such as tactile, auditory, and vestibular senses in place of vision can bring positive emotions to the user, and the infinite possibilities of multisensory joint compensation pathways should be actively explored and applied to a wide variety of scenarios.

3.3. Multimodal Interaction Design System under Sensory Compensation

- Interaction scenarios for the visually impaired

User, behavior, tool or medium, purpose, and scenario are the five basic elements of interaction design [14]. Scene is an extremely important element in the interaction system, and it is an important goal of interaction design to study user behavior in a specific scene, and to plan and design user behavior logic for the corresponding scene. The large scene is relatively macroscopic, which can overview the user's macroscopic needs; while the small scene is more focused and concrete, which can provide insights into the more specific needs of the user, as well as reflecting the user's specific behavioral processes and detailed experience of the product, which facilitates the designer's targeted design under the target scenario [15].Based on the above, this paper subdivided the game viewing scenario into five small scenarios, namely, at home, on the way, outside the stadium, during the game, and after the game, and investigated the five basic elements of the interaction of visually impaired people in the five small scenarios, namely, the user, the behavior, the tool or medium, the purpose, and the scenario, to summarize the pain points, opportunity points, and needs of the visually impaired people who are currently facing the game viewing, as shown in Fig. 2.

Figure 2. Design Challenges for Visually Impaired People in Game Viewing Scenarios.

• Multimodal Interaction System Design

Seeking the goal of hassle-free viewing for the visually impaired based on accessibility, research and practical experience have shown that the implementation of multimodal interaction design has facilitated changes in service delivery. Together with the use of assistive technology, inclusive practices, and multisensory surrogates, it can improve the behavior and socialization of visually impaired people during game viewing, in addition to reducing wasted time. Combined with the above research on user pain points, opportunity points and needs, the user needs are categorized into four modules: tournament, navigation, barrier-free viewing and calling, and set as the main entrance of the user interaction interface, categorize the 15 user needs mentioned above according to these four modules as the first-level content, match the relevant technology according to user needs as the second-level content, and ultimately decide to form a visually-impaired people's tournament-viewing system by the interaction app end and the device end.

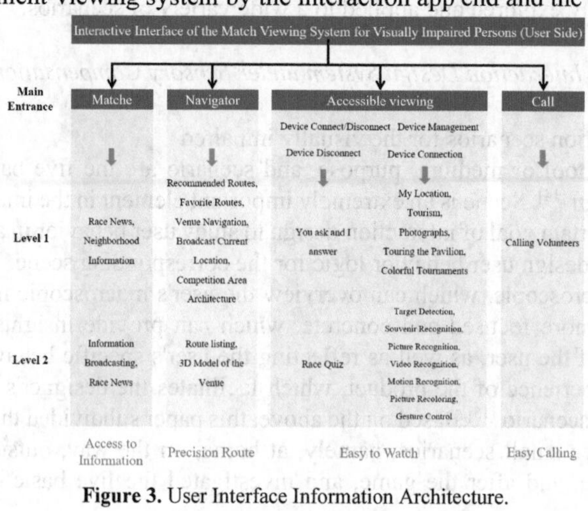

Figure 3. User Interface Information Architecture.

Four modules are constructed according to the requirements module in the information architecture diagram, as input user requirements, task operation, output results and completion of user requirements, in order to complete the flowchart of the interactive interface of the viewing system for visually impaired people.

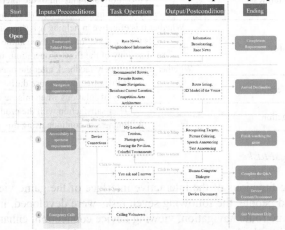

Figure 4. Flowchart of the user interface.

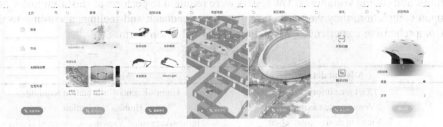

Figure 5. Interactive system interface diagrams.

4. Usability Testing of Interactive Interfaces for Visually Impaired Game Viewing Systems

Usability testing is an important part of the design practice to test the usability of the interactive interface of a multimodal visually impaired crowd viewing system under the theory of sensory surrogacy.

4.1. Selection of test subjects

A total of 6 visually impaired were invited to test the interactive interface of the game viewing system for the visually impaired, including 2 blind and 4 visually impaired people aged between 20-40 years old. The above six visually impaired have the ability to operate smart phones and are interested in sports events. By inviting target users to use the prototype, observing their performance and recording their ratings on the four test specifications, namely, user friendliness, validity, fault tolerance, and satisfaction, we can obtain effective feedback and continuously improve the interaction design of the viewing system for the visually impaired.

Table 1. Test metrics.

Test dimensions	Test metrics
User friendliness	Is the product easy to operate and learn
	Is the information layout of the interface clear
	Are there steps in the interface that are not understood
Validity	Whether it is effective in helping users accomplish their tasks
	Is there a good function guide in the interface
	The simplicity of the flow of operations in the interface
	Whether there is timely feedback after the operation is completed
Fault tolerance	Is there frequent misuse during use
	Clarity of solutions when misuse occurs
Satisfaction	User satisfaction with the product
	Willingness to continue using this product

4.2. Designing test tasks

According to the functions of the interactive interface of the game viewing system for visually impaired people, the following seven tasks were developed, including get race information, venue route navigation, viewing device connection, enhanced color vision for the visually impaired, take a picture to recognize objects, venue tours and guided tours, and calling volunteers. The testers were required to perform at least four tasks, and upon completion, they were asked to give their feedback and feelings according to the Comprehensive Experience Completion Task Evaluation Form.

Table 2. Test tasks

Mission details	Mission path
1.Get race information	Home--Events--Information Reading
2.Venue route navigation	Home - Navigation
3. Viewing device connection	Home--Accessible Viewing--Connected Devices
4. Enhanced color vision for the visually impaired	Home--Accessible Viewing--Colorful Viewing
5. Take a picture to recognize objects	Home--Accessible Viewing--Picture Taking
6. Venue tours and guided tours	Home--Accessible Viewing--Accessible Venues
7. Calling volunteers	Home--Emergency Call

4.3. Test Methods and Analysis of Results

The interface prototype for this test was created by Axure RP. After production, a QR code containing the address is generated by uploading it to the Axure cloud, and the QR code was scanned with a smartphone for simulation testing of the interface prototype. The Likert scale method was first introduced by psychologist Rensis A. Likert in 1967 and has been widely used in quantitative research in the social sciences. The method is based on constructing a series of declarative sentences describing the situation of a certain viewpoint or behavior and asking the tested users to choose one answer among five levels, where 5 is the highest score representing very satisfied, 4 is quite satisfied, 3 is average, 2 is dissatisfied, and 1 is very dissatisfied, to obtain the user's attitudes and evaluations of the viewpoint or behavior and to collect the results of the ratings, so as to summarize the strengths of the system's design and the areas that need to be improved.

After the completion of the above tests, all the test results were organized, which shows from the data that the users evaluated the various dimensions of the system interface well. The highest rating among the four dimensions is the user satisfaction with the product, and most users indicated that they have a good overall feeling about the product and are willing to continue to use it; the effectiveness score is 4.6, and users indicated that they can complete the expected tasks and have a good feedback mechanism; due to the existence of multiple operation steps in the same interface, which leads to misoperation of the visually impaired people, it is possible to set up uneven cell phone planes to help the visually impaired people differentiate the function positions, or adopt the pop-up confirmation frame and auditory guidance interaction to improve the fault tolerance of the visually impaired people's operation process. In terms of overall ratings, the design solution for this topic largely met expectations.

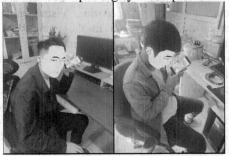

Figure 6. Usability Testing Process.

Table 3. Test results.

Test dimensions	Test metrics	Average score for each	Average score
User friendliness	Is the product easy to operate and learn	4.8	4.4
	Is the information layout of the interface clear	4.5	
	Are there steps in the interface that are not understood	4.0	
Validity	Whether it is effective in helping users accomplish their tasks	4.6	4.6
	Is there a good function guide in the interface	4.7	
	The simplicity of the flow of operations in the interface	4.3	
	Whether there is timely feedback after the operation is completed	4.8	
Fault tolerance	Is there frequent misuse during use	4.0	4.1
	Clarity of solutions when misuse occurs	4.2	
Satisfaction	User satisfaction with the product	4.6	4.7
	Willingness to continue using this product	4.7	

5. Conclusion

With the continuous development of technology, scholars have found that tactile or auditory compensatory modes can realize the visually impaired people's perception and communication of visual images, and the abdomen, back, thighs, forehead or tongue can be used as the sensory organs for visual input. Combined with the technologies of target detection and motion recognition, it can provide visually impaired with diversified information perception modes, and the multimodal interaction mode, which integrates visual enhancement and visual substitution and other sensory compensatory methods, can better satisfy the obstacles and needs of the visually impaired in the game-viewing scenarios than the single-sensory interaction mode. When designing the viewing system for the visually impaired, in addition to meeting the functionality, more attention should be paid to the interaction needs of the visually impaired to optimize the user's sensory experience and service level.

This study provides guidance for solving the problem of game-viewing for visually impaired and constructing multimodal interaction modes, and also proposes multimodal interaction design modes for different scenarios. Visual enhancement and auditory compensation interaction modes are used in the game viewing scenarios; visual enhancement and tactile compensation interaction modes can be used for navigation in open scenarios; and auditory and tactile multimodal interaction modes can be used in relatively quiet and closed scenarios. It also provides a reference for the accessibility design in future scenarios. With the continuous optimization and updating of interaction modes in product design, exploring the multimodal interaction modes of products for the visually impaired and their user experience research will become one of the hot spots of design research, and the multimodal interaction design modes of products for the visually impaired will be more diversified and perfect in the future.

Acknowledgments. This work was supported by Supply and Demand Matching Employment Program of Ministry of Education of the people's Republic of China ("Human Factors and Ergonomics Specialization", 2021).

References

[1] Guillié, S. Essai sur l'instruction des aveugles. Paris: C.L.F. Panckouke (1817),31.
[2] Levy, W. H. Blindness and the Blind or: a treatise on the science of typhlology. London: Chapman & Hall(1872),63.
[3] Bach-y-Rita P. Vision substitution by tactile image projection. Nature(1969),963-964.
[4] Collins CC, Bach-y-Rita P. Transmission of pictorial information through the skin. Adv Biol Med Phys 14(1973),285–315.
[5] Zappe A-C, Maucher T, Meier K, Scheiber C. Evaluation of a pneumatically driven stimulator device for vision substitution during fMRI studies. Magn Reson Med 51(2004),828–834.
[6] Meijer PBL. An experimental system for auditory image representations. IEEE T Biomed Eng 39(1992),112–121.
[7] Burton H, Snyder AZ, Diamond JB, Raichle ME. Adaptive changes in early and late blind: A fMRI study of verb generation to heard nouns, J Neurophysiol 88(2002),3359–3371.
[8] Sugiyama H, Ayabe-Kanamura S, Kikuchi T. Are olfactory images sensory in nature? Perception 12 (2006),1699-708.
[9] S. Di, J. Jin, G. Tang, X. Chen and R. Du. The fabrication of a multi-spectral lens array and its application in assisting color blindness. International Journal of Optomechatronics 10 (2016),14-23.
[10] O. Després, V. Candas, A. Dufour. Spatial auditory compensation in early-blind humans: Involvement of eye movements and/or attention orienting? Neuropsychologia 43(2005),1955-1962.
[11] Karmel A., Sharma A., Pandya M., Garg D. IoT based assistive device for deaf, dumb and blind people. Procedia Comput 165(2019),259-269.
[12] Kilian J, Neugebauer A, Scherffig L, Wahl S. The unfolding space glove: a wearable spatio-visual to haptic sensory substitution device for blind people. Sensors 22(2022),1859.
[13] Hendrik N. J. Schifferstein & Pieter M. A. Desmet. Tools Facilitating Multi-sensory Product Design. The Design Journal 11(2008),137-158.
[14] Xin Xiangyang. Interaction design: From physical logic to behavioral logic. Decoration 01(2015),58-62.
[15] Wang Yumei, Hu Weifeng, Tang Jin, & LI Shiguo. Research on scene theory in product interaction design. Packaging Engineering 38(2017),76-80.

Design Studies and Intelligence Engineering
L.C. Jain et al. (Eds.)
© 2024 The Authors.
This article is published online with Open Access by IOS Press and distributed under the terms
of the Creative Commons Attribution Non-Commercial License 4.0 (CC BY-NC 4.0).
doi:10.3233/FAIA231496

To Improve the Students' Learning Motivation of Vocational Colleges Through Design Thinking

Qianqian LIN [a,1] , Zhenghong LIU [a,2], and Yuanbo SUN[b]

ª *Beijing Polytechnic*
ᵇ *Beijing Institute of Technology*

Abstract. This study aims to introduce design thinking intervention into vocational education classes to improve students' learning motivation. Through the literature research on design thinking and learning motivation, researchers choose to implement design thinking intervention in vocational college students' career planning courses. To test the results of the intervention, the paired sample t-test was used to demonstrate whether there were statistically significant differences for the quasi-experiment group before and after design thinking intervention in learning motivation. The results show that design thinking plays a positive role in improving students' learning motivation in vocational college.

Keywords. design thinking, learning motivation, vocational education

1. Introduction

China attaches great importance to the development of vocational colleges and points out in the " "National Medium- and Long-Term Education Reform and Development Plan" that improving the quality of vocational education is the core of the reform and development of national vocational education [1]. However, vocational education still has many problems and challenges at this stage. Previous studies and literature studies have found that at present, students in higher vocational colleges generally have the problem of low learning motivation, lack of interest in learning, and poor self-control ability [2], which seriously affect the teaching effect.

Learning motivation plays a key role in students' learning effect, and if educators can stimulate students' learning motivation, it will be of great help to students' learning [3]. At the same time, learning motivation has a direct impact on learning performance, which is conducive to students' positive emotions in the learning process can improve students' learning satisfaction, and is the main factor that enables students to maintain continuous learning [4]. Studies have shown that students with high learning motivation are more active in learning, more willing to explore new knowledge, and brave to face various difficulties and challenges in the learning process [5]. Students with high learning motivation are more satisfied, confident, and exploring in learning, and have a good experience in the learning process [6].

---

[1] Corresponding Author.

[2] Corresponding Author.

At this stage, design thinking as a mature method and thinking model, has been widely used in engineering, management, education, and other fields, and has derived a variety of tools and models, such as Stanford University's five-step design thinking and the British Double Diamond Model. Design thinking is goal-oriented, emphasizes interdisciplinarity, and is committed to cultivating students' thinking methods. It has been proven to effectively improve student engagement in class [7] and has also been proven to help cultivate students' innovative abilities and higher-order thinking [8].

Thus, this study aims to introduce design thinking into vocational education classes to improve students' learning motivation. Accordingly, this study intends to explore the following research question (RQ):

RQ: What are the differences in students' motivation before and after design thinking intervention?

Based on the above research questions, the researchers define the research objective (RO) as follows:

RO: To determine the differences in students' motivation in class between before and after teaching by design thinking intervention.

This research paper consists of five parts. Section 2 provides a detailed review of the literature. In Section 3, the research methodology is explained. In Section 4, the findings with the research objectives were compared. In Section 5, the research contributions to theory and practice are presented, and Section 6 concludes the research paper by stating limitations and suggesting future directions.

2. Literature review

2.1. Design thinking

Design thinking was first proposed by Simon in 1969. After decades of development, design thinking has been widely used in many fields. This study focuses on the research of design thinking in the field of education.

Design thinking emphasizes goal orientation, pays attention to the cultivation of innovative thinking, and mainly focuses on practical projects in the implementation process, which is consistent with the educational concept of vocational education focusing on learning in practice. At the same time, design thinking breaks through the teacher-centered teaching mode in traditional education, and can provide mature concepts, methods, and tools, which is also recognized by the modern education circle. Razzouk and Shute discuss and summarize the research on design thinking and apply the findings to education to improve students' problem-solving skills [9]. Lin introduced design thinking into vocational college students' career planning courses and found that this mode could improve students' career planning abilities[7]. Wang and Wang combine case analysis and design thinking to propose a teaching method called the Joint Analysis Process (JAP) [10]. Lin and Shen believe that design thinking helps to enhance people's higher-order thinking[8]. Luka introduced the attributes and processes of design thinking into the teaching process, emphasizing a human-centered problem-solving approach to bring interdisciplinary innovation and creative outcomes[11].

2.2. Learning motivation

Learning motivation includes two psychological processes: motivation and orientation, which are the keys for learners to maintain the learning process continuously. It means that learners have clear goals, and learning initiative, and are willing to make efforts for them. A commonly used model of learning motivation is the Attention, Relevance, Confidence, and Satisfaction (ARCS) model. ARCS model is based on the expected value theory[12], which points out that to stimulate students' learning motivation, it is necessary to: (1) make students' attention focus and keep it continuously; (2) Students should think that what they are learning is relevant to their needs and goals; (3) Make students confident and believe that they can succeed; (4) Students can feel satisfaction and pride in learning. The four components are defined as.

- Attention refers to the degree of continuous attention to things in a period [13], which is manifested by students' positive attitude towards learning, conscious attention to learning content, and the ability to generate interest and desire for the breadth and depth of learning exploration.
- Relevance means that the learning content is relevant to the student's goals and needs, has value for the student's future development, and the student is willing to put practical effort into it. Students need a classroom with practical value and a purposeful learning process[14]. What students learn needs to be relevant to them and worthy of their time and attention[15].
- Confidence means that students affirm their strengths and merits, have the belief that they can achieve the learning goals they want to achieve, and are willing to make full preparations to meet challenges before achieving the learning goals. According to Jiang, self-confidence is related to success, satisfaction, and happiness. Self-efficacy, self-esteem, and self-identity are the three factors that affect the level of self-confidence[16]. Self-confidence also refers to students' perceived likelihood of success through individual effort and control[13].
- Satisfaction refers to the sense of honor that students feel when they reach the expected goal in the learning process, or the inner satisfaction after being praised by classmates and teachers. Satisfaction positively impacts learning and is also an important factor in maintaining learning motivation[12].

2.3. Research Framework

Following the design thinking steps commonly developed by Stanford's d 'school, the design thinking process can be divided into five processes: empathy, definition, ideation, prototyping, and testing. Numerous tools are used in each process, such as groupings, interviews, brainstorming, user research, blueprints, and reports. These methods can mobilize the enthusiasm of students, help students set goals, and improve students' attention, to improve the learning motivation of vocational students. Therefore, researchers introduced design thinking into the curriculum to improve students' learning motivation and the action research framework can be seen in Figure 1.

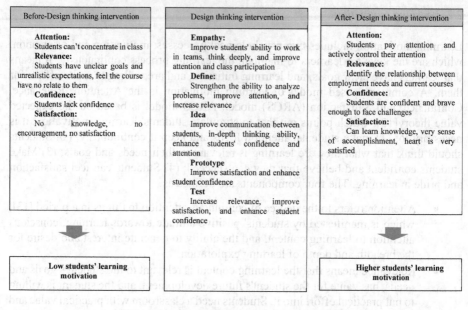

Before-Design thinking intervention	Design thinking intervention	After- Design thinking intervention
Attention: Students can't concentrate in class **Relevance:** Students have unclear goals and unrealistic expectations, feel the course have no relate to them **Confidence:** Students lack confidence **Satisfaction:** No knowledge, no encouragement, no satisfaction	**Empathy:** Improve students' ability to work in teams, think deeply, and improve attention and class participation **Define:** Strengthen the ability to analyze problems, improve attention, and increase relevance **Idea** Improve communication between students, in-depth thinking ability, enhance students' confidence and attention **Prototype** Improve satisfaction and enhance student confidence **Test** Increase relevance, improve satisfaction, and enhance student confidence	**Attention:** Students pay attention and actively control their attention **Relevance:** Identify the relationship between employment needs and current courses **Confidence:** Students are confident and brave enough to face challenges **Satisfaction:** Can learn knowledge, very sense of accomplishment, heart is very satisfied
Low students' learning motivation		Higher students' learning motivation

Figure1 Action research framework (researcher, 2023)

3. Methodology

3.1. Research design

This study adopts a combination of qualitative and quantitative research methods, mainly using questionnaires, interviews, self-reports, and classroom observation. The study samples were 68 sophomores majoring in media design at Beijing Polytechnic (BP). The questionnaire design was based on the ARCS model of learning motivation, see Table 1. The 5-point Likert scale was used to set answers, ranging from strongly disagree to strongly agree. The questionnaire was used to test students' attention, confidence, relevance, and satisfaction before and after the design thinking intervention.

Table 1. Sample questionnaire adapted from M. Keller (John Keller's ARCS model. 1987).

Dimension	Items
Attention	1. This class captures my attention.
	2. I listen attentively and think carefully in class.
	3. My attention is often caught by questions about topics in class.
	4. My attention is often caught by the goals I want to achieve in this class.

Relevance	5. I think carefully about what I expect to learn
	6. I actively search for the professional skills needed for employment.
	7. I know how the knowledge learned in this course will be applied in my work in the future.
	8. I discussed the relationship between this class and the future with the teacher and other students.
Confidence	9. I feel confident that I will do well in this course.
	10. Although the course is challenging, I think I can solve it and face it bravely.
	11. I think I am a valuable person.
	12. I think I have a lot of advantages.
Satisfaction	13. I learned what I wanted to learn in class.
	14. This course gives me a sense of satisfaction.
	15. I enjoy working on this course.
	16. I would recommend this course to other students.

To test the validity of the questionnaire, the researchers invited three experts in design thinking to rate it. Among the scores given by the three professors, except for the fifth and eighth items, the average score is 0.8, and the average score of the others is 1, and the validity test meets the standard. To test the reliability of the questionnaire, 32 respondents participated in a pilot test. After the 32 respondents completed the questionnaire, Research Technic conducted Cronbach's Alpha test on the reliability of the data, and the results are shown in Table 2, and the reliability test meets the standard.

Table 2. The Reliability Test Result (N=32).

Student's motivation	Cronbach's Alpha
Attention	0.956
Relevance	0.933
Confidence	0.930
Satisfaction	0.975

3.2. Research sampling

This study selected 68 sophomores majoring in media design from BP as research samples. The sample was moderately male-female and ranged in age from 18 to 25. The reason why the researcher chose sophomore students is that freshman students have fewer majors' courses, and junior students have more internships outside the school. The quasi-experimental group is shown in Table 3.

Table 3. Demographic Characteristics of Respondents.

Content		Frequency	Percentage
Gender	Male	33	48.53%
	Female	35	51.47%
Age	18-25	68	100%
Major	Media design	68	100%
Grade	Sophomore year	68	100%

3.3. Procedure

Before the design thinking intervention, the researchers interviewed 5 students. In the interviews, the students repeatedly mentioned the status quo of inattention, and the students generally lacked goals and learning motivation. To better study the learning motivation, the researchers conducted a questionnaire survey on the students.

The design thinking intervention consists of empathy, definition, ideation, prototyping, and testing. The researchers first introduced the steps and implementation of design thinking to the students. Then, the researcher guided students to set goals. Each student wrote down what they wanted to achieve in 5 years. Teachers grouped students by the goals they set and grouped students into one group that shared a common goal, each group contained 4-5 students. (1)Empathy: In the first stage, students introduced themselves to each other to increase mutual understanding. In the second stage, teachers guided students to collect information from recruitment websites and government public information networks to understand the employment environment. (2)Definition: In the third stage, the group conducted brainstorming and focused groups based on early self-understanding and environmental understanding to identify feasible goals that were in line with the actual situation. (3) Prototyping: Worked in groups to develop plans and strategies to achieve set goals. (4)Test: Each group reported the plans to teachers and classmates and modified and improved the plan after they put forward relevant suggestions.

After the design thinking intervention, the same questionnaire was used in the quasi-experiment group as the quantitative research, self-reflection reports, and 8 semi-structured-open questions also used as qualitative research to measure students' learning motivation in class.

4. Results

The researchers used a paired sample t-test to analyze the questionnaire data, and the differences in the mean scores of students' learning motivation before and after the design thinking intervention were summarized as follows: The results are shown in Table 4.

Table 4. Paired samples t-test on Students 'Motivation.

Pairs	Paired (Mean SD)		Difference (1-2)	T	P
	Pair1	Pair2			
Q1:This class captures my attention	2.81 1.11	4.24 0.81	1.43	8.237	0.000**
Pair1 Pair2					
Q2:I listen attentively and think carefully in class.	2.78 1.13	4.34 0.73	1.56	9.132	0.000**
Pair1 Pair2					
Q3: My attention is often stimulated by the questions asked or the problems given on the subject matter in this class	2.76 1.07	4.18 0.86	1.41	8.473	0.000**
Pair1 Pair2					
Q4: My attention is often stimulated by the goals I want to achieve in this class .	2.85 1.12	4.37 0.79	1.51	9.002	0.000**
Pair1 Pair2					
Attention	2.80 1.01	4.28 0.73	1.48	9.454	0.000**
Pair1 Pair2					
Q5:I think carefully about what I expect to learn.	2.99 1.13	4.44 0.72	1.46	8.938	0.000**
Pair1 Pair2					
Q6:I actively search for the professional skills needed for employment.	2.93 1.18	4.37 0.73	1.44	8.085	0.000**
Pair1 Pair2					
Q7:I know how the knowledge learned in this course will be applied in my work in the future.	2.87 1.13	4.44 0.70	1.57	9.514	0.000**
Pair1 Pair2					
Q8:I discussed the relationship between this class and the future with the teacher and other students.	2.63 1.14	4.31 0.87	1.68	9.034	0.000**
Pair1 Pair2					
Relevance	2.85 1.02	4.39 0.68	1.54	9.714	0.000**
Pair1 Pair2					
Q9:I feel confident that I will do well in this course.	2.94 1.06	4.43 0.74	1.49	9.785	0.000**
Pair1 Pair2					
Q10:Although the course is challenging, I think I can solve it and face it bravely.	2.90 1.15	4.47 0.70	1.57	8.654	0.000**
Pair1 Pair2					
Q11:I think I am a valuable person.	2.96 1.32	4.41 0.80	1.46	7.748	0.000**
Pair1 Pair2					
Q12:I think I have a lot of advantages.	2.88 1.22	4.37 0.83	1.49	7.951	0.000**
Pair1 Pair2					
Confidence	2.92 0.99	4.42 0.70	1.50	9.881	0.000**
Pair1 Pair2					
Q13:I learned what I wanted to learn in class.	2.78 1.13	4.27 0.70	1.52	9.088	0.000**
Pair1 Pair2					
Q14: This course gives me a sense of satisfaction.	2.80 1.12	4.27 0.72	1.55	8.854	0.000**
Pair1 Pair2					
Q15: I enjoy working on this course.	2.86 1.31	4.38 0.80	1.56	9.246	0.000**
Pair1 Pair2					

Q16: I would recommend this course to other students. Pair1 Pair2	2.78	1.06	4.27	0.77	1.47	8.746	0.000**
Satisfaction Pair1 Pair2	2.78	1.06	4.27	0.72	1.49	9.125	0.000**

p<0.05.

According to the t-test results of paired samples results in the above table, the Sig value of students' attention, relevance, confidence, and satisfaction are all less than 0.05. This information implies a significant difference in students' learning motivation between before and after design thinking intervention.

The researchers designed semi-structured-open questions, there are 8 questions. The researchers selected representative responses as follows:

"There's a lot of interaction in the class that doesn't allow your mind to wander... ", "I became aware of my lack of concentration and tried not to touch my phone...", "What you learn now is what you'll need to hire in the future...", "I can learn difficult lessons, and I feel accomplishment after solving a problem."

In the reflection report, students mentioned that after teaching by design thinking, they can pay more attention in class, be more aware of the relationship between the knowledge they have learned in class and the skills they should have in the future, and have more confidence to face difficulties and accept challenges.

5. Conclusion and discussion

5.1. Conclusion

This study aims to investigate the current situation of BP and try to improve students' learning motivation by implementing design thinking interventions. Combined with the previous literature study, the researchers implemented a design thinking intervention for BP students. The research objectives were achieved through the use of quantitative and qualitative analysis. The results of semi-structured interview, reflective paper, observation, and paired sample t-test all prove that design thinking can promote students' learning motivation. The data of quantitative analysis results show that the significance value is less than 0.01, indicating a statistically significant difference compared with before the implementation of design thinking intervention. It is also proved that design thinking intervention can promote the improvement of students' learning motivation.

5.2. Discussion

To determine the differences in students' motivation in class before and after the design thinking intervention, the researcher designed a design thinking intervention based on the preliminary diagnosis, literature review, and vocational college students' characteristics. It contains empathy, define, idea, prototype, and test. In this research, the findings supported the same or similar results of relevant studies done by previous researchers.

Previous research has shown that design thinking can enhance communication and collaboration among students, and improve relevance and creativity[17]. After interventions, students mentioned in their reports that the classroom atmosphere is good, and they are more willing to engage in the class, by clarifying their goals through group discussions, they found the relationship between the course and future employment, their attention is improved, and they are more willing to devote their energy to the class. Ewin et al. believe that design thinking methods can improve empathy, proactively face challenges, and improve self-confidence and satisfaction to a certain extent[18]. After intervention, students feel that they can solve problems more clearly, and the probability of success is increased through the test process, which makes them more confident. Razzouk and Shute believe that design thinking can improve students' problem-solving abilities[9]. Mosely, Wright, and Straker found that design thinking will improve the experience in the learning process and realize the value of learning[19]. After the intervention, students reported that they were satisfied during the learning process because there was a lot of classroom interaction, and their concentration was high. They used design thinking to solve many problems and their self-confidence improved. These behaviors have obvious changes in students. The research report of the three observation teachers also proved that fewer students played on their mobile phones in class showed their attention is concentrated, and they would like to express themselves showed they are more confident than before.

These findings are consistent with data from quantitative studies. Quantitative analysis of variables with a sig value less than 0.5 proved that students' attention, relevance, self-confidence, and confidence were improved after design thinking intervention. The results of this study are consistent with previous literature, suggesting that design thinking can enhance students' learning motivation.

Previous studies have shown that design thinking has been applied in the field of education and has a positive impact on students. The results of this study not only strengthen the positive role of design thinking in education but also show the application of design thinking in a new field of education - vocational education. Therefore, the research process and results can provide theoretical and practical references for improving the learning motivation of vocational college students. In the future, the researchers can further study to form a design thinking-oriented intervention model, which can be extended to more vocational education schools.

6. Heading

To continuously stimulate students' learning motivation, the researchers put forward the following suggestions:

School level. Schools should promote design thinking throughout the school. Previous studies have shown that design thinking has been proven to improve students' innovative ability and problem-solving abilities, and this study also proves that design thinking can improve students' learning motivation. Schools should hold design thinking promotion classes for students and teachers, encourage teachers to apply design thinking in curriculum design, and encourage students to apply design thinking in study and life.

Teacher level. The teacher should let the students be the master of the class. By setting goals for students, and organizing groups, plans, and discussions, we can find solutions to problems that are more effective than simply inculcating knowledge through lectures. Teachers should encourage students to think more, express more, and praise students without stinginess, which can improve students' learning motivation.

Student level. Students should pay attention to the improvement of personal ability, especially in the improvement of self-control and employability. Students can learn more about attention maintenance and future employment, which can enhance self-control, help students set goals, and prepare for the changing and complex society in the future.

Limitations of the study:

The study has some limitations. First of all, design thinking is applied in career planning courses, because the content of career planning courses contains content that "future employment is related to current courses", which may affect the intervention effect in "relevance". Second, the sample size of this study is not large, and it is only conducted in the School of Art and Design, so the results obtained may not apply to other schools. Third, due to the limited duration of the intervention, the current study is only short-term, and it remains to be seen whether it will yield long-term results.

Recommendations for future research:

The intervention in this study showed some improvement in students' learning motivation, but due to the short duration of the intervention, it is uncertain whether it can have a long-term lasting effect. Future studies should extend the intervention process and continue to observe and test the effects of the intervention for a longer period. Secondly, the samples of this study are students from the same college and major, and whether the research results apply to students from other majors remains to be verified. Therefore, future research should select a larger sample size and more students from more majors, so that the research results will be more applicable.

Acknowledgment: The authors would like to acknowledge the teachers and students of Beijing Polytechnic, and this study is supported by the " *Project of Cultivation for young top-notch Talents of Beijing Municipal Institutions*", and the Key Project of Beijing's 14th Five-Year Plan for Education Science in 2022: "*Research on Project Teaching Reform of Design Thinking Integrating Technical Courses in High Schools*".

References

[1] Ministry of Education of the People's Republic of China, the 2018 National Vocational College Evaluation Report was released, Retrieved November 27, 2019, from http://www.moe.gov.cn/jyb_xwfb/gzdt_gzdt/s5987/201911/t20191127_409905.html.

[2] Zheng, Jian, Summary and analysis of "China Vocational Education Observation Report" by Mercator China Research Center, Germany. *Chinese Vocational and Technical Education* 33 (2016), 78-86.

[3] P. R. Pintrich, A motivational science perspective on the role of student motivation in learning and teaching contexts, *Journal of Educational Psychology* 4 (2003), 667–686.

[4] F.Paas, J. E.Tuovinen, J. J. G.Merriënboer, & van and A. A.Darabi, A motivational perspective on the relation between mental effort and performance: Optimizing learner involvement in instruction, *Educational Technology Research & Development* 3 (2005), 25–34.

[5] R.Martens, J. Gulikers, & T. Bastiaens, The impact of intrinsic motivation on e-learning in authentic computer tasks. *Journal of Computer Assisted Learning* 5 (2004), 368–376.

[6] U. Schiefele, Interest, learning, and motivation. *Educational Psychologist*, 26 (1991), 299–323.

[7] Lin, Qianqian, and Yuanbo Sun. "A Teaching Experience of Service Design Course Supported by Design Thinking." Advances in Ergonomics in Design: Proceedings of the AHFE 2021 Virtual Conference on Ergonomics in Design, July 25-29, 2021, USA. Springer International Publishing, 2021.

[8] Lin Lin, Shen Shu-sheng. The Connotation and Training Strategies of the Design Thinking. *Modern Distance Education Research* 6 (2016), 18-25.

[9] R.Razzouk, & V.Shute, What is design thinking and why is it important? *Review of Educational Research* 3 (2012), 330–348.

[10] S.Wang, & H.Wang, Teaching design thinking through case analysis: Joint analytical process. *Decision Sciences Journal of Innovative Education* 9 (2011), 113–118.

[11] I.Luka, Design thinking in pedagogy. *The Journal of Education, Culture, and Society* 2 (2014), 63–74.

[12] J. M. Keller, *Motivational design for learning and performance: The ARCS model approach.* Springer Press, 2009.

[13] S.Wongwiwatthananukit, Applying the arcs model of motivational design to pharmaceutical education. *Libri* **2** (2015), 188-96.

[14] G.Claxton, Expanding young people's capacity to learn. *British Journal of Educational Studies* **2** (2007), 1-20.

[15] J. D. Willms, (2009). Student Engagement at School: A Sense of Belonging and Participation. Results from PISA 2000. Paris: Organization for Economic Co-operation and Development (OECD). Accessed October 2010 from http://www.unb.ca/crisp/pdf/0306.pdf.

[16] Jiang, Xianglin., Zeng, Jiansheng. & Liu, Shaisheng., On the Cultivation of self-confidence of students in higher vocational colleges, *Journal of Jiujiang Vocational and Technical College* **1** (2008), 71-73.

[17] C.Lee, & R.Benza, Teaching innovation skills: Application of design thinking in a graduate marketing course, *Business Education Innovation Journal* **7** (2015), 43–50.

[18] N.Ewin, J.Luck, R.Chugh, & J.Jarvis, Rethinking project management education: A humanistic approach based on design thinking, *Procedia Computer Science* **12** (2017), 503–510.

[19] G.Mosely, N.Wright, & C.Wrigley, Facilitating design thinking: A comparison of design expertise, *Thinking Skills and Creativity* **27** (2018), 177–189.

Design Studies and Intelligence Engineering
L.C. Jain et al. (Eds.)
© 2024 The Authors.
This article is published online with Open Access by IOS Press and distributed under the terms
of the Creative Commons Attribution Non-Commercial License 4.0 (CC BY-NC 4.0).
doi:10.3233/FAIA231497

Research on the Color Design of Hospital Inpatient Wards Under the Concept of Color Empowerment

Wei-lin QIU [a,b,1]

a. College of Mechanical and Electrical Engineering, Guangdong University of Petrochemical Technology, Guangdong Maoming 525000, China
b. City University of Macau, Macau, 999078, China

Abstract: The concept of color empowerment is a recent study that combines color with architecture, industry, and product design. The concept of color empowerment emphasizes the influence of color on the physiological and psychological aspects of people's existence, and strengthening the design of color empowerment can help hospital inpatient wards to sort out their functions, explore the potential functions of color, and explore the positive impact of color on the hospital inpatient environment. By analyzing representative and positive hospital designs with case studies, we can extract the color characteristics, combine color with the needs of hospital users, find more functions brought by color, create a good medical environment, relieve patients' psychological stress and enhance the body's ability to resist disease, and help patients recover as soon as possible. In practice, it is necessary to combine the actual situation and clarify the main points and attention to the application of color in the interior design of medical buildings, so as to lay a solid foundation for the subsequent work and improve the effect and level of ward design.

Keywords: Color empowerment; Hospital inpatient wards; Interior design; Tone

1. Introduction

Under the influence of the COVID-19 virus epidemic, the capacity, equipment and environment of modern hospitals are gradually changing, and humanistic care and psychological guidance in inpatient wards have become one of the focuses of attention. The color environment design of hospitals has become an important element in influencing people's psychology. In the past, the medical space design in the use of color and ornamental characteristics of a single, cannot meet the patient in the hospital in the heart of the demand and requirements. Considering the special characteristics of the inpatient ward environment, reasonable color empowerment can create a better medical building environment, enhance the image and efficiency of the hospital, ease the emotions of patients, their families and medical staff, and reduce psychological pressure.

2 Design Impact Analysis of Color Empowerment Theory

Empowerment is a concept that was firstly proposed in the business operation and management circles, and its original meaning is that enterprises release power from the

---

[1] Corresponding Author. Qiu Weilin, Lecturer of Guangdong University of Petrochemical Technology, Guangdong Maoming; E-mail: 258605246@qq.com

top down and give employees the power to work independently under certain principles and rules. Empowerment is a kind of management concept that subverts the traditional incentive mechanism of enterprises, which is different from the previous mode of "company employment-hierarchical management", and is more inclined to the innovative mode of "gathering elites - resource sharing", which creates a suitable atmosphere and supportive environment to give full play to the creativity of the creative elites. It creates a suitable atmosphere and supportive environment to give full play to the creativity of the creative elites, quickly perceive the needs of customers, and happily create corresponding products and services. This concept of participation in creation extends to psychology, where empowerment is equivalent to "awakening", which refers to giving energy to others through words, deeds, attitudes, and even the design and change of the environment, so as to change the negative state of others. Empowerment in psychology includes self-empowerment and external empowerment. Self-empowerment is through self-promotion, burning up one's own inner motivation, looking for the direction of positive efforts to stimulate personal energy; external empowerment refers to the use of words, attitudes, behaviors, or environmental modification, etc., to ignite the energy of others or awaken others. It can be seen that empowerment is to stimulate the potential energy of people, things and objects in a certain environment or mechanism, and to bring this energy into active play, so that it can produce new functions and effects.

The research on color psychology has a long history, and there are scientific experimental results on the effects of color on people's physiology and psychology. The most representative researches on the influence of color system include the Menzel Color System, NCS Natural Color System and PCCS Color System of Japan Color Research Institute, whose researches mainly include the characteristics of color, the interrelationship between colors and the influence of colors. By combining the effects of color on people's bodies and minds with empowerment theory, we can construct a pyramid of color empowerment (Figure 1).

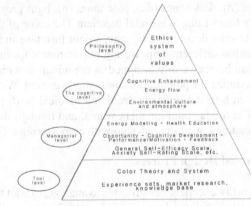

Figure 1 Color Empowerment Pyramid

The bottom layer of the pyramid belongs to the tool layer, which is the most basic part, including the use of color-related research theories and systems as an empowerment tool; the second layer is the extension of the application of the concept of color empowerment from management science, including the study of the impact of color on people's emotions, physical state and other aspects of the assessment criteria will be involved in the commonly used emotional assessment scales, including self-management ability scale, general self-efficacy scale, anxiety self-assessment scale and self-assessment scale. The assessment criteria will be intervened in commonly used emotional assessment scales, including self-management energy scale, general self-efficacy scale, anxiety self-assessment scale, depression self-assessment scale, etc., and also intervene in targeted, self-developed scales in different departments according to the actual situation; the third layer belongs to the cognitive part of the contents of the negative emotions, such as anxiety, depression and agitation, which seriously affects the clinical rehabilitation of somatic diseases and the prognosis of the disease1. Under the role of color empowerment, the changes in the emotional factors of depression, anxiety, and agitation of the subjects are studied, as well as the role of these factors in terms of work status, rehabilitation status, and health resources. The highest level as the philosophical level, which affects the overall ethical relationships and values, is the ideological level of color empowerment. This is an overview of the current basic setting for the theory of color empowerment.

Through the analysis of the PCCS color system into the color empowerment pyramid, in the overall environment design of hospital wards, mainly through different hue, lightness, purity and hue to convey different perceptions, bring different emotions and mental states, but also make the hospital inpatient wards environment to produce different semantic and emotional value. Therefore, in the design of hospital inpatient wards, the three attributes of color and the design of tone are the main elements that produce design impact. Hue produces various associations, cold colors produce a sense of cleanliness, warm colors produce a sense of friendliness and warmth, and the brightness of colors affects the overall environmental space.

Brightness and purity in the PCCS color system is divided into twelve shades, which are vivid tones (V), strong tones (S), bright tones (B), light tones (It), light tones (sf), dark tones (dp), cloudy tones (d), dark tones (dk), pale tones (p), light grey tones (ltg), grey tones (g), and dark grey tones (dkg), hospital inpatient The color of the ward contains several aspects such as interior decoration, signage, indoor furniture and decorative color matching, and each part has different empowering requirements for hues. The color of each part of the ward can be reasonably designed in combination with its contents and materials in order to maximize the potential of color empowerment. We study the effects of color empowerment in hospital inpatient wards on medical staff, patients, patients' families and other staff in the hospital inpatient wards, and through the study of visual patterns and color associations, we form a design with empowering effects.

3 Color Empowerment-led Design Process

Combine the existing world's excellent design cases to analyze, extract the design theme, and select the corresponding color scheme according to the design theme, adjust the matching hue of the color scheme, so as to produce the color impact. First, investigate the world's classic hospital design cases, extract the relationship between their design themes and design colors, and provide design directions for designing the color scheme of hospital inpatient wards. Secondly, design research is conducted to collect users' needs, construct an imagery map and analyze it. Finally, the color empowerment design scheme for hospital inpatient wards is established.

The color empowerment analysis is carried out on the 12-tone scheme in the PCCS color system, and the perceptual law is applied to match the color tone with the hard furnishings, signage design, soft furnishings and other aspects, so as to design a design scheme with the effect of color empowerment. Due to the special nature of the hospital ward environment, the 3 shades of gray are not used. In the process of investigation, it was found that the general public could not accurately distinguish the closer tones among them, so bright tones (B) and light tones (It) were combined into bright and clear tones, and turbid tones (d) and light gray tones ((ltg) were combined into intermediate tones. Finally, the five tones most suitable for the hospital ward environment are extracted, which are distinct, bright and clear, light and weak, dark and intermediate, and are expressed in warm and cold colors respectively (Figure 2).

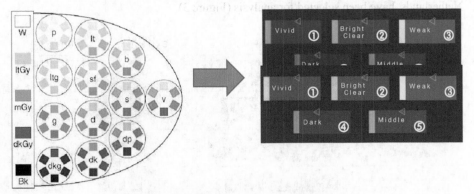

Fig. 2 PCCS color system hue extraction

These five shades were combined with the hue, purity and lightness elements of color empowerment in a questionnaire survey to find out the direction of the public's highest acceptance of color empowerment in the hospital's impression.

4 Design practice

4.1 Design purpose

Ulrich proposed the theory of supportive design in 1991. Unlike the concept of healing environments, which emphasizes the elimination of environmental features that cause stress or negative emotions, supportive design theory takes an important step forward by emphasizing the addition of resources for coping with stress, anxiety, and other negative emotions in healthcare environments, and the improvement of healthcare procedures to enhance the positive emotions of patients2.

The purpose of color empowerment design is to redesign the colors of hospital inpatient rooms to have a color empowerment effect. Hospitals are public institutions that provide patients with necessary medical examinations, therapeutic measures, nursing techniques, reception services, rehabilitation equipment, rescue and transportation services, etc. Their design is unique in that, in addition to meeting medical and nursing care, it also includes duties such as stabilizing the working conditions of medical staff, stabilizing patients' emotions, and reducing the burden on patients' families.

4.2 Classic Case Study

4.2.1 Classic Hospital Color Empowerment Analysis

Hospitals have special design needs in terms of patient care, especially inpatient wards, which are different from outpatient clinics in that users, especially patients, need to stay in the environment for a long time, so the design of this environment is more complex than that of outpatient clinics and other places. In this paper, the most influential hospitals in the design of medical environments, such as the Basel Neurological Rehabilitation Hospital in Switzerland, the Asahikawa Red Cross Hospital in Japan, the Cleveland Medical Center in the U.S., and the Zaandam Medical Center in the Netherlands, have been selected for analysis (Figure 3).

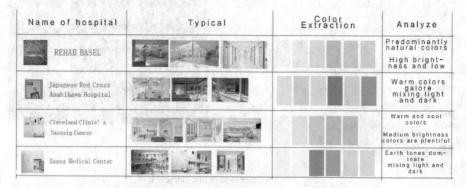

Name of hospital	Typical	Color Extraction	Analyze
REHAB BASEL			Predominantly natural colors High brightness and low
Japanese Red Cross Asahikawa Hospital			Warm colors galore mixing light and dark
Cleveland Clinic' s Taussig Cancer			Warm and cool colors Medium brightness colors are plentiful
Zaans Medical Center			Earth tones dominate mixing light and dark

Figure 3 Classic Hospital Color Empowerment Analysis

NO1-REHAB BASLE: Built in 1999 and completed in 2002 by HERZOG & DE MEURON, the architecture draws on the concept of town planning to introduce natural light and landscape into the hospital environment. The concept of color empowerment is that color frames the hospital space in a way that affects everyone who comes to the hospital, including healthcare professionals, patients, visitors and caregivers. Color design is mainly expressed by color schemes, material textures, light effects, and patterns. In order to match this design concept, a large number of natural elements are selected from building materials to colors. For example, the corridors, staircases, and halls of the hospital are all wrapped with original wood-colored wood grain boards and wooden floors, and the wooden columns, beams, and doorframes are all original colors with white latex paint and cement self-leveling, and all the windows in the public space are set as floor-to-ceiling full-surface glass windows, which provide sufficient light, and the lush greenery in the courtyard through the large area of transparent glass adds an extra colorful empowerment to the wards and makes people in the rooms feel that they are in good hands. The lush greenery of the courtyard adds an extra colorful touch to the rooms, allowing people in the rooms to feel the abundant life force. Black handles in the nurses' station and corridors of the inpatient unit are designed to harmonize the brightness of the overall space. One of the hospital's healing features is the spa courtyard, which uses medium shades of blue to create a serene and elegant space. Basel Neurological Rehabilitation Hospital introduces natural elements of color to patients to assist in the treatment, but also for the psychological adjustment of the companions, medical staff, the use of varying shades of wood and high purity of green and white with the use of inpatient wards close to nature, increasing affinity. The use of this color, so that when people walk into the hospital, did not feel that this is a hospital space, but like in the forest, in the park, color empowerment to give the Basel Neurological Rehabilitation Hospital, a "hospital, not like a hospital" effect.

NO2-RED CROSS ASAHIKAWA in Japan: Built in 2017 with a floor area of 48,225 square meters, the designer is the Hospital Bedding Research Group, whose inpatient wards have a total of 514 beds. Asahikawa Red Cross Hospital was the first hospital in Hokkaido, Japan to have an intensive care center, and the first to develop an image of medical care support. The color scheme of the Asahikawa Red Cross Hospital's design is similar to that of the Basel Neurological Rehabilitation Hospital in that it also incorporates nature, but its use of color is consistent with local Japanese values in order to create a sense of calm and positivity. Asahikawa Red Cross Hospital's most prominent use of color empowerment is in the design of its inpatient logo, which won the 43rd SDA Award for Excellence in Signature Design in Category E. This design is a great example of the use of color empowerment. This design is a subtle expression of color empowerment, which makes people feel a sense of emotional calm.

In its original design, the signs in the inpatient wards were not color-coded, and the contents were handwritten in black and white, which led to a high rate of errors in the process of care and treatment by medical staff and patients' families. This is not a cure for the patient, but fatal. So the hospital commissioned the designer to redesign the entire hospital signage, especially the bedside signage in the inpatient wards, into four categories: A, B, C and D. Category A is for patient information, attending physician information, allergy history (special precautions), and the nurse-in-charge, which is represented in black and white/graphic. category B is for supplementing the graphic symbols and precautionary character information required by the hospital/clinic department, and is usually preceded by a yellow triangular warning message. preceded by a warning sign with a yellow triangle, with specifics in black letters on a white background.Category C is the risk level resulting from a risk assessment. The blue logo is for level A care, indicating a low level of care, the patient can basically take care of themselves; the yellow logo is for level B care, indicating a medium level of care, the patient needs assistance; the red logo is for level C care, indicating a high level of care, the red color with the exclamation point symbol, in the wards to always remind the caregiver's attention. category D logo is a graphic pattern of black and white, partially with red to warn reminders, is the patient movement, posture, rows and rows, and is the patient movement, posture, rows and rows. The D logo is a black and white graphic pattern, partly with red color for warning reminders, and is a pictogram list of patients' movement, posture, excretion, meals, drinks, relevant restrictions and support methods. Reasonable use of color enables healthcare workers and caregivers to understand the patient's condition at the first time, which reduces their burden to a great extent. At the same time, the rational use of color can play a calming and soothing role in the recovery of the patient's psychology.

NO3-Cleveland Clinic's Taussig Cancer in America: Cleveland Clinic's Taussig Cancer was founded on February 28, 1921 as one of the most prestigious medical institutions in the world. It is legendary not only for combining "clinical and nursing care" with "research and education," but it is also known as a hospital that heals through art. At the Cleveland Clinic's Taussig Cancer Institute, for example, almost all of the exterior walls are designed with high, floor-to-ceiling windows that let in a great deal of light. In the reception hall, waiting room, negotiation room and other spaces, a large area of white wall base, determine the high brightness of the interior color tone, with bright and clear colors, color scheme lively and rich artwork, Jiayi decorative chandeliers, so that the hospital wards space a sweep of the depressing. Meanwhile, most of the partitions in the Institute are designed in a calm and low-key dark walnut color with beige seats, adjusting the space for activities through color combined with the placement of furniture. The entire Cleveland Clinic series uses color empowerment to achieve the purpose of enhancing the healing effect and improving the quality of life of the users, and the rich colors not only come from local artists and community artwork, but also often conducts art and medical related research, and has achieved remarkable results.

NO.4-ZAANS MEDISCH CENTRUM: Zaans Medisch Centrum was built in 2016 with a floor area of 39,000 square meters by Mecanoo Architecten, with the design concept of "freeing the building from the constraints of a medical institution and presenting a pleasant living atmosphere". It is also the most typical hospital design with "regional" design features. The designer treats the entire hospital as a mythological picture book, and combines the hospital decoration with regional "picture book" design, which not only increases the hospital's "livability" but also increases the hospital's "livability". This not only increases the "livability" of the hospital, but also adds character and culture to the environment.

In the design of Zaans Medisch Centrum, the spacious lobby provides a sense of welcome. The entire lobby is white as the background color of the walls, with a beige wooden ceiling and a semi-circular skylight, a light wooden floor with brightly colored sofas, and a haze blue and light grass green color scheme, adding a lively flavor to the space. The wall painting depicts the history and culture of Zaans with thin black lines, and the glass partition runs through the whole building, bringing in abundant light. In the design of the wards, a large number of dark blue lines are used to emphasize the element of water in the space, and the wards use high brightness blue and green to create a space that blends with the rich wood color.

By analyzing the four most distinctive medical institutions, we can see the role of color empowerment in hospital ward design. Color empowerment makes hospital furniture and signs have more functions, can clearly divide the area in the ward, can quickly get the information of patient's needs, can optimize the movement of medical staff, reduce the work pressure and error rate, can relax the user's mood, calm down the emotions, and help the patient's recovery.

And we extracted the trend of color empowerment from the classic case studies, most of which are dominated by the colors of nature, and the overall design is mostly in high brightness tones, while avoiding the psychological anxiety caused by high-color and strong contrasting colors, and enriching the space with medium-color colored with high-brightness colorless colors, such as the blue color of the water to give people a sense of intimacy. Different brightness and purity of green in the hospital will create a vibrant, energetic atmosphere.

4.2.2 User Needs Analysis

Users of hospital wards include patients, healthcare workers, patients' families, and, in recent years, caregivers. They have physical and psychological needs in using the ward environment (Figure 4).

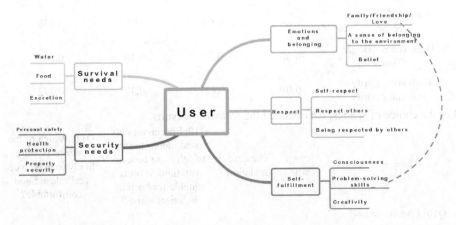

Figure 4   Analysis of user needs

Adopted a field visit way to carry out a survey of user needs, in the field survey of hospitals, most hospitals as a public facility, per capita use area is small, patients often feel embarrassed and depressed in the hospital. And the medical staff belongs to the high intensity of work, medical furniture storage does not distinguish between the use of each part of the purpose of the use. For example, inpatient wards of the nurses' station, due to the nurses are shift system, utensils storage cannot be handed over one by one, in fact, to the medical and nursing work to increase the burden. Due to the intense workload of the medical staff, many patients' families also do not have access to timely information related to nursing care.

The physiological needs of users include basic physiological needs and safety needs, and the psychological needs include emotional needs, respect needs and self-actualization needs. In developed countries, some hospitals to high-end, privatized hospitals as the main business, such as the United States of America's Cleveland Hospital, is the hospital to hospitalization, color empowerment of the most representative design cases. Inside the Cleveland Hospital, color empowerment gives users great satisfaction in terms of psychological needs, and at the same time, color empowerment integrates medical care space, which can optimize medical and nursing actions and reduce workload.

4.2.3 Design element extraction

In conjunction with the field visits to the inpatient wards of the hospital, a questionnaire survey was conducted for the color-enabled design, which resulted in imagery values regarding hue, lightness, and purity of the colors in the inpatient wards.

Project	Factor 1	Factor 2	Factor 3	Commonality
Pure White - Colored	0.82	0.05	0.26	0.747
Single color--Multi-color	0.85	-0.14	-0.19	0.776
Warm colors - cool colors	0.03	-0.02	0.92	0.848
Dark Tones - Bright Tones	-0.00	-0.71	-0.40	0.662
High color purity - low color purity	-0.08	0.82	-0.30	0.772

For the choice of shades, we obtained the following results.

Project	Average value	Standard deviation	Q10: Five commonly used indoor tones, which color tone do you think is more suitable for hospital inpatient wards?	Q11: Which of the options is more likely to make you feel relaxed and comfortable?
Q10: Five commonly used indoor tones, which color tone do you think is more suitable for hospital inpatient wards?	2.80	0.76	1	
Q11: Which of the options is more likely to make you feel relaxed and comfortable?	2.86	1.14	0.13	1
* p<0.05 ** p<0.01				

According to the results of the questionnaire survey, we can draw two conclusions.

First, in terms of hue, Q1 influence factors are all positive, showing that people prefer multi-color matching; Q2 influence factors have two falling on the negative axis, showing that people prefer multi-color matching. According to the survey, it can be seen that people prefer warm colors as the main color and cold colors as the supplementary multi-color matching.

Secondly, brightness and purity are integrated as the direction of hue in PCCS, and the influence factor falls on the part of medium color and high brightness color. Too bright colors are easy to cause visual fatigue, and too muddy colors will depress emotions, so most of the respondents chose medium colorful colors.

From the conclusion of the survey, it can be seen that the overall color scheme of inpatient wards is most popularly favored by the public with high brightness and medium chroma colors as the overall color direction. After discussion among designers, medical staff, patients and family members, it was determined that green and wood colors were chosen as the main colors for hard furnishings, and light and weak tones were chosen as the main colors with haze blue for tonal enrichment, in which the main operation area was distinguished by light green.

4.3 Design Program

Based on the survey results, the hospital inpatient ward space was designed and remodeled. The color empowerment design scheme for the outer-hung window ward and inner-hung window ward were designed respectively to combine color with the overall decoration, furniture, medical supplies and materials used, retaining the original colors of most wooden or wood-like materials, i.e., original wood color, chicken-wing wood color, and walnut color; beige was chosen for the floor and part of the wall, so as to make the whole space maintain clean tones and at the same time, to give a sense of friendliness to the people. Based on the results of the case study and market research, combined with the psychological needs that color empowerment needs to address to people, a natural theme was chosen for the design (Figure 5). The colorful part of the choice is green as the main tone, the green will reduce the purity, the color gradient effect on the wall, more in line with the visual effect caused by natural light. Lighting is provided by floor-to-ceiling windows and overhead lights, with artwork decorated in the same color.

Figure 5 Color empowerment based ward color palette design

Furniture in the interior is mainly in original wood color, and wood color is still used as the main color in the wards. Modular design is used, so that different hospitals or departments can be assembled according to the specific ward design and operational needs. Color empowerment design also includes furniture design for patients' families, mostly in dark colors to differentiate the furniture used by patients. This color differentiation avoids mixing of furniture and has the effect of improving the experience and preventing infection.

In terms of signage color design, male ward door signs are blue and female ward door signs are pink; pipe labels and signage are marked with different brightness colors according to the part, function and role, such as arteries→red, veins→blue, fistula tubes→brown, and other pipelines→purple. Dietary identification cards and risk identification cards also use different shades and brightness of color for functional division, together with pictures for representation, to provide tips for medical and nursing staff and caregivers, to reduce the workload and safety risks.

4.4 Program Evaluation

After the completion of the program, it participated in the Third China Top Ten Hospital Interior Design Program, was selected as a finalist and finally won the 13th place. It participated in the 6th DIA China Design Intelligence Competition and was shortlisted as a finalist. To a certain extent, it proves the feasibility of the program.

5 Conclusion

Color empowerment is a sublimation on the basis of color psychology, which has a positive visual and functional promotion effect on the hard decoration design, furniture design, soft decoration design and signage design of hospital inpatient wards. It can be applied functionally for healthcare personnel, can be used for emotional relief and physiological recovery for patients, can relieve anxiety for patients' family members, and can reduce the workload for nursing staff. Color empowerment is a comprehensive study of color science, material science, psychology, aesthetics and other aspects of science. In the near future the function of medical buildings will be more enriched, in addition to the medical function, it will also cover the prevention and rehabilitation and other aspects of the function. Therefore, the hospital space should focus on the reasonable use of color empowerment to improve the medical environment, in order to have a positive impact on the public's psychology, to improve the negative emotions of patients, to promote the recovery of patients' health, and to save health resources.

References

[1] ZHANG Yan, TANG Lian, WANG Yanyan, YIN Tong, LI Bo. Psychological care of hospitalized patients with cardiovascular disease with anxiety and depression. China Rehabilitation Theory and Practice,2010,16(05):425-426.
[2] Li Wenxu. Trial analysis of the application of color in landscape design. Construction and Budget,2021(08):62-64.
[3] Zhang Fuhui. The role of humanized design in modern medical building design. Fujian Architecture,2006(01):81-83.
[4] TAO Lijing. Research on the application of "general sense" in furniture design. Jiangnan University,2009.
[5] Editorial Planning Department. Color art in hospital architecture. China hospital building and equipment,2013(10):23.
[6] Chen Qiwei. Color design of hospital buildings. Engineering and Construction,2010,24(06):747-749.
[7] Huang Wenting. Analysis of indoor light environment and color design of hospital buildings--Taking Chongqing Peace Hospital and Southwest Hospital as Examples. Interior Design,2008(02):12-20+25-27.
[8] LIU Chunchun, ZHANG Guangqing. Research on color of hospital buildings from the perspective of color psychology--taking Beijing as an example
[9]. China Hospital Building and Equipment,2021,22(05):95-99.

Design Studies and Intelligence Engineering
L.C. Jain et al. (Eds.)
© *2024 The Authors.*
This article is published online with Open Access by IOS Press and distributed under the terms
of the Creative Commons Attribution Non-Commercial License 4.0 (CC BY-NC 4.0).
doi:10.3233/FAIA231498

Combining Contemporary Design Principles with the Craftsmanship of Ancient Chinese Architecture

Guangzhou LI[1] and Porncharoen RATTHAI[2]

[1] *Suzhou Arts and Design Technology Institute, Suzhou, 215104, China*
[2]*Faculty of Decorative Arts, Silpakorn University, Bangkok,10200, Thailand*
*E-mail: [1]*liguangzhou2022@163.com,* [2]*ratthai6654@gmail.com*

Abstract. This study delves into the area of traditional Chinese architecture, evaluating its historical, cultural, and artistic relevance as well as its integration into contemporary design methods. This research seeks to build a link between the traditions of the past and the innovations of the present in architectural design by a thorough examination of architectural features, craftsmanship, and symbolic representations. This study analyzes the rich heritage of traditional Chinese architecture using qualitative research approaches such as 16 semi-structured interviews with experienced architects and an exhaustive survey of current literature. The interview data was subjected to a rigorous three-step coding analysis, which included open coding, axial coding, and selective coding, made possible by the use of the MAXQDA-2020 software for efficient data administration and analysis. The research findings shed light on several prominent themes, including the intricate craftsmanship and design principles inherent in traditional Chinese architecture, the historical and archaeological significance embedded within architectural elements, the innovative adaptation of traditional techniques within contemporary design practices, and the challenges and opportunities associated with preservation and revitalization efforts. This research emphasizes the need of reinterpreting traditional workmanship by seamlessly incorporating historical and archaeological significance into modern design techniques. It also emphasizes the essential need of preserving traditional Chinese architecture in the face of rising urbanization and cultural globalization. The findings obtained from this research are useful for many stakeholders like architects, designers, politicians, and scholars involved in the protection, rehabilitation, and long-term development of architectural cultural heritage.

Keywords. Traditional Chinese Architecture, Craftsmanship Design, Archaeological Significance, Innovation, Adaptation, Preservation, Revitalization, Bridging Tradition, Modernity.

1. Introduction

Architecture reflects a society's cultural character powerfully, capturing its values, beliefs, and goals inside physical buildings (Sagiv & Schwartz, 2022). Traditional Chinese architecture, recognized for its rich past and deep significance, shows the country's historical culture and creative talent (Xu & Wang, 2021). Its meticulous workmanship, harmonious design principles, and historical importance have earned it worldwide acclaim and adoration, making it an enthralling study topic (Feng, 2020).

The goal of this research is to dig into the area of traditional Chinese architecture and investigate its many facets. We want to obtain a better knowledge of the historical, cultural, and aesthetic dimensions of this architectural legacy by investigating its application in modern design approaches. A substantial amount of research has been devoted to traditional Chinese architecture, giving insight on its architectural components, cultural meaning, and historical history. These studies have produced vital insights into the delicate link between architectural form, cultural values, and society ideas via painstaking research of historical documents, architectural drawings, and cultural references.

Furthermore, investigated the symbolic value of traditional Chinese architectural components such as the dougong system and the usage of fortunate motifs. These research have shown the deep-rooted symbolism contained within each design decision, highlighting the cultural and spiritual components of ancient building techniques.

While prior study has greatly contributed to our knowledge of traditional Chinese architecture, there are still certain gaps and research prospects. This project intends to fill these gaps and contribute to current knowledge by concentrating on the important research issues listed below: To begin, there is a need to investigate the reinterpretation of historic workmanship in traditional Chinese architecture, as well as its impact on current design processes.

Traditional architecture in China acts as a physical connection to the past, signifying the continuation of cultural practices through generations. It embodies the knowledge, skill, and aesthetic expressions of ancient builders while also reflecting the nation's historical progress and cultural evolution. Furthermore, traditional Chinese architecture is firmly ingrained in the Chinese people's cultural memory and awareness. It fosters a deep link between people and their cultural heritage by evoking feelings of pride, cultural identification, and belonging. Thus, preserving and renewing traditional architecture is critical for sustaining cultural continuity and instilling a feeling of cultural pride and identity in the Chinese populace. Furthermore, the significance of traditional Chinese architecture goes beyond its cultural worth. Traditional architectural preservation and promotion are so important for the tourist sector, contributing to local economies and cultural exchange. Therefore, the key objectives of this study was to explore the following knowledge areas:

- To investigate traditional Chinese architecture in depth, taking into account its historical, cultural, and artistic components.

- To investigate the reinterpretation of traditional Chinese architecture's historic craftsmanship and its influence on current design techniques.

- To incorporate the historical and archaeological relevance of traditional Chinese architectural features into modern design approaches.

- To address the challenges and opportunities related with traditional Chinese architectural preservation and revival.

- Contribute to the larger area of architectural studies by offering insights and recommendations for the long-term development and adaptation of traditional architectural heritage.

- The aim of this research is to equip architects, designers, policymakers, and scholars with the necessary knowledge and tools to safeguard, rejuvenate, and sustainably develop architectural cultural heritage.

2.Literature Review

Craftsmanship has always been seen as a sacred component of human history, and the study of past techniques has enormous importance in inspiring contemporary design. The dovetail joint structure and the dougong system have piqued the interest of designers and scholars in the context of traditional Chinese architecture. These architectural features not only display excellent craftsmanship, but they also have historical and archaeological significance. For generations, woodworkers have used the dovetail joint to attach pieces of wood flawlessly. Its unique interlocking architecture gives the created things extraordinary strength and endurance. The dovetail junction has been widely used in traditional Chinese architecture, contributing to the structural integrity of structures such as temples, pagodas, and ancestral halls . Exploring the origins, history, and variants of this joint offers light not only on the workmanship of ancient Chinese artisans, but also on the engineering principles and cultural importance linked with these constructions.

The dougong system is another fascinating component of traditional Chinese architecture (Pei et al., 2023). This one-of-a-kind architectural element consists of interlocking wooden brackets that sustain the roof's weight and distribute it equally to the pillars below (Yan, 2020). The dougong system not only demonstrates extraordinary precision and engineering prowess, but it also represents the balance of nature and human innovation. Its ornate and graceful design has become a symbol of traditional Chinese architecture, and it may be found gracing palaces, temples, and other massive monuments . Designers can incorporate historical and cultural value into their creations by reinterpreting the craftsmanship hidden within these ancient architectural features . This investigation has the potential to result in the development of unique goods that bridge the gap between tradition and modernity, paying attention to the legacy of craftsmanship while embracing current aesthetics and functionalities.

This study is significant because it has the potential to encourage designers and architects to delve further into the rich heritage of traditional Chinese craftsmanship. Practitioners can embrace the essence of traditional approaches and adapt them to the demands of today's design landscape by getting a full understanding of the dovetail joint structure and the dougong system. This project not only fosters a deep respect for traditional workmanship, but it also promotes the preservation and revitalization of cultural heritage. Finally, the study of the dovetail joint structure and the dougong system in traditional Chinese architecture opens the door to the unsurpassed workmanship of ancient artists. We may honor our cultural history while encouraging creativity by reinterpreting and merging these components into contemporary design. This study opens the way for a peaceful synthesis of heritage and modernity, expanding the creative landscape and motivating future designers.

3.Methods

This study used a qualitative method to look into "Reinterpreting Ancient Craftsmanship: Designing Creative Products Inspired by the Historical and Archaeological Significance of Dovetail Joint Structure and Dougong in Traditional Chinese Architecture." The main way that information was gathered was through 16 semi-structured conversations (see table 1). The builders who were chosen to take part in the talks were professionals who had worked on projects related to the study's topic, as the title says.

Table 1. Background Information of Participants

Respondent	Gender	Age	Years of Experience	Expertise	Relevant Projects
R1	Male	45	20	Architectural	Renovation of ancient temples
R2	Male	38	12	Interior Design	Restoration of historical palaces
R3	Male	52	25	Structural	Preservation of traditional courtyard houses
R4	Male	42	18	Landscape	Integration of traditional gardens in modern design
R5	Male	41	15	Architectural	Repurposing historic buildings for cultural centers
R6	Female	37	10	Urban Planning	Revitalization of traditional marketplaces
R7	Male	49	22	Architectural	Conservation of ancient city walls
R8	Female	36	8	Interior Design	Adaptive reuse of traditional residences
R9	Male	47	17	Structural	Preservation of ancient pagodas
R10	Female	39	11	Landscape	Redesign of historical parks
R11	Male	44	19	Architectural	Restoration of traditional teahouses
R12	Female	43	16	Urban Planning	Renovation of historic city squares
R13	Male	50	23	Architectural	Conservation of traditional wooden structures
R14	Female	35	7	Interior Design	Modernization of traditional guesthouses
R15	Female	48	21	Structural	Preservation of ancient bridges
R16	Female	40	13	Landscape	Incorporation of traditional elements in modern parks

In order to get useful information from the collected data, the analysis process consisted of three steps of code analysis. Open coding, axial coding, and selected coding were all parts of the coding study. During the open-coding stage, the data were carefully looked at, and applicable concepts, ideas, and themes were found and named (see figure 1).

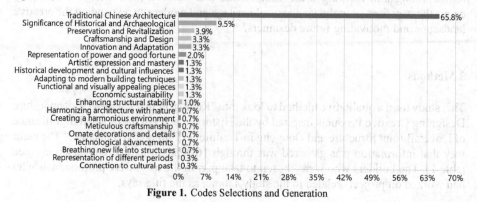

Figure 1. Codes Selections and Generation

During the axial coding process, links and relationships between the discovered codes were set up (see figure 2). This made it possible to create a complete coding system. In the last step, selective coding, the most important and relevant codes were chosen to make a story that makes sense and pull out the key results. MAXQDA-2020 software was used to make the process of analyzing data easier. This program had useful tools and features for gathering, recording, and analyzing the interview data. This made sure that the analysis process was accurate and quick.

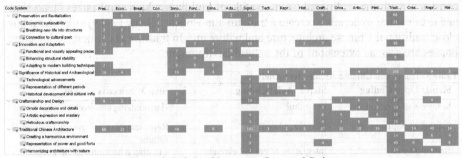

Figure 2. Relationships among Generated Codes

The survey respondents were selected through a technique known as purposive convenience sampling. Architects who had worked on projects connected to the topic of the study were picked on purpose to make sure that the data collected would be very useful and informative (see table 2). In short, this qualitative research study asked 16 architects who had worked on projects related to the research topic to take part in semi-structured interviews. Coding analysis was done on the collected data in three steps: open coding, axial coding, and selected coding. MAXQDA-2020 software was used to organize and analyze data in an effective way.

Table 2. Interview Questions to Study Participants

Interview Questions

1. Can you provide an overview of your experience and expertise in traditional Chinese architecture?

2. How have you incorporated traditional Chinese architectural elements in your past projects?

3. What are your thoughts on the significance of craftsmanship and design in traditional Chinese architecture?

4. Can you discuss any specific examples where you have utilized the dovetail joint structure or dougong system?

5. In your opinion, how can traditional Chinese architecture be adapted and innovated for modern designs?

6. What are the challenges and opportunities in preserving and revitalizing traditional Chinese architecture?

7. Have you encountered any unique situations where you had to balance tradition with modern requirements?

8. How do you envision traditional Chinese architecture's future and its impact on innovative product design?

9. Do you have any particular ideas or thoughts to give about this study topic?

4. Statistical Analysis and Findings

In this part, the results and analysis are based on the answers from 16 semi-structured interviews with architects who have worked on projects connected to the study topic. The interviewers and other people who have written about traditional Chinese building have given appropriate examples to back up these answers.

4.1. Traditional Chinese Architecture

Upon reviewing the interview responses, it became evident that the architects shared a consensus regarding the distinctive features of traditional Chinese architecture and its significance to Chinese culture (see table 3). According to Interviewee 1, traditional Chinese architecture demonstrates a great reverence for the natural environment. The structures are intended to fit in with their environment without standing out. It is consistent with the traditional Chinese style of building, which emphasizes "feng shui" and uses natural materials to create a tranquil atmosphere. Zhang (2019) talks about how close traditional Chinese architecture and nature are. In traditional Chinese architecture, houses are seen as extensions of the natural environment.

Table 3. Traditional Chinese Architecture Analysis

Step 1: Open Coding	Step 2: Axial Coding	Step 3: Selective Coding
Seamless integration	Feng shui	Harmonizing architecture with nature
Symbolic motifs	Dragons, phoenixes	Representation of power and good fortune
Nature-inspired	Integration of natural elements	Creating a harmonious environment

Also, Interviewee 3 brought up the symbolic importance of traditional themes and fortunate symbols in Chinese architectural design by saying, "Traditional Chinese architecture includes symbolic elements like dragons and phoenixes, which represent power, prosperity, and good fortune." Literature from the past (see table 4) that looks at the symbolic meanings of the detailed carvings and artistic patterns on traditional Chinese buildings backs up this finding. Zhang and Lee (2022) talks about what these patterns mean symbolically and how they show national beliefs and values.

Table 4. Traditional Chinese Architecture

Interview Responses	Literature Support
There is a profound regard for the natural environment in traditional Chinese architecture, and structures are built to blend with the natural setting in which they are located.	Guo et al. (2020) focuses attention on the tight link that exists between traditional Chinese architecture and environment. In this kind of architecture, structures are seen as extensions of the natural landscape.
"Traditional Chinese architecture incorporates symbolic elements like dragons and phoenixes, which represent power, prosperity, and good fortune."	describes the symbolic significance of these motifs and their representation of cultural beliefs and values in traditional Chinese architecture.

4.2. Craftsmanship and Design

The builders were always impressed by the high level of handiwork in traditional Chinese buildings (see table 5). Interviewee 7 talked about the complex construction methods used in traditional wooden structures. He said, "The dovetail joint structure used in traditional Chinese architecture is a testament to the careful craftsmanship of the craftsmen who made them." This fits with what is written about traditional Chinese architecture, which says that it takes a lot of skill and accuracy to make the joints and links in these buildings look smooth and fit together well. Pan and Zhang (2021) talks about the technical skills of traditional Chinese workers and how they were able to make building systems that were very complicated.

Table 5. Craftsmanship and Design Analysis

Step 1: Open Coding	Step 2: Axial Coding	Step 3: Selective Coding
Intricate joinery	Dovetail joint structure	Meticulous craftsmanship
Attention to detail	Carvings, paintings	Artistic expression and mastery
Exquisite craftsmanship	Precision and skill	Ornate decorations and details

Also, Interviewee 12 liked how traditional Chinese architecture paid attention to detail, especially in the cutting and painting methods. They said, "The intricate carvings and brightly colored paintings in traditional Chinese architecture are proof of the craftsmen's creativity and skill." This finding fits with what has been written in the past (see table 6) about how traditional Chinese buildings are decorated with elaborate decorations and small, detailed details. Xu et al. (2020) looks at the artistic parts of traditional Chinese building. He points out how the carvings, paints, and decorations show skill and artistic expression.

Table 6. Craftsmanship and Design

Interview Responses	Literature Support
"The dovetail joint structure used in traditional Chinese architecture is a testament to the meticulous craftsmanship of the craftsmen who created them."	Xingbo and Peijun (2023) discusses the technical prowess of traditional Chinese craftsmen and their ability to create complex joinery systems.
"The intricate carvings and vibrant paintings found in traditional Chinese architecture are a testament to the artistic expression and mastery of the craftsmen."	In his article "Exploring the Artistic Aspects of Traditional Chinese Architecture," examines the workmanship and creative expression that are evident in the carvings, paintings, and decoration of traditional Chinese buildings.

By combining the information from the interviews with what is already known about traditional Chinese architecture, this research study gives a full picture of the themes (see figure 3) it looks at: Traditional Chinese Architecture, Craftsmanship and Design. The study shows how important traditional Chinese architecture is in terms of culture, art, and history. It also shows how important it is to change and keep these architectural practices in a modern setting.

5. Discussion

Traditional Chinese architecture has long been admired for its distinctive characteristics and cultural importance. The interview results verified the significance of seamless integration with nature, which has been continuously stressed in previous studies. The respondents emphasized the harmonious link between traditional Chinese architecture and nature, highlighting the usage of feng shui principles and the use of natural materials in design. This is consistent with the current body of research that acknowledges the close relationship between traditional Chinese architecture and nature.

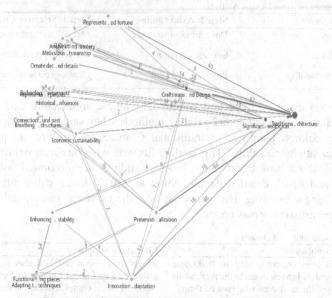

Figure 3: Codes Relation Model derived through Analysis

Furthermore, both the interview answers and previous research emphasized the symbolic elements utilized in traditional Chinese architecture, such as dragons and phoenixes, which symbolise strength, wealth, and good fortune. The relevance of these symbolic aspects in transmitting cultural ideas and values via architectural design was stressed by the respondents. This conclusion is consistent with previous research on the symbolic meaning of motifs in traditional Chinese architecture.

The interview results reinforced the praise for the great skill demonstrated in traditional Chinese architecture in terms of craftsmanship and design. Interviewees commended the sophisticated woodworking skills, particularly the dovetail joint structure.

Several major observations arise from comparing the findings of this study to other investigations. The findings of the interviews support and expand on the existing body of knowledge on traditional Chinese architecture, highlighting the seamless integration with nature, the symbolism embedded in architectural design, the exceptional craftsmanship displayed in joinery and artistic expression, the historical and archaeological significance of architectural elements, the potential for innovation and adaptation, and the importance of preservation and revitalization. The correspondence between interview answers and previous literature improves the validity and dependability of the results, emphasizing the continuity of the issues investigated in this study.

6. Conclusion

Finally, this research looked at the reinterpretation of historic workmanship in traditional Chinese architecture and its effect on the design of creative items. The study examined key themes such as traditional Chinese architecture, craftsmanship and design, historical and archaeological significance, innovation and adaptation, preservation and revitalization, and the bridging of tradition and modernity through qualitative interviews with 16 experienced architects and designers.

The study's results demonstrated the lasting relevance of traditional Chinese architecture and its ability to effortlessly interact with the natural surroundings. Symbolic motifs used in architectural design, like as dragons and phoenixes, were recognized as potent expressions of cultural ideas and values. It also showed the possibilities for invention and adaptation, illustrating how these old processes may be blended into current designs to produce useful and aesthetically beautiful buildings and furnishings.

The study stressed the need of maintaining and reviving traditional Chinese architecture in the face of contemporary challenges. This study, through linking tradition and modernity, sheds light on how traditional Chinese architecture may inspire and influence the design of innovative items. The study adds to the current body of knowledge by verifying and building on previous research, showing the relevance and importance of traditional craftsmanship in a continuously changing society.

It is anticipated that the conclusions of this study would motivate architects, designers, and politicians to respect and embrace the rich history of traditional Chinese architecture. The sample size of 16 respondents, although varied in their knowledge, may not reflect the whole range of viewpoints within the subject. Future study should include increasing the sample size and integrating different approaches to increase our grasp of the issue.

This research emphasizes the lasting significance of historic craftsmanship in traditional Chinese architecture, demonstrating its capacity for creativity, adaptation, and the construction of inspired and culturally meaningful designs. By understanding and embracing these ideas, we can bridge the gap between tradition and modernity, assuring the preservation and revival of traditional Chinese architectural legacy for future generations to enjoy and take inspiration from.

Future research might add user opinions and impressions of traditional Chinese architecture to supplement the results of this study. Researchers may acquire insights on the influence of traditional architecture on people's experiences, cultural identity, and sense of place by integrating the perspectives of inhabitants, tourists, and other stakeholders.

References

[1]Feng, W. (2020). *Intercultural Aesthetics in Traditional Chinese Theatre*. Springer.
[2]Guo, Y., Tong, L., & Mei, L. (2020). The effect of industrial agglomeration on green development efficiency in Northeast China since the revitalization. *Journal of Cleaner Production, 258*, 120584.
[3]Pan, Y., & Zhang, L. (2021). Roles of artificial intelligence in construction engineering and management: A critical review and future trends. *Automation in Construction, 122*, 103517.
[4]Pei, W., Lo, T. T. S., & Guo, X. (2023). Integrating Virtual Reality and interactive game for learning structures in architecture: the case of ancient Chinese dougong cognition. *Open House International, 48*(2), 237-257.
[5]Sagiv, L., & Schwartz, S. H. (2022). Personal values across cultures. *Annual review of psychology, 73*, 517-546.
[6]Xingbo, L., & Peijun, A. (2023). Construction. In *Chinese Handicrafts* (pp. 227-296). Springer.
[7]Xu, C., Huang, Y., & Dewancker, B. (2020). Art inheritance: an education course on traditional pattern morphological generation in architecture design based on digital sculpturism. *Sustainability, 12*(9), 3752.
[8]Xu, Q., & Wang, J. (2021). Recognition of values of traditional villages in southwest China for sustainable development: A case study of Liufang Village. *Sustainability, 13*(14), 7569.

[9]Zhang, D. (2019). Cultural symbols in Chinese architecture. *Architecture and Design Review*, *1*(1), 1-17.
[10]Zhang, Y., & Lee, T. J. (2022). Alienation and authenticity in intangible cultural heritage tourism production. *International Journal of Tourism Research*, *24*(1), 18-32.

Design Studies and Intelligence Engineering
L.C. Jain et al. (Eds.)
© *2024 The Authors.*
This article is published online with Open Access by IOS Press and distributed under the terms
of the Creative Commons Attribution Non-Commercial License 4.0 (CC BY-NC 4.0).
doi:10.3233/FAIA231499

841

Research on the Design of Tourism Cultural and Creative Products from the Perspective of Semiotics

Zhenzhen Wang[a,1], Yu WANG[b]

[a] *School of Art and Design, Ma'anshan University, Ma'anshan, An Hui, China*
[b] *New Media School, Beijing Institute of Graphic Communication, Beijing, China*

Abstract. Under the background of cultural tourism economy, this paper explores the design methods of tourism cultural and creative products. Guided by the theory of semiotics three-in-one model, using FAHP and CRITIC model, combined with game theory, this paper screens and weighs cultural symbols, and discusses their application in tourism cultural and creative product design. Taking Caishiji as an example, this paper analyzes cultural symbols from four dimensions: shape, pattern, color and material, and applies them to the design practice of tourism cultural and creative products. The evaluation results show that this design method based on cultural symbols can effectively improve the design efficiency and scientificity, and the obtained tea set design scheme can also meet the needs of users. This study is of great significance for designers to understand and use regional symbols and improve the design effect of tourism cultural and creative products.

Keywords. Semiotics; Trinity model; Tourism cultural creation; FAHP; CRITIC

In recent years, the rapid development of cultural tourism economy has given birth to local cultural and creative industries, and tourism cultural and creative products have also become the research focus of scholars. The design research of tourism cultural and creative products is mainly carried out in two aspects: on the one hand, based on design theory, qualitative research is carried out from the generation mode and logic of cultural form symbols [1]. For example, Liu Yang et al. [2], Shi Aiqin et al. [3], Huang Wenqing et al. [4]; On the other hand, quantitative research based on user demand and big data drive discusses the design method of tourism cultural and creative products. For example, Yang Xiaoyan et al. [5], Xiao Derong et al. [6], Sun Binbin et al. [7]. Qualitative research is richer in explaining the formation of cultural content, but it lacks rational data support and insufficient conclusions. Quantitative research in the design practice of tourism cultural and creative products, it is more convincing to digitize design factors, but in practice, it lacks the guidance of design theory and is not logical. Therefore, taking the Caishiji scenic spot in Ma'anshan as an example, this paper intends to adopt the method of combining qualitative research with quantitative research, taking the semiotics triple integration model as the theoretical research basis, combining FAHP model, CRITIC model and game theory, and using fuzzy comprehensive evaluation method to verify the

---

[1] Corresponding author, School of Art and Design, Ma'anshan University, No. 8 Huangchi Road, Dangtu County, Ma'anshan City, Anhui Province, 243100; Email: 302667806@qq.com

feasibility of the design method, so as to explore the innovative design method of tourism cultural and creative products and provide reference for tourism cultural and creative design.

1. Theoretical introduction

1.1 Overview of Semiotic Three-in-One Model

Semiotics is a system of constructing cultural images in semantic field. At the philosophical level, Pierce proposed a three-element model of semiotics to explain the essence of semiotics theory. Ternary relation is a theoretical model composed of objects, symbols and explanatory items. Its principles have two points: 1. A true symbol must contain an irreducible ternary relation related to its objects and explanatory items; 2. The explanatory term of a symbol itself can also be used as a symbol, and another explanatory term can be deduced in principle to infinity.

1.2 Overview of FAHP and CRITIC Theory

AHP (Analytical Hierarchy Process, AHP), proposed by Professor Saaty. T. L. of America, is a system analysis method combining qualitative and quantitative analysis. FAHP (Fuzzy Analytic Hierarchy Process, FAHP) introduces fuzzy mathematics theory on the basis of AHP, and combines fuzzy complementary matrix to calculate index weight, which mainly solves complex problems with unclear boundary and multi-role participation, and helps users analyze problems and make decisions.

CRITIC is a more comprehensive objective weighting method than entropy weight method and standard deviation method. It comprehensively measures the objective weight between indexes by the contrast intensity of evaluation indexes and the conflict between indexes, in which the contrast intensity is expressed by standard deviation, and the greater the standard deviation, the higher the weight; The conflict between indicators is based on the correlation between indicators. If there is a strong correlation between two indicators, the smaller the conflict, the lower the weight.

2. The design process of tourism cultural and creative products under semiotics

The design process of tourism cultural and creative products is mainly carried out in three stages: early symbol extraction, mid-term symbol application and later design achievement evaluation.

2.1. Image symbolic extraction

The regional cultural characteristics of Caishiji are mainly natural landscapes. Therefore, this study collects design samples from multiple angles according to the order of scenic gate, Cuiluo Bay, Cedar Forest, Taibai Building, Li Bai Memorial Hall and Pavilion. At the same time, five product design teachers and five product managers were invited to form an expert group, among which five product design teachers served as design groups in the expert group. Through field investigation, 127 valid photos were obtained. After preliminary selection, six final samples were obtained by the expert group according to the characteristics of scenic spots, which constituted the design sample database.

This paper analyzes the design samples from three aspects: objects, symbols and explanatory items of the ternary model, and carries out symbolic design of sample scenic spots' shapes and patterns [8]. See Table 1 for the various explanatory item elements obtained.

By consulting the literature of tourism cultural and creative design and combining with the opinions of the expert group, the explanatory items are translated into the design symbols of tourism cultural and creative products according to four aspects: shape, pattern, color and material, as shown in Table 1. Morphologically, the outer contour of the sample photo is taken as the shape of the scenic spot photo sample; Patterns with internal characteristic lines as sample symbols; In terms of color, among the 3-4 colors of each scenic spot sample, the first two are selected as the main colors according to the principle of high and low voting results; On the material, the style presented according to the material characteristics is used as the material symbol.

Table 1. Interpretation item resolution

	scenic gate	CuiluBay	Cedar Forest	Taibai Building	Li Bai Memorial Hall	Pavilion
morphology						
Pattern						
Color						
Material						

2.2. Determine the index system

According to the relevant theories of FAHP and the symbol induction of tourism cultural creation, the form, pattern, color and material are regarded as the criterion layer B of tourism cultural creation product design, namely form B1, pattern B2, color B3 and material B4. On the basis of the criterion layer screened by the expert group, the design elements of Caishiji tourism cultural and creative products are obtained, that is, scheme layer C. Material, there are stone, wood, porcelain clay three. After the market category investigation of Wenchuang products and the discussion of the expert group, it is concluded that the material of Stone is not suitable for Wenchuang products, so the material selection is composed of wood and porcelain clay. In terms of color, there are two main colors in the color samples of each scenic spot. After comparing and analyzing the colors of each scenic spot, it is found that the colors of the scenic gate and Li Bai Memorial Hall are similar, both of which are white and black; The fir forest and the pavilion are similar in color, both brown and black; Cuiluo Bay is blue and black; Taibai Building is red and black. To sum up, the highest occurrence probability of black is 6 times, brown is 2 times, white is 2 times, red is 1 time and blue is 1 time. Therefore, black, brown and white are selected according to the occurrence frequency from high to low. See Figure 1 for specific elements.

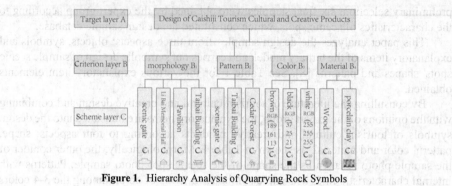

Figure 1. Hierarchy Analysis of Quarrying Rock Symbols

2.3. FAHP Determines Subjective Weight of Indicators

Firstly, the fuzzy complementary judgment matrix is established. Using the calibration method of 0.1-0.9 (Table 2), the importance of the design evaluation index of Caishiji tourism cultural and creative products at the same level is compared in pairs, and the judgment matrix is constructed. Its properties are shown in Equations (1) and (2):

$$A = (a_{ij})_{n \times n}$$

Table 2. Scale of Judgement Matrix

Scale	Importance Level	Meaning
0.5	be of equal importance	I and J are equally important to the specified attribute
0.6	Slightly important	Factor i is slightly more important than factor j
0.7	Obviously important	Factor i is significantly more important than factor j
0.8	Strongly important	Factor i is more important than factor j
0.9	Absolute Importance	Factor i is absolutely more important than factor j
0.1, 0.2, 0.3, 0.4	Reverse comparison	If the element ai is compared with the element aj to obtain a judgment rij, the judgment obtained by comparing the element aj with the element ai is rji=1-rij

$$a_{ij} + a_{ji} = 1 \text{, (1)}$$
$$a_{ii} = 0.5 \text{, (2)}$$

In order to get more objective weight results for each index feature, the scale of numerical value is completed by the expert group.

Secondly, the weight of fuzzy judgment matrix is calculated. The fuzzy judgment matrix is summed according to the equation (3), the fuzzy complementary judgment matrix is transformed into a fuzzy consistent matrix according to the equation (4), and the weight of each fuzzy judgment matrix is obtained according to the equation (5):

$$r_i = \sum_{k=1}^{n} a_{ik}, i = 1, 2, \cdots, n \text{, (3)}$$

$$r_{ij} = \frac{r_i - r_j}{2(n-1)} + 0.5 \text{, (4)}$$

$$\omega_i = \frac{\sum_{j=1}^{n} r_{ij}}{\sum_{i=1}^{n}\sum_{j=1}^{n} r_{ij}} = \frac{\sum_{j=1}^{n} a_{ij} + \frac{n}{2} - 1}{n(n-1)}, i = 1, 2, \cdots, n$$

, (5)

The weight vectors of each fuzzy judgment matrix are: = (0.300, 0.267, 0.233, 0.200); = (0.250, 0.217, 0.250, 0.283); = (0.300, 0.317, 0.383); = (0.350, 0.383, 0.267); = (0.4, 0.6). $\omega_A \ \omega_{B_1} \ \omega_{B2} \ \omega_{B3} \ \omega_{B4}$

Thirdly, the consistency test of fuzzy judgment matrix. By calculating the consistency of fuzzy judgment matrix, it is tested whether the weight obtained by formula (6) is reliable. The weight vector is used to construct the characteristic matrix W= (ij) n of the fuzzy judgment matrix, where ij is calculated by equation (6), and the compatibility index between the paste judgment matrix and its eigenvalue matrix is calculated by equation (7). When the compatibility index is ≤ 0.1, the fuzzy judgment matrix is reasonable.

$$\omega_{ij}^* = \frac{\omega_i}{\omega_i + \omega j}(i, j = 1, 2, \cdots, n)$$

, (6)

$$I(A, W^*) = \frac{\sum_{i=1}^{n}\sum_{j=1}^{n}\left| a_{ij} + \omega_{ji} - 1 \right|}{n^2}(i, j = 1, 2, \cdots, n)$$

, (7)

The calculated characteristic matrix,According to the formula (7), I (A, WA*) = 0.083 < 0.1, I (B1,) = 0.050 < 0.1, I (B2,) = 0.062 < 0.1, I (B3,) = 0.094 < 0.1, I (B4,) = 0.050 < 0.1. $W_{B_1}^* \ W_{B_2}^* \ W_{B_3}^* \ W_{B_4}^*$

Table 3. Calculation results of FAHP index weight

Target layerA	Criterion layer (B)	B weight	Sub-criterion layer (C)	C weight	comprehensive weight
Design of Caishiji Cultural and Creative Products	morphology	0.300	scenic gate C1	0.250	0.075
			Li Bai Memorial Hall C2	0.217	0.065
			Pavilion C3	0.250	0.075
			Taibai Building C4	0.283	0.085
	Pattern	0.267	scenic gate C5	0.300	0.080
			Taibai Building C6	0.317	0.085
			Cedar Forest C7	0.383	0.102
	Color	0.233	brown C8	0.350	0.082
			black C9	0.383	0.089
			white C10	0.267	0.062
	Material	0.200	Wood C11	0.400	0.080
			porcelain clay C12	0.600	0.120

2.4. CRITIC determines the objective weight of indicators

First, construct the initial evaluation matrix. Firstly, eight cultural and creative product enthusiasts are invited to assign values to each index in scheme layer C by using Likert scale method (grade 1-9), and establish an initial evaluation matrix, as shown in Table 4.

Table 4. Initial evaluation matrix of CRITIC

Users	target											
	C1	C2	C3	C4	C5	C6	C7	C8	C9	C10	C11	C12
User1	7	5	2	7	5	4	6	7	7	6	7	9
User2	5	6	4	9	6	7	5	4	5	5	8	8
User3	6	6	2	4	7	6	3	7	8	6	6	5
User4	7	7	5	7	4	6	9	5	6	6	7	8
User5	5	4	5	4	4	5	6	4	8	4	8	7
User6	7	9	4	5	5	4	7	6	9	4	8	6
User7	6	8	5	4	6	4	5	6	5	8	9	5
User8	6	7	6	6	7	6	8	8	6	6	8	4

Second, calculate the coefficient of variation:

$$\begin{cases} \overline{x_j} = \dfrac{1}{n}\sum_{i=1}^{n} x_{ij} \\ \\ S_j = \sqrt{\dfrac{\sum\limits_{i=1}^{n}(x_{ij}-\overline{x_j})^2}{n-1}} \end{cases} \quad , (8)$$

Where Si is the standard deviation of the J-th index; xj is the average difference of j indexes.

Thirdly, the correlation coefficient and quantitative index value between each index are calculated according to equations (9) and (10):

$$q_{ij} = \frac{Cov(x,y)}{\sqrt{Var[x]Var[y]}} \quad , (9)$$

Where: Cov (x, y) is the covariance between the index x and y; Var [x] is the variance of x; Var [y] is the variance of y.

The conflict between item j and other indicators is as follows:

$$f_j = \sum_{i=1}^{n}(1-q_{ij}) \quad (10)$$

Fourth, calculate the amount of information contained in the J index according to Equation (11):

$$c_j = \delta_j \sum_{i=1}^{n}(1-q_{ij}) \quad (11)$$

Fifth, calculate the weight of the J index according to equation (12):

$$\omega_j = \frac{c_j}{\sum_{i=1}^{n} c_j} \quad (12)$$

According to equations (8), (9), (10), (11) and (12), the relevant calculation results of CRITIC are obtained, as shown in Table 5

Table 5. Related calculation results of CRITIC

term	Indicator variability	Indicator variability	Indicator variability	Weight
C1	0.835	10.230	8.537	0.046
C2	1.604	9.745	15.627	0.084
C3	1.458	10.594	15.444	0.083

C4	1.832	10.655	19.523	0.104
C5	1.195	11.300	13.506	0.072
C6	1.165	11.787	13.732	0.074
C7	1.885	9.761	18.401	0.098
C8	1.458	10.512	15.323	0.082
C9	1.488	13.355	19.873	0.106
C10	1.302	10.909	14.209	0.076
C11	0.916	11.277	10.331	0.055
C12	1.773	12.653	22.432	0.120

2.5. Calculation of comprehensive weight based on game theory combination weighting method

FAHP and CRITIC have subjective and objective characteristics. In order to balance the defects between them and optimize the weighting decision-making scheme, the weight results of the two subjective and objective weighting methods obtained by FAHP and CRITIC are comprehensively analyzed by using the game theory combination weighting method. Through the combination of subjective weight and objective weight, the advantages of FAHP and CRITIC are combined, and finally a relatively balanced comprehensive weight is obtained.as shown in Table 6.

Table 6. Weight of each evaluation index

evaluating indicator	C1	C2	C3	C4	C5	C6	C7	C8	C9	C10	C11	C12
FAHP	0.075	0.065	0.075	0.085	0.080	0.085	0.102	0.082	0.089	0.062	0.080	0.120
CRITIC	0.046	0.084	0.083	0.104	0.072	0.074	0.098	0.082	0.106	0.076	0.055	0.120
comprehensive weight	0.049	0.082	0.082	0.103	0.073	0.075	0.099	0.082	0.105	0.075	0.058	0.120

The weight of each index is obtained by calculation. Calculated by FAHP model, the index weights from big to small are porcelain clay C12, fir forest pattern C7, black C9, Taibailou shape C4, Taibailou pattern C6, etc. Calculated by CRITIC model, the index weights from big to small are porcelain clay C12, black C9, Taibai building shape C4, fir forest pattern C7 and so on. It can be seen that the results calculated by the two models are not much different, and the data are reasonable. At the same time, the game theory is used to calculate the comprehensive weight of each symbol. According to the size of the comprehensive weight, the design elements are used to represent the product design, forming new explanatory items and realizing the expression of cultural creativity.

2.6. Design Practice

According to the calculation of comprehensive weight, the obtained comprehensive weight values of design elements from large to small are C12, C9, C4, C7, C2, C3, C8, C6, C10, C5, C11 and C1, among which the highest weight is C12 porcelain clay. Starting with the material porcelain clay, the product positioning is carried out, and combined with the market research of tourism cultural and creative products and the discussion of the expert group, the final design theme is determined: starting with the life of young people, drawing up the scene of leisure tea tasting, and designing a tourism cultural and creative product teapot made of porcelain clay. According to the relationship of semiotics ternary model, according to the four dimensions of shape, pattern, color and material, the design elements are represented on the teapot of tourism cultural and creative products, so as to realize the product representation of Caishiji cultural symbols.

3. Fuzzy comprehensive evaluation of design results

Fuzzy comprehensive evaluation method is to evaluate the uncertain information digitally in a scientific way, so as to obtain reliable data as a support and determine the feasibility of Caishiji tourism cultural and creative design scheme. Ten university design teachers and ten enterprise designers from different backgrounds were invited to comprehensively evaluate the design scheme. According to the principles and methods of scheme evaluation, the 20 university design teachers and enterprise designers from different backgrounds can evaluate from a professional perspective, which ensures the accuracy and objectivity of the design scheme.

Determine the final score of the evaluation scheme. Therefore, the fuzzy evaluation results of teapot design scheme are between very satisfactory and satisfactory. This scheme design has been recognized by the public in the combination of product design and cultural genes, and has a high level, which shows that the design method is effective.

4 Conclusion

In Pierce's pragmatic study, semiotics theory constructs the structural relationship of symbolic ternary representation, which is infinitely deductive in the logic of symbolic representation. In the process of cultural creative design, it guides the generation and translation of cultural symbols and the design process of tourism cultural and creative products, and provides a method for the formation and reconstruction of cultural symbols in the stage of cultural creativity. In the process of transforming symbol genes into the design of cultural and creative products, the logic and process of image transformation should be more rigorous, and the transformation mode should be more reasonable. Therefore, in the follow-up research, we should also explore the rationalization mode of symbol transformation logic in the process of cultural symbol translation.

Acknowledgments

This paper is one of the phased achievements of the key school-level quality engineering project of Maanshan University in 2022 (No. 202205); One of the achievements of Anhui Province excellent young teacher cultivation project.

References

[1] ZHOU Yan. Research on cultural and creative products of Shaanxi History Museum from the perspective of semiotics Chongqing Business University, 2020.
[2] LIU Yang, WANG Jia-hui. Analysis on the design of industrial tour culture and creative products--Taking Shougang Park as an example Packaging Engineering, 2022, 43 (24): 294-301.
[3] SHI Ai-qin, CHENG Cheng, LIU Jia-xin, etc. Cultural and creative development strategy of festival tour based on regional characters Social Scientist, 2021, 295 (11): 55-60.
[4] HUANG Wen-qing, XU Yan-ting. Cross-domain culture and creative products development model based on "space-time coordinates"-take the design of tour culture and creative products in Heilongjiang as an example. Art Watch, 2020, 293 (01): 75-76.
[5] YANG Xiao-yan, LIU Xiao. Spring Festival cultural theme element extraction and derivative design. Packaging Engineering, 2019, 40 (04): 93-98.

[6] XIAO De-rong, LIU Wei, DING Zi-rui. Research on gene construction and design application of the basket culture in western Hunan. Forest Products Industry, 2022, 59 (12): 73-78.

[7] SUN Bin-bin, DU He-min. Research on tourism culture and creative product design based on consumption value theory. Packaging Engineering, 2022, 43 (22): 333-340.

[8] CHARLES S P, Collected Papers. Cambridge Mass: Harvard University Press, 1932.

Design Studies and Intelligence Engineering
L.C. Jain et al. (Eds.)
© 2024 The Authors.
This article is published online with Open Access by IOS Press and distributed under the terms
of the Creative Commons Attribution Non-Commercial License 4.0 (CC BY-NC 4.0).
doi:10.3233/FAIA231500

Modern Design Thinking and AIGC Intervention

Yu WANG[a,1], Zhenzhen WANG[b] and Ruirui MU[a]

[a]*New Media School, Beijing Institute of Graphic Communication, Beijing, China*
[b]*Art Design School, Ma Anshan College, Ma Anshan, China*

Abstract. Modern Design Thinking is a series of constantly developing heuristic methodologies that advocate for human-centered, collaborative, interdisciplinary, and iterative design research. This article traces the development of modern Design Thinking through literature research. Designers should understand the current Design Thinking mode and its limitations and speculate and develop Design Thinking based on continuous design practice and philosophical abstraction. Designers should actively face the intervention of AIGC, regard it as their tool and assistant, work together with it, and jointly promote design innovation development. Designers must maintain their advantages in creativity and personalization, constantly learn and update their skills and knowledge, establish emotional connections with users, and provide better design services.

Keywords. Modern Design Thinking, traceability, design process, AIGC

1. Introduction

The extension of design in modern society is constantly expanding, with the fields of design ranging from visual design, product design, and environmental design to service design, experience design, organizational design, and system design. As an exclusive term, Design Thinking is not exclusive to design studies. It has permeated the development of various industries, such as sociology, management, and engineering. From the perspective of keyword search popularity on the Google platform, the global search of "Design Thinking" shows a growth trend. The search volume was low from 2004 to 2010, and then the popularity rose. The increase was not significant during the COVID-19 epidemic. Then, the search popularity remained high (see Figure 1; "Remarks" in the figure is the Google data system update node).

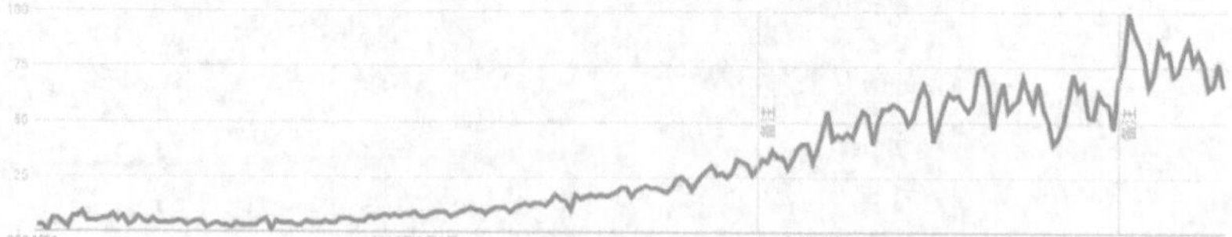

Figure 1. "Design Thinking" search popularity (Google Trends)

---

[1] Corresponding Author. New Media School, Beijing Institute of Graphic Communication, 1st Section 2 Xinghua Street, Daxing District, Beijing China, 102600; E-mail: wangyu@bigc.edu.cn; bank925@qq.com

Richard Buchanan (1992), a professor at Carnegie Mellon School of Design, proposed that Design Thinking is a new synthesis of symbols, things, behaviors, and environments, emphasizing humans' specific needs and values in diverse environments (see Figure 2):

- Symbol and visual communication design includes both traditional graphic design and the communication field of film and television media.
- It is the design of objects, including the shape and appearance of objects, and the new construction of multiple physical, psychological, social, and cultural relationships between products and people.
- Organized service and event planning and design include traditional logistics management content, physical resource integration, decision-making, strategic planning, and how Design Thinking can achieve satisfactory and meaningful smooth experiences in specific contexts.
- It is the design of complex systems or environments of living, working, entertainment, and learning and exploring the role of design in continuously developing ecological and cultural systems, meeting people's needs, and meeting expected environments.

Symbols, things, behaviors, and ideas are interconnected and permeated and are integrated into contemporary Design Thinking, playing a significant role in innovation. The effectiveness of design depends on the designer's ability to integrate the three rational thinking of product ingenuity, product functional logic, and personal and social value realization [1].

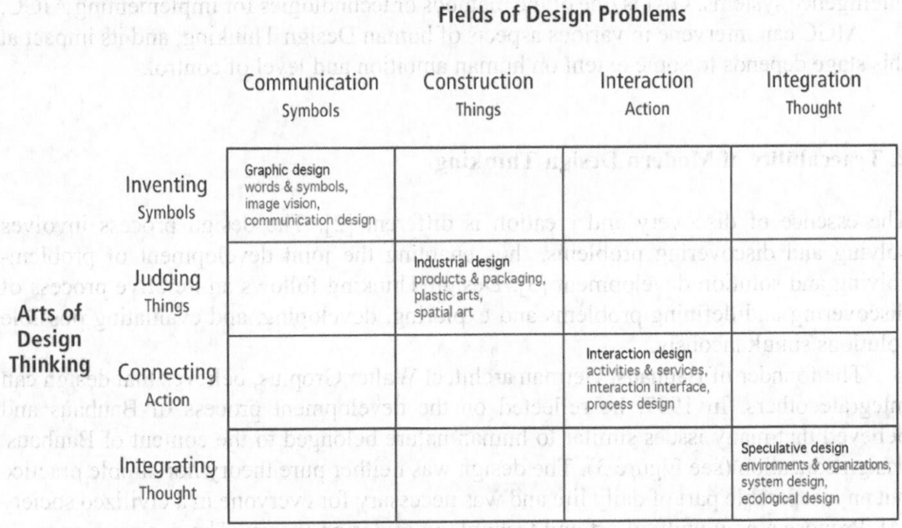

Fields of Design Problems

		Communication Symbols	Construction Things	Interaction Action	Integration Thought
	Inventing Symbols	Graphic design words & symbols, image vision, communication design			
Arts of Design Thinking	Judging Things		Industrial design products & packaging, plastic arts, spatial art		
	Connecting Action			Interaction design activities & services, interaction interface, process design	
	Integrating Thought				Speculative design environments & organizations, system design, ecological design

Figure 2. The four orders of design. (Richard Buchanan)

Design Thinking is a people-oriented, problem-solving-oriented methodology emphasizing participatory and iterative design processes, aiming to collaborate across multiple disciplines and discover and solve complex problems. The complexity of design objects determines the extension and transformation of Design Thinking. However, some scholars in China currently confuse "Design Thinking" with "design creativity" or believe that designers cannot produce eye-catching and touching creative products through rigorous deduction of Design Thinking. The reason is that they need to understand the development context of Design Thinking. Design Thinking has become a systematic methodology for people-oriented collaborative innovation (an independent concept); design creativity (Ideas/Inspiration/Creation) is not a theoretical term but can be understood as the intuitive expression of designer inspiration based on narrative, symbolism, and semantics.

In 2022, AIGC broke out, causing competition from the technology and industry sectors. AIGC (Artificial Intelligence Generated Content) is an artificial intelligence system based on machine learning, deep learning, and other technologies that can perform search, screening, summarization, reasoning, and synthesis of new data from big data. It can assist or replace humans in analysis, research and development, and decision-making. AIGC is a new production method for digital content generation and interaction, following PGC (Professionally Generated Content) and UGC (User Generated Content), such as AI graphics, audio and video, AI code, and virtual human, object, and field content.

Generative AI (GAI) is an artificial intelligence technology that can generate new, deceptive content by learning and simulating data distribution characteristics. Generative AI can generate various types of content, including images, audio, videos, text, and more. AIGC refers to content automatically generated by artificial intelligence systems. This type of content can be generated using GAI technology or other artificial intelligence technologies such as natural language processing or image recognition. AIGC can include articles, news reports, works of art, music, and more. Therefore, GAI is a technology used to generate content, while AIGC refers to content generated by artificial intelligence systems. GAI is one of the methods or technologies for implementing AIGC.

AIGC can intervene in various aspects of human Design Thinking, and its impact at this stage depends to some extent on human ambition and level of control.

2. Traceability of Modern Design Thinking

The essence of discovery and creation is different [2]. The design process involves solving and discovering problems, thus enabling the joint development of problem-solving and solution development [3]. Design Thinking follows an iterative process of discovering and defining problems and exploring, developing, and evaluating possible solutions simultaneously.

The founder of Bauhaus, German architect Walter Gropius, believes that design can integrate others. In 1937, he reflected on the development process of Bauhaus and believed that many issues similar to human nature belonged to the content of Bauhaus' design education (see Figure 3). The design was neither pure theory nor simple practice but an inseparable part of daily life and was necessary for everyone in a civilized society [4]. Propose a new unity of art and technology in design theory. The design purpose is people rather than products. The design follows natural and objective laws for curriculum reform and teaching practice.

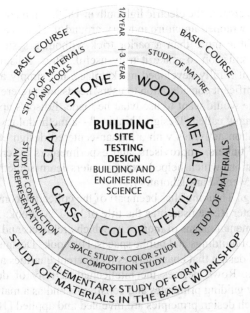

Figure 3. Bauhaus curriculum wheel.

In the early stages of World War II, Brehon B. Somervell, the General of the US Army Supply Services, attempted to unify the dispersed procurement activities of the Army and Navy, establishing an integrated Army Supply Plan (ASP), which controlled the entire procurement process from contracts and production schedules to delivery and distribution to the battlefield. In order to manage the complex procurement process, ASP introduced a military supply management system in early 1944, which consisted of a carefully designed set of tables and records. All necessary procurement information for each project was gathered for the first time to collect and record the latest information at various stages of ASP operation. Although people did not consider this system to be a product of Design Thinking at the time, it was considered a pioneer in later system design in the design community (such as systems used to handle large-scale projects similar to the Apollo program in the 1960s and early 1970s) [5].

John Dewey (1964) believes that inquiry is a controlled transformation that transforms uncertain states into states with relatively certain classifications and relationships, transforming the various constituent elements of the original state into a unified whole [6]. Under this definition, the exploration strategy is to find theoretical, practical, or productive solutions to problems, guiding people's knowledge progress in cognitive and behavioral aspects [7]. Dewey described the five stages of thinking logic in "How We Think": First, identifying difficulties and difficulties; Second, Positioning and defining the problem; Third, Possible answers and solutions; Fourth, Reasoning associations; Fifth, Further observation and experimentation to validate beliefs [8]. It can be seen that the exploration process is consistent with the logical thinking. These five stages are closely related, and reciprocating iterations will occur during the process. When people gather information to answer a question and solve a problem, it is called conducting research work [9]. Design research has a certain degree of complexity and resistance to solution, and each stage of the research process may repeatedly verify and solve problems, ultimately solving problems in a spiral ascending form as a whole. Dewey's "inquiry theory" also applies to the design field.

Thomas Edison created the electric lightbulb in 1879, often considered his signature invention, and then wrapped an entire industry around it. However, Edison understood that the bulb was little more than a parlor trick without a system of electric power generation and transmission to make it truly useful. Thus, Edison's genius lay in his ability to conceive of a fully developed marketplace, not simply a discrete device. He invariably gave significant consideration to users' needs and preferences and was able to envision how people would want to use what he made. Edison's approach was an early example of what is now called "Design Thinking"—a methodology that imbues the full spectrum of innovation activities with a human-centered design ethos. He surrounded himself with gifted tinkers, improvisers, and experimenters by creating a team-based approach to innovation, which helped experimenters learn something new from each iterative stab in his Menlo Park laboratory.

The term "Design Thinking" has been part of the collective consciousness of design researchers since Peter Rowe used it as the title of his 1987 book. According to Rowe, Design is the fundamental means of inquiry by which architects and planners realize and give shape to ideas of buildings and public spaces. His book "Design Thinking" provides a general portrait of design that characterizes its inherent qualities and sets it apart from other inquiry forms. Rowe defines the intellectual activity of designing as rational inquiry governed by guiding principles and constraints and as a matter of the conviction and impulse by which design principles are invented and applied [10].

Jonathan Cagan, Craig M. Vogel (2002) emphasized that development teams should collaborate and collaborate across disciplines on the basis of balancing the needs and desires of target users and other stakeholders, and proposed the Design Thinking process of Integrated New Product Development (iNPD), which includes four stages: opportunity identification stage, explicit and ambiguous early stage, insight into user needs and product development requirements; In the opportunity understanding stage, understand the relationships between stakeholders and the opportunity points throughout the entire process of accessing products/services, and translate them into overall design specifications; In the conceptualization stage of opportunities, value opportunities are transformed into functional, user-friendly, and attractive product/service conceptual models, and iterative optimization is repeatedly tested; In the opportunity realization stage, clarify the product brand identification and promotion marketing plan, and comprehensively carry out production, processing, and marketing (see Figure 4). INPD is a process that can guide specific practical operations and help development teams clarify the "fuzzy early stage." It is a systematic method that combines strategic planning, design, development, and brand management and integrates physical product and service design [11], which has been widely applied in the industry.

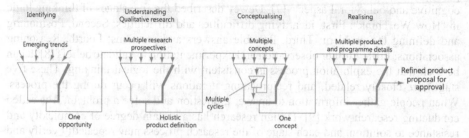

Figure 4. iNPD process (Jonathan Cagan, Craig M. Vogel, 2002)

Professor David Kelly, one of the founders of IDEO, Stanford University, founded d.school in 2004, using Design Thinking as a way of thinking and a code of conduct. He offers design courses for the entire school, dedicated to cultivating students' innovative thinking and problem-solving abilities. IDEO CEO Tim Brown (2008) proposed that Design Thinking is an innovative human-centered design approach that draws inspiration from the methods and tools adopted by many designers, integrating human needs, technological possibilities, and the conditions required to achieve business goals [12]. Design Thinking focuses on social issues, empathizes with user needs, defines problems, goals, and impacts, analyzes stakeholder relationships, envisions solutions, prototype tests, implements, and iterates products (see Figure 5). The socialized thinking advocated by Design Thinking is a method of design attitude, thinking, and communication with people. Design Thinking is just such an approach to innovation: a human-centered, creative, iterative, and practical approach to finding the best ideas and ultimate solutions [13].

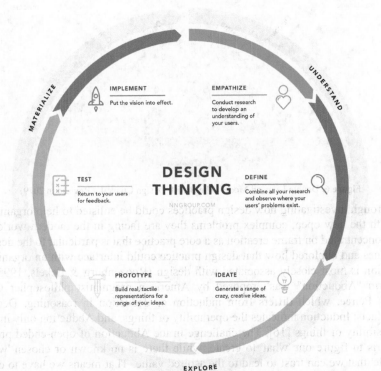

Figure 5. Design Thinking (NNGROUP.com)

The Double Demand Model was created by The British Design Council (2005) and describes the mindset used by designers, mapping the divergent and convergent stages of the design process. Design Thinking starts with a trigger, which may be an idea, some insights, market changes, or macroeconomic changes [14]. Stage 1: Identify issues. Understanding phenomena and current situations, exploring new issues, and identifying opportunities for further reflection. Stage 2: Define the problem. Integrate information and knowledge into insights, define real problems, focus on opportunities, and develop plans. Stage 3: Development exploration. Through the iterative process of exploration and verification, the design solution is evolved into an executable development solution. Stage 4: Delivery Plan. Analyze and validate potential solutions, and after the solution is determined, begin implementing the deliverable solution (see Figure 6).

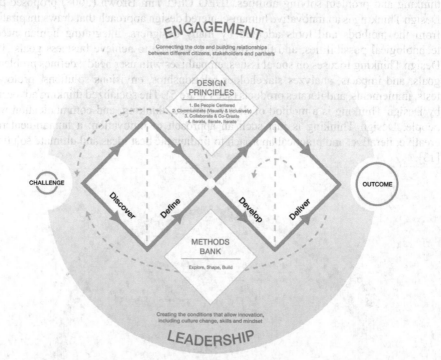

Figure 6. Double Demand Model (The British Design Council, Revised in 2019)

Through investigating how design practices could be enlisted to help organizations deal with the new open, complex problems they are facing in the modern world, Kees Dorst concentrated on frame creation as a core practice that is particular to the designing disciplines and explored how that design practice could interface with an organization. Abduction is most closely associated with design (Roozenburg & Eekels, 1995) [15]. The term "Abduction" was proposed by American pragmatist philosopher Charles Sanders Peirce, which differs from induction or deduction in reasoning. Deduction proves facts; Induction indicates the operability of things, and Abduction only indicates the possibility of things [16]. The challenge in the Abduction of open-ended problem-solving is to figure out 'what' to create, while there is no known or chosen 'working principle' that we can trust to lead to the aspired value. That means we have to create a 'working principle' and a 'thing' (object, service, system) in parallel (see Figure 7) [17].

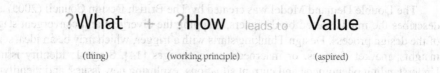

Figure 7. Abduction of open-ended problem-solving (Kees Dorst, 2011)

We can see that from Dewey's exploration theory, Integrated New Product Development, IDEO's Design Thinking, to The British Design Council's Double Demand Model, there is a common understanding of the "Design Thinking" process, which involves drawing threads and cocoons from the chaotic and fuzzy early stages to define real problems, designing prototypes, iteratively testing and implementing solutions, and analyzing problems through agile iteration to obtain the best solution during the process.

3. AIGC Intervenes in Modern Design Processes

Design Thinking follows the principle of putting people at the center. ISO 9241-210:2010 provides requirements and recommendations for human-centered design principles and activities throughout the entire lifecycle of computer interaction systems, aimed at being used by those who manage the design process, focusing on the software and hardware of the interaction system to enhance the way people interact with the system. This type of design research has a typical architecture, an iterative research cycle typically characterized by observation, definition, rapid prototyping, and testing. Each iteration is built on the lessons learned from the previous cycle, and the process terminates when the results are appropriate or the deadline is reached [18]. AIGC has changed the speed and efficiency of the design process. Traditional design processes typically require significant time and effort to complete various stages, such as requirements analysis, creative development, design production, and review. However, AIGC can automatically generate design content, significantly shortening the time of the design process. Designers can quickly create preliminary design plans using design elements and templates generated by AIGC and make further adjustments and optimizations. This way, designers can respond to customer needs faster and provide more efficient design services.

3.1. Background Research and Requirement Insight Stage

Design Thinking starts with understanding, and the design process starts with deeply understanding the client's background, behavior, and experience. Using empathy to view the world from the perspective of others is the key to collaborating with stakeholders and utilizing different perspectives to plan better solutions. However, people inevitably have certain cognitive biases or are constrained by the information cocoon effect, which narrows our horizons and makes it difficult for us to empathize with people who are different from ourselves. However, AIGC can help designers understand market trends, user preferences, and industry dynamics by analyzing a large amount of data and information. Designers can use AIGC-produced data analysis reports and trend predictions to guide design direction and decision-making. In this way, designers can more accurately grasp market demand and provide design works that meet user expectations. AIGC can also help designers understand users' evaluations and needs for design works by analyzing user behavior and feedback data. Designers can utilize user feedback and insight reports generated by AIGC to understand user preferences, pain points, and expectations, thereby optimizing design works. This way, designers can better meet users' needs and provide design solutions with a more user experience.

3.2. Collaborative Innovation and Problem Definition Stage

The design research process requires designers, organizations, and stakeholders to engage in Participatory Design or Co-Design. In the process of open innovation, people from different fields share and integrate ideas, ideas, and knowledge to meet the needs of various stakeholders [19]. The complexity and diversity of problems are something only some can handle, and this process still requires designers to take the lead, highlighting designers' professionalism in controlling design research. AIGC can achieve a more efficient innovation process through collaborative work with designers. Designers can interact and collaborate with AIGC in real time, raise questions, seek advice, and receive timely feedback through dialogue. This interactive design process can help designers better understand user needs, utilize AIGC-produced design works as creative inspiration and reference, and quickly generate diverse design solutions. Generative AI intervenes in co-creation, analyzing stakeholders' knowledge background and practical needs more profoundly and comprehensively, thereby making designer decisions more objective, generating efficient, high-quality, low-cost solutions, and jointly promoting innovation and progress in design works. AIGC can help designers define design problems more accurately by analyzing and processing a large amount of data. Designers can provide AIGC with some essential information and parameters, and AIGC can analyze this data to help designers better understand user needs and pain points. AIGC can provide in-depth insight and understanding of design issues based on user feedback and behavioral data, assisting designers in defining and solving problems better.

3.3. Creation Developing and Concept Setting Stage

In traditional design processes, the creative and conceptual stages typically require designers to conduct extensive research and brainstorming to generate ideas and concepts. AIGC can provide rich creative inspiration and reference resources, helping designers obtain more inspiration and references during the design and research stage. Designers can broaden their design ideas and enhance the innovation and uniqueness of their designs. AIGC can also automatically generate ideas and concepts by analyzing a large amount of data and information. Designers can use the creativity and concepts generated by AIGC as a starting point for further development and optimization. In this way, designers can create ideas and concepts faster, improving the efficiency of the design process.

AIGC can increasingly participate in creative digital content generation work, assisting designers in continuously generating, iterating, and validating innovative solutions through human-machine collaboration. AIGC has been involved in the production of various media forms such as text, images, music, videos, virtual humans/objects/fields, and completed the creation of specific themes under the guidance of humans. AIGC can automatically generate design prototypes and sketches. Designers only need to provide some basic design parameters and requirements. AIGC can quickly generate multiple design solutions, helping designers explore different creative directions faster and allowing them to gain more creativity and choose the best solution. AIGC can automatically complete repetitive and tedious design tasks, such as graphic generation, layout, and color selection. This way, designers can devote more time and energy to creative and strategic work, improving design efficiency.

3.4. Review and Feedback Stage

AIGC provides automated design review and optimization functions, allowing designers to use these tools to check their designs' accuracy, consistency, and compliance. Designers can quickly identify and fix problems in their designs, improving the quality of their designs. AIGC can automatically evaluate designs based on design specifications and best practices and provide suggestions for improvement. AIGC can simulate user behavior, provide feedback on design usability, usability, and satisfaction, evaluate the user experience of design solutions, and automatically generate different versions of design solutions to help designers optimize strategies to meet customer requirements and improve user experience. AIGC can use simulation and simulation techniques to predict the performance and effectiveness of designs under different conditions, validate and optimize designs, and help designers identify and solve potential problems before production, which helps to reduce errors and inconsistencies in design and improve design quality and efficiency.

Although AIGC can skip many steps in the human Design Thinking process and directly provide solutions, we still hope to use AIGC to support and assist in various stages of the Design Thinking process to control the research direction and form of results accurately (see Figure 8).

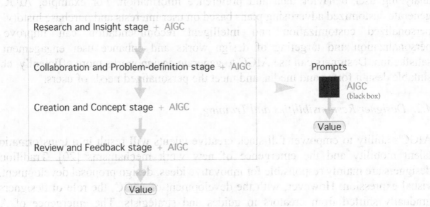

Figure 8. Design Thinking Process + AIGC.

4. AIGC Changes Modern Design Services

Here, we will discuss it from two aspects: the design object and the design subject.

4.1. Design Form and Media

AIGC has improved the design process and processes in modern design services. It can provide insight, automatically generate design solutions, automate review and optimization, and interact and collaborate with designers in real time, thereby improving design efficiency and quality and helping designers create excellent design works more efficiently. Designers can use AIGC as a starting point and reference resource to further develop and improve their design work. At the same time, AIGC can help designers quickly identify and fix design issues, improving the quality and accuracy of design works.

The application of AIGC in design form and media provides designers with automated design generation, multimedia design and interactive experience, personalized customization, and intelligent recommendation services. AIGC can automatically generate design works through deep learning and algorithm models. By inputting essential information and parameters, designers can enable AIGC to generate design works that meet the requirements automatically. For example, AIGC can automatically generate product models and rendered images with usage scenarios. This automated design generation can significantly reduce designers' workload and time costs and improve design efficiency. AIGC can help designers provide more decadent choices and creativity in multimedia design and interactive experience. AIGC can generate diverse design forms and media presentation methods by analyzing many multimedia materials and interaction design cases. For example, AIGC can generate web page templates with different styles and layouts, helping designers quickly build website interfaces. In this way, designers can more flexibly choose and apply various design forms and media to meet the needs of different user groups. AIGC can provide intelligent design customization and recommendation services based on users' personalized needs and preferences. AIGC can generate personalized design works tailored to users by analyzing user behavior data and preference information. For example, AIGC can generate customized advertising plans based on user interests and purchase history. This personalized customization and intelligent recommendation can improve the personalization and targeting of design works and enhance user engagement and satisfaction. Designers can use AIGC to generate design works more efficiently, choose suitable design forms and media, and meet the personalized needs of users.

4.2. Designer Responsibilities and Training

AIGC's ability to empower full-stack creative talents will result in a transformation of talent mobility and the emergence of new work mechanisms [20]. Traditionally, designers are mainly responsible for innovative ideas, design proposal development, and visual expression. However, with the development of AIGC, the role of designers has gradually shifted from creators to guides and strategists. The emergence of AIGC redefines the roles and responsibilities of designers. Designers must collaborate with AIGC technology as tools and resources to expand their creative abilities and Design Thinking. Designers need to understand and master the principles and applications of AIGC technology to communicate and collaborate with it effectively. Designers need to learn how to utilize the design content and creativity generated by AIGC to provide customers with more strategic and innovative solutions. The role of designers has gradually shifted from creators to guides and strategists. Designers must consciously guide their development direction when using AIGC to meet customer needs and goals. Designers need to possess strategic thinking and innovative abilities, be able to combine the design content generated by AIGC with their professional knowledge and experience and provide more creative and valuable design solutions. Although AIGC can automatically generate design content, it lacks human emotions and personality. Designers can customize and personalize the design content generated by AIGC through in-depth communication and understanding with customers to meet their unique needs and brand image.

Design education is an essential part of cultivating designers, and the emergence of AIGC has brought new challenges and opportunities to design education. Designers need to adapt to the skills and tools of using AIGC to better collaborate with artificial intelligence. Therefore, design education must update course content and teaching methods, strengthen training on related knowledge such as artificial intelligence and machine learning, and enable students to use AIGC technology to assist design work flexibly. At the same time, design education must cultivate students' creativity and Design Thinking. Although AIGC can automatically generate design content, it must partially replace designers' creativity and unique perspective. Therefore, design education must focus on cultivating students' creativity, critical thinking, and problem-solving abilities, enabling them to collaborate with AIGC to create more innovative and strategic design solutions. In addition, design education also needs to pay attention to ethical and moral issues. Using AIGC may raise ethical and moral issues such as intellectual property, data privacy, and social impact. Therefore, design education must teach students how to use AIGC technology correctly, follow ethical norms, and be aware of design's social responsibility and impact.

Overall, the emergence of AIGC has profoundly impacted modern design services and design education. It has changed the positioning and blame of designers, improved the efficiency of the design process, broadened the diversity of design outputs, and prompted design education to update courses and cultivate students' creativity and problem-solving abilities.

5. Problems and Challenges

AIGC's involvement in the Design Thinking process brings some problems and challenges to designers. Firstly, the design works generated by AIGC may need more uniqueness and personalization, as they are generated based on a large amount of data and algorithms. Designers must know this by conducting in-depth research on user needs and market trends, seeking unique creative inspiration, and creating more personalized and innovative design works. Secondly, designers need to adapt to the collaborative work style with AIGC. Designers can use AIGC as their tool and assistant to repeatedly interact and adjust with AIGC to generate design solutions quickly. At the same time, designers must filter and modify the designs generated by AIGC to ensure that they meet user needs and brand image. Once again, designers need to constantly learn and update their skills and knowledge, understand the latest design trends, and adapt to the development of AIGC technology. Designers can pay attention to relevant technologies and algorithms and understand their principles and application scenarios. Finally, the design works generated by AIGC may lack the emotional and human touch and cannot establish deep emotional connections with users. Designers can inject unique humanistic characteristics into their design works by incorporating personal creativity and emotional elements. Designers can also engage in in-depth communication and feedback with users, understand their needs and emotional experiences, and create more infectious design works.

Although AIGC still has much room for development in details, accuracy, and extreme event handling, its initial performance is impressive, with some achievements comparable to those of experienced creators. Generative AI is undergoing rapid innovation and will become a new life form in the digital world with unlimited potential.

References

[1] Richard Buchanan, Wicked Problems in Design Thinking, *Design Issues* **8** (1992), 5-21.
[2] Richard Buchanan, Declaration by Design: Rhetoric, Argument, and Demonstration in Design Practice, *Design Issues* **2**(1985), 4-22.
[3] Bryan Lawson, *How Designers Think: The Design Process Demystified*, Elsevier, Amsterdam, 2006.
[4] Walter Groupius, *Scope of Total Architecture*, Krill Book Publishing, New York, 1956.
[5] Victor Margolin, The United States in World War II: Scientists, Engineers, Designers, *Design Issues* **29**(2013), 14-29.
[6] John Dewey, *Logic: The Theory of Inquiry*, Holt, Rinehart and Winston, New York, 1964.
[7] Richard Buchanan, Think about Design: An Historical Perspective, *Philosophy of Technology and Engineering Sciences* (2009), 409-453.
[8] John Dewey, *How We Think*,2nd ed. Heath Press Inc, Royal Oak, 1933.
[9] Booth, C. Wayne, Gregory G. Colomb and Joseph M. Williams, *The Craft of Research*, 3rd ed. The University of Chicago Press, Chicago, 2008.
[10] Peter G. Rowe, *Design Thinking*, The MIT Press, Cambridge, 1987.
[11] Jonathan Cagan, Craig M. Vogel. *Creating breakthrough products: revealing the secrets that drive global innovation*, 2nd ed. Pearson Education Inc., NJ., 2013.
[12] Tim Brown, Barry Katz, *Change by Design: How Design Thinking Transforms Organizations and Inspires Innovation*, Harper Business, New York, 2009.
[13] Tim Brown, Design Thinking, *Harvard Business Review* **86**(2008), 84-92.
[14] Design Council, *Double Demand Model* [EB/OL], https://www.designcouncil.org.uk, 2019.
[15] Norbert F. M. Roozenburg and Johannes Eekels, *Product Design: Fundamentals and Methods*, John Wiley & Sons, Chichester,1995.
[16] Bruno Latour and Steve Woolgar, *Laboratory Life: The Construction of Scientific Facts*, 2nd ed. Princeton University Press, NJ.,1986.
[17] Kees Dorst, The Core of 'Design Thinking' and its Application, *Design Studies* **32**(2011), 521-532.
[18] Donald A. Norman, Roberto Verganti, Incremental and Radical Innovation: Design Research Vs. Technology and Meaning Change, *Design Issue* **30**(2014), 78-96.
[19] Xiang Y. Xin, Xi Wang. The Uncertainty of Co-creation and Service Experience in Service Design, *Decoration* **4**(2018), 76-78.
[20] Ming Y. Feng, Rui Cao, Qing J. Chen, The Transformation and Reconstruction of Art Design Education under the Impact of AIGC: Opportunities, Paradigm and Response, *Industrial & Engineering Design* **5**(2023), 47-58.

Design Studies and Intelligence Engineering
L.C. Jain et al. (Eds.)
© 2024 The Authors.
This article is published online with Open Access by IOS Press and distributed under the terms
of the Creative Commons Attribution Non-Commercial License 4.0 (CC BY-NC 4.0).
doi:10.3233/FAIA231501

863

Design of Fast-Growing Plant Material Woven Furniture Products Based on Sustainable Concepts

Beibei JIA[a]

[a] *Department of Art and Design, Beijing City University, Beijing, China*

Abstract. In today's society, with the growth of population and energy consumption, various natural resources are rapidly depleted, and traditional handicrafts are on the verge of being lost because they do not meet the needs of modern life. Fast-growing wood product weaving is a social activity made by artificial weaving using bamboo, rattan, willow, grass, hemp, palm, etc. as raw materials. Woven furniture made of fast-growing wood is a new type of furniture with great development prospects. It is environmentally friendly, has aesthetic appeal, and has cultural connotations. Starting from the aspects of green environmental protection, culture, fun, simplicity, etc., it provides an idea for the innovative design of this type of furniture. Taking bamboo as an example to illustrate sustainable furniture design strategies.

Keywords. Sustainable concept; fast- growing plants; furniture design

1. Sustainable design concept and overview

In 1987, in the article "Our Common Future" published by the United Nations World Commission on Environment and Development, "sustainable development" was defined for the first time as: sustainable development that effectively meets the needs of the present without affecting the needs of future generations. This shows that on the premise of achieving economic development and people's prosperous lives, we can fully realize the protection of the ecological environment and the rational use of natural resources [1]. Liang Ting, a scholar at the Hong Kong Polytechnic University, explained the concept of sustainable design: Sustainable design is different from design that usually only uses physical products as output. Instead, it establishes and develops sustainable design that meets the special needs of customers by combining products and services.

Sustainable design is based on sustainable development and strives to achieve sustainable development of humans, nature, society and ecology. Furniture is ubiquitous in people's lives and cannot be separated from it. From production to use to disposal, it is closely related to the ecological environment and inseparable from sustainable development. Sustainable furniture design refers to the application of sustainable development concepts in the furniture design process. This article will analyze the design forms of rapidly growing plant material woven furniture products based on the concept of sustainability, and propose corresponding solutions using bamboo furniture nas a example.

2. Fast-Growing Plant Materials for Woven Furniture

The materials for weaving furniture from fast-growing wood materials are easy to obtain, and there are many materials to choose from. The weaving methods of various materials will have some subtle differences, and the final results will also have some subtle differences. Bamboo is exquisitely woven, rattan is exquisite, willow is rough, and straw is soft. All kinds of materials can be combined with each other. It is a kind of furniture with great development potential. Depending on the softness, suppleness, toughness, and thickness of the woven materials, their strengths and weaknesses can be exploited. In the process of making furniture and daily necessities, bamboo and rattan combinations and willow grass combinations are more commonly used. Using short-cycle plants as raw materials, we weave a green and environmentally friendly product, which is a product that is very popular among contemporary consumers. In addition, this type of furniture is both creative and beautiful in its woven patterns.

Bamboo woven furniture is made of bamboo as the main body. It is a household item that uses other materials as the skeleton and bamboo as the veneer to fill the skeleton. It is usually made of a combination of bamboo and wood or bamboo and rattan [2]. Its types include bamboo dining tables and chairs, sofas, coffee tables, side tables, screens, etc. Compared with willow and rattan furniture, the processing procedures of raw materials such as bamboo strips, bamboo strips, and bamboo strips are much more complicated. Although the bamboo decorative surface made by this method is more refined, the cost and labor are relatively high. In the creative design of contemporary furniture, bamboo is an important structural form, which proposes a new idea for the fusion of traditional and modern furniture. There are various ways to connect the frames of bamboo furniture, inheriting the wisdom of traditional Chinese handicrafts. As shown in the following diagram, it can be generally divided into three methods: bending, wrapping, and inserting.

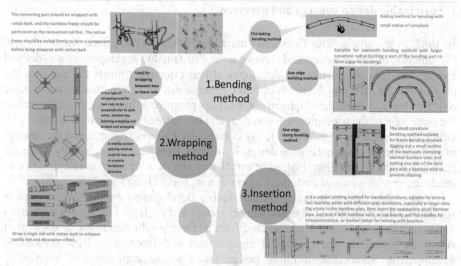

Figure 1. Joining methods for bamboo furniture frames

With the development of the times, various new technologies for bamboo materials are rapidly developing, new products are constantly emerging, and the scale of industrialization has significantly increased. Bamboo bending furniture, which is deeply loved by consumers, has emerged in the market. Bamboo curved furniture is usually composed of several bamboo curved components and connectors, demonstrating a sense of curve and softness in form. However, due to the different unit compositions of bamboo furniture, there are also differences in its processing methods. According to the different classifications of furniture materials, their bending components usually come in different forms such as round bamboo tubes, bamboo strips, bamboo strips, and bamboo laminated timber. The addition of bamboo bending technology not only makes furniture decorative, practical, and interesting, but also adds a unique cultural atmosphere. As shown in Figure 2.

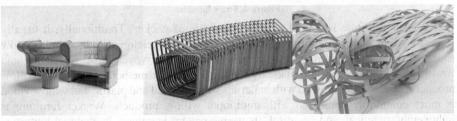

Figure 2. Bamboo furniture

Rattan furniture, also called "rattan big pieces", is a kind of furniture made of thick rattan as a frame and wrapped with rattan bark and stem core. It includes chairs, stools, sofas, beds, tables, tables, shelves, and cabinets, cabinets, screens, etc., are all elegant and exquisite. In addition to rattan leather furniture, rattan core furniture, rattan furniture, and polished rattan furniture, there are also many kinds of rattan furniture such as rattan bamboo, rattan wood, and rattan steel, which are durable and durable. Rattan furniture is made from fast-growing plants and has the most types and styles. This is mainly because the thickness of rattan materials is different. Thick rattan can be used as bones, while thin rattan can be used for weaving [3]. Nowadays, some people use paper, plastic, leather and other materials to imitate the rattan craftsmanship to create "imitation rattan furniture", which is very similar in visual and aesthetic terms, is low in price, and has great development potential. As shown in Figure 3.

Figure 3. Rattan furniture

Straw weaving is a handmade product made of various soft herbs, with wheat straw, corn husks, and cattail woven as the main materials. Straw furniture is mainly small furniture such as poufs, futons, and low tables. Air-dried water hyacinth is a good textile material, but its production process is complicated and requires drying of the material. The water hyacinth house has sofas, chairs, stools, lamps, beds, flower utensils, etc. The materials are naturally rough, the color is elegant, and the texture is thick. It is not only green and environmentally friendly, but also brings a sense of leisure and wildness to the room. Currently, this type of furniture is mostly available in foreign furniture markets, but its popularity in China is not high. As shown in Figure 4.

Figure 4. Straw furniture

Wicker furniture is a kind of furniture made of wicker. Traditionally, it usually refers to willow composite furniture. It uses wood as the skeleton, uses the whole willow as the warp, and the willow bark to weave the weft. It is woven through weaving and two-way. A kind of furniture made by latte art and other methods [4]. Modern willow products can also be combined with materials such as metal and plastic, but willow wood is more commonly combined with traditional willow products. Wicker furniture is lightweight, practical, and beautiful. Its weave pattern is unique, its material texture is natural, and it has a great decorative effect. Wicker furniture can be roughly divided into tables, chairs, cabinets, shelves, beds, outdoor leisure, etc. With the changes in modern people's lifestyles, wicker furniture is dominated by casual style. As shown in Figure 5.

Figure 5. Willow furniture

When it comes to woven furniture made of fast-growing wood, the first thing that comes to mind is rattan and bamboo furniture. The development of these two types of furniture has attracted more attention, and willow products are more famous. However, from the perspective of raw materials, rattan is highly moisture-loving and mainly grows in the tropics and subtropics. However, my country's rattan resources are relatively scarce and harvesting is difficult, and the processing process of bamboo is relatively complicated, resulting in high production costs. Qiliu is a plant that is relatively easy to survive. It likes fertilizer, water and rain, and its growing season is very short. It can be harvested twice a year. It has a wide range of growth, its raw materials are much cheaper than rattan bamboo, and its processing is relatively simple. In addition, wicker products are elegant in color, durable in the sun, come in various patterns, and are beautiful. Under the current dual background of "green environmental protection", "traditional craft protection" and "humanistic care", the art of "willow weaving" has huge space for innovation and huge market value.

3. Analysis of fast-growing plant material woven furniture design

3.1 Environmentally friendly

Environmentally friendly furniture is a whole process from raw materials to production, use to recycling. It causes less pollution, wastes less energy, and can be degraded and recycled. During use, the material factors of the product cause minimal damage to the human body. From the functional perspective of furniture, it can reduce unnecessary functions and will not waste resources.

It is made from fast-growing tree species and natural materials. Its growth rate is faster than ordinary wood, which can realize the sustainable utilization of raw materials and is easy to decompose naturally after being discarded. We use green, fast-growing plants as raw materials to design woven furniture, and summarize the design points into two aspects: material and function. The materials used can be divided into: woven raw materials and auxiliary frame materials. In terms of woven materials, try not to dye or spray them as much as possible to retain the original color of the plant and reduce the pollution of colorants [5]. You can choose metal or logs as auxiliary frames. The wood uses a traditional willow frame, which can be more flexible when weaving, but avoid using plywood that releases formaldehyde. The metal frame is combined by welding. When designing, you must consider the focus point of the weaving in advance to ensure that each side has four sides, or a closed side weaving frame. If necessary, you need to discuss it with the craftsman. communicate. The structure of the product should be very simple, minimize unnecessary functionality, and combine environmental protection with simple beauty.

The "straw stock" created by Juan Cappa uses natural fast-growing material straw combined with a simple metal frame to create a sustainable and environmentally friendly furniture design.

Figure 6. Straw furniture by Juan Cappa

3.2 Cultural type

Cultural design is to integrate the culture of weaving raw materials, weaving equipment culture, traditional ecological culture and traditional culture into furniture modeling. This type of furniture culture is carried out at the subconscious level and introspection level. It awakens or increases human memories of culture through changes in the external form of furniture. At the same time, it can also use the surrounding atmosphere to It creates an emotional interaction between people and objects (woven furniture), thereby conveying thoughts on consumer culture.

Culture makes people think deeply and settle their souls, while living space is a place where people can rest physically and mentally. Through cultural decoration, people's emotions can be improved, and at the same time, culture can bring People's spiritual satisfaction and happiness make products resonate emotionally with consumers. However, unlike the bedroom, the living space is a window that communicates between the inside and the outside of the home, which allows this type of home cultural design to develop in the direction of decoration, with aesthetics as the main purpose and practicality as the auxiliary. In the cultural design of furniture made of fast-growing plant materials, the selection of culture is an important link. It must match the material according to its characteristics and combine it with the cultural form that it adapts to. Simply pile them up, but look for cultural connotations that can inspire people. Try to think about the combination from the perspective of the reflective layer, analyze different cultural groups, and "prescribe the right medicine".

3.3 Simple type

The admiration for simple design is also due to the development of society. In this era of extremely abundant materials, there are many things to choose from, and the same is true for external stimulation. "Five colors make people blind, five tones make people deaf, and five flavors make people taste bad." It's cool. Things are born for people and used by people. When it becomes an obstacle that prevents you from doing things, it will become easier and easier.

Dazzling excitement and products also encourage people to tend towards simple designs, and some people have begun to pursue a simple life. Less is more, more is more confusion. The simple design of fast-growing plant woven furniture is to meet the most fundamental needs of users. It is not only an expression of the simple furniture form that people choose, but also affects people's lives.

The specific design performance is to cut off unnecessary functionality, decoration and interest in the furniture to achieve the purpose of moderation. Secondly, we must abandon some unnecessary things. Because human energy is limited, the shapes of furniture that can be used are also limited. Things that are unnecessary or not suitable for your own development should be abandoned. When designing, and try to avoid useless furniture. Finally, to liberate people from dependence on items, this requires furniture to adhere to its proper functions and bring maximum appeal to users. The design of simple and fast plant material woven furniture should follow the concept of "less is more", maintain basic functions, focus on function, and pursue the texture of the product in the few places where the design effect can be achieved.

4. Sustainable Design Strategies for Bamboo Furniture

4.1 The strength of bamboo

Bamboo material itself has high mechanical strength and is very easy to split. From the data in the table below, it can be seen that the tensile strength of bamboo can reach about twice that of wood, and the compressive strength is more than 10% higher than that of wood. Even under the same unit weight, the tensile strength of bamboo can even exceed that of steel by 2-3 times. From this, it can be seen that bamboo is very suitable for making furniture in terms of mechanical properties.

Table 1. Strength Comparison of Bamboo, Wood, and Steel

Type		Tensile strength (Mpa)		Compressive strength (Mpa)	
		Weight	Average	Weight	Average
Bamboo	Moso bamboo	1947.9		642.0	
	Steel bamboo	2835.6		541.8	
	Lacquered bamboo	1822.4	2086.3	358.9	488.5
	Hemp bamboo	1952.3		411.5	
Wood	Cedarwood	713		404	
	Chestnut wood	985	1008	359	427
	Pine	1302		527	
	Birch	1035		428	
Steels	Mild steel	3780-4251			
	Semimild steel	4400-5000	5170-5563	The tensile strength of metal materials is called compressive strength.	
	Semihard steel	5200-6000			
	Hard steel	7300			

Bamboo has high mechanical strength, strong compressive and tensile properties, and bending resistance. From a physical property perspective, as long as suitable material selection and processing methods are used, bamboo is very suitable for furniture production.

4.2 Design strategies to cope with changes in color texture

The so-called natural bamboo utensils are bamboo utensils that use bamboo as raw materials and then undergo physical treatment. The color of such bamboo is difficult to grasp. The color of bamboo is not cyan as seen from the outside, but some are yellow, some are white, and some are black.

As long as they are natural-colored bamboo utensils, during long-term storage and daily use, their colors will generally range from green (white) to yellow (yellow), and then to reddish brown. This is because of the characteristics of bamboo itself, which will change according to the environment. Change with change. Therefore, we cannot conclude just from the color that yellow is the bamboo inside, green is bamboo green, and bamboo green is not necessarily cyan. To judge whether it is bamboo green, it depends on whether there is a layer of sodium-like substance on its surface. Things, this red represents old things, or it may be an old color. This is a kind of high-quality natural bamboo that will change color after some changes; from green to yellow, then to black [7]. The reason why they become dark is because these bamboo utensils did not have time to dry during storage and use, or were soaked in water for too long, or were made of tender bamboo or Yinshan bamboo, so these bamboo utensils will not be used in the future. They will become moldy and black. Such bambooware has no collection value, and most of them are defective products that have passed the test of time. This is also a problem we want to avoid when designing.

The color and texture of bamboo itself will change with age, and it will also be affected by the surrounding environment. As the age of the tree increases, the yellow and red colors of the bamboo will become darker and darker. At the same time, the brightness of the bamboo will also decrease, and the color will become more stable, from green to yellow-green, then to yellow, and finally Black spots appear. The bamboo furniture meticulously designed by German designer Stefan Dietz in Figure 7 gradually changes its processing surface from light green to gray, restoring the true color of bamboo as much as possible and allowing users to see the age of the product. The original bamboo, with the passage of time, will present a buckwheat color and become more distinctive in this type of bamboo furniture.

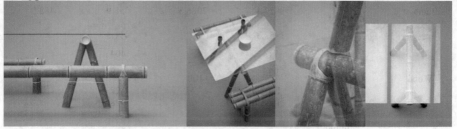

Figure 7. Bamboo furniture by German designer Stefan Dietz

4.3 Design strategies to deal with bamboo cracking and damage

After a set of bamboo furniture is completely damaged, it can be disposed of reasonably even when the bamboo is broken. For example, a broken bamboo strip can also be modified according to your own needs, including bamboo strips, bamboo strips, bamboo filaments, etc.

Composed of different types of bamboo, after the existing form changes, the same material can produce more and more novel effects. The bamboo sticks are handmade with no other connection methods, subtly expressing the characteristics of bamboo and looking both vivid and interesting. During manufacturing, the designer will split one end of the bamboo in half, then hammer it to form a dandelion shape, and then carefully stack each piece of bamboo together to form a huge Ottoman-style structure. The originally hard material became extremely soft at this moment. After careful design in figure 8 by Stefan Dietz, bamboo furniture consists of a bamboo bench and a pair of brackets, which can be fixed together with a single rope to support the entire desktop. If there is any damage, reassemble it again to restore its use status.

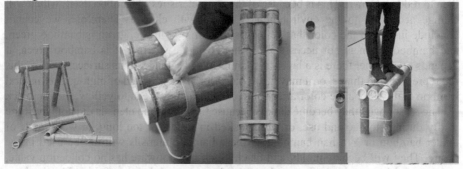

Figure 8. Design strategies for furniture cracking and damage

4.4 Design strategies for convenient packaging and transportation

During the handling and packaging process, the sustainable development of bamboo furniture is expressed as the smallest possible size, lighter mass, and less easily damaged parts, which embodies the sustainable design concept, including the energy consumption during transportation. Consumption, labor handling cost, occupied space, damage rate during transportation, consumption of packaging materials, etc. Stefan Dietz's bamboo furniture can be packaged flat, solving the problem of large and heavy handling space. Soba reinterpreted the traditional bamboo bench by incorporating clever twisting structures into the bamboo structure, making it easy to assemble bamboo furniture and achieving flat packaging. Using powerful fiber ropes and wooden handles at both ends, the joints need to be tightened for assembly. A connecting strip is left around the top of the leg stick of the bracket, which can be assembled in just a few minutes, making packaging and transportation convenient and easy.

Therefore, reasonable design must be carried out based on the physical and chemical properties of bamboo in the early stage of design. It's cleverly designed to fit all parts into a small space.

Figure 9. Strategy for assembling components

4.5 Design strategies for bamboo recycling

With the reduction of global forest resources and the strengthening of environmental protection awareness, finding low-carbon, environmentally friendly, and sustainable materials has become a top priority in the field of materials research in various countries. Bamboo materials are renewable resources with a short growth cycle of 4-5 years, while wood typically has a production cycle of over 15 years. As the world's preferred alternative to wood resources, bamboo will usher in important development opportunities. Compared to wood, bamboo has stronger regeneration ability, clear bamboo grain, beautiful board surface, natural color, pleasant bamboo fragrance, and more elegant texture, making it an ideal substitute for wood and other materials Secondary utilization of waste bamboo, such as crushing it and processing it to make it into new composite materials; realizing the secondary utilization of its value in the weaving process and making full use of its value.

Although bamboo grows rapidly, it is not an inexhaustible resource. Therefore, the secondary utilization of waste bamboo, such as crushing and processing it into new composite materials; Realizing the secondary utilization of its value during the weaving process and fully utilizing its value will be particularly important. In cities, companies related to discarded furniture and second-hand furniture can be set up to recycle and reuse furniture materials that can still be used but have been thrown away, dismantle damaged furniture, and reassemble recyclable parts. It is hoped that with the assistance of the government, this information can be properly disposed of and the concept of sustainable development can be promoted on a larger scale.

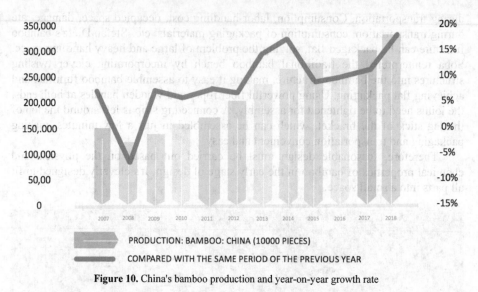

Figure 10. China's bamboo production and year-on-year growth rate

5. Conclusion

Under the concept of sustainable development, research on rapidly growing plant materials needs to be continued to make woven furniture product design more possible. In this process, it is necessary to fully tap the advantages of each material, deeply tap its technological potential, combine traditional handicrafts with new processes and technologies, and serve society and people's lives, using concise visual formal language for innovative design. This article studies and briefly elaborates on the design application forms in the field of sustainable bamboo woven furniture, and proposes corresponding solutions from different perspectives.

References

[1] Zhou Haoming, Sustainable design ideas and methods based on "full life cycle assessment", *Industrial Engineering Design* **2** (2020), 25-34.
[2] Dong Ziyu, *Research on structural design of original bamboo furniture*, Hebei University of Science and Technology, 2020.
[3] Wei Yang, Wang Zhiyuan, Chen Si, Research progress on reinforcement technology of bamboo flexural members, *Transactions of the Chinese Society of Forestry Engineering* **6** (2021), 9-17.
[4] Wang Yang, Research on the application of green materials in modern woven furniture, *Western Leather* 41(2019) ,2.
[5] Cao Ruirui, Application and innovation of traditional rattan weaving technology in home design, *Tomorrow's Fashion* **6** (2022), 89-92.
[6] Wang Jiaqi, Bai Yumei, Feng Yanli, Design of waste fabric woven furniture under the low-carbon concept, *Screen Printing* **7** (2023), 39-41.
[7] Qin Yuhua, Research on the application of plant patterns in chair-type furniture, *Art Appreciationm* **5** (2020), 218-219.

Design Studies and Intelligence Engineering   873
L.C. Jain et al. (Eds.)
© 2024 The Authors.
This article is published online with Open Access by IOS Press and distributed under the terms
of the Creative Commons Attribution Non-Commercial License 4.0 (CC BY-NC 4.0).
doi:10.3233/FAIA231502

Research on Knowledge Transfer-Oriented Intelligent Assistance Design Communication System for CNC Machine Tools

Xiaoli NIU[a], Honghai LI[a,1], and Xiaobin SHI[a]

[a] *Beijing Information Science & Technology University*

Abstract. In product design, the most critical part is collaboration and communication with different stakeholders with different expertise and knowledge. Sketches and scheme drawings are the medium for design communication and interpretation among different groups of people. However, due to the different knowledge backgrounds of different groups of people, there will be understanding errors and communication barriers in design communication, slowing down the entire design cycle. To improve the efficiency of communication in design projects, this paper proposes a knowledge communication mechanism based on design knowledge research to support professional industrial design processes. Inspired by intelligent technology and generative design, an intelligent assistance design communication system architecture for CNC machine tools is constructed for knowledge transfer. We concept an intelligent design tool from the user's perspective for usability testing. We hope to realize design knowledge transfer and collaboration through the system, assist in completing the appearance design for CNC machine tools, and provide users with a good experience.

Keywords. Knowledge transfer, Design communication, Intelligent assisted design, CNC machine tools, Interactive design

1. Introduction

Design is essentially a process of knowledge flow, integration, competition, and evolution [1], and its core is the acquisition and application of knowledge. In the current mainstream industrial design process of CNC machine tools, the essence of the design process can be understood as the process of knowledge transfer and integration between user knowledge of the 'problem and demand carrier', designer knowledge of the 'industrial design carrier' and engineer knowledge of the 'engineering data carrier'.

The traditional industrial design method of CNC machine tools is generally a project commission system and personalized customization. The demand side expresses its design vision by proposing project requirements to the design side. In the early stage, the design side needs to conduct a lot of design research on the demanding enterprise or communicate with the demanding enterprise to make a preliminary design judgment. However, due to the knowledge and cognitive differences between the demand side and

---

[1] Corresponding Author. Honghai Li, Beijing Information Science & Technology University, China, E-mail: Lihonghai@bistu.edu.cn.

the design side, it is easy to cause cognitive bias and low communication effectiveness between the two sides, which in turn leads to the delay of the design process and the reduction of design efficiency.

Communication is the core of knowledge exchange between stakeholders with different technical and social backgrounds. Zhinan Zhang et al. proposed a method to systematically improve the understanding of the target object, including the composition of the object, the nature of the object, and the tools to support its related communication and promote knowledge communication and collaboration between stakeholders in the product design process by improving communication efficiency [2]. Rajaratnam Dilakshan et al. assessed how AR can be used to overcome design communication issues in the early stages of architectural projects. They believe that AR can be used for architectural design communication, and AR toolkit models can improve users' cognitive ability of knowledge and design experience [3]. Collaboration and communication with stakeholders with different knowledge backgrounds are the most critical aspects of the design phase, and solving design communication problems is the key to improving design efficiency.

Intelligent design, as a design trend driven by artificial intelligence technology, can realize in-depth exploration, analysis, processing, and application of design data and knowledge. An intelligent assistance design communication system will become a guiding role in the process of transferring design knowledge. Therefore, analyzing, acquiring, and expressing knowledge in the process of CNC machine tool industrial design, and constructing a knowledge-assisted design communication system are the hotspots of research and application of intelligent technology in industrial design and concept design.

2. Research status of intelligent-assisted design

Intelligent design refers to the application of modern information technology, using computer simulation of human thinking activities to improve the intelligence level of computers so that computers can more and better undertake various complex tasks in the design process, and become an important auxiliary tool for designers. Fang Liu et al. argue that intelligent design or design intelligence usually refers to the introduction of artificial intelligence methods in design work, to help designers or other creators perform more efficient or more creative work. Through literature review, it is found that the intelligent design system has mainly experienced four stages of development.

2.1. System KBS is based on a knowledge database (expert system)

For example, Jiuxi Li et al. applied artificial intelligence theory and expert system technology to the field of product design, proposed a product design expert system framework structure, and realized the organization of information and materials through intelligent agent technology. According to the shape analysis method, the system realizes auxiliary innovative design [5].

2.2. Scheme creation and screening platform (vision-based)

For example, the AutoDraw sketch drawing platform generates a series of detailed images through sketch drawing.

2.3. Intelligent system that combines the designer's thinking and cognitive processes

For example, Ali AI Graphics, through inputting needs, platform generation and output, adjustment of detailed elements, and selection of design schemes, completes the design process. This process combines AI generation with the designer's thinking process and can improve the quality of design works to a certain extent.

2.4. Intelligent collaborative system for AI, designers, and engineers

For example, JD Linglong, in addition to providing a series of intelligent image generation tools, also provides development frameworks, intelligent code platforms, front-end development workstations, and design collaboration platforms.

In recent years, research on intelligent-assisted design has focused mainly on sketch drawing, visual communication design, interaction and interface design, 3D modeling, and AI art creation design. Through the use of artificial intelligence, the design process can be completed from text to image, from sketch to image, from sketch to 3D model, from 2D design diagram to 3D model diagram, and also layout retrieval and reformatting, trend analysis, and automatic generation of creative text and graphics can be realized. It can be seen that artificial intelligence technology applied in different scenarios can assist in completing users' personalized needs, help users improve the efficiency of information acquisition, and shorten the product design cycle.

3. Knowledge transfer-related research and traditional CNC machine tool industrial design process overview

3.1. Knowledge transfer-related concepts

- Explicit knowledge and tacit knowledge

Based on different acquisition channels, knowledge can be divided into explicit knowledge and implicit knowledge. The design process is mainly composed of implicit knowledge, including intangible skills, judgment, and intuition possessed by human experts, as well as designers' personal insights, inspiration, visual perception, and experience. In CNC machine tool industrial design, background research must first be conducted to understand the product itself and user needs. Then, through their knowledge system, designers use sketch and effect drawings to express design knowledge. The essence of this process is knowledge transformation and externalization. In the industrial 4.0 era, the development of artificial intelligence technology will further promote the explicit transformation and dissemination of knowledge.

- Explicit knowledge and tacit knowledge

Knowledge transfer is an activity between knowledge subjects with knowledge differences, first proposed by Titus in 1977, focusing on the economic development phenomenon brought about by knowledge production based on technology transfer [6]. Knowledge transfer is a deterministic knowledge activity that is evident in its clear goals, determined knowledge senders, receivers, and intermediaries, and mostly carried out in controlled environments and processes [7]. Some scholars summarize it as five factors, including source, information, channel, receiver, and context [8]. Traditional knowledge transfer models focus on the process of knowledge transfer, with classic models such as

Gilbert and Cordey-Hayes' five-stage model of knowledge acquisition, communication, application, acceptance, and assimilation [9].

- Knowledge visualization

In 2004, Martin J. Eppler and Remo A. Burkhard first proposed the concept of knowledge visualization, considering it as an application of knowledge representation used to improve knowledge creation and transfer between two or more people [10]. Knowledge visualization is a graphical method that can be used to build and convey complex insights, emphasizing how to promote the transmission of knowledge between people and teams.

In product design, sketches, and model effect drawings are mediums for different people to exchange and explain designs, but due to differences in knowledge backgrounds among different groups, there may be understanding errors and communication barriers in design exchanges. Effective knowledge transfer and knowledge visualization models can promote the process of integrating different knowledge and solve problems related to communication barriers in design exchanges.

3.2. Traditional CNC machine tool industrial design process overview

The traditional industrial design process is based on the design process evolved from IDEO Company in the United States and Olivetti Company in Italy [11]. It mainly includes four parts: exploration stage, development stage, iteration stage, and implementation stage.

In the exploration stage, designers collect essential information to support their design concept from a large number of information systems. For CNC machine tool industrial design, the exploration stage mainly includes background research (market, competitors, society) and user analysis (user needs, user roles), and extracts and screens the results, analyzes and converts the needs.

The development stage is the core stage of industrial design. Based on the concept formed in the first stage, develop design ideas and conduct preliminary design. In the early stage, collect design inspiration, and stimulate creative thinking through brainstorming; the design process is to express design ideas through design thinking and methods, including sketches, model diagrams, effect diagrams, scene diagrams, and necessary descriptive text.

The iteration stage mainly includes design evaluation, design decisions, and iteration optimization. Based on the preliminary design solution, select the optimal solution, improve the design solution based on user and expert opinions, and finally output the complete design product. Generally speaking, the development stage and iteration stage are carried out simultaneously, and the design process requires repeated review and optimization.

The implementation stage involves putting the design results into production, which requires the first three stages to focus on maximizing user satisfaction.

From these four stages, the traditional CNC machine tool industrial design process has several special problems: including a long product update cycle, more design solutions constrained by technology, and customization of processing methods. This determines CNC machine tool design needs more communication with engineers.

4. Knowledge system in intelligent assistance design communication

4.1. Knowledge classification in industrial design of CNC machine tools

According to the design role, the knowledge system in CNC machine tool industrial design includes designer knowledge, engineer knowledge, and user knowledge. Based on the acquisition path, the knowledge system can be classified into explicit knowledge and implicit knowledge. Based on the characteristics of CNC machine tool industrial design and combining the knowledge classification method based on roles and acquisition path, the knowledge system in CNC machine tool industrial design is further divided into usage knowledge and experiential knowledge.

- Usage knowledge

Usage knowledge refers to knowledge that is explicitly expressed and can be used directly. It includes design object knowledge and user knowledge. The design object knowledge for the CNC machine tool is the design language in exterior design, mainly including structural layout style, morphological characteristics, presentation details, overall color, material texture, processing technology, etc. The user here refers to the operators who directly use the machine tool and the workers. User knowledge includes aesthetic elements, operation methods, human-machine engineering, and other contents of CNC machine tools.

- Experiential knowledge

Experience knowledge refers to the knowledge that designers and engineers accumulate over a long period in their work, which cannot be clearly expressed. It includes problem-solving strategies, skills, and aesthetic potential of CNC machine tool designers and engineers. Problem-solving strategies and skills experience can reflect the logical thinking process of solutions, and aesthetic potential can infer mainstream solutions. Experience knowledge can be transferred and converted into useful knowledge through a conversion mechanism.

4.2. Knowledge communication mechanism

Based on the research method of structured expression of knowledge in engineering design communication [2], combined with the five factors of knowledge transfer mentioned earlier, the communication mechanism in CNC machine tool industrial design is divided into the following five parts.

- Communication node

Stakeholders in design communication, including the source and receiver. Here, it refers to designers, users, and engineers, among which users also include novice designers.

- Communication object

The information processed in the communication process, which here refers to design knowledge. To solve the communication barriers in the design process, different knowledge integration methods must be realized through different knowledge transfer ways, with a focus on expressing design knowledge in different ways.

- Communication channel

Composed of asynchronous and synchronous communication methods that connect the source and receiver, which can promote design communication. Based on the assistant system, knowledge transfer among different communication nodes in the CNC machine tool industrial design process is realized through artificial intelligence methods.

- Communication mode

The knowledge expression methods of different communication nodes. The communication modes of different nodes are as follows: designers-sketches and design diagrams; engineers-data and structure; users-emotional descriptions and scenarios.

- Communication context

Use contextualization. In the design communication process, product design thinking must be carried out in a system of people, objects, and environment throughout the product lifecycle.

As shown in Figure 1, design communication involves knowledge transfer. During the design communication process, the assistant system based on artificial intelligence technology encodes the design knowledge of different groups, and decodes and outputs it through the system. Knowledge transfer of CNC machine tool design knowledge is carried out based on the visualization of CNC machine tool design knowledge. The source of knowledge transfers design knowledge to the receiver in a visualized way and stores it in the knowledge base.

Figure 1. Knowledge communication mechanism in intelligent assisted design for CNC machine tools.

5. Construction of intelligent assisted design communication system for CNC machine tools

5.1. System architecture

Based on the research on CNC machine tool industrial design knowledge and the proposed knowledge communication mechanism, in combination with the five-stage model of knowledge transfer, a knowledge transfer-oriented intelligent assisted design system architecture is proposed, as shown in Figure 2. Group knowledge communication, knowledge application, and knowledge acceptance together, because in the intelligent assistant system, these three stages are performed at the application layer, while knowledge acquisition and knowledge assimilation are both based on the knowledge base in the data layer.

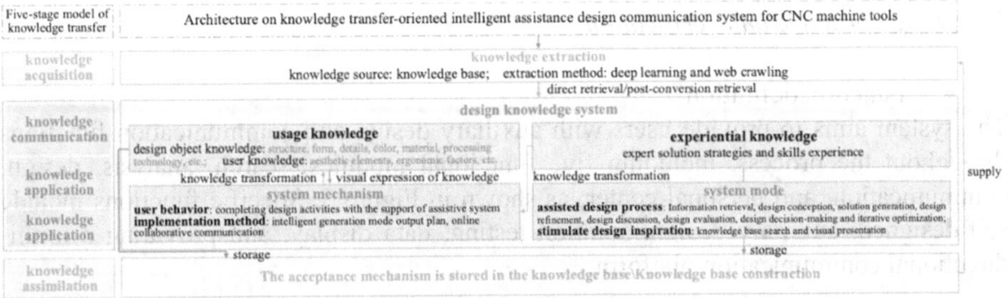

Figure 2. System architecture.

- Knowledge extraction and knowledge base construction

Knowledge extraction uses methods such as machine learning and natural language processing to extract specific information from different data, which is the foundation of building a knowledge base [12]. The CNC machine tool knowledge base can provide designers with design information to choose from and help make design decisions. The methods of knowledge extraction and knowledge base construction can refer to the research of scholars in the field, and in the system construction, the interfaces based on existing technologies are accessed.

- Research on design knowledge system

This section mainly focuses on the research of the knowledge system in intelligent assisted design for CNC machine tools. The core of the research on the design knowledge system revolves around knowledge communication and the communication mechanism. The use of knowledge in the system can be directly expressed through knowledge visualization and is divided into functional modules in the system design. Experience knowledge in the system can be transformed and materialized into usable knowledge through knowledge conversion. After acquiring, communicating, applying, and accepting design knowledge, it is stored and expanded in the knowledge base to provide for the next knowledge retrieval.

- System position

The positioning of the system operation end includes the system mechanism and system mode. The system mechanism refers to the implementation method of user behavior and the operation end, where user behavior refers to user design communication and completion of design activities supported by the system. The corresponding implementation method is to automatically generate a large number of design schemes through intelligent technology and provide a large number of design cases to assist in online collaborative communication. The system mode is the main function of the system, which is to assist designers in their industrial design activities and solve design communication problems. The system provides both assistance in the design process and a mechanism to stimulate design inspiration. The assistance process includes users' input design requirements and conducting information retrieval in the application layer, using the design modules for creative ideas and intelligent generation of design schemes, and using the communication module to conduct design evaluation and optimize the design scheme through iterative design.

5.2. Design practice and verification

- Function definition

The system aims to provide users with auxiliary design and communication functions throughout the process, including five functional modules: search, analysis, design, communication, and personal center, as shown in Figure 3. Specific functions include self-designed, auxiliary design, solution testing, data display, and providing a multi-directional communication platform.

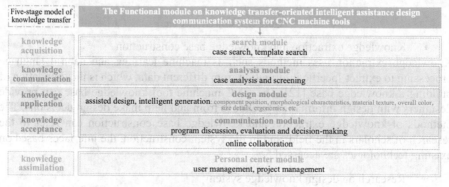

Figure 3. Function modules.

- Scheme design

The interface prototype is the external manifestation form of functional and interaction architecture. By drawing the interface prototype, abstract functional requirements can be visualized [13]. Prototype design unfolds from functional interaction flow and visual design, as shown in Figure 4. The interface prototype can be used for preliminary interaction operations. Through usability evaluation of the prototype, user satisfaction and opinions on the interface prototype can be obtained, and the prototype solution can be iteratively optimized based on the feedback results.

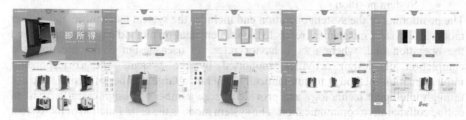

Figure 4. Prototype solution.

- Design practice verification

Carry out usability testing on the preliminary prototype solution, including eye-tracking experiment and 5-level Likert scale scoring. Quantitative analysis of the user's operation effectiveness and operation efficiency can be conducted using eye-tracking experiment, and qualitative analysis of user satisfaction can be conducted using the 5-level Likert scale. The two can be combined to comprehensively evaluate the usability of the system's interactive interface and functions. Content is shown in Table 1. After completing the eye-tracking test, the user is scored from 1 to 5 points from the three dimensions of usability, effect of the generated scheme, and degree of design knowledge transfer.

Table 1. Test contents

Test task	Test type	Test question
1. Find the design entrance on the homepage and enter. 2. Browse the design interface and select the content of the machine tool design module in sequence.	Usability	Q1: This system is simple and easy to use. Q2: The content displayed by the system is clear. Q3: The interface of the system makes me feel comfortable.
3. Generate a scheme and select one for optimization. 4. Browse the design optimization interface, adjust the details of the scheme, and exit.	Effect of the generated scheme	Q4: The system can quickly output schemes. Q5: Using the system can shorten the design cycle. Q6: Quick generation can save discussion time.
5. Enter the user management interface and browse, enter the file exchange details, and browse.	Degree of design knowledge transfer	Q7: Online collaboration can reduce communication problems. Q8: Using this system can obtain knowledge of machine design. Q9: The system can improve the reuse rate of design knowledge.

A total of 10 effective experimental data were collected. As shown in Table 2, according to the track map obtained by the eye-tracking experiment, the visual search trajectory meets expectations, no important information is missing, and the acquisition rate is relatively high. Through the heat map, it is found that the heat map distribution is concentrated, and the color contrast is obvious, with many focus points on graphic information. Among them, the layout of collaborator information in interface six interferes with the identification of main content and needs to be optimized later. The eye movement tracks and focus areas of most pages are on the main information, the function buttons and interface information are unambiguous, and the interface usability is good.

Table 2. Eye-tracking heat map and track map (partial)

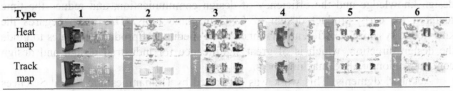

Type	1	2	3	4	5	6
Heat map						
Track map						

The Cronbach's alpha reliability coefficient value of the scale is 0.838, which is relatively high. Further analysis of the scale data found that the coefficient of variation of the questions is less than 0.15, and there are no abnormal values in the test data. The results can be directly described and analyzed by averaging the results. The specific results are shown in Table 3. From the data in the table, it can be seen that the mean of the questions is all above 4 points, and the average values of the three content dimensions are 4.367, 4.267, and 4.300, which are all in the high score range. This indicates that the descriptive statements in the scale are all positive, which means that the usability and use effect of the intelligent assistance design communication system interface and function for knowledge transfer are ideal. The system can be further optimized and iterated based on this scheme.

Table 3. Data analysis of test results

Dimension	Question number	Average value	Standard deviation	Average value of dimension
Usability	Q1	4.3	0.483	
	Q2	4.3	0.483	4.367
	Q3	4.5	0.527	
Effect of the generated scheme	Q4	4.3	0.483	
	Q5	4.4	0.516	4.267
	Q6	4.1	0.568	
Degree of design knowledge transfer	Q7	4.1	0.568	
	Q8	4.4	0.516	4.300
	Q9	4.4	0.516	

6. Conclusion

This article explores the knowledge communication mechanism among designers, engineers, and users in the industrial design process of CNC machine tools from the perspective of design knowledge and knowledge transfer and proposes an intelligent assisted design communication system architecture oriented to knowledge transfer based on the design knowledge transfer process. An intelligent assistance design communication system that helps different stakeholders with different knowledge backgrounds to efficiently acquire, reuse, and transform design knowledge is constructed. The system aims to intelligently generate CNC machine tool product design schemes and provide many design cases to assist online collaborative communication. Through preliminary user testing, it can be known that the system can improve the reuse rate of design knowledge and the efficiency of design communication, and reduce the time required for early product design of CNC machine tools. This paper regards the knowledge systems of different personnel as the medium of product attributes to guide the design direction, which is of great significance for industrial design and design communication of CNC machine tools.

Acknowledgments. This work was supported by Humanities and Social Sciences Foundation of Ministry of Education of the people's Republic of China ("A Study of Practice-Based Design Research Models from a Knowledge Production Perspective", Grant Number: 18YJC760039).

References

[1] Xie Youbai. Design Science. Journal of Shanghai Jiaotong University, 2019, 53(07): 873-80.
[2] Zhang, Z., Liu, J., Evans, R.D., et al. A Design Communication Framework Based on Structured Knowledge Representation. IEEE Transactions on Engineering Management, 2021, 68(6): 1650-62.
[3] Rajarnam D, Weerasinghe D M L P, Abeynayake M, et al. Potential use of Augmented Reality in pre-contract design communication in construction projects. Intelligent Buildings International, 2021, 14(6): 661-78.
[4] LIU Fang, WANG Zun-fu, LIANG Xiao-ting. Review on Cultural Big Data and Intelligent Design Platform. Packaging Engineering, 2021, 42(14): 1-8+39.
[5] Li Jiuxi, Wang Chunshan, Zhao Shupeng, et al. Research of expert system for product design. Packaging Engineering, 2005, (06): 176-8.
[6] Teece D J. Technology transfer by multinational firms: The resource cost of transferring technological know-how. The economic journal, 1977, 87(346): 242-61.
[7] Liu Changle, Ren Xu, Hao Shengyue. Survey of knowledge transfer research in project environment. Research on Library Science, 2015, (14): 19-25.

[8] Szulanski G. The process of knowledge transfer: A diachronic analysis of stickiness. Organizational behavior and human decision processes, 2000, 82(1): 9-27.

[9] Gilbert M, Cordey-Hayes M. Understanding the process of knowledge transfer to achieve successful technological innovation. Technovation, 1996, 16(6): 301-12.

[10] Eppler, M J, Burkhard R A. Knowledge visualization: towards a new discipline and its fields of application. Università della Svizzera italiana, 2004.

[11] Chen Huabo, Zhang Haimin. Research on innovation process of industrial design guided by TRIZ theory. Journal of Jilin Provincial Institute of Education, 2020, 36(03): 116-9.

[12] Wang Liping, Zhang Chao, Cai Enlei. Knowledge extraction and knowledge base construction method from industrial software packages. Journal of Tsinghua University (Science and Technology), 2022, 62(05): 978-86.

[13] Chen Hao. Web Design of Human Factors & Interaction Experience Studio. Hunan University, 2015.

Design Studies and Intelligence Engineering
L.C. Jain et al. (Eds.)
© 2024 The Authors.
This article is published online with Open Access by IOS Press and distributed under the terms
of the Creative Commons Attribution Non-Commercial License 4.0 (CC BY-NC 4.0).
doi:10.3233/FAIA231503

Laser-Induced Colourization on Metal Surface for Product Design

Fangyuan JI [1], Jiandan ZENG, Zhigang TANG, and Xibin WANG
College of FineArt, Zhaoqing university

Abstract. Colour generation by laser-induced colourization has several advantages compared to dye technology, such as higher resolution, minimal pixel areal and fastness colours. However, current colourization methods need to be pre-designed and the mechanism of laser-induced colourization are still need understanding. Here we investigate the effects of laser parameters on metal surface colourization. Different processing parameters induced transient local heat generation on metal surface that leads to different heat accumulation and oxide compound, which caused different interference with white light and then generating different colour appearance. The colour transition process also obeys the paint theory. This work provides a better way for product designer, engineer and surface researchers.

Keywords. Laser-induced colourization, nanosecond laser pulse, repeated frequency, product design.

1. Introduction

Laser has been widely used in drilling, ablation, and surface treatment. Laser-driven excitation of surface colourization on metal product design opens a new toolbox to product design. However, the interaction of laser-materials is the essential nature in all every application on metal material. As a bright technology for surface treatment, laser-induced colourization contributed a higher resolution with fastness colours on metal surface. A remarkable property for laser-induced colourization is plasmons that leads to exhibit scattering properties and producing colours by exploiting plasmonic effects on surface. Another feature for laser-induced colourization is that the thermal effect produced by nanosecond laser generated a large of metallic oxide on metal surface, which interference with the white light source and then presented a different colour. Therefore, this technology can be used in any metal colouring or any other applications where paint or pigments are not allowed.

Owing to the requirement on ablation characteristics and cold processing, the ultra-short laser have been used for materials colourization. From nanosecond pulse to femtosecond pulse, researchers still working on this topic. Jean-Michel Guay et. al investigated the colourization process on silver coins weighing up to 5kg, they find that the colours are related to parameter and accumulated fluence [1]. Xiaolong Zhu et al studied a printing method on nanoimprinted plasmonic meta surfaces, they find that the pulse energy density and surface morphologies can generates different colour appearances [2]. Fan at al investigated the picosecond laser on copper colourization, they find that lower scanning speed causes a denser distribution of nanoparticles with a nearly constant mean radius, where each colour can be generated by a set of parameters [3,4]. Wu

---

[1] Corresponding Author.

et al studied the influence of picosecond laser such as scanning gap, scanning speed and pulse energy on colouring effects [5]. However, the picosecond laser [6,7] raised a high cost for customer, it is of great meaning to investigate the application of nano laser on metal colourization [8,9]. The biggest challenge for nanosecond laser is that the large clusters and chunks produced by nano pulse processing [10-12], which means the application of laser-induced colourization with nanosecond laser is still need exploration. Here, we investigate the effects of parameters on colours generation, and analyze the mechanism of laser colourization on metal surface. Finally, we designed a gradient picture on metal surface with a set of parameters, which means that the application of nanosecond laser on colourization is capable for product design.

2. Experimental setup

As presented in Figure 1, the experimental system consists of a laser, fiber, scanning system and focus lens. Nanosecond laser pulse generated by the laser machine, and the two of scanning galvanometers are controlled by an industrial computer where can read the scanning path or text. A stainless steel was fastened on the focal position of laser beam that is for the colourization experiments.

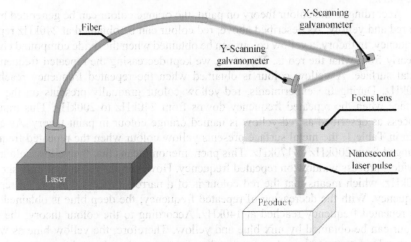

Figure 1. Experimental system for laser-induced colourization on metal surface.

$$E = f_{repeated\,frequency} \times P_{power} \times W_{pulse\,width} \quad (Eq.\ 1)$$

In order to investigate the effects of repeated frequency of nanosecond pulse on colourization, we firstly kept the pulse width, laser power, focal position, scanning gap and speed as 8ns, 40W, 0mm, 0.001mm, 1000mm/respectively. The repeated frequency was set from 350kHz to 140kHz with a10kHz step. The different repeated frequency generates the changing of laser energy, this can be described in Eq.1 which $f_{repeated\,frequency}$ is the repeated frequency of pulse laser, E is the input energy of laser beam, P_{power} is the power of laser beam, $W_{pulse\,width}$ is the pulse width of each nanosecond pulse.

A microscope was used to capture the colours on metal surface.

3. Analysis and discussion

As described in section 2, the effects of repeated frequency on colour firstly studied for a better understanding on laser-induced colourization. The experimental results are presented in Table 1.

As shown in Table 1, 350kHz repeated frequency generated a blue on metal surface. With the decrease of repeated frequency, the colour trends to change from blue to purple colour. When the repeated frequency downs to 310kHz, the colour presents a purple on the metal surface. This phenomenon can be explained by the fact that the change of repeated frequency decreased the laser energy on metal surface, which means that the heat accumulation has been changed and caused a variation on the degree of oxidation. Finally, the presented colour been changed into a purple. According to the colour theory on paint, the purple can be generated by mix the blue and red. This also can be certified by the next experiments. As the continuous decreasing on repeated frequency, a purple-red colour starts to shown on the metal surface when the repeated frequency reach at 270kHz. This phenomenon can be explained by the fact that the interference characteristics of oxide compound is changed due to the variation on heat accumulation. With the decrease of repeated frequency, the colour trends to become red on the metal surface. The colour is completely changed into red when the repeated frequency reached at 240kHz.

According to the colour theory on paint, the orange colour can be generated by mix the red and yellow. As described above, red colour can be obtained at 240kHz repeated frequency. In theory, a yellow colour can be obtained when the oxide compound changes linearly from what the red is. Therefore, we kept decreasing the repeated frequency on metal surface. A yellow colour is obtained when the repeated frequency reached at 200kHz. During the experiments, red-yellow colour gradually presents on the metal surface when the repeated frequency downs from 240kHz to 200kHz. This transition process as described as red-yellow is named orange colour in paint theory. As can be seen in Table 1, the metal surface presents yellow colour when the repeated frequency changed from 200kHz to 170kHz. This phenomenon means that the yellow colour have a widest process window on repeated frequency. However, the red colour only shown at 240kHz, which means that the red colour is of a narrow process window on repeated frequency. With the decreasing of repeated frequency, the deep blue is obtained when the repeated frequency reached at 140kHz. According to the colour theory, the green colour can be obtained by mix blue and yellow. Therefore, the yellow-blue as well as green colour starts to present on the metal surface when the repeated frequency changed from 160kHz to 150kHz.

The oxide compound can be influenced by the heat accumulation on the metal surface, and the repeated frequency defines the heat accumulation when keep the heat dissipation condition as constant during the experiments. As discussed above, different colours can be obtained by changing the repeated frequency of nanosecond laser. Furthermore, the colour transition process of laser-induced colourization obeys the colour theory in paint when changing the repeated frequency for generating different colours.

Table 1. Different repeated frequency of nanosecond laser corresponding to different colours

Repeated frequency/kHz	Colour picture	Colour description
C350		Blue
340		Blue
330		Blue
320		Blue
310		Blue-Purple
300		Purple
290		Purple
280		Purple
270		Purple-Red
260		Purple-Red
250		Purple-Red
240		Red
230		Red-Yellow/Orange
220		Red-Yellow/Orange
210		Red-Yellow/Orange
200		Yellow
190		Yellow
180		Yellow
170		Yellow-Blue
160		Yellow-Blue

150   Yellow-Blue/Green

                                                       Deep-blue
140

Besides the repeated frequency, there are still have many parameters on colourization during the laser-metal interaction. As is presented in Figure 2, non-fading colours can be obtained by adjusting processing parameters. Cyan is generated as described in Figure 2(a) by increasing the laser power to 45W from blue colour mentioned above. For obtaining a high-resolution colour, a golden colour can be generated in Figure 2(b) by decreasing the repeated frequency to 175kHz from yellow colour mentioned above. A green colour is obtained by increasing the input energy of laser pulse as shown in Figure 2(c). Blue colour still be obtained in Figure 2(e) when decreasing the power to 30W while a 40W generated the same colour. This phenomenon means that the repeated frequency is the key factor to generate blue colour. A brown colour can be generated by downing the input energy of laser pulse as shown in Figure 2(d). A purple can also be obtained by increasing the repeated frequency to 600kHz as shown in Figure 2(h), and the same colour is generated when the repeated frequency down to 140kHz. This is because that the input energy is decreased when the repeated frequency change to extremely high or low.

As is shown in Figure 3, an example of gradient design on product surface which means that the design method with nanosecond laser can be used to generate different colours with a set of parameters, and the scanning galvanometer can draw different patterns that controlled by industrial computer. Firstly, the relationship between colour and processing parameters should be obtained by a lot of experiments, and then the different colour area should be set on different layer with different processing parameters. Finally, we can get a product with different colour on metal surface.

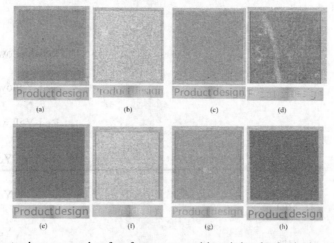

Figure 2. Different colours on metal surface from nanosecond laser-induced colourization. a) Cyan with 1000mm/s, 8ns pulse width, 350kHz frequency and 45W power; b)Yellow with 1000mm/s, 8ns pulse width, 175kHz frequency and 40W Power; c) Green with 800mm/s, 8ns pulse width, 300kHz frequency and 50W power; d) Brown with 0.003mm scanning gap, 1000mm/s, 8ns pulse width, 145kHz frequency and 50W power; e) Blue with 900mm/s, 8ns pulse width, 300kHz frequency and 30W power; f) Golden with 1000mm/s, 8ns pulse width, 200kHz frequency and 45W power; g) Pink with 1000mm/s, 8ns pulse width, 240kHz frequency and 40W power; h)Purple with 1000mm/s, 4ns pulse width, 600kHz frequency and 40W power;

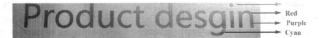

Figure 3. Example of gradient design with laser-induced colourization

4. Conclusions

This work studied the effects of processing parameters on colour generation during laser-induced colourization on stainless-steel product surface. Firstly, different colours is generated by setting different repeated frequency of processing pulse. This phenomenon can be explained by the fact that the different repeated frequency caused the difference on heat accumulation, which resulting the different interference between surface oxide compound and white light and then presents a different colour. Furthermore, the colour transition obeys the paint theory, which means that researchers and engineer can obtain an ideal colour by high-precision adjusting parameter when they know the base colour from paint theory. This work presents a convenient way to fast obtain a non-fading design on product, and this technology can be used in engineering as well as scientific research.

References

[1] Jean-Michel Guay, Antonino Cala Lesina, Guillaume Cote, Martin Charron, Daniel Poitras, Lora Ramunno, Pierre Berini, Arnaud Weck. Laser-induced plasmonic colours on metals, Nature communications 8(2017),16095

[2] Xiaolong Zhu, Mehdi Keshavarz Hedayati, Soren Raza, Uriel Levy, N. Asger Mortensen, Anders Kristensen, Digital resonant laser printing: Bridging nanophotonic science and consumer products, Nano Today,19(2018),7-10.

[3] Peixun Fan, Minlin Zhong, Lin Li, Patrick Schmitz, Cheng Lin, Jiangyou Long, Hongjun Zhang. Angle-independent colorization of copper surfaces by simultaneous generation of picosecond-laser-induced nanostructures and redeposited nanoparticles, Journal of Applied Physics 115(2014),1-7.

[4] Peixun Fan, Minlin Zhong, Lin Li, Patrick Schmitz, Cheng Lin, Jiangyou Long, Hongjun Zhang, Sequential colour change on copper surfaces via micro/nano structure modification induced by a picosecond laser, Journal of Applied Physics 114(2013), 1-5.

[5] Wu Yonghua, Yang Baoping, Kang Xianmin, Effects of processing parameters of ultra-fast laser on surface coloring of stainless steel, Chinese Journal of Lasers 44(2013),0302005.

[6] Li Yangbo, Bai Feng, Fan Wenzhong, Zhao Quanzhong, Color difference analysis of femtosecond laser colorized metals, Acta Optica Sinica, 36(2016), 0714003.

[7] Wang Haozhu, Yang Fenghe, Yang Fan, Nie Meitong, Yang Jianjun, Investigation of femtosecond-laser induced periodic surface structure on molybdenum, Chinese Journal of Lasers, 42(2015),0103001.

[8] Liu Zhongmin, Zhang Qingmao, Guo Liang, Lv qitao, Yang Kun, Influence of laser process parameters on color obtained by Marking, Chinese Journal of Lasers 41(2014),0403011.

[9] Wang Hanzhang, Yin Yanrui, Dou Zhiqiang, Tian Kang, Lu Jingqi, Laser coloring of stainless steel, Laser and Optoelectronics Progress,60(2023),0916001.

[10] M S Tillack, D W Blair, S S Harilal, The effect of ionization on cluster formation in laser ablation plumes, Nanotechnology, 15(2004),390-403.

[11] P Balling, J Schou, Femtosecond-laser ablation dynamics of dielectrics: basics and applications for thin films. Reports on Progress in Physics, 76(2013), 036502.

[12] Chantal Boulmer-Leborgne, Ratiba Benzerga, Jacques Perriere, Nanoparticle formation by femtosecond laser ablation, Laser-surface interaction for new materials production, Springer,2009.

Design Studies and Intelligence Engineering
L.C. Jain et al. (Eds.)
© *2024 The Authors.*
This article is published online with Open Access by IOS Press and distributed under the terms
of the Creative Commons Attribution Non-Commercial License 4.0 (CC BY-NC 4.0).
doi:10.3233/FAIA231504

Application of Biofeedback Technology in Human-Computer Interaction in Video Games

Shenglin XU[a], Zekun QIN[a] and Xin LYU[a1]

[a] *the School of Animation and Digital Arts, Communication University of China*

Abstract. From the birth of video games until today, players have interacted with video games via controllers. However, with the maturation of biofeedback technology, players can now obtain brand-new interactive gaming experiences. The commands input to the game are no longer merely from the buttons on the game controller. Biofeedback technology uses sensors to read the physiological signals of the game player, enabling the game to directly perceive the player's physiological state through data such as heart rate, eye movement, and facial emotions when they are playing the game and match the next step in the game progress. Compared to traditional games, video games based on biofeedback technology provide specific, real-time feedback to individual players, creating an immersive gaming experience through embodied interactions, guiding game designers better. When artificial intelligence technology combines with biofeedback technology, AI will learn and analyze a large amount of user physiological data collected by biofeedback technology, making the interaction between the game and the players more intelligent and personalized.

Keywords. Biofeedback technology, human-computer interaction, video games, artificial intelligence

1. Introduction

Since the birth of video games, players have mainly interacted with video games through input devices such as game controllers, mice, keyboards, etc. Although there were more updated and complex controllers like steering wheels and joysticks before long, the essence of the human-computer interaction in video games was players actively inputting commands into the video games, while games were hardly output based on the physiology of the player's actual gaming state.

Biofeedback technology has been applied to video games with the development of biological sensors. The game begins to capture the player's physiological reactions, such as heart rate and eye movement via sensors in real-time. The game system determines the player's physiological state based on the signal data and adjusts the game content. Biofeedback games focus more on the real-time input from the player and create a more dynamic gaming experience. It adds new interactivity and immersion, making games more attractive than in the past. It gives games a deeper ability to understand and adapt to players' needs, providing players with a different experience compared with traditional

---

[1] Corresponding Author, the School of Animation and Digital Arts, Communication University of China, Beijing, China; E-mail: lvxincuc@163.com

games. Biofeedback technology changed how video games interact with players, enhanced the player experience, and transformed video games tremendously.

Specifically, biofeedback technology makes role-playing games or strategy games more immersive by changing the plot or difficulty of the game. Applying biofeedback in health games helps players understand and manage their physiological states, such as stress management and relaxation training. It makes biofeedback an effective health intervention and opens the door to a broader range of physical and mental health solutions.

2. The Principle of Biofeedback Technology and Applied to Video Games

2.1. The Principle of Biofeedback Technology

Biofeedback technology is a technology that measures, records and feeds back various physiological data to the user's body. The biocybernetic loop formed by the user and the sensor is an essential component of the biofeedback system [2][3], in which the user's physiological signals are acquired through the sensor, and then the results are fed back to the user after processing [4][5]. Specifically, biofeedback technology involves various biofeedback methods that can monitor the user's responses and transmit the data to the software system through wireless transmission. Afterward, the software processes these data, determining the user's real-time status.

2.2. Biofeedback Technology Applied to Video Games

In recent years, more affordable and reliable sensor technology and more open gaming platforms have promoted the development of biofeedback technology [2]. Navarro et al. [2] believe that biofeedback technology applied to games can be classified according to two major criteria: *a. the player's physiological control* and *b. the type of physiological data captured.*

For *a. the player's physiological control*, Kuikkaniemi et al. [6] studied first-person shooter (FPS) games applying biofeedback technology, in which biofeedback modulated game mechanics related to the player's character. They classified the game into explicit and implicit biofeedback according to whether the player is aware of the biofeedback technology when playing the game and pointed out that the player prefers explicit biofeedback. Nacke et al. [7] categorized the game into direct physiological control (physiological signals can be controlled by the player at will) and indirect physiological control (physiological signals cannot be controlled by the player and change in response to other physiological activities) according to the player's control of the game through changing the physiological signals. They found that the player preferred direct physiological control and suggested that "direct physiological sensors should be mapped intuitively to reflect an action in the virtual world" and "indirect physiological input is best used as a dramatic device in games to influence features altering the game world" [7].

As for *b. the type of physiological data*, the biofeedback technology applied in video games involves methods such as electroencephalogram (EEG), electrocardiogram (ECG), eye-tracking (ET), electrodermal activity (EDA), and electromyogram (EMG). Navarro et al. [2] retrieved 437 publications that applied biofeedback technology in video games and selected 45 papers that covered six different biofeedback methods. They analyzed the specific interactive technologies corresponding to each biofeedback method, as shown in the table below.

Eye tracking manufacturer Tobii is co-developing the brain-computer interface platform Galea with the game company Valve and the brain-computer interface team OpenBCI [10]. A series of biofeedback technologies are being used in Galea, such as eye-tracking, EEG, EMG, EDA, EOG, etc., in order to determine the user's data from the body in real time and feeding it back to the platform [11]. In the foreseeable future, biofeedback technology will be more widely used in games.

Table 1. Biofeedback Methods and Interaction Techniques, collated from Navarro et al. [2]

EEG	ECG	ET	EDA	EMG	Multi-Modal
Mental commands	Dynamic heart-rate adaptation	Pointing Selecting	Arosual response	Gestures grammar	Mechanic enhancement
Mental state adaptation	Breathing manipulation	Smooth pursuits Gaze awareness		Direct movement mapping	Affective adaptation
		Aligning		Expression recognition	Physiological control

3. The impact of biofeedback technology on human-computer interaction in video games

3.1. Game Content: Immediate and Specific Feedback to Individual Players

Biofeedback technology lets the game capture the player's playing state in real-time and carry out different game progresses accordingly.

The content of games without biofeedback comes from the game designer's analysis of different potential players' preferences, predicting their behavioral decisions while playing the game, and evaluating their game-playing abilities. The state of individual players cannot get specific and timely feedback on the game content during the game. In contrast, biofeedback technology can observe the player's physiological state, read the physiological data, and take them into the game as input signals. The game progress changes at the game content level according to the physiological state of the player's play. Biofeedback games respond to the user's biofeedback and make changes in real-time [1], meaning that the player's physiological state becomes part of the game.

For example, the game may affect the attributes and skills of the game character based on the player's physiological state. The character's strength and speed may increase when the player's heart rate increases and blood pressure rises. The game can also develop the plot according to the player's physiological data. A more joyful and uplifting plot could be presented when the user feels happy or excited during the game. The game content can adjust difficulty by monitoring the player's physiological signals. When the player is highly stressed or relaxed, the game could automatically adjust the difficulty, making the content more adaptable. Overall, biofeedback games offer more ways for players to participate in game content than traditional games.

3.2. Game players: Embodied Interaction and Immersive Experience

Biofeedback technology allows players to interact with the game personally and obtain an immersive gaming experience. It has a positive impact on improving players' physical and mental health.

First is the aspect of game interaction. Although interacting with games through buttons on the controllers has matured after years of development meanwhile players are accustomed to such operations, this kind of human-computer interaction brings players a low sense of embodiment. The concept of "embodiment" comes from the theory of "embodied cognition", which means that our knowledge and understanding are based on our physical experience and are closely related to our body and body movements. The interaction of games applied in biofeedback technology is a kind of embodied interaction. It closely links the player's operation of the game with the player's body movements, expressions, emotions and other factors affected by the game, and increases the game experience and immersion by making full use of the player's physical experience.

Second is the aspect of game experience. Biofeedback technology inputs the player's emotions, heart rate, and other physiological states caused by game content into the game. The game uses the player's real-time status to change the game's progress and results. this means the game feedback obtained is based on the player's actual physiological and psychological conditions. The game whose change in progress comes from the player's own gameplay, its experience is bound to be more immersive.

One of the applications of biofeedback technology's embodied interaction that brings an immersive gaming experience is to help players with physical exercise and health management. For example, some games aim to train meditation or manage emotions, helping players understand and manage their own physiological state. Players use biofeedback technology to read and control their own breathing and heartbeat to relax, lower their heart rate, or improve their concentration while playing games. Another easily overlooked point is that it was difficult for players to pay attention to the real-time condition of their bodies when playing games in the past. Games using biofeedback technology can monitor the player's heart rate, blood pressure, and other data in real-time, reminding the player to make timely adjustments if abnormalities are found. It is not difficult to see that biofeedback technology applied to games has the potential to become an effective health intervention.

3.3. Game Designers: More Data Sources and New Tools for Game Design

Using biofeedback technology as a form of human-computer interaction in games provides designers with more user data for player analysis and new tools for game design.

For traditional games, game designers mostly use subjective self-reports to obtain player feedback during game development. After being put into the market, game designers adjust the game based on the player's performance and community comments. Designers cannot obtain objective, real-time player experience data and behavioral responses. Biofeedback technology adds a new dimension to player data collection. Designers can now obtain players' physiological data, such as heart rate, eye movements, etc., which directly reflect the players' physical and mental reactions, providing designers with a reliable data source for better user experience research and game design. For example, by collecting the player's heartbeat data through a heart rate sensor, developers can understand when the player is nervous, excited, or scared and the specific degree of these feelings. In Nacke's view [8], evaluating players' emotions plays an essential role in game user research. McStay [1] believes that the availability of biofeedback technology can help developers understand which parts of the game are boring or exciting. Undoubtedly, biofeedback technology will guide designers in further iterations of games.

Biofeedback technology has become a "new tool" for game designers to create more possibilities for game design and is used to design novel game mechanisms and experiences [9]. Game designers can create more diverse gameplay and plots for games by integrating biofeedback from players. Players' control of the body's physiological state has become a gameplay method. Influencing the direction of the game through the player's own eyes, expressions, and heartbeat is something that game designers could not imagine or achieve before biofeedback technology.

4. Case Study

4.1. Background

In order to examine the interaction of biofeedback technology applied in gameplay impacts the game experience more immersive, a case study was conducted by collecting feedback from participants playing *Nevermind* which is "the first commercial biofeedback-enhanced adventure thriller game to use consumer-level biosensors" [12][13]. *Nevermind's* biofeedback algorithm will monitor players' feelings of stress and fear moment-to-moment using biofeedback technology. The game will become harder if the fears get the best of players, while the game will be easier if players can calm down facing terror[13].

Figure 1. The change in game difficulty is mainly reflected in the reduction of picture clarity, dimming of light, and changes in scene content. The figure 1 shows playing *Nevermind* with (right) /without (left) biofeedback.

Nevermind can be played with biofeedback technology, while it is acceptable to be played without biofeedback technology. The game currently responds to emotion-based biofeedback with a standard webcam via Affectiva's Affdex technology and/or physiological-based biofeedback via a supported heart rate sensor [14]. When the physiological-based biofeedback is working, the emotion-based biofeedback would enhance the experience.

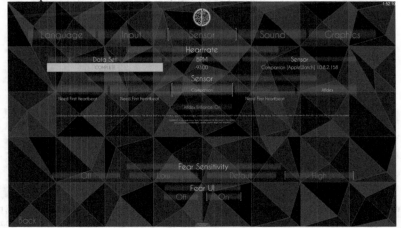

Figure 2. Game settings interface after connecting with biofeedback technology devices. Affectiva's Affdex technology enhances physiological-based biofeedback.

4.2. Methods

- Participants

A total of 34 participants were recruited for the experiment, 15 males and 19 females, whose ages ranged from 18 to 25 years. They were all undergraduate or graduate students majoring in game design or digital arts. 3 participants (Male=1, Female=2) who have played *Nevermind* before were ruled out of the data according to the prespecified exclusion criteria.

- Apparatus

A standard webcam was implemented using Logitech C270 for emotion-based biofeedback. Physiological-based biofeedback was supported by an Apple Watch Series 5 as the heart rate sensor, connecting to an iPhone 12 Pro Max. A capable gaming PC (Intel Core i7-11700 CPU, NVIDIA GeForce GTX 3070, 16 GB RAM) ensured fluent gameplay. All self-reported measures were assessed on a separate computer using the online survey tool Wenjuanxing [15].

- Measures

We assessed the players' sense of immersive with the *Immersive Experience Questionnaire* (IEQ) [16]. The questionnaire consists of 5 dimensions: (1) Challenge, (2) Control, (3) Real world dissociation, (4) Emotional involvement, and (5) Cognitive involvement, measuring a mixture of person factors (1)-(2) and game factors (3)-(5) [16]. All 31 questions were rated on a 7-point Likert scale. After 31 questions, an extra question "How immersed did you feel?" will be asked as an additional measure to check whether the IEQ is reliably reflecting the participant's immersive experience according to [17]. IEQ is widely used in assessing player immersive experience in the game research field. The paper that reports the development of IEQ has been widely cited [17].

Figure 3. Emotion-based biofeedback (left-up), Physiological-based biofeedback (left-down is a screenshot of Apple Watch and middle is a screenshot of iPhone). Logitech C270 was used for emotion-based biofeedback and Apple Watch Series 5 was used for Physiological-based biofeedback (right).

- Procedure

After filling in a demographics questionnaire, an initial tutorial level was played by every participant in order to be accustomed to game controls before the trial started. The study used a two-condition (play *Nevermind* with/without biofeedback) within-subjects design. Both two conditions were presented using a randomized ordering and were played by all participants. According to [18], each condition was played for 10 minutes or until the end of the level (10-35 min), which is widely recognized playing time in the game research field. Before operating the biofeedback condition trial, the heart rate sensor and webcam were recalibrated for every participant. After each condition, participants completed IEQ. All participants were debriefed and thanked for their participation after finishing both two conditions.

4.3. Results and Discussion

Initially, a normality test was applied to the 31 sets of valid experimental data. This assessment utilized the Shapiro-Wilk test for normality. While a subset of the data displayed minor deviations from the assumption of normality ($p > .05$), the overall data met the criteria for normality: the absolute value of skewness was less than 10 and the absolute value of kurtosis was below 3. Subsequently, a one-way ANOVA was employed to analyze the differences among the groups (see Table 2).

- Challenge: A significant main effect of Biofeedback on perceived challenge was identified ($F = 9.671$, $p = 0.003$). Participants perceived gameplay incorporating biofeedback to be more challenging ($M = 4.90$, $SD = 0.83$) compared to gameplay without biofeedback ($M = 4.23$, $SD = 0.88$) ($p < .05$).
- Control: We found a significant main effect of Biofeedback on perceived Control ($F = 38.396$, $p = 0.000$). Participants rated Control to be higher in gameplay with biofeedback ($M = 5.23$, $SD = 0.92$) than without biofeedback ($M = 3.65$, $SD = 1.08$) ($p < .05$).
- Real World Dissociation: A significant main effect of Biofeedback on Real World Dissociation was established ($F = 22.012$, $p = 0.000$). Participants

perceived more dissociation from the real world with biofeedback (M = 4.90, SD = 0.94) than without biofeedback (M = 3.68, SD = 1.11) (p < .05).

- Emotional Involvement: A significant main effect of Biofeedback on Emotional Involvement was identified (F = 53.262, p = 0.000), indicating that participants involved more emotion in the gameplay with biofeedback (M = 5.45, SD = 0.93) than without biofeedback (M = 3.61, SD = 1.05) (p < .05).
- Cognitive Involvement: We observed a significant main effect of Biofeedback on Cognitive Involvement (F = 53.648, p = 0.000), indicating that participants involved more cognition in the gameplay with biofeedback (M = 5.71, SD = 0.82) than without biofeedback (M = 4.10, SD = 0.91) (p < .05).

Moreover, the result of the Additional Measure question (How immersed did you feel?) shows the IEQ is reliably reflecting the participant's immersive experience.

Our results indicate that the interaction of biofeedback technology applied in gameplay should be considered as a positive choice for it impacts the game experience more immersive. All questions of Control, Emotional involvement, and Cognitive involvement factors showed significant difference. Except for questions Challenge2, Challenge3, Real World Dissociation5, all questions of Challenge and Real World Dissociation factors showed significant difference.

Challenge2 (Were there any times during the game in which you just wanted to give up?) and Challenge3 (To what extent did you find the game easy) showed no significant difference. It's understandable for people to want to give up and find the game difficult while playing an adventure thriller game. The game levels are the same in two conditions, while biofeedback changes the game clarity, brightness and several specific scenes. It is possibly indicated that biofeedback could auxiliarily affect the extent of the challenge, but does not change the essence as the adventure thriller game. No significant difference to the question Real World Dissociation5 (To what extent did you notice events taking place around you?). This may be due to the limitations of the form of the video game that biofeedback cannot make up for shortcomings of the game interaction media. Since there is a VR version of *Nevermind*, comparing the form of the game (video game version and VR game version) with changing conditions with or without biofeedback may be the future research of this study.

Table 2. The table shows the results of a one-way ANOVA

	Condition (Mean±Std. Deviation)		F☐	p☐
	1.0(n=31)	2.0(n=31)		
Challenge1	3.52±1.39	4.90±1.27	16.809	0.000**
Challenge2	4.68±1.38	4.61±1.75	0.026	0.872
Challenge3	3.74±1.24	4.16±1.63	1.297	0.259
Challenge4	4.00±1.21	5.32±1.28	17.535	0.000**
Control1	3.90±1.47	5.06±1.41	10.067	0.002**
Control2	3.77±1.31	5.77±0.96	47.185	0.000**
Control3	3.23±1.45	5.06±1.15	30.440	0.000**
Control4	3.68±1.30	5.13±1.31	19.164	0.000**
Control5	3.58±1.43	4.97±1.38	15.098	0.000**
Real World Dissociation1	3.84±1.49	5.39±1.12	21.533	0.000**
Real World Dissociation2	3.81±1.66	4.68±1.33	5.202	0.026*
Real World Dissociation3	3.61±1.67	5.13±1.12	17.691	0.000**
Real World Dissociation4	3.77±1.15	4.58±1.36	6.369	0.014*
Real World Dissociation5	3.61±1.52	4.35±1.47	3.808	0.056

Table 2. The table shows the results of a one-way ANOVA

	Condition (Mean±Std. Deviation)		$F\square$	$p\square$
	1.0(*n*=31)	2.0(*n*=31)		
Real World Dissociation6	3.65±1.28	5.29±1.13	28.772	0.000**
Real World Dissociation7	3.16±1.46	4.90±1.40	22.961	0.000**
Emotional Involvement1	3.68±1.45	5.19±1.30	18.816	0.000**
Emotional Involvement2	3.52±1.21	5.26±1.37	28.311	0.000**
Emotional Involvement3	3.87±1.20	5.71±0.94	45.000	0.000**
Emotional Involvement4	3.35±1.36	5.32±1.22	36.056	0.000**
Emotional Involvement5	3.61±1.33	5.52±1.12	36.979	0.000**
Emotional Involvement6	3.61±1.31	5.19±1.30	22.737	0.000**
Cognitive Involvement1	4.23±1.09	5.71±1.01	31.118	0.000**
Cognitive Involvement2	4.00±1.44	5.74±0.86	33.620	0.000**
Cognitive Involvement3	4.87±1.65	6.16±1.42	10.929	0.002**
Cognitive Involvement4	3.87±1.52	5.42±1.09	21.229	0.000**
Cognitive Involvement5	3.84±1.37	5.39±0.95	26.687	0.000**
Cognitive Involvement6	3.84±1.16	5.39±1.05	30.316	0.000**
Cognitive Involvement7	4.68±0.98	5.55±1.15	10.306	0.002**
Cognitive Involvement8	4.03±1.17	5.87±1.09	41.127	0.000**
Cognitive Involvement9	3.68±1.28	5.68±1.14	42.491	0.000**
Additional Measure	5.13±1.80	7.77±1.41	41.472	0.000**
Challenge	4.23±0.88	4.90±0.83	9.671	0.003**
Control	3.65±1.08	5.23±0.92	38.396	0.000**
Real World Dissociation	3.68±1.11	4.90±0.94	22.012	0.000**
Emotional Involvement	3.61±1.05	5.45±0.93	53.262	0.000**
Cognitive Involvement	4.10±0.91	5.71±0.82	53.648	0.000**

* *p*<0.05 ** *p*<0.01

5. Potential Problems of Biofeedback Technology Applied to Games

Biofeedback technology breaks through the traditional human-computer interaction method in games, bringing a new gaming experience to players and opening up new paths for innovation and development in the gaming field, but potential problems still exist. The present study discusses two aspects, *privacy and regulations, accuracy and cost.*

5.1. Privacy and Regulations

While biofeedback technology helps improve the gaming experience, it also raises privacy concerns. Biofeedback technology needs to collect and analyze players' physiological data, which may violate players' privacy if the data is improperly handled. Meanwhile, different countries and regions have different regulatory requirements for collecting and using citizens' personal physiological data. A game that utilizes biofeedback technology may raise local legal issues in different parts of the world. In this regard, game designers need to understand and comply with local laws and regulations on physiological data. When collecting and using players' physiological data, game designers should clearly inform and obtain players' consent and authorization, ensure that the physiological data is only used for the purpose of enhancing the game experience and not for other purposes, and encrypt the data to ensure data security.

5.2. Accuracy and Cost

Although many sensor devices claim to be able to accurately measure physiological data, such as heart rate, facial expressions, etc., the accuracy of these devices is actually not high enough. The use of expensive sensors in pursuit of high accuracy will raise the cost of gameplay, resulting in a certain degree of inequality as some players are unable to obtain a complete game experience because they don't have enough money to purchase a game device. In this regard, on the one hand, game designers can balance the relationship between the accuracy of physiological data and the game experience by choosing hardware devices with relatively acceptable prices for players and high accuracy for the game experience. On the other hand, game designers can provide more diversified choices, such as non-biofeedback versions of the game or biofeedback devices that sacrifice a little bit of accuracy but are more economical and affordable so that more players can enjoy the fun of the game.

6. The future of combining AI and biofeedback technology

Although biofeedback technology applied in video games makes the player's different physiological states elicit corresponding gameplay feedback, this logical causal link between the player and the game is still not divorced from the game designer's pre-setup for the game. With the development of biofeedback technology and AI technology, the game industry is about to enter the period of AI biofeedback technology. Combining biofeedback technology and AI technology will make the game's feedback to the player more intelligent. Introducing biofeedback technology opens a whole new chapter in video games, while AI technology will provide a more personalized gaming experience based on user physiological data. It will not only be able to process and parse the massive amount of data from biofeedback technology but also change the game progress according to this data. Specifically, this is mainly reflected in two aspects: *Intelligent NPC* and *Personalized experience*.

6.1. Intelligent NPC

Introducing AI will make the game's non-player characters (NPC) more intelligent. Firstly, AI can allow NPCs more natural language interaction capabilities and complex decision-making logic, improving the player's gaming experience. Secondly, AI can be combined with biofeedback to read and understand the player's emotional and physiological state, allowing NPCs to adapt better and respond to player behavior. For example, if the player is emotionally agitated, NPCs may act more helpful or aggressive, adding challenges or providing assistance depending on the game's settings.

6.2. Personalized experience

AI can understand the player's personal preferences by analyzing biofeedback data, such as the player's favorite game style, characters, etc., thereby adjusting the game's story direction and elements to match the player's style and creating a personalized gaming experience. For example, if the player's heart rate increases and the expression is happy in specific plots, the AI can determine that the player likes this part and recommend more similar content in the future. Unlike the past's fixed plot lines, the open narrative empowered by AI combined with biofeedback technology can make each player's gaming experience unique and make timely changes based on player behavior and feedback.

References

[1] McStay. Andrew, *Emotional AI: The Rise of Empathic Media,* SAGE Publications Ltd, London, 2018.
[2] Navarro D, Sundstedt V, Garro V, Biofeedback methods in entertainment video games: A review of physiological interaction techniques, *Proceedings of the ACM on Human-Computer Interaction* 5 (CHI PLAY) (2021), 1-32.
[3] Alan T Pope, Edward H Bogart, and Debbie S Bartolome, Biocybernetic system evaluates indices of operator engagement in automated task, *Biological Psychology* 40 (1995), 187–195.
[4] Jennifer Allanson and Stephen H. Fairclough, A research agenda for physiological computing, *Interacting with Computers* 16, 5 (2004), 857–878.
[5] Stephen H. Fairclough, Fundamentals of physiological computing, *Interacting with Computers* 21 (2009), 133–145.
[6] Kuikkaniemi, K., Laitinen, T., Turpeinen, M., Saari, T., Kosunen, I., and Ravaja, N., The influence of implicit and explicit biofeedback in first-person shooter games, *Proc. of CHI'10*, ACM (2010), 859–868.
[7] Lennart E. Nacke, Michael Kalyn, Calvin Lough, and Regan Lee Mandryk, Biofeedback game design: using direct and indirect physiological control to enhance game interaction. *Proceedings of the SIGCHI Conference on Human Factors in Computing Systems* (2011), 103-112.
[8] Lennart E. Nacke, *An Introduction to Physiological Player Metrics for Evaluating Games*, Springer London, London, 585–619, 2013
[9] Eduardo Velloso, Carl Oechsner, Katharina Sachmann, Markus Wirth, Hans Gellersen, Arcade+: A Platform for Public Deployment and Evaluation of Multi-Modal Games, *CHI PLAY '15* (2015), 271-275.
[10] https://www.media.mit.edu/posts/galea/
[11] https://www.immersivelearning.news/2021/02/09/tobii-valve-openbci-collaborate-on-galea-vr-brain-computer-interface/
[12] https://www.flyingmollusk.com/projects
[13] https://nevermindgame.com/about
[14] https://nevermindgame.com/sensors
[15] https://www.wjx.cn/
[16] Charlene Jennett, Anna L. Cox, Paul Cairns, Samira Dhoparee, Andrew Epps, Tim Tijs, Alison Walton, Measuring and defining the experience of immersion in games, *International Journal of Human-Computer Studies* (2008), 641-661.
[17] https://uclic.ucl.ac.uk/people/anna-cox/research-group/ieq
[18] Kivikangas, J. M., Ekman, I., Chanel, G., Järvelä, S., Salminen, M., Cowley, B., Henttonen, P., Ravaja, N. Review on psychophysiological methods in game research. *Proc. of 1st Nordic DiGRA*, DiGRA (2010).

Design Studies and Intelligence Engineering
L.C. Jain et al. (Eds.)
© 2024 The Authors.
This article is published online with Open Access by IOS Press and distributed under the terms
of the Creative Commons Attribution Non-Commercial License 4.0 (CC BY-NC 4.0).
doi:10.3233/FAIA231505

Analysis on the Predicament of Future Law and Its Solution Under the Background of Artificial Intelligence

Xiaoying RUAN[a,1] and Hongfu CHEN[b]

a *Law School of Minjiang University, Fuzhou, Fujian, 350001, China*
b *Foreign Language College of Minjiang University, Fuzhou, Fujian, 350001, China*

Abstract: In order to study the potential, unknown and unpredictable legal risks of content technology generated by artificial intelligence, the future legal dilemma and its solution path analysis under the background of artificial intelligence are put forward. The rapid development of ChatGPT has faced legal difficulties in the fields of technology monopoly, algorithm bias, false information, intellectual property rights and data security, so it is not only necessary but also urgent to think calmly about ChatGPT from the perspective of legal regulation. Because risks and regulations often go hand in hand, we should carry out comprehensive management of the whole data life cycle and the whole chain, study and analyze the forward-looking system design, prevent the possible anti-competitive risks such as algorithmic monopoly and abuse of market dominance of AIGC, build a multi-dimensional supervision system including the external supervision and self-supervision of AIGC, create a systematic supervision ecology, establish a standardized supervision system, and adopt appropriate advanced system design. AIGC represented by ChatGPT can be used not only by human beings, but also by human beings.

Keywords: ChatGPT; AIGC; Legal response; Legal dilemma; copyright

1 Introduction

Chatgpt (Chat Generative Pre-trained Transformer) is a chat robot program released by OpenAI, an American artificial intelligence research laboratory, on November 30, 2022. As an artificial intelligence language model, once it was launched, it immediately became the "top stream" in the field of science and technology, and it was successfully out of the circle. Bill Gates bluntly said: "ChatGPT has no less influence than the birth of the Internet and personal computers!" For a time, all kinds of information related to ChatGPT have spread all over the network. At the same time, the advent of ChatGPT set off a new wave of AI Generated Content, AIGC). Since 2018, artificial intelligence technology has emerged in industrial development and social change, and its potential has been widely recognized by countries around the world [1]. The strategic layout of artificial intelligence in developed countries has been continuously upgraded, which

---

[1] Corresponding Author.

shows that the development of artificial intelligence is attracting global attention and moving towards a new global pattern. In 2019, a series of events, including the US technology blockade, the start of new infrastructure construction, and epidemic prevention and control, had a far-reaching impact on the development of China's artificial intelligence technology industry [2]. The 14th Five-Year Plan [3] adopted in 2020 pointed out that we should aim at frontier scientific and technological fields such as artificial intelligence, implement a number of strategic national major scientific and technological projects, and at the same time promote the deep integration of big data and artificial intelligence, so as to promote healthy economic development. Artificial intelligence will undoubtedly play an important role in promoting the high-quality development of the national economy.

The world has been "stunned" by waves of AIGC, which not only brings convenience to people's work and life, but also adds fun. However, the embedding of AIGC into multiple social application scenarios makes social life face both opportunities and risks. With the continuous evolution and iteration of technology, AIGC is about to usher in more "anthropomorphic" substitutes, and human society will also encounter profound and multi-dimensional changes [4]. The advance of technology will inevitably lead to potential, unknown and unpredictable technical risks and legal risks. At the same time, at the existing legal level, a few people are driven by interests and knowingly commit crimes, so the legal problems faced by AIGC cannot be underestimated.

2 Literature review

From the perspective of rights protection and incentive effect, some scholars have come to the conclusion that they are opposed to protecting the copyright of artificial intelligence products through copyright law. For example, on the one hand, the rights and interests of programmers have been realized in software copyright protection, and the copyright protection of their output content has the potential risk of hindering public access; On the other hand, in the era of big data, end users enjoy commercial benefits, and whether the works generated by artificial intelligence are protected by copyright or not will not affect the rate of users using programs and publishing works [5]. Therefore, it is unnecessary to obtain copyright protection for works generated by artificial intelligence. The creation of works requires creative labor input, but also requires the creation to reach a certain height [6]. They believe that a work is the crystallization of the author's wisdom and emotion, and it is the manifestation of his ideological personality.

Distinguishing Authors-in-Fact from Authors-in-Law was recognized by scholars in the last century. They think that the factual author and the legal author of the same work are not necessarily the same person. They recognize the authorship of the machine but not its legal status. This is the basic principle of the Fictional Human Author Theory. It holds that if the content generated by computer software can meet the objective requirements of the work, it should be recognized as a work in the legal sense, and at the same time, the computer software should be given the identity of the author, but this identity is not accompanied by the de facto relationship of rights and obligations, strictly speaking, it is only a virtual one. The winner of the ultimate substantive right is determined by the copyright bureau or the referee considering various factors [7]. This practice is more flexible, and it can take into account the interests of many subjects comprehensively, which has been recognized by many experts in the field. In addition, relevant researchers believe that artificial intelligence should be encouraged to obtain new legal person status and become the winner of rights and interests, so as to make up for the deficiency of the existing system in solving the problem of copyright ownership of works created by intelligent machines [8]. After analyzing the contribution of the main participants in the process of intelligent generation one by one, it is found that it mainly includes programmers, users and intelligent algorithms themselves. And in the framework of English law, the advantages and disadvantages of distributing power to the above three are summarized, but in the end, the only answer to the ownership of rights is not obtained [9].

The essence of artificial intelligence "creation" is a "mechanical" implementation process, which is more a passive reflection of the outside world and can only be a writing behavior, lacking the embodiment of basic ideas and the output of the author's emotions. This feature will lead to the loss of the essence of creative behavior and the accumulation of boring words [10]. Some studies believe that the study of the properties of intelligent products should be based on the delineation of the scope of research objects. For example, products that are not recognized as works will no longer be studied in terms of their properties [11]. On this basis, we insist on denying the nature of the works of intelligent products. In his view, the product is only the operation result of an intelligent program, which has no basic thoughts and feelings, let alone the extension of the author's personality, and does not meet the basic conditions for becoming a work [12].

AIGC has also triggered a continuous hot discussion and thinking about artificial intelligence around the world, either praising it, belittling it, loving it or fearing it. However, human beings have been unable to escape from the Wang Yang Sea of AI. As a legal person, it is not only necessary but also very important to think calmly about ChatGPT from the perspective of legal regulation.

3 Technology Rush and Legal Dilemma

We can understand the generation of artificial intelligence products as the intelligent output of an anthropomorphic algorithm model: firstly, based on massive data materials, we use super computing power to explore the hidden characteristics and their relationships in a large number of data, and finally form an algorithm model similar to the thinking mode of human brain for specific problems to output intellectual achievements. The core stage in this process is deep learning. Figure 1 is a flow chart of artificial intelligence from input to learning to output, to help us understand the operation principle more intuitively.

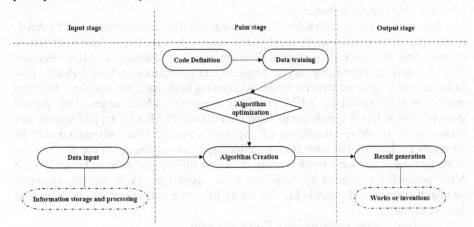

Figure 1 Operation mechanism of artificial intelligence

The negative impact of AIGC on market competition, technological innovation, consumer rights and national security is ultimately manifested in potential legal risks such as technology monopoly, capital expansion, data abuse, algorithm discrimination, privacy infringement and legal dilemmas that are difficult to overcome at the moment.

3.1 Legal Dilemma of Technology Monopoly

The rapid development of high technology will inevitably attract the pursuit and capital blessing of investment institutions. Enterprises with scientific and technological heads can not only quickly graft the original market influence to AIGC track, and then take a dominant position in the new market, but also maintain their dominant position in the new market field by adopting unfair competition behaviors such as technology monopoly and data monopoly [13]. Technology monopoly will not only lead to unfair competition, but also lead to a series of legal problems such as market competition failure, limited consumer choice, unfair price and decreased innovation ability.

3.2 legal problems of algorithm bias

Algorithm governance is related to national political security, economic security, cultural security and the protection of citizens' rights and interests. How to effectively prevent and eliminate the harm of algorithm application is the main goal of algorithm governance at present, and it is also a compliance problem faced by algorithm developers and designers. At present, there are still some technical problems in the algorithm of AIGC [14,15]. For example, the algorithm of AIGC relies on the statistical laws in the training database and cannot crawl the real-time data on the Internet. At the same time, AIGC can't identify and verify the source of data, which is prone to algorithm discrimination and algorithm abuse, thus causing legal problems such as data compliance. In addition, because the training data is limited by the types and contents of the data, if the neutrality and integrity of the data are incomplete, the database is prone to the wrong value tendency, and when the user needs the relevant "answer", the "answer" output by AIGC algorithm may have the wrong content or biased guidance. For example, if the data training set contains discriminatory data such as gender, age, country, belief and race, it will mislead AIGC to make a discriminatory reply and regard the discriminatory reply as the "correct answer" [16]. Therefore, the decision made by AIGC is also discriminatory. Moreover, algorithm bias can easily lead to potential legal risks such as national political security and cultural security.

3.3 Legal risks of false information

Associated with algorithm bias, the problem of false information caused by AIGC is also difficult to overcome. To identify and control the problem of false information, we must first overcome the technical dilemma and legal dilemma of AIGC. Because AIGC is based on the existing natural language text information (corpus) behind AI for probability statistics, the answers to the questions it feeds back are actually "statistical results". In many questions, AIGC may "talk nonsense", which seems to be "correct answers", but in fact it is outrageous false information. If AIGC is applied to customer evaluation or customer complaints of goods or services, false information will be extremely misleading and even lead to serious legal consequences. At present, in view of the fact that AIGC can't break through the above difficulties in the technical level, if AIGC products represented by AIGC are to be applied to search engines, customer complaint systems and other fields, the whole life cycle and full chain compliance of data are essential.

3.4 Legal Debate on Intellectual Property Rights

At present, the discussion on the intellectual property rights of the content generated by AIGC is extremely fierce. At present, the focus of discussion is mainly on two aspects.

One is whether the reply (paper) generated by AIGC is original, that is, the ownership of the copyright of the paper generated by AIGC; The second is whether the reply (paper) generated by AIGC constitutes academic misconduct or infringement.

3.4.1 Can AI become the copyright owner?

According to Article 3 of China's Copyright Law, a work refers to an intellectual achievement that is original and can be expressed in a certain form in the fields of literature, art and science. Obviously, in the framework of China's intellectual property system, originality is the core criterion to judge whether AI can become a copyright owner [17]. At present, in the intellectual property system of most countries, including China, the author of the work can only be a natural person, and AI cannot be the author of the work, which is also confirmed by the relevant judicial precedents in China.

As shown in Figure 2, the court held that one of the controversial focuses of the case was whether the article involved constituted a legal person's work, and the controversial focus was the judgment of the ownership of the artificial intelligence product rights. The court held that the articles involved were presided over by the plaintiff as a legal person and organized relevant teams to form the overall intelligence and then complete the creation. It can be considered that the whole reflects the plaintiff's creative needs and intentions. At the same time, the court held that "this article was written automatically by the robot" at the end of the article involved was an act of signing the work, which had a clear and specific subject orientation, so it could be considered that the article involved was the responsibility of the development company [18]. In combination with the provisions of Article 11 and Article 12 of the Copyright Law, in the absence of clear evidence to the contrary, the court held that the article involved belonged to a legal person work organized and hosted by the plaintiff company, which reflected the plaintiff's needs and intentions and the plaintiff company assumed relevant responsibilities.

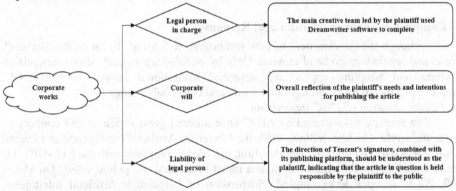

Figure 2 Mind Map of Legal Person's Works Confirmed by the Court

3.4.2 AIGC constitute infringement?

The copyright issue of the content generated by AIGC has also brought great impact to the academic circle, and the possible infringement caused by AI has aroused heated debate and discussion among scholars. At present, some countries and regions have given feedback at the academic level. For example, in order to deeply explore the potential risks that the large language model (LLMs) of AIGC may bring to the academic community and the academic chaos it will cause, the British magazine Nature published two analytical articles on AIGC in a week. Whether there is potential infringement of AIGC and how to effectively regulate the legitimate use of AIGC are the focus and difficulty of current controversy. In addition, for articles that cite artificial intelligence writing tools as references, the author needs to provide detailed citation arguments. At present, whether AIGC will constitute infringement is still inconclusive [19]. The mainstream view is that AIGC should be regarded as a tool and object used by human beings, and has no personality in the legal sense. Therefore, AIGC itself cannot bear the corresponding legal responsibilities. If the content generated by AIGC infringes on the copyright or privacy of others, the right holder or user of AIGC should bear the corresponding legal responsibilities.

3.5 Legal Concerns about Data Security

Massive data support is the premise and foundation of AIGC operation, and its data mainly comes from reptile data set and human language data set. Although AIGC has taken necessary precautions in data compliance, the inherent technical model of AIGC and the risks in data security are difficult to overcome. First of all, although AIGC will strictly abide by the existing privacy policies and safety regulations when obtaining and storing training data, data security will still be threatened by network attacks and data crawling due to technical limitations, and the security protection of data related to national security, business secrets and personal privacy in the process of flow and sharing should be paid special attention to. Secondly, because AIGC needs to rely on massive database information, if users enter sensitive confidential information such as national security, business secrets and personal privacy during chatting, AIGC will automatically obtain such information and store it in the background, and AIGC will also incorporate confidential sensitive data into the corpus for training [20]. Therefore, AIGC may lead to the legal risk of violating national security and revealing personal privacy and business secrets. Finally, because AI needs to capture data to repeatedly train the algorithm, whether the data captured by AI is legal and whether the capture behavior is infringing will also involve the issue of whether the data is compliant.

4 Compliance Supervision and Legal Response

Although the development of new technology will bring "Colin Grics dilemma", risks and regulations go hand in hand. Only by establishing a standardized supervision system and adopting appropriate advanced institutional innovation can AIGC, represented by AIGC, be brought into a safe and controllable range.

4.1 Basic situation of AIGC supervision

The security risks caused by AIGC have aroused great vigilance and concern all over the world. On March 30th, 2023, the Center for Artificial Intelligence and Digital Policy (CAIDP), a non-profit organization, has filed a complaint with the FTC-GPT-4 is biased and deceptive, which will pose a threat to privacy and public safety. On March 29, 2023, an open letter entitled "Suspension of Large-scale Artificial Intelligence Research" attracted widespread attention around the world. The open letter was signed by more than 1,000 recognized and well-known scientific and technological experts around the world, and the signers included not only the Turing Prize winner Yoshua Bengio. It also includes Elon Musk, CEO of Tesla, Stephen Wozniak, co-founder of Apple, ZacharyKenton, a senior research scientist, and other well-known entrepreneurs, scholars and executives of well-known enterprises in the AI field [21].

Although the appeal of the above-mentioned celebrities may not stop the progress of AIGC, AIGC cannot grow wildly. The global AIGC industry is still in the stage of order adjustment, and the legal policies of various countries are still being explored, and the policies of various countries show obvious differences. For example, only a few states in the United States have issued laws and regulations on deep composition technology, and these laws and regulations are aimed at regulating the deep composition that affects elections and the deep composition of pornographic works or false information. Through the revision of the Digital Services Law, the European Union requires the platform to carry out deep composition tagging. The EU is relatively cautious about AI, and it hopes to bring the development and application of AI into a definite legal framework, which holds a regulatory attitude. The EUs artificial intelligence path advocates "human-centric", which promotes the development and innovation of artificial intelligence while building a supervision system to prevent risks and protect citizens bas ic rights and safety. At present, the EUs supervision and governance of artificial intelligence focuses on respecting personal dignity, personal freedom and protecting data and privacy. The latest legislative progress is the revision of the Law on Artificial Intelligence by the European Parliament on June 14th, 2023. The method adopts the "risk-based method" to classify artificial intelligence systems into four categories, and sets different compliance requirements. Among them, the generative artificial intelligence system generally belongs to finite risks artificial intelligence system, which needs to comply with the minimum transparency obligation, but it may fall into the category of high-risk artificial intelligence system because of its applicable field and generated content [22]. At the same time, the law also stipulates the compliance obligations of different subjects such as providers, importers, distributors, deployers, and providers of basic models related to general and generative artificial intelligence. According to the nature and severity of the infringement, the relevant parties who do not comply with the Artificial Intelligence Law may be punished with administrative fines of different scales.

In the technical governance of AIGC in the world, Chinas legislation and supervision are not backward. At the policy level, China has successively issued a series of programmatic documents to promote and standardize the development of the artificial intelligence industry, including the Development Plan for the New Generation of Artificial Intelligence, the Ethical Code for the New Generation of Artificial Intelligence, the Guiding Opinions on Accelerating Scene Innovation to Promote High-quality Economic Development with High-level Application of Artificial Intelligence, and the Notice on Supporting the Construction of a New Generation of Artificial Intelligence Demonstration Application Scenes. On the legal level, China has promulgated the Network Security Law of the Peoples Republic of China, the Data Security Law of Peoples Republic of China (PRC), the Personal Information Protection Law of Peoples Republic of China (PRC), the Civil Code of Peoples Republic of China (PRC), the Copyright Law of People s Republic of China (PRC) and other legal provisions, which provide a basic system for the supervision and governance of AIGC. The Regulations on the Administration of Internet Information Service Algorithm Recommendation came into effect in March 2022, and there are specific regulations on the supervision of generating synthetic algorithms in this regulation [23]. On January 10, 2023, the Regulations on the Management of Deep Composition of Internet Information Services came into effect. In view of the importance and high risk of deep composition technology, deep composition has become the first algorithm service type in Chinas algorithm governance. The National Network Information Office, together with the National Development and Reform Commission, the Ministry of Education, the Ministry of Science and Technology, the Ministry of Industry and Information Technology, the Ministry of Public Security and the State Administration of Radio, Film and Television, promulgated the Interim Measures for the Administration of Generative Artificial Intelligence Services, which came into effect on August 15, 2023, aiming at promoting the healthy development and standardized application of generative artificial intelligence. With the rapid iteration of artificial intelligence, the legal supervision of generative artificial intelligence in China has gradually deepened.

However, both the legal supervision in European and American countries and the legislative practice in China are currently in the exploration stage of laws and policies. Even if the existing legal policies are gradually improved at the legislative level, based on the consideration of political, economic and social rule of law, whether the existing legal policies are feasible and operable remains to be tested by practice [24]. At present, the organization responsible for algorithm filing, evaluation and supervision is mainly the Network Information Office (Network Management Technology Bureau of the Central Network Information Office). At the same time, the telecommunications authorities and public security departments will also be responsible for supervision and management according to their duties. The main compliance obligations for generative artificial intelligence are shown in Fig. 3:

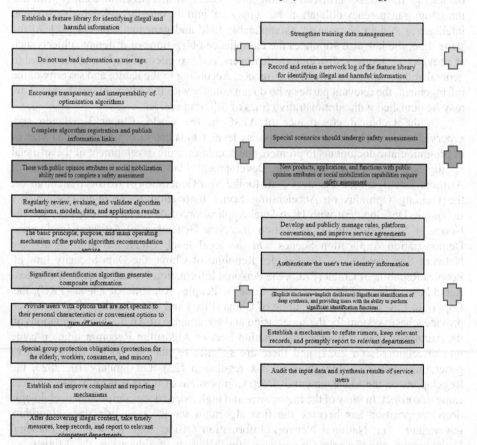

Figure 3 Main compliance obligations of AIGC

As shown in Fig. 4, after the indirect intelligence achievements are recognized in the generation process and the objective criteria for evaluating the products are defined in the generation results, the artificial intelligence products can obtain the status of works and become objects protected by law. In this way, the rights, obligations and ownership of artificial intelligence products are another key to solving rights disputes and adjusting the interests of all parties.

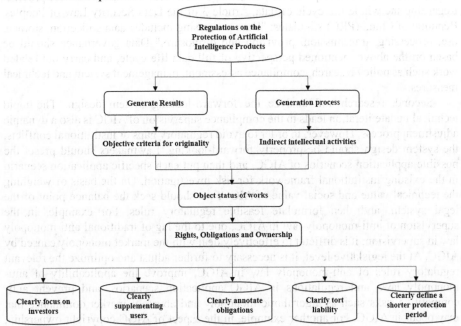

Figure 4 Mind Map of Rights, Obligations and Ownership

4.2 Legal Response to AIGC Supervision

In the face of the rapid development of AIGC technology, the existing institutional regulations are scattered, and there is often "piecemeal" selective legislation in legislative practice, and a scientific regulatory ecosystem has not yet been formed at the level of regulatory implementation. Therefore, in order to effectively prevent the legal risks of AIGC, scientific and reasonable legal regulatory rules must be set up.

First, carry out comprehensive management of the whole chain. In view of the control dilemma of AIGC, it is necessary to start from the whole life cycle of AIGC, from the construction of language model, the establishment of corpus, the labeling of corpus and the training of language model to compliance supervision, and at the same time, the updating iteration of AIGC products after they are put on the market and the exit of the system also need compliance management of the whole chain. Article 13 of the Interim Measures for the Management of Generative Artificial Intelligence Services clearly requires: "Providers should provide safe, stable and continuous services in the course of their services to ensure the normal use of users." In addition, the supervision of AIGC must also combine algorithm supervision with data supervision, and explore the algorithm governance mechanism of scenario and refinement [25]. Article 7 of the Administrative Regulations on Algorithm Recommendation for Internet Information Services stipulates: "An algorithm recommendation service provider shall implement the main responsibility of algorithm security, establish and improve management systems and technical measures such as mechanism review, scientific ethics review, user registration, information release review, data security and personal information protection, anti-telecommunication network fraud, security assessment and monitoring, and emergency response to security incidents, formulate and disclose relevant rules of algorithm recommendation service, and equip professionals and technical support commensurate with the scale of algorithm recommendation service." This regulation clearly defines the main responsibility of the algorithm recommendation service provider. Regarding the whole life cycle of data, Article 3 of the Data Security Law of Peoples Republic of China (PRC) stipulates: "Data processing includes data collection, storage, use, processing, transmission, provision and disclosure." Data governance should be based on the above-mentioned perspective of full data life cycle, and carry out related work such as policy research, compliance assessment, management system and technical measures.

Second, research and analyze the forward-looking system design. The rapid technical update iteration leads to the compliance supervision of AIGC is also a dynamic adjustment process. However, in order to avoid regulatory gaps or institutional conflicts, the system design should be properly forward-looking. Lawmakers should preset the possible application scenarios of AIGC, and then put each specific application scenario in the existing institutional framework for risk investigation. On the basis of weighing the technical value and social value of AIGC, we should seek the balance point of the legal system, and then formulate feasible regulatory rules. For example, in the supervision of anti-monopoly law in AIGC, due to the lag of traditional anti-monopoly law in supervision, it is difficult to effectively deal with the market monopoly caused by AIGC. At the legislative level, it is necessary to further adjust and optimize the relevant regulatory rules of anti-monopoly law in AIGC, improve the applicability of anti-monopoly laws and regulations in AIGC application scenarios, and prevent anti-competitive risks such as algorithmic monopoly and abuse of market dominance that may occur in AIGC. For another example, in the aspect of AIGC copyright ownership, because AI cant be the copyright owner, we can combine the relevant provisions of Chinas existing copyright law to explore how to determine the copyright owner of AIGC works according to the role of different subjects on the generated content.

Third, build a multi-dimensional supervision system. Constructing diversified supervision system is an important guarantee for effective supervision of AIGC. The diversified supervision system includes two dimensions: the external supervision of AIGC and the self-supervision of AIGC. The external supervision of AIGC mainly refers to the administrative supervision from government agencies. For example, the supervision of the national network information department in the field of Internet information security, the supervision of public security organs on crimes against citizens personal information and computer crimes, and the supervision of the market supervision bureau on safeguarding consumers legitimate rights and interests are all within the supervision scope of relevant administrative departments. In addition, the supervision and feedback from AIGC users also belong to outsourcing supervision. The self-supervision of AIGC includes both internal and external aspects. Internally, there are potential legal risks in data compliance, technical iterative updating and algorithm optimization. AIGC service providers need to establish a series of internal control systems for risk prevention, including key work such as safety operation and maintenance, training and learning, emergency plan, after-the-fact resumption and internal accountability. Externally, AIGC service providers need to establish an early warning system for public use. When public users use AIGC to engage in illegal and criminal acts, AIGC service providers have the obligation to delete or stop these infringements or illegal acts. Article 14 of the Interim Measures for the Administration of Generative Artificial Intelligence Services has a similar provision: "If a provider discovers illegal content, it shall promptly take measures such as stopping generation, stopping transmission and eliminating, take measures such as model optimization training for rectification, and report to the relevant competent department. If the provider finds that the user uses the generative artificial intelligence service to engage in illegal activities, it shall take measures such as warning, restricting functions, suspending or terminating the provision of services to him according to law, keep relevant records and report to the relevant competent authorities. " Only when external supervision and internal supervision participate together, and the government and the platform coordinate and supervise each other, can we build an effective mechanism to prevent the potential legal risks of AIGC.

As shown in Fig. 5, it is necessary to formulate special protection regulations for artificial intelligence products in combination with the technical characteristics of artificial intelligence, so as to solve its legal problems more pertinently and improve the existing copyright law system. Item 9 of Article 3 of the newly revised Copyright Law sums up "other intellectual achievements that conform to the characteristics of works" in the category of works. This major revision is to change the mode of "statutory types of works" implemented in the original Copyright Law into the mode of "open types of works". It is not impossible for artificial intelligence products that meet the characteristics of works to obtain the object status of works. Although artificial intelligence products are not clearly defined as works by legal provisions, as long as the content expression of artificial intelligence products does not violate the legal provisions, does not harm public interests, and conforms to the characteristics of works required by the Copyright Law, they can theoretically be recognized as "other intellectual achievements that conform to the characteristics of works" and thus become the object of legal adjustment and protection.

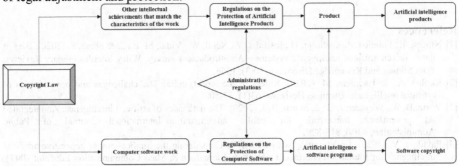

Figure. 5 Mind Map of Formulating Special Protection Regulations

Fourth, build a systematic regulatory ecology. The potential risks brought by AIGC technology cant be fundamentally solved only by the system construction at the legal level, and at the same time, it cant be supervised by the temporary supervision moveme nt overnight. In the AI era, it is necessary to give full play to the internal driving force of technical governance and the external regulation of legal regulation, and at the same time give full play to the value orientation led by culture, create a multi-dimensional systematic supervision ecology of technology, law and culture, and build a solid guarantee system for the safe application of AIGC with a benign and interactive supervision ecology. First of all, we can give full play to the advantages of the technology itself and set up an internal monitoring system when developing AIGC application scenarios and related products. For example, the self-monitoring function of the system can be realized by embedding corresponding algorithms, programs or codes to mark and report suspected forged false information when capturing input data and generating digital content. Secondly, in view of the inherent risks of technology-driven, it is necessary to accelerate the special research on artificial intelligence legislation at the legal level, and promote legislation and law revision on the basis of learning from the legislative achievements of artificial intelligence in the United States and the European Union. Finally, in order to further create the cultural atmosphere of AIGC risk prevention, AIGC developers should promote the cultural system construction of network security and data security, enhance the awareness of legal risk prevention of relevant institutions and personnel through cultural construction, and lead the value pursuit of AIGC products with risk prevention culture.

5 Conclusion

The rolling wheel of technology development is unstoppable. AIGC technology represented by ChatGPT has great development prospects, and more people are willing to accept and embrace the convenience and new development opportunities brought by technology. In this rapidly changing era, people are more willing to believe that technology will bring happiness to mankind rather than disaster, but we must also face up to the potential legal risks behind ChatGPT explosion. If human beings cannot effectively prevent and resolve the potential risks behind technology, technology development may also evolve into disaster. AIGC, represented by ChatGPT, has become a new competition track in the AI field in the world. Mastering the right to speak and make rules in AI governance and forming new national competitive advantages first has become the goal of all countries. On this track, China should not lag behind, but should be at the forefront of the world.

References

[1] Ntoutsi, E., Fafalios, P., Gadiraju, U., Iosifidis, V., Nejdl, W., Vidal, M. E., ... & Staab, S. (2020). Bias in data‐driven artificial intelligence systems—An introductory survey. Wiley Interdisciplinary Reviews: Data Mining and Knowledge Discovery, 10(3), 1356.
[2] Kaplan, A., & Haenlein, M. (2020). Rulers of the world, unite! The challenges and opportunities of artificial intelligence. Business Horizons, 63(1), 37-50.
[3] Wirtz, B. W., Weyerer, J. C., & Sturm, B. J. (2020). The dark sides of artificial intelligence: An integrated AI governance framework for public administration. International Journal of Public Administration, 43(9), 818-829.
[4] Pavlik, J. V. (2023). Collaborating with ChatGPT: Considering the implications of generative artificial intelligence for journalism and media education. Journalism & Mass Communication Educator, 78(1), 84-93.
[5] Murdoch, B. (2021). Privacy and artificial intelligence: challenges for protecting health information in a new era. BMC Medical Ethics, 22(1), 1-5.
[6] Asatiani, A., Malo, P., Nagbøl, P. R., Penttinen, E., Rinta-Kahila, T., & Salovaara, A. (2021). Sociotechnical envelopment of artificial intelligence: An approach to organizational deployment of inscrutable artificial intelligence systems. Journal of the Association for Information Systems (JAIS), 22(2), 325-252.
[7] Biswas, S. (2023). ChatGPT and the future of medical writing. Radiology, 307(2), 223312.
[8] Dwivedi, Y. K., Hughes, L., Ismagilova, E., Aarts, G., Coombs, C., Crick, T., ... & Williams, M. D. (2021). Artificial Intelligence (AI): Multidisciplinary perspectives on emerging challenges, opportunities, and agenda for research, practice and policy. International Journal of Information Management, 57, 101994.
[9] Wu, T. (2019). Will artificial intelligence eat the law? The rise of hybrid social-ordering systems. Columbia Law Review, 119(7), 2001-2028.
[10] Lin, T. C. (2019). Artificial intelligence, finance, and the law. Fordham L. Rev., 88, 531.
[11] Felzmann, H., Fosch-Villaronga, E., Lutz, C., & Tamò-Larrieux, A. (2020). Towards transparency by design for artificial intelligence. Science and Engineering Ethics, 26(6), 3333-3361.
[12] Loureiro, S. M. C., Guerreiro, J., & Tussyadiah, I. (2021). Artificial intelligence in business: State of the art and future research agenda. Journal of business research, 129, 911-926.

[13] Carter, S. M., Rogers, W., Win, K. T., Frazer, H., Richards, B., & Houssami, N. (2020). The ethical, legal and social implications of using artificial intelligence systems in breast cancer care. The Breast, 49, 25-32.

[14] Veale, M., & Zuiderveen Borgesius, F. (2021). Demystifying the Draft EU Artificial Intelligence Act—Analysing the good, the bad, and the unclear elements of the proposed approach. Computer Law Review International, 22(4), 97-112.

[15] Ali, S., Abuhmed, T., El-Sappagh, S., Muhammad, K., Alonso-Moral, J. M., Confalonieri, R., ... & Herrera, F. (2023). Explainable Artificial Intelligence (XAI): What we know and what is left to attain Trustworthy Artificial Intelligence. Information Fusion, 99, 101805.

[16] Taeihagh, A. (2021). Governance of artificial intelligence. Policy and society, 40(2), 137-157.

[17] Grover, P., Kar, A. K., & Dwivedi, Y. K. (2022). Understanding artificial intelligence adoption in operations management: insights from the review of academic literature and social media discussions. Annals of Operations Research, 308(1-2), 177-213.

[18] Paranjape, K., Schinkel, M., Panday, R. N., Car, J., & Nanayakkara, P. (2019). Introducing artificial intelligence training in medical education. JMIR medical education, 5(2), 16048.

[19] Smuha, N. A. (2019). The EU approach to ethics guidelines for trustworthy artificial intelligence. Computer Law Review International, 20(4), 97-106.

[20] Eling, M., Nuessle, D., & Staubli, J. (2021). The impact of artificial intelligence along the insurance value chain and on the insurability of risks. The Geneva Papers on Risk and Insurance-Issues and Practice, 1-37.

[21] Re, R. M., & Solow-Niederman, A. (2019). Developing artificially intelligent justice. Stan. Tech. L. Rev., 22, 242.

[22] Helbing, D., Frey, B. S., Gigerenzer, G., Hafen, E., Hagner, M., Hofstetter, Y., ... & Zwitter, A. (2019). Will democracy survive big data and artificial intelligence?. Towards digital enlightenment: Essays on the dark and light sides of the digital revolution, 73-98.

[23] Surden, H. (2019). Artificial intelligence and law: An overview. Georgia State University Law Review, 35, 19-22.

[24] De Bruyn, A., Viswanathan, V., Beh, Y. S., Brock, J. K. U., & Von Wangenheim, F. (2020). Artificial intelligence and marketing: Pitfalls and opportunities. Journal of Interactive Marketing, 51(1), 91-105.

[25] King, T. C., Aggarwal, N., Taddeo, M., & Floridi, L. (2020). Artificial intelligence crime: An interdisciplinary analysis of foreseeable threats and solutions. Science and engineering ethics, 26, 89-120.

Design Studies and Intelligence Engineering
L.C. Jain et al. (Eds.)
© 2024 The Authors.
This article is published online with Open Access by IOS Press and distributed under the terms
of the Creative Commons Attribution Non-Commercial License 4.0 (CC BY-NC 4.0).
doi:10.3233/FAIA231506

Indoor Color Planning Based on Color Image Coordinate System

Can ZHOU[a, 1]

ᵃCollege of Furniture and Art Design, Central South University of Forestry & Technology

Abstract: Because the color configuration in most indoor space design is not ideal, in order to meet people's physiological and psychological needs, indoor color planning based on color image coordinate system is put forward. Design an indoor color configuration system based on RGB-D image. In terms of system hardware, TCS3415 color sensor is used to design color acquisition module, and Kinect equipment is used to design RGB-D image acquisition module. In system software, RGB-D image information extraction function and indoor color configuration function are designed. The experimental results show that: according tor²The distribution table shows that when the significance level is 0.05. When the degree of freedom is 2, r^2The critical value of is 5.89. Conclusion: There is no obvious difference between the system in this paper and the color scheme designed by professional designers, which verifies the effectiveness of the system.

Keywords: RGB-D image; Color configuration; Indoor color; system design

1 Introduction

It is very difficult to unify everyone's feelings about color. The uncertainty of personal aesthetics makes it impossible for us to find a "universal" formula to apply when designing interior colors. "Although the lamb is beautiful, it is difficult for everyone to adjust." For the same thing, people will make different choices according to their own artistic accomplishment and aesthetic taste. Similarly, people's choice of color will vary according to their own needs. It is precisely because of the infinite possibility of color that designers pay more and more attention to it, but the professional knowledge and content of color are too complicated for many designers to understand and master. More often, designers do color design work with their own perceptual knowledge [1]. In fact, the application of color in interior design is not irregular. The understanding of color should also be based on the establishment of good cognition, and constantly explore more possibilities of color. Color theory can guide us to match colors scientifically and reasonably, but in the process of interior design, colors are designed in three-dimensional space, which makes color matching more complicated. Usually, space function and decorative materials will get more attention in interior design, but the collocation of indoor color relations often gets less attention. Most people are usually inexperienced in color matching, and everyone's preference for colors in the space leads to the neglect of the overall color relationship in the indoor space, which makes the colors in the space messy. Although

---

[1] Corresponding Author.

many designers are constantly trying to use colors, the interior designers' grasp of the color relationship is always unsatisfactory, so it is urgent to study a set of rigorous and practical application methods of interior color design [2]. The continuous development and progress of social life, people's attention to the beautiful living environment and the influence of the environment on people's emotions all put forward new requirements for interior design. Compared with other design elements, color has more urgent practical needs in interior design. What kind of color collocation can bring what kind of visual and psychological experience to the interior space is the theme of the current interior design color discussion.

2 Literature review

Westerners attach importance to the research and development of color theory and occupy a certain active position in the field of color. Color matching theory of color; The physicist Newton's research on spectral color promoted the development of color theory, and since then, color theory has entered the stage of scientific development. Various painting schools in the field of modern western art painting have made a very mature discussion on color. The application fields of color are getting wider and wider from painting to design, which is wider than before. Especially in the field of interior design, color has brought new design ideas for interior space design with its creative advantages [3]. Since 1980s, color trend report has been extended to the field of interior design. Personalized design of household products, humanized treatment of indoor space colors and color coordination of indoor environment are constantly expanding the extension of indoor design. In terms of design practice, foreign interior designers are bold and unique in the use of color, and interior design is no longer simply supporting the artistic embellishment of the space derived from architecture. If architecture determines the initial form of space, then color is the second way to change the appearance of space [4]. In recent years, there are many successful cases of interior color design. After extensive analysis and research, the division of labor and cooperation between space design and product design, the combination of space and art, the update of technology and decorative materials, and the personalized development of users' subjective needs make the interior color design abroad show cross-disciplinary characteristics [5].

In terms of related theories, there is no research method of its own color theory and color system in China. The reason is that the academic circles in China pay much attention to color research, but the theoretical research is still in the superficial understanding stage. Due to the complexity of color theory, academic circles have not comprehensively and systematically combed it. However, the understanding of color embodied in China's ancient cultural system is very different from the current situation in China. In ancient China, the understanding of color was very rational, and he had made unique discoveries in color vision, emotion and collocation changes. The color understanding of "ink is better than multicolor" mentioned in China's traditional paintings is also highly praised in modern China art circles, so many artists in China seem to have a negative emotion towards color. Looking at the field of interior design, although there is no systematic theoretical guidance for interior color design in China, there are also some research attempts made by researchers, designers and artists. From the perspective of color geography, this paper explores the methods and laws of landscape color design, and obtains a deeper color theory achievement [6]. No matter a designer or an artist, it is inseparable from the continuous practice and understanding of color. As an interior designer, the related practice of color is also a very challenging work and research.

Today, China's indoor color configuration design is mature, but the research on indoor color configuration system is still less. The goal of this paper is to combine theory with practice and design an indoor color configuration system to contribute to creating a more comfortable living environment for residents.

3 research methods

3.1 Hardware Design of Indoor Color Configuration System

3.1.1 Color acquisition module

The basis of indoor color configuration system is color acquisition. In this paper, color sensor is mainly used to design the color acquisition module of the system. This sensor belongs to a digital color light sensor, which can not only accurately collect the chromaticity and illuminance of ambient light, but also have a digital output with 16-bit resolution. The specific parameters are shown in the following table 1:

Table 1. Parameter Table of Color Sensor

project	parameter
output	300kHz
Operating temperature/°C	-10~50
Operating voltage /V	2.1~3.4
encapsulation	CS
pin	GND、VCC、SCL、SDA

When the color sensor senses external light, the external light will be filtered by the infrared blocking filter of the sensor, and useless IR and UV signals will be weakened, thus obtaining visible light, which will enter their respective channels after passing through the RGB and Clear filters of the sensor, thus outputting digital signals [7]. After the color sensor collects the color, it will directly transmit the color data to the main control chip of the system. At this time, the main control chip will process the RGB value of the color and transmit the processed information to the upper computer for display.

3.1.2 RGB-D image acquisition module

The hardware of RGB-D image acquisition module of color configuration system is mainly composed of Kinect devices,which are RGB camera sensors and depth sensors, as shown in Figure 1:

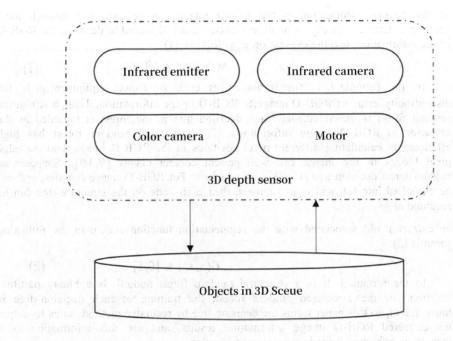

Figure1. overall structural diagram of Kinect equipment

When the RGB-D image acquisition module of the color configuration system acquires the RGB-D image of an object in a 3D scene, the infrared emitter of Kinect equipment willemit infrared light, which will be reflected on the surface of the object, thus forming laser speckle, including object pattern information, and then the infrared camera will capture the reflected infrared light. Because there is a certain displacement between the laser speckle and the baseline of the infrared camera, Therefore, the parallax set of object pixels will be generated, so as to obtain the infrared depth image of the object in the 3D scene. At the same time, the color camera of Kinect equipment will automatically collect the RGB image of the object, and then get the indoor RGB_D image [8]. The resolution of RGB image obtained by Kinect equipment can reach 640×480, and the resolution of infrared depth image can reach 320×240, which can help the color configuration system designed in this paper to have the most direct understanding and cognition of indoor environmental information.

3.2 Software design of indoor color configuration system

3.2.1 RGB-D image information extractionfunction

The characteristic information of RGB-D images can well present the indoor scene characteristics, thus helping the color configuration system to better grasp the indoor scene information. Therefore, this paper has set up the RGB-D image information extraction function in the color configuration system, and here this paper uses the structural forest to extract the outline information of RGB-D images. Each pixel on the RGB-D image not only contains color information, but also reflects the three-dimensional coordinate information of the indoor scene, so the contour information of the RGBD image can be extracted through local geometric features. Firstly, a nonlinear noise model M isused to describe the RGB-D image information, and the expression is as follows (1):

$$M = |Y_0| \in D^2|Y_1| \tag{1}$$

In the formula,γ_0 Is the measurement error of Kinect equipment;γ_1 Is the discontinuity error of RGB-D image;D RGB-D image information. Then, a structured random forest is generated, and each decision tree in the forest is regarded as the extractor of RGB-D image information. The structured random forest has high efficiency in calculating different pixel positions in the RGB-D image, and the edge pixel blocks in the image can well present contour details [9,10]. Suppose the random forest decision tree is s(x), in which x For RGB-D image samples, and can be classified into left and right subtrees, then each node on the structure tree can be regarded as

an extractor and associated with the segmentation function shown in the following formula (2):

$$G(x, s_i) \in \{0,1\} \tag{2}$$

In the formula,i It is a structural random forest node;G Is a binary partition function. In the structured random forest, the training of each decision tree is independent, so this paper trains the decision tree by recursive method, so as to output the extracted RGB-D image information results, and use this information as a theoretical reference for indoor color configuration.

3.2.2 Indoor color configurationfunction

Indoor color configuration function is the key function of the system designed in this paper, which needs to be realized on the basis of strictly following the corresponding rules. Firstly, the extracted RGBD image information and the collected color information are quantized to reduce the difficulty of configuration, and a reasonable color configuration table is constructed according to the quantization results [11]. On the basis of the color table, the indoor color configuration is realized according to the following process: firstly, the RGB-D image color is divided by the median splitting method to find the smallest color value among all colors in the image, and the color dimension components of all pixels of the image are sorted according to the color values, and the indoor colors are configured according to the component order, and soon until the color configuration of all indoor space areas is completed; Then set a standard RGBD image color template, which is mainly used to compare the difference between indoor color configuration and template, and obtain the average and variance of RGB-D image color by threshold method, as shown in the following formula (3):

$$C = \mu \cdot \left(\frac{S}{N}\right) \tag{3}$$

In the formula,C Is the standard RGB-D image color; Is the difference factor of standard RGB-D image color; Configure an offset index for the best color;NIs the number of colors that meet the configuration conditions [12]. Then statistically average the color average calculated by Formula (3) and the pixel value of RGBD image, and take the result as the standard color configuration template. Finally, referring to the RGB-D image color configuration template, the indoor space color is configured. Considering the configuration accuracy and configuration speed, this paper designs a system to obtain the color difference between them through visual communication technology, and the expression is shown in the following formula (4):

$$T = \sum C \otimes \frac{\alpha}{\beta} \qquad (4)$$

In the formula,T An indoor space with colors to be configured;c Is the color to be configured; To configure the chromatic aberration of the color. According to Formula (4), after determining that there is no obvious difference between the color configuration of the actual indoor space and the RGB-D image color configuration template, define the indoor color configuration style and record the configuration results.

4 Result analysis

4.1 Example application

In this paper, a residential district is taken as the design object, and its color configuration is designed by using this system. The whole district has 12 buildings and 1200 rooms, and this time only one room is used for color configuration.

This paper will evaluate and analyze the color scheme, so as to judge whether the system designed in this paper is feasible. The evaluation of color scheme is mainly carried out in the form of experiments, and the seven - level Likert scale is used as the evaluation questionnaire of color scheme [13,14].

The indoor color scheme designed by the system is displayed on the computer, and 20 owners are invited to watch and score the color scheme by using the questionnaire in the table. At the same time, the 20 owners were shown the color scheme designed by professional designers, and the questionnaire was also used for scoring. After collecting all the questionnaires, use SPSS software to analyze the questionnaire evaluation results, and the analysis method is Friedman test, as shown in the following formula (5):

$$F^2 = \frac{12}{nm(m+1)} \sum H_i^2 - 3n(m+1) \qquad (5)$$

In the formula,F^2For Friedman's two-way rank variance;n In order to evaluate the number of observations in the questionnaire;m To evaluate the number of questionnaires; H_i Weidi i Rank sum of three evaluation questionnaires. After calculating the statistics of the evaluation questionnaire according to the above formula, the output results of seven groups of semantic phrases in SPSS software are shown in Table 2:

Table 2. Evaluation Results of Color Configuration Scheme

Word meaning phrase	F^2
Open-narrow	5.34
Urgency-slowness	6.03
Hot-cold	7.11
Easy-heavy	5.39
Kindness-alienation	6.18

Excitement-calmness	5.99
Bright-dim	6.13

according toF^2The distribution table shows that when the significance level is 0.05. When the degree of freedom is 2,F^2The critical value of is 5.89, and the values of each semantic phrase in the evaluation results of color scheme obtained in the above table areF^2Both of them are greater than the critical value, which shows that there is no obvious difference between the color perception brought by the color configuration scheme designed by this system and the color perception brought by the color configuration scheme designed by professional designers, which further verifies the feasibility of the system designed in this paper, and the system can provide color configuration schemes that meet the needs of users.

4.2 Research object of dominant color in interior design

In the choice of research objects, it can't coverall interior designers or design institutions at home and abroad. The reference for the choice of research objects comes from the number of Baidu search results, so if these conclusions are taken as the research basis, it will be insufficient. At the sametime, due to time and geographical constraints, it is impossible to collect color information directly from interior design cases, which will have a certain impact on the objectivity of the research results of leading colors in interior design. Because there is almost no information about the dominant color in interior design at home and abroad, the research on the dominant color in interior design in China is not only in the exploratory stage, and there are also a few designers and scholars who think that the dominant color does not exist at all. Therefore, in the choice of research objects, in addition to considering the quantitative factors of Baidu search results, we should try our best to choose the design works of representative interior designers and design institutions that are familiar to the industry [15,16].

4.2.1 Liang Zhitian Interior Design Case Analysis

Liang Zhitian, one of the top ten designers in Hong Kong, founded Liang Zhitian Architects Co., Ltd. and Liang Zhitian Design Co., Ltd. in 1997 [17]. Through the collection and analysis of RGB data of Liang Zhitian design cases, we can get the pie chart of "RGB numerical analysis of color sampling in Liang Zhitian interior design cases" and "percentage of RGB average value of color sampling in Liang Zhitian interior design cases" (see Figure 2). After rounding, the average values of RGB values in design cases are R (red) 124,G (green) 96,B and B (blue) 70. According to the principle of RGB color mode, red, green and blue Three Lamps District lights are superimposed on each other, and the colors are mixed. When the value of one light is greater than the other two lights, the color mixing result will be biased towards the color tone with the largest value. According to the above RGB data and charts, the average value of RGB values in Liang Zhitian design case tends to warm color.

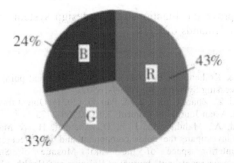

Figure 2. Percentage of RGB average value of color sampling in Liang Zhitian interior design case

4.2.2 Gao Wenan Interior Design Case Analysis

GaoWenan, a senior interior designer in Hong Kong, is known as the father of interior design in Hong Kong and won the Lifetime Achievement Award of the Hong Kong Interior Design Association. Through the collection and analysis of RGB data of GaoWenan design cases, we can get the corresponding pie chart of "RGB numerical analysis of color sampling of Gao Wenan interior design cases" and "percentage of RGB average value of color sampling of Gao Wenan interior design cases" (see Figure 3). After rounding, the average values of RGB values of design cases are R (red) 132,G (green) 109,B and B (blue) 92. According to the above RGB data and charts,

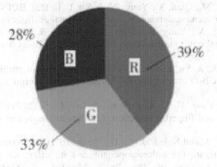

Figure 3. Percentage of RGB average value of color sampling in Gao Wenan interior design case

5 Conclusion

Color allocation in indoor space design is the key factor to create a good environment atmosphere, which can improve the health of residents from two aspects: psychological efficacy and physiological efficacy. Therefore, on the basis of following the human visual characteristics and the principles of indoor color allocation, this paper introduces RGB-D images to design an indoor color allocation system. And the application results of an example show that the system can provide users with a satisfactory indoor color configuration design scheme, and can also provide guidance for the color configuration design of other functional spaces in China. Of course, the design of indoor color configuration is a complicated study. In the future, the author will continue to improve the functions of this design system in combination with the actual psychological demands of users.

References

[1] Yin, T., Zhou, X., & Krähenbühl, P. (2021). Multimodal virtual point 3d detection. Advances in Neural Information Processing Systems, 34, 16494-16507.

[2] Hu, J., Zhang, H., Li, Z., Zhao, C., Xu, Z., & Pan, Q. (2021). Object traversing by monocular UAV in outdoor environment. Asian Journal of Control, 23(6), 2766-2775.

[3] Sadeghi Habibabad, A., MahdiNejad, J. E. D., Azemati, H., & Matracchi, P. (2022). Using neurology sciences to investigate the color component and its effect on promoting the sense of spirituality in the interior space of the Vakil Mosque of Shiraz (using quantitative electroencephalography wave recording). Journal of Religion and Health, 61(3), 2398-2415.

[4] Mahajan, H. B., Uke, N., Pise, P., Shahade, M., Dixit, V. G., Bhavsar, S., & Deshpande, S. D. (2023). Automatic robot Manoeuvres detection using computer vision and deep learning techniques: a perspective of internet of robotics things (IoRT). Multimedia Tools and Applications, 82(15), 23251-23276.

[5] Berrio, J. S., Shan, M., Worrall, S., & Nebot, E. (2021). Camera-LIDAR integration: Probabilistic sensor fusion for semantic mapping. IEEE Transactions on Intelligent Transportation Systems, 23(7), 7637-7652.

[6] AbdelRaouf, A. (2021). A new data hiding approach for image steganography based on visual color sensitivity. Multimedia Tools and Applications, 80(15), 23393-23417.

[7] Chen, Y., Wang, L., Galloway, K., Godage, I., Simaan, N., & Barth, E. (2021). Modal-based kinematics and contact detection of soft robots. Soft Robotics, 8(3), 298-309.

[8] Brachmann, E., & Rother, C. (2021). Visual camerare-localization from RGB and RGB-D images using DSAC. IEEE transactions on pattern analysis and machine intelligence, 44(9), 5847-5865.

[9] Zhou, W., Zhu, Y., Lei, J., Wan, J., & Yu, L. (2021). CCAFNet: Crossflow and cross-scale adaptive fusion network for detecting salient objects in RGB-D images. IEEE Transactions on Multimedia, 24, 2192-2204.

[10] Zhou, W., Yue, Y., Fang, M., Qian, X., Yang, R., & Yu, L. (2023). BCINet: Bilateral cross-modal interaction network for indoor scene understanding in RGB-D images. Information Fusion, 94, 32-42.

[11] Yu, L., Xiong, J., Fang, X., Yang, Z., Chen, Y., Lin, X., & Chen, S. (2021). A litchi fruit recognition method in a natural environment using RGB-D images. Biosystems Engineering, 204, 50-63.

[12] Zhou, W., Pan, S., Lei, J., & Yu, L. (2021). TMFNet: Three-input multilevel fusion network for detecting salient objects in RGB-D images. IEEE Transactions on Emerging Topics in Computational Intelligence, 6(3), 593-601.

[13] Tran, D. S., Ho, N. H., Yang, H. J., Kim, S. H., & Lee, G. S. (2021). Real-time virtual mouse system using RGB-D images and fingertip detection. Multimedia Tools and Applications, 80, 10473-10490.

[14] Sadeghi Habibabad, A., MahdiNejad, J. E. D., Azemati, H., & Matracchi, P. (2022). Using neurology sciences to investigate the colorcomponent and its effect on promoting the sense of spirituality in the interior space of the Vakil Mosque of Shiraz (using quantitative electroencephalography wave recording). Journal of Religion and Health, 61(3), 2398-2415.

[15] Ghasemian Dastjerdi, P. (2023). The Psychological Effect of Color on Fashion and Interior Decoration (Case study: Pantone's Color of the Year). Journal of Studies in Color World, 13(2), 201-213.

[16] Laksitarini, N. (2021). INFLUENCE OF COLOR ON INTERIOR ELEMENTS CHILD-FRIENDLY DENTAL CLINIC ON THE PSYCHOLOGY OF VISITORS. Jurnal PATRA, 3(1), 48-52.

[17] Saidjon, Q., & Bakhrom, U. (2021). The Influence Of Interior Psychology On Uzbek Architecture. The American Journal of Interdisciplinary Innovations and Research, 3(06), 31-35.

[18] McGee, B., & Park, N. K. (2022). Colour, light, and materiality: biophilic interior design presence in research and practice. Interiority, 5(1), 27-52.

[19] Zhang, K. (2021). Research on the Application of Traditional Architectural Decoration Elements in Modern Interior Design. Learning & Education, 9(5), 148-149.

[20] Pishva, A., & Kianersi, M. (2023). Physical and Functional Changes in the Interior Design of. Journal of Fine Arts: Performing Arts & Music, 28(1), 13-29.

Design Studies and Intelligence Engineering
L.C. Jain et al. (Eds.)
© 2024 The Authors.
This article is published online with Open Access by IOS Press and distributed under the terms
of the Creative Commons Attribution Non-Commercial License 4.0 (CC BY-NC 4.0).
doi:10.3233/FAIA231507

Artificial Intelligence Driven Promotion of Cultural Heritage Protection in the Context of Harmony Rural Construction

Xiujuan WU[a,b,1]

a Citi University

b School of Art, Hu Zhou University

Abstract: In order to use digital technology to protect intangible cultural heritage and regional culture, the innovative digital design of intangible cultural heritage is put forward from the perspective of Internet. This paper puts forward a collaborative innovative design method of "root carving technology+digitalization". Taking "Zhu Zhanghuis lecture" in Yuelu Academy as the representative, this paper explores the innovative methods of developing scene-based root carving products by regional culture. The results show that the acceptance of using light-cured resin as the accessory of root carving is not high, and the proportion of people in the industry who appreciate or accept it is only 71.3%. Developing the design around the basic model is conducive to improving production efficiency, ensuring the improvement of efficiency while retaining the uniqueness of hand-made. The whole root carving product has a certain artistic conception, and can appreciate the connection with the concept of time, but the specific story can be strengthened. Conclusion: Integrating the situational story method into the root carving design of Hunan School can enhance the overall atmosphere and story of the root carving works, enhance the story of the root carving cultural and creative products of Yuelu Academy, and be conducive to the promotion and dissemination of regional root carving culture and academy culture.

Keywords: root carving; Digitization of intangible heritage; Digital design; collaborative design

1 Introduction

The trend of the combination of culture and industrial manufacturing in China puts forward the actual demand for creative design, that is, to study the common key technologies based on China style, take cultural heritage (especially intangible cultural heritage) as a typical sample, study the cultural ecology, cultural forms and expression methods of Chinas historical development, as well as regional cultural differences and cultural values, comprehensively analyze the design elements of Chinas aesthetic characteristics, construct a framework model of China style, and realize the development of Chinese style design to intelligence and high-end. Intangible cultural heritage preserves national individuality and national aesthetic habits in a "living" state, and contains the unique spiritual value, thinking mode, imagination and cultural consciousness of the Chinese nation, which is the basic basis of Chinas design style and the classic cultural elements and prototype [1]. Because of its intangible, dynamic, spatio-temporal characteristics, the increasing and accelerating globalization and

---

[1] Corresponding Author.

modernization process have led to great changes in domestic cultural ecology, and the protection and development of intangible cultural heritage with sound, image and skills as the means of expression has encountered great challenges. In recent years, through database construction, digital application and big data analysis, digital technology provides a technical platform for the recording, preservation and dissemination of intangible cultural heritage in China, and also provides a new way for the inheritance, innovation and development of intangible cultural heritage. At the same time, many problems still exist, such as: ① the research topics of intangible digital protection are relatively scattered, and there is no scientific protection model for the whole life cycle management of intangible digital information from the overall view of intangible resources; (2) Pay attention to presenting intangible cultural forms, and lack the display of intangible cultural structure and significance to explore the internal mechanism of non-genetic inheritance and innovation; ③ It is difficult to show the vitality of intangible cultural heritage and reflect the cultural creativity of inheritors [2]. In order to inherit and develop intangible cultural heritage, realize the activation and creative utilization of intangible cultural heritage, the concepts of participatory digital protection and productive protection came into being, which supported giving inheritors and owners the right to participate in digital protection, fully exploring the potential social and economic value of intangible cultural resources, and promoting the development of cultural industries through the transformation of creativity, creativity and innovation [3].

2 Literature review

Due to historical reasons in Italy, many intangible cultural heritages are scattered in private and church hands, which leads to many difficulties in practical protection. In order to solve this problem, Xu, Z. and others set up a society to manage and strengthen the sharing of these resources. The main work is registration, sorting and other control work, which makes further protection more convenient. For example, the "Internet Cultural Heritage Project" was established to provide people with resources that can be queried online. The system can integrate the resources of libraries and other related cultural institutions, and facilitate people and other institutions to obtain digital resources of intangible cultural heritage through online platforms and other channels [4].

The digital protection of French intangible cultural heritage in its national library has developed well. In 2003, the digital project Gallica completed the historical introduction of thousands of illustrations and related documents, nearly 10 million books and hundreds of thousands of still images. Kró l, K. and others started "Digitization of Cultural, Scientific and Educational Contents", which belongs to the project of "Investing in the Future" and planned digital cultural skills, mainly in the fields of books, music and images [5].

The research on intangible cultural heritage in China started late, starting in 2003, when the UNESCO Committee of the National Peoples Congress drafted the Draft Law on the Protection of Traditional Ethnic and Folk Cultures in Peoples Republic of China (PRC), which was later renamed the Law on the Protection of Intangible Cultural Heritage in Peoples Republic of China (PRC) (draft). In 2004, China became the sixth country to join the Convention for the Protection of Intangible Cultural Heritage, and it was not until recently in 2011 that the Peoples Republic of China (PRC) Intangible Cultural Heritage Law was formally implemented. As people pay more and more attention to intangible cultural heritage, relevant theoretical works on intangible cultural heritage are also emerging one after another. Xie, R. and others have expressed their opinions. For example, The Paradox and New Path of the Protection of Intangible Cultural Heritage, The Origin, Current Situation and Related Issues of the Concept of Intangible Cultural Heritage, and Intangible Cultural Heritage Towards the Concept of Discipline have all sorted out and understood the definition and concept of intangible cultural heritage. For example, Protection and Utilization of Intangible Cultural Heritage, Re-understanding of the Characteristics and Protection of Intangible Cultural Heritage have made their own interpretations on how to protect intangible heritage [6]. The research on intangible cultural heritage abroad started earlier than that in China. Nikolakopoulou, V. and others first put forward the concept of "intangible cultural wealth" and promulgated the Law on the Protection of Cultural Property to define its category [7]. Cui, C. and others also promulgated relevant laws in 1962 to regulate their countrys cultural property. It was not until the adoption of the Convention for the Protection of the World Cultural and Natural Heritage in 1972 that the worldwide protection activities officially began. In this Convention, the proposal on intangible cultural heritage was put forward for the first time. Although the proposal was rejected at that time, with the development of time, the concept of intangible cultural heritage was put forward and put on the agenda again with the attention of relevant government departments. It was not until 2003 that UNESCO promulgated and adopted the Convention for the Protection of Intangible Cultural Heritage, in which the connotation of intangible cultural heritage was clearly defined [8].

The main purposes of this product survey are: to understand the acceptance of "Zhu Zhang Zhi Hui" in the root carving industry; Discover the shortcomings of the product; Find the part with high user recognition and analyze the competitive advantage of the product. In this digital scene root carving design, the design method is quite different from traditional root carving products, and there is some innovation in the application of materials with scene root carving products. It is very important to investigate the market acceptance of innovative products.

3 Research methods

3.1 sketch design

Sketch is a key link in the initial stage of design, and it is an informal form used to describe the general idea of design. Based on the investigation, analysis and derivation process mentioned above, the project team will fully imagine and associate with the user perception model and product positioning, and complete the preliminary modeling design of root carving products with full conceptual sketch design.

3.1.1 Concept sketch scheme

In the design process, the design requirements are often put forward in the form of keyword description and oral communication, or by collecting excellent similar designs to form an image version [9]. Designers need to use fragmented information and elements to guide the direction of subsequent design, and at the same time, they need to decompose and integrate the fragmented information elements semantically to form a complete design scheme.

The purpose of conceptual sketch scheme design is twofold. First, the important innovation of this root carving design is the application and integration of resin materials, which need to be integrated in conceptual design [10]. Secondly, the focus of the scene-based root carving is to make the theme of the story clear, and the conceptual design should be carried out under the principle of ensuring cultural identity and recognition, reflecting the core spirit of Zhu Zhanghuis speech. There are two basic types of root carving suitable for the theme of Zhu Zhanghuis lecture: ring type and tree type. It is necessary to complete the conceptual modeling design by constantly updating, iterating and trying the sketches around the two basic types and related design elements.

The design elements mainly focus on the relevant intention extraction of Zhu Zhanghui. In the story told by Zhu Zhanghui, in the category of humanistic elements, there are two people, Zhu Zhanger and the audience, and the architectural elements include lecture hall and Hexi platform. There are many text elements in inscriptions and poems. Among the natural elements, there are ginkgo leaves in the autumn of Yuelu Mountain, which contain the meaning of time and study; There is Ziyang Cinnamomum camphora planted by Zhu Xi for Meiji learning ambition; White horses led by people who drink horses [11,12]. By following the above design principles and using elements reasonably, we can design related scene root carving products around the story.

According to the images related to Zhu Zhanghuis lecture, the relevant elements were extracted and iterated, and three preliminary conceptual sketch schemes were formed through the design of elements and root carvings.

Conceptual sketch scheme 1 mainly revolves around the concept of "applying the practice". This design hopes to integrate the concept of "thousand-year inheritance and applying the practice" mentioned by Zhu Zhanghui into the works, which tells the story of the Millennium changes of an academy after Zhu Zhanghuis speech. The basic form of the whole modeling uses a ring shape, hoping to create an atmosphere that crosses just visiting. Looking back at the past years through the traces of old trees, after thousands of years, the spirit will last forever [13]. The works mainly embody three elements, namely, Ginkgo biloba, Ziyang camphor and Zhu Zhang, all of which are associated with the event of "Zhu Zhang will speak".

The second concept sketch scheme is to reproduce the core scenes of speaking. This scheme takes Zhu and Zhang as the core design elements, adds simplified elements that can reflect the school scenes, uses tree-shaped modeling as the basic form, and restores the speaking scenes with minimalist language. I hope to restore the scene told by Zhu Zhanghui simply and directly. The past events turned white and remained in my memory, and the old trees at that time stood here and made people forget history.

The inspiration of the concept sketch scheme 3 is the influence on the generations of the academy after the lecture. This scheme hopes to depict the passage of time after Zhu Zhanghuis lecture in a more subtle way, but the spirit of the lecture will last forever. The white horse symbolizes that time passes like a white horse, and it is also the unprecedented grand occasion of drinking horse pond in front of the academy when Zhu Zhanghui speaks.

3.1.2 Concept sketch scheme evaluation

After the above conceptual sketches were evaluated and reviewed by the project team, the first creative scheme was finally chosen, that is, the design around the concept of "practical application".

The members of the project team believe that the design of the first scheme can intuitively express the theme of Zhu Zhanghui, and the elements used are also familiar to the target audience. The whole scene has a certain sense of time travel, the composition is more creative than the second scheme, and the story is more clear than the third scheme. Although the story of the second scheme is clear, the overall design language is too straightforward, and the craftsmanship of the root carving part is not as good as other schemes. The overall artistic conception of the third scheme is good, but the white pony is used to show the grand occasion of many horse drinkers when Zhu Zhanghui speaks, and it implies the concept of time passing, which has certain connotation, but the story is obscure, which does not highlight the advantages of situational root carving in telling stories, and the story is too weak for readers to watch. To sum up, the first concept is the design direction of this root carving design.

Deepen the connotation and form design of the elements in Scheme 1, and the specific meanings of the elements used are:

1. Ginkgo biloba in the Academy: When Zhu Zhanghui talked about it, it was in the autumn of Lushan, and ginkgo was in full bloom. At the same time, Ginkgo biloba means "eternal", and it is an eternal witness when the essence of traditional culture is scattered and passed down from generation to generation [14].

2. Ziyang camphor tree: Zhu Xi planted a camphor tree behind the school after Zhu Zhanghuis lecture. After thousands of years, it has become a towering tree. It happens that this material is a hollow old camphor tree. Both of them have the meaning of growth, development and inheritance. The material and story are very appropriate. Moreover, Zhu Xi once planted camphor trees in his hometown and became famous. The element of camphor trees bears Zhu Xis spirit of constantly pursuing and surpassing himself in academics, and it is also a response to his parents expectations, which is integrated with the spirit of an academy in a Millennium university.

3. Zhu and Zhang: Zhu and Zhang are the soul figures of this story and the founders of the academys thousand -year history. Characters are the core part of the scene root carving, so it is necessary to restore the posture that Zhu and Zhang can speak as much as possible.

Through the deepening process of element connotation and form design, the preliminary design scheme is obtained. The elements used are Ginkgo biloba leaves, Zhu Zhang and Ziyang Cinnamomum camphora in an academy, and the root carving style adopted is ring-shaped.

3.2 root carving renderings design

Rendering design is a common design display method in the early stage of design, which can transform conceptual design into concrete and visible visual expression and help designers express and spread their own design ideas. The ultimate goal of renderings design is to transform the conceptual design into the final product according to the realization of renderings [15]. The cost of trial and error can be effectively reduced by designing the renderings for root carving products. According to the evaluation results of the conceptual sketch scheme, the project team took the deepened design scheme as the prototype and designed the renderings after shooting the physical drawings of the root wood. The environment of the renderings is set in a scene that reflects certain soothing emotions, and the overall color is warm, highlighting the wooden texture and natural softness of root carving products.

3.2 Digital model design of root carving

According to the design of the sketch of the creative idea, the selected ring root material is measured to facilitate the fitting of the size and proportion in the subsequent application of related elements. The production of 3D digital model will be divided into two parts, which are modeled and rendered by digital technology on the computer respectively.

Image source: The first part of the authors self -drawing is the rough root mould showing the overall product space structure, and the rough root mould is modeled on the computer with C4D software. The main purpose of making a rough heel model is to facilitate the subsequent adjustment of the proportion, collocation and size of different elements, and to find the most suitable spatial structure of the root carving product.

The second part is to make printable models of some characters or elements and integrate them into the scene root carving products as innovative elements in the root carving products. The model that can be printed is different from the rough model, so it needs to be made into a high-precision model, which is called high-precision model for short. The model must be a complete solid model with wall thickness, and the accuracy requirement is relatively high. There are three elements involved in the work: Zhu and Zhang, Ginkgo biloba in the Academy and Cinnamomum camphora in Ziyang. In this innovative design method, the resin material model is combined with root carving products, and the rough model of the above three elements in the material library of an academy built in the previous article can be used, and then further fine-tuning and adaptation can be carried out. Among them, Zhu Zhang and Xueyuan Ginkgo need to print, so they need to make a high mold. Ziyang Cinnamomum camphora is realized by traditional carving, and the final effect is uncertain with the materials. Therefore, the model only needs to be used to make the overall effect diagram of the product, because it needs to be refined and modified on the basis of the rough mold in the material library.

The combination and construction of ginkgo leaves were carried out. Firstly, the preliminary modeling is completed by C4D software. Because of the need for 3D printing in the future, it is necessary to refine the model to ensure that the ginkgo leaf is a model with solid and wall thickness, and the thickness should not be too thin. Secondly, because the leaves have a certain thickness, they need to be combined and deleted on the computer in advance, and the shape needs to be matched reasonably. After many combinations and adjustments, the design of the whole ginkgo leaf shape has been completed [16]. Finally, because the Ginkgo biloba leaves are thin and small in size, there is no need to hollow out the model, and after the combination of the models, you can wait for the subsequent printing and effect presentation.

The rough models of Zhu and Zhang were extracted from the material database of the project team, and the model was modeled by reverse engineering in the preliminary research of the "Virtual Academy" project. After model refinement, reduction and combination adjustment, and hollowing out, the model design of Zhu and Zhang was completed. Finally, the rough model of root material modeling is combined with the model of material, and the three-dimensional structure effect of the whole scheme is obtained.

3.3 Product physical display

After the completion of the work, the product display map is photographed, and the whole photographic environment conforms to the characteristics of the product. The key words of product positioning are soothing, culture, creativity, Zen, academy stories, wood and so on. As a whole, a warm yellow tone is adopted, and traditional cultures such as root carving products and tea culture can be well integrated, and integrated with the whole environment of log tone, creating a peaceful and quiet Zen.

3.4 Dynamic interactive display process

After the design of dynamic interactive program is completed, the pictures and model materials that need to be used should be integrated to present better visual effects. The key words of product positioning are soothing, culture, creativity, Zen, academy stories, wood, etc. Combined with the final effect of product positioning, the warm yellow color tone is adopted in the design of the whole interactive process, and the photographed product physical map is put into the environmental effect map which conforms to the characteristics of the product. In the process of interaction, we should add some dynamic graphic display elements in visual design. Through the addition of dynamic graphics, the positioning of root carving products can be strengthened, giving the whole quiet, warm and soothing mood, so as to enhance the emotional experience of users. In terms of interaction, the function needs to be as simple as possible, mainly showing the appearance and function of the product clearly. Based on the above analysis, it is designed that the "Zhu Zhang Zhi Hui" dynamic interaction is the emotional version of visual design.

Combining the product positioning of "Zhu Zhang Zhi Hui" with the users use scene, the background picture of the scene used in this dynamic interactive exhibition and the decorative elements used are made in photoshop software through partial shooting and partial drawing.

The static frame of the dynamic interaction process finally output by the computer display program is divided into the following processes:

1. After loading, enter the cover page and click the "Learn More" button to enter the subsequent physical display section.

2. The user is prompted with the function of the products incense burner by words, and the user moves the sandalwood on the desktop to the incense mouth at the top of the root carving product and lights the backflow sandalwood.

3. After the user lights sandalwood, the smoke slowly floats out with time.

4. Smoke wafts out and gradually becomes rich. At this time, users can view the three-dimensional model of the product from multiple angles through text prompts, and users can enter the viewing screen of the three-dimensional model by rotating the model.

5. After entering the model display screen, the user can rotate and watch the 3D model within a limited angle by zooming in, zooming out and rotating. After 10 seconds, the prompt button "Return to Home Page" appears.

Through this dynamic display process, users can appreciate the details of the product, and at the same time, they can understand the product functions more intuitively and feel the usage scene of the product.

4 Result analysis

4.1 User feedback survey

4.1.1 User product feedback

The main positioning of this product is nature, Zen and leisure, and the user groups are mainly tourists, traditional culture lovers and root carving product lovers. According to the theory of usability testing, it takes 15 test users to find out all the existing problems in the product testing. According to this theory, 15 young tourists, fans of Hanfu, Chinese studies and tea culture were invited as typical representatives of user groups to experience products and interactive programs.

The users experience process is divided into two parts, the first part is the experience of interactive programs, and the second part is the evaluation and suggestion of the final works. Summarize the suggestions given by users as follows:

1. Some details of digital sculpture design are not enough, and the reduction degree of characters can be further improved. As a root carving product, there are few hand-carved parts, so the craftsmanship of the details can be stronger [17].

2. In the animation part of the function demonstration, the incense is put into the incense mouth and automatically ignited, which can increase the link of users own ignition, and design the matching ignition tool to improve the whole experience process.

3. The operation of the interactive program is slightly stuck, which is not smooth and natural enough, and the smoke effect produced in the animation is not realistic

enough, which affects the overall atmosphere and sense of substitution. Collect and sort out the feedback data of 15 users, and get the user feedback table in Figure 1.

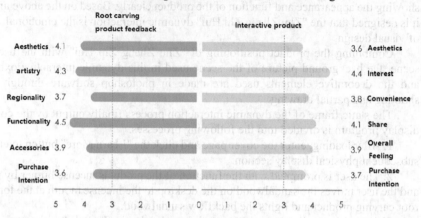

Figure 1. User experience feedback

4.1.2 Root carving industry feedback survey

At the same time of design innovation, it may cause destructive innovation, and it is impossible to gain the sense of identity of specific culture-related enthusiasts, practitioners and inheritors. The attitude of craftsmen towards technical intervention and the sense of innovation are an important part of the collaborative innovation process of handicrafts and digital technology [18]. In the design of root carving products in this innovative scene, the materials and design flow are quite different from other root carving products, and there will be many new performances in the final presentation effect. Therefore, it is necessary to visit people in the root carving industry for evaluation and suggestions for subsequent improvement and creation.

Use questionnaires and face-to-face interviews to conduct a comprehensive return visit survey. Firstly, in the form of questionnaire, a survey questionnaire was distributed to 80 root carving craftsmen, root carving market merchants and root carving collectors, with a recovery rate of 100% and an effective rate of 100%. Because of the innovative application of resin materials in this paper, the acceptance of traditional root carving art practitioners is highly uncertain, so it is evaluated and the acceptance table of resin/nylon and other 3D printing materials by root carving industry practitioners is obtained [19]. Synthesize the contents of other investigations related to this root carving product, sort out and analyze the data, and get the basic identification degree, artistic evaluation, commodity evaluation and other data of this product as shown in Table 1. Evaluation scoreS_iCalculate according to the following formula (1):

$$S_i = \frac{\sum_{i=1}^{80} s_i}{80 \times 5} \tag{1}$$

Among them,s_iRepresents the score of an evaluation index. According to the results, several practitioners with very different views were selected for further follow-up interviews. The representative evaluations and suggestions obtained are as follows:

Table 1. Feedback data of root carving industry insiders on "Zhu Zhangzhihui"

evaluating indicator	score
Aesthetics	4.1
artistry	4.0
territoriality	3.6
functionality	4.2

Fitting acceptance	3.7
buying inclination	3.4

1. The acceptance of using light-cured resin as the accessory of root carving is not high, and the proportion of people in the industry who appreciate or accept it is only 71.3%. The insiders suggest that this accessory can be made into a detachable part or an alternative scheme of ceramic parts can be provided to provide users with more choices, which should get better feedback from the root carving market.

2. Developing the design around the basic pattern is beneficial to improve the production efficiency, and the requirements for the skill threshold of craftsmen are lower, but the artistry is also reduced. In the application of elements in a single part, more design schemes should be provided according to the different details of root materials, and the adjustable range should be expanded to ensure the improvement of efficiency while retaining the uniqueness of hand-made.

3. The whole root carving product has a certain artistic conception, and can realize the connection with the concept of time, but the specific story can be strengthened.

4.2 Outlook: "Handicraft+Digitalization" Collaborative Innovation to Build a Regional Cultural Ecology

The so-called regional cultural ecology is a system that integrates many internal and external factors that constitute the regional cultural system and the interaction between them. The value of studying and constructing regional cultural ecology lies in that the intangible cultural heritage can be developed and passed down naturally and healthily through production and lifestyle, which is more dynamic and open than the independent inheritance of culture. Therefore, constructing regional cultural ecology is an effective method to revitalize regional culture at present [20].

Through the mode shown in Figure 2 below, handicrafts and digitalization work together to build a regional cultural ecology. In this collaborative innovation process, handicrafts and digital technology depend on each other, handicrafts can provide value support and cultural support for digital technology, and digital technology can enhance the execution of traditional handicrafts, and innovation and scientific and technological strength complement each other and innovate together.

Taking the root carving in Hunan as an example, digital technology has been incorporated into the traditional technological process, and the communication efficiency in the design demand stage can be improved by quickly drawing conceptual sketches; Through real-time collaborative design, the direction of the conception and deepening stage is ensured to be accurate, and the cost in the modification process is correspondingly reduced; Through digital technology, the types of root carving materials, artistic forms and display methods are improved in the design and implementation stage.

In the future development, through the similar collaborative innovation design method of "handicraft+digitalization" in this paper, digital technology can be more deeply involved in the design and production process of handicrafts, further enrich and improve the cultural ecological construction of different regional cultures, attract more human and material resources to invest in it, produce a more perfect design and production process, and produce more products with the unique ingenuity of traditional handicrafts and the aesthetic and value orientation of modern people.

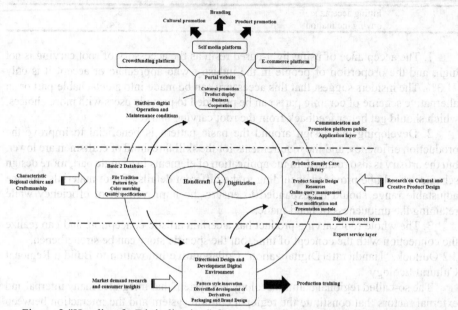

Figure 2 "Handicraft+Digitalization" Co-constructing Regional Cultural Ecology

5 Conclusion

(1) "Handicraft+Digitalization" collaborative innovation design

This paper summarizes the problems existing in the current root carving industry, analyzes the feasibility and advantages of digital design involved in root carving product design, and puts forward the method of "root carving technology+digitalization" to jointly build the regional cultural ecology of Huxiang. Taking "Zhu Zhanghuis lecture" in an academy as a representative, this paper explores the innovative methods of developing scene-based root carving products in Huxiang regional culture. At the same time, three-dimensional printing products are innovatively added to the root carving design, which enriches the expression forms of products.

(2) The situational story method is applied to the root carving design of an academy.

Integrating the situational story method into the root carving design of an academy enhances the overall atmosphere and story of the root carving works, which can enhance the story of the root carving cultural and creative products of an academy and provide reference for the development of other products. At the same time, the style of root carving in Hunan is used in the products, which is conducive to the promotion and dissemination of root carving culture in Hunan and the culture of an academy.

(3) Study on the basic type of root carving.

Through market visits and online surveys, the characteristics of root wood suitable for the scene were found, the characteristics of several basic types were summarized, and the method of integrating design elements and product functions into the basic types was put forward to ensure the batch production of root carving products while maintaining the ingenuity and natural beauty.

(4) Interactive program design for handicraft exhibition.

The dynamic interactive display design of handicraft product function and shape is carried out, and the interactive program is built by TouchDesigner. Through the dynamic display process, users can appreciate the details of handicraft products, and at the same time, they can understand the product functions more intuitively and feel the usage scene of the products.

References

[1]   Hou, Y., Kenderdine, S., Picca, D., Egloff, M., & Adamou, A. (2022). Digitizing intangible cultural heritage embodied: State of the art. *Journal on Computing and Cultural Heritage (JOCCH)*, *15*(3), 1-20.

[2]   Yue, M., Wang, G., & Li, Z. (2022). The Digital Protection and Inheritance of Intangible Cultural Heritage:--Taking the Qing Dynasty horse-face skirt as an Example. *Highlights in Art and Design*, *1*(3), 83-87.

[3]   Liu, Y. (2022). Application of digital technology in intangible cultural heritage protection. *Mobile Information Systems*, *2022*, 1-8.

[4]   Xu, Z., & Zou, D. (2022). Big data analysis research on the deep integration of intangible cultural heritage inheritance and art design education in colleges and universities. *Mobile Information Systems*, *2022*, 1-12.

[5]   Król, K. (2021). Digital cultural heritage of rural tourism facilities in Poland. *Journal of Cultural Heritage Management and Sustainable Development*, *11*(4), 488-498.

[6]   Xie, R. (2021). Intangible cultural heritage high-definition digital mobile display technology based on vr virtual visualization. *Mobile Information Systems*, *2021*, 1-11.

[7]   Nikolakopoulou, V., Printezis, P., Maniatis, V., Kontizas, D., Vosinakis, S., Chatzigrigoriou, P., & Koutsabasis, P. (2022). Conveying Intangible Cultural Heritage in Museums with Interactive Storytelling and Projection Mapping: The Case of the Mastic Villages. *Heritage*, *5*(2), 1024-1049.

[8]   Cui, C., Zhao, Y., & Wang, L. (2021). Protection and dissemination of Chinese intangible cultural heritage based on digital games. *International Communication of Chinese Culture*, *8*, 483-491.

[9]   Chatzigrigoriou, P., Nikolakopoulou, V., Vakkas, T., Vosinakis, S., & Koutsabasis, P. (2021). Is architecture connected with intangible cultural heritage? reflections from architectural digital documentation and interactive application design in three aegean islands. *Heritage*, *4*(2), 664-689.

[10]   Aljaberi, S. M., & Al-Ogaili, A. S. (2021). Integration of cultural digital form and material carrier form of traditional handicraft intangible cultural heritage. *vol*, *5*, 21-30.

[11]   Turillazzi, B., Leoni, G., Gaspari, J., Massari, M., & Boulanger, S. O. M. (2021). Cultural heritage and digital tools: The ROCK interoperable platform. *International Journal of Environmental Impacts*, *4*(3), 276-288.

[12]   Skublewska-Paszkowska, M., Milosz, M., Powroznik, P., & Lukasik, E. (2022). 3D technologies for intangible cultural heritage preservation—literature review for selected databases. *Heritage Science*, *10*(1), 1-24.

[13]   Wu, C., & Wu, X. (2021). The Art-Craft Boundary in Contemporary Central China: The Case of Root Carving. The Journal of Modern Craft, 14(2), 141-154.

[14]   Wang, B. (2021). Digital design of smart museum based on artificial intelligence. Mobile Information Systems, 2021, 1-13.

[15]   Meron, Y. (2021). Terminology and design capital: examining the pedagogic status of graphic design through its practitioners' perceptions of their job titles. International Journal of Art & Design Education, 40(2), 374-388.

[16]   Huda, A., Azhar, N., Almasri, A., Wulansari, R. E., Mubai, A., Sakti, R. H., ... & Hartanto, S. (2021). Augmented Reality Technology as a Complement on Graphic Design to Face Revolution Industry 4.0 Learning and Competence: The Development and Validity. Int. J. Interact. Mob. Technol., 15(5), 116-126.

[17]   Chen, L., Tong, T. W., Tang, S., & Han, N. (2022). Governance and design of digital platforms: A review and future research directions on a meta-organization. Journal of Management, 48(1), 147-184.

[18]   Marion, T. J., & Fixson, S. K. (2021). The transformation of the innovation process: How digital tools are changing work, collaboration, and organizations in new product development. Journal of Product Innovation Management, 38(1), 192-215.

[19]   Zhang, Y., Meina, A., Lin, X., Zhang, K., & Xu, Z. (2021). Digital twin in computational design and robotic construction of wooden architecture. Advances in Civil Engineering, 2021, 1-14.

[20]   Ng, M. S., Graser, K., & Hall, D. M. (2023). Digital fabrication, BIM and early contractor involvement in design in construction projects: A comparative case study. Architectural Engineering and Design Management, 19(1), 39-55.

Design Studies and Intelligence Engineering
L.C. Jain et al. (Eds.)
© *2024 The Authors.*
This article is published online with Open Access by IOS Press and distributed under the terms
of the Creative Commons Attribution Non-Commercial License 4.0 (CC BY-NC 4.0).
doi:10.3233/FAIA231508

A New Bio-Inspired Tool for Visual Design: A Cognitive Protocol Analysis

Yiwen WANG[a], Nannan LI [a], and Biao LI [a]
[a]*Dalian Polytechnic University*

Abstract. Designers are always looking for inspiration. Many disciplines use inspiration from nature to create something new, a practice often referred to as " bio-inspired bio-inspired ". Biology-inspired design has been widely applied and studied in engineering, architecture, products and many other disciplines, but in the field of visual design, although there are some works but few research. This article through the review of existing literature on bio-inspired design thinking, and bio-inspired interdisciplinary design development and trend of bio-inspired design in the future, in order to investigate the existing bio-inspired design tools whether can fit for visual designers, and provides a new tool for visual designers and students develop their creative development space.

Keywords. Bio-inspired, analogies, designer's toolkit, visual communication design, inspiration

1. Introduction

Bio-inspired has been widely applied into engineering, architecture, products and other fields (Vattam et al., 2010; Cheong et al., 2010; Volstad & Boks, 2012; Fu et al., 2014; Badarnaha, 2015; Al-Obaidi, 2017). Generally, biologists lack knowledge of design and engineering, while engineers and designers are laymen of biology. Thus, connecting the interdisciplinary knowledge transfer, communication and creation becomes the key that should be considered in the field of bio-inspired thinking (Vattam, 2008; Vattam, 2013; Cohen, 2016). In the past decade, growing efforts have been devoted to interdisciplinary research that can connect biology and other disciplines, and many bio-inspired design strategies from relevant disciplines have been formulated (Bogatyreva et al., 2002; Vattam et al., 2010; Baumeister, 2012; Badarnaha, 2015). However, there is no definite research on applying bio-inspired into visual design.

As for the application of bio-inspired design, Benyus (1997) divided it into three levels from shallow to deep, including mimic of natural surfaces (forms), mimic of natural processes, and simulation of natural ecosystems (Belletire, 2005). Compared with other disciplines, though bio-inspired design has been applied into visual design, the applications are mostly at the shallow (surface) level, and there is no profound thinking or research on the knowledge transfer between biology and visual design.

When bio-inspired design methods are used into creative thinking, bio-inspired design databases (AskNature, 2008) are indispensable tools for designers. So far, online searching (AskNature, 2008), interactive software (Vattam et al., 2010; Chakrabarti, 2005), bio-inspired cards (Volstad, 2012; Bio-inspired 3.8, 2016) and other databases have been exploited and developed, which can be used as tools in engineering, architecture, products and packing. When bio-inspired design is used into different disciplines, however, the languages adopted, the views concerning design, the limitations to design issues, and the sources used to realize abstract design concepts all differ to some extent (Vattam, 2007). For instance, the focus in the field of architecture is how to use the physical space and building structures, but how to optimize functions, values, appearance and material quality in the fields of engineering and product design, and is how to optimize information transfer in the field of visual design. Thus, when designers from different disciplines use bio-inspired databases, they have similarity in some areas, but also emphasize differently and use different connection languages. However, so far, there is no specific bio-inspired tool for visual design.

Given the above analysis and the interdisciplinary interaction of future design (Oxman, 2016) and since bio-inspired design is a promising discipline in the future (Gamage & Hyde, 2012), we find the applications of bio-inspired into the vision field are superficial, but not profound or comprehensive. The problems to be solved in this study are: bio-inspired design is a tool for vision designers to exploit creativity and innovation potential, but are the existing bio-inspired design tools developed in the fields of engineering, architecture and product design feasible to visual design? If yes, will the tools help to enhance the novelty and profundity of visual designers? If not, what characteristics should be possessed by bio-inspired design tools that are feasible to visual design?

2. Methodology and Steps

Here, cognitive protocol analysis was adopted, which consisted of three steps. Step 1-- test 1: no-bio-inspired design experience visual designers were asked to use three ways of thinking (no-bio-inspired inspired thinking, thinking assisted by bio-inspired resource cards, thinking assisted by bio-inspired design cases) during visual design. Step 2-- test 2: have bio-inspired design experience visual designers were asked to use the three thinking ways as in step 1 during visual design. Step 3: Tests 1 and 2 were compared for discussion and analysis.

This study was aimed to explore whether the existing bio-inspired design tools would help the subjects during creative conception and to explore the feasibility of these tools. Given the advances of design thinking in recent decades, Cross (1999) reorganized the existing research methods. Of them, 'oral analysis' was a complete observation of the design processes of designers (Suwa & Tversky, 1997). Oral information is the source of scientific data and the basis of studying the problem-solving process of subjects (Ericsson et al., 1980). Oral analysis is the best way to acquire oral data for studies on 'thinking aloud' in the design field (Ginsburg et al., 1983; Stewart, 1983; Finegold & Mass, 1985). The oral data reflect the process how a subject finishes the design objectives (Ericsson et al., 1980) and can be used to extract the complex structure of problem solving and to uncover the hidden internal mechanisms (Ginsburg et al., 1983). Thus, in this study, 'thinking aloud' was used as an experimental method. The whole processes were audio- and video-recorded, and photos were taken.

2.1. Step 1: No Bio-inspired Inspired Designer

2.1.1 Subjects

All subjects enrolled had sufficient experience in designing. In step 1, two no-bio-inspired inspired vision designers with more than 15 years of experience in visual design were selected.

Since this study was aimed to differentiate the effects of some creative conception tools on the conception of the subjects, the test topics should be operated by the same subjects.

2.1.2 Design Topics

As for selection of topics, visual design covers graphic design, ad design, commercial design and other aspects, and graphic design is subdivided into logo design, book design and inset design. Given that none of the above different classifications can fully manifest visual design, we, after comprehensive analysis, selected poster design as the direction of test topics. This is because poster design covers many aspects of vision design, and posters are widely-accepted popular transmission ways and are aimed at information delivery.

In this study, three topics were used to test the subjects. The subjects should be the same, which avoided between-topic interference due to continuous thinking. As for topic design, topic 1 and topic 2 were parallel, but the themes were different, and topic 2 and topic 3 both involved bio-inspired design and thus the directions were largely different.

Topic1: [Future] themed poster design (the subjects were encouraged to break through two-dimensionality and paper media and to use multi-sensory factors into creation, but not to use bio-inspired design thinking).

Topic 2: [Environmental protection] themed poster design (in addition to the encouragement in topic 1, the subjects were provided bio-inspired resource cards to help with the inspired creative conception).

Topic 3: [Break] themed poster design (in addition to the encouragement in topic 1, the subjects were provided bio-inspired design cases to help with the inspired creative conceiving). Since topic 2 and topic 3 both involved the inspired creative conceiving and to avoid the interference of topic 2 on topic 3, we set them at different aspects of thinking, while ensuring both were poster design. Thus, topic 3 was an abstract concept of [break], so the subjects can comprehend it as [break through] or [break down] according to their conceptions.

2.1.3 Design Tools

Topic 1: The plotting tools (including drawing sheets, pencils, marker pens, colored pencils) and computers (as demanded by the designers) were all commonly-used by the subjects.

Topic 2: Bio-inspired resource cards were also provided in addition to those in topic

Topic 3: Bio-inspired design cases were also provided in addition to those in topic 1.

2.1.4 Experimental Operation

Since the subjects should be the same person, the subjects may also be interfered by the memory from the previous topic he/she had finished, in addition to the between-topic interference. Thus, to avoid such interference from previous tests, certain intervals were set: one week between topics 1 and 2, and one month between topics 2 and 3.

Topic 1: During this no-bio-inspired design, the subjects conceived topic 1 without using bio-inspired design and were informed with the instruction prior to the test. During the test, the subjects creatively conceived and drafted within 30-60 minutes. The whole processes were audio- and video-recorded, and photos were taken, and the conception and drafting were photographed by digital cameras.

Topic 2: During this bio-inspired design, the subjects conceived topic 2 by using **biomimicry resource cards** (Figure1.) and were familiarized with the cards in advance. During the test, the subjects creatively conceived and drafted within 30-60 minutes. The whole processes were audio- and video-recorded, and the conception and drafting were photographed by digital cameras.

Figure 1. biomimicry resource card.

Topic 3: During this bio-inspired design, the subjects conceived topic 3 by using bio-inspired design cases and were familiarized with the cases in advance. During the test, the subjects creatively c onceived and drafted within 30-60 minutes. The whole processes were audio- and video-recorded, and the conception and drafting were photographed by digital cameras.

Figure 2. bio-inspired design cases.

2.2 Step 2: Bio-inspired Designer

In step 2, the two subjects enrolled should be vision designers with experience of bio-inspired design, with more than 15 years of experience in visual design, and with experience of using bio-inspired design to think in the past 3 years. Design Topic, design Tools and experimental Operation, are the same as step 1.

3. Results and Discussion

Totally 12 groups (4 subjects × 3 topics) of data were obtained, including audio records, videos, drafts and photos. Firstly, the oral data were transcribed into literal data, which were then segmented, and finally each segmentation was encoded. During the transcription, the videos and drafts from the designing process were used, and the segmentation was based on each design idea as a unit. The segmentations were encoded according to an encoding system, and the feasibility of the bio-inspired tools was discussed on basis of the results.

The results were comprehensively compared to investigate whether they can be used as effective supplementary tools by vision designers for the creative conception. If yes, we discussed how to use these tools during the design process so as to improve the novelty and depth of vision designers during the creative conception. If not, we discussed how to adjust these tools so they would become usable for vision designers.

Table 1. Subjects receives inspiration

Subjects		Topic 1	Topic 2	Topic 3
Bio-experience	Subjects1	⊗	◖	◑
	Subjects2	⊗	◐	●
No Bio-experience	Subjects3	⊗	◖	●
	Subjects4	⊗	◖	◐

⊗ no more inspired   ◖ a little inspired   ◐ commonly inspired   ● more inspired   ◑ very inspired

4. Conclusions

The analysis of test data shows that none of the existing bio-inspired tools are fully feasible for vision design, so we propose three directions or recommendations for the development of new tools. 1 Many bio-inspired cases suggest biological data are very helpful for inspired designers, but the major challenge in vision design may be that the existing tools focus on the combination of biological data with engineering and structures, but rarely on the combination with vision design language. Thus, using vision language to link biology knowledge will make the tools more effective. 2 Since the bio-inspired research often involves multiple disciplines, when it is used into vision design, relevant research cases will endow designers with more direct vision experience and make them more clearly inspired. Thus, more interdisciplinary cases involving bio-inspired should be offered to vision designers. 3 When the existing bio-inspired design tools and relevant databases are to be used by vision designers as supplementary tools in creative thinking, the biology knowledge and relevant cases should be summarized and classified using the vision design language, so that the knowledge can be effectively and rapidly used by vision designers according to their demands.

References

[1] Al-Obaidi, K. M., Azzam Ismail, M., Hussein, H., & Abdul Rahman, A. M. (2017). Biomimetic building skins: An adaptive approach. Renewable and Sustainable Energy Reviews. 79(4), 1472–1491.

[2] AskNature. (2018). A project of Bio-inspired 3.8. Accessed Octuber 2018. www.asknature.org.

[3] Austin, S., Steele, J., Macmillan, S., Kirby, P., & Spence, R. (2001). Mapping the conceptual design activity of interdisciplinary teams. Design Studies. 22(3), 211-232.

[4] Benyus, J. (1997). *Biomimicry: Innovation Inspired by Nature*, New York, William Morrow.

[5] Bogatyreva, O., Pahl, A.-K. & Vincent, J. (2002). Enriching TRIZ with Biology. TRIZ future. Proceedings ETRIA world conference. 301–308. Strasbourg.Belletire, 2005)

[6] Baumeister, D. (2012). Biomimicry Resource Handbook: A Seed Bank of Knowledge and Best Practices. Missoula: Biomimicry 3.8.

[7] Badarnaha, L., & Kadrib, U. (2015). A methodology for the generation of biomimetic design concepts. Article in Architectural Science Review. 58(2), 120–133.

[8] Biomimicry 3. 8 (2016). A project of Biomimicry 3.8, Accessed October 2016. www.biomimicry.net

[9] Chakrabarti, A., Sarkar, P., Leelavathamma, B., & Nataraju, B. (2005). A functional representation for aiding biomimetic and artificial inspiration of new ideas. *Artificial Intelligence for Engineering Design, Analysis and Manufacturing. 19*(2), 113-132.

[10] Cohen, Y. H. & Reich, Y. (2016). The Biomimicry Design Process: Characteristics, Stages and Main Challenge. In: Biomimetic Design Method for Innovation and Sustainability, Springer, London. 19-29. Ericsson et al., 1980

[11] Gamage, A., & R. Hyde. (2012). A Model Based on Biomimicry to Enhance Ecologically Sustainable Design. Architectural Science Review. 55 (3), 224–235.

[12] Oxman, N. (2016). Age of Entanglement. Journal of Design and Science. https://doi.org/ 10.21428/7e0583ad.

[13] Vattam, S., Helms, M. E., & Goel, A. K. (2007). Biologically-Inspired Innovation in Engineering Design: A Cognitive Study. *Technical Report GIT-GVU-07-07, Graphics, Visualization & Usability Center, Georgia Institute of Technology.*

[14] Vattam, S., & Goel, A. (2013). Biological Solutions for Engineering Problems: Cross-Domain Textual Case-Based Reasoning in Biologically Inspired Design. *Procs. 21st International Conference on Case-Based Reasoning. 7*, 343-357.

[15] Vattam, S., Helms, M., & Goel, A. (2010). A content account of creative analogies in biologically inspired design, *AIEDAM. 24* (4), 467-481.

Design Studies and Intelligence Engineering
L.C. Jain et al. (Eds.)
© *2024 The Authors.*
This article is published online with Open Access by IOS Press and distributed under the terms
of the Creative Commons Attribution Non-Commercial License 4.0 (CC BY-NC 4.0).
doi:10.3233/FAIA231509

The Development of a University Express Packaging Recycling System Based on Service Design

Meidan DENG[a], Di WANG[a], Shanglu ZHAO[a], and Biyun ZHU[a1]

[a] *Department of Art and Design, Beijing City University, Beijing, China*

Abstract. Based on the theoretical framework of the principles and methodologies of service design, this study adopts the express delivery points in universities in Beijing as the research subject. Through field visits and interview-based investigations, this paper analyzed the handling of express packaging. This investigation aims to systematically resolve the significant issues caused by the improper utilization of express packaging—such as extensive accumulation and waste—through a well-thought-out service system design. The ultimate goal is to promote a sustainable design for the express packaging recycling system in universities. In the end, a comprehensive online and offline recycling system was established to improve the circular use of express packaging and materials and to reduce the consumption of paper resources. This study hopes to provide valuable insights for the overall express packaging recycling system design in the country.

Keywords. Service design; express packaging; recycling system; sustainable design

1. Introduction

With the rapid development of technology in China and the significant growth of internet technologies, especially under the current context of the ongoing pandemic, more and more Chinese people are turning to online shopping. This trend has also stimulated the rapid growth of the e-commerce industry. According to data from the National Postal Bureau, annual express service volume in China has grown nearly 18 times over the past decade, ranking top for nine consecutive years worldwide. In 2020 alone, the total express deliveries reached 833 million parcels(as shown in Table 1). By 2023, the daily processing capacity exceeded 700 million, with an average annual parcel count of nearly 80 per person. However, the ubiquity of online shopping has led to significant resource waste, and most importantly, the issue of accumulating packaging waste is becoming increasingly severe. One of the primary sources of this packaging waste is university express delivery stations.

---

[1] Corresponding Author.

Against the backdrop of such waste, the Chinese government has proposed green logistics and green packaging industry standards and requirements. However, due to the current resource constraints, the primary goal should be shifted from green deliveries to a more critical problem of resource recycling. Thus, enhancing the recycling rate of express packaging and reducing the consumption of paper resources is a potential direction for the express industry.

Table 1. National Express Delivery Volume from 2010-2020.

Year	National Express Delivery Volume (in 100 million pieces)	Year-on-Year Growth (%)	Express Delivery Revenue (in 100 million yuan)	Year-on-Year Growth (%)
2010	23.4	25.9	574.6	20.0
2011	36.7	57.0	758.0	31.9
2012	56.9	54.8	1055.3	39.2
2013	91.9	61.6	1441.7	36.6
2014	139.6	51.9	2045.4	41.9
2015	206.7	48.0	2769.6	35.4
2016	312.8	51.4	3974.4	43.5
2017	400.6	28.0	4957.1	24.7
2018	507.1	26.6	6038.4	21.8
2019	635.2	25.3	7497.8	24.2
2020	833.6	31.2	8795.4	17.3

2. An Overview of Service Design

Service design is effective in planning and organizing all aspects related to a service—people, infrastructure, communication, materials, etc.—to enhance user experience and service quality. By establishing a user-first service standpoint and tracking all touchpoints in the experience flow, the aim of service design is to create an excellent user experience. The express packaging recycling system needs to consider everyone involved in the express service as well as workers at express delivery points, infrastructure, communication, tangible materials, etc. In this connection, express packaging serves as the central element linking all stakeholders.

3. The Current Situation of University Express Packaging Handling

Statistics show that university students are one of the primary online shopping demographics, making university express deliveries a potential market under the booming e-commerce industry. Currently, there are various operating models for university express deliveries, including proprietary operations by courier companies, centralized pickups, scattered pickups, automated pickups, campus O2O, and crowd-sourced deliveries. The primary materials used for packaging are plastic bags, paper packaging, foam, and fillers. Among these, paper-based packaging is the most used one, leading to the most waste and environmental pollution.

Taking a particular university in Beijing as an example, a survey of 150 students revealed that 72.5% of students shop online 1 to 5 times a month, 25% do so 5 to 10 times a month, and 2.5% shop online more than 10 times a month(as shown in Table 2).

Table 2. Online Shopping Frequency of Students from a University in Beijing (Based on a Sample of 150 Students).

Monthly Online Shopping Frequency	Number of Students	Percentage
1 - 5	108	72.%
5 - 10	39	26%
Over 10	3	2%

At the northwest entrance of the campus, there is a venue of concentrated express delivery points from various companies for the convenience of the staffs and students to pick up package. However, these points often have littered packaging waste around them, not only tarnishing the aesthetics of the campus but also resulting in significant resource wastage(as shown in Figure 1). Most of the discarded packaging ends up at waste disposal sites, with only a small portion being reused by couriers. This waste issue stems from two main factors: a lack of recycling awareness among students and an absence of a systematic recycling infrastructure.

Given that Beijing has millions of university students generating tens of millions of express parcels annually, it signifies the production of an equal number of packaging materials, which in turn leads to immense packaging waste.

Figure 1. The Current Situation of Packaging Accumulation at an Express Station of a University in Beijing.

4. University Express Packaging Recycling System Based on Service Design

Given the current situation of express packaging in universities in Beijing, this study adopts the principles and methodologies of service design and proposes a comprehensive online and offline recycling system. This system provides students with self-service express packaging recycling bins, coupled with a points reward and supervision mechanism to encourage students to actively recycle their packages. This is done to improve the circular use of express packaging and materials, reduce the consumption of paper resources, and thereby refine the university express packaging recycling system(as shown in Figure 2 and Figure 3).

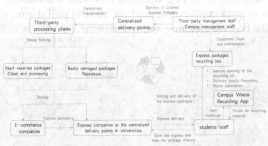

Figure 2. University Express Packaging Recycling Service System.

Figure 3. Blueprint of the University Express Packaging Recycling System Service.

4.1. Establishment of Offline Self-Service Recycling Bins

The bins owned by third-party companies are set up at central express delivery points within the university. Students can classify and drop off their used express packages. The third-party companies either assign dedicated personnel or collaborate with university logistic staff for managing these recycling bins. Managers can monitor the storage status of these bins in real-time via an app, ensuring timely cleanup and transport of the collected materials to processing facilities. Here, well-preserved packaging is either reused or reprocessed into new express packaging, which is then sold to e-commerce businesses or courier companies.

According to the common materials for express packaging, the recycling box is equipped with four recycling barrels, namely paper packaging, plastic packaging, foam packaging materials and fillers(as shown in Figure 4). And based on the daily production volume, the capacity of the recycling bucket is divided, with the largest capacity being the paper packaging recycling bucket and the smallest being the filling material recycling bucket. The overall height of the recycling box is 185cm, and the height range of the delivery window on the front of the recycling box is 115-170cm. The delivery range is around 110-120cm, which is comfortable for people to stand and reach for objects. The entire window is convenient for users to drop the packaging without lifting it, reducing delivery difficulties. At the same time, there is also a screen on the front of the recycling bin, which mainly functions to connect QR codes, view user information, view the remaining amount of the recycling bin, and provide online feedback and messages. On the back of the recycling box, there is an electrical box area, a heat dissipation zone, and four recycling box entrances and exits. The height of the handle of the recycling bin is 105cm, which is less than the distance from the waist of an adult to the ground, making it convenient for staff to pull the recycling bin from the inlet and outlet of the box for cleaning and maintenance(as shown in Figure 5).

Figure 4. Design Drawing of Express Packaging Recycling Box.

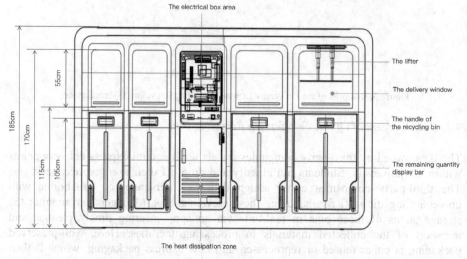

Figure 5. Dimension diagram of express packaging recycling box.

4.2. Online Behavior Tracking and Incentive Mechanisms

Before depositing their express packaging into the recycling bins, students can either scan a QR code or use an app to connect with the system. The system then records the details of the deposit and calculates the points the student earns based on the type and weight of the packaging material. Once they accumulate enough points, students can redeem various items from an in-system store. By integrating online behavior tracking with incentive mechanisms, a comprehensive online-offline service model is realized, fostering a sustainable express packaging recycling system.

4.3. Recycling System Workflow

The Campus Green Station APP is an app configured for the recycling system, which allows students and management personnel to learn about the information of the recycling bin and complete related operations for express packaging recycling. Through the app login page, you can enter user mode and administrator mode respectively.

- Workflow for user

The overall framework of the user mode is divided into four modules: Home, Mall, Me, and Know-how. "Home" is the first and core scenario of the app, which focuses on searching for nearby collection points, selecting and opening collection boxes, and recording delivery information. "Mall" is the main scenario of the app, focusing on the functions of points record, query, redemption and so on. "Me" includes functions such as personal information modification and software settings, etc. "Know-how" mainly includes functions such as pushing environmental protection knowledge such as how to classify and recycle, and redeeming points through learning.

After unpacking their parcels, user can scan a QR code or use an app to connect with the system. They then choose the appropriate bin for their packaging material, and upon confirmation, the corresponding bin opens. After depositing their packaging, the system scans and compresses the material, weighs it, and logs the details. Points are then awarded to the user based on the type and weight of the deposited material. Once the points are credited, the bin closes, completing the deposit process. The system store displays items that user can redeem with their accumulated points(as shown in Figure 6).

Figure 6. User app interface display.

- Workflow for Administrator

The overall framework of the administrator mode is divided into four modules: Capacity View, Information Feedback, Repair Record, and Add Device. "Capacity View" can show the remaining capacity of the equipment. "Information feedback" includes summarizing and viewing equipment information. "Repair Record" displays real-time repair requests and past maintenance records. "Add Device" is the function of adding devices and inputting device location, data, name and other related information.

Administrator can visually inspect the amount of waste in each bin through transparent sections on the bins. Additionally, they can use the app to monitor the storage status in real-time. When the bins are full, they promptly clean and package the waste by type, transporting it to central collection points. These materials are then sent to processing plants for sorting and repurposing. If a bin malfunctions, the app sends a warning notification, prompting the manager to address and resolve the issue(as shown in Figure 7).

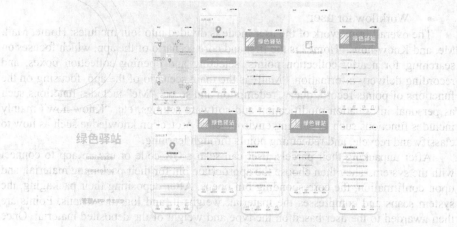

Figure7. Administrator app interface display.

5. Conclusion

With the rapid rise of e-commerce and express delivery industries, improper handling and disposal of express packaging have led to vast amounts of waste and accumulation. However, these challenges can be properly addressed through employing effective design principles. By championing the cause of sustainable express packaging recycling systems and enhancing the recyclability of express packaging and materials, the paper consumption can be minimized efficiently. The findings and proposals of this paper can serve as valuable references for devising recycling systems for express packaging countrywide.

References

[1] Hu Hong. Jin Yuxin. Zhou Zhoufeng, Design of a courier packaging recycling system based on service process optimization,   Industrial Design, January 2020.

[2] Liu Manli, Research on Improving and Applying the Quality of Express Delivery Services in Universities, Tianjin University of Technology, January 1,2021.

[3] Zeng Boya. Bao Yimei, Research on the Recycling and Reuse of Packaging Materials for Express Delivery in Colleges and Universities - Taking Tianjin Universities as an Example, Chinese Market, July 5, 2021.

[4] The Development Path of Recyclable Express Packaging . China Packaging, 2021.

[5] Zhou Xiaochen, Research on the Problems and Countermeasures of Packaging Recycling in University Express Delivery under the Background of Green Logistics - Taking Anhui Normal University Wanjiang College as an Example , Fortune Times, 2021.

[6] Liang Huiping. Li Jiagui, Design of Intelligent Express Packaging Recycling Service , Design, 2021.

[7] Li Jinyu, Research on Incentive Mechanism for Express Packaging Recycling Based on Post Station Service Platform, Dalian University of Transportation Learning, 2020.

[8] Cao Xing, Research on Consumer Behavior Intention in Express Packaging Recycling, Xi'an University of Electronic Science and Technology, 2019.

[9] Luo Shijian. Zou Wenyin, Current Status and Progress of Service Design Research, Packaging Engineering, 2018.

[10] Zhang Yi, Research on Logistics Cost and Benefit Allocation of Express Packaging Recycling in Universities, Southwest Jiaotong University, 2018.

[11] Zhang Xijian, Research on Green Systematic Design of Express Packaging, Beijing University of Technology, 2016.

[12] https://www.doc88.co

Design Studies and Intelligence Engineering
L.C. Jain et al. (Eds.)
© 2024 The Authors.
This article is published online with Open Access by IOS Press and distributed under the terms
of the Creative Commons Attribution Non-Commercial License 4.0 (CC BY-NC 4.0).
doi:10.3233/FAIA231510

Computational Interpretation of the Difference Between the 5 Writing Styles of Chinese Calligraphy

Yangzi FU[a], Ruimin LYU[a,1], Guoying YANG[b], Baixi XING[c] and Lekai ZHANG[c]

[a] *School of Artificial Intelligence and Computer Science, Jiangnan University*
[b] *Goldsmiths College, University of London*
[c] *Zhejiang University of Technology*

Abstract. Visual art works contain a lot of tacit knowledge that is difficult to accurately express in words. If they are expressed quantitatively in a computable form, it helps to apply this part of tacit knowledge to a wider field. Chinese calligraphy style carriers have tacit knowledge of Chinese cultural characteristics, which our research quantitatively interprets. In our study, 33 interpretable features were designed and summarized, and the random forest classification was adopted. As a result, we found that only 8 computational features with concise mathematic form were needed to interpret the differences between the five writing styles of Chinese calligraphy with an accuracy of 66.7 %. Based on these features and the evaluation of five calligraphy styles, we find that some combination of features can cause people's perception of a particular style and establish the relationship between objective features and people's subjective feelings. The results can provide inspiration for the creation of artists and designers, and have potential applications in the fields of psychology, design, and human-computer interaction.

Keywords. Visual perception, Chinese calligraphy, Interpretable features, Computational aesthetics

1. Introduction

Language cannot fully capture all knowledge, and many researchers argue that artistic works often contain implicit knowledge that far surpasses the explicit knowledge described in language[1]. This is particularly true for the vast reservoir of visual knowledge embedded within visual art, which remains largely untapped and underutilized[2]. Visual art serves as a crucial medium for recording the perceptual facets of these concepts. Human society has evolved numerous forms of visual art, such as sculpture, painting, animation, calligraphy, and more. These art forms coexist in an irreplaceable ecological balance due to their unique strengths in capturing and expressing visual knowledge. How to transform unique visual knowledge from a culturally specific art category such as calligraphy into an interpretable quantitative form is the main thrust of this study.

Chinese calligraphy contains a rich reservoir of visual knowledge and appreciation materials that have evolved and accumulated throughout the history of Chinese cultural

---

[1] Corresponding Author: Ruimin Lyu, ruiminlyu@jiangnan.edu.cn

development, and some scholars believe that it contains the unique gene of Chinese culture[3]. The usability of calligraphy has been validated in certain studies[4], If we could transform this knowledge from experiential expression into a quantitative form, it may allow this knowledge to transcend cultural barriers and be applied more widely.

The development of emerging fields such as empirical aesthetics, computational aesthetics, and self-explanatory models has brought about possibilities for exploring visual knowledge within various art forms. Existing research categories include: color composition[5], low-level visual features[6], visual complexity[7], web design[8], packaging design[9].

In recent years, machine learning plays a very important role in the quantitative research of calligraphy style. However, the existing work mainly attempts to train artificial intelligence models to achieve style classifications[10][11], rather than explaining calligraphy styles. Only a few studies have discussed the interpretability of calligraphy style. Sun et al. [12] proposed a calligraphy scoring model, SRAFE, which combines calligraphy aesthetic features with deep learning and discusses the correlation between these aesthetic features and subjective human aesthetics. Rongju Sun et al. [13] proposed certain aesthetic features based on classical calligraphy rules, unveiling the relationship between these aesthetic features and human aesthetic preferences. Kaixin Han et al. [14] proposed some computational features related to the visual complexity of calligraphy and discusses the connection between visual complexity in calligraphy and subjective human aesthetic perceptions. However, these studies did not delve into specific stylistic impressions within calligraphy. Kaixin Han et al. [15] introduced the stylistic impressions of squares and circles in calligraphy, explaining how the objective features of calligraphy fonts impact human perceptions of squares and circles' aesthetic appreciation. Based on the above-mentioned research, it is evident that establishing a relationship between interpretable features and calligraphy styles is feasible, though relevant research remains scarce.

In view of this, this study aims to provide a quantitative explanation of calligraphy style, rather than improving the style discrimination ability of AI models. As a result, the following two contributions have been made:

- We built a new calligraphy database, which contains five styles of calligraphy, and extracted 1600 characters from 130 calligraphy works. Then we extract 33 interpretable features from morphology, structure, and contour, which cover the features proposed by previous studies, and we propose some new ones.

- We examined the interpretability of these features for five calligraphy styles using random forest classification and found that only eight simple, intuitive interpretable features, such as aspect ratio, contour entropy, etc., were needed to interpret the differences between the five styles with an accuracy of 66.7%. In the end, we delved into the relationship between calligraphy styles and these features, uncovering that certain combinations of features can influence how people perceive specific styles. This not only validated existing calligraphy knowledge but also established a connection between objective features and individuals' subjective aesthetic experiences.

2. Dataset For Experiment

This experiment selected a total of 130 works, including five basic calligraphy styles: seal script, official script, regular script, running script, and cursive script, and then randomly selected about 6 to 18 characters from each work as original materials.

Before extracting features, it is necessary to perform data normalization on the materials. Firstly, we convert the artwork images into binary format, which results in black characters on a white background. Many historical books contain varying levels of noise. To address this issue, we first apply median blur to reduce some of the noise. After the initial computer-based processing, we proceed with manual adjustments.

To ensure uniform character size, we use the outer rectangle of the font to split the characters, scale the longer sides of the split character image to 200 pixels equally, and finally align the center of each word to a 260×260 canvas.The processed character samples are shown in Figure 1.

Figure 1. Processed character samples

3. Feature Extraction

In this section, based on the aesthetics of calligraphy, we have summarized 33 interpretable objective features from three perspectives: morphological features, structural features, and contour features. Subsequently, we applied these features to the character materials processed in the previous section. Finally, we calculated the average feature value of individual characters in each artwork to describe the characteristics of each piece.

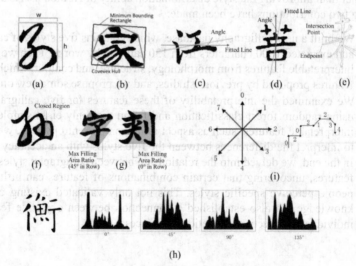

Figure 2. Illustrations of some features

3.1. Morphological features

This section presents several fundamental morphological features derived from convex hull, skeleton, and other basic geometric shapes.

f1: Aspect ratio. It is used to describe the width and narrowness of a character, as shown in Figure 2(a), where w represents the width of the character's bounding rectangle, and h represents the height of the character's bounding rectangle. The calculation method for f1 is as Eq. (1).

$$f1 = w / h \tag{1}$$

f2: Rectangularity. It is used to describe the degree of approximation between a character and a rectangle. As shown in Figure 2(b), we introduce the convex hull to describe the basic shape of the character. P_{con} represents the perimeter of the character's convex hull, and P_{min} represents the perimeter of the character's minimum bounding rectangle. The definition of f2 is as Eq. (2).

$$f2 = P_{con} / P_{min} \tag{2}$$

f3: Roundness. This metric assesses how closely a character's convex hull approximates a circle, with C denoting the character's area. The calculation formula is as Eq. (3).

$$f3 = 4\pi C / P_{con} \tag{3}$$

f4: Eccentricity. It is used to calculate the eccentricity of the character's minimum bounding rectangle. Eccentricity values range from 0 to 1, with 0 indicating the minimum eccentricity for a circle, and 1 indicating the maximum eccentricity for a straight line. Here, a represents the semi-major axis, b represents the semi-minor axis, and the formula for calculating eccentricity is as Eq. (4).

$$f4 = \sqrt{1 - (b / a)^2} \tag{4}$$

f5, f6: The inclination angle of the fitted line and slope, which describes the character's tilt degree. We employ the least squares method to calculate the optimal fitted line, where k represents the slope of the line and b is the intercept. The Angle denotes the minimum angle between the fitted line and the x-axis, defined as Eq. (5).

$$\text{Angle} = |180 \sec k / \pi| \tag{5}$$

If Angle is less than 45°, f5 measures the angle between the fitted line and the x-axis, as shown in Figure 2(c). However, when Angle exceeds 45°, f5 determines the angle between the fitted line and the y-axis, as illustrated in Figure 4(d). The definitions of f5 and f6 are as Eqs. (6) and (7).

$$f5 = \begin{cases} \text{Angle} , & \text{Angle} < 45 \\ |90 - \text{Angle}|, & \text{Angle} \geq 45 \end{cases} \tag{6}$$

$$f6 = k / w \tag{7}$$

f7, f8: Skeleton Endpoint Count and Intersection Point Count. As shown in Figure 2(e), the font's skeleton is extracted, removing short skeleton branches. Then, the skeleton is traversed, with endpoint pixels being defined as black pixels with only one adjacent black pixel, and intersection pixels as black pixels with three adjacent black pixels. The counts of these endpoints and intersection points are recorded.

f9, f10: Average Width and Variance. The average width and thickness variation of strokes can be obtained from the medial axis of the character.

f11, f12: The Count and Area Proportion of Enclosed Regions. While writing characters, a multitude of enclosed areas is generated, as shown in Figure 2(f). We quantify the number of these enclosed regions within the character as f11. Furthermore, f12 provides insights into the size of these areas, where Cn signifies the area of enclosed regions, and A represents the convex hull area. This is defined as Eq. (8).

$$f12 = Cn / A \tag{8}$$

3.2. Structure features

From the perspective of calligraphy aesthetics, we introduce some structural features.

f13: Space Utilization. It describes the relationship between ink usage and the space occupied by the font. C represents the character area, and it is defined as Eq. (9).

$$f13 = C / A \tag{9}$$

f14~f17: Pixel Projection Variances. Illustrated in Figure 2(h), these metrics provide insights into the stroke distribution characteristics of the character. They compute the variances of the character's vertical projections at 0°, 45°, 90°, and 135° angles, respectively.

f18~f22: Ink Distribution. Create a new coordinate system with the center of the convex hull as the origin. Then, calculate the convex hull area to ink ratio for the four quadrants. f22 is the variance of f18~f21.

f23: Fitted Line Segmentation Area Ratio. The fitted line divides the convex hull into two regions, calculating the ratio between the smaller area Cmin and the larger area Cmax.

$$f23 = Cmin / Cmax \tag{10}$$

f24, f25: Maximum GAP Proportion and Average GAP Proportion. Utilizing a straight-line scan through the character, it traverses the character and fills the spaces between characters, as shown in Figure 2(g). These areas are instrumental in characterizing the spacing between characters. gap(i) represents the gap when characters are scanned with a line at an angle of i degrees.

$$f24 = \max\{gap(i)/gap(i) + C\}, i=1,2,3,....,90 \tag{11}$$

$$f25 = \sum_{i=0}^{90} gap(i)/gap(i) + C / 90 \tag{12}$$

f26~f31: Elastic Mesh Layout. To achieve this, we uniformly divide the ink strokes of the font into four equal parts in both the vertical and horizontal directions using four lines, and then calculate the relative positions of these four lines.

3.3. Contour Features

This section extracts some features from the outline of the character.

f32: Corner Count. Utilizing the Shi-Tomasi algorithm, we detect and quantify the sharper regions within the character contours.

f33: Contour Entropy. Illustrated in Figure 2(i), we utilize Freeman encoding to traverse the font's contour, generating a sequence based on the relative positions of the current pixel and the next pixel, and subsequently calculate its contour information entropy.

4. Feature Selection

To validate the interpretability of font styles, we employed these interpretable features to classify five calligraphy styles (Seal Script, Clerical Script, Regular Script, Running Script, and Cursive Script). We initially standardized the data through z-score normalization and used 90% of the original dataset as our training set. We compared the performance of various classifiers and found that the random forest classifier had the best performance, with an accuracy of 73.6% on the five-fold cross-validation model, indicating that these features we introduced could distinguish the five calligraphy styles to a certain extent.

Table 1 lists the features and meanings that are also in the top ten of MeanDecreaseAccuracy and MeanDecreaseGini, and a total of 8 features are screened. The random forest classifier trained on only eight features can achieve 66.7% accuracy on the five-fold cross-validation model, indicating that these eight features can interpret most of the style differences.

Table 1. Eight features that influence the differences in calligraphy styles.

Feature	Definitions	MeanDecreaseAccuracy	MeanDecreaseGini
f1	Aspect ratio	26.90	9.86
f16	Pixel projection variance at 90°	19.48	5.72
f33	Contour entropy	17.77	6.04
f7	Skeleton endpoint count	17.31	4.96
f32	Corner count	11.01	3.59
f11	Area proportion of enclosed regions	12.27	3.76
f12	The count of enclosed regions	5.38	2.22
f5	The inclination angle of the fitted line	10.48	3.89

5. Analysis

Based on the eight interpretable features selected, we correlate existing calligraphic evaluations to these features and discuss the characteristics of each style and the differences between styles.

5.1. Analysis of the characteristics of five calligraphy styles

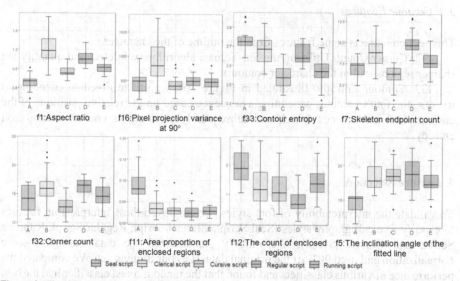

Figure 3. The presentation of how the five calligraphy styles are distributed across various features. A corresponds to Seal Script, B to Clerical Script, C to Cursive Script, D to Regular Script, and E to Running Script.

The distribution of the five calligraphy styles in different characteristics is shown in Figure 3. Seal Script exhibits higher values in features f33, f11, and f12, suggesting greater shape complexity with strokes often concealing their endpoints, forming closed areas. In contrast, features f1 and f5 have lower values, indicating Seal Script's characteristic slender shapes and even ink distribution, aligning with its description of elongated forms, uniform lines, and symmetrical complexity.

Clerical Script displays elevated values in features f1, f16, and f33, indicating its characteristic wide characters with a substantial variation in the 90° projection and a high level of complexity in its outlines. This aligns with the typical evaluation of Clerical Script, known for its broad, flat characters, emphasis on horizontal strokes, and diverse stroke patterns.

Cursive Script typically exhibits lower values in features f33, f7, and f32, suggesting fonts in this style tend to have simpler outline shapes with fewer endpoints and corners. This aligns with the general impression of Cursive Script, characterized by its fluidity, abundance of connected strokes, and a high degree of simplification.

In Regular Script, the values of feature f1 tend to cluster around 1. Additionally, there are elevated values for features f7 and f32, while feature f12 exhibits lower values. This indicates that fonts in this style tend to have square and well-defined shapes, with more endpoints and corners and fewer enclosed areas. This corresponds to the typical view of Regular Script, known for its regular, clear characters with distinct edges.

Running Script, which is a type of font that falls between Regular Script and Cursive Script. Our results indicate that the majority of feature values for Running Script are distributed between those of Regular Script and Cursive Script.

5.2. Analysis of the characteristics of five calligraphy styles

To further discuss the unique characteristics of each calligraphy style, we paired them up and used random forest classification to distinguish their characteristics. We then visualized these differences in Figure 4.

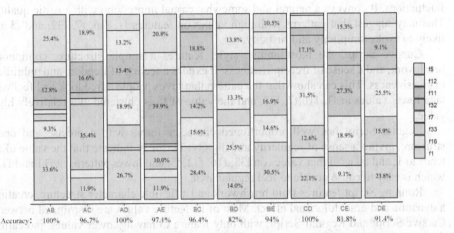

Figure 4. The visualization of feature importance obtained through random forest classification for each pair of script styles, with feature importance determined by MeanDecreaseAccuracy. A corresponds to Seal Script, B to Clerical Script, C to Cursive Script, D to Regular Script, and E to Running Script. Accuracy represents the classification accuracy obtained after five-fold cross-validation

Seal Script (A) showed distinct differences in features f1, f11, and f5 when compared to other styles, highlighting its slender character shapes, balanced structures, and consistent line thickness. Clerical Script (B) stood out from most other styles in features f1 and f16, emphasizing its elongated character shapes and exaggerated horizontal strokes. Cursive Script (C) differed in features f33 and f7 from most other styles, underscoring its simplified character shapes. Regular Script (D) showed significant differences in feature f7, primarily characterized by clear and distinct brushstrokes. Semi-Cursive Script (E) did not display pronounced feature differences when compared to other styles. However, Cursive Script and Running Script (CE) had similar features, resulting in lower accuracy in binary classification, primarily differing in feature f32.

Traditionally, people describe calligraphy features using language, but our research provides strong, objective evidence for distinguishing the unique traits of different calligraphy styles.

6. Discussion

Figures 3 and Figures 4 illustrate the unique characteristics of each script style based on these objective features. These five script styles have well-established guidelines for style appreciation. By mapping these features to how people perceive calligraphy styles, we can establish a link between interpretable features and individuals' subjective style perception. The corresponding relationships are explained as follows.

In terms of subjective evaluations, Seal Script is characterized by elongated character forms, smooth and consistent strokes, and a balanced, stable structure. It conveys a sense of refinement and solemnity, appealing to a careful and serious impression. This can be interpreted by the high values on features f33, f11, and f12, along with low values on features f1, f7, and f5 is easy to cause people's delicate and solemn style perception.

The Clerical Script is flat and criss-crossed, emphasizing horizontal stroke fluctuations. It conveys a natural and somewhat casual impression with a rustic quality. This may suggest that patterns with high values on features f1, f16, f7, f32, and f5 are likely to evoke simplicity and rusticity.

Cursive Script, the most unique style, features a simple structure, continuous brushwork, and a sense of free-spiritedness. It exudes a feeling of freedom and unbridled expressiveness. This can show that the pattern that gives people a free look and feel will take lower values at f1, f16, f7, f33, and the value of f5 is clustered at a relatively high value.

Regular Script has well-proportioned character forms with a precise and open structure, giving a sense of regularity and dignity. This may indicate that the value of f1 tends to 1, and takes higher values on f33, f16, f32, f5, and lower patterns at f11 and f12, which is easy to cause people to feel regular style.

Running Script features fluid brushwork and a flexible character structure, creating a dynamic and graceful visual effect. Most of its feature values are distributed between Cursive Script and Regular Script, with only feature f5 having lower values, indicating that no matter how the lines vary in Running Script, the ink distribution tends to balance. This provides evidence for the perception of stability and liveliness in Running Script. This indicates a pattern that gives a stable but lively impression, with moderate eigenvalues and low f5.

7. Conclusions and future work

Calligraphy is not only a form of subjective expression but also a graphic art. In this study, we aim to extract unique visual information from calligraphy, select 1600 characters from 130 works as experimental datasets, summarize 33 interpretable features, and finally screened out 8 interpretable features that have a significant impact on people's visual perception. Additionally, we have revealed the relationship between objective features and people's subjective perception of style. This contributes to a better understanding of how humans perceive information and can be used to guide artists in their creative process. Furthermore, it offers new perspectives for the study of other forms of art. In the future, the dataset and features obtained in this paper can be used to develop style and emotion recognition models. How to specifically apply these models in design and psychology will be a significant focus of future research.

Acknowledgement

This work was supported by the 2022 Open Project of Jiangsu Key Laboratory of Media Design and Software Technology (Jiangnan University), and Humanities and Social

Sciences Foundation of Ministry of Education of China (18YJC760123), and the National Natural Science Foundation of China (72304249), and Fundamental Research Funds for the Provincial Universities of Zhejiang (GB202003008).

References

[1] P.J, and Silvia, Emotional Responses to Art: From Collation and Arousal to Cognition and Emotion, *Review of General Psychology* **9** (2005), 342-357.

[2] G.E. Myers, and R. Arnheim, Art and Visual Perception: A Psychology of the Creative Eye. *Philosophy and Phenomenological Research* **16** (1956), 425-426.

[3] R. Li, X.F. Jia, C.l. Zhou, and J.S. Zhang, Reconfiguration of the brain during aesthetic experience on Chinese calligraphy—Using brain complex networks, *Visual Informatics* **6** (2022), 35-36.

[4] W. Hou, and G. Festi, Cultural Dynamics of Chinese Calligraphy from a Semiotic Gaze. A Design-Oriented Platform to Valorize Cultural Heritage, *Design in the Era of Industry 4.0* **3** (2023), 61-72.

[5] D. Kang, H. Shim, and K. Yoon, A method for extracting emotion using colors comprise the painting image. *Multimedia Tools and Applications* **77** (2018.), 1-18.

[6] J.L. Liu, E. Lughofer, X.Y. Zeng, Could linear model bridge the gap between low-level statistical Features and aesthetic Emotions of Visual textures, *Neurocomputing* **168** (2015), 947-960.

[7] Dai, L., Zhang, K., Zheng, X.S. et al., Visual complexity of shapes: a hierarchical perceptual learning model, *Vis Comput* **38** (2022), 419–432.

[8] J.Kim, J.Lee, and D. Choi, Designing emotionally evocative homepages: an empirical study of the quantitative relations between design factors and emotional dimensions. *International Journal of Human-Computer Studies* **59** (2003), 899-940.

[9] C. Spence, and G.V. Doorn, Visual communication via the design of food and beverage packaging, *Cognitive Research: Principles and Implications* **7** (2022), 42.

[10] Y.B. Wen, and S. Juan, Chinese Calligraphy: Character Style Recognition based on Full-page Document, *In Proceedings of the 2019 8th International Conference on Computing and Pattern Recognition* (2019), 390-394.

[11] P.C. Gao, G. Gu, J.Q. Wu, and B.G. Wei, Chinese calligraphic style representation for recognition. *International Journal on Document Analysis and Recognition* **20** (2017), 59-68.

[12] M.W. Sun, X.Y. Gong, H.T. Nie, Iqbal, M. Minhas, and B. Xie, SRAFE: Siamese Regression Aesthetic Fusion Evaluation for Chinese Calligraphic Copy, *CAAI Transactions on Intelligence Technology* (2022), 1077-1086.

[13] R.J Sun, Z.H. Lian, Y.M. Tang, and J.G. Xiao, Aesthetic visual quality evaluation of Chinese handwritings. *In Proceedings of the 24th International Conference on Artificial Intelligence* (2015), 2510-2516.

[14] K.X. Han, W.T. You, S.H. Shi, H.H. Deng, and L.Y. Sun, The Doctrine of the Mean: Chinese Calligraphy with Moderate Visual Complexity Elicits High Aesthetic Preference, *International Journal of Human-Computer Interaction* (2022), 1-14.

[15] K.X. Han ,W.T. You, S.H. Shi , and L.Y. Sun, The Impression of Round and Square: Chinese Calligraphy Aesthetics in Modern Type Design. *International Journal of Human-Computer Interaction* (2023), 1-14.

Design Studies and Intelligence Engineering
L.C. Jain et al. (Eds.)
© *2024 The Authors.*
This article is published online with Open Access by IOS Press and distributed under the terms
of the Creative Commons Attribution Non-Commercial License 4.0 (CC BY-NC 4.0).
doi:10.3233/FAIA231511

Research on Creative Design Reasoning Model Based on Cultural Elements

Xin TIAN [a,b,1] and Shijian LUO[a] and Yao WANG[a]

[a]*Department of Industrial Design, College of Computer Science and Technology, Zhejiang University, Hangzhou 310027, China*
[b]*College of Management, Guizhou University, Guiyang 550025, China*

Abstract. Creative reasoning is an important part of product creative design. To help designers clarify their reasoning thinking in the design process, this paper proposes a manual craft product creative design reasoning model based on traditional animal pattern cultural elements. This model combines the form, color, and semantics of traditional animal patterns with traditional intangible cultural heritage and uses semantic reasoning to assist creative design. The cultural elements in animal patterns are combined with modern products and objects, personalized requirements, and scenarios to generate random sentences, which helps designers in creative design reasoning. This model can effectively guide designers to integrate cultural elements into creative design, provide ideas and practical methods for the inheritance and innovation of traditional patterns and handicrafts, and improve the cultural connotation and market competitiveness of handmade products.

Keywords. Animal pattern, Cultural element, Creative design

1. Introduction

Creative design is the process or outcome of extending, presenting, and interpreting innovative ideas and concepts through the medium of design [1]. It is a design approach that emphasizes innovation, transformation, and enhancing user value, highlighting the integration of design with technology, culture, and market in multiple domains. Based on specific design requirements, designers constantly seek creative solutions through analogies drawn from reality and past experiences. The creative design comprises two processes: creative reasoning and creative expression [2]. During the process of creative reasoning, designers establish associations between patterns and products based on design objectives. In the process of creative expression, designers utilize the various associative relationships obtained from reasoning to sketch product designs, thereby completing the creative design process. The process in which people draw inspiration from one domain and apply it to another is known as analogy[3]. By employing analogies and associations between patterns and products, designers can enhance the fluency of their conceptualization during the process of creative expression. This enables the designed products to convey the cultural imagery and aesthetic beauty inherent in the patterns[4].

Common strategies for creative reasoning include inductive reasoning, deductive reasoning, concept combination techniques, and case-based reasoning. Inductive

---

[1] Corresponding Author. 9204290@qq.com

reasoning helps designers draw inspiration from existing handicrafts, while deductive reasoning transforms abstract ideas into concrete design solutions. Concept combination techniques support creative thinking[5]. Common strategies for creative reasoning include inductive reasoning, deductive reasoning, concept combination techniques, and case-based reasoning. Inductive reasoning helps designers draw inspiration from existing handicrafts, while deductive reasoning transforms abstract ideas into concrete design solutions. Concept combination techniques support creative thinking[6]. Case-based reasoning (CBR) facilitates the identification of creative and valuable ideas[7]. However, these creative reasoning methods have limitations. They do not facilitate the in-depth exploration of cultural elements during creative reasoning for designers. The reasoning search results are limited to precise search terms and cannot generate randomly combined sentences, making it difficult to consider various cultural elements such as pattern form, color, materials, craftsmanship, and art. As a result, they fail to generate creative designs that represent the cultural connotations of patterns.

This paper presents a creative design reasoning model based on the five cultural elements of "form, color, material, craftsmanship, and art" using traditional animal patterns as an example. The main contributions are as follows:

We integrate the cultural elements of form, color, and craftsmanship from traditional animal patterns with modern products, personalized needs, and scenarios. The model generates random sentences to assist in creative design. This combination provides new ideas and practical approaches for innovation in traditional patterns and handicrafts.

We conduct random reasoning and associations between keywords representing cultural elements from traditional animal patterns and other relevant concepts to help designers generate more creativity.

We integrate the cultural elements of traditional patterns into modern products and life scenes, allowing users to perceive the cultural symbols and connotations, such as ethnic aesthetics, values, and graphic semantics, contained within animal patterns.

The integration of cultural elements from traditional animal patterns with modern life scenes helps protect and inherit traditional pattern designs. It effectively guides designers in incorporating traditional cultural elements into creative design, providing an innovative approach and promoting the fusion and development of traditional culture and modern design.

2. Analysis of cultural elements of traditional animal prints

The cultural significance and diverse representation techniques of animal patterns, particularly those based on ethnic totem designs, make them the most profound aspect of ethnic pattern art [7]. Animal patterns hold a significant position in traditional Chinese culture, not only possessing high artistic value but also reflecting the histories, cultures, and lifestyles of various ethnic groups. These patterns are commonly used in the textiles, embroidery, and clothing of China's ethnic minorities, featuring animal motifs and patterns with a strong natural style. The designs and patterns often depict animals such as lions, tigers, deer, horses, cattle, birds, etc., showcasing strong decorative and ethnic characteristics.

Figure 1 extracts common animal motifs, such as birds, tigers, snakes, fish, butterflies, dragons and so on, from the ethnic patterns of Chinese ethnic minorities according to the categories of "birds, beasts, reptiles, fish and insects, totems", and sums up the cultural elements of these motifs in terms of the specific animal forms, colour compositions, commonly-used objects, implied meanings, commonly-used techniques and so on. The keywords of these patterns are summed up from specific animal forms, colour composition, common objects, implied meanings, common techniques and other aspects to form the five cultural elements of "form, colour, object, meaning, technique and technology".

Patterns category	Shape (specific animal)	Color (color)	Object (item)	Meaning (significance)	Technology (traditional craft)
Avian	Mandarin ducks	Red, green	children's clothing, couples clothing and supplies	Beauty, love, fidelity	Paper-cutting, batik, embroidery
	Bird	Red, blue, green	Clothes Sling piece	Free, beautiful	
	Crane	White, gray	Costumes, decorative paintings, etc.	Elegance, peace, longevity and good fortune	
	Rooster	Red, yellow, orange	Costume, embroidery, etc.	Courage, strength	
Walking animals	Tiger	Orange, black	child hat, etc.	Mighty, brave	
	Bull	Brown, black	black Clothing, decoration	Stability, endurance	
	Horse	Brown, black, white, gray	Hat, headband	Freedom Success	
	Sheep	Brown, white	Costume, decoration	Beautiful	
	Dogs	Brown, White	Costume, decoration	Loyalty, fraternity	
	Deer	Brown or gray	Costume, decoration	Happiness, prosperity	
Reptile	Snake	Yellow, green	Costume, decoration	Survival and reproduction, wisdom	
Fish and insects	Butterfly	Red, yellow, blue	Women's Clothing Wedding Shoes	Spirit of all things, beauty, double life	
	Fish	Red, golden yellow	Costume, decoration	Seeking to conceive many children, harvest, abundance	
	Cicada	Green, brown	Costume, decoration	Life force	
	spider	Black, brown	Costume, decoration	Fulfillment of wishes, removal of diseases	
Mysteries	Dragon	Red, Yellow	Costume, decoration	Power, mystery, spirituality	
	Phoenix	Red, Yellow	Costume, decoration	Auspiciousness, happiness	

Figure 1. Keyword table of some cultural elements of animal prints.

The animal motifs in Figure 1 vividly reflect the traditional cultural characteristics of China's ethnic minorities. These motifs are entirely derived from nature and people's perception of life, as well as folk tales, legends and totem worship, and contain rich cultural connotations.

For example, the butterfly pattern contains unique graphics that convey the distinct semantic connotations of the history, culture, and aesthetic consciousness of China's ethnic minorities. The unique graphics conceal unique semantic connotations of the Minority history and culture, esthetic consciousness, etc[8]. The morphological characteristics of butterfly patterns present realistic or abstract graphics of butterflies. The butterfly's wings typically have complex patterns and designs, and the pattern composition has aesthetic features such as orderliness and symmetry [9]. Usually, bright colors such as red, yellow, blue, etc., are used to increase visual impact. Butterfly patterns often appear on the chest of women's clothing and wedding shoes, symbolizing beauty and happiness. They are also considered to protect people from evil and misfortune, representing love, beauty, and freedom. How to develop innovative product design based on the original cultural connotations of ethnic motifs, rather than simply pasting the motifs onto the product in a raw manner, is a problem that must be solved by creative reasoning for ethnic cultural and creative products.

3. A two-way creative reasoning experiment between animal prints and modern products

3.1. Experiment 1: Creative Reasoning from Product to Animal Patterns

Experimental Objective: Explore designers' commonly used creative reasoning patterns.

Participant Selection: 12 industrial design graduate students with more than four years of product design experience were selected as participants (5 males and 7 females, aged 22-29).

Stimuli: The goal was to cover as many categories and usage environments of products as possible. Eight common products were selected: drones, eye masks, pillowcases, sunglasses, notebooks, cars, chairs, and speedboats, covering both complex and simple products.

Experimental Procedure: Assuming that the participant is researching product design ideas, they were asked to write down as many animal words as possible based on the eight stimuli. After completing the reasoning task, the participants were required to write a brief sentence explaining the reason for each product and animal combination. Only the product words were presented throughout the entire reasoning process.

Experimental Results: The results showed that each participant inferred about three corresponding animals for each product. The common reasoning patterns from product to organism can be divided into "product-animal emotional perception reasoning", "product-animal form reasoning", "product-animal function reasoning", "product-animal scene occurrence reasoning", and "product-animal material reasoning". Tables 1-5 show six reasoning patterns.

Table 1. Affective perception reasoning of "product -Animal"

Produc	Animals	Reason
Chairs	Horse	Gentle horses give people a feeling they can rely on.
Sunglasses	Fish	Light and smooth for a lighter feel.
Car	Tiger, Lion	Some brave and fast animals - design cars.

Table 2. Morphological Reasoning of "product -Animal"

Product	Animals	Reason
Unmanned aircraft	Crane	The way it flies in the sky.
Pillowcase	Cicada	The pillowcase is similar to the wings of a cicada.
Notebook	Butterfly, Cicada	Wings and pages are very similar to the book, and can be opened and closed.

Table 3. Function Reasoning of "product -Animal"

Product	Animals	Reason
Pillowcase	Dogs	Held in the body are soft and very comfortable.
Speedboat	Mandarin ducks, Crane	All can float on the surface of the water, the palms of the feet flapping forward.
Eye Mask	Spider	Eye patch brings darkness, spiders like darkness.

Table 4. Environment Reasoning of "product -Animal"

Product	Animals	Reason
Speedboat	Fish, Snake	All can go fast in the water.
Drones	Bird	live in the sky.
Speedboat	Fish, Snake	All can go fast in the water.

Table 5. Material reasoning of "product -Animal"

Product	Animals	Reason
Chairs	Horse	Gentle horses give people a feeling they can rely on.
Sunglasses	Fish	Light and smooth for a lighter feel.
Car	Tiger, Lion	Some brave and fast animals design cars.

3.2. Experiment 2: Creative Reasoning from Animal Patterns to Products

Experimental Objectives and Participant Selection are consistent with Experiment 1.

Stimuli: The goal was to cover as many animal patterns as possible. Eight common animal patterns were selected: birds, tigers, sheep, fish, snakes, spiders, dragons, and butterflies, covering different categories of traditional patterns. In Luo and Dong's 2017 study, they found that text descriptions can achieve higher innovation in creative design processes [10]. Therefore, only the key names of the animal patterns were provided during the reasoning process.

Experimental Procedure: Assuming that the participant is researching product design ideas, they were asked to write down modern product words associated with the eight stimuli and explain the reasoning behind each animal pattern and its corresponding product in one sentence.

Experimental Results: The results showed that each participant inferred two corresponding modern products for each animal pattern. The common reasoning patterns from animal patterns to products can be divided into "animal-product form reasoning", "animal-product emotional perception reasoning", "animal-product function reasoning", and "animal-product material reasoning". Tables 6-9 show six reasoning patterns and examples.

Table 6. Form reasoning of "Animal - product"

Animals	Produc	Reason
Spider	Refrigerator,sticker	Refrigerator stickers and spiders are shaped like a small..
Bird	Scissors	The bird's wings and scissor handles are similar in outline.
China Dragon	Whip	China Dragon.

Table 7. Affective perception reasoning of "Animal - product"

Animals	Produc	Reason
sheep	Cold repellent supplies	Sheep look warm.
Bird	Infinity Headphones	Free as a bird.
Tiger	King's Crown	Majestic, dignified.

Table 8. Function reasoning of "Animal - product"

Animals	Produc	Reason
Snake	Fans	Winter can not be used to hibernate.
Butterfly	Seeder	Butterfly pollen collection is similar to sowing seeds with a seeder..
Spider	Mosquito Killer	Both can eliminate mosquitoes.

Table 9. Material reasoning of "Animal - product"

Animals	Produc	Reason
Tiger	Leather and fur products	The tiger's fur pattern is very characteristic.
Fish	Necklace	Fish scales have the same shine as jewelry.
Sheep	Sweaters, Blankets	Same hair texture.

During the bi-directional creative reasoning from animal patterns to modern products experiment, it was found that each participant could infer about three matching animal patterns for each product and about two corresponding modern products for each animal pattern.

In the experiment, some participants had a relatively narrow range of reasoning methods, focusing only on emotional perception or functional reasoning. In addition, some participants' reasoning methods also involved cultural connotation interpretation. For example, when thinking of butterfly patterns, they associated it with mothers and inferred baby products accordingly.

It was found in the experiment that emotional perception and form reasoning are the most commonly used reasoning patterns in creative reasoning. However, in the creative design process of traditional ethnic patterns, if animal patterns and modern products are matched one-to-one based solely on emotional perception reasoning, image reasoning, function reasoning, and environment reasoning, the inspiration for creativity is limited.

The historical culture, color characteristics, semantic connotations, and other cultural elements contained in animal patterns cannot be extracted. Moreover, these cultural elements cannot be appropriately combined with traditional crafts to present them on products, and the five cultural elements of "form, color, material, technique, and art" contained in animal patterns cannot be integrated into the design, as summarized in Table 1. Therefore, this paper proposes a creative design reasoning model based on cultural elements.

4. Concept of creative reasoning model based on cultural elements

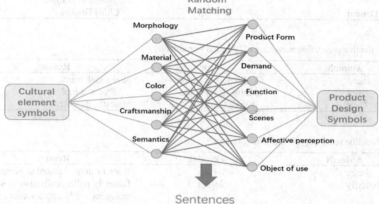

Figure 2. CRPS creative reasoning model based on cultural elements..

To avoid the limitations of creative inspiration brought by one-to-one correspondence between animal patterns and modern products in bi-directional creative reasoning, this paper proposes a "CRPS Creative Design Reasoning Model" based on the five cultural elements of animal patterns: "form, color, material, technique, and art", which encompass the historical culture, color characteristics, semantic connotations, and other cultural elements contained in ethnic animal patterns.

This reasoning model extracts keywords for "Morphology", "Material", "Color", "Craftsmanship", "Semantics", "Product Form", "Function", and "Affective Perception" based on the cultural element symbols of animal patterns and product design symbols. In addition, three keywords from personalized user requirements, "Object of use", "Demand", and "Scenes", are added to the product design symbol dimension. By inputting the animal pattern keywords and corresponding product keywords from Experiments 1 and 2 into the model, along with other cultural element keywords corresponding to the animal patterns and user use keywords, random sentences were generated in the order of "animal pattern, color, craftsmanship, material, product, scene, function, user, emotional expression" to complete creative reasoning based on the five cultural elements of animal patterns: "form, color, material, technique, and art". The generated random sentences were further filtered based on the conditions that the selected manual craft techniques can achieve, helping designers incorporate the cultural elements of patterns and personalized user requirements into product creative design. This model extends the combination of cultural factors in theory, practice, and design process, providing a comprehensive and effective framework for incorporating cultural elements into creative design.

In the specific application of the model, traditional crafts that can present products were used as limiting conditions. In the model validation, the combination of butterfly patterns and eye mask products was selected. The reasoning result of the random sentence generated by the "CRPS Creative Design Reasoning Model" included "butterfly", "blue and white", "batik dyeing", "silk", "eye mask", "resting place", "sleep aid", "mother", and "care". A new creative product combining animal patterns and modern products was designed, as shown in Figure 2. The cultural implication of "Butterflies give birth to all things" was deeply explored in the product promotion concept, positioning the emotional expression of the product as the theme of "attachment" and expressing love and high praise for mothers.

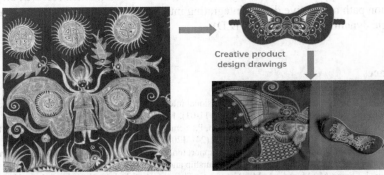

Figure 3. Case diagram of the use of CRPS creative reasoning design based on..

Using this reasoning pattern for creative product design not only allows traditional cultural elements to be incorporated into modern products, enabling users to perceive the cultural symbols and connotations of ethnic aesthetics, values, graphic semantics, and other elements contained within animal patterns but also supports traditional handicraft artisans through the use of traditional manual processing techniques, empowering the inheritance of handicrafts.

5. Conclusion

This article mainly studies the reasoning pattern between traditional animal patterns and modern products, and their application in the creative design of cultural and creative products. This paper proposes a reasoning pattern for creative design that combines the cultural elements of traditional animal patterns with traditional handicrafts and is based on individual user requirements. By identifying the relationship between cultural elements and user requirements, selecting appropriate traditional manual techniques, and generating creative designs based on randomly generated statements according to the reasoning pattern, this study explores an innovative path combining animal pattern graphic cultural elements with modern product creative reasoning. The CRPS creative reasoning pattern was used to practice modern product creative reasoning design for butterfly-patterned animal patterns. By combining user requirements with animal pattern cultural elements, the creative design reasoning preserved the cultural connotations of traditional patterns while allowing pattern graphics and traditional handicrafts to enter people's daily lives in the form of modern products, facilitating their inheritance and development. Therefore, we believe that a product creative design reasoning pattern based on cultural elements is a method worth exploring and applying. In the future, we can further study the relationship between cultural elements and handicrafts, find more cultural elements to apply to creative reasoning, promote innovation and reform of traditional handicrafts, and enable them to play a greater value in modern society.

Acknowlegment

The work was supported by the Zhejiang Social Science Foundation, research on the realization path of creative design integrating intelligent technology to enhance new economic dynamics(No. 21XXJC01ZD).

References

[1] Shijian, L., Cong, F., Shan, P.: The four-dimensional intelligent creative design system in the era of group intelligence innovation. Design Art Research 11(01), 1-5+14 (2021).
[2] Bian, Z., Shijian, L., Zheng, F., Wang, L., Shan, P.: Semantic Reasoning of Product Biologically Inspired Design Based on BERT. Applied Sciences 11(24), 12082 (2021).
[3] Siemon, D., Robra-Bissantz, S.: A creativity support tool for cognitive idea stimulation in entrepreneurial activities. International Journal of Entrepreneurship and Small Business 33(4), 532-552 (2018).
[4] Alipour, L., Faizi, M., Moradi, A. M., Akrami, G: The impact of designers' goals on design-by-analogy. Design Studies 51, 1-24 (2017).
[5] Christensen, Bo T., and Linden J. Ball.: Dimensions of creative evaluation: Distinct design and reasoning strategies for aesthetic, functional, and originality judgments. International Journal of Human-Computer Studies 63(3), 383-404 (2005).
[6] Wu, M. C., Lo, Y. F., Hsu, S. H. : A Case-Based Reasoning Approach to Generating New Product Ideas. The International Journal of Advanced Manufacturing Technology 30(1-2), 166-173 (2005).
[7] Wang, Q.: The cultural connotation of ethnic pattern art. Guizhou Ethnic Studies 39(03), 119-122 (2018).
[8] Peng, Z., Deng, K., Wei, Y., Wang, Z.: Study on the factors affecting the embroidery pattern style of Miao in Leishan. Asian Social Science 17(12), 1-81 (2021).
[9] Yunjuan, L., Siting, Z., Yingjin, G.:The artistic characteristics and cultural connotations of animal patterns in traditional Hakka costumes. Journal of Minjiang College, 42(01),106-112(2021).
[10] Shijian, L., Ye Nan, D.: Role of cultural inspiration with different types in cultural product design activities. International Journal of Technology and Design Education, 27(3),499-515(2017).

Design Studies and Intelligence Engineering
L.C. Jain et al. (Eds.)
© 2024 The Authors.

967

doi:10.3233/FAIA231512

Study on the Design of Children's Home Oral Protection Based on Perceptual Engineering

Yanan ZHANG[a], Weijia GUAN[a], and Yi LIU[a,*][1]

[a] *Fashion Accessory Art and Engineering College,*
Beijing Institute of Fashion Technology, Beijing, P. R. China

Abstract: This paper describes the process and method of designing children's home oral protection products based on perceptual engineering theory. Representative product samples and key perceptual vocabulary are selected through various analysis methods such as survey research. Combined with the semantic differential method for quantitative analysis, the data of users' perceptual cognition of the sample products are obtained, so as to obtain the perceptual vocabulary of the typical samples. Using SPSS factor analysis and principal component analysis, we obtained the variance diagram, fragmentation diagram, rotated factor loading coefficient diagram and component matrix diagram of the typical sample perceptual vocabulary data, and extracted four key perceptual vocabularies affecting the design of children's household oral protection products: "cartoon", "experience ", "warmth", and "texture". The method satisfies children's perceptual needs and provides a reference for product design research in children's groups.

Keywords. perceptual engineering; children's oral cavity; semantic differential method; principal component analysis

1.Introduction

Perceptual engineering is widely used in several fields, including medical assistance, smart products, education and healthcare, and digital arts. In the design of assistive devices for the elderly and disabled, perceptual engineering and the KANO evaluation method are combined to focus on user needs and create products that meet user expectations, such as smart medicine boxes. Perceptual engineering is also used in the smart home field to extract design elements to meet users' emotional needs by analyzing user needs and semantic differential methods, such as Bluetooth speakers. In addition, perceptual engineering helps to satisfy users' emotional needs in the design of medical devices, such as forearm and elbow mobilizers, by establishing the connection between emotional needs and perceptual vocabulary through factor analysis and semantic differential method, which guides the design of product styling. Perceptual engineering provides critical support for product design in different fields.

---
* Liu Yi ,gxyly@bift.edu.cn

2.Design process

Perceptual engineering is a methodology for obtaining users' perceptual imagery of product attributes and incorporating it into the design process to guide and evaluate the design. The methodology consists of three phases: perceptual imagery acquisition, data analysis, and design output. In the case of children's oral protection design, these phases include:

(1) Perceptual imagery acquisition: screening perceptual vocabulary through principal component analysis expert evaluation, selecting key perceptual adjectives through questionnaire survey, and establishing a product intent styling evaluation system to understand the intentional needs of the target group of children for the product.

(2) Analyzing data: analyzing and organizing the evaluation of representative sample data through the use of semantic differential scales and other tools.

(3) Design output: Develop design principles and product design, analyze and organize data results by analyzing and organizing data results.

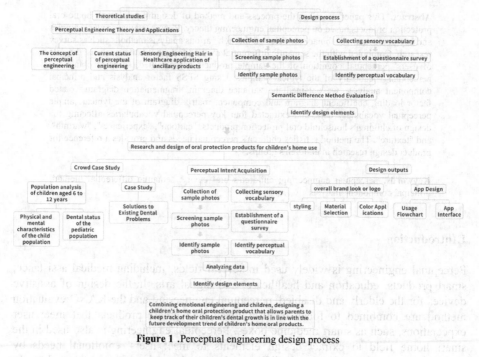

Figure 1 .Perceptual engineering design process

3.Physical and psychological characteristics of children

6-12 years old is the critical period of children's oral development, milk teeth are replaced by permanent teeth, need to pay special attention to children's oral and facial health, teeth in accordance with the "left-right symmetry, first down then up" order of replacement, about 6 years.

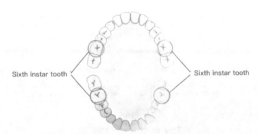

Figure 2 Sixth instar tooth

In the stage of psychological development of children aged 0-12 years, including early childhood, preschool and elementary school, cognitive ability develops gradually, physical strength is limited, and the world is understood mainly through sensory and visual cognition. Therefore, the cognitive characteristics and physiological conditions of children in different age groups need to be considered in product design (As shown in Table 1).

Table 1. Three stages of children's cognitive development

Cognitive development	psychological characteristic	Behavioral characteristics
0-2 years sensory-motor steps	Apply actuality to what is currently being felt	Various reflexive behaviors Simple motor habits around one's body mimic familiar behaviors
Pre-operational stage 2-7	Thought irreversibility, lack of constancy structure self-centeredness begins to diminish	To engage in "thinking" with a variety of simple language and symbols, one needs to be guided
Concrete operations stage, ages 7-12	Logical thinking, arithmetic skills, conceptual systems used for concrete things, gradually able to apply conservative principles	To engage in "thinking" with a variety of simple language and symbols, one needs to be guided

In addition, many children are squeamish about dental treatment, with high prevalence rates ranging from 39.90% to 43.4%. This poses a challenge to oral care and treatment and needs to be addressed early to avoid any impact on dental treatment in adulthood.

4.Research process

Applying the perceptual engineering method to design the styling of children's home oral protection products, the steps include establishing the correlation between the children's perceptual library and the product design elements, constructing a perceptual engineering system, conducting perceptual analysis including design concepts, sketches, and schemes, and finally establishing a process for predicting users' perceptual responses, which is illustrated in Figure 3.

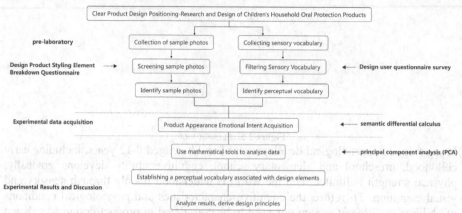

Figure 3 Specific operational procedures for children's home oral protection products

4.1. Establishment of a Typical Sample Bank

The purpose of this experiment is to understand children's preference for the styling of household oral protection products. Through market research and product picture collection, representative oral product styling pictures were selected based on factors such as visibility, clarity, product shooting angle, and product styling similarity in order to further analyze the preferences of the target consumer group.

Figure 4 Sample images

Four design experts extracted nine representative samples from a sample of children's home oral products and analyzed them using the semantic differential method based on factors such as design style, functional features and usage experience, in order to understand the target group's perceptual intention towards existing products and provide a basis for subsequent design research.

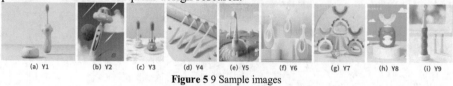

(a) Y1   (b) Y2   (c) Y3   (d) Y4   (e) Y5   (f) Y6   (g) Y7   (h) Y8   (i) Y9

Figure 5 9 Sample images

4.2. Sensory vocabulary collection

A perceptual vocabulary base was created, with an initial collection of 100 words (shown in Figure 6), and 20 words related to children's oral products were retained after screening. Next, a questionnaire survey was conducted including 8 experts, 24 product designers and 30 children aged between 6-12 years. The survey was conducted using adjective pairs, and 10 groups of adjectives with the most votes were finalized (as shown in Table 2).

1. stable 2. soft 3. environmentally friendly 4. balanced 5. curved 6. safe 7. stress–reducing 8. creative 9. growing 10. rich 11. quirky, 12. pleasing to the ear 13. playful 14. interesting 15 intelligent 16. cozy 17. flexible 18. interactive 19. quiet 20. sedate 21. explorable 22. patient 23. immersive 24. Effective 25. Cartoon 26. Frosted 27. Design 28. Popular 29. Bright 30. Wear–resistant 31. Skeletonized 32. Natural 33. Simple 34. Balanced 35. Drop–resistant 36. Substantial 37. Professional 38. Versatile 39. Experiential 40. Plastic 41. Smooth 42. Ease of use 43. Morphing 44. Bionic 45.Convenient 46.Clean 47.Intelligent 48.Time–saving 49.Comfortable 50.Universal 51.Delicate 52.Relaxing 53.Coordinated 54.Fun 55.Active 56.Practical 57.Reasonable 58.Relaxing 59. Smooth 60.Long–lasting 61.Changing 62.Practical 63.Affectionate 64.Warm 65.Good 66. Technological 67. Innovative 68. Popular 69. Growing 70. Adaptable 71. Kind 72. Energetic 73. Safe 74. Rounded 75. Dexterous 76. Expensive 77. Mobile 78. Intelligent 79. Efficient 80. Aesthetically pleasing 81. Advanced 82. Harmonized 83. Leisurely 84. Favorite 85. Tender 86. Beautiful 87. 88 energetic 89. sturdy 90. unique 91. popular 92. popular 93. retro 94. innovative 95. old–fashioned 96. light 97. changing 98. realistic 99. growing 100. unchanging

Figure 6 100 sensory words

Table 2. Sentimental Intention Adjectives Ranked in the Top 10 by Votes

conjunctions	vote	conjunctions	vote
funny thing	39	experiential	35
cartoon	39	wearable	34
warm	39	textured	32
growing	36	popular	31
interactive	35	colorful	30

Through market research and picture collection, 9 children's oral protection products were selected, combined with 10 groups of perceptual vocabulary for questionnaire survey. 28 experts and designers rated the products, and then statistically drew conclusions to provide reference for future product design. Examples of questionnaires are shown in Figure 7.

Figure 7 Sample of children's oral products Y8 Sample questionnaire

4.3. Experimental data acquisition phase

The expert ratings of the different adjectives in each sample were counted by principal component analysis, according to the computational formula of the additive principal component analysis:

Let there be a comprehensive semantic indicator $F_i(i = 1,2,\ldots,m)$, coefficients $a_{ij}(j = 1,2,\ldots,m)$, $(m \leq n)$ initial indicator variable X_{jo}. then the linear combination of comprehensive semantic indicator and indicator variable is.

$$\begin{cases} F_1 = a_{11}x_1 + a_{12}x_2 + \ldots + a_{1n}x_n \\ F_2 = a_{21}x_1 + a_{22}x_2 + \ldots + a_{2n}x_n \\ \cdots \\ F_m = a_{m1}x_1 + a_{m2}x_2 + \ldots + a_{mn}x_n \end{cases} \quad (1)$$

The results are as follows:

KMO value		0.723
	approximate chi–square (math.)	179.460
Bartlett's test of sphericity	df	45
	p–value	0.000

Figure 8 KMO and Bartlett's test

Using principal component analysis for information enrichment research, the KMO value was 0.723 (greater than 0.6), which meets the prerequisite requirements for principal component analysis, and the data can be used for principal component analysis research. At the same time, the data passed the Bartlett sphericity test (p<0.05), which is suitable for principal component analysis.

Table 3. Table of variance explained

serial number	characteristic root			principal component extraction		
	characteristic root	Variance explained %	Cumulative %	characteristic root	Variance explained %	Cumulative %
1	5.254	52.544	52.544	5.254	52.544	52.544
2	1.376	13.759	66.303	1.376	13.759	66.303
3	1.181	11.808	78.111	1.181	11.808	78.111
4	0.682	6.816	84.927	-	-	-
5	0.554	5.537	90.464	-	-	-
6	0.315	3151	93.615	-	-	-
7	0.242	2.423	96.038	-	-	-
8	0.231	2.307	98.345	-	-	-
9	0.090	0.896	99.240	-	-	-
10	0.076	0.760	100.00	-	-	-

Three principal components were extracted by principal component analysis with eigenroot values greater than 1. The variance explained was 52.544%, 13.759%, and 11.808%, respectively, and the cumulative variance explained was 78.111%. The weights of the three principal components were 67.27%, 17.61% and 15.12%, respectively.

Table 4. Table of factor loading coefficients after rotation

name (of a thing)	ingredient			Commonality (common factor variance)
	ingredient1	ingredient2	ingredient3	
funny thing1	0.785	0.440	0.066	0.814
cartoon2	0.894	0.111	-0.110	0.823
warm3	0.152	0.865	-0.139	0.791
growing4	0.675	0.563	0.095	0.782
interactive5	0.881	0.186	0.037	0.812
experiential6	0.920	0.150	0.102	0.880
wearable7	0.236	0.391	0.718	0.724
textured8	-0.110	-0.179	0.817	0.803
popular9	0.529	0.439	0.074	0.477
colorful10	0.285	0.887	0.190	0.904

The commonality values of all study items were higher than 0.4, indicating strong correlations with the study items and factors. Factor 1 is strongly correlated with experience, cartoon, and interaction; Factor 2 is strongly correlated with bright, fun, and growth; and Factor 3 is strongly correlated with texture and wear.

Table 5. Matrix of component score coefficients

name (of a thing)	ingredient		
	ingredient1	ingredient2	ingredient3
funny thing1	0.178	0.044	0.001
cartoon2	0.319	−0.180	−0.108
warm3	−0.187	0.507	−0.172
growing4	0.099	0.150	0.016
interactive5	0.290	−0.141	−0.004
experiential6	0.314	−0.179	0.047
wearable7	−0.035	0.123	0.504
textured8	−0.008	−0.145	0.668
popular9	0.078	0.116	0.012
colorful10	−0.148	0.458	0.070

In the component matrix obtained from principal component extraction, perceptual adjectives are mainly influenced by component 1, with consumers paying most attention to "cartoon", "experiential" and "interactive". Constituent 2 also has a strong influence on perceptual adjectives, with users valuing "warm" and "brightly colored". Constituent 3 is less influential on perceptual adjectives, with users focusing on "texture".

4.4. Design principle outputs

Based on the results of statistical analysis, cartoon, experiential, warm, textured, were finally selected as the characterization of the new product design.

5.Design program

The perceptual goals of oral protection products for children aged 6-12 years include a cartoon appearance and warmth, as well as experiential interaction and material textures.

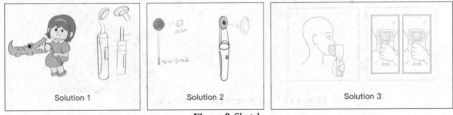

Solution 1   Solution 2   Solution 3

Figure 9 Sketch

Solution 1 uses two parts, a toy model and a dental monitor, with an app to view 3D images of teeth;

Solution 2 is designed in the shape of a lollipop with a built-in high-definition camera for oral inspection, and parents can view the images on an app;

Solution 3 is designed for the preventive detection of dental caries, using a specific infrared camera to make early caries visible.

All of these design solutions aim to improve the accuracy and efficiency of children's oral inspection, while taking into account children's perceptual needs and fear factors.

5.1.Final Solution

This children's home oral protection product takes into account children's sensory preferences and oral health needs. It is produced under the design principles of "cartoon, experience, warmth and texture".

The design adopts the cartoon shape and lollipop shape, the cute candy probe attracts children and facilitates oral examination, and the size refers to the national standard (Figure 10). The handle adopts the second form according to the experiment (Figure 11) streamlined design, textured material and non-slip design to enhance the grip experience. In terms of functionality, the product has a built-in high-definition camera, LED lights to remind the oral condition, parents can view dental images through the APP, and provide interactive elements to ease children's fear. Food-grade silicone and medical plastic are used to ensure safety. Colorful children's favorites that inspire creativity. The comprehensive design aims to create a product that is appealing to children and effective in monitoring oral health.

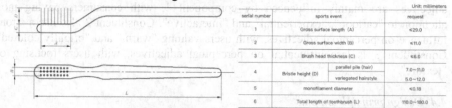

serial number	sports event		request
			Unit: millimeters
1	Gross surface length (A)		≤29.0
2	Gross surface width (B)		≤11.0
3	Brush head thickness (C)		≤6.0
4	Bristle height (D)	parallel pile (hair)	7.0~11.0
		variegated hairstyle	5.0~12.0
5	monofilament diameter		≤0.18
6	Total length of toothbrush (L)		110.0~180.0

Figure 10 Children's toothbrush sizes

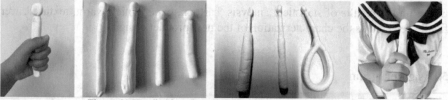

Figure 11 Handheld product experiment for children's products

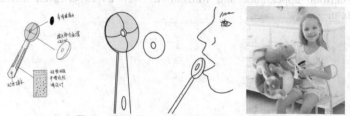

Figure 12 Final program presentation drawing

Figure 13 Schematic model diagram

6.Conclusion

The study addresses the emotional needs of children aged 6-12 years old and the overall design of the form, function and human-machine interface of home oral protection products. Steps include:
(1) In-depth understanding of the behavioral and psychological characteristics of the target group;
(2) Establishing a perceptual vocabulary database and collecting the target group's perceptual intention adjectives for oral protection products;
(3) Repositioning the product's form design through principal component analysis;
(4) Utilizing computer-aided design software to carry out the product form design, and at the same time perfecting the product's function, structure and use details.

Acknowledgement

This research was financially supported Beijing Institute of Fashion Technology College of 2023Graduate Research Innovation Project and this paper is sponsored by the Humanities and Social Sciences of Ministry of Education Planning Fund "Research on Digital Design and Communication of National Fashion Clothing from the Perspective of Cultural Confidence" (22YJAZH037) and Postgraduate Education and Teaching Reform Project of Beijing Institute of Fashion Technology (NHFZ20230188).

References

[1] QI Hao,CHEN Jinglian. A design method of elderly home medicine box integrating KANO and perceptual engineering. Packaging Engineering **43** (2022), 6, 49-55.
[2] ZHANG Bao,HU Angguo, ZHANG Di. Research on CMF design method of Bluetooth speaker based on perceptual engineering. Packaging Engineering **42** (2021), 8, 156-161.
[3] FU Xiaoli,CUI Ruchen. Design of forearm and elbow joint mobilizer based on perceptual engineering. Industrial Design **06** (2022), 28-30.

Design Studies and Intelligence Engineering
L.C. Jain et al. (Eds.)
© 2024 The Authors.
This article is published online with Open Access by IOS Press and distributed under the terms
of the Creative Commons Attribution Non-Commercial License 4.0 (CC BY-NC 4.0).
doi:10.3233/FAIA231513

Research on Style Transfer of Artistic Images Based on Artificial Intelligence

Jian WANG[1]

Changsha University of science and technology, School of Design Art, Changsha, 410114, China

Abstract: In order to solve some inherent defects of generative confrontation network model in artistic image processing, such as unstable training, gradient disappearance and pattern collapse, the research on artistic image style transfer based on artificial intelligence generative confrontation network is put forward (overall method). On the basis of generative countermeasure network, the network model structure is optimized, and the spectral normalization processing is introduced and the residual structure is improved. Normalization constrains the parameter learning range of the network model, accelerates the learning speed of the model, and has a certain regularization effect; In the generator network, a new residual structure is used to optimize the signal propagation and reduce the training error. Through the treatment of identity mapping, ResNet network alleviates the problems of gradient disappearance and network degradation caused by deep network layers. The experimental results show that 10 subjects, aged between 22 and 30, including 3 females and 7 males, were invited to participate in the test. They had never been exposed to 30 pictures in the two groups, and the corresponding model of each group was unknown. From the results, the stylized pictures using the model proposed in this paper are more popular among young people, with an evaluation rate of 58% and better visual experience. Conclusion: Experiments show that the improved algorithm is better than the original algorithm in image style conversion.

Keywords: image style transfer; Deep learning; Generative countermeasure network; Artistic images

1 Introduction

Visual art is a visible work of art, which is ubiquitous in our daily life, ranging from a sculpture and a building to a dress and a photo. Using the current scientific and technological means to analyze visual art images can not only help non-art majors better understand and appreciate art, so as to enhance their aesthetic ability and cultivate their sentiment, but also help art theory researchers, artists and other types of artists to interpret art works from different angles, analyze the development law of art history, and even stimulate creative inspiration. The basis of using computer to analyze artistic works lies in the classification of visual artistic images.

In recent years, peoples material life has developed rapidly, and more and more people have gradually improved their pursuit of spiritual and cultural life. Museums, art galleries and other places have been widely welcomed by people [1]. Works of art are

---

[1] Corresponding Author.

very common in peoples daily life. Tall and magnificent buildings, colorful costumes, exquisite and lovely handicrafts and so on are all part of art. Peoples understanding and preference for works of art also reflect their unique aesthetic to a certain extent. In fact, peoples yearning for and pursuit of art can be traced back to tens of thousands of years ago. As early as ancient times, people began to draw murals on mountain walls. Up to now, more and more people are willing to participate in artistic activities (such as photography), and appreciating art has become a daily pastime and temperament-cultivating activity. With the gradual improvement of the construction of art websites, modern digital art galleries and other materials, many people have begun to use network resources to learn art-related knowledge [2]. Therefore, how to use computer technology to process and analyze a large number of works of art, so as to help people better understand and appreciate art has become particularly important.

2 Literature review

Markov Random Field (MRF) model, that is, using nonparametric sampling texture generation method, selects the most similar texture segment from the sample texture picture and fills the original image with pixels. However, every pixel needs to traverse the texture fragment, so even a small texture patch takes hours or days to generate [3]. Inspired by MRF method, the running speed of the model is improved by two orders of magnitude by using tree-structured vector quantization (TSVQ). Take an example texture sample and a random noise image with a user-specified size as input. According to the position and color value of each pixel in the random noise image, an example texture region similar to it is selected for filling [4]. The user directly inputs the interactive control of the texture synthesis process, that is, the color selected from the input texture is used to draw the target image. The algorithm can also generate candidate textures through different iterations to provide users with choices. However, this algorithm is not suitable for any texture, and only includes many repeated patterns in nature, such as pebbles, leaves, shrubs, flowers and branches [5]. Related researchers have developed a texture transfer algorithm based on image gradient. Considering the gradient direction, L-shaped is added to evaluate the similarity of the neighborhood to improve the effectiveness of the algorithm [6]. Wu, Q and others put forward a method of re-coloring and nonlinear image filtering, which can quantize the color image according to the main color of the image and generate an image with oil painting style. In addition, through the interactive interface with the user, the color, brightness, contrast and other attributes of each pixel are processed separately to achieve the effect of local thinning of the generated image [7]. Singh, A. et al. proposed a facial style transfer algorithm based on local multi-scale style transformation [8]. Wang, L. and others think that the direct application of general style transformation will deform the face of a character, so the style transformation can be realized by locally capturing spatial changes and processing facial textures of different scales, but the generated results are easily influenced by masks, and there may be cases of input noise amplification [9].

In this paper, the network model structure is optimized on the basis of the production countermeasure network, and the spectral normalization processing is introduced and the residual structure is improved. Normalization constrains the parameter learning range of the network model, accelerates the learning speed of the model, and has a certain regularization effect; In the generator network, a new residual structure is used to optimize the signal propagation and reduce the training error. Through the treatment of identity mapping, ResNet network alleviates the problems of gradient disappearance and network degradation caused by deep network layers. Finally, the algorithm model is verified by experiments, and the evaluation standard of the algorithm model is put forward. Experiments show that the improved algorithm has improved the effect of image style conversion compared with the original algorithm.

3 research methods

3.1 Cycle Consistency Generation Countermeasure Network Model

The proposal of generating countermeasure network has brought a different ray of light to deep learning, and GAN has also been used more and more in the field of image migration style. Some improved models for generating countermeasure networks, including WGAN, DCGAN, CGAN and Pix2Pix, have been mentioned above, but these networks require Paired training data sets, that is, the data sets must be paired. If a scene is converted from day to night, it is required to provide the image data set of day and night in the same scene, which is more demanding [10]. Therefore, CycleGAN came into being and can be trained with unpaired data sets. As shown in fig. 1a, the cyclic consistency generative countermeasure network consists of two groups of generative countermeasure networks, and X and Y represent image data sets from different domains.

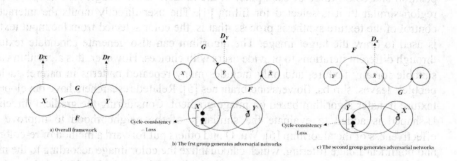

a) Overall framework   b) The first group generates adversarial networks   c) The second group generates adversarial networks

Figure1 .CycleGAN network model

The task of image style transfer can be regarded as the mapping from one kind of image set to another. X and Y are unpaired two sets of image data sets in different fields. Different from the native GAN network, CycleGAN network structure defines two generators, namely $G: X \rightarrow Y$ and $F: Y \rightarrow X$. The two generators are cyclically consistent, namely: $F(G(x)) \approx x$ and $G(F(y)) \approx y$. As shown in figs. 1b and 1c, take the first generation countermeasure network as an example, which includes a generator G and a discriminator. D_Y Used to judge the image data x Does it belong to the field? Y. One of the generators G sends the data x generate Y Data in the domain $\hat{Y}$, another generator F will $\hat{Y}$ Restore to the original domain $\hat{x}$ For the sake of consistency, x and $\hat{x}$ They should be as close as possible, and the distance between them is called Cycle-consistency Loss. For the whole network, the two groups generate the loss function of the countermeasure network as follows (1) and (2):

$$
\begin{aligned}
L_{GAN}(G, D_Y, X, Y) \\
= E_{y \sim p_{\text{data}}}(y)[\log D_Y(y)] \\
+ E_{x \sim p_{\text{data}}}(x)[\log (1 - D_Y(G(x)))]
\end{aligned}
\tag{1}
$$

$$
\begin{aligned}
L_{GAN}(F, D_X, X, Y) \\
= E_{x \sim p_{\text{data}}}(y)[\log D_X(x)] \\
+ E_{y \sim p_{\text{data}}}(y)[\log (1 - D_X(F(y)))]
\end{aligned}
\tag{2}
$$

For the loss of cyclic consistency, the generator G is forward cyclic consistency, that is: $x \to G(x) \to F(G(x)) \approx x$, generator f is the reverse cycle consistent, namely: $y \to F(y) \to G(F(y)) \approx y$ The loss with cyclic consistency adopts L1 norm, and its total cyclic consistency loss can be written as the following formula (3):

$$
\begin{aligned}
L_{cyc}(G, F) = E_{x \sim p_{\text{data}}}(x)[\| F(G(x)) - x \|_1] \\
+ E_{y \sim p_{\text{data}}}(y)[\| G(F(y)) - y \|_1]
\end{aligned}
\tag{3}
$$

Therefore, the total loss function is the following formula (4):

$$
L(G, F, D_X, D_Y) = L_{GAN}(G, D_Y, X, Y) + L_{GAN}(F, D_X, Y, X) + \lambda L_{cyc}(G, F)
\tag{4}
$$

Among them, λ The correlation between the generated data is characterized. The larger the value, the closer the generated content is to the conditional image, and the final optimization function is similar to that of the native GAN, so it is necessary to solve the minimax problem, namely the following formula (5):

$$
G^*, F^* = \arg \min_{G,F} \max_{D_X, D_Y} L(G, F, D_X, D_Y)
\tag{5}
$$

In the network structure, the generator network consists of three parts: coding layer, conversion layer and decoding layer, and the discriminator network consists of convolutional neural network to judge whether the input image belongs to a certain classification.

3.2 Image Style Migration Method Based on CycleGAN

3.2.1 Normalization of the model

In the early stage of training, the discriminator can often accurately discriminate the false sample data output by the generator, and the generator will quickly fail, so this paper studies the performance control of the discriminator. In order to better control the output performance of the discriminator, it is necessary to satisfy the Lipsey continuity, which is a smoother condition than the usual continuity [11,12]. Specifically, it is desirable to limit the speed at which the function of the discriminator changes, that is, it is necessary to limit the modulus of the function gradient of the discriminator D to fluctuate within a controllable range, and also to make the function smoother. In order to achieve control purposes, it is conventional to regularize functions, such as L^1 Regularization, L^2 Regularization and sparseness, etc. In this paper, spectral normalization is introduced to limit the function gradient of the neural network. Spectral normalization constrains the Lipsey constant of the discriminator by constraining the spectral norm of the weight matrix of the discriminator network, so that any input X will not be stretched, specifically, every time the network parameter matrix W is updated, it will be divided by the maximum singular value.$\sigma(W)$, as shown in the following formula (6):

$$W \leftarrow \frac{W}{\sigma(W)} \tag{6}$$

The advantage of this method is that it can limit the function gradient of neural network without destroying the proportional relationship between parameters. However, in order to calculate the maximum spectral coefficient of the discriminant neural network, the singular value decomposition of the parameter matrix must be carried out for each layer of the network in each training iteration, especially when the weight dimension of the network is relatively large, heavy calculation will waste a lot of computing resources. Therefore, in order to reduce the calculation amount and speed up the operation efficiency, the singular value is approximately obtained by using the power iteration method. Let a be a matrix, and its maximum singular value (a) is satisfied, as shown in the following formula (7):

$$\sigma(A) > \frac{\| A\xi \|_2}{\| \xi \|_2} \tag{7}$$

The power iteration method can be briefly summarized as follows: firstly, a non-zero initial vector v is selected, and after an iteration sequence is constructed, the approximate solution of the unit principal eigenvector is obtained by mutual iteration of equations 3-7, and then the following equations (8) and (9) are transformed:

$$\hat{u} \leftarrow \frac{W_T \hat{v}}{\|W_T \hat{v}\|_2} \tag{8}$$

$$\hat{v} \leftarrow \frac{W_T \hat{u}}{\|W_T \hat{u}\|_2} \tag{9}$$

$$\sigma(W) \approx \hat{v} W_T \hat{u} \tag{10}$$

3.2.2 Residual structure of the model

With the complexity of the model, problems such as over-fitting, too heavy calculation and network degradation began to appear. Some scholars thought that the above problems might be caused by the deep network. Later, others put forward the residual structure, that is, adding a group of direct connections from input to output. The residual structure convolves the difference between output and input, and both input and output are normalized in batches, which has achieved certain results. After that, it is improved on the basis of ResNet, and an improved residual network ResNetV2 is proposed. In the initial ResNet, because the batch normalization is placed after the addition operation, the signal propagation is hindered and the error decreases slowly at the initial stage of training, while the linear rectification function is placed after the addition operation, which makes the output constant and affects the representation ability of the model [13]. ResNet adopts a structure of pre-activated residual network, which reduces the limitation of residual function value domain and has better performance than the previous residual network. The structure of pre-activated residual network is shown in Figure 2. In the next experiment, different residual structure combinations will be used to verify the improvement effect of the residual model on the generation of countermeasure networks.

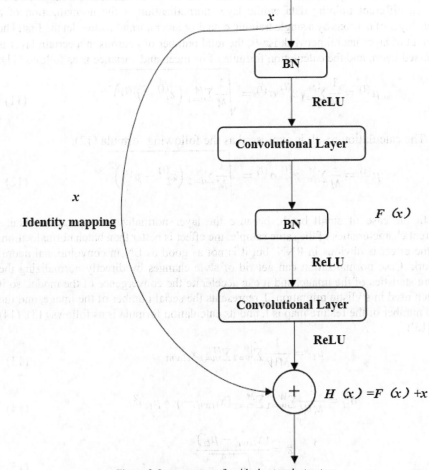

Figure 2. Improvement of residual network structure

3.2.3 Structure of generator model and discriminator model

The original cyclic consistency generation countermeasure network uses the original residual network structure in its coding layer. Based on the traditional network architecture, this paper improves the generator and adopts a new residual network in its coding layer. The BN-Inception network model with batch normalization processing and related normalization models, the normalization goal is to make the data distribution consistent, and the selection of normalization function will bring certain influence to the network performance.

Batch normalization usually calculates the mean and variance of each batch along the channel, then normalizes and adjusts the data to a normal distribution with a mean of 0 and a variance of 1. Normalization can make the data distribution consistent and improve the problem of gradient disappearance [14]. However, BN is sensitive to the size of batch. If batch is too small, the calculated mean and variance of batch normalization can not well reflect the distribution of data.

Layer normalization is to normalize CHW in the channel direction, and to normalize all neurons in a certain layer in the network structure, regardless of the size of batch and the depth of input sequence. Batch normalization is the normalization of a single neuron between different training data, while layer normalization is the normalization of a certain layer of neurons by a single training data. For layer normalization, let the first$l$The net input of layer neural network is$z^{(l)}$, the total number of neurons in a certain layer is expressed by m, and the calculation formula of its mean and variance is as follows (11):

$$\mu^{(l)} = \frac{1}{M}\sum_{i=1}^{M} z_i^{(l)} \quad \sigma^{(l)} = \sqrt{\frac{1}{M}\sum_{i=1}^{M}\left(z_i^{(l)} - \mu^{(l)}\right)^2} \tag{11}$$

The calculation result is expressed as the following formula (12):

$$\mu^{(l)} = \frac{1}{M}\sum_{i=1}^{M} z_i^{(l)} \quad \sigma^{(l)} = \sqrt{\frac{1}{M}\sum_{i=1}^{M}\left(z_i^{(l)} - \mu^{(l)}\right)^2} \tag{12}$$

In the case of small batch, because the layer normalization operation obtains different characteristics of the same sample, the effect is better than batch normalization, and the effect is obvious in RNN, but it is not as good as BN in convolutional neural network. Case normalization can get rid of style changes by directly normalizing the feature statistics of the image, and it can accelerate the convergence of the model, so it is often used in stylistic migration. T represents the serial number of the image, and the serial number of the feature map is I, and its calculation formula is as follows (13), (14) and (15):

$$\mu_{ti} = \frac{1}{MW}\sum_{w=1}^{W}\sum_{m=1}^{M} x_{tiwm} \tag{13}$$

$$\sigma_{ti}^2 = \frac{1}{MW}\sum_{w=1}^{W}\sum_{m=1}^{M}(x_{tiwh} - \gamma * \mu_{ti})^2 \tag{14}$$

$$\tilde{z} = \frac{(x_{tiwh} - \mu_{ti})}{\sqrt{\sigma_{ti}^2 + \varepsilon}} \tag{15}$$

Adaptive normalization combines batch normalization, layer normalization and case normalization, and gives corresponding weights. The network adaptively learns to allocate each normalized ratio, which has the best effect, but the training is more complicated and requires a lot of calculation. To sum up, this paper adds the instance normalization structure to the generator network to improve the generator performance. The generator network structure consists of coding layer, conversion layer and decoding layer. In the coding layer, the instance normalization structure and ReLU activation function are added, which are expressed in the form of Conv+IN+ReLU, where the first layer has a step size of 1, the convolution kernel size of 7*7 and the number of channels is 64, while the next two layers have different convolution kernels, with a step size of 2 and the number of channels of 128 and 228 respectively. In the transfer floor structure, nine improved ResNetV2 residual networks are used. The structure uses the case normalization model to process the characteristic diagram, and the pre-activation function uses the constant linear rectifier function ReLU. Finally, the convolution kernel with the size of 3*3 is used for convolution, the step size is set to 2, and the number of channels is unchanged. The process of IN-ReLU-Conv is repeated, and the feature image obtained after IN+ReLU+Conv operation is added with the feature image of identity mapping [15]. The decoding layer structure is composed of two layers of De Conv-IN-ReLU structure and one layer of Conv-IN-ReLU structure. The size of transposed convolution kernel in the first two layers is 3*3, the step size is set to 2, and the number of channels is 256 and 128. The last layer uses 7*7 convolution kernel, the step size is 2, and the number of channels is 3. The residual network structure is easy to train and has strong feature extraction ability.

The above is the generator structure of the model, which realizes the migration from the source domain image to the target domain image. The discriminator discriminates between the real image in the target domain and the pseudo-target transferred from the source domain style, and outputs a judgment quantity to measure the similarity between the generated image and the image set in the target domain. Markov discriminant is adopted in this model, which can ensure the detail and clarity of the image, so it has been widely used in image style transfer [16]. Finally, the Markov discriminator will output a one-dimensional map to discriminate the image, and each output of the one-dimensional map corresponds to a receptive field in the original image. In addition, the parameter matrix of the network is often regularized to ensure the smooth function curve. In this model, spectral normalization function is used instead of batch normalization function after convolution layer to obtain better regularization effect. The discriminator model consists of five layers of networks, and the convolution layer uses a convolution kernel with the size of 4*4. The step size of the first three layers is set to 2, the number of channels is 64, 128 and 256 respectively, and the slope of the Leaky Relu function is set to 0.2.

4 Result analysis

4.1 Experimental Data and Platform

The experimental platform of this paper adopts Intel Xeon series E5-2620V4,8-core 2.1GHz frequency, 16G DDR4 memory, 512G SSD and NVIDIA GTX series 1080Ti GPU. The operating system is Ubuntu version 18.04, and the experiment is mainly based on TensorFlow learning framework, which contains a complete ecosystem of various development and project research. It is an open source deep learning framework with version 1.6.0,CUDA CUDA version 9.0, and the programming language used is Python. The main experiment in this paper is based on the artistic image data set, including the artistic image data set downloaded from wikiart and Flickr, and compared with the original CycleGAN. In order to ensure the independence of the training and the accuracy of the data, a Matlab program was written to process the pictures, and the images with specifications larger than 256,256 were cut, and the edge values were removed, and the images with specifications smaller than 256,256 were discarded. In total, four types of subdivided artistic works were adopted, namely Van Gogh, Monet, Cezanne and Japanese genre paintings. Among them, there are 350 works of Van Gogh, 561 works of Monet, 497 works of Cezanne and 659 works of Japanese color ukiyo-e.

In addition, about 8,000 landscape pictures were crawled by the crawler program, and the images with the size of 256,256 were also processed by Matlab and the data smaller than this specification were discarded, and 5,200 effective image data sets were obtained. 200 pieces of landscape images are randomly selected to form a test set, and all kinds of art works are separately formed into a training set A, which is divided into Van Goghs training set, Monets training set, Cezannes training set and Ukiyo -e training set, and the remaining landscape images are used as a training set B.

In training, Adam(Adaptive Moment Estimation) optimization algorithm is used to optimize the model parameters. The initial learning rate is fixed at 0.0002, and all the batch sizes of the experiment are set to 1, with a total of 200 iterations. In the training process, each iteration will randomly sample an image from training set A and training set B, feed forward the two images first, and calculate the reconstruction loss, content loss, confrontation loss and identity mapping loss respectively, and carry out gradient back propagation [17]. During the experiment, the value in the cyclic consistency loss function is set to 10, and the activation function of the convolution layer in the discriminator network uses the Leaky-ReLU function with a slope of 0.2.

4.2 Experimental evaluation criteria and methods

In the evaluation criteria of image style transfer quality, it can be generally divided into two categories, namely subjective evaluation criteria and objective evaluation criteria. Subjective evaluation criteria lay particular stress on humans intuitive feeling as the standard to measure image quality, which is closely related to visual sensory experience; The objective evaluation standard pays more attention to eliminating the influence of subjective factors as much as possible, and uses a unified standard algorithm or function to evaluate the correlation or error between the picture and the real picture as a quantitative evaluation index to evaluate the generated image. The commonly used objective evaluation criteria include Mean Square Error,MSE) and Peak Signal-to-Noise Ratio,PSNR). However, the above methods are all based on the errors of corresponding pixels, and the evaluation results may be similar but quite different from the actual effect or experience, which cannot fully represent the results of image evaluation, so it is necessary to add the indicators of humanoid visual evaluation to measure them together [18]. Brightness, contrast and structure are one of the elements of an image. Structural SIMilarity,SSIM) measures the similarity of images from the above three aspects, taking objective indicators as the main body and taking into account human visual preferences to some extent. In this paper, PSNR and SSIM are used to evaluate the stylized quality of images. The higher the value of PSNR and SSIM, the higher the stylized quality of images is. Among them, structural similarity is used to measure the similarity of images. Set two$m \times n$Image collection of$I$and$K$For any I and J, the peak signal-to-noise ratio can be defined as the following formula (16):

$$MSE = \frac{1}{mn}\sum_{i=0}^{m-1}\sum_{j=0}^{n-1}[I(i,j) - K(i,j)]^2 \tag{16}$$

Where MSE is the mean square error and is defined as the following formula (17):

$$PSNR = 10\log\left[\frac{(2^n - 1)^2}{MSE}\right] \tag{17}$$

Given two images X and y,SSIM is defined as the following formula (18) and (19):

$$SSIM\ (x,y) = [l(x,y)]^\alpha \cdot [c(x,y)]^\beta \cdot [s(x,y)]^\gamma \tag{18}$$

$$l(x,y) = \frac{2\mu_x\mu_y + C_1}{\mu_x^2 + \mu_y^2 + C_1} \quad c(x,y) = \frac{2\delta_x\delta_y + C_2}{\delta_x^2 + \delta_y^2 + C_2} \quad s(x,y) = \frac{\delta_{xy} + C_3}{\delta_x\delta_y + C_3} \quad (19)$$

Respectively representing image brightness comparison, image contrast comparison and image structure comparison, wherein,μ_x, μ_y bexand$y$The average value,σ_x, σ_y for x, y The standard deviation,σ_{xy} be x, y Covariance of.$C_1 = (k_1L)^2$, $C_2 = (k_2L)^2 C_3 = C_2/2$ Is used to maintain a stable constant, and the dynamic range of pixel values is used in the formula. L Express. In practical application, it is often used $\alpha = \beta = \gamma = 1$ Substituting (3-17) into (3-16) gives the following formula (20):

$$\text{SSIM}(x,y) = \frac{2\mu_x\mu_y + C_1}{\mu_x^2 + \mu_y^2 + C_1} \cdot \frac{2\delta_{xy} + C_2}{\delta_x^2 + \delta_y^2 + C_2} \quad (20)$$

On the subjective evaluation method, the ablation experiment is carried out for the proposed model to verify the effect, that is, one part of the improved model is replaced one by one, and the generation effect of each model is compared to verify the actual effect and function of this part. The experimental control group is CycleGAN network. In addition, an artificial random perception test experiment is designed to evaluate the image effect.

4.3 Experimental Comparison and Analysis

The effect diagram of ablation experiment, four groups of experiments were set up. In the first group, the residual structure of the generator used ResNetV1; The second group uses spectral normalization (SN) instead of batch normalization (BN) in the discriminator on the basis of the first group. The third group uses ResNetV2 in the residual structure of the generator; The fourth group is similar to the second group. On the basis of the third group, the batch normalization is replaced by spectral normalization in the discriminator. The ablation experiment is first tested in a kind of picture styles, namely, inputting pictures, using the cyclic consistency of the original structure to generate a countermeasure network and the improved network model proposed in this paper. The group using the improved residual structure is more effective than the control group in restoring the details of the image, retaining the structural information more completely, and the picture effect is better than other groups. Then this paper uses PSNR and SSIM indicators to evaluate the effect of image style transfer.

As shown in Figures 3 and 4, the improved residual structure and different discriminator structures are used to generate the countermeasure network compared with the initial cyclic consistency, and the indexes of PSNR and SSIM models are improved, indicating that the authenticity of the image samples generated by the improved network structure is improved. They are stylized images of several kinds of masters works. The leftmost image in each row is the input image, the right side is the improved model, and the middle group is the image processed by CycleGAN model [19]. The improved model is better than the original model in detail structural information and color conversion effect. However, some structural information in the original image is lost, resulting in a small-scale model collapse. In subjective evaluation, the improved model has a certain improvement in image generation quality compared with the original model. In terms of objective evaluation, the test results of PSNR and SSIM are shown in Figures 3 and 4, and the two indexes are obviously improved compared with Baseline.

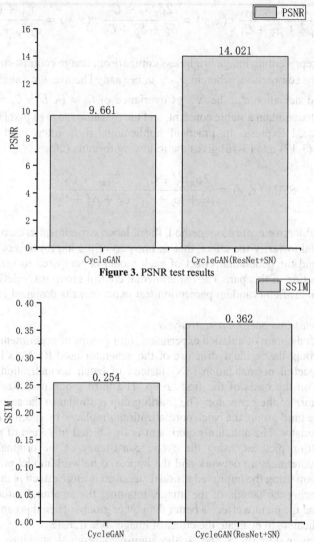

Figure 3. PSNR test results

Figure 4. SSIM test results

On the subjective evaluation, the visual experience test is also designed, which is compared with CycleGAN and the improved model proposed in this paper. Fifteen pictures are randomly selected from the test set and stylized by two stylization methods respectively, and the two image sets obtained are marked as set i and set ii. During the test, the subjects randomly selected the same set of stylized pictures from the I and II sets, so that the subjects could judge which one was better in visual sense experience. A total of 10 subjects, aged between 22 and 30, including 3 women and 7 men, were invited to participate in the test. They had never been exposed to 30 pictures in the two groups, and the corresponding model of each group was unknown. As shown in Table 1, the stylized images of the same original picture are extracted from the I and II sets at the same time every time. If one set is considered to be more visually effective than the other set, the evaluation number will be increased by 1, and the other set will not be operated. After extracting 15 sets of images, the evaluation rate will be obtained by dividing the evaluation number obtained from each set by the total evaluation number. As shown in Table 1, from the results, the stylized pictures using the model proposed in this paper are more popular among young people, with an evaluation rate of 58% and better visual experience.

Table 1 Visual Experience Test

Image collection	Evaluation number	Evaluation rate
Set I	63	42%
Set II	87	58%

5 conclusion

In this paper, the model of cyclic consistency generation countermeasure network is introduced, and the model structure is improved on this basis. In view of the image transfer of artistic works style, in the construction of generator, it is proposed to optimize signal propagation and reduce training errors by improving the residual structure, thus alleviating the problems of gradient disappearance and network degradation caused by the increase of network depth. The introduction of spectral normalization in the discriminator controls the learning range of neural network parameters and improves the stability of the network model. Finally, the subjective and objective evaluation criteria are put forward, and the model is trained on four different styles of data sets, and the results of the model generation are verified and analyzed by experiments. The experiments show that the samples generated by this method perform well, and the authenticity of the generated images is enhanced. Compared with the original network model, it has certain advantages and improves the visual effect of image style transfer.

references

[1]   Liu, Y. (2021). Improved generative adversarial network and its application in image oil painting style transfer. *Image and Vision Computing*, *105*, 104087.

[2]   Li, R., Wu, C. H., Liu, S., Wang, J., Wang, G., Liu, G., & Zeng, B. (2020). SDP-GAN: Saliency detail preservation generative adversarial networks for high perceptual quality style transfer. *IEEE Transactions on Image Processing*, *30*, 374-385.

[3]   Kang, Y., Gao, S., & Roth, R. E. (2019). Transferring multiscale map styles using generative adversarial networks. *International Journal of Cartography*, *5*(2-3), 115-141.

[4]   Gao, X., Tian, Y., & Qi, Z. (2020). RPD-GAN: Learning to draw realistic paintings with generative adversarial network. *IEEE Transactions on Image Processing*, *29*, 8706-8720.

[5]   Zhang, F., & Wang, C. (2020). MSGAN: generative adversarial networks for image seasonal style transfer. *IEEE Access*, *8*, 104830-104840.

[6]   Chen, H., Wang, Z., Zhang, H., Zuo, Z., Li, A., Xing, W., & Lu, D. (2021). Artistic style transfer with internal-external learning and contrastive learning. *Advances in Neural Information Processing Systems*, *34*, 26561-26573.

[7]   Wu, Q., Zhu, B., Yong, B., Wei, Y., Jiang, X., Zhou, R., & Zhou, Q. (2021). ClothGAN: generation of fashionable Dunhuang clothes using generative adversarial networks. *Connection Science*, *33*(2), 341-358.

[8]   Singh, A., Jaiswal, V., Joshi, G., Sanjeeve, A., Gite, S., & Kotecha, K. (2021). Neural style transfer: A critical review. *IEEE Access*, *9*, 131583-131613.

[9]   Wang, L., Chen, W., Yang, W., Bi, F., & Yu, F. R. (2020). A state-of-the-art review on image synthesis with generative adversarial networks. *IEEE Access*, *8*, 63514-63537.

[10] Li, B., Zhu, Y., Wang, Y., Lin, C. W., Ghanem, B., & Shen, L. (2021). Anigan: Style-guided generative adversarial networks for unsupervised anime face generation. *IEEE Transactions on Multimedia*, *24*, 4077-4091.

[11] Liu, S., & Zhu, T. (2021). Structure-guided arbitrary style transfer for artistic image and video. *IEEE Transactions on Multimedia*, *24*, 1299-1312.

[12] Ubhi, J. S., & Aggarwal, A. K. (2022). Neural style transfer for image within images and conditional GANs for destylization. *Journal of Visual Communication and Image Representation*, *85*, 103483.

[13] Sun, L., Chen, P., Xiang, W., Chen, P., Gao, W. Y., & Zhang, K. J. (2019). SmartPaint: a co-creative drawing system based on generative adversarial networks. *Frontiers of Information Technology & Electronic Engineering, 20*(12), 1644-1656.

[14] Ma, Z., Li, J., Wang, N., & Gao, X. (2020). Semantic-related image style transfer with dual-consistency loss. *Neurocomputing, 406*, 135-149.

[15] Chong, C. K., & Ho, E. T. W. (2021). Synthesis of 3D MRI brain images with shape and texture generative adversarial deep neural networks. *IEEE Access, 9*, 64747-64760.

[16] Shahriar, S. (2022). GAN computers generate arts? a survey on visual arts, music, and literary text generation using generative adversarial network. *Displays, 73*, 102237.

[17] Ni, Z., Yang, W., Wang, S., Ma, L., & Kwong, S. (2020). Towards unsupervised deep image enhancement with generative adversarial network. *IEEE Transactions on Image Processing, 29*, 9140-9151.

[18] Alotaibi, A. (2020). Deep generative adversarial networks for image-to-image translation: A review. *Symmetry, 12*(10), 1705.

[19] Ma, Z., Li, J., Wang, N., & Gao, X. (2020). Image style transfer with collection representation space and semantic-guided reconstruction. *Neural Networks, 129*, 123-137.

Design Studies and Intelligence Engineering
L.C. Jain et al. (Eds.)
© 2024 The Authors.
This article is published online with Open Access by IOS Press and distributed under the terms
of the Creative Commons Attribution Non-Commercial License 4.0 (CC BY-NC 4.0).
doi:10.3233/FAIA231514

Research on the Method of Artistic Image Restoration Based on Artificial Intelligence

Jian WANG[1]

Changsha University of science and technology, School of Design Art, Changsha, 410114, China

Abstract: In order to improve the current inpainting algorithm for natural art images, an artistic image inpainting model is proposed by integrating artificial intelligence and embedding multi-scale attention expansion convolution. According to the uniqueness of artistic images, the network structure of DMFB is improved, and its repair model combines two plug-and-play optimization modules: extended convolution block and coordinate attention mechanism. The extended convolution module is used to capture multi-scale context information, and the coordinate attention mechanism is used to improve the remote migration ability of features of the repaired network. The combination of the two makes the repair results meet the visual visibility and semantic rationality. The experimental results show that ablation experiments are carried out to evaluate the effectiveness of each module in this model. In this paper, the hybrid extended convolution and coordinated attention mechanism are used to train the network, and the effectiveness of MADC is verified. When the expansion rate changes to 2, 4, 6 and 8, the method in this paper will lead to moderately distorted structure and fuzzy texture. On the contrary, there is no coordination attention. In the branch of mechanism, the output of this method shows texture defects and discontinuities. By using these two branches, the method in this paper has achieved good results in structure and texture. The quantitative evaluation of branches without coordinated attention mechanism is given when the expansion rate is fixed at 2, 4, 6 and 8. Conclusion: The results restored by this method are more consistent with the real image in human senses, and the objective evaluation of PSNR, SSIM and MSE has also been improved to some extent.

Keywords: image inpainting, deep learning, attention mechanism, artistic image

1 Introduction

Culture and art play a very important role in the development of human civilization. Painting is an important cultural and artistic form. It is an important part of Chinese culture, rooted in the soil of national culture, and reflects a wide range of real-life content through beautiful artistic forms, thus reflecting the cultural outlook and aesthetic taste of all ethnic groups. It is a unique and important way for human beings to observe and express the world. For thousands of years, China has produced a large number of paintings. The study of these paintings is an important means for people to understand the development history of human history, culture, art and science and technology, thus further promoting the development of human civilization. These paintings span

---

[1] Corresponding Author.

thousands of years and contain rich cultural, artistic, scientific and historical values. However, due to natural disasters (earthquakes) and natural weathering, as well as more and more economic activities of human beings, some paintings are more or less damaged or missing, which seriously affects the appreciation, cultural creativity and cultural communication based on these paintings. Therefore, how to use the latest scientific and technological means to digitally repair these damaged or missing artistic images is of great significance.

With the development of computer collection technology and hardware and the states emphasis on the protection of cultural heritage, with the support of relevant state departments, the relevant cultural protection departments have carried out a large number of high-precision digital collection projects of painting works (artistic images), such as typical projects such as the painting series of past dynasties, the complete works of Song paintings and the complete works of Yuan paintings, and accumulated a huge amount of artistic image data [1]. These digitized data provide a data base for intelligent analysis and processing of artistic images. At the same time, computer artificial intelligence technology, especially deep learning technology, has made a major breakthrough, such as the accuracy of image classification based on deep learning has reached 96%, and the accuracy of face recognition has reached more than ninety-seven percent. The development of computer artificial intelligence technology provides technical feasibility for digital restoration of artistic images. In addition, at present, Chinas per capita GDP has exceeded $10,000. According to international experience, when the per capita GDP reaches $10,000, the demand for cultural and entertainment consumption will explode. Therefore, the restoration of artistic images is of great significance to the current cultural industry in China [2].

2 Literature review

The image inpainting algorithm based on PDE was first put forward by the concept of image inpainting technology [3]. Anantarisirichai, N. et al. put forward a fast marching algorithm based on BSCB, which can completely repair the image by determining the direction of the isochromatic line in the area to be repaired and progressing layer by layer [4]. Zhang, Z. and others put forward an algorithm to keep the direction of the isochromatic line by using Euler-Lagrange equation and anisotropic diffusion, which is called total variation (TV) [5].

Traditional image inpainting usually uses the redundancy of the image itself, that is, the information of the known area is used to complete the unknown area. The approximate method is to search the pixels around the unknown area and select a pixel with higher reliability to complete it. However, due to the low efficiency of this method, it is difficult to be competent for the task of artistic image restoration. With the vigorous development of deep learning, many researchers began to apply deep learning to the task of artistic image restoration. In the task of repairing old photos, two encoders are trained to project old photos and high-definition photos into hidden space, and a hidden space mapping module is designed to transform the feature distribution of old photos into the feature distribution of high-definition photos, so as to realize the repair of old photos [6]. Focusing on the task of Dunhuang frescoes restoration, the researchers put forward a method of Dunhuang frescoes restoration based on structure guidance. They used the representation of color in high-dimensional feature space to improve the quality of regional color restoration, making the overall color of the restored Dunhuang frescoes relatively smooth [7]. In addition, by constructing two restoration paths, namely, the path to predict the prior distribution of missing areas and the path to generate conditions, good results have also been achieved in the natural scene image restoration task [8]. With the rapid popularization of the new generation of artificial intelligence science and technology and products, the application scope of artificial intelligence is more and more extensive, which can be applied to medical impact analysis, investment analysis, agricultural robots, self-driving cars, virtual reality and other fields. The structure of artificial intelligence industry can be divided into application layer, platform interface layer, technology layer and foundation layer. At present, the technological innovation of most scientific researchers mainly focuses on the technical layer and the basic layer, while the project innovation of enterprises mainly focuses on the application layer. However, the platform interface layer, which integrates algorithms and provides interfaces for the application layer, has relatively little work. This part of the work is of great significance for promoting the development of artificial intelligence industry and the transformation of scientific research results. If the algorithm is limited to the laboratory and cannot be transformed into a tool to facilitate peoples lives, then the practical significance of this work is quite limited. Through the intervention of the platform interface layer, many developers who have no experience in artificial intelligence can simply and quickly use mature artificial intelligence algorithms for application development, thus promoting the popularization and application of artificial intelligence technology. At present, more and more large enterprises around the world have begun to build their own artificial intelligence platforms. In addition to the purpose of profit, I also hope to expand the companys own popularity in this way to attract more outstanding talents.

In recent years, the image inpainting method based on deep learning has shown good inpainting results in the task of inpainting large missing areas. The existing methods are mainly aimed at natural images, but the restoration effects of structural distortion, inconsistent lines and blurred textures are often output on artistic images. The main reason is that artistic images are generally unstructured data, which have complex line drawing, rich colors and abstract content. Therefore, in order to solve the above problems, this paper proposes an artistic image restoration method embedded with multi-scale attention expansion convolution.

3 research methods

In order to make the natural image inpainting model better applied in artistic images, this paper proposes an artistic image inpainting model embedded with multi-scale attention expansion convolution. The model structure is improved on the basis of generating countermeasure network. The generator is an encoding-decoding network, and the discriminator has two branches-global discriminator and local discriminator. The generator generates natural and reasonable restoration images, and the discriminator performs network countermeasure training to assist the generator to generate more credible restoration images. The proposed network structure and loss function will be described in detail below.

3.1 Generation Network

The generated network adopts a coding-decoding structure, in which the characteristic coding network shown in Table 1 consists of a series of 3×3 convolution layers and multiple attention expansion convolution. In this network, a 5×5 convolution kernel is used in the first convolution layer, which can fully extract the potential information features of the input image [9,10]. Then, a multi-scale attention expansion convolution module (MADC) is embedded behind the convolution layer. This module combines the advantages of extended convolution and attention mechanism, which can not only expand the receptive field, but also effectively extract the interesting features of the image. In addition, the convolution layer with 3×3 convolution kernel and the combination module of multiple attention expansion convolution are used continuously in this paper, which makes more image feature details remain in the encoding process and makes the decoding process generate images with consistent content and reasonable semantics.

Table 1. Coding network structure

Layer number	Layer type	Convolution kernel size	dilatation coefficient	step	Output size	Number of output channels
1	Convolution layer	5*5	2	1	256*256	64
2	Convolution layer	3*3	1	2	128*128	128
3	MADC					
4	Convolution layer	3*3	1	1	128*128	128
5	MADC					
6	Convolution layer	3*3	1	2	64*64	256
7	MADC					
8	Convolution layer	3*3	1	3	32*32	512
9	MADC					

At the same time, Table 2 gives the detailed architecture of the decoding network. The decoding process consists of a 3×3 convolution layer, three consecutive up-sampling layers and a 3×3 convolution layer, in which the last two up-sampling layers use ReLU activation function to output information, and the last convolution layer uses Tanh activation function to output information [11]. A series of up-sampling and convolution layers continuously map the features extracted from the coding network to the real image, thus generating a credible restoration image.

Table 2. Decoding network structure

Layer number	Layer type	Convolution kernel size	dilatation coefficient	step	Output size	Number of output channels
1	Layer type	3*3	1	1	32*32	512
2	Convolution layer	3*3	1	2	64*64	256
3	Up-sampling	3*3	1	2	128*128	128
4	Up-sampling	3*3	1	2	256*256	64
5	Up-sampling	3*3	1	1	256*256	3
6	Convolution layer	3*3	1	2	64*64	256

3.2 Multi-scale attention expansion convolution

Multi-scale attention expansion convolution (MADC) is a plug-and-play optimization module, which combines the mixed expansion convolution block with the coordination attention layer, as shown in Figure 1. It uses extended convolution to expand the receptive field without increasing the amount of calculation, and at the same time uses attention mechanism to retrieve interested information and suppress useless information [12]. The following two parts will be introduced in detail.

(1) Extended convolution block

The extended convolution is an improvement on the standard convolution, which is a special extended convolution with an expansion rate of 1, while the extended convolution with an expansion rate greater than 1 can expand the receptive field and extract background information on different scales, and at the same time, it does not need to introduce additional computational overhead in the feature extraction process. By expanding the acceptance domain of the network, expanding convolution is also very important for the image inpainting task, because it does not need to downsample or increase the number of model parameters [13,14]. Firstly, the serial layer with increased expansion rate is used to expand the receptive field of output neurons. However, the use of large expansion rate information may only benefit some large areas, but it may have disadvantages for small areas. Here, this paper uses the idea of DMFB, which consists of four consecutive convolution layers, and the expansion rates in DMFB are 1, 2, 4 and 8 respectively. However, the convolution kernel of the expanded convolution is not continuous, and not all pixels participate in the calculation, so adopting the expansion rates of 1, 2, 4 and 8 will lose the continuity of information and cause the grid effect. When using multiple expansion convolution, it is necessary to design the expansion coefficient of each convolution kernel so that it can just cover the underlying features [15]. Using different expansion coefficients of 1, 3, 5 and 7 can ensure that the receptive field is equally large and more information can be used, otherwise grid effect will occur, and the following ablation experiments prove the effectiveness of expansion coefficients of 1, 3, 5 and 7. Therefore, this paper changes the expansion rate to 1, 3, 5 and 7. Specifically, the first convolution layer on the left in MADC reduces the number of channels of input features to 64, which is used to reduce parameters, and then sends these processed features to four branches, and extracts multi-scale features through expanded convolution with different expansion factors, which is recorded as $x_i (i = 1,2,3,4)$. except x_1, each x_i Has a corresponding 3 x 3 convolution, using $K_i(\cdot)$ Express. By cumulative addition, various sparse multi-scale features are combined to obtain dense multi-scale features. This article uses y_i express $K_i(\cdot)$ The output of. The specific combination mode is as follows (1):

$$y_i = \begin{cases} x_i, & i = 1 \\ K_i(x_{i-1} + x_i), & i = 2 \\ K_i(y_{i-1} + x_i), & 2 < i \leq 4 \end{cases} \tag{1}$$

The next step is to simply use 1 x 1 convolution to fuse the connected features. In a word, the extended convolution layer increases the receptive field of general extended convolution, and its parameters are less than those of general convolution kernel.
(2) Coordinate attention mechanism
Coordinate attention mechanism uses more effective methods to capture location space information and channel relations, so as to enhance the feature representation ability of mobile networks. In the coordinate attention mechanism, two-dimensional channel attention is decomposed into two independent one-dimensional feature codes, and both coding processes perform feature aggregation operations along the spatial direction, as shown in Figure 1. One of the one-dimensional feature coding processes can capture the long-distance dependence between features along the spatial direction, and the other can retain the accurate location information of features. Then, the feature maps extracted from the two branches are fused and encoded into a set of joint feature maps with both direction perception and accurate position information. The complementary application of feature maps to the input feature map can improve the

representation of the feature map of interest [16]. It plays an important role in image restoration network. Therefore, coordinate attention is inserted into the network of this paper to guide image restoration. In order to verify the effectiveness of coordinate attention, this paper uses Grad-CAM as a visualization tool to visualize it. Compared with the two attention mechanisms of CABM and coordinate attention, coordinate attention mechanism can emphasize the relative position of the most interesting background area in human senses, and the color of the background block of interest is brighter and more obvious.

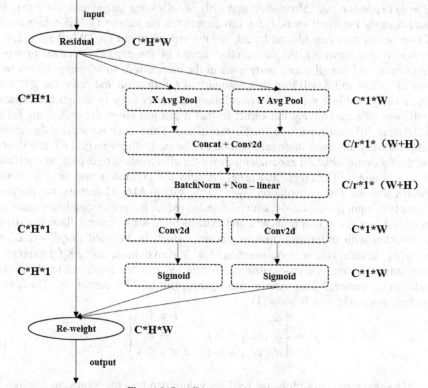

Figure 1. Coordinate Attention Model

3.3 Authentication Network

In order to make the image repaired by the generator network consistent with the original image structure and texture, this paper uses RaGAN to pursue a more realistic generated image. The identification network consists of a global discriminator and a local discriminator, which ensures the consistency between local and global contents. The global discriminator consists of six convolution layers, with a convolution kernel size of 5, an expansion coefficient of 2 and a step of 2. The local discriminator consists of five convolution layers, with a convolution kernel size of 5, an expansion coefficient of 2 and a step of 2. Except for the last layer, Leaky ReLu with a slope of 0.2 is used, as shown in Table 3. In this paper, VGG is used to extract the feature space of the picture, and the discriminator is used to calculate the anti-loss on this feature space, which can better help the generator understand the image information. In addition, the network adopts spectral normalization to realize the training of network stability, thus making the generated image more realistic and reasonable [17,18].

Table 3 Identification network structure

Branch type	Layer type	Convolution kernel size	dilatation coefficient	step	Output size	Number of output channels
Global discriminator	1	Convolution layer	5*5	2	128*128	64
	2	Convolution layer	5*5	2	64*64	128
	3	Convolution layer	5*5	2	32*32	256
	4	Convolution layer	5*5	2	16*16	512
	5	Convolution layer	5*5	2	8*8	512
	6	Convolution layer	5*5	2	4*4	512
Local discriminator	1	Convolution layer	5*5	2	64*64	64
	2	Convolution layer	5*5	2	32*32	128
	3	Convolution layer	5*5	2	16*16	256
	4	Convolution layer	5*5	2	8*8	512
	5	Convolution layer	5*5	2	4*4	512

3.4 Loss function

In order to improve the training efficiency of the generator, this paper adopts four loss functions, including reconstruction loss, perception loss, style loss and confrontation loss, which are introduced as follows.

(1) Reconstruction loss: Reconstruction loss is very useful for the regional convolution filter to learn and generate meaningful content in different regions, so this paper uses L1 reconstruction loss to ensure that the restored image is consistent with the real image, and its calculation formula is as follows (2):

$$L_{\text{rec}} = \left\| I_{\text{out}} - I_{\text{gt}} \right\|_1 \tag{2}$$

In the above formula (2), I_{out} Its an image of network repair, I_{gt} Is a real image;

(2) Perceptual loss: The perceptual loss formula is used to extract the advanced semantic features between the real image and the inpainted image, and to perceive the quality of the inpainted image. In this paper, the perceptual loss function that has been defined on the VGG-16 network and pre-trained on ImageNet is used, as shown in the following formula (3)]:

$$L_{\text{prec}} = E\left[\sum_i \frac{1}{N_i} \left\| \Phi_i(I_{\text{out}}) - \Phi_i(I_{\text{gt}}) \right\|_1 \right] \tag{3}$$

In the above formula (3), Φ_i It is the first in the VGG16 network diagram. i The activation diagram of the layer, in this experiment. Φ_i Corresponding to ReLu1_1, ReLu2_1, ReLu3_1, ReLu4_1 and ReLu5_1.

(3) Style loss: The convolution layer transposed from the decoder will bring artifacts similar to chessboard. In order to alleviate this influence, this paper introduces style loss, which is widely used in image inpainting and style transfer tasks, and is also an effective

tool to fight against "checkerboard" artifacts. The given size is $C_j \times H_j \times W_j$, its calculation formula is as follows (4):

$$L_{style} = E_j \left[\left\| G_j^{\Phi}(I_{out}) - G_j^{\Phi}(I_{gt}) \right\|_1 \right] \tag{4}$$

(4) Relative average LS countermeasure loss: Antagonistic loss is the catalyst to repair the missing area. The discriminator in this paper adopts relative average LS countermeasure loss and uses local and global discriminators. Both local discriminator and global discriminator use spectral normalization to realize stable training. For generators, antagonistic losses are defined as:

$$L_{adv} = -E_{xr} \left[\log \left(1 - D_{ra}(x_r, x_f) \right) \right] - E_{xf} \left[\log \left(1 - D_{ra}(x_f, x_r) \right) \right] \tag{5}$$

In the above formula (5), $D_{ra}(x_r, x_f) = \text{sigmoid} \left(C(x_r) - E_{xf}[C(x_f)] \right)$ and $C(.)$ indicates that the last layer has no local or global discriminator with sigmoid function, (x_r, x_f) They are real images and network-generated images.

(5) The total loss function is the following formula (6):

$$L_{total} = \lambda_r L_{re} + \lambda_p L_{prec} + \lambda_s L_{style} + \lambda_{adv} L_{adv} \tag{6}$$

among $\lambda_r, \lambda_p, \lambda_s, \lambda_{adv}$ Is the balance parameter.

4 Result analysis

4.1 Experimental environment

In order to verify the superiority of this model in restoring artistic images, NVIDIARTX2080Ti graphics card is selected as the experimental platform, and Pytorch 1.10.2 architecture is used to build a restoration network with 32 GB of memory. In this paper, the model is qualitatively and quantitatively compared with DMFB, RFR, PRVS, CSA and MEDFE algorithms on art image data sets, and ablation experiments are designed to prove the effectiveness of the MADC optimization module in this model. The motives for choosing these methods as comparison algorithms are as follows: (1) Inspired by the work of DMFB, this paper has made some improvements in the network structure. In the DMFB literature, multiple DMFBs with expansion rates of 1, 2, 4 and 8 are used continuously in the repair network to obtain a larger and more effective receiving domain. In this method, the expansion rates are changed to 1, 3, 5 and 7, and the interest characteristics of the four combined branches are enhanced by combining the CA attention mechanism, so the DMFB and the DMFB are combined. (2)RFR module, like MADC, is also an image inpainting method based on attention mechanism. The difference is that the attention mechanism in RFR is knowledge consistency attention mechanism, while MADC is coordinate attention mechanism, which can verify the effectiveness of this attention mechanism. (3) In 3)PRVS, a series of visual structure reconstruction layers (VSR) are superimposed in the encoding and decoding stages, and the structural information is integrated into the reconstructed feature map, and the visual structural features are alternately reconstructed in a gradual way. Using structural diagram to guide the generation of the next feature diagram is an image inpainting method based on structural information. Artistic images usually have complex topological structures, so a masterpiece based on structural information is selected for comparison [19]. (4)CSA is an image inpainting based on coherent semantic attention mechanism, which is different from this paper. Comparing the two can verify the effectiveness of this papers attention mechanism; (5)MEDFE recombines the deep features of the encoder into structural features and the shallow features into texture features, and balances the output features in the channel domain and the spatial domain. Similar to the structure in this paper, it is a single-stage network, so MEDFE is compared with the experimental results in this paper.

4.2 Construction of artistic image data set

At present, most of the public data sets used in the field of image restoration are natural images. However, due to the important cultural value of artistic images to the nation, most of them are distributed in national museums, art galleries, cultural centers and other places, and some of them are in the hands of private collectors, so there are few authoritative public data sets for the restoration research and application of artistic images in deep learning. With the world paying more and more attention to the protection of cultural heritage, with the support of the relevant state departments, the relevant cultural protection departments have carried out a large number of high-precision digital collection projects of paintings (artistic images). Typical projects, such as the painting series of past dynasties, the complete works of Song paintings and the complete works of Yuan paintings, have accumulated a huge amount of artistic image data, and research teams in some universities have also collected and built databases based on artistic images. These digitized data provide a data base for intelligent analysis and processing of artistic images.

I have obtained the data set of China traditional landscape painting opened in Chinese-Landscape-Painting, which contains 2192 pieces. Besides Chinas landscape painting, I also collected the artistic images of famous foreign painters. Including Alfred Sisley, eugene boudin, claude monet, Pierre Auguste Renoir, Henri Rousseau and Vincent Van Gogh, there are 464, 549, 937, 583, 80 and 934 works, with a total of 3,574 works (oil painting data source is https://www. wikiart。 org/)。 At present, there are few open art image data sets. In order to enlarge the data set as much as possible to verify the effectiveness of the model, this paper cuts the traditional high-definition landscape painting in China into several images with rich contents. Finally, a total of 21,000 pictures were collected, all of which were 256x256x3. In order to ensure the randomness and uncertainty of the damaged area, the position of the mask in the image is random, and the size of the damaged area is also random.

4.3 Qualitative comparison

In this paper, the method is used to inpaint images with different scale masks. From the figure, it can be found that the inpainting results of images with mask ratio of 0-20% are no different from the real images in human senses, and the structure is consistent and the texture is reasonable. However, with the expansion of the damaged area, the semantic information of the image is missing too much, and there will be discontinuous lines, and the detailed texture is blurred and inconsistent with the real image.

In order to show the superiority of the art image inpainting method, the inpainting results of this method and five schemes, such as DMFB, RFR, PRVS, CSA and DEM Fe, are qualitatively evaluated. As a result of RFR, PRVS, CSA and DEMFE, there are obvious visual artifacts in the missing area, including image blur and distortion (shown in the white box). Among them, when there is face information with rich semantic information in artistic images, although DMFB produces more pleasing content, there is a lack of correlation between the cavity area and the background area in its restoration map, such as line discontinuity [20]. Compared with the above two methods, MADC method has a good visual effect, can effectively generate results with real texture, and has a high correlation between the repair area and the background area.

4.4 Quantitative comparison

In this paper, different mask ratios are used for numerical evaluation on artistic image data sets. During training, the data set is divided into training set, verification set and test set in the ratio of 8:1:1. 1000 pictures were randomly selected from the art image data set for testing. For the evaluation indicators, this paper follows the use of SSIM, MAE and PSNR evaluation indicators. The evaluation results are shown in Figure 2 and Table 4. Fig. 2 is a quantitative evaluation and comparison between the method in this paper and five methods: DMFB, RFR, PRVS, CSA and MEDFE. Table 4 compares the repair results of this method under different scale masks. From the two tables, it is found that the quality of image restoration in this paper is better than the existing methods in pixel level, structure level and perception level. At the same time, this method has a good effect on filling irregular holes under different scale masks.

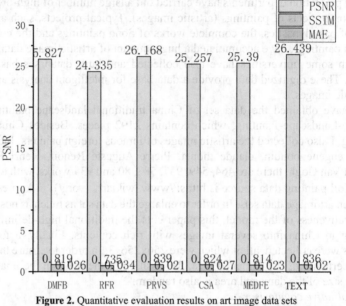

Figure 2. Quantitative evaluation results on art image data sets
Table 4. Quantitative evaluation results of different scale masks

Mask	10%-20%	20%-30%	30%-40%	40%-50%
PSNR	29.902	27.3 82	26.439	24.579
SSIM	0 .927	0.867	0.836	0.761
MAE	0 .011	0.021	0.027	0.032

4.5 Ablation experiment

Finally, this paper conducts ablation experiments to evaluate the effectiveness of each module in this model. In this paper, the hybrid extended convolution and coordinated attention mechanism are used to train the network, and the effectiveness of MADC is verified. When the expansion rate changes to 2, 4, 6 and 8, the method in this paper will lead to moderately distorted structure and fuzzy texture. On the contrary, there is no coordination attention. In the branch of mechanism, the output of this method shows texture defects and discontinuities. By using these two branches, the method in this paper has achieved good results in structure and texture. The quantitative evaluation of branches without coordinated attention mechanism is given when the expansion rate is fixed at 2, 4, 6 and 8.

5 conclusions

In this paper, an artistic image inpainting method embedded with multi-scale attention expansion convolution is proposed. In the coding stage of the network, there are five convolution layers, four of which are followed by an optimization module, and the optimization module consists of several attention expansion convolutions (MADC), and the missing content is roughly extracted by re-creating loss training. In the decoding stage, three upsamples and two convolution layers are used to generate a natural and reliable restored image. In the loss function, four different loss functions, namely reconstruction loss, style loss, perception loss and confrontation loss, are combined to train and generate the confrontation network. In the mixed expansion convolution, this paper fuses four expansion convolution blocks with expansion rates of 1, 3, 5 and 7 respectively, and obtains dense multi-scale features. At the same time, the coordination attention layer is inserted into the network to enhance the expression ability of interested features, improve the remote migration ability of features embedded in the network, and make the repair results meet the visual visibility and semantic rationality. Experiments verify the effectiveness of this method.

references

[1] Willemink, M. J., & Noël, P. B. (2019). The evolution of image reconstruction for CT—from filtered back projection to artificial intelligence. European radiology, 29, 2185-2195.

[2] Jin, Z., Iqbal, M. Z., Bobkov, D., Zou, W., Li, X., & Steinbach, E. (2019). A flexible deep CNN framework for image restoration. IEEE Transactions on Multimedia, 22(4), 1055-1068.

[3] Koonjoo, N., Zhu, B., Bagnall, G. C., Bhutto, D., & Rosen, M. S. (2021). Boosting the signal-to-noise of low-field MRI with deep learning image reconstruction. Scientific reports, 11(1), 8248.

[4] Anantrasirichai, N., & Bull, D. (2022). Artificial intelligence in the creative industries: a review. Artificial intelligence review, 1-68.

[5] Zha, Z., Yuan, X., Zhou, J., Zhu, C., & Wen, B. (2020). Image restoration via simultaneous nonlocal self-similarity priors. IEEE Transactions on Image Processing, 29, 8561-8576.

[6] Muckley, M. J., Riemenschneider, B., Radmanesh, A., Kim, S., Jeong, G., Ko, J., ... & Knoll, F. (2021). Results of the 2020 fastMRI challenge for machine learning MR image reconstruction. IEEE transactions on medical imaging, 40(9), 2306-2317.

[7] Knoll, F., Murrell, T., Sriram, A., Yakubova, N., Zbontar, J., Rabbat, M., ... & Recht, M. P. (2020). Advancing machine learning for MR image reconstruction with an open competition: Overview of the 2019 fastMRI challenge. Magnetic resonance in medicine, 84(6), 3054-3070.

[8] He, W., Yao, Q., Li, C., Yokoya, N., Zhao, Q., Zhang, H., & Zhang, L. (2020). Non-local meets global: An iterative paradigm for hyperspectral image restoration. IEEE Transactions on Pattern Analysis and Machine Intelligence, 44(4), 2089-2107.

[9] Zhang, Y., Tian, Y., Kong, Y., Zhong, B., & Fu, Y. (2020). Residual dense network for image restoration. IEEE transactions on pattern analysis and machine intelligence, 43(7), 2480-2495.

[10] Arabi, H., AkhavanAllaf, A., Sanaat, A., Shiri, I., & Zaidi, H. (2021). The promise of artificial intelligence and deep learning in PET and SPECT imaging. Physica Medica, 83, 122-137.

[11] Racine, D., Becce, F., Viry, A., Monnin, P., Thomsen, B., Verdun, F. R., & Rotzinger, D. C. (2020). Task-based characterization of a deep learning image reconstruction and comparison with filtered back-projection and a partial model-based iterative reconstruction in abdominal CT: a phantom study. Physica Medica, 76, 28-37.

[12] Mei, Y., Fan, Y., Zhang, Y., Yu, J., Zhou, Y., Liu, D., ... & Shi, H. (2023). Pyramid Attention Network for Image Restoration. International Journal of Computer Vision, 1-19.

[13] Pan, X., Zhan, X., Dai, B., Lin, D., Loy, C. C., & Luo, P. (2021). Exploiting deep generative prior for versatile image restoration and manipulation. IEEE Transactions on Pattern Analysis and Machine Intelligence, 44(11), 7474-7489.

[14] Pan, J., Dong, J., Liu, Y., Zhang, J., Ren, J., Tang, J., ... & Yang, M. H. (2020). Physics-based generative adversarial models for image restoration and beyond. IEEE transactions on pattern analysis and machine intelligence, 43(7), 2449-2462.

[15] Malik, J., Kiranyaz, S., & Gabbouj, M. (2021). Self-organized operational neural networks for severe image restoration problems. Neural Networks, 135, 201-211.

[16] Lu, J., Li, N., Zhang, S., Yu, Z., Zheng, H., & Zheng, B. (2019). Multi-scale adversarial network for underwater image restoration. Optics & Laser Technology, 110, 105-113.

[17] Hou, G., Pan, Z., Wang, G., Yang, H., & Duan, J. (2019). An efficient nonlocal variational method with application to underwater image restoration. Neurocomputing, 369, 106-121.

[18] Zhang, K., Li, Y., Zuo, W., Zhang, L., Van Gool, L., & Timofte, R. (2021). Plug-and-play image restoration with deep denoiser prior. IEEE Transactions on Pattern Analysis and Machine Intelligence, 44(10), 6360-6376.

[19] Yu, K., Wang, X., Dong, C., Tang, X., & Loy, C. C. (2021). Path-restore: Learning network path selection for image restoration. IEEE Transactions on Pattern Analysis and Machine Intelligence, 44(10), 7078-7092.

[20] He, W., Yao, Q., Li, C., Yokoya, N., Zhao, Q., Zhang, H., & Zhang, L. (2020). Non-local meets global: An iterative paradigm for hyperspectral image restoration. IEEE Transactions on Pattern Analysis and Machine Intelligence, 44(4), 2089-2107.

Design Studies and Intelligence Engineering
L.C. Jain et al. (Eds.)
© 2024 The Authors.
This article is published online with Open Access by IOS Press and distributed under the terms
of the Creative Commons Attribution Non-Commercial License 4.0 (CC BY-NC 4.0).
doi:10.3233/FAIA231515

Research on Crowdinnovation Design Methods and Models for Internet Platforms Based on the Innovation Value Chain

Cong GU [a,1] and Fei WANG [b]

[ab] *China Academy of Art, Hangzhou, China, 310002*

Abstract. One prominent characteristic of the knowledge economy era is the widespread participation of the general public, harnessing collective intelligence for networked distributed innovation. However, the theoretical discourse on crowdsourcing tends to idealize collective intelligence and its role in solving innovation challenges. Forms such as crowdsourcing and freelancing introduce certain limitations and drawbacks, leading to criticisms regarding the quality, efficiency, and issues surrounding intellectual property within crowdsourced innovation. This emphasis on public participation often undervalues and overlooks the expertise and value contributed by professionals.The author believes that the general public plays a significant role in online platform innovation, but they cannot entirely replace the leadership of professionals and experts in the innovation process. Therefore, based on the different characteristics of the general public, professionals, and experts, the author expands the value chain model of internet platform product innovation on the foundation of the innovation value chain theory. To achieve this, the author proposes and constructs a crowd innovation design method and model, harnessing the strengths of various participants in the innovation process and implementing crowdinnovationin different stages to address complex innovation problems. This approach aims to enhance the quality of creative production, improve the innovation value, and boost the innovation capabilities of internet product innovation platforms.

Keywords. Crowdinnovation, Design methods, Knowledge economy, Product innovation, Internet Platform, Innovation value chain

1.Introduction

With the development of internet technology, creative thinking and connections through online platforms have become a reality. Crowd creation (Zhong Chuang) has increasingly become a new way of thinking and an innovative approach in the internet field. Crowd creation, crowd sourcing, and crowd-funding service models have been widely applied. The rapidity, ubiquity, asynchrony, anonymity, interactivity, low entry barriers, and the ability to support various forms have made the internet an excellent medium[1] to promote creative participation. Mass participation in online collaboration and the utilization of crowd wisdom have resulted in many successful cases. For instance, Starbucks' "ideas.starbucks" community, Lego's creative community,

---

[1] Corresponding Author: Cong Gu; Mailing Address: China Academy of Art, Hangzhou, Zhejiang 310002, China; Email: guc@caa.edu.cn.

Wikipedia, and the regular T-shirt design contest platform of the wireless T-shirt company Threadless, which solicits creative ideas from consumer users. Many enterprises obtain solutions through open innovation platforms from the internet's mass collaborative innovative approach.

Internet platform crowd creation can be divided into two types: one is a spontaneous innovation community of the masses, where the platform organization is loose, and the masses spontaneously participate in the community through various drivers. They exchange knowledge, skills, and experience to meet innovation needs, such as K68, Upwork, Freelancer, Behance, Core77, and more. The other type is organized mass innovation. It utilizes enterprise-built open innovation platforms or third-party service platforms, publishes requirements to platform users, and involves the masses in providing answers and solutions. This is done through crowd-sourcing, rewards, and competitions. Examples include P&G and IBM, as well as open innovation platforms like InnoCentive, Ninesigma, yet2.com, and Yourencore. Crowd creation is essentially the democratization of individual innovation development led by elite culture. However, it also has its limitations. Academia's view of crowd wisdom and its grassroots value is often overly idealistic. The internet's anonymity and low entry create a large amount of useless information on platforms, and the quality of crowd creation has been criticized. Additionally, issues related to the protection of intellectual property rights exist.

Internet platform crowdinnovation can be classified into two primary types. The first type involves spontaneous innovation communities where the platform is loosely organized. The masses participate voluntarily through different incentives, engaging in the exchange of knowledge, skills, and experiences to fulfill their innovative needs. Prominent examples include platforms like K68, Upwork, Freelancer, Behance, Core77, and others.The second type is organized mass innovation, where enterprises establish open innovation platforms or leverage third-party service platforms to post requirements for platform users. This enables the crowd to contribute solutions through crowd-sourcing, rewards, and competitions. Companies such as P&G and IBM utilize these open innovation platforms, including InnoCentive, Ninesigma, yet2.com, and Yourencore.

The essence of crowd creation is the democratization of individual innovation led by elite culture. Nevertheless, it has inherent limitations. Academic perspectives on crowd wisdom and its grassroots value are often overly idealistic. The internet's anonymity and low entry barriers lead to an abundance of useless information on platforms, creating quality concerns within crowd creation. Additionally, issues surrounding the protection of intellectual property rights persist[2].

The development of internet technology has underscored the immense value of online platforms as vehicles for innovation and resource interfaces. Industrial design services characterized by product innovation have entered the realm of internet platforms. They facilitate the alignment of creative needs with creative production through the internet. These platforms aggregate a wealth of creative design resources and employ network technology, collaborative tools, and service management to facilitate the synchronization of design with business needs. They offer services like intellectual property services, product technology development, and channels for market conversion, forming a model for implementing product innovation on internet platforms. Examples include platforms such as LKKER, Taihuoniao SaaS, and Lai Sheji (Figure 1).The service process typically involves the following steps: requirement posting, service matching, design service, evaluation acceptance, project assessment, and follow-up conversion services. These product innovation platforms to some extent reduce the innovation costs for businesses. They act as third-party service providers, providing service guarantees and reducing the investment risks for both creative producers and consumers. This, in turn, enhances the efficiency of product innovation.

While implementing product innovation on internet platforms may be more challenging compared to other crowdinnovation platforms, these product innovation platforms are essentially traditional 1-to-1 closed design service models. They are often viewed as a "window" for information search and requirement contact, failing to harness the full potential of crowd wisdom participation on the internet. This hinders the creation of large-scale, high-value crowd network innovation activities. Compared to the mass participation in crowd innovation models, these platforms primarily consist of designers, which limits their personnel structure, making them predominantly youthful. The platforms lack high-end experts and other innovation resources, ultimately hindering their ability to generate high-quality and market-potential ideas. These platforms primarily focus on simple product appearance design and cannot address complex innovation needs of businesses. This study presents a theoretical model designed to address the issues in creative production on internet platforms.

Figure 1: LKKER Platform Design Tasks
Image Source: LKKER Platform Official Website (http://www.lkker.com/)

2. Theory

The theory underpinning the development of the crowdinnovation design method and the perspective of this study is the Innovation Value Chain theory. The Innovation Value Chain (IVC), as conceived by Morten T. Hansen and Julian Birkinshaw, builds upon Michael E[3]. Porter's value chain theory, merging innovation seamlessly with the value chain.

While Porter's value chain theory delves into the process of value creation, the Innovation Value Chain theory centers on the analysis of value creation within a chain-like innovation process and structure.

The Innovation Value Chain theory regards the entire process, from ideation to the eventual transformation into a product, as a cohesive chain-like structure. It categorizes innovation into three stages: idea generation, idea transformation, and idea dissemination. Within these three stages, businesses must engage in internal adoption, cross-departmental adoption, and external procurement to generate ideas. Further, they need to navigate through six pivotal activities, including idea screening, idea development, and idea diffusion, to unlock the value of innovation (Figure 2). By scrutinizing the chain-like innovation process and phases within their organizations, business managers can assess their strengths and weaknesses in innovation and customize best practices to address issues and deficiencies. This approach empowers them to formulate strategies, seek solutions, and enhance the implementation of innovation within the enterprise, ultimately leading to value addition. The Innovation Value Chain serves as a comprehensive research framework tailored to these objectives[4].The Innovation Value Chain illustrates the complete innovation process within enterprises and underscores the interplay among crucial elements during the innovation process[5].

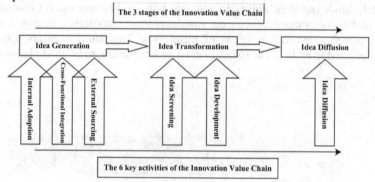

Figure 2: Basic Model of the Innovation Value Chain
Image source: Compiled based on the original content of "The Innovation Value Chain" by Morten T. Hansen and Julian Birkinshaw.

3. Methods and Models

3.1 Innovation Value Chain Model for Product Innovation Platforms

The Innovation Value Chain theory, initially developed within the context of manufacturing enterprises, forms the foundation of this study. Drawing upon a comparative analysis of innovation in traditional enterprises and innovation within internet platforms (Table 1), the author, in conjunction with Geoffrey G. Parker, Marshall V. Van Alstyne, and Sangeet Paul Choudary's delineation of the three core interactive functions in the platform value creation process: "pull," "facilitate," and "match" [6] (Parker, G. G., Van Alstyne, M. V., & Choudary, S. P., 2019), has put forth the Innovation Value Chain model for internet product innovation platforms (Figure 3). This model extends the existing Innovation Value Chain theory.

In this research, the Innovation Value Chain model for product innovation platforms is introduced, breaking down the innovation process of these platforms into four distinct stages: creative resource integration, creative production, creative transformation, and creative diffusion. These four stages constitute critical components of the activities surrounding product innovation carried out through platform services. They represent the fundamental innovation framework of product innovation platforms. The four stages within the Innovation Value Chain for product innovation platforms encompass a total of eight key elements.

Table 1: A Comparison between Enterprise Product Innovation and Platform-Based Product Innovation
Source of Information: Created by the author

		Enterprise Product Innovation Process	Platform-Based Product Innovation Service Process
Value Orientation		Profit-driven pursuit of innovation through product innovation.	Value creation via the service product innovation process.
Basis of Innovation		Organization of production factors.	Integration of supply and demand resources.
Agents of Innovation		Entrepreneurs.	Participants in the platform (multi-stakeholder).
Form of Innovation		Design - Manufacture - Sale.	Achieving design - manufacture - sale through platform's "pull, facilitate, match" functions.
Stages of Innovation	Creative Generation	Generated internally by the enterprise or jointly with external parties.	Matched with creative service providers by the platform, resulting in creative generation by service providers
	Creative Transformation	The enterprise selects and invests in the creative idea.	The adopters accept the creative ideas, and they may be developed and produced through the platform's resources or other means.
	Creative Diffusion	Internal consensus within the enterprise on innovative concepts.	The platform assists in promoting creative outcomes and collaborates on sales channels.

Product Innovation Platform Innovation Value Chain consists of 4 stages

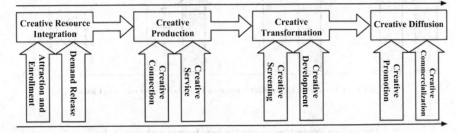

the 8 key activities of the Product Innovation Platform Innovation Value Chain

Figure 3: Innovation Value Chain Model for Internet Product Innovation PlatformsSource of Information: Created by the author

Integration of Creative Resources: The platform aggregates various innovation resources and attracts participants to join. Demand-side users post creative requirements on the platform, forming value units that both parties can interact with[7]. The more and larger resources the platform attracts, the greater its potential becomes.

Creative Production: Creative production involves two key components: creative connection and creative services. Demand-side users publish innovative requirements, and eligible supply-side providers sign up and engage in collaboration through the platform. Once the connection is established, supply-side providers start providing creative services as per the requirements, with the platform facilitating communication and coordination to varying degrees between both parties, and providing relevant internet-sharing tools to enhance online collaboration.

Creative Transformation : Creative transformation consists of two key activities: creative screening and creative development. After the supply-side providers complete the creative solutions, the platform and demand-side users need to evaluate and select the most valuable and market-promising creative solutions for further development. The resources gathered by the product innovation platform also include technical development, production partners, etc., who provide support for technical development, prototyping, and manufacturing.

Creative Diffusion: Creative diffusion refers to the platform's promotion and investment in creative outcomes, connecting to sales channels and providing commercial services. It also brings funding and sales channel support for creative incubation, further promoting the diffusion of creative outcomes.

In the innovation process, the most critical stage to achieve the maximum innovation value and return on investment in the market is the early creative generation stage. Morten T. Hansen and Julian Birkinshaw also emphasized the importance of focusing on the right connections. To gain more value, companies need to choose creative solutions with higher market potential and value for development. This study will focus on the first three stages and the five key components of the product innovation platform's innovation value chain (Figure 4).

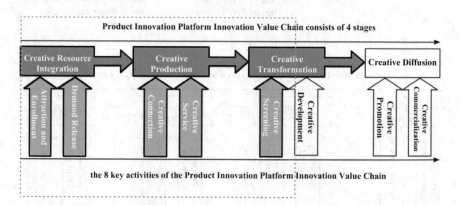

The Internet Product Innovation Platform Innovation Value Chain

Figure 4: Key Research Areas of the Product Innovation Platform's Innovation Value Chain
Image source: Created by the author

3.2 Product Innovation Platform crowdinnovation Design Method

Professors Steven D. Eppinger and Karl T. Ulrich have summarized the new product development process into six stages: Planning, Concept Development, System Design, Detailed Design, Testing and Refinement, and Pilot Production and Scaling (Figure 5)[8]. This model illustrates that product innovation is a sequential, phased innovation process. Idea generation marks the starting point of the innovation process, determining whether innovation can bring greater value and market returns to the enterprise. How to generate better and more valuable ideas on the platform becomes a key aspect of innovation [9]. While a diverse crowd can indeed provide a wealth of different creative ideas and concepts, it may not suffice for the chain-like innovation process of a product. Professional designers are needed to carry out a series of conceptual and detailed design processes. Moreover, for the different design proposals collected on the platform, experienced industry experts are required to guide and assess the innovative design direction to meet the needs of innovation development. Based on this chain-like product innovation process, collaborative cooperation should be carried out in stages and objects, employing different methods for different innovation stages, and capitalizing on the respective strengths of the participants in each stage.

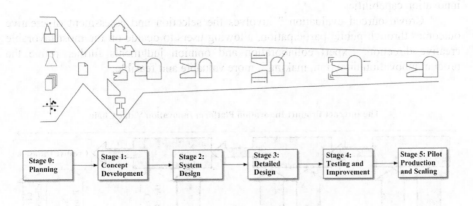

| Stage 0: Planning | Stage 1: Concept Development | Stage 2: System Design | Stage 3: Detailed Design | Stage 4: Testing and Improvement | Stage 5: Pilot Production and Scaling |

Figure 5: Basic Product Development Process
Image Source: Karl T. Ulrich and Steven D. Eppinger. Product Design and Development[M]. Translated by Yang Qing and Yang Na. Beijing: China Machine Press, 2018: 13.

Therefore, in the Internet platform crowd-creation design method proposed by the author, the main participants are composed of mass innovators (non-design professionals), professional designers, industry experts, and even enterprises are required to participate in the collaboration. Diversified public group thinking can solve the problem of limitations of the creative breadth of a single group. The participation of professional designers can ensure the implementation of creative professional design, and the participation of experts can guide and grasp decision-making in creative directions.

Based on the innovation value chain theory, the author constructed a crowd-creation design method. It is based on the chain structural characteristics of product innovation and focuses on the innovation needs of enterprises. It involves designers, experts, non-design professional mass innovators and other groups to participate in creative implementation to solve the problem of enterprise innovation. Regarding the complex issues of innovation, it is a "creative processing factory" that solves the problem of creative production. The crowd-creation design method includes the diverse thinking linking method of "Crowdsourced Linking", the multi-element and staged collaboration method of "Crowdsourced Collaboration", and the multi-level, multi-objective and multi-angle screening and evaluation method of "Crowdsourced evaluation" (Figure 6).

" Crowdsourced Linking" creates the conditions for collaboration, emphasizing the involvement of both the general public and professional designers. The diversity and heterogeneity of collective thinking provide a broader range of creative proposals and problem-solving solutions.

" Crowdsourced Collaboration" aims to enhance the quality of creative ideas by promoting collaboration between the general public, designers, and experts. This approach stands in contrast to the "1-on-1" platform innovation service model and aligns better with the spirit of openness, sharing, and collaboration on the internet. Collaborative participation enhances the quality of creative ideas, thereby improving the platform's ability to address complex innovation challenges and enhancing its innovation capabilities.

" Crowdsourced evaluation " involves the selection and assessment of creative outcomes through public participation, allowing users to decide on the most favorable creative direction. Expert collaboration and opinion judgments further refine the product innovation direction, making it more valuable and feasible.

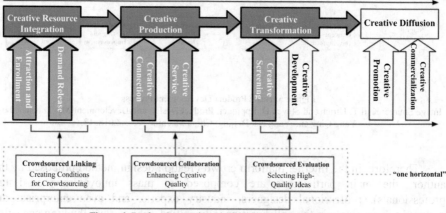

The Internet Product Innovation Platform Innovation Value Chain

Figure 6: Product Innovation Platform Collaborative Method
Image Source: Created by the Author

3.3 Product Innovation Platform Crowdsourced Design Model

The crowdsourced design model is based on a chain-like innovation structure, with different innovation actors playing various roles at different stages of product innovation to produce high-quality creative content with greater market potential and value. Based on the six stages of the product innovation process and the three core interactive functions of platform value creation (attract, facilitate, match) [10], the author divides the crowdsourced design model into eight steps: "attract residents, publish demands, solicit problems, propose ideas, identify innovation opportunities, professional design, concept selection, and creative development" (Table 2, Figure 7).

Table 2: Content of the 8 Stages of crowdinnovation Design

phase	Content	Purpose
1	Attraction of Participants	Attracting the general public to participate in crowdsourced innovation
2	Demand Release	Expecting the help of the wisdom of the crowd
3	Problem Collection	Formulating the needs and pain points of the general users
4	Creative Proposals	Gaining insights into the expectations of new products from the general users
5	Innovation Opportunity Identification	Defining the innovative direction for new product development
6	Professional Design	Creating product conceptual ideas
7	Concept Selection	Realizing product concepts into actual products
8	Creative Development	Realizing product concepts into actual products

Source of information: Compiled by the author

On one side, various diverse groups enter the platform, forming diverse thinking, while on the other side, companies participate in the platform and release innovation propositions. The general public discusses innovation problems from a user perspective online and filters and focuses the content through user self-voting (liking), thus forming core problem points A with extensive and universal relevance. Based on core problem A, the platform again solicits solutions from the general public, aiming to predict future new products at the user level. Users, through voting (liking), filter and focus the content once again, generating creative proposals with a user-demand foundation. These creative proposals undergo analysis and discussion by professionals and experts, forming the development direction B for new products. Subsequently, professional designers work on professional design around development direction B, and the platform organizes experts, companies, and users to collectively participate in the evaluation and selection of design outcomes, ultimately establishing the design scheme for product innovation, and the product enters the subsequent development stage.

In the process of crowdinnovation design, the general public plays a dual role of user innovation and self-filtering, providing both extensive creative thinking and focusing on problems. Professional designers, based on the creative ideas from the general public, further focus on design proposals. Experts can provide guiding and decisive recommendations on creative issues, product innovation directions, and design proposals, leading to optimization and enhancement of the design plan. Diverse innovation entities leverage their respective strengths in the chain-like innovation process to collaboratively drive high-quality creative output.

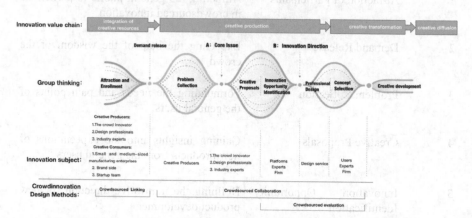

Figure 7: Crowdinnovation Design Model Image Source: Created by the author

4. Conclusion and Discussion

The process of crowdinnovation design introduces the general public in the early stages to participate in problem research and creative collection, implementing an innovation model guided by user needs and user participation. Through three rounds of problem research, creative proposals, and professional design, the process casts a wide net, involving the general public and obtaining the most extensive and diverse array of solutions. This is achieved through self-selection by users, forming a funnel-based focusing approach (Figure 8). Combining professional service providers' design expertise with collaborative assessments involving users, experts, and those with demands, it achieves a design innovation model.

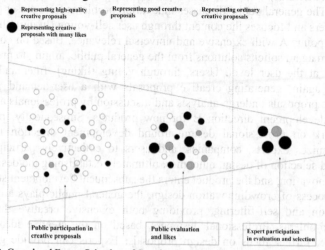

Figure 8: Crowd and Expert Selection of Creative Proposals Image Source: Created by the Author

The process of crowdinnovation design embodies the integration of divergent and convergent thinking, representing a funnel-shaped process of continuous divergence and convergence of thought. Divergent thinking aims to increase possibilities to create new choices, while convergence is aimed at arriving at a single best solution (Figure 9). As Linus Pauling, a two-time Nobel laureate, once said, "To have a good idea, you must first have a lot of ideas."[11]

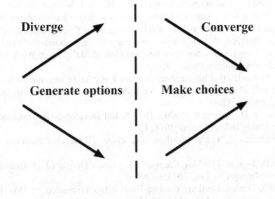

Figure 9: Divergence and Convergence
Image Source: Tim Brown. "Change by Design: How Design Thinking Transforms Organizations and Inspires Innovation." Translated by Hou Ting. Beijing: Beijing United Publishing Media Group Co., Ltd., 2011, pp. 62-63.

Crowdinnovation design method is a new approach to product innovation activities in the Internet age. It also needs to address three important questions and establish relevant mechanisms: first, how to attract a wide range of the general public to participate in platform innovation; second, how to facilitate collaborative efforts among various platform user groups; third, through what means and mechanisms can the general public evaluate and filter creative proposals and results.

This study introduces the innovation value chain theory to Internet platforms. Based on changes in the Internet innovation scene and innovation methods, it not only extends the innovation value chain theory but also proposes crowdinnovation design methods as a research perspective and approach. It emphasizes that in the Internet age, despite changes in the innovation process, the general public cannot replace the leadership role of professionals and experts. Excellent and high-value innovations require the collaborative participation of diverse groups, with different stages of the process involving cooperative innovation.

Acknowledgments

This article received support from the "Design-AI Lab," the Philosophy and Social Sciences Lab of the Ministry of Education.

References

[1] Daren C. Brabham. "CROWD SOURCING 众包." Translated by Yu Weishen and Wang Xu. Chongqing: Chongqing University Press, 2015, pp. 21-22.

[2] Zhao Fuzeng, Ding Xuewei. "Research on Mass crowdinnovation Based on Internet Platforms" in China Soft Science, 2009(05): 63-72.

[3] Zhang Xiaolin, Wu Yuhua. Analysis of the Innovation Value Chain and Its Effective Operation Mechanism. Journal of Dalian University of Technology (Social Sciences Edition), 2005(03): 23-26.

[4] Hansen M T, Birkinshaw J. The innovation value chain. Harvard Business Review, 2007, 85(6): 121-122.

[5] Priyadarshini A，O'Gorman C，Gao Y. Adopting an open innovation paradigm: managerial perceptions and the in- novation value chain. June 3-6,2014. R&D Management Conference, Stuttgart, Germany,2014.

[6] Geoffrey G. Parker, Marshall V. Van Alstyne, and Sangeet Paul Choudary. "Platform Revolution: How Networked Markets Are Transforming the Economy and How to Make Them Work for You." Translated by Zhipeng. Beijing: Machinery Industry Press, 2019, p. 44.

[7] A value unit refers to the detailed information about each service or item posted on the platform, which is information that is beneficial and exchangeable for users. Examples include YouTube videos and Uber's availability of vehicles, among others.

[8] Karl T. Ulrich, Steven D. Eppinger. Product Design and Development. Translated by Yang Qing and Yang Na. Beijing: Machinery Industry Press, 2018: 13.

[9] Hansen M T, Birkinshaw J. The innovation value chain. [J].Harvard Business Review, 2007, 85(6): 121-122.

[10] Tim Brown. IDEO, Design Thinking Change Everything. Translated by Hou Ting. Beijing: Beijing United Publishing Media Group Co., Ltd., 2011: 62-63.

[11] Tim Brown. IDEO, Design Thinking Change Everything. Translated by Hou Ting. Beijing: Beijing United Publishing Media Group Co., Ltd., 2011: 62-63.

Design Studies and Intelligence Engineering
L.C. Jain et al. (Eds.)
© 2024 The Authors.
doi:10.3233/FAIA231516

Knowledge Collaboration Mechanism and Validity Assessment Based on Design Awards: A Case Study of Design Intelligence Award

Jihong ZHU[a,1], Peiwen PENG[a], Zhouping XU[a], and Yixin ZHANG[a]

[a]Zhejiang University of Technology, Hangzhou, China

Abstract. The essence of design award lies in the curation of outstanding design cases. Through the organizational mechanisms established by award organizers, it can serve as an exceptional platform for knowledge exchange, dissemination, and innovation. This paper introduces the concept of Design Award Knowledge Network (DAKN), taking Design Intelligence Award(DIA) for example, elucidates the collaborative mechanisms of knowledge dissemination and innovation within the DAKN, notably facilitated through the D·will Lecture and DI Project Workshops. Additionally, surveys were conducted among faculty and students participating in the series of events initiated by DIA. The findings underscore the prominent advantage of a 'stimulative policy environment' within this network, while revealing the need for improvements in the 'accessibility of knowledge resources.' This paper proposes that enhancing the vitality of DAKN rely on the diversification of knowledge, interdisciplinary approaches, and organizational collaboration. This entails the aggregation of talent from various universities, institutions, and enterprises to establish collaborative innovation teams. Through collaborative governance, the integration of diverse foundational capabilities, data information, and tool skills from various stakeholders should be orchestrated to achieve effectiveness in knowledge exchange.

Keywords. design award, design award knowledge network (DAKN), collaborative innovation, knowledge management

1. Knowledge in design award

The primary purpose of design awards is to acknowledge best design cases, serving as a proactive and professional guiding force in the developing industry. In the era of knowledge-driven economy, design awards have evolved into a vital activity that propels economic and societal progress, enhances product quality, and enlightens the public. They have also become an integral part of a nation's innovation ecosystem. By evaluating and recognizing innovative and creative works, design awards amass a reservoir of outstanding design knowledge resources. It can be said that the award evaluation process itself constitutes a knowledge aggregation mechanism that attracts

---

[1]Corresponding Author: Zhu Jihong, Postal address: School of Design and Architecture, Zhejiang University of Technology, Hangzhou, China,310023; E-mail: jhzhu@zjut.edu.cn.

outstanding design works. Additionally, design awards offer numerous opportunities for acquiring new knowledge. This kind of knowledge is not confined solely to the databases of awarded works but predominantly resides within designer community interactions, design exhibition events, and activities that afford participants adequate space for engagement. This mode of knowledge exchange facilitates the more effective dissemination of tacit knowledge, which is pivotal in enhancing competitive innovation.

2. Design award knowledge network

It's necessary to propose the concept of Design Awards Knowledge Network(DAKN). DAKN is a complex adaptive system that selects outstanding works based on the evaluation criteria of design awards, connecting design works and designers. Starting from the basic data of submitted works, through the evaluation of outstanding works, and extending to various activities within the award platform, it integrates scattered information into organized knowledge, such as annual design trend reports, yearbook, magazines, editions and websites. This represents the explicit output of the values of design awards, reflecting the ethos of design awards. The award evaluation process itself is a progression from design data to the formation of design wisdom, serving as a significant manifestation of the knowledge value of design awards.

Through knowledge exchange activities, DAKN connects actors with the knowledge entity, creating a network where design knowledge is acquired, shared, and recreated among individuals. Structurally, DAKN consists of two subsystems: the knowledge's resource network and the actors' social network. In terms of relationships, it refers to the interactive coupling between actors and knowledge.

In a knowledge society, no individual or organization possesses a sufficient amount of knowledge to independently undertake the diverse and intricate tasks required on a daily basis. Achieving organizational objectives necessitates collaborative efforts within the system. It is evident that knowledge networks inherently serve a collaborative function. This holds particularly true for the DAKN, where the knowledge resource serves as the foundational element. However, the most critical component within the network is the actors involved. Connecting the knowledge resource with the actors are the various exchange activities within design awards. For instance, the database of award-winning works by iF award, which represents a collection of knowledge resources pertaining to award-winning works, cannot be considered a comprehensive iF knowledge network (iF-KN). The essence of iF-KN is primarily embodied in the connections between knowledge and individuals. This is seen through international and domestic scientific conferences, hearings, research activities conducted by the iF Foundation, as well as activities related to education and professional training. Similarly, DIA-KN extends beyond the database of awarded works and exhibits from previous years. It is further reflected in the various events associated with its "Academy Award" positioning. These events include annual academic forums, themed design exhibitions, D·Will Lectures, DI Project Workshops, and others. The dynamic coupling of knowledge and individuals within these activities promotes the dissemination, reutilization, and innovation of design award knowledge.

3. Knowledge collaboration mechanism based on design awards

DAKN is essentially a value innovation process centered on knowledge, which involves information acquisition, knowledge production, knowledge integration, and knowledge diffusion and application through excellent award-winning cases, as well as dynamic development and continuous change. The knowledge in the excellent design cases gathered during the award is disseminated through the D · Will Lecture in the DIA-KN, and innovative application of knowledge is achieved through the DI Project, resulting in a spiral evolution of knowledge value.

Unlike traditional workshop-based collaborations and collaborations between industry schools and research institutions, DI Project, as a collaborative model based on design awards, brings together a wealth of valuable case resources and numerous innovators. DI Project promotes knowledge exchange among various actors in the network, establishing significant relationships for mutual creation and growth, resulting in multidimensional interactions among different roles and deeper knowledge collaboration.

In the first DI Project named Neural Symbol Universal AI Concept Design Camp, the DIA-KN platform try to conduct a new mechanism of industry-university-institutes collaboration. By utilizing a project-based collaborative approach and involving novice designers, it establishes a three-party collaboration involving enterprises (marketing specialists, technical engineers, product managers, designers), universities (arts and design departments), and institutions (laboratory scientists, DIA research team). This industry-university-institute collaboration framework differs from the traditional one. It is a model of collaborative framework driven by the DIA-KN, based on individuals and knowledge coupling (Fig.1). The uniqueness of this framework is primarily reflected in its future-oriented approach, fluid participant management, integrated knowledge resources, and a flexible, open innovation ecosystem.

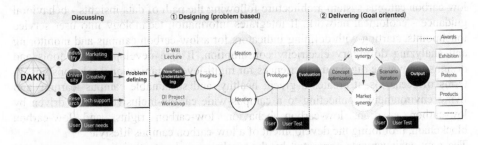

Figure 1. Industry-University-Institute Collaborative framework of DI Project led by DIA-KN

Under this framework, the China Academy of Art collaborated with DIA and worked alongside the participating company Alibaba Cloud to conduct a series of workshops, including *New Vision of Smart Life* and *Low-Carbon Campus* with subsequent application and validation. These workshops were centered around the concept of "Art+Technology" and utilized big data and AI technologies to explore systematic solutions for future life scenarios through the collaborative efforts of industry, university and institute, fostering knowledge co-creation. They made excellent use of the knowledge resources within the DIA-KN and facilitated knowledge collaboration among various actors, resulting in remarkable knowledge outputs.

The workshop of *New Vision of Smart Life* leverages digital twin technology to explore the digitization of traditional scenarios, unearthing smart life scenarios for the future. This injects imagination and new technology into everyday life scenarios, delivering novel experiences and value. It has generated multiple solutions, including smart communities (Fig.2), digital campuses, digital museums, intelligent elderly care communities, and smart supermarkets. By employing digital twin technology to dynamically present the behaviors and processes of physical scenes, it enhances management efficiency and user experiences within life scenarios.

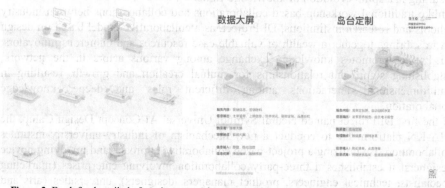

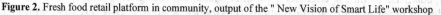

Figure 2. Fresh food retail platform in community, output of the " New Vision of Smart Life" workshop

The workshop of *Low-Carbon Campus* is an innovative project aiming to campus carbon neutrality. This project proposes the design concept of *Campus as a community, Low-carbon as fashion* with the aim of exploring sustainable solutions for a low-carbon campus. It encourages students to conduct low-carbon activities and constructs a low-carbon campus system architecture following the path of data insights - behavioral guidance - ecological network. It integrates information technology into user service touchpoints, starting with defining indicators for a low-carbon campus and monitoring and analyzing dormitory electricity consumption. It also develops digital tools and designs innovative digitized experiences for multi-level organizational relationships. In terms of scenarios, it creates a green, healthy, and sustainable campus learning and living environment, connecting to a campus-wide carbon-inclusive system driven by low-carbon creation, low-carbon behavior, low-carbon rights, and low-carbon blockchain, promoting the development of a low-carbon campus lifestyle.

The new achievements generated by the workshops, due to their innovativeness and cutting-edge nature, have not only resulted in numerous invention patents, utility model patents, and design patents but have also garnered favor from various awards, receiving multiple design awards. These innovative outcomes from DI Project have become valuable case resources for multiple design awards, enhancing the high recognition from businesses and widespread social impact of the DI Project industry-university-institute collaborative innovation model initiated by the DIA.

4. Assessment of the co-validity of knowledge in DIA-KN

It is only with the full participation of actors that a knowledge network can demonstrate its overall validity. Therefore, this paper firstly summarizes the structural indicators based on organizational elements and outcome evaluation through literature research and interviews with scholars and experts. Four important indicators were established: the synergy of actors, the accessibility of knowledge resources, the incentive of the policy environment, and the optimization degree of performance construction. The evaluation indicators of knowledge synergy effectiveness of the DIA-KN were screened out. Subsequently, we analyzed and extracts 15 key utility indicators (first-level indicators). The utility evaluation model below (Table 1) is summarized to evaluate the effectiveness of DIA-KN.

Table 1. DIA-KN Utility Evaluation Model

	Evaluation indicators		Evaluation indicators		Evaluation indicators		Evaluation indicators
Actors	Knowledge acquisition capacity	Resources	Knowledge representation capability	Policy	Expected goal perception	Performance	Organizational creativity
	Knowledge absorption capacity		Knowledge retention capability		Incentive system setup		Knowledge quality enhancement
	Knowledge transfer capacity		Knowledge retrieval capability		Exchange platform building		Organizational change capacity
	Knowledge innovation capacity		Knowledge dissemination capacity		Knowledge sharing culture		

According to the utility evaluation index of DIA-KN, 32 related questions were designed for knowledge providers and knowledge recipients (Table 2), and the 5-point Likert scale was used to evaluate the recognition of the evaluation index of knowledge synergy validity by DI Project participants. In order to conduct a more accurate quantitative examination of each indicator, the author designed 2-3 questions for each indicator, and implanted some reverse examination questions to make the questionnaire results more reliable and obtain a real and effective overall evaluation.

Table 2. Correspondence problem of DIA-KN utility evaluation indicators (excerpt)

Framework	indicators	Indicator correspondence issues
Synergy of actors	Knowledge acquisition capacity	During the DI Project, you have effective access to complementary resources and expertise through the DIA-KN.
		During the DI Project, you make greater use of contacts and expertise gained from non-DIA collaborative network resources.
	Knowledge absorption capacity	During the DI Project, you were able to fully understand and assimilate the knowledge, experience and methodology shared by tutors and participants.
		The new knowledge you gain in DI Project can be effectively applied to subsequent work and contribute directly to the outputs.
		There are large cognitive differences in DI Project projects where you are unable to understand the perspectives and experiences of other team members.
	Knowledge transfer capacity	In DI Project, you can use a variety of tools to communicate effectively so that others understand your design intent.
		You will be able to communicate well with your team members and reach a consensus on DI Project.
	Knowledge innovation capacity	You will be able to integrate and create new designs as you learn and assimilate new knowledge.
		You have gained more inspirational ideas and enhanced your design thinking and creativity after participating in the DI Project workshops.

	Knowledge indicates ability	In DI Project, there is a structured presentation of design knowledge, such as design methods, design techniques, design specifications, design processes, design principles, and other aspects of knowledge outputs. The workshop initially provided lectures through the D`Will Lecture, which provided a good foundation for subsequent collaborative workshops
Accessibility of knowledge resources	Knowledge retention capacity	Knowledge contained in the DI Project (e.g. background information, technical principles, etc.) is shared on the web platform and available. DIA's award-winning cases over the years are kept in a database in a filtering, categorical and searchable way for access.
	Knowledge retrieval capacity	You'll search the DIA's award-winning casebook for valuable design inspiration. Documents and information related to each issue of DI Project are organized and preserved in a standard manner to facilitate future retrieval.
	Knowledge dissemination capacity	Through the DI Project, you know more about the outstanding winning cases of DIA and are willing to share with others. New knowledge outputs produced through DI Project have gained a more far-reaching dissemination impact than typical knowledge outputs.

The validity evaluation questionnaire was distributed and collected through the *wjx.cn* platform, taking the participants of the DI Project as the main respondents. In this survey, 56 questionnaires were finally recovered, including 9 tutors and 47 students. After screening out the invalid questionnaires with the same score or short answering time, 46 valid samples were retained, including 8 tutors and 38 students, with an effective recovery rate of 82%. In the questions listed in Table 2, the evaluations were scored on a 5-level Likert scale, corresponding to five levels: very dissatisfied, dissatisfied, uncertain, satisfied, and very satisfied. Finally, the relevant data were imported into SPSS for statistical analysis and collation.

This questionnaire mainly explores the main aspects of the effectiveness of DIA-KN. Firstly, the average data of the 4 primary evaluation indicators and 15 secondary evaluation indicators of the questionnaire were ranked (Fig.3).

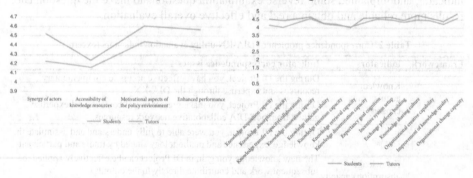

Figure 3. Line chart of the average of the primary and secondary indicators in DIA-KN

According to the data results, all indicators of DIA-KN are in the range of 4 or above, indicating that all indicators have played a good role in promoting the knowledge network. Among the first-level evaluation indicators, "the stimulus of the policy environment" is the most significant advantage of the DIA knowledge network, while the "accessibility of knowledge resources" needs to be enhanced. Among the specific secondary indicators, the trainees and tutors generally believe that the "knowledge innovation ability" in the DIA knowledge network is the most effective, while the "knowledge retrieval ability" needs to be improved. In addition, respondents also rated "knowledge-sharing culture" and "organizational change ability" as highly arguing, demonstrating that both play a key role in the operation and improvement of the DIA knowledge network. Then, the mean, maximum and minimum values of each question in this questionnaire were statistically organized (Table 3).

Table 3. Descriptive statistics of DIA-KN performance

Indicators	Serial number	Students			Tutors		
		Mean value	Max. values	Min. value	Mean value	Max. values	Min. value
Knowledge acquisition	H1a	4.11	5	2	4.50	5	4
Knowledge absorption	H2a	4.05	5	2	4.00	5	4
	H2b	4.05	5	1	4.00	5	4
	H2c	3.97	5	2	5.00	5	5
Knowledge transfer	H3a	4.11	5	2	4.50	5	4
	H3b	4.37	5	2	5.00	5	4
Knowledge innovation	H4a	4.55	5	2	4.00	5	4
	H4b	4.53	5	2	5.00	5	4
Knowledge indicates	H5a	4.21	5	2	4.00	5	3
	H5b	4.24	5	2	4.50	5	4
Knowledge retention	H6a	4.05	5	1	4.00	5	2
	H6b	4.18	5	2	5.00	5	3
Knowledge retrieval	H7a	4.16	5	1	4.50	5	3
	H7b	3.92	5	1	4.00	5	2
Knowledge dissemination	H8a	4.39	5	2	4.50	5	4
	H8b	4.26	5	1	5.00	5	4
Expected goal perception	H9a	4.50	5	2	5.00	5	4
	H9b	4.55	5	2	5.00	5	4
Incentive system setup	H10a	4.61	5	2	5.00	5	4
	H10b	4.34	5	1	5.00	5	3
Exchange platform building	H11a	4.32	5	1	4.50	5	3
	H11b	4.32	5	2	5.00	5	4
Knowledge sharing culture	H12a	4.53	5	2	5.00	5	4
	H12b	4.42	5	2	5.00	5	4
Organisational creativity	H13a	4.45	5	3	5.00	5	4
	H13b	4.34	5	2	5.00	5	4
	H13c	4.47	5	3	5.00	5	4
Knowledge quality enhancement	H14a	4.37	5	2	5.00	5	3
	H14b	4.03	5	1	4.00	5	3
Organisational change	H15a	4.50	5	2	5.00	5	4
	H15b	4.58	5	3	5.00	5	4
Cronbach's reliability analysis							
Alpha		Cronbach's Alpha			N of Items		
0.898		0.953			31		

The Cronbach's alpha coefficient was 0.953 in the reliability test, which was of high reliability quality and could be used for further analysis. According to the results of the chart, the minimum values of each question showed that the students had low scores in six aspects: "knowledge absorption ability", "knowledge preservation ability", "knowledge retrieval ability", "incentive system setting", "communication platform construction" and "knowledge quality improvement", which indicated that there was a large knowledge potential gap between the students and lecturers in the workshop, and it was necessary to improve the knowledge absorption ability of the students through relevant measures. The survey also found that the database of DIA award-winning cases over the years is incomplete, which affects the information retrieval and preservation of students, and it is necessary to improve the construction of the network platform of the DI Project, improve the connection between the DIA work database and the design workshop, and standardize the file storage mechanism of the DI Project. DIA-KN has resource characteristics but needs to be further improved. The economic and social benefits of the workshop results is not obvious yet.

In order to better explore the correlation between the performance construction of DIA knowledge network and actors, knowledge resources and policy environment, this study also analyzed the correlation of four evaluation indicators of DIA knowledge network through Pearson index and Sig. index (Table 4).

Table 4. DIA-KN Performance Correlation Statistics

		Knowledge indicates ability	Knowledge retention capacity	Knowledge retrieval capacity	Knowledge dissemination capacity
Knowledge quality enhancement	PCC	.465**	.684**	.623**	.624**
	Sig. (bobtail)	0.003	0.000	0.000	0.000
	Cases Number	38	38	38	38
		Knowledge absorption capacity	Knowledge transfer capacity	Knowledge innovation capacity	Knowledge acquisition capacity
Organisational creativity	PCC	.531**	.419**	.608**	.491**
	Sig. (bobtail)	0.001	0.009	0.000	0.002
	Cases Number	38	38	38	38
		Desired target value	Incentive system setup	Exchange platform building	Knowledge sharing culture
Organisational change capacity	PCC	.724**	.829**	.761**	.591**
	Sig. (bobtail)	0.000	0.000	0.000	0.000
	Cases Number	38	38	38	38

**. The correlation is significant at the 0.01 level (two-tailed).

In the chart above, the larger the Pearson index, the higher the correlation between the two indicators; The smaller the Sig. index ratio of 0.01, the more significant the correlation is demonstrated. As far as the Sig. index as a whole, the correlation values between all indicators are less than 0.01, indicating that there is a certain correlation between the indicators of the DIA-KN. Based on the two judgments, there exists high correlation between "knowledge quality improvement" and "knowledge preservation ability", "organizational creativity" and "knowledge innovation", also between "organizational reform ability" and "incentive system setting". Therefore, in order to solve the problem of the above-mentioned descriptive statistical results, the organizational structure and operational capacity of the DIA-KN can be further improved by improving the indicators that are highly relevant to each other.

5. Results and Discussion

Based on this questionnaire study, it can be found that the industry-university-institute collaboration of "art + technology" based on DIA-KN can play a very important role in the innovation of technology application scenarios. Although the participants in the workshop gave DIA-KN a low score in terms of knowledge absorption, knowledge preservation, and knowledge retrieval ability, they still believed that "the stimulus of policy environment" was the most significant advantage of DIA-KN, and there was a high correlation between organizational creativity ability and knowledge innovation ability. From the perspective of the subject of organizational creation, enterprises and universities have completely different organizational behavior characteristics and work goals, but the innovation resources they have are highly complementary or interdependent. A comprehensive team like Alibaba Cloud, which integrates marketing, scientific research and design, has strong applied research capabilities. For those powerful subsystems like Alibaba, the collaborative participation of multiple design universities could be external knowledge source system. Due to the potential difference between universities and enterprises in heterogeneous knowledge, the novelty, challenge and complementarity brought by this technological difference have effectively stimulated the interest and motivation of interactive learning between them and established a trusting cooperative relationship. This trusting relationship, backed by the knowledge collaboration mechanism of the design award, is an important factor in the ongoing cooperation between Alibaba Cloud and the China Academy of Art on the DIA-KN.

According to such a characteristic, DI Project form a supply and demand market for cooperative innovation of industry-university-institute. Enterprise needs the help of external knowledge sources to promote technological innovation, and the DIA-KN provides new impetus for enterprise creative innovation activities through the excellent award-winning work resource and the design collaboration of college design students with rich artistic imagination. University students who lack experience in technical information and markets also need to be supplemented by corporate knowledge, and DIA-KN provides an effective connection from excellent design knowledge to actor partnerships.

6. Conclusions and future work

Overall, DIA-KN, which is formed by the link between D·Will Lecture and DI Project, is a chain that promotes knowledge exchange, dissemination and innovation. The absorption, integration and creative combination of knowledge achievements by industry-university-institute increase the possibility of transforming knowledge achievements into productivity. There are many similar industry-university-institute supply and demand relationships in the DIA-KN, so the construction of industry-university-institute interaction through the design award platform is a response to this similar cooperation. This kind of cooperative relationship can reflect the resource complementarity and reorganization advantages of multi-party participants with knowledge resources. Industry-university-institute cooperation derived from design award is an effective mechanism for knowledge upgrading in DAKN innovation system, which is of great significance for industrial innovation. How to give full play to the subjective initiative of each subject and make DIA-KN a fluid, growing and dynamic network is the key issue to be considered by the DIA as an Academy Award. Therefore, design awards are more than just awards for excellent products. It is not only a system to evaluate the merits of design, but also to obtain new discoveries through evaluation, the application of new materials and technologies emerging from excellent award-winning cases, the highlighting of new views and new insights, the expansion of new scenarios and new services, and the design awards to share them with the public, and then guide the next creative mechanism. The design award should focus on the interpretation, guidance and publicity of innovative thinking, the establishment of diversified innovative communication methods, and the formation of innovative consciousness of communication. By gathering talents from different universities, scientific institutions and enterprises to form a collaborative innovation design team, we can promote the upgrading and recreation of innovative knowledge from the excellent award-winning cases.

References

[1] Liu P L, Tsai C H. Using analytic network process to construct evaluation indicators of knowledge sharing effectiveness in Taiwan's high-tech industries. Asian Journal on Quality, 2008.

[2] Zhang Aiqin, Chen Hong. Research on Evaluation of the Coordination Innovation of Knowledge Innovation Network among Industries, Universities and Research Institutes. Journal of North University of China (Social Science Edition),2009,25(04):44-47.

[3] He Renke. He Renke: International Design Competition is the Gateway for Chinese Products to the World. Design, 2021,34(02):50-53.

[4] Hang Jian. Systemic: Everything is "Design". Zhuang Shi,2021(12):12-16.

[5] Lou Yongqi. New Environmental Design in the Global Knowledge Internet Time. Journal of Nanjing Arts Institute (Fine Arts & Design),2017(01):3-9+224.

[6] Li Dan, Yu Zhuchao,Fan Zhiping. The analysis for construction processes of knowledge networks. Studies in Science of Science,2002(06):620-623.

[7] Amy C. Edmondson. Teaming: How Organizations Learn, Innovate, and Compete in the Knowledge Economy. Beijing: Publishing House of Electronics Industry,2019.6

[8] Gemser G, Wijnberg N M. The economic significance of industrial design awards: A conceptual framework. Academic Review, 2002, 2(1): 61-71.

[9] Sahin D, Calguner A, Yavuzcan H G. Design awards as a design promotion activity: International design awards. Press Academia Procedia, 2017, 4(1): 134-142.

[10] Watanabe M, ONO K, Wu Y, et al. Expansion of Design Fields Based on The Trends in Design Award. Journal of the Science of Design, 2020, 4(1): 167-174.

[11] Guan J, Liu N. Exploitative and exploratory innovations in knowledge network and collaboration network: A patent analysis in the technological field of nano-energy. Research policy, 2016, 45(1): 97-112.

[12] Phelps C, Heidl R, Wadhwa A. Knowledge, networks, and knowledge networks a review and research agenda. Journal of Management, 2012, 38(4):1115-1166.

Design Studies and Intelligence Engineering
L.C. Jain et al. (Eds.)
© 2024 The Authors.
This article is published online with Open Access by IOS Press and distributed under the terms
of the Creative Commons Attribution Non-Commercial License 4.0 (CC BY-NC 4.0).
doi:10.3233/FAIA231517

Research on the Elements of Tourist Experience Demands in Archaeological Site Parks Based on Grounded Theory

Yizi CHEN [a,b,1] and Zihan DENG [b]

[a] *College of Art, Zhejiang University of Finance & Economics, Hangzhou, China, 310018*
[b] *School of Industrial Design, China Academy of Art, Hangzhou, China, 310024*

Abstract. This study refines the tourists' five main demand categories of "perceptual presentation demand", "behavioral interaction demand", "scene narrative demand", "content perception demand" and "main goal demand" in the archaeological site parks, through choosing the tourist experience of archaeological site parks as the research object, taking their review texts in the Internet as the basic data, and using the basic research procedures of open coding, spindle coding, selective coding of grounded theory, then verifying the results by the reliability test and the matrix method in social network analysis. The elements of visitor experience demand in archaeological site parks extracted from this study have good credibility to support for the design of visitor experience in archaeological site parks and experience optimization of subsequent related products.

Keyword. Archaeological site parks, Tourist experience, Demand elements, Grounded theory

1. Introduction

In recent years, the cultural industry and tourism industry have accelerated their integration under the support of intelligent technology, and archaeological site parks have begun to pay attention to the physical operation, emotional needs, and cognitive thinking of tourists in the process of visiting. The author attempt to explore the possibility to make tourists feel, share and participate in the historical and cultural landscape in the archaeological site comprehensively through taking tourist experience demands as the guide, and supported by the digital technology. Compared with the traditional tourist experience in archaeological site parks, the design based on the actual tourist experience demands is more realistic, and the in-depth study of the actual problems and demands of tourists is of great significance to improve the quality and value of their experience in archaeological site parks. This research can provide a data base for the tourist experience in archaeological site parks, to provide a theoretical basis for the tourist experience design of archaeological site parks.

---

[1] Corresponding author: Yizi Chen; Postal address: College of Art, Zhejiang University of Finance & Economics, Hangzhou, China, 310018; Email address: chenyz-1@163.com.

2. Research Design

2.1 Research Method

Grounded theory, as a research method based on data to discover clues, is a typical research method with theoretical exploratory function, which can encode and generalize unstructured large amounts of data and produce corresponding categories, to establish a scientific and effective user experience element. Therefore, according to the review text of the Archaeological Site Park, this study coded original data at three levels through grounded theory, including open coding, spindle coding and selective coding, so as to obtain the core category of tourist experience. Extracting the factors of concern for tourist experience demands in the archaeological site park, and studying the relationship between the core categories, can provide practical reference for the enhancement and improvement of tourist experience in the park.

2.2 Research Process

2.2.1 Data Collection

The collection and collation of textual data is carried out from tourists' online comments and in-depth interview. On the one hand, this study took Liangzhu Ancient City Archaeological Park as an example, and semi-structured interviews to tourists there was collated into textual form. On the other hand, according to the APP index ranking provided by iResearch, Ctrip.com is ranked first because of its wider coverage and more active users, so this study takes it as the data source of the tourists' comment texts.

In the process of searching the texts, firstly, based on the list of three batches of established national archaeological site parks released by the State Administration of Cultural Heritage, keyword searching was carried out on Ctrip.com in turn, then a total of 35 national archaeological site parks were searched, except for 1 archaeological site park could not be retrieved the relevant attraction information. Among them, 7 archaeological site parks have no tourist comments on Ctrip.com, and the relevant data cannot be obtained.

In the end, this study collected a total of 32,480 online comments from tourists on 28 national archaeological site parks on Ctrip.com up to 10 September 2022, which was used as the raw text data for the sample.

2.2.2 Data Collation

In order to ensure the accuracy and representativeness of the selected text data, this study selects and arranges the retrieved comment texts according to the following principles: Deleting the duplicated tourists' comment contents in the text data;

Eliminating the overly simplified and non-substantial contents.

Deleting the contents that do not directly evaluate the tourists' experience of the archaeological site park.

Eventually, through the collation and selection of text data, as well as the adjustment and improvement of text data collection results, a total of 21,571 valid comments were obtained, which were used as the text content of the study. (Figure 1)

Summary.date.comments
A free attraction in Sanming, the Lingfeng Cave on the mountain is not open, only the smaller sail cave and museum are open.
Feature or lack of point, if on the way to go.
It is located in the northeast corner of Sanxingdui Site, a national key cultural relic protection unit, and is located by the Duck River in the west of GuangSeoul.
Sanxingdui Ruins is the ancient Shu cultural site with the largest scope, longest duration and richest cultural connotation found in Southwest China so far.
The museum is divided into a comprehensive hall and a bronze hall, where you can enjoy a large number of unearthed gold, pottery, ivory and other cultural relics, all of which have distinct
Sanxingdui Ruins tells us a thousand years of history, and it is recommended that you must go there. Let us understand the civilization of Samsung and the current situation of society at that time, it
Located in the northeast corner of the national key cultural relics protection unit Sanxingdui Site, located in the west of the Duck River of Seoul, 40 kilometers from Chengdu in the south, 26
kilometers from Deyang in the north, it is a modern museum of special sites in China. Sanxingdui Museum has two pavilions, with an exhibition area of nearly 12,000 square meters.
Children like Sanxingdui, so the first stop in Chengdu to go to Sanxingdui, Sanxingdui must have a guide, as long as 3 hours of explanation is very worthwhile. The only fly in the ointment is the air
conditioning in the museum, the cooling effect is really worrying, the summer vacation is too hot, in the museum is also more than sweat.
worthwhile, although the legs are a little unbearable, but the spirit has been satisfied.
It is very shocking, there is a strong visual impact. Different from the ordinary Central Plains culture, it has its own characteristics. Experience. The ancient Shu people's wisdom and feel the
powerful strength of the ancient Shu State at that time, it is recommended to find a guide, can feel the history and culture of Sanxingdui more deeply.
It is very recommended to come, Guanghan North station taxi 17 yuan,10 minutes less can go to Sanxingdui Museum, two museums plus a cultural relics protection center, at least spend 3 hours to
visit, the second phase of the project is being built, later cultural relics may be more rich, the only way is to return to a enthusiastic "taxi to slaughter, received 24.5.
Have also seen the mask and bronze sacred tree reported by the media before, see the real thing, just know what is spectacular! What is shock, what is the thick sense of history!
Sanxingdui Museum is highly recommended.
Recommended reasons: With a history of 3,000 to 5,000 years, Sanxingi is an ancient city, ancient country and ancient Shu cultural site with the largest scope, longest duration and richest cultural
connotation found so far in Southwest China. Sanxingdui site is known as one of the greatest archaeological discoveries of mankind in the 20th century.
Recommended points:
1 Sanxingdui culture is necessary to explain the public number to buy 10 yuan, but it is recommended to find a docent.
2. Sanxingdui culture is rich in connotation. It is recommended to record it in your own way.
3. Children recommend watching the animation in Sanxingdui Hall No. 1 to better understand Sanxingdui culture.
One person, one day tour. The guide narrated very well and was conscientious and responsible. Sanxingdui now top traffic, the day is very hot, there are many people, but it is worth the trip, to see
Sanxingdui Museum is a modern museum of thematic sites. The museum was opened in October 1997. The museum area covers an area of about 530 mu, with the first exhibition area of 4,200
square meters and the second exhibition area of 7,000 square meters. The shape of the pavilion pursues the god of combination with geomorphology, historical sites.
The facilities are basically complete, the rented automatic explanation equipment has no power control, and it can not be rented when it is lower than how much, so as to avoid holding a no power
Always want to see for a long time, find a explanation, little sister people very gentle explanation is also very fine, and finally from the pavilion out of the souvenir shop, but also bought hundreds of
It is worth going to shock the ancients casting advanced, exquisite craft. A line of three people made an appointment in advance of the docents 300 yuan, speak very in place, the No. 1 hall to
accompany the explanation for one and a half hours. Ctrip booked the ticket immediately have staff contact, the service is very serious and intimate. Special reminder: the elderly have 18 old age
Sanxingdui Culture in Guanghan, Sichuan
Sanxingdui culture is an ancient culture of the same period as the Xia, Shang and Zhou cultures in Central Plains. It is the product of the integration of Qiang, Yi and other tribes, with its own unique
history of myths and legends, totem beliefs and tribal culture. Sanxingdui culture records a thick, splendid and unique history of tribal culture, which appears brilliantly but disappears mysteriously.
I still know very little about the history of ancient Shu and the course of Sanxingdui civilization. As the national treasure fever continues to ferment, our understanding of the civilization of
It's a great experience! I've been to Sanxingdui before, but I didn't know much about it systematically. This time, I brought my children with me. At 10:30 in the morning, Xu spoke very well and was
very professional. He used his own PAD from time to time to search some pictures for us to better explain the archaeological significance of some cultural relics. Xu is very dedicated, the whole 3
hours full of dry goods, and the language is humorous, the children do not feel boring, very good! But this time, because CCTV came to live broadcast, all the places were closed, we could not visit
the repair center. But when we learned that Hall 3 is under construction,
It will open in October next year. Come back next year!

Figure1. Tourist comments on the National Archaeological Site Park (Image source: Ctrip.com data, compiled by the author)

2.2.3 Analysis Method

The analysis method were divided into four main steps as follows:

Open coding: the initial analysis and conceptualization to the primary data. It requires the researcher to initially integrate all the data without bias and give them the appropriate concepts. Maintaining the habit of writing analytical memos needs to be aware of during the open coding process, which enhances the analysis and reflection on the primary sources.

Spindle coding: to discover and establish connections between individual concepts and categories. Since the connection between data is crucial to the final construction of the theory, the researcher needs to be clear about the intrinsic connection between concepts so as to analyse the problem from the broadest perspective.

Selective coding: the process of constructing a theory around core categories. With the deepening of the analysis, the researcher has a clear understanding of the core categories that are the most important in the research problem. The primary and secondary relationships between the categories have been very clear, then, the researcher needs to focus on the main core to carry out the study, so as to form a new theory.

Reliability and validity test: verify the reliability and validity of the coded content analysis. The same method was used to measure on the same object repeatedly, and if the results obtained were the same, it would be able to prove the consistency, reliability and stability of the research experiment.

3. Data Analysis

According to the grounded theory, the analysis of the research data consisted of four main parts: open coding, spindle coding, selective coding, and reliability and validity test.

3.1 Open coding analysis

Open coding requires the researcher to hold an open attitude in the initial study, and gradually generalize the concepts with the same attributes and similar meanings in the original data into certain categories to establish the relationship from phenomenon to category, the open coding process of this study is as follows:

- Screening of the collected text data, paragraph splitting of the commented texts therein, and integrating them into a single document as the basis of the next step of the study.
- Coding the processed text statements and summarizing the specific concepts appearing in the statements.
- Integrating all the concepts and summarizing the categories.

The following table demonstrates some of the specific processes and concepts of open coding.

Table 1. Example of open coding demonstration (Table source: self-making)

No.	Original Record	Concept
1	The inside of the Daming Palace is very large, and the buildings inside are very characteristic, and a lot of cultural relics are here, it is well worth a visit.	Architectural style
2	The use of modern restoration technology, fully demonstrated the glory of Tang Dynasty, 3D film is very good, focusing on the restoration of Tang Dynasty.	Sound and light technology
3	Seeing the masks and the bronze god tree in real life, one realizes what is spectacular! What is shocking, what is the sense of historical heaviness!	Mind-blowing
4	The Sun God Bird, an icon of China's historical and cultural heritage, was unearthed here, it's necessary to hiring a tour guide, there's plenty of backstory to listen to.	On-site Explanation
5	The scenery is beautiful, and the air is good!	Natural scenery
6	You can see the museum exhibitions as well as the Lantern Festival, which is held everywhere during the Chinese New Year, with snacks and performances.	Festive atmosphere

Based on the coding principles and specific steps of grounded theory, this study carefully and individually analyzed and generalized all the tourists' textual data, and combined with the characteristics of archaeological site parks, 62 concepts and 25 categories of cultural tourism experience to archaeological site parks were finally summarized as below.

Table 2. Open coding results (Table source: self-making)

No.	Category	Concept
A1	Visual perception	Natural scenery, colors, forms
A2	Auditory perception	Nature sounds, local dialect
A3	Tactile perception	Material texture, weather and climate
A4	Olfactory perception	Fresh air, floral odour
A5	Taste perception	Local food, delicious food
A6	Aesthetic perception	Cultural features, architectural styles, manufacturing techniques
A7	Escape perception	Forget worries, escape from reality, mental relaxation
A8	Intelligent terminal	VR display, video introduction, sound and light technology
A9	Product function	Path navigation, content expansion, interactive media
A10	Interactive interface	Function distribution, interface style
A11	Human-computer interaction	Difficulty of operation, high learning cost
A12	Interactive participation	Participation in activities, on-site discussion, network sharing
A13	Cultural landscape	Special attractions, geographic features
A14	Story Scene	Reducing historical events, rendering story atmosphere
A15	Local atmosphere	Sense of place, festive atmosphere
A16	Task guidance	Narrative clue guidance, role-playing, character interaction
A17	Excursion activities Festivals	archaeological simulation, cultural project experience
A18	History and culture	Ethnic spirit, religious beliefs
A19	People and customs	Living habits, customs and rituals
A20	Storyline Plot	development, story line connection
A21	Education and popularization of science	On-site explanation, knowledge learning, cultural education
A22	Leisure and recreation Camping	picnicking, playing and walking
A23	Cultural identity	Value identity, national self-confidence, national sentiment
A24	Emotional resonance	Soul shock, understanding the rise and fall of history, local attachment
A25	Heart-flow experience	Whole-body concentration, passage of time, strong sense of immersion

3.2 Spindle Coding

The results of open coding are independent of each other, spindle coding can specify and scope the categories and dimensions of the concepts, and reorganize them to form a certain coherence, to summarize and merge them into the main category and the secondary category, the coding of this part is mainly to get the secondary category of the concepts mentioned above.

In this paper, by spindle coding of the constituent elements of cultural tourism experience in archaeological site parks, 8 secondary categories are finally summarized, including perceptual presentation, interactive products, interactive behaviour, narrative scenarios, activity tasks, content needs, tour goals, and experiential feelings as below.

Table 3. Results of spindle coding (Table source: self-making)

Secondary category	Category
B1 Perceptual presentation	A1 Visual perception, A2 Auditory perception, A3 Tactile perception, A4 Olfactory perception, A5 Taste Perception, A6 Aesthetic Perception, A7 Escape Perception
B2 Product interaction	A8 Intelligent terminal, A9 Product function, A10 Interaction interface
B3 Interaction mode	A11 Human-computer interaction, A12 Interactive participation
B4 Narrative Scene	A13 Cultural Landscape, A14 Story Scene, A15 Local Atmosphere
B5 Activity tasks	A16 Task guidance, A17 Tour activities
B6 Cultural output	A18 History and culture, A19 Humanities and customs, A20 Storyline
B7 Tour Goal	A21 Science Education, A22 Leisure and Recreation
B8 Experience Feeling	A23 Cultural Identity, A24 Emotional Resonance, A25 Heart Flow Experience

3.3 Selective Coding Analysis

Selective Coding is the process of category theorizing, whereby the primary categories are deepened and compared with the initial categories, a core theory is developed to validate the relationships between the categories, and primary sources and developed labels, concepts, and categories are used to illustrate the full range of phenomena.

According to the content of this paper, the author chooses to use the tourists' experience in the National Archaeological Site Park as the story line of selective coding and try to analyze the tourists' experience demands in the whole process of touring the park. When tourists enter the park, they will get the sensory experience of sight, hearing and touch firstly, as well as the perceptual experience of the architecture aesthetic style of the site and the escape from real life. Secondly, tourists interact with tourism products, participate in interactive projects, and communicate with other tourists. Thirdly, tourists will participate in the tour activities and complete the corresponding tasks according to the guidance of the activity tasks, to build up the overall story scene and atmosphere and generate the great experience.

Table 4. Selective coding results (Table source: self-making)

Core category	Secondary category	Category
C1 Perceptual Presentation Demand	B1 Perceptual Presentation	A1 Visual Perception, A2 Auditory Perception, A3 Tactile Perception, A4 olfactory perception, A5 taste perception, A6 aesthetic perception, A7 Escape perception
C2 Behavioral Interaction Demand	B2 Product Interaction	A8 Intelligent Terminal, A9 Product Function, A10 Interaction Interface
	B3 Interaction mode	A11 Human-computer interaction, A12 Interactive participation
C3 Scene Narrative Demand	B4 Narrative Scene	A13 Cultural Landscape, A14 Story Scene, A15 Local Atmosphere
	B5 Activity tasks	A16 Task guidance, A17 Excursion activities
C4 content perception Demand	B6 cultural output	A18 history and culture, A19 humanities and customs, A20 storyline

C5 Main goal Demand	B7 Park visit goal	A21 Science education, A22 Leisure recreation
	B8 Experience Feeling	A23 Cultural Identity, A24 Emotional Resonance, A25 Heart Flow Experience

According to the above table, this article proposes 5 core demand categories of "perceptual presentation demand", "behavioral interaction demand", "scene narrative demand", "content perception demand" and "Main goal demand".

3.4 Reliability and Validity Tests

In order to verify the reliability and validity of this coded content analysis, the same method will be used to measure the same object repeatedly to verify the degree of consistency, reliability and stability of the results obtained. According to the validation method proposed by Glaser, the author selected 25% of the samples from the text data for the reliability test, 2 coders negotiated and coded the text data at the same time, and then the reliability test of the data will be conducted according to the Holsti interaction discriminant formula.

The Holsti interaction discriminant reliability formula is:

$$R = \frac{sn \times K}{1 + (n - 1) \times K}$$

"R" is the discriminant reliability, "n" is the number of coders, "K" is the average mutual agreement between coders, when R>0.8, it means that the coding result is "acceptable", R>0.9, it means that the coding result is "good". Since there were 2 coders in this study, the formula for calculating the average mutual agreement was:

$$M = \frac{2M_{AB}}{N_A + N_B}$$

Where "MAB" denotes the number of codes that were identical for both coders, and "NA" and "NB" denote the number of codes for each of the two coders. During the open coding process, both coders coded 21571 tourist comments, i.e., NA=NB=21571; the number of data categorized as identical by both was 20385, i.e., MAB=20385.

Through formula (2), the average mutual agreement $K_{AB} = \frac{2 \times 20385}{21571 + 21571}$=94.5% can be obtained; then substituting it into formula (1), discriminant reliability

$R = \frac{2 \times 0.945}{1 + (2-1) \times 0.945}$=0.972 can be calculated.

The calculation found that the Kappa coefficient of the open coding reliability R of this study is 0.972, which passes the Holsti Interactive Discriminant Reliability Test, indicating that the elements of cultural tourism experience in archaeological site parks distilled in this study have a good credibility.

4. Element Extraction of Tourist Experience Demand in Archaeological Site Parks

Social network analysis is a method to analyze the degree of correlation between factors within a system and the degree of influence of each factor in the whole system. The social network analysis method can be used to explore and analyze the structural characteristics of the mixed experience elements in archaeological site parks.

In this paper, we constructed a social relationship matrix with mixed experience elements and converted it into a visual social relationship network diagram with Ucinet6 software, so as to show the social network members and their relationships and structural characteristics more clearly and explicitly.

Overall, it is mainly divided into three steps:

First, the co-occurrence matrix is constructed based on the 25 mixed experience elements of archaeological site parks refined above as nodes, i.e., the number of times two mixed experience elements appear in a comment at the same time, so as to depict the inter-relationships between these two mixed experience elements.

Second, the co-occurrence matrix of the mixed experience elements is then converted into a 0-1 co-occurrence matrix, i.e., when the two elements co-occur is greater than 1, the corresponding matrix cell is assigned the value of 1, and vice versa is 0, and the binary matrix of the mixed experience elements is finally obtained.

Third, Using Ucinet software to calculate the overall density of this binary matrix, and the calculation result was 0.9067, that is, there is a close connection between the mixed-experience elements of the archaeological site park as refined above.

On this basis, the Net Draw function of Ucinet was used to visualize the relationship between the mixed experience elements, and the specific results are shown in Figure 2.3.

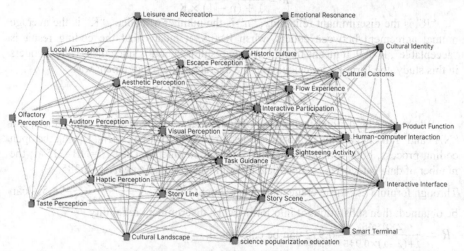

Figure 2. Structural network of mixed experience elements in archaeological site parks
(Source: Ucinet, compiled by the author)

Core node is the association relationship generated by the relationship between each node element and other elements, if a node element is directly associated with many other node elements, the node is more important in the whole social network, and its influence on the mixed experience is also greater.

According to the figure above, the network of mixed experience elements in archaeological site parks has the characteristics of multi-core and high-density. In general, the core nodes of mixed experience elements in archaeological site parks mainly include the following five aspects:

- the perceptual presentation demand with the needs of visual perception, auditory perception, aesthetic perception, etc.

- the behavioral interaction demands the needs of interactive participation, excursion activities, and human-computer interaction;
- the scene narrative demands the needs of task guidance and story scenes as the core.
- the content perception demands the needs of history and culture, cultural scenery and storyline as the core.
- the main goal demands the needs of cultural identity, emotional resonance, and heart flow experience as the core.
- The above five dimensions together reflect the core demands of tourists for archaeological site parks.

5. Analysis of tourists' experience demand elements in archaeological site parks

Based on the grounded theory and the basic research procedures of open coding, selective coding and theoretical coding, this paper examines and discusses the tourists' experiential demands in archaeological site parks. Finally, it refined the 5 main demand elements of "perceptual presentation demand", "behavioral interaction demand", "scene narrative demand", "content perception demand" and "main goal demand" in archaeological site parks.

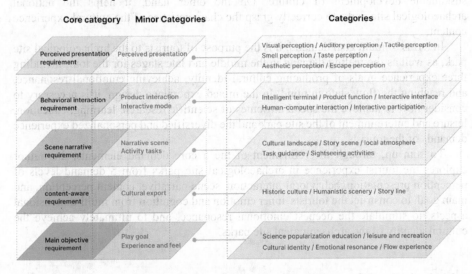

Figure3. Grounded theory research results and tourists experience demand element model of archaeol ogical site park (image source: self-making)

In terms of perceptual presentation demand, it is the key channel for tourists to obtain the experience content, including sight, hearing, taste, touch, smell and other sensory perception. The way in which tourists perceive archaeological site parks is no longer single, and tourists can obtain the experience content through a variety of perceptual channel. Tourists are brought into specific cultural contexts to understand culture and are provided with personalized narratives and itineraries to create a mixed scene space of reality.

In terms of behavioral interaction demand, the objects that tourists communicate and interact with in archaeological site parks include tourism experience products and interfaces, scene experience facilities and other tourists. Tourists can actively communicate and interact with the park through behavioral interactions driven by intuition and the experience products set up by the segmentation to produce two-way interactions at the sensory and behavioral levels, and at the same time, produce an invisible emotional resonance and cultural identity for the park in the process of interaction.

In terms of scene narrative demand, tourists in archaeological site parks have the demand to feel the scene culture and participate in the cultural story. According to the experience motivation, experience needs and knowledge structure of different tourists, the richness and complexity of the scene narrative content is set hierarchically in this way; on this basis, the narrative content and story text are opened up, prompting tourists and other groups to become the interpreters of the scene narratives, and the narrative co-creation is carried out through the whole process of the tourist's experience, thus realizing the constant updating and continuous iteration of the narrative content.

In terms of content perception demand, on the one hand, it helps tourists to tap into the feelings and perceptions of the history and culture, to achieve content iteration from tourists' production, updating and optimization for periodically providing cultural content input for the national archaeological site parks, and to achieve benign and sustainable development of culture. On the other hand, it helps the national archaeological site parks to correctly grasp the characteristics of the cultural experience content.

In terms of main goal demand, it is the purpose of tourists to the archaeological site park, as well as the feeling demand in the middle and late stages for the tour, including three experience goals of producing cultural identity, achieving emotional resonance, and reaching the flow state in mind. In the mixed experience design, it is necessary to consider how to achieve the social attributes of scientific research, learning, education, leisure and entertainment of the site park and the diversified and personalized experience demands of the tourists.

To sum up, through the refinement of the 5 core demand elements, the author explores the tourist experience in archaeological site parks from 5 demand levels of perception presentation, behavioral interaction, scene narrative, content perception, and main goal, to construct the tourists' inner emotion and cognition from multi-dimensional aspects, to stimulate the deepest emotional resonance, and to ultimately achieve the cultural identity of the archaeological site parks.

6. Limitations and Prospect

Due to the limitations of research time, energy and ability, the research still should be improved and explored.

1. The samples of the data on tourist demand in archaeological site parks is relatively little, and some of the data in archaeological site parks could not be obtained, thus the analysis result may be biased, and the bias can be corrected in the subsequent study through more samples and more rigorous analysis.

2. This paper takes Ctrip.com comments as the sample, but tourists' characteristics are not obvious and the content is not clear, which may affect the accuracy of the analysis of tourist experience demand in archaeological site parks to a

certain extent, so in the follow-up study, the questionnaire could be designed to quantify the system of the demand component factors, in order to test and adjust the elements of the tourist experience demand in this paper.

It is hoped that there will be more and better methods for the research on the elements of tourist experience in archaeological site parks in the future, which will have far-reaching significance for how archaeological site parks can provide tourists with good service and product experience and thus create the value of their own products under the environment of the experience economy and the Internet.

Acknowledgment

This paper is supported by "Research on the Development Strategy of Zhejiang Digital Tourism Cultural and Creative Products Based on Cultural Identity", the 2021 General Scientific Research Project of Zhejiang Provincial Education Department (Y202147412).

References

[1] Csikszentmihalyi M. Finding flow: The psychology of engagement with everyday life, New York: Basic books, 1997.
[2] Jenkins, Participatory culture: interview, John Wiley & Sons, 2019.
[3] Nina Simon, The Participatory Museum: Museum 2. First Edition (US). 2018.
[4] Polly McKenna- Cress, Janet A. Kamien. Creating Exhibitions: Collaboration in the Planning, Development, and Design of Innovative Experiences, Zhenjiang University Press, 2021.
[5] M. Wilson, Six Views of Embodied Cognition, Psychonomic Bulletin & Review, 2002.
[6] Marto A, Melo M, Gonçalves A, et al. Multisensory augmented reality in cultural heritage: impact of different stimuli on presence, enjoyment, knowledge and value of the experience, IEEE Access, 2020, 8: 193744-193756.
[7] Shan Jixiang, Protection of Large Archaeological Sites, Tianjin University, 2015.
[8] XI Yueting, Research on Cultural Tourism of National Archaeological Site Park, Science Press, 2020.
[9] Li Lijuan, Research on Co-creation of Tourism Experience Value, Tourism Education Press, 2013.
[10] Li Ruyo, Research on Value Co-creation Mechanism of Tourists' Participation in Tourism Experience, Zhejiang Gongshang University, 2012.

Design Studies and Intelligence Engineering
L.C. Jain et al. (Eds.)
© 2024 The Authors.
This article is published online with Open Access by IOS Press and distributed under the terms
of the Creative Commons Attribution Non-Commercial License 4.0 (CC BY-NC 4.0).
doi:10.3233/FAIA231518

Virtual Simulation Experimental Teaching Method and Practice Based on BOPPPS Teaching Model: An Example of Virtual Simulation Experiment Platform of Jiajiang Bamboo Paper Making Skills

Fangyu LI[a] and Jiayi LI[b,1] and Yefei LI[c]

[a] *School of Design, Southwest Jiaotong University*
[b] *Art Design Dept, The Engineering&Technical College of Chengdu University of Technology*
[c] *School of Mechanical and Electrical Engineering, University of Electronic Science and Technology of China*

Abstract. Based on the research of intangible cultural heritage, this study summarizes and organizes the non-heritage knowledge of the bamboo paper making techniques of the JIJIANG River, takes the characteristics of virtual simulation experiment into reasonable consideration, and carries out the design of the virtual simulation experiment platform of the bamboo paper making techniques of the JIANG River based on the BOPPPS teaching model and task-driven teaching method. The platform includes the integration of the theoretical basic knowledge of the technique of making bamboo paper and the establishment of a 3D virtual scene of the paper-making workshop one by one. By combining the techniques of paper making with virtual simulation technology, students can be highly immersed in the "experiment" and motivated and motivated to learn. At the same time, it enriches the way of preserving and passing on the craft, leading users to explore it actively and enhancing their sense of participation. It also provides a reference for the preservation and transmission of other intangible cultural heritage, especially traditional crafts, in the virtual simulation experiment environment.

Keywords. Virtual simulation experiment, BOPPPS teaching mode, intangible cultural heritage, Jiajiang bamboo paper making skills

1. Introduction

Virtual simulation experiments integrate virtual reality, multimedia, human-computer interaction, databases, network communications and other technologies, and are the main direction of the informatization construction of experimental teaching in my country [1]. Li Ping and other scholars gave a detailed description of the characteristics of the virtual simulation experiment center, pointing out that the essential characteristics of the virtual

---

[1] Corresponding Author: Jiayi Li, 1027268187@qq.com

simulation experiment consist of information technology features, highly simulated experimental environments and objects, and meeting undergraduate teaching requirements[2]. In 2018, the Ministry of Education pointed out in the "Opinions of the Ministry of Education on Accelerating the Construction of High-level Undergraduate Education and Comprehensively Improving Talent Training Capabilities" that we should vigorously promote the construction of virtual simulation experiments. In 2019, the Ministry of Education pointed out in the "Implementation Opinions of the Ministry of Education on the Construction of First-Class Undergraduate Curriculum" that the professional layout is reasonable, the teaching effect is excellent, and openness and sharing are effective. Among them, the five major categories of first-class courses include virtual simulation experimental courses, and a national virtual simulation experimental teaching course sharing platform (http://www.ilab-x.com/) has been built and is open to the public.

2. Research status of virtual simulation experimental teaching construction

2.1. Overview of research on virtual simulation experimental teaching construction

"Virtual simulation experiment" was first proposed in 1989 by Professor William Wolfe of the University of Virginia in the United States. Since its introduction, it has been widely used in various professional fields. In the early days, it was mainly used for teaching basic courses in engineering colleges, such as the Microelectronics Online Laboratory of the Massachusetts Institute of Technology, the Surgical Simulation Laboratory of the University of North Carolina, the Virtual Physics Laboratory of the University of Houston, and the Dynamic fluid virtual simulation experimental system at George Mason University, etc. [3]. Wang Weiguo and others have done some research on the current situation and development of virtual simulation experimental teaching in foreign universities and pointed out some new trends worthy of attention[1]. According to the content of cultural heritage and different experimental purposes, Zhu Kerong divided the virtual simulation experimental teaching center related to cultural heritage inheritance into comprehensive cultural protection and display, national-level "intangible cultural heritage" skill inheritance, cultural heritage scene reproduction and application, innovative application of cultural heritage tourism industry, and proposed a "two-level, three-link, four-module" virtual simulation experimental teaching system[4]. Zhu Kerong analyzed the current situation of the construction of virtual simulation experimental teaching centers in the liberal arts in 2016. Due to the late start of liberal arts laboratory construction and the limited application of virtual simulation technology in the liberal arts field, the overall construction level is relatively low[5].

2.2. Overview of research on virtual simulation experimental teaching construction

In the development of virtual simulation experiments in the field of cultural heritage, in 2010, P.A. Fishwick and others built the Second China Project as a hybrid immersive, knowledge-based software platform for Chinese cultural training[6]. E. Selmanovi c and others added interactive digital stories to a virtual simulation system related to the diving tradition of the Old Bridge in Mostar, and conducted a user experience evaluation to prove that this method can create empathy among participants[7]. Marilena Alivizato and others took the i-treasures project as an example to study the establishment of a virtual learning environment for cultural heritage.It also verified that this platform is not only used as a "scientific experiment", but also requires intangible cultural heritage practitioners to participate in the design, research and implementation process, in order to stimulate the potential of intangible cultural heritage[8].Our country's research focus is mainly on technology exploration and the design and development of virtual simulation experiment platforms.For technology exploration, Chen Jianqiang used NGRAIN technology to improve the quality of real-time display images of 3D models[9].A three-dimensional model library system of ethnic minority costumes for clothing design teaching and learning has also been established through the combination of VR (virtual reality) and AR technology[10]. Zhou Hua and others used high-precision three-dimensional laser scanning and texture mapping technology to model the three-dimensional model of Tang Sancai for research on virtual simulation experimental teaching of cultural relics appreciation[11]. On the national virtual simulation experimental teaching course sharing platform, you can see virtual simulation courses related to intangible cultural heritage from many universities. Sichuan Normal University independently developed a virtual simulation experimental teaching project for traditional building mortise and tenon structures. This project uses 3D high-precision modeling to fully restore the East Hall of Foguang Temple, a wooden building in the Tang Dynasty, and creates 8 traditional building mortise and tenon joint production and combination experiments to demonstrate the exquisiteness of the mortise and tenon joint structure. Zhengzhou University of Light Industry has developed a virtual simulation experimental teaching project for Jun porcelain firing. Under the guidance of teachers, students conduct independent experimental operations, in-depth observation, experience and learning on the entire process of Jun porcelain firing in wood kilns in the form of 3D real scenes. Those type of virtual simulation experiment simulates different types of culture, effectively solving the problem of users being unable to "immerse themselves", and also contributing to the protection and inheritance of intangible culture.

Scholars' design and development of virtual simulation experiment platforms mainly focus on teaching method design, experimental system construction, experimental process design, interactive interface design, assessment system design, etc., mainly in order to solve the problems of high teaching costs, low student participation, and vulnerability to seasonal and venue factors.

3. Overview of the BOPPPS Teaching Model

The BOPPPS teaching model is the theoretical basis of ISW, a widely implemented teacher skills training system in Canada. This model emphasizes the student-centered teaching concept and modularizes the classroom teaching process. In the teacher training process, micro-teaching methods are used to conduct drills, allowing teachers to re-examine and improve the teaching process through small-scale, short-term, high-intensity drills, thereby ensuring the effective realization of the established course teaching objectives[12].

The BOPPPS teaching model divides the course into six modules: Bridge-in, Objective, Pre-assessment, Participatory learning, Post-assessment, and Summary. Because this teaching model emphasizes student-centeredness, pays attention to student participation, and has a clear structure and is easy to operate. Therefore, this model is not only used to train teachers' teaching skills, but has gradually been widely used in all types of teaching and has been highly recognized. With the development of online teaching, many scholars combine the BOPPPS teaching model with online teaching. Li Qi and other scholars studied the implementation of classroom teaching activities based on the BOPPPS teaching model throughout Rain Classroom to improve classroom efficiency, and verified its effectiveness through teaching effect analysis[13]. Feng Yongwei combined the BOPPPS teaching model with the Lanmoyun class APP to solve practical problems such as the low efficiency of the existing classroom and the weak sense of student participation[14]. Wu Changdong successfully verified the effectiveness of this model through real application[15].

The BOPPPS teaching model emphasizes student participation, interaction and feedback, and can be well applied to teaching methods with highly experimental and operational teaching content. It is suitable for teaching virtual simulation experiments, and students can conduct in-depth learning during the participation process. The combination of BOPPPS teaching model and virtual simulation experiment can improve the efficiency of the experiment and ensure the quality of the experiment. First, it can realize a closed loop of the experimental process to ensure that nothing is missed during the experiment and a virtuous cycle is formed. Second, it can greatly improve students' participation, be student-centered, goal-oriented, and guide students to learn independently. Third, it can help teachers analyze the teaching process based on subsequent real experimental results, thereby designing teaching content more effectively and improving teaching quality.

4. Design of virtual simulation experimental teaching model of Jiajiang bamboo paper skills based on BOPPPS

The BOPPPS teaching model focuses on student participation, and the task-driven teaching model embodies the idea of "teaching as the leader and learning as the main body". According to the teaching process of BOPPPS, the "Bridge-in" and "Objective" are introduced to lead students to learn the background information and basic knowledge related to Jiajiang bamboo paper making techniques. Through the pre-assessment phase, students' mastery of the learning content is tested and used as a basis for whether students can enter the next stage. The participatory learning stage is the key, using simulation production experience to allow students to participate in the process of making Jiajiang bamboo paper. The Post-assessment phase generates an experimental report based on students' performance in the participatory learning phase, and invites students to self-evaluate their learning satisfaction in this experiment. In the summary stage, students are guided to review the learning content and stimulate students to think. Through analysis, the teaching plan of the Jiajiang Bamboo Paper Skills Virtual Simulation Experiment Teaching Platform was obtained. As shown in Figure 1, according to the teaching model that combines the BOPPPS teaching model and task-driven teaching, students enter the virtual simulation experimental teaching platform. Through the textual declarative knowledge designed by the developer, students have a clear understanding and positioning of the learning content. Students can clearly understand the overall goal and task of the experiment and improve their learning motivation. After students complete the study of basic knowledge, assessments will be used to evaluate their mastery of knowledge. Passing the test proves that students have the basic knowledge background required for the experiment and have clarified the specific content of the task, and can enter participatory learning that focuses on operations. In the process of participatory learning, students are required to complete multiple operational tasks using the basic knowledge learned in the early stage and combined with experimental requirements. After completing all tasks, obtain the corresponding experimental report and summary. Abandoning the traditional one-way indoctrination teaching model, the entire process is controlled by students independently. Through different multimedia means, information exchange is made more abundant and natural, allowing students to learn in a relaxed, free, pleasant and positive environment, and realizing a truly student-oriented teaching model.

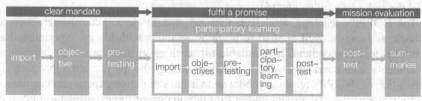

Figure 1. Virtual simulation experimental teaching model based on BOPPPS.

The BOPPPS teaching model runs through the task-driven teaching method, refining and supplementing the entire task-driven process. This method can strengthen interactive links, obtain timely feedback, and improve teaching efficiency. The specific teaching construction framework is shown in Figure 2.

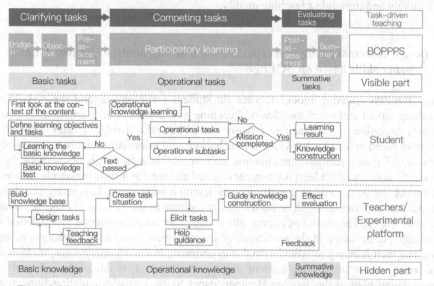

Figure 2. Virtual simulation experimental teaching construction framework based on BOPPPS.

5. Design of the Jiajiang bamboo paper making skills virtual simulation experiment platform

5.1. Information architecture

Based on the summary of key knowledge points and research on the teaching model of the virtual simulation experiment of Jiajiang bamboo paper making techniques, the information architecture is divided into two major sections: "knowledge popularization" and "process". They correspond to the two parts of "basic knowledge" and "operational knowledge" in the teaching model. And based on this, the design of the entire information architecture is carried out, as shown in Figure 3.The specific contents of the two modules are as follows.

- Knowledge popularization: In this module, students can independently view and learn the detailed graphic content of historical evolution, masters and celebrities, and papermaking raw materials. They can also take assessments in the knowledge quiz module. Passing the assessment indicates that they have mastered the basic knowledge.
- Process: In the process stage, students can first recognize and learn the tools and understand the overall process of Jiajiang bamboo paper production. After learning, students can move and view independently in the three-dimensional simulated papermaking environment. They can click on raw materials and tools during the roaming to experience the overall process of papermaking.

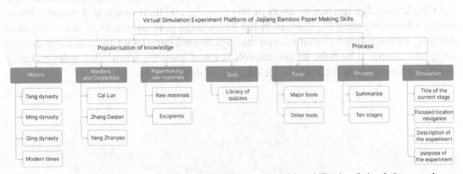

Figure 3. Information architecture of the Jiajiang bamboo paper making skills virtual simulation experiment platform.

5.2. Process design

The process design clearly displays the interactive process of the entire experiment. The operation process is designed based on the process in the teaching framework, the information architecture of the Jiajiang bamboo paper making skills virtual simulation experiment platform and the actual needs of users, as shown in Figure 4.

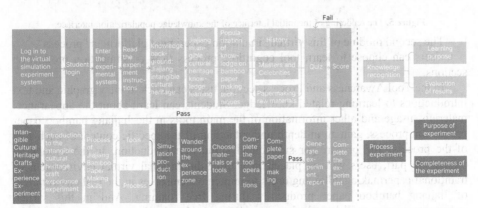

Figure 4. Operational flow chart of the Jiajiang bamboo paper making skills virtual simulation experiment platform.

5.3. Main module design

The first module of the Jiajiang Bamboo Paper Making Techniques Virtual Simulation Experiment Platform is "Knowledge Popularization". In this module, users can select and view relevant knowledge about Jiajiang Bamboo Paper Making Techniques by clicking. It can be divided into three parts: historical evolution, masters and celebrities, and papermaking raw materials, as shown in Figure 5. The main teaching objectives are to let students understand the historical development and cultural connotation of Jiajiang bamboo paper making techniques, understand the celebrities and stories related to Jiajiang bamboo paper making techniques, and master the raw materials, accessories and their functions of Jiajiang bamboo paper making. In the knowledge popularization interface, users can click to switch between different knowledge points for repeated learning. After the user self-assesses their learning and meets the standards, click to participate in the knowledge contest. The questions in the knowledge quiz are derived from the knowledge learned by users of this module, and their function is to test whether students have mastered the content in the knowledge popularization. If the user passes the quiz, it proves that he has mastered the background knowledge and can enter the next stage of learning. If he fails, he can consolidate and learn the knowledge independently, and then participate in the knowledge quiz again until he passes.

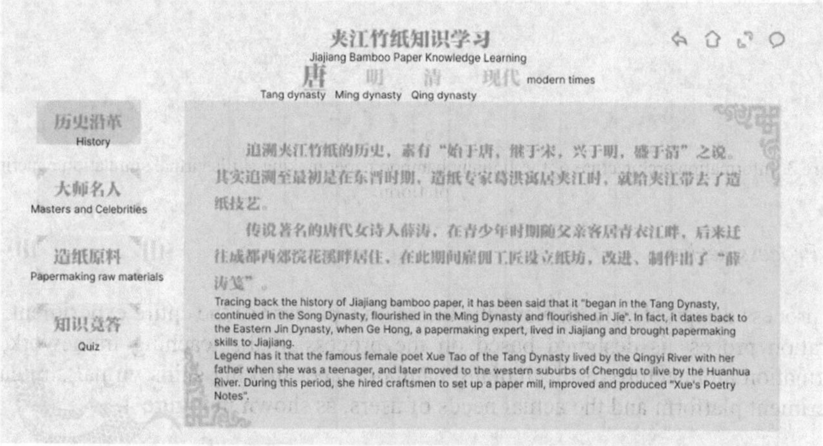

Figure 5. The rendering of the initial interface of the knowledge popularization interface.

The second module of this virtual simulation experiment platform is "process".

Users can choose to learn tool cognition, process flow or simulation production sections.

In the Tool Awareness and Process section, users can click to view graphic and text introductions to learning-related knowledge. Students can learn about the appearance, materials, usage and other information of the main tools in the Jiajiang bamboo paper production process, gain an in-depth understanding of the specific content of each step of the process, and prepare for subsequent simulation production. In the simulation production part, users will be placed in a three-dimensional virtual environment of traditional papermaking, allowing users to immerse themselves in the real environment of Jiajiang bamboo paper production during free roaming. And in this virtual environment, users will be asked to complete staged tasks. Users can experience the specific steps of Jiajiang bamboo paper production in depth, which will help users master the overall production process of Jiajiang bamboo paper.

After selecting tool cognition, the user enters the tool cognition interface, which is divided into two parts. The left side is the first-level navigation. In this part, users can quickly select the tool they want to view based on the tool name. The right side is the information display part, which will display the picture and text information of the selected item according to the user's selection on the left. The effect is shown in Figure 6. If you select other tools, a secondary navigation will appear on the right, and users can select the corresponding small tool according to its name to view and learn.

Figure 6. Rendering of the tool awareness section (drawn by the author).

After selecting the process flow interface, an overview of the process flow will be displayed first, and the relevant knowledge content of the process flow will be briefly introduced in text form. After entering, the interface is divided into upper and lower parts. The ten stages of the process flow are arranged in sequence at the top, and users can click to select different stages for learning. After selecting a certain stage, the picture and text information of that stage will be displayed, as shown in Figure 7.

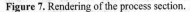

Figure 7. Rendering of the process section.

In order to provide users with the best experience, this experiment is implemented using the Unity engine. Build and adjust the model material and scene model in Unity to make it closer to the real effect, as shown in Figure 8 and Figure 9.

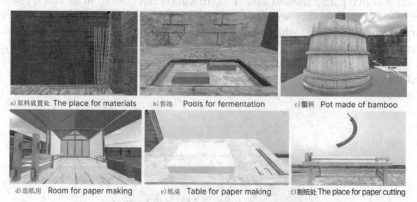

a)原料放置处 The place for materials   b)窖池 Pools for fermentation   c)篁锅 Pot made of bamboo

d)造纸房 Room for paper making   e)纸桌 Table for paper making   f)割纸处 The place for paper cutting

Figure 8. Partial rendering of the scene.

Figure 9. The process of scene building and animation production in Unity.

6. Conclusion

Through the analysis and combination of the BOPPPS teaching model and the task-driven teaching method, this paper determines the virtual teaching model of Jiajiang bamboo paper skills virtual simulation experiment, and designs a specific teaching construction framework. In the virtual simulation experiment, the BOPPPS teaching model is combined with the task-driven teaching method. Through the setting of total tasks and sub-tasks, students can better master the basic knowledge, operational knowledge and summary knowledge in Jiajiang bamboo paper making techniques in the process of completing the tasks. This virtual simulation experiment platform can lead students to experience the charm of ancient bamboo paper making techniques and inspire students' sense of identity and protection awareness of intangible cultural heritage. This platform can also carry out repetitive simulation exercises anytime and anywhere, helping the digital protection of Jiajiang intangible cultural heritage bamboo paper making skills and the dissemination and popularization of Jiajiang bamboo paper making skills.

Acknowledgments

Funding Supported by the New Interdisciplinary Cultivation Fund Program of Southwest Jiaotong University (YG2022002) .The First Batch of Provincial Research and Reform Practice Projects of New Liberal Arts in Sichuan Province--Multidisciplinary Integration of Interaction Design Curriculum and Teaching Material System in the Context of "New Liberal Arts + Intelligence". Ministry of Education Industry-University Cooperation Collaborative Education Program

References

[1] Wang Weiguo, Hu Jinhong, Liu Hong, Current Status and Development of Virtual Simulation Experimental Teaching in Foreign Universities, *Laboratory Research and Exploration* **34** (2015) , 214–219.

[2] Li Ping, Mao Changjie, Xu Jin, Carry out the Construction of a National Virtual Simulation Experimental Teaching Center to Improve the Informatization Level of Experimental Teaching in Colleges and Universities, *Laboratory Research and Exploration* **32** (2013), 5–8.

[3] Wu Juan, Sun Yuemin, Lei Wei, Xu Chunhong, Qin Yizhen, Song Aiguo, Planning Ideas and Progress in the Construction of the Electromechanical Comprehensive Virtual Simulation Experimental Teaching Center of Southeast University, *Experimental Technology and Management* **31** (2014), 5–9.

[4] Zhu Kerong, Construction of Virtual Simulation Experimental Teaching Center for Cultural Heritage Inheritance Application, *The Road to Digitalization of Museums* (2015), 132–135.

[5] Zhu Kerong, Issues and reflections on the construction of virtual simulation experimental teaching center for liberal arts, *Modern Education Management* **01** (2016), 87–91.

[6] P.A. Fishwick, A.J. Coffey, R. Kamhawi and J. Henderson, An experimental design and preliminary results for a cultural training system simulation, *Proceedings of the 2010 Winter Simulation Conference* (2010), 799-810.

[7] Selmanovic E, Rizvic S, Harvey C, et al, VR Video Storytelling for Intangible Cultural Heritage Preservation, *Eurographics Workshop on Graphics and Cultural Heritage* (2018).

[8] Alivizatou, Marilena, Digital Intangible Heritage: Inventories, Virtual Learning and Participation, *Heritage & Society* **12** (2019), 116–135.

[9] Chen Jianqiang, Research and implementation of desktop 3D VR system for national cultural heritage based on NGRAIN technology, *Journal of Guizhou University for Nationalities (Philosophy and Social Sciences Edition)* **06** (2017), 80–91.

[10] Chen Jianqiang, Application of VR and AR technology in teaching ethnic minority clothing design, *Laboratory Research and Exploration* **36** (2017), 111–113.

[11] Zhou Hua, Zhang Ziying, Huang Kejia, Zhang Junna, Han Jianye, Feng Xiaobo, Research on virtual simulation experimental teaching of cultural relics appreciation - taking the appreciation of Tang Sancai as an example, *Laboratory Research and Exploration* **35** (2016), 77–82.

[12] Cao Danping, Yin Xingyao, Canadian BOPPPS teaching model and its inspiration for higher education reform, *Laboratory Research and Exploration* **35** (2016), 196–200+249.

[13] Li Qi, Yang Mei, Han Qiufeng, Smart teaching design and application based on Rain Classroom - Taking "College Computer Fundamentals" as an example, *Computer Engineering and Science* **41** (2019), 139–143.

[14] Feng Yongwei, Research on the teaching model of advertising major under the intelligent Internet technology + BOPPPS model - taking the "Advertising Copywriting" practical training class as an example, *Media* **08** (2019), 79–82.

[15] Wu Changdong, Jiang Hua, Chen Yongqiang, Research and application of BOPPPS teaching method in MOOC teaching design, *Experimental Technology and Management* **36** (2019), 218–222.

Design Studies and Intelligence Engineering
L.C. Jain et al. (Eds.)
© 2024 The Authors.
This article is published online with Open Access by IOS Press and distributed under the terms
of the Creative Commons Attribution Non-Commercial License 4.0 (CC BY-NC 4.0).
doi:10.3233/FAIA231519

Requirement Analysis of Smart Kitchen Dietary and Social Service System Based on Older Adults Mental Models

Fangyu LI[a], Lin ZHU[a], Zheng LIU[b,1], and Lin LI[a]

[a] *School of Design, Southwest Jiaotong University*
[b] *Cultural, Creative, Design and Manufacturing Collaborative Innovation Center,*
China Art College

Abstract. Using kitchen life as an entry point and the theory of mental modelling, we carried out a study on the needs analysis of a smart kitchen diet and social service system, aiming to meet the new needs of the elderly in terms of health and social interaction. Through questionnaires and user interviews, we collected and analyzed the mental data of the elderly and created a mental model of "diet and social interaction" as well as user requirements. The Analytic Hierarchy Process was used to identify the importance of dietary and social needs, covering the four demand directions of diet and nutrition, health management, social interaction, and health awareness. This study highlights the potential of user-centred research methodology in the health and social care of older people and provides useful guidance and insights for the design of future smart kitchens and related products.

Keywords. Mental Modelling, Eating Healthy, Smart Kitchen, Social Service System

1. Introduction

The "14th Five-Year Plan" period is a critical period for China in addressing the challenges of ageing. By 2020, China's elderly population aged 60 and over will reach 264 million, accounting for 18.7 per cent of the total population, and the elderly population is growing rapidly year by year. Society is paying more and more attention to the quality of life of the elderly, and is actively responding to the concept of "active ageing" put forward by the World Health Organisation (WHO), which emphasises the importance of social participation of the elderly. The kitchen, as an important space for daily activities, carries most of the needs of family life, affects the quality of life of the users, and even influences the harmony of family social interaction [1]. The study of intelligent kitchen dietary and social service system can not only meet the dietary needs of the elderly, but also provide a space for social interaction and improve the quality of life of the elderly [2]. From the perspective of mental modelling theory, we think about how to make smart kitchens more age-friendly, so as to improve the life satisfaction and well-being of the elderly, and provide more dietary social service support for the elderly.

---

[1] Corresponding Author: Zheng Liu, aliu6@126.com

2. Relevant studies

Kitchen plays an important role in human history and is one of the main living spaces of human beings [3]. Starting from the "Frankfurt Kitchen" project in 1926, the concept of modern whole kitchens began to be designed by manufacturers, with more emphasis on user convenience and optimization of the operation process.In the 1990s, with the rapid development of information technology, the prototype of smart kitchens appeared to create multifunctional composite spaces covering parenting, entertaining, and socializing, etc. In 2013, New Zealand kitchen brand Fisher &Paykel organized the "Social Kitchen" design competition, which gave a new meaning to the concept of "social kitchen". In the kitchen scene, we can see the evolution from a material-supportive to a spiritual-emotional kitchen service system.

While about 80% of the elderly in China suffer from chronic diseases, 40% of them suffer from multiple chronic diseases at the same time [4]. Due to the low importance of dietary nutrition among the elderly, it increases the risk of developing multiple diseases in their lives [5]. Smartphone applications can provide appropriate dietary advice. For example, researchers such as Lina Ma developed a dietary program for the elderly, which can achieve effective management of their diets.

3. Acquisition of mental models based on diet and socialisation of older people

3.1. The role of mental models

The theory of mental models was proposed by British psychologist Kenneth Craik in the 1940s[6], who advocated that mental models are the human individual's view of the way the external real world works and are transformed by self-perception to form an internal mental model, which guides human behavioural activities in real life. Mental models can better help us understand users' behaviour and cognition, and deeply explore users' intrinsic needs for products. Zhang Wan yu et al[7] determined the users' cognitive needs through the construction of a mental model and designed a robot service design solution that meets the users' cognition.Abdul Razak F H et al[8] obtained the elderly's expectations for the use of reminder systems through the construction of a mental model for elderly users. The above studies show that the construction of mental models helps to clarify the real needs of users and bring a good experience for them.

3.2. Mindfulness information collection on eating and socialising among older people

The construction of the mental model first needs to fully obtain the user's mental information in the process of using the product, and we conducted a questionnaire survey around the elderly's diet and social interaction in the kitchen. A total of 140 questionnaires were distributed to the elderly in Chengdu city who are over 55 years old, and 120 questionnaires were received. The questionnaires included personal information, Internet habits, diet and health status. The results of the study show that

In terms of social interaction, most of the elderly choose to live with their partners or family members. About 89.67% of the elderly used smartphones to contact friends and relatives, browse news, relax and shop online. 48% of the elderly felt lonely in their daily lives and had relatively little social interaction, but 66.6% were willing to take part in social activities to satisfy their mental entertainment needs.

In terms of diet and health, 45.83 per cent of the elderly suffer from chronic diseases and are therefore concerned about diet and health. About 64.17 per cent of the elderly have adopted healthy dietary measures. Elderly people usually obtain health advice through television, internet and books. They preferred dietary health products providing features such as healthy recipes, dietary health education and cooking instructions.

When it comes to cooking, older adults usually shop at supermarkets or food markets, with very few ordering online. Older people also pursue the pleasure of cooking, but there is a lack of organised storage of ingredients. Therefore, they hope that the kitchen equipment can provide functions such as ingredient management and partitioned storage of ingredients.

Based on the questionnaire survey, we conducted user interviews with four elderly people. The interviews were conducted in terms of Internet use, smart device use, social habits, interaction, diet and nutrition, and kitchen equipment use, in order to address the behavioural and psychological activities of the elderly in the process of diet and health and social interaction.

3.3. Analysis of the Psychological Needs of Older People for Eating and Socialising

Clustering method is to cluster and classify the information of research and investigation according to the degree of similarity, in the case of different degrees of similarity of the research object, the high degree of similarity will be classified, according to the different degree of similarity to complete the clustering of the research object is the principle of clustering method of classification [9]. Studying the behavioural characteristics of the elderly in the process of diet and social interaction as a demand standard, classifying and clustering the information according to the user's behaviour and the need to use the information in the process of information processing, and then classifying and adjusting and diffusing the information after the clustering is completed, helps us to intuitively understand the behavioural information of the elderly users in the process of diet and nutrition, social activities, etc., and to sort out the relationship between the different demand structures.

3.4. Eating and Social Mental Modelling for Older Users

In the mental model construction stage, we adopted the "affinity diagram" method proposed by Young [10], which is a complete description of the attitudes and perceptions formed by users when using the product. We divided the collected requirements into three parts: ingredient procurement, diet and nutrition, and health knowledge, and then analysed the specific tasks in each part to analyse the problems that older people might encounter in task-heavy tasks, so as to find opportunities for design improvement. Based on user interview data, we learnt that older people usually purchase ingredients from supermarkets or farmers' markets, and sometimes their children assist them in purchasing online. Therefore, when designing the service system, we can consider phone ordering to provide one-click delivery service. In addition, the elderly may encounter problems such as unhygienic operation, not knowing how to cook, and storage of ingredients during the cooking process, so we can provide services such as advice on healthy recipes, partitioning of refrigerator ingredients, and voice-video guidance. Given the limited dietary and nutritional knowledge of the elderly and the high number of patients with chronic diseases, we can therapeutic recipes, and information. To increase the social aspect of eating and cooking, we can also support collaborative cooking. These analyses build a mental model of eating and social behaviour of elderly users.

Finally, according to the psychological space formed by the classification of the needs and activities of the elderly, the logical relationship between the psychological space is determined and clustered into "diet and nutrition", and finally the psychological model of diet and social interaction is formed, as shown in Figure 1.

Figure 1. mental model

4. Access to core requirements for smart kitchens for the elderly

4.1. Analytic Hierarchy structural modelling

Analytic Hierarchy Process (AHP) is a quantitative way of thinking about decision-making, by quantitatively analysing the qualitative issues in the study, the objective reality judgments of the relevant experts and users are transformed into quantitative weights, so as to get the importance ranking of the object content [11].

User demand hierarchy is carried out. Based on the user's mind space, the research will determine the relationship between the needs of food and social services, and divided into four subsystems, according to the importance of its different elements to make an evaluation to objectively quantify the needs of food and social services. Setting the target layer A as the importance of dietary and social factors; guideline layers B1, B2 and B3 represent diet and nutrition, health management and social interaction, respectively; programme layer C contains factors C1-C11, and the construction of programme layer factors needs to take into account the operational needs, emotional needs and cognitive abilities of the elderly in addition to the functional needs of the product, and finally establish the demand hierarchy model shown in Figure 2.

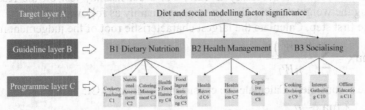

Figure 2. Hierarchical Analytical Structural Model of Dietary and Social Needs.

Constructing a judgement matrix. Experts are invited to compare the importance of the elements in the hierarchical model of dietary and social needs, and relevant data are obtained to construct a comparative judgement matrix. According to the theory of fuzzy mathematics, the elements in the hierarchical model are rated and quantified by the scale method, and the importance of the elements is assigned by the expert rating method. Experts are invited to assign the weights of C1-C9 to the specific programmes under the guideline layer Bk according to their relative importance, i.e., constructing the pairwise comparison judgement matrix C=(Cij)n×n, and the form of the judgement matrix is shown in Table 1, in which Cij is the importance value of element i and element j relative to the target, and the factor comparison scale is shown in the table 2.

Table 1. Judgement matrix form

B_K	C_1	C_2	C_3	C_4	... ...	C_n
C_1	C_{11}	C_{12}	C_{13}	C_{14}	... ...	C_{1n}
C_2	C_{21}	C_{22}	C_{23}	C_{24}	... ...	C_{2n}
C_3	C_{31}	C_{32}	C_{33}	C_{34}	... ...	C_{3n}
C_4	C_{41}	C_{42}	C_{43}	C_{44}	... ...	C_{4n}
... ...	... ...	... ...	... ...	... ...	... ...	... ...
C_n	C_{n1}	C_{n1}	C_{n1}	C_{n3}	... ...	C_{nn}

Table 2. factor contrast scale

serial number	Importance level	Cij Assignment
1	The two elements ij are equally important	1
2	Element i is slightly more important than element j	3
3	element i is significantly more important than element j	5
4	element i is more important than element j	7
5	element i is definitely more important than element j	9
6	Between the importance levels	3,4,6,8
7	If the ratio of the importance of element i to element a, then the ratio of the importance of element j to element i is 1/a	1/2, 1/3, 1/5, 1/7, 1/9

A total of 12 experts and professional caregivers related to research on elderly users were invited to score this study, including three PhDs, seven masters and two undergraduate students. The importance of each factor was discussed and analysed, and the final evaluation results converged.

Calculate the weights and perform consistency test. Calculate the relative weight values, obtain the weight vector W=[wi]1*n, calculate the weight of each element, and obtain the hierarchical single sorting results of A,B1,B2,B3.

$$W_i = \frac{1}{n} \sum_{J-1}^{n} \frac{1}{\sum_{i=1}^{n} a_{ij}} (i, j = 1,2,3......n) \tag{1}$$

In order to ensure the consistency of the experts' thinking on the evaluation of various factors in the evaluation process, and to ensure the reasonable validity of the weight calculation, it is necessary to carry out a consistency test on the results after calculating the weight results. The test steps are mainly as follows:

In the first step, Calculate the largest characteristic root of the judgement matrix:

$$\lambda \max = \sum_{i=1}^{n} \frac{(AW)i}{nWi} \tag{2}$$

In the second step, Calculate the consistency indicator: CI:

$$CI = \frac{\lambda \max - n}{n-1} \tag{3}$$

where λmax is the maximum eigenvalue of the judgement matrix and n is the order of the judgement matrix.

In the third step, Calculate the consistency ratio CR.

$$CR = CI / R \tag{4}$$

Where CI is the judgement matrix consistency index, RI is the random consistency index, and the values of RI for different orders are shown in the table 3.

Table 3. RI values for different orders

1	2	3	4	5	6	7	8	9
0	0	0.58	0.90	1012	1.24	1.32	1.41	1.45

When CR<0.1, the judgement matrix has satisfactory consistency, when it does not meet the standard, it is necessary to re-adjust the judgement matrix scores and test, after the consistency of the calculation of the results are less than 0.1, the judgement matrix are through the consistency test, with validity. The results of hierarchical single sorting and consistency test are shown in Table 4.

Table 4. Hierarchical single-ranking weights and consistency tests.

pairwise comparison matrix	Sorting weight vector	Maximum eigenvalue	CI	Consistency CR
A	W=(0.6144, 0.2684, 0. 1172)	λmax= 4. 10751	0.0358	0.0402
B1	W1=(0. 192, 0.2534, 0. 1342, 0.2748, 0. 1455)	λ max= 5.3211 1	0.0802	0..716

The weights of each level of indicators to the overall target level were further calculated for a composite weight ranking and are shown in Table 5.

Table 5. Table of Weighting Results for Catering and Social Services System.

normative layer			programme level		Combined weights
Content		Weight 1	Content	Weight 2	
B1	Dietary Nutrition	0.614	Culinary Instruction	0.192	0.118
			Nutritional Assessment	0.2534	0.1557
			Dietary Management	0.1342	0.0828
			Healthy Recipes	0.2748	0.1688
			Ingredients Ordering	0.1455	0.0894
B2	Health Management	0.2684	Health Profile	0.3108	0.0834
			Health Education	0.4934	0.1324
			Cognitive Games	0.1958	0.0525
			Cooking Exchange	0.4934	0.0578
B3	Socialising	0.1172	Interest Gathering	0.3108	0.0364
			Offline Educational Activities	0.1958	0.023

4.2. Functional Requirements for the Dietary and Social Services System for the Elderly

Based on the hierarchical analysis, we derived a hierarchy of needs for food and social functions and analysed the needs for service system functions in the following four areas .First of all, diet and nutrition needs to be analysed for dietary nutrient composition, nutritional intake, analysis of nutritional health data, recommended dietary nutritional recipes, food delivery services, remote assistance for dietary meals, and storage and management of food materials. In terms of health management, it is mainly to record daily drinking water, store and manage medication, learn nutritional and health knowledge, and provide remote assistance. In the aspect of health cognition, it is mainly dietary health counselling, cognitive game training, and multimedia dissemination of health counselling. Finally, in the area of social interaction, there is a social platform for diet and emotional sharing, integrated community activity information, and family communication assistance.

5. Needs analysis of older persons

Based on previous research on the mental models of the elderly and the sorting of their needs using hierarchical analysis we propose the following needs analysis for the Smart Kitchen dietary and social service system:

Dietary and Nutritional Needs: they need the system to provide dietary composition analysis, record nutritional intake and analyse health data. In addition, the system should recommend appropriate dietary recipes. Elderly people may need fresh ingredient delivery service. and need remote assistance from caregivers or children. In addition, the system should provide ingredient storage and management functions to help the elderly better manage their ingredients.

Health Management Requirements: The system should record data about the user's body and diet to create a personal dietary health profile. This helps in tracking health conditions. The system can also record the user's daily water intake and provide storage and management of related items. In addition, the system needs to provide health counselling to help the elderly better understand diet and health.

Social Interaction Needs: The elderly want the system to provide a platform for social interaction and emotional sharing. They are eager to share their dietary experiences with other seniors, as well as socialise with people through the system. The system should also integrate information on community activities to facilitate social interaction.

Health Cognitive Needs: Older adults need the system to provide diet and health counselling services to answer their questions about health and diet. Cognitive training games should also be developed. In addition, health awareness among older adults can be raised by providing information on chronic disease treatment and related videos.

6. Conclusion

Against the backdrop of an ageing society, the quality of life and spiritual needs of the elderly are increasing, and the daily dietary and nutritional needs of the elderly are also receiving much attention. The daily dietary nutrition, physical health and socialisation needs of the elderly are also of great concern. Behind the demand analysis of smart kitchen service system based on mindfulness model is to meet the unique dietary and social needs of older adults and to serve their physical health and mental health. This study aims to gain a deeper understanding of the lifestyles of older adults thereby constructing a mental model. By weighting the needs of the elderly, it helps us to better analyse and summarise their demand tendencies. The smart kitchen based on diet and socialisation takes on the function of diet and health while promoting communication between the elderly and their families through gathering and entertainment, interactive communication, etc., forming a living space that meets the diet and socialisation needs of the elderly and creates an atmosphere of family communication. This research helps to address the challenges of an ageing society, promotes technological innovation and extends mental modelling approaches to other fields.

Acknowledgments

Funding Supported by Zhejiang Provincial Key Laboratory of integration of healthy smart kitchen system(Grant NO: 2019F06), the New Interdisciplinary Cultivation Fund Program of Southwest Jiaotong University (YG2022002), Key Research Base of Philosophy and Social Sciences in Sichuan Province of Modern Design and Cultural Research Center(Grant NO: MD21E025)

References

[1]   Bell G, Kaye JJG. Designing technology for domestic spaces: A Kitchen Manifesto. 2002;2(2):46-62.
[2]   Xu Z, Dong H. Developing future kitchen for older adults: a model and participatory design approach based on literature review and ethics framework. 2023.
[3]   Gürata D. What a Kitchen Can Be: A Food-Centric Approach: Bilkent Universitesi (Turkey); 2021.
[4]   Ding J, Wang NP, Luo CY, Tian H, Qin WQ, Li Rong, Hu XY, Chinese Journal of Gerontology Xu J. Survey and analysis of dietary nutrition and health status of middle-aged and elderly people in urban communities. 2014(7):1950-1951.
[5]   Li Lin, Li Fangyu, Packaging Engineering Art Edition Liu J. Exploring the Development Trend of Intelligent Kitchen and Design for Elderly in the Context of Active Ageing. 2022;43(2):72-81, 89.
[6]   Achinstein P. The nature of explanation. Oxford University Press, USA; 1983.
[7]   Zhang Wanyu, Yu Suihuai, Mechanical Design Liu J. Intelligent robot service design based on mental model measurement. 2018;35(5):105-110.
[8]   Abdul Razak FH, Sulo R, Wan Adnan WA. Elderly mental model of reminder system. 2012. p 193-200.
[9]   Li HT, Intelligence Theory and Practice Song J. Selection and application of mental model measures of user use of websites. 2015;38(2):11-16.
[10] Young I. Mental models: aligning design strategy with human behavior. Rosenfeld Media; 2008.
[11] Brunelli M. Introduction to the analytic hierarchy process. Springer; 2014.

Design Studies and Intelligence Engineering
L.C. Jain et al. (Eds.)
© 2024 The Authors.

doi:10.3233/FAIA231520

Research on the Performance Assessment of CMF Design Curriculum Based on Fuzzy Comprehensive Evaluation: Taking the CMF Design of Passenger Interface of High-Speed Train Dining Car as an Example

Jun DU, Ning DAI, Fangyu LI, Tianjiao ZHANG, and Xiaoyan WANG
School of Design, Southwest Jiaotong University

Abstract. The purpose of this study is to integrate the fuzzy comprehensive evaluation method into the design scheme evaluation of art and design students and explore the method to improve the course work assessment. On the basis of determining the objectives of curriculum cultivation, the research group proposed a fuzzy comprehensive evaluation method of a curriculum design scheme. Taking CMF design of the passenger interface of a high-speed train as an example, the study attempts to improve the previous issues of difficulty in determining the weights of course design evaluation methods and inaccurate evaluation results. The evaluation index system is established according to the characteristics of CMF curriculum design and the need for teaching reform. The application of fuzzy comprehensive evaluation to CMF design coursework assessment is an innovative attempt for the course teaching reform of art design majors, which has important popularization and application value.

Keywords. fuzzy judgment, CMF design, Passenger interface design, Teaching reform, Course assessment

1. Introduction

In view of the construction of the university-level first-class course "CMF Application and Design", the research group of product design major of Southwest Jiaotong University explores the course design and assessment. CMF literally stands for color, materials and surface treatment processes. CMF design is a key factor in creating emotional products [1]. CMF course, as an important part of the compulsory courses for product design major, mainly teaches the basic knowledge of CMF systematically, guides and cultivates students' design thinking, and the final CMF design scheme becomes the key content of the assessment of students' learning and practical ability. In view of this, the research group tried to apply the fuzzy comprehensive evaluation method to students' CMF design work assessment of the passenger interface of high-speed train dining car and explored the evaluation method of art design course work.

2. Design scheme and fuzzy comprehensive evaluation method

The reasonable selection of assessment methods and evaluation methods for art and design course assignments in universities is two key factors that determine the success or failure of teaching work.

2.1. Selection of assessment scheme

At the beginning of the course, the teacher constructs a theoretical model of CMF design to guide students to conduct in-depth analysis of the concept and function of CMF design, as shown in Figure 1[3]. Combined with the relevant elements involved in CMF and the basic characteristics of its knowledge structure, it can be summarized into four levels: physical culture, cultural symbols, functional experience, and emotional resonance, so that students can initially form the design direction of "from material form to interactive form".

Secondly, the research group selected the passenger interface CMF design of the dining car of the high-speed train CR400BF, which runs from 3 to 8 hours, as the research object. Passenger interface refers to the internal environment formed by a variety of in-car facilities such as interior wall panels, interior roof panels, doors and Windows, seats, and hardware in the train cabin [4]. The existing standardized train space environment is subject to many restrictive factors. At present, A group of trains only has a sales bar in the second-class passenger car, as shown in area A in Figure 2, and some of its seating area and luggage rack area are respectively shown in areas B and C in Figure 2. The corresponding status quo is shown in Figure 3-A, Figure 3-B and Figure 3-C. Failure to provide passengers with a complete and comfortable dining space alone can lead to awkward, cramped and other psychological states during the use of space [5].

2.2. Scheme assessment method

The fuzzy comprehensive evaluation method is used to evaluate things because things often have multiple attributes, so it is necessary to take into account all aspects when evaluating things, which means multiple evaluation indicators need to be selected, and the properties of these indicators are often fuzzy, therefore, this comprehensive evaluation is called fuzzy comprehensive evaluation [6]. Therefore, the research team consulted three teachers with years of experience in mathematics teaching to give suggestions, and selected four aspects of "innovation, practicality, aesthetics and standardization" as the evaluation indicators. Then, two product design experts from the business community were invited to discuss with the head of the teaching department of the college, and finally agreed to adopt fuzzy comprehensive evaluation in the process of job review.

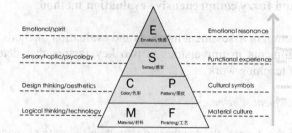

Figure 1.CMF design theoretical model

Figure 2. Layout of dining car

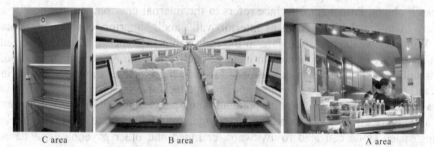

C area   B area   A area

Figure 3. Current situation of areas A, E and F

3. Fuzzy comprehensive evaluation

Fuzzy comprehensive evaluation is a method of educational evaluation using fuzzy mathematics [7]. Fuzzy mathematics was born in the 1960s, it can be used to consider the influence of various factors related to the things being evaluated, and make a general evaluation of things with the help of the fuzzy transformation principle and maximum membership principle.

3.1. Evaluation mechanism

Since the cognitive process of human beings is from simple to abstract thinking, its cognitive goals are divided into six main categories: knowing, understanding, applying, analyzing, synthesizing and evaluating [8]. The set of proposed comments (the set representing levels, classifications, etc.) as $R = \{r_1, r_2, ..., r_m\}$, with a total of m levels; The set of factors is $V = \{v_1, v_2, ..., v_n\}$, a total of n factors. Take the single factor evaluation of the NTH factor as R_n, which can be used as a fuzzy subset on V, where r_{nm} represents the membership degree of the *nth* factor evaluation for the *m* level. The total evaluation matrix R of n factors is:

$$R = \begin{pmatrix} R_1 \\ R_2 \\ M \\ R_n \end{pmatrix} = \begin{pmatrix} r_{11} & r_{12} & \Lambda & r_{1m} \\ r_{21} & \Lambda & \Lambda & r_{2m} \\ \Lambda & \Lambda & \Lambda & \Lambda \\ r_{n1} & \Lambda & \Lambda & r_{nm} \end{pmatrix}$$

When the comprehensive evaluation must consider the effect of each factor on the evaluation level, the evaluation effect forms A fuzzy subset A on the set of factors,

$$A = (a_1, a_2, ..., a_n)$$

a_i is the membership degree of v_i to A, which is a measure of the effect of factors on the evaluation grade, indicating the ability to evaluate the grade according to a single factor v_i; The value is given based on experience.

After determining A and R, a comprehensive evaluation can be carried out. The operation form is $B = A\sigma R$, σ is a fuzzy composite operator. The overall process is represented by the block diagram as follows:

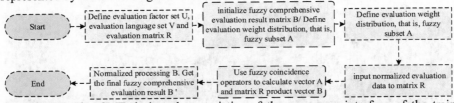

According to the CMF design characteristics of the passenger interface of the train restaurant [9], the research group adopts a special "weighted average type" fuzzy comprehensive evaluation, whose fuzzy composite operator is $\sigma = (\bullet \oplus)$, where $\oplus$ represents the ring sum, defined as $|\alpha \oplus \beta| = \min\{1, \alpha + \beta\}$ and the ring sum does not exceed 1. $\overset{n}{\underset{i=1}{\oplus}}$ represents the sum of *n* numbers under the $\oplus$ operation,

$$b_j = \oplus_{i=1}^{n} a_i \cdot r_{ij} = \min\left\{1, \sum_{i=1}^{n} a_i r_v\right\}$$

Where bj∈B.

```
# Make a fuzzy comprehensive judgment
def fuzz_synthesis(evaluation_matrix, weights):
    # Calculate the membership of each element
    single_values = np.zeros(len(evaluation_matrix))
    for i in range(len(evaluation_matrix)):
        for j in range(len(evaluation_matrix[i])):
            single_values[i] += weights[j] * evaluation_matrix[i][j]
    # Normalizes membership values
    single_values /= np.sum(single_values)
    # Calculate the comprehensive evaluation results
    synthesis_value = np.sum(weights * single_values)
    return synthesis_value
```

3.2. Case Evaluation

Figure 4 and Figure 5 show the students' work design scheme of "CMF design of high-speed train restaurant passenger interface". First of all, students adjusted the existing layout in Figure 2, and changed the original three sections A, B and C in Figure 2 into four sections E, F, T and O in Figure 4 to meet the needs of passengers for the dining car. In order to facilitate the study, this paper selects the virtual reality renderings of F and E regions for evaluation, as shown in Figure 5.

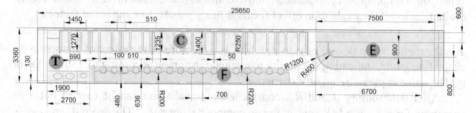

Figure 4. Dining car layout of the modified CR400BF high-speed train

E area   F area

Figure 5. Renderings of areas E and F

Assignment requirements for high-speed train passenger interface design: Students need to design a comfortable, beautiful and ergonomic interior space from the perspective of color, material, surface treatment, etc[10].

Table 1. Figure 5-F transcript

	CMF innovation u_{11}	Practicality u_{12}	Aesthetics u_{13}	Standardization u_{14}
Review Teacher 1	92	95	93	100
Review Teacher 2	95	94	97	90
Review Teacher 3	98	95	93	95

For the redesigned dining area environment shown in Figure 5-F, the course team selected three reviewing teachers to give numerical evaluation, as shown in Table 1; The teacher made three rating levels: "excellent, good, medium"; The weight distribution is given: innovative 40%, practical 35%, aesthetic 20%, normative 5%.

①Determine the set of first-level factors as u1={innovation, practicality, aesthetics, standardization}

② Determine the weight distribution of first-level factors, that is, the fuzzy subset of evaluation weights is

A_1= (0.40 0.35 0.20 0.05)

③ Determine the evaluation language set as

v_1= {Excellent, Good, Acceptable}

For the normalization of the single score in Table 1, it is divided by a full score of 100 (as the maximum membership degree 1), there is

$$u_{11}=\{innovation\}= (0.92\ 0.95\ 0.98)$$
$$u_{12}=\{practicality\}= (0.95\ 0.94\ 0.95)$$
$$u_{13}=\{aesthetics\}= (0.93\ 0.97\ 0.93)$$
$$u_{14}=\{standardization\}= (1.00\ 0.90\ 0.95)$$

According to the above data, the fuzzy relation matrix is formed,

$$R_1 = \begin{pmatrix} 0.92 & 0.95 & 0.98 \\ 0.95 & 0.94 & 0.95 \\ 0.93 & 0.97 & 0.93 \\ 1.00 & 0.90 & 0.95 \end{pmatrix}$$

Calculate $B_1=A_1\sigma R_1$,

$$B_1 = (0.40\ \ 0.35\ \ 0.20\ \ 0.05)\sigma \begin{pmatrix} 0.92 & 0.95 & 0.98 \\ 0.95 & 0.94 & 0.95 \\ 0.93 & 0.97 & 0.93 \\ 1.00 & 0.90 & 0.95 \end{pmatrix} = (0.94\ \ 0.95\ \ 0.96)$$

After normalization processing, we get:

$$B_1'= (0.330\ \ \ 0.333\ \ \ 0.337)$$

According to the "maximum membership principle", the corresponding evaluation grade is very good.

Table 2. Figure 5-E transcript

	CMF innovation u_{11}	Practicality u_{12}	Aesthetics u_{13}	Standardization u_{14}
Review Teacher 1	good	good	acceptable	excellent
Review Teacher 2	good	good	good	acceptable
Review Teacher 3	excellent	good	acceptable	good

For the redesigned high speed train dining car bar as shown in Figure 5-E, the reviewing teachers took language as the evaluation method, as shown in Table 2; The teacher set three assessment levels: "Excellent, very good, good"; The weight distribution is given: innovative 40%, practical 35%, aesthetic 20%, normative 5%.

As shown above,

①Determine the set of first-level factors as u_2={innovative, practical, aesthetic, normative}

(2) Determine the weight distribution of first-level factors, that is, the evaluation weight

The fuzzy subset is A_2= (0.40 0.35 0.20 0.05)

③Establish that the evaluation language set is V_2={excellent, very good, good}

For the normalization of individual results in Table 2, there is

$$u_{21} = \{innovative\} = \begin{pmatrix} \dfrac{1}{3} & \dfrac{1}{3} & \dfrac{2}{3} \end{pmatrix} \quad u_{22} = \{practical\} = \begin{pmatrix} \dfrac{1}{3} & \dfrac{1}{3} & \dfrac{1}{3} \end{pmatrix}$$

$$u_{23} = \{aesthetic\} = \begin{pmatrix} \dfrac{0}{3} & \dfrac{2}{3} & \dfrac{0}{3} \end{pmatrix} \quad u_{24} = \{normative\} = \begin{pmatrix} \dfrac{2}{3} & \dfrac{0}{3} & \dfrac{1}{3} \end{pmatrix}$$

According to the above data, the fuzzy relation matrix is formed,

$$R_2 = \frac{1}{3} \begin{pmatrix} 1 & 1 & 2 \\ 1 & 1 & 1 \\ 0 & 2 & 0 \\ 2 & 0 & 1 \end{pmatrix}$$

Calculate $B_2 = A_2 \sigma R_2$,

$$B_2 = (0.40 \quad 0.35 \quad 0.20 \quad 0.05)\sigma \frac{1}{3} \begin{pmatrix} 1 & 1 & 2 \\ 1 & 1 & 1 \\ 0 & 2 & 0 \\ 2 & 0 & 1 \end{pmatrix} = \frac{1}{3}(0.85 \quad 1.15 \quad 1.20)$$

After normalization processing, we get:

$$B_2 = (0.266 \ 0.359 \ 0.375)$$

According to the "maximum membership principle", the corresponding evaluation grade is good.

Table 3. Evaluation of Figure 5-F by ordinary weighting method

	CMF innovation	Practicality	Aesthetics	Standardization
Individual average score	95	95	94	95
evaluation weight	0.40	0.35	0.20	0.05
total score		0.40*95+0.35*93+0.20*94+0.05*95=94.1		

3.3. Evaluation and Discussion

In the evaluation of CMF design work, if the "ordinary weighting method" is adopted, then the results of Figure 4-F are shown in Table 3: it is very obvious that the final score corresponds to the evaluation level of excellent (stipulated: excellent is not less than 90 points, good is 80 to 89 points, and good is less than 80 points). It is two levels higher than the conclusion of "fuzzy comprehensive evaluation". Therefore, in theory, a fuzzy comprehensive evaluation is "better" than the ordinary weighted method, and the conclusion is more reliable and scientific. Although the "general weighted scoring method" assigns different weights to evaluation indicators, its calculation is still a simple total score addition method in essence, so it is difficult to truly reflect the difference in weights. "Fuzzy comprehensive evaluation method" is the extension of the "general weighted method", which has the characteristics of more accurate and more subdivided. It can not only reflect the value of weight, but also reflect the comprehensive impact of various factors. For the language evaluation method used in Figure 4-E, the final evaluation can only be completed through the conversion process of "language evaluation → score value → language evaluation". In this process, the uncertainty of the information content of the evaluation index is inevitably increased, and it is difficult for students to understand and improve.

4. Conclusion

The evaluation of the CMF design course contains a lot of emotional factors [11], which makes the evaluation difficult to quantify. Taking the interface design of passenger dining cars for high-speed trains as an example, the research group found that it was difficult to explain the substantial difference between the 83-point design scheme and the 88-point design scheme by using score evaluation; The use of language evaluation methods can make the evaluator overlook many valuable information in the homework, and the evaluation results are often not objective and accurate enough, leading to a dilemma in homework assessment. However, the introduction of fuzzy mathematics into the coursework assessment can optimize the evaluation method. In art design course assignment, the fuzzy comprehensive evaluation method can not only overcome the difficulty of evaluation, but also evaluate the design scheme objectively, or it will become a new choice of art design evaluation mode.

Acknowledgement

This paper is supported by the "Key Project of 2022 University-level Undergraduate Education and Teaching Research and Reform (20220317)", "2021 Southwest Jiaotong University First-class Undergraduate Curriculum Construction Project" and "Degree and Graduate Education and Teaching Reform Research Project (YJG5-2022-Y037)" of Southwest Jiaotong University.

References

[1] Zhan Yuhao, Record of Young Leading Talents Summit on Industrial Revolution Driven by Design Innovation (PartII), Design Research 9 (2019), 1-7.
[2] Li Yiwen,Huang Mingfu.CMF Design Tutorial, Chemical Industry Press, Peking, 2019.
[3] Du Jun, Research of Teaching Practice of CMF design Course Based on Online and Project, Design 06(2020), 136-138.
[4] Xiang Zerui,Zhi Jinyi,,et.al, Methodology and Cases of Industrial Design for Rail Vehicles, China Machine Press, Peking, 2019.
[5] Du Jun, Zhi jinyi,et.al, Interior Environment Design of High-speed Train Dining Car Based on the Characteristics of Reception Psychology, PACKAGING ENGINEERING 41(2020),31-36.
[6] FAN Tai-hua,FENG ri.Implementation of Theory of Fuzzy Evaluation in Online Education Excellent Courses, Zhuangshi 19(2009): 78-91.
[7] SHEN Shusheng, Deng Yansheng, Construction and Empirical Study of Teaching Quality Evaluation System under the Background of Emerging Engineering Education, e-Education Research 44(2023), 103-107.
[8] Luo Lixuan, Hong ling.Kansei Engineering Design, Tsinghua University Press, Peking, 2015.
[9] XU Bo-chu, LI Yang, Rail Car Styling Design, Science Press,Peking, 2012.
[10] Zuo Hengfeng, Yan Yang, Discussion on Subjective Experience of CMF: Material Textures, Zhuangshi 08(2017), 118-121.
[11] Becerra,Liliana, The fundamental principles of cmf design, Frame Publishers BV, Netherlands, 2020.

Design Studies and Intelligence Engineering
L.C. Jain et al. (Eds.)
© 2024 The Authors.
This article is published online with Open Access by IOS Press and distributed under the terms
of the Creative Commons Attribution Non-Commercial License 4.0 (CC BY-NC 4.0).
doi:10.3233/FAIA231521

Research on the Design of Red Cultural and Creative Products in Hongyuan County Based on Regional Characteristics

Sinuo CHEN[1], Ning DAI[1], Jun DU[1], Fangyu LI[1], Jingyu HE[2], and Yuqing WANG[1]

[1] *School of Design, Southwest Jiaotong University*

[2] *School of Economics and Management, Southwest Jiaotong University*

Abstract. Purpose Combining regional and red cultural and creative products, product innovation design exploration from the perspective of design, breaking through the shackles of the homogenization of existing red cultural and creative products. **Method** Taking Hongyuan County as an example, the existing regional language and red cultural elements were collected, analyzed, summarized and refined. The hierarchical analysis method was used to make hierarchical comparison of the design elements, and the importance of the design elements was ranked through scientific score calculation and weight evaluation, so as to determine the design requirements and target direction. **Conclusion** Scientific analysis and evaluation of demand red cultural elements through analytic hierarchy process can effectively improve design efficiency, further avoid the interference of subjective factors on design, form diversified design concepts, and provide reference value for the same type of design needs.

Keywords. Analytic hierarchy process; Red culture; Cultural and creative design; Hongyuan county

1. Introduction

Red culture is a precious spiritual wealth in the great historical process of the Chinese nation. Red culture contains rich cultural connotation and profound philosophical significance. The Outline of the 14th Five-Year Plan (2021-2025) for National Economic and Social Development and Vision 2035 of the People's Republic of China, it is pointed out that revolutionary culture should be carried forward and the red gene should be inherited [1]. Red culture should focus on promoting the protection of revolutionary cultural relics and red sites, and promote the development of mutual integration of culture and tourism in red tourism. China's vast territory, the formation of various places have significant regional characteristics. Reasonable integration of regional characteristics into red culture will break through the current situation of uniformity of cultural and creative products and form distinctive red cultural elements.

Because the country attaches great importance to red culture and users' demand for product styles, the market of red cultural creative products has developed rapidly. At the same time, red cultural creative products also show problems. First, there is a convergence of product design styles. Red cultural products in different regions appear similar in style and content. Secondly, there is the problem of aesthetic fatigue among consumer users. This problem weakens the advantage of red cultural value with regional characteristics. Therefore, in the design of red culture with regional characteristics, it is necessary to innovate red cultural and creative products to meet the needs of consumers and start the popularity of regional red cultural characteristics. This is a major challenge. To sum up, this paper will take Hongyuan County as an example to study the red cultural creative products with regional characteristics based on the perspective of design. At the same time, the paper will use the analytic hierarchy process to analyze the data information of red culture in Hongyuan County. Using the method of scientific calculation, this paper analyzes the design requirements of red culture in Hongyuan County. This method will help to explore the design path of red cultural creative products with regional characteristics.

2. Regional Characteristics and Red Cultural and Creative Products

2.1. Regional identity

Regional characteristics are mainly reflected in regional location, terrain, folk culture, economic conditions, historical background and other factors. These factors will affect the local people's way of life and cultural identity as well as their values. Such influence will enable the region to form a cultural symbol with regional characteristics. For Chinese red culture, regional characteristics can bring personalized and differentiated content to red revolutionary old base areas. Red cultural products with regional characteristics can promote the development of red tourism and help stimulate local economic growth[2].

2.2. Red cultural creative products

Red cultural creative products are based on Chinese revolutionary history and culture. Products take design creativity as the core demand, tangible or intangible presentation form as the carrier. The purpose of red cultural creative products is to shape IP with Chinese revolutionary history and culture, and carry forward the spirit of red culture. Red culture can give creative products high cultural added value. The resources of red Revolution history are designed into creative derivatives of red culture through creative innovation[3]. Such products have outstanding cultural communication significance and social and economic value.

2.3. Connection between regionalism and red cultural and creative design

The development of red culture is characterized by distinct regional features. The occurrence of major events in Chinese revolutionary history and the development of characters are closely associated with specific regions. These regional characteristics reveal the personalized and diverse content of red culture in each region. By integrating regional elements into the design of red cultural creative products, we can create unique and diverse items that possess greater vitality and charm. The differentiation brought about by regional characteristics plays a vital role in avoiding market product homogenization. Paying significant attention to the application of regional characteristics in the creative design of red culture can render our design decisions more forward-looking[2].

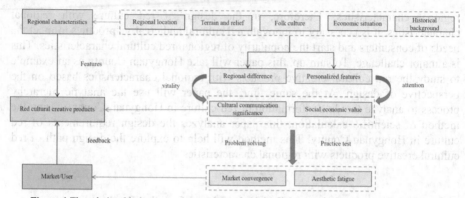

Figure 1. The relationship between regional characteristics and red cultural creative product design.

3. Research Methods and Path Analysis

This paper analyzes the design path of red culture with regional characteristics. From the perspective of user demand analysis, we should pay attention to the user's demand experience and market value. It requires clear design tendency and cultural focus to give full play to the advantages of regional characteristics. In order to better complete the design path analysis, this paper takes Hongyuan County, Sichuan Province, China as an example, and uses the analytic hierarchy process to conduct target screening and weight analysis on the red cultural design elements in Hongyuan County. It is hoped that scientific computing can be used to clarify the needs of users and clear the direction of design.

3.1. Analytic hierarchy process

The Analytic hierarchy Process (AHP), proposed by the American operations research scientist, is a hierarchical weight decision analysis method using the network system theory and the multi-objective comprehensive evaluation method.[5].
The systematic and modular analysis method can effectively reduce the subjectivity and one-sidedness of complex problem analysis.

3.2. Design path analysis

This paper takes Hongyuan area as the carrier of red culture, analyzes its design needs and cultural needs. First of all, the user market to conduct a variety of forms of research activities. User demand samples can be obtained through user research. Secondly, the samples are screened and integrated. Through the analytic hierarchy process, we scientifically construct the layered model of sample elements. Finally, the weight of all elements is calculated and analyzed. Analyze users' needs according to factor weight, infer design demand trend, and locate cultural focus. This method can improve the design efficiency and enhance the enabling effect of regional red culture. The detailed design path analysis diagram is shown in Figure 2.

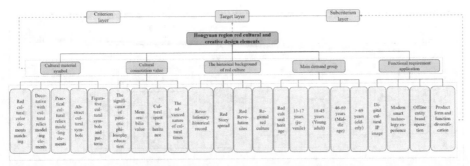

Figure 2. Design research methods and paths.

4. Practice of red cultural and creative design process in Hongyuan region

Through the research and analysis of the design of red cultural creative products with regional characteristics in Hongyuan County. From the demand point of view to the actual research of users. The analytic hierarchy process was used to analyze and evaluate the survey data. The corresponding factor weights are calculated and compared to avoid the interference of subjective consciousness to the design, improve the design efficiency and innovate the design content. So as to complete the design practice of regional red cultural creativity.

4.1. Element positioning and system construction

Firstly, the paper analyzes the demand elements of Hongyuan County in the aspect of red cultural creative design. The team adopted field investigation, literature review, actual interview, case evaluation, shadow follow-up and other research methods. A sample of the requirement elements is obtained through these methods. Secondly, from the perspective of design, the different requirements are transformed into a unified design model language. This process requires the summary, induction and classification of the design elements. Finally, the hierarchical model of design elements is constructed and analyzed[8]. It is necessary to conduct a qualitative analysis of the design elements and establish a multi-level evaluation index system of red cultural creative products with Hongyuan regional characteristics.

According to the needs of users in the early stage, a total of 155 samples of questionnaire information were collected. Using the hierarchical construction method of analytic hierarchy process, the index framework of the creative design elements of red culture in Hongyuan region is established. The evaluation system is divided into three parts: target layer, standard layer and sub-standard layer. According to the previous research, the standard layer mainly includes five aspects: cultural material symbol, cultural connotation value, red historical background, main demand groups and functional demand application. From the 5 criterion layers, 22 scheme layers are derived. As shown in Figure 3.

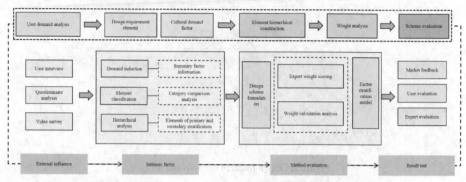

Figure 3. Hongyuan region red cultural and creative design elements.

4.2. Factor index and weight calculation test

The discriminant matrix of criterion layer and scheme layer is established according to analytic hierarchy process. It is stipulated that the index set of the evaluation system is:$U=\{u_1, u_2, u_3 \ldots u_n\}$, Experts use 1-9 scoring scale method to complete the scoring, and determine the corresponding weight coefficient. The set of factor weights is obtained:$A=\{a_1, a_2, a_3 \ldots a_n\}$.By assigning weights to the importance of different evaluation indicators, the pairwise discrimination matrix of the criterion layer is established through pairwise comparison, as shown in Table 1.

Table 1. Pairwise discriminant matrix.

Z	A1Cultural material symbol	A2Functional requirement application	A3The historical background of red culture	A4Main demand group	A5Cultural connotation value
A1Cultural material symbol	1	1/2	2	5	1/6
A2Functional requirement application	2	1	3	7	1/5
A3The historical background of red culture	1/2	1/3	1	3	1/7
A4The historical background of red culture	1/5	1/7	1/3	1	1/9
A5Cultural connotation value	6	5	7	9	1

The maximum feature root of the criterion layer matrix is obtained based on the score data:$\lambda_{max} = \sum_{i=1}^{n} \frac{[AW]}{nw_i}$ =5.226856161. To verify the consistency index, RI is the average randomness index of pair-to-pair discriminant matrix, which is brought into the consistency test formula CR=CI/RI. The weight vector of the index is calculated as follows:

$$RI = 1/12, n = 5$$

$$CI = \frac{\lambda_{max} - n}{n-1} = (5.22685616 - 5)/(5-1) = 0.0567$$

Thus, CI=0.0567; CR=CI/RI=0.050637536/1.12=0.050637536 and CR=0.050637536 < 0.1, the judgment matrix passed the consistency test. The index weights of the criterion layer are obtained. After the index weights of the criterion layer are determined, the judgment matrix is constructed for the indicators of the scheme layer respectively, and the consistency test is carried out to calculate the index weights of the scheme layer. For details, see Table 2-6

Table 2. Discriminant matrix and weight calculation of cultural material symbol layer

A1Cultural material symbol	Red cultural color elements matching	Decorative with cultural relics modeling elements	Practical cultural relics modeling elements	Figurative cultural symbols and patterns	Abstract cultural symbols	ω_i	λ_{max}	CR
Red cultural color elements matching	1	1/4	2	1/2	3	0.1412		
Decorative with cultural relics modeling elements	4	1	6	2	6	0.4572		
Practical cultural relics modeling elements	1/2	1/6	1	1/5	1/2	0.0583	5.1250	0.0279
Figurative cultural symbols and patterns	2	1/2	5	1	4	0.2674		
Abstract cultural symbols	1/3	1/6	2	1/4	1	0.0760		

Table3. Discriminant matrix and weight calculation of functional requirements application layer

A2Functional requirement application	Digital cultural IP image	Modern smart technology experience	Offline entity brand operation	Product form and function diversification	ω_i	λ_{max}	CR
Digital cultural IP image	1	3	1/2	5	0.2808		
Modern smart technology experience	1/3	1	1/7	2	0.0951		
Offline entity brand operation	2	7	1	9	0.5686	4.0165	0.0049
Product form and function diversification	1/5	1/2	1/9	1	0.0556		

Table 4 . Discrimination matrix and weight calculation of red historical background layer

A3 Historical background in red	Revolutionary historical record	Red story spread	Red Revolution on sites	Regional red culture	Red cultural heritage	ω_i	λ_{max}	CR
Revolutionary historical record	1	5	9	3	7	0.5004		
Red story spread	1/5	1	6	1/3	3	0.1406		
Red Revolution sites	1/9	1/6	1	1/7	1/3	0.0338	5.2656	0.0593
Regional red culture	1/3	3	7	1	5	0.2583		
Red cultural heritage	1/7	1/3	3	1/5	1	0.0669		

Table5. Discriminant matrix and weight calculation of the main demand group layer

A4 main demand groups	Age 18 or younger	19 to 39 years	40 to 59 years	Age 60 or above	ω_i	λ_{max}	CR
Age 18 or younger	1	1/3	1/5	3	0.1216		
19 to 39 years	3	1	2	7	0.4454	4.1704	0.0507
40 to 59 years	5	1/2	1	9	0.3852		
Age 60 or above	1/3	1/7	1/9	1	0.0479		

Table6. Discriminant matrix and weight calculation of cultural connotation value layer

A5 Cultural connotation value	The significance of patriotic philosophy education	Memorabi lia value	Cultural spirit inheritance	The advanced nature of cultural times	ω_i	λ_{max}	CR
The significance of patriotic philosophy education	1	7	3	4	0.5538		
Memorabilia value	1/7	1	1/3	1/4	0.0614		
Cultural spirit inheritance	1/3	3	1	1/2	0.1595	4.1195	0.0356
The advanced nature of cultural times	1/4	4	2	1	0.2253		

From the results presented in Table 2-Table 6, it can be seen that the consistency of the judgment matrix in the analysis and evaluation meets CR < 0.1, that is, it passes the consistency test standard. Based on the accuracy of the result, the comprehensive weight of the elements of the scheme layer is calculated, and the final weight value is obtained. For details, see Table 7.

Table7. Summary of the comprehensive weights of the elements of the scheme level

First-level indicators	second-level indicators		The weight value of synthesis
	0.1255	Red cultural color elements matching 0.1412	0.0177
		Decorative with cultural relics modeling elements 0.4572	0.0574
A1Cultural material symbol		Practical cultural relics modeling elements 0.0583	0.0073
		Figurative cultural symbols and patterns 0.2674	0.0336
		Abstract cultural symbols 0.0760	0.0095
	0.1956	Digital cultural IP image 0.2808	0.0549
A2Functional requirement application		Modern smart technology experience 0.0951	0.0186
		Offline entity brand operation 0.5686	0.1112
		Product form and function diversification 0.0556	0.0109
	0.0765	Revolutionary historical record 0.5004	0.0383
A3The historical background of red culture		Red story spread 0.1406	0.0108
		Red Revolution sites 0.0338	0.0026
		Regional red culture 0.2583	0.0051
	0.0349	Age 18 or younger 0.1216	0.0042
A3The historical background of red culture		19 to 39 years old 0.4454	0.0156
		40 to 59 years old 0.3852	0.0135
		Age 60 or above 0.0479	0.0017
	0.5675	The significance of patriotic philosophy education 0.5538	0.3143

A5Cultural connotation value	Memorabilia value	0.0614	0.0348
	Cultural spirit inheritance	0.1595	0.0905
	The advanced nature of cultural times	0.2253	0.1278

The comprehensive weight value of each element of the scheme layer can be obtained from Table 7, and the comprehensive weight value is calculated by consistency test:

$$CI=0.034678281 \tag{1}$$
$$CR=CI/RI=0.03467828/1.12=0.030962751<0.1 \tag{2}$$

The obtained result CR=0.030962751 < 0.1 means that the comprehensive index of the matrix model passes the consistency test principle, and the calculated results are scientifically reasonable and meet the design reference requirements.

4.3. Weight analysis of demand factors

Based on the analysis of the red cultural design elements of Hongyuan County, the comprehensive weights of each level are sorted and evaluated, as shown in Figure 4. First of all, with the continuous expansion of the cultural and creative market in the field of red culture, the audience of red cultural creative products with regional characteristics shows a younger development trend. Secondly, users' demand for cultural and creative design continues to escalate. Users' demand for cultural products is developing towards more life and visualization. Last but not least, users pay more attention to the unique spiritual and cultural value brought by regional cultural products and the transmission of regional cultural value with The Times. To sum up, the product not only needs to have the representation of red cultural objects, but also needs to have profound cultural deposits as a support to show profound and powerful cultural spiritual values.

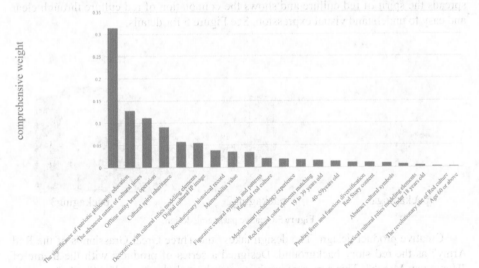

Figure 4. User requirements weight bar chart.

5. The design strategy of red cultural creative products in Hongyuan County

5.1. Analysis of design elements of red culture in Hongyuan County

Based on the scientific weight analysis conclusion, designers should pay more attention to the expression of regional red culture. In the design process, the local characteristics are integrated into the design of red cultural elements. First, the designer transformed and refined the red historical resources of Hongyuan County in the design process, and transformed the abstract culture and spirit into concrete visual cultural symbols. Second, designers should disassemble and reorganize the design elements of red culture, and extract the red cultural symbols with regional characteristics with unique connotation and high cultural added value. Through the design method of "creative products tell red stories", the design effect of "object and self empathy" can be achieved.

5.2. Hongyuan County red cultural creative product design practice

This paper will start from three aspects of creative packaging design, creative product design, and creative IP design. It will combine local red culture content to carry out a design practice for Hongyuan County.

Creative packaging design. Combining Hongyuan County local characteristic products: yak milk, Tibetan sheep, Sichuan traditional Chinese medicine and other three categories as packaging design goals. In the design idea, the selection of Hongyuan County classic red culture stories including: "Golden fishhook", "temple gift of food", "Little Red Army on horseback" and other three as creative cultural heritage support. The spiritual connotation of the red story is refined and presented in a symbolic and symbolic way. Red culture takes characteristic products as the carrier, spreads the spirit of red culture and shows the connotation of red culture through clear and easy to understand visual expression. See Figure 5 for details.

packaging1   packaging2   packaging3

Figure 5. Creative packaging design

Creative product design. The design takes "the Three Great Grasslands of the Red Army" as the red story background. Designed a series of products with the theme of "Hongyuan March". This series of products mainly includes "broad", "flow", "imprint" three sub-themes. The characteristics of the Hongyuan region such as "Hongyuan prairie", "marshland" and "Moon Bay" are combined with the historical spirit of the Red Army's Long March. On the other hand, through the abstract red culture and local scenery, the regional red cultural color is defined, including "travel red", "flow green", "ink yellow".The visual creative design of cultural and creative products is accomplished through the abstraction and re-empowerment of elements. See Figure 6 for details.

Product 1   Product2   Product3

Figure 6. Creative product design

Creative IP design. The purpose of the design is to reflect the profound "civil-military relationship" in Hongyuan area. With "yak revolution" as the red background, the Red Army and Hongyuan County residents as the IP image. Combined with the image features of Tibetan sheep, Tibetan yak and Long March military uniform, it shows the relationship between the military and the people and the historical characteristics of Hongyuan County. Let the design work bear the unique red culture of Hongyuan. See Figure 7 for details.

Figure 7 Creative IP design

6. Conclusion

This paper takes the user demand as the starting point and takes the AHP as the scientific method. Explore the design path of red culture combined with regional characteristics in creative design from the perspective of design. Taking Hongyuan County as an example, this paper practices the elements of red culture design demand in Hongyuan region. Starting from the two dimensions of design demand and cultural demand, the user demand is integrated, and the analytic hierarchy process is used to complete the analysis of the factor weight. Finally, using the analysis conclusions, Hongyuan County red cultural creative products to complete the design practice. The practice is carried out from various aspects such as color representation, symbolic image and product modeling. The spiritual and cultural needs are transmitted to People's Daily life in the form of images. To achieve the purpose of cultural communication by meaning and meaning. At the same time, it also has the effect of regional red culture revitalization. Ahp brings design closer to the will of the market. Scientific methods can improve the efficiency of design and increase market satisfaction. It provides reference value for the design and research of red culture helping rural revitalization.

Acknowledgments. This paper is supported by the Fundamental Research Fund of Central University, the Undergraduate SRTP National Innovation Project (202210613056) of SWJTU, 2022 SWJTU Research Projects on Teaching Reform of Degree and Graduate Education (YJG5-2022-Y037), and 2022 Sichuan Old Revolutionary Areas Development Research Center Project.

References

[1] Outline of the 14th Five-Year Plan (2021-2025) for National Economic and Social Development and Vision 2035 of the People's Republic of China,People's Publishing House, Peking, 2021.

[2] Xu Dan.,A study on Folk Culture Tourism in The Former Central Soviet Area of Southern Jiangxi Province,Jiangxi Social Sciences34(2014),229-232.

[3] Tang Yi,Chen Ziying,Communication of Red Culture Creative Products in Museums Prospected in the Context of Metaverse,Southeast Culture(2022),174-178.

[4] Liu Weishang,Wang Zeyi,Sun Bingming et al,Design of Regional Red Cultural IP Product Based on Qualia Theory,Packaging Engineering44(2023),368-378.

[5] Saaty TL,How to make a decision:The analytic hierarchy process,Interfaces48(1994),9-26.

[6] HUA Tianqi, Shen Huan, Li Zhou et al.,Implementation of SAS/IML module of analytic hierarchy process ,China Health Statistics34(2017),839-841.

[7] Zhou Qi, Niu Yanan, Bi Weilong,Roduct Design of Shadow Play Based on Analytic Hierarchy Process,Packaging Engineering43(2022),217-224.

[8] Song Shuliang, Luo Xiaohuan,Problems and Strategies in the Design of Red Cultural and Creative Products,Design Art Research8(2018), 116-122.

[9] Zhu Xiaofei,Wang Yongjun,Li Dajun,The Effectiveness Test of the Maximum Membership Principle in Fuzzy Comprehensive Evaluation,Surveying, Mapping and Spatial Geographic Information39(2016),135-137+143.

[10] Xu Li.,Digital Protection and Innovative Development Path of Red Cultural Resources,People's Forum1(2021),139-141.

[11] LIU Y T,Research on Red Culture in Hunan Regional Product Packaging Design,Packaging Engineering44(2023),378-383.

[12] Kang, Xinhui Nagasawa, Shin'ya,Integrating kansei engineering and interactive genetic algorithm in jiangxi red cultural and creative product design,Journal of Intelligent and Fuzzy Systems44(2023),647-660.

[13] Chen Xiang,Research on cultural and creative product design based on regional red culture,Geography Teaching Reference for Middle Schools7(2022),I0002

Design Studies and Intelligence Engineering
L.C. Jain et al. (Eds.)
© 2024 The Authors.
This article is published online with Open Access by IOS Press and distributed under the terms
of the Creative Commons Attribution Non-Commercial License 4.0 (CC BY-NC 4.0).
doi:10.3233/FAIA231522

1071

The Design of Undergraduate Students' Learning Product Service System Based on User Behavioural Persuasion

Zhule ZHANG [a,b,1] and Ningchang ZHOU [a,2]

ᵃ *South China Agricultural University, Guangzhou, China*
ᵇ *The Hong Kong University of Science and Technology, Hong Kong, China*

Abstract. The article investigates the application of user behavior and persuasive design theories in product design and develops a design model based on user behavioral persuasion. The research collects data on study habits observed from undergraduate students and subsequently examines the patterns and variations within this cohort. The investigation leads to the development of a product service system that integrates motivational education to encourage undergraduate students to cultivate positive study habits and enhance the overall quality of their learning experience. The study builds a logical and efficient design model and hits the pain points of undergraduate students learning behaviors, delivering effective design solutions and improving the match between product strategies and design requirements by combining with motivational education.

Keywords. User behavior, persuasive design, motivational education, product service system design

To realize the ambitious goal of the great rejuvenation of the Chinese people, it is imperative for China, a nation with a large population, to transition into a talent-rich country. In this regard, the pivotal role and profound significance of education, particularly at the undergraduate level, cannot be overlooked, where undergraduate education serves as a crucial mechanism for identifying and nurturing talented individuals. However, the realm of undergraduate education is today plagued by prevalent problems such as diminished student enthusiasm, unfavorable attitudes, and substandard learning quality. Most of the current solutions aimed at enhancing student learning quality mostly employ punitive mechanisms or untargeted incentive strategies without concrete product support and specific positive measures, hence significantly diminishing their effectiveness in implementation. To address the limitations, it is essential to apply design and educational theories to propose efficacious design strategies and outcomes base on real cases and data. This article presents a design model that is guided by theories of user behavior and persuasion design, analyzing the learning behavior of undergraduate students, introducing the

---

[1] Zhule Zhang, 5598, The Hong Kong University of Science and Technology, Clear Water Bay, Sai Kung, Hong Kong; Email: zzhanghd@connect.ust.hk.

[2] Corresponding Author: Ningchang Zhou, 202, Block 17, Furniture Center, South China Argicultural University, 510640 Guangzhou, China; Email: 93890290@qq.com.

concept of educational incentives to summarize the strategies for designing product service systems, which are to enhance the overall learning quality of undergraduate students, that align with the learning habits of two distinct types of students.

1. Design Model Construction

1.1. Design Method Based on User Behavior

According to Maslows hierarchy of needs theory, individuals are driven by their self-needs to develop behavioral motivations. Through their actions, they strive to fulfill increasingly higher levels of requirements until they ultimately attain the highest degree of psychological needs associated with self-identification. Therefore, when designing based on user behavior, it is essential to comprehend, compile, and analyze user needs, motivations, and behaviors in order to deliver design solutions that meet user expectations and needs.

Various scholars employ diverse methodologies centered upon user behavior in their research and product design processes. The research conducted by Song Xianping et al. focused on user behavior analysis, operational methodologies, and psychological motives when utilizing products, aiming to explore the design needs and implement innovative designs for household fire extinguishers [1]. Yu Ruyang et al. conducted an analysis of user behavior pertaining to the utilization of domestic floor-cleaning robots, where they successfully assessed the degree of satisfaction associated with diverse user requirements, subsequently formulating tailored strategies intended for enhancing the overall user experience [2]. Li Xin et al. conducted a study to investigate the behavioral features of women engaging in fitness exercises during pregnancy to examine the challenges and needs by acquiring user behavioral data in a suitable manner, employing scientific analysis techniques to discern requirements and formulate design strategies [3].

1.2. Related Theories of Persuasive Design

Persuasive technology is a multidisciplinary domain encompassing the fields of computer science and psychology. This discipline centers on the utilization of research, analysis, and design methodologies to change consumers attitudes, beliefs, and patterns of usage, as well as the intended functions of products. The application of persuasive technology has been observed in many sectors such as education, healthcare, commerce, and product design. The concept of persuasive design, initially introduced by Professor B.J. Fogg from Stanford University, involves a design approach that leverages persuasive technologies to effectively change user behavior or attitudes with design where it underscores the attainment of alterations and the direction of user conduct without resorting to coercion [7].

Simultaneously, Professor B.J. Fogg introduced the widely recognized FBM model of behavior persuasion. He noted that the three dimensions of motivation, capability, and trigger factors are the causes of conscious behavior. The model places emphasis on the necessity for individuals to possess adequate motivation, corresponding abilities, and triggering conditions to execute a particular behavior [5]. It elucidates the process through which behavior undergoes transformation as a result of the influence exerted by these elements. Furthermore, it provides guidance to designers and researchers, encouraging them to adopt a systematic approach when considering the potential factors that can bring about behavioral change.

1.3. Design Model Construction Based on User Behavior and Persuasive Design Theory

Based on the preceding discourse, while analyzing user behavior, it is crucial to collect information regarding to user needs, motivations, and actions. Conversely, when conducting persuasive design, it is vital to concentrate on user motivations, abilities, and triggers. Indeed, there is a substantial overlap and reciprocal reinforcement between these two fields of study. The trigger factors and abilities considered within the framework of persuasive design theory can be matched with the requirements and behaviors identified in user behavior research. Thus, when establishing the design model, it is important to zero in solely on three key components: user demands and trigger factors, motivation, and behavior and abilities (see Fig. 1).

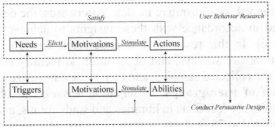

Figure 1. Relationship between user behavior research and persuasive design theory

In the data insights of these three parts, it is required to capture user behavior and analyze relevant data, sorting and defining the user journey along with activity chain, and focusing on optimizing the user experience. By gaining a deep understanding of user behavior, it is feasible to effectively categorize different user types, develop comprehensive personas, and analyze the user behavior chain which enables the identification of pain points and supports the exploration of design opportunities. On the basis of the findings, it can be achieved to provide specific solutions and design strategies, and to advance theoretical advancements towards the process of productization. Based on the aforementioned procedures, it is conceivable to develop a design model comprising three distinct levels, namely data gathering, theoretical proposal, and practical production. Each level operates as an autonomous unit, generating outcomes, while simultaneously advancing and establishing an interconnected and close-loop system (see Fig. 2).

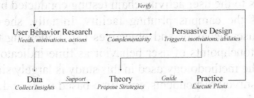

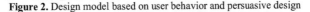

Figure 2. Design model based on user behavior and persuasive design

2. Insight Collection of Undergraduate Students' Learning Process

Prior to proposing design strategies, it is fundamental to collect the needs, triggering factors, motivation, behavior, and capabilities of the target users. Within the framework of this article, the requirements and triggers refer to enhancing the quality and reinforcing the achievements of learning. The research will collect data by interview and observation which will then be subjected to summarizing and testing with the goal to derive representative conclusions, and subsequently guide the development of practical and the outputs of design strategies.

2.1. Establishment of Typical User Roles

User role research is a systematic procedure that involves investigating the underlying user characteristics and associated attributes of the target audiences. This is accomplished through multiple methods, including engaging in conversations and conducting surveys where the findings of the research are subsequently conveyed to designers through multimedia platforms such as websites, text documents, reports, or illustrative models. Afterwards, the design elements are iteratively refined in accordance with these insights to achieve a comprehensive design solution [6]. In this research, it is undertaken through the utilization of interviews, questionnaire surveys, and observation to identify commonalities and variances within the collected samples, and thereafter summarize the results.

Segmentation of user groups. Observation was used to observe the study methods of 10 self-study locations in libraries and study rooms, and a questionnaire survey was distributed to 75 students to analyze statistically their study methods.

Definition of user categorization. The learning approach can generally be categorized into the two user categories.

Time-based users are individuals who engage in learning strategies that prioritize activities such as reading and memory. This type of user typically spends time studying with watching and reading while less time on writing.

Quantity-based users are individuals who engage in learning approaches that prioritize the act of writing and documenting information. This particular kind of users typically engages in extensive written learning events and writes more.

Statistics on Sample Group Classification. The undergraduate student group was split into two categories, time-based users (time-based) and quantity-based users (quantity-based), accounting for 44% and 56% of the group, respectively.

2.2. Establishment of User Behavior Chain

This section refers to the user activity chain testing conducted by He Xuemei in the service design of the campus printing facility. Initially, she conducted a rough segmentation of user behavior and objectives [7]. Following that, the researcher documented key touchpoints of user behavior as time indicators to draw the user behavior chain. The methodology used in this study is largely similar.

From the 75 survey respondents, five time-based users and five quantity-based users are selected and assigned tasks with certain restrictions to serve as the information source for establishing the user behavior chain based on their activities. Peer communication is evaluated based on the quality of learning from various completion methods of the same user type.

Group 1: Five time-based users are segregated and given two 100-word articles to memorize and dictate. The assessment of learning quality is based on the criteria of total time and dictation performance.

Group 2: The five time-based users same as group 1 are grouped together and given two new 100-word articles to memorize and dictate. Discussion is permitted among individuals during the preparatory phase, but it is prohibited during the dictation phase. The assessment method of learning quality is the same as group 1.

Group 3: Five quantity-based users are separated and given two hours to accomplish a writing assignment. The completion quality indicators encompass both the quantity of words and the level of writing which are also applicable to group 4.

Group 4: The five quantity-based users same as the group 3 are grouped together and given two hours to complete a writing assignment. Discussion is facilitated among individuals involved in the process.

The evaluation examining the impact of peer communication is based on learning quality by comparing the results between Group 1 and Group 2, and between Group 3 and Group 4 as well. During the phase of completing Groups 2 and 4, the researchers diligently documented their behaviors, time nodes, and the fluctuations in user emotions to build a comprehensive behavior chain where the following codes shown on table 1 were employed.

Table 1. User behavior codes

User Behavior	Code
List Agenda	A
Read Material	B
Start Learning	C
Discuss with peers	D
Finish Preparation	E
Use Mobile Phone	F
Encourage each other	G
Take a rest	H
Check timing	J
Complete	K

Table 2. The behavior record and result upon completion of Time-based users (Remarks: The unit of duration is minutes, less than one minute is counted as one minute and rounded up in the statistics of user's time length, and the average time is retained as one decimal. The total score is presented in the percentage system with two parts where the total time (50%) in order of priority were assigned points 50, 45, 40, 35, 30 and the results of the score (50%) according to the wrong word each deduct one point.)

Category	Group	User I	User II	User III	User IV	User V	Average
Learning Process	1	A-B-C-H- J-E-K	B-C-H-J- H-E-K	B-C-H-J- E-K	A-B-C-E- J-K	A-B-C-H- J-E-K	-
	2	A-B-C-D- F-H-G-J- E-K	B-C-D-H- G-F-G-J- E-K	A-B-C-D- F-G-J-E- H-K	A-B-C-D- J-E-K	A-B-C-D- F-G-J-E- K	-
Total Duration	1	28	34	27	22	30	28.2
	2	23	24	23	19	22	22.2
Non-study Duration	1	3	9	2	1	6	4.2
	2	3	3	2	1	2	2.2
Score	1	86	65	95	98	80	84.8
	2	89	75	90	100	95	89.8

Table 3. The behavior record and result upon completion of Quantity-based users (Remarks: The unit of duration is minutes, less than one minute is counted as one minute and rounded up in the statistics of user's time length, and the average time is retained as one decimal. The score is presented in the percentage system.)

Category	Group	User VI	User VII	User VIII	User VI	User X	Average
Learning Process	3	B-C-H-J-H-J-K	B-C-J-H-K	B-C-H-J-K	A-B-C-H-J-K	A-B-C-J-K	-
	4	B-D-C-H-G-K	A-B-D-C-F-G-J-K	B-D-F-G-C-H-G-K	A-B-D-F-G-C-J-H-G-K	A-B-D-C-J-K	-
Non-study Duration	3	32	12	20	8	1	14.6
	4	10	5	12	8	1	7.2
Score	3	60	90	90	92	100	84.8
	4	85	92	90	94	100	92.2

2.3. Analysis of Group Behavior During User Learning

The examination of the learning outcomes between different groups in each user type experiment reveals that the inclusion of peer contact yields a noteworthy enhancement in the overall quality of learning. In the conducted tests involving Group 1 and Group 2, it was observed that the mean duration of non-learning intervals among users dropped from 4.2 minutes to 2.2 minutes. Simultaneously, the average score exhibited an increase from 84.8 points to 89.8 points. The members of Group 2 were able improve their approaches to learning, identify areas of difficulty, and enhance the overall quality of their learning experience through effective communication. The average non-learning time in tests on Groups 3 and 4 dropped by over 50.68%, while the average score climbed noticeably from 84.8 to 92.2 points. This phenomenon can be attributed to the fact that users were able to decrease non-learning behaviors through peer support and supervision, and acquire more effective learning strategies through communication, resulting in an overall enhancement in the average learning quality of the entire group.

3. Solution Proposal

The utilization of electronic media, including as television, computers, and mobile phones, for educational purposes, commonly referred to as e-learning, has undeniably emerged as a prevailing trend and area of growth. However, Zheng Yanfu adopted the independent sample t-test method to experimentally examine the gathered data and discovered that the observed impact of e-learning is not deemed sufficient [8]. The analysis of the survey revealed that students who utilize paper-based materials for studying have a comparatively profound comprehension of the subject matter and demonstrate enhanced proficiency in written language expression, resulting in superior performance on examinations. According to the research conducted by Pan Hui, it was seen that the overall reading comprehension score was marginally higher when assessed on paper as compared to a computer screen. Additionally, the analytical ability score was found to be slightly higher in the paper-based group compared to the e-learning group. Meanwhile, the scholars discovered that mobile reading is conducive to dispersed and transitory learning, whereas paper reading is more conducive to in-depth learning.

Furthermore, with the proper cultivation of incentive spirit and mechanism, undergraduates have the potential to develop a sound ideology of striving and demonstrate a willingness to exert themselves towards its realization. The synergistic impact of this phenomenon on the objective of the present study necessitates the use of suitable incentive strategies. Incentive education refers to an educational approach wherein educators utilize specific incentive principles and appropriate methods to stimulate the motivation of students, correct their thinking and motivation, enhance their ideological consciousness, and mobilize their enthusiasm, initiative, and creativity. This method is based on educational goals and takes into account the needs and characteristics of the learners, aiming to guide them towards the predetermined educational objectives.

Drawing upon the scholarly contributions and theoretical frameworks posited by the aforementioned academics, alongside an examination of the findings derived from user research, the proposed design strategy shall commence with the utilization of conventional paper-based pedagogical approaches. This would be supplemented by the integration of incentive-based educational methodologies, culminating in the comprehensive design and development of the product-service system.

3.1. Overall Framework Proposal

By delineating typical user roles, constructing user behavior chains, and assessing the correlation between peer communication and the quality of learning, the pain points are investigated and anticipated requirements are formulated under the acquirement of pertinent data. Following the process of screening and integration, the design opportunities can be succinctly categorized into five distinct content items that are the quantification of learning quality for quantity-based users, the quantification of learning quality for time-based users, the implementation of timed reminders for work and rest intervals, instant peer messaging, and enabling the sharing of learning progress. The five solutions can be formed from the five functions: word count statistics, time recording, timed reminders, peer communication, and real-time data sharing. Furthermore, the five functions can be categorized into four different components, including data gathering, data processing, data feedback, and social system.

The process of data collecting is facilitated by the utilization of various writing tools and specific supplementary hardware. Data processing serves as a bidirectional transmission platform allowing the exchange of information between the stages of data gathering and data feedback. The transmission of data feedback primarily depends on networking or other connectivity mechanisms to relay information to external platforms where feedback is then visually displayed on mobile applications. The social system operates through using collected and analyzed data, including rankings, which foster competitiveness and motivation among users, encouraging changes in their learning attitudes and behaviors. Additionally, the system enhances communication and interaction among users. The design of the mobile application and smart pen module originates from the aforementioned four components which serves as the foundation for the further development of the product framework and subsequent product design.

3.2. Design of Data Collection End

Based on the identification of typical user roles and the formulation of potential solution, the module of data collection consists of two modules, namely word count statistics and usage time recording.

The module for word count statistics incorporates a data collection method for periodic triaxial acceleration behavior, which can be measured and executed using an accelerometer. Jiang Bo introduced a novel approach for detecting steps using waist-mounted microelectromechanical systems (MEMS) accelerometers [9]. This algorithm combines three thresholds, including peak, zero-crossing, and valley, to assess the movement condition of pedestrians. The reduction of noise interference in the accelerometers false peak value is achieved by sequentially detecting the three thresholds. The process of writing is characterized by the generation of triaxial acceleration fluctuations and short breaks occurring between successive words, resulting in exhibiting periodic patterns akin to those observed during walking. Hence, the act of writing can be seen as a behavioral pattern characterized by periodic triaxial acceleration fluctuations, which can be identified by the utilization of a MEMS accelerometer. The calculation of the number of words written can be achieved by the analysis of the acquired image, where it can provide an indicator of the learning outcomes for quantity-based users.

In addition, the module can get usage time values by analyzing the image derived from the acceleration data. This particular value can serve as one of the foundational elements for time statistical analysis. Plus, the time recording feature can be initiated and terminated manually with the help of a time chip, which is used to quantify the learning achievements of time-based users.

3.3. Design of Data Transmission and Processing End

The data transmission and processing component is capable of evaluating and converting the acquired acceleration change data into word count and duration data. This helps the visualization and analysis of user settings gained from the data feedback component, which then transmits the information to the data collection component to aid in the completion of user settings. The processor is responsible for carrying out the data processing tasks, while the transmission function is facilitated by means of Bluetooth technology, where data can be disseminated among users in order to achieve the process of peer sharing and motivating.

The data feedback endpoint facilitates the visualization of processed data, enabling users to quantitatively assess their learning outcomes, make comparisons with other users, and gain a partial understanding of their learning progress, which has a motivational impact.

3.4. Design of Social System

Interaction and communication between users play a significant role in influencing user behavior in online communities [10]. The social system is an integral component of the incentive system, which provides users with stimulation and motivation and encourages them to set personal objectives. The primary modules of the social system are learning achievement ranking and instant messaging. Users can select a quantification approach that aligns with their preferred learning style, time-based or quantity-based. Additionally, they can exchange data with peers within the groups they participate in, and receive diverse visual virtual incentives based on their ranking outcomes. Furthermore, users have the opportunities to engage in discussions and send messages which can augment the motivational impact by interaction among peers (see Fig.3).

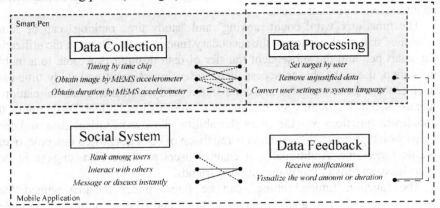

Figure 3. The structure of the product system

3.5. Design Strategy Proposal of Mobile Application

The interaction between users and products is not limited to the physical characteristics of the product, but also includes a process consisting of a series of behaviors, which is a system service platform mediated by the product [11]. Hence, it can be argued that the inclusion of digitalization holds major significance in the realm of persuasive design [12]. The utilization of a mobile application as a visual medium for representing the product system enables an illustration of the users current status, goals, and achievements.

The mobile application integrates many features outlined in the FBM model to effectively generate triggering factors for users. The main motivating factors in online communities are rewards, which include various forms of recognition, prestige, and respect. Users demonstrate a willingness to uphold their reputation and social standing by consistently making valuable contributions to the community [13]. Therefore, while the implementation of virtual incentives, showcasing user achievements, and adding interactive features could increase user motivation. Besides, users have the option to set personal targets and allocate time accordingly, taking into account their unique learning abilities and habits. Additionally, the inclusion of a conversation and communication feature, such as instant messaging, allows users to promptly address their learning inquiries, thereby enhancing their proficiency in utilizing the platform. Furthermore, it is possible to send daily reminders at a designated time and disclose the top three outcomes of the daily rankings, which can effectively stimulate user engagement and enhance their excitement for learning, leading to an improvement in the quality of learning.

4. Design Strategy Practices

4.1. Design of Mobile Application "Track"

"Track" is one of the outputs of this product design, which is a mobile application with four primary features: word count ranking, study time ranking, timing setting, and interactive communication.

The functions "word count ranking" and "study time ranking" can be found inside the "statistics" section of the secondary function area. Through the utilization of a smart pen and the subsequent transfer of data through Bluetooth to a mobile application, users are able to access their present word count and study time data, which enables them to engage in a comparative analysis of their ranks in relation to other users, thus facilitating the attainment of a motivational effect. Furthermore, the subordinate functions provide users the ability to view historical data and form groups which provides the seamless comparison of ones quantified outcome over a specific timeframe. Additionally, it enables users to share data, engage in peer supervision, and foster motivation among friends.

The function "timing setting" can be found under the area named "Me". Users can set their own goals in the application and receive automated reminders when the designated time arrives. This feature has the potential to enhance learning motivation by setting goals and reinforcing the motivational impact of the system.

The instant messaging function is situated under the "Notification". Users can discuss and communicate with friends in various groups in real time, as well as obtain information such as likes from other users (see Fig. 4).

4.2. Design of the Smart Pen

The smart pen serves as the medium for collecting data and executing user instructions within the product. The proposed concept involves the integration of electronic component modules into stationery items, offering several benefits such as recyclability, compactness, user-friendly operation, and affordability. The users activity-related data is captured using an accelerometer and a time chip, and the specific outcomes are derived through the data processing component. In the meantime, the smart pen can send out visual reminders at the designated time set in the application "Track" (see Fig. 5).

Figure 4. The interface of mobile application "Track" in Chinese

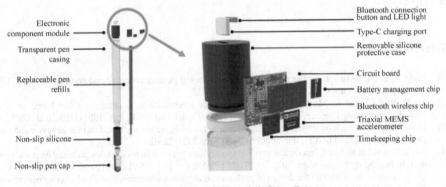

Figure 5. Exploded view of the Smart Pen

5. Conclusion

The role of education, particularly at the undergraduate level, holds enormous significance in the realm of social development. Nevertheless, due to shifts in the social milieu and alterations in students attitudes and self-perception, certain students exhibit diminished motivation for learning and a decrease in enthusiasm. Consequently, there is a deterioration of the quality of their education, which is detrimental not only to their personal development but also to the long-term progress of society and the nation. In turn, educators are currently grappling with an urgent need to address challenges related to enhancing the educational standard, revamping the learning environment, and fostering a better atmosphere for learning. Through the execution of external interventions and the facilitation of students self-transformation, the collective can be motivated towards change, hence presenting a promising avenue for exploration.

This article defines typical user roles, delineates the customary user behavior chains and user journey maps, and scrutinizes the experimental findings. Subsequently, the study delves into the areas of discomfort and anticipated outcomes, and proceeds to develop appropriate design approaches. By making slight alterations to traditional products and integrating them with mobile devices that enable data visualization and foster community engagement, a product is developed that is underpinned by persuasive theory and user behavior. The aforementioned product acquires data from an individual user and utilizes it for the purpose of facilitating the sharing of information between group circles. Drawing upon persuasive theory, this approach facilitates the process of integrating individuals into cohesive groups, hence fostering the creation of a reconfigured environment. This study is grounded in the context of everyday life, aligning with the specific usage scenarios and social needs of individual users to achieve optimal outcomes through incremental modifications. Nonetheless, it is important to acknowledge certain limitations in the research process, such as a limited sample size and inadequate experimental design. These shortcomings should be duly considered in later stages of investigation, allowing for further refinement and iterative updates. The ultimate goal is to develop a comprehensive and representative product that fulfills its intended purpose effectively.

References

[1]   Song X, Li M. Research on fire extinguisher design based on user behavior and context. Design. 2022 Feb; 5(2):122-125, doi:CNKI:SUN:SJTY.0.2022-02-028

[2]   Yu R, Wang J, He R, Ma C. Application experience optimization of sweeping robot based on user behavior. Packaging Engineering. 2022 Feb;43(2):90-97, doi:10.19554/j.cnki.1001-3563.2022.02.012.

[3]   Li X, Shen J. Research on the design of fitness products during pregnancy based on user behavior analysis. Design. 2021;34(22):118-121, doi:CNKI:SUN:SJTY.0.2021-22-024

[4]   Bai Z, Yan F, Pei H, Liu S. Interactive cervical spondylosis prevention product design based on persuasive design. Packaging Engineering. 2020 Dec;41(24):79-84, doi:10.19554/j.cnki.1001-3563.2020.24.011

[5]   Du Y, Gong M. Research on the design of professional cognitive education based on behavior persuasion. Design. 2021;34(04):118-121, doi:CNKI:SUN:SJTY.0.2021-04-037

[6]   Tan H, Feng A. Research methods based on user roles. Packaging Engineering. 2017 Aug;38(16):83-86, doi:10.19554/j.cnki.1001-3563.2017.16.020

[7]   He X, Song N. Campus print center service design based on user behavior. Packaging Engineering. 2020 Jan;41(2):166-174, doi:10.19554/j.cnki.1001-3563.2020.02.025

[8]   Zheng Y. Deliberate on E-Learning Style. China Metallurgical Education. 2019 Dec;2019(06):115-120. doi:10.16312/j.cnki.cn11-3775/g4.2019.06.036

[9]   Jiang B, Fu L. Multi-threshold step detection algorithm based on waist MEMS accelerometer. Electronic World. 2020;2020(06):45-46, doi:10.19353/j.cnki.dzsj.2020.06.025

[10]   Guan T, Wang L, Jin J, Song X. Knowledge contribution behavior in online Q&A communities: An empirical investigation. Computers in Human Behavior. 2018;81:137-147.

[11]   Xin X. Interaction design: from logic of things to logic of behaviors. Zhuangshi. 2015;2015(01):58-62. doi:10.16272/j.cnki.cn11-1392/j.2015.01.012

[12]   Lou S, Deng R, Cao H. Visualization methods research of persuasive design in APP. Packaging Engineering. 2017 Jul;38(14):85-88. doi: 10.19554/j.cnki.1001-3563.2017.14.020

[13]   Zhang J, Qiu S. Research of user behavior persuasion design. Design. 2014 Sep;2014(09):188-189. doi:CNKI:SUN:SJTY.0.2014-09-090.

Design Studies and Intelligence Engineering
L.C. Jain et al. (Eds.)
© 2024 The Authors.
This article is published online with Open Access by IOS Press and distributed under the terms
of the Creative Commons Attribution Non-Commercial License 4.0 (CC BY-NC 4.0).
doi:10.3233/FAIA231523

1083

Research on Intelligent Assistant Teaching System for National Musical Instruments Based on PSS

Na LU[1]

Zhejiang University of Finance and Economics, Hangzhou, 310024, China

Abstract: In order to improve the efficiency and quality of the teaching service of the national musical instruments, a design method of product service system (PSS) for national musical instruments is proposed to build a tool for integrating teaching resources, autonomous practice feedback, and social interaction. The basic characteristics of the national musical instruments of the balance between the improvement and the inheritance of traditional music is summarized, the shortcomings of digital transformation of national musical instruments under the condition of smart technology are compared and pointed out, there is still room for development in precision teaching services. Based on the design method of PSS, the musical instrument products and teaching services are integrated into an overall solution, a model of teaching service and value co-creation is constructed. A service process is formed with the song as the basic teaching unit and gesture skill training as the key. The human-smart system collaboration mode is analyzed. The smart product subsystem and teaching service subsystem are established. The relationship among the stakeholders is discussed. The prototype scheme of the smart assistant teaching system of Pipa based on this method is built up to verify.

Keywords: product service system, musical instrument design, Intelligent Instrument, human- system collaboration, digital transformation

1. Introduction

With a long history and profound cultural accumulation, national Musical Instruments are important cultural treasures of the Chinese nation. The education of national Musical Instruments is not only a key path to understand the history and culture of the nation, but also a solid foundation [1] for the inheritance, innovation and cultural confidence of China's aesthetic education culture. However, in China's music education market, there is a huge gap between Chinese and western instrument education and training scale. Compared with the largest number of piano children in the world, the scale of national musical instrument training represented by zither, pipa and erhu is still small and its influence is insufficient [2]. One of the important reasons is that the traditional teaching of national Musical Instruments focuses on music inheritance and cultural precipitation, and the digital transformation of education is relatively lagging behind, and the lack of docking with digital platforms and intelligent technologies. In 2017, the Notice of The State Council on the Issuance of a New Generation of Artificial Intelligence Development Plan was released, which focused on the intelligent education scene and emphasized the promotion of the whole process application [3] of artificial

---

[1] Corresponding Author. 34971313@qq.com

intelligence in teaching, management, resource construction and other aspects, and the intelligent development of national musical instrument teaching was imperative.

Product Service System (PSS) is a business model and design concept that creates value for users by organically combining products and services, generating personalized services through data connection, and providing new development space [4] for the industry. Based on PSS, this paper constructs an intelligent assistant teaching system for national Musical Instruments. Through comparison, it shows that the intelligent design of national Musical Instruments is insufficient and puts forward intelligent teaching service process and human-machine collaborative division of labor to enhance learning efficiency. By defining the intelligent system, the service blueprint is constructed to coordinate multi-stakeholder resources to improve the learning experience. Research on testing the prototype system in pipa teaching to assist efficient autonomous practice.

2. Overview of musical instrument design

2.1 Design of national Musical Instruments

The design of national Musical Instruments is a process of integrating many aspects such as music culture, music performance, instrument appearance and production technology to create a unique device that conforms to the characteristics of national temperament. Musical instrument design is not only influenced by music theory, instrument performance, music history, music education and other theories, but also related [5-6] to acoustics, mechanics, materials science and other basic theories, through the combination of ergonomics, formal aesthetics, material technology manufacturing and other design theories to achieve productization [7]. The design and transformation of ethnic Musical Instruments such as Erhu, Guqin and pipa focus on the needs of players, composers and audiences, and seek a balance [8-9] between improvement and innovation and inheritance of the characteristics and traditions of ethnic music. On the one hand, the traditional timbre and shape characteristics of the instrument are maintained. On the other hand, it has made a qualitative leap in the performance of intonation, range, and volume. As a complex system evolution, the design of national Musical Instruments ADAPTS to the needs of contemporary music and the impact of market development trends, combined with sensors, multimodal data, music analysis algorithms and other intelligent technologies become inevitable.

2.2 Current situation of intelligent Musical Instruments

Intelligent musical instrument is a comprehensive product service system solution [10] that combines artificial intelligence and other technologies with the classical acoustics and playing skills of traditional Musical Instruments through instrument ontology, sensors, intelligent algorithms and network links. Intelligent musical instrument system integrates audio analysis, automatic playing, instrument learning and other functions to improve the learnability, usability and performance [10 11] of Musical Instruments. Firstly, combining with the original musical instrument playing mode, mechanical and electronic technology and digital synthesis technology, the new timbre, pitch and rhythm of electronic music are added to form a new music rendering style. Secondly, screen interaction, keyboard equipment and human-computer interaction are used to virtualize, providing different customized performance modes of traditional Musical Instruments and performances combined with a variety of art forms. Finally, through cameras and sensors, timely feedback is provided to users, adaptive teaching is provided, and the learning efficiency of Musical Instruments is improved. On the other hand, the intelligent musical instrument system uses APP to extend the whole life cycle value and commercial closed loop of Musical Instruments, and adds personalized services such as game teaching, interest community, and network broadcast. It plays an increasingly important role in the development and promotion of modern music culture, as shown in Table 1.

Table 1. Intelligent musical Instrument Products and Their Service Features

Type	Typical products	Service Features
	Smart guitar, smart ukulele Typical brands: Take Fire, Populele, etc	Guitar fingerboard light guide, instrument body has inlaid type LED display system. APP online guidance and question answering, community interaction, software tuning, gamification practice.
Smart string instrument	Stringless guitar Typical brands: Kitara, Strandberg, etc	Multimedia touch screen, elastic rubber, the number of strings and sound effects can be adjusted according to the user's wishes, and headphones and loudspeakers can also be connected. With an app, you can combine a digital instrument with an emulator.
	Intelligent zither, intelligent pipa Typical brands: Dunhuang · Luo LAN, Yi Guzheng, Chenyu, etc	The instrument is equipped with Bluetooth device and APP connection, forming prompts and feedback. The APP also provides music lovers with functions such as online video learning, consultation and appointment with teachers.
Smart keyboard Instrument	Smart piano Typical brands: Yamaha, The ONE, Find, Baldwin, etc	The piano is equipped with an indicator light to display the key position synchronously and practice with the light. APP built-in professional teaching videos, series of tutorials from shallow to deep, gamified piano practice, timbre changes.
Intelligent blowing instruments	Electric blowpipe Typical brands: Ielts Lok, Roland, etc	The blowpipe comes with 10 timbres, one key to octave, intelligent sound, and comes with 2 fingers.
	Electric harmonica Typical brands: Mozca, etc	The harmonica has 78 built-in timbres, rich playing skills and rich interfaces.
Smart Percussion Instrument	Electronic percussion instruments Typical brands: Roland, Cherubs, etc	The instrument is connected to the APP through Bluetooth to learn, simulate the real drum percussion effect, and the interface is rich and widely compatible.
	Somatosensory percussion instrument Typical brand: AeroBand	Self-created exclusive teaching APP, MIDI software adaptation.

In short, intelligent Musical Instruments have made innovations in timbral communication, performer creation, learner practice, and interaction freedom. However, the proportion of intelligent systems based on Chinese national Musical Instruments is relatively low, the construction of systems with teaching as the core function is still not perfect, and there are still many opportunities for the development of intelligent assistant supported by multimodal data. It has become an important direction[12] to build a precise teaching service scene, improve man-machine collaborative teaching, and promote the new teaching mode of Musical Instruments.

3. Construction of an intelligent system for national Musical Instruments

3.1 Product Service System Approach (PSS)

Product service system approach (PSS) is a design concept [13] that integrates products and services to form an overall solution and realize user value at a deeper level. Intelligent technology promotes the evolution of product service system, further strengthens the coupling degree of tangible products and intangible services to form a digital ecosystem[14], and creates value [15] in many aspects of economy, experience and industrial ecology. The auxiliary teaching system of national Musical Instruments based on PSS is a musical instrument learning platform combining software and hardware formed by this design concept, which is a tool for integrating teaching resources, autonomous practice feedback and social interaction. The research of the system breaks through the limitation of the single function design of the traditional musical instrument system, introduces a variety of high-quality educational resources more widely, reshapes the interactive experience between teachers and students, and can play the following three roles:

1) To construct a co-creation model of musical instrument teaching service and value. On the one hand, intelligent auxiliary system perceives user data and brings value to users. On the other hand, users increase teaching content and data, which is conducive to the iterative development of intelligent system.

2) Improve the efficiency of musical instrument teaching. Artificial intelligence based on data analysis can partially replace the repetitive labor work of guidance and feedback, which can solve the problems of high cost and low efficiency of the original one-to-one music teaching.

3) form multi-level resource linkage[16] of stakeholders. Through the network platform, business, resources and man-machine are widely connected to promote the evolution of industrial ecology and new folk music culture that keep pace with The Times.

The construction of the assistant teaching system of national Musical Instruments mainly includes five aspects: service process, human-machine collaboration mode, intelligent system, stakeholders and service blueprint. The following sections discuss one by one.

3.2 The construction of intelligent service process

According to the characteristics of musical instrument teaching objectives and teaching cognitive process, the intelligent teaching service process is constructed by taking single music teaching as the basic teaching unit and focusing on playing movement skills training. The design of the service process can determine the system function, sort out the core business, and optimize the user experience, which is mainly divided into four stages:

● Stage 1: Music theory knowledge learning, students contact with Musical Instruments. In familiarizing with music score, rhythm, pitch and other conceptual foundations, students experience the melody, timbre and harmony of music, understand the historical context behind the music, and lay the foundation for the training of playing movement skills. The teacher's main task is to teach the main points of knowledge, and students need to master the basic concepts for later application of coordinated movements.

- Stage 2: teachers play demonstration, students feel the essentials. The teacher plays the instrument for demonstration, and the students are required to observe the sequence of the teacher's actions. In the process of students' own operation, the teacher prompts students by refining words to help students pay attention to the key points of the instrument in rhythm, movement and posture.
- Stage 3: Autonomous training of playing movement skills, students associated with the application. Students were trained independently by combining music theory knowledge, teacher's playing demonstration, their own experience and other information. In the process of playing movement skills training, students need to maintain the sensitivity to rhythm, strengthen the control of arm, wrist, shoulder and waist posture, and effectively coordinate and control finger types, shapes, and left-hand coordination.
- Stage 4: Instrument learning community interaction, students exchange and share. In the process of musical instrument learning and performance, students use to upload their own videos and various learning resources to learn from each other, learn from and share with each other, and form a mutually promoting learning atmosphere.

3.3 Man-machine collaborative teaching mode

On the basis of building the service process, the human-machine division of labor is further refined and analyzed. The human-machine collaboration relationship established by teachers, students and AI systems is a form[17] of development of hybrid enhanced intelligence, and is one[18] of the key links to realize the personalized, accurate and large-scale teaching mode centered on students, which lays the foundation for the formulation of the teaching mode under the conditions of intelligent technology, as shown in Table 2.

Teachers led the teaching process and paid attention to cultivating students' humanistic feelings and interest in learning. Teachers complete the multi-level demonstration and teaching of social and psychological attributes, emphasize the cultivation of music quality and aesthetic concept, and strengthen the contact with students while dealing with students' emotions, attitudes and values. At the same time, students can master the playing skills by themselves, and enhance the learning ability[19] of independent design, monitoring, adjustment and reflection through metacognition and self-assessment. In the process of communication with teachers and peers, students can obtain humanistic care and social interaction, and improve their comprehensive quality of music. Under the guidance and collaboration of AI in autonomous learning, students 'personalized learning experience is improved.

AI takes the advantages of the fineness, quantity and efficiency of machine processing information, and runs diagnosis, feedback, intervention and reflection through the teaching process[20], and supports both teaching activities of teachers and students. AI acts as a teaching assistant on the teacher side, supporting the integrated teaching design, learning emotion awareness, and ability evaluation in the big data environment, and optimizing the teaching effect. Through semantic retrieval, big data mining and other intelligent technologies, AI forms the knowledge service ability of national Musical Instruments and enhances students 'interest in learning music knowledge. AI acts as a learning partner on the student side, realizes message recommendation, resource recommendation and learning path planning, feeds back learning situation, and improves learning efficiency. AI forms strategy guidance through artificial intelligence technologies such as gesture recognition and emotion recognition, traces back the root causes of problems such as music recognition, rhythm, and finger-pointing, gives targeted tips and feedback to students' shortcomings in autonomous learning, and adjusts the practice focus individually.

Table 2. Cooperative teaching mode of teachers, students and AI system

	Students	Teachers	AI Technical support
Stage 1	Students learn before class, master the basic music theory foundation, clarify the operation corresponding to the concept, carry out the pre-class test, and reflect on the remedy	Teachers split teaching objectives, optimize the key points of knowledge, import and review excellent teaching resources, and organize pre-class tests	**Teachers:** assist the overall preparation of lessons, help the course test, through the course test can find students' individual differences and problems **Student side:** provide teaching resources and provide analysis of test results
Stage 2	Students listen to lectures collectively, observe the key points of musical instrument playing, conduct group study, and experience musical instrument playing in person	Teachers demonstrate and teach in person, accurately diagnose students' performance tips and feedback, fully interact with students, and give individual guidance according to the situation	**The teacher side:** created AR and VR teaching environment, increased teaching video demonstration data records, student behavior records, and analyzed the learning situation of teaching key points **and difficulties** **Student side:** AI-assisted demonstration forms tips and feedback, 3D animation strengthens the content information, and reduces the work burden of teachers
Stage 3	Students practice independently and fully apply the knowledge points and performance skills learned in class. Individual study, through variant practice, strengthen the standardized training of playing gestures and so on	Combined with data feedback, teachers found specific problems in students 'independent practice, and gave strategy guidance and personalized task direction. Teaching reflection was carried out to form new teaching strategies	**Teachers:** feedback students' autonomous training and learning status to teachers through multimodal data. For the evaluation of autonomous practice test, variant practice suggestions were put forward **Student side:** assisted autonomous practice in the arrangement of learning content, frequency, intensity and timing. The training efficiency was improved by tracing the root causes of problems such as music recognition, rhythm and fingering
Stage 4	Students make use of different online and offline environmental conditions to communicate, gain mutual support from peers, and gain all-round improvement through the discussion of experiences, opinions, and knowledge	Teachers cultivate folk music culture and ecology, guide students' music aesthetics, and realize the pleasant feeling of learning and spirit	**Teachers:** build a social network based on musical instrument playing interest, use web crawler technology to collect public opinion data, and activate online communities and user viscosity **Student side:** recommend online communities, forums and learning partners according to students' interests and learning priorities

3.4 The construction of intelligent support system

Based on determining the process and man-machine mode, the system framework of auxiliary teaching of national Musical Instruments is formed based on PSS, and the corresponding functional service business is completed. The assistant teaching system of national Musical Instruments consists of two parts: product subsystem and service information subsystem. The product subsystem completes the functions of basic playing, interface interaction and multimodal data acquisition, which includes the following three parts:

● National musical instrument ontology. Based on continuing the traditional characteristics of national Musical Instruments, maintaining the sound principle, material structure and operation mode of the existing Musical Instruments, the instruction and data exchange equipment are added to form the playing basis.

- Interactive display equipment. Based on regular natural interactive operation, the teaching content is vividly displayed through the display device.
- Data acquisition sensors. Multi-modal data of students are collected through video, audio, electromyography, and other sensors, which lays the foundation for software services. Among them, the gesture playing of the ethnic pluck instrument is very rapid and complex, and the gesture data are collected by data gloves, forearm sensors and distance sensors. The camera is used to obtain the learners' facial expression and body posture data to comprehensively understand the playing state. Wearable devices were used to understand heart rate, electroencephalogram (EEG), electrodermal signal, and user activity and engagement.

According to the intelligent service process, the service information subsystem establishes multiple ports such as students, teachers, and comprehensive management for support, and the characteristics of data storage and intelligent analysis in the whole process. Taking students as the main service object, this paper focuses on the self-training module of playing movement skills in the service information subsystem, which mainly includes three parts:

- Autonomous training adjustment system. Set teaching strategies and contents according to the teaching objectives of plucking instrumental music and arrange the learning and training process. According to the collection of individual training feedback system, personalized adjustment and revision of stage goals were carried out to match personal ability and based on gradually breaking through the learning comfort zone.
- Self-directed training prompt system. In the process of autonomous practice, multi-channel prompts such as monitors, wearable devices and speakers can reduce students 'cognitive load and strengthen their memory. According to the score teaching procedure, multiple intuitive prompts for language, rhythm and key points are set to facilitate the training of collaborative skills such as remote ensemble and music.
- Independent training feedback system. Through the information collection system, the individual characteristics of rhythm, fingering, and body posture in the playing process of the music are collected, and the shortcomings compared with the expert teachers are quickly pointed out, and the reasons for the playing problems are reasoned, to reduce the ineffective training. The feedback includes comparing the errors in the playing sub-items and the differences in the overall playing analysis.

3.5 Stakeholder analysis

Due to the significant increase in the complexity of product service systems, the auxiliary teaching system of national Musical Instruments cannot be completed by a single party. Therefore, identifying and analyzing the organizations and individuals with important interests in the system will play an important role in optimizing resource allocation, establishing cooperative relationships, and reducing system risks. The stakeholders of the national musical instrument teaching assistance system include four levels: core users, product service providers, ecological chain enterprises and social environment, as shown in Figure 1. In the service process, the data flow organically coordinated multiple stakeholders, and the system integration formed a significant value spillover effect [21], which promoted the positive iteration of the ecology of the instrument education industry.

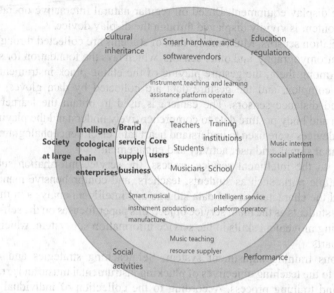

Figure 1. Schematic diagram of core stakeholders

3.6 Blueprint of Intelligent Teaching services

The service blueprint shows the whole picture [22] of the system service user process through the user behavior layer, the foreground layer and the background layer, as shown in Figure 2. According to the specific scene of musical instrument teaching, it is extended to student behavior activity layer, teacher behavior layer and background intelligent support layer, which illustrates the relationship between teacher and student activities, the connection between online and offline links, and the support relationship of intelligent system.

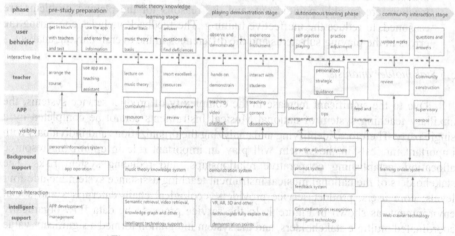

Figure 2. Blueprint for Intelligent Teaching Services

4. Intelligent auxiliary teaching system for Pipa

4.1 Teaching background of pipa

The pipa is a traditional plucped musical instrument with a history of more than 2,000 years in China. Its playing skills are complex and varied, among which fingers directly affect the timble, range, volume and emotional expression of the performance [23]. The teaching of the lute is still mainly based on the traditional mentoring system, which is based on the one-to-one, hand-by-hand and tone-to-tone teaching mode. It takes a long time to practice the playing details of the fingering movement, strength, and string touching way, which leads to [24] the high cost of lute enlightenment teaching and the difficulty of teaching promotion. The study uses user portraits to construct a typical user model, as shown in Table 3, which reflects that the core problems focus on the lack of effective feedback and supervision after class practice, resulting in low practice efficiency and difficulty in skill improvement. The intelligent assistant teaching system for lute is constructed around the key features of user portraits, which improves the efficiency and interest of autonomous practice of lute playing skills and extends the teacher's offline teaching to autonomous learning after class.

Table 3. Typical User Portrait of Pipa Teaching

	• Age: 12, Gender: Female • 6 months experience in learning the pipa with some interest • Family members have no relevant music background and cannot provide the necessary background knowledge and learning resources
Needs and Goals	• Feel and experience the pipa playing, enrich the life after school, and hope to become the main way and channel to be happy and relaxed in my spare time • Master the pipa playing proficiently, practice one skill, participate in the artistic performance activities sponsored by the school, and make new friends • Make full use of your potential to prepare for the exams, competitions and further studies
User Behavior Characteristics	• Go to the training class near your home every week, and learn from the teacher for 3 hours • After class, you need to arrange time to complete the practice homework required by the teacher • Keep practicing the piano for more than half an hour every day under the supervision of parents
User pain points and obstacles	• Fingering is complex, and the knowledge points taught by the teacher are easy to forget. It is hoped that there will be professional guidance after class • I cannot get corresponding support without teaching resources. I want to know the situation of other friends playing Musical Instruments • After class, I don't know whether my fingers are correct or not. Blind practice misses the opportunity for growth • The high cost of pipa teaching makes it an important expenditure for interest cultivation

4.2 Pipa intelligent auxiliary product subsystem

The pipa product subsystem is shown in Figure 3 on the basis of the intelligent technical support system in Section 2.4, which includes the following three aspects: First, the intelligent pipa retains the original musical instrument characteristics, adds indicators and microphones, and exchanges data with the smart TV through Bluetooth; Secondly, wearable devices represented by data glove and forearm bracelet are used to capture the motion characteristics of fingers and forearm more accurately, which is the premise of intelligent fingerings recognition. Finally, smart TV with a camera not only connects smart terminals with the cloud, but also provides an immersive learning environment.

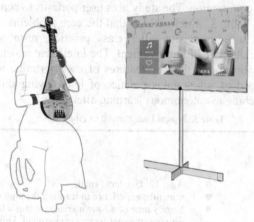

Figure 3. Pipa product subsystem

4.3 PIPA intelligent auxiliary information service subsystem

The lute information service subsystem is mainly composed of four basic functional modules, including lute music theory knowledge learning, playing demonstration, movement training and autonomous training, and instrument learning community interaction. The system is oriented to children or adult beginners. The design of the TV interactive interface adopts the layout of magnetic disk to highlight the use function. The interface color style is soft and elegant Chinese ancient style, creating an elegant national artistic atmosphere, as shown in Figure 4.

Select from the above four modules to focus on the autonomous training service process of playing movement skills. A user journey diagram is constructed from the perspective of students, and the changes of student-centered lute teaching mode are illustrated through user goals, behaviors, system service contact points, emotional states and system support [25], as shown in Figure 5.

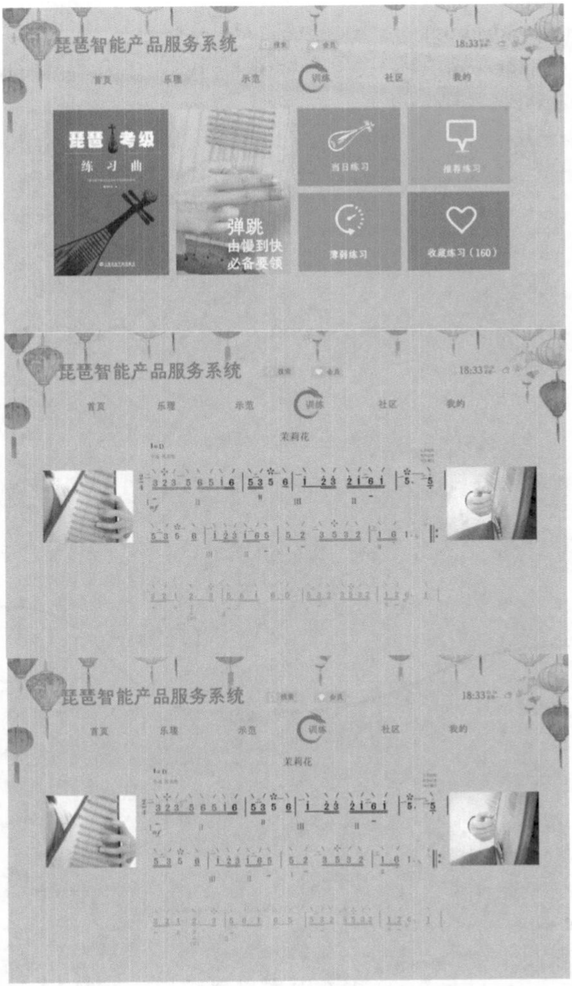

Figure 4. Pipa service subsystem autonomous training interface (adjustment, prompt, feedback)

5. Conclusion

China's national Musical Instruments have a long history and rich cultural connotation. The education and popularization of national Musical Instruments is one of the important links in inherits and carries forward the excellent traditional culture and cultural power. The intelligent product service design method provides a new development space for the intelligent and digital transformation of national musical instrument teaching. The design of national Musical Instruments needs to break through the limitations of playing devices and evolve and develop toward the ecological evolution and development [26] of teaching service industry based on intelligent technology. Taking the pipa instrument as an example, this paper establishes an intelligent musical instrument product service system and scheme, which provides new ideas for the intelligent universal teaching of ethnic plucking instruments by obtaining multimodal data. It is foreseeable that with the deepening of intelligent technology into the teaching scene, the teaching quality and service experience of national Musical Instruments will be further improved and developed.

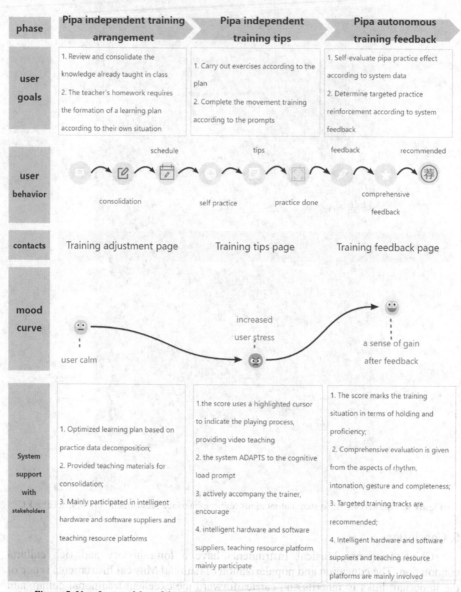

Figure 5. User Journey Map of the Autonomous Practice Module for Pipa Playing Action Skills

References

[1]   China Musical Instrument Association. *China Musical Instrument Yearbook (2021)*. Beijing: China Light Industry Press, 2021.

[2]   LIU Liu. *A Brief Talk on Multi-music Enlightenment Education* [M] Social Science Literature Press, 2014

[3]   THE STATE COUNCIL. *Notice of the State Council on Printing and Distributing the Development Plan for the New Generation of Artificial Intelligence.* Bulletin of the State Council of the People's Republic of China, 2017 (22): 7-21

[4]   SUN Xiaohua, Zhang Yiwen, Hou Lu, etc *Overview of research on AI product and service system* Packaging Engineering, 2020 (10) :49-61.

[5]   ZHANG Dongsha. *Research on the improvement strategy of musical expressiveness in pipa performance* House of Drama, 2021 (34): 77-78.

[6]   ZHANG Shiwei, Zhang Xuhua. *Research on the innovative design of national bass plucked instruments introduced into industrial design* Packaging Engineering, 2020, 41 (20): 290-297.

[7]   CHEN Liqing. *Carrying forward the performance and teaching of traditional plucked music from the perspective of national culture -- A review of "Research on the performance and artistic style of Chinese traditional plucked music".* China Journal of Education, 2020 (08): 141.

[8]   YU Zhengyue, Deng Xiaowei, Yao Weiping, Zhou Li. *Research on Chinese traditional musical instruments from the perspective of mechanics.* Electroacoustic Technology, 2017,41 (11): 74-79.

[9]   FU Lu. *Aesthetic Research on the Modeling of Chinese National Musical Instruments.* National Art Research, 2010 (4): 56-61.

[10]   CHEN Renyu. *Research on the experience design of intelligent electric pipa under the concept of modernization of national musical instruments* [D]. Shanghai Jiaotong University, 2020.

[11]   ZHANG Dongsha. *Research on the improvement strategy of musical expressiveness in pipa performance* House of Drama, 2021 (34): 77-78.

[12]   FANG Haiguang, Kong Xinmei, Li Haiyun, et al. *Theoretical research on human-machine collaborative education in the era of artificial intelligence.* Modern Education Technology, 2022,32 (07): 5-13

[13]   JIANG Shaofei, Feng Di, Lu Chunfu et al. *Evolutionary design method from product-to-product service system.* Computer Integrated Manufacturing System, 2018,24 (03): 731-740

[14]   HU Ying, Zhou Zihan, Chen Duoyi, et al. *Research on the design of data-driven intelligent medical product service system* Packaging Engineering, 2022, 43 (24): 28-38.

[15]   LI Ruiqi, Li Yajun, Gao Xingxing. *Optimization design method of product service system driven by user evaluation.* Mechanical Design, 2020,37 (10): 121-127.

[16]   ZHENG Maokuan. *Research on the theory and method of intelligent product service ecosystem.* Shanghai Jiaotong University, 2018.

[17]   WANG Lianghui, Xia Liangliang, He Wentao. *Return to precise teaching of pedagogy - towards human-computer collaboration.* Research on Audio-visual Education, 2021,42 (12): 108-114.

[18]   ZHANG Xuexin, Li Guoli. *The construction of the four-level model of capability evaluation* Teaching Research, 2022, 45 (1):1-7

[19]   CHEN Kaiquan, Han Xiaoli, Zheng Zhanfei, et al. *Scene construction and application mode analysis of intelligent education from the perspective of human-computer collaboration -- a review of research on human-computer collaborative education at home and abroad in the past decade.* Journal of Distance Education, 2012,40 (02): 3-14.

[20]   CHENG Hong, Huang Rui, Qiu Jing, et al. *Overview of the progress of human-computer intelligence technology and system research.* Journal of Intelligent Systems, 2020,15 (02): 386-398.

[21]   FANG Haiguang, Kong Xinmei, Li Haiyun, et al. *Research on human-computer collaborative education theory in the era of artificial intelligence.* Modern Education Technology, 2022,32 (07): 5-13.

[22]   LI Miao. *Research on the theory and method of product ecosystem design for user experience.* Shanghai Jiaotong University, 2016.

[23]   LUO Jianqiang, Zhang Yanping, Peng Yongtao. *Research on process improvement of service-oriented manufacturing system based on service blueprint.* China Mechanical Engineering, 2018,29 (18): 2250-2258.

[24]   XU Jia. *Analysis of the performance art and music personality of national plucked instruments.* Contemporary Music, 2022 (12): 89-91.

[25]   LUO Yun. *On the application of "flip", "wheel" and "hearing" in pipa teaching* Journal of Chifeng University: Natural Science Edition, 2012 (10): 253-254.

[26]   XIONG Jingjing, Huang Yunyun, Wang Weishuai, et al. *Research on mobile O2O outpatient medical service process based on service blueprint theory.* China Hospital Management Journal, 2021,41 (02): 65-69.

[27]   WANG Yiyan, Zheng Yonghe. *Human-machine collaborative learning in the era of intelligence: value connotation, representation form and practical approach.* China Audio-visual Education, 2022 (09): 90-97.

Design Studies and Intelligence Engineering
L.C. Jain et al. (Eds.)
© 2024 The Authors.
This article is published online with Open Access by IOS Press and distributed under the terms
of the Creative Commons Attribution Non-Commercial License 4.0 (CC BY-NC 4.0).

Subject Index

3D modeling	20
adaptation	831
age-appropriate	663
air quality analysis	333
analogies	934
analytic hierarchy	478
analytic hierarchy process	
(AHP)	1060, 467, 507
animal pattern	958
app interface design	436
archaeological significance	831
archaeological site parks	1023
architectural innovation	81
art education	58, 216
artificial intelligence (AI)	333, 890
Artificial Intelligence Generated	
Content (AIGC)	404, 713,
	850, 901
artistic creation	148
artistic image(s)	976, 989
ask aloud protocol	225
attention mechanism	989
augmented reality	148
authenticity verification	137
autoencoder	373
automotive front face	295
bathing facilities	663
behavioral design	415
bio-inspired	934
biofeedback technology	890
biomaterials	81
biometric security	259
blind box	478
blockchain	137
BOPPPS teaching mode	1034
BP neural network	703
brand	683
bridging tradition	831
card-based Tools	205
caregivers	362
ceramic bottle	703
characteristics	595
ChatGPT	901

children gesture design	148
children's oral cavity	967
Chinese calligraphy	948
Citespace	47
clustering	373
CMF design	1052
CNC machine tool skill training	789
CNC machine tools	873
co-design	595
coding analysis	595
collaborative design	382, 923
collaborative innovation	1013
color configuration	914
color empowerment	820
computational aesthetics	948
computer aided design	713
computer-aided diagnosis	304
computer-aided Putonghua test	278
control	486
copyright	901
correlation analysis	436
course assessment	1052
craftsmanship	10
craftsmanship design	831
creative design	958
creative ideation	205
creativity	58
creativity measurement	764
CRITIC	841
crowdinnovation	1001
cultural and creative	
design	205, 1060
cultural and creative	
products	635, 732
cultural and tourism products	507
cultural element	958
cultural imagery	497
culture and creative products	478
data mining	393
deep learning	976, 989
deepfake	304
deepfake medical image	304
defect detection	373

definition of innovation direction 70
demand analysis 137
demand description 322
demand elements 1023
DEMATEL 467
dementia 459
design 1
design award 1013
design award knowledge network
   (DAKN) 1013
design communication 873
design for social innovation 595
design images 322
design layout 251
design methods 1001
design process 850
design structure matrix 312
design thinking 583, 673, 809
designer's toolkit 934
detection 626
device design 540
diet management system 549
digital design 382, 923
digital personality 191
digital sport 164
digital transformation 1083
digitization 775
digitization of intangible
   heritage 382, 923
disabled elderly of mild and
   moderate type 362
disorder detection 641
DMC model 164
driving 486, 614
eating healthy 1044
elderly 39
elderly volunteer service 652
electric power system 179
emergency products 524
emotional design 732
end-of-life treatment 28
entropy weight method 436
ergonomics 723
ESG 754
evaluation grid method (EGM) 39
evaluation method 467
explainable artificial intelligence
   (XAI) 333
express packaging 940

extension model 393
fake vein attack 259
fashion capital 605
fast-growing plants 863
FBM behavior model 549
Feitian element 404
female design 560
finger exercises 241
finger vein authentication 259
fintech 673
first order motion 216
flow theory 286
Fogg behavioral model 415
furniture design 863
fusion design 449
future development 605
fuzzy analytic hierarchy
   process (FAHP) 663, 841
fuzzy hierarchical analysis 97
fuzzy judgment 1052
gamification 789
gamification design 241
gamification theory 164
Gaussian mixture model 179
generalized regression neural
   network (GRNN) 507
generating a countermeasure
   network 322
Generation Z 789
generative countermeasure
   network 976
genetic algorithm 312
gesture recognition technology 241
graph construction 70
green design 540
grounded theory 663, 1023
growth distribution 694
Guangzhou Nanhuaxi Street
   Historic District's 571
H5 interactive advertising 286
Hongyuan county 1060
hospital inpatient wards 820
human-AI co-creation 20
human-computer interaction
   (HCI) 560, 614, 890
human-machine interaction 191
human-machine system 614
human-system collaboration 1083
hunchback correction 560

icon design	97	legal dilemma	901
icon recognition	97	legal response	901
iconography	97	life circle	436
image inpainting	989	light intervention	530
image style transfer	976	LIME	333
immersive	58	live e-commerce broadcast	683
improved KJ method	436	localization	775
indoor color	914	low-carbon campus	415
industry-education integration	10	machine learning	127
information platform	754	maintenance of cultural facilities	652
innovation	108, 754, 831	map analysis	571
innovation design	164	Maslow's hierarchy of needs	732
innovation value chain	1001	maximum entropy model	267
innovative design	10	"Mechanical Weaving	
innovative design method	28	Technology" course	1
innovative design of outdoor		medical image processing	304
seating	449	medical syringe	373
inspiration	934	memetics	635
intangible cultural heritage	20, 1034	mental health app	97
intangible cultural heritage		mental model	524
handicraft	117	mental modelling	1044
intelligent assisted design	873	metric correlation	764
intelligent instrument	1083	minimal path	251
intelligent shoe washing machine	467	Miryoku engineering	39
intelligent wheelchair	362	mobile Chinese food cart	723
interaction design	486, 789	mobile sales vehicle	683
interactive design	873	model central	486
interactive narrative design	497	modern design thinking	850
interactive place	683	modernity	831
interface design	415	modularity	754
interface female	486	motivation affordance	789
interior design	820	motivational education	1071
intermediate knowledge	205	motor imagery	88
Internet of Things	626	multi-modal	641
internet platform	1001	multi-sensory	517
interpretable features	948	multicentered	614
irrational user model	524	multidimensional random	
jewelry design	47, 404	variables	179
Jiajiang bamboo paper making		multimodal interaction design	799
skills	1034	multitasking	614
Jiangnan Sizhu	497	muscle fatigue	241
Jingchu pattern	713	museum creativity	764
knowledge economy	1001	music therapy	459
knowledge management	1013	musical instrument design	1083
knowledge map	47, 595	nanosecond laser pulse	884
knowledge transfer	873	network urban analysis	571
large language models	673	NFT	20
laser-induced colourization	884	Northern Wei Feitian	404
learning motivation	809	Nuo cultural	478

object detection 88
offshore trade 137
olfactory display 517
online shopping users 507
operating space 723
optimization algorithms 251
painting synthesis 216
palm leaf sheath fibers 694
parametric 775
participatory design 225
passenger interface design 1052
passive 267
PAT Model 286
patent knowledge 70
PCMI 764
perceptual engineering 967
persuasion theory 549
persuasive design 1071
physiology signal 127
plastic waste 540
playground AI 47
possible state 267
practice teaching 10
presentation attack 259
preservation 831
principal component analysis 967
problems 278
process optimization 312
product design 28, 108, 191, 322, 362, 703, 764, 884
product family DNA 295
product innovation 1001
product innovation design 673
product innovation design method 583
product life cycle 28
product service system 1083
product service system design 1071
product system thinking 583
product-service system 28
public toilets 742
Qianmen Street 342
quantification theory type I 39
question-asking 225
recycling system 540, 940
red culture 1060
rehabilitation 459
relevance 179
repeated frequency 884

requirements management 673
residential planning 251
revitalization 831
RGB-D image 914
root carving 382, 923
rural idle primary schools 530
rural revitalization 652
self-attention mechanism 486
semantic differential method 967
semiotics 841
senility 449
sensing technology 626
sensor 641
sensor devices 560
sensory characteristics 404
sensory compensation 799
service design 652, 742, 940
SHAP 333
shape grammar 295
shopping cart 39
signage system 605
simulation 312
smart kitchen 1044
social innovation design 117
social service system 1044
space interaction 148
spatial experiment 225
spatial renovation 742
spirit of place: historical performance 342
spoofing 259
statistical machine translation 267
strategies 278
stroke patients 88
styling design 295
sub-obese people 549
supernumerary robotic limb 88
sustainability 754
sustainable 530
sustainable concept 863
sustainable construction 81
sustainable design 28, 940
sustainable development 117
symbol perception 497
system design 914
systematic thinking 583
tangible interaction 148
task model 524
tea 626

teaching reform	1052
technological humanization	191
temporomandibular joint disorder	641
tensile properties	694
text classification	393
text-to-image	713
the country	449
think aloud protocol	225
third-person pain	127
TODIM decision making	703
tone	820
tourism cultural creation	841
tourist experience	1023
traceability	850
traditional Chinese architecture	831
traditional culture	108
traditional handicrafts	732
trinity model	841
uncertainty analysis	179
university	436
urban block	742
urban form	571
urban furniture	775
user behavior	1071
user demand	342, 732
user experience	286, 393, 517, 635, 789
user-friendly design	723
user imagery	703
user profile	507
user requirement	362
user research	524
vascular biometrics	259
video games	890
virtual reality	58
virtual simulation experiment	1034
visual communication design	934
visual errors	1
visual perception	948
visually impaired people	799
vocational education	809
voice interaction	191
wearable	517
wearable device	641
wind power	179
woven fabrics	1
Wuyi Overseas Chinese Hometown	775
Yarn development	10
Yungang Grottoes	404

Design Studies and Intelligence Engineering
L.C. Jain et al. (Eds.)
© *2024 The Authors.*
This article is published online with Open Access by IOS Press and distributed under the terms
of the Creative Commons Attribution Non-Commercial License 4.0 (CC BY-NC 4.0).

Author Index

An, C.	799	Hemanth, D.J.	259, 304
Bai, Z.-w.	393	Hong, L.	373
Balas, V.E.	v	Hong, X.	663
Chakraborty, S.	333	Hou, J.	694
Chang, R.	20	Hou, X.	530
Chen, D.	322	Hu, J.	47, 70, 404, 467, 486
Chen, H.	560, 626, 641, 683, 901	Hu, L.-x.	362
Chen, H.-F.	137	Hu, X.	507
Chen, L.	478, 775	Hu, Y.	286, 312, 322
Chen, M.	614	Huang, J.-J.	39
Chen, Q.	342	Huang, L.	1, 10, 251
Chen, S.	1060	Huang, Y.	549
Chen, X.-l.	703	Huang, Z.	560, 626, 641, 683
Chen, Y.	415, 1023	Huo, H.	47, 70, 404, 486
Chen, Z.	251, 295, 775	Jain, L.C.	v
Cheng, D.	732	Ji, F.	884
Cheng, H.	764	Jia, B.	863
Cui, Z.	88	Jiang, H.	524
Dai, N.	1052, 1060	Kuang, Y.	97, 635
Deng, M.	524, 723, 940	Lai, Z.	251
Deng, Z.	1023	Lakshmi, D.	304
Dey, N.	333	Lee, S.-l.	732
Ding, J.	88	Li, B.	540, 934
Ding, W.	517	Li, C.	47, 486
Du, J.	1052, 1060	Li, F.	549, 1034, 1044, 1052, 1060
Duan, J.-j.	393	Li, G.	393, 831
Feng, B.	497	Li, H.	571, 873
Feng, F.	626	Li, J.	1034
Feng, R.	415	Li, L.	1044
Feng, W.	683	Li, M.	703
Fu, J.	164	Li, N.	934
Fu, Y.	948	Li, Q.	312
Gao, B.	286	Li, R.	652
Gao, Z.	97, 635	Li, S.	436
Gu, C.	1001	Li, T.-s.	789
Guan, W.	967	Li, W.	754
Guan, Z.	595	Li, W.-l.	362
Guo, Y.-x.	703	Li, Y.	1034
Han, J.	108, 117	Li, Z.	530, 540, 775
He, B.	641	Liang, Y.	652
He, J.	1060	Liao, R.	58
He, T.	342	Lin, M.	614
He, X.	295, 614	Lin, Q.	809

Lin, Y.	1, 10, 164	Song, X.	127
Liu, F.	47, 70, 404, 467, 486	Song, Y.	278
Liu, H.	605	Sun, B.	652
Liu, J.	148	Sun, X.	524, 723
Liu, L.	295	Sun, Y.	809
Liu, M.-y.	789	Tan, Y.	732
Liu, X.	478, 549, 694	Tang, E.	560, 626, 641, 683
Liu, Y.	967	Tang, H.	517
Liu, Z.	459, 809, 1044	Tang, L.	205, 225
Lu, C.	342	Tang, M.	216
Lu, D.	1	Tang, Z.	88, 216, 241, 884
Lu, J.	47, 70, 267, 404, 467, 486	Thomas, N.J.	259
Lu, N.	1083	Tian, X.	958
Lu, S.	605	Wang, D.	940
Lu, X.	436	Wang, F.	1001
Luo, S.	958	Wang, H.	88
Lyu, R.	948	Wang, J.	976, 989
Lyu, X.	890	Wang, K.	127
Ma, B.	295	Wang, Q.	81
Ma, M.	382	Wang, S.	137, 225, 251
Man, S.S.	81	Wang, W.	673
Mao, Y.	251	Wang, X.	373, 571, 884, 1052
Mei, S.	663	Wang, Y.	191, 713, 841, 850, 934,
Meng, L.	583		958, 1060
Meng, S.-K.	39	Wang, Z.	10, 841, 850
Misra, B.	333	Wang, Z.-f.	362
Mu, R.	850	Wei, Z.	97
Niu, X.	873	Weng, J.	47, 70, 404, 467, 486
Pan, D.	47, 486	Wu, A.	20
Pan, M.	295	Wu, M.	775
Pan, X.	560, 626, 641, 683	Wu, Q.	342
Pan, Y.	127	Wu, Q.	v
Pang, S.	241	Wu, X.	923
Peng, J.	560, 626, 641, 683	Wu, Y.	47, 70, 404, 486
Peng, P.	1013	Wu, Z.	694
Qi, Y.	694	Xie, Y.	560, 626, 641, 683
Qiao, Y.	742	Xie, Z.	373
Qin, Z.	890	Xing, B.	127, 216, 241, 673, 948
Qiu, W.-l.	820	Xu, S.	890
Qiu, X.	764	Xu, W.	117
Qiu, Y.	595	Xu, Y.	507
Ratthai, P.	831	Xu, Z.	241, 1013
Ruan, X.	901	Yan, F.	373
Sheng, C.-x.	362	Yan, T.	1, 10
Shi, F.	v	Yang, B.	81
Shi, S.-S.	137	Yang, F.	164, 614
Shi, X.	873	Yang, G.	948
Shi, Y.	1, 10, 127	Yang, J.	754
Song, Q.	652	Yang, W.	28

Yang, Y.	635	Zhang, M.	47, 70, 404, 467, 486
Yang, Z.	295	Zhang, R.	583
Yao, C.	459	Zhang, T.	179, 1052
Yao, J.	497	Zhang, W.	742, 799
Yao, Y.	560, 626, 641, 683	Zhang, Y.	614, 967, 1013
Ye, D.	583	Zhang, Z.	342, 449, 1071
Yin, F.	267	Zhao, H.	342
Yin, J.	205	Zhao, S.	940
Ying, F.	459, 560, 626, 641, 683	Zheng, J.	560, 626, 641, 683
Yu, J.	216	Zheng, X.	164
Yu, S.	47, 70, 404, 467, 486	Zhou, C.	914
Yu, X.	108	Zhou, N.	1071
Zeng, J.	884	Zhou, X.	404, 467, 486
Zhan, J.	560, 626, 683	Zhou, Z.	742
Zhang, B.-Y.	39	Zhu, B.	723, 940
Zhang, F.	393	Zhu, D.	635
Zhang, H.	216, 241	Zhu, J.	1013
Zhang, J.	507, 641, 694, 723	Zhu, L.	1044
Zhang, L.	88, 137, 148, 164,	Zhu, X.	517
	191, 948	Zou, P.	216, 241